THIS BELONGS

Terry
with love
Diana

WE ONLY SING WHEN WE'RE FISHING
GRIMSBY TOWN F.C.
THE OFFICIAL HISTORY
1878 - 2000

By Dave Wherry

Published by:
Yore Publications
12 The Furrows, Harefield,
Middx. UB9 6AT.

British Library Cataloguing-in-Publication Data.
A catalogue record for this book
is available from the British Library.

ISBN 1 87442778X

Printed and bound by
Bookcraft, Midsomer Norton, Bath.

Dedication

Bunt Wherry and Sid Woodhead

If it were not for the encouragement of these two great men,
the author of this book would never have required a publisher.

Both of these kind gentlebeings sadly passed on within days
of each other in the Autumn of 1997, after a lifetime of supporting
Grimsby Town Football Club.

Subsequently they both attended Wembley
that following Spring in spirit, rather than in person.

We Only Sing When We're Fishing
as They Listen Above The Clouds.

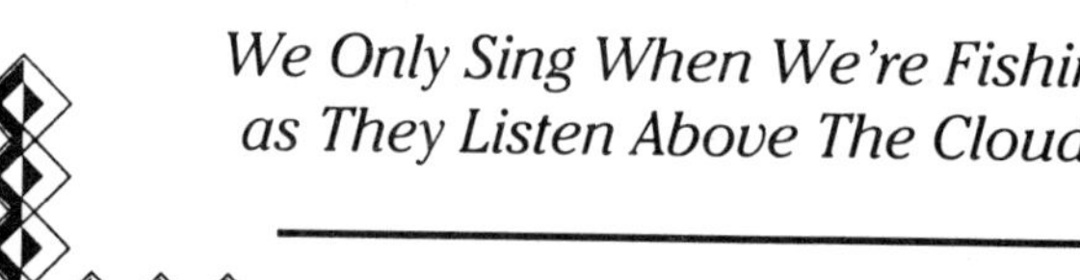

Acknowledgements

Firstly I owe a great deal of thanks to Tony Brown who suggested my name when Dave Twydell of Yore Publications was searching for an author for a Grimsby Town book. Dave contacted me in February 2000 and invited me the opportunity to write the club's history, for which I am extremely grateful. Not only has Dave produced a book that I am proud of but he has made it possible with 100% encouragement and trust in someone's abilities he knew nothing of previously. His co-operation, flexibility and calmness through eight months of hard graft and at times panic and frustration was an overriding factor that the printer's deadline was met.

Although it is my name on the cover of the book, many people have kindly assisted me along the way, none more so than Club Historian Rob Briggs. Rob not only supplied many photographs and snippets of information from his wide collection of Grimsby Town memorabilia, but took the time to visit the Library and proof read all the statistics on my behalf, as well as providing worthwhile information and ideas which were used in the final production. Thanks Rob, I couldn't have done it without you.

Statisticians Les Triggs, Derek Hyde, Ian Nannestad, Tommy Barnes, Peter Kellett, David Steele, David Downes, Michael Norton and Steve Emms have all added facts which lie within these pages, plus Doug Lamming and Charles Ekberg and other authors whose books have been referred to in order to confirm many factual details. Barrie Kirk, who along with Rob Briggs inherited much of the late Sid Woodheads marvellous collection, was more than generous with his time and assistance allowing precious items to be borrowed and sent to Yore Publications to be scanned.

I have contacted and met several former players and their families in my research, which was probably the most satisfying and rewarding work as I began compiling this book. Numbering around 300 whom all appear during the following pages, special credit must lie with 1930's reserve Albert Armitage of Sheffield, plus Wally Taylor, Stan Lloyd, Brian Hill, Malcolm White, the 'young' Jimmy Bloomer, Bobby Ross, David Lewis (son of Arthur), Vic Barney, Jimmy Thompson, Clarry Williams, John Cockerill, Harry Wainman, Clive Wigginton, and Dave Boylen who provided tales to accompany photographs from their personal albums.

Supporters John Robinson, Dave Wagstaff, Jim. Connor, Jack Westerby, Brendan Clarke, the Hawson brothers, Tim Kingswood, Simon Rowbotham, Bill Armstrong, and Lee Taylor also deserve a mention.

Co-operation from Doug Everitt and Grimsby Town Football Club, Grimsby Central and Louth Libraries, Peter Moore Editor of the Grimsby Telegraph and photographer Jonathan Moscrop was also most appreciated. In the majority of cases the photographs reproduced were not identified as to copyright holder, although no doubt many originated from the Grimsby Telegraph, and I therefore apologise should copyright have inadvertently been infringed.

Finally and most importantly, my family who have been behind me from day one, the patience shown by my wife, Lisa and daughter Jade has been my motivation. Now all the decorating and gardening can commence and Jade can have her playroom and computer back. Thanks to you all, and if anyone as been forgotten I apologise unreservedly.

Dave Wherry
October 2000

Foreword

By John Cockerill, Assistant Manager Grimsby Town

I was sitting at home in Cleethorpes on a mid-summer's evening when I received the telephone call that changed my life. *"Cockers, it's Alan Buckley here. Do you fancy turning professional and joining us?"* Within a few days I had met the Gaffer, signed on the dotted line, and began a (so far) 13-year association with my home-town club that I had supported since being a young lad.

It was, then, with a great amount of pleasure that I accepted the invitation to write the foreword for this book - chronicling the great club that is Grimsby Town.

I grew up with black and white running through my veins. My father, Ron, joined the club in 1958 before retiring due to injury in 1968. While I only remember his testimonial match against Sunderland (I was six at the time), I soon realised how good a player "Cannonball Ron" was. I thought life as a professional footballer had passed me by. My mum and dad's house overlooked Reynolds Street School's playing fields - my first school - and I would dream about pulling on the black and white shirt. My mates and I would stand in the Imperial or Constitutional Avenue corners cheering on the mighty Mariners week-in, week-out. There were some big games that stick in my mind: 20,000 plus saw Norwich, while I was in the Pontoon for the famous game against Exeter when Lawrie McMenemy led the team to promotion from the old Fourth Division. I was therefore deeply disappointed to be told, when I was at Lindsey School in Cleethorpes and playing for Grimsby Boys, I was "too small to make a pro footballer".

While my brother Glenn went on to join the professional ranks and enjoy a terrific career at the highest level, I signed up for the RAF. I was actually lorry driving when Alan called in 1988 and playing part-time in the Vauxhall Conference League for Stafford Rangers. He had tried to sign me for Kettering a couple of times beforehand. He had only been at Blundell Park two or three weeks and he paid £21,250 for my services which broke the bank at Blundell Park as the club was in a financial mess. He was offering the chance of a lifetime and even the fact I would have to take a pay cut was not going to get in the way of fulfilling a dream. So I followed in my father's footsteps and made my Football League debut as centre half in the first game of the 1988-89 season at Cambridge.

But the less said about that the better, I made my home debut against York in midfield. I was fortunate to score in a 2-0 win and did not look back. The following year we were promoted with memorable scenes in the old directors' box after the Wrexham game when we won 5-1. We went on to have more highlights the following season. The big home win against Huddersfield when I scored twice and created a third - was probably my best game in a black and white shirt. Then there was the final game of the season against Exeter. What a day that was. I drove in at 1 p.m. and the streets were packed with Grimsby people going to the game. And when we came out to warm-up the ground was already full with more than 14,000 soaking up the atmosphere. It was unforgettable and, when I got the winning goals in the 2-1 win that saw us promoted to the old second division, I was in dreamland in front of the last big crowd at Blundell Park. Those memories more than make up for the disappointment of having to quit prematurely because of injury. It was Alan who gave me a chance at Blundell Park away from playing when he put me forward as the club's first Football in the Community Officer. When he left in 1994 to go to West Brom. I was suddenly left as caretaker boss. I was fortunate to get some favourable results and the fans were right behind us.

After that I enjoyed a good spell in charge of the youth team and it is easy to forget that eight of those lads went on to make the professional grade including John Oster, Danny Butterfield and Daryl Clare. When Alan came back I was proud to be asked to be his right-hand-man. The fairytale continued with the two Wembley appearances less than 12 months later. I have been fortunate to play a role in the fortunes of the Mariners, but there are many who have similar memories to my own. I'm sure the following pages will help rekindle them.

My thanks to Nigel Lowther at the Telegraph for help in compiling this foreword.

CONTENTS

Chapter One

THE FORMATION OF GRIMSBY PELHAM FOOTBALL CLUB

1878-1892

1878/79

A meeting was held in an upstairs room above the Wellington Arms public house on Freeman Street, which was attended by several members of the local Worsley Cricket Club, several weeks after their summer season had been completed. The date was Friday 20 September 1878, and the gathering had been assembled with the intention of forming a football club, to occupy winter afternoons until cricket began again the following season. That autumn evening, the decision was made to form a club by the name of 'Grimsby Pelham'. Pelham was the family name of the Earl of Yarborough, a large landowner in the area, who became patron to the club. Included in this band of local gentlemen, the founders of the club, were Sir John Astley - who was elected Club President, John Wintringham (Vice President), S.Huxley, a player who also became the club's first secretary, and a local schoolmaster, Charles Horn, who became the club's inaugural custodian. Horn was voted team captain, for it is believed that it was he who first introduced *"a large bag of wind"* to his Cricketing friends several weeks earlier on Clee Park. The foundations for Grimsby Town Football Club had been dug.

Published in the local newspaper, the *Grimsby News,* on 27 September 1878 was an announcement heralding the formation of the new football club and informing that the season would start with a practice game to be played on Saturday 5 October 1878 at Clee Park, a public area, which had been secured for this purpose. A Captain's XI beat a Vice Captain's XI 7-3 on the day, when several keen participants and spectators alike attended.

1878
Back: Lammin (Secretary), Hall, Lincoln, G.Atkinson, Evans, Asling, Read
Front: Noble, Warner, T.Atkinson, Monument, Fanthorpe

Pelham's first ever match was played on 2 November 1878 away to Britannia and Brigg, which was possibly a combination of two teams. This first match was lost by a narrow 2-0 scoreline, which was considered not too disappointing all things considered. Pelham had only been formed seven weeks prior, and their experience consisted of only practise sessions once every week. In addition the match was played in familiar surroundings for the home side. In those early days, football in the north adopted the Association (Sheffield) rules which enabled sides to be comprised of 12 players each, but Pelham managed to field only 11, one of which, George Haddlesey, was drafted in at the last minute; he had only travelled as a spectator, to support his brother Sam!

The Grimsby players for this initial contest were: Charles Horn, captain and goalkeeper, J.C.Coates, A.Ousley, S.Huxley, R.Chapman, W.Bridge, F.Long, Arthur Mountain, F.Charlton, plus brothers Sam and George Haddlesey. Pelham played in their then official club colours of blue with white horizontal stripes, and this included Horn in goal.

The first home game was played on Clee Park against the Brigg club again, which Pelham lost 4-1, with forward Mountain gaining the distinction of scoring the club's first ever goal. The grand sum of 6/9d. (33p) was taken on the gate. Strangely, it would appear that these were the only two fixtures completed during the club's first season, no doubt in part due to a severe winter that year. Despite lack of matches the clubs accounts for the first term held them in credit, and a balance reading of £3-18s.-5d took them into their second season.

1879/80

R.Chapman took over the duties of secretary from team-mate Huxley during the summer months, and the club started the season as 'Grimsby Pelham'. But early victories over the two premier clubs in the town convinced the committee that they should change the name to Grimsby Town Football Club. The two main rivals were Pelham white Star, who were established prior to the Pelham club and had on one occasion entertained the Nottingham Wanderers club whilst they were holidaying in Cleethorpes, and the other outfit was a side known as Wanderers. The Wanderers later became attached to the Grimsby Town F.C. organisation when they were adopted as the second eleven.

1879
Back: Read, Hall, Lincoln, Marshall, Warner, Ousey, Lammin (Secretary)
Front: Noble, Monument, France, T.Atkinson, Lowe

Also, Clee Park became Town's official home after a lease was purchased in the close season at a cost of 10 shillings (50p) per annum. The ground was situated where parts of Daubney Street and Barcroft Street now run, just a short distance from the future home at Blundell Park, on the opposite side of Grimsby Road in Cleethorpes. Clee Park had no stands or other amenities at this time.

The team in those early days was made up of a local contingent of professional gentlemen or with business interests in the Grimsby area, opposed to laymen with humble backgrounds whom later became the players of future sides. Head teacher Charles Horn, who later became a JP and a club director, plus solicitor Sam Haddlesey, both continued to play in 1879/80, whilst timber merchant Joe Barker, medical officer Doctor Grange, and a Captain Bennett also figured in the side. Bob Lincoln, the estate agent, was another notable player, and became involved with sport in an official capacity in the town for many years; he was also the author of the book, *Reminiscences of Sport in Grimsby*. Aaron Burnham, a founder-member of the club, also later became a member of the board of directors when the club turned professional and became a limited company.

Arthur Mountain scored the club's first goal after the name change, in a 2-1 defeat to Hull Town in the second game of the season. Most home games were played at Clee Park, although at this time the venue was still a public park and not a permanent ground, but a field near where the Dock Station is situated was also used. All matches played were still of a 'friendly' nature for it was to be some years before points could be won, therefore just a great deal of pride was at stake. Record gate receipts of nine shillings (45p) for one match was realised. The playing record for the season (September 1879 to May 1880), read: Played 15, won 6, drawn 3, lost 6, goals for 23 goals and against 15.

1880/81

In 1880, the club had moved their headquarters from the Wellington Arms rooms to the more sensible surroundings of Drings Hotel (where the *Grimsby Evening Telegraph* Offices now stand).

This season Town had some popular men amongst the ranks, players who became pioneers of the footballing hero status, which the club have continued to produce over the years. Men such as winger George F.Grant, Sam Noble, and Charlie Hall, the latter who played for several seasons and later served the club as trainer. Utility man George Atkinson, who usually played in goal, was injured after colliding with an opposing attacker from Louth and broke his collar bone, he thus became Town's first serious playing casualty. Two clergymen also starred during the season, namely full-back, Rev J.F.Flowers who was also a keen Cricketer, and Rev F.C.Marshall.

The 1880/81 playing record was: Played 12, won 6, drew 4, lost 2, a marked improvement on the previous two seasons.

1881/82

The Lincolnshire Football Association was formed in the summer of 1881, and a knock-out tournament was organised, the winners of the final being awarded with a trophy. Many of the teams in the county entered the competition in its inaugural season including Grimsby Town. In more modern times defeating the likes of Brigg Town, Spilsby and Gainsborough Trinity, with respect, would not cause much effort, but in the 1880's it was a far different story. All clubs were new to competitive football and all were inexperienced, thereby making for a more even playing field.

Town were drawn to play yet another side from Brigg, on 14 January 1882, on this occasion it was to be Brigg Ancholme on their own ground. Town ran out comfortable 6-3 victors, assisted by Atkinson and Marshall who scored a brace each, to place Town into the second round, where they met a team from Louth. This February tie was drawn 2-2, being replayed at Clee Park the following week, and Grimsby Town progressed, this time with a 3-0 win. Brigg Town were drawn away in the semi-finals, a team, whom Town had found difficult opponents in the past.

Brigg unceremoniously swept Grimsby away with a 5-0 thrashing. The cup had brought new interest to football in the area at that particular time, and the following season would bring more cup adventures.

On the personnel side, the Rev Flowers had taken over the captaincy from Horn in September, and W.T Lammin who had been working on the administrative side of the club since its formation, became the sole secretary. The record for 1881/82 read; Played 19, won 9, drawn 3, lost 7, 49 goals for and 42 against.

1882/83

Grimsby Town entered the English Cup (as it was known then but later to be the more familiar F.A.Cup) for the first time. The F.A. had provided a competition as early as 1871, but it was only now that the 'Fisherman' from Grimsby felt they could compete, but a shock was in store. In the early eighties, clubs from all over Britain were open to enter, including teams from Scotland and even Ireland. Town received a plum tie in the first round versus such a far-flung club, for they were drawn at home to the great Queens Park from Glasgow, the reigning Scottish Cup holders for the previous two years. But Town were to progress without kicking a ball as the Scots refused to travel such a long distance to the English east coast. Town therefore received a walkover to round two, and faced a Rotherham works side, the little known Phoenix Bessemer, at Clee Park. For Town's historic first national cup game played on 25 November 1882, they fielded the following; H.Evans in goal, team skipper Flowers, W.Jenkinson, T.Warner, Charlie Hall, Sam Noble, John Tonge, C.Chapman, C.France, Harry Monument and R.Ousley.

Expectations were high, and a good crowd had gathered despite the entrance fee being raised to the princely some of six pence (2½p). But the enthusiasm soon died, for effort alone was not going to win this cup-tie, and it was soon evident that Town were not going to win the Cup that particular year. They were hammered 9-1 in front of their local crowd, by a Yorkshire side which showed no little skill.

On the bright side, the scoreline was never to be matched again (bar an Arsenal thrashing in 1931) and this still remains the club's record F.A.Cup defeat and record home reversal. What would the outcome have been if the highly talented Queens Park had fulfilled their first round fixture? Another fact from that embarrassing day that will be held in the club records for ever, is the name of the scorer of the club's first F.A.Cup goal, a certain Harry Monument. Harry, became a well known local player and had sporting letters published in the local press under the pseudonym 'Old Monny'.

The Lincolnshire Cup brought false hope after a semi-final defeat, once again at the hands of rivals Brigg Town, on this occasion a 3-0 away defeat.

Brigg used the then more modern playing formation of 2-3-5, a transition from the original 2-2-6, which most clubs had previously adopted, and which Town were soon to follow. Other results that season included the beating of Louth Town, twice by 6-0 and 6-1, and losing 7-0 at Nottingham Forest.

A very small but important upgrade was made to the Clee Park ground- the addition of changing rooms! These were not exactly rooms but bathing vans borrowed from the nearby Cleethorpes sea-front, obviously not in demand during the winter months.

1883/84

At the Annual General Meeting of 1883, Mr Charles Frederick Carter (a local Coal Salt businessman) became club President. He was to reign for the next decade, taking the club into the Football League, and making many decisions that would eventually lead the 'Fishermen' to greater achievements.

The English Cup threw Grimsby and already staunch rivals, Hull Town, together in the first round. Hull Town, were not the forerunners of Hull City F.C., but an independent organisation. The team from the other side of the Humber had visited Grimsby several times in the past, and were actually the first club from outside Lincolnshire to play Grimsby Town. Grimsby earned their first ever victory in this cup, with a 3-1 win played 'across the water' on 3 November 1883. Unfortunately, towards the end of the same month, they were knocked-out of the competition by a useful Grantham side, by a 4-0 scoreline.

But, for the first time of many, Town reached the final of the Lincolnshire Cup. After defeating Market Rasen by a then record 10-1 (5 of the goals coming from the Atkinson brothers) in the first round, they beat Brigg Town 3-1 away, a sign of improvement over the earlier seasons. Barton and Gainsborough Trinity were then overcome, and Town faced Spilsby in the April final which was played at Brigg. Despite goals from winger Sam Noble and Harry Monument, Town lost 4-2.

New players for the season included centre-half G.Kimpson, who became club captain, half-back A.H.Read, and T.Garnham an inside-right. Continuing to have a fixture programme made up of 'friendlies' and cup matches, Towns opponents however were now attracted from farther afield, for Nottingham Forest beat Town 5-1 on their first visit to Clee Park, and others included Lincoln City, Sheffield Pybank and Manchester Greenways. A profit of £15 was made from a total income of £153 for the season.

1884/85

A complete change of playing strip was worn for the first time in 1884, from blue and white hoops to a new chocolate brown and blue halved jersey and white knickers.

The Grimsby Borough coat of arms was also displayed on the left breast, depicting the three boars' heads and black chevron, which is still within the club's logo today.

Admission fees for a season ticket at Clee Park rose to five shillings (25p), plus two shillings and sixpence (12½p) for a view from the newly erected grandstand. The money for this stand was donated by club patron, Alderman Henry Smethurst of the firm Henry Marrows, and had a capacity for around 500 spectators, despite regular gates of around only 1,000

Blackburn Olympic played Town in a friendly on 20 September at Clee Park, which was lost 9-0. Olympic (not Rovers) were the first northern club to win the F.A.Cup, in 1883. Admission for this game was raised to 1/6d. (7½ p), due to the attractiveness of the opposition. Some rewarding cup runs were enjoyed this season, for Town reached the semi-final stage of the Lincolnshire Cup, missing out on a final place following a defeat at the hands of Gainsborough Trinity, after beating M.S.& L.Railway Steamship Dept., Barton and Louth. The team also progressed the furthest in the F.A.Cup to date. A first round win over Grantham, albeit after a replay, was achieved, then a 3-0 victory against Redcar of the north-east, and a single goal conquest of Lincoln City in the third round. This run pitched Town into the fourth round versus Old Carthusians, an away match in London, which is believed to be Town's first visit to the capital. The game was played on Wandsworth Common, and for the match a 'football special' was ordered to take 200 supporters from Grimsby station by rail to 'the smoke'. Unfortunately Town were defeated 3-0 and didn't reach this stage of the competition again until 1908. The reversal was no disgrace as Old Carthusians were one of the country's top sides around this period and actually won the cup in 1881.

1884/85 Season
Back: Lammin (Secretary), Taylor, Asling, Taylor
Middle: Hall, Kimpson, Mundahl
Front: Noble, Garnham, Raynes, Monument, Read

Steady progress was being made each season, and notably ten clubs from the Nottinghamshire area appeared at Clee Park in an eight week spell during the season. One of the new players, Jack Taylor, was signed from Spilsby, having been poached by Town after he had assisted in the construction of the new grandstand in his job as a joiner. It should be remembered that Grimsby Town were an amateur club in those days, therefore it was illegal to pay players, but with the boom of the fishing industry in full swing, many men were invited to play for Town with the added bonus of a full-time job, in the town.

Other new signings included local man, Harry Mundahl, and forward Bob Raynes. The 1884/85 playing record was: Played 33, won 17, drawn 5, lost 11, 86 goals for and 61 against.

1885/86

The club played in the same colours but a change from woollen jerseys to a button up shirt was introduced. Meanwhile the improved form continued with a trophy to show for the team's efforts in 1885/86. The club had really developed in these early years, and they now had a regular reserve side and even a third team called the 'Colts'. Interest in the club was growing locally and the town's population was booming with the jobs provided by the fishing port; at the turn of the century Grimsby was to become one of the largest fishing ports in the world.

In the F.A.Cup, Town made a third round exit, losing narrowly 2-1 to Middlesbrough Ironopolis at the quaintly named Paradise Ground. In the previous round they thrashed Ironopolis' neighbours Darlington 8-0, at Clee Park, with Harry Monument scoring four of the goals and J.Seal bagging a hat-trick. This was a record F.A.Cup victory for the club, with Monument scoring the most in a single tie, at a time when new records were almost annual occurances. Indeed the Town players can count themselves lucky to have reached thus far unscathed, for in the first round tie played in October, they won 2-0 at Lincoln City's home at that time, the 'Cow Paddle'. After the final whistle had been blown, the visiting players fled for their lives to the changing room shed as hostile City fans chased them off the pitch. Luckily the door of the shed could be locked from within and the players were saved by a band of Grimsby dockers who came to the rescue brandishing sticks and lumps of timber!

An excellent run in the Lincolnshire Cup saw Town win their first trophy, but not without problems from old friends (or foes), Lincoln City, again! After victories over Grantham Victoria, Lincoln Rangers and Grantham Town, the 'Fishermen' were awarded a home semi-final tie versus Lincoln City on 13 March 1886. The largest crowd to date was drawn to Clee Park, when an attendance of 5,000 gathered to hopefully see the old rivals beaten. The game finished 1-1, whereupon the City directors called for 30 minutes extra time to be played, which Town refused.

Grimsby were eventually awarded the tie, but not until after an F.A. hearing. Apparently the committee who made the decision were previously presented with boxes of fish.....from Grimsby! The 'Fishermen' met Lincoln Lindum in the final at Grantham and won 2-0, but the trophy was withheld until the following season, following further enquiries.

Later in the season the Clee Park attendance record was broken again with a 6,000 crowd when Manchester Greenways were overcome 4-0. R.Sharman from Notts County, master shipwright Harry Smith, aged 23, and William Hopewell, later of Middlesbrough, all made appearances during the season, when the full record read; Played 38, won 30, drawn 6, lost 2, 118 goals for and 27 against.

1886/87

Preston North End were invited for a friendly during 1886/67, although one of the top clubs in the country they were yet to win the FA Cup but at the season's end they reached the semi-final and were just beginning a period of greatness, which eventually gave them the nickname 'The Invincibles'. The game, played on 24 November, was lost 3-0 and afterwards there was a grand banquet held at the Town Hall. On 11 December, Town entertained even bigger opposition in the form of current F.A.Cup holders Blackburn Rovers. Rovers had held the Cup for the previous three years, but Town managed a creditable 1-1 draw on Clee Park, in front of a 4,000 gate.

The club failed to retain the Lincolnshire Cup, sadly losing to arch-enemy Lincoln City in a final replay at Gainsborough, unluckily losing 2-0 and the services of hit-man Monument with an injury. The first final match, also played at Gainsborough, attracted a crowd of 8,000. In earlier ties Town achieved record victories, 15-0 over Lincoln St. Swithins, then in the second round an even larger win, 19-0, over Morton St.Pauls, the match being played on Grimsby Rangers' ground; this result remains a club record score.

In the F.A.Cup, the team was knocked out in the second round, the opponents being Nottingham Forest, a 1-0 replay defeat after a 2-2 draw played on the Gregory Ground in Lenton, Notts. Town had beaten Yorkshire side Sheffield Heeley 4-1 at home in round one, despite the 'Yorkies' being drawn at home, the tie was reversed and played at Grimsby. The seasons full record was: Played 42, won 26, drawn 6, lost 10, scored 152 and 50 against.

1887/88

In the close-season of 1887, the club headquarters moved to the Ship Hotel in Flottergate. Also that summer several top Scottish players signed for the Town, namely International forward, Bob McBeth, from Edinburgh St.Bernards, who became club captain, Dave Riddoch from Berwick Rangers, the International full-back Jim Lundie (vice-captain) from Hibernian and the very fast and robust striker Fred Geary, who signed from Nottingham Rangers, a future England player in his later days with Liverpool and Everton. Among these were probably, unofficially, Town's first professional players, for professionalism was not yet permitted.

Old foes, Lincoln City, received information that Grimsby had obtained some very useful new signings, who were probably too good for the club at that stage. Sensing something untoward, the F.A. received reports that illegal payments had been made at Grimsby. The F.A., probably informed by a jealous City messenger, took up the matter but could find no wrong-doings at Clee Park and apologised. Word has it though that certain Town officials spent the previous evening amending the books!

Town continued to improve on the field, aided by the new Scottish signings, plus Cooper from Derby County, the former England International. Friendlies versus top sides were arranged but the season's cup competitions were little to write home about. After being knocked out of the F.A.Cup by a side named Old Foresters in the third round, the Lincolnshire Cup season was aborted. Despite Town reaching the final, with victories over Lincoln Rangers, Horncastle United, Gainsborough Trinity and Cleethorpes Town, the Town committee briefly resigned from the Lincolnshire F.A. and the final was never played. New developments were on the horizon. The Playing record for the season read: played 47, won 31, drawn 4, lost 12, 156 goals for and 56 against.

1888/89

The club headquarters changed once again, this time involving a move to the White Hart, after only a year at The Ship. More Scots were signed in Adam Ogilvie, from Forfar Athletic, a utility player who played in every position for Town - including goal - and Donald Sutherland. Walter Reid signed in November, followed by Danny Doyle in December from Newcastle East End. Doyle became a Scottish international, also captaining his country from his full-back position. By now, Town had a large Scottish contingent in the club.

This season Grimsby Town won their first points in a league match. A competition called 'The Combination' was formed by officials from several Midlands and Lancashire clubs, but could not emulate the success of the Football League (first played for this same season). With no headquarters or administrational support the Combination folded by May with many fixtures not being completed.

The first competitive (non-cup) game was played on 1 September 1888, away at Long Eaton Rangers, which Town lost 3-1. There was a large gap in this competition allowing the F.A.Cup qualifying games to take priority, and Town's second Combination game wasn't until 8 December 1888, at Clee Park, against county rivals Gainsborough Trinity, when the homesters gained their first points in a 4-2 win.

The final record in the Combination read; 13 played, 8 won, 2 drawn, 3 lost, 41 for and 17 against.

Town were forced to qualify for the F.A.Cup 'proper' as the F.A. had received applications for that season's competition from 149 clubs and decided to introduce qualifying rounds. Through October and November, Town progressed to the first round of the Cup after beating Lincoln City, Newark and Cleethorpes Town, which brought Sunderland Albion to Clee Park in December. Sunderland were despatched of comfortably, by 3-1, including a *"smart pair"* from McBeth the skipper.

Danny Doyle

Before the next Cup round was played Town played a friendly against Derbyshire side Staveley on 12 January 1889 at Clee Park. During the game full-back Danny Doyle made a challenge for a high ball against Staveley winger and Derbyshire Cricketer William Cropper. Doyle accidentally caught his opponent in the midriff with his knee, resulting in Cropper leaving the action. Cropper to the shock of everyone died the next day, his injury being an undetected bowel rupture. Sheffield Wednesday among others refused to play Town fearing for the safety of their players.

Mr I.J.Patmore became club secretary in January, before round two of the F.A.Cup drew Town against 'The Invincibles' Preston North End. This match was played in front of a Clee Park record attendance of 8 to 10,000 on 16 February 1889. Grimsby thought they had taken a second half lead with a Riddoch goal, but the referee disallowed it for no good reason, to the great disappointment of the large crowd. Town allowed their heads to drop after this harsh decision and eventually conceded two late goals. Preston went on to win the Cup and the League that season, thus becoming the first 'double' winning side in history. However there was success in the County cup, Town beating Grantham Rovers 3-1 in the final at Boston, with goals from Hunt (2) and Doyle.

Doyle moved to Bolton Wanderers in May, carrying the guilt of Cropper's death with him, although he eventually came through and gained success after joining Everton and Celtic. When he officially turned professional he earned the top wages of his day and was heralded a 'star'.

During April experimental friendly floodlit matches were organised versus Rotherham Town and Boston, Grimsby winning both, by 8-0 and 5-1 respectively.

A 'Wells' lighting system was used with eight pylons placed around the pitch. Tar barrels were located under each pylon and then pumped up under pressure to a gas burner. Town were one of several floodlight pioneers, although the tests in Grimsby only lasted for these two games. This was to be the final season at Clee Park as the lease was not renewed in the May for the coming season.

1889/90

Town applied, but failed to obtain membership to the Football League, receiving no votes (along with three other hopefuls), when the four clubs for re-election were all successful in their bids.

With the Combination folding towards the tail end of 1888/89, a new league was formed, and known as the F.A.Alliance. At a meeting on 28 May 1889, the Alliance was born and Grimsby Town was invited to join which they gladly accepted, although not all present at the meeting were happy with their inclusion. Clubs from the Midlands opposed Grimsby becoming new members, Sunderland Albion met opposition too. Grimsby and Sunderland were far-flung places a time when travelling was difficult, but Grimsby agreed to pay half towards the visitors costs, which was welcomed with open arms.

This season Town would have a new home, for they were offered a site on grounds, for rent, by owner Edward Heneage, the MP for Grimsby, whom later became Lord Heneage. The new ground was to be called Abbey Park, due to the close proximity of the old Wellow Abbey. Stands from Clee Park were dismantled and re-erected at the new ground during the summer months, the cost of relocation costing in excess of £300.

The exact position of Abbey Park was situated off Welholme Road, where Peoples Park and Farebrother Street now stand. The old grandstand was rebuilt on the Welholme Road side, running along the side of the pitch. On the opposite side was a huge open banking which could hold around 8000 spectators. The second stand was moved from Clee Park, a smaller one, which was erected behind the goal at the Cleethorpes End, and had 300 seats. The opposite goal was known as the Park End. A fine stadia indeed, which had a capacity for around 10,000. Season tickets sold for a guinea in the grandstand (£1-05), and 10 shillings (50p) elsewhere. The opening game was played on 30 August 1889 versus twice F.A.Cup finalists and a member of the Football League, West Bromwich Albion.

The visitors beat Town easily, 6-1. This result, seen as a national sporting shock, was played on one of the best little grounds in the Country.

Grimsby's first Alliance game was at Abbey Park, when they again opposed Long Eaton Rangers, on this occasion winning 4-1. The first goal was scored by Riddoch, then debut goals followed from David Black, Johnny MacKnight and McDill - all Scotsmen! Black was signed from Hurlford who just a month earlier had won a full International cap versus Ireland.

Town did not lose until November, their first defeat coming at home to Sunderland Albion by 2-1. As well as League fair, Scottish opposition was attracted during the festive period in the form of Clyde and Motherwell. Town continued to improve and thrashed Newton Heath, 7-0 in February, this club being the former name of Manchester United. The final five League games of the season were all won, the team boosted with the excellent signing in March of full-back Ambrose Langley, from Boston. Langley was born in Horncastle and made his Town debut versus Sheffield Wednesday; he went on to make over 300 appearances in a ten year spell after leaving Grimsby. Town finished the season in a creditable 4th position in competition with strong opposition.

1890/91

On the 20 May 1890, Grimsby Town Football Club, became a Limited Company, this came about when a share capital of £1,800 in one pound shares was made available, although only 400 of these original shares were bought up.

Another successful season was achieved on the pitch. No big names were brought in during the summer and the same squad, bar skipper McBeth who departed for Accrington, was used. Cosgrove was probably the top scorer in the 22 Alliance matches, although with only eight goals (several goalscorers remain unknown, due to scant reporting in those days) from his inside-left position. This total included an opening day hat-trick, when Newton Heath were defeated 3-1 at Abbey Park. Despite the lack of goals the Town managed a final placing of third, winning eight of their last nine games, and remained undefeated at home throughout the Alliance campaign.

The F.A.Cup became a farce of a competition in the early stages this season, when once again Town had to endure the qualifying rounds. In protest Town sent a Reserve XI to play at Ecclesfield, in the inaugural qualifying round, where the second team were soundly beaten 8-2.

Jimmy Lundie was rewarded for his loyalty and consistency at right-back with a Testimonial during the season, which earned him £50. The Scot, who was at this time club captain, had not missed a league or cup game for Town during four full seasons and was reported to have never fouled an opponent whilst playing for Town! His last game for the club was in 1895, and he remained living in Grimsby until his death in 1942, aged 85.

1891/92

This was to be Grimsby Town's third and final Alliance season. Ambrose Langley left for Middlesbrough Ironopolis, being replaced by new captain and left-back, Ramsay Gray from Doncaster Rovers, whilst winger, Black moved on to the other Middlesbrough, making way for a new inside-left, Jack Ackroyd from Heanor Town. Also of note was the flourishing partnership of the Rose brothers who dominated the right hand side of 'The Fishermans' attack. With 'Hickey' Rose at inside-forward and Alfie on the wing these brothers were extremely popular with the growing crowds. The pair were seen as locals, despite originating from the Suffolk port of Lowestoft, but their father had brought them to Grimsby as youths when he was attracted by the fishing boom in the town. The only game of the season Town did not field a Rose, at Burton Swifts in January, was the first match the Frith brothers played together in the first team. Charlie and Tom Frith were to become the first brothers to represent Town in the Football League.

A record F.A.Cup victory was recorded in October (which still stands), when Boston Town were defeated 10-0. Dave Riddoch scored the club's first ever penalty-kick after its introduction this season, in the 3-3 draw at Newton Heath in March. New forward, Ackroyd proved a success in his first season with 13 Alliance (including four in the 6-1 win over Lincoln City in March) and three F.A.Cup goals, and he ended the season top scorer. Town finished a poor 10th but good news was to follow.

Lapel pin-on paper 'favours' were popular from the early 1890's.

Usually multi-coloured there were often several designs printed for different clubs.

Chapter Two

1892 - 1903

1892/93

Grimsby Town at last became a member of the Football League. During the summer months a decision was made for the rival Alliance League to more or less become the new Division Two. The Football League now boasted 28 members (amazingly none situated south of Birmingham), of which the Second Division contained 12, including GrimsbyTown. Promotion would not be automatic, but a series of so-called 'Test-Matches' were to be contested between the clubs finishing in the last two places in Division One and the top pair in Division Two, this scheme was abolished in 1899 making way for automatic promotion and relegation.

In this season of much importance, the club made their priority quality new signings, but they had little money to throw around. Three players were signed from the Midlands, Jimmy Whitehouse and Sandy Higgins from Birmingham St.George's, and Harry Fletcher from Albion Swifts. Will Fairley joined from St.Mirren, soon to be followed in October by ex-team mate Matt Mullen. Former Sheffield Wednesday and England International, Teddy Brayshaw, was secured as was Charlie Henderson from Middlesbrough club, South Bank.

Town's first Football League match was played at Abbey Park, versus Northwich Victoria, on 3 September 1892, when they won 2-1 with a couple of goals from Dave Riddoch, who thus became the club's first Football League goalscorer. The historic side read; Wheelhouse; Lundie, Frith; Murrell, Walker, Ogilvie; Higgins, Henderson, Brayshaw, Ackroyd and Riddoch. Riddoch was robbed of a hat-trick by the officials as another 'goal' was considered to be offside. The game was attended by around 2,000 supporters, which is thought to be about the average gate for that season. The next three games were lost, but Town recovered to finish the season in 4th position. When Grimsby lost, they lost heavily; 3-5 in the return at Northwich, 3-8 at Champions Small Heath (later named Birmingham City), plus 1-6 and 1-5 to Darwen and Burton Swifts respectively.

Grimsby's largest victories were saved for the Cup. After thrashing both Lincoln City and Stockton, 5-0 each, they went out 0-2 at Darwen. Other points of note during this season's cup campaign, were incidents in the 2nd qualifying round game at Doncaster Rovers.

The first match ended 1-1 and was abandoned due to bad light, and Doncaster also had a goal disallowed. The re-match again took place at Doncaster, almost three weeks later and in front of a hostile 'Yorkie' crowd who were feeling somewhat robbed in the first encounter. Sadly Tom Frith left the field with a broken leg, but Town were victorious with 10 men, winning 2-1 on the day, but with a suspicious second goal. As the Town players left the pitch at the final whistle, they were bombarded with stones from angry home supporters.

Ackroyd again top-scored in the League with 12 goals, and at this time was thus the club's record League goalscorer. Higgins finished his first season as overall highest marksmen, with six cup goals and eight in the League, which included scoring all three on 1st October versus Small Heath in a 3-2 win; he thus became the clubs first scorer of a Football League hat-trick.

1893/94

A new Club President was announced, F.B.Coulson who was a serving Director. A very satisfactory first campaign in the Football League, gave little reason for personnel changes in the pre-season period. Henderson had left mid-season, and utility man Ogilvie moved to First Division and F.A.Cup semi-finalists Blackburn Rovers - as goalkeeper, despite playing all 21 of his League games in 1892/93, as an out-field back. Ogilvie was well qualified though as he had appeared for Town constantly through the Alliance years before Whitehouse's arrival between the'sticks'. Others to leave were two Scots, Mullen (returned north) and Walker (to Everton).

New arrivals all came from the North Yorkshire region. Three of the new men, Crawford, Graham and Welshman Jack Jones, came from the previous season's F.A.Cup opponents Stockton. Another, centre-forward ,Tommy McCairns, came from Whitby Town and became a scoring sensation. The new man scored 20 goals in an amazing 11 consecutive League and Cup games between October and December, a feat since matched by no player at Grimsby.

McCairns completed the season with 18 League and nine F.A.Cup goals (a club record F.A.Cup scorer in a season), whilst playing just 30 games.

Goals came easy for Town all season, scoring five or more goals on no less than nine occasions, including a then record League win on the opening day versus Northwich Victoria, 7-0, and a record away win, at Middlesbrough Ironopolis by 6-2 - no doubt Town's Teesside contingent felt much at home! Crawford scored a very creditable, seven goals in eight matches during his brief two month stay, before presumably returning to the north-east. The Frith brothers became the first Football League kinsmen to represent the club, in September versus Burton Swifts.

In 5th place, Town finished one place lower than the last season, although the Division now contained 15 clubs opposed to the previous 12.

Jones left for Sheffield United, after being an ever-present on the left flank. He went on to make 21 appearances for Wales and captained 'Spurs first F.A.Cup winning side of 1901, as well as becoming their first ever full Internationalist. Another loss in the summer of 1894 was loyal servant Jack Ackroyd who joined Rotherham Town. Jack had been rewarded with a Benefit game in September, when a Notts XI was beaten 5-1. Russell returned to his native Scotland after only one season, having missed only three games and scoring a hat-trick on his debut in the first game of the season. He later transformed successfully from a forward to left-half shortly after McCairns arrival.

1894/95

In the close season there was much incoming activity. Defenders were signed from Merseyside - Jim Stott (Liverpool) and Billy Lindsay (Everton) - both originating from the Middlesbrough area, as were Cooper (Middlesbrough), Fairbairn (Ironopolis) and Frost (South Bank). Town obviously had many contacts in that area of the country at that time, although it does seem as though many clubs recruited players from the north-east in the nineties as the popularity of the game grew among the working class, indeed the north-east remains a hot-bed of footballing talent even today. Joe Murray (Dundee) and Jim Waterson (Arbroath) completed the, now expected, Scottish influx. Inside-right Eccleston was also recruited, from Preston North End, whilst a new Trainer was obtained from Stoke, namely William Allen.

A home win on the opening day of the season against Leicester Fosse, with a 4-3 victory courtesy of an own goal winner by Bailey, in front of a 5,000 Abbey Park crowd, raised already high expectations. Between October and January, Town recorded a then club record, eight straight wins in the League, but gradually form turned against them. They had a relatively poor second half to the season, winning only two of the last six games, but the team again finished a respectable 5th. All League games at Abbey Park were won, bar one, losing 1-0 to 'Test Match' participants, Notts County in February. This was a replayed game as the original fixture was abandoned with Town leading 3-2; the pitch having become unplayable.

The re-arranged game was the only occasion that Town failed to score in front of their own public. Admission fees had been raised in the summer and stood for the 1894/95 season at the following; 5/6d. (27½ p) for a child, ladies 7/6d, and men 10/6, for season tickets. The price inflation did not put the fanatics off, indeed the average gate increased due to the quality of entertainment, no doubt. Town by now had a reputation as a very good home side, and on their travels were noted as playing hard but fair and above all being good sports, which in these early days meant that Town could draw a good crowd to their opponents grounds.

Front men Eccleston, Fletcher and McCairns all achieved double figures in goals, the latter scoring 18 in the League for the second consecutive season. Of the new signings Lindsay had an excellent first season and was ever-present, with Stott and Eccleston missing only one game each. Unfortunately, as finances were tight, Town decided to sell both these players after they impressed during the season. Stott went to Newcastle United (£15) and Eccleston returned to Preston (£20, then reported as a record fee for Town).

During 1894, the demands of financially supporting a professional club competing in the Football League were almost too great. Fund-raising and charity events for the cause of the club helped, but without personal donations from three of the club's Directors, things could have turned out so differently, in particular the gesture by William H. Bellamy who gave £150 to pay off the debtors and keep the club alive.

Mr Bellamy later became club Chairman, having been involved with the running of the club since 1890. He was to serve as Director until 1906, a role which included Honorary Financial Secretary, Treasurer and Team Selector. He was also a member of the Lincolnshire F.A., and later the English F.A., committees, becoming Vice-Chairman (January 1929) then Life Vice-Chairman (1941) of the latter, and Football League Committee member from 1896-1900. He was also the linesman for the F.A.Cup semi-final in 1902 between Southampton and Nottingham Forest, and the performed the same role for the 1905 final played at the Crystal Palace Stadium. Men such as Mr Bellamy have been in great demand by the club ever since, and the supporters plus the players of the day owed him a great debt.

1895/96

Other players to leave during the close season with Stott and Eccleston were Frost (Middlesbrough) and Murrell (Newark Town). Long-serving forward Dave Riddoch retired after eight years with the club, eight years in which he had seen the club grow and establish itself in the Football League, and now playing on one of the best grounds in the country and a whisker away from attaining top flight football.

The Abbey Park Ground in 1897, possibly a trial match between the First Team and Reserves. 'Popular Jim' emblazed across the roof of the stand refers to a local brand of cigarette available from Tierneys Tobacconists. The Terraced houses behind the stand are in Welholme Road.

In no season thus far were Town so close in attaining First Division status as they were for the ensuing 1895/96 campaign, for they had established themselves as one of the stronger sides in the Division over the past few years. Players who joined the ranks in the 1895 close season were backs Davis from Ilkeston, grabbed from under the noses of First Division Nottingham Forest, and Burnley's Stuart Munn. New wingers came in the form of Jack Bell (Wolves) and Bob Gray (Aston Villa) who were reserves surplus to requirements with their top flight clubs.

The season began in mediocre fashion with four wins, five losses and a draw in the opening two months. Then a tremendous run from November until the end of the season produced a great deal of realistic hope for everyone connected with the club. Losing on only three occasions in 20 League games, and only drawing one of those, it would have seemed that Town must at least reach the Test Matches, but they didn't, missing out by one spot, finishing third and four points behind Liverpool and Manchester City who tied on 46 points each.

Town again won all their games at home, bar one, this time remaining unbeaten with a draw versus Woolwich Arsenal in April being the only blemish. A new goalscoring club record was achieved with 82 for the season. For the third consecutive season Tommy McCairns scored most with 26, in just 28 League games. In November, McCairns became the club's first honoured player when he played up front for the Football League XI versus the Irish League, in only the seventh such representative fixture.

He and Sandy Higgins were selected as reserves for the full England squad in April to play Scotland. McCairns capped a very good season for himself by recording a club record six goals in the 7-1 trouncing of Leicester Fosse on the final day of the season, this stood as a record for Division Two until 1957.

At the season's end, Preston North End again poached a Grimsby inside-right, on this occasion Tom Pratt, who had only signed from Fleetwood Rangers the previous summer, and had only missed one match in the League programme, scoring a creditible 15. Another to depart was the popular custodian, Jimmy Whitehouse, when Aston Villa paid a near national record for a goalkeeper, £200, shattering Town's previous record of just £20, which was created just the season before! Whitehouse did not miss a single League or Cup game whilst on Grimsby's books. The following season he won Football League Championship and FA Cup winning medals with a Villa side which won the 'Double'. Could Town replace such a player? Whitehouse had also established the club's appearance record becoming the first player to make 100 League appearances, departing on 110, and having appeared in all of the club's Football League games to that date.

1896/97

The sale of Whitehouse and increasing attendances in 1895/96 meant Town could survive financially for at least another season. The sale of one of the club's best assets to balance the books set a growing trend for the 'Fishermen' and may strike a cord with the modern day fan.

As a replacement, Tom Cain was signed from Southampton, for a then record £20 fee (one tenth the fee received for Whitehouse; would he be ten times less of a keeper?). Cain came with a good reputation having kept goal for Stoke and Everton in the First Division, and presumably he came on the recommendation of Trainer William Allen whom had been at Stoke with Cain. Despite Town winning and drawing their first two games, Cain was then dropped and never seen again - apparently he was very poor. The 'keeper's slot was taken by 'Nune' Wallace, who was signed from Attercliffe. Having let eight in against Town in the 1894 F.A.Cup tie, this performance was hardly a good reason to sign him! The team lost 5-1 at Burton Wanderers on Wallace's debut. However they carved out some decent victories despite some erratic goalkeeping from Wallace, and it appears that he showed brilliant form on occasions and was known as a showman. The player was popular with regular visitors to Abbey Park, but the last straw came in an F.A.Cup game against Bolton Wanderers.

Town had been included in the first round proper for the first time since the formation of the Football League and fancied their chances against their Division One opponents. A 0-0 draw at home in which Wallace performed superbly, required a replay which was also drawn 2-2. A third match was required and this was played at Sheffield United's Bramall Lane Ground. Town were leading by the odd goal until disaster struck. Wallace conceded two simple late goals and Grimsby were knocked out of the Cup. Wallace was accused of cheating and receiving a 'bung'- his innocence was never established, and he never played for Town again.

Another goalkeeper signed from Yorkshire played the final six games, George Hardy of Mexborough, who became the new record signing in February, for a fee of £50. His stay also ended prematurely, when he returned to Mexborough in May - for free!

Although it was not a season for goalkeepers the other players performed remarkably well. Lindsay again had a consistent season at right-back, and the half back line of Munn, Higgins and Tommy Chapman was solid. Chapman had arrived from Manchester City where the Welshman had impressed in the previous season's Test Match side. Inside-right Hugh Morris was another Welshman signed from the Manchester club. Both players became Town's first full Internationalists when they appeared in the Welsh side which lost 4-0 to England at Bramall Lane, Sheffield, on 29 March 1897. Tragically, Morris died in September 1897, after signing for Millwall Athletic.

Outside-right Joe Rogers was also a success, described as one of the best players the club has ever had. Rogers came with goalkeeper Cain, from Southampton, and finished the season with 13 goals from 26 starts in the League. Sadly Sandy Higgins departed for Bristol City, thereby leaving a large gap in the Town rearguard.

For the third consecutive season Town had three forwards who all scored double figures, this time Harry Fletcher gaining pole position with 17, over McCairns' 15. Town's form may not have been as great as 1895/96, but the same final position of 3rd was attained, therefore they missed out on a Test Match place, by only a single point on this occasion - 38 compared to Newton Heath who finished 2nd with a tally of 39. Town entered the Lincolnshire Cup for the first time in six seasons and won the trophy convincingly with a 6-2 victory over old rivals Lincoln City in the April final.

1897/98

In the previous five seasons in which Town had been members of the Football League Division Two the lowest final position was fifth, yet they never appeared in the Test Matches. Consistently doing well in the League campaigns but never receiving any awards, the supporters were rightly expecting great things for the coming 1897/98 season.

Barton, Richardson and new goalkeeper Walter Whittaker were all brought in from Manchester side Fairfield. Whittaker was signed for a reported £60 - Town had therefore established new record signings three times in a year, and all on goalkeepers! Winger Jack Bell left for Swindon Town in the summer, but in January a centre-half by the same name arrived from Lancashire side Bacup. Their individual achievements in the past have usually been confused, the two having been classed as one player.

Major participants in this campaign were other new signings, half-back Jock McLean from Liverpool, and at inside-right another Scot, Ted Goldie, from Motherwell. McLean was a very hard player indeed and came with a great reputation as one of the finest backs in the land, he never missed a game in which, sadly, turned out to be his only season as a 'Mariner'.

The season began badly with a disappointing 4-1 beating at Woolwich Arsenal, but Town won the next two games convincingly at 'fort' Abbey Park. Matches were won and lost, with Town not fielding a settled side, through injuries and transfers, as they had done previously. A grand 7-0 thrashing over bottom of the table Loughborough Town in December, which equalled the club's biggest League win, briefly raised spirits, but only a fortnight later they lost at home to Manchester City 4-3; this was only the third League defeat at Abbey Park since March 1894. Town uncharacteristically lost another four home games in the next four months, including two in the space of a week against Woolwich Arsenal and Walsall.

The club signed former Sunderland Championship medalist, left-half Harry Johnston, from Aston Villa in October but he only stayed for eight games, leaving in February. Munn was allowed to move to rivals Manchester City in November, (Newcastle United) and Fletcher (Notts County) departing in February and March respectively.

Jock McLean.

Walter Whittaker record £60 buy.

Ted Goldie

Three stars of the period

Lindsay had been an influential figure at right-back for four seasons missing only six games in that time. In May, he assisted Newcastle United to achieve First Division status for the first time in that club's history when they finished 2nd in the League and were promoted through the final Test Matches ever played. Lindsay captained the 'Magpies' in that inaugural season in the top flight. The departure of Fletcher was an even bigger blow to take. The last occasion a Town side failed to have Fletcher's name on the team sheet was in October 1893, for he had played in every match since, mainly at inside-left, scoring 63 League goals in a then record 154 League appearances. It is difficult to understand why Town received no official fee for this talented group.

In the F.A.Cup, Town were drawn away at Nottingham Forest and lost 4-0 to that season's eventual winners, when Derby County were beaten 3-1 in the final at the Crystal Palace. In the League, Grimsby Town totalled a very disappointing 24 points and finished in a lowly 12th position. The club used 26 different players during this campaign, which told its own story.

1898/99

A mass clear-out in the summer saw Whittaker and Goldie join Reading, Rogers teamed up with Lindsay at Newcastle United, and Chapman moved to Kent club Chatham. Another three all relocated in the Bristol area, flanker, Bob Gray (Bedminster), McLean (Bristol City, from whom Town received £40) and scoring legend Tommy McCairns (Bristol Rovers). McCairns left, setting a then club goalscoring record of 86 League goals. Ten of the most regular appearance makers had left, and only local man Tom Frith remained with previous January signing Bell.

The club recruited a whole new team, 14 players in all, and amongst them were a sprinkling of locals. Grimsby-born Jim Bagshaw (from Gainsborough Trinity) spent the season in goal, new full-backs Pennington (Bristol Rovers) and Stewart (Newcastle United) played only one game each before another local, 'Bodge' Mountain made the right-back position his own, with another new signing, Boston born Fred Nidd (Lincoln City) on the left. New half-backs Cherry (Hamilton Academicals), Griffiths (Aston Villa) and Paddy Gray (Liverpool) rotated, taking turns to partner 'Happy' Nelmes (Middlesbrough) who became the most consistent performer in the whole defence. New forwards included, Jenkinson and Ratcliffe (both from Sheffield United), a certain Herbert Chapman (Rochdale) who moved little ground as a player, but later masterminded Huddersfield Town's greatness in the 1920's and Arsenal's reign on top of the football world in the 1930's.

Chapman's stay at Abbey Park was brief, for he played only 10 games before moving to Swindon Town in January. Pangbourne (Bury), Greenwood (Warmley) and centre-forward Cockshutt (Reading) complete the squad that started the season. Cherry and Gray were the only 'Jocks' on the club's books with the rest coming from Grimsby/Lincolnshire, the Midlands, Yorkshire, Lancashire and only two from the north-east.

In the season's opener, Town lost heavily, 7-2, at future Champions Manchester City, and didn't record their first victory until 8 October, a 2-0 home win over Small Heath from Birmingham. Grimsby had only won four League matches by the New Year, but could add a further three victories to their tally as they progressed through the qualification rounds of the F.A.Cup.

They eventually lost 7-0 at Preston. Many of the pre-season signings were disappointing, half of them playing only a handful of games. Two extra newcomers were drafted in after Christmas with Charlie Richards arriving from Nottingham Forest in January, and Jim Lockie from Newcastle United the following month. Richards was a great success at inside-right, having come with a good reputation after winning a Cup-winners medal and a full England cap the previous season; his high quality shone. Richards finished the season with a record that read, 13 goals in 20 games.

The month of April, proved to be uplifting. On April fools day, visitors Luton Town were soundly beaten 5-0 in front of 5,000 locals, the following Saturday a short rail journey to old rivals Lincoln City saw Town equal their previous best away win with a resounding 6-1 victory, which was very satisfying in those days when rivalry between the two clubs was at its most heated. The following Saturday was one to savour.

Only 2,500 spectators were attracted to Abbey Park for the visit of bottom of the table Darwen, when the homesters had nothing to loose or gain from their safe mid-table position. They drafted in three reserve team players, against a side who were already destined to seek re-election. Darwen had previously only scored four goals away from home all season, and had conceded 100 in total. At the end of the 90 minutes, Jenkinson and Cockshutt had both scored hat-tricks, and the team had achieved a club record League victory of 9-2, a record that looks favourite to stand for all-time. The margin could have easily been wider if it had not been for some excellent saves by the opposing 'keeper McIver, and Town's Bagshaw letting the opposition's only two shots on goal in the second half just roll past him into the net. In the summer Darwen were not re-elected as expected and never regained their Football League status again.

Town completed the season with mixed fortunes, for they lost on the last day of the season 5-1 to Gainsborough Trinity, the match played at Lincoln. They then went on to beat the same Gainsborough side 4-0, on the same ground the following Saturday to win the Lincolnshire Cup for the fourth time. The team finished mid-table at 10th, a slight improvement from a year earlier, and with a new team. Cockshutt proved a success top-scoring with 16 League goals, followed by Richards 13, Jenkinson 12 and Greenwood 11.

Grimsby Town retained most of the regulars, when only ever-present Bagshaw moved up the coast to Scarborough, and centre-half Bell went to Chesterfield. Sadly Tom Frith was forced to retire during the season after a career dogged by injuries.

The Darwen game was to be the last at Abbey Park as the lease had already ran more than its full distance.

Original agreements in 1889 stated that the lease would be for a strict period of seven years and would not be renewed in 1896. But Mr Heneage, the site owner kindly extended the permit for a further three years, however the land would prove more profitable to him for use for new housing developments. Happy memories were taken from Abbey Park; 102 Football League matches were played at the venue, of which 78 were won, 9 drawn and only 15 lost. Some 301 goals were scored compared to only 104 conceded. Town only failed to score at Abbey Park on nine occasions. Many clubs records were set and broken on this ground, some which remain intact one hundred years later. Gates of 10,000 were achieved during the 1896/97 campaign, versus Newcastle United and on the last day of the season against Woolwich Arsenal, when Town almost reached the First Division.

The Committee had received plenty of notice to make new ground arrangements, and steps were already being considered. Mr J.H.Alcock was building what was to be the new Imperial Hotel in Cleethorpes, and the club was interested in the land next to the site owned by the Sidney Sussex College, which Mr Alcock also leased. The two parties struck a deal, the club taking over Mr Alcock's lease on the land and transferring all equipment from Abbey Park to the new site. The new venue was situated on the main route between the fish docks at Grimsby and the sea front and growing resort of Cleethorpes. The new ground would be known as Blundell Park, after the nearby road of Blundell Avenue, which in turn took its title from one Peter Blundell, who in 1616 donated money to establish the Sidney Sussex College.

The Abbey Park stands were re-erected, the grandstand now known as the Abbey Park Stand, being reconstructed on the side of Blundell Park which was later to be the home of the Barrett then Findus/John Smiths Stands. Another stand was transferred to the Cleethorpes end of the ground, which became known as the Hazel Grove Stand. A new stand was constructed at the Dock end of the ground, adopting the name 'Pontoon', from the recently built Alexandria Dock. The Pontoon End was to house the more fanatical, less reserved local supporter. The playing surface was laid and everything was in place for a new season on a new ground.

1899/1900

Supporters were not one hundred percent behind the ground move and were especially displeased with the club's Directors in not buying the ground outright. Despite these thoughts excitement grew as the first game approached. The board attempted to soften the blow of the upheaval by re-signing old favourite, 'keeper Jimmy Whitehouse, from Bristol club Bedminster, and First Division Burnley's, Beveridge. Both were to figure in that opening match. Luton Town were the first visitors to Blundell Park, on 2 September 1899. The team that represented Town on that historic day, in front of a 4,000 crowd, read:-

Wheelhouse; Beveridge and Nidd; Griffiths, Gray and Nelmes; Jenkinson, Richards, Cockshutt, Ratcliffe and Greenwood.

Jimmy Cockshutt didn't take long to place himself in the clubs annals, scoring the first ever goal at Blundell Park, when Town took the lead after only 7 minutes, and went in at the interval 3-0 up. The new playing surface was tested for durability after Town's third goal, when torrential rain threatened to cut the game short. Luton obviously dealt with the difficult conditions better and the game ended 3-3.

A total of 99 League and Cup goals were seen at Blundell Park in that inaugural season, 65 having been scored by Town. Impressive victories over Lincoln City (5-2), Barnsley (8-1), Burton Swifts (6-0), and on the last day of the season Leicester Fosse (6-1) saw Town finish in a much improved 6th spot. Unfortunately a Boxing Day encounter with Newton Heath was lost at home 7-0, which established a new club record League defeat. If it was not for a poor run of results in the festive period things could have been different, when three consecutive games were lost, including two at home, and no goals were scored. Another new attendance record was set with the attractive visit of Champions-elect Sheffield Wednesday, and 7,000 fans saw Town narrowly lose 2-1 in this April match. An unusual feature to the season was that of full-back Nidd who was also used in goal, playing seven of his 21 League games in that position. Town were only served by a handful of such versatile talents. Nidd was the only player to depart in the summer, leaving for Watford.

Grimsby were once again knocked out of the F.A.Cup by Nottingham Forest, but retained the Lincolnshire Cup for the first time in the their history, after beating Lincoln Adelaide 6-2. Richards finished the season as top marksman with 20 League goals.

1900/01

Grimsby Town brought in more new players, and hence strengthening the squad for an assault on promotion to the First Division. Goalkeeper 'Bogey' Harris replaced Whitehouse, who was soon to leave for Newton Heath being unhappy at losing his place for the opening games of the season. New captain, Joe Leiper (Derby County) replaced Nidd at left-back, with 'Swappy' Leigh (Aston Villa), Harry Mellor (Stoke) and Tom Lakey (from old favourites, Stockton) coming in to the forward line. Others to move on because they couldn't get a game after the new signings were, Greenwood, Cockshutt, and then Ratcliffe; not one of the trio played a single game in the 1900/01 season.

Town started the season with some inconsistent performances to say the least, for they lost 3-0 and 4-0 at Burnley and Leicester Fosse respectively, yet between these two games they won convincingly 6-1 and 5-2 at home to Port Vale and New Brighton Tower.

However, the defeat at Leicester in mid-September was to be the last of the year until a record-breaking run came to an unceremonious end, with a 5-0 trouncing at New Brighton in January. The players created a club record of 17 games without defeat, which ironically started and finished against the same opponents, New Brighton Tower. In this time Town had reached the top spot in the table by late November and shared it with Small Heath towards the end of the season. Indeed another unbeaten run was enjoyed after the New Brighton defeat, consisting of six victories and two draws, until they visited rivals Small Heath in Birmingham on 1 April. In a close game Town were narrowly defeated 2-1 and lost the pole position.

The team began to show signs of nervousness with just four games remaining, two each at home and away. They could only draw 0-0 with locals Gainsborough Trinity and lost at Newton Heath, thankfully Small Heath too found life at the top stressful. In the penultimate game, Town just needed to win to gain promotion, at home to Glossop, who themselves were no mugs, but the desired victory, a narrow 1-0 result, was recorded, courtesy of 'Swappy' Leigh's 8th goal of the season.

Now there was every chance of clinching the title in the final match of the season. Level on 48 points with Small Heath, both sides had difficult away fixtures - Town playing at 5th placed Middlesbrough and Small Heath at Burnley who were 3rd. On 27 April 1901, Grimsby grafted hard for a 0-0 draw, but could not laugh or cry until news came through of Small Heath's fate at Burnley. Communications being not as they are today, it was some time before Burnley's victory was confirmed. Town were the Champions of Division Two.

After a 23 year history, GrimsbyTown would next season be playing in the First Division. The whole mood in the area at that particular time changed in a short period. The port was growing rapidly, jobs were readily available, trips to the seaside were becoming more popular, and the booming population could be proud of living in the home of a First Division club. The turn of the century had brought good fortune upon Grimsby and Cleethorpes.

On the playing side Scottish 'cap', Rab MacFarlane, signed from New Brompton, replacing Harris in goal in February. 'Bodge' Mountain and Leiper were regular full-back partners. Griffiths, Gray, Nelmes and Hemingfield, rotated to produce the half-back line of three. The wingers were replaced by two of the best players to have turned out for the club at this stage.

The fans favourite Harry Fletcher was recalled from Notts County in late September and took over the duties from Jenkinson wide on the right. Welsh International Alf Watkins moved from Aston Villa, scoring a brace on his debut on the left wing in the 5-2 win over Burton Swifts, in February.

The inside-forwards were Richards and Mellor with Leigh in the centre. Surprisingly not one attacker scored more than nine goals, Richards and Lakey sharing the honours with this number, a poor return by Championship standards. One of Town's few disappointments that season came in the F.A.Cup, when they lost 1-0 in the qualifying round at home to Middlesbrough.

Yet more records were broken during the campaign. In the scoreless draw at Blundell Park versus Gainsborough Trinity on Good Friday, a new high attendance figure was set for the ground. The biggest crowd at the ground, 8,000 spectators, paid a record £277 on admission. Harry Fletcher's return meant that he could continue to add to his reigning record of League appearances for the club. 49 points achieved was a club record at the time, and 20 wins equalled the 1896 effort. Town also achieved a unique double in winning the Championship as well as the County trophy, capturing the Lincolnshire Cup for the third year on the trot.

Unfortunately three stars moved on in the summer. MacFarlane returned to Scotland, signing for Celtic, the influential Charlie Richards went to Leicester Fosse, and Alf Watkins had an even shorter stay than MacFarlane when he moved to Millwall Athletic. All three had previously won full 'caps' for their respective countries.

Town had worn a slightly different style strip for the promotion season. The chocolate and blue halves, were replaced by quartered shirts, with a then 'modern' lace-up colour. White knickers remained, but the Coat of Arms didn't, and an emblem of any kind on the 'home strip' did not return until 1978! Takings for the Championship season were £4,360, against spending costs of £4,185; the club were therefore £174 in credit on the season. Each player received a Championship medal as well as a cash bonus of £200 to share amongst the team.

1901/02

Ground improvements got under way in the summer to bring the reasonably new Blundell Park up to First Division standards. For the past two seasons there had been poor changing and press facilities, so a new stand was built on the Harrington Street side of the ground, referred to as the Main Stand, which housed proper Dressing Rooms, a Press Box and a Directors Box. A roof was also constructed over the then Pontoon Terrace.

Grimsby Town's first ever season in the First Division opened with a home match with a Derby County side who had finished a mid-table 12th the previous season. A good attendance of around 7,000 (paying £234), saw Town compete well in a 1-1 draw. The side for the clubs first top flight action, included six new signings and read; Goalkeeper Billy Tennant (from Walsall); Mountain and Leiper; Hemingfield, 'Baby' Bellingham and Nelmes; Alf Dean (Nottingham Forest), George Harper (Wolves), Duncan Ronaldson, 'Swappy' Leigh and Andy Gardner (Clyde). Bellingham and Ronaldson, plus Alex McConnell, Clutterbuck and Skinner, were all obtained from Queens Park Rangers. 'Swappy' Leigh not only scored the goal which clinched promotion to Division One, but also gained the distinction of scoring the club's first goal in Division One.

In the next game Town lost 3-1 at Sheffield Wednesday after leading 1-0 for a large part of the game. Alex McConnell only lasted 10 minutes before being carried off, and Town hung on to their lead until the final minutes, the defence finally caving-in and conceding three late goals. An 8,000 home crowd saw Town gain their first win, 1-0, over Nottingham Forest in the next game, with a Ronaldson goal.

The next two home matches were won, against Bury and Blackburn Rovers, but they only achieved one more victory before the New Year. Then a League run produced just one defeat in the first 11 games of the year, including seven wins, which provided hope of First Division survival, although safety at this stage was not yet assured. The run came to an end with a 3-1 defeat at eventual Champions Sunderland. Town had two remaining home games but three away in the April run-in. Both home games were won, 3-0 over 3rd placed Newcastle United and another fantastic result with the 4-1 beating of Aston Villa. In the Villa game, the latest goalscoring hero, William Appleyard, scored the club's first Division One hat-trick.

Town were left with two away games, firstly at relegation rivals Stoke, and then versus Liverpool on the final day; a result was needed in at least one match. Town lost 2-0 at Stoke, when the team were victims of some dubious refereeing and a violent physical attack from Stoke fans, with several players and officials requiring treatment after being struck by stones and other missiles. So the pressure was on at Anfield. Town clung on to a 2-2 draw and survived. The relief was so great in the town that the result sparked off celebrations to match the previous year's promotion party! The players returned to Grimsby, by rail, on the Sunday morning and were greeted at the station by 1,000 supporters and a brass band which escorted them through the streets to the Lincoln Arms where a meal and refreshments were waiting.

The club's improved form coincided with the arrival of five players who were selected regularly from the turn of the year. Walter Whittaker was reintroduced in goal after returning from Blackburn Rovers in December, signing for a record £150, this being the second occasion he had broken the club's incoming transfer fee. Full-back McConnell replaced the injured Leiper, for the New Years Day game at Bury and kept his place until the end of the season. The draw which was gained at Gigg Lane kick-started the good run. Harry Fletcher returned on the right wing in the Bury game and also kept his place for the next 16 matches.

Appleyard - known locally as Willie or 'Tich', or more familiarly in footballing circles as Bill or 'Cockles'- joined Town in the close season from local side Grimsby Tradesmen. A former Fisherman, the Cleethorper made an impressive debut on Christmas Day at Blackburn's Ewood Park, despite Town losing 2-0 on the day. He made 19 consecutive League appearances scoring nine goals by the season's end (together with his FA Cup goal versus Portsmouth he was the joint top scorer with Ronaldson). He went on to become one of the footballing characters of the Victorian period and known throughout the land.

The fifth and final ingredient to the survival cake was the introduction of the Scotsman, Jimmy Long, in February at inside-left, who achieved a scoring debut in the 2-2 draw at Sheffield United. Long was bought from Clyde - left winger Gardner's former club - for a fee of £70, and he joined his ex-colleague on the left side of attack for the rest of the season.

In the F.A. Cup, Town were held 1-1 by the strong Southern League side Portsmouth at home in a January first round tie. A large and confident home crowd at Blundell Park produced record gate receipts of £374. Town disappointingly lost 2-0 in the replay, but a total income from the F.A.Cup totalled a tidy sum of £950. The gate receipt record was broken again only five games after the cup-tie, when Newcastle United were the visitors in a League match. £410 was taken for the Good Friday fixture which Town won 3-0, in front over 7,000 fans. Quoted attendance figures taken from match reports around this time varied wildly as the Portsmouth Cup gate was estimated at 10,000 yet the Newcastle game was given as 7,000, although it is possible that a reduced price was available for the Cup game against non-League opponents.

The club's Reserve side competed in a competition for the first time when it was decided to enter the Midland League in the summer of 1901. They finished in 4th place with a fairly experienced squad. Representing the 'stiffs' were a mixture of players recovering from injury (of which Town had many this season) or out of favour first-teamers and up and coming locals. In the summer, Town allowed both Dean and Leigh to join Bristol City, with Reserve 'keeper Clutterbuck and Joe Leiper both moving to Chesterfield. Billy Tennant, who had spent part of the season in goal, joined the club's coaching staff as Reserve Team Manager.

1902/03

Town had survived their first season in Division One and to bolster the side for another tough campaign the board paid £250 for record-signing Newcastle United captain Dave Gardner, a former Scottish 'cap', who was described as being a gentleman on the field of play, an elegant and intelligent full-back, and was a crowd favourite at Newcastle especially when he produced one of his famous back-heeled passes. Andy Gardner (no relation) moved in the opposite direction when he joined the Gallowgate club. Outside-left Gardner had performed well during his only season with Town, missing just three early games due to injury. Other new signings included four more Scots, Atherton (Dundee), experienced defender Archie Dunn (Millwall Athletic), Alex Glen from Clyde, and Everton reserve forward Glasgow-born Peter Paterson. Also from the Liverpool team's reserves came the only anglo signing Harry Singleton. Singleton was to take over from the departed Andy Gardner on the left flank. Paddy Gray and 'Happy' Nelmes were beginning their fifth season in the half-back line, and were joined by Bill Hemingfield.

Despite some useful new signings this season was always going to be one of struggle. The campaign started a week late for Town, as their involvement in the uncivilised scenes at Stoke towards the end of the previous season, innocent or not, warranted a one week ban by the League Committee. Eventually an opening day defeat at home to Nottingham Forest proved the club's more pessimistic followers right.

1902/03- Action v Stoke October 1902. Town forwards (coloured shirts) await a corner at the Cleethorpes End. Note the referees attire and the new, but now (100 year-old) almost unrecognisable Main Stand. This end of the stand was extended to join the Cleethorpes End in 1931. The glass partitioning and wooden supports still survive.

The second home game however produced a 4-1 win over Blackburn Rovers. Although Rovers had finished the previous season in 4th spot, this was not the Rovers side of old for they could only finish 3rd from bottom come the following spring. Besides this victory Town only won once more in 1902, with a 4-1 festive victory over Derby County.

Despite the introduction of Sunderland's Bobby Hogg and Colin McLatchie to the forward line for their debuts at Liverpool in early December, Town lost by a record 9-2 score. Both these players had been swapped for Grimsby's George Harper on 12 November. Hogg had previously represented the Football League, exactly two years earlier, and scored a hat-trick against the Irish in his only appearance. He and McLatchie had played exactly 200 League and Cup games between them for Sunderland, including around 20 each in the last season's Championship side. Both came with excellent pedigrees, but unfortunately also injuries. Neither were impressive as Town players, and both moved on after just a handful of games each.

Grimsby Town opened the New Year with a 1-0 victory at Bolton, their first away win of the season. The players were treated to a short break in Matlock in January, and the next home game, versus Bury, was won. No doubt compensating for money spent on the Matlock visit, prices were raised at the turnstiles for the Cup fixture with Newcastle United, which was not appreciated by the loyal supporters, who deserved better treatment for standing by their club in this stormy season. Despite a feeling of slight injustice a crowd of 7,000 attended the tie, with healthy gate receipts of £337. On the field, Town beat Newcastle 2-1, setting up a second round home tie with Notts County. A much needed £495 was taken on the gate - a new club record - but Town sadly lost 2-0.

League fare continued, a marginal improvement on the first part of the season, and consecutive victories over Liverpool and West Bromwich in April gave a little hope. But when the final game arrived, as with the previous season, Town again needed a result to be safe. Aston Villa had to be overcome at Blundell Park, providing fellow strugglers Blackburn Rovers were defeated. But Town lost 2-0, and so also lost their First Division status; the result was irrelevant as Blackburn won their game.

But bad feeling surrounded Town's first ever relegation. Blackburn Rovers were a powerful force at the turn of the century, much more powerful than unfashionable minnows Grimsby Town, and there is reason to believe that Blackburn's survival was not achieved fairly and squarely. Evidence suggests that a 'Lancashire Ring' was involved in Town's demotion. Towards the end of the season Blackburn beat a safe mid-table Everton 3-0 at Goodison Park, yet despite the scoreline Rovers had played poorly and it was clear for all to see that something was amiss. Another game was played with Bury who allegedly gifted both points to Rovers, and thus helped to ensure the playing of local 'derbies' with their north-western friends the following term.

As Grimsby was somewhat of an outpost for opponents to travel to, and only attracted small attendances in First Division competition, they did not really fit in with the 'big boys' and were made to feel unwelcome. It was even suggested that refereeing decisions had unjustly gone against the club during the previous two years. Town appealed for an investigation to be made by the authorities, and as a result of the inquiry Blackburn's Secretary Mr Walmsley was banned from involvement with the running of a professional football club for life, for his attempt at match-rigging. This was no victory for Town however, as League placings were unaltered, for Everton and Bury were cleared of the accusation of bribes acceptance. And Grimsby Town were still relegated. Reflecting upon the season it appears that Town were just not good enough, despite the talk of being treated unfairly; unlucky possibly.

Lack of finances through loss of First Division status hit the club hard. Fourteen players were allowed to leave during the summer, the only fees being received for Appleyard (£350 from Newcastle United), Glen (Notts County), Ronaldson (Bury), Mountain (Leicester Fosse), Whittaker (a club record £400 move to Derby) and Ben Hall (also to Derby County); the latter had replaced the injured centre-back Gray since the previous November. The total sum received for these players was a meagre £1,260, plus Hemingfield who rejoined newly crowned Champions Sheffield Wednesday for nothing. All bar Mountain rejoined top flight clubs.

Chapter Three

THE LOST  YEARS

1903 - 1919

1903/04

So Town returned to the Second Division after an absence of only two years. New players to replace the many who left included Roberts and Freddy Wilkinson from Bishop Auckland. 20-year-old Charlie Roberts was to become one of the best defenders in English history, although he sadly only spent one excellent season with Town before joining Manchester United, eventually captaining them to their first Championship and F.A.Cup wins. He made his Town debut in the opening match at home to Bradford City which Town won 2-0, with goals from Dunn and Rouse.

Others to play their first games for the club in this match were John Nichol at right wing, also signed from north-east amateur circles, Willie Miller from Edinburgh St.Bernards was centre-forward (it was reported that Miller was very poor and out of his class, and he soon returned to Scotland). The other debutant was outside-left Harry Lappin from Manchester United.

Other newcomers soon to figure were the Airdrie half-back George McDiarmid, who went on to serve Town well, 18-year-old forward Bert Hodgkinson from Derby County's reserves, and John McConnell who joined his brother, from Kilmarnock.

A swift return to Division One was not attained, although the team held its own, finishing in 6th spot. The squad had change considerably within the previous year- players at the best stages of their careers allowed to leave being replaced by those of inexperience or of a lesser standard, with the exception of the 'gem of a find', Charlie Roberts.

Town's home record was as good as their away form was poor. They were undefeated at home, which must have been a welcome relief for locals, but only two games were won away from Blundell Park, which would need improving for success to return. The highlight of the season was the 5-1 drubbing of Barnsley on Boxing Day. Alex McConnell was the only ever-present, despite 'keeper Martin Spendiff, Rouse, and Long all appearing in more than 30 games.

In the summer playing assets were again sold, and two successes of the past campaign left for pastures new. Top goalscorer, with 13 in the League, Freddie Rouse (who also played a handful of games towards the end of the 1902/03 season), established himself as Town's main striker during the season, but moved on to First Division Stoke for around £150. Charlie Roberts became an England International after moving to Manchester United for a club record £700, this was a substantial fee considering Roberts had only turned professional 12 months earlier.

1904/05

The season began with new club colours for the Barnsley game. Plain salmon pink tops were selected, which was a complete contrast to the 'old' chocolate and blue quartered shirts - how fashions have changed! To accompany the new kit a new forward line was selected; right-winger John Reynolds (from Burton United), 'Langfly' Baker from Norwich City who had played seven games towards the end of the previous season, Herbert Morley in the centre signed from Kiveton Park of Sheffield, Jim Turner from Brentford, and outside-left Ross arrived from Notts County. But this front line was not a success.

Town had a poor season, after a reasonable start produced hope, when only one match was lost in the first six games. But in the final 24 games, from late October to April, the team failed to score in 14 games (at the time the record for a season); netting only 33 goals all season was another dismal record!

The McConnell brothers began the season as full-backs, until the elder and more experienced Alex was badly injured in October. Morley signed as a forward, dropped to right-back, and never ventured to his advanced position again. In fact Morley along with McDiarmid were the season's only ever-presents. Several locals were tried with little success; Ayre, Elkins, Cartledge, Oakes, Ab Thompson and 'Punch' Padley all joining from the Grimsby League. Other notables to serve in this disappointing season were, half-backs Gordon Coles (Woolwich Arsenal) and Jimmy McGregor (from Queens Park). Another Scot, Charlie Mochan, came from Strathclyde in November, only to leave for Brighton & Hove Albion in the summer. Further acquisitions included Martin Higgins, and in March centre-forward Jack Butler. Grimsby returned to Bishop Auckland and Kiveton Park for these respective signings.

A rare 4-0 win was recorded in March against Bristol City, Butler scoring a brace on his debut. Highest goalscorers for the season were Ross and Harry Phillips with a very poor seven each, and Town finished 13th in the final table.

1905/06

The Football League decided in the summer to extend both divisions by two teams each, therefore there was no relegation from the First, with Liverpool and Bolton Wanderers joining the top Division. New League members who joined the Second were Burton United, Clapton Orient, Stockport County (who had been missing for a season) and a certain Hull City, who had only been formed a year earlier.

During the close-season, Town had lost the services of Phillips (New Brompton), Reynolds (to Sheffield Wednesday for a £275 fee), first choice 'keeper Martin Spendiff who joined new members and neighbours Hull City, Wilkinson to Norwich City and Ross to Glossop; the latter was soon to be followed by McDiarmid who also joined the Derbyshire club. Replacing these players, once again, were those with no experience of football played at this level. Of eight new signings only forward Jimmy Swarbrick, signed from Southern League Brentford, had played in the Football League before - having made 15 appearances for Blackburn Rovers - and Algernon Pynegar who turned out just once for Derby County the previous season.

A surprising start to the season at Chesterfield saw Town winning comfortably by 4-1, but the first home game against Manchester United was lost 1-0. That initial victory was the best for sometime and again Town struggled to score goals. However, one of the most pleasing set of results came in the first professional 'Humber Derby' played at Anlaby Road, Hull on 16 December 1905. Grimsby won 1-0 thanks to a Joe Johnson goal, and the return match at Blundell Park produced the same score, this time with a goal from Fred Robinson to complete the 'double' over Hull City.

Old favourite Harry Fletcher returned for a third and final spell at the club in October, after moving back from Brentford. He once again continued to add to his club appearance record, and amazingly equalled Tommy McCairns' League scoring record when netting his only goal of the season at home to Bristol City the day after Boxing Day. His League record for 'The Mariners' at the season's end read; played 244, goals 86.

The first three games of the New Year threw up some unusual results. Firstly a visit to Bank Street, Clayton saw Town lose 5-0 to Manchester United on the January 6th. In the next game Grimsby were unceremoniously dumped out of the Cup, 6-0, in the first round by Newcastle United at St.James' Park. The following week, Town regained some dignity with their largest win of the season after a 5-0 victory over Burslem Port Vale; all three games in the space of a fortnight. The club was originally drawn at home to Newcastle United in the Cup-tie, but sacrificed home advantage to generate more money, with the expected bigger crowd that would be attracted further north.

Town finished the season in a much improved 8th position. Right-half Jimmy McGregor was the only player to appear in all 38 League matches, with 'Langfly' Baker completing the season with 10 goals before he returned to Norfolk. Others to leave that summer were John McConnell (Brentford) and the long-serving 'Happy' Nelmes (Burton United). Nelmes had made over 200 appearances in his eight year stint as a Mariner.

1906/07

New signing - Dickie Morris

As fortunes had not changed by playing in salmon pink, the club opted to change colours again, selecting to play in white shirts with red yoke around neck and shoulders, red cuffs and a lace-up collar. Shorts were red and stockings were black with a red hoop on a white band on the turnover. The new strip made its debut in the first game of the season at home to Nottingham Forest. Players making their debuts that day were two new signings from Leeds City, left-back John MacDonald (who replaced the departed McConnell) and Dickie Morris at inside-left. Morris was a current international and already held 10 Welsh caps. Scottish right- winger Tom Rodger was signed from Preston North End and centre-forward Tom Hakin from his home town club Mexborough. Forest were beaten 3-1, with the impressive Morris scoring on his debut, in front of a 7,000 crowd.

Again a good first result was spoilt by the disappointing away form which followed, with losses at Leicester Fosse and Lincoln City. Town managed a 3-1 away win at Chesterfield though, in late September, with three of the new forwards scoring - Hakin, Morris and Rodger. Narrowly losing 3-2 at Port Vale in the next game, Fletcher scored one of the goals in that defeat, the 87th League goal of his Town career breaking Tommy McCairns' League scoring record in the process. Burnley were beaten 1-0 in a home game in early October at Blundell Park courtesy of a McGregor penalty. Sadly only two of the next 11 games were won, the final match in the poor run being lost 6-1 at West Bromwich on Christmas Day.

The following day Town broke the bad sequence and redeemed themselves with a 2-0 home win over local rivals Gainsborough Trinity. The club's home-grown goalkeepers Cartledge and Horner (who had shared the custodian's spot for the past 18 months) gave way to new signing from East Stirling, Harvey Carmichael. Another introduction to the side was a local, Tom Morris, a 22-year-old centre-half from Grimsby Rovers. The recent re-introduction of Burnett at centre-forward brought further success, for including the Gainsborough win Town won 10 out of the next 14 in the League, although they were knocked out of the Cup at Woolwich Arsenal during this period.

The Morris pair had impressed greatly in this run, although both were soon destined to leave. Dickie won his 11th cap for Wales, scoring his first international goal in February in a 3-2 win in Ireland, and Tom showed good strength and distribution at the back having made the transition from park football to competing at a professional level look remarkably easy. Unfortunately Town won only one of the final six games to finish a disappointing mid-table 11th. That final win came in a 2-1 victory versus Glossop in front of a Blundell Park crowd who paid a total of only £32, thought to be the lowest amount taken for a League match at Blundell Park; apparently the weather was atrocious with bitterly cold driving wind and rain.

Town used 27 different players during the campaign, and employing a squad of such numbers very rarely brings success. A mass exodus was to follow. Baker (Norwich City) and Hooper (Nottingham Forest) had left in February, followed by the influential Herbert Morley in March, when he moved to Notts County for £600. Morley went on to win an England cap in 1910. Moves at the season's end included full-back MacDonald (to Q.P.R.), Dickie Morris and Butler (Plymouth), plus Burnett and Tom Morris (Brighton & H.A.), and once again the club's top scorer that season with 13, Tom Rodger, who went to Reading. Swarbrick (Oldham), McGregor (Glossop), Milnes (Bradford) and Openshaw (Salford) were amongst the others.

1907/08

If the 1906/07 season proved disappointing, the following campaign was to prove no better. Virtually a new squad was signed to accompany the inexperienced reserve players who were left from the previous season. An amazing total of 13 newcomers were signed in the summer months, plus Athersmith, the former Aston Villa and England winger who was installed as Trainer. Athersmith came with a great pedigree, gaining 12 International Caps and winning five Championship medals, plus an F.A.Cup winners medal, with the Villa team of the late 1890's. Six of the new men made their debuts in the season opener at home to Gainsborough Trinity, which was lost 4-1, and the following away games also ended in defeat, at Lincoln and Stockport, which set the tone for a season of struggle.

The next three games were surprisingly won, but then Town's victory against Stoke, by 1-0, was the only success in a run of 17 games.

Only Carmichael, Lee, Higgins and Hakin had previously appeared for Town in the opening couple of games. 'Chopper' Lee was selected as first choice right-half after only four appearances during the whole of the previous season. Of the new signings only young right-back Sidney Wheelhouse (who had been signed with Paddy Stokes) from Shildon Athletic showed any consistency. Jack, Hakin, Kilbourne and local amateur Chris Young had all been tried at centre-forward in the early stages with limited success. Not until summer signing Bob Blanthorne was given his chance, in late October, did Town find a regular goalgetter. The, by now, 34-year-old Harry Fletcher made a welcome return to the side in 1907/08 after missing most of the previous season with injury problems. He did, however, score a hat-trick against Glossop in a 4-0 win on 28 September, but this trio of goals were to prove his last of the campaign and his professional career, despite him playing a further 20 League games in an attacking role.

The run of depressing results lasted until a win at Glossop in late January. During that sequence McDiarmid (Clyde) and John McConnell (Brentford) had returned from spells away, but both struggled to keep a place in the side or to turn results around. December proved to be the worst calendar month on record with all six games played being lost, although five were away from home. Nine consecutive losses during this particular spell is still a club record. Although a Cup run was to prove a welcome distraction and League form picked up a little in the coming months.

In the Cup, Town beat Bristol City after a replay. In the second round a then non-League Carlisle United were overcome convincingly 6-2 at Blundell Park, with Bob Blanthorne scoring five, which is still an individual F.A.Cup scoring record for the club. Crystal Palace were the next Cup visitors to Blundell Park, attracting a 9,000 crowd paying record receipts of £524-10s.-9d. Town won this match 1-0 with Blanthorne again scoring. So, the quarter-final (fourth) round was reached for the first time in the club's history and they were drawn away to a very strong Newcastle United. In a few short years a large gulf had opened between the fortunes of Newcastle and Town. Newcastle were reigning Football League Champions and riding high in the First Division, whereas Town were a struggling Second Division outfit with no money. Ten years earlier both clubs were competing at the same level, as two of the better sides in Division Two, but soon to gain promotion Newcastle survived, won trophies, and attracted large gates. Town, who had failed to hold on to their top division status, were further back than when they started their League Career. On Cup-tie day, 7 March 1908, the gulf showed, Newcastle winning easily 5-1, and went on to eventually lose in the final to Wolves.

Town won six of the following games after the Cup run but still only finished in 18th position from 20, and had to apply for re-election to the Football League, which was duly granted. No doubt credit was given to the Cup run, and their total of 30 points, compared to the 23 of Chesterfield and Lincoln City's 21.

31 players had been used during this campaign, 12 of them on less than five occasions each. The season had only produced one player who could be said to have come through with full credit - the outstanding centre-forward play of Bob Blanthorne. Birkenhead-born Blanthorne had played just two games for Liverpool, in April 1907, before joining Town as a 23-year-old. He then had to wait until the 10th match of the season to grab his chance, which he did with both hands, scoring both goals in a 2-2 draw with Blackpool; he only missed one game from-there-on-in. Blanthorne finished the season with 14 goals from 28 starts in the League, plus seven Cup goals. As previously related, Town struggled to keep their top goalscorers in this period, and Blanthorne's case was no different, for he was transferred to the north-east, to the great Newcastle United, but for a paltry £350. Blanthorne sadly badly broke his leg on his debut for the Magpies the following season and never played professionally again.

As was soon to be seen by the Blundell Parkites, many of the side who would run-out on to the pitch in the following September would be new faces. A large majority of the squad left in the summer including Martin Higgins (Bristol Rovers), who had made around 100 appearances for Town in the previous four years as a half-back.

1908/09

For the 1908/09 season Town changed club colours again, reverting back to the Chocolate and Blue quarters of old, plus long white shorts and black stockings with a Chocolate and Blue hoop on the turnovers - at least there was no fear of clashing colours with opponents!

New signings included Newcastle United reserve men Crosby Henderson and Harry Leonard, who no doubt moved in part exchange for Blanthorne, although neither had played at Football League level prior to signing. Bill Forster and Isaac Owens both transferred from Southern League Crystal Palace, making their Town debuts in the opening game of the season against Stockport County, which was won 3-0. The three goals were all scored by debutants, Owens, Harry Springthorpe from Northampton Town, and new left-winger Tommy Coxon who had signed from Stoke. New Captain Andy Davidson, from First Division Bury, made an impressive debut at centre-half by showing an excellent turn of speed.

After a promising start, things were soon to turn sour once again. That first day win was to be the only victory until mid-October, when Bradford were beaten 2-0 at Park Avenue, then Wolves visited Blundell Park and another victory was recorded, 3-0. But another lean spell followed until Christmas, despite 'Cockles' Appleyard coming 'home' from Oldham Athletic, but unfortunately he was not the same player that had left. Town won all three of their festive fixtures, before losing the following trio without scoring, the heaviest defeat being 7-0 at West Bromwich. A first round F.A.Cup exit, at home to Stockport County, was disappointing in this period, especially after the previous season's showing in the competition.

One particular player was attracting media attention. Goalkeeper Walter 'Buns' Scott was getting quite a reputation as a penalty stopper as Burnley found to their cost on the 13 February. In just six days, over New Year, Scott had saved four penalties in three matches; on 28 December versus Lincoln City in the Lincs. Cup Final, Town winning 2-1, twice at Stockport on New Years Day ensuring Town went home 1-0 winners, and another at West Bromwich the following day, although Town lost 7-0. The best was yet to come.

Town lost 2-0 at Burnley, but everyone who saw the game didn't go home talking about the result, they were talking about that Grimsby goalkeeper. Scott saved an amazing three of four penalties taken against him that day. In that game several records were established; the most penalties a team has been awarded in a match, the most penalties missed by a team in a match, and the most penalties saved by a 'keeper in one match. By May, Scott had saved an incredible 14 from 17 penalties! Despite his heroics it was the forwards at the other end of the pitch that caused the problems. Town finished below halfway, in 13th, scoring only 41 goals in 39 League and Cup matches. Although Coxon and Leonard played well throughout the season they only scored six goals each, but were the leading marksmen, and the other forwards failed to impress. Satterthwaite and Appleyard were the biggest culprits, the former - an inside-forward - scored a paltry two from 21, after signing from Woolwich Arsenal in November, and Appleyard did little better with two from 13. In the final five games, when four were won, Town were undefeated, and they pulled clear of the re-election zone.

Nine of the squad left, including the impressive Captain Andy Davidson who had marshalled his defence well. Davidson, a Scot, joined Southampton but soon returned to the Grimsby area to live, spending the rest of his days there. The final results were encouraging and produced a little hope for the following season.

1909/10

A mixture of injuries, inadequate signings, and in the end very unfortunate luck all conspired to 1909/10 as being one of the Mariners darkest of seasons. Never fielding a settled side was Town's biggest downfall, principally through injuries to key players such as 'Chopper' Lee and Albert Hatton. Davidson's replacements were poor, for these three players together made up the half-back line that had shown to be strong in front of Scott the previous season. In fact it was a great relief when, in October, Davidson returned after he failed to impress in his short stay at Southampton. Town only won once in 14 games before December, and had to wait until 27 December to name the first unchanged side of the season; 30 different players had been used in just the first 18 games! Two spells, one of 11 games (from September to November) and another of 10 (December to February) produced no victories at all. In the latter spell, Town once again exited the Cup at the first hurdle, a replica of the season before, losing 2-0 at home this time to Bristol Rovers. 'Buns' Scott was sold in January for a club record £750 to Everton, after being the only ever-present up until this time, and his understudy, Tommy Lonsdale, replaced him in goal.

From late February there was a marked improvement, when the final 12 games read: won 6, drawn 2, lost 4. five of the six victories were reasonably large 4-0, 4-2, 3-0, 5-3 and the last home game produced a 7-0 thrashing of Barnsley. At last Harry Leonard had found his scoring boots, netting 13 goals in his final 11 appearances, including hat-tricks against Glossop and Burnley. Leonard finished the season with a creditable total of 17 goals from 24 League appearances.

Despite the late rally, the Mariners still only finished a point above bottom placed Birmingham, and had to apply for re-election again. There was little worry from the club's officials as they arrived at the Imperial Hotel, London, for the League A.G.M. on 13 June. After all they had enjoyed a good couple of months and had just beaten 6th placed Barnsley 7-0 and also won 4-2 at Birmingham in March. Chesterfield had finished top of the Midland League and were looking to regain their Football League status, which had only been lost the season before, and the other contenders - Stoke, Hartlepools United and Huddersfield Town - all stood only a narrow chance of gaining enough votes.

It came as a great surprise when Huddersfield received 26 votes to Grimsby's 12; Birmingham polling most votes with 30. The situation was seen as even more ridiculous, for the Mariners reserve team had beaten Huddersfield's first team twice during the Midland League fixtures! The votes stood, and the Mariners were no longer members of the Football League, being force to drop down into the Midland League.

During the 1909/10 season Town had used a club record 34 different players, including reserve team Manager Harry Fletcher who played his last game for the club on 22 January at Clapton Orient, having made his Town debut some 17 years earlier. He finished his playing career with both club scoring and appearance records in the Football League - 273 appearances and 92 goals - plus the most F.A.Cup games for the club, 33, which record still exists.

1910/11

All change as the new season approached. Over half of the 34 players from the previous season had left, either during the campaign or offloaded in the summer. Town would be playing in the comparative humiliating surroundings of the Midland League, where a mixture of Football League Reserve sides and top non-League teams in the area made up the League. The Mariner's First XI took the place of the reserve team, which was scrapped for this season, having no League to play in, and this factor accounted for the huge staff clear-out during the close-season. The club changed playing strip once again, the idea of reverting to the quartered shirts a few seasons earlier having backfired, for it was believed that the First Division days would return with that earlier style and colours. This time the black and white vertical striped shirts, were introduced for the first time, colours in which the club are still proudly associated with, albeit in this first season they were accompanied with white shorts.

With no Reserve side the size of the squad was kept to a minimum. The team that played at Nottingham Forest Reserves on 1 September read; Lonsdale in goal; Sid Wheelhouse, with a new full-back partner in Tony Arrowsmith, a former miner, signed from Worksop Town; Tom Kelly (signed the previous summer from Denaby United) was joined in the half-back line by newcomers Jim Gordon who had played two games the previous season as an amateur, and Henderson a Scot from Bradford City. The new combination on the wings was Hobson from New Brompton on the right, and Worth from Rochdale on the left. Forwards Leonard and schoolteacher Tom Bell were joined by new man Jackson. This first game, to great relief, was won 1-0,. The first home game versus Barnsley Reserves was only drawn and the next game at Castleford was lost 2-0. The side had remained unchanged for the those three games, but the inclusion of 'Chopper' Lee and Harry Springthorpe for the next home match improved the side, and they beat a Leicester Fosse reserve team emphatically 8-1, with Leonard scoring five of the goals.

Confidence was high at the beginning of the season with the club full of determination to force the hand of the Football League members to allow them back in. But there was no room for complacency, for Town really needed to do well this season and appeared capable enough to impress sufficiently. Only one game was lost between the 8-1 victory and defeat at Barnsley Reserves on 27 December, this being at top of the table Hull City Reserves, 0-1, in mid-October. A run of six straight wins in November and December saw big victories over Mexborough (6-0) and Worksop Town (7-0). In that Mexborough win the recent signing from Norwich City - 'Ranji' Hubbard - made his debut at inside-right, scoring two of the goals.

Town were now established in the top three and were only denied the first spot due to Hull's second eleven and Wednesday's Reserves having played more games.

The good League form transferred over to the Cup in January when Croydon Common were thrashed 8-1, and Crewe Alexandra were beaten 5-1 on their own ground in round two. In the next round the Mariners lost to eventual F.A.Cup winners Bradford City.

In late March the more than impressive displays of Harry Leonard were enough for him to transfer to First Division Middlesbrough, having scored 28 goals in 28 games that season. In the final run-in local forwards Chris Young and Gus Huxford were introduced, with great success. April began with just 8 games to play and Town were well in contention for the Championship. During those remaining games the team was undefeated, beating top of the table Sheffield Wednesday Reserves 2-0 at Blundell Park on Good Friday in front of a 7,000 crowd. A point dropped at Rotherham Town meant Town had to produce decent results in the final two games. Worksop Town were again thrashed, this time 6-1 on their ground courtesy of a Hubbard hat-trick. The championship was clinched on the final day of the season at home to Rotherham County, when a Chris Young hat-trick, secured a 4-0 victory.

Harry Leonard

The club had to wait until the Football League A.G.M. on 29 May to see if their campaign for a return was successful. Finishing bottom of Division Two were the old enemy Lincoln City, and they received 17 votes to Grimsby Town's 18. The Mariners were back. In reflection the loss of Football League status had done the club little harm, and the small squad had coped well all season, whilst success had renewed interest in the club's fortunes. In contrast to the previous season the Mariners could boast four ever-presents - the full-back pairing of Wheelhouse and Arrowsmith, centre-half Gordon and winger Hobson.

1911/12

Grimsby Town entered the 1911/12 season with a great deal of optimism. Only 'Chopper' Lee (New Brompton), amateur Chris Young (Gainsborough Trinity) and Hobson departed in the summer. The nucleus of the squad had been kept with seven good acquisitions made in the close-season. Included in these were left-half Frank Martin (£85) from Hull City, and the club's first foreigner, the German born right-half Max Seeburg, who signed from Burnley. Prior to joining Burnley in 1910, Seeburg had spent his 'teens' in the Tottenham area of North London were he learned a trade as a Carpenter, and had been associated with Tottenham Hotspur when they entered the Football League in 1908. Staniforth of Bristol City was signed to replace Hobson on the right wing. Other new forwards included John Hodgkinson from Nelson, George Rampton from Walsall and Arthur 'Pecker' Mounteney from Preston North End. Mounteney was one of the rare breed of footballing cricketers, having played an impressive 144 First class matches for his home County of Leicestershire upon retiring in 1924.

The season started steadily against tougher opposition. A 0-0 draw with Wolves in the opening game was a good footing to build from, then a 2-0 victory at Leicester Fosse was achieved. The following three matches were drawn, the first defeat coming in the 6th game with a narrow 1-0 reversal at Nottingham Forest. Chelsea and Bristol City were beaten at Blundell Park. Chelsea were leading with just three minutes remaining, but very late goals from Huxford then a winner from Staniforth reversed the scoreline, although most of the 7,000 crowd had already gone home thinking Town had lost. New record signing Tommy Mayson, who had a hand in the Bristol victory on his debut, had been signed for £350 from Burnley in October. Mayson was introduced at inside-left with Mounteney and Hubbard also in the central positions. Mayson soon moved to the wing with impressive ease, after Albert Worth and his understudy Huxford were both injured in December. Experienced Hull City right-half George Browell was signed and came straight into the side in November, replacing the injured Seeburg. Town continued to accumulate points without really compiling a decent run to speak of.

14 October 1911: The Mariners take the field at Millfields, Clapton Orient's Ground (A 1-0 defeat was the result).

The first game of the New Year brought Leicester Fosse to Blundell Park, and the Mariners recorded their most emphatic win of the season with a 4-0 victory - but there was more to the match than just the scoreline. Fosse were 3-0 down when their players began to complain about the atrocious weather conditions, presumably in an attempt to have the match abandoned. The referee ignored the plea and two Leicester players left the field in disgust. Play continued and by the time the final whistle blew, they were left with only five players, the others deciding also to protest and sit out the remainder of the match!

Inside-forward 'Pip' Rippon was introduced in January, scoring the only goal of the game on his debut against Burnley. An impressive Mounteney hat-trick at Fulham on the final day, in a 3-1 away victory, secured the Mariners the 9th spot of 20 - the highest the club had finished for six years. Consistency of results proved a slight problem throughout the season but all-in-all not a bad rebirth. 'Ranji' Hubbard top scored with 14 goals, but he soon moved to Lincoln City. Again the side which was selected was in part unchanged, with mid-season signings Mayson and Browell fitting-in well, but unfortunately the latter retired injured in the summer.

1912/13

Replacements for the departures came in the form of Irish International right-half Billy Andrews from Glentoran and forwards Jock Quin and Birch, both signed from Eccles Borough. Quin replaced Hubbard at centre-forward, with Birch filling the position on the left wing left vacant by Worth moving to Luton Town, and Mayson reverted to his inside role.

A poor start was made, with the team not winning until the fourth game, 2-1 against Fulham. But good home form was consistent throughout the season, although too many games were drawn - winning 10, sharing the points on eight occasions, and losing only once, to Clapton Orient, in late November. In contrast the away form was generally poor. Apart from excellent results on their travels around New Year, with three consecutive away games won at Leeds City, Huddersfield Town and Fulham, Town struggled to gain points. Only two more victories on their travels, in the Spring, were recorded all season - ironically the best result was 3-1 at Clapton Orient, the only side to win at Blundell Park!

The defence was solid and the line-up rarely changed from Lonsdale in goal, full-backs Wheelhouse and Arrowsmith, and the half-back line of Andrews, Gordon and Martin. Mounteney moved south in December taking with him reserve outside-right Ashton, and Duncan, a Scottish winger, took over the duties as reserve cover, moving from Portsmouth in return. 'Pip' Rippon established himself in Mounteney's place, and he never missed a game from then on, finishing the season with 14 goals, one behind top scorer Mayson on 15.

Mayson had an unfortunate finish to the season when breaking his leg in the gallant 2-1 victory at Nottingham Forest, Town finishing the game with 10 men. An improved final position of 7th was attained.

1913/14

Only winger Fred Staniforth left the club of the regular first teamers in the summer, joining First Division Liverpool. Several new players were brought in to bolster the squad as fortunes improved. Of those, wingers Jack Scott and Jimmy Miller were both signed from Newcastle United's reserves for £50 each. Scott operated on the left and was the most experienced of the two, with a mere eight first team appearances in three years, opposed to Miller who made his senior debut with Grimsby. Miller failed to impress at Blundell Park, figuring in six early games of the season, then never to be seen again at Grimsby. During the war he signed for Everton, later playing League Football for several clubs, until 1926 with Luton Town aged 37.

Other inclusions were the return of Martin Spendiff from Millwall, in goal, displacing the unfortunate Lonsdale who later moved to West Ham United, Scot Dave Kenny came as a centre-forward with full-back Tom McKenna both from Barrow. Strangely both served Town better in different positions and later became partners in the half-back line the following season, with Kenny in the central role. Rochdale's inside-forward Alf Gregson was another to sign.

The Mariners began the campaign poorly despite some useful signings on paper. The only victory in the first seven games came in a 1-0 win over Wolves. Then followed three straight wins - the best run of the season - which stretched to the usual good form at Christmas. Including those consecutive victories, Town only lost three in 10. But scoring goals was becoming a problem. Will Rippon, brother of 'Pip', joined from Hamilton Academicals in October for a club record fee of £450. He performed well at centre-forward becoming the top scorer for the season with 12 goals in 23 starts, while 'Pip' scored nine goals from inside-right; the Rippons between them scored half of the paltry 42 goals for the season. A poor first half of 1914 saw only four wins and 11 losses, when the team scored in only one of the final eight games. Again Town's back six were solid with the problems being at the other end of the field, and a final place of 15th was disappointing. The last main event of the season saw top goalscorer Will Rippon move to Rotherham Town in July.

1914/15

Great Britain declared war on Germany on the 4 August 1914, just four weeks before the Football League fixtures were due to commence, on the first day in September. A meeting was called on 6 August, when the current affairs were discussed, with the war situation mentioned only briefly. It is thought that the League Committee were of the opinion that the war would be short-lived and everything would be back to normal in a few months, so there was no need for drastic measures so far as football was concerned. A percentage of funds generated by football was to be allocated towards the cost of war and the entertainment was allowed to continue to boost morale. If you were a Grimsby supporter the latter didn't work, for many locals joined the Navy and the football was far from entertaining, even at a cost of 2d. (1½p).

The Football League games began as scheduled with Town drawing 2-2 at home to Preston North End, which featured new signings, 'keeper Percy Summers (from Chesterfield Town) and speedy winger Tommy Spink (Rochdale) starring, but 'Pip' Rippon missed a penalty in a hotly contested game. In the return match at Preston just five days later, Town lost 3-0, and both Town's Frank Martin and Morley of Preston were dismissed for fighting, a feud believed to have been carried on from the opening day game. Home form was mediocre and on their travels it was very poor, with only one win during the campaign, surprisingly at promotion candidates Wolves on 3 October, with a 'Pip' Rippon goal. Only 12 goals were scored away from Blundell Park all season, with big losses at Woolwich Arsenal (5-0) and Bristol City (7-0) before New Year.

The New Year started well with a 4-0 win over Nottingham Forest, before the following Saturday when Northampton Town were the visitors in the F.A.Cup. For the fourth consecutive year the Mariners were knocked-out at this first round stage, losing 3-0 to their Southern League counterparts. Frank Martin among others received his marching-orders for the second occasion that season. Martin was dealt a hefty two month suspension.

As war was continuing, the first real sign of change for Grimsby Town as a club came with the results of the recruitment drive of the Army's 17th Middlesex Regiment - known as the Footballers Battalion. In February, Dave Chalmers, Alf Gregson, Kenny, Martin and Sid Wheelhouse all signed-up, with Percy Summers and Tom McKenna soon to follow, although all bar Chalmers and Gregson continued to figure in first team action until the end of the season.

On 20 February, Stockport County were well beaten with the largest win of the year, 6-1, aided with a George Rampton hat-trick and an excellent start when Billy Andrews scored after just 15 seconds (surely some kind of record for a defender), from a corner when Andrews had moved up-field. Good home wins were recorded over Woolwich Arsenal (1-0), and pleasingly Lincoln City were defeated 5-1, (with another Rampton trio). The 1-0 victory over Bury on Easter Monday proved to be Town's last win in Football League competition for the next four years, as in the summer the decision was taken to suspend Football League games until the end of the war. Grimsby had not performed well, adding to the problem of poor away form was a glut of dismissals and penalty misses, of the latter both Rippon and Wheelhouse were guilty. Rampton top scored with 18 goals, and Town finished 4th from bottom.

The Great War 1915-19

Despite the Football League being suspended, regionalised competitions were formed and the club continued to entertain the Grimsby public, although the F.A.Cup and County Cups were also suspended as was professionalism. Town entered into the Midland Section of the Wartime League and players representing the side were a mixture of local amateurs, plus soldiers and sailors who were based locally, which included many professionals attached to other clubs but who were allowed to make 'guest' appearances. Town were rarely able to call upon the services of their signed players regularly, only when they were based within travelling distance or on leave.

In the first game of the **1915/16** season, the Mariners entertained a Nottingham Forest team, which was as unrecognisable as Town's side, being made up of a similar mixture of personnel. Pip Rippon was the only Grimsby player to have appeared in the last game of the previous season, with Sid Wheelhouse and Ernie Whitchurch the only other members of the team from that earlier squad. Mariners of old, Albert Hatton, Nat Johnson, Chris Young, 'Toy' Coulbeck and Will Rippon returned to help their former club out, whilst Burnley's 'keeper Ronnie Sewell and the Manchester City left-back Pat McGuire 'guested'. Reserve winger Walsh made up the first wartime team. The Mariners drew 1-1 with a goal from Cleethorper Chris Young who had just returned home since his release from Burslem Port Vale.

On 3 November 1915, the S.S.Mercian was torpedoed and sank in the Mediterranean, on board was former Grimsby player Harry Springthorpe, who lost his life serving with the Lincolnshire Yeomanry.

26 games were played in the first part of the season from September until the end of February, Town finishing 2nd to bottom of the principle competition. During March and April, the team played 10 games against similar opposition in a Subsidiary Competition which they actually won. Regulars (using that term loosely), were Sewell in goal, McGuire who was serving with the 3rd Battalion of the Manchester Regiment, and full-back Frank Webster formerly of Chelsea.

The Manchester Regiment provided many of Town's 'guest' players during the war, being based in the town with H.M. Minesweepers and the Dublin Fusiliers. The half-back line saw the return of Billy Rushby, who had left the club a year earlier, Scot Alec Ormiston of Chelsea, and Grimsby's very own Whitchurch. Wingers were other ex-players Billy Hooper, whose home was in the town although he was serving with the Army Service Corps whom he had served before becoming a professional footballer, and Gus Huxford who had been appearing for Goole Town more recently. A combination of Coulbeck, Young and the Rippon brothers made-up the inside positions.

Will Rippon 'guested' from his club Rotherham Town, and Young scored 28 goals from 30 games, including five in the 7-1 win over Rotherham County. The 36 players to play for the club was a large number compared to previous seasons, but was nothing in comparison to the coming war years. In April 1916, 'keeper Percy Summers was badly wounded in the hand and stomach by a grenade. Town winger and Grimbarian Ralph Thompson was killed on 1 July 1916 whilst serving with the Lincoln 'Chums'- the 10th Battalion of the Lincolnshire Regiment - and soon to follow, on 18 September, was the popular full-back Sid Wheelhouse killed in action whilst with the Footballers Battalion in France.

The start of the **1916/17** season saw Sewell, Webster and Ormiston still making regular guest appearances for the club until December. Former York City goalkeeper Sutcliffe, eventually took over from Sewell, but not before the unusual circumstance of Trainer 'Tee' Holden keeping goal at Park Avenue, Bradford on 18 November. Sewell unexpectedly couldn't make the game, which needless to say the Mariners lost, with the emergency 'keeper picking the ball out of the net no less than nine times. Sewell had played 44 times for the Mariners, had won a Cup medal with Burnley in 1914, and went on to gain a single England cap in 1924.

The trend of borrowing players on the day of the match was becoming more regular for away matches. When Town played at Barnsley on the first day of the season, Phil Bratley reported to the Oakwell Ground hopeful of being selected to play. Play he did, but as a Mariner against his own club, when Town arrived short. Likewise Sheffield United's Fred Charles played for Grimsby in the following away game at Bramall Lane, and actually scored against his regular team-mates. There was much confusion in these days of war so far as team planning was concerned. The team selectors were often unaware of a player's availability until sometimes just before kick-off. Even if players were declared available and had to travel independently from where they were stationed, unpredictable rail links often proved a downfall to them reaching a match on time.

The reverse also regularly occurred, for if a player was not attached to a club or served as a club reserve, he would often attend a game carrying his boots in the knowledge that his services may be called upon. One instance of this practice was when locals 'Punch' Padley and Colin Stainsby attended a game at Blundell Park on 6 January 1917, and both represented visitors Leicester that day aiding Fosse to win 3-1, with Padley scoring one of the goals.

Another example was a game played at Birmingham on 3 May 1917. Goalkeeper Sutcliffe successfully made the journey to St.Andrews, along with former Town player Jack Butler who had been playing regularly during 1916/17. But the nine other players had to be poached from the touch-line. Five from Aston Villa and several top amateur players from the Midlands area were drafted in to the Grimsby side. In fact the only player attached to Grimsby Town was forward George Rampton, having played very few games for Town during the war due to him returning to live in Walsall! Also towards the end of this season it is recorded that the Mariners fielded father Bill and son Jack Butler in the same team in six games, and in five of those games the Rippon brothers also appeared together. Jack Butler had been a Town player 10 years earlier, before more recently playing for Plymouth Argyle. Jack was aged 31, so his father at this time, could have quite possibly been in his fifties!

On 31 March, Town entertained a Chesterfield side which won 3-2. The visitors team contained three of Grimsby's reserves, including Alf Cooper Junior, son of the Mariners Chairman. The club remained in a low position in both competitions all season, for it was only the lucky clubs who could field settled sides that could give any true consistency in their performances.

1917/18 continued in the same vein, with Town being the last club in the country to gain their first point, a draw against Sheffield United on the 20 October. Results improved slightly, but with many different players representing the club success on the field was unlikely. An amazing 93 different players were used during the season, and only 24 goals were scored in the Principle Competition, which included losses at Notts County (8-0) and Hull City (7-1) in consecutive matches over Christmas. Surprisingly though, for the second time, the six game subsidiary competition was won, which was competed against Lincoln City, Gainsborough Trinity and Hull City. Again the trip to Birmingham proved to be the fixture which stood out. Town's Dave Kenny made a rare appearance on leave from the Footballers Battalion, and he was the only signed Grimsby player sharing the field with unfamiliar team-mates. West Bromwich and England full-back Jesse Pennington was the Grimsby captain for the day, when the Mariners won 1-0, despite fielding several of the Birmingham reserve side.

The first day of the **1918/19** season saw the Mariners travel to Coventry City, and in an amazing game Town lost 4-7. With the Great War concluding in November 1918, several players returned; Frank Martin, Dave Kenny and Alf Thompson reporting back safely from the war, with 'keepers Martin Spendiff and Percy Summers both making an appearance before the season's end. Grimsby finished second from bottom of the Principal League, and in the summer months there was a real worry that their Football League status would be lost due to poor displays throughout the war.

192 different players had been used in the last four seasons, and they scored 191 goals in 142 matches. Many of these players only played at most a couple of games for the Mariners, and also this period tragically marked the end of Ralph Thompson and Sid Wheelhouse's lives. The years to come would be ones of change for Great Britain and Grimsby Town Football Club. For many these were 'Lost Years', and now it was time for a change for the better........... but not immediately.

Chapter Four

CHANGE FOR  THE BETTER

1919 - 1928

1919/20

The return of peace-time Football to Blundell Park was not to be a simple transition. On the plus side the Mariners maintained their Second Division status, but on the minus side no players had been signed from which to choose a team. Trial matches were arranged in the summer months and players who impressed were given contracts. Martin Spendiff, Dave Kenny, Ernie Whitchurch, Tommy Spink and Gus Huxford were all re-engaged for the 1919/20 season, with 'Pip' Rippon and Frank Martin joining their old team-mates after demobilisation from the Army in October. Newly signed players included utility man Wally Battiste (Shirebrook), Sid Dawson (Northampton Town), Harry Storer (Eastwood) and locals Ernie Gray and Bill Broom all of whom had played for the Mariners in the war. Right-back Grant McEachran (Barrow) was joined by winger Albert Smith from Rochdale, plus Clark and Martin Golightly, both from Durham City, as the other new signings.

The Football League had decided to begin the season in August from now and in the future, and to play home and away games against the same opposition within a week of each other. The Division was now made up of 22 teams playing 42 games. The new clubs in Division Two were Tottenham Hotspur who had been voted out of Division One after they finished bottom in 1915, and new boys Coventry City, Rotherham County, South Shields and West Ham United, plus the reinstated Stoke.

The new era started in the worst possible fashion. Town's first game was at home to Stockport County, and they found themselves 1-0 down after about 30 seconds, probably the worst start to a season ever. They went on to lose the game 3-0. In the next game Wolves brushed Town aside comfortably with a 6-1 win at Molineaux. Stockport were then beaten on their own Edgeley Park, for Grimsby's first win of the season, with a brace from the young and impressive Harry Storer, but new boys West Ham and Rotherham County both completed the double over the Mariners by mid-November. By this time, two new acquisitions had been captured from the Leeds City auction- George Affleck (for a club record £500) and Arthur Wainwright (£200). Leeds were expelled from the Football League on 13 October 1919 for allegedly paying their players illegal payments during the war. As Leeds would not produce their accounts for the Committee's inspection their records were expunged and after eight games, Port Vale continued playing Leeds' fixtures.

In December and January a spell of 10 consecutive games without a win, including an F.A.Cup exit at home to Bristol City in the inaugural round was recorded. Two 1-0 victories against Nottingham Forest and Barnsley showed a flicker of hope, but the poor form continued. Despite the final four home matches being won it was a case of too little too late. To bolster the defence, former keeper 'Buns' Scott (who returned from Worksop) and mid-season newcomers Affleck plus right-half Wilf Gillow, were introducted.

Top Scorer - Harry Storer

Sid Dawson

Albert Smith - from Rochdale

But it was in the forward line where the Mariners failed. The inside-forwards squandered dozens of good chances during the season, on many occasions Town outplaying their opponents but not winning through poor finishing. Storer top scored with 12, from a total of 34 goals, an unfortunate club record for a Football League season. The highest position the Mariners had achieved was just 17th, for one week. Town finished in bottom place, despite beating Champions 'Spurs in April. Once again the club had to apply for re-election, arguably this had been Grimsby Town's worst season to date.

1920/21

At the June Football League A.G.M. the fate of Grimsby Town was once again out of their own control. Town, second from bottom Lincoln City, Cardiff City, and the newly formed Leeds United were all in contention for two places. Newcomers Cardiff and Leeds were voted in, whilst Lincoln and, once again, Grimsby were out. But the Mariners were soon after provided with a lifeline. The Committee of the Southern League had been campaigning for a number of years to be recognised as members of the Football League, and thankfully for Town their admission was accepted too, for Grimsby were invited to take the final available place through gaining more votes than Lincoln in the failed re-election campaign. The Southern League's quality was thought to be as high as the Second Division around this time, so Town were not really expected to challenge for Promotion.

(Above) record-signing George Affleck, and (below) Frank Martin who served Town from 1911- 21, captaining the side during WW1.

So for the 1920/21 season Grimsby found themselves in the unfamiliar surroundings of the newly formed Third Division. In preparation for the new season a team Manager would be appointed for the first time. Until this point in time a selection committee of club Directors had picked the playing side and negotiated transfer dealings, assisted by the footballing knowledge of the Trainer, but this system was considered somewhat dated in the early 1920's, and the club's supporters voiced their wishes for a Manager. The first man to be honoured with the title of 'Grimsby Town Manager' was former Welsh International and Birmingham schoolteacher, Haydn Price.

Price had grown-up in the Glamorgan village of Mardy, firstly playing for the village side before signing for Cardiff City, then Aberdare Athletic, Aston Villa, Burton United, Wrexham, Leeds City and Shrewsbury Town. He won 5 full caps for Wales, then became secretary for Walsall before returning to Wales to manage Mid-Rhondda. He arrived at Blundell Park in July 1920 bringing with him a former Villa team-mate, the veteran England International Joe Bache, as captain and Player/coach from Mid-Rhondda.

Other players moving from Rhondda were 'keeper Harry Moody, centre-half Jimmy Carmichael, Dai Collier and later Albert Irvine, in all costing a combined sum of £200. Other new signings were another goalkeeper, Whalley, plus Tom Broome (both from Gillows old club Preston North End), Frank Smith from Swansea Town, and Irish International forward Jimmy Macauley from Leicester.

The first game of the season was played at Blundell Park against Northampton Town (who were playing their first Football League game), on 28 August 1920. Town won 2-0 with both goals scored by debutant Macauley in front of a 10,954 attendance paying a record £681-0s.-5d. in gate money. The following game was also won, 1-0 against Southend United, with 40-year-old captain Bache scoring his only goal for the Mariners. Following three consecutive defeats, Town found that they were not going to find this League as easy as first thought. Only three more wins and six defeats saw the abrupt end of Price. The first Manager, having been appointed only in the Summer, by November and 15 games later he resigned his post! Price wasn't happy with the interference by the board on team selections.

Again the board took control of team affairs, until March, when former Lincoln City half-back and Manager, Scot, George Fraser took over in the hot-seat. In the meantime, the Hull City centre-half Charlie Deacey was signed for a club record £750.

Five consecutive draws were recorded in the League over the festive period with Town progressing in the F.A.Cup by beating Kettering Town and Norwich City. A third round tie at home to Southampton on 29 January drew a record crowd of 14,025 to Blundell Park, with new record gate receipts of £1,294 being paid. Town lost 3-1 to the top of the (Third Division) table Southampton.

Fraser took charge in March but the form failed to improve, not helped by the sale of excellent prospect Harry Storer who was sold for a club record £4,500 to Derby County, which shattered the previous record of just £750 and kept the club financially solvent. Storer went on to play for England and became a successful Manager with Coventry City, Birmingham and later Derby County. Storer was one of the few sparks of enjoyment in this season of change for the club. Another point of note in February concerned Dai Collier who was called up for his only Welsh Cap, when he appeared against Scotland; his side lost 2-1, but he scored his country's goal. Town finished a disappointing 13th, although on reflection this was seen as a great improvement on the previous campaign. The close season brought change again.

1921/22

Although the Mariners had performed well enough to maintain their Football League status they found themselves changing Divisions once more. Towards the end of the 1920/21 season, the final selections for another Division Three - North - was formed. Grimsby shifted from the newly titled Third Division South to the more accessible Northern Section. The long rail journeys had done Town no favours on their travels down South the previous season, when they gained few points.

Ashington were the first opponents on the opening day, Town losing 1-0 away at Portland Park - the most northern geographical point at which the club had appeared at that time, but only had to wait a week for revenge, the Mariners winning 6-1 in the first game of the season at Blundell Park. Young Scot Jock Miller, scored a hat-trick on his home debut, after his close-season signing from Greenock Morton. The side was unchanged for the first four games with only Miller not appearing for the club previously. Moody in goal; full-backs Affleck and McEachran; halves Gillow, Captain Deacey and Jack Bradford; wingers Spink and Albert Smith; inside-men George Morrall and former back Carmichael supporting centre-forward Miller. A disappointing 7-1 thrashing came at Southport in October, then in the following set of matches the double was recorded over eventual Champions Stockport County, and also Rochdale, in consecutive games. Stockport went on to lose only six matches all season - two against Town. By the turn of the year form had begun to pick-up.

Hat-trick hero Jock Miller

One man deserves to be mentioned at this stage. Jimmy Carmichael was brought to the club by previous Manager Haydn Price as a centre-half, where he played consistently missing only one game of the first 22 played in 1920/21, but his form , although fair, was far from eyecatching. After Price departed, Carmichael's form dropped, and he was replaced by record signing Deacey in the middle of defence. Carmichael did not figure in first team action again until new boss George Fraser played him at inside-right for the final three games. He scored a goal, performed well and gained himself another year's contract with the club, which had seemed unlikely until the experiment of moving him into the forward line.

The new season began with Carmichael installed at inside-right from the outset, and he scored eight goals in 15 games. But not until he moved into the centre-forward position for the Tufnell Park Cup replay in December did he really find the goal trail. In the next game he scored all four in a 4-1 victory versus Halifax Town. Miller had moved to inside-left with great success and both continued to score goals freely.

With a successful combination up front, Town won 12 of 13 games in the League from January to late April, which placed them in contention for the Championship, but in the end it was a case of the run arriving too late in the season to catch Stockport. Town finished 3rd, level on points with runners-up Darlington who had a better goal average. With only the Champions of the League being promoted to Division Two the Mariners were unfortunate to miss out, despite keeping their undefeated home form intact all season.

Carmichael however had placed his name in club folklore. He finished the season with 37 League goals in as many games, plus one in the F.A.Cup and another in the County Cup. The 37 League goals was the highest scored by any individual in the country that season, which also set a new club seasonal record and established a Divisional record for the Northern Section. He scored 11 goals within six consecutive games in January and February, and recorded his second four of the season against Barrow. During this time Miller also played well, and he gained another hat-trick in the 5-2 win over Durham City, finishing the season with 13 League goals. Another bright spark was the emergence of 20-year-old left-back and former miner Billy Felton, who had been signed from Jarrow the previous season. The reserves also had a good campaign , finishing runners-up in the Midland League, their best showing to date, with local Tommy Talks scoring 24 goals.

Match action in 1922: The roof was changed and the stand extended towards the Cleethorpes End in 1931.

1922/23

The nucleus of the squad had been re-signed for the new season with no major newcomers, relying instead on the further influx of young talent from the footballing hotbed of the north-east. Squad players Cook, Graver and the most successful Frank McKenna were signed from such amateur circles, joining Felton, Joe Laws and Casson, having progressed to the first team after making previous similar moves from the shipyards and coal mining areas of the Tyne and Durham.

The Mariners found the quality of the opposition in the Northern Section was not as good as the Southern Section. Even in those days Town were known for their pretty approach play and had the reputation as the best footballing side in this section, which was on occasions their downfall as the majority of the northern clubs favoured the more robust kick and rush tactics.

An excellent start to the season started with a 4-0 home victory over Wrexham, with the Scottish forward connection, Carmichael and Miller, continuing where they had left off the previous campaign and scoring a brace apiece to defeat the Welsh team. Undefeated for the first five games the momentum had continued and confidence was high, indeed Town were top of the table in these early stages. Then a spell of indifferent form came before losing all four games played in November.

In fact Town only won once more before February, including an early exit from the F.A.Cup at home to Midland Leaguers Worksop Town. The win though was worthy of note as it was a crushing 7-1 demolition of Accrington Stanley, who were to finish well above Town in the final positions. Inside-right Frank McKenna scored a hat-trick in this Christmas morning game. Town then began to improve once more towards the end of the season. Carmichael scored four in the 7-4 victory over Ashington in late February, which was followed by away wins at Darlington and Lincoln City in April. The Imps were beaten again the following Saturday with a McKenna goal, when they visited Blundell Park.

Town finished a disappointing 14th; so where did it all go wrong? The reason is difficult to detect, although the support play of the right hand side of attack was of poorer quality than the previous season. The spaces left by the departure of Spink (Worksop) and Morrall (Redditch) were not filled adequately. Kirsopp and Ritchie were both signed from Bury to fill these positions but their expected good understanding was not forthcoming. Again scoring goals was not a problem, yet reports of the day suggest many more should have been taken than the 55 recorded.

Carmichael again excelled, becoming club and Divisional top goalscorer for the second consecutive season, finishing with a total of 23 in the League, supported well by Miller with 11. Another point of note was the January sale of Felton, who moved to Sheffield Wednesday for £1,500, went on to play for England in 1925, and achieved regular First Division football with Wednesday, Manchester City and 'Spurs.

1923/24

The board were not happy with the performances during the previous season, and personnel were changed in erratic fashion. 11 players left in May replaced by a new eleven by August. The first few games showed little progress with one win from the first four games, Bradford Park Avenue being defeated at Blundell Park by a couple of Miller goals. The new men who appeared in the inaugural games were right-back Jack Ackroyd, signed from Exeter City, Harry Leddy and Billy Marshall (both from Chesterfield), and wingers Flanaghan plus Honeyman who arrived from Maidstone United. Inside-right Doug Thomson was captured from Aberdeen, with Wilf Gillow returning to the club for a second spell from Lancaster Town.

Of these Marshall and Gillow were to prove the most influential. Form was inconsistent with only one of the first six home games won by November, on the other side of the coin, two 3-1 away wins were recorded in September at Halifax Town and ancient rivals Lincoln City - with Carmichael scoring all three - at Sincil Bank. Throughout the campaign only Carmichael found the net with any regularity.

Wilf Gallow, who returned, and soon became Player/manager.

Nine games without a win ended in March with a single goal victory against highflyers Rochdale. In this spell Town had been knocked-out of the Cup at Exeter. During March, came also the loss of Miller to Manchester United, Jack Bradford to eventual Northern Champions Wolves, and the not surprising resignation of George Fraser. It was a well known fact that the Manager had suffered the same interferences that Price had endured regarding team selection and squad strengthening. He at least left the club with credit for the transformation of Carmichael's fortunes. Carmichael again reached 20 goals for the season in the League when Town finished in mid-table at 11th. Other successes were the progression of 20-year-old Fred Hilton at centre-half and 19-year-old back Charlie Wilson. Wilson was from Cleethorpes and had earlier captained Grimsby Boys. Flying winger Marshall was a success on the left-wing and goalkeeper Jock Archibald became an ever-present after making his debut in October, after signing from Newcastle United Reserves in the summer. Incidentally this was the season Town first wore Black shorts with striped shirts.

1924/25

In June 1924 the board made the brave decision to make player Wilf Gillow the first team Manager, and with his playing contract also renewed this made him the first Player/manager in the Club's history. The season started in unspectacular fashion with a 2-0 home loss to a strong Darlington side, whom by May were to be crowned Champions. Good wins away at Park Avenue (Bradford) and at Accrington Stanley mirrored the start of the previous season with poor home form. Only the third home win of the campaign came, against Walsall, on Christmas Day. Town were at the foot of the table when a string of wins in January, losing only one in seven, lifted them, only to lose the next four straight games by early March.

Then seven consecutive games were unbeaten, including five wins and two draws, which saw the Mariners rise to mid-table and away from the re-election zone. Town finished 12th, with definite signs of improvement in the Spring. During these matches Jimmy Carmichael etched his name further into the annuls of Grimsby Town's history, when scoring his 93rd League goal for the Mariners at Barrow on 7 March, thereby breaking Harry Fletcher's record. Carmichael, the following month, became the first forward to score 100 League goals for the club, when scoring the third of his hat-trick in the final home game of the season in the 4-0 win against Wigan Borough.

This season also saw the initial introduction of Joe Cooper and young forward Joe Robson. Joe Cooper was a Schoolteacher during the week and creative inside-forward come the weekend. He was signed from First Division Notts County in September 1924 for £1,000, making his Town debut versus Chesterfield - the Derbyshireman's first club - in the scoreless draw at the end of that month. Despite combining teaching and playing, Cooper came to Grimsby as an experienced 25-year-old with plenty of games under his belt with his previous clubs. Robson on the other hand was introduced as a raw centre-forward, small in stature but tough and fast. He came to Grimsby, his first professional club, after scoring over 200 goals in amateur leagues in his native Gateshead, and would certainly be one to watch in the future. In their only seasons as Mariners, half backs Bob Coverdale and Dick 'Rusty' Field gained credit.

1925/26

With improved form during the latter part of the past season, it was hoped that Town could achieve great things this campaign, providing the strong-looking squad could stay injury free, a downfall of the previous campaign.

Improvements to Blundell Park were carried out before and during this season. The Abbey Park stand was replaced by a new wooden terraced stand with a roof. This stand became the Barrett Stand (named after Alderman Frank Barrett who donated funds for the new structure). Both open corners either side of the Hazle Grove Stand (Cleethorpes End) received new timber terracing also. Yet all this work was undertaken while the club was still leasing the Park.

Doncaster Rovers were beaten 3-0, Blundell Park's visitors for the first game in August, and a 5-1 thrashing of Walsall followed a few days later, with McKenna scoring a hat-trick. A tremendous start to what turned out to be a memorable season. Carmichael had added to his record haul by scoring in all of the clubs first six games, that sixth match being an emphatic 8-0 win over Tranmere Rovers on 1 October, with Joe Cooper scoring a hat-trick. Continuing to gain wins at home and the odd point away, Town hit a sticky patch around November, when only one game was won in six, including two bad losses, 1-4 at both Lincoln City and Wrexham, within the space of a fortnight.

This spell was convincingly ended with six straight wins in December and January. The inexperienced Joe Robson hit the goal trail claiming two hat-tricks in a week, with 4-1 wins at New Brighton (in only Robson's second game of the season), then a 3-0 victory over leaders Bradford Park Avenue on Christmas Day. The leaders were also beaten the following day 1-0 by Town at Park Avenue, and these precious four points gained in 48 hours proved to be the turning point of the season.

Local man Charlie Wilson.

The fine form continued into the New Year when the only blemishes came with a third round Cup exit at First Division Birmingham in January, and a disappointing 5-2 reversal at fellow Championship contenders Rochdale in February. Undefeated in March, Easter approached with challengers Chesterfield visiting on Good Friday. Town won 1-0 with a Marshall goal (against his former colleagues), scored in the opening minute, in front of a record Blundell Park who saw the Mariners reach top spot. In fact due to the speed of the strike and the size of the crowd many supporters actually missed the goal! Ashington were beaten 3-1 the following day, the only blot coming on Easter Monday when Town crashed 2-0 at Saltergate. With just five games remaining Town had a tricky run-in as three were away. But bottom of the table Barrow were swept aside 3-0 as were Nelson. A re-arranged game at Doncaster was successful, resulting in a 4-1 win, but only a draw was earned at Crewe.

The final and deciding game came on May Day with the visitors being New Brighton, whilst closest rivals Bradford were at home to Wigan Borough. Town had to win to become Champions, or rely on Bradford losing. New Brighton 'keeper, Mehaffy had not read the script and the game entered the 75th minute goalless, with the visiting custodian having stopped everything that Town threw at him. Then Carmichael latched onto a loose ball in the box and scored his 33rd goal of the season to send the crowd into ecstasy. The Blundell Parkites new if Town could hang-on to victory the Championship was theirs, and hang-on they did.

The season was a success for many reasons. Firstly Manager Wilf Gillow decided to retire from playing at the season's outset to concentrate on the management side. Some excellent new players were drafted in during the summer, such as Captain Jack Hardy, who was salvaged from Derby County's reserves, left-back Hughie Jacobson (Blyth Spartans), half-back John Pugsley from his native Cardiff, right wingers Jackie Foster (Halifax Town) then Charlie Devan (South Shields). If the side did suffer injuries the reserve replacements were the strongest the club had ever had.

Charlie Wrack was brought in as cover, as was Joe Robson, neither looking out of place in the first team and both unfortunate to have their appearances restricted due to the form of their seniors. The November injury to regular right-back Harry Arch was overcome with the acquisition of right-half Fred McLachlan from Coventry City, which resulted in Charlie Wilson moving to the full-back position with great ease.

As far as honours and records go, many fine achievements were registered for the first time in 1925/26. The reserve side captured both the Midland Combination League and Cup; a record number of 61 points for a season was set, Town being undefeated at home, and only dropping one point to Wigan Borough; just eight goals were conceded at Blundell Park. Attendances were the highest they had ever been, with an average gate of 9,418. League record gate receipts were established three times during the season, in October v Rochdale when they were top of the table (£733-14s.-1d.), then on Christmas Day when Bradford were in pole position (£857-7s.-9d.). The Good Friday game against Chesterfield attracted a record attendance of 16,086 paying another new record £1,065. (Although none of these gate receipts surpassed the record figure received for the Cup game in the 1920/21 season). The future now looked bright.

1926/27

Although the club and the local area were on a high, the 1926/27 season was seen as one in which the Mariners must consolidate, and the priority was to avoid slipping back into the Northern Section rather than dreaming of a quick return to the top flight. The six new players who were signed in the summer were only squad strengtheners rather than stars.

The season began with the same starting line-up that clinched the title the previous May. But early injuries to both Wilson and McKenna, meant new signing Cec Harris from Aston Villa filled-in for Wilson, and 'Gladys' Cooper swapped to inside-left in McKenna's absence. Bill Gardner was the reserve inside-right. Joe Cooper adopted the nickname 'Gladys' as he was *"very delicate and caring with the ball."*

The campaign opened disappointingly and Town struggled to find their feet in this higher class environment. On the first day of the season the worst luck was had at Barnsley. Right-back Charlie Wilson was injured in the first half and failed to appear after the half time interval, to make things worse Frank McKenna also left the field later in the game, Town eventually lost 2-1, with nine men. A good away win at Darlington in the fifth game came as a relief, but the first home victory didn't arrive until 2 October when Fulham were beaten 2-0.

Good support had continued and the record attendance had been broken again in only the second home game when Manchester City visited Cleethorpes. The large crowd were attracted by the presentation of the Championship Shield and medals to the Mariners, plus no doubt the quality of the opposition. City had just been relegated from the First Division and were to prove one of the strongest sides in the Division. Town managed a 2-2 draw, Carmichael equalising in the final minutes, in front of 16,559.

The Fulham success was only a flash in the pan as Town failed to win in any of the following seven League games, including a 6-1 thrashing at Port Vale. However, steady progress was made in the Cup competition, when home ties against Halifax Town and York City were won, which placed the side in the third round. Four straight wins, including the 2nd round Cup victory, were enjoyed in December which lifted the hopes of the supporters. One game of note in this spell was the 0-0 draw with Chelsea. Chelsea were awarded a penalty from which they 'scored', but as the ball firmly struck the rear stanchion the referee waved play-on thinking the ball had rebounded off the post, to much annoyance from the Londoners! Later in the game Chelsea had a player dismissed, and Town gained a point which shouldn't have been.

Grimsby were unfortunate with injuries all season, Joe Robson grasping his chance with both hands as hero of the terraces when Carmichael was not fit. A new inside-right was signed from Rotherham United in November, and he went straight into the side, scoring on his debut, with town progressing on to win his first three games. The player, Jackie Bestall, was a diminutive character, standing at only 5'-5''and weighing around 9st. But he became a giant of talent in the years to come. In 1926/27 he began to show his tremendous array of skills and endeared himself to the Blundell Park faithful; they knew that here was a special 'gem'.

Despite Town having the best squad for years, the poor results continued. The Mariners lost at Blackpool 6-2 on 27 December, and a run of nine games saw only a single point gained and a Cup exit. The biggest point of concern was the amount of goals being leaked, 21 being conceded in just four games in February. Drastic measures were taken and things improved in the short term.

Goalkeeper Jock Archibald was made the scapegoat, with a new centre-half signed from Birmingham the previous month, Billy Hunter. Both were dropped, Archibald never to play for the first team again. This was a sad end to the 'keeper's Town career as he had played well in the majority of his 100 plus games for the club. Archibald was one of nine players placed on the transfer list after the 5-2 home defeat to Oldham Athletic, and this proved to be the final straw as this setback was the fourth consecutive heavy home loss.

A 5-0 away win immediately followed at Fulham, with stand-in Joe Robson scoring his second hat-trick in 10 days. Home fans were treated to a rare 5-2 victory in the next against Preston North End, and a very pleasing 3-2 win, over the Humber was recorded in Hull. Results at last began to turn around, as the defence had plugged the leaks, and a few points were being picked-up here and there, before safety was secured with a few games to spare. The loyal supporters were rewarded with a final day 6-0 victory against Wolves, when Robson scored four, taking his tally to 24 goals in just 26 League appearances. He had finally claimed the centre-forward spot and made it his own. Carmichael who had struggled with injuries scored 11.

Town finished 17th in the table, after what had been an unsettled season. Manager Gillows changes in February saw Hardy (Oldham) leave and several new men brought in. Goalkeeper Bill Cowell was signed from Derby County, replacing Archibald. Meanwhile Charlie Wilson returned from injury and Charlie Wrack performed excellently when given his opportunity at centre-half. The inspired signing of Bestall before Christmas was followed by the capture of Sunderland attackers Jack Prior and Steve Coglin. Both were class acts who had struggled to gain regular places in a Sunderland side that was at that time one of the best in the land. Coglin had actually scored seven goals in 12 Division One matches for Sunderland that season, including a hat-trick in October. Strangely, neither player appeared to have commanded a transfer fee.

A whole host of players departed in the end of season clear-out. Championship regulars McLachlan (Bury), Pugsley (Bristol City), McKenna and Devan (both Fulham), plus Jimmy Carmichael (Worksop Town). Carmichael left after becoming a goalscoring legend. He had scored a record 137 League goals for the Mariners, including three fours and four threes in 227 starts. He became the first of the prolific strikers that were to grace Blundell Park in future years, spending time with understudy Joe Robson and teaching him the tricks of his trade. He was awarded a Testimonial match towards the end of the Championship season, and after hanging-up his boots he returned to live in Grimsby, where he worked on the docks.

Support at the gate increased again, with a record attendance of 18,040 for the 1-0 Reading defeat in late April, and the average in the League saw a rise of 3,000 to 12,556.

1927/28

Good news came on 13 July 1927, when it was announced that Grimsby Town Football Club had bought their leased Blundell Park Ground. This was a certain sign of assurance for the fans, proving the Club's Directors were moving towards building for the future. Alderman Barrett had raised funds for the purchase and made a reasonable donation, but ultimately it was the supporters who bought their home.

New half-backs arrived in Peter Cowper (West Ham), Billy Powell (Sheffield Wednesday), Jim Calderwood and the return of local 'Baggy' Coupland (both from Manchester City). Prior and Marshall were wingers, with Bestall and Coglin supporting Joe Robson up-front. Unfortunately Joe Cooper failed to maintain his first team place in such a strong forward line and became first reserve.

Despite a strong squad, the season started poorly with the first win of the campaign not arriving until 15 October, but it came in style with a 1-0 victory at local rivals Hull City. The first home win followed during the following week with a 3-2 victory over Leeds United. The club took a nine game run into December, losing only once. Gus Meikle, a summer signing from Portsmouth, deputised for the injured Prior on the right in this spell. Any injuries to the backs was usually covered by the versatile Calderwood.

A 2-1 home defeat to Swansea Town ended the sequence, but the following game, on Boxing Day, attracted a record Blundell Park crowd of 18,630 (paying a record £1,248 receipts) to see highflying visitors Chelsea. The game ended 1-1 with a Coglin penalty scored for Town. Two excellent away wins over the New Year were enjoyed, Clapton Orient being beaten 2-1, and Blackpool - an amazing 5-4 victory - with Bestall netting four himself, and reserve centre-forward Ben Twell getting the other.

But the following sequence of results were a crushing blow. West Brom won 6-0 at Blundell Park, followed by a 0-4 Cup exit at Reading, then a visit to Southampton proved fruitless with a 5-0 defeat; 15 goals conceded in just three games. Again Gillow showed he was not one to stand for poor performances and wholesale changes were made for the 1-0 win against Notts County in the next game on 11 February. Goalkeeper Cowell made way for reserve custodian Tommy Read, who had waited since the summer to make his Mariners debut. Calderwood at right-back was dropped for Harris, Robson returned from injury as did Wilson, and Cooper was reinstated at Coglins expense.

Stalwart Jackie Bestall, later to appear for the Football League XI

Apart from the initial match the gamble failed, for only four more games were won, and the final three of the season were lost. However, in those final games Robson's goalscoring touch returned in abundance, scoring 13 in the final eight games including a hat-trick at Barnsley in a 4-1 win, then on the final day he netted the quickest hat-trick ever seen at Blundell Park with three in three-and-a-half minutes; but opponents Preston North End still ran-out 6-4 winners! Robson top-scored with 26, Coglin came next with 11, and Bestall managed 10, during the season when Town were finally placed 11th in the table. Summer signings Coupland (Caernarvon Town), Cowell (Millwall) and Cowper (Lancaster Town) all departed in May.

In almost 10 years since the end of the Great War, the club had seen many changes. The Football League's confusing Divisional reconstruction and the playing on many different Grounds against varied opponents, team selections by team Managers, and the development of Blundell Park. Although the Mariners only finished in mid-table during 1927/28, the best years were just on the horizon, and the changes that were to be made would be for the better.

Chapter Five

1928 - 1939

1928/29

There were no clues to suggest that this Golden Anniversary season was going to be any different to the previous two years, and during pre-season, plus early in the season, there was nothing special to report. It was known that the Mariners had a good team but in the past, if injuries struck, form suffered.

Chelsea right-half, Jock Priestley was the only new signing as the season began. Priestley came to Blundell Park as a vastly experienced campaigner appearing 200-plus times for the Londoners. He proved to be the key figure in the Mariners defence which had been missing in previous years.

The opening day game saw a 2-2 draw at Bristol City with Robson scoring both. A 2-1 win in the first home game versus Barnsley was welcome, although Nottingham Forest earned a point at Blundell Park several days later through a dubious goal from Robson which is thought to have entered the goal via the side netting! Town's first defeat came at West Bromwich by the narrowest of margins, when a disputed penalty was scored against the Mariners. Town had won just one of the first four games, hardly the start required for a promotion season.

Some impressive results were recorded up to December, Clapton Orient being beaten 6-1, with four goals from Coglin, a 2-1 away win at Stoke City, Robson scored a hat-trick in the 4-2 win over Bradford Park Avenue, followed by a 4-0 victory versus Reading. In the meantime, arch-rivals Hull City became the first visitors to win at Blundell Park in late September. December was a poor month with only one of six won, including three consecutive 4-1 defeats, at Millwall and those at home to Middlesbrough, plus Blackpool on Christmas Day. The Mariners entered the New Year in a mid-table position.

The season seemed to be heading nowhere, when a run of 13 League matches saw 12 victories, and catapulted the side up the Second Division table into the promotion race by late March, with seven games remaining. Grimsby were indeed becoming the surprise package of the Division, and although unfashionable, they began to receive praise on opponents grounds for the attractive football they displayed.

On 29 March 1929, the first ever 20,000 plus gate was attracted to Blundell Park, against Chelsea, with the Mariners lying in second place. 23,644 supporters (paying record receipts of £1,573-16s.-7d.) saw a Jackie Bestall goal clinch victory. The excellent form came to an end in the return at Stamford Bridge, Town losing 3-2. After a 3-1 defeat at Southampton in the next game, decent results were required in the final five matches.

Sure enough three consecutive wins over Wolves, Notts County and Millwall meant that promotion to the Top Flight was assured. But two difficult away games remained in order to clinch the Championship. The first, at third placed Bradford Park Avenue, and the final match against the only challengers Middlesbrough. Town lost 1-0 at Park Avenue, and going into the Middlesbrough game both teams were on level points with 53 each - the winners of this match would be crowned Champions. 36,500 'Boro fanatics packed into Ayresome Park and roared their Middlesbrough side to a 3-0 victory, and the title was theirs. Though disappointing, Town had the huge consolation of joining them in Division One as runners-up, 26 years after the Mariners previous brief flirtation in the big time.

Manager Wilf Gillow was fortunate in the fact that he could select basically the same team week-in and week-out. The eleven players whom featured in the first day draw at Bristol City all appeared in over 30 games. Indeed only 13 different players had been selected by Christmas, and come May only five more had been added.

Tommy Read established himself as a crowd favourite in goal, rejoicing in the nickname 'Rocket', which described the speed in which the 'keeper would leave his line to thwart any approaching danger. Read missed only one match - through injury- that being the final fixture at Middlesbrough. Understudy, Tom Poskett, who signed from Crook Town in December, deputised, making his senior debut and stepping into the cauldron of fire. Unfortunately Poskett was understandably nervous and two of the goals were scored through the 'keeper's mistakes. Right-back Jim Calderwood was ever-present until February when Charlie Wilson took-over. Left-back Hughie Jacobson made his 100th Mariners' appearance during the season and was the only overall ever-present.

The half-back line consisted of Priestley (Captain), Wrack and Powell. Wingers Jack Prior and Billy Marshall were outstanding with inside men Jackie Bestall and Steve Coglin scoring 11 each. Top Scorer was Joe Robson with a prolific 32 League Goals in 36 starts.

A new and impressive centre-forward, Tim Coleman, replaced Robson during the run-in scoring seven goals in his first eight appearances. Coleman had been signed from Halifax Town in the February for a club record £1,250. But with Town and Joe Robson producing some outstanding performances, Coleman had to wait almost two months for his Mariners debut when Robson became injured. Coleman duly scored the winner in that first game versus Oldham Athletic.

Another record signing:
Goalscorer Tim Coleman

Billy Marshall and Charlie Wilson were both rewarded for their loyalty to the club in the promotion season with a joint benefit which raised £371 each from the gate money received from the Oldham game, which was played on Easter Saturday. Both had been with the club for six seasons at this point. One sad note of the season was the Cup exit at West Bromwich, with ten men after Joe Cooper was carried off the field following a wild challenge from a Baggies back. Consequently, Cooper was out of the game for the next 10 months.

1929/30

The First Division campaign began with a more than encouraging start. With no new signings in the summer, Gillow allowed the squad who had earned the club their new premier status the chance to show their skills and competitiveness at this highest grade.

Of the players who appeared in the first match of the season at Sheffield United, only Priestley (Chelsea), plus Prior and Coglin (Sunderland) had performed at this level previously. Town produced a tremendous result with a 3-2 win at Bramall Lane, goals coming from Marshall and Bestall (2).

A near 20,000 crowd welcomed the side, as they ran out for the first home game of the season against the previous season's F.A.Cup finalists Portsmouth, and the team gained a creditable 1-1 draw. The following week Newcastle United visited Cleethorpes and were comfortably swept aside, Town winning 4-0 in front of a 22,000-plus crowd. Goalscoring legend Hughie Gallacher missed a penalty for Newcastle, much to the joy of the locals. The return at Portsmouth again finished in a 1-1 draw, before Town lost the first game of the season, their fifth match, unceremoniously at Blackburn Rovers by 4-1. The next home game saw rivals Middlesbrough again defeat the Mariners at Blundell Park, 3-0, the first home defeat in 14 matches. A 4-2 win over Huddersfield Town and a 5-2 win at Old Trafford in October put the form temporarily back on course. Then a poor run of results saw only one won and one drawn in the next eleven matches up to Boxing Day. The heaviest defeat of 6-0 came at then leaders Leeds United, and an entertaining game was had at eventual runners-up Derby County when Town lost 5-4.

Bad luck continued in the following match on Christmas Day, when Leicester City won 4-1 at Blundell Park, for during this festive game Town lost the services of both centre-back Harry Swaby and outside-right Harry Barley, both locals, to injury. Barley sustained a broken leg, leaving the nine men to struggle on regardless. This left Town bottom of the Division. This ill-fated game also saw the Town debut for their new record signing, a left-half from Leeds United named Teddy Buck, who cost a fee of £2,000, a princely sum for one who had only appeared in the Yorkshire club's team on eight occasions. The 'double' was achieved over Sheffield United with a 4-1 win, goals coming from Coglin with a brace of penalties and Robson with another pair.

The F.A.Cup produced a humiliating result, with defeat at Third Division (South) Brighton & Hove Albion in a replay after drawing 1-1 at Blundell Park. A good recovery saw Blackburn Rovers (5-3) and Liverpool (3-2) beaten, with Coglin scoring all three against the latter. In the third consecutive home game eventual Champions Sheffield Wednesday showed their quality in a 5-0 win. Superb wins at Middlesbrough (5-1) and that versus relegation rivals Burnley (4-0) were all too rare as the Mariners struggled to gain points.

A final run of five wins in the final six matches saw the club finish in 18th position, three places, but just one point above relegated Burnley, who went down with Everton.

The Mariners helped seal Everton's fate in an encounter at Goodison Park on 12 April, when 23 goal centre-forward Joe Robson travelled to Merseyside, but felt he was unfit to play on arrival. One of the club's Directors heard of the news and invited Robson to have a seat in the stand in the Directors box, so they could watch 'a real' centre-forward in action - Everton's Dixie Dean. The deliberate ploy by the Director saw Robson make a miraculous recovery and take to the field for kick-off. The final result ended; Everton 2- Robson 4! The legendary Dixie Dean, then a current England International, failed to score and Everton were later relegated. Making his senior debut for Town at Goodison was a 20-year-old reserve right-half, Alec Hall.

Robson finished the season with 30 First Division goals from 41 games, thereby establishing a new club record for goals scored in the highest division.

Changes during the season saw Powell injured in October, and failing to regain his place when fit, he moved to Southend United in the following summer. Calderwood was also injured and retired at the season's end. The good news was that talented youngsters were waiting in the wings. The reserve side finished 4th in their league, with locals Bateman, Hall, Barley and Swaby all gaining First Division experience during the season. Other promising reserves who figured in the First Team were Tim Coleman, playing out of position on the right-wing, and centre-forward Glover who appeared in just one game, at West Ham. This 19-year-old former Welsh Schoolboy International scored an astonishing 71 Midland League goals for the reserves in 1929/30 - an all-time record for the Midland League and also that for a Grimsby Town Reserve Team. Read and Charlie Wilson were ever-presents with Robson and Priestley missing only one game each.

1930/31

Once again the survivors were not joined by any major new signings, just several squad players who in the beginning would operate mostly in the reserves, although 'Ginger' Hall was promoted from the 'stiffs'. The initial results of the campaign were disappointing, starting with Chelsea who were victorious visitors in the opening game, in front of a 20,000 Blundell Park crowd. Only one victory in the first seven matches was recorded, that at Newcastle United courtesy of a Robson brace in a 2-1 win. The first home success arrived on 4 October when West Ham were beaten 4-0, after Town's victory at Old Trafford, again, the previous Saturday.

George Pearce - the club's longest serving Chairman (1931 - 1955).

During September, two events are worthy of reflection. Firstly Joe Robson moved onto Huddersfield Town for a club, and near national record £8,000. Robson had been incredibly popular at Grimsby, with the crowd shouting *"give it to Robbie"*, whenever the Mariners broke from defence. Robson scored 123 League goals in just 161 games, and went on to add a further 18 in 23 starts for Huddersfield Town during the rest of the season, before injury dogged his career. In the Manchester United match, outside-left Billy Marshall took to the field, becoming the club's new Football League appearance record-holder, his 274th game surpassing Harry Fletcher's 20-year-old record; both Marshall and Fletcher were Birmingham born.

Despite the loss of Robson, Town were not about to spend any of the substantial windfall on a replacement, as Tim Coleman and young Pat Glover were both waiting for their chance to prove themselves in the central striking role. The supporters were angry and upset at the release of Robson, but there was no need to worry. Coleman had been playing on the right-wing whenever first choice Jack Prior was sidelined, but due to Robson's consistency, the replacement had only made sporadic appearances in the middle. His first goal came at Old Trafford, and he went on to five in the space of three games. On 1 November, Leicester City were beaten 8-2 with Coleman scoring four, the first three of the Mariners goals arriving within 10 minutes of the kick-off.

December was again a poor month for the club, when they won only once, against Sheffield United, on the 13th, and the next League victory was not recorded until 31 January, nine games later. A mini F.A.Cup run gave welcome relief from poor League form as Midland League Scarborough and Manchester United were both defeated, placing Town in the fifth round for the first time since the competition had been in its then present format.

Sadly, a club record 9-1 defeat at future Champions Arsenal was then suffered, fortunately a score never repeated since. Ironically, this was a re-arranged fixture after the initial match was abandoned earlier in the season due to thick fog, when the referee called a premature end to the game in the 62nd minute, with Town leading 1-0! Only five of the final 16 games that followed were lost, not including the fifth round Cup exit at Everton, in an exciting game which ended 3-5. The 65,534 attendance at Goodison Park was the largest crowd up to then that had witnessed a Grimsby Town side in action.

By now, Tim Coleman had certainly settled in to his central role. In a spell from February to April, he scored in a club record-breaking 11 consecutive matches, totalling 19 goals. This included a pair of hat-tricks, one at West Ham and the other against Cup-finalists Birmingham. In the 6-2 win over Blackpool, in late April, Coleman scored another threesome, taking his total to a record 35 First Division goals, in 38 games. His goals helped the Mariners to finish in a respectable 13th position - another new club record. Summer signing, winger Horace Fielding from Stockport County, acquitted himself well when Marshall moved to inside-left, during a mid-season period of 17 games. The promising Reserve side won the Midland League title, scoring some 174 goals during their successful campaign.

1931/32

After a solid start to 1931 during the previous season, the only problem was to find an inside-left for the start of the new one. Cooper had displaced Coglin, and the latter departed for Notts County. When Cooper became injured, and with no suitable reserves, Town bought in Scot Bill Chalmers, a lightweight forward from Newcastle United for £1,000. Although he endured only a brief spell at Blundell Park, Chalmers later became Coach for Italian giants Juventus.

Off the field, the Blundell Park main stand was altered. In the close season, the stand was continued to join-up with the Hazle Grove Stand at the Cleethorpes end, and a brand new style roof was fitted, giving the ground a different look. Despite these new look surroundings a poor start to the season saw a draw and four defeats, including a 7-0 thrashing at Villa Park in September, no thanks to the Mariners being reduced to 10 men when hot-shot Coleman left the field with a broken arm.

Changes were made for the next game with former Liverpool reserve right-half Gardner and local centre-half Harry Betmead coming in for their debuts, whilst Glover and Cooper were given further chances to impress. Two wins without conceding a goal were recorded with home victories over Bolton and Leicester. Gardner and Betmead both went on to play for England.

Jackie Bestall was honoured in September by being the first Mariner to represent the Football League XI since the days of Higgins and McCairns in the mid-1890's. Bestall played against the Irish League at Blackpool and the Scottish League at Celtic's ground. A further honour was gained when reserve Pat Glover won his first Welsh 'cap' in October. Despite Town losing four straight games in October, Glover had taken his chance well with first choice striker Coleman sidelined with injury. In seven starts Glover scored the same number of goals for Town, and played for Wales with just 11 first team games experience, during which he scored a total of nine goals. In those days, before floodlights, Internationals were played on regular Saturdays during the season, with the League programme continuing regardless. Town played at Blackburn Rovers whilst Glover was on international duty, and although Town lost 3-2, Coleman returned to the centre-forward role in Glover's absence, scoring both Town goals, and retaining his place on the Welshman's return!

Ten losses in the League from November to mid-January placed the Mariners in troubled waters. A 5-1 win over Liverpool in February, with a Coleman hat-trick, raised hopes, but form was going to have to dramatically alter for survival. The squad was depleted with injuries, and March arrived with just seven victories all season.

Tim Coleman signed for reigning Champions Arsenal in March, although it is unclear if the transfer fee surpassed that of Robson's £8,000 a year earlier. The Mariners are thought to have received between £5-9,000 for Coleman, although Arsenal's centre-half Billy Seddon came to Blundell Park just four days later, presumably as part of the package in a deal that could also have been a club record fee in its own right, for Seddon was certainly a class act and valued at £2,500. The blow of Coleman's loss was softened by the knowledge of the emergence of Glover. Also in March, the Mariners confusingly signed a second Charlie Wilson. Already on the books with that name was the regular right-back from Cleethorpes who had given good service, when left-half Charlie 'Tug' Wilson was signed from Sheffield Wednesday and joined him. The first game in which both Charlie Wilsons' played was on 19 March 1932 at Portsmouth.

After a 4-2 defeat at Champions-elect Everton, Manager Wilf Gillow resigned from his position, although he continued running the side until the end of the season. Gillow, the most successful Manager in the Club's history, was sorry to see his side's slump into Division Two.

The final three games were won but it was all for nothing for although the players raised themselves off bottom spot, they were still relegated, finishing in 21st place and a point away from safety. If results on the final day had gone the Mariners way, First Division status would have been maintained. Town needed to win, with both Blackpool and West Ham losing - West Ham lost but Blackpool won at Sheffield United, thus condemning Town to the Second. This had been an unlucky season, with many believing the squad were good enough to have stayed up, and injuries appeared to be the downfall, for 29 players were used in the League. Although the overall reason for relegation in reality was that the side did not perform.

Glover was the premier marksman with 16 League and Cup goals, including all four in the Cup win over Exeter City. One unusual feature of the relegation side, is the fact that no less than five different players scored hat-tricks during the season. Glover, Coleman and Fielding were joined by Max Holmes and Jimmy Dyson in an amazing penultimate game played at West Bromwich. In a see-saw game at The Hawthorns, the Mariners won 6-5, with both latter mentioned players gaining three-a-piece.

Holmes was only playing his seventh first-team game, after signing in the summer from his hometown Spalding. Right-winger Dyson had signed for a reported club record £2,350 from Oldham Athletic in March and was also playing his seventh game for the club. Full-back Arthur Bateman played in goal for part of the match as Town were reduced to 10 men for a spell when 'Rocket' Read received treatment off the pitch. After saving a penalty he collided with Edwards, who knocked in the rebound for Albion's fourth goal, to make it 3-4 at that stage. Read later returned to the fray when Town were 4-5 down.

The proceeds of the Middlesbrough game on Good Friday were donated to Jackie Bestall in Testimony to his loyal service.

1932/33

Many players who had served Town well in the top flight departed during the summer. Notable were long-serving Joe Cooper (Lincoln City) and Billy Marshall (Reading). Marshall set a club record 340 League appearances before leaving, being Town's left-winger for the previous decade. Swaby (Barnsley), Priestley (St.Johnstone) and Jack Prior (Ashington) all left, plus Bill Bell and Tom Gardner who both joined Hull City.

New Manager Frank Womack was installed in May, a veteran Captain and right-back for Birmingham from 1908-28, and who still to this day holds the club record League appearance record for the Brummies, having played 491 matches, not including Cup and War games. Womack had spent the previous two years managing lowly Division Three (South) club Torquay United. He applied for the Blundell Park job because of the lack of ambition shown by the Torquay board to progress.

Torquay right-back, Jimmy Wright became the only pre-season signing following his manager 'up north', Womack deciding to work with what he had, but no doubt another reason for this tactic was the lack of funds the club had for transfers. Reserves Arthur Bateman, Matt Moralee, Jack Hodgson, and Charlie Craven were given early opportunities. Winger Dennis Jennings became the first major signing when joining from Huddersfield Town.

Skipper Jackie Bestall leads the side out.

An instant return to Division One seemed just a distant dream as Christmas approached. Just six wins had been recorded, with only three of those at home. The humiliation of further relegation was a distinct possibility at this stage. The main problems seemed to be the defence leaking goals and failure to maintain an early lead. One prime example of this came in the Preston North End match in October. Pat Glover scored an amazing four goals in the first 12 minutes, only for Preston to return to Lancashire with a point in an incredible 5-5 draw. Never in the club's history had Town played out such a score, but unbelievably, it was repeated when playing Charlton Athletic just seven home games later!

Winger Cyril Lewis dons his Welsh Amateur Cup , in May 1933. Days later he turned professional with the Mariners.

In nine games from December to February no League wins were recorded, despite a shock 3-2 Cup victory over First Division Portsmouth in the middle of this poor form, although the forwards were still scoring well. Jennings scored a hat-trick in a 3-3 draw at Blundell Park against Lincoln City, the week following the Cup victory, and Craven scored three in the 5-1 win over Oldham Athletic. In an amazing turn of form the Mariners failed to lose any of the final 11 games, and finally secured 13th position in the table.

The defence became more solid allowing their strikers goals to at last count for something, and the side became more settled as they hit a rich vain of form. Read continued in goal although young George Tweedy made his debut in November. Jimmy Wright was the most consistent right-back until losing his place to March signing from Barrow, Jim Kelly. Hughie Jacobson and Alec Hall were as reliable as ever, with Betmead and Buck displacing the poor performances of the experienced Seddon and 'Tug' Wilson who moved on to Luton Town and Aston Villa respectively. Dyson and Fielding were the principle wingers with new signing Jennings making plenty of appearances covering on both wings. Captain Bestall and revelation 'Swerver' Craven supported Glover well up-front.

Scoring goals was not a problem, Glover netting 24, Craven 17 and Jennings 14 (a club record for a winger), although 84 were let in. After a bad start, the finish was impressive with a 6-1 final day win over Port Vale, and hence carrying hope for the 1933/34 season.

1933/34

Although a good conclusion to the previous season had resulted, few could have envisaged what was in store for the new season. No improvements had been made to the squad, only the addition of Welsh Amateur International Cyril Lewis, who became the reserve team winger. Horace Fielding had moved to Reading in the summer, so, reserve Les Dodds played at outside-left for the opening games. The first game was won 1-0 against Burnley, with a goal by Jennings, and a strong Bolton side visited in the next game, having just descended from Division One.

Town lost this match 3-2, but excellent away win s at Oldham (5-1) and the Bolton return (4-0), were followed by an encouraging 3-0 home win over Preston North End. Another home defeat came in late September, but a combination of good away form and a tight defence at home saw the Mariners as surprise early promotion candidates.

On 11 November Lincoln City were beaten 3-0 at Cleethorpes and Town went top of the table. December approached, with Town still winning, and sitting on top, after accumulating seven straight wins. The festive period normally brought about a downturn of form, and supporters were sceptical about their side's early success.

Although a slight hitch came with Bradford City winning 4-1 at Cleethorpes, the Mariners remained clear at the top. Rivals Blackpool had been beaten 4-3 at Bloomfield Road, and the double was achieved versus Manchester United over Christmas with Glover scoring a hat-trick at Old Trafford in a 3-1 victory. On Boxing Day the Mariners were runaway 7-3 victors, with all forwards scoring, including Bestall and Glover who excelled with a brace each. The goals kept pouring in, and the side was as consistent as the results. Only the more than capable 'keeper Tweedy and outside-left Holmes were newcomers from the side that started the season in August.

Welsh International Pat Glover, who played no small part in the Championship season with his record number of goals.

All games in January were won bar the Cup game at Portsmouth, and Town were now red hot favourites for the title as they continued to run away from the chasing pack. Glover scored his third hat-trick of the season in the 5-2 Millwall win in mid-March, then a 2-0 home victory over Bury and an away victory at Brentford set-up a match to clinch the championship as early as 7 April, at rivals Hull City, with four weeks of the season left to run. Top scorer Pat Glover was injured, but reserve Wally Ponting replaced him and scored the only goal of the game. The Mariners had emphatically won the Second Division Championship.

The team played out their remaining fixtures and saved the best until last as Blackpool were hammered 7-0 in the final home game of the season (taking the goals tally over the 100 mark), and Max Holmes scored a hat-trick from centre-forward. The season ended with Preston North End, also promoted as runners-up, finishing seven points behind Champions Grimsby. The Mariners were by far the best side in the Division as the results had proved, strong in the rearguard and artistic and creative in attack, they won many plaudits on their travels with top class performances.

12 games were won away from home, with an especially good record when visiting Lancashire, and this was the best travelling return of any club in the country. Indeed they had remained top from the Lincoln match in November. Astonishingly all the players were on the clubs books the season before, when the team nearly dropped into the Third Division.

The players who represented the Champions were: In goal, 'Rocket' Read, with George Tweedy deputising for 12 games mid-season. One of the main reasons of the team's success was the consistency of the defence, where amazingly Jim Kelly and Hughie Jacobson (full-backs) plus Hall, Betmead and Buck (half-back line) were all ever-presents.

The exciting young prospects of locals 'Ginger' Hall (aged 24) and Harry Betmead (21) had played exceptionally well throughout the campaign with Teddy Buck. This solid defensive line conceded few goals, allowing the prolific forward line to score a club record 103 goals. Dennis Jennings appeared the most on the wing, with the immaculate Bestall and Craven, also ever-presents, at inside-forward, both scoring and providing many goals for the side.

Pat Glover made a second appearance for Wales in November scoring in a 1-1 draw in Ireland, and he ended the season with an all-time club record 42 League goals in just 39 appearances. Many of the goals were supplied by the intricate work of skipper Bestall and his fellow creator Charlie Craven. Bestall scored 11 himself, whilst Jennings recorded 13, with Craven netting a club record 18 for an inside-forward.

To cap the finest season as yet, the club's reserves won the very competitive Midland League to form a unique double. The reserves clinched their title on the same day as the first team, also against Hull City (Reserves), and both by 1-0!

Gates rose steadily, but the end of season euphoria was not as one would expect, due to Town clinching promotion so early on, for interest peaked at Easter with a 23,000 attendance against Brentford. The change in fortunes had a great deal to do with the tactics enforced by Manager Womack. The team worked to a plan all having individual tasks on the field, with each strength and weakness being studied about their opponents before the plans were created.

The players obviously reacted well to Womack's ideas on the game, which proved successful; 27 games won was a club record.

1934/35

The all-conquering Mariners squad rejoined the First Division with the most impressive promotion side the club had ever produced. Now the test would come to see if they could compete and impress at the highest level. Many hoped they would, but the realists expected another year of top flight struggling.

Again no major signings were required, only outside-left Ben Burley was brought in by Womack from Southampton. The first two games saw Cyril Lewis operating on the right-wing, though no win was recorded over Preston or Sunderland or goals scored. The first victory came in a 3-0 win against Portsmouth, which also saw the club League appearance record broken by Hughie Jacobson playing his 341st game. Jacobson had been the first choice left-back for the previous nine seasons. An excellent 5-1 win at Huddersfield Town came in mid-September, with Glover scoring four of the goals. Wolves were beaten and Aston Villa lost 5-1 at Blundell Park with a Craven hat-trick. Another fine away win, at Derby (4-1 with a Glover threesome) came the following week and the nation began to take notice.

The home match with Champions Arsenal attracted a record League attendance to Blundell Park, when 26,288 (at that time the highest attendance for a League match, paying a record £1,771-11s.-9d.) crammed in to witness a 2-2 draw, with Glover converting a penalty in the final minute. Another draw at Liverpool and a home win over Leeds United saw Town climb to 4th place by the end of October. The year ended with the Mariners still unbeaten at home, and good wins against Sheffield Wednesday, 'Spurs and Preston over the festive period. Form dipped a little as seven games were lost after New Year, including a Cup defeat at Everton. A draw at Highbury, at the height of Arsenal's powers began a nine game unbeaten run-in as the season closed. The Mariners finished in 5th position the club's highest ever final placing, and thereby answering pre-season pessimists.

Tweedy replaced Read in goal and was ever-present between the sticks, while Kelly and Jacobson continued in the full-back positions although both suffered spells of injury; Summer signing from Stockport County Ned Vincent covered from New Year. Hall, Betmead and Buck were again superb, reserve Jack Hodgson filling-in well on the occasions of Betmead's absence in the centre. The only slight disappointment was the consistency of the wingmen, for many said of the Mariners that if they were as strong on the flanks as the inside-forwards they would be unstoppable. However, Dyson (right) and Burley (left) performed to the best of their abilities as Lewis and Jennings struggled with injuries. Bestall, Glover and Craven were not only renowned as the most complete forward line the Mariners had ever had, but were one of the strongest in the country at the time.

Bestall was at last capped by England, against Ireland in February, assisting in a 2-1 win at Goodison Park. Bestall was 34-years-old when making his international debut and must have been one of the shortest, lightest and oldest England debutants ever! Bestall was also the first ever Mariner to win a full cap for England. Craven too, was selected by England for a game in Holland a couple of weeks after the season had finished, though he only travelled as 12th man and his services were not required. Glover scored 34 First Division goals, but failed to impress the Welsh selectors during this campaign, and was unable to add to his two Welsh caps. Glover was ever-present in the Mariners attack with Craven and Bestall missing just one game each. Again the success of the half-back line impressed.

1935/36

The Mariners had done far more than survive, they had become a well respected side. But they would have to prove themselves consistently to stay one of the better teams in the country.

Burley moved on to Norwich City and the long serving Read (Crystal Palace) and Jacobson (Doncaster Rovers) left. Jacobson departed leaving the League appearance record standing at 360. Reserve players Vic Dodsworth and Ronnie Ferrier joined Manchester United, despite neither figuring in the Mariner's First Division side. Forward Max Holmes went to Hull City, and replacing Burley on the left flank was Jimmy Smailes from Blackpool, who rivalled Bestall as Town's smallest player.

The first home game saw Arsenal visit Cleethorpes, and attracted another 26,000 crowd. The Gunners had been crowned League Champions for the previous three years, though Town added to their own growing reputation with a Craven goal sealing a 1-0 victory. This result was to produce false hope as Arsenal won 6-0 in the return several days later, and the next match at Liverpool was lost 7-2. Until Boxing Day not a single game had been drawn, with Town winning just seven and losing thirteen of the twenty played. Glover was still scoring goals however and had notched two hat-tricks (versus eventual Champions Sunderland and Brentford) and a 'four' at troubled Aston Villa in a 6-2 win. Glover was rewarded with a third Welsh cap in October.

With the New Year came the third round of the F.A.Cup in which the Mariners had shown little progression in recent seasons. Indeed Hartlepools United were drawn away and put up a great fight to earn a draw against their First Division opposition. Town won the replay 4-1, then produced a terrific 4-0 win at Port Vale in round four. Meanwhile in the League results also began to improve. A 3-0 win at Manchester City on New Years Day was followed by a 2-0 victory at Chelsea just three days later. In fact the Mariners only lost once in a run of 13 games (including Cup-ties).

That 13th game was the F.A.Cup 5th round tie at home to Manchester City. New record receipts of £2,270-1s.-0d. were paid as the Mariners reached the Quarter-finals with a 3-2 win - but not without problems. Town took the lead with an early goal from Lewis, but City equalized. Then Lewis left the field to receive attention to a cut eyebrow, reappearing with a large plaster above his eye, to score his and Town's second. City scored again bringing the scores level at 2-2. Lewis in his all action display left the field once more, after a clash, with left his arm hanging limp.

Raring to go for the Semi-final:
Glover, Lewis, Baldry, Tweedy, Betmead and Bestall with Trainer Mo Atherton.

The Mariners were down to 10 men, yet Glover scored the winner. Lewis reappeared once again with his arm strapped to his body with a white bandage around his chest and still sporting a patch on his face from the earlier incident. Indeed Lewis almost added to the score after producing a run down the centre of the pitch and finishing with a rasping shot which troubled the City 'keeper. The vision of Lewis, swathed in medical tape, on a present day football pitch would be difficult to envisage. Reports released the next day revealed that Lewis had in fact dislocated his shoulder and would be unfit for several weeks. Again a home tie was drawn, this time the visitors were Middlesbrough who were dispatched of comfortably with a 3-1 win.

This resulted in Betmead missing the Semi-final through suspension. Despite the chance of a Wembley appearance the League form took a dive and relegation became a strong possibility. The Mariners had experienced a miserable run in the League, and a 5-1 defeat at 'Spurs occurred the Saturday before meeting Arsenal at Huddersfield Town's Leeds Road ground for the Semi-final. Form had been poor and although Arsenal won by just 1-0, they had dominated the game and went on to win the Final when beating Sheffield United.

Arsenal's Cliff Bastin scores the only goal in the Semi-final. When Town came the closest they have ever come to reaching the Final. Kelly, Tweedy and Buck watch in vain.

Town had reached the Semi-final of the F.A.Cup for the first time in the club's history, but not without loss. Betmead, the Mariners centre-half had clashed with former team-mate Tim Coleman, who was now a Middlesbrough forward, and the result ended with both players being dismissed.

Although disappointed not to reach Wembley, the reality, was that performances must improve or the Mariners would be playing Second Division football come the autumn. Five good wins came in the final nine matches as Town pulled clear of the relegation zone, finally finishing four points clear at 17th.

Changes during the season were minimal with reserves Baldry, Robertson, Tomlinson, Theaker and Crack all making sporadic appearances, plus right-winger George Baldry who broke into the first team in November and played in 20 League games plus all the Cup matches; all six players were Lincolnshire born and bred.

Reserve centre-back Jack Hodgson successfully converted to a left-back early in the season after injury to Kelly, and when he returned it was as right-back for the injured Vincent. The wings caused some concern again. Smailes broke his leg in a reserve game and Lewis was already in the wars, having displaced a cartilage in his knee in a pre-season practise game, and couldn't play until December - before the Cup injury. Baldry, Dyson, Moralee and Jennings (who joined Birmingham in January) filled the wing roles without great success. Glover again had an excellent scoring record with 35 goals in 40 League and Cup games.

'Unfashionable' Grimsby are recruited for an advert!

More club records were established during the season with Bestall passing the 360 match mark at Derby in December and Glover surpassed Carmichael's scoring feats when bagging the second goal of a hat-trick in the 4-1 win over Derby in April, this being his 138th League goal for the Mariners. The 3-0 win over Stoke City at Easter doubled as a Benefit match with loyal servants Betmead, Buck, Craven and Ponting sharing the £1,306 gate money.

It was an inconsistent but memorable season, for the Mariners had occupied 8th position in February and also been at rock bottom twice in October. Hall, Buck and Craven were ever-present in the 48 League and Cup games. Baldry and Annables moved over the river to Hull, with Smailes and reserve Walton joining Stockport County. Wally Ponting was released to Chesterfield and at last could prove his worth at first team level, after being Glover's understudy. Indeed Ponting scored an impressive 26 Second Division goals during 1936/37 for the Derbyshire club.

1936/37

The Mariners had another event filled season in 1936/37. Two losses in the two opening games gave early cause for concern especially when Teddy Buck was not fit for the second at Chelsea, and was destined to be out for three months; he had not missed a single game since 11 March 1933, a run of 149 games. Then the following two games were won, followed with a crushing 7-0 defeat at Liverpool.

An excellent run of seven games with just one defeat saw the Mariners rise to the dizzy heights of second place by mid-November, and they could brag of having the First Division's top scorer at that stage; not Pat Glover but fellow Welshman, winger Cyril Lewis with 14. A feat which not many wingers achieved in those days, never mind one from Grimsby! All this was achieved despite losing Manager Frank Womack who was poached by ambitious Leicester City.

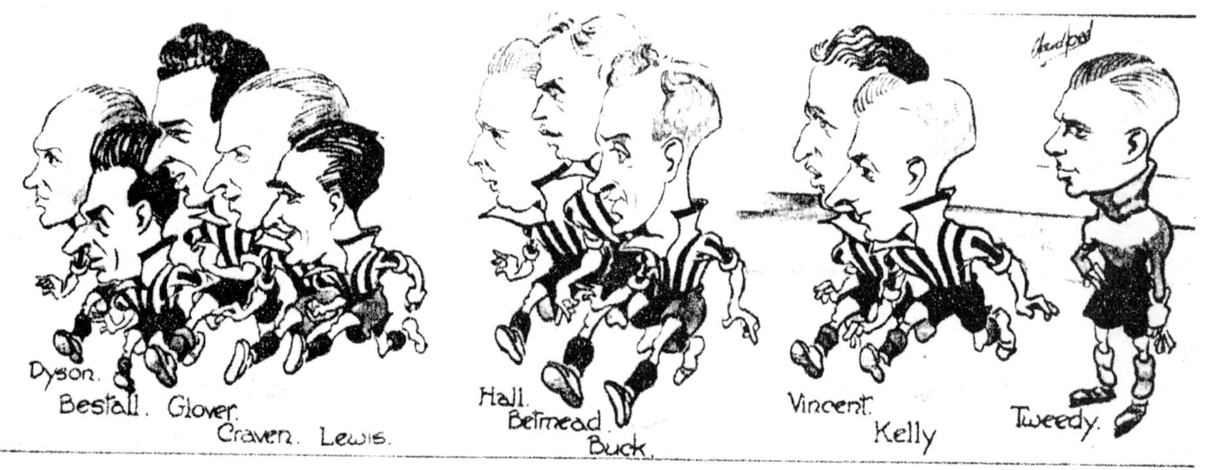

A caricature of one of the club's greatest teams.

Womack went on to lead Leicester to the Second Division Championship by the end of the season, just as he had with the Mariners. Trainer Mo Atherton was placed in temporary charge until a new manager was appointed.

Manager Charlie Spencer giving some advice to winger Cyril Lewis.

A 6-4 win over Preston (Lewis scoring four) at Blundell Park in the last match in October was followed by a 6-2 (Lewis three) victory over Manchester United in the very next home game. United were so impressed with the 'Welsh Wonders' Lewis and Glover that it was reported that Town were all but offered a blank cheque to secure the two players, and thereby break the national transfer record to take both players to Old Trafford. But the Town board stood firm and declined the generous offer.

Life at the top was shortlived, as Town's form was inconsistent to say the least, in losing 5-1 at reigning Champions Sunderland, to thrashing the future Champions, 5-3, on Christmas Day. The only away point won in a spell of five months was again versus Manchester City in a 1-1 draw at Maine Road; Grimsby were rapidly becoming City's bogey side. Cup wins against lowly Cardiff City and Walsall in January saw Town gain an easy entry in to the 5th round of the Cup. Wolves were drawn at home and Blundell Park's largest ever attendance was recorded, no doubt many supporters thinking Town's name was already on the Cup. 31,651 (paying a record £2,772-10s.-9d.) saw a 1-1 draw, but the Mariners were thrashed in the replay 6-2 at Molineux, after the Wolves' Manager controversially ordered the pitch to be heavily watered prior to kick-off.

Only one game had been won in the last seven when the decision was made to appoint former Newcastle United and England pivot Charlie Spencer as Manager. Spencer had the best possible start with a 5-1 home win against 'Yorky' rivals Sheffield Wednesday.

Although results did not completely turn around, a spell of three consecutive wins placed Town in mid-table come the end of the season, in what was an unusually tight Division with few points separating many clubs. In those three final victories Pat Glover scored five in the 6-0 win over Sunderland, who had reached the Cup Final. Huddersfield Town were beaten 3-0 at Leeds Road and Everton lost 1-0 at Blundell Park. Town finished in 12th, level on points with Birmingham, Chelsea and Preston.

Glover again finished as the club's top marksmen - for the fifth season running - with 33 League and Cup goals. Lewis' early scoring form subsided, for he scored only once after New Year, but his record of 19 League and a further three in the Cup was enough to shatter the previous club record for a wingman and was impressive by any standard.

As a team, Town only had periods of success, but certain individuals were honoured at the highest level. Goalkeeper George Tweedy had an outstanding season as did Harry Betmead who both made their debuts for England that season. Lewis was due to play for Wales, being selected with Pat Glover for the England game in October, but Town Chairman George Pearce made an eleventh hour decision to deny Lewis his debut, and instead he played and scored in the 2-0 home win over Brentford. Lewis never did make that Welsh debut despite being named as reserve once more and missing another chance through injury. However, Glover's international season was quite the reverse, for he played in all three of the Home Championship Shield games and scored in all three games; two against Scotland and Ireland, plus one in the 2-1 win over England at Ninian Park. His five goals helped Wales win the trophy. Finally Jackie Bestall again represented the Football League XI in Ireland in September at the age of 36.

Back on a more local level, reserve Frank Wattam replaced the injured Buck during his three month absence, so the half-back line of Hall, Betmead and Wattam was proudly one of Grimsby-born players representing the club in the top flight. Another local was introduced for his debut before the season's end, that of winger Jack Swain, who appeared on the opposite side to February signing Dennis Quigley from Brechin City.

1937/38

Manager Charlie Spencer began his first season in charge, a season that was to be one with few highlights and many disappointments, but eventually and ultimately survival.

The opening game saw the Mariners travel to Preston North End. The 4-1 defeat was a bad enough start, but a tragic knee injury to star performer Pat Glover before the interval set the tone for the rest of the campaign. Without Glover, and Bestall now past his best, the Mariners struggled to score goals, this problem had not troubled a Grimsby side for the past 15 years with the likes of Carmichael, Robson, Coleman and of course, Glover in attack. Reserves Reg Tomlinson and Tom Hinchcliffe took over Glover and Bestall's places in the pre-Christmas period.

The Mariners first win came as late as the 10th game, a 2-1 home victory over Middlesbrough in October. In the next game, new signing Irish International winger Jackie Coulter came from Everton and scored the winner on his debut at Huddersfield. On Coulter's home debut he again scored the winner, against his former club Everton. These three consecutive 2-1 victories were rare indeed, and a 5-1 home defeat to Stoke City on Christmas Day dampened spirits further. The Mariners would certainly need their usual turn of form at New Year, though it was a little late arriving this season - Easter in fact - but a saving run of points were eventually accumulated.

Star signing Hughie Gallacher

Town were knocked out of the F.A.Cup with an embarrassing defeat to Third Division (South) side Swindon Town. The Wiltshire club held the Mariners to a 1-1 draw at Blundell Park before winning the replay 2-1 after extra time. The first victory of 1938 came in February with an unexpected 4-0 win over Birmingham. By now the side was gradually changing. Two reserve summer signings, both named Shaw (not related), unusually made their first team debuts together in a 1-1 draw at Leeds in late January. Also making his Mariners debut at Leeds was the legendary Scot Hughie Gallacher.

Unfortunately Gallacher was signed by Grimsby at the end of his illustrious scoring career, although he still commanded a club record fee of £4,000 which was paid to Notts County. He had scored over 400 first class goals, mainly for Newcastle United and Scotland, on arriving for a short spell at Blundell Park, now aged 35. He was one of the most famous players of the late 20's and early 30's, having managed several goals against the Mariners in the past, including hat-tricks for Chelsea and Derby County.

For the Birmingham win Cam Theaker deputised for the injured Tweedy in goal and another £4,000 buy, inside-right Jock Beattie, made his debut and scored. Beattie and Tom Hinchcliffe moved in opposite directions earlier that week, as Hinchcliffe joined Huddersfield Town, and Dyson had already left for Nottingham Forest. Beattie was playing for his third First Division club that season having started with Birming-ham, and by the end he had also played against all three clubs!

1937/38 season - Action at Highbury. Arsenal's Swindin gathers the ball from (unseen) Gallacher. Charlie Craven (right) is ready to pounce.

Glover returned from injury in April to save the Mariners from relegation, when five wins in the final seven games coincided with his return.

The final day of the season saw the club rise from bottom in the morning to two points clear of the relegation zone, finishing in 20th position, by the evening. The Mariners beat Chelsea 2-0 with goals from Beattie and Glover, as both Manchester City and West Bromwich failed to win and were relegated instead.

Freddie Howe and Tom Jones (right) attack the Chelsea goal in the victorious F.A.Cup Quarter-final tie at Stamford Bridge.

Survivors from previous years proved to be the rocks of the side. Tweedy, Hodgson, Hall, Betmead, Buck and Charlie Craven were all the most consistent performers. Stars Coulter (who played twice for Northern Ireland whilst with the Mariners that season) and Gallacher, both played their part in Town retaining First Division status, despite their ageing years.

May saw survival but several players had made their last appearances for the Club. Coulter (Chelmsford City) and Gallacher (Gateshead) moved on after brief stays. Then came the loss of two of the club's longest serving servants, Jim Kelly and the great Jackie Bestall. Kelly moved on to Bradford Park Avenue after six seasons with Town, and played in both the Championship and Cup Semi-final sides. Bestall decided to retire, and became the trainer at Birmingham, having set a club League appearance record of 427 games.

It is believed that legends Robson, Coleman and Glover would not of had such reputations for scoring if Bestall had not been on hand to provide their many chances. Bestall arguably stands alone as the club's greatest ever servant and most talented player; a Cleethorpes road was even named in his honour. Another huge loss in the summer was Charlie Craven.

Craven was signed by newly promoted Manchester United for £6,000, and finished his final season as a Mariner as top scorer with 12 goals, due to the absence of Glover in the centre.

1938/39

The Mariners were fortunate indeed to be facing such a club as Aston Villa on the first day of the new season, for it looked, for long periods during the previous campaign, that they would possibly be playing the likes of Chesterfield and Plymouth in the coming months.

The return to fitness of Glover produced a little hope, but many thought the writing was on the wall, especially before the curtain-raiser, when Glover went down with rheumatism in his other knee, in which he had suffered an injury the previous season. With Craven and Bestall missing Town would again struggle. Spencer's replacements were wingers Jimmy Boyd, the former Scottish Cap and Newcastle Cup winner who signed from Dundee, and Bradford City's Roland Bartholomew. Inside men were Tommy Jones from Blackpool and Billy Temple from Carlisle United.

The first two games were lost, against Villa and at Everton, and only two were won in the first 10. Then an unexpected run of 10 games without defeat followed the best spell the club had ever seen in the First Division, taking them up to Christmas Eve established in the top half of the table. In that excellent run, wins were recorded at Blundell Park against Birmingham, Chelsea, Charlton, Leeds and Leicester, with a victory at Stoke.

By October it was obvious that the Mariners required a decent centre-forward and the signing of Manchester City's Freddie Howe coincided with the club's upturn in form; Howe scored four in the 6-1 win over Leicester. But four straight defeats in the League saw the club drop to midway as the F.A.Cup third round awaited.

Town won that tie easily, 6-0 against the club bottom of Division Two, Tranmere Rovers. A draw at Millwall in the next round then saw Town win the replay 3-2. In the fifth round Grimsby were drawn at Sheffield United. The Blades were a Second Division club in contention for the Championship, and Town escaped from Bramall Lane with a 0-0 draw, played in front of a partizan 62,000 crowd. A Freddie Howe goal won the replay.

The Mariners were drawn away for the third tie on the trot - this time at Chelsea who were struggling in the League.

The Mariners were drawn away for the third tie on the trot - this time at Chelsea who were struggling in the League. Grimsby won 1-0 with a goal from winger Freddie Crack. Yet the following Saturday, Town visited Stamford Bridge again, this time in a First Division match, and lost 5-1! Crack's winner at Chelsea placed the Mariners in the Cup Semi-final again for the second time in the 30's. A record (still standing) 76,962 Old Trafford attendance saw Grimsby Town play Wolverhampton Wanderers for a place in the F.A.Cup Final. But as the game unfolded it became obvious that the Mariners would have to wait for at least another year to reach Wembley.

Things were against Town before the match even started, for first choice 'keeper George Tweedy was declared unfit with flu, and Cam Theaker the regular reserve custodian had moved to Newcastle United just before Christmas. So, George Moulson, untried at first team level, came in for his debut in the Semi-final. Moulson was a local lad, despite being born in Ireland, and joined the Mariners staff after a spell in the Army. The Mariners made the better start to the game, but on 20 minutes tragedy struck. Stand-in Moulson collided with Wolves' striker Dorsett, and both players lay motionless before stretchers were called for. Moulson suffered concussion and did not continue. Left-back Jack Hodgson donned the number one jersey for the remainder of the game; what a baptism for poor Moulson. After 90 minutes Wolves had reached Wembley with a not surprising score of 5-0. The Mariners had battled well but the obvious disadvantage took its toll, especially when Dorsett re-emerged shortly after being stretchered off.

The Semi-final defeat caused further goalkeeping problems in the First Division matches that followed. Centre forward Pat Glover was forced to start in goal at Charlton, despite just returning from injury, and for the following game amateur 'A' Team 'keeper Tom Anderson made his only first team appearances (with credit) in a 1-1 home draw with Bolton. Anderson was the fifth goalkeeper to be used during the season (sixth if you count Hodgson), before the welcome return of Tweedy.

GRIMSBY TOWN
FOOTBALL CLUB

OFFICIAL
FIXTURE LIST
SEASON 1939—1940.
Fixture List Copyright by the Football League Ltd., reproduced by permission.

With the Compliments of The Chairman and Agents of
Court
"Children of the Forest"
No. 3710.
Ancient Order of Foresters
Held at
THRIFT HALL, Pasture Street,
(End Room of Passage)
Every alternate Tuesday

Burnetts (Gy.) Ltd., Printers, Strand Street.

The season that never was!

On the final day of the season the Mariners beat Champions Everton 3-0 to finish 10th in the League. With the addition of the Cup run, this was on paper Grimsby Town's best ever season

The defence of Tweedy, Vincent, Hodgson, Hall, Betmead and Buck had been at its most solid. The regular forward line of Boyd, Beattie, Howe, Jones plus any of the outside-lefts Bartholomew, Swain, Lewis or Crack had all performed with an immense degree of credit. Twenty-seven players had been used in the first team, despite the side being fairly settled, and Howe top-scored with 21 League and Cup goals. Harry Betmead capped another marvellous season by being selected to tour South Africa with an F.A. XI, and playing in two of the three games. The reserves also had a successful season with a record score of 17-0 against Denaby United, when Freddie Kurz netted seven goals. Kurz played just three first team games despite his 37 goals in 24 Midland League games.

The attendance at Old Trafford in the Semi-final remains the largest audience to which Grimsby Town have performed. Freddie Howe became the first wearer of the number 9, in the Semi-final, as Town wore numbered shirts for the first time, although this did not become compulsory until after the A.G.M. three months later.

Two significant players to leave for Plymouth Argyle during the close-season were Pat Glover and Cyril Lewis. Both had been hampered by injuries in the previous couple of years which affected their performances and limited appearances. Lewis still held the record goals in a season for a Grimsby winger, and Glover left behind a string of club records which were all still in existence some 60 years later. His seventh and final Welsh cap came in March when he scored in the 3-1 win over Ireland at Wrexham. He holds the record international appearances and goals (seven) for a Mariner, most goals in a season, and a record total of 180 aggregate League goals. His total goal haul of 208 (including F.A.Cup and Lincs. Cup) for the club, seems never likely to be beaten.

Chapter Six

WAR AND DECLINE

1939 - 1951

The **1939/40** season became the shortest Football League season in history. New players were signed in Winstanley, a full-back from Stoke City, Fred Reeve a right-half from Rochdale and new wingers Jack Johnson (Huddersfield Town) and Billy Wardle (Manchester City). The question of how successful this squad with the new signings, would be was never answered, as three games into the new season, League Football was abandoned with the outbreak of the Second World War.

Grimsby's opening game at Old Trafford was lost 4-0, and on the following Tuesday a 0-0 draw with Wolves at Blundell Park saw the opening of the new Osmond Stand at the Cleethorpes end, replacing the final memories of the old Abbey Park ground with the demolition of the Hazle Grove Stand. The new stand had been built at a cost of £4,500. Preston were beaten 2-0 on Saturday 2 September 1939 with both goals from Howe, and war was declared against Germany on the very next day.

The first of the Mariners staff to be called up for war service were Freddie Kurz, Sam Hodgson (a reserve half-back and brother of Jack), Turner (another reserve back) and Crack, into the Army, and new signing Jack Johnson who joined the R.A.F. Kurz, being Grimsby-born turned out in several games for his home town club whilst on leave, but played the majority of his football in London as he was based at the Woolwich Arsenal with the Royal Artillery, and represented Charton, Chelsea, Watford, Fulham, Millwall, Clapton Orient and finally Crystal Palace, for whom he later signed permanently. Boyd and Fred Reeve never played for the club during wartime, with Winstanley even failing to make his debut.

Several Friendlies were arranged, before the Football League decided to organize regionalised divisions as in the First war. The Mariners were in an East Midland Division, joined by the only other First Division side Sheffield United. The League got underway on 21 October, against Mansfield Town. Town won 2-1 with reserve centre-forward Roberts scoring on his debut. During this season the team was heavily represented by members of the 1938/39 reserve side. As in the first world war 'guest' players were permitted with several former Mariners again appearing in the black and white stripes. Ponting, Ike Robinson (both with the Grimsby Borough Police), Lumby, Moralee, Holmes (by now a Grimsby Schoolteacher), Bestall and former reserve Tommy Ward, now on the books of Mansfield Town, all made appearances in this first season.

A two-legged cup competition was also organized in the absence of the F.A.Cup, in which a Middlesbrough side defeated Town in the first round. An unusual instance occurred with Ned Vincent being a Grimsby ever-present but also finding time to make one appearance for Bradford City! Bradford was the northern headquarters for fire training, and Vincent was in the city on a course.

The strong back-line of Tweedy, Vincent, Jack Hodgson, Betmead and Hall was amazingly kept intact for the majority of the **1940/41** season; Scunthorpe United's pivot Mal Millington was eventually called-up in Betmead's place. This feat was achieved by Hall, Buck and Vincent being in the A.F.S. (Auxiliary Fire Service) in the town and Harry Betmead was an Army P.T.I. (Physical Training Instructor) based at nearby Lincoln, until his unavailability when he was transferred to Aldershot Garrison. Tweedy and Jack Hodgson were serving as War Reserve Policemen in Grimsby, with Hodgson also being employed on *"work of national importance"*, and on the docks.

For the first game of the season at Lincoln City, a 2-2 draw, former reserves Connie Holland and Wally Annables appeared for Town with future Scotland and Arsenal star Jimmy Logie at outside-right. The League positions for this season would be merited on goal average, not points, with form counting towards qualification for a War Cup competition.

A Mariners side entertained a Bradford City side in front of just 600 spectators in November, but because of poor attendances and the threat of Luftwaffe air raids upon Blundell Park with its east coast location, the Bradford match was the last to be played at Blundell Park until 1944. Instead Scunthorpe United agreed to host the Mariners matches at their Old Showground. The first occasion Town played there as a 'home' side was versus Chesterfield on 30 November. The game was lost 5-4 which must have been great entertainment for the Scunthorpe neutrals. Scunthorpe United were not members of the Football League until 1950, so this higher class action was welcome.

During the ensuing war seasons many of Scunthorpe United's Midland League side guested for the Mariners at the Old Showground. Included in the line-ups was centre-forward Harry Johnson who had scored a record 69 goals in 1938/39 as the 'Knuts', as they were then known (the nickname of the Iron came later), claimed the Midland League title.

The Second leg of a War Cup game versus Barnsley, which had been extended into extra time, had to be abandoned after 161 minutes play as the referee had to return for his R.A.F. duties. The game was all level at 2-2, and 3-3 on aggregate, yet Barnsley progressed into the next round through having a better record than Grimsby in the League campaign.

One Mariner who made his first team debut this season was reserve goalkeeper Jack Frost. Frost had been signed in July 1939 from North Shields and kept goal for the Mariners in two away games in the north-east whilst he was on leave at his Wallsend home in December. Frost was serving with the 4th Royal Engineers and by the war's end had become the most decorated professional footballer in Britain. Only 11 players were decorated for their war efforts, in 1945, Frost being the only player to receive two such honours. He received the M.B.E. and the Lloyds Medal for Gallantry at sea. He only played three war games for the Mariners in nine years service with the club, before moving on to Darlington in July 1948 where he made 45 League appearances for them having also made a 'guest' appearance for the Quakers during the war.

Harry Johnson continued his excellent goalscoring form with 16 from 16 in League competition, scoring in all eight of his first games for the Mariners. Dougie Witcomb (West Bromwich and Wales) and Tom Swinburne (the Newcastle United and England 'keeper) guested for Town during 1941/42 both playing in War Internationals for their countries. Vincent was again an ever-present for the Mariners but also played once for Doncaster Rovers.

1941/42 saw a 7-1 win over Sheffield United in late November with Tom Rudkin (the Peterborough United winger) and Ron Ferrier (Oldham Athletic, ex-Mariner and Cleethorpes-born striker) both scoring hat-tricks. The Mariners reached the Semi-final of the League War Cup in May, and after two-legged victories over Barnsley, Nottingham Forest and Norwich City, saw Town face Sunderland. After a 0-0 draw at Roker Park, in front of a 20,000 plus gate (by far the largest attendance the Mariners played before during these war years). The Mariners were favourites to win through, attracting a then Old Showground record crowd of 11,896 for the 2nd leg, but they unfortunately lost 3-2.

The season also saw the introduction, briefly, of the Moore brothers - Norman and Roy. Neither played prolifically for the Mariners, but in the 1980's Roy's sons Kevin, Dave and Andy all had lengthy service with the club. Roy was actually a 6 feet plus half-back for Town's reserves when called in to first team service for a couple of games against Rotherham United, as goalkeeper! He also guested once for Hull City in goal before the war ended. Norman was an excellent goalscorer, netting many with his head, who could also play in the half-back line if required. He spent his most successful period as an out-and-out goalscorer over the Humber with Hull City after the war, and guested for no fewer than nine sides during this period as he moved around the U.K. He joined the Royal Engineers, later becoming a P.T.I. based in North Wales, and appeared mostly for Wrexham, and also Chester, but was later stationed in London and East Anglia where he guested for other clubs. Billy Wardle made a brief appearance at York City for the Mariners in January, and had played for the British Army of the Rhine Team.

The **1942/43** season opened with an away match at Chesterfield which was lost 2-0. Appearing for the Mariners for the first time was Manchester City and Irish International Peter Doherty. He appeared several times for the Mariners as he was based in Lincolnshire with the R.A.F., as were many of the club's 'guest' players.

Regulars in the side for this season were still Vincent, Hodgson, Hall, and Buck, plus Millington. Tweedy had now joined an Infantry Regiment with the Army, with Sheffield United's Jack Smith keeping goal mostly for Town. Wingers Billy Davies (Watford) and Jack Ranshaw (from Nettleham, near Lincoln) rarely missed matches, in fact Ranshaw top-scored with 16 goals. Matt Moralee, the former Mariner, scored all five in the 5-2 win over Doncaster Rovers in January, and the week before, Scottish International Andy Black scored a hat-trick for Town in the 3-3 draw with Rotherham United. Black, although on the books of Hearts, had seen much war service with Portsmouth prior to his spell with Grimsby, and he played for Northern Command in his spell with the Mariners. R.A.F. fighter pilot and Burnley and England Amateur International Peter Kippax played for the Mariners whilst stationed in the area during the autumn. Teddy Buck emulated Vincent's earlier feat of appearing in all of Town's matches as well as appearing for Bradford City.

1943/44 saw 'keeper George Moulson establish himself as an ever-present in Tweedy's absence. Moulson had the distinction of playing alongside his elder brother Con in a game at Sheffield United in January. Con was a former reserve team half-back at Blundell Park in the late 1920's, but went on to play for Bristol City, Lincoln City, Notts County and Ireland in the thirties; the Moulson brothers both appeared around 100 times for Lincoln as war guests. Unusually Dickie Dorsett, the Wolves forward, and Moulson, who collided in the 1939 Cup Semi-final became team-mates during this season, when the former guested for Town on 12 occasions.

Another set of brothers played in the same team when Sam Hodgson made his Mariners debut in November, in defence with Jack. Sam, although on Town's books was based at Catterick, North Yorkshire as a P.T.I. and had guested regularly for Darlington, York City and Middlesbrough. Local youngsters Len Rook, 'Nooky' Roberts, Stan Vinson and Freddie Browning were all given a first-team try. The first instance of a coloured player appearing for the Mariners came when Wrexham's Peter Baines guested during the season, and he went on to play 16 games before the end of the war. Adding to the Moores', Moulsons' and Hodgsons', the local brothers of George and Lou Ely and Ray and Ken Moody also appeared during the hostilities. Only Ken, of the latter four players, made any impression on League Football when peace resumed.

The return to Blundell Park came on New Years Day with a 1-1 draw against Doncaster Rovers, when Dorsett scored for Town. Unfortunately the game was abandoned 10 minutes from the end as 'Ginger' Hall refused to leave the pitch after the referee attempted to dismiss him. Apparently Hall was innocent of any crime and protested. One highlight of the season was Leeds United's Len Dunderdale scoring a hat-trick for the Mariners in a 3-2 away win at Sheffield Wednesday in October.

The **1944/45** season saw the highest turnover of representatives, 62 in all, many of whom did not play for the club before or after. Local centre-forward Ken Reeve made a goalscoring start to the season, bagging three in the first couple of matches. These were his only appearances of the season as he was on leave from the Royal Marine Commandos. Winger Billy Pearson had been playing for Town and eventually signed the Irishman having been spotted playing locally for the R.A.F. Another member of the Air Force, Jim Johnson from York City, signed for the club around the same time.

A local winger appeared in April 1945, he was signed on amateur forms throughout the war but had been serving with a Bomb Disposal Unit. His name was Billy Harvey, who later became Manager of the Mariners some 23 years later, although he never made a Football League peacetime appearance for the club. Another raw recruit who was impressive during 1945 was forward Joe Rodi. Rodi was of Italian parents who moved to Glasgow where Joe was born. He signed for Town from East Fife, scoring 13 goals in his first 10 appearances, and ended the season as top scorer.

Another familiar face returned after Christmas, defender Arthur Bateman. Grimsby-born Bateman, played seven games in the unfamiliar roll of inside-left. Bateman signed professional forms for the Mariners in 1927 and captained Town's reserves before moving onto Southend and Brentford. Whilst with Brentford he skippered their Second Division Championship side of 1935, then in the First Division played regularly at right-back. Bateman returned at the outbreak of war to join the Grimsby Borough Police Force, and had been playing in his new forward position with Grimsby Hotspurs in the very strong local league which included all the local R.A.F. stations. Camps such as Waltham, North Cotes, Manby and Binbrook all had excellent teams with many Football League players at their disposal, and other teams came from the Fire Service, Police and Army.

With the war in Europe ending in May 1945. The organisation of Football returned to something like normal for **1945/46**, although the Football League fixtures would not be reinstated for another season, due to there still being a great deal of unrest, and the war in Japan did not cease until September, after the season had started.

Grimsby Town

Football Club, Ltd.

OFFICIAL

FIXTURE LIST

SEASON 1945-6.

This List has been authorised by the Directors of the Grimsby Town Football Club, Ltd., and printed by Richardsons and Coppin, Ltd. Printers, Victori

C. W. SPENCER, Sec./Man

A return, to a degree of normality

Grimsby were to play in a War North League which had much stronger opposition than the local regionalised Leagues in which they had been performing for the past few years. Clubs from Lancashire and the North-East were now in competition, and the F.A.Cup was reinstated.

The matches were paired, as in the early 1920's, with home and away games against the same club being played on alternate weekends, whilst the F.A.Cup rounds were played over two-legs for the only season in history.

The Mariners started well in this League, with a narrow 3-2 defeat at Blackburn Rovers, before winning four consecutive games. Attendances were now better all over the country as the risk of air-raids had diminished, and morale was up. Players started returning to their clubs after serving their nation in all manner of ways.

Grimsby's side had seen many changes over the passed few years, but as the end of the season approached more and more familiar, but older, faces returned to first team action. In goal George Moulson continued to be the regular choice before the return of Tweedy in April, and the full-backs were still Ned Vincent and Jack Hodgson. Sam Hodgson returned from Army duties at right-half, alongside Betmead or Charlesworth and Buck. Vincent, Jack Hodgson and Buck were the only players to have played in over 200 war games, while Hall topped 180.

The best 'guest' service came from Scunthorpe United's Mal Millington, who played 150 games for the Mariners - some loan spell!

Harry Chadwick from Lancashire performed well at outside-right after signing from Blackpool reserves, although Crystal Palace's Glyn Lewis finished the season on the wing. Norman Moore was at inside-right, before the signing of Newcastle United's Harry Clifton who played for England in a war international in 1939. Many centre-forwards were tried before Freddie Howes return from the Royal Navy. Joe Rodi was at inside-left but had to make way for Royal Engineer Tommy Jones, who had returned to his former trade during the war. Left-wingers were Billy Davies, who returned to Watford, Billy Pearson, then Billy Wardle. The top overall wartime goalscorer was winger Jack Ranshaw who netted 30 goals, followed by Scunthorpe United's Harry Johnson with 29.

The end of the war seasons saw Teddy Buck announce his retirement, having been Grimsby's left-half since 1929. In 17 years with the club he amassed 590 first team appearances (including 354 in the Football League), more than any other Mariner, though his 202 war appearances are ignored in most statistical references. A stalwart of the 1934 Championship side and both Cup Semi-finals, Buck remained on the Coaching staff at Blundell Park, for a short while.

235 war matches in League and Cup had been played with some 179 different players representing the club during those seasons, and Grimsby Town Football Club supplied a total of 58 members of staff to the Armed Forces between 1939 and 1945.

1946/47

Normal Football League action at last returned, with the League deciding to use the same fixture lists that had been made for the aborted 1939/40 season.

Pre-season training saw the return of many of the 1939/40 squad, though obviously all by now were seven years older. Some youngsters had progressed to first team level during the war, but the main bulk of the side were of an age which many pundits of the day thought was too old. The Mariners started as the nation's favourites to be relegated in this first post-war season. Most of the other top flight squads had been bolstered by expensive signings, but the Mariners had spent no money in the transfer market, just releasing Freddie Howe to Oldham Athletic, and signing six free transfers.

The first match marking the return to First Division action was played at Maine Road against Manchester United, for Old Trafford was under reconstruction after being bombed during the war. The Mariners fielded the following - 'veteran' side (age in brackets); Tweedy (33); Vincent (37), Jack Hodgson (32); Sam Hodgson (27), Stan Charlesworth (26), Fred Reeve (28); Jack Johnson (27), Harry Clifton (32), Jim Johnson (23), Jim McGowan (22) and Wardle (28).

The only new signing to figure in the first game was McGowan from Dumbarton, and this was to be Charlesworth's final appearance before joining Barnsley. His only other League outing for the club was on 19 April 1939, therefore his two Football League appearances were more than seven years apart, although he had played 40 games during the war. Of these players only new man McGowan and Fred Reeve had not played for the Mariners during the hostilities. Reeve played in the abandoned 1939/40 season, therefore his last appearance for the club was seven years previously. Reeve had guested for Southend United during 1939/40, as well as for Millwall and Clapton Orient, whilst the Londoner was on leave from the forces.

That first game in Manchester was lost 2-1 with McGowan scoring on his club debut. Sam Hodgson was actually making his Football League debut, some 10 years and 7 months after initially signing professionally for the Mariners, in January 1936!

1946/47- The first of many more to come.
Billy Cairns scores his first goal for the club on his debut versus Portsmouth in October

A scoreless home draw with Wolves saw the return of Betmead and Tom Jones, with left-half Tom Blenkinsopp making his Football League debut, some seven years after signing for the club. The first win came in the fifth game, 2-1 at home to Chelsea, in front of a 22,000 crowd, but the next Blundell Park match was lost 6-1 to future Champions Liverpool. An excellent 2-1 win at Sunderland saw the successful conversion of Blenkinsopp, who scored both goals in an experimental debut at centre-forward. In the following game, the last in October, new signing inside-left Billy Cairns made a scoring debut in the 3-2 victory over Portsmouth. Cairns, despite being aged 34 when he signed from Gateshead in May, was to provide the club with excellent service in the coming years, scoring goals a plenty. Blenkinsopp continued his goalscoring form with seven in his first six games.

Horace Wallbanks arrived from Aberdeen in November, playing on the right wing for six consecutive matches. The player had already made five guest appearances for the Mariners in 1944.

Town hit a sticky patch in form, from 16 November, beating only Charlton Athletic (3-1 on Christmas Day) and Sheffield United (2-1 in January) in an 18 match spell, which ended with a 1-0 win at Brentford on 29 April. Six of the games were drawn, and the heaviest defeat in this period, of 5-0, came once again versus Liverpool at Anfield, and prior to this League match the Mariners had been knocked out of the Cup by the Scousers.

As Spring emerged from the bad winter that season, Billy Cairns found his goalscoring touch, bagging 13 goals in the final 13 games, including a hat-trick in the 4-1 win on the last day against already relegated Leeds United. The Mariners finished a creditable 16th, after everybody had, the previous summer, written off their chances of survival. Cairns finished the season as top scorer with 18 League plus four Cup goals. Grimsby's lack of success in the bad run was put down to the problem of not maintaining an initial lead on nine occasions.

The visit of Stoke City on 4 April established a Blundell Park record League attendance when Town were beaten 5-2 in front of 26,537 (receipts of £2,409-3s.-3d.). The reserves won the Midland League title for the fifth time. Of the 29 players used in the League campaign, an amazing 19 were also on the club's books in 1939. Joining Sam Hodgson and Blenkinsopp in making late Football League debuts were Frank Mouncer, Norman Penrose, Ken Reeve, Norman Moore, Freddie Fisher and George Moulson. Fisher was the most successful of this band, making 38 appearances at full-back. All, bar Penrose, had made first-team war appearances.

Of those to leave in the summer were Tom Jones and Ned Vincent to retirement, whilst Norman Moore joined Hull City, and Moulson finally went to Lincoln City permanently, having made around 100 guest appearances for the Imps during the hostilities.

1947/48

Manager Charlie Spencer brought 32-year-old winger Albert Wilson, from Rotherham United and rookie forward Tommy Briggs from Plymouth Argyle to Blundell Park in the close-season.

The Mariners started the campaign with a convincing 3-0 win over Aston Villa, in front of a 20,500 Cleethorpes crowd. So impressed with the performance were many supporters, that upon their journey home talk was of a successful season. Then reality struck with tremendous force as the next game was lost 8-1 at Wolves, after a Cairns goal had put Town 1-0 up! In fact the Wolves game started a five game run of straight defeats when only three goals were scored. Wins against Manchester City and Huddersfield Town reinstated false beliefs, for only one match was won and one drawn in the next 11 games up to December. That single success came in a 4-3 victory at Cup-winners and League runners-up Manchester United, with Cairns scoring three of the goals.

In came two more ageing stars to bolster the weak defence, Tom Galley (32) from Wolves for £1,250, and Eric Sibley (32), from Blackpool at a cost of £3,000. Both were top First Division defenders before the war with Galley winning two England caps. Two wins in December, none in January or February, one each in March and April, then an 8-0 May day thrashing at new Champions Arsenal completed a miserable season which tells its own story. Town had finished rock bottom of the First Division on just 22 points. To be safe of relegation they needed a further 15 points to finish above third from bottom Sunderland. Falling to bottom place in January the team remained there until the seasons end.

Although it would seem the defence was to blame for a terrible season this was not the case. Tweedy was the club's unofficial player of the year in goal, with Blenkinsopp and Fisher also claiming credit. The defence was placed under extreme pressure at times through other sections of the team failing to work as a unit and squandering possession on countless occasions.

Several unwanted club records were sadly established this season; The only time the club had finished bottom of the First Division..... a record 28 League defeats..... conceding a record 111 goals..... gaining 22 (fewest) points in a season.....only eight games (fewest) were won..... with a record poor run of home form which stretched from a win on 17 September until the next victory on Good Friday (26 March) - 13 consecutive home games.

Harry Betmead retired in December, and is still the only Grimbarian England International to have played for his home-town club. Betmead was by far the most successful centre-half the area has ever produced, and 'Ginger' Hall made his final appearance for the club in the 5-1 defeat at Huddersfield in September. Many suggested that Hall would have represented his country if on the books of a more popular club than Grimsby. He had been a part-timer throughout his playing career despite most of it being at the top level, working as a joiner during the week. Hall hung up his boots in May 1948.

Reporting for Training in 1948, newly appointed Trainer -Tom Dawson - addresses the 'troops', including Moody, Taylor, Briggs, McGowan , Galley, Sibley, Fisher, Cairns, Penrose, Tweedy, Bircham, Vincent, Dawson, Clifton and Pearson

The Mariners completed their final season in the top flight, a position they have yet to regain and may be some distance away from attaining again. Despite average gates of around 15,000-16,000, every season the Mariners played in the First Division, from 1934-48, their average was the lowest in the Division. Regardless to what some old timers may have you believe the Mariners have never been a large or wealthy club. Their spell with the elite was a constant struggle, bar the odd couple of memorable seasons. However their survival at this level is to the credit of the players, management and supporters of the era.

Long serving left-back Jack Hodgson left for Doncaster Rovers in January, therefore the back line of Vincent, Hodgson, Hall, Betmead and Buck, which had represented the club over a period of 12 years, (the half backs for 16 years) had disbanded within 12 months, leaving only 'keeper George Tweedy.

Club record signing Lew Armitage was signed in January from Rotherham United for £5,000 to boost the goalscoring figures, but unfortunately suffered a career ending injury only eight games into his spell as a Mariner, damaging his kidneys in a collision with the Manchester United 'keeper, Crompton, in March.

The only real success during this worst season on record was the form of Blenkinsopp in his usual position as a half-back. He was rewarded with a call-up to play for the Football League against the League of Ireland in April. Sadly the following month he moved to Middlesbrough for a club record £12,000. Others to leave were Sam Hodgson (Mansfield Town), Jack Johnson (Shrewsbury Town), Freddie Reeve (Reading), Ken Reeve (Doncaster Rovers), Dick Taylor (Scunthorpe United), Billy Wardle (Blackpool, for £10,000) and Albert Wilson (Boston United).

Tom Jones retired in the summer, playing his last first team drawn game in the Cup versus Reading on January 11th. Tom was aged 39 years, turning 40 in March, and one of the oldest of players to have played in the League up to this time.

1948/49

The new season in the Second Division began in the worst possible fashion with two opening home defeats to Fulham and Nottingham Forest. Although a win at Plymouth was achieved in the first away game, with Tommy Briggs scoring against the club that had released him to the Mariners. New signings were halves, Tom McKenna from Reading (who had arrived in exchange for Fred Reeve) and Ernie Forrest from Bolton Wanderers. New wingers Stan Lloyd, a new record £6,000 signing from Sunderland, and Jimmy McStay (Dundalk) also figured in the early matches.

The first home win came in the fifth match at Blundell Park by 4-1 over Q.P.R. Although the side contained some promising individuals, they appeared disjointed. Only one match in a run of 10 was won, on Christmas Day, with a welcome 3-0 victory over Yorkshire rivals Barnsley. Missing from the Grimsby side was McGowan, who broke his leg at West Bromwich a fortnight earlier. Some more poor results continued up until February, including a Cup exit at home to Third Division rivals Hull City at Blundell Park. The gate receipts for the Cup game broke previous records with £2,819-5s.-9d. being paid.

The Mariners were to emulate the form of the 1932/33 season when Town had been relegated from the First Division, for they struggled in the first half of the season, only to be saved by an excellent run-in. Further new signings were introduced in February/March which proved a revelation. Reserve Wilf Chisholm had replaced George Tweedy in goal after a poor showing by the former international in a 6-3 defeat at Elland Road in late October.

1948/49: Early morning training on the front at Cleethorpes.
The leading group of players are Wilf Chisholm, Tom Dawson (Trainer), Jimmy Johnson, Wally Taylor, Billy Pearson, Jim Duthie and Jim McStay.

Local man Ken Moody and Fisher were established full-backs, with McKenna ever-present at right-half. The ageing Galley and Sibley had made way for Forrest at centre, who was himself replaced by the impressive Duncan MacMillan, recently signed from Celtic for £3,500. Other new signings in the latter stages of the season, were Paddy Johnston at left-half, Jock Shearer a Bradford City inside-right (£2,000), and outside-left Geordie Hair, costing another £6,000 from Newcastle United. It's easy to guess where Paddy, Jock and Geordie originally came from! Irishmen Johnston arrived from Middlesbrough as compensation for centre-back Norman Robinson who had been signed in the summer. It is thought that the Teessiders off-loaded Robinson, without disclosing the defender's career-ending injury. With the new signings in place and the experienced Cairns nurturing young Briggs up-front, the Mariners only lost four of the final 14 games.

New signings- February 1949. Jock Shearer (from Bradford City), Geordie Hair (Newcastle U) and Paddy Johnston (Middlesbrough).

Finishing a mid-table 11th was seen as a success compared to the early season form. Tommy Briggs had established himself in the number 9 shirt, scoring 26 in 34 League games, and Cairns, who was the provider of many, bagged 12 himself. Some of the older players departed in the summer - Clifton, Forrest and Galley - whilst Sibley and out of favour winger Pearson both moved to Chester.

1949/50

The new season started at Southampton with Manager Charlie Spencer keeping faith in the same eleven who had finished the previous season. Briggs began the season where he had left off, scoring both Town's goals in a very worthy 2-0 victory. Sadly this excellent away win was to be a rarity as the season unfolded.

In the first home game Coventry City were beaten 3-2 with Briggs scoring all the Mariners goals, and he went on to net all of the club's initial nine. Good home victories were recorded over Sheffield United (4-0), their neighbours Wednesday (4-1, with a Lloyd hat-trick), Chesterfield (5-2) and Leicester City (2-1), though there were no further away wins.

A spell of eight games without a win before Christmas proved a worry since the run included five consecutive losses. Form picked up on entering the New Year with a 2-1 success at Q.P.R., and a 6-1 home victory over Luton Town.

July 1949 - Manager Charlie Spencer greets his new summer signings: Laurie Mackenzie a recent capture from Sheffield Wednesday, plus new forwards Jimmy Bloomer (Hull City) and Vic Barney (Bristol City).

Tommy Briggs scores one of his two goals in the 2-1 victory over Swansea Town, (September 1949). Skipper Billy Cairns (centre) looks on. This pair scored an amazing total of 221 goals between them for 'The Mariners'.

Briggs scored in the last three - and the following week, at Luton in the Cup, they won 4-3. The League victory was the most emphatic since the war, though a 7-2 defeat came in the next game at Barnsley.

Veteran goalkeper, George Tweedy, passes on some of his vast knowledge, to Chisholm, Garbutt and Bircham take note.

The summer signings by now had been introduced for spells. Winger Vic Barney (Bristol City), Jimmy Bloomer (Hull City), Laurie Mackenzie (Sheffield Wednesday), Don Harnby (Spenny-moor), Johnny Mulholland (Ply-mouth) and Jim Duthie (R.A.F.). Bloomer, Mackenzie, Mulholland and Duthie were all Scots-men joining MacMillan, McKenna, McGowan and Shearer. Manager Spencer, Trainer Dawson, Assistant ex-full-back Hughie Jacobson, Tweedy, Chisholm, Lloyd, Cairns, Hair, Bircham, Jimmy Johnson, Rankin and Don Harnby were all from the North-east. Moody and Mouncer were Grimsby-born and together with Wally Taylor from Kirton-in- Lindsey, these three were the only locals.

A mediocre season with, mediocre results saw the club finish in 11th position again. Home form was good though with plenty of goals coming from Briggs and Cairns.

The average home League attendance was the highest in the club's history at 18,238. Blundell Park's first ever all-ticket game came with the visit of neighbours Hull City in February. With the Humber rivalry at its peak, a 26,500 crowd witnessed a Cairns header which claimed a victory for the homesters. Briggs was becoming the star of the side as Captain Cairns took a more reserved roll as provider. Briggs scored 36 League goals, by far the highest in England for 1949/50, and Cairns was credited with 17. Briggs was rewarded for his fine scoring form by way of an England 'B' appearance against Switzerland at Hillsborough; England won 5-0 with every player in the forward line scoring a goal.

The lack of success on their travels proved the team's downfall with just three wins and a trio of draws. A 5-0 Cup thrashing was endured at Fratton Park, handed out by First Division Champions Portsmouth. Johnston and Cairns were ever-present, with Briggs missing just one game. Bircham, McKenna and Barney subsequently all departed to non-League football in the south.

1950/51

Charlie Spencer had been taken seriously ill in the close-season and the club did not know if or when he would be fit enough to return to his managerial duties. George Tweedy, who had recently announced his retirement from playing, had been appointed Assistant Manager and took over the running of the first team in a Caretaker capacity; the omens were not good.

Welsh inside-right Frank Squires was a record buy from Plymouth Argyle for £8,500, joining former team-mates Glover and Mulholland. Squires went straight into the first team line-up for the season's opener against Cardiff City. Other new men, Alf Barratt, Leicester City's reserve back, winger Jimmy Maddison (Darlington) and reserve 'keeper George Turnbull (Alnwick Town) all had to wait a while for their debuts.

The first three games were drawn, which began an opening run of eight games before the first victory, when Bury were beaten 2-1 on 23 September, with goals from Squires and Cairns. In this poor start the Mariners at least drew credit from one of those matches. Manchester City were the visitors to Blundell Park, and although City took the lead, the scores were all level at 2-2 by half-time. Just as the second half began disaster struck as Jock Shearer made his final contribution ever in a black and white shirt, when he collided with City 'keeper Trautmann. Shearer came off worst, being stretchered of with a broken leg. It is said that the impact of the challenge could be heard all around the ground.

1949- Laurie Mackenzie, Tom McKenna, Paddy Johnston and Vic Barney in training.

A 4-0 home defeat by Champions Preston North End saw the debut in goal of Stan Hayhurst who had signed from Barrow, but was from the Preston area himself.

This was also the last occasion Tweedy selected a side as he stepped down, and former Manager Frank Womack was recalled from his retirement in nearby Caistor. Spencer was still in a Norfolk hospital when Womack, aged 62, was appointed on a part - time basis, in late January.

With Town now down to 10 men (still no subs. in those days), City regained the lead scoring two goals, and making the score 4-2. The Mariners looked dead and buried as the final five minutes approached, but amazingly late goals by MacMillan and Briggs secured a draw, against all the odds. City were early table leaders at this stage and were duly promoted come May.

Immediately after the first win, Town lost 7-1 at Q.P.R. By the time the following victory came, Tweedy had been forced to experiment with reserves, as many of the first XI had been struck down by injury. Bloomer moved to the centre-forward position from the right, as Briggs was injured for a spell, and he settled extremely well with all four goals in a 4-2 win over Southampton. Then Brentford were beaten 7-2 in the following home game in November, this time Bloomer netted three. But the defence was playing poorly and leaked goals. Reg Scotson, the Sunderland half-back was drafted-in, and Briggs then returned, but not for long, playing his last Mariners game on Christmas Day, in a home defeat to Leicester City. Briggs later signed for Coventry City for a club record £19,550 (this fee was the fifth highest paid between British clubs at the time). The fans, not for the first or the last time, were outraged at the club's decision to sell their most prized asset. Briggs had scored 83 goals in 121 first team games.

Without Briggs the season, which was already turning into a struggle, became worse. Exeter City, bottom of the Third Division South, gained a draw at Blundell Park, before knocking Town out of the Cup, winning the replay 4-2.

Cairns took over the mantle of chief goal-getter, scoring eight in seven consecutive games, but the Mariners only won two of those matches. Five consecutive defeats saw the Mariners as bottom club with two games remaining. The final games, which were both away, were ironically not lost; a 3-1 victory at Swansea (including two goals from debutant Kevin Wood) and a 2-2 draw at promoted Manchester City.

The final game before the players broke-up for their summer break was the occasion of the first ever foreign team to play at Blundell Park. Saarücken of Germany were a touring side who visited England as part of the Festival of Britain series of matches, and they beat the Mariners 2-1.

Cairns top scored with 16 goals, and the Mariners team would need rebuilding as the playing staff was almost totally cleared out. Fifteen players with first team experience departed, following Briggs and Jim Johnson who had left in March, and Manager Charlie Spencer announced he would not be returning due to his ill-health. So the club were about to embark on a new era with no Manager and a new playing staff required, as they had dropped from the heights of the First Division - with visits to Highbury, Old Trafford and Anfield et al, with prospects now of playing at Workington and Accrington Stanley; and all in the space of three short seasons.

Chapter Seven

THE CHILTON CHICKS

1951 - 1961

1951/52

The new Manager appointed was one Bill Shankly. Shankly had been a Scottish International in his playing days with Preston North End and came to Grimsby after Managing Carlisle United for the previous couple of seasons. He brought with him winger and fellow Scot Alex McCue from Brunton Park. Other members of this new side were centre-half Bill Bellas, signed from Southport in exchange for Wally Taylor, Alf Barratt and £1,000. Shankly's former Preston team-mate Bill Brown was installed as Captain at right-back after joining from Elgin City where he was Player/manager. Other Scotsmen were signed too in Wally Galbraith from New Brighton, who had also been the Player/manager, Don McKenzie a Glasgow Rangers reserve forward, Wally Freeburn from East Stirling and Jim Hernon an inside-left from Bolton Wanderers. Nottingham-born former paratrooper Roland Wheatley also arrived from Southampton.

Not the best of starts was had with a 3-1 defeat at Chesterfield, then old rivals Lincoln City won 3-2 at Blundell Park, the Mariners being heavily handicapped when 'keeper Stan Hayhurst left the field with a broken finger, and right-back Brown replaced him in goal. Later in the game McCue, making his home debut, broke his leg, leaving the Mariners with only nine men and no goalkeeper to speak of. Billy Cairns scored his fifth goal in the first three games as Bradford Park Avenue were beaten 3-0, with George Tweedy, still on the coaching staff, who was recalled from his playing retirement.

Billy Cairns, Tom Dawson, Jimmy Maddison, Stan Lloyd and Paddy Johnston pictured in the Main Stand during 1951.

An excellent 2-0 revenge at Lincoln was achieved in the next match, this time with young Grimbarian Tom Daley making a clean sheet debut in goal. The Mariners were now making good progress winning most home games and picking-up odd points on their travels, though several were dropped due to forced changes. Shankly was proving a popular choice as Manager with the supporters, and making the most of Blundell Park's new public address system by speaking to the crowd before home games and informing supporters of the club news.

An excellent festive period was enjoyed with the beating of new Football League members Scunthorpe United in both

League matches, on Christmas Day by 3-2, then the following day 3-1 at the Old Showground. The clubs had met many times in the past in County Cup matches, Friendlies and the Town's reserves in the Midland League, but this was the first pair of matches that the North Lincolnshire clubs had met in Football League combat. These results were particularly welcome as the other locals, Lincoln City, were above Town at the top of the League and had just knocked the Mariners out of the F.A.Cup. Halifax Town were then trounced 8-1 to end the year on a high note.

From mid-January the team made a tremendous assault on the Championship in their attempt to catch the leaders Lincoln City. In fact the side was only beaten once more in the remaining 20 games, including a club record run of 11 straight wins. The biggest victory came in the final game with a 5-0 thrashing of Workington. The excellent form however achieved nothing as far as honours were concerned, for Lincoln had also continued to win, and the Mariners finished runners-up, thereby failing to gain promotion as only the Champions were promoted; despite the accumulation of a club best 66 points. If 'Lady Luck' had been playing for Town in that autumn Lincoln defeat, then the season may well have panned-out differently.

For the winning run Tweedy had returned as regular 'keeper with full-backs Brown and Galbraith in front. The half-back line read; Scotson, MacMillan and Johnston - who were all outstanding. Lloyd on the right-wing impressed, with Maddison on the left, whilst new inside-left Hernon showed excellent skills and a nose for goal, as did the other forwards Cairns and Bloomer. The highest League gate was broken at Blundell Park when nearest rivals at the top of the table, Stockport County, visited on Good Friday, a game which attracted 26,605 (receipts of £2,554).

Cairns top scored with 31 in the League, plus four in the Cup. He netted hat-tricks in the 4-0 Cup win over Darlington and the 4-1 Southport game, in which he became only the fourth man in the club's 74 year history to score 100 League goals for the club, following Carmichael, Robson and Glover. Not bad form for a 39-year-old! Bloomer and Hernon scored 17 and 16 respectively. Another interesting 'Friendly' game came at the end of this season when the Mariners were invited to play in the Paisley Cup against St.Mirren at Love Street. This was the most Northern stadium in which the club had appeared.

1952/53

Shankly initially kept faith with his players, signing only youngsters and squad players to strengthen the Championship challenge; John Millar and Ray Robson, both from Bradford City were two such additions. Everyone was confident that Town could regain their status as a Division Two side. Chairman George Pearce entered his 20th season as Chairman, and the first official Grimsby Town Supporters Club was formed in June with the backing of both Shankly and Pearce.

The Mariners had a flying start, the best ever to a season, when winning the first five (two against Scunthorpe), drawing two away games, then winning a further pair, before losing at Carlisle in the 10th match. That defeat was only a slight hiccup as Town were undefeated again for the next seven outings. Unfortunately, Jimmy Bloomer broke his leg at Darlington in the F.A. Cup and would be out for a year. An away loss at Gateshead was countered in the next game, when Hartlepools were thrashed 7-0, in mid-November. The recent £4,000 signing from Manchester City, Fred Smith, scored four of the goals in a seven minute spell!

Although the Mariners remained on course for the Championship, Christmas and New Year provided the worst set of results, including the loss of their unbeaten home record, to Bradford, in the first Blundell Park match of the year. But impressive wins against Chester (5-4) and Mansfield Town (5-1) in consecutive home games put confidence back in the side.

February approached with the Mariners still in with a good chance, but a terrible end to the season saw only four victories in the final 14 games. Only Macmillan remained within the pre-Christmas strong defence, as Brown, Galbraith, Scotson and Johnston all had spells on the sidelines during the final months.

A promising but inexperienced back guard saw reserves Tom Daley, Freeburn, Ray Robson, Roy Player, Ed Grant and Arnold Walker all fill-in. Long term injuries to Bloomer, and then Fred Smith, caused problems up-front. The side finished in 5th position which was disappointing after the tremendous start. As the Championship slipped out of their grasp several youngster were tried, including locals Wally Lord, Denis Smith and Ken Jenkin.

On 9th March, the first match under permanent floodlights was played when Town's reserves took-on Gainsborough Trinity in a Midland League game, in front of a 6,379 gathering. The floodlights had been paid for by Director Roy Osmond whose father had earlier instigated the building of the Osmond Stand in 1939. High profile Friendlies that followed saw visits from Blackburn Rovers and Scottish 'A' Division side Falkirk, which were attended by an aggregate crowd of 21,649.

On the 3 April, George Tweedy stood-in for the injured Hayhurst, and played his final game for the club at the ripe old age of 40 years and 84 days. However up-front that day was Billy 'Peter Pan' Cairns who was even older at 40 years and 179 days. Surely the only occasion the club has fielded two 40-year-olds in the Football League. Tweedy made his Mariners debut in November 1932, over 20 years earlier! McCue had returned from injury to top the club's scoring charts with 13, closely followed by Smith on 12 and Cairns with 10.

Pre-season weigh-in 1953. Skipper Billy Cairns' weight is recorded by physio Jimmy McCoy. Others present are (L-R), Hemon, Nicholson, Tom Dawson, Robson, Jacobson (Asst Trainer) and Bloomer.

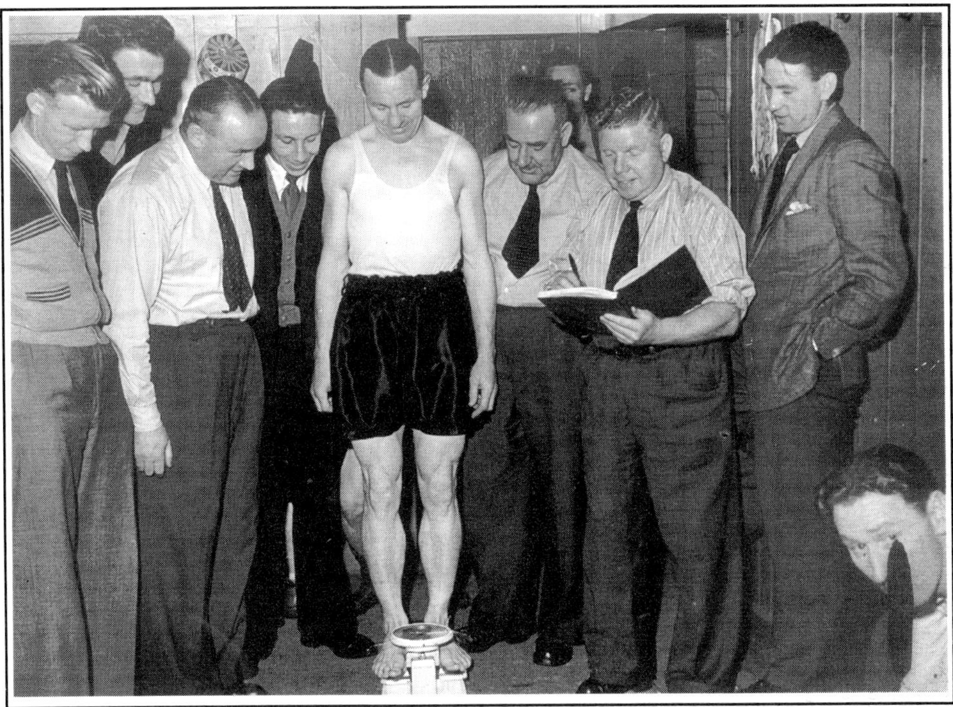

In the close season Wally Galbraith left to become manager of Accrington Stanley taking reserve pivot Joe Cadden with him as his first signing. Hayhurst, Lloyd and Harry Hart all dropped into non-League football, with McCue joining Shrewsbury Town.

1953/54

Inside-forward Archie Wright arrived from Blackburn Rovers and right-winger Derek Stroud from Bournemouth, both for small fees. The season started with a good 3-0 win over York City with a youngster from the Doncaster area, Clarry Williams, impressing in goal, but 'Scunnie' earned their first ever League points against Town with a 1-0 victory in the local derby at Blundell Park five days later.

Billy Cairns was selected for the last time in the 3-1 defeat at Accrington on 16 September, aged 40 years and 324 days, setting a club record for the oldest League player. Cairns had proved great value for money with excellent service, top scoring on several occasions as well as Captaining the side, Cairns was renowned for his superb heading ability, seeming to be able to hang in the air for that split second longer than his marker. After retiring in the summer of 1954 Cairns became landlord of the Freeman Arms on Freeman Street for many years.

The Mariners reached Christmas Day with a poor run of six games without a win, though all three of the festive matches were won. Scoring goals became a problem with no adequate replacement found for the ageing Cairns at centre-forward. By this stage of the season it was obvious that promotion would not be attained this time round, and Shankly resigned in January, to take up a fresh challenge at lowly Workington. It was not until 1959 that he became Manager of Second Division Liverpool and hence became one of the greatest managers of all-time, turning the Reds into one of the best clubs in the world.

Shankly left partly because of lack of money in the coffers, as the average gate had dropped to below the 10,000 mark for the first time since the war, and there were no funds available to delve into the transfer market. Shankly was a football man through and through and highly competitive. During his time at Grimsby, five-a-side matches were arranged in training with the Town squad being split into Scotland v England; Shankly was deeply patriotic, always captaining Scotland in these practise games. It is a well known fact the man detested Sundays, as there were no matches or training sessions.

In January, an interesting Cup-tie unfolded against Second Division Fulham. The Mariners had reached the third round by defeating Rochdale and non-League Witton Albion (albeit only after a replay) earlier. Town were drawn at home with the Londoners, which produced an amazing 5-5 draw, with a Bloomer header entering the net off the underside of the bar in the final minute to clinch a replay and also complete his hat-trick. The replay was abandoned at Craven Cottage at half-time scoreless, due to torrential rain causing a waterlogged pitch, but Town finally lost out 3-1 at the third attempt.

Shankly's replacement was former Manchester City half-back, 32-year-old Billy Walsh, who was actually appointed as Player/manager, though he only turned out for the reserves and never the first team. He was born in Dublin but moved to Manchester with his family when he was just six, playing for England Schools before signing as an amateur for Manchester United. A year later he turned professional for rivals City, playing over 220 in the war and a further 109 peacetime games . He also won caps for Eire (nine), and Northern Ireland (five). He came to Grimsby after Managing Chelmsford and Canterbury.

Many changes were forced upon Walsh, losing both 'keeper Clarry Williams and Paddy Johnston to cartilage injuries, within weeks of taking up his new post. Hernon returned from a lengthy injury but was never the same player, Fred Smith and Bloomer would also suffer in this way, whilst many of the players drafted into the side were not really up to the task or were inexperienced. With no finances to strengthen the squad Walsh was always going to struggle. Heavy defeats came at Mansfield Town (5-1) and Gateshead (7-1), the latter courtesy of four goals by Grimbarian Billy Watkin who Town released to Andover Town, without making the first team at Blundell Park. Watkin was an England Schools International and was released by Town as he was on National Service with the R.A.F.in Hampshire. The Mariners finished in 17th position, their lowest ever League ranking.

Wright joined Galbraith at Accrington, with Hernon (Watford), Rayner (Bury) and Fred Smith (Bradford City) all departing. Also the training staff of Tom Dawson and his assistant Hughie Jacobson left.

1954/55

Walsh began the new season knowing that the club was running at a loss financially with little hope of quality new signings, instead having to rely on rough diamonds such as his first signing, Johnny Archer in goal, who was signed from the Kent non-League scene which the Manager new well. A whole team of inexperienced players arrived from various clubs and backgrounds, plus Ron Harbertson who came from Valley Parade in exchange for the departed Fred Smith. Walsh realised the coming season would be a hard slog.

The first game was won convincingly 3-0 at Rochdale with new striker Arthur Hughes scoring two on his debut, and another new man, Ray De Gruchy, adding the third. The season began with Archer in goal (Williams was still recovering from injury), and at the back, Bill Brown with a new partner, the experienced George Higgins who had signed from Bolton Wanderers. Scotson, MacMillan and young Dick Conner, began the season in the half-back line. Derek Stroud was the only old boy of the attack, alongside inside-forwards Bill Pringle (Liverpool Reserves) and Hughes who had previous League experience and was signed from Walsh's former club Canterbury City. 33-year-old Ray Harrison, formerly of Burnley and Doncaster Rovers appeared at centre-forward, whilst outside-left De Gruchy was a Channel Islander and signed from Nottingham Forest reserves.

Pringle was soon dropped and replaced by Brian Lowry a young winger who had been an amateur with Manchester United. Roy Player came in for the injured MacMillan. Five straight defeats came around October, and not another away win arrived until the day after Boxing Day, when Barnsley were beaten 3-1. That Barnsley win came after the Tykes had won 3-1 at Blundell Park on Christmas Day.

The poor display pressed Walsh into making several changes. Debuts were given to Tom Redding, signed who from Brigg Town, with Brian Slater and Albert Stokes who both played up front, each being natives of Sheffield; Stokes scored on his debut.

In the 2nd round of the F.A.Cup, victory came against Southampton by 4-1, with Harbertson and Harrison scoring two each. The 3rd round saw Wolverhampton Wanderers drawn to play at Blundell Park. Wolves were reigning League Champions and were in the kind of form that would see them challenging for the title again, while Town were in the lower reaches of Division Three. Almost 26,000 fans crammed into Blundell Park paying record receipts of £3,435. Town were surprisingly leading 2-0 at half-time when an injury to Skipper Higgins forced him to remain on the field as a passenger for most of the second half. Wolves eventually ran-out 5-2 victors.

Back to life in the League, and a home defeat to Chesterfield saw Walsh lose his job after a year in charge. He departed on 1st March, and was asked to leave on medical grounds by new Chairman Mr Would, the pair not seeing eye-to-eye. Walsh and his side had tried, but were simply not good enough, especially on their travels.

The Board had attempted to bring a little continental style to Blundell Park with the appointment of Emilio Berkessy as Trainer in November. Berkessy was of Transylvanian birth, and had played most of his football in Hungary, where he became an international player then National Coach, before spells at club level coaching in Italy and Spain. He had come to England hoping to find a touch of success at Grimsby but after just a one month stay he was asked to leave the country with his application for a work permit being refused.

Walsh emigrated to New Zealand in 1956, then to Australia a decade later, where currently he still lives. Amazingly he made a playing return and was capped by New Zealand at International level, making his last appearance against Australia in 1966 aged 45! Incredibly he represented four different countries at football, spanning 32 years!

On 15th March, the Manchester United and England centre-half Allenby Chilton was appointed Player/manager. Chilton unable to turn things around winning only two and drawing one of 13 matches before the season came to a close, and scoring just seven goals. This was hardly inspiring form by the players to impress their new boss, and by finishing 23rd in the final table, Town were forced to apply for re-election, which was granted at the June A.G.M.

Bloomer and MacMillan had left mid-season, with Harbertson, Harrison and Hughes departing after just a year. Hughes top scored with 12 in the League, before returning to Kent and joining Gillingham, and Harrison joined Bloomer at Kings Lynn.

Salt was rubbed into the supporters wounds even further when their side only managed to score 47 goals. Former striker Tommy Briggs was the country's top marksman scoring 33 League goals for Blackburn Rovers, including a record seven in one game against Bristol Rovers, which still stands as a Second Division record, whilst Grimsby failed to score in 18 of their matches!

Despite the clubs lowly status, Mr Arthur Drewry, a Mariners Director, was appointed Chairman of the Football Association in May, and left his seat on the Football League Committee.

1955/56

Allenby Chilton certainly had his work cut out and had a big task in front of him. However he was a strong and determined man, and was well prepared for the season ahead as he had been at the club since March, rather than just the few weeks close-season. Although funds were extremely limited, Chairman Arthur Would promised as much cash as possible for Chilton to reconstruct his side.

Inside-right Billy Evans was signed for £3,000 from Gillingham, part of the deal which saw Hughes join the Gills. £2,000 was spent on winger Gerry Priestley from Exeter City, and Hull City centre-forward Bob Crosbie cost £1,425.

New signing - Bob Crosbie.

Dave Richardson, a left-half from Leicester City Reserves, came for a £500 fee, and Rotherham United's 21-year-old inside-left Tony Reeson arrived on a free. All the newcomers went straight into the side with only Jim Maddison remaining in attack from the previous regime. Other new additions were Chilton himself at centre-half, with a new left-back in Ray De Gruchy. De Gruchy had been signed the previous season as an attacker but only with average ability, however Chilton converted him into a left-back during the summer and thrust him into the side in the opening fixture.

Other important new signings were Trainer Bill Lambton and his assistant Ron Humpston, both originating from the East Midlands. Each had been only mediocre goalkeepers in their playing days, Lambton with Nottingham Forest, Exeter City and Doncaster Rovers, Humpston with Portsmouth and Huddersfield Town. During the war they had both been P.T.I.'s in the Armed Forces and physical strength and fitness methods similar to the Military were introduced at Blundell Park.

It was thought that both Chilton and his Trainers were in agreement that if the players were fitter and stronger they would withstand the weekly knocks better and would be able to perform at a higher standard come the winter months and soggy pitches. Training routines involved plenty of speed work and concentrated on developing muscles that were not directly used in playing football, to help with less pulls and strains and to provide better balance. These revolutionary ideas on Training were Lambton's brainchild and Grimsby soon gained the reputation as a 'super fit' team. Chilton and Lambton had both been labelled 'Iron Men' in their day, and inscribed above the home changing room door was the motto *'Keep Fighting'*, with a pair of boxing gloves beneath.

32 players had been used in the previous campaign, and now consistency would be the key. Chilton vowed in a pre-season interview that *" There is no question of Grimsby Town hoping for a better season than last. We are going to have a better one"*. And a better one was had.

The opening game saw a 1-1 home draw with Rochdale, Evans scoring on his debut, followed by a fantastic 6-1 thrashing of Chester, when Crosbie netted four and Reeson the other two. This installed tremendous confidence at such an early stage, with all three new attackers also opening their accounts for the club.

Player/manager Allenby Chilton leads out his side, in front of a packed Main Stand paddock.

Bill Brown defends, as Southport attack in front of a packed Blundell Park. A 2-0 victory ensured the fans went home happy, for the Championship was won.

Two away defeats followed, but the Mariners soon became unstoppable with a run of 16 games producing 13 wins, two draws and just one defeat, which placed them top of the table after the away win at Darlington. And that is where they stayed until January. Dick Conner replaced the injured Paddy Johnston at half-back in late September, but that was the only major change to the side before December. All forwards were scoring regularly with Reeson bagging a hat-trick in a 4-3 win at York City, despite Crosbie being sent-off.

Town had two good Cup wins in the early rounds, versus non-League Netherfield 5-1, and Southport 3-2 in a replay. The first two League games in December were lost at Wrexham and Rochdale, but a Crosbie hat-trick beat Chesterfield on Christmas Eve. If the season had a bad month it was January. No wins from the four games played knocked the Mariners out of the Cup at First Division Portsmouth, and they lost their undefeated home record to Workington. Apart from the first day draw, the Mariners had won all their previous 15 home games and conceded just four goals at 'fort' Blundell Park. Top spot was also temporarily lost. The Cup defeat at Fratton Park was the first occasion the club had played under floodlights in a competitive match, when they were turned on in the second half. Floodlights had not yet been used in League matches, and this was one of the first major matches in which they were used in England.

Five straight wins were recorded, starting another Crosbie threesome in the 5-1 victory against Oldham Athletic. But Scunthorpe United stole a 1-0 win at Blundell Park in front of over 23,000 supporters in late March, and for the next match injuries in the back line saw Roy Player replace Chilton, and Paddy Johnston recalled for Richardson, who had been ever-present. Crewe, were then swept aside, Crosbie scoring his second foursome of the season in another 5-1 victory. Mansfield Town, Wrexham and Darlington were all beaten with a point obtained at Workington. With three games remaining the Mariners needed just two points to be certain of promotion and the Championship, as nearest rivals Derby County had been dropping some vital points.

23,056 supporters created a tremendous atmosphere as Town dominated the Southport match, but the breakthrough didn't arrive until the 50th minute, when a 30 yard Billy Evans thunderbolt entered the Pontoon net. The noise inside Blundell Park was deafening and became even louder when Bob Crosbie scored the second with a well placed header. The Mariners became the first club in history to become divisional Champions a year after re-election. The crowd streamed onto the pitch in jubilant mood, from all four sides of the Ground, as the final whistle blew.

Allertby Chilton receives the Third Division North Championship shield from Mr Richards, the vice-chairman of the Football League.

The remaining two matches were both won and the Mariners were presented with the Championship Shield after the 2-0 defeat of Bradford City. The team that won the Championship was one of little change as 11 players each made over 35 starts, namely Williams, Brown, De Gruchy, Conner, Chilton, Richardson, Priestley, Evans, Crosbie, Reeson and Maddison; nine of these made over 40 appearances, with Williams and Priestley ever-presents, whilst Chilton captained his charges.

The change of fortune had never been so rapid in the club's history and this success was remarkable. Many records were again established and broken; 25 clean sheets were enjoyed by ever-present 'keeper Clarry Williams, and the team leaked only 29 goals all season. 68 points was the most the club had ever accumulated, Bob Crosbie scored 35 goals in 42 starts as he topped the scoring charts for the Mariners and the whole of Division Three North. Record receipts for a League match were paid when £3,034 was received for the Scunthorpe match, and the return match at the Old Showground several days later ensured the Mariners neighbours established their League records for both attendance and gate receipts.

To cap this fine season Director Arthur Drewry was promoted to Chairman of F.I.F.A. in June.

1956/57

The 'Chilton Chicks' were born in 1956/57, and they continued to grow with the further addition of young Manchester United reserve Johnny Scott, who had been with Chilton under the guidance of Matt Busby. Chilton was under no delusions knowing this was a time for the club to make as a priority survival and stability.

The Second Division was to prove a far more difficult competition in which to gain success. An away point at Bristol Rovers was a good start, though this was followed with a narrow 1-0 defeat at Stoke City. Both initial home games were won, with Scott scoring on his debut versus Notts County, and Evans netting a brace in the 4-1 victory in the Stoke return match. Reserve Roy Player came in for the injured Manager Chilton, who decided to retire from playing and concentrate on managing. Five games without a win in September was then corrected with a 5-0 victory over Swansea Town. More injury problems struck during October and November, notably Roy Player, who fractured his skull in a collision with Tommy Briggs in the Blackburn defeat, although Malcolm Tucker remained ever-present at centre-half. De Gruchy (his place was taken by Richardson who successfully moved to left-back), Reeson and Crosbie had all been missing for spells at this stage. Crosbie's understudy was Brian Hodgson, son of thirties stalwart Jack Hodgson.

Away wins were achieved at West Ham, Bristol City and Notts County as Christmas approached, yet the first win of the New Year didn't arrive until February.

New forward Ron Rafferty was given his chance in the early part of the year after his signing from Portsmouth. He impressed on his debut scoring in the 5-3 Cup defeat at West Ham, and he kept his place with Reeson and Crosbie both missing games through injury during the run-in.

Winning four of the last five games resulted in a safe 16th final position. With more injuries than the season before, reserves had been introduced, including local half-back Keith Jobling and flying winger Jimmy Fell. Irish winger Johnny Scott had been the find of the season, producing excellent skill, speed and crosses from the right flank, he top-scored with 11 League goals, closely followed by Evans, Crosbie and Rafferty (plus his debut goal in the Cup), all on 10. Bill Brown, the only ever-present was reinstated as captain upon Chilton's retirement, although the Manager's leadership qualities were missed in the centre of defence. Crosbie returned north of the border to his native Scotland, signing for Queen of the South.

The past three seasons had been ones of great contrast, but Chilton had been true to his word in his predictions.

1957/58

The new season began with Ron Stockin being the only major signing when he joined from Cardiff City for a fee of £5,000. He made his debut in the opening game of the season at home to Leyton Orient, and what a start. Town won 7-2 with the new man scoring one of the goals.

Colin Tinsley played 12 games in goal, with new professional full-back Bernard Fleming appearing after leaving the R.A.F. in the summer; the pair were originally from the Middlesbrough area. Another promising youngster also made his debut in the early stages of the season, left-half Don Welbourne, who had just turned 17 when he first appeared in the 4-1 win against Huddersfield Town in September. The Huddersfield victory was no fluke as Lincoln City were beaten 4-1 at Sincil Bank the following Saturday.

Although some good results were achieved, others were not so encouraging, as the side struggled to find consistency. Four consecutive defeats prompted Chilton to sign one of the most talented young defenders in the country, when Manchester United's Jeff Whitefoot surprisingly joined the Mariners for £8,000 in November. Whitefoot was United's youngest debutant when appearing during the 1949/50 season aged just 16 years and 105 days. Upon joining Town he was only 23, having won England honours at schoolboy and Under-23 levels, plus a Championship medal in 1956, although he had failed to make a subsequent appearance in their all-conquering side. What such a talent, still in his prime, was doing joining the struggling Second Division Grimsby Town was a mystery, but Allenby Chilton's Old Trafford connections had proved their weight in gold once more. Whitefoot played in all the remaining games and his class was outstanding.

Fulham's Jimmy Hill goes close with his shot at a misty Blundell Park. Town's 'keeper Williams, plus Roy Player and Don Donovan look on anxiously.

The Mariners could brag of players with real flair such as Whitefoot, Scott, young Jimmy Fell and Rafferty, though consistency as a team continued to be a problem all season. A 7-0 thrashing of Bristol Rovers on their own Eastville ground was recorded in mid-December, when all the forwards scored and Rafferty missed a second penalty. This was, and still is, Town's largest ever away victory and was the club's fourth consecutive win. Yet in the next game the Mariners were themselves taught a footballing lesson, dealt out by Leyton Orient when the Londoners won 5-1, to make amends for the opening game.

Form continued to yo-yo as four excellent home wins over Liverpool, Charlton Athletic, Rotherham United and Lincoln City sandwiched a 5-1 Cup defeat at Sheffield United. Six consecutive games were lost in February and March, with only one goal being scored, and 18 leaked. Tony Reeson had moved on to Doncaster Rovers, only to be replaced by a striker who would have probably been at the top of the supporters' wanted list.....former favourite Tommy Briggs. Briggs was now aged 34 but had been hugely successful in his spell at Blackburn Rovers,

Scoring fortunes failed to change with Briggs in the side, despite a hat-trick in a rare 4-1 win against Middlesbrough in April. Although only five victories were salvaged from 19 games since the New Year, Town finished an improved, but disappointing 13th.

Ron 'Chips' Rafferty (nicknamed after the Australian actor), scored 26 League goals with Fell scoring 14 in his first full season at professional level.

On the completion of the League campaign the players were not immediately released for their summer break, in fact John Scott only managed a few weeks rest before he reported for training again in July. The reason for the delay being the club's first trip to foreign soil as the Mariners made a three week tour to Czechoslovakia. The trip was arranged by Chairman Arthur Would, who apparently had a business interest in producing ornaments and gifts made of cut glass, for which a cheap but skilled market had been established in Czechoslovakia. Sales, it was hoped, would be successful in Britain.

The Mariners first game was played in Bratislava against the Czech National side who were due to play in the World Cup finals in Sweden at the end of the month. With great credit the Mariners drew 1-1 in a game which was screened live on State television, thus becoming the first ever live TV

1957/58- Captain Bill Brown leads out his Mariners, followed by Clarry Williams and Johnny Scott. Note the presence of Towns first match day mascot Pontoon Pete, complete with an early version of 'Harry the Haddock'.

broadcast involving the Mariners. The tour was a great success but on the field the Mariners failed to win in the five matches played.

Johnny Scott, on his return from Czechoslovakia, met up with the Northern Ireland World Cup squad in Belfast, then travelled to the finals in Sweden to make his International debut, as the Irish made their first appearance on the world stage against, none other than...... Czechoslovakia! Scott made two appearances as the Irish reached the Quarter-finals, and he is the only serving Mariner to play in the World Cup Finals.

1958/59

The squad had something of a makeover on their return from overseas. Departures included several who had served the club well. Bill Brown had applied and was successful in becoming Barrow's new manager, and players who started the 1957/58 season in the side but lost their places included De Gruchy (Chesterfield), Walker (Walsall), Tinsley (Darlington) and Tucker (Skegness Town), who all moved on. The most expected, but least wanted move was that of Whitefoot. He brought in £11,000 when transferring to Nottingham Forest, and finished the season as an F.A.Cup medal winner. He spent 10 years at the City Ground, grossing 285 first class appearances for Forest.

Several quality players were brought in to replace those who left. Costing £8,000 each were defenders Don Donovan, the Everton and Eire right-back, and Ron Cockerill from Huddersfield Town who was a long striding left-half. Luton Town's Scottish cap Mike Cullen was also signed, replacing Billy Evans who had joined the Town's coaching staff. Two reserve 'keepers in Alec Bell and Malcolm White were also signed, with reserve forwards Ritchie and Barrett joining from southern non-League football.

The opening day of the season saw Town visit Anfield, and an outstanding performance by Town winger Jimmy Fell against Liverpool gained him an award presented by a national newspaper. Fell had already scored as Town 'keeper Clarry Williams became injured and couldn't continue. The outfielder donned the 'keeper's jersey and gloves and saved a point for the Mariners in a 3-3 draw. The Daily Mirror provided Fell with an 'Andy Capp' award for performance of the week.

Town continued this promising start with 4-2, 3-2 and 4-4 results. The 4-4 draw was at Lincoln City with Rafferty scoring all the Mariners goals. Home form continued to be good, and the first defeat arrived in curious circumstances in mid-October, in a friendly against Prague Dynamo of Czechoslovakia. The 1-0 reverse came by way of a huge clearance from the Czech 'keeper, Doeljst, which was wind-assisted and bounced clean over the unsuspecting Malcolm White's head.

It is very likely that this was the first ever goal by a goalkeeper from a full-length clearance. Another unfortunate incident occurred to young Malcolm White just days later. With Williams and Bell injured, the 17-year-old White made his Football League debut in goal at Hillsborough against future Champions Sheffield Wednesday. Town were hammered 6-0, which was bad enough for White, but his own defender, Roy Player, was credited with two of the goals. White, who had been an apprentice bricklayer for British Rail in the Midlands, didn't play in the first team again for another two years!

In fact from that point on the Mariners had a terrible season. They had a contrasting match at Bristol Rovers compared to a season earlier, for they lost 7-3, and only five more wins were recorded all season, as the team fell totally apart. Another 'keeper, Alan Barnett, was signed from Portsmouth as all the incumbents were struggling with form and injury. Barnett made his debut on the last ever Christmas Day fixture, when the Mariners lost 2-1 at home to Sheffield United. No League games were played in January and only the Cup games survived the weather.

In the Cup, Town drew Manchester City at home in the third round, a team struggling in the League, but none the less they were still from the First Division. Town drew 2-2 in front of a 15,000 crowd and were not expected to win the replay at Maine Road. But two tremendous strikes from Ron 'Cannonball' Cockerill gave the Mariners a surprise 2-0 victory. The fourth round unfortunately provided no shocks as Nottingham Forest swept the Mariners aside 4-1 with an impressive display.

Town recovered well from their Cup defeat and beat Cardiff City 5-1 in February, though the next victory did not come until seven games later, at 'Sunny Scunny', when the Mariners restored some local pride with a 3-1 away win over their neighbours. With 10 games left there were sufficient chances to get the team out of its perilous position, but the warnings were not heeded, nor action taken. Two games were drawn and the next six were lost. A 4-1 win against Leyton Orient produced a little hope, but the Mariners had to get a result at Stoke in the final game, or rely on other results for their own safety. Preparations for the Stoke encounter were not exactly ideal, as Chilton resigned three days before the game, after being informed that his contract would not be renewed in the Summer. Trainer Bill Lambton was in charge as the Mariners crashed 4-0, and were relegated, finishing a point behind survivors Rotherham United.

This was to be the only season that saw all three Lincolnshire clubs grace the Second Division, but Lincoln and Scunthorpe survived, and Barnsley were relegated with the Mariners to the new Third Division, after a Fourth Division had been formed in place of the regional Divisions. With such good players at the club it is difficult to find a reason why the team failed to perform during the second half of the season. Rafferty top scored with 19 in the League and Keith Jobling was the only ever-present. Loyal winger Jimmy Maddison, moved to Chesterfield in March as he failed to regain his place from the impressive Fell. Briggs had been disappointing upon his return to Grimsby and departed to manage Irish outfit Glentoran, with Dick Conner moving south to Southampton. Roy Player also left, for Oldham Athletic, and the close-season was one of uncertainty as the club remained Managerless.

1959/60

Former Sergeant-Major, Trainer Bill Lambton, was still in charge of training, tactics and team selection as the new season opened in Division Three, with the board of Directors unable to find a suitable replacement for the departed Chilton. Lambton had only recently returned for a second spell at Blundell Park, in April, after short spells in charge at Leeds United (3 months) and Scunthorpe United (just three days). His troops knew what to expect of him with his disciplinarian ruling of the squad.

New signings, left-half Joe Birbeck from Middlesbrough and striker Ralph Hunt from Derby County, both appeared in the first game of the season at home to Chesterfield. Birbeck was signed due to the long term injury of Ron Cockerill. The season started almost as well as the previous as Town romped to a 5-1 victory with the strong strike force of Cullen, Rafferty and Hunt all scoring. Hunt can probably claim the feat of scoring the quickest debut goal, as the Mariners recorded the first of the season after just 90 seconds! In fact the Mariners were unbeaten going into the sixth game having beaten Colchester and Accrington, 4-1 and 4-0 respectively in the previous weeks, and Hunt bagging himself a hat-trick in the Colchester win.

Then a run of 10 games with only one victory was endured into mid-October, this sequence ending with another unbeaten period of nine League games, and still under Lambton's 'temporary' leadership! In the mid-November to December period of the season, the Mariners played their F.A.Cup matches. A first round tie saw them pull Cheshire League opponents, Rhyl - away - out of the hat. This potential banana skin was overcome courtesy of two own goals by the Welsh side, as Town came away lucky 2-1 victors. Wrexham were drawn at home in the next round, and as they were struggling at the wrong end of Division Three, Town were expected to win this one too. However Wrexham triumphed 3-2 and that was the end of the Cup exploits for the season.

No games were won of the five played in December as the Mariners continued their up and down season. Brian Keeble, a 21-year-old signing from Holbeach United, settled in to first team football with ease, when he filled in at right-back, the position vacated by Donovan's move to the half-back line, as both Welbourne and Birbeck had spells of absence. Despite the lack of consistent results two players who were showing consistency were Hunt and Rafferty who were both lethal in front of goal.

After just one win in January, Bill Lambton finally stepped-down from his caretaker position, allowing a new boss - Tim Ward - to take the reigns; the club had waited 10 months before appointing Chilton's successor. Lambton had done a good job and was unfortunate not to have secured the position himself, but he stayed on as Trainer. Ward, appointed as late in the season as February, steadied the ship and the Mariners finished the season well, losing only once at home in the remaining games, and being undefeated in the last six games which were played against difficult opposition.

Ward had been a half-back with Derby County, England and Barnsley, and also managed the latter. With injury problems in defence, Keeble and latterly local part-timers Johnny Pearce and Tony Knights, both aged 20, all performed remarkably well for Ward. The Mariners finished in 5th spot, level on points with Coventry City.

The Third Division was a very open one that season with nothing much between any of the sides at the top and bottom, for Champions Southampton won only 7 games away from home...the same amount as bottom club Accrington! Town finished 7 points behind second place Norwich City who were also promoted. If the Mariners had taken a little more care when playing the lower clubs these extra points would have been earned. Of the four sides relegated, York City, Mansfield Town and Wrexham all took two points each from Town. On the other hand, of the four clubs finishing above Town, only Shrewsbury Town beat Grimsby (one game out of eight); on that occasion Town were 2-0 up, but finally lost 5-2 as an the injury-struck Mariners were reduced to only nine fit men.

The defence had worked hard among the disruptions, but the main praise had to be given to forwards Ralph Hunt and Ron Rafferty. Between them they scored 59 goals - Hunt 34 and Rafferty 25 - and both were in the Divisional 'Top Ten' goalscorers list, although Hunt was beaten into third place; Southampton's Derek Reeves was top, with 45. Skilful winger Johnny Scott chipped in with 14 goals. Departures included Clarry Williams (Barnsley), Dave Richardson (Swindon Town), with Birbeck and Stockin retiring to non-League circles in their native areas.

1960/61

No major new signings were made as Ward had faith in the players that he had 'adopted' for a promotion bid. A new decade and era began with a completely new playing strip, new floodlights were erected at Blundell Park, and the Mariners were to take part in the newly created Football League Cup, which was to start before Christmas.

For the first game, against Chesterfield, the Mariners appeared from the Main Stand tunnel in plain white short sleeved tops, with a black 'v' at the neck and armlets; shorts and socks were red, with not a black stripe in sight. The game was drawn 0-0.

Unlucky goalkeeper Malcolm White had been given a chance again in the pre-season games and had performed well enough to be selected for the season's start. His defence included captain Keith Jobling at centre-half with Pearce and Knights alongside him, and Donovan plus Keeble were the regular full-backs. The forward line remained Scott, Rafferty, Cullen, Hunt and Fell, Cullen being switched to the central role to hopefully improve his goal tally.

Malcolm White shows a safe pair of hands as Don Donovan covers during the 3-1 home win versus Walsall in October 1960.

A second draw was played at Colchester when the forwards failed to score again. The third game produced the first win of the season at no better place than Boothferry Park, Hull. The Mariners won 3-2, the Tigers having been relegated from Division Two in May. In fact unbeaten until the 11th match was the best start to the season in the Mariners history. In the following eight games, seven were won, the other, a goalless drawn match at Coventry finished with 10 men after Johnny Scott had been sent-off.

On the downside, Trainer and former player Billy Evans tragically died from Cancer in August, aged 38, and a Benefit match was organized in his memory later in the season. Hunt and Knights had been lost in these early games to injury, and Welbourne was recalled at half-back, with three local youngsters who were tried in Hunt's position, before Derek Williams proved a success. The youngsters were Alec Brader (of Horncastle), plus Laverick and Sinclair who had both played together at Holme Hill Junior School in Grimsby as infants; Derek Williams was the brother of former 'keeper Clarry.

Another point of note in these early stages was the switching-on of the new Floodlights. The Supporters Club had paid £9,000 for their installation during the summer months and they were first used for the reserves' game against Sunderland on Tuesday 13 September. The following Tuesday saw their use for the first time in a League Match, when Newport County were beaten 2-1.

An indifferent spell in the League was completed with an unusual week late in October. The Mariners beat Halifax Town 6-1 on the Saturday, before travelling to First Division Bolton Wanderers for their first ever game in the League Cup, on the Tuesday. Town had received a bye in the first round and attended Burnden Park in high spirits after their good start to the season. 2-0 up at one stage the Mariners eventually lost 6-2.

The following game saw another away trip, this time to Tranmere Rovers, where they won 6-3, with Derek Williams scoring four! The next two League games were both won, athough, either side of a disappointing F.A.Cup exit at Fourth Division Darlington. Unusual and unpredictable results continued, in particular Port Vale's visit to Blundell Park in early December when they beat Town 5-0. Grimsby were still at the top end of the Division but not many sides gain promotion by losing by such a large scoreline at home.

A Rafferty hat-trick at home to Barnsley secured a 3-2 win over the Tykes, though the score was reversed at Oakwell the following week. 1961 started badly as the Mariners fell-out of the Promotion race. No victory in January, but a couple of consecutive wins in February raised hopes for the remaining 14 games, yet only two were won, and the Mariners sank to 6th. Those two victories were marked with hat-tricks from Rafferty, against Tranmere, and Hunt in the Torquay game. The bad form coincided with the departure of Jimmy Fell to Everton in March for £18,000.

Attendances dropped dramatically from well over 10,000 at the start of the season to below 4,000 for the final home game against Southend, the lowest gate at Blundell Park in peacetime since official records were kept by the Football League in 1925. The reason for this slump was not just the poor showings, but the addition of the disquiet felt by many supporters concerning the sale of Fell, plus price increases which were levied following the Footballers maximum wage being abolished.

Rafferty top-scored with 24 in Division Three, followed by Derek Williams with 17. Hunt had endured a disappointing season, first with injury then being unable to displace any of the forwards for a permanent first team recall. He scored just six in the League, but was the reserves' top goalscorer with 10. Rafferty gained two worthy honours during the season. Firstly he scored six goals in a first team game, achieving this feat in the 8-3 defeat of Lincoln City in the County Cup in November, then the first goal of his hat-trick against Tranmere in March was his 100th League goal for the club.

If it hadn't have been for the poor finish the Mariners would have returned to Division Two, they would have to try their luck again. 1959/60 and 1960/61 were almost identical seasons, would 1961/62 be the same?

Chapter Eight

THE RISE AND FALL OF THE SWINGING SIXTIES

1961 - 1971

1961/62

The close-season saw three new players arrive at Blundell Park. Hunt had left for Swindon Town in exchange for Welsh winger Freddie Jones who moved from Wiltshire, to replace the void left by Fell's departure on the left wing. Port Vale's striker Cliff Portwood was brought in to replace Hunt, who cost £6,000. The Nottingham Forest reserve full-back Barry Wealthall was the other new recruit.

Legs Up !!! Brian Clifton, Freddie Jones, Mike Cullen, Cliff Portwood, Barry Wealthall and 'keeper Malcolm White, limber-up on the wall bars.

The season started with a 2-0 win at Newport County, both goals coming from Cullen. The Supporters Club had funded the building of the new Pontoon Stand during the summer, which would continue to house the most vocal fanatics at Blundell Park. The stand was opened for the first home game of the season when Torquay United spoiled the atmosphere of the 11,000 Mariners followers, as they stole a 3-2 victory. The return was won in Devon, the following Wednesday.

Town began to record some useful results, including a 4-0 win versus Reading, with a hat-trick from Rafferty, and a 4-1 victory over ancient rivals Lincoln City, Portwood scoring a trio on this occasion. Then Town were unable to win for five consecutive games, including a 7-0 thrashing at Northampton. Gates were again down on previous seasons as Town had been knocked-out of both Cups at the first stages, by Fourth Division sides, and lie 12th in the League at Christmas with the future looking unspectacular. The year finished by losing both the festive games, 2-0 at Southend and Coventry.

However, the New Year brought with it some new found fortune. The side was the same but a run of seven straight victories saw the Mariners creep up the table to become outsiders in the promotion frame. A slight hiccup came with a 1-1 draw in the Lincolnshire derby at Sincil Bank, then a 3-2 defeat at promotion rivals Q.P.R., after Town had been 2-0 up with goals from Rafferty. Rangers equalised with 12 minutes left and then scored a winner from a cross which appeared to have ran out of play before going in the net off defender Tony Knights.

The Mariners picked themselves up again and went on another unbeaten run of six games, before losing 1-0 at Hull City. With just four games left, Bradford Park Avenue were first beaten home and away. Top of the table Portsmouth, who were already promoted, were to be joined by either Q.P.R. or the Mariners as the final promotion place for Division Two would be decided in the final two games.

Grimsby entertained Watford and after leading 4-1 they eventually won 5-3 in front of a 15,000 Blundell Park crowd. Rangers also won so the final promotion spot was not yet secured. The Mariners only had a tricky away game at relegation candidates Brentford on Tuesday 1st May, whilst Rangers had two games left after the weekend, playing Lincoln on the Monday and Halifax on the Thursday. Rangers won 5-0 at Lincoln on the Monday with many Mariners followers present, and over 19,000 fans attended Griffin Park on May day, including many Q.P.R. supporters to cheer on Brentford in order that their team could finish ahead of the Mariners.

It was not until the second half that a Scott free-kick, just outside the Bees box, ricocheted off the wall of players and into the path of Portwood, who scored from a tight angle with a powerful drive. With nine minutes remaining Rafferty scored another to send the Mariners back into Division Two, a remarkable feat as they looked no-hopers at Christmas.

That final goal of the season was Rafferty's 34th in the League campaign, setting a new club record for Division Three, another remarkable feat for this season as he had continued playing injured since early March. The players that were instrumental in the club's success were Barnett in goal, Donovan and Keeble as full-backs who had been consistent all season. Jobling and Knights with either Pearce (this trio were all Grimsby-born) or Cockerill as a third partner. Scott had local deputy John Waite on the right wing, and Freddie Jones on the left. The change which probably brought the success was the shuffling of the forward line, around January. Portwood moved from inside-right to centre, Rafferty from number 9 to 10, and Cullen from inside-left to inside-right. Portwood had a good first season with a scoring return of 14. Everyone at the club had really pulled together in the last four months, with Ward allowing the players to enjoy their success before an end of season tour of Czechoslovakia.

Sixteen players travelled to eastern Europe, including reserve striker Dick Young who had just finished his national service with the Durham Light Infantry and turned professional on demobilisation after a trial spell. He came from the north-east and joined his cousins Derek Williams and Jimmy Thompson on the club's staff, and scored five in the first two games of the six game tour, including a hat-trick in the second versus Slovan Liberec. Town won 4-0 and this was Televised live across Czechoslovakia, the game being played on a Sunday, the first occasion the Mariners had done so.

This tour was more of a success on the field than the previous, for only one game was lost. This was also the last time Tim Ward would see his side in full flight, as before pre-season training commenced, he was invited to take-over the hot seat at his former club Derby County.

1962/63

Ward decided to return to manage his first love Derby County, after unbelievably not receiving the offer of a new contract at Blundell Park. The board soon announced the appointment of Rotherham United supremo Tom Johnston. Johnston, had narrowly failed to reach the top flight with the Millers, who were also finalists in the first League Cup. He had previously been a winger with both Nottingham clubs in his playing days and had coached in Finland.

Trainer Lambton had left in January to Manage Chester, with his assistant and former full-back George Higgins becoming Trainer. Another former player returned in the summer, Clarry Williams who became assistant to Higgins. Clarry's brother Derek in the meantime had joined Bradford Park Avenue.

The season started with a defeat at Plymouth, a draw at home to Portsmouth, then the first victory in the local derby versus Scunthorpe United, by 3-0 at Blundell Park. Then seven consecutive defeats saw Town still to win a League Cup game and rooted at the bottom of the Division; they certainly found the step-up a difficult one. White replaced Barnett in goal, whilst the defence selected was the same as the previous season, though they had performed poorly. Youngsters Young and winger Brian Hill were introduced early on, before centre-forward George McLean was signed from Norwich City. Young produced a remarkable hat-trick at Tim Ward's Derby when Town won 4-2 in late September.

Ronnie Foster in action soon after his signing from Orient.

As New Year approached Town were still bottom with just four wins, the other pair of successes being a 3-1 victory at Charlton and 4-1 at home to Southampton. By this stage Johnston had made a further addition to the side in Southampton's Brian Clifton, who was unfortunate enough to be injured on his debut in October and was out until February.

In December inside-left Ronnie Foster came in for a record £11,500, from First Division Leyton Orient, while Ward had taken Cullen to Derby County. After the New Year further misery came with the Mariners again being knocked out of the F.A.Cup at the first hurdle, this time by eventual finalists Leicester City. A bad winter meant that Town didn't return to League action until mid-February.

The return was a welcome one as Clifton scored the only goal on his comeback when Town defeated high flying Middlesbrough at Ayresome Park. In this game debutant Charlie Wright produced heroics in goal, having been signed from Workington that month. The 'double' was achieved with a 2-1 win over Charlton in the next game, and the Mariners continued to win most at home and draw away as safety was assured in the final match when Bury were thrashed 5-1, George McLean scoring four. 19th position was poor but so had been the performances, Town had not been out of the bottom six all season, so survival had to be seen as a mark of success.

McLean top-scored with 15 as goals from Rafferty and Portwood dried-up at this level. The side now read; Wright, Jimmy Thompson, Donovan, Cockerill, a much improved Jobling, and Clifton. Scott had been struggling with injury and form and was replaced by another new signing, Jimmy Pennington from Crewe Alexandra in early April, plus Foster, McLean and Rafferty with Brian Hill consistent on the wing. Young Hill had lightning speed and had taken his chance well. All the youngsters tried during the season had been brought to the club by Tim Ward.

1963/64

Town certainly had to improve this season or suffer the consequences. Johnston had a clear-out in the summer when 12 players with first team experience left, including Scott (York City), Rafferty (Hull City), 'keepers Barnett (Exeter City) and White (Walsall), plus reserve Dick Renwick who joined Aldershot. Gil Wheaton met up with an old friend, Bernard Fleming, at Bill Lambton's Chester.

Two new men were brought in, both Scotsmen, winger Malcolm Bogie from Hibernian, and a slim forward from Airdrieonians, Matt Tees. The preferred black and white stripes were reinstated for the new season also, although throughout the sixties they were not quite as bold. White socks were worn as opposed to red, and overall the kit displayed more white than black.

Tees impressed in his first games as he scored after just 10 seconds in his debut in a pre-season friendly against Gordon Banks and Leicester City. He followed this with the goal in the draw at Swansea in the first League game. The first seven games passed without a win including the expected exit from the League Cup, and in this spell Middlesbrough beat Town 6-0. Another Scot, Don Walker, was signed by Town after the Middlesbrough game, from that club.

Young returned to the side and scored in the first win of the season over Newcastle United. This result was especially pleasing for cousins Young and Thompson as they came from the Gateshead area and the former player had been released by the Magpies in his teens. Town's result was even more remarkable as Young was later stretchered off and Clifton was nothing more than a passenger as he continued with a groin strain. The season reached December with only one win, 3-1 over Norwich City, in the previous 11. The biggest victory of the season then came when Northampton were beaten 4-1, with Cockerill and McLean scoring a brace each. Now playing at left-back was a youngster from Scunthorpe, named Graham Taylor.

All the new signings were disappointing with Bogie playing just once, Walker suffering from injury, and Tees had managed just three goals by February, although the other forwards had done little better. A much needed win came courtesy of a 3-1 victory over Middlesbrough, but just one more in the next nine dampened any cinders that were still smouldering. That success was an unexplained 4-0 victory at Maine Road against Manchester City on an off-day, and four straight losses followed.

The Mariners needed a miracle to survive with just five games left. A good start was made with a 2-2 draw at Portsmouth. Then relegation rivals Scunthorpe were beaten 2-0, and another home game followed, against Cardiff. The Mariners, although full of effort, failed to have any luck in front of goal and Cardiff broke away and scored twice. The last away game was won 2-1 at Northampton Town, leaving the Mariners and 'Scunnie' as favourites to go down as the final game approached. Town could only manage a 2-2 draw with the already promoted Sunderland in front of a 16,500 crowd at Blundell Park, a game remembered for the outstanding performances by Wright and Montgomery in goal.

Other results were gathered and it worked out the Mariners had been relegated by a goal average difference of just 0.045. Plymouth scored 45 letting in 67. Town had the same 32 points as Plymouth and finished with a record of 47 for, 75 against. If tables relied on goal power instead of difference the club would have survived, but they didn't, and so a return had to be made again to Division Three after just two seasons.

Top scorer was Cliff Portwood with 11, and Charlie Wright was the only ever-present, in goal. Bogie (Aldershot), Walker (Workington), Knights (Luton Town) and Portwood (Portsmouth) all departed in the summer.

1964/65

Johnston remained in charge and no major recruits were taken on in the summer. Town made the best possible start to dismiss any relegation blues, by hammering Oldham Athletic on their own ground 5-1 with a foursome from McLean, who had only managed seven goals during the previous season.

Town drew and then won consecutive home games, before being beaten 5-3 at Bristol Rovers. But the results were generally going the Mariners way, including an unbeaten home run, and they had reached the top of the table by October.

Oldham were beaten again as the Mariners at last won their first ever League Cup game after four years of trying. A 3-1 victory saw them face First Division Leicester City in round two, at home, but they lost 5-0, as 18-year-old England Youth International John Lakin appeared for the only time in his Mariners career.

Three generations of Towns great goalkeepers.
First team regular Charlie Wright is given some pointers from former 'keeper, assistant trainer Clarry Williams, as a youthful Harry Wainman looks-on. Between them they kept goal for Town on over 800 different occasions.

Tom Johnston then dropped the bombshell that he was leaving to become Manager at Second Division Huddersfield Town. Johnston had hardly enjoyed a successful time at Grimsby, but as the side were currently flying high it was thought he was the man to bring instant promotion. Trainer George Higgins was placed in temporary charge and could count himself unlucky not to have landed the job permanently as he maintained the team's form at the top of the table, when they failed to lose any of the seven games in which he was in charge. The only career of a Grimsby manager never to lose a match!

Late November saw Glaswegian, Jimmy McGuigan appointed, and he took charge in his first match against Shrewsbury Town, with the Mariners lying in second spot. The game was drawn and the next was won against Oldham Athletic once again, this time by 3-1. Not a bad start for McGuigan, a former wing-half with Hamilton, Sunderland, Stockport, Crewe and Rochdale. He then hung up his boots and became the Coach, then Manager in his fifth term at Gresty Road, before receiving an invitation to lead the Mariners. He immediately brought Billy Haydock with him and signed Ray Lancaster from Rotherham United. Haydock also made an impressive start to his Mariners career scoring two of the goals in the latest Oldham win.

But then something went drastically wrong as the Mariners plummeted down the table at an alarming rate. A Cup exit came at Stockport County, after a three match epic with Barrow, and an abandonment in the first encounter in the second round.

After beating Oldham on 12 December, McGuigan's second win didn't arrive until April 6, 18 games later! Half of those games were drawn however, producing a club record run of five on the trot in February.

Thankfully four of the final six games were won, including a 3-0 win over Scunthorpe, but Town finished a very disappointing 10th.

Youngsters who impressed during the season were again full-backs - Thompson and Taylor. Cockerill, Jobling and Clifton were the experienced half-back line, and 17-year-old Harry Wainman appeared on four occasions in goal as Wright was injured. Summer signings Les Barratt (Barrow) and Keith Allen (Portsmouth) were only given brief chances at first team level. The skilful Dougie Collins, first brought to the club by Tom Johnston on his release from Rotherham United, showed nice touches in the final matches after he was rewarded with a first team place following his 18 goals in the reserves. Hill, Jobling and Jimmy Thompson were ever-presents, and the forwards put up a better show with McLean netting 20, Foster 11 and Tees 10.

With the club again struggling financially several players were off-loaded in the summer months. Young, Allen, then Haydock, all joined Stockport County. Pennington (Oldham), Barratt (Southport), Keeble (Darlington) and McLean (Exeter City) left, with Don Donovan becoming Manager at Boston United and taking with him Lakin, Billy Howells and most of the reserve side, as the Mariners couldn't raise enough funds to finance a second team for 1965/66.

1965/66

With no reserve side, the young players had to rely on appearances in Clarry Williams' Northern Intermediate junior team. Among these teenagers were Wainman and Dave Boylen, Nottinghamshire lads John Wilkinson and Dave Morgan, Brian Kerry from South Yorkshire, and three Scots - Georgie Taylor, Peter Beckers and Angus Davidson - who all came from the Angus region. Locals Jimmy Bloomer (son of the 1950's striker) and Dave Garland made up the numbers, all of whom were to make first team appearances during the next couple of seasons.

New experienced signings were centre-forward, Rod Green from Gillingham and utility man Bobby Ross from St.Mirren. The Football League brought in the use of substitutes for the first occasion this season, one to be pre-named and used at any time during the game but, initially, only to replace an injured player. Future England Manager Graham Taylor was selected as Team Captain aged only 20.

The Mariners started their season with a 1-1 draw at home to Bristol Rovers, Tees scoring Town's only goal. Ray Lancaster was named as the club's first substitute though he didn't appear on this occasion, but later became the first for the club when replacing Matt Tees on 27 August at York. Six straight wins in October saw Town become during the early season likely promotion candidates. Tees and Green hit good form including their two goals each in a 4-1 win at Oldham.

Impressive League form was enhanced in the other competitions as Second Division Crystal Palace (away), Bolton and Preston were beaten 1-0, 4-2 and 4-0 respectively in the League Cup, and Barrow and Barnsley were overcome in the F.A.Cup. The League Cup victories led to West Ham United visiting Cleethorpes in the Quarter-final in December. 17-year-old Angus Davidson made his senior debut as Bobby Ross was pronounced unfit before kick-off. West Ham were European Cup Winners holders and fielded England Captain Bobby Moore, Martin Peters and Geoff Hurst.

But strikers Tees and Green again proved their worth with a goal each as Town led 2-1 with 20 minutes remaining. Then Hurst equalised and the match finished 2-2. This was and an excellent show from the Mariners which earned them a replay, although it was felt that their opportunity had surely passed. During the replay the match remained goalless until Hurst again struck late to knock the gallant Mariners out. West Ham reached the Final losing to West Bromwich over two legs, and in the summer the three West Ham players were World Cup winners.

In the F.A.Cup, after their two earlier round victories, Town drew Second Division opponents again - Portsmouth. A 0-0 draw at Blundell Park in early January, set-up the chance of a tremendous 3-1 victory at Fratton Park in the replay. In the fourth round though Manchester City were too strong for the Mariners, winning 2-0.

March 1966 at Walsall. Rod Green saves well from a young Allan Clarke, as full-back Jimmy Thompson closes-in. Regular centre-forward, Green, replaced the injured 'keeper, Charlie Wright, who was carried off earlier in the game.

The Cup exit coincided with a slump in League form and the club's wafer thin squad was being stretched to its limits. Charlie Wright was stretchered off with concussion at Walsall with Rod Green taking over in goal. This was to be crowd-pleaser Wright's final appearance for the club, as he was transferred to Charlton Athletic on recovery from his injury.

Home form was excellent, the team being unbeaten until the Easter weekend when they lost both home games in the space of 24 hours, to Scunthorpe and Mansfield. However their away form in the League was constantly poor with only two victories, at Brighton and Oldham, in October, yet amazingly three games had been won away in the F.A.Cup.

A final place of 11th was finally achieved, after many of the Junior side were fielded due to first-team injuries in the later games. The addition of winger Johnny Fielding injected pace to the forward line when he was secured from Brentford, scoring on his debut in December at home to Swindon Town. Due to the successful run in the Cup competitions, which caused a fixture backlog, eight matches were played in the month of May.

Tees top-scored with 36 League and Cup goals, his only hat-trick of the season coming in the Preston Cup win. His form blossomed, with the aid of partner Green who netted 15. Brian Clifton was the only major departure moving down the A16 to play for Don Donovan's Boston United.

1966/67

The reserve side were reinstated and joined the Midland Counties League, and two early signings made by McGuigan were Billy Rudd, a scheming front man from York City, and Dave Worthington a play anywhere man from Barrow. Losing 2-1 at Workington on the opening day preceded a 2-1 win at Barnsley in the League Cup, before Walsall were beaten 3-1 in the first game at Blundell Park, Worthington, at centre-forward, scored in both of his first two games.

The following home game saw local rivals Scunthorpe United thrashed, 7-1, when both Green and Hill scored hat-tricks against a startled 18-year-old Ray Clemence. A successful September was enjoyed when four straight wins and an away draw in the return at Scunthorpe was recorded, and a second round cup victory over Bradford Park Avenue saw Town then beat Workington 3-0. The usual good start soon petered out by November, with bad defeats to Q.P.R.(5-1), 4-0 at Colchester and 6-0 at Reading.

At this stage Town had lost the services of Brian Hill, who had joined Second Division Huddersfield Town for a club record £22,000, and again this was a decision taken by the board which angered supporters. Geoff Martin was signed from Workington to replace Hill. Welshman Graham Rathbone arrived from Newport County and went straight into the side at centre-half, and these two dealings left only £5,000 of the money from Hills' transfer.

4-1 wins over Workington and Doncaster were rare highlights in December, before five games without a win followed into February. Ray Lancaster moved to Lincoln in January being replaced by Scunthorpe's Bobby Smith. Another controversial decision by the board was taken with the sale of front pair Rod Green and Matt Tees to Charlton Athletic for a combined fee of £23,000. The motive would appear to be for much needed cash, but replacements cost £20,000 in Gary Moore from Sunderland and Dave Wilson from Carlisle United.

The average Blundell Park attendance was now well under 5,000, with many fans staying away through poor displays and lack of trust in the board. Hill, Green, Tees and Wright who were four of the most popular players to represent the club during this period were now gone. The supporters barracked the new front men Moore and Wilson during their initial games, though Wilson scored seven goals in 16 starts, including a hat-trick against Gillingham in front of a 3,658 gate, the smallest in the League at Blundell Park since 1925!

Pre-season training at Peakes Lane in 1966: Hill, Bloomer, Graham Taylor, Tennant, Hayes, Burgess, Worthington, Morgan, Lancaster, a local athlete and another unknown runner, Kerry, Beckers, Wainman, Jobling, Wilkinson and Thompson all prepare for the coming season.

Goalscoring Legend Matt Tees in menacing mood during the1966/67 season.

Town finished 17th, avoiding relegation to Division Four by just four points, five having been picked-up in the final four matches. Despite leaving in February, Green (13) and Tees (12) finished the season as the highest marksmen. Highlights had been the inclusion of reserve players, winger Stuart Housley and Dave Boylen, in the final months, the former having scored 17 goals for the second XI. Another point of note during this poor season was the trial of Friday night games to boost attendances at Blundell Park which proved unsuccessful.

The season ended on a sombre note when Manager Jimmy McGuigan departed as Manager. All out-going transfers had been made without his knowledge or approval and the board were not willing to renew his contract because of the lack of success; the Manager was give little alternative but to resign. Many players, including Graham Taylor who was later to become a successful manager himself, considered Jimmy McGuigan as the finest Manager they had played under. Jimmy Thompson and John Fielding both left to try their luck with Port Elizabeth in South Africa.

1967/68

Don McEvoy was appointed McGuigan's successor in July. As a player he had appeared at centre-half with Huddersfield Town and captained Sheffield Wednesday to the Second Division title in 1956. Manager at Barrow since 1964, McEvoy had just lead Barrow to promotion from the Fourth Division, and it is thought he was employed by the Mariners because his coaching methods were to the liking of the board. Being short of cash, just one free signing was brought in, and although McEvoy was restricted, he said that within the squad he had *"great potential"* from the outset. Goalkeeper Chris Harker was signed from Bury to deputise for Harry Wainman.

Wins over Walsall, Stockport, Scunthorpe and Brighton, plus three draws in the first 10 games, was a reasonable start, though a League Cup defeat at Bury was suffered. Blundell Parkites witnessed a first defeat of the season on home soil, ironically by a Barrow side built by McEvoy himself. Sadly the Brighton win on 4 October was the last to be seen for a long time, apart from a 3-1 revenge over Bury.

Bobby Ross scores from the spot at a snowbound Blundell Park. This goal against Bradford Park Avenue (in 1967) earned Town an F.A.Cup replay, only to go out two days later by 1-4. The attendance at Blundell Park was just 2,388.

A 7-1 trouncing by a mediocre Watford was the low point, as November and December passed with no victories. Despondency summed up the mood in the camp, and McEvoy resigned with the club at the bottom of the table, having won just once in the previous 17 games. McEvoy had not seen eye-to-eye with the board and was critical of his players spirit; he jumped before he was pushed.

The 1968 New Year saw Town Managerless at the bottom of Division Three, until the surprise appointment of little known local man Bill Harvey. Harvey was born and raised in Grimsby, had attended Harold Street School, and also played for the Grimsby Boys side. He was actually on the club's playing staff as an amateur from 1936-46, but his first team appearances were limited to a few in the war years, despite making his reserve team debut at 16. He played Midland League football for Boston United and Scarborough before gaining his F.A.coaching badge in 1956 whilst playing for Spalding United. He became Reserve Team Trainer at Bristol City, then managed Luton Town from July 1962 to November 1964, having gained that position after an extremely successful interview, where he impressed the Luton board with his bubbly personality. He coached at Swindon Town and Bristol City once more before coming home in January 1968.

Harvey must have certainly lifted the players as he got off to a flying start with a 3-0 away win at Scunthorpe United, and form improved with the picking up of points at home and winning further games away, at Colchester, Southport and Tranmere, in the run-in to the season's end. With Peterborough United already demoted through the Football League deducting them of 19 points due to illegal payments to players, the Mariners lifted themselves from bottom spot and amazingly could still survive as the final game approached.

The last game of the season was against Swindon Town, where a good win was required providing other clubs' results went their way. Colchester and Scunthorpe were already down with Peterborough, but Town could mathematically still catch Mansfield Town, providing the Field Mill side lost and Grimsby beat Swindon by at least two clear goals. The best performance of the season saw Town 3-1 up with minutes remaining when Swindon scored from a corner. Relegation by goal difference of 0.08 was hard to take after this good win, especially with Mansfield having lost by three clear goals at Bournemouth. Harvey had transformed the spirit within the players, but he would have to lift them once more as the club faced their first season in the Fourth Division.

Injuries to Moore and Boylen didn't help the survival cause in the latter part of the season, and neither did some strange refereeing decisions, one worthy of mention being a 'goal' Gary Moore scored with a header on the stroke of half-time in the home game with Oxford United in March; the match official decided that the ball had entered the net after the whistle had blown and it did not stand - Town lost 1-0.

After the final game of the season the players made one last attempt to gain a success as they qualified for the finals of a national 5-a-side tournament played at the Empire Pool, Wembley. Lincoln City were beaten by a goal from Collins, but they then lost 5-4 on penalties in the Semi-finals to Charlton Athletic.

Wilson and Moore achieved double figure goal scores for the season, and a further disappointment came in the close season with the loss of captain Graham Taylor to Lincoln City, following his attendance at an F.A. Coaching course in Zambia. Martin returned to his home-town club Chesterfield and Harker moved to Rochdale, to join up with Billy Rudd.

1968/69

Harvey had found three useful 'free' transfers as full-back John Duncliffe and utility player Mike Hickman were exchanged for Bobby Smith, who went to Brighton, and goalkeeper John Macey signed from Shrewsbury Town. Centre-half Graham Rathbone was named Captain for the season.

The season started promisingly with a 3-0 win over Newport County in the club's first Fourth Division game. The Mariners were now one of the few clubs to have played in five Divisions of the Football League.

After the initial good result against Newport, the second League win didn't arrive until seven matches later against Notts County, who Town had also defeated in the first round of the League Cup. The next round brought early season excitement to Blundell Park as First Division Burnley were drawn. In the first leg the Fourth Division Mariners held their superior opponents to a 1-1 draw, with Hickman scoring for Town before Burnley equalised late on. Unfortunately the second leg was lost 6-0, the heaviest defeat the club has suffered to date in this competition, when the void between classes was exposed. Skilful displays by Dougie Collins on the left-wing in these ties prompted Burnley to make a £27,500 offer which the board simply couldn't refuse, thereby breaking Grimsby's transfer record.

Forwards Dave Wilson (Walsall, £10,000) and Gary Moore (Southend United £8,000) had also moved on by November, despite Town already struggling to score goals whilst they were in the side. Further gloom came with the news that Ron Cockerill's injury problems had forced him to retire.

Gates had by now slumped to 2-3,000 the transfer fees allowing the club to just survive. A little over £50,000 had been received in transfer money since May but gates of over double the normal numbers were necessary for the club to break even. Harvey was allowed a little cash to bolster his flagging attack as firstly Graham Oates, a winger who had First Division experience with Blackpool, was signed, plus Stuart Brace of Peterborough United who was bought in.

Drafted into the centre-forward position was 6'-5" giant Gordon Walker, signed from Sheffield works side Stocksbridge. Town could at least claim to have the tallest and the shortest players in the country as Walker partnered 5'-3" Dave Boylen. Three draws were followed with an away win at Scunthorpe, and a 3-0 home victory against York. Walker scored on his debut against Port Vale in another draw, which showed signs of improvement, but still not enough points were being won.

Walker scored a brace in a 2-0 win over Rochdale, only for the team to lose 6-1 at Spotland in the return just a month later in the first game of the New Year. Harvey signed another Yorkshireman, Keith Cockburn from Bradford Park Avenue, but this was to be his final signing for the Mariners. Any Manager would have struggled, being restricted by such financial restraints, and Harvey was informed after a board meeting on Friday 17 January by newly appointed Chairman Roy Osmond, that the club was considering bringing in a Player/manager. Harvey resigned, agreeing to take charge of the side the following day at York City, but not informing the players of his decision until after the match so as not to disrupt the pre-match arrangements. Harvey had been boss for exactly one year to the day.

Ironically the best performance of the season followed with a 5-2 away win, Brace scoring a hat-trick. Harvey's announcement in the Bootham Crescent changing rooms came as a shock to the players after such a result, for the boss was popular with his staff. The new man the Directors had in mind was Bobby Kennedy of Manchester City. However Kennedy was not immediately released from his contract and it wasn't until March that he was installed in the hot-seat, City demanding a £10,000 transfer fee. In the meantime George Higgins again took control in a Caretaker roll. But his four game spell in charge proved disastrous compared to his short stint in 1964/65. All four games were lost, including home defeats to Scunthorpe and a 5-1 thrashing by Bradford City.

The first six games that Kennedy was in charge saw four draws and two wins, the newcomer himself playing in all of those games. Showing excellent composure on the ball - a Scottish Under-23 international in his prime - Kennedy shone in the basement division.

Only two points were gained in the final seven games as Town finished in 91st place in the Football League and had to face the humiliation of re-election. In the Brentford game of 3 May only 1,833 witnessed a dour 2-0 defeat, this attendance being the lowest officially recorded for a Football League match at Blundell Park. The club had reached rock bottom and it was difficult to see a bright future ahead. Promising youngsters Jimmy Bloomer, Housley and Davidson, were all released through financial shortages. Davidson went on to play over 350 games for Scunthorpe United.

Keith Jobling, who signed for the Mariners as a professional in July 1953, decided to retire in the summer after some 16 years service in the first team. He made his 428th League appearance for the Mariners at Doncaster in November, surpassing Jackie Bestall's 31-year-old record. Currently, Jobling is still the holder of the club record for League starts with 450 (although John McDermott who began the 2000/01 season as a regular, required just 31 to pass the record).

1969/70

Bobby Kennedy signed full-back Dave Mobley from Sheffield Wednesday's reserves and Rochdale's 1967/68 top goalscorer Joe Fletcher, who came on a three month trial.

A scoreless draw at Workington opened the season, followed by an early exit from the League Cup, by 2-0 at home to Doncaster Rovers, though a same score win followed over Hartlepool. Brace scored a hat-trick in a 3-1 win at Southend; coincidentally Town's last victorious away success was also at Southend (with a Brace strike), early in the previous April. A 4-1 win over Chester was the highlight of September, Brace featuring once again by scoring another couple of goals.

The local derby with Scunthorpe was to prove the main talking point around this time. A hard fought game at Blundell Park saw Town trailing 1-0 into the closing stages, after Heath had converted a penalty for the Iron. Following the goal, minor incidents began to occur in individual battles around the pitch and it seemed that it would not be long before these would come to a head. Don Welbourne and Town's Graham Rathbone had an altercation, leaving Welbourne requiring treatment, and both were sent-off . At the restart Brace sprinted up field to score a last minute equaliser, which was celebrated by a pitch invasion. The dismissed players were reprimanded by the F.A., and each was sentenced to long bans of two month, being made examples in a new discipline clampdown. The only good to come from the ban was the introduction to the centre of defence of 19-year-old Clive Wigginton, nephew of Ron Cockerill, who deputised well and made over 20 appearances in his first full season as a professional.

Paddy Hamilton was made Chairman in October. Highly respected and popular with all those he worked with, his election set the foundations for immediate survival and future success for the club. An Irishmen, and 'adopted' by Grimsby, with whom he had become a successful Skipper, then hardware shop owner in the Town, he was a season ticket holder at Blundell Park for 25 years before being elected to the board in 1966.

A run of three consecutive wins at Exeter, Oldham and at Chesterfield, lifted spirits, though Brace seemed to be the only player in the side capable of scoring.

Although times were hard in this period, both Bobby Ross (left) and Dave Boylen (right) were excellent servants to the club amassing almost 650 first team games between them.

They first met each other at Doncaster railway station as they changed train and travelled to Cleethorpes together; they soon became colleagues when they signed for Town later that day!

Fletcher's trial was unsuccessful, and Walker, who didn't get many chances under Kennedy, was also released after a barren spell up front. Mike Hickman was next tried in the number 9 shirt where he proved more successful than his predecessors. Tony Marsden a former Blackpool striker became the club's first ever temporary loan signing when playing a couple of games in a month long stay, before returning to his club, Doncaster Rovers, in November.

The small squad hit an injury crisis in January, and 18-year-old Lincoln lad Benny Williams plus local amateur Kenny Chapman were fielded at Sincil Bank in the County derby. Town lost 2-0 and before the end Williams left the field being replaced by the only other fit player on the club's books, reserve goalkeeper John Macey, who Kennedy was forced to name as substitute. Macey played up-front for the final 20 minutes!

Shortly after the Lincoln match, Jack Lewis agreed to sign for the Mariners from the Imps, although he hardly set Blundell Park alight in his first few games. Duncliffe had been recalled at full-back in favour of Mobley, and Rathbone returned. A couple of wins at the end of February saw Lewis score his first goals for the club which was some reward, but the finest result came on the final day as Town thrashed Colchester United 5-3, Hickman scoring a hat-trick with Oates providing the other two.

The Mariners finished in 16th position, an improvement on the previous year, and several plus points were realised during the season. Wainman, Worthington and Brace all had their best season so far for the club and were each ever-presents, while Kennedy, Ross, Boylen, Hickman and Oates all made over 40 appearances. Hickman scored 13 goals from centre-forward with his non-stop running and 100% effort. The goalscoring efforts of dashing Stuart Brace received most praise. His 25 League goals surpassed Cyril Lewis' 33-year-old scoring record for a winger, although Lewis was playing against the best full-backs in the country and he played less games than Brace, but the man from the West Country scored almost half of the Mariners total account, as the club struggled at the wrong end of the League.

Summer departures included Duncliffe (Peterborough United), Macey (Newport County), Mobley (Altrincham) and Cockburn (Bangor City).

1970/71

Kennedy signed new replacements, in left-back Jim Kirkland from Aberdeen and winger Alan Woodward from non-League Alfreton Town. Both impressed in an encouraging 4-1 win over Oldham Athletic, Woodward providing the fourth on his League debut. Although the day before the League campaign began Town lost 2-1 to Lincoln City in the League Cup.

The Mariners were still in serious financial trouble as the past lack of success on the field had failed to bring paying punters back on the terraces, the vicious circle revolving as no money could be spent on improving the squad.

Bobby Ross secured a 1-0 victory at Newport with his second penalty of the season, though disaster struck in the next game at Southport. Harry Wainman left the field injured with full-back and Captain Dave Worthington taking over in goal, whilst an apprentice, substitute Paul Crampton took over his position, and Town lost 1-0. Mick Gadsby of York City was drafted in on loan for a couple of games while Wainman regained fitness, and made his debut in goal behind new defender Stewart Gray from Doncaster Rovers.

Results were once again inconsistent as the club continued to struggle on and off the pitch. A 2-0 win over Southend and a victory at Town's favourite away ground, courtesy of two goals from Scunthorpe lad Graham Oates at the Old Showground, was followed with a 5-0 beating at Chester. Then future Champions Notts County were defeated 2-1 at Blundell Park in mid-October. Three good home wins were followed by three away defeats, including an F.A.Cup exit at Bury.

The victory treble in October coincided with a trio of transfer moves. An Irish League player, Alan Campbell, had moved from the troubles of Belfast's notorious Shankill Road, seeking safety in Grimsby as he stayed with relations who lived in the town. He worked on the docks for a while until Chairman Paddy Hamilton heard of Campbell's circumstances and asked his club, Coleraine, if he could have a trial with the Mariners. The Irish club allowed Campbell to sign for Town, on the condition he would be released back to Coleraine upon his return to Irish shores.

Graham Oates was allowed to join up-and-coming non-League side Wigan Athletic, before Hamilton instigated another transfer coup, with the successful return of the former hero of the Pontoon, the free-scoring Matt Tees who was signed from Luton Town after three years absence. Both of these in-coming deals were master strokes by Hamilton, and 3,000 additional fans immediately returned to see Tees' homecoming, the Scot obliged with a goal in a 2-0 victory over new boys Cambridge United.

Free-scoring winger Stuart Brace in action.

Most of the fans returned for the next game when Tees scored again, in the victory over Barrow. Unfortunately this brief spark of interest soon died, as only three of the next 16 games were won over a terrible Christmas and New Year period, which saw a 5-1 defeat at Darlington on Boxing Day, and Brentford inflicted the same scoreline at Blundell Park in March.

In this period Town played in three consecutive games where each attracted under 2,000 spectators, albeit only one of them in Cleethorpes. An amazing turn of form, with no warning, arrived during the final run-in as Town rose from the re-election zone up to 19th position after losing only once in the final 11 games, including the winning of the final four (albeit all at home).

In the final month there were signs of hope at last despite the team's lowly position. New men Woodward, Gray, Tees and Campbell had all looked impressive in spells, as did the ever consistent Worthington, Rathbone, Brace and Boylen. It is difficult to explain the lack of success this side of the late 1960's had, for on paper and on their day, as individuals, they were very capable players and above Fourth Division standard, yet lack of luck and consistency had cursed them. Kennedy himself was a more than useful performer though the best spell he had as Manager came when he was injured and out of the side, in April 1971, and therefore able to concentrate on running the team.

Perhaps if he had chosen to retire from playing earlier he may have been a more successful Manager, yet that chance never arose at Blundell Park as just two days after his most successful spell at the club came to an end, so did his career as Manager of Grimsby Town. The board decided it was time for a change and Kennedy was on his way.

Chapter Nine

1971 - 1980

1971/72

The board appointed a new Manager in the May, former Coldstream Guard, and standing tall at 6'-4", Lawrie McMenemy. Gateshead born McMenemy never played in the Football League, although he was associated with Newcastle United as a junior. After his spell in the Army he was employed by the Tyneside Council in the Recreation department, and also on the coaching staff for Gateshead and Bishop Auckland. He became a full-time coach at Sheffield Wednesday in 1966, before managing Doncaster Rovers to the Fourth Division Championship in his first season as a Manager in 1969. Thankfully for Grimsby Town, Doncaster were relegated in 1971 and McMenemy was sacked.

New Manager:
Lawrie McMenemy

Paddy Hamilton was impressed with McMenemy's attitude in his job interview, and he had produced a Championship winning side before in similar circumstances at Belle Vue, who also had financial restraints. McMenemy was given his chance to turn the club around, although he was under no contract at this stage.

The club were all but rock bottom and were losing money every week. McMenemy reported for training with a squad of just 12 players, and it seemed unlikely that success would be immediate. Jim Thomson a Newcastle United reserve and Owen Simpson (Darlington) were secured on free transfers, plus several others were given trials. Scotsmen Jim Clunie (Trainer) and John Fraser (Physio) were also brought to the east coast, the pair knowing each other from earlier days at Raith Rovers.

A good start was made when the Japanese national side visited Blundell Park in August for a pre-season friendly. The Mariners produced a confidence building 7-2 victory which included a Mike Hickman hat-trick. A good tally of goals, backed McMenemy's tactics that the side would be an attacking one, although he also stated that if success was to be had, hard work and commitment would be needed by everybody involved with the club.

The season opened with a 4-1 victory over local rivals Scunthorpe United, courtesy of a Matt Tees hat-trick, then Doncaster were beaten 4-3 the following Tuesday in the League Cup, much to the satisfaction of Mr McMenemy. The first away game of the season also saw a 4-3 win, at Exeter City. The first week had produced 12 goals and three wins, an impressive start. The goals continued to flow, with Town sitting in 2nd place in the table by mid-October, after three consecutive wins, the last occurring at Scunthorpe, with another brace from Tees.

Then a bad spell saw three games lost (two at home), as November approached, though a 1-1 home draw with future Division Two Champions Norwich City was recorded in the fourth round of the League Cup, although the replay was lost 3-1. The first cup game attracted 22,000 fans to Blundell Park, and despite Grimsby fielding a weakened side, they performed miracles, and scored with a Stewart Gray header.

November only saw one win from five played as Town also made an exit from the F.A. Cup. A slight injury crisis didn't help matters with Harry Wainman, the only 'keeper on the club's books, unfit, and Campbell, Rathbone and Woodward were also all out for spells. Woodward's injury was most serious as sadly he never played for the first team again.

The New Year came with the Mariners still in 6th position, and a consistent run of good results was required to stay with the promotion pack. The team was unbeaten in January, and suffered just one loss, at Southport, in February. Experienced campaigners Lew Chatterley, a midfielder from Northampton Town, and winger Allan Gauden of Darlington were introduced around this time, and goalkeeper cover came in the form of Huddersfield Town's reserve Ian Turner.

Wins generally continued into March, but a home game in thick fog was abandoned against Exeter City, when king-pin of the defence Graham Rathbone dislocated his shoulder which put him out of the side until the following season. Home gates for the season had been good and were getting bigger and louder as the season came to a close. Five consecutive games were won as Town went top of the table with just six games left.

A nervous 3-3 draw at home to Aldershot was followed by a relieving 1-0 win at Colchester. Promotion was clinched in the following game at Bury with a courageous performance by Rathbone's deputy Clive Wigginton, when he headed the all important goal before leaving the field with a nasty head wound later in the 1-1 draw. A 2-1 defeat at Doncaster was followed by another Wigginton goal in a 3-2 win against the 'Posh' of Peterborough. The Championship was still not confirmed, and Town's final game came with the rearranged Exeter City match, when just a point was required. The Mariners won 3-0 with goals from Tees, Hickman and Chatterley, and at the end the 22,489 crowd spilled on to the pitch in jubilation. Champions.

Stuart Brace - in his first season with Grimsby had a double figure goal tally. With more to follow!

A simply amazing season had ensued. Just 12 months earlier, barely 4,000 supporters watched the final games of the season as Town struggled to 19th. Now under the guidance of a new Manager, virtually the same players performed miracles to achieve the Championship, and in some style. 88 League goals were scored with a further 12 in cup matches, thereby totalling 100 for the season. In the League, Tees had scored 27, Brace 19 and Hickman 13. The Mariners had totalled the most goals in England during the campaign.

The support was tremendous, and McMenemy took every opportunity to whip-up enthusiasm as regular visits to schools, local industries and the docks were made by him and his squad. The idea was to attract more people to games, and also at the same time to create a good team spirit, and send a strong message to his players that they lived a charmed life for Dockers and Factory workers grafted much harder.

Graham Rathbone in action at Scunthorpe in September 1972.

Some of the money they earned was spent paying the players wages. McMenemy installed belief in everyone, his players, backroom staff, supporters and the local community.

Blundell Park attendances improved so much, that record receipts were broken on no less than five occasions during the season: In January (v. Lincoln £4,329), March (v. Reading £4,617) and against Exeter (£6,214). Cup records in October (v. Gillingham £4,563 and Norwich (£7,005) were also achieved. Town had played some very entertaining football, scored plenty of goals, and the supporters responded both home and away. The Supporters Club presented a 'Player of the Year Trophy' for the first time that season, as fans voted for their star man. Despite the side being attack-minded and scoring plenty of goals, 'keeper Harry Wainman received the first accolade. The squad stayed together for an assault on the Third Division.

1972/73

McMenemy secured the signing of Barnsley left-back Dave Booth for the new season, and midfielder Barry Lynch returned from a spell in America, having previously been a team-mate with Lew Chatterley at Aston Villa in the 60's. Everyone believed Town were on a roll and anything was possible.

A deceiving start saw just two wins in the first six League games, both at home, but September was an excellent month as five consecutive games were won in Division Three, though a loss at Bury meant no League Cup run this season. A 6-2 defeat at Swansea City was the heaviest in four years as the Mariners settled into life in the higher league.

The coffers were now much healthier thanks to the promotion season and Town splashed out a record £20,000 on striker Phil Hubbard from Norwich City in October. Good home victories continued - 3-1 over Southend and 6-2 against Oldham .

In the latter match, Stuart Brace scored four, three of them in the space of just five minutes 55 seconds! Then Notts County (Hubbard hat-trick), Brentford and Scunthorpe were all beaten as Town's excellent form at Blundell Park continued as the New Year approached. Progress was also made in the F.A.Cup, which saw non-League Wigan Athletic and Chesterfield fall to the Mariners.

With January came a 100% League record as Bristol Rovers, Watford and Walsall were all beaten in entertaining games. The Bristol game saw the referee disallow three Grimsby goals and one of the opponents' efforts when Town won 2-0, and Watford were beaten at Vicarage Road with a couple from Tees, whilst Chatterley grabbed a hat-trick as Walsall lost 6-2. Two excellent results against Second Division Preston North End, provided a rare F.A.Cup run. A 0-0 draw in front of 16,000 at Blundell Park produced a hard fought 1-0 victory through an Allan Gauden strike.

Then First Division Coventry City were drawn away in the fourth round. 12,000 travelling supporters descended upon Highfield Road expecting a shock result, but unfortunately a late and disputed penalty finished the Mariners after they had held the First Division side at bay for almost all of the game.

A finale of only two wins in the last 13 games, saw Town drop from the promotion frame, but none the less finishing a creditable 9th; Brentford and Scunthorpe who had both been promoted with Grimsby were relegated. The poor form coincided with the loss of key members due to injury and Rathbone had moved to Cambridge United.

Brace scored 18 as Hubbard took over Tees' mantle in attack. The ageing Scot struggled to score regularly and finished his Football League career when he moved on to non-League Boston United in the summer. His 109 competitive goals had produced many happy memories in his two spells with the club; currently, he still lives in Cleethorpes and is stil remembered as a hero. Shortly after McMenemy first became Manager he was amazed by Tees' build, *"He could hardly stand up in training. He didn't look strong enough"*, but with guts and determination he defied his frail appearance.

Sadly Tees was not the only member of staff to leave the club as McMenemy himself not surprisingly moved onto better things, with Southampton, where he was taken in the Summer, and groomed for the Manager's hot-seat in November. Southampton were relegated, but soon regained First Division status after winning the F.A.Cup as a Second Division side under McMenemy's leadership. He became a well known T.V. pundit and a respected character in the game, becoming the Northern Ireland National Team Manager in 1998. Lynch (Scunthorpe United), Gauden (Hartlepool United) and Campbell (Coleraine) also moved on.

1973/74

In July the surprise choice of Scunthorpe United's Ron Ashman as manager became official. Ashman had served Norwich City for 22 years as a player (over 650 first team appearances - a club record), captain, coach and Manager. He had been boss at the Old Showground for six years prior to arriving at Blundell Park and was highly thought of in Scunthorpe despite their recent relegation.

Ashman's new signings were right-back Don Beardsley (Hull City), who replaced the out of favour Worthington., Frank Sharp (Barnsley) who took over Gauden's place on the wing, and Frank Barton arrived from Blackpool, although he was educated quite locally at Barton upon Humber. Grimsby born Keith Brown was signed from Nottingham Forest where he had played with the reserves.

Dave Worthington was having contractual problems with the club and never made another appearance. He led the side in both the darkest periods and also the brightest - Championship - season. He went from April 1967 to October 1972, missing only one first team game, as he settled in the side as a right-back; this was a sad way to see the end of his Blundell Park career.

Ashman did not have the best of starts to his Grimsby leadership, although it was never going to be easy following McMenemy. 10,709 fans saw a disappointing start to the season when Third Division new boys Hereford United won 3-1 at Blundell Park. The next game was lost at Chesterfield followed by a home draw, after Northampton Town had been beaten in the League Cup.

Goalscoring winger Stuart Brace left for Southend United and Worthington was loaned out to home town club Halifax, after Town recorded their first League win of the season - 4-1 against the Shaymen. Worthington soon joined Brace at Roots Hall. Frank Barton, who had earlier been under Ashman at Scunthorpe moved on to the right wing, and Grimsby Schoolteacher and forward Rod Fletcher was bought from the Iron in November. One win in the first eight League games was followed by five good victories, and although Ashman's style produced fewer goals the defence became tighter. Many games were drawn and most games were decided by the odd goal, in contrast to McMenemy's flamboyant attacking style.

Six of the next eight were drawn as Town were placed at the turn of the year in 13th position. Home performances were far from convincing, though the away form had been well above average. The League Cup had brought a little success with Town drawing Second Division highflyers Luton Town, and a 1-1 draw at Kenilworth Road was followed by a 0-0 replay at home; a third match decider was also played at home, but was lost 2-0 in front of an expectant 15,000 crowd. Luton were later promoted to the top flight.

An even bigger Cup draw came with the visit of Burnley in the F.A.Cup third round, when again a large home crowd was attracted, and again unfortunately witnessed a defeat.

Ashman's tactics altered the appearance of the side considerably. By the New Year the team was playing how he wanted with precise approach play, which was possibly not as attractive to watch but probably more successful at Third Division level. Wainman still in goal, with full-backs Beardsley and Booth, plus Wigginton in the centre of defence with firstly Gray then Czuczman. A midfield of Chatterley and Barton changed to Hubbard and Boylen, Hubbard moving back into a midfield role, and allowing Jack Lewis to forge a partnership with Hickman up front. Barton and Sharp appeared on the wings, later Boylen taking Sharp's place.

A 5-0 win over Tranmere then a 5-1 victory against Rochdale, both in January, rekindled a little more interest though four straight defeats followed. The problem of a regular goalscorer was solved in March and without the expenditure of a big transfer fee. Ian Turner and Lew Chatterley had left to join McMenemy at Southampton, as new reserve 'keeper Neil Freeman from Arsenal arrived. Grimsby League forward Jimmy Lumby was signed from local side Ross Sports.

Lumby had almost slipped the net as he had been released from a trial three month contract by McMenemy in January 1973 and played for Boston United and Boston F.C. before rejoining his first club, Ross, in the October. The Mariners snapped him up again in March and Ashman thrust him straight into the first team partnering Jack Lewis. The 19-year-old Lumby scored a hat-trick in only his 7th League game and ended the season with nine from 16 starts. An excellent run-in provided only three defeats in the final 13 games with Town finishing in 6th.

Despite the higher League ranking, the crowds had gradually began to slip away as the euphoria of McMenemy's days faded. Booth, Wigginton and Barton were ever-presents and Lewis top scored with 13 in the League. Frank Sharp was the only departure, leaving for Port Vale.

The season ended on a high note as the Mariners performances earned a cash reward. By their scoring of 67 League Goals, Town were the highest goalscorers who were not promoted from the Third Division, and they were awarded a cheque for £4,000, from Brewery Watney Mann in a competition the company had organised.

Martin Young first came on the scene during the 1974/75 season.

1974/75

No new signings were made in the close season although one new face in the starting XI was that of 18-year-old Scot Bobby Cumming. Cumming had actually played a few Scottish League games whilst a schoolboy with Albion Rovers but had been a member of Town's Junior and Reserve side for a year. He took the place of the injured Booth for the first game at home to Blackburn Rovers which was lost 2-1. One win (3-0 against Port Vale) in the first eight games was disappointing after the finale to the previous season, and a defeat at Chesterfield saw an early exit in the League Cup.

Form improved in October as youngsters Brown and Martin Young were introduced along with new midfield signing Roy Coyle who had played for Sheffield Wednesday and Northern Ireland. Home points were picked-up and two away wins at Wrexham and Bournemouth followed, but a 5-0 defeat at Colchester was offset by an excellent 3-1 victory at leaders Peterborough United on Boxing Day.

A poor run of six games without a win saw Ashman sacked along with Trainer Colin Appleton, after the 3-1 defeat at Tranmere in January. Ashman had just strengthened the squad with new centre-half Steve Govier from Brighton for £16,000, although he was soon struck down with injury. Ron Wigg scored in the Tranmere defeat just after he had been signed from Rotherham United for £17,000, whilst Hickman was sold to Blackburn Rovers for £10,000.

Physio John Fraser took over for three games until Coventry City coach Tom Casey was appointed Manager in February. Casey had been a Northern Ireland international as a wing-half and had been principally with Newcastle United in the 1950's. Appointed Casey's Trainer was George Aitken who had been a player with Middlesbrough and more recently the manager at Workington. The Mariners failed to score in the first four games under Casey, so striker Malcolm Partridge was signed in mid-March from Leicester City to solve the problem. Though by the end of the season results had improved, Partridge failed to score in his 11 starts!

Town rallied to finish in 16th place, but gates continued to drop and money was as tight as ever. If anyone had been a success during this season of struggle it was rejuvenated forward Jack Lewis, who had been signed in 1970, but it was only in the last 18 months that he had been given a regular run in the side. He scored 21 League goals in 1974/75, although was pipped by Frank Barton as the fans 'Player of the Year'.

The Juniors' season ended on a high as they were invited to play in a Youth Tournament in Breda, Holland in May. A record of played 5, won 5, scored 15, against 5 was enough to win the competition. The side included Captain Martin Young, Jim Lumby, Keith Brown, Bob Cumming, Allan Marley, Ian Walton and a 17-year-old Kevin Moore who all went on to represent the first team. Lumby was released to Boston United, Clive Wigginton was allowed to join Scunthorpe United, and Beardsley and Fletcher were also released.

1975/76

With no money to strengthen the side Casey was going to have a season of troubles ahead of him, and his spell as Manager was full of bad luck.

A 2-0 win over newly relegated Cardiff City, was a good start to the season, though Steve Govier was lost to injury. The next game at Doncaster Rovers in the League Cup was lost 3-1 after 'keeper Neil Freeman left the field injured, and as first choice Harry Wainman was already recovering from injury, Oxford United's reserve Keith Baker made his only League appearance the following week whilst on loan.

As the injuries mounted up, Casey had little choice but to upgrade from within. Aged 16 years and 143 days, coloured winger Tony Ford became the youngest ever Mariner when he made his debut as a substitute at Walsall in October, and he continued to figure in the first team throughout the season. Ford, born in the Nunsthorpe area of Grimsby, had only left Wintringham School in the June, and was just three months into his apprenticeship. Bob Oldridge was also drafted in for his senior debut, joining from local junior side Immingham Old Boys, though he had been playing for the Mariners Juniors.

Town reached the half-way stage unbeaten at home in the League, despite a blemish on the home record when non-League Gateshead won 3-1 in the first round of the F.A.Cup. In contrast the away form was woeful, and by March just one win and one draw were recorded on the team's travels. This dismal record included the fixture at Port Vale in December when Town were 3-0 up, only to concede four goals in a 10 minute spell. The one draw was secured at Millwall in January, courtesy of a goal from 'loanee' Joe Waters on his debut. The diminutive Waters was signed on loan from Leicester City and impressed greatly in Midfield in his four game spell. Supporters were outraged when he returned to Leicester without the club making an offer for him. He eventually was signed a couple of weeks later for £8,000, although in order to afford him a donation of £2,000 from the Supporters Club was made.

Further bright news also came in February, as the continuing good form of Jack Lewis earned him a Welsh Under-23 cap and a full squad call-up, though his 'over-age' appearance against Scotland at the Intermediate level was his only reward.

Two consecutive home games were lost in March (the first of the season), which saw Town slip closer to the relegation spots. With just three wins in the final 14 games, Town narrowly escaped the drop, finishing in 18th with 40 points, and only one more than relegated Aldershot. The Mariners only won seven points in total on their travels. Lewis was again top marksmen with 15, as Harry Wainman excelled at the other end, and again won the fans award for best player.

Casey was forced to sell, and £16,000 was collected with the sales of Barton (Bournemouth), Hubbard (Lincoln) and Czuczman to Scunthorpe United, this latter transfer being Ashman's first signing on his return to the Old Showground. Freeman (Southend United) and Marley (Louth United) were also allowed to leave.

1976/77

The experienced Colin Blant (Darlington) and Norman Whitehead (Chester) were drafted into the squad in close-season. Youngsters Kevin Moore, Nigel Batch (Derby County apprentice) and Terry Donovan (Louth United) signed their first professional contracts; none of the threesome waited long before their debuts. Former fifties player Dick Conner returned to Blundell Park as Trainer.

A poor pre-season, was continued into a League Cup exit and two League defeats. Govier was badly injured in the first League game at Bury, with Booth being crocked in the next match at home to Crystal Palace, and this was the beginning of the end for both players as Govier never played again whilst Booth was eventually forced to retire after never regaining full fitness. The Palace game was the first match to be sponsored at Blundell Park when local estate agent, G.M.Barton, offered financial support, Bobby Charlton was the sponsor's guest of honour when Town lost 1-0.

Jack Lewis in action against Brighton in September.

Teenagers Ford (17) and Donovan (18) were called-up for first team duty, joining Bobby Cumming (20), Kevin Moore (18), Martin Young (21) and Bob Oldridge (18) already in the starting line-up. Terry Donovan and Kevin Moore, both sons of ex-Mariners Don and Roy, had played for England Under-18 Schoolboys the previous season. A 3-0 defeat at Mansfield Town saw further changes with Mike Brolly and Steve Harding (both signed from Bristol City) making their debuts in the first win of the season against Brighton, although a 5-2 defeat transpired at Oxford in the next game. Joe Waters became the first Mariner to win a full international cap since Johnny Scott in 1958, and scored in the 3-3 draw for Eire in Turkey.

Just three wins in the first 16 games was enough to see Tom Casey sacked in November. Casey, often credited with giving youth their chance at Blundell Park, in reality had little choice, and youth team Trainer, Bernard Fleming, should be given most credit for the juniors progressing, making sure all signed for the club in the first instance. But the truth of the matter is that whoever had been in charge, the club were extremely fortunate to be able to select from a wealth of such talented locals, which would have been be difficult for any Manager to ignore; most went on to have lengthy professional careers.

Results immediately improved, when four straight wins came in late November under the temporary control of Dick Conner - a 5-3 win in the F.A.Cup replay against Cheshire League Droylsden, then League victories over Portsmouth, Wrexham and Reading, all of which were at home. Speculation was rife as to who the next boss would be until the appointment of the Exeter City Manager John Newman. Newman had seen Town in action in Christmas games against Lincoln City and Sheffield Wednesday (when Nigel Batch made his debut in goal), neither of which was won.

Not the most impressive start to the Manager's Blundell Park career was made, as only three games were won in 21. A late run of two draws and three wins came too late as the Mariners were relegated, finishing in 23rd place, and finally going down 2-0 on the final day at Reading. 25 players had been used, many of whom were under 25-years-old, therefore, though talented, there was no real experience in the side.

Summer signings Blant and Whitehead each only played a few disappointing games before leaving soon after. Centre-half Keith Hanvey was a good signing from Rochdale in February, and striker Garry Liddell joined from Leeds United, scoring on his debut versus Rotherham United in the 1-1 draw in March, as Newman attempted to remould the side. Liddell replaced Ron Wigg who had left for Barnsley the week before. Another local youngster, 16-year-old apprentice Kevin Drinkell, made an impressive start to his League career, with two goals in a defeat at Wrexham.

1977/78

Jack Lewis' on-off transfer finally went ahead when he joined Blackburn Rovers for £15,000 in August. Stewart Gray, Bob Oldridge and Steve Govier also left as Newman built a side to regain Third Division status, although many thought it could take quite a while.

Free signings were made to bolster the defence, with bald centre-half Geoff Barker from Reading and Paul Cooper, a Huddersfield Town reserve full-back, being recruited, plus young Shaun Mawer turning professional. Both legs of the first round of the League Cup were played before the Division Four games began. Hartlepool being beaten twice (3-0 and 2-1), with Waters scoring a hat-trick in the first leg.

The previous season's top scorer Malcolm Partridge was asked to start the season in the centre of defence after Hanvey recovered from injury, and Shaun Mawer soon took over the right-back spot from Cooper. A sound start was made with several home wins and away games produced victories at York, Barnsley and Huddersfield on the team's Yorkshire travels. Long-serving midfielder Dave Boylen, played his final games for the club before leaving in October.

Keven Moore stretches for the ball, while Malcom Partridge lends support. In the local derby versus Scunthorpe United.

Boylen had given excellent service to the club, known for his tigerish abilities despite his lack of height and no little skill, he had shared highs and lows at the club since he signed in 1965, a winner of the 'Player of the Year' award in 1974, he received a Testimonial year in 1975.

Town placed in a mid-season position reached the F.A.Cup third round by beating Workington and Barnsley, and were drawn against Lawrie McMenemy's Southampton, who were flying high in Division Two. The team produced some excellent fighting spirit as it took three games for the Saints to overcome the Mariners, eventually by 4-1 at Leicester City's Filbert Street Ground.

The Mariners' performances continued to improve after the Cup exit losing only once at home to Northampton Town in late March and the away form was good. As the season closed the Mariners finished in 6th place, just three points short of promoted Brentford. Eleven losses away from home proved the downfall, but the young squad had gained invaluable experience which they would take into the following season. The impressive Terry Donovan scored 14 League goals, whilst Waters and Brolly were ever-presents. Attacker Mike Lester had been signed from Washington Diplomats of America, having previously been on Manchester City's staff. Keith Hanvey (Huddersfield Town) and Paul Cooper (Nuneaton Borough) left the club in the Summer months.

1978/79

The club celebrated their Centenary this season, '100 years of Grimsby Town Football Club', this was a magnificent milestone to achieve, considering the club had probably had slightly more downs than ups. An exhibition was held at the Grimsby Library to mark the occasion amongst several other events organised during the season, and the club badge was introduced on to the breast of the team shirts for the first time since the three boars heads were worn for the 1936 Cup Semi-final.

Incoming personnel included former Lincoln City Manager George Kerr, replacing Dick Conner as first team Coach, and he instigated the superb capture of the Imps' defender Dean Crombie on a free transfer, also midfielder Bobby Mitchell joined from Blackburn Rovers. Pre-season training began on a sour note as long-serving goalkeeper Harry Wainman, who was about to start his 24th season as a professional at Blundell Park, fractured his wrist. Although Wainman did eventually regain fitness, he could not displace the impressive Nigel Batch, and never played for the first team again, becoming stuck on the 420 League appearance mark for the club. Had it not been for this unfortunate injury he would have no doubt claimed the club record, which stood at 450.

The campaign started well with League Cup wins home and away versus York City, though Reading won on the League's opening day at Blundell Park. Wigan Athletic didn't enjoy their first ever Football League game at home as Town ran-out 3-0 winners. Four straight wins in the League (three away from home), were only upset by losing 2-0 at First Division Manchester City in the League Cup second round. Three points were then dropped in two home games though a good 3-0 win was enjoyed at Crewe, the slight inconsistency coming due to a bout of injuries; long term suffers Wainman and Dave Booth were joined by Donovan, Cumming and Lester.

December approached with Garry Liddell, Young and Partridge all missing with injury as the Mariners struggled to keep a settled side. Kevin Moore's younger brother Dave came into the side at the expense of right-back Shaun Mawer, whilst Cumming, Mitchell and Lester all returned, as Town began to pick-up points.

1978/79 season: Joe Waters dispatches this penalty in the 2-2 draw with Wimbledon.

Cumming playing in midfield scored all three against York, and the transformation of Tony Ford to centre-forward worked wonders as he celebrated with a hat-trick in the 5-1 demolition of Bradford City, having previously only scored one goal during the campaign. In the next home game a third player scored plenty of goals with Mike Lester hitting four in the 7-2 defeat of Darlington. Town were 6-0 up at half-time, and Lester also missed a penalty as the rampant Mariners hit form.

Now lying in 4th position, despite injury problems, a slight hiccup came at Hartlepool when they were beaten 1-0 for the third time that season. A 3-1 away win at fellow promotion contenders Portsmouth in front of the 'Match of the Day' cameras proved to be a turning point in the season and the team never looked back. Old favourite Clive Wigginton made a return from Lincoln City in the centre of defence in March as the Mariners continued to win. A 4-0 thrashing at future Champions Reading was the only loss in a 19 match run, and a Joe Waters header clinched promotion in the 2-1 win at Northampton. Grimsby were the first club in the country to gain promotion that year when they sat proudly at the top of the Fourth Division table, and with three matches to play, the Championship was a distinct opportunity. A 1-1 draw at Newport was recorded, though a 4-3 home defeat dashed any dreams of top spot, as Doncaster's former Mariner Jack Lewis bagged a hat-trick, ironically, a feat he had failed to achieve in Cleethorpes. The final game became an anti-climax, when 7,000 travelling fans visited Barnsley on the final day, for Reading had already been crowned Champions. Town lost 2-1, and Barnsley were also promoted, in front of a 21,000 Fourth Division crowd.

Classy displays since the turn of the year, saw the Mariners produce attractive and successful football that was acknowledged on many opponents' grounds. Kevin Moore and Joe Waters were merited in the Divisional Select XI, and the transition of Ford to a central striker was rewarding with a total of 16 League goals, as defences failed to harness his electrifying pace, despite only a single goal prior to January. Waters and Cumming totalled double figures each from midfield, in a season when goals were spread evenly throughout the side; Kevin Moore netted seven from left-back by January, most of which were headed from corners and free-kicks; the Mariners being very successful from dead-ball situations. The team formed a trademark line of four of five players on the edge of the box, all being excellent headers of the ball, splitting as the corner or free-kick was in flight and causing havoc in the opponents defence as they struggled to successfully mark the Mariners. This move had been introduced by Newman and Kerr, and was well rehearsed in training.

Newman was a popular Manager, having worked exceedingly hard for the club's cause, and was respected by players and supporters alike. Meanwhile the gates had crept back-up to the five figure mark towards the season's end. Many thought this young side which had been carefully crafted would be a surprise package in the coming Third Division campaign. Batch, Kevin Moore, Crombie and Waters were ever -present, with Ford and Brolly also playing over 40 games. Donovan recovered from injury only to move on to Aston Villa for a record £75,000 fee, which would have risen to £150,000 after an agreed number of appearances, but which was never achieved. Donovan played in the First Division and Europe and became an International with Eire whilst at Aston Villa, although injury was to cruelly cut his career short. Partridge (Scunthorpe United), Barker (Bridlington), and Booth finished their playing careers with the Mariners, the latter becoming Youth Coach after retiring through a persistent knee problem.

Finishing runners-up and promotion was a fitting end to the Centenary celebrations. One final item to celebrate was the revamped Matchday Programme which won the best programme in Division Four award, and the most improved in the Football League, along with that of Manchester United.

1979/80

John Newman who had done such a fine job guiding the club back to Division Three, was approached by Colin Addison, the newly appointed Derby County Manager to become his Assistant. Newman accepted, knowing he would be leaving the club with a sound future, and coach George Kerr well capable of taking charge. Kerr was eventually made Manager after the players had shown great support for him. The new Manager's first new signing was John Stone of Darlington for a club record £22,500, a good piece of dealing by Kerr as Darlington had turned down a £30,000 offer only months before.

The season began well with Scunthorpe United being knocked out of the League Cup, their attacker Kevin Kilmore impressing and making the short trip to Blundell Park the following month in another record-breaking deal, on this occasion of £60,000. Impressive wins over Exeter City (4-1) - Cumming scoring within the first minute of the first League game - Blackpool (4-3) and Huddersfield Town (4-1 away in the League Cup) were recorded in the early matches. Batch was excellent in goal, as the family Moore partnership flourished in the full-back positions. Stone and Wigginton clicked in central defence though Crombie was soon recalled. Captain Waters and Mitchell were creative in midfield, Brolly on the right crossed with accuracy as the courageous Cumming raided down the left in his unorthodox fashion. Liddell and Ford started up-front, though Kilmore and Drinkell probably proved the stronger pairing.

Town chairman Paddy Hamilton sadly passed away in late September, black arm bands being worn as a mark of respect in the following home game against Notts County in the League Cup (retired Glass Merchant, Dick Middleton took over as Chairman).

Second Division County were easily beaten 3-1 as the Mariners marched on. October was completed in excellent fashion with First Division Everton visiting in the fourth round of the League Cup. Brian Kidd opened the scoring for the Merseysiders' only for unsung hero Mike Brolly to score both Town's goals as they progressed to the Quarter-finals in fine style in front of 22,000 at Blundell Park.

Dave Booth was granted a Testimonial match against Derby County, which attracted a 13,000 plus crowd. Although Booth was popular, the attendance was particularly large as vouchers that were given out guaranteed Cup tickets for the next League Cup game. Captain Joe Waters made a second appearance for Eire, against the 'North' in Belfast, and Mike Lester moved to Barnsley for £20,000.

Town were continuing to win in the League and also in the F.A.Cup, losing only once in the six November games, then just another single defeat in nine games in December, that reverse coming at the hands of First Division Wolves. Wolves had been drawn at home in the League Cup Quarter-Final, and Town were unfortunate not to win when Kevin Moore struck the underside of the Pontoon bar in the closing minutes. But the game remained goalless in front of a the largest crowd at Blundell Park, 23,115, since 1956. The Molineux replay saw another heroic draw as the Mariners were saved by a Palmer own goal under a challenge from Liddell, then Brolly struck the crossbar in extra time. A second replay was required which was played at Derby County's Baseball Ground. Town eventually losing 2-0, assisted by a controversial Hibbitt penalty after Wigginton had committed a foul **outside** the penalty area! Wolves went on to win the trophy beating Nottingham Forest in the final.

Mike Brolly scores the first in the 5-1 thrashing of Brentford on the way to the title.

The first game of the 1980's was played in front of 50,000 spectators when the Mariners visited Liverpool in the third round of the F.A.Cup. Liverpool were at the height of their dominance and Town lost 5-0, though they did not disgrace themselves.

Cup distractions out of the way, the Mariners could once again concentrate solely on the Third Division title race. A disappointing home defeat to challengers Blackburn Rovers (the first occasion that shirts advertising Findus were worn), was soon forgotten about as the side started a tremendous run that was worthy of Champions. Only one more defeat came in the final 20 games.

A 3-0 win at Blackpool, with Town going into pole position, was followed by the 5-1 thrashing of Brentford and an important 3-2 victory at promotion-chasing Chesterfield. This match was best remembered for the unfair dismissal of Kevin Moore and a bullet header by Drinkell, which almost burst the net at the end where the 5,000 Town supporters stood. March saw more important goals by Drinkell, as Gillingham, Millwall and Southend were beaten at Blundell Park. An away draw at Hull was achieved, before a tremendous 6-3 away victory at Wimbledon, assisted by a Kilmore hat-trick. Kerr and Secretary David Dowse surprisingly both resigned in February, only to reconsider their decision just a few hours later.

A 1-0 win at Barnsley, in front of another huge travelling black and white army at Oakwell, was obtained from a fantastic Brolly free-kick, although Kilmore sadly broke his leg. Draws against Hull at home and Reading away were followed with a 2-0 win over Oxford. A hard fought goalless draw at Mansfield finally clinched promotion in front of the ITV cameras, leaving just one point required in the final match at home to Sheffield United to become Champions. In glorious May sunshine the Mariners provided a superb performance for the supporters as a Drinkell hat-trick and another goal from Waters finished the season in perfect style. Many of the 19,000 fans poured onto the pitch to celebrate with their heroes.

Town were worthy Champions, Kerr having continued the momentum that Newman had started. The squad was still young but now had experience also. The 92 League and Cup goals had again arrived from all areas of the team with Drinkell (16), Kilmore (15) and Cumming (14) scoring most in the League. Waters and Kevin Moore were both rewarded for their consistency by being selected for the Divisional side once more. Dean Crombie was voted by the fans as 'Player of the Year', and Kerr voted 'Third Division Manager of the Year' What a season. The side were considered well capable of holding their own in the Second Division, but only the future would tell. Town were back after an 16 year absence, which had seen the club almost go out of existence. Survival has, and probably always will be the name of the game in this part of the world.

Chapter Ten

KERR, BOOTH AND THEN .... TO THE LYONS!

1980 - 1988

1980/81

The summer of 1980 saw Blundell Park change dramatically, with all seating areas renewed in the Osmond and Main Stand, and seats added to the Standing Paddock in the latter; new plastic red seats replaced the old wooden versions, as ground improvements were enforced for Second Division regulations.

No new players were signed, though Ron and Dudley Ramsden became Directors. Before Second Division action began, Town had Anglo-Scottish and League Cup-ties to compete in. Unconvincing performances against Notts County (1-0 and 3-0 defeats) in the League Cup and just one victory out of three versus lesser opponents in the Anglo-Scottish Cup was not the best beginnings to this new era.

Three draws and the first victory over Wrexham in the initial four games was enough to take the club's unbeaten League record to 19 games without defeat, the run stretching back to the loss at Colchester in early February. The defence was switched around which was fairly successful, though problems lay up front, with just six goals scored in the first 15 games.

At the back, Stone began at right-back, in place of Dave Moore, and brother Kevin moving to the centre of defence with Wigginton.

Kevin Kilmore leads the Bristol City defence a merry dance.

Young Phil Crosby and old boy Mike Czuczman (returning after a spell in the U.S.A.) were tried, before Crombie settled at left-back. Waters and Mitchell continued in midfield, with Drinkell, Liddell, Kilmore and Ford all struggling to score, as Town languished in the lower reaches of the Division.

Goals finally began to flow with a 3-1 win over Cambridge United, which started with the club's fastest ever goal, when Waters finished a three man move in the first 10 seconds. Cambridge were a goal down without even touching the ball. A 4-2 win came in the next match at Preston, then former England and Ipswich Town striker, Trevor Whymark was a surprise December signing from Vancouver Whitecaps for a club record £80,000. He scored in his home debut in an excellent 2-0 win against Chelsea as the Mariners began to rise up the table.

In fact a run of 12 games with just one defeat saw them catapulted into the promotion frame by the end of March. With the 2-1 beating of Notts County and Swansea City 1-0 at Blundell Park, Grimsby were amazingly in third spot with just seven games remaining, and still unbeaten in the League at home. Could the inconceivable be achieved with a third consecutive promotion, and a return to the top flight with a Fourth Division squad?

Unfortunately the bubble burst and burst badly.

Just one of those final games were won, 2-1 at Sheffield Wednesday, the club's first ever win at Hillsborough. Defeats came at Q.P.R., a 5-1 home loss to Champions West Ham (David Cross scoring four), and the season finished disappointingly with another 5-1 defeat, at Cambridge. A final place of 7th was a tremendous achievement with a squad which had cost just £200,000, including 12 former Juniors amongst the 19 players. Just two defeats were witnessed at Blundell Park, when only 10 goals were conceded - half of those coming in the West Ham game! Waters and Batch were again ever-presents.

Garry Liddell moved onto Hearts in February, as youngsters John Steeples and Gary Beacock were blooded. Sadly Shaun Mawer finally lost his battle to injury and retired, aged only 21.

1981/82

The 1981/82 season was to be an unusual one on and off the field. In the summer the Barrett Stand was condemned, being deemed unsafe by Safety Officers, so work began on the erection of the new impressive £1 million Findus Family Stand, and continued during the season, when three points were to be awarded for a win for the first time. Experienced former Lincoln City striker John Ward was signed from Watford on a free transfer.

A brand new shiny Adidas kit was introduced for the new season, which sported a red trim on shirt, shorts and socks. Pre-season had been successful with a 100% record in the newly formed Football League Group Cup. The first game of the season was against newly relegated First Division Leicester City. Town gaining a creditable 2-2 draw, with a certain Gary Lineker scoring for the opposition.

The following three games were won (two of these at Watford and Orient) as Town became early promotion contenders, though this form was not to last.

Grimsby had a terrible run of 18 games without a win in the League which was finally ended in a 1-0 victory over Derby County, courtesy of a Kilmore strike. Circumstances had changed in those 18 matches, in particular with some howling individual mistakes, and at this level they were punished. A 6-0 thrashing came at Luton as Town slipped from top to bottom in a matter of weeks.

The popular, though outspoken George Kerr was sacked in January, less than a week after Town had demolished Millwall 6-1 at the Den in the third round of the F.A.Cup, after the Mariners were a goal down at half-time. It was a well known fact that Kerr and more than one Director did not see eye to eye, and the Manager was dismissed with Town in bottom place following a 2-1 home defeat to Orient.

Former Captain and then Reserve Team Coach Dave Booth moved through the ranks again to become the new Manager after a spell as Caretaker boss. His first game in charge was the Group Cup Semi-final against Shrewsbury Town, which after making the worst possible start, going 1-0 down in the 2nd minute, Kevin Kilmore scored a last minute winner, which took the club to the Final. Another fine Cup win came in Booth's second match when Town won 2-1 at Newcastle in the F.A.Cup, and Town reached the fifth round for the first time since the war. However, League form failed to improve with results at home continuing to be a problem. Grimsby Town played their first game on synthetic turf with two visits to Q.P.R's Loftus Road, and lost on both occasions, one in the League the other in F.A.Cup fifth round.

Tony Ford in action v Leyton Orient
(note The O's played in Town's away shirts!).

Several squad changes came in March with experienced goalkeeper Peter Grotier replacing Harry Wainman in the reserves, after signing from Cardiff City, and Barnsley's Scottish defender Neil Cooper replaced the out of favour Clive Wigginton, who with reserve Graham Cawthorne finished the season at Doncaster Rovers. Ward (Lincoln City) and Czuczman (York City) also departed.

April proved an impressive month as the first week produced three straight wins including the beating of Wimbledon in the Final of the Group Cup at Blundell Park, plus another win at Newcastle, and a 5-1 demolition of Shrewsbury Town, which saw the Mariners hit form at a vital time.

The new £1m. Findus Stand nears completion

Safety was assured with a tremendous 2-1 away victory at promotion chasing Leicester City, when a brace from Whymark took his League total to 11 goals for the season as Town finished 17th, two points clear of the relegation zone. Batch was excellent in goal and was voted 'Player of the Year' for the second season running and having been ever-present for his fourth consecutive year. Waters was injured for a spell in late October which allowed young Andy O'Dell to make his mark. Mitchell missing in Midfield during the closing months saw Beacock, Kevin Moore and John Stone all tried without great success.

Brolly (Derby County), Mitchell (Carlisle United) and Wigginton (Torquay United) were all allowed free transfers in the summer as Booth attempted to form his own squad. These three had given superb service to the club and in particular Brolly who was a surprise choice for release. The ever growing construction of the Findus Stand was one point of interest for supporters as the season progressed.

1982/83

Booth spent over £100,000 in the summer with the signing of experienced midfielders Phil Bonnyman from Chesterfield (£80,000) and Micky Speight from Blackburn Rovers (£25,000) both having been thorns in the Mariners side in the 1979/80 season. Speight was a former England 'B' international and Sheffield United Captain.

Pre-season began on the right footing as Kevin Drinkell bagged a hat-trick at Sheffield United in the 3-1 Football League Trophy win, and a 16,137 crowd witnessed the Bank Holiday visit of First Division drop-outs Leeds United who were held to a 1-1 draw, despite their side bristling with internationals. A weekend marred by crowd trouble and fighting in Cleethorpes by the large Yorkshire following also saw the grand opening of the Findus Family Stand (minus Executive Boxes, which arrived a year later). Scunthorpe were knocked out of the Milk Cup (formerly the League Cup) as the Mariners became the campaign as unlikely leaders of Division Two, drawing against Leeds and winning the next six matches, including a 5-1 defeat of Blackburn Rovers and a 4-1 win at Middlesbrough.

Life at the top was shortlived as Town lost 5-2 at Chelsea the following week. Just one victory in eleven games during October and November saw Town slip down the table and unceremoniously knocked out of the Milk Cup by Sheffield United (5-1), despite another Drinkell hat-trick in the 3-3 first-leg.

Drinkell's third hat-trick of the season came in the 4-1 defeat of Crystal Palace. It seemed that Dave Booth would have his work cut-out to keep his star striker, whose all-round game had really developed him into becoming one of the most sort after goalscorers in the country. Amazingly Drinkell finished the season with 26 goals in total, despite the Mariners plummeting to 19th position in the League. Town won none of their final 14 games as relegation threatened, and they survived again by just two points, with the final three games all drawn. Just 45 League goals were scored, with Drinkell's 17 thus accounting for over one third of them. An unwanted club record was created when five games passed without scoring (into May), and just five goals were scored overall in the poor run from February.

The side had been bolstered by loan signings Mark Whitlock (Southampton) and Mike Saxby (Luton Town) during the season and in May, free transfers were given to Andy O'Dell, Kilmore and Crosby, who all joined George Kerr's former band of Mariners at Rotherham United. John Stone soon joined them with Kerr also signing former favourites Terry Donovan and Bobby Mitchell for the 1983/84 season. Dave Moore (Carlisle United), Beacock (Hereford United) and John Steeples (Scarborough) also left.

Speight, who had been signed as captain, was disappointing and missed most of the season through injury. On the other hand 18-year-old striker Paul Wilkinson was a refreshing introduction when he scored within minutes of making his

League debut, coming on as a second half substitute to salvage a point in the January 1-1 draw with Charlton Athletic.

Goal Machine Kevin Drinkell in action v Crystal Palace.

1983/84

New signings came in the shape of Northern Ireland and Southampton veteran centre-half Chris Nicholl, Middlesbrough striker Dave Shearer, and former Wintringham and Grimsby Schools winger Paul Emson, who returned home after hitting the headlines with his pace at Derby County. Another signing of note was the promotion of local England Schoolboy international Gary Lund. None of the newcomers cost a transfer fee.

The opening day saw Drinkell open his account for the season with a text book header against Shrewsbury Town, only for Nigel Batch to drop a rare clanger when allowing an upfield punt to bounce over him and into the Pontoon net in the 1-1 draw. Drinkell scored with a powerful long range shot in a Tuesday night victory against Leeds, as Town made a promising start to the season. Wilkinson was given his chance from the outset to partner Drinkell as Shearer rarely got a look-in. The side were consistent and solid as well as deadly up-front. Bobby Cumming, a man for all seasons and positions, had finished the previous season on the left-wing, but was now performing well at right-back. Nicholl and Kevin Moore struck-up an immediate understanding in the middle of defence as 'Drinks' and 'Wilkie' had done further up-field. Nicholl won his 50th, and final (51st) caps for Ireland whilst a Mariner.

York City were beaten over two-legs in the Milk Cup, before First Division Coventry City were held in the next round. The previous season F.A.Cup finalists Brighton & Hove Albion were thrashed by a rampant Grimsby forward line with Wilkinson (2), wingers Ford and Emson, plus home debutant Gary Lund all scoring in the 5-1 win. Town were in fine form losing only once, 4-0 at Portsmouth, in a long spell, before meeting Portsmouth once more at Blundell Park in March, when Pompey were victorious with the odd goal in seven. The only other defeats in this spell came in the second round second leg of the Milk Cup, (1-2 at Coventry City) and by the same score in the F.A.Cup to bogey side Portsmouth, again.

The Mariners were playing some high quality entertaining football which took them to third place before the Portsmouth defeat. December had been an extremely successful month with a 1-1 draw in the club's first League game played on a Sunday, at Blackburn, a 3-2 win, at Champions-elect Chelsea on the 17th, and a 1-0 win against eventual runners-up Sheffield Wednesday on Boxing Day. Still in with a chance of promotion the good form took a dip at a vital stage. Home wins over Barnsley, 1-0, and a Drinkell hat-trick in the 3-0 win victory over Swansea City were acquired, but a poor Easter included a narrow defeat at Promotion rivals Sheffield Wednesday. The season was well and truly lost when bottom of the table Cambridge United denied Town victory on one of those days where the ball failed to enter the net, despite the Mariners having almost all the possession and chances. For the final game Chelsea won the championship with a Kerry Dixon header when Town lost 1-0 at Blundell Park. The Mariners finished in 5th position their highest in the Football League since losing their First Division status in 1948.

The high positioning was pleasing, especially with the introduction of several juniors into the team who had contributed to the winning of the Northern Intermediate title. Lund scored three goals in two final games, the youngest Moore brother, Andy, Juniors captain Gary Henshaw, and Irish Youth International Paul Agnew all made their debuts, and the future certainly looked bright.

Departures had seen Neil Cooper join St.Mirren for £12,000 in November, and Whymark leave for Southend United in January, as the veteran struggled to regain his place in the very strong forward line. Shearer (Gillingham) and Speight (Chester City) moved on, both players having unfortunately provided their best form before arriving in Cleethorpes. The saddest departure was that of popular Irish skipper Joe Waters, who decided to emigrate and coach in the North American Indoor League after a tremendously loyal and consistent career with the Mariners. His skill, determination and leadership would be sorely missed.

Drinkell again top-scored, netting 15 League goals, with the emerging Wilkinson close behind. Tony Ford had his most consistent season to that date, for he was an ever-present and 'Player of the Year' for the first time. Nigel Batch in goal also never missed a game, for a club record 5th season.

1984/85

Hopes were high for the coming season. Booth had lost the experience of Waters and Speight and replaced that with promising youngsters. Steve Foley replaced Waters in the number four shirt with Chris Seagraves arriving as a right-back. Both had been reserve players with Liverpool in their all-conquering Central League side, but had failed to break into the fantastic Liverpool side of the era. Two other First Division youngsters came in the form of Sheffield-born Mike Rowbotham (Manchester United) and Richard Dawson (Stoke City youth team 'keeper). Only Foley had experienced League football of these newcomers, when he had appeared in a brief loan spell with Fulham.

The season started well with a 1-0 victory over Barnsley, before losing 3-0 at promotion favourites Manchester City on August Bank Holiday Monday. An injury to Cumming at Maine Road provided Seagraves with his League debut when he came on as substitute. He began the next game at Middlesbrough when the Mariners produced an amazing 5-1 win. Confidence was high and Charlton fell 2-1 to the Mariners in the next game. Three losses in the League came as a shock especially when two were at home, to Leeds and new boys Oxford United. The Oxford game saw one of the unluckiest debuts of all-time for new Mariner signing Neil Robinson who arrived from Swansea City. With his first kick he sliced a clearance past Nigel Batch, in only the second minute, and into the Pontoon net in front of the astonished fans.

Barnsley were swept aside in the Milk Cup, and a top-draw hat-trick from Gary Lund secured all three points in a 3-2 win at Bramall Lane against Sheffield United. Oldham were then beaten 4-1. The homegrown partnership of Wilkinson and Lund was so strong that the talented Drinkell was forced to watch from the subs. bench for the early part of the season.

Another good away win, 4-2 at Cardiff, was enjoyed, before another high scoring week in November saw Rotherham United first thrashed 6-1 (when all the midfield, wingers and forwards scored one each on Tuesday night Milk Cup duty). The momentum was carried into the League on the Saturday when Wolves were beaten 5-1. During the following week Gary Lund made his debut for the England Under-21's in Turkey, after making only 12 starts in League Football for Town. Wilkinson had also been selected but withdrew through injury and never travelled with the squad.

Form was slightly inconsistent, though the Mariners were still capable of some tremendous results on their day, none more so than the Milk Cup fourth round tie at Goodison Park. Everton were F.A.Cup holders, and sitting at the top of the First Division (before going on to become Champions of England and winners of the European Cup Winners' Cup that year). When the Mariners visited on a wet and cold November, the form book read true as Everton staged wave after wave of attacks, but Town's defence stood firm with heroics from Batch and goal-line clearances from Captain Kev Moore, Nicholl and Scouser Seagraves.

By now a replay was expected as Town's defence had survived. Then, in a rare foray up-field in the dying minutes, Everton conceded a free-kick. Bonnyman lofted the free-kick into the box which to everyones amazement Paul Wilkinson connected with, and a looping header which left the stunned Southall helpless saw Town record a famous victory, against all the odds. The Mariners had reached the Quarter-finals, but again only to lose 1-0 to future winners - this time Norwich City - at a frost covered Blundell Park in January.

A shot, in acrobatic fashion, from Paul Wilkinson in the Oldham Athletic match; Paul Emson looks-on.

New Years Day had been greeted with a 5-1 thrashing of Huddersfield Town in the League before F.A.Cup games were played against Notts County. Town, drawn away, looked likely winners as they took a 2-0 lead, only for Notts County super sub. Ian McParland to come on and score two late goals. The replay on the Tuesday night saw Lund record his second hat-trick of the campaign and Wilkinson net at both ends in a 4-2 victory. The fourth round was played at home against First Division Watford. Town took the lead with a Steve Foley drive before Watford ran away 3-1 winners, with reserve 'keeper Peter Grotier looking vulnerable from a leg injury.

A slight injury crisis struck with Batch (stomach) and Grotier (leg) both out, but young Richard Dawson kept a clean sheet on his debut in a scoreless draw at Leeds, before David Felgate arrived on loan from Lincoln City. Felgate's signing was followed with three straight wins including a 6-3 beating of Cardiff City and a 1-0 win at Wolves; the latter result provided a 'double' over their old bogey side, a team they hadn't previously beaten home or away since 1938. Further injuries struck in March as the midfield consisted of Rowbotham and Mark Hine both making their debuts in the Oldham defeat.

Wilkinson finally made his debut for the England Under-21's at Portsmouth, against Eire, and scored; three days later he signed for Everton in a club record £300,000 deal. The player's qualities were his tireless running and heading ability as well as his obvious eye for goal.

April arrived with Town completely outclassing Manchester City in a marvellous 4-1 win, and a 2-0 victory on the final day at Crystal Palace saw the Mariners finish 10th. If Booth could have just created that missing consistency then surely Town would have been in with a chance of promotion. Neil Matthews, Henshaw and Andy Moore were given further chances in the final months, the Manager not being afraid to turn to youth.

Foley and Seagraves spent just one season in Cleethorpes and Player/Assistant Manager Chris Nicholl succeeded Lawrie McMenemy as Southampton boss. After several years of speculation Kevin Drinkell finally moved on. Norwich City were the lucky club who obtained the player for a tribunal set fee of £105,000. Norwich had indeed got themselves a bargain as Drinkell went on to become the Second Division top scorer the following season when his goals shot the Canaries back to Division One. He was a superb header of the ball, possessed a tremendous shot, was an accurate passer and holder of possession, and therefore had all the attributes of a great striker. Drinkell, Wilkinson and Lund all were home grown and all scored double figures in the 1984/85 Division Two scoring charts.

1985/86

Booth made some interesting moves into the transfer market as the new season approached. Dave Felgate signed permanently for £27,500, along with team-mate Gordon Hobson (£35,000 - also from Lincoln City) who Town had been watching for a while. The club's first £100,000 signing arrived in August, in Watford centre-forward Jimmy Gilligan, but that record lasted just one week before Andy Peake arrived for £105,000 from Leicester City. Gilligan and Hobson were taken on to replace Drinkell and Wilkinson. Reserve trialist Tony Barratt of Billingham Town also signed.

Record-signing Andy Peake

Peake's first game as a Mariner came in a friendly match against his former colleagues just a day after signing for Town, and Gilligan scored in a 1-1 draw with Leicester City. The first League game saw a point rescued from the long haul down to Brighton as new boy Hobson left the bench and equalized in the final minute to make the score 2-2.

The Mariners had to wait until the eighth game of the season for the first win, with a blistering volley from Peake in the Friday night defeat of Carlisle United. Town had drawn five of their previous games of which two were lost. Peake's goal was scored in front of the Osmond End, where for this season, disgruntled Pontoonites stood. The Police had advised the club to make the change as away supporters would be easier to Police at the Grimsby end of the ground. This decision to move home fans was, not surprisingly, unpopular. The away fans also had the luxury of having seats which had been installed at the back of the Pontoon. The move lasted for just two years.

In October, the surprise news came that Dave Booth was to resign from his position as Manager, and turning his back on football, become a Property Developer in Tenerife. Booth had been a good team boss with the Mariners, having stabilised the club in the Second Division. His farewell game was a 3-2 win over Middlesbrough, when ironically his summer signing Gilligan had by far his best game as a Mariner, scoring twice.

Former 'keeper Peter Grotier took temporary charge of the side as the board looked for a replacement. Boardroom movements had also been made with Dudley Ramsden, Tom Bygott then Ron Ramsden (father of Dudley) all becoming Chairman within the October/November period. With gates barely averaging 5,000, the club was losing money every week, and although the on the field performances had been satisfactory, supporters sensed something bubbling under the surface.

Grotier's first League game in charge was against Millwall and Town won 5-1 with a Hobson hat-trick. Hobson was proving a bargain up front, for he was highly skilful and gave !00% effort, matching this with the experience of winding-up his opponents at any given opportunity; not a dirty player but devilishly cunning.

Despite this fantastic start, the Directors had already earmarked a replacement and once again, as in bygone years, they opted for a Player/manager. Ex-Liverpool and England player Phil Neal was first choice of Dudley Ramsden, but on his refusal, Sheffield Wednesday and former Everton Captain Mike Lyons was chosen by new Chairman Ron Ramsden, and he became the club's 21st Manager. A wholehearted player Lyons installed his old Everton team-mate Terry Darracott as assistant, before his first game, versus Portsmouth. Things started well with a 1-0 win, Lyons having a good game alongside Skipper Kevin Moore in the centre of defence. Red socks were immediately replaced with white ones, as Lyon's made the first of many strange changes. A narrow defeat at Norwich City, 3-2, followed, then Blackburn were hammered 5-2 in the last game of November. December provided no wins as Lyons made some unpredictable changes as he experimented with his squad, including hard tackling centre-back Andy Moore replacing the creative Andy Peake in the centre of midfield.

Due to lack of finance, Lyons had the unenviable task of releasing no less than seven of the club's youngsters just before New Year, and coaches and former players Peter Grotier plus Alan Woodward also left. Perhaps the largest loss to the club was that of Commercial Consultant Alec King, to Sunderland. Renowned as being the best in the business, King had been the brain behind all the club's fund-raising schemes, which had generated over a million pounds worth of business to Blundell Park during his eight year stay.

The New Year began with a 3-1 win over Shrewsbury Town, Lyons scoring two. Arsenal were drawn at home in the F.A.Cup third round, which produced a classic as a reinstated Lund hooked home an early goal for Town, before Arsenal equalized soon after. A Charlie Nicholas hat-trick saw off Town, but not before a Lyons conversion and a Peake penalty produced an eventual 4-3 Town defeat. Both Moore brothers had missed the Cup game with legs in plaster.

Lyons had attempted to strengthen the bond between the club and the local community with visits to the Docks, schools and hospitals, as Lawrie McMenemy had done 14 years prior. On the pitch, results were pleasing with three consecutive 1-0 wins in February and early March, which lifted the club into 9th position, yet a poor run-in saw Town finally finish 15th.

The poor end of season run coincided with no fewer than 10 first-teamers being placed on the transfer list, and Felgate, Ford and Bonnyman were loaned out during the final months. This was a decision which bemused supporters as Ford had not missed a single game for three straight seasons and himself and Bonnyman had both deputised as Captain in Kevin Moore's absence. Speedy winger Paul Emson was dropped then released (to Wrexham), along with Mark Hine (Darlington), and 'Young Player of the Year' Tony Barratt (Billingham Town). Local favourites Ford (Stoke City) and Lund (Lincoln City) were allowed to leave with Gilligan (Swindon Town) for deals worth just £40,000 each. Havelock schoolboy winger Chris Grocock was blooded in the final game at Blackburn. Whether any of these strange decisions lie with financial restraints, the board, Lyons or a combination of all three, the supporters were not happy.

1986/87

New players were signed to make up a squad following the departures. A pre-season Icelandic Tour provided a confidence booster when defender Dave Burgess (Tranmere Rovers) and former Welsh International forward Ian Walsh (Barnsley) showed up well, with Town winning all three games. Other successes of the tour were trialists Neil Horwood (a Grimsby lad, and former Hereford School pupil) and Ian Straw (former Southampton apprentice) who were both offered terms. Phil Turner arrived from Lincoln City in exchange for Lund, and the experienced Don O'Riordan left troubled Middlesbrough. Locals Andy Dixon then Peter Rawcliffe also signed professional contracts. Terry Darracott returned to Everton, with Lyons selecting players Bonnyman and O'Riordan as first team coaches.

The side was unchanged for the first few matches with Batch in goal, and Burgess plus Cumming as full-backs. Kevin Moore and Lyons completed the defence line. Neil Robinson replaced Ford, wide on the right, with new signing Turner out on the left, but it soon became apparent to all, bar Lyons, that neither were effective wide players. Both players performed better given opportunities in central midfield, although Robinson was also a useful right-back. With Peake and O'Riordan in central midfield, Walsh and Hobson were the main strikers and neither could be classed as target men even though Lyons had adopted a direct style of play.

The first home win didn't arrive until November, although only one had been lost in six away games. By the time of the first win, 22 players had already been used, as Lyons juggled with personnel. By then Peake had moved to Charlton Athletic for £75,000, and Des Hazel and Brian Rice had been signed on loan. Winger Hazel was a success, he had lightning pace and scored the 'goal of the season' at Portsmouth after skipping past the entire Pompey team, however he soon returned to Wednesday's reserves, with Town unable to afford him.

Gordon Hobson comes close with a shot in the Leeds United match

Only six of the 22 games had been lost by New Year, though nine had been drawn. Dave Moore returned, doubling up as Youth Coach, so for a few fleeting months all three Moore brothers were in the club's first team pool, however they were never selected in the same side. In the meantime, star forward Gordon Hobson had gone on strike, of a different kind, when the club refused to let him talk to First Division Southampton. He eventually signed for the Saints in a £125,000 deal in November.

Garry Henshaw celebrates his goal versus West Brom with ex-Pontoonites behind the Osmond End goal.

Dave Felgate (to Bolton Wanderers, for £16,000) and Kevin Moore (£100,000, to Oldham Athletic) left as Lyons further reshaped his side for promotion. Moore was team captain and it was the consensus that he should never have been allowed to leave; he went on to captain Southampton in the top flight. Though reckless changes to the playing side continued, a 3-1 win in early March lifted Town to 8th, just a few places off a promotion spot, with 10 games remaining. Mick Halsall was signed from Carlisle United replacing Moore as Captain, and later Scott McGarvey also arrived from Cumbria, with loan signing Mark Prudhoe being preferred to Batch in goal.

During those final 10 games the unthinkable happened when just two points from a possible 30 were won as the Mariners slipped from 8th to 21st, and were relegated. The indignity of relegation came with a 2-2 draw at home to Hull City, when three points were required; the Mariners neighbours were also relegation-threatened, but survived. The final game saw Town hammered 5-1 at Stoke City, a ground where they had already been beaten 6-0, earlier in the season in the F.A.Cup. All Lyons' plans had backfired, and he was as shocked as the supporters. The board's decision to employ an inexperienced Manager in the first place was highlighted as a poor decision, and Lyons was dismissed as late as mid-June, which was an odd time for it left little time for a new Manager to prepare.

A mass exodus then occurred with Batch, Cumming and Andy Moore all dropping out of the League and moving to neighbours Lincoln City. Henshaw and Crombie joined Felgate at Bolton, Bonnyman met up with old boss Dave Booth, who had returned to football at Darlington. Halsall (Peterborough United), Horwood (Cambridge United), Matthews (Halifax Town) and Straw (Burton Albion) also left. The name of Mike Lyons still leaves a sour taste in the mouths of true Mariners, but the question was, was he solely to blame?

1987/88

New Manager Bobby Roberts was given the unenviable task of building a squad which would lift the club back into Division Two at the first attempt. He had just a few weeks to prepare for the season and the squad he had inherited were still battlescarred and shellshocked. Roberts had been a player with Motherwell and Leicester City before Managing Colchester United and Wrexham, and joined the club from a coaching position in Kuwait.

Scott McGarvey in action.

Goalkeeper Steve Sherwood was signed on a free transfer from Watford, as the only player left on the books in this position was youngster Lee Pratt. Reserves from Liverpool, Ian Toale and Preston North End's Steve Saunders arrived on trial with loanees Marc North (Luton Town) and Trevor Slack (Rotherham United). All where members of Roberts' first squad at Doncaster Rovers, which lost 1-0. The omens were bad as Fourth Division Darlington, with Grimsby connections, won in the Littlewoods Cup.

A 3-1 win at Preston was encouraging, with Saunders scoring his first goal for the club against the side which had released him, and young trainee Tommy Watson made his debut. Another away day at Bury saw McGarvey score both goals in the 2-0 win. Just one home win, against Gillingham, was recorded before York City were thrashed 5-1 in late November. By now, North (£40,000) and Slack (£10,000) had both been signed permanently.

Youngsters John McDermott, Watson, Grocock and Dixon were now all regulars as the club plunged further into financial ruin, and playing now in front of 2-3,000 Blundell Park gates, with sponsors reluctant to support a club which seemed to have an unpromising future. A 5-0 defeat at Fulham saw Town drop into the bottom five, despite former tormentor Terry Curran making his Mariners debut. Centre-forward North scored a hat-trick in the 3-0 Port Vale win in the last game of the year, but Town remained at 20th in the table.

Walsh moved to Cardiff City (£16,000) and Slack transferred to Northampton Town (£10,000), and a deal in which Phil Turner moved to Leicester City, saw Kevin Jobling arrive at Blundell Park in exchange. Shaun Cunnington arrived from Wrexham the same day in February. The season was coming to a close and the Mariners had not been higher than 20th since November. Lack of goals and confidence were the major factors in the Mariners failure.

Free-scoring Nottingham Forest reserve Billy Stubbs came on loan to boost the flagging forward line for the end of season run-in, when the form improved slightly, but too many games were drawn which should have been won. Off the field the club faced a £30,000 tax bill with no money to pay it. Appeal funds were organised and the urgently required money was generated.

A tremendous win at Wigan Athletic, which included a Sherwood penalty save gave the Mariners a glimmer of hope before going into the final game at home to Aldershot. The Shots took an early lead which Marc North equalised, but he turned villain when he had a second half penalty saved.

And so Town were relegated for the second consecutive season and would be playing in the Fourth Division once more. Roberts was sacked just two days after the Aldershot defeat as new Chairman Peter Furneaux searched for a very special man to turn things around.

Dave Moore and Neil Robinson both joined Booth at Darlington. Burgess (Blackpool), Curran (Chesterfield), and the highly impressive Don O'Riordan (Notts County) all departed. O'Riordan was actually voted 'Player of the Year' and also 'Sunday People Defender of the Division' after he had moved from midfield to the back four with great ease. He was captain on the field and coach and ambassador off it. He was somewhat disappointed at not gaining the hot-seat on Roberts' dismissal.

In just a little over 18 months the club went from winning 3-0 at Crystal Palace to failing to beat the likes of Aldershot and Doncaster Rovers, and in front of seriously diminished attendances. Could Grimsby Town Football Club bounce back again?

Chapter Eleven

THE ARRIVAL OF....  BUCKLEY (PART 1)

1988-1994

1988/89

The man employed to ensure the club's very existence was one Alan Buckley. He arrived in June from GM Conference outfit Kettering Town. Buckley installed Arthur Mann, one of his former players, as his assistant and together they schemed to build a squad on a shoestring budget.

Alan Buckley

Seven new players came in from non-League circles or on free-transfers. The new captain was the highly experienced defender Tommy Williams from Birmingham City. Steve Stoutt arrived from Wolves and one of Buckley's old Walsall men, Richard O'Kelly, signed from Port Vale. Kettering Town youngsters 'keeper Paul Reece (£10,000) and centre-back Andy Tillson followed Buckley, with other Conference stars Keith Alexander (£11,500) of Barnet and local John Cockerill (£21,250) who signed from Stafford Rangers. John, the son of former favourite 'Cannonball' Ron, grew-up in Cleethorpes but had failed to break into professional football in his teens due to his size. He joined the R.A.F. and also spent a couple of years lorry driving in Australia before coming home, aged 27. Alexander was a draughtsman in South Lincolnshire and Tillson a Market Gardener. The most expensive summer signing was that of the £30,000 Electronic Scoreboard at he Osmond End, which was donated by an unknown benefactor!

The season opened with a 4-1 defeat at Cambridge United and a Littlewoods Cup exit, when both legs were lost 1-0 to Rotherham United. Hardly inspiring form. The first win came in the Torquay home game courtesy of a Marc North strike. An away draw at Glanford Park, Scunthorpe, provided some encouragement, but this was just a prelude to further letdowns, when big home defeats to Rotherham United (4-0) and Rochdale (3-1) followed. Scott McGarvey was swapped with Bristol City's proven marksmen Tony Caldwell.

However, the former Bolton hitman only stayed for a month before moving to Stockport County, without scoring a goal. Two shock results came in November with a 5-0 win against Doncaster Rovers, then a Cockerill goal scored directly from a corner-kick, which was enough to beat Wolves, who were sitting at the top of the Third Division, in the first round of the F.A.Cup.

Buckley's side was far from settled, losing both Stoutt and Williams with lengthy injuries in the early stages. The positions of Williams and Cockerill, who began the season in the centre of defence, were now filled by the inexperienced Tillson and 18-year-old Mark Lever. Cockerill had moved into central midfield with Shaun Cunnington, whilst Alexander and O'Kelly were working together well up front. The unorthodox 'King Alex', becoming something of a cult hero; the coloured striker with his 6'-4'' rangy build was surprisingly better on the ground rather than in the air.

Division Four form was still inconsistent, though the side were to put an F.A.Cup run together that would be talked about for years to come. After Third Division leaders Wolves, Fourth Division leaders Rotherham were beaten in the next round, before First Division Middlesbrough were drawn away. With Town placed 88th in the League and Middlesbrough just 13th there seemed to be only one outcome. Manchester United had lost at Ayresome Park just five days earlier, so when Town went in at half-time 1-0 down, it was no surprise. The second half saw the Mariners come more into the game, and with just 20 minutes remaining Buckley introduced substitute Marc North. Town finished winning 2-1 with North scoring both, one with his first touch, and the other from a diving header, with just three minutes remaining, to produce the shock of the round.

Cup fever struck the area when Third Division Reading were drawn at home which gave the Mariners a good chance of further progression. North scored again as Town drew 1-1, and they were again the underdogs for the replay. Jobling this time appeared from the bench to score the winner after Cunnington had scored earlier, in a final 2-1 win. A 2-0 win at Rochdale in the League boosted hopes, as the Mariners, still placed 18th in Division Four, visited Cup holders Wimbledon in round five. The away terracing at Plough Lane was packed with a 7,000 following, and a sea of inflatable Harry Haddocks. Only 2,000 had attended the first game of the season at Blundell Park, so 7,000 travelling to the capital was a success of its own. Unbelievably the Mariners took the lead through Alexander, only for the Dons to claw their way back and win 3-1. The dream was over, but still the memory lingers on.

The Cup form created interest in the club once more and League results were transformed. York were beaten 3-0 away, and then Scunthorpe and Lincoln visited Cleethorpes. Scunny went away with a draw, but Lincoln were defeated by a Richard O'Kelly strike; Lincoln-born Dave Gilbert made his debut with 'loanee' Dale Banton.

A 5-0 thrashing at Leyton Orient was a set-back, but only one of the final nine games were lost as Town shot up the table and just failed to reach a play-off place, finishing 9th. The introduction of the tricky Gilbert on the left, proved a master stroke after his £55,000 capture from Northampton Town, and the 30-year-old Alexander was a success in his belated entry to the professional ranks, scoring 14 in the League. Saunders and O'Kelly also netted double figures. O'Kelly unfortunately broke his leg at Doncaster and never played again.

Grocock and Pratt joined Boston United, Dixon (Southend United) and Saunders (Scarborough) also left. Saunders had been an honest, hard working attacker, but will probably be most remembered for chances missed rather than scored as well as his, 'Eddie the Eagle' looks!

1989/90

The previous season showed distinct signs of promise and the side began to play neat attractive football. The squad was strengthened further with three excellent signings in forward Tony Rees, a former Welsh cap, who arrived from Barnsley, and skilful winger Gary Childs from Birmingham City. The biggest coup of all was that of former Nottingham Forest and England striker Garry Birtles from Notts County. Birtles was in the twilight of his career but his class still shone in the Fourth Division.

The season started well, when a 0-0 draw at home to Cambridge was followed by a 3-0 away win at Torquay and a 4-1 beating of Colchester United. Second Division Hull City were defeated over two legs in the Littlewoods Cup, Childs scoring the winner deep into extra time. Coventry City were drawn in the next round, the home leg being won convincingly 3-1, as Town regained their reputation as a Cup side under Buckley. Unfortunately a large expectant following saw a farcical second leg as fiery Welshman Rees was dismissed after just four minutes for retaliating in response to early rough treatment that was dished out by the First Division side. Playing most of the game with just 10 men Town went down 3-0, Kevin Drinkell scoring on his Sky Blues debut with an overhead kick in front of his former fans.

Results took an inexplicable dive in the League with just one win in eight, including four straight defeats. That one victory came against Gillingham with youngsters Chris Hargreaves and Paul Smaller making their full debuts. Consecutive away wins at Wrexham and York City helped turn the tide, and 17-year-old Hargreaves scored both goals in the F.A.Cup win at York.

The New Year began well with a 4-2 victory over Stockport, though January was not the best month with the departure from the F.A.Cup at Huddersfield Town, and the failure to score in three other games. Then Keith Alexander, who had now been dropped to the subs. bench, had the distinction of coming on and scoring in three consecutive matches. Ian Knight was signed from Sheffield Wednesday on loan, scoring in the 4-2 win over Burnley, he then had the misfortune of breaking his leg in his first game after his £15,000 permanent transfer, in the defeat at Colchester. Knight, at one time an England Under-21 cap, had previously badly broken his leg whilst with the Owls.

March sparked off an incredible run of seven straight wins, conceding only two goals, as the crowds returned to Blundell Park and Town were looking strong in 2nd place, with Buckley receiving the 'Manager of the Month' award. A Gilbert penalty was enough to beat Lincoln in front of an 11,000 plus gathering, and a 2-2 draw at Halifax followed before Town flopped in front of expectant home fans against Peterborough United. Wins at Stockport and Southend and a home victory in the Scunny 'derby', maintained 2nd position with three games left. The 2-0 win at Fourth place Southend virtually clinched promotion and a scoreless home draw with spoilers Hartlepool United was enough. Exeter City took the Championship, with the Mariners having a tremendous promotion party as 'Player of the Year' Garry Birtles helped himself to a hat-trick in a 5-1 win over Wrexham.

Gary Birtles

The squad overall was versatile, fitting in to a system that rarely changed. Sherwood was in goal with Paul Reece deputising, with full-backs John McDermott and Paul Agnew. The latter had spells of injury with a troublesome hamstring, being replaced by firstly teenager Geoff Stephenson, then with Jobling dropping back successfully from midfield. Lever and Tillson were flourishing in the centre though Knight and Birtles had spells filling-in. Cockerill and Cunnington were a rock solid partnership in the middle of the park, both being hard tacklers who loved forward charges. Childs and Gilbert were by far the best wide men in the Division. Two from Rees, Alexander or Birtles appeared up-front, and goals arrived from all areas of the squad, with the promise of more excitement to come. The unlucky O'Kelly, Stoutt and Williams all left after injury troubles. Young coloured forward Roger 'Harry' Willis joined to soon-to-be Conference Champions Barnet.

1990/91

Buckley deemed the squad to be as good and large enough to succeed in the Third Division. The only newcomer was Bradford City's out of favour striker Neil Woods who came on loan, although Rees and Birtles suffered slight injuries as the season was about to start.

How right Buckley was. From day one they pressed for promotion, the first three games were won and Town were early leaders. Woods was signed for £90,000 after scoring four goals in those first three wins at Preston, Crewe and at home to Wigan. Crowd favourite Alexander failed to gain a place in the winning side and soon moved on to Stockport County. The momentum continued as Town played some delightful attacking football accompanied by a tight defence. Just one defeat, at Brentford, in the first 15 games, saw the side in the top three for the first half of the season, vying for the leadership with other new boys Southend United.

A slight hiccup came in November when Bolton won at Blundell Park and three points were lost to rivals Southend. This was not a year for Cup success as all were exited at the first stage. Crewe in the Littlewoods Cup, Blackpool in the F.A.Cup and to York City and Darlington, 3-1 each, in the Leyland DAF Cup. Rees and Tommy Watson were both dismissed in the Darlington game..... for arguing with each other!

Good wins against Bournemouth (5-0) and Fulham (3-0) came at critical times as the side were having an indifferent spell. A 4-1 win versus Preston in mid-January coincided with Ian Baraclough and veteran Paul Futcher making their debuts, as the Mariners struck an injury crisis in defence. Baraclough had been on loan for a month from Leicester City and could play anywhere, and Futcher, who also originally came on loan after appearing for Halifax Town's reserves, was a cultured centre-back with skills and tricks of a silky midfielder.

Shaun Cunnington in action versus Stoke City.

The composure of Andy Tillson had been spotted by Queens Park Rangers who bought him for a club record £500,000 - not a bad return for a free transfer from non-League just 17 months earlier! Town originally had cover but injuries to Knight, Birtles, Cockerill and Agnew forced the temporary signing of Futcher.

A 2-0 win at Bradford City saw Town go top, though only briefly, but thirteen games passed with just one defeat, including another undefeated March, which included four straight wins, one of which was against rivals Southend who like the Mariners had not left the top positions. Cockerill returned from injury only for the club to lose Childs. Futcher had been secured permanently for the bargain fee of just £10,000 and wing cover came in the form of Huddersfield Town's Mark Smith for £55,000 on transfer deadline day. The good run had seen Town return to pole position with just nine games remaining.

April was a nervous month as good results began to falter. Just two wins came, one over Cambridge United and the other, a vital 2-0 victory at Leyton Orient, just as Town looked to be dropping into the play-off zone. With two games left a large travelling army embarked on the Victoria Ground of Stoke City. The game was halted as Stoke fans caused a pitch invasion, the score remained goalless, and the Mariners gained a point.

Southend United, and a late rally from Cambridge United, saw the pair already promoted with Town favourites for the third automatic spot, though they needed a result in the final game at home to Exeter City. A 14,225 (record receipts of £53,958-40p) home crowd roared the Mariners to victory, as local boy John Cockerill was hero of the day scoring both goals in a famous 2-1 victory.

John Cockerill strikes against Exeter City in the promotion decider

All three clubs that were automatically promoted were in the Fourth Division the previous season.

Buckley had achieved the unimaginable feat of a swift return to Division Two against all the odds, and with a club record 83 points. Sherwood and Captain Cunnington had been ever-presents, though the squad as a whole had been magnificent. Gilbert, Woods and Rees all scored double figures as again the goals were shared around the side. Now for Division Two.

1991/92

Experienced midfield anchor-man Jim Dobbin was signed from Barnsley (£50,000) on the same day as Exeter City's centre-forward Murray Jones (£75,000) arrived. Baraclough, who had been on loan the previous season was released by Leicester City and returned to Blundell Park to assist in the club's stabilising season to retain Second Division status.

The season opened in exciting fashion when Cambridge United were once again opponents, but far removed from the 0-0 draw that had opened the previous season.

Blundell Park in the early 1990's.

On this occasion the air-raiding Cambridge side with Dion Dublin up front stole the victory in a 4-3 win. Town were without the injured Cunnington and Childs, and Rees was soon to join them. This season was not going to be easy because of the great difference in quality of clubs in the Second compared to the Third.

Kevin Jobling.

Rotherham United were easily passed in the first round of the Rumbelows Cup and three points were won at Oxford United in the League, with goals from Cockerill and McDermott. The first League home win came by 2-1 against Plymouth Argyle and a tremendous, morale-boosting victory at big spending Sunderland in late September saw the Mariners rise to 8th position. The next game was against Aston Villa in the Rumbelows Cup in front of a 13,000 plus Blundell Park crowd. Town drew the first leg 0-0 and was expected to go out upon their visit to Villa Park. A 'Diddy' Dave Gilbert penalty put Town in the lead with Sherwood in inspired form in goal. Villa equalised, but Town hung on through extra time to win with the away goal. 'Spurs and their all-star side were drawn in the third round, and in that match England legend Gary Lineker was kept quiet all night by Futcher and the much improved Lever, but the Mariners still went down 3-0 in front of the largest crowd at Blundell Park for over 11 years. 17,017 paid record receipts of £97,000 to see this all-ticket tie.

A hard time was had in the League as injuries began to upset the side, with every player in the first team pool being absent at one time or another, as the squad became depleted. Just one win in October, one in November and another in December saw Town drop to second from bottom. Consecutive away draws at millionaire club Derby County and Tranmere Rovers, between Christmas and New Year, provided a little hope, but troubles had again struck on the Wirral as 'keeper Paul Reece left the field injured. Tony Ford scored in this 1-1 draw, returning after a five year absence when he signed from West Bromwich Albion (£35,000); he could now also play a useful game at right-back, as well as in attack.

Tony Rees

With January came the arrival of centre-back Graham Rodger and nippy striker Clive Mendonca, both on loan from Luton Town and Sheffield United respectively. Their arrival sparked two straight wins against Oxford and at high flying Cambridge United, when the newcomers replaced the injured Futcher and Woods.

Summer signing Jones had been signed as a target man to be used if tactical options required change, but alas he was not of Second Division standard and remains Buckley's least successful signing, though the money spent on him was recouped when he was sold to Brentford.

Only four wins came in the following 16 games, and the best possible result in a tricky away game at Port Vale was required to survive. Thankfully a Tommy Watson goal stole all three points as the Mariners escaped the drop, finishing 19th. The season had been one of struggle, but the lowly position was attained unfortunately through the endless injury list.

1992/93

The League was reorganised for this season with the inception of the F.A. Premier League which took over the title of the 'old' Division One. The other Divisions of the Football League were renamed accordingly, so on paper the Mariners had moved from the Fourth to the First Division in three consecutive seasons!

Sadly, Knight, Birtles and Cockerill never played for the club again all being released due to injury problems. Shaun Cunnington left for big spending Sunderland in a £600,000 deal, and with the Cunnington money Buckley signed three new players. Paul Groves replaced Cunnington in midfield, when he came from Blackpool for a record £150,000, Mendonca signed eventually for £85,000 after two loan spells. Rhys Wilmot became the new goalkeeper, after a tribunal set fee of £87,500, from Plymouth Argyle. Reece left for pastures new, eventually settling at Oxford United, and veteran Sherwood would still continue to play after recovering from injury, despite entering his 39th year.

A 3-1 defeat at Charlton Athletic was not the desired start, but the squad was still riddled with injuries. Then the 3-2 win over Watford saw Tommy Watson become the first player to score goals in the Fourth, Third, Second and now First Division for the club. The centre of defence became even more depleted, Futcher and Lever both missing the first games with Rodger and Baraclough standing in at Charlton. Left-back Agnew moved into the centre for the Coca Cola Cup-tie at Barnsley and for the live TV encounter at Birmingham City alongside debutant Peter Handyside. The Oakwell game was won by Town on penalties and the Birmingham match lost 2-1 with a disputed winner. The Brummie attacker appeared yards offside.

Another youngster came into the side at full-back, and former favourite Andy Tillson returned for a month's loan to help out his old buddies. Three consecutive League defeats saw Town drop to 19th and knocked out of the Coca Cola Cup by QPR, a tie again decided on a penalty shoot-out, the first ever witnessed at Blundell Park. But the Mariners recovered well with an unbeaten run of seven including six wins. The best result came at runaway leaders Newcastle United, where Kevin Keegan's side had a 100% record having won all eleven League games, prior to the visit of 'minnows' Grimsby Town. The largest crowd of the day in England saw Jim Dobbin rifle a tremendous shot into the top corner of the net in the final minutes, as Town broke Geordie hearts with a 1-0 win. Making his debut that day for Town was former England 'keeper Dave Beasant who had been borrowed from Chelsea just the day before. He was a class act and it was no coincidence that the side's good run came in the same period as Beasant's all too brief stay, for he departed in late November, and Town lost the next four matches.

Scottish Under-21 International Peter Handyside (his first game in March), on 'National Service'.

At home to Derby County the game was lost 2-0 in the first live League TV match staged at Blundell Park, which was also the first League game there on a Sunday. A superb rally in the New Year saw Town reach 7th spot as the side began to show some consistency, despite still being dogged by injuries to key players during January and February. Captain Graham Rodger scored three goals in as many games in forays forward, and Paul Groves recorded his second hat-trick of the season, from midfield, in the 3-3 draw with Notts County. Dobbin and Groves were settling into a neat combination in the centre of midfield, not as swashbuckling as Cunnington and Cockerill but still useful, and scoring more than their fair share of goals.

Tony Daws was signed from Scunthorpe United (£50,000) in March, and his first four starts saw as many straight wins as he fitted into the attack which had appeared to be lacking in confidence. Town's final home game was against Champions-elect Newcastle United, when Andy Cole opened the scoring in the 2-0 defeat for Town. A 14,402 crowd swelled by thousands of Geordies paid record receipts for a League game of £81,200.

The Mariners were everybody's favourites to be relegated at the season's outset, but not only had they survived, they had produced some of the most skilful possession football in the Division and could outclass big spenders such as Newcastle, West Ham, Wolves, Derby, Leicester and Birmingham. Buckley must take full credit for the side finishing 9th in such a competitive Division, with small gates, and no money for large transfer fees or wages. He had built a squad which could compete at this high level, an amazing achievement if compared to the humble beginnings of the 1988/89 season.

The evergreen Steve Sherwood was released to Northampton Town and Mark Smith moved to Scunthorpe United for £20,000.

1993/94

With the new season came a newly designed home strip; white, with red collar and thin black stripes, keeping the black shorts, but returning to white socks. The previous season's kit had included much more black, and the new outfit was strikingly different.

Buckley again turned to one of his old Walsall favourites when Craig Shakespeare (£115,000) signed from West Bromwich Albion in the summer, and was joined by free transfer 'keeper Paul Crichton who joined from troubled Doncaster Rovers.

Both new men began in the attractive opening fixtures at home to Bolton and away at Nottingham Forest. A goalless start against Bolton was offset at the City Ground a week later in an amazing game which Town lost 5-3 to a very strong side. Crichton committed a howling mistake when he completely miskicked a Futcher back pass and saw the ball roll agonisingly into the Trent End net; to make matters worse Forest had been Crichton's first club. The player recovered from this set-back, and was later voted the fans 'Player of the Year', remembered for some incredible saves he made during the season, though his kicking improved little.

The first four home games were drawn which was to set the tone for the season. The back line was solid but the forwards were guilty of missing many chances that were created. Woods was carried off against Middlesbrough in the Anglo Italian Cup game, when the Mariners played Boro of the park in the first half, in front of just 996 supporters. An away win at Peterborough was secured with a tremendous strike from Groves late in the game.

Forest favourites Gary Crosby and Nigel Jemson provided temporary assistance early in the season as once again the treatment room was full.

Hartlepool United had been beaten 5-0 on aggregate in the Coca Cola Cup before Tranmere Rovers outplayed Town in the next round with a 4-1 win. Scoring for the Mariners that night was new cult hero former Nigerian International Chima Okorie. Despite never starting a game, his appearance from the subs. bench with a goal, sparked Chima fever amongst the loyal travelling band. Named substitute for the following games, the Pontoon would chant his name in times of trouble. Some of his tricks and skills in the pre-match warm-up were worth the entrance fee alone. He broke a leg in a reserve game and then quietly moved on to Torquay in March.

Southend were thrashed 4-0, and it should have been more, with a brace each from Mendonca and Childs. A Centre-forward with a good goalscoring record, Chelsea's Steve Livingstone, arrived on loan in October, but he too was guilty of not converting chances that the side were readily creating, though he was signed permanently in January. His first home game after his £130,000 transfer was the F.A.Cup fourth round tie against the mighty Aston Villa. A first goal for the emerging starlet Gary Croft in the previous round against Wigan, made the visit of Villa possible. After only 20 minutes, punches were exchanged between 'Livvo' and Shaun Teale and they were both dismissed. Town showed up better, but Villa took the lead with a breakaway goal, although Paul Groves scored the equaliser after a tremendous battling run towards the Pontoon End. Sadly Villa's quality showed with a Dwight Yorke strike in a game in which Town had the Lions share of possession and chances. The money taken on the gate surpassed that of any previous Blundell Park match at £119,799.

Undefeated in the month of March (undoubtably Buckley's boys favourite month), Town lifted themselves from their false lowly position to 11th, though they soon slumped back to a final placing of 16th, with just one win from the last 10 games. The side had probably played the best quality football under Buckley this season, but poor finishing allowed many potential victories to finish as draws. The 20 one-pointers over the season, with 16 at home, frustrated supporters, and this was reflected on the season's average attendance. The high number of draws was a club home and overall record. A scoreless draw with Forest in the penultimate game was enough for the former European Champions to return to the Premier League after just one season.

Crichton had been a superb ever-present in goal, and McDermott, Croft, Futcher, Gilbert and Groves all produced top quality performances week-in week-out. Mendonca had taken the mantle of Pontoon hero, though he should have possibly doubled his total of 14 strikes when considering the number of chances that were provided. Buckley became frustrated with the ever-growing injury list and the lack of crowd support in numbers shown for his side.

Tony Ford finally departed in the Summer after a more than useful contribution in his 14th season for the club, moving on to become Scunthorpe United's player-coach, alongside old school friend Dave Moore. Unbelievably, although Ford received an M.B.E. in the 2000 New Year Honours list for services to football, he never received a Testimonial from his home town club whom he served so well. Tony became the British record holder for most League appearances for an outfield player during 1999/2000, and still performing consistently for Rochdale.

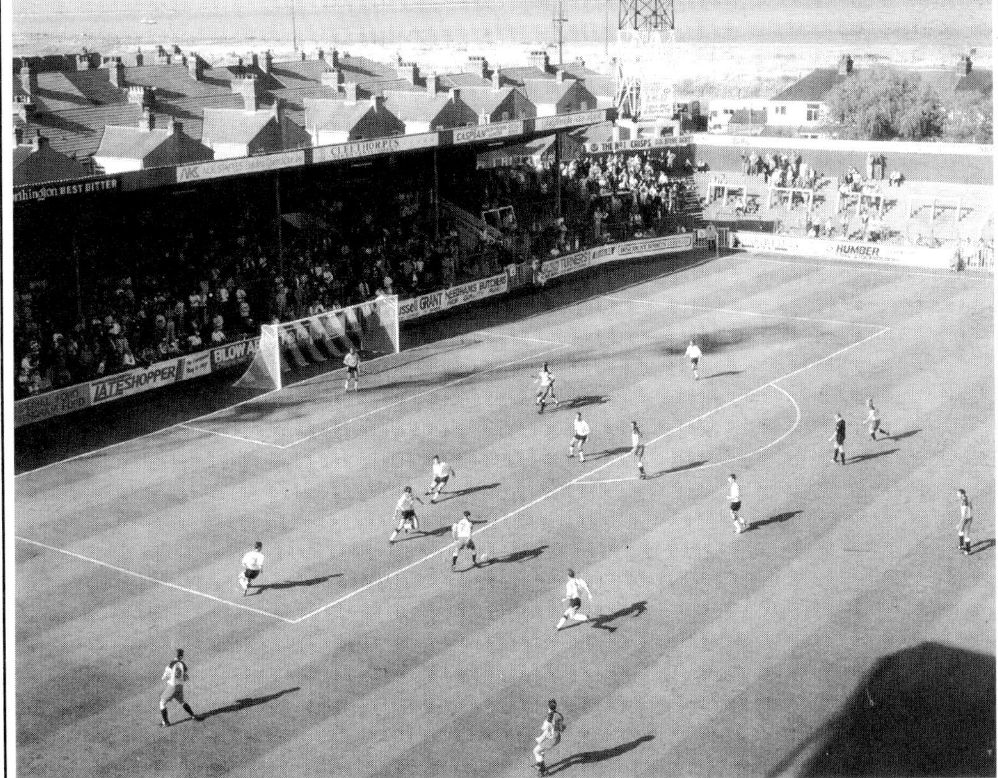

An unusual shot of Blundell Park taken from the TV gantry at the Watford match.

Chapter Twelve

LAWS, BONETTI  AND SWAIN

1994 - 1997

1994/95

The pre-season period passed well with all of the squad regaining fitness and recording a 100% record on a tour of Northern Ireland. Buckley made no new signings in the summer, although he realised a slight profit by selling reserve 'keeper Rhys Wilmot to Crystal Palace for £80,000, even though Wilmot had not played first team football for over a year; this was typical of the Manager's eye for good business. Buckley had announced that this was the best squad of players he had ever had and there was no better time to 'gatecrash' the Premiership. Backed by Chairman Peter Furneaux a ground move was also high on the agenda as the implications of the Taylor Report took effect.

Bolton were again the visitors for the opening game, and Clive Mendonca started the season with a hat-trick in a 3-3 draw. Away draws at Watford and Sunderland followed, with the first win coming in a 3-1 victory over Tranmere Rovers.

Brian Laws

Town lost to Bradford City in both legs of the Coca Cola Cup, though Port Vale were beaten 4-1 in the League, but in front of just 3,216 supporters. Portsmouth were also overcome, 2-0, in front of another poor crowd before the shock news came on 20 October that Buckley and his backroom staff of Mann and O'Kelly had accepted new jobs at West Bromwich Albion. With no coaching staff left, Chairman, Peter Furneaux, immediately placed Football in the Community Officer John Cockerill in charge of first team affairs with senior players Futcher and Rodger to assist him until a new boss was found. In an incredible caretaker spell Cockerill took Town up to 5th spot, losing just one in seven games, and he was the firm favourite of the fans to take the job. The situation was dealt with on 29 November when Nottingham Forest full-back Brian Laws was unveiled as the new boss, with Kenny Swain brought in as his assistant. Cockerill became Youth Team coach a job he was pleased to accept.

Laws' first game saw the Mariners win 2-1 at Bristol City and move into 4th spot, although none of the following five games produced three points, and the team soon slipped to 13th. Laws who had no coaching experience had not arrived as a Player/manager, but he soon found himself signing a contract in case of emergencies. He made his first appearance in late January and it was soon apparent that he still had plenty of skill, pace and determination left.

First Tony Rees, then Paul Agnew, moved on to West Bromwich, to add to the fans fury with Buckley's decision to leave, with many branding him a moneygrabber. Yet in reality Buckley took the job at the Hawthorns because there was unlimited resources to reach the very top, whereas in Cleethorpes, hampered by poor attendances, he was always going to be financially restricted.

Bill Carr became the new club Chairman, and as squad players 'keeper Jason Pearcey from Mansfield Town and Sheffield United's reserve defender Ashley Fickling became Laws' first signings, followed by the Leeds United diminutive striker Jamie Forrester, who was loaned to the Mariners. The team played with more haste than Buckley's outfit, though with basically the same players played in a slightly more direct fashion. Many argued that Laws' marginally more cavalier style was more attractive to watch, as opposed to Buckley who was at times criticised for producing pretty but punchless performances. A 5-0 win over Wolves and a 3-1 TV game victory against Sunderland were the best examples of Laws' work, when Town finished 10th at the end of a turbulent season.

The final home game, a 0-0 draw with Wolves, was the last occasion that fans would be able to stand to at Blundell Park, as work in the summer cut the capacity to 8,607 and seats were installed throughout, including the Pontoon Stand - watching Town would never be the same again.

1995/96

Another successful tour of Northern Ireland was enjoyed as the Mariners returned to a new look Blundell Park. The Imperial and Harrington Street Corners were flattened and tarmac covered. Fans took their seats in the new Pontoon and Lower 'Stones Best Bitter' Stands (formerly Findus) for the first game of the season. The match, against Portsmouth, saw Town win 2-1 with goals from Laws and Croft, and witnessed one of the Manager's rough diamonds, winger Nicky Southall, make an impressive home debut after his £70,000 move from Hartlepool United.

Paul Futcher. The arrival of Laws, spelt the end for cult favourite Futcher, who simply oozed class in his successful spell with Town.

Southall replaced the immaculate 'Diddy' Dave Gilbert who joined Buckley at West Bromwich with physio Paul Mitchell. Bestall, Boylen, Waters and Gilbert had all served the club well down the years and all impressed despite their small stature. Laws was confident that the Play-offs could be reached if the squad stayed injury free.

Top scorer Mendonca would be out for months and the consistent left-back Kevin Jobling broke his leg in only the third match, at Derby, whilst centre-backs Rodger and Lever also suffered set-backs. Richard Smith arrived on loan from Leicester City and impressed greatly, with Forrester eventually signing on a 'free' from Leeds, after the Yorkshire club had asked 'silly money' for his transfer the previous season.

Laws attempted to secure quality signings for the club by searching new areas for talent. Premier League reserve teams and lower divisions had been scoured, before Laws stumbled across an Italian who had played for Juventus, but was tied to an American Sports Agency. His name was Ivano Bonetti. Bonetti was more than just another player, for he was one with magic in his boots who could inspire others, and he was 'adopted' by the football fans of North Lincolnshire like no other player before him. He repaid the supporters with some memorable performances and a love affair between Bonetti, the club and the fans was wonderful to be a part of. Four straight wins with Bonetti saw Town reach 2nd place in the table, and the dream was well on course.

Ivano Bonetti brought national attention to Blundell Park in his all too brief spell as a 'Mariner'.

Bonetti scored his first goal in no better way than beating the much disliked West Bromwich at Blundell Park; this was expected to be Bonetti's final home game for the club as his agents had set a date for the end of the loan period that was soon to arrive. He performed an emotional lap of honour after the final whistle blew, the board not being able to afford the £100,000 asking price.

However, an appeal was set-up which was successful, and the money was scraped together by sponsors and supporters and he was eventually released from his contract and free to rejoin his beloved Mariners. His goal at Tranmere took Town to 2nd place once again. Bonetti was an ambassador for Italians who were trapped by contracts, and arranged for several to travel to Grimsby to have trials, including Enzo Gambaro and Luca Pelligrini.

Four consecutive draws over the festive period saw Town slip to 10th, but they then embarked on a glorious F.A.Cup venture. Luton Town were hammered 7-1 in the third round, setting-up a fourth round tie at West Ham. The Saturday game was called off due to snow, with Town gaining a well earned draw in the rearranged tie, with a goal from Laws.

Before the Cup replay, surprise news reached the fans which related to an incident in the changing room after an away defeat at Luton. Laws and Bonetti, it was reported, had an altercation in which the Italian received a fractured cheekbone. Bonetti was therefore out injured and despite Laws' inevitable concern regarding the outcome of the incident, and against all the odds outclassed the Hammers with a 3-0 victory. The Multi-million pound Chelsea were due in town for the next round, and were held to a goalless draw, but the bubble finally burst, 1-4 at Stamford Bridge, in the replay.

Returning to the League, Town dropped to 19th as uncertainty rang around Blundell Park. Gary Croft joined Blackburn Rovers for a club record sale of £1,000,000, whilst Tony Gallimore, the £200,000 Carlisle United left-back (a club record buy), and Richard Smith (£50,000) became Mariners. Arsenal reserve winger Mark Flatts arrived on loan and impressed as little as Vance Warner had done in a similar deal from Nottingham Forest the previous month.

Graham Rodger former Player of the Year and Captain.

Darren Wrack a local born attacker came home from Derby County for £100,000. Nottingham Forest's former England favourite Neil Webb was given a short contract and a chance to prove his fitness, as Laws once again built for promotion.

Wolves visited on the first day, with Town going down 3-1 to a Steve Bull hat-trick, a result not helped by Laws, who appeared to be unfit, after returning prematurely to first team duty following a groin injury. Steve Livingstone appeared in the back four as Richard Smith was dogged by injury. The first win of the season came against Swindon Town, 2-1, as Mendonca attempted to shoot the side to victory single-handedly, with Derby County's Paul Trollope, on loan, impressing; his only goal for the Mariners came in a 6-1 thrashing at Bolton. After five games without a win, including two 3-0 defeats - the last at home to bottom of the table Oldham - Laws was fired, with Town placed firmly in the relegation zone.

The only bright point of note as the season closed was the return of Clive Mendonca who had been out with a mysterious back problem. He scored all three against his 'favourite' opponents Ipswich, when Town won 3-1, and they eventually survived relegation with a lowly 17th placing.

Bonetti unsurprisingly left, despite recovering from his injuries, soon signing for Tranmere Rovers, and team captain Groves (£600,000) plus, eventually, Crichton (£250,000) left for The Hawthorns. Dobbin (to Rotherham United) and Watson (retired injured) were free to leave at the end of another most eventful season.

John Cockerill was asked once again to take temporary control of the first team, which he did for the 4-2 home defeat to Sheffield United, after this he was apparently rejected by the board for squad strengthening ideas, and 'Cockers' stood down with Kenny Swain taking over, ambitiously promising to keep the club from relegation without needing to spend on squad improvements.

1996/97

Laws, despite his part in the Bonetti incident, was awarded with a new contract which seemed a strange decision by Bill Carr and his board at the time, for the team boss had obviously lost some credibility - would the players and supporters stand by the Directors and the Manager?

Pre-season was spent in Scotland, as Laws continued his search for untapped talent. Promising new signings were made with wide man Kingsley Black, who had played at the very top with Nottingham Forest and Northern Ireland (for an undisclosed fee but thought to be around £25,000) and record capture Tommy Widdrington from Southampton (£300,000).

Paul Crichton. The last Mariner Buckley signed for West Brom.

Swain was amazingly confirmed as the man for the job after a 7-1 thrashing at Sheffield Wednesday in the F.A.Cup, at which time the club sat firmly on the bottom of the Division. To his credit Swain did not hesitate to give youth a chance and Jack Lester and the incredibly skilful Skegness teenager John Oster were now Town's best performers. 'Keeper Jason Pearcey struggled with confidence and local Andy Love was provided with an opportunity to prove his worth. An important 4-3 win at relegation rivals Bradford City in early March provided hope as the Mariners moved out of the bottom three for the first time since Laws' departure. All action midfielder Michael Appleton enjoyed a 10 match loan spell before returning to Manchester United.

Another loanee, Jason Lee, arrived from Nottingham Forest and became an instant hero as he scored the winner against Ipswich Town after coming on as sub., but the Mariners were still in the danger zone, and regularly swapping places with Bradford City.

Town had a difficult run-in with five of the final seven games away from home, but unfortunately only the home game with Reading was won, before the last game of the season came at home to Southend United. Town, sitting in the undecided relegation spot, had to win and hope Bradford lost. A season's best performance in the 4-0 win versus the already relegated Essex side was of no use as Bradford beat Q.P.R. 3-0. Swain and his players almost made it, but not quite.

Super Clive Mendoca pictured after scoring his last goal for the Mariners

© Copyright Jonathon Moscrop..

Demonstrating fans called for the board to resign before, during and after the final game, yet it was Swain who became the scapegoat and lost his job, just five months after taking over.

Oster and Mendonca had been plus points in a depressing season, but both were to leave. Out of favour Jamie Forrester joined old boss Brian Laws, now at Scunthorpe United in March (£50,000), and immediately hit the goal trail. He was joined by Jimmy Neil plus Craig Shakespeare who were signed by The Iron on free transfers. Mendonca scored 20 League goals during the season, the first Mariner to do so since Jack Lewis in 1975, but he joined ambitious Charlton Athletic for £700,000, and young Oster joined Premiership Everton for a deal approaching £2,000,000 - after just 22 starts and less than 12 months as a professional.

Could there be only one choice to save the club............again?

Surprise choice for Manager Kenny Swain... but not for long!

The third of this trio to leave.... Craig Shakespeare.

Chapter Thirteen

BUCKLEY'S RETURN  AND BEYOND?

1997 - 2000

1997/98

Alan Buckley had been sacked by a demanding West Bromwich board in January and was unemployed. He had left Cleethorpes on a sour note in October 1994, but things had become much worse at Blundell Park since then and most were willing to forgive him! He was confirmed the new Manager in May and asked John Cockerill to be his assistant, knowing what it would take to get the club back on the right tracks, although not all the supporters had complete faith in his ability.

Players familiar to Buckley's methods were installed. Captain Groves returned (£250,000) and exciting winger Kevin Donovan (£300,000) came with him from the Hawthorns. Mendonca's replacement, Lee Nogan (who came from Reading for £170,000) and goalkeeper Aidan Davison (Bradford City, a free transfer) also arrived. Davison was soon to play his third game for his adopted nation Northern Ireland against Germany after only three first class games for Town.

Pre-season friendly games produced encouraging wins over Aberdeen and Hearts, and the Division Two campaign began with a 1-1 home draw against a much fancied Bristol City side. The following two games were also drawn and then two defeats followed, the first League win coming in a terrific 2-0 result at Fulham, with both goals scored by Livingstone. In the meantime a Jack Lester hat-trick in the first 11 minutes saw off Coca Cola Cup opponents Oldham Athletic in a 5-0 first round second leg encounter.

The first home League win didn't arrive until the 10th match, a 2-1 victory over Wigan Athletic, courtesy of a couple of Donovan penalties. Town had also been victorious at Bournemouth the previous week, but at the end of October they languished in 17th place, despite becoming Giantkillers in the Coca Cola Cup with their defeat of Premiership Sheffield Wednesday and Leicester City. The Owls were beaten over two legs less than a year after the 7-1 massacre, and Leicester were completely outplayed in the 3-1 victory, with the goals arriving from substitutes Livingstone (2) and the Foxes old boy Kevin Jobling in his Testimonial year.

Former favourite Gilbert and Holsgrove (Reading) on loan assisted in these early months. Southend were thrashed 5-1 as Town had a much better November. Burnley were beaten 4-1 in the League, Shrewsbury Town, 4-1 in an F.A.Cup replay, but with losses arriving at Chesterfield 1-0 in the League, and by a 3-0 Coca Cola Cup defeat, which saw Michael Owen's inaugural first team hat-trick at Liverpool. The Burnley win kick-started a 13 match unbeaten run as League form improved and progress was made in the F.A.Cup. Undefeated in December, included revenge wins at Chesterfield in the Auto Windscreens Shield and an F.A.Cup second round (after a replay) that sandwiched an excellent 4-0 win at Bristol Rovers. Town finished the year on a high note beating Preston 3-1 which elevated them to 4th position. Youngsters Danny Butterfield and Daryl Clare notably impressed when called upon.

The Mariners entered the New Year firing on all cylinders. First Division Norwich City were shown no mercy as they were easily beaten 3-0, with Donovan scoring the final goal despite missing a penalty. It took mighty Leeds United to knock Town out in the next round. Local rivals Hull City and Scunthorpe United were defeated in the Auto Windscreens Shield as distant dreams of Wembley were first envisaged. Town were taught a footballing lesson in a 4-1 defeat at Ashton Gate by Bristol City and rectified this by beating Brentford 4-0 the following week, with new signing David Smith scoring with a tremendous strike on his debut. Wayne Burnett, a cultured midfielder, also arrived in January, on loan. Smith came from West Bromwich - at £200,000 - and Burnett was rescued from Huddersfield Town's reserves, his move soon being made permanent for £100,000, much to the delight of the fans.

Away victories in the League at Millwall and Wigan kept the ball rolling, and the Northern Final of the Auto Windscreens Shield was reached with a late Burnett header in front of an 8,000 plus crowd against Blackpool. Bournemouth and Blackpool were also both beaten in the League, as promotion and a Wembley appearance looked distinct possibilities.

Buckley's favourite month March arrived, and points continued to be picked up, with the only defeat coming at Burnley. Town were now 3rd, with Watford and Bristol City already looking certainties for the only two automatic promotion places. Burnley's Turf Moor was not only the ground at which Town lost their only game in March, but just 11 days before the League encounter it was an arena where the Mariners made club history.

A 1-1 draw at Blundell Park meant that all the stops would have to be pulled out when Burnley were visited in the second leg of the Northern Final of the Auto Windscreens competition for them to reach Wembley. It was a memorable night for all those travelling fans, as a header from Nogan and a vicious volley from Donovan saw Town progress to the coveted Twin Towers for the first time in the club's existence.

Cup fever struck North Lincolnshire like never before and everyone in the area was talking about Grimsby Town and Wembley. The anticipation was fantastic for everyone, but their was still a job to do in the League, and form hit a sticky patch before the Wembley visit on Sunday 19 April against Bournemouth. Just one win, against Plymouth, and including two consecutive home defeats occurred in the eight games between qualification for Wembley and the game itself. Town had to set their sights on reaching Wembley for a second time, as the play-offs now seemed to hold the only key to First Division football again.

The Wembley day came and what a special day it was. An amazing Black and White Army, 31,000 strong, screamed the Mariners onto the hallowed turf as they emerged from the famous tunnel. The early play was even, before a mix up in the Town defence gifted Bournemouth's John Bailey an easy tap-in after half hour, and in front of the Town supporters. McDermott cleared off the line as Town came under further pressure.

One down at half-time, and the Mariners needed to find an early goal. When this didn't arrive, Black and Livingstone entered the fray from the subs. bench. 'Man of the Match' right-back John McDermott became an attacking force with a long range effort really testing the Cherries 'keeper, and Town began to press further, before a deep cross from McDermott was met at the back post by Black, who nodded the ball down. The ball entered the net off 'keeper Jimmy Glass' legs. which was met with an explosion of noise, and great relief from the Mariners fans. Town now pushed for a winner but after 90 minutes it was still all square. The first half of extra-time came and went, as tired legs led to mistakes; then entered Wayne Burnett. A Kevin Donovan corner on the left evaded everyone, and it reached Burnett, who arrived late into the box. He made an awkward but solid contact on the ball, and steered it in for an unforgettable 'Golden Goal' winner. The celebrations carried on late into the night for the supporters, but the players were playing at Carlisle just 48 hours later, with an important job to do.

A Donovan penalty won the Carlisle game, and a 0-0 draw at Champions-elect Watford, meant Town were assured a two-leg play-off place against Kevin Keegan's Fulham. The last League game was lost embarrassingly at home to Oldham, which was hardly a perfect preparation for the pair of games to come, and the celebrations were somewhat stifled.

The first play-off leg was in London and ended all square at 1-1, after David Smith equalised a Peschisolido penalty. The Fulham centre-forward and Lever left the action late in the first half; Lever on a stretcher, and Moody dismissed for the crude challenge which put the Grimsby player there. Buckley was pleased with a draw, and just one more winning game would see the Mariners return to Wembley. Tension was high at Blundell Park, for the whole season was at stake for both sides.

A Happy team group and Officials celebrate victory.

Town held the advantage being the home side, and unbelievably Peschisolido committed the same offence as Moody had in the first leg by scything down a player, Handyside on this occasion, with a late challenge during the first half. Fulham's most talented striker left the referee no option but to show him the red card.

© Copyright Jonathon Moscrop. Back to the First Division: Donovan slips the ball past the Northampton 'keeper.

A frantic half saw plenty of chances but no goals, until Donovan raced through the middle to slip an 81st minute winner past Maik Taylor. The scenes at Blundell Park were magical as the Mariners had earned themselves another Wembley appearance. It had taken 120 years to get there (or more accurately 55 since the Stadium first opened), and just 35 days to make a return visit! Northampton Town stood between the Mariners and a perfect season. 40,000 'Cobblers' followers compared to 20,000 from Grimsby descended on Wembley, though the Black and White Army was not to be out-sung. It took only 16 minutes for Donovan to score his 21st goal of the season, when he struck what became the only goal, which returned Town to Division One.

Lever was the 'Man of the Match', in defence, and it capped what was arguably the most enjoyable season that any Grimsby Town Supporter had ever had. It was like a Fairy Story and all was made possible by the return of one man.... Alan Buckley. His summer signings of Donovan and Davison had been revelations in a side which showed little if any weakness. Thirty-five clean sheets from 68 games played was indeed a great achievement, with skipper Paul Groves being the only man to play in all of those games in this marathon of seasons.

The summer was one of Champagne and Roses, but before long it was again back to the familiar war of survival.

1998/99

Financial stability followed the Wembley season, with the revenue and interest supplied by the Cup runs in all competitions and eventual promotion. The summer saw seven departures as Buckley reshaped for the future. Pearcey and physio Gerry Delahunt joined Brentford, Fickling moved to Scunthorpe United, Jobling went to Shrewsbury Town, plus Darren Wrack (Walsall), Neil Woods (York City) and Graham Rodger (eventually retiring injured) all left.

The club played their part in the prestigious pre-season Isle of Man Tournament before Stacy Coldicott (£125,000) and Lee Ashcroft eventually arrived after 'on-off' transfer speculations. Both had played under Buckley at West Bromwich, although Ashcroft arrived via Preston, and for a record £500,000. Jim Dobbin, from Scarborough, was another Buckley old boy, who returned to captain the reserves.

Davison and Donovan were both struggling with injuries as the new season kicked-off, and a live TV game against Ipswich Town was first on the agenda as Town returned to the big time - what a difference a year can make - with a goalless draw. A visit to Bolton's new Reebok Stadium proved fruitless, though a 5-1 thrashing of arch rivals West Bromwich was most pleasing, with Town's former Baggies having something to prove against their former club. Three consecutive defeats were offset with a six game unbeaten run which took Town to 5th, after beating Bristol City 2-1 in late October. But the Mariners lost 2-1 after extra-time at Sunderland's impressive Stadium of Light in the Worthington Cup, after defeating Preston North End and Sheffield United in earlier rounds.

A slump in November was forgotten when seven from 10 were won in a run which ended in February that had taken the team to 7th in the table. Could the impossible dream still be realised? No was the short answer!

A poor run with just six goals scored in the final 17 matches saw the goal dearth result in the Mariners finishing 11th, which on reflection was a creditable position when the strength and the spending power of the club's opponents was taken into account. It just seemed disappointing after the euphoria of the previous season's achievements.

Fans favourite Jack Lester.
Not an outstanding goalscorer for the club, but his shielding, battling qualities and mazy runs in the box, endeared him to the crowd.

The talented Jack Lester was by far Town's most troublesome striker but he only scored on four occasions in the League, whilst Nogan and Donovan's form was not that of a year earlier. Donovan amazingly failed to score a single goal, and Ashcroft found it difficult to settle. Livingstone was called into the back four and Clare provided a little spark up-front but was rarely given a lengthy run in the side.

Injuries to Donovan, Burnett, Richard Smith and Lever came at vital times, and goalkeeping hero Davison had struggled with form. After failing to sign an improved contract, Buckley banned the 'keeper from Blundell Park and he never played for the club again. Paul Groves had another good season in front of goal, scoring 14 from midfield, and with safety assured but the play-offs too far to reach, youngsters were given chances in the final games.

Butterfield and Love were given extended runs, Matt Bloomer, Ben Chapman, rookie 'keeper Steve Croudson and Buckley junior, Adam, all made League debuts during the season. Croudson took the eye with a clean sheet debut at home to Wolves, and their single point from the game meant the big spending Midlanders missed out on a play-off place.

One-time Record signing
Tommy Widdrington moved on.

Widdrington joined Port Vale after a successful loan spell, Nogan (Darlington), Dobbin (Gainsborough Trinity) then eventually Davison - who decided to sign for Sheffield United - all left on the new 'Bosman' instigated rules.

1999/2000

One look at the fixture list and it was obvious that this really would be a season for survival. Bury, Oxford and Bristol City were relegated as Fulham, Manchester City and Walsall took their places. Sunderland, Bradford and Watford attained Premiership status with Charlton, Blackburn and Nottingham Forest dropping down. This was surely the strongest ever 'second' tier division in history, with Grimsby again favourites for relegation. But as before Buckley had different ideas.

Disaster struck on the pre-season tour of Northern Ireland when reliable centre-back Peter Handyside broke his ankle in a freak accident when he caught his studs in the turf whilst making a clearance. Burnett and Richard Smith again both struggled with fitness and would be out for lengthy periods.

Buckley signed Welsh international cap Danny Coyne from Tranmere Rovers to replace Davison in goal, and striker Bradley Allen from Charlton Athletic, who both arrived on free 'Bosman' transfers. York City's Alan Pouton came on loan and was eventually signed for £150,000.

Ashcroft and Allen began the season up front, though neither scored in the early games, and the latter was replaced by Lester. Lester bagged a hat-trick in the 6-0 Worthington Cup win over Carlisle United, but once again struggled to find the net in the First Division. Allen gained a reputation as a super sub. when coming off the bench to score at Port Vale, then the winner at home to Walsall, before scoring both goals in the 3-2 defeat at Tranmere Rovers. He was rewarded with a starting place against Birmingham and scored in the 1-1 draw. In the meantime, with consecutive 2-1 wins at Portsmouth and at home to Ipswich Town, the Mariners were placed 9th in October.

Attentions turned to off-field activities, when Daryl Clare and Buckley had an altercation after a reserve game; Clare immediately went on loan to Northampton Town, the Eire Under-21 starlet becoming an instant hit at Sixfields. December saw the complete board removed in the A.G.M., Bill Carr's position being filled by former Director Doug Everitt, and backed by Bryan Huxford and former Chairman Dudley Ramsden.

Consistent left-back Tony Gallimore.

Six figure buy Stacy Coldicott.

The finances were reviewed and it was decided that the club must sell to survive, and so Jack Lester moved on to Nottingham Forest, but for a paltry £300,000, in January.

Ashcroft and Lester were just hitting form as Town began a six game unbeaten spell with a 4-3 win over Forest, when Lester scored the winner in his final game, at Fulham. A rejuvenated Daryl Clare reappeared and showed good form, then more ructions came about with a reported training ground bust-up between Ashcroft and Buckley, which resulted in the forward being dropped. Mark Nicholls, a loanee from Chelsea, partnered Clare but the pair lacked punch. Just five goals were scored in the final 15 games including a club record six game blank run.

The final 11 games produced no victories, but four consecutive draws in April, which just saved the club from relegation, and a final poor, but safe, 20th place in the table.

All the summer signings became popular with the fans after nervous starts, and Mark Lever became the king-pin at the back with some assured performances. Unfortunately his contract ended in the summer and failing to agree on a new deal the 'Player of the Year' left for Bristol City, again on a 'Bosman ruling', after 13 years a Mariner.

Unsurprisingly Ashcroft also left, leaving for Wigan Athletic for an undisclosed fee, but well below the £500,000 the Mariners had paid for him.

It is difficult to see what lies ahead for Grimsby Town Football Club. At the time of writing, plans are still in hand for a new ground, and a new era already began, with a new board and a new Manager in Lennie Lawrence, after Buckley's shock sacking just two games into the 2000/01 season.

One thing is for certain, if the club survives for another 122 years, there will still be optimists and pessimists voicing their opinions, whatever the weather. Lets all hope the club has a bright future in which many more memories can be created and enjoyed.

CLUB PERSONNEL & PLAYERS' AWARDS

CHAIRMEN

Sir John Astley	(President 1878)
Charles F.Carter	(President 1883-93)
F.B.Coulson	(President 1893-?)
Chris White	(late 1890's)
William H.Bellamy	(1900)
Alf. W.Cooper	(1910's)
Jim Plastow	(early 1920's)
J.W.Stookes	(1928-31)
George Pearce	(1931-55)
J.W. 'Fish'	(1953 -55)
F.Arthur Would	(1955- Dec 68)
L.Roy Osmond	(Dec 1968- Oct 1969)
H.C. 'Paddy' Hamilton	(Oct 1969- Sep 1979)
R.K. 'Dick' Middleton	(Sep 1979- Jan 1985)
Dudley B.Ramsden	(Jan- Oct 1985)
Tom W.Bygott	(Oct- Nov 1985)
W.Ron Ramsden	(Nov 1985- Oct 1987)
Peter W.Furneaux	(Oct 1987- Dec 1994)
W.H. 'Bill' Carr	(Dec 1994- Dec 1999)
Doug P.Everitt F.C.A.	(Dec 1999- present)

SECRETARIES

S.Huxley	(1878-79)
R.Chapman	(1879-81)
William T.Lammin	(1881- Jan 1889)
I.J.Patmore	(Jan 1889-93)
J.Shephard	(1893-95)
F.Hazlegrove	(1895-98)
Harry N.Hickson	(1898- Mar 1932)
William Hooton	(Mar 1932-39)
Charlie W. Spencer	(1939-46)
J.R.Atkinson	(1946-49)
Cyril Hammond	(Jun 1946- Jun 1952)
R.Byron Robinson	(Jun 1952 - 1967)
David M.Wroot	(Aug 1967-Jul 1970)
George Siddon	(Jul - Nov 1970)
Dorothy Edwards*	(Jul 1971 - Jun 1974)
Franklyn Wilson	(Jun - Nov 1974)
Dorothy Edwards	(Nov 1974 - Jan 1977)
H.C. 'Paddy' Hamilton	(Jan- Jun 1977)
David J.Dowse#	(Jun 1977 -1982)
Bernard J.Fleming	(Oct 1982 - Oct 1986)
Ian Fleming	(1986 (Chief Exe.1996)-present)

Position no-longer known as Secretary. * First female Secretary of a Football League Club.
Youngest Secretary of a Football League Club (aged 20 when appointed).

MANAGERS	Birthdate/place	Record (League & Cup) P	W	D	L	F	A
Haydn Price (Jul - Nov 1920)	1885, Mardy	15	5	1	9	18	28
George Fraser (Mar 1921 - Mar 1924)	1874, Elgin	129	51	31	47	183	161
Wilf Gillow (Jun 1924 - May 1932)	08/7/1892, Preston	355	143	68	144	624	639
Frank Womack (May 1932 - Oct 1936)	16/9/1888, Wortley ^	190	87	35	70	371	315
Mo Atherton (Caretaker, Oct 1936 - Mar 1937)	1884, Ince	25	8	7	10	48	52
Charlie Spencer* (Mar 1937 - May 1951)	04/12/1899, Washington	281	93	64	124	419	533
George Tweedy (Caretaker, Jul 1950 - Jan 1951)	08/1/13, Willington	29	4	10	15	46	71
Frank Womack (Part-time, Jan - May 1951)	^	15	4	3	8	20	30
Bill Shankly (Jul 1951 - Jan 1954)	02/9/13, Glenbuck	129	66	27	39	229	165
Billy Walsh (Feb 1954 - Mar 1955)	31/5/21, North Wall, Dublin	47	14	11	22	56	79
Allenby Chilton (Mar 1955 - Apr 1959)	16/9/18, South Hylton	240	94	41	105	369	384
Bill Lambton (Caretaker, Apr 1959- Feb 1960)	02/12/14, Nottingham	33	12	11	10	64	57
Tim Ward (Feb 1960 - Jun 1962)	17/10/17, Cheltenham	112	55	21	34	190	160
Tom Johnston (Jul 1962 - Oct 1964)	30/12/18, Coldstream	107	30	32	45	140	182
George Higgins (Caretaker, Oct - Nov 1964)	16/6/25, Dundee "	7	3	4	0	10	4
Jimmy McGuigan (Nov 1964 - Jul 1967)	01/3/24, Addlewell	137	48	38	51	191	193
Don McEvoy (Jul 1967 - Jan 1968)	30/12/28, Golcar	30	6	7	17	30	52
Bill Harvey (Jan 1968 - Jan 1969)	1920, Grimsby	53	16	15	22	61	75
George Higgins (Caretaker, Jan - Mar 1969)	"	4	0	0	4	3	12
Bobby Kennedy (Mar 1969 - May 1971)	26/3/37, Motherwell	111	35	28	48	125	153
Lawrie McMenemy (May 1971 - Jul 1973)	26/7/36, Gateshead	108	55	20	33	175	135
Ron Ashman (Jul 1973 - Feb 1975)	19/5/26, Whittlesey	87	31	25	31	114	114
John Fraser (Caretaker, Feb 1975)	20/9/32, Montrose	3	1	1	1	5	4
Tom Casey (Feb 1975 - Nov 1976)	11/3/30, Comber	79	23	21	35	89	115
Dick Conner (Caretaker, Nov - Dec 1976)	13/8/31, Jarrow	7	4	1	2	12	7
John Newman (Dec 1976 - Jul 1979)	13/12/33, Hereford	132	59	28	45	181	153
George Kerr (Aug 1979 - Jan 1982)	09/1/43, Alexandria	131	59	35	37	173	142
Dave Booth (Jan 1982 - Oct 1985)	02/10/48, Kexborough	196	72	54	70	280	279
Peter Grotier (Caretaker, Oct - Nov 1985)	18/10/50, Stratford (E.London)	4	2	0	2	9	7
Mick Lyons (Nov 1985 - Jun 1987)	08/12/51, Everton	77	21	21	35	82	107
Bobby Roberts (Jul 1987 - May 1988)	02/9/40, Edinburgh	54	15	15	24	57	70
Alan Buckley (Jun 1988 - Oct 1994)	20/04/50, Mansfield +	281	110	74	97	358	320
John Cockerill (Caretaker, Oct - Nov 1994)	12/7/61, Grimsby <	7	4	2	1	8	7
Brian Laws (Nov 1994 - Nov 1996)	14/10/61, Wallsend	99	30	28	41	121	146
John Cockerill (Caretaker, Nov 1996)	<	1	0	0	1	2	4
Kenny Swain (Caretaker, Nov 1996 - Jan '97, appt. Jan - May 1997)	28/1/52, Birkenhead	30	8	9	13	43	52
Alan Buckley (May 1997- May 2000) (plus 2 games 2000-01)	+	173	67	44	62	191	186

(John Cockerill - Caretaker for 2 games, Aug 2000, before Lennie Lawrence appointed 28 Aug 2000)

*Charlie Spencer's record does not include the war years (1939/40-1945/46), or season 1950/51 - absent throughout, due to illness.

TRAINERS AND COACHES

William Allen (Trainer 1894-97)
W.Leach (Trainer May 1897-99)

George Craddock Trainer May 1899-03)
Jack Wheeler (Trainer May 1904-07)
Charlie Athersmith (Trainer Jun 1907-09)
Alex McConnell (Res.Team Man. 1906-08)
Tom'Tee'Holden (Trainer May 1909-19)
Jimmy Lundie (Trainer c/s May 1919-20)
Martin Golightly (Trainer c/s Nov 1920 -23)
D.Hanlon (Trainer Jun 1923-)
Pervey (Trainer Jun 1926-27)
Jerry Jackson (Trainer cs.1927) - Died before taking up post.
Herbert Woods (Trainer Jul 1927-31)
Bill Hopkins (Trainer 1931-Dec 1933)
Mo Atherton (Trainer Jan 1933-Oct 1939)

Johnny McIlwarne (Trainer Jun 1945-48)

Tom Dawson (Trainer Jul 1948- Feb 1955)

Billy Cairns (Ass.Man Jul 1954)

Bill Lambton (Trainer Jul1955-Nov 1957)
Ron Humpston (Trainer Nov 1957-59)
Bill Lambton (Trainer Apr1959-Jan 1962)

George Higgins (Trainer Jan 1962-Jan 1971)

McCormack (Ass. Trainer 1894)
R.C.Hall (Ass. Trainer 1895)
H.Colbrook (Ass.Trainer 1899-04)
Billy Tennant (Res. Team Manager Sep 1903)

E.Betmead (Ass.Trainer 1907-08)
Harry Fletcher (Aug 1908-09)

Joe Bache (Player-coach Jul-Nov 1920)
W.G. McMillan (Ass.Trainer Nov 1921-23)
Bill Hemingfield (Ass.Trainer ?-1928)

Martin Golightly (Ass.Trainer 1929-31)

Tom'Tee'Holden (Ass.Trainer 1936/7)
John McIlwarne (Ass. Train Jul 1937-45)
Ted Buck (Ass.Trainer 1945)
Hughie Jacobson (Ass.Trainer Jul 1946-May 1955)
Ron Ferrier (Ass.Manager Jul1948-50)
George Tweedy (Player/Ass.Manager Jun 1950-53)
Frank Mouncer (Res.Team Trainer Jul 1954)
Emilio Berkessy (Coach Nov-Dec 1954)
Ron Humpston (Ass.Trainer Jul 55-Nov 57)
Billy Evans (Ass.Trainer May 1958-Aug 1960)

George Higgins (Ass.Trainer Aug 1960-Jan 1962)
Clarry Williams (Ass.Trainer Jul 1962-May 1967)
Roy McLaren (acting Trainer Jul 1967-May 1968)

Doug Holden (Trainer-coach Jan-Sep 1971)
Jim Clunie (Trainer-coach Sep 1971-Oct 1973)
Colin Appleton (Trainer-coach Oct 1973-Feb 1975)
George Aitken (Trainer-coach Feb 1975-May 1976)
Dick Conner (Coach Jul 1976-May 1978)
George Kerr (Coach Aug 1978-Aug 1979)
Dave Booth (Coach Aug 1979-Jan 1982)

Trevor Whymark (Player/coach Mar1982-Jan 1984)
Peter Grotier (Player/coach Mar 1982- Jul 1985)

Chris Nicholl (Play/Ass.Man. Aug 1983-Jul 1985)
Peter Grotier (Ass.Manager Jul-Dec 1985)
Terry Darracott (Ass.Man. Nov 1985- Aug 1986)
Don O'Riordan (Play/Ass.Man Aug1986-Jun1988)

Phil Bonnyman (Play/coach Aug 1986-May 1987)

Arthur Mann (Ass.Man. & Res.Team Coach Jun 1988-Oct 1994)
Kenny Swain (Ass. Man. & Res. Team Coach Nov 1994-Jan 1997)
Andy King (Res.Team Manager Jan-May 1997)
John Cockerill (Ass.Man. & Res.Team Coach May 1997-present)

YOUTH COACHES

The term 'Youth Coach' did not arrive at Blundell Park until the arrival of new boss Lawrie McMenemy in the summer of 1971. Previously the running of the club's junior sides was the responsibility of the Trainer, his assistant, Reserve Team Manager or Scout. Forerunners not otherwise mentioned, include BillyWebb (1950's) and physio Jimmy McCoy (1960's).

Bernard Fleming (Jul 1971-Jan 1979)
(Asst. Brian Stratford)
Dave Booth (Jan-Aug 1979
(Became Reserve & First Team Coach)
Harry Wainman (Feb 1981-Mar 1982)
Alan Woodward (Jul 1982-Dec 1986)

Gordon Simmonite (Dec 1985-Nov 1986)
Dave Moore (Nov 1986-May 1988)
Arthur Mann (see Trainers/coaches)
Richard O'Kelly (May 1991-Oct 1994)
John Cockerill (Nov 1994-May 1997)
Ian Knight (Jul 1997-present)

FOOTBALL IN THE COMMUNITY OFFICERS

Former players Bobby Mitchell (from Mar 1988-May 1991) and Richard O'Kelly (May 1991-Apr 1993) where heavily involved with promoting Grimsby Town F.C. in the local community, tasks including coaching at schools and working with children with disabilities, but, neither were labelled with the official title of - 'Football in the Community Officer'.

John Cockerill (Apr 1993-Nov 1994)
Ian Knight (Jan 1995-Oct 1996)
Mark Ellis (Dec 1996-Mar 1997)
(Adrian Parrish & Matt Franklin temp. in charge Mar-Jun 1997)

Julian Winter (Jun 1997-Jul 1998)
(Adrian Parrish & Matt Franklin temp. in charge Jul-Nov 1998)
Graham Rodger (Nov 1998-present)

PHYSIOTHERAPISTS

The term 'Physio' also arrived at the club in 1971. 'The Man with the Magic Sponge' was in earlier times the club Trainer. But, for an amazing 52 years from 1919-1971, Jimmy McCoy MSM, MSF was employed by the club. A former amateur boxer and First World War stretcher barer from Manchester, Jimmy McCoy served 'The Mariners' as masseur and was often placed in charge of the Colts and 'A' team. As sports science progressed, Town introduced their first full-time physiotherapist.

John Fraser	(Sep 1971- May 1988)	Ken Reed	(Aug 1992-May 1994)
Bert Loxley	(Temporary Jan-May 1988)	Paul Mitchell	(Jul 1994-Jul 1995)
Mark Geeson	(Jun 1988-Jun 1989)	Gerry Delahunt	(Jul 1995-Jul 1998)
Peter Jellett	(Jul 1989-May 1992)	Paul Mitchell	(Jul 1998-present)

SCOUTS

For many years professional clubs have required the use of Scouts, to find talented players, locally or farther afield. Over the years 'The Mariners' have received information about thousands of potential players from hundreds of different Scouts. Obviously they are too numerous to mention, but a few people have consistently provided a lead to a signing for the club. Former player **Jimmy Boyd**, scouted for Town in the north-east immediately after the second world war. Another former player **Lew Armitage** was employed as Chief Scout during the fifties. Different Managers came and went during the 1960's each having their own scouting networks all over the UK. In the 1970/80s Grimsby produced many youngsters whom went on to play in the Football League. Names such as **Brian Stratford, Martin Teanby, Ray Gooch** and **Geoff Bartholomew** have passed on many youngsters to the club from local circles. During more recent times **Ronnie Mann** was Alan Buckley's chief informer at junior, non-league and senior level.

PLAYER OF THE YEAR AWARDS

The first Grimsby Town Player of the Year trophy was presented at a Dinner/Dance organised by the GTFC Supporters' Club, on May 8th 1972, to 'keeper Harry Wainman for his outstanding performances during the successful championship campaign of 1971/72. A trophy has been awarded every season since, with the addition of a 'Young Player' award in 1975. In later seasons the ceremony has grown to include trophies presented by individual local sponsors and organisations, which totalled 28 different titles for the awards in May 2000.

Below, is a list of the winners of the main *Supporters' Player* and *Young Player of the Year* awards, the competitions in which all supporters can vote.

	Supporters' Player of the	**Young Player of the Year**
1972	Harry Wainman	-
1973	Dave Booth	-
1974	Dave Boylen	-
1975	Frank Barton	Ian Walton
1976	Harry Wainman	Tony Ford
1977	Joe Waters	Kevin Drinkell
1978	Geoff Barker	Shaun Mawer
1979	Joe Waters	Dave Moore
1980	Dean Crombie	Phil Crosby
1981	Nigel Batch	Andy O'Dell
1982	Nigel Batch	John Steeples
1983	Kevin Drinkell	Paul Wilkinson
1984	Tony Ford	Gary Lund
1985	Tony Ford	Andy Moore
1986	Gordon Hobson	Tony Barratt
1987	Neil Robinson	John McDermott
1988	Don O'Riordan	Tommy Watson
1989	Shaun Cunnington	Mark Lever
1990	Garry Birtles	John McDermott
1991	Dave Gilbert	Mark Lever
1992	Paul Futcher	John McDermott
1993	Paul Futcher	Gary Croft
1994	Paul Crichton	Gary Croft
1995	Gary Croft	Gary Croft
1996	Paul Groves	Jamie Forrester
1997	Graham Rodger	John Oster
1998	Kevin Donovan	Daryl Clare
1999	Paul Groves	Danny Butterfield
2000	Mark Lever	Danny Butterfield

-Programme Parade-

A selection of programme covers throughout the years
1886/87 to 2000/01

1886/87
Season

At:
The Northolme
Gainsborough Trinity

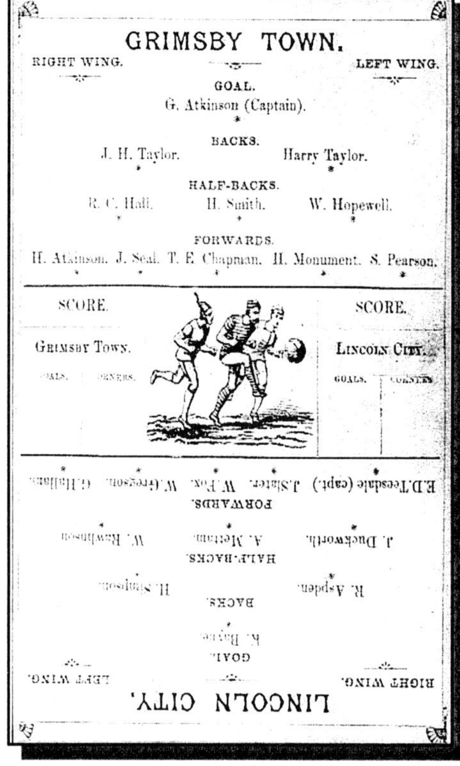

The earliest
known programme
featuring
Grimsby Town F.C.

GRIMSBY TOWN
VERSUS
SHEFFIELD WEDNESDAY
ON THE
Old Show Ground, Scunthorpe,
Saturday, October 30th. Kick-off 3 p.m.

GRIMSBY TOWN.
1 Moulson
2 Vincent 3 Hodgson
4 Hall 5 Millington 6 Buck
7 Johnson 8 Forsyth 9 Dunderdale 10 Baines 11 Ranshaw

Referee: Mr. JESSUP (Hull).

Linesmen: L. Robinson G. Thompson

11 Burton 10 Ward 9 Wright 8 Robinson 7 Fox
6 Cockcroft 5 Millership 4 Herbert
3 Ashley 2 Whitchurch
1 W. Drury
SHEFFIELD WEDNESDAY

PROGRAMME :: :: ONE PENNY

Any alterations before the match will be notified on board.

RICHARDSONS & COFFIN, LTD., PRINTERS, GRIMSBY.

1943/44

1929/30

Pre 1950

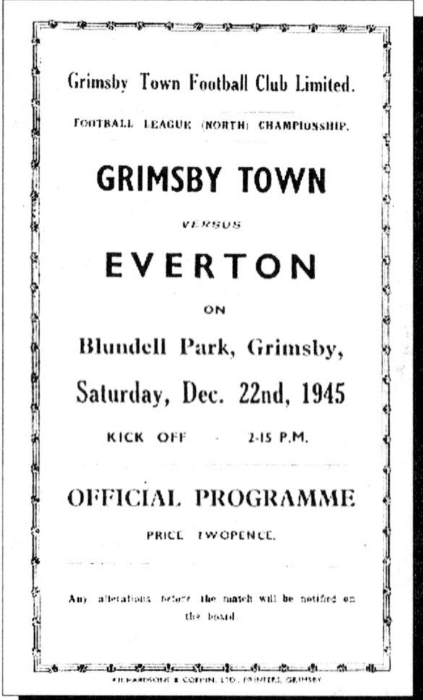

1945/46

1947/48

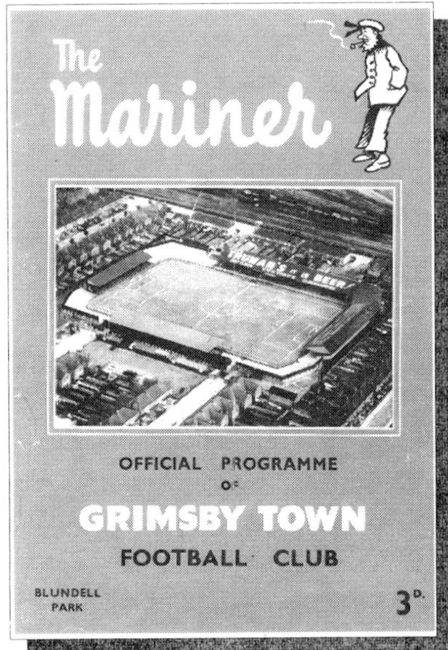

Early 1950's

№ 973

"THE MARINER" — 3d.

GRIMSBY TOWN FOOTBALL CLUB, LIMITED.

THIRD DIVISION, FOOTBALL LEAGUE.

SATURDAY, Mar. 3rd, 1962

GRIMSBY TOWN

versus

NORTHAMPTON TOWN

KICK-OFF 3-0 p.m.

NEXT HOME MATCH

NORTH REGIONAL LEAGUE

Reserves v. BRADFORD P.A. Res.

Saturday, Mar. 10th, 1962. Kick-off 3-0 p.m.

GRIMSBY TOWN FOOTBALL CLUB

1955/56

THE MARINER

GRIMSBY TOWN FOOTBALL CLUB LTD.

FOOTBALL LEAGUE FOURTH DIVISION

SATURDAY, FEB. 1st, 1969

BRADFORD CITY

KICK-OFF 3.0 P.M.

Town v. BARNSLEY

PRICE NINEPENCE

GRIMSBY TOWN FOOTBALL CLUB

1969/70

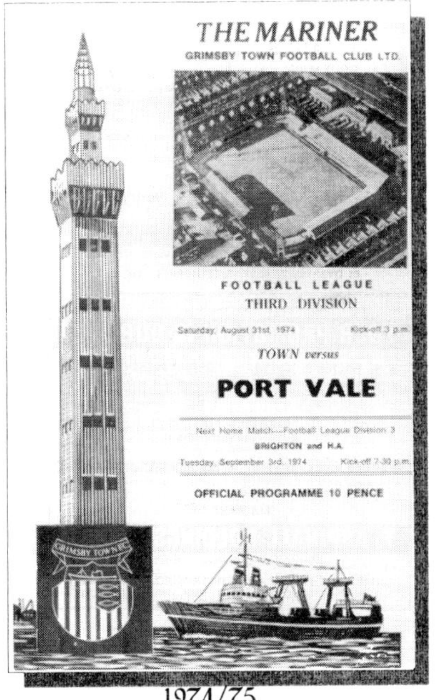

1974/75

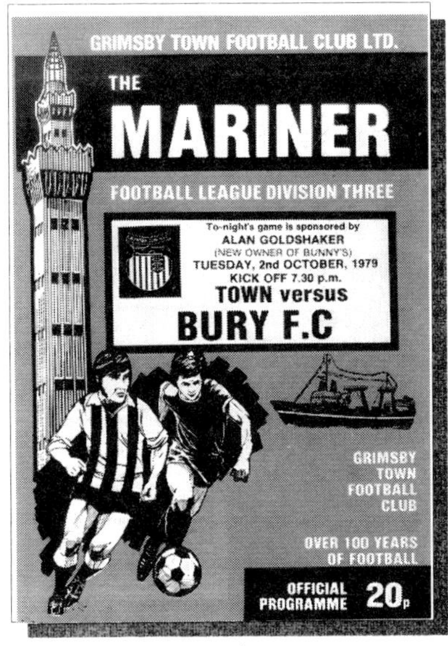

1979/80

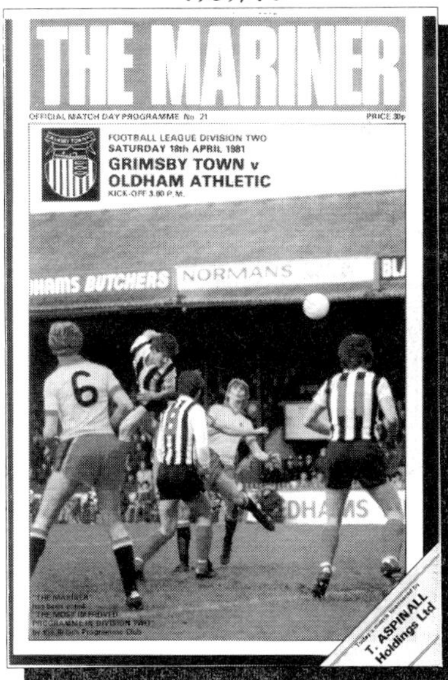

1980/81

1981/82

1982/83

1983/84

1984/85

1985/86

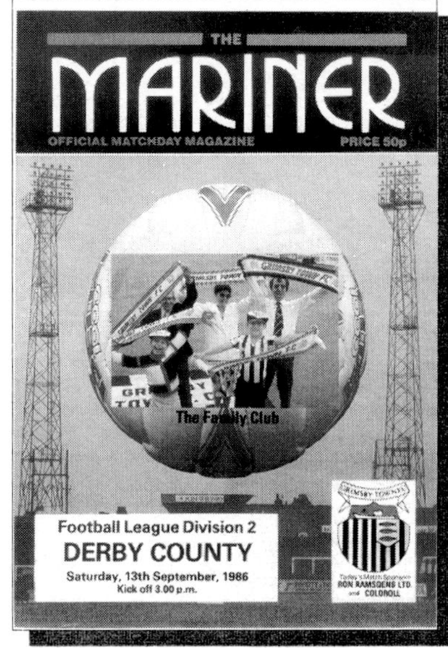

1986/87

1987/88

1988/89

1989/90

1990/91

1991/92

1992/93

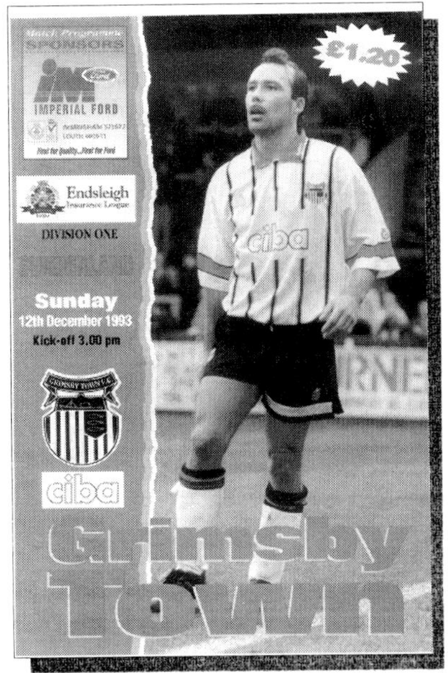

1993/94

1994/95

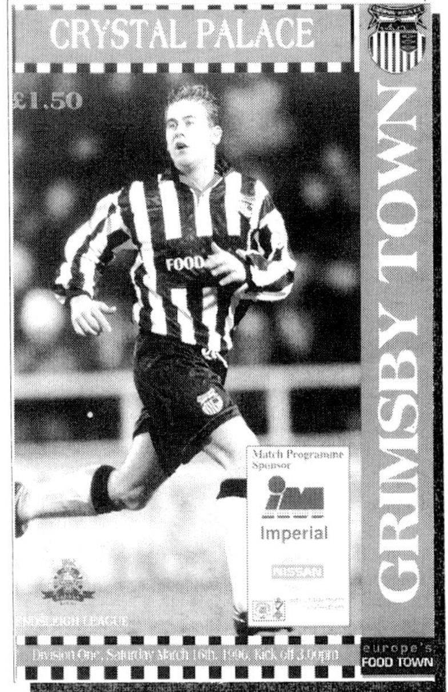

1995/96

1996/97

1997/98

1998/99

1999/2000

2000/01

INTERNATIONAL MARINERS

The following is a list of players whom have represented their countries, during the period they were on the books at Grimsby Town. *Gained more Caps with other clubs.

FULL CAPS

ENGLAND

Bestall JG (1) 6 Feb 1935 v N Ireland (Everton) won 2-1
Betmead HA (1) 20 May 1937 v Finland (Helsinki) won 8-0 Scandanavian Tour
Tweedy GJ (1) 2 Dec 1936 v Hungary (Arsenal) won 6-2
(Higgins W and McCairns T were uncapped reserves, 4 Apr 1896 v Scotland (Glasgow) lost 1-2)
(Craven C -uncapped reserve-18 May 1935 v Holland (Amsterdam) won 1-0)

WALES

Chapman T (5*) 24 Feb 1894 v Ireland (Swansea) won 4-1
12 Mar 1894 v England (Wrexham) lost 1-5
24 Mar 1894 v Scotland (Kilmarnock) lost 2-5
16 Mar 1895 v Ireland (Belfast) drew 2-2
23 Mar 1895 v Scotland (Wrexham) drew 2-2 (scored)
Collier DJ (1) 12 Feb 1921 v Scotland (Aberdeen) lost 1-2 (scored)
Glover EM (7) 31 Oct 1931 v Scotland (Wrexham) lost 2-3
4 Nov 1933 v N Ireland (Belfast) drew 1-1 (scored)
5 Oct 1935 v Scotland (Cardiff) drew 1-1
17 Oct 1936 v England (Cardiff) won 2-1 (scored)
2 Dec 1936 v Scotland (Dundee) won 2-1 (scored both)
17 Mar 1937 v N Ireland (Wrexham) won 4-1 (scored 2)
15 Mar 1939 v N Ireland (Wrexham) won 3-1 (scored)
Morris H (1*) 29 Mar 1897 v England (Sheffield) lost 0-4
Morris R (1*) 23 Feb 1907 v Ireland (Belfast) won 3-2 (scored)
(Lewis AC, uncapped res. 17 Oct 1936 v England (Cardiff) won 2-1)

IRELAND

Andrews W (2*) 15 Feb 1913 v England (Belfast) won 2-1
15 Mar 1913 v Scotland (Dublin) lost 1-2

NORTHERN IRELAND

Coulter J (2*) 10 Nov 1937 v Scotland (Aberdeen) drew 1-1
16 Mar 1938 v Wales (Belfast) won 1-0
Davison AJ (1*) 20 Aug 1997 v Germany (Belfast) lost 1-3
Scott J (2) 17 Jun 1958 v Czechoslovakia (Malmo) won 2-1
19 Jun 1958 v France (Norrkoping) lost 0-4
(both World Cup Final matches in Sweden)
Nicholl CJ (2*) 21 Sep 1983 v Austria (Belfast) won 3-1
12 Oct 1983 v Turkey (Ankara) lost 0-1
(Agnew P- N Ireland XI v Tottenham H XI for Danny Blanchflower's Benefit match):
1 May 1990 at White Hart Lane- received no cap.)

REPUBLIC OF IRELAND

Waters JJW (2) 13 Oct 1976 v Turkey (Ankara) drew 3-3 (scored)
21 Nov 1979 v N Ireland (Belfast) lost 0-1 (sub)

ST. LUCIA

Alexander K (2) May 1990 v Guadaloupe, won 2-1
May 1990 v St.Vincent, drew 1-1

FOOTBALL LEAGUE AND FA REPRESENTATIVES

FOOTBALL LEAGUE

Bestall JG (3) 23 Sep 1931 v Irish League (Blackpool) won 4-0
7 Nov 1931 v Scottish League (Celtic) lost 3-4
23 Sep 1936 v Irish League (Belfast) lost 2-3
Blenkinsopp TW (1*) 14 Apr 1948 v League of Ireland (Preston NE) won 4-0
Higgins W (1) 7 Nov 1896 v Irish League (Belfast) won 2-0
McCairns T (1) 9 Nov 1895 v Irish League (Stoke) drew 2-2
Bellamy WH Committee 1896-1900
(Football League contd.)
Drewry A Committee 1940-49, President 1949-55
Would FA Committee 1963-75, Life Member 1975-95

FOOTBALL LEAGUE (Barclays First Division)

Futcher P (1) 21 Oct 1992 v Italian 'Serie B' (Bristol C) won 3-1

FA XI

Betmead HA 1939 v S Africa (twice)
Dawson T (Trainer) 1949 on Canadian Tour

OTHER INTERNATIONALS

ENGLAND 'B'

Briggs TH (1) 18 Jan 1950 v Switzerland (Sheffield W) won 5-0 (scored)

ENGLAND UNDER 21

Croft G (4) 6 Jun 1995 v Brazil, lost 0-2
(All played 8 Jun 1995 v Malaysia, won 2-0
in Toulon) 10 Jun 1995 v Angola, won 1-0
12 Jun 1995 v France, lost 0-2
Lund GJ (1) 13 Nov 1984 v Turkey (Bursa) drew 0-0
Wilkinson P (1*) 25 Mar 1985 v Rep.of Ireland (Portsmouth) won 3-2 (scored)

SCOTLAND UNDER 21

Handyside PD 22 Mar 1993 v Iceland (Kilmarnock) drew 1-1
(* Played in 8 Jun 1993 v Bulgaria, won 1-0 *
Toulon) 10 Jun 1993 v Mexico, won 2-0 *
14 Jun 1993 v England, lost 0-1 *
15 Nov 1994 v Russia (Cumbernauld) won 2-1
6 Sep 1995 v Finland (h) won 5-0
14 Nov 1995 v San Marino (h) won 1-0

WALES UNDER 21

Oster JM (4*) 30 Aug 1996 v San Marino (Barry T) won 4-0 (sub)
4 Oct 1996 v Holland (Cardiff C) lost 0-2 (sub)
13 Dec 1996 v Turkey (h) lost 0-3
28 Mar 1997 v Belgium (a) won 1-0

WALES UNDER 23

Lewis FJ (1) 4 Feb 1976 v Scotland (Wrexham) lost 2-3 (overage player.

NORTHERN IRELAND 'B'

Black KT (1*) 9 Feb 1999 v Wales (Wrexham) lost 0-1
Scott J (1) 23 Oct 1957 v Romania (Belfast) won 6-0 (scored)

NORTHERN IRELAND UNDER 23

Agnew P (1) 15 May 1990 v Rep. of Ireland (Portadown) lost 2-3 (sub)

REPUBLIC OF IRELAND 'B'

Clare DA (1) 9 Feb 1999 v FA of Ireland (Bray) won 4-3 (scored 2)

REPUBLIC OF IRELAND UNDER 21

Clare DA (6) 18 May 1998 v Scotland (Ballyboffy) won 3-0
4 Sep 1998 v Croatia (Kilkenny) drew 2-2
13 Oct 1998 v Malta (Arklow) won 2-1 (scored)
27 Apr 1999 v Sweden (Birr) lost 0-3
31 Aug 1999 v Yugoslavia (h) lost 0-2
3 Sep 1999 v Croatia (a) lost 1-5 (sub.)

ENGLAND AMATEUR

Blanchard WS (1) 17 Feb 1912 v Wales (Bishop Auckland) won 3-0
Springthorpe HT (1)19 Feb 1910 v Wales (Huddersfield) won 6-0

ENGLAND YOUTH

Butterfield DP (1) 12 Feb 1998 v Israel (Northwich V) won 1-0 (sub)
Clare DA (1) 1996 v Wales - went on to represent Eire.
Crosby PA (4) 3 Oct 1981 v Cameroon, won 2-0 *
(* Youth World 5 Oct 1981 v Argentina, drew 1-1 *
Cup Finals (Sydney) 8 Oct 1981 v Australia, drew 1-1 *
Australia) 11 Oct 1981 v Egypt, won 4-2 *
Lakin JT & # 25 Jan 1964 v N Ireland (Belfast) won 3-1
Wainman WH # # 22 Feb 1964 v Scotland (Middlesbrough) drew 1-1
14 Mar 1964 v Wales (Leeds) won 2-1
Waite JA (6) 27 Feb 1960 v Scotland (Newcastle) won 1-0
19 Mar 1960 v Wales (Canterbury) drew 1-1
2 Apr 1960 v E Germany (Portsmouth) drew 1-1
16 Apr 1960 v Bulgaria (Graz) lost 0-1
18 Apr 1960 v Poland (Graz) won 4-2
20 Apr 1960 v Austria (Vienna) lost 0-1

UNOFFICIAL YOUTH

Butterfield DP (1) 1998 v Manchester U Yth (Bisham Abbey)
Wigginton CA (2) 1969

SCOTLAND YOUTH

Handyside PD 1993
(Selected to play for England Youth v Gambia, on 16 Nov 1992, but chose to represent his native Scotland.)

WALES YOUTH

Oster JM Jan-May 1996 (inc tournament in N Ireland, May 1996)

ENGLAND SCHOOLBOYS -UNDER 18

Grocock CR (2) 6 Apr 1987 v Switzerland (Bradford C) drew 1-1
9 May 1987 v Scotland (Hamilton A) won 1-0
Lester JW (6) 2 Mar 1994 v France (Gillingham) lost 1-2
27 Mar 1994 v Wales (Berne) won 3-0 (scored)
31 Mar 1994 v Switzerland (Berne) won 3-0 (scored 2)
19 Apr 1994 v Austria (Gloggnitz) drew 1-1
21 Apr 1994 v Slovakia (Bratislava) lost 0-4
3 May 1994 v Holland (Norwich C) won 2-1 (scored)
Lund GJ (3) 27 Apr 1983 v Scotland (Doncaster R) drew 0-0
May 1983 v Scotland (Falkirk) lost 1-2
May 1983 v Wales (Shrewsbury T) won 5-0 (scored 3)
Moore TK (2) Mar 1976 v Wales (Swansea C) won 4-0
10 Apr 1976 v Scotland (Blackburn R) drew 2-2

ENGLAND GRAMMAR SCHOOLS

Brader A (1) 1960 v Scotland (Celtic) lost 0-1

ENGLAND SCHOOLS -UNDER 16

Bloomer MB (1) Nov 1995 v Wales

ENGLAND SCHOOLS -UNDER 15

Dixon WH (2) 1919 v Scotland (Glasgow) lost 0-5
1919 v Wales (Liverpool) won 3-0
Mouncer FE (1) 1937 v N Ireland (Middlesbrough) won 6-0
Watkin WTS (2) 1947 v Scotland (Everton) drew 1-1
1947 v Republic of Ireland (Dublin) lost 3-8

INTERNATIONALS BEFORE AND AFTER

The following is a list of players who represented their countries - either prior to joining, or after leaving, Grimsby Town. * Appearances made with Grimsby Town included.

FULL CAPS (Only)

ENGLAND
Bache JW (1903-11, 7 caps-4goals)
Beasant DJ (1989, 2 caps)
Birtles G (1980, 3 caps)
Brayshaw E (1887, 1 cap)
Chilton AC (1950-51, 2 caps)
Felton W (1925, 1 cap)
Galley T (1937, 2 caps-1 goal)
Gardner T (1934-35, 2 caps)
Morley H (1910, 1 cap)
Richards CH (1898, 1 cap)
Roberts C (1905, 3 caps)
Spencer CW (1924-25, 2 caps)
Storer H (1924-27, 2 caps)
Ward TV (1947-48, 2 caps)
Webb NJ (1987-92, 26 caps-3 goals)
Whymark TJ (1977, 1 cap)
Wartime Clifton H (1939, 1 cap-1 goal)

MANAGERS Graham Taylor (Manager) and Lawrie McMenemy (Asst. Manager), from July 1990 until November 1993.

SCOTLAND
Boyd JM (1933, 1 cap)
Cullen MJ (1956, 1 cap)
Gallacher HK (1924-35, 21caps-25 goals)
Gardner DR (1897, 1 cap)

(Scotland contd.)
Lundie J (1886, 1 cap)
MacFarlane R (1896, 1 cap)
Shankly W (1938-39, 5 caps)
Wartime Shankly W (1940-43, 7 caps-1 goal)

WALES
Chapman T (1894-97, *7 caps-2 goals)
Coyne D (1996, 1 cap)
Felgate DW (1983, 1 cap)
Hodgkinson AV (1908, 1 cap)
Jones JL (1895-04, 21 caps)
Morris R (1902-08, *11 caps-1 goal)
Morris H (1894-97, *3 caps-2 goals)
Nogan LM (1992-95, 2 caps)
Oster JM (1997-99, 4 caps)
Price H (1907-09, 5 caps)
Pugsley J (1930, 1 cap)
Rees AA (1984, 1 cap)
Trollope PJ (1997-98, 5 caps)
Walsh IP (1979-82, 18 caps-7 goals)
Watkins AE (1898-1904, 5 caps)
Wartime
Glover EM (1939, 1 cap-1 goal)
Squires F (1942-45, 2 caps)

IRELAND
Andrews W (1908-13,* 3 caps)
Macauley JL (1911-13, 6 caps-1 goal)

NORTHERN IRELAND
Black KT (1988-94, 30 caps-1 goal)
Casey T (1956-58, 12 caps-2 goals)
Coulter J (1933-38,*11 caps-1 goal)
Coyle RI (1973, 5 caps)
Davison AJ (1996-97,*3 caps)
Nicholl CJ (1974-83,*51 caps-3 goals)
Walsh WJ (1947-48, 5 caps)

REPUBLIC OF IRELAND
Donovan DC (1954-57, 5 caps)
Donovan TC (1979, 1 cap)
Moulson GB (1948, 3 caps)
Moulson C (1936-37, 5 caps)
Walsh WJ (1946-50, 9 caps)

HONG KONG
Wright CG (1960, 2 apps- during National Service)
ITALY
Bonetti I (1986, 1 cap)
NEW ZEALAND
Walsh WJ (1966, 1 cap)
NIGERIA
Okorie CE (1990-91, 9 caps)
SOUTH AFRICA
Rowbotham MG (1993-94)
ST. KITTS
Hazel DS (1998)

PLAYERS... THE TOPS

APPEARANCES:
The following players are the 25 who have all topped 300 appearances (in all games including Lincs. Cup but not 'Friendlies' and minor cup competitions) - number shown in brackets. The full breakdown of players' records are shown in the general 'Who's Who section. Players noted * Retained for the 2000/01 season and therefore their totals have increased.

(399)
Mark Lever
(389)
Bobby Cumming
(382)
Hughie Jacobson
(378)*
Paul Groves
(378)
'Ned' Vincent
(372)
Dean Crombie
(363)
Billy Marshall
(355)
Harry Betmead
(336)
Clive Wigginton
(329)
Dave Worthington
(322)
Ron Cockerill
(306)
Harry Fletcher
(303)
Dave Gilbert

GOALSCORERS

The following players are the 10 who have all scored over 100 goals (in all games bar 'Friendlies' and minor cup competitions) - number shown in brackets. The full breakdown of players' records are shown in the general 'Who's Who section.

GRIMSBY TOWN FOOTBALL CLUB

Founded: 1878
Turned Professional/Limited Company: 1890

Grounds	Clee Park	1880-89
	Abbey Park	1889-99
	Blundell Park	1899-present

Honours (Note: Re-classification of Divisions for 1992/93 season)

Founder Members of Football League Division Two 1892/93

Highest League placing (Div.1)	1934/35	5th
Division Two Champions	1900/01, 1933/34	
promoted	1928/29, 1997/98	
Division Three Champions	1979/80	
promoted	1961/62, 1990/91	
Div 3 (North) Champions	1925/26, 1955/56	
Division Four Champions	1971/72	
promoted	1978/79, 1989/90	
Midland Lge Champions	1910/11, 1930/31	
	1932/33, 1933/34	
	1946/47	

F.A. Cup Semi-final	1935/36, 1938/39
League Cup Quarter-final	1979/80, 1984/85
FL Group Cup Winners	1981/82
Auto Windscreens Shield Winners	1997/98
Lincolnshire Cup Winners	37 times
League War Cup Semi-final	1941/42

Most League points in a season	1955/56	68
(3 points for win)	1990/91	83
Least	1947/48	22
Most League goals in a season	1933/34	103
Least	1904/05 (34 games)	33
	1919/20 (42 games)	34
Most League goals conceded	1947/48	111
Least	1955/56	29
Most clean sheets in a season (Lge)	1955/56	25
Most League wins in a season	1955/56	31
Least	1902/03, 1947/48	8
	1950/51	8
Most League draws in a season	1964/65	17
Least	1892/93,1894/95	1
	1895/96	1
Most League defeats in a season	1947/48	28
Least	1900/01	5

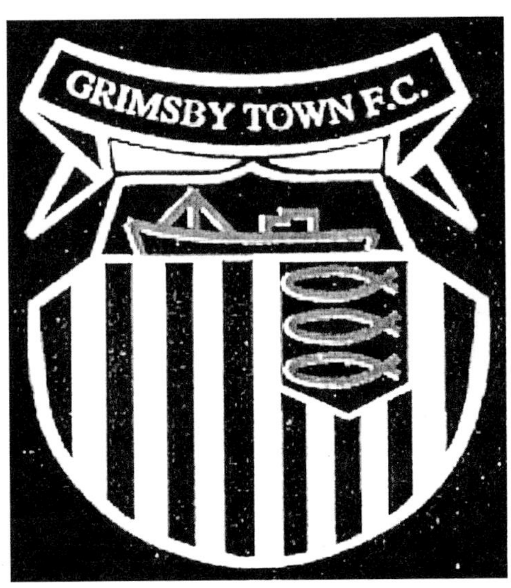

Best League home win	9-2	1898/99	v. Darwen
Biggest League home defeat	0-7	1899/00	v. Newton Heath
Best League away win	7-0	1958/59	v. Bristol Rov.
Biggest League away defeat	1-9	1930/31	v. Arsenal
Best F.A.Cup win	10-0	1891/92	v. Boston T.
Biggest F.A.Cup defeat	1-9	1882/83	v. Phoenix Bessemer
Best League Cup win	6-0	1999/00	v. Carlisle U.
Biggest League Cup defeat	0-6	1968/69	v. Burnley
Best Lincs Cup win	19-0	1886/87	v. Morton St.Paul's

Least players used in a season	1893/94	17
Most	1909/10	34

GRIMSBY TOWN IN THE THE FOOTBALL LEAGUE

Grimsby Town's record versus the 121 clubs played in Football League Competition.
Clubs who have changed name(s), have been collectively listed under their most modern title, e.g. Small Heath = Birmingham City

		HOME					AWAY				
OPPONENT	P	W	D	L	F	A	W	D	L	F	A
ACCRINGTON S	22	11	0	0	36	6	5	0	6	14	17
ALDERSHOT	22	5	4	2	13	11	1	4	6	13	19
ARSENAL	42	11	6	4	31	26	1	4	16	18	76
ASHINGTON	10	4	0	1	21	9	1	0	4	5	8
ASTON VILLA	20	4	1	5	20	16	2	3	5	19	29
BARNSLEY	94	26	9	12	95	53	12	11	24	60	87
BARROW	26	12	0	1	30	4	2	4	7	11	22
BIRMINGHAM C	66	18	8	7	46	35	8	9	16	40	65
BLACKBURN R	54	12	7	8	56	41	0	9	18	20	57
BLACKPOOL	58	16	9	4	57	29	7	7	15	46	68
BOLTON W	52	9	10	7	38	26	7	6	13	30	56
BOOTLE	2	1	0	0	3	0	0	0	1	1	3
BOURNEMOUTH	30	8	4	3	21	10	4	4	7	14	18
BRADFORD C	44	10	5	7	29	28	8	6	8	29	32
BRADFORD PA	44	13	5	4	42	18	6	3	13	23	41
BRENTFORD	52	16	4	6	58	28	10	0	16	27	51
BRIGHTON & HA	30	6	3	6	27	21	4	4	7	15	25
BRISTOL C	48	15	4	5	43	28	2	6	16	17	56
BRISTOL ROV	30	7	5	3	23	15	4	3	8	18	31
BURNLEY	40	14	2	4	37	18	1	4	15	12	44
BURTON S	18	8	0	1	38	9	4	1	4	12	16
BURTON U	8	3	1	0	7	1	1	0	3	3	5
BURTON W	6	3	0	0	12	3	0	1	2	2	7
BURY	52	18	4	4	49	20	4	9	13	31	53
CAMBRIDGE U	24	7	3	2	19	9	3	2	7	12	24
CARDIFF C	24	4	4	4	18	13	2	2	8	17	29
CARLISLE U	28	10	3	1	22	9	6	4	4	21	22
CHARLTON ATH	50	9	7	9	41	42	8	5	12	30	40
CHELSEA	40	10	5	5	28	21	3	2	15	19	52
CHESTER C	28	9	4	1	29	13	6	1	7	15	21
CHESTERFIELD	70	17	12	6	60	34	11	6	18	48	57
COLCHESTER U	28	7	3	4	30	19	3	3	8	12	23
COVENTRY C	16	5	0	3	17	9	1	3	4	5	11
CREWE ALEX	46	12	6	4	44	21	8	8	7	25	30
CRYSTAL PAL.	32	8	2	6	20	14	4	0	12	13	33
DARLINGTON	36	11	3	4	32	13	7	5	6	20	22
DARWEN	12	5	0	1	25	6	1	1	4	8	17
DERBY CO	64	13	8	11	47	41	5	7	20	37	71
DONCASTER R	30	9	4	2	33	16	6	3	6	23	21
DURHAM C	10	4	1	0	11	4	3	1	1	7	7
EVERTON	22	4	3	4	12	14	2	1	8	16	32
EXETER C	22	8	1	2	21	9	3	3	5	13	21
FULHAM	48	11	5	8	33	36	7	4	13	29	47
GAINSBOROUGH T	26	6	4	3	22	16	4	2	7	19	25
GATESHEAD	16	5	3	0	16	5	1	1	6	8	19
GILLINGHAM	26	9	4	0	23	7	4	3	6	11	16
GLOSSOP	26	9	4	0	24	3	1	3	9	7	25
HALIFAX T	44	13	5	3	48	18	6	6	9	23	28
HARTLEPOOL U	34	13	6	3	49	19	6	7	9	25	30
HEREFORD U	12	1	3	2	4	7	2	0	4	8	10
HUDDERSFIELD T	66	16	12	5	58	37	9	8	16	35	47
HULL CITY	46	10	7	6	29	21	7	5	11	32	50
IPSWICH T	16	3	2	3	11	11	1	4	3	3	8
LEEDS CITY	18	4	1	4	16	13	2	0	7	11	29
LEEDS UTD	38	10	5	4	35	21	2	5	12	11	34
LEICESTER C	68	20	8	6	80	37	6	6	22	25	59
LEYTON ORIENT	46	11	8	4	47	24	7	5	11	23	35
LINCOLN C	78	19	12	8	87	51	14	10	15	65	64
LIVERPOOL	36	8	5	5	26	23	0	5	13	21	64
LOUGHBOROUGH T	10	5	0	0	25	1	3	1	1	9	4
LUTON T	32	7	5	4	32	16	4	5	7	23	35

		HOME					AWAY				
OPPONENT	P	W	D	L	F	A	W	D	L	F	A
MAIDSTONE U	2	0	0	1	2	3	0	1	0	2	2
MANCHESTER C	50	13	8	4	62	37	4	2	19	30	58
MANCHESTER U	37	10	4	4	37	26	4	2	13	26	42
MANSFIELD T	30	7	3	5	25	17	1	6	8	13	29
MERTHYR T	2	0	1	0	1	1	0	0	1	1	3
MIDDLESBROUGH	56	17	4	7	59	47	6	4	18	28	56
MIDDLESBROUGH IRON	2	1	0	0	2	1	1	0	0	6	2
MILLWALL	30	9	3	3	25	11	4	2	9	10	19
NELSON	8	3	0	1	8	3	0	2	2	2	6
NEW BRIGHTON	6	1	1	1	3	3	1	1	1	6	4
NEW BRIGHTON TOWER	6	1	1	1	8	6	0	0	3	1	9
NEWCASTLE U	36	8	7	3	28	16	6	2	10	18	36
NEWPORT CO	20	7	2	1	16	6	3	2	5	9	12
NORTHAMPTON T	24	6	2	4	20	15	3	1	8	13	28
NORTHWICH VIC	4	2	0	0	9	1	1	0	1	4	5
NORWICH C	20	3	3	4	12	15	0	4	6	8	18
NOTTINGHAM F	34	8	6	3	26	17	4	2	11	23	36
NOTTS CO	54	15	9	3	48	31	8	3	16	28	48
OLDHAM ATH	62	18	5	8	62	40	10	5	16	40	47
OXFORD U	22	5	2	4	10	9	3	2	6	12	19
PETERBOROUGH U	32	6	7	3	25	20	4	4	8	21	26
PLYMOUTH ARG	28	5	8	1	24	15	3	3	8	15	28
PORTSMOUTH	58	15	6	8	37	31	5	2	22	33	65
PORT VALE	78	23	10	6	89	41	11	6	22	44	76
PRESTON N E	53	11	10	6	50	41	4	3	19	24	53
QUEENS PARK RGRS	32	9	7	0	29	14	3	2	11	11	36
READING	42	12	5	4	39	18	6	7	8	23	38
ROCHDALE	34	11	4	2	37	15	8	2	7	28	30
ROTHERHAM CO	6	1	1	1	4	3	0	0	3	2	8
ROTHERHAM T	6	3	0	0	15	2	0	0	3	5	8
ROTHERHAM U	30	8	2	5	27	22	1	4	10	11	24
SCARBOROUGH	4	2	0	0	5	1	1	0	1	4	5
SCUNTHORPE U	42	11	5	5	35	20	9	7	5	32	24
SHEFFIELD U	44	6	3	13	28	34	4	5	13	26	47
SHEFFIELD WED	38	9	4	6	34	23	1	2	16	10	47
SHREWSBURY T	38	12	3	4	33	21	6	3	10	25	35
SOUTHAMPTON	24	6	4	2	26	16	2	3	7	9	32
SOUTHEND U	52	19	6	1	52	17	5	5	16	17	46
SOUTHPORT	30	10	1	4	24	12	3	2	10	14	32
STALYBRIDGE CEL	4	1	1	0	4	1	0	0	2	2	6
STOCKPORT CO	54	20	2	5	59	22	6	10	11	28	40
STOKE CITY	50	9	10	6	37	32	3	6	16	14	51
SUNDERLAND	48	6	6	12	33	37	3	6	15	27	59
SWANSEA C	44	13	3	6	39	23	3	6	13	19	35
SWINDON T	36	12	3	3	32	16	1	5	12	14	39
TORQUAY U	16	5	2	1	15	7	2	2	4	10	13
TOTTENHAM HOT	14	4	1	2	14	8	1	0	6	10	19
TRANMERE ROV	54	15	10	2	54	16	10	6	11	42	45
WALSALL	54	18	4	5	59	27	1	5	21	16	51
WATFORD	40	7	7	6	27	25	5	4	11	25	40
WEST BROMWICH A	44	11	6	5	43	33	3	3	16	28	60
WEST HAM U	26	6	3	4	21	16	2	0	11	15	30
WIGAN ATH	8	3	0	1	9	7	3	0	1	6	2
WIGAN BOR	10	1	4	0	7	3	0	2	3	4	11
WIMBLEDON	10	3	1	1	8	5	2	2	1	10	9
WOLVERHAMPTON W	65	17	7	9	46	29	6	5	21	28	87
WORKINGTON	24	6	2	4	17	8	1	5	6	10	17
WREXHAM	46	12	7	4	32	13	6	4	13	23	42
WYCOMBE W	2	0	1	0	0	0	0	1	0	1	1
YORK C	36	12	4	2	36	14	6	10	2	27	21

Largest Blundell Park attendances:

31651	20/2/37	v. Wolves (F.A.Cup)
26605	11/4/52	v. Stockport Co. (League)

Lowest Blundell Park attendance:

1833	03/5/69	v. Brentford (League)

Largest Attendances involving Grimsby Town:

76962	25/3/39	v. Wolves (F.A. Cup Semi-final)
65534	14/2/31	v. Everton (F.A.Cup Rd 5)
63210	21/3/36	v. Arsenal (F.A.Cup Semi-final)
62988	23/5/98	v. Northampton T (Play-off Final)
62432	19/4/98	v. Bournemouth (AWS Final)
62022	11/2/39	v. Sheffield U (F.A.Cup Rd 5)
51202	24/10/36	v. Arsenal (Div 1)

Seasonal Average Attendances	
1925/26	9418
1926/27	12556
1927/28	11228
1928/29	12297
1929/30	14724
1930/31	13084
1931/32	11953
1932/33	8358
1933/34	10852
1934/35	13706
1935/36	11496
1936/37	11501
1937/38	12288
1938/39	12066
Second World War	
1946/47	15602
1947/48	16059
1948/49	16602
1949/50	18238
1950/51	15914
1951/52	14855
1952/53	14246
1953/54	9589
1954/55	8313
1955/56	14837
1956/57	15159
1957/58	13964
1958/59	12788
1959/60	10564
1960/61	9698
1961/62	9272
1962/63	11218
1963/64	9515
1964/65	7143
1965/66	7237
1966/67	5809
1967/68	4292
1968/69	4005
1969/70	4376
1970/71	4142
1971/72	11163
1972/73	10657
1974/75	7239
1975/76	5809
1976/77	5373
1977/78	4314
1978/79	4489
1979/80	10404
1980/81	11069
1981/82	8036
1982/83	7745
1983/84	7601
1984/85	6415
1985/86	5152
1986/87	4603
1987/88	3412
1988/89	4302
1989/90	5984
1990/91	7478
1991/92	6915
1992/93	6091
1993/94	6199
1994/95	5921
1995/96	5865
1996/97	5640
1997/98	5271
1998/99	6698
1999/00	6155

Official Attendances from the Football League only available from 1925

MISCELLANEOUS RECORDS

(* Indicates still with club)

Appearances (Most):

Football League

(Progressive Club record holders)

Jimmy Whitehouse	1892-96	110
Harry Fletcher	1892-10	273
Billy Marshall	1923-32	340
Hughie Jacobson	1925-35	360
Jackie Bestall	1926-38	427
Kevin Jobling	1954-69	450
John McDermott	1987-	419 *

F.A.Cup

Harry Fletcher	33
Teddy Buck	32
'Ginger' Hall	31
Jackie Bestall	30
Dave Riddoch	29
*John McDermott	28 (3)*
Jimmy Lundie	27
Kevin Moore	25
George Tweedy	25

League Cup

Kevin Moore	41
Nigel Batch	33
Tony Ford	32 (3)
Harry Wainman	32
*John McDermott	30 (2)*
Joe Waters	29
Bobby Cumming	26 (3)
*Paul Groves	26 (1)*
Dave Worthington	23
Clive Wigginton	22 (1)
Mark Lever	21 (2)

Consecutive

Jimmy Whitehouse	110 Sep. 1892	Apr. 1896	(League)
'Ginger' Hall	162 Mar. 1933	Nov. 1936	(Lge & Cup)
Dave Worthington	245 Dec. 1967	Oct. 1972	
Joe Waters	265 Nov. 1976	Oct. 1981	
Paul Groves	353* Aug. 1992	Nov. 1999	

(1996-97 season with W.B.A.)

In a Season

Paul Groves	68	1997/98	(Lge & Cup)

Goals (Most):

Football League

(Progressive club record holders)

Jack Ackroyd	1892-94	18
Tommy McCairns	1893-98	86
Harry Fletcher	1892-10	92
Jimmy Carmichael	1920-27	137
Pat Glover	1930-39	180

F.A.Cup

Tommy McCairns	18
Pat Glover	17
Dave Riddoch	10
Billy Cairns	9
Harry Fletcher	8
Sandy Higgins	8
Bob McBeth	7
Harry Monument	7
Bob Blanthorne	7
Jackie Bestall	7
Charlie Craven	7
Jimmy Bloomer	7

League Cup

Matt Tees	10
Kevin Drinkell	8
*Paul Groves	7
Jack Lester	6
Rod Green	5
Stuart Brace	5
Bobby Cumming	5
Joe Waters	5
Tony Ford	5
Paul Wilkinson	5
Clive Mendonca	5

Lincolnshire Cup

Joe Robson	19
Harry Monument	15
Jimmy Carmichael	15

Consecutive games

Tommy McCairns	1893/94
11 games	20 goals
Tim Coleman	1930/31
11 games	19 goals

~ INTRODUCTION TO THE STATISTICAL SECTION ~

PLAYERS 'WHO'S WHO' (Pages 135 - 154)

Every player who has appeared in a competitive match for 'The Mariners' since the club entered the Football League (1892/93) is included, plus (shown in 'other column'), pre-Football League (1888-92) and war appearances (1915-19 and 1939-46).
Key (All details where known, and all applicable to Grimsby Town):
Player: Surname followed by initials, and most commonly known first name (in some cases shorter versions or nicknames).
Birthplace: The most accurate description of a players birthplace is given (i.e. local district).
D.O.B. Full dates of birth are listed, in some instances month and year, or year only, where full details have not been traced.
From: Previous club or last known league. Alternatively, 'App' (Apprentice) or 'Trainee' indicate previously on a junior contract. Former junior club or school is noted, where applicable, even if signed amateur or on association schoolboy forms.
Season: The first (only one in some cases) and last season in which the player made a first team appearance for 'The Mariners'. Example: 1967-72 indicates debut in 1967-68, last appearance(s) in 1972-73 (regardless of any apps. during interim seasons). Pre-League seasons are shown for a player who played a competitive match for the club prior to the 1892/93 season and also played in the Football League for 'Town'. War seasons are included if the player was at that time on the club's books. However, if not on Grimsby Town's books but appeared as a 'guest', his appearances are shown in the 'other' column, but the seasons apply to the peace-time period only.
F Lge = Football League record **FA Cup** = FA Cup record
FL Cup = Football League Cup record (including all sponsored versions of the trophy: Milk Cup, Littlewoods Challenge Cup, Rumbelows Cup, Coca Cola Cup and Worthington Cup).
Other = Record in one or more of the following: The Combination (1888/89), Football Alliance (1889-9 1), Midland League (1910/11), World War One league competitions (1915-18), abandoned 1939/40 Football League season, World War Two league or cup competitions, plus Anglo Scottish Cup (1980/81), Football League Group Cup (1981/82), Football League Trophy (1982/83), Full Members' Cup (1985/87), Sherpa Van Trophy (1987/89), Leyland DAF Cup (1989/91), Zenith Data Systems Cup (1991/92), Anglo Italian Cup (1992/94), Auto Windscreens Shield and Division Two Play-offs (both 1997/98), but does not include Friendlies, Testimonials, Tours, or other cup matches.
A = full appearances (started match) **S** = Made a sustitute appearance **G** = goals scored
Next: Details of the next move or reason why no more apps. were made.
Additional line entries are given where apps. have been made in more than one spell with the club, (with the exception of 'loan' players whom the club later signed). The apps/goals record shown is the aggregate record of all spells with 'Town'.

✣ ✣ ✣ ✣ ✣ ✣ ✣ ✣ ✣ ✣ ✣ ✣ ✣ ✣ ✣ ✣ ✣ ✣ ✣

SEASONAL STATISTICS SECTION (pages 162 - 316)

Generally this section is self-explanatory.

The left hand column gives the match number (league) or cup round, e.g. P or Pre = Preliminary and Q = qualifying round. R2 = Round 2. R1L1 = Round 1, 1st leg. R12r = Round 1, 2nd replay. SF = Semi-Final, etc.
2nd column is the fixture date.
3rd column is the opposition (upper case, capitals, is a home game, lower case is an away game).
4th column is the result (Grimsby score first).
5th column Grimsby goalscorers (where known); OG = own goal, pen = penalty.
6th column is the match attendance (where known), prior to 1926 these were generally not 'official' and usually based on newspaper estimates.
7th column (right hand section) are the match line-ups; The shirt numbers worn or position are shown. Prior to shirt numbering, the generally accepted numbering for positions are shown, e.g. 1 = goalkeeper, 4 = right half, 7 = right winger, etc. (the 1999/00 season identification is shown on the appropriate page). * indicates the player was substituted by no.12, ^ by no.13, and + by no.14, although these are not necessarily the actual shirt numbers worn by the substitutes. (unused substitutes are not shown).

PRE- FOOTBALL LEAGUE PLAYERS (1882/92)

Player	Pos	Comb		F Allnc		FA Cup		Player	Pos	Comb		F Allnc		FA Cup	
		A	G	A	G	A	G			A	G	A	G	A	G
ACKROYD Jack*	IL			20	3	3	2	McDILL	OR			3	2		
ARNOLD	IR			1				MacKNIGHT H Johnny	CF			19	10	2	
ASLING W	G					6		McNICHOL	OR			4			
ATKINSON C	OL					3		McURICH CH	IR			1			
ATKINSON George	U					9		MAY	CF			4	2		
ATKINSON Harry	OR					9	2	MONUMENT Harry	OL					10	7
ATKINSON T	CF					2		MORTON H	CF					1	
BECKETT C 'Wag'	IL	1						MUDIE H	OR	1	1			4	
BELLAMY	F			3				MUNDAHL Harry S	U			4		5	2
BLACK David G	OL			42	12	2	1	MURRELL Aubrey J*	HB			22		2	
BLYTHE Tom H*	OR	1						NOBLE Sam	OR					8	
CHAMBERS H	LH					5		OGILVIE Adam*	U	5		58		11	
CHAPMAN C	IR					1		OUSLEY R	OL					1	
CHAPMAN JE	CF					3	1	PEARCE C 'Neal'	OL	1					
CHILD A	LH					2		PEARSON Sammy	IL					3	3
CHRISTIAN F	G					1		PLUMTREE	HB	2					
COSGROVE	IL			13	8			RAYNES R Bob	CF					5	1
CROFT	IR	1						READ AH	IL					8	
DEVLIN	OR			11	1	2	2	REID William*	FB	12	1	58	9	7	3
DORE	IL			1				RIDDOCH David*	CF	11	4	55	14	15	3
DOYLE Danny	LB	7	7			4		ROSE Alf	OR			22	3	1	
ELLEMAN AR	OL			8	4			ROSE THT 'Hickey'*	OR			44	12	3	2
EVANS H	G					3		ROSS W	OR			5	1	1	
FINDLEY J	CH			4		1		SANDERSON	OL	3	1				
FLOWERS JF (Revd)	LB					2		SEAL J	CF	7	3				
FRANCE C	CF					1		SHARMAN Richard	IL					3	1
FRITH Charlie*	LH			11		2		SHAW	CH			3			
FRITH Tom*	LB			14		1		SMALLEY	OR			2	3		
GARNHAM T	IR					12	4	SMITH Harry	CH	13		35		13	1
GRAY J Ramsay	LB			11		3		SMITH Harry jnr	G					1	
GUNNER	OL					1		SMITH Wally*	OR					1	2
HAINES W 'Nigger'	IF			19	4	3	2	SOAMES C	OL					1	
HALL R Charlie	RH	1				9		STOVIN T	G			2			
HARVEY W	RH					1		SUTHERLAND Donald	HB	11	4	27	2	9	3
HOLLINGSWORTH	IR					1		TAYLOR Harry	LB	1				15	
HOLTBY J 'MacBrog'	G	11				9		TAYLOR Jack H	RH	13		33	1	22	
HOPEWELL William T	LH	4		4		9		TAYLOR Jack jnr	OR	7	1			3	1
HUGHES H	IF			3	2	2		THICKETT	RH	1					
HUNT J	IL	12	4			8	2	TONGE John	OR					1	
JENKINSON W	LB					2		TURNBULL J	G			12			
KIMPSON George	CH					10		TWYMAN	G	1					
LANGLEY Ambrose	LB			25	1			WALKER Jack*	RH			40	2	3	
LEE Johnny	IF	2				7	6	WALTON R	LH				1		
LOWE GLW	IL					1		WARING T	CH				1		
LUNDIE Jimmy*	RB	13		64		16	2	WARNER T	RH				1		
MacBETH G	OL			1		1		WINTER Joe	RB				1		
McBETH Bob	IL	9	4	19	16	11	7								

*Also made F Lge apps for 'The Mariners'

Who's Who: Football League Players

Player		Birthplace	D.O.B.	From	Season	F Lge			F A Cup			F L Cup			Other			Next
						A	S	G	A	S	G	A	S	G	A	S	G	
Abbott W	Walter	Birmingham	1899	Birmingham Jnr Lge	1919	5												Chesterfield Muni
Ackroyd J	Jack	Heanor	1868	Heanor T	1891-93	38		16	13		6				20		3	Rotherham T
Ackroyd JW	John	Rotherham	1895	Exeter C	1923	6												
Affleck G	George	Auchendinny	01/07/88	Leeds C	1919-24	197			13									Rotterdam (Holland)
Agnew P	Paul	Lisburn	15/08/65	Cliftonville (N.Ire)	1983-94	219	23	3	23	1		17			12	2		West Brom Alb
Ainsworth C	Charlie	Ashbourne	1885	Derby Co	1909	3												
Alexander K	Keith	Gedling	14/11/58	Barnet	1988-90	64	19	26	8		1	4	2	1	4	1	1	Stockport Co
Allen BJ	Bradley	Harold Wood	13/09/71	Charlton Ath	1999*	12	19	8		2	1		4					*
Allen K	Keith	Newport (IOW)	09/11/43	Portsmouth	1964	6		1										Stockport Co
Anderson JE	John	Rochester	07/06/31	Langold CW (Notts)	1955	3												C Palace
Anderson TD	Tom	Gateshead		Hull Amat Lge	1938	1												
Andrews W	Billy	Kansas City, U.S.A.	1886	Glentoran (Ire)	1912-18	105		2	3						6		1	Darlington
Annables W	Wally	Swinton	31/10/11	Mexborough Ath	1932-34	6									1		1	Hull C
Appleton MA	Michael	Salford	04/12/75	Manchester U	1996	10		3										(loan)
Appleyard W	Cockles	Cleethorpes	16/11/78	Grimsby Tradesmen	1901-02													Newcastle U
				Oldham Ath	1908	57		21	4		1							Mansfield Mechanic
Arch WH	Bill	Tipton	29/11/94	Willenhall	1923-25	91			5									Hartlepools U
Archer JG	John	Whitstable	09/04/36	Whitstable T	1954	10												Whitstable T
Archibald J	Jock	Strathaven	23/08/95	Newcastle U	1923-26	111			10									Darlington
Armitage LC	Lew	Kingston upon Hull	15/12/21	Rotherham U	1947	8		2										Retired injured
Armstrong JB	John	Gateshead	1890	Shildon Ath	1912	4		1										
Arrowsmith JT	Tony	Staveley	06/09/87	Worksop T	1910-14	137			7						38			Chesterfield
Ashcroft L	Lee	Preston	07/09/72	Preston NE	1998-99	52	9	15	1			7		2				Wigan Athletic
Ashton E		Lancashire		Haslingden	1911-12	8												Portsmouth
Atherton TH	Tom	West Derby	1879	Dundee	1902	2												Brentford
Atkin FW	Fred	Cleethorpes	1887	Kingston upon Thames	1914	12			1									
Atter JT	Jack	Dinnington	09/05/01	Dinnington Main	1922-25	48			1									Rotherham U
Ayre HW	Herbert	Grimsby	1882	Grimsby St. Johns	1904	3												Grimsby Amat. Lge.
Bache JW	Joe	Stourbridge	08/02/80	Mid-Rhondda	1920	5		1										Trainer in Germany
Bacon CG	Buzz	Grimsby	1889	Louth Grammar Sch	1908-11	11									1			Goole T
Bagshaw JE	Jim	Grimsby	1874	Gainsborough Trin	1898	34			5									Scarborough
Bailey W	Wally	Birmingham	1876	Grimsby Amat Lge	1895	2												Grimsby Amat. Lge.
Baker K	Keith	Oxford	15/10/56	Oxford U	1975	1												(loan)
Baker L	Langford	Lowestoft	29/03/79	Norwich C	1903-05	59		16	3		1							Norwich C
Baldry GW	George	Cleethorpes	26/05/11		1935	20		7	6		2							Hull C
Banton DC	Dale	Kensington	15/05/61	Walsall	1988	3	5	1										(loan)
Baraclough IR	Ian	Wigston	04/12/70	Leicester C	1990-92	2	3											Lincoln C
Barker GA	Geoff	Kingston upon Hull	07/02/49	Reading	1977-78	66		1	6			6						Bridlington Trin
Barley HF	Harry	Grimsby	01/02/05	Humber U	1929-30	5		1										Hull C
Barnett GAS	Alan	Croydon	04/11/34	Portsmouth	1958-62	116			7			1						Exeter C
Barney VC	Vic	Bethnal Green	03/04/22	Bristol C	1949	7			1									Headington U
Barr J	John	Lanemark	1885	Motherwell	1906	2		1										
Barrass C	Chris	South Shields	11/02/98	Jarrow	1921	4												
Barratt AG	Alf	Weldon	13/04/20	Leicester C	1950	23			2									Southport
Barratt A	Tony	Salford	18/10/65	Billingham T	1985	20	2		1			3			2			Billingham T
Barratt LE	Les	Nuneaton	13/08/45	Barrow	1964	4		1	2		1	1						Southport
Barrett RH	Ron	Reading	22/07/39	Maidenhead U	1958	3												Poole T
Bartholomew R	Roland	Great Harwood	15/01/15	Bradford C	1938-39	12		4	1						6		3	
Bartlett TR	Terry	Cleethorpes	30/08/48	Clee Park Rgrs	1967	1												Whitby T
Barton F	Frank	Barton-upon-Humber	22/10/47	Blackpool	1973-75	123		15	8		2	5	1					Bournemouth
Barton H	Harry	Lancashire		Fairfield	1897	3		1										
Batch NA	Nigel	Huddersfield	09/11/57	Derby Co	1976-86	348			22			33			15			Lincoln C
Bateman A	Arthur	Grimsby	15/03/08	Cleethorpes T	1929-32	18									7		1	Southend U
Battiste W	Wally	Worksop	11/06/92	Shirebrook	1919	31			1						16		6	Gillingham
Beacock GC	Gary	Scunthorpe	22/01/60	VV Ripperda (Holland)	1980-82	10	7		1	1					1	2	1	Hereford U
Beadling W	William	Sunderland	1885	Ashington	1908													Northampton T
				Northampton T	1909	35		5										
Beardsley DT	Don	Alyth	23/10/46	Hull C	1973-74	66			6			5						Louth U
Beasant DJ	Dave	Willesden	20/03/59	Chelsea	1992	6												(loan)
Beattie JM	Jock	Newhills	28/05/12	Huddersfield T	1937-44	56		13	7		2				14		4	Walsall
Beckers P	Peter	Dundee	03/10/47	Craigmore Th	1964	1												Skegness T
Bell AS	Alec	Auchinleck	13/03/31	Exeter C	1958	8												Retired injured
Bell J	Jack			Wolverhampton Wndrs	1895-96	48		11	9		3							Chesterfield
Bell J	Jock	Dundee	1877	Bacup	1897-98	28		3	3									Swindon T
Bell JJ	Jack	South Shields	02/03/91	Merthyr T	1920	3												Nottingham F
Bell TD	Tom	West Stanley	1885	West Stanley	1909-11	32		9							21		6	Scunthorpe &LU
Bell WT	Billy	North Seaton	1905	Sheffield U	1930-31	11			2									Hull C
Bellas WJ	Bill	Great Crosby	21/05/25	Southport	1951	5									1			Barry T
Bellingham FJ	Baby	Stirlingshire	1878	Queens Park Rgrs	1901	4												Brentford
Bemrose FE	Teddy	Caistor	20/10/35	Caistor	1959-60	2												Louth U
Bestall JG	Jackie	Beighton	24/06/00	Rotherham U	1926-37	427		76	30		7				2			Birmingham (coach)
Betmead HA	Harry	Grimsby	11/04/12	Haycroft Rov	1931-46	296		10	19						40		5	Retired

Player		Birthplace	D.O.B.	From	Season	F Lge			F A Cup			F L Cup			Other			Next
						A	S	G	A	S	G	A	S	G	A	S	G	
Beveridge D	David	Scotland		Burnley	1899	5		2										
Bidmead WH	Bill	West Bromwich	12/1882	Leyton	1908	1												Brierley Hill Alliance
Binks L	Louis	Sheffield	23/10/98	Coventry C	1922	3									1			Rotherham Co
Birbeck J	Joe	South Moor	15/04/32	Middlesbrough	1959	18			2									South Shields
Birch W	Billy	Rainford	1887	Eccles Bor	1912-13	34		1	1						5			Gainsborough Trin
Bircham B	Barnie	Philadelphia	31/08/24	Chesterfield	1949	8			2									Colchester U
Bird WS	Walter	Hugglescote	1891	Notts Co	1919	7		2										Bristol Rov
Birtles G	Garry	Chilwell	27/07/56	Notts Co	1989-91	54	15	9	4	1		2	3	2	2	1		Scunthorpe U (trial)
Bisby F	Fred	Mexborough	1880	Kilnhurst T	1905-07	12		1										
Bisby JC	John	Rotherham	1877	Sheffield U	1906-07	7		1										Denaby U
Black KT	Kingsley	Luton	22/06/68	Nottingham F	1996-*	87	49	8	5	2		14			2	5	1	*
Blackburn R	Bob	Edinburgh	1885	Aberdeen	1909	6												
Blair J		Glasgow		Glasgow Benburb	1895	1			1									
Blake E	Ernie	Grimsby	1896	Grimsby Rov	1920	7												Grimsby Rov
Blanchard WS	Billy	Grimsby		Grimsby Jnr Lge	1907-12													Fulham
				Fulham	1913-14	11												Retired
Blant C	Colin	Rawtenstall	07/10/46	Darlington	1976	9						1						Workington
Blanthorne R	Bob	Birkenhead	08/01/84	Liverpool	1907	28		14	5		7							Newcastle U
Blenkinsopp TW	Tom	Witton Park	13/05/20	West Auckland	1942-47	74		10	4						7		1	Middlesbrough
Bloomer J	Jimmy	Rutherglen	10/04/26	Hull C	1949-54	109		42	11		7							Kings Lynn
Bloomer JM	Jimmy	Rutherglen	22/08/47	Apprentice	1965-68	48	4		3			3	1					Worksop T
Bloomer MB	Matt	Grimsby	03/11/78	Franklin College (Gy)	1997-*		6									1		*
Blythe TH	Tom	Grimsby	1872	Grimsby All Saints	1891													Grimsby All Saints
				Cleethorpes Swifts	1897-98	4		1							1			Grimsby All Saints
Bogie MM	Malcolm	Royston Mains	26/12/39	Hibernian	1963	1												Aldershot
Bonetti I	Ivano	Brescia (Italy)	01/08/64	Torino (Italy)	1995	19		3	2		1	1						Tranmere Rov
Bonnyman P	Phil	Maryhill	06/02/54	Chesterfield	1982-86	146	6	16	9			13		2	5		1	Darlington(Pl/coach)
Booth D	Dave	Kexborough	02/10/48	Barnsley	1972-77	199	1	7	13		1	12						Youth Coach
Boulton R	Ralph	Grimsby	22/07/23	Grimsby Jnr Lge	1947-48	3												Goole T
Bowden JW	Jim	Wolverhampton	08/1880	Southampton	1907	19			3									Hyde
Boyd JM	Jimmy	Glasgow	29/04/07	Dundee	1938-39	37		9	7		1				3			Retired
Boylen D	Dave	Macclesfield	26/10/47	Gorton BC	1966-77	370	14	34	20	1	2	18	2	1				Drewery Sports
Boylen J	John	Wishaw	1898	Wigan Bor	1923	4												Armadale
Brace SC	Stuart	Taunton	21/09/42	Peterborough U	1968-73	205	1	81	9	1	2	12		5				Southend U
Brader A	Alec	Horncastle	06/10/42	Horncastle Gram Sch	1960	2												Skegness T
Bradford J	Jack	Paisley	09/04/95	Hucknall Byron	1920-23	108			10									Wolverhampton W
Bradley M	Martin	Wolstanton	1886	South Kirkby	1907	28		6	1									Mexborough T
Bradley P	Percy	Kingston upon Hull	1887	Day Street OB	1910-12	6			1						14			Goole T
Bratley CT	Tony	Grimsby	30/04/39	Armstrong St. Sch (Gy)	1958	2			1									Gainsborough Trin
Brayshaw E	Teddy	Kirkstall	1863	Sheffield Wed	1892	2												Retired
Briggs TH	Tommy	Chesterfield	27/11/23	Plymouth Arg	1947-49													Coventry C
				Blackburn Rov	1958	135		87	5		5							Glentoran (N.Ire)
Brocklesby HE	Bert	Grimsby	1879	St. James U	1897	3												Grimsby All Saints
Brolly MJ	Mike	Galston	06/10/54	Bristol C	1976-81	246	8	27	16		1	16		2	7	1	2	Derby Co
Brooks AF	Arthur	Henstead	04/10/91	Norwich C	1909	4		2										
Brooks JE	Ernie	Heanor	20/11/92	Langley Heanor	1919	3												Shirebrook
Broom W	Billy	Grimsby	26/02/95	Box Company	1918-19	3		2							2			Brigg T
Broome TA	Tom	Pendleton	1892	Preston NE	1920	7												Bolton Wndrs
Browell G	George	Wallbottle	1884	Hull C	1911	23												Retired injured
Brown K	Keith	Nunsthorpe	23/09/54	Nottingham F	1973-75	32	7	5	2			1						Louth U
Brown WF	Bill	Larkhall	20/10/22	Elgin C	1951-57	265		1	18									Barrow (Man)
Brumley E	Edward	Grimsby	02/1878	Grimsby All Saints	1900-02	5		2										Reading
Buck T	Teddy	Dipton	29/10/04	Leeds U	1929-45	354		4	32		2				204		7	Retired (Ass. Train)
Buckley AC	Adam	Nottingham	02/08/79	West Brom Alb	1998-*	8	7		2				1					*
Burgess DJ	Dave	Norris Green	20/01/60	Tranmere Rov	1986-87	66	3		4			6			3			Blackpool
Burkinshaw JDL	Jack	Kilnhurst	12/05/90	Kilnhurst T	1907	5		3										Rotherham Co
Burley B	Ben	Sheffield	02/11/07	Southampton	1934	22		5										Norwich C
Burley WRE	Bill	Devonport	03/01/99	Peterborough &FU	1924	5												Peterborough &FU
Burnett JJ	Jim	Scotland		Dundee	1905	51		13	3									Brighton &HA
Burnett J	John	Market Rasen	24/06/39	Gainsborough Trin	1958	1												
Burnett W	Wayne	Lambeth	04/09/71	Huddersfield T	1997-*	42	9	3				3	2		8		3	*
Burnett WJ	Billy	Pelaw	01/03/26	Wardley CW	1947	10			1									Hartlepools U
Burton R	Ridley	Amble	21/12/93	Close Works	1919	13												
Bush GE	George	West Ham	1883	Leyton	1907	12		2										
Butler J	Jack	Sheffield	1885	Kiveton Park	1904-06	44		2	3						20			Plymouth Arg
Butler PJF	Peter	Halifax	27/08/66	Notts Co	1995	3												(loan)
Butterfield DP	Danny	Boston	21/11/79	Trainee	1997-*	34	14		1	2		6	1		1	1	1	*
Cadden JY	Joe	Glasgow	13/04/20	Liverpool	1952	1												Accrington Stan
Cain T	Tom	Sunderland	1869	Southampton	1896	2												Hebburn Arg
Cairns WH	Billy	Newcastle-upon-Tyne	07/10/12	Gateshead	1946-53	221		120	10		9							Retired
Calderwood JC	Jim	Busby	19/12/98	Manchester C	1927-29	74			2									Retired injured
Caldwell A	Tony	Salford	21/03/58	Bristol C	1988	2	1											Stockport Co
Campbell D	Doug	Kirkintilloch	14/12/22	Barrow	1951	6			2									Peterborough U

Player		Birthplace	D.O.B.	From	Season	F Lge			F A Cup			F L Cup			Other			Next
						A	S	G	A	S	G	A	S	G	A	S	G	
Campbell F	Frank	Dunkeld	23/12/50	Dundee Jnr Lge	1968	4												Chorley
Campbell TA	Alan	Shankill Rd. (Belfast)	11/09/43	Coleraine (N Ire)	1970-72	84	1		3			4						Coleraine (N Ire)
Carmichael HW	Harvey	Tillicoultry	20/08/84	E Stirlingshire	1906-07	36			4									Millwall Ath
Carmichael J	Jimmy	Bridgeton	14/12/94	Mid-Rhondda	1920-26	227		137	17		5							Worksop T
Carrington A	Andy	Grimsby	14/11/36	Welholme Sch (Gy)	1959-60	4												Boston U
Carroll M	Mike	Aberdeen	10/09/52	Liverpool	1971		1											Louth U
Cartledge SH	Sam	Basford	1882	Grimsby St. Johns	1904-06	52			1									Worksop T
Cassidy PJ		Ireland		Shelbourne (Ire)	1912	1												
Casson W	Walter	Blyth	1895	South Shields	1921-23	19		5										Pontypridd
Catley JW	Jack	Grimsby	16/03/45	Cleethoe Rgrs	1962	2												Barton T
Cawthorne GJ	Graham	Doncaster	30/09/58	Harworth CW	1979	1												Doncaster Rov
Chalmers D	David	Buckhaven	1891	York C	1913-14	5												Gillingham
Chalmers W	Bill	Bellshill	1913	Newcastle U	1931	6		1										Bury
Chantry H	Harry	Grimsby	21/11/85	Grimsby Rov	1906	4												Grimsby Rov
Chapman B	Ben	Bottesford	02/03/79	Trainee	1997-*	1	1		1							1		*
Chapman HG	Herbert	Kiveton Park	19/01/78	Rochdale	1898	10		4	2									Swindon T
Chapman KFR	Kenny	Grimsby	16/11/48	Louth U	1969	6	1											Burnley (trial)
Chapman T	Tommy	Newtown	1871	Manchester C	1896-97	50			4									Chatham
Charlesworth JSF	Stan	Conisborough	10/03/20	Wath Wndrs	1938-46	2			1						38		1	Barnsley
Chatburn FW	Fred	Grimsby	1878	Grimsby All Saints	1897-98	2		1										Grimsby All Saints
Chatterley LC	Lew	Birmingham	15/02/45	Northampton T	1971-73	72	1	16	9			5		1				Southampton
Cherry T	Tom	Torphichen	1873	Hamilton Acad	1898	7			2									
Childs GPC	Gary	Kings Heath	19/04/64	Birmingham C	1989-96	204	28	26	15		1	16		1	7	2		Winterton Rgrs
Chilton AC	Allenby	South Hylton	16/09/18	Manchester U	1954-56	63			4									Retired (Manager)
Chisholm W	Wilf	Hebburn	23/05/21	Newcastle U	1946-50	92			2									Spennymoor U
Clare DA	Daryl	St. Helier (Jersey)	01/08/78	Trainee	1995-*	28	34	9	1	4			5	1	4	2		*
Clark J	John	Annfield Plain		Durham C	1919-20	39		12	2									Leadgate Park
Clifton B	Brian	Whitchurch	15/03/34	Southampton	1962-65	104		5	6			6						Boston U
Clifton H	Harry	Marley Hill	28/05/14	Newcastle U	1945-48	69		23	2						13		5	Goole T
Clutterbuck HJ	Harry	Wheatenhurst	01/06/73	Queens Park Rgrs	1901	1												Chesterfield T
Cockburn K	Keith	Barnsley	02/09/42	Bradford PA	1968-69	15	4	2	1									Bangor C
Cockerill J	John	Grimsby	12/07/61	Stafford Rgrs	1988-91	99	8	19	11		2	6			6		2	Retired injured
Cockerill R	Ron	High Green	28/02/35	Huddersfield T	1958-67	293	1	28	15		3	14		2				Retired
Cockshutt JW	Jim	Darwen	1873	Reading	1898-99	61		21	8		4							Nelson
Coglin S	Steve	Willenhall	14/10/03	Sunderland	1926-30	118		39	3									Notts Co
Coldicott S	Stacy	Worcester	29/04/74	West Brom Alb	1998-*	77	4	2	3			7		1				*
Coleman E	Tim	Blidworth	04/01/08	Halifax T	1928-31	87		57	7		1							Arsenal
Coles FG	Gordon	Nottingham	1875	W Arsenal	1904-07	44												Haessche VV (Holl)
Collier DJ	Dai	Llwynypia	12/04/94	Mid-Rhondda	1920-21	44		13	6		1							
Collins JD	Dougie	Newton (Derbys)	28/08/45	Rotherham U	1963-68	96	7	9	8			10	1	1				Burnley
Conner RJ	Dick	Jarrow	13/08/31	South Shields	1953-58	186		8	9		1							Southampton
Cook J	James	Kilbirnie	1885	Airdrieonians	1906-08	8												Plymouth Arg
Cook RJ	Jim	Herrington	1904	Chester-le-Street	1922	5												West Stanley
Cooper J	Joe	Newbold	1899	Notts Co	1924-31	154		47	13		1							Lincoln C
Cooper N	Neil	Aberdeen	12/08/59	Barnsley	1981-83	47		2	2			5			3			St. Mirren
Cooper PT	Paul	Birmingham	12/07/57	Huddersfield T	1977	3						3						Nuneaton Bor
Cooper R	Robert	Southend-on-Sea		Middlesbrough	1894	2												
Coulbeck T	Toy	Cleethorpes		Cleethorpes T	1907-09	13		4	1						26		3	Gainsborough Trin
Coulter J	Jackie	Whiteabbey	1912	Everton	1937	25		11	2									Chelmsford C
Coupland CA	Baggy	Cleethorpes	29/05/00	Haycroft Rov	1921-22													Mansfield T
				Manchester C	1927	56		2	6		1							Caernarvon T
Coverdale WR	Bob	West Hartlepool	16/01/92	Hull C	1924	30		1										Bridlington
Cowell W	Bill	Acomb (Northmbrlnd)	07/12/02	Derby Co	1926-27	39			1									Millwall
Cowper PP	Peter	Tyldesley	01/09/02	West Ham U	1927	4												Lancaster T
Coxon T	Tommy	Hanley	10/06/83	Stoke	1908-09	61		6	2									Leyton
Coyle RI	Roy	Douglas St.(E Belfast)	31/01/48	Sheffield Wed	1974	24		1	2									Linfield Pl/man
Coyne D	Danny	Prestatyn	27/08/73	Tranmere Rov	1999*	44			1			4						*
Crack FW	Freddie	Lincoln	12/01/19	Lincoln OB	1935-45	28		7	3		1				11		4	Lincoln OB
Crampton P	Paul	Nunsthorpe	28/01/53	App	1970		1											Bournemouth (trial)
Crapper C	Chris	Rotherham	1884	Sheffield Wed	1907	3												Retired (injured)
Craven C	Charlie	Boston	02/12/09	Boston U	1930-37	256		95	17		7							Manchester U
Crawford W		Middlesbrough		Stockton	1893	7		6	1		1							
Crichton PA	Paul	Pontefract	03/10/68	Doncaster Rov	1993-95	133			8			7			2			West Brom Alb
Croft G	Gary	Burton-upon-Trent	17/02/74	Trainee	1990-95	139	10	3	8	2	1	7			3			Blackburn Rov
Crombie DM	Dean	Lincoln	09/08/57	Lincoln C	1978-86	316	4	3	17		1	27			12			Bolton Wndrs
Crosbie RC	Bob	Glasgow	02/09/25	Hull C	1955-56	65		45	3		3							Queen of the South
Crosby G	Gary	Sleaford	08/05/64	Nottingham F	1993	2	1											(loan)
Crosby PA	Phil	Leeds	09/11/62	App	1979-82	34	5	1	1			3			2	1		Rotherham U
Croudson SD	Stevie	Grimsby	14/09/79	Trainee	1998-*	4	1		1			1						*
Crozier J	Joe	Middlesbrough	04/12/89	Bradford PA	1922	14												Trainer in Germany
Cuff PJ	Pat	Middlesbrough	19/03/52	Middlesbrough	1971	2												(loan)
Cullen MJ	Mike	Glasgow	03/07/31	Luton T	1958-62	178		35	7		1	3						Derby Co
Cumming DD	David	Glasgow	1900	Dundee	1922	6												

Player		Birthplace	D.O.B.	From	Season	F Lge			F A Cup			F L Cup			Other			Next
						A	S	G	A	S	G	A	S	G	A	S	G	
Cumming R	Bobby	Airdrie	07/12/55	FA forms	1974-86	338	27	58	19	1	2	26	3	5	6	2	1	Lincoln C (pl/coach)
Cunnington SG	Shaun	Bourne	04/01/66	Wrexham	1987-91	182		13	11		3	11			9			Sunderland
Curran E	Terry	Kinsley	20/03/55	Grantham T	1987	10	1		1						1			Chesterfield
Czuczman M	Mike	Carlisle	07/05/53	Preston NE	1971-75													Scunthorpe U
				San Jose E'quakes (US)	1980	116	6	6	4			6			3	1		York C
Daley TE	Tom	Grimsby	15/11/33	Elliston St. Sch (Clee)	1951-53	14												Huddersfield T
Dart E	Eli	Chesterfield	12/03/80	Skinnigrove	1909	3												
Davidson AC	Andy	Auchinleck	24/02/78	Bury	1908													Southampton
				Southampton	1909	59			2									Grimsby Rov
Davidson AG	Angus	Forfar	02/10/48	Arbroath LC	1965-68	46	5	1	2			5						Scunthorpe U
Davies GA	George	Prescot	19/01/97	Merthyr T	1923-24	12		1										
Davis FC	Felix	Wolverhampton	1870	Ilkeston	1895-96	29		1	5		1							
Davison AJ	Aidan	Sedgefield	11/05/68	Bradford C	1997-98	77			7			10			10			Sheffield U
Daw EC	Teddy	Doncaster	23/01/75	Hexthorpe Wndrs	1896	2												Barnsley
Daws A	Tony	Sheffield	10/09/66	Scunthorpe U	1992-93	14	2	1				2			1	1	1	LincolnC
Dawson R	Richard	Nether Edge	12/04/67	Stoke C	1984	1												Gainsborough Trin
Dawson S	Sid	Mexborough	1893	Northampton T	1919-20	48			1						29			Denaby U
Deacey C	Charlie	Wednesbury	06/10/89	Hull C	1920-22	90		4	8									Pontypridd
Dean A	Alfie	West Bromwich	02/01/77	Nottingham F	1901	17		1										Bristol C
De Gruchy RP	Ray	St Helier (Jersey)	18/05/32	Nottingham F	1954-57	74		2	4									Chesterfield
Dent GH	George	Kingston upon Hull	09/03/99	Humber Graving Dock	1923-24	24		12	1									Cleethorpes T
Devan CF	Charlie	Girvan		South Shields	1925-26	50		12	5		1							Fulham
Dixon A	Andy	Louth	19/04/68	App	1986-88	35	3		1	1		1			1	1		Southend U
Dixon WH	Billy	Grimsby	1905	Welholme Sch (Gy)	1923-25	9												Barrow
Dobbin J	Jim	Dunfermline	17/09/63	Barnsley	1991-95													Rotherham U
				Scarborough	1997-98	155	15	21	7	1	1	13	1	3	5		1	Gainsborough Trin
Dodds LS	Les	Patishead	20/09/12	Newcastle Swifts	1931-33	14		1							11			Hull C
Dodsworth VE	Vic	Mexborough	02/10/11	Gainsborough Trin	1932	4		1										Manchester U
Donaldson DE	Dave	Selby	28/02/11	Selby T	1931	1												York C
Donovan DC	Don	Northside (Cork)	23/12/29	Everton	1958-64	238		1	12			3						Boston U (Pl/man)
Donovan K	Kevin	Halifax	11/12/71	West Brom Alb	1997-*	114	1	19	9		1	11	1	2	9		3	*
Donovan TC	Terry	Liverpool	27/02/58	Louth U	1976-78	52	12	23	5		2	6		3				Aston Villa
Dow HC	Hugh	Herrington	04/04/06	Sunderland	1931	2												Darlington
Drinkell KS	Kevin	Grimsby	18/06/60	App	1976-84	242	30	89	12	5	5	20	4	8	10		6	Norwich C
Dubois JM	Joe	Monkstown	27/12/27	Bedford T	1953	6		1										Halifax T
Duff WFA	Billy	Rochdale	16/12/38	Scunthorpe U	1959	3		1										Toronto W E (Can.)
Duke J	Jock	Mauchline			1919-20	6												Scunthorpe U
Duncan AL		Glasgow	1891	Portsmouth	1912	2												
Duncliffe MJ	John	Brighton	17/09/47	Brighton &HA	1968-69	71	1		1			4						Peterborough U
Dunn A	Archie	Bridgeton	14/12/76	Millwall Ath	1902-03	45		1	4									Welling Bor
Duthie J	Jim	Trumperton Farm	23/09/23	RAF	1948-50	40			4									Hull C
Dyson JM	Jimmy	Middleton	04/03/07	Oldham Ath	1931-37	139		38	8		1							Nottingham F
Eccleston W	Bill	Preston	1873	Preston NE	1894	29		13	4		1							Preston NE
Elkins A	Arthur	Grimsby	1880	Grimsby Amat Lge	1903-04	18		7	1									Grimsby Amat Lge
Emson PD	Paul	Lincoln	22/10/58	Derby Co	1983-85	90	7	15	3	1		12		1	1	1		Wrexham
Evans CJH	Charlie	Cardiff	31/01/97	Northampton T	1925	5												
Evans WE	Billy	Aston	05/09/21	Gillingham	1955-57	102		28	6		2							Retired (Ass. Train)
Fairbairn J	Jim	Stockton on Tees	1872	Middlesbrough Ironopolis	1894	2		2										
Fairley W	William	Scotland		St. Mirren	1892	17			2									
Faulkner RA	Ray	Horncastle	26/05/34	Horncastle T	1954	5		1										Skegness T
Felgate DW	Dave	Blaenau Ffestiniog	04/03/60	Lincoln C	1984-86	36			1			2						Bolton Wndrs
Fell JI	Jimmy	Cleethorpes	04/01/36	Waltham	1956-60	166		35	7			1						Everton
Felton W	Bill	Heworth	01/08/00	Jarrow	1921-22	43			3									Sheffield Wed
Ferguson EB	Eddie	Whitburn	10/09/49	Rotherham U	1971	1	1											(loan)
Ferguson JJ	Jack	Rowlands Gill	1904	N East Amat Lge	1926	3			1									
Fickling AS	Ashley	Sheffield	15/11/72	Sheffield U	1994-96	26	13	2	2	1		2	1					Scunthorpe U
Fidler DJ	Dennis	Stockport	22/06/38	Port Vale	1961	9		3	1									Halifax T
Field R	Rusty	Sunderland	02/08/91	Norwich C	1924	32			1									Accrington Stan
Fielding HL	Horace	Heywood	14/10/06	Stockport Co	1930-32	69		12	4									Reading
Fielding JA	John	Speke	02/09/39	Brentford	1965-66	29	1	8				1						Port Elizabeth (S.Afr)
Finlayson E	Evan	Scotland	1876	Glasgow Rangers	1899	5			1									
Fisher FT	Fred	Wednesbury	14/01/20	Fallings Heath	1938-50	166			8						2			Rochdale
Flanaghan HN	Harry	Nottingham	1896	Maidstone U	1923	3												Denaby U
Flatts MM	Mark	Haringey	14/10/72	Arsenal	1995	4	1											(loan)
Fleet A	Albert	Grimsby		Grimsby Rgrs	1906	4												Grimsby Amat Lge
Fleming BJ	Bernard	South Bank	08/01/37	RAF Binbrook	1957-60	22						1						Workington T
Fletcher HH	Harry	Birmingham	20/06/73	Wolverhampton W	1892-97													Notts Co
				Notts Co	1900-02													Fulham
				Brentford	1905-09	273		92	33		8							Retired (Res. Train)
Fletcher JR	Rod	Preston	23/09/45	Scunthorpe U	1973-74	9	3	1	1									Immingham T
Fletcher JM	Joe	Longsight	25/09/46	Rochdale	1969	11		1				1						Barrow
Foley S	Steve	Kirkdale	04/10/62	Liverpool	1984	31		2	3		1	6		2				Sheffield U

Player		Birthplace	D.O.B.	From	Season	F Lge			F A Cup			F L Cup			Other			Next
						A	S	G	A	S	G	A	S	G	A	S	G	
Ford T	Tony	Nunsthorpe	14/05/59	App	1975-85													Stoke C
				West Brom Alb	1991-93	380	43	58	18	4	2	32	3	5	9	2	3	Scunthorpe U
Forrest E	Ernie	Sunderland	19/02/19	Bolton Wndrs	1948	33		1	2		1							Millwall
Forrester JM	Jamie	Bradford	01/11/74	Leeds U	1994-96	34	16	7	3	1	3		1					Scunthorpe U
Forster W	Billy		1882	C Palace	1908	5												
Foster JFT	Jackie	Southwick	21/03/03	Halifax T	1925	10		1										Bristol C
Foster RE	Ron	Islington	22/11/38	L Orient	1962-65	129		24	12		2	8		2				Reading
Freeburn WO	Bill	Burnbank	07/04/30	E Stirlingshire	1951-52	34			1									Spalding U
Freeman N	Neil	Northampton	16/02/55	Arsenal	1973-75	33			4			1						Southend U
Frith C	Charlie	Grimsby	1868	Grimsby Amat Lge	1890-93	9		1	2						11			Grimsby Amat. Lge.
Frith T	Tom	Grimsby	1870	Humber Rov	1890-98	125			18						14			Grimsby Amat. Lge.
Frost W	Walter	Middlesbrough		South Bank	1894													Middlesbrough
				Middlesbrough	1897	16		5	3		4							
Fulljames W	Bill	Cleethorpes	1889	Grimsby Rov	1911	1												Scunthorpe U
Futcher P	Paul	Chester	25/09/56	Halifax T	1990-94	131	1		6			9			3			Darlington (Man)
Gabbiadini R	Ricki	Newport (Gwent)	11/03/70	Sunderland	1989	3		1										(loan)
Gadsby MD	Mick	Oswestry	01/08/47	York C	1970	2												(loan)
Galbraith WM	Wally	Glasgow	26/05/18	New Brighton	1951-52	77			5									Accrington Stan
Gallacher HK	Hughie	Bellshill	02/02/03	Notts Co	1937	12		3										Gateshead
Galley T	Tom	Hednesford	04/08/15	Wolverhampton Wndrs	1947-48	32		2	1									Kidderminster Hrs
Gallimore AM	Tony	Nantwich	21/02/72	Carlisle U	1995-*	161	8	4	9			14		1	10			*
Gambaro E	Enzo	Genoa (Italy)	23/02/66	Bolton Wdrs	1995		1											Italian football
Gardner A	Andy	Oban	26/09/77	Clyde	1901	31		4	2									Newcastle U
Gardner DR	Dave	Glasgow	31/03/73	Newcastle U	1902-03	51			3									West Ham U
Gardner T	Tom	Huyton	28/05/09	Liverpool	1931	13												Hull C
Gardner W	Bill	Langley Moor	07/06/93	Ashington	1925-26	20		4	2									Darlington
Garland D	Dave	Grimsby	18/06/48	Armstrong St. Sch (Gy)	1965	2												Scunthorpe U
Gates GJ	George	London		C Orient	1909	17		2	1									Merthyr T
Gauden A	Allan	Langley Park	20/11/44	Darlington	1971-72	54	1	12	6		2	3						Hartlepool U
Gilbert DJ	Dave	Lincoln	22/06/63	Northampton T	1988-94													West Brom Alb
				West Brom Alb	1997	264		41	11		2	19		4	9			(loan)
Gildea H	Harry	Broxburn	1890	Hibernian	1909	3												Bristol C
Gilligan JM	Jimmy	Hammersmith	24/01/64	Watford	1985	19	6	4		1		3		2	2			Swindon T
Gillow WB	Wilf	Preston	08/07/92	Preston NE	1919-21													Lancaster T
				Lancaster T	1923-24	103		5	5									Retired (Manager)
Gimblett AJ	Arthur	Merthyr Tydfil	1889	Merthyr T	1913	4												
Glen A	Alex	Kilsyth	11/12/78	Clyde	1902	13		1	2									Notts Co
Glennon JE	Teddy	Whitwick	1889	Kilnhurst T	1907-08	10												Denaby U
Glover EM	Pat	Swansea	09/09/10	Swansea T	1929-38	227		180	18		17							Plymouth Arg
Godwin V	Verdi	Blackburn	11/02/26	Middlesbrough	1951	1												Brentford
Goldie E	Edward	Motherwell	15/05/73	Motherwell	1897	26		5	1									Reading
Golightly M	Martin	Lintz	1891	Durham C	1919	9												Retired (Trainer)
Gordon JT	Jimmy	Barking	1886	Barking	1909-14	126		7	7		1				38		7	Retired
Govier S	Steve	Watford	06/04/62	Brighton &HA	1974-76	23	1					2						Retired injured
Graham J	James			Stockton	1893-96	84		2	15		2							New Brompton
Grant EA	Eddie	Greenock	01/10/28	Sheffield U	1952-53	15		5										Corby T
Grant W	Walter	Cleethorpes	1883	Grimsby Rgrs	1903-05	9		2										Chesterfield T
Graver F	Fred	Craghead	08/09/97	Shildon	1922	6		1	1									West Stanley
Gray AE	Ernie	Cleethorpes	10/03/94	Cleethorpes T	1918-19													Cleethorpes T
				Cleethorpes T	1924-26	6		1							6			Grimsby Amat. Lge.
Gray GJP	George	Sunderland	07/07/25	Derby Co	1950	3												Swindon T
Gray P	Paddy	Glasgow		Liverpool	1898-02	121		5	11		1							Fulham
Gray RSM	Bob	Stirling	27/02/72	Aston Villa	1895-97	69		25	11		3							Middlesbrough
Gray SA	Stewart	Doncaster	16/10/50	Doncaster Rov	1970-76	263	1	2	19		1	17		1				Frickley Ath
Green HR	Rod	Halifax	24/06/39	Gillingham	1965-66	65		20	8		3	9		5				Charlton Ath
Green K	Ken	Kingston upon Hull	20/11/29	Selby T	1951	1												
Greenwood W	Wilson	Padiham	1868	Warmley	1898-99	57		13	7		2							Newton Heath
Greetham H	Harry	Grimsby	07/03/30	Hardy Rgrs	1950	4												Skegness T
Gregory G	George	Hyde	1873		1893	1												
Gregson A	Alf	Bury	1889	Rochdale	1913-18	49		12	1						3		1	Bury
Griffiths JE	John	Aston	1876	Bilston T	1898-01	85		5	11		3							Northampton T
Grocock CR	Chris	Grimsby	30/10/68	Havelock Sch (Gy)	1985-88	18	24	1	1	2					1	1	1	Boston U
Grotier PD	Peter	Stratford (E London)	18/10/50	Cardiff C	1981-84	10			1			2				1		Retired (Asst Man)
Groves P	Paul	Derby	28/02/66	Blackpool	1992-95													West Brom Alb
				West Brom Alb	1997-*	318	1	62	20		3	26	1	7	14		3	*
Hair G	George	Ryton	28/04/25	Newcastle U	1948-50	68		8	2									Peterborough U
Hair W	Billy	Edinburgh	1904	Glasgow Rangers	1928	6		2										
Hakin JT	Tommy	Mexborough	1882	Mexborough T	1906-07	58		16	4									Plymouth Arg
Hall AF	Alec	Grimsby	17/09/09	Cleethorpes T	1929-47	358		4	31						183		22	Canada
Hall B	Ben	Ecclesfield	06/03/79	Sheffield Amat Lge	1900-02	39		4	2						2			Derby Co
Halsall M	Mick	Bootle	21/07/61	Carlisle U	1986	12												Peterborough U
Ham RS	Bobby	Bradford	29/03/42	Gainsborough Trin	1963	2		1										Bradford PA
Hamilton IR	Ian	Stevenage	14/12/67	Sheffield U	1999	6		1										(loan)

Player		Birthplace	D.O.B.	From	Season	F Lge			F A Cup			F L Cup			Other			Next
						A	S	G	A	S	G	A	S	G	A	S	G	
Handyside PD	Peter	Dumfries	31/01/74	Trainee	1992-*	164	7	3	11			15	1		13	1		*
Hansen E	Edwin	Denmark	21/01/20	Koge KB (Denmark)	1946	1												Danish football
Hanvey K	Keith	Newton Heath	18/01/52	Rochdale	1976-77	54		2	5									Huddersfield T
Harbertson R	Ron	Seghill	23/12/29	Bradford C	1954	26		6	3		2							Ashington
Hardie G	George	Stanley	1873	Mexborough	1896	6												Mexborough
Harding SJ	Steve	Bristol	23/07/56	Bristol C	1976	8												(loan)
Hardy JJ	Jack	Sunderland	10/02/99	Derby Co	1925-26	46		4	5		1							Oldham Ath
Hargreaves C	Chris	Cleethorpes	12/05/72	Trainee	1989-92	15	36	5	1	2	2	2	2		2	4		Hull C
Hargreaves WV	William	Wombwell	1888	Darfield U	1908-09	18		1	1									Mexborough T
Harker CJ	Chris	Shiremoor	29/06/37	Bury	1967	10												Rochdale
Harmsworth F				Newcastle U	1903	5												
Harnby DR	Don	Kelloe	20/07/23	Spennymoor U	1949-51	34			3									Spennymoor Utd.
Harper CG	Colin	Ipswich	25/07/46	Ipswich T	1976	3												(loan)
Harper G	George	Birmingham	01/05/77	Wolverhampton Wndrs	1901-02	21		3	2									Sunderland
Harris CV	Cecil	Grantham	01/09/96	Aston Villa	1926-27	47		1	1									Gainsborough Trin
Harris G	George	Redditch	1875	Wolverhampton Wndrs	1900	13												Portsmouth
Harrison P	Percy	Huthwaite	1902	Notts Jnr Lge	1921	8			1									Denaby U
Harrison RW	Ray	Boston	21/06/21	Doncaster Rov	1954	38		7	2		3							Kings Lynn
Hart H	Harry	Sheffield	29/09/26	Coventry C	1952	13		3										Frickley CW
Hatton A	Albert	Nottingham	1879	Sutton Junction	1907-09	74		2	5						1			Crystal Palace
Haydock WE	Billy	Salford	19/01/36	Crewe Alex	1964	21		4										Stockport Co
Hayhurst SM	Stan	Leyland	13/05/25	Barrow	1950-52	62			5									Weymouth
Hazel DS	Des	Bradford	15/07/67	Sheffield Wed	1986	9		2										(loan)
Hemingfield WE	Bill	Wortley	1875	Sheffield Wed	1899-02	94		9	7		1							Sheffield Wed
Henderson C	Charlie	Co Durham		South Bank	1892	12			2									Leith Ath
Henderson CG	Crosby	South Hylton	12/05/85	Sheffield U	1908-09	65			2									Birmingham
Henderson WP	Bill	Dundee	1883	Bradford C	1910-11	4									23		2	Scunthorpe U
Henshaw G	Gary	Leeds	18/02/65	App	1983-86	46	4	9	2			4	2		1			Bolton Wndrs
Hernon J	Jimmy	Cleland	06/12/24	Bolton Wndrs	1951-53	91		23	4									Watford
Hickman MFT	Mike	Elstead	02/10/46	Brighton &HA	1968-74	247	7	48	14		3	17		3				Blackburn Rov
Higgins G	George	Dundee	16/06/25	Bolton Wndrs	1954-56	47			3									Scarborough (Pl/mn)
Higgins M	Martin	Co Durham	1883	Bishop Auckland	1904-07													Bristol Rov
				New Brompton	1911	96		8	9									Scunthorpe &LU
Higgins W	Sandy	Smethwick	1870	Birmingham St George's	1892-96	126		27	22		8							Bristol C
Hill B	Brian	Mansfield Woodhouse	15/12/42	Parkhall U	1960-66	180		26	12			13		2				Huddersfield T
Hilton F	Fred	Sheffield	08/07/03	Sheffield Amat Lge	1922-24	71			6									Notts Co
Hinchcliffe T	Tom	Denaby	06/12/13	Denaby U	1936-37	27		5	1									Huddersfield T
Hine M	Mark	Middlesbrough	18/05/64	Whitby T	1984-85	20	2	1	1			1			2			Darlington
Hobson G	Gordon	Pitsmoor	27/11/57	Lincoln C	1985-86	50	2	18	1			7		2	1		2	Southampton
Hodgkinson AV	Bert	Pembroke Dock	04/08/85	Derby Co	1903	16		4	1		1							Plymouth Arg
Hodgkinson JC	John	Stockport	1886	Nelson	1911	12		3										
Hodgson BG	Brian	Cleethorpes	29/01/36	Askern Welfare	1956	7		1										Workington
Hodgson J	Joe		1894		1913	1												
Hodgson JV	Jack	Seaham Harbour	30/09/13	Seaham CW	1932-47	212		2	22						232		4	Doncaster Rov
Hodgson S	Sam	Seaham Harbour	21/01/19	Seaham CW	1943-47	21			2						21			Mansfield T
Hogan W	Bill	Aldershot	1871	Leicester F	1896	1												
Hogg R	Bob	Whitburn (Co Durham)	1879	Sunderland	1902	3		1										Blackpool
Holmes MM	Max	Pinchbeck	24/12/08	Spalding U	1931-34	37		17	2						15		1	Hull C
Holsgrove P	Paul	Cosforth	26/08/69	Reading	1997	3	7											(loan)
Honeyman JW	Jack	Middlesbrough	29/12/93	Maidstone U	1923	21		1	1									Maidstone U
Hooks VR	Vic	Springfield Rd(Belfast)	04/07/55	Manchester U	1972		1											Went to sea
Hooper WG	Billy	Lewisham	20/02/84	Army Service Corps	1905-06	33		6	2		1				15		4	Nottingham F
Horner J	James	Grimsby		Grimsby Amat Lge	1903													Grimsby Rov
				Grimsby Rgrs	1905-06	14												Grimsby Rov
Horwood NK	Neil	Peterhead	04/08/64	Kings Lynn	1986		1						1			1		Cambridge U
Housley S	Stuart	Dunscroft	15/09/48	App	1966-68	34		3	2		2							Yeovil T
Howe F	Freddie	Bredbury	24/09/12	Manchester C	1938-45	29		15	6		6				20		11	Oldham Ath
Howells WM	Billy	Grimsby	20/03/43	Cleethoe Rgrs	1963	6												Boston U
Hubbard A	Ranji	Leicester	07/02/83	Norwich C	1910-11	25		13	4		5				26		13	Lincoln C
Hubbard PJ	Phil	Lincoln	25/01/49	Norwich C	1972-75	144	2	37	12	1	1	7						Lincoln C
Hudson CH	Charlie	Birmingham	1872	Birmingham Amat Lge	1895	5			1									
Hughes A	Arthur	Linlithgow	23/11/27	Canterbury C	1954	25		11	2		1							Gillingham
Hughes J	Joe	Porth		Bristol C	1921-22	31												
Hunt RRA	Ralph	Portsmouth	14/08/33	Derby Co	1959-60	53		39	1		1							Swindon T
Hunter R	Robert	Filey	1883	Yorks Amat Lge	1904	8		1	1									
Hunter W	Bill	Cardenden	16/08/00	Birmingham	1926-27	6												Coventry C
Huxford AT	Gus	Brixham	29/07/89	Grimsby St Johns	1909-19	18		2	1						90		20	Charltons (Gy)
Hyde LJ	Len	Birmingham	06/05/76	Kidderminster Hrrs	1897	4												Wellingborough
Irvine AW	Albert	Leith	24/02/95	Mid-Rhondda	1920	3												Boston T
Jack S	Sam	Scotland	1884	Third Lanark	1907	1												
Jackson E	Ernie	Sheffield	1903	Boston T	1925-26	20			3									Mansfield T
Jacobson H	Hughie	Hepscott	20/02/03	Blyth Spartans	1925-34	360		1	22									Doncaster Rov
Jemson NB	Nigel	Hutton	10/08/69	Sheffield Wed	1993	6		2							1			(loan)

Player		Birthplace	D.O.B.	From	Season	F Lge			F A Cup			F L Cup			Other			Next
						A	S	G	A	S	G	A	S	G	A	S	G	
Jenkin K	Ken	Grimsby	27/11/31	Hardy Rgrs	1950-53	23		6										Retired injured
Jenkinson TI	Tom	Yorkshire		Sheffield U	1898-00	66		24	10		4							Retired injured
Jennings DB	Dennis	Habberley Valley	20/07/10	Huddersfield T	1932-35	99		29	3									Birmingham
Jennings W	Walter	Grimsby	20/10/97	Welholme OB	1919	2			1									Swansea T
Jewell P	Paul	Walton	28/09/64	Bradford C	1995	2	3	1				1						(loan)
Jewell W	Bill		1884	Royal Engineers	1907	19		2										
Jobling KA	Keith	New Waltham	26/03/34	New Waltham	1953-68	450		5	24			19						Boston U
Jobling KA	Kevin	Sunderland	01/01/68	Leicester C	1987-97	251	34	10	10	4	2	13	4	1	7	7		Shrewsbury T
Johnson J	Jim	Stockton-on-Tees	26/02/23	York C	1944-49	6		1							17		6	Carlisle U
Johnson JW	Jack	Newcastle-upon-Tyne	12/02/19	Huddersfield T	1939-47	44		2	2						15		3	Shrewsbury T
Johnson J	Joe	Rossendale	1882	Rossendale U	1905	19		3										Carlisle U
Johnson NV	Nat	Gateshead	1887	Windy Nook	1912	1									52		3	Castleford T
Johnston CP	Paddy	Dublin	16/07/24	Middlesbrough	1948-56	250		16	11		2							Skegness T
Johnston H	Harry	Glasgow	1871	Aston Villa	1897	8												Gravesend
Johnston H	Henry	Manchester		Port Vale	1920	1												
Jones FG	Freddie	Gelligaer	11/01/38	Swindon T	1961-62	58		9				2						Reading
Jones JL	Jack	Rhuddlan	1866	Stockton	1893	28		6	5		1							Sheffield U
Jones ML	Murray	Bexleyheath	07/10/64	Exeter C	1991	14	14	3		1		1	2	1		1		Brentford
Jones T	Tommy	Stanton Hill	1889	Huthwaite Colliery	1921	3			5						17		4	New Hucknall Cllry
Jones TW	Tom	Oakengates	23/03/07	Blackpool	1938-46	48		8	10		1							Retired
Keeble BB	Brian	Holbeach	11/07/38	Holbeach U	1959-64	172		1	5			4						Darlington
Keeble WFW	Fred	Coventry	30/08/19	Albion Rov	1946	7		1	2		1							Notts Co
Kelly JE	Jim	Seaham Harbour	29/12/07	Barrow	1932-37	160		3	14									Bradford PA
Kelly T	Tom	Tunstall		Denaby U	1908-10	26		3	3						31		2	Silverwood T
Kemp G	Gil	Wallasey	1888	Coventry C	1919	9		1										Doncaster Rov
Kennedy R	Bobby	Motherwell	23/06/37	Manchester C	1968-70	84		1	2			2						Nottingham F(scout)
Kenny D	David	Maybole		Barrow	1913-19	58			1						18		1	Bristol Rov
Kent PW	Percy	Manchester	1897	Blackpool	1920	1												
Kerry BP	Brian	Maltby	18/12/48	App	1965		1											Huddersfield T
Kettle WW	Billy	South Shields	10/09/98	Southend U	1922	16		3										Southport
Kilbourne A	Amos	Long Eaton	1881	Bury	1907-09	66		16	6		2							
Kilmore K	Kevin	Frodingham	11/11/59	Scunthorpe U	1979-82	70	32	27	4	1	2	4			4	3	2	Rotherham U
Kirkland JW	Jim	Bedford	30/10/46	Aberdeen	1970	12						1						Scottish Amat. Lge.
Kirsopp WHJ	Billy	Liverpool	21/04/92	Bury	1922	6		2	1									New Brighton
Kitching H	Harry	Grimsby	09/05/00	Municipal College (Gy)	1923	16		1										Boston T
Knight IJ	Ian	Hartlepool	26/10/66	Sheffield Wed	1989-91	16	5	2				1				1		Carlisle U
Knights AF	Tony	Grimsby	13/03/40	Chelmsford Sch (Gy)	1959-63	75		1	1			1						Luton T
Kurz FJ	Freddie	Grimsby	03/09/18	Grimsby YMCA	1938-45	3									17		10	Crystal Palace
Lakey TF	Tom	Stockton-on-Tees	1874	Stockton	1899	30		12	1									
Lancaster R	Ray	Catcliffe	17/08/41	Rotherham U	1964-66	16	2					1						Lincoln C
Lappin HH	Harry	Manchester	01/01/79	Newton Heath	1903	20		4	1									Rossendale U
Laverick PH	Peter	Cleethorpes	29/01/39	Welholme Sch (Gy)	1957-60	4												Bristol C
Laws B	Brian	Wallsend	14/10/61	Nottingham F	1994-96	30	16	2	4		1	2						Darlington
Laws JM	Joe	Cornsay Colliery	06/07/97	Spennymoor U	1921-22	53		5	2									Worksop T
Leafe AR	Dick	Boston	1891	Boston T	1909	1												Boston T
Leaning J	Joe	Grimsby	1874	Grimsby All Saints	1897													Grimsby Rov
				Grimsby Rov	1900	5			1									Grimsby Rov
Leddy H	Harry	Dublin	1895	Chesterfield	1923	13												
Lee A	Chopper	North Staveley	1884	Darfield U	1906-10	86			9		1				28			New Brompton
Lee JA	Alfie	Rotherham	01/02/92	Rotherham U	1913-18	15									17			West Ham U
Lee JB	Jason	Forest Gate	09/05/71	Nottingham F	1996	2	5	2										(loan)
Leigh WH	Wally	Yardley	01/11/74	Altrincham	1900-02	48		12	1									Bristol C
Leiper J	Joe	Partick	1873	Derby Co	1900-01	46												Chesterfield T
Leonard HD	Harry	Sunderland	01/07/86	Newcastle U	1908-10	53		23	2		4				26		24	Middlesbrough
Lester JW	Jack	Millhouses	08/10/75	High Storrs Sch (Sheff'ld)	1994-99	93	40	17	8	1	2	13	4	6	4	4		Nottingham F
Lester MJA	Mike	West Gorton	04/08/54	Washington Dips (US)	1977-79	45	3	10		1		3	1	2				Barnsley
Lever M	Mark	Beverley	29/03/70	Trainee	1987-99	343	18	8	17	3		21	2		18			Bristol C
Lewis AC	Cyril	Trealaw	10/04/09	Tranmere Rov	1933-38	75		31	10		6							Plymouth Arg
Lewis FJ	Jack	Long Eaton	22/03/48	Lincoln C	1969-76	231	27	74	8	5	2	12	3	1				Blackburn Rov
Liddell G	Garry	Stirling	27/08/54	Leeds U	1976-80	90	15	22	5	1	1	9	3	1	1	1		Heart of Midlothian
Lindsay WA	Billy	Stockton-on-Tees	10/12/72	Everton	1894-97	106		1	14									Newcastle U
Linton J		Scotland		Dundee	1892	1												
Livingstone SC	Steve	Middlesbrough	08/09/68	Chelsea	1993-*	178	46	33	9	5	4	13	6	4	4	3		*
Lloyd WS	Stan	Shildon	01/10/24	Sunderland	1948-52	148		23	5									Worksop T
Lockie JC	Jim	Newcastle-upon-Tyne	04/01/74	Newcastle U	1898	6												Hebburn Argyle
Long J	Jimmy	Scotland	1881	Clyde	1901-03	57		13	2									Reading
Lonsdale TS	Tommy	Bishop Auckland	21/09/82	Bishop Auckland	1908-13	87			4						24			West Ham U
Lord W	Wally	Grimsby	01/11/33	Hardy Rgrs	1952-53	7		1										Lincoln C
Love AM	Andy	Grimsby	28/03/79	Trainee	1996-98	12												Ilkeston T
Lowe WC	William	Boston	1877	Grimsby All Saints	1898	2												
Lowry BT	Brian	Ancoats	12/12/36	Manchester U	1954-55	12		1										Aldershot
Lumby JA	Jim	Grimsby	02/10/54	Ross Sports	1973-74	28	3	12				1						Boston U
Lumby WCW	Walter	Milton Regis	16/01/15	Sittingbourne	1937	3									12		2	Stockport Co

Player		Birthplace	D.O.B.	From	Season	F Lge A	F Lge S	F Lge G	F A Cup A	F A Cup S	F A Cup G	F L Cup A	F L Cup S	F L Cup G	Other A	Other S	Other G	Next
Lund GJ	Gary	Cleethorpes	13/09/64	Havelock Sch (Gy)	1983-85	47	13	12	4		5	6	2	1	2		1	Lincoln C
Lundie J	Jim	Edinburgh	20/04/57	Hibernian	1888-94	50			27		2				77			Retired (Asst Train)
Lynch JB	Barry	Northfield	08/06/51	Atlanta Chiefs (US)	1972	10	4											Scunthorpe U
Lynn F	Frankie	Black Hill	29/05/29	Tow Law T	1948	2												RAF
Lyons MJ	Mike	Everton	08/12/51	Sheffield Wed	1985-86	50		4	4		1	3						Everton(Res Coach)
Macauley JL	Jim	Portarlington	1889	Leicester C	1920	16		4	2									Lancaster T
McAvoy J	John	Scotland	1878	W Arsenal	1899-00	26			2									Scottish football
McCairns T	Tommy	Low Dinsdale	22/12/73	Whitby	1893-97	137		86	17		18							Bristol Rov
McClennon JW	James	Tynemouth	16/12/00	Tyneside Amat Lge	1923-25	11												Brentford
McConnell A	Alex	Glenbuck	1875	Queens Park Rgrs	1901-04	84			4									Retired (Res Train)
McConnell J	John	Glenbuck	1881	Kilmarnock	1903-05													Brentford
				Brentford	1907	55			1									
McCue AB	Alex	Greenock	25/11/27	Carlisle U	1951-52	37		15	4		1							Shrewsbury T
McDermott J	John	Middlesbrough	03/02/69	Trainee	1986-*	419	18	8	28	3	2	30	2		21			*
McDiarmid G	George	Scotland	1880	Airdrieonians	1903-04													Glossop
				Clyde	1907	71		1	4									
MacDonald J	John	Ayr	1882	Leeds C	1906	16												Queens Park Rgrs
McEachran G	Grant	Barrow-in-Furness	1894	Barrow	1919-21	66			4									Doncaster Rov
Macey JRT	John	Bristol	13/11/47	Shrewsbury T	1968-69	36	1		1			1						Newport Co
MacFarlane R	Rab	Greenock	1875	New Brompton	1900	18			1									Celtic
McGarvey ST	Scott	Easterhouse	22/04/63	Carlisle U	1986-88	49	1	7	3		1	2	1	1	3		1	Bristol C
McGowan J	Jimmy	Cambuslang	12/01/24	Dumbarton	1946-48	34		4										Southampton
McGregor J	Jim	Scotland		Queens Park	1904-06	93		3	5									Glossop
McHardy G		Scotland		Dundee	1892	3												
McKenna FC	Frank	Walker	09/12/02	Wallsend	1922-26	114		31	10		3							Fulham
McKenna T	Tom	Paisley	11/11/19	Reading	1948-49	50		2	2									Chelmsford C
McKenna TP	Tom	Dublin	01/10/91	Barrow	1913-14	16												Belfast U (Ire)
McKenzie DC	Don	Glasgow	08/06/27	Glasgow Rangers	1951	4												
Mackenzie ML	Laurie	Old Kilpatrick	07/07/24	Sheffield Wed	1949-50	58		11	2		1							Gainsborough Trin
McLachlan F	Fred	Kirkcudbright	21/08/99	Coventry C	1925-26	52			3									Bury
McLatchie C	Colin	New Cumnock	02/11/76	Sunderland	1902	9		1										Lanemark
McLean GR	George	Paisley	16/09/37	Norwich C	1962-64	91		41	3			2		1				Exeter C
McLean JC	Jack	Port Glasgow	22/05/72	Liverpool	1897	30		2	1									Bristol C
MacMillan D	Duncan	Old Kilpatrick	18/01/22	Celtic	1948-54	188		2	12									Dundee U (trial)
McStay JG	Jimmy	Newry	04/08/22	Dundalk (N.Ire)	1948-51	61		2	4									Boston U
Maddison JP	Jimmy	South Shields	09/11/24	Darlington	1950-58	272		40	19		4							Chesterfield
Marklew RK	Roger	Sheffield	30/01/40	Accrington Stan	1960	6		1	1			1						?
Marley A	Allan	Carrville	29/02/56	App	1974-75	39	1	2	1									Louth U
Marlow F	Freddie	Walkley	09/11/28	Buxton	1951	12		6										Goole T
Marsden AJ	Tony	Bolton	11/09/48	Doncaster Rov	1969	2												(loan)
Marshall WE	Billy	Birmingham	01/10/98	Chesterfield	1923-31	340		60	23		3							Reading
Martin F	Frank	Gateshead	03/01/87	Hull C	1911-20	159		1	5						58		5	Aberdare Ath
Martin GP	Geoff	New Tupton	09/03/40	Workington	1966-67	71		5	2			3						Chesterfield
Matthews N	Neil	Humberston	19/09/66	App	1984-86	9	2	1										Halifax T
Mawer SK	Shaun	Ulceby	06/08/59	App	1977-79	57	3		5			3						Retired injured
Mayson TF	Tommy	Whitehaven	08/12/86	Burnley	1911-15	85		28	4		1				1			Everton
Meikle AM	Angus	Coalburn	07/02/00	Portsmouth	1927	13		2	1									
Mellor H	Harry	Stoke-on-Trent	1878	Stoke	1900	33		4	1									Retired injured
Mendonca CP	Clive	Tollington	09/09/68	Sheffield U	1991-96	161	5	61	8		2	10	1	5	2		1	Charlton Ath
Millar H	Hugh	Glasgow	24/05/98	Gillingham	1921-23	26			5									
Millar JW	John	Auchterderran	31/12/27	Bradford C	1952	5		2	2		1							Llanelli
Miller AJ	Alan	Epping	29/03/70	Middlesbrough	1996	3												(loan)
Miller J	Jimmy	Percy Main	10/05/89	Newcastle U	1913	6		1										Everton
Miller J	Jock	Greenock		Greenock Morton	1921-23	89		32	9		4							Manchester U
Miller WL	Willie	Scotland	1880	Edinburgh St Bernards	1903	4												
Mills KD	Keith	Egham	29/12/42	Englefield Green Rov	1960	2												Yiewsley
Milnes C	Charlie	Manchester	01/07/85	Doncaster St Johns	1905-06	35		1										Bradford PA
Mitchell R	Bobby	South Shields	04/01/55	Blackburn Rov	1978-81	142		6	9			16		1	8	1	1	Carlisle U
Mobley DL	Dave	Oxford	24/08/48	Sheffield Wed	1969	26	1		1			1						Altrincham
Mochan C	Charlie	Scotland		Strathclyde	1904	12			2									Brighton &HA
Moody JH	Harry	Rochdale	12/03/96	Mid-Rhondda	1920-21	33			1									Rochdale
Moody KG	Ken	Grimsby	12/11/24	Humber U	1941-50	114			2						12			Peterborough U
Moore AR	Andy	Cleethorpes	14/11/65	App	1983-86	62	3	1				4			2			Lincoln C
Moore AP	Tony	Scarborough	04/09/47	Chesterfield	1970	2	1											(loan)
Moore DC	Dave	Grimsby	17/12/59	App	1978-82													Carlisle U
				Blackpool	1986-87	139	1	2	9			9			6	1		Darlington
Moore G	Gary	South Hetton	04/11/45	Sunderland	1966-68	52	1	15	1			6						Southehd U
Moore NW	Norman	Grimsby	15/10/19	Armstrong St. Sch (Gy)	1941-46	7		1	2		1				36		9	Hull C
Moore TK	Kevin	Grimsby	29/04/58	Wintringham Sch (Gy)	1976-86	397	3	28	25		3	41		3	11		2	Oldham Ath
Moore TR	Roy	Grimsby	18/12/23	Armstrong St. Sch (Gy)	1941-49	3									3		1	Spalding U
Moralee MW	Matt	Mexborough	21/02/12	Gainsborough Trin	1931-35	27		5							29		17	Aston Villa
Morgan AN		Grimsby		Grimsby All Saints	1902	1												Grimsby All Saints
Morley H	Herbert	Kiveton Park	01/10/82	Kiveton Park	1904-06	93		3	5									Notts Co

Player		Birthplace	D.O.B.	From	Season	F Lge			F A Cup			F L Cup			Other			Next
						A	S	G	A	S	G	A	S	G	A	S	G	
Morrall GA	George	Birmingham	1893	Hull C	1920-21	65		8	6									Redditch
Morris H	Hugh	Chirk	1872	Manchester C	1896	23		1	1									Millwall Ath
Morris R	Dickie	Newtown	1879	Leeds C	1906	24		7	2									Plymouth Arg
Morris TH	Tom	Grimsby	1884	Grimsby Rov	1906	28			2									Brighton &HA
Moulson GB	George	Clogheen	06/08/14	Army	1936-46	1			3						107			Lincoln C
Mouncer FE	Frank	Grimsby	22/11/20	Humber U	1945-48	22			3						2			Retired
Mount E	Edward	Cambuslang	18/01/75	Cambuslang Hibs	1897	4												
Mountain G	Bodge	Grimsby	1874	Waltham Hornets	1895													Went to sea
				Grimsby All Saints	1897-02	152		4	12									Leicester F
Mounteney A	Pecker	Belgrave	11/02/83	Preston NE	1911-12	45		17	1									Portsmouth
Mulholland JR	John	Jamestown	07/12/28	Plymouth Arg	1949-50	2												Scunthorpe U
Mullen M	Matt	Scotland		St. Mirren	1892	16		6	6		6							
Munn S	Stuart	Glasgow	22/08/73	Burnley	1895-97	63			9		1							Manchester C
Murray J	Joe	Aberdeen		Dundee	1894	2												
Murrell AJ	Aubrey	Grimsby	1870	Grimsby Amat Lge	1890-93													Grimsby All Saints
				Grimsby All Saints	1894	35		1	9						22			Newark
Neil JD	Jimmy	Bury St. Edmunds	28/02/76	Trainee	1995-96	1	1											Scunthorpe U
Nelmes A	Happy	Bristol	1871	Middlesbrough	1898-05	219		14	15									Burton U
Newton B	Ben	Grimsby	10/10/34	Elliston St Sch (Gy)	1953	3												Grimsby Amat. Lge.
Newton W	Billy	Quebec	06/08/98	Leicester C	1926	14			1									Stockport Co
Nichol J	John	Morpeth	1879	Morpeth Hrrs	1903	16		3	1									
Nicholl CJ	Chris	Wilmslow	12/10/46	Southampton	1983-84	70			1			8						Southampton (Man)
Nicholls M	Mark	Hillingdon	30/05/77	Chelsea	1999	6												(loan)
Nicholson GH	Harry	Wetheral	25/01/32	Carlisle U	1953	17												Nottingham F
Nidd GF	Fred	Boston	1869	Lincoln C	1898-99	50		1	8									Watford
Nogan LM	Lee	Cardiff	21/05/69	Reading	1997-98	63	11	10	4		2	9	1	2	8		2	Darlington
North MV	Marc	Ware	29/05/66	Luton T	1987-88													Leicester C
				Luton T	1991	64	4	17	8	1	5	4		2	6		1	Leicester U
Oakes F	Fred	Gainsborough		Grimsby St. Johns	1904	1												
Oakley N	Norman	Norton (Middlesbro.)	04/06/39	Swindon T	1966	15												Boston U
Oakton AE	Eric	Kiveton Park	28/12/06	Kiveton Park	1924	2												Rotherham U
Oates G	Graham	Scunthorpe	04/12/43	Blackpool	1968-70	80	1	9	2			1	1					Wigan Ath
O'Dell A	Andy	Kingston-upon-Hull	02/01/63	App	1981-82	18	2		2				2		1			Rotherham U
Ogilvie A	Adam	Scotland	1867	Forfar Ath	1888-92	21			17						63			Blackburn Rov
O'Kelly RF	Richard	West Bromwich	08/01/57	Walsall	1988	38	1	10	6			2			2	1		Port Vale (Com.Off)
Okorie CE	Chima	Izomber (Nigeria)	08/10/68	Peterborough U	1993		5						1	1				Torquay U
Oldridge AR	Bob	Barton-upon-Humber	17/11/57	Immingham OB	1975-76	9	6					1						Immingham OB
Openshaw W	Bill	Manchester	1881	Hooley Hill	1905-06	5												Salford U
O'Riordan DJ	Don	Dublin	14/05/57	Middlesbrough	1986-87	86		14	6			6			3			Notts Co
Oster JM	John	Boston	08/12/78	Trainee	1996	21	3	3		1	1							Everton
Owens I	Isaac	Darlington	1881	C Palace	1908	6		3	1									Darlington
Padley G	Punch	Grimsby	1882	Grimsby St. Johns	1904-05													Worksop T
				Worksop T	1915	18		8	1									Grimsby Amat. Lge.
Pangbourne T	Tom	Birmingham	1870	Bury	1898	3												New Brompton
Parker A	Snowy	Grimsby		Grimsby Rov	1897	1												Grimsby Rov
Parkin TA	Tommy	Gateshead	01/02/56	Ipswich T	1975	6												(loan)
Parry FT	Frank	Aigburth	14/06/98	Everton	1926	1												Accrington Stan
Partridge M	Malcolm	Calow	28/08/50	Leicester C	1974-78	134	4	25	9		2	7						Scunthorpe U
Paterson P	Peter	Glasgow	1880	Everton	1902	2												
Pattinson JB	John	Worksop	1886	Sheffield U	1907	19		2										Doncaster Rov
Paul T	Tommy	Grimsby	14/05/33	Immingham St. Andrews	1958	1												Spalding U
Peake AM	Andy	Market Harborough	01/11/61	Leicester C	1985-86	39		4	1		1	5			1			Charlton Ath
Pearce JA	Johnny	Grimsby	29/02/40	Grimsby Tech Sch	1958-61	48			1			2						Gainsborough Trin
Pearcey JK	Jason	Leamington Spa	23/07/71	Mansfield T	1994-97	49			1			3						Brentford
Pearson JC	John	Dudley	14/03/96	Brentford	1924-25	5			3									Retired injured
Pearson WGA	Billy	Clonmel	23/10/21	RAF	1946-48	35		8							25		4	Chester
Pell D	Dennis	Normanton	09/04/29	Rotherham U	1955-56	3		1	1									Frickley Colliery
Pennington A		Stoke-on-Trent	1875	Bristol Eastville Rov	1898	1												Folkestone
Pennington J	Jimmy	Golborne	26/04/39	Crewe Alex	1962-64	89		8	5		1	3						Oldham Ath
Penrose N	Norman	Consett	10/03/22	Medomsley	1946-47	9												Blyth Spartans
Phillips HG	Harry	Staffordshire		Lincoln C	1903-04	21		9	2									New Brompton
Phillips MS	Mike	Skares	18/01/33	Cumnock Jnrs	1954	6		1										Cheltenham T
Pickering FG	Frank	Burton-upon-Trent	1890	Sutton T	1912	2									12		4	Sutton T
Player PRI	Roy	Portsmouth	10/05/28	RAF	1952-58	57			3									Oldham Ath
Ponting WT	Wally	Grimsby	23/04/13	Humber U	1930-35	12		3	1						7		1	Chesterfield
Porter J	John	Stockton-on-Tees	1886	Skinnigrove	1909	1												
Portwood CE	Cliff	Salford	17/10/37	Port Vale	1961-63	92		35	3		1	2						Portsmouth
Poskett TW	Tom	Esh Winning	26/12/09	Crook T	1928-30	2												Lincoln C
Pouton A	Alan	Newcastle-upon-Tyne	01/02/77	York C	1999-*	19	17	1	1	1		3	2					*
Powell WMP	Billy	Sutton-in-Ashfield	21/01/01	Sheffield Wed	1927-29	78		1	3									Southend U
Pratt LS	Lee	Cleethorpes	31/03/70	Trainee	1986	1												Boston U
Pratt TP	Tom	Fleetwood	28/08/73	Fleetwood Rgrs	1895	29		15	7		1							Preston NE
Priestley G	Gerry	Halifax	02/03/31	Exeter C	1955-58	110		11	6		2							Crystal Palace

Player		Birthplace	D.O.B.	From	Season	F Lge			F A Cup			F L Cup			Other			Next
						A	S	G	A	S	G	A	S	G	A	S	G	
Priestley J	Jock	Johnstone	19/08/00	Chelsea	1928-32	139		7	7									St. Johnstone
Pringle WA	Bill	Walton	24/02/32	Liverpool	1954	2												Rhyl
Prior J	Jack	Choppington	02/07/04	Sunderland	1926-31	160		34	8		2							Ashington
Prout GW	George	Dalton-in-Furness	03/11/02	Preston NE	1926	4			1									Carlisle U
Prudhoe M	Mark	Washington	08/11/63	Walsall	1986	8												(loan)
Pugsley J	John	Grangetown	01/04/00	Cardiff C	1925-26	80		6		1								Bristol C
Purvis WYR	Willie	Berwick-upon-Tweed	14/12/38	Berwick Rgrs	1961-62	7		2										Doncaster Rov
Pynegar A	Algernon	Heanor	1883	Derby Co	1905	2												
Quigley D	Dennis	St. Andrews	07/12/13	Brechin C	1936-38	23		2										Hull C
Quin WJJ	Jack	Barrhead	1890	Eccles Bor	1912-14	61		5	1									Clyde
Raby WL	Walter	Lincoln	23/09/02	Lincoln C	1921	2		1	2									Clapton Orient
Rafferty R	Ron	South Shields	06/05/34	Portsmouth	1956-62	264		145	10		3	3		4				Hull C
Rampton G	George	Brighton	28/10/88	Walsall	1911-14	73		30	3						8		1	
Ramsden E	Ernie	Sheffield	1882	Brentford	1909	5												Midlands non-League
Rankin J	Jim	Gateshead	08/09/27	Brighton &HA	1949-50	5		1										
Ratcliffe GA	George	Hanley	1877	Sheffield U	1898-99	57		19	7		1							West Ham U
Rathbone GC	Graham	Newport (Gwent)	22/08/42	Newport Co	1966-72	232	1	11	6			17						Cambridge U
Rawcliffe P	Peter	Grimsby	08/12/63	Louth U	1986-87	9	13	2		2			1		2	1		Scunthorpe U (trial)
Rayner JP	Jimmy	Cornsay	31/03/35	Langley Park Jnrs	1952-53	12		3	3		5							Bury
Read TA	Rocket	Carters Green	02/04/00	Stockport Co	1927-33	247			12									Crystal Palace
Reay H	Harry	Sunderland	1896	Preston NE	1924	1												
Redding TR	Tom	Grimsby	17/03/32	Brigg T	1954-56	4												Scarborough
Reece PJ	Paul	Nottingham	16/07/68	Kettering T	1988-91	54			5			3			4			Doncaster Rov
Rees AA	Tony	Merthyr Tydfil	01/08/64	Barnsley	1989-93	124	17	33	8	1		11	2	2	5		3	West Brom Alb
Reeson MA	Tony	Rotherham	24/09/33	Rotherham U	1955-57	76		20	5		3							Doncaster Rov
Reeve FW	Fred	Clapton	01/05/18	Rochdale	1939-47	46			1						2			Reading
Reeve KE	Ken	Grimsby	13/01/21	Humber Jnrs	1939-47	24		5							29		15	Doncaster Rov
Reid W	Walter	Scotland	1869	Scottish Jun. Foot.	1888-92	10			11		3				70		10	
Reynolds JW	John	Manchester	23/09/81	Burton U	1904	29		3	2		1							Sheffield Wed
Reynolds W	William	Manchester	1878	C Orient	1905	6												Swindon T
Rice B	Brian	Bellshill	11/10/63	Nottingham F	1986	4												(loan)
Richards CH	Charlie	Burton-upon-Trent	09/08/75	Nottingham F	1898-00	80		42	5		2							Leicester F
Richardson D	Dave	Billingham	11/03/32	Leicester C	1955-59	175		1	11									Swindon T
Richardson W	William	Denton	20/10/78	Fairfield	1897-98	2												
Riddoch D	Dave	Edinburgh	1864	Berwick Rgrs	1888-94	59		18	29		10				66		18	
Rippon T	Pip	Beighton	04/02/88	Derbys Amat Lge	1911-19	121		37	2		1				67		21	Lincoln C
Rippon W	Willis	Beighton	15/05/86	Hamilton Acad	1913	23		12							43		11	Rotherham T
Ritchie T	Tommy	Bangor (Co Down)	10/07/30	Bedford T	1958	1												Barrow
Ritchie W	William	Renton		Bury	1922	25		4										Retired
Roberts C	Charlie	Rise Carr	06/04/83	Bishop Auckland	1903	31		4	2									Manchester U
Robertson AC	Chris	Mablethorpe	1915	Lincs Amat Lge	1935-37	5												Chester
Robinson A	Alf	Grimsby	1887	Grimsby Rov	1909	2												Grimsby Amat. Lge.
Robinson F	Fred	Belper	1881	Belper T	1905-06	33		8										Rotherham Co
Robinson HJ	Hervey	Grimsby	1874	Grimsby All Saints	1893-98	10		9										Grimsby All Saints
Robinson I	Ike	Bishop Auckland	1915	Scarborough	1936	3									1			Grimsby Police
Robinson JN	Norman	Middlesbrough	15/01/21	Middlesbrough	1948	5												Retired injured
Robinson N	Neil	Walton	20/04/57	Swansea C	1984-87	109		6	6			4			3	1		Darlington
Robinson RW	Ray	Blaydon	1895	Sunderland	1921	9									2			Sunderland
Robinson SB	Sam	Grimsby	1878	Grimsby Rov	1899	1												Grimsby Rov
Robson J	Joe	Gateshead	21/03/03	Saltwell Villa	1924-30	161		123	6		1							Huddersfield T
Robson TR	Ray	Westerhope	11/08/28	Bradford C	1952-54	58		2	5									Wisbech T
Rodger G	Graham	Glasgow	01/04/67	Luton T	1991-97	134	12	11	12		1	5	1		3			Retired injured
Rodger T	Tom	Scotland	1882	Preston NE	1906	34		13	2									Reading
Rogers JJ	Joe	Coventry	05/11/74	Southampton	1896-97	53		23	4		1							Newcastle U
Ronaldson DM	Duncan	Scotland	1879	Queens Park Rgrs	1901-02	64		19	4		1							Bury
Rose THT	Hickey	Lowestoft	1870	Grimsby All Saints	1888-95	34		7	9		2				44		12	Grimsby All Saints
Ross RC	Bobby	Craigmillar	09/09/41	St. Mirren	1965-70	208	4	18	7		1	15		1				Gainsborough Trin
Ross W	William	Kiveton Park	1874	Notts Co	1904	32		7	2									Glossop
Rouse FW	Fred	Cranford	28/11/81	Shepherds Bush	1902-03	37		15	2									Stoke
Rowbotham MG	Mike	Sheffield	02/09/65	Manchester U	1984	3	1						1					Gainsborough Trin
Rowston CE	Scratty	Grimsby	1887	Cleethorpes T	1909	15		1	1									Cleethorpes Town
Rudd AC	Archie	Nottingham	1887	Notts Olympic	1907	1									1			
Rudd WT	Billy	Moss Side	13/12/41	York C	1966-67	59	1	9	3			8		1				Rochdale
Rushby W	Billy	Cleethorpes	18/11/88	Cleethorpes T	1912-18	5									38			Cleethorpes Town
Russell J	James	Scotland		Scottish Jun. Foot.	1893	25		4	5									
Sankey T	Tom	Nuneaton	24/10/94	Huthwaite Colliery	1920	4			2		1				33		8	
Satterthwaite JN	Joe	Cockermouth	1885	W Arsenal	1908	20		2	1									New Brompton
Saunders SJP	Steve	Warrington	21/09/64	Preston NE	1987-88	70	6	13	9				2		4	1	2	Scarborough
Saxby MW	Mike	Clipstone	12/08/57	Luton T	1982	10												(loan)
Scotson R	Reg	Stockton-on-Tees	22/09/19	Sunderland	1950-54	164		4	12		2							Skegness T
Scott J	Johnny	Belfast	22/12/33	Manchester U	1956-62	240		51	8		2	1		1				York C
Scott JG	Jack	Rosehill	1890	Newcastle U	1913-14	47		1	2						2			Non-League

Player		Birthplace	D.O.B.	From	Season	F Lge			F A Cup			F L Cup			Other			Next
						A	S	G	A	S	G	A	S	G	A	S	G	
Scott W	Buns	Worksop	1886	Worksop T	1907-09													Everton
				Worksop T	1919	99			5									Gainsborough Trin
Seagraves CA	Chris	Bootle	07/10/64	Liverpool	1984	22	1		3			6						Hong Kong
Seddon WC	Bill	Clapton	28/07/01	Arsenal	1931-32	20		1										Luton T
Seeburg MP	Max	Leipzig (Germany)	19/09/84	Burnley	1911	20			1									Reading
Shakespeare CR	Craig	Great Barr	26/10/63	West Brom Alb	1993-96	84	22	10	5	3		6	1			1		Scunthorpe U
Sharp F	Frank	Edinburgh	28/05/47	Barnsley	1973	26	3	2	4			4		1				Port Vale
Shaw AE	Basher	Co Durham		Chilton Colliery Rec	1923	5												Chilton Colliery Rec
Shaw H	Bert	Sheffield	1919	Boston U	1937-38	15		3										Chelmsford C
Shaw J	Jack	Oldham	02/10/16	Mossley	1937-38	7												Birmingham
Shaw JF	Joe	Durham	1882	Hull C	1909	6												
Shearer DJ	David	Caol	16/10/58	Middlesbrough	1983	1	3											Gillingham
Shearer JM	Jock	Dunfermline	08/07/17	Bradford C	1948-50	34		7	1									Retired injured
Sherwood S	Steve	Selby	10/12/53	Watford	1987-92	183			9			12			8			Northampton T
Short M	Maurice	Grove Hill	29/12/49	Oldham Ath	1970	10												(loan)
Sibley ES	Eric	Christchurch	17/11/15	Blackpool	1947-48	23			3									Chester
Simpson O	Owen	Mickley	18/09/43	Darlington	1971	6	1		1			3	1					Boston U
Sinclair MJ	Mike	Grimsby	13/10/38	Carr Lane Sch (Gy)	1957-60	6		1										Ards (N.Ire)
Singleton HB	Harry	Prescot	1877	Everton	1902	18		2	2									New Brompton
Skinner H	Harry	Middlesex	1875	Queens Park Rgrs	1901	1												
Slack TC	Trevor	Peterborough	26/09/62	Rotherham U	1987	21			1			2			2			Northampton T
Slater JB	Brian	Lower Handsworth	20/10/32	Sheffield Wed	1954	4												Rotherham U
Smailes J	Jimmy	South Moor	09/06/07	Blackpool	1935	10			2		1							Stockport Co
Smaller PA	Paul	Scunthorpe	18/09/70	Trainee	1988-89	1	1											Bridlington Town
Smith A	Albert	Burnley	28/04/87	Rochdale	1919-21	89		15	9		4							
Smith D	David	Stonehouse	29/03/68	West Brom Alb	1997-*	81	3	7	2			6	3	1	7		1	*
Smith DN	Denis	Grimsby	23/12/32	Hardy Rgrs	1952-53	4												Goole T
Smith F	Frank	Darnall	22/11/1887	Swansea T	1920-21	5			1									Retired
Smith FE	Fred	Draycott	27/05/26	Manchester C	1952-53	50		24	4		1							Bradfovrd C
Smith MC	Mark	Norton (Sheffield)	19/12/61	Huddersfield T	1990-92	37	40	4	1	3		2	3		2	1		Scunthorpe U
Smith RG	Richard	Lutterworth	03/10/70	Leicester C	1995-*	78	3		2			10						*
Smith R	Rob	Kingston-upon-Hull	25/04/50	Hull C	1971	10	1		1									Hartlepool
Smith RW	Bobby	Prestbury	14/03/44	Scunthorpe U	1966-67	48	4	1	2			1	1					Brighton &HA
Smith W	Wally	Grimsby		Grimsby All Saints	1890-92	2		1	1		2							Grimsby All Saints
Smith WE	Walter	Leicester	25/03/84	Plymouth Arg	1922	10									1			
Southall LN	Nicky	Linthorpe	28/01/72	Hartlepool U	1995-97	55	17	6	4	3	2	3	3	1				Gillingham
Sowerby WHR	Roy	Kingston-upon-Hull	31/08/32	Wolverhampton Wndrs	1953-54	12		1										
Speak G	George	Blackburn	07/11/90	Darwen	1911-12	4												Gainsborough Trin
Speight M	Micky	Upton	01/11/51	Blackburn Rov	1982-83	35	3	2	1			3			2			Chester C(Pl/coach)
Speight W	Wally	Elsecar	1881	Yorks Amat Lge	1903	6		1										Rotherham T
Spendiff MN	Martin	North Shields	24/06/80	North Shields Ath	1902-04													Hull C
				Millwall Ath	1913-19	123			7						4			Retired
Spink TW	Tommy	Dipton	13/11/87	Rochdale	1914-21	116		3	5		1				30		1	Worksop T
Springthorpe HT	Harry	Tinwell	28/04/86	Northampton T	1908-12	25		6	4		2				11		8	
Squires F	Frank	Swansea	08/03/21	Plymouth Arg	1950	36		2	2		1							Merthyr Tydfil
Staniforth FW	Fred	Kilnhurst	1884	Bristol C	1911-12	67		8	2									Liverpool
Steeples J	John	Doncaster	28/04/59	Pilkington Rec	1980-81	4	3									2		Scarborough
Stephenson G	Geoff	Preston (Tyne&Wear)	28/04/70	Trainee	1987-89	19	2					1			1			Boston U
Stevenson J	Jimmy	Paisley	1876	Newcastle U	1901	8		1										Leicester F
Stevenson R	Robert	Craigneuk	1898	Motherwell YMCA	1921-22	8			1									
Stewart TG	Tom	Lanarkshire		Newcastle U	1898	1												
Stockin R	Ron	West Bromwich	27/06/31	Cardiff C	1957-59	49		14	4		1							Wisbech T
Stokes AW	Albert	Darnall	26/01/33	Hampton Sports	1954-56	16		3	1		1							Scunthorpe U
Stokes P	Paddy	Stockton-on-Tees	1883	Shildon Ath	1907													Non-League
				Non-League	1908	14		2	5									Oldham Ath
Stone JG	John	Carlin How	03/03/53	Darlington	1979-82	89	5	2	8			11			7			Rotherham U
Storer H	Harry	West Derby	02/02/98	Eastwood	1918-20	64		18	4		2				8		2	Derby Co
Stott J	Jimmy	Darlington	08/10/08	Liverpool	1894	29		4	4		2							Newcastle U
Stoutt SP	Steve	Halifax	05/04/64	Wolverhampton Wndrs	1988-89	3		1				2						Lincoln C
Straw IE	Ian	Sheffield	27/05/67	Southampton	1986	7	3					1			1			Burton Alb
Stroud DNL	Derek	Wimborne	11/02/30	Bournemouth &BA	1953-54	71		12	8		1							Dorchester T
Stubbs W	Billy	West Hartlepool	01/08/66	Nottingham F	1987	2	5	2										(loan)
Summers P	Percy	Chesterfield	1889	Chesterfield T	1914-18	34			1						1			Luton T
Swaby HN	Harry	Grimsby	22/01/06	Cleethorpes T	1926-31	44		2	4									Barnsley
Swain JS	Jack	Grimsby	13/04/14	City of Leeds College	1936-38	22		6	1									Scunthorpe U
Swarbrick J	Jim	Lytham St. Anne's	1881	Brentford	1905-07	67		12	3									Oldham Ath
Sykes AB	Arthur	Grimsby	1897	Grimsby Rov	1920	1												Grimsby Rov
Talks T	Tommy	Lincoln	15/05/97	Grimsby Rov	1920-21	15		4	1									Boston T
Taylor F	Fred	Grimsby	01/04/77	Grimsby All Saints	1897	1												Grimsby All Saints
Taylor GJ	Georgie	Dundee	23/10/48	Dundee Jnr Lge	1965-67		1		1			1						New Imperial (Grim.)
Taylor G	Graham	Worksop	15/09/44	Scunthorpe U	1961-67	189		2	12			14						Lincoln C
Taylor RE	Dick	Wednesfield	09/04/18	Midlands Jun. Lge.	1938-47	36			4									Scunthorpe U
Taylor WB	Wally	Kirton in Lindsey	30/10/26	Hibaldstow	1944-50	21			2						1			Southport

						F Lge			F A Cup			F L Cup			Other			
Player		***Birthplace***	***D.O.B.***	***From***	***Season***	**A**	**S**	**G**	**A**	**S**	**G**	**A**	**S**	**G**	**A**	**S**	**G**	***Next***
Tees M	Matt	Johnstone	13/10/39	Airdrieonians	1963-66													Charlton Ath
				Luton T	1970-72	196		93	14		6	17		10				Boston U
Temple W	Bill	Barlow	12/12/15	Carlisle U	1938-45	2									1		1	Gateshead
Tennant W	Billy	Wolverhampton	12/07/65	Walsall	1901	13												Retired (Res Train)
Thain JW	Jack	Gateshead	1903	Peterborough &FU	1924	26		4										
Theaker CA	Cam	Spalding	08/12/12	Spalding Utd.	1935-38	5												Newcastle U
Thompson AJ	Ab	Louth	1885	Grimsby Amat Lge	1904	2												Grimsby Amat. Lge.
Thompson A	Alf	Padiham	1891	Grimsby Rov	1918-19	3		1	1		1				17		4	Charltons (Gy)
Thompson EG	Ernie	Bradford	1892	Bradford PA	1924	7			1									
Thompson JB	Jimmy	Windy Nook	07/01/43	St. Marys BC	1962-66	156		2	12			12						Port Elizabeth (S Afr)
Thompson RM	Ralph	Grimsby	1892	Grimsby Amat Lge	1913-14	12												Grimsby Amat. Lge.
Thomson D	Doug	Dundee	10/08/91	Aberdeen	1923	25		3	4		1							Aberdeen
Thomson JA	Jimmy	Glasgow	28/06/48	Newcastle U	1971	23	3	4	1		2	3	2					Greenock Morton
Tillson A	Andy	Huntingdon	30/06/66	Kettering T	1988-90													Queens Park Rgrs
				Queens Park Rgrs	1992	108	1	5	10			8			6			(loan)
Tinsley C	Colin	Grove Hill	24/10/35	Redcar BC	1954-57	24												Darlington
Toale I	Ian	Walton	28/08/67	Liverpool	1987	16	4		1			1			2			Caernarfon T
Tomlinson RW	Reg	Sleaford	02/07/14	Horncastle T	1935-37	20		2	2		2							Southampton
Trollope PJ	Paul	Swindon	03/06/72	Derby Co	1996	6	1	1										(loan)
Tucker M	Malcolm	Hartford Village	12/04/33	4 N's (Newcastle)	1953-57	40			1									Skegness T
Turnbull GF	George	Gateshead	04/02/27	Alnwick T	1950	2			2									Accrington Stan
Turner I	Ian	Middlesbrough	17/01/53	Huddersfield T	1971-73	26			1			1						Southampton
Turner PJE	Jim	Brentford	01/11/79	Brentford	1904	14												
Turner P	Phil	Sheffield	12/02/62	Lincoln C	1986-87	62		7	6			6			3		1	Leicester C
Tweedy GJ	George	Willington	08/01/13	Willington T	1932-52	347			25						72			Retired (Asst Man)
Twell B	Ben	Temple Normanton	30/08/03	Grassmoor Ivanhoe	1927	3		1										Southport
Tyler W	Bill	Bradford (Manchester)	28/05/00	Bournemouth &BA	1927	1												Hurst
Vincent NE	Ned	Prudhoe	03/03/09	Stockport Co	1934-46	144		2	15						219		21	Retired
Vincett JH	John	Hastings	24/03/83	Hastings & St. Leonards	1907	32			5									Leicester F
Wainman WH	Harry	Kingston-upon-Hull	22/03/47	App	1964-78	420			20			32						Retired (Yth Coach)
Wainwright AH	Arthur	Tinsley	01/11/94	Leeds C	1919	8		2										Grsley Rov
Waite JA	John	Grimsby	16/01/42	Wintringham Sch (Gy)	1961-62	8		1										Gainsborough Trin
Walker A	Arnold	Haltwhistle	23/12/32	Appleby-Frodingham	1950-57	65			6									Walsall
Walker DH	Don	Edinburgh	10/09/35	Middlesbrough	1963	15		1										Workington
Walker J	Jack	Alexandria	1869	Vale of Leven	1889-92	13			8						40		2	Everton
Walker J	Johnny	Robroyston	12/12/73	Clydebank	1995-96	1	2	1										Mansfield T
Walker JG	Gordon	Hillsborough	26/11/45	Stocksbridge Works	1968-69	25	2	5				1						Matlock T
Wallace AJJ	Nune	Sheffield	1874	Attercliffe	1896	20			3									
Wallbanks WH	Horace	Chopwell	04/09/18	Aberdeen	1946	9		1	2						5		1	Luton T
Walsh IP	Ian	St. David's	14/09/58	Barnsley	1986-87	36	5	13	3		1	6		4	2		1	Cardiff C
Walton IJ	Ian	Goole	17/04/58	App	1975	2		1					1					Scunthorpe U
Ward JP	John	Lincoln	07/04/51	Watford	1981	2										2		Lincoln C
Wardle W	Billy	Sunniside	20/01/18	Manchester C	1939-47	73		11	6						22		2	Blackpool
Waring J	Jack	Wombwell		Wombwell	1933	2												Crewe Alex
Warner VJ	Vance	Leeds	03/09/74	Nottingham F	1995	3												(loan)
Warren RA	Bob	Newhall	1886	Derbys Amat Lge	1909	1												
Waters JJW	Joe	Limerick	20/09/53	Leicester C	1975-83	356	1	65	20		5	29		5	12		3	Tacoma Stars(USA)
Waterson J	Jim	Scotland		Arbroath	1894	20		3										
Watkins AE	Alf	Llanwnog	01/06/78	Aston Villa	1900	11		5										Millwall Ath
Watson TR	Tommy	Walton	29/09/69	Trainee	1987-95	134	38	24	3			10	5	2	8	2		Boston T
Wattam F	Frank	Grimsby	12/11/08	Louth T	1932-40	27									20		1	Consolidated (Grim.)
Wealthall BA	Barry	Radford	01/05/42	Nottingham F	1961-62	9						1						York C
Weatherall L	Len	Middlesbrough	21/05/36	Redcar BC	1954-55	10		1										Alford T
Webb NJ	Neil	Reading	30/07/63	Nottingham F	1996	3	1					1						Aldershot T
Welbourne D	Duncan	Scunthorpe	28/07/40	Scunthorpe U	1957-63	130		3	5			2						Watford
Welsh W	William	Grimsby		Grimsby Amat Lge	1919	5												Grimsby Amat Lge
Whalley FH	Fred	Salford	09/10/98	Preston NE	1920	23			3									Leeds U
Wheatley R	Roland	Radford	20/06/24	Southampton	1951	5												Halifax T
Wheaton GJ	Gil	Mickley Square	01/11/41	Mickley Square Wlf Jnrs	1962	7												Chester
Wheelhouse S	Sid	Darlington	1888	Shildon Ath	1907-15	234		3	13						40			WW1 Killed in action
Whelpton JI	Jimmy	Sheffield	1887	Guildford Utd.	1913	1												
Whitchurch E	Ernie	Sheffield	07/08/91	Sharrow Reform	1912-19	30									65		1	
White M	Malcolm	Wolverhampton	24/04/41	Coseley Amat	1958-62	65			1			2						Walsall
Whitefoot J	Jeff	Cheadle	31/12/33	Manchester U	1957	26		5	1									Nottingham F
Whitehead NJ	Norman	Fazakerley	22/04/48	Chester	1976	3	1											Bangor C
Whitehouse J	Jimmy	Birmingham	04/73	Birmingham St. Georges	1892-95													Aston Villa
				Bedminster	1899	137			24									Newton Heath
Whitfield J	Jim	Kingston-upon-Hull	18/05/19	Humber U	1946-48	29		7	4		2							Scunthorpe U
Whitlock M	Mark	Portsmouth	14/03/61	Southampton	1982	7	1											(loan)
Whittaker W	Walter	Manchester	20/09/78	Fairfield	1897													Reading
				Blackburn Rov	1901-02	75			2									Derby Co
Whymark TJ	Trevor	Burston	04/05/50	Vancouver Whtcps (Can)	1980-83	83	10	16	6		1	5		1	9		1	Southend U
Widdrington T	Tommy	Walkergate	01/10/71	Southampton	1996-98	75	19	8	3	1		10	3		1			Port Vale

Player		Birthplace	D.O.B.	From	Season	F Lge			F A Cup			F L Cup			Other			Next
						A	S	G	A	S	G	A	S	G	A	S	G	
Wigg RG	Ron	Great Dunmow	18/05/49	Rotherham U	1974-76	51	12	12	3		1	4		1				Barnsley
Wigginton CA	Clive	High Green	18/10/50	App	1968-74													Scunthorpe U
				Lincoln C	1978-81	286	9	8	21			22	1		7			Torquay U
Wilkinson F	Freddy	Bishop Auckland	1882	Bishop Auckland	1903	16		2	1		1							Norwich C
Wilkinson J	John	Worksop	01/04/49	App	1965-67	8	1		1									Nantwich T
Wilkinson P	Paul	Grimoldby	30/10/64	App	1982-84	68	2	27	4	2	1	10		5				Everton
Williams ABF	Benny	Lincoln	14/04/51	App	1969	2												Lincoln U
Williams C	Clarry	Wardley	13/01/33	Doncaster Rov	1952-59	188			14									Barnsley
Williams D	David	Hillsborough	07/10/31	Beighton Miners Welfare	1953	5												Gainsborough Trin
Williams D	Derek	Wardley	28/01/37	Sheffield Wed	1956-61	44		19	1									Bradford PA
Williams TE	Tommy	Winchburgh	18/12/57	Birmingham C	1988-89	19	1					4						Retired injured
Williams T	Trevor	Grimsby		Grimsby Rgrs	1903	4		1	1						2		1	Grimsby Rgrs
Williamson J	John	Fauldhouse	16/10/96	Preston NE	1926	1												Lancaster T
Willis RC	Harry	Sheffield	17/06/67	Dunkirk (Notts)	1989	1	8						1					Barnet
Wilmot RJ	Rhys	Rogiet	21/02/62	Plymouth Arg	1992	33			4			4			2			Crystal Palace
Wilson A	Cowboy	Rotherham	28/01/15	Rotherham U	1947	17		1										Boston U
Wilson C	Tug	Heeley	20/07/05	Sheffield Wed	1931-32	27		2										Aston Villa
Wilson CH	Charlie	Cleethorpes	10/02/04	Cleethorpes T	1923-32	273		2	19									Bournemouth &BA
Wilson DEJ	Dave	Dunstall Park	04/10/44	Carlisle U	1966-68	63		22	2			4						Walsall
Wood K	Kevin	Armthorpe	03/11/29	Worksop T	1950-51	3		2										Peterborough U
Woods NS	Neil	York	30/07/66	Bradford C	1990-97	175	51	42	8	2	3	11	4	2	8		1	York C
Woodward A	Alan	Stanton Hill	19/06/47	Alfreton T	1970-71	54		13	1			5		1				Boston U
Worth A	Albert	Manchester	1888	Rochdale	1910-11	20		2	4		2				36		11	Luton T
Worthington D	Dave	Halifax	28/03/45	Barrow	1966-72	292	1	14	12		1	23		4				Southend U
Wrack C	Charlie	Boston	28/12/99	Cleethorpes T	1925-30	125		2	5									Hull C
Wrack D	Darren	Cleethorpes	05/05/76	Derby Co	1996-97	5	8	1								1		Walsall
Wright AW	Archie	Glasgow	23/11/24	Blackburn Rov	1953	39		9	5		1							Accrington Stan
Wright CG	Charlie	Govan	11/12/38	Workington	1962-65	129			11			8						Charlton Ath
Wright J	Jim	Okehampton	11/09/10	Torquay U	1932-34	27			3									Sheffield Wed
Wright N	Norman	Ushaw Moor	27/12/08	Esh Winning	1927-29	17		3										Crewe Alex
Yates D	Dave	Barnsley	08/03/53	Barnsley	1976	10												(loan)
Young C	Chris	Cleethorpes	26/05/86	Cleethorpes T	1905-10	5		2	1						54		41	Gainsborough Trin
Young M	Martin	Grimsby	09/04/55	FA forms	1974-78	87	7	4	4			4						Retired injured
Young R	Dick	Felling	13/07/39	South Shields	1962-64	33		13	2			3		4				Stockport Co

Appeared in FA Cup only

Player		Birthplace	D.O.B.	From	Season	F Lge A	F Lge S	F Lge G	F A Cup A	F A Cup S	F A Cup G	F L Cup A	F L Cup S	F L Cup G	Other A	Other S	Other G	Next
Chadwick H	Harry	Werneth	25/01/19	Blackpool	1940-45				1						25		6	Tranmere Rov
Cleator					1893				1		1							
Harvey W	Bill	Grimsby	1920	Grimsby YMCA	1944-45				1						3			Boston U
Morgan D	Dave	Nottingham	01/08/48	App	1965				1									Arnold Town
Rodi J	Joe	Glasgow	23/07/13	East Fife	1944-45				2		1				32		20	Rochdale
West A					1893				1									

Appeared in Football League Cup only

Player		Birthplace	D.O.B.	From	Season	F Lge A	F Lge S	F Lge G	F A Cup A	F A Cup S	F A Cup G	F L Cup A	F L Cup S	F L Cup G	Other A	Other S	Other G	Next
Lakin JT	John	High Green	21/08/46	Stocksbridge Works	1964							1						Boston U

Appeared in Midland League 1910/11 only

Player		Birthplace	D.O.B.	From	Season	F Lge A	F Lge S	F Lge G	F A Cup A	F A Cup S	F A Cup G	F L Cup A	F L Cup S	F L Cup G	Other A	Other S	Other G	Next
Hobson JD		Ecclesfield		New Brompton	1910				3						38		5	
Jackson					1910										9		2	
Nocton		Grimsby		Grimsby Rgrs	1910										1			Grimsby Rgrs

Non-Playing Substitutes only

Player		Birthplace	D.O.B.	From	Season	F Lge A	F Lge S	F Lge G	F A Cup A	F A Cup S	F A Cup G	F L Cup A	F L Cup S	F L Cup G	Other A	Other S	Other G	Next
Clohessy MJ	Mark	Dublin	28/08/75	Trainee - G	1993	14*			2*									Irish football
Colgan NV	Nick	Drogheda	19/09/73	Chelsea - G	1994	6*												(loan)
Dickins MJ	Matt	Sheffield	03/09/70	Blackburn Rov -G	1994	6*												(loan)
Gowshall J	Joby	Louth	07/08/75	Trainee - D	1995							1*						Boston U
Green PG	Peter	Northampton	17/12/65	Louth U - F	1986	1*												Pretoria (S Africa)
Quy AJ	Andy	Harlow	04/07/76	Derby Co - G	1996	1*												Stevenage Bor
Trinder JL	Jason	Leicester	03/03/70	Friar Lane OB - G	1993	3*									1*			Leicester U
Welton GE	Guy	Grimsby	04/05/78	Trainee - G	1994	1*												Notts CCC (Cricket)

*The number of occasions the player was named as a substitute, but never made an appearance.

Players of the First World War (1915-1919)

Sheet 1 **Allott to Forman**

Player		Pos	Years	War Details	A	G
Allott H		OR	1917	War apps for Barnsley	6	1
Andrews W*	Billy	RH	1917-18	Grimsby T. Belfast U 'guest'	2	
Ashling SG		CF	1916-18		12	1
Atkinson A		FB	1917-18	Grimsby T Res	5	
Bailey T	Tom	RH	1919	Gresley Rov	1	
Ballance H		CF	1918	Gainsborough	7	2
Barraclough		LH	1917	Bradford PA	1	
Battersby		CF	1917	vs. Birmingham (a)	1	
Battiste W*	Wally	HB	1919	Shirebrook. Later signed.	16	6
Bavin A	Arthur	OL	1918	Ruston Aircraftmen. Ex-Lincoln C	1	
Beach S		LH	1918	Sheffield Wed	1	
Bell		IL	1917	vs. Birmingham (a)	1	
Benfield TC	Tom	IF	1916-18	Derby Co. Leics Rgmt (L Corp). K.I.A.	10	5
Bertie		OR	1918	vs. Nottm F (a)	1	1
Beswick J		OR	1918	vs. Huddersfield T (a)	1	
Binks L*	Louis	LB	1918	Tinsley Amats. Later Coventry C & GTFC	1	
Birch W*	Billy	OL	1915-16	Gainsborough. Ex-Grimsby T	5	
Black		OR	1918		1	
Booth JW		OL	1919	vs. Rotherham Co (a)	1	
Booth R	Bob	RH	1917	Blackpool	1	
Branston JH	Jim	G	1918-19	Notts Co	46	
Bratley C		IL	1916	Rawmarsh area. Brother of Phil	1	
Bratley H		RH	1916	Barnsley area. Brother of Phil	2	
Bratley PW	Phil	LB	1916	Rawmarsh. Liverpool	6	1
Brelsford C		LB	1919	Sheffield Wed	1	
Brooks S		OL	1917	'Guested' for Birmingham WW1	1	1
Broom W*	Bill	CF	1919	Box Company.Later signed.	2	
Brown		OR	1918	Lincoln C	1	
Bryan JJ	John	CH	1917	Notts Co,Lincoln C & Shirebrook	1	
Burkinshaw R	Ralph	IR	1918	Barnsley. Brother of Jack (Ex-GTFC)	1	1
Burton E		OR	1917	Birmingham area. Leicester F 'guest'	1	
Butler J*	Jack	RB	1916-17	Ex-Grimsby T. Son of Bill	20	
Butler R		IF	1916	Middlesbrough area. L Corp in 2/1st Nth Cyclists Corps	3	
Butler W	Bill	RH	1917-18	Father of Jack. From Sheffield area	15	1
Cavanagh JA	John	IR	1918	Lincoln C. Ex-Ashington	1	
Charles F	Fred	IR	1916	Sheffield U	1	1
Cheetham		LH	1917	Stockport Co. 3rd Mancs Rgmt (Pte), Pheasley	1	
Clarke H	Horace	LH	1917-19	Grimsby T. Ex-Scunthorpe signed from Sheffield Wed	46	2
Codd TH	Tommy	OL	1917	Leicester F. Footballer's Battalion. Ex-Goole T.	1	
Colebrook W		OL	1916-17	Grimsby T. From Haycroft Rov	15	6
Cooke		OL	1918	Apps inc.vs. Nottm F (h&a)	4	
Cookson SP	Sam	LB	1918	Manchester U. 3rd Mancs Rgmt (Sgt)	2	
Cooney J		OL	1916	Rawmarsh area	3	
Cooper A (jnr)	Alf	LB	1916	Grimsby T.Son of Chairman. Army Cadet	1	
Cooper E	Ed	OR	1918	Newcastle U. W Yorks Rgmt. Ex-Glossop.	4	1
Cooper JC	Jack	G	1916-18	Barnsley,then Sheffield W. WW1'Gunner'	2	
Cordall S		CH	1917-18	War apps for Everton	7	
Coulbeck T*	Toy	IL	1915-16	Gainsborough. Ex-Grimsby T	26	3
Crane		LH	1918	vs. Coventry C (a)	1	
Crutchley J		CH	1917	Halesowen T	1	
Danesborough		IR	1918	vs. Gainsborough (a)	1	
Davis AG	Arthur	IR	1919	Evesham T. Later of Coventry C	2	
Dawson F		RH	1917-18	Pte in HM Minesweepers	2	
Dawson S*	Sid	LB	1918-19	Northampton T. Later signed.	29	
Day		RH	1918	3rd Mancs Rgmt (Sgt)	1	
Dodds		OL	1918	Borrowed vs. Sheffield U (a)	1	
Ducat A	Andy	RH	1917	Aston Villa & England Int. Cricket star also	1	
Dunn R		OL	1918	Notts Co	2	
Elvin		RH	1917	vs. Hull C (a)	1	
Farrah		OL	1919	vs. Bradford C (a)	1	
Fearnley E	Eric	IF	1916-18	Bradford C & PA amat. Journalist	9	
Fenney A		CF	1917	vs. Leicester F. (h)	1	1
Finneran		OR	1918	Army Pte	1	
Forman GA		OR	1917-18	Local. WW1 'Stoker'	5	

Player		Pos	Years	War Details	A	G
Gaskell		LB	1917	4th Mancs Rgmt (Corp)	1	
Gladwin		OR	1917	vs. Chesterfield (a)	1	
Goodfellow		CF	1917	Sgt in Army	5	1
Graham DC		LH	1915-18	GTFC Res. Borrowed by several clubs whilst at Blundell Park	8	
Gray AE*	Ernie	OL	1919	Cleethorpes T. Later signed.	6	
Gray G	Baggy	RB	1918-19	Cleethorpes T	23	
Green H		RB	1915	'Sapper' in Army	1	
Gregson A*	Alf	IL	1919	GTFC	3	1
Hall B*	Ben	LB	1916-17	South Shields.Ex-GTFC & Leicester F	2	
Hall E	Ellis	CH	1917	Ex-Huddersfield T.Brother of Ben, Harry & Fretwell	5	
Halley R		CH	1917		2	
Harris G		OR	1917		7	
Harrold S	Sid	OR	1917	Wednesbury. Later Leicester F	1	
Hatton A*	Albert	RH	1915	Ex-GTFC	1	
Hawley F	Fred	RH	1917	Sheffield U	1	
Heath E	Ernie	G	1916	Bradford C (ex Gainsborough Trin)	1	
Henderson J	Jimmy	CF	1918	Cardiff C. Lancs Fusiliers (L Corp)	1	
Hendrie R		CF	1917-18	Signaller in HM Minesweepers.	12	3
Hesseltine C		RH	1915	'Sapper' in the Army	2	
Hill G		OR	1918	Scunthorpe &LU	3	
Hinton		G	1917	Local, Humber Graving Dock	1	
Hobson		IL	1917-18	3rd Mancs Rgmt (Corp)	7	
Holden TH	Tom	G	1916	Grimsby T Trainer	1	
Hollings		IR	1917	Scunthorpe &LU.From Rawmarsh area.	4	1
Holt A		OR	1919	Lancs Lge. Distillery(Ire)WW1.Mancs Rgt	5	
Hooper W*	Billy	OR	1915-18	Ex-GTFC. Driver in Army Service Corps	15	4
Horton		IR	1919	vs. Notts Co (a)	1	
Howarth		OL	1918	Pte in Army.vs. Lincoln C (a)	1	
Humphries	Howard	IL	1917	Aston Villa	1	
Huxford AT*	Gus	OL	1915-19	Goole T. Ex-GTFC, re-signed after war.	82	12
Isherwood R		OL	1917	Bradford PA. 3rd Mancs Rgmt (Pte)	7	1
Johnson N*	Nat	CH	1915-18	Charltons (Gy Lge), ex-Grimsby T.	52	3
Kenny D*	Dave	CH	1917-19	GTFC. Army service until Feb 1919	18	1
Kirkman S	Sam	OL	1918	Sheffield Wed. Army Pte served in France	2	
Kitchen JE	Joe	OR	1918	Sheffield U. Grimsby born.	1	1
Knighton T	Tom	CF	1917-19	Tottenham H. Man U guest WW1.A Lieut	12	7
Langley T		CH	1917	vs. Notts Co (a)	1	1
Lawrence GW	George	G	1919	Derby Co	1	
Laws		IL	1918	Signaller in Army	1	
Lee JA*	Alfie	FB	1915-16	GTFC	17	
Lee JW		LB	1915-16	L Corp in Army	4	
Lees JWD	Joe	IL	1917	Barnsley.'Sapper' in Army. Later RUFC	3	
Lyons T	Tom	RB	1917	Aston Villa	1	
McDermott R		IL	1917-18	Oldham Ath. Pte in Army	4	
McGuire P	Pat	LB	1915-16	Manchester C.3rd Mancs Rgmt (L Corp)	31	6
McIver N		OR	1916	Nottm F& Brad PA WW1. (Blackburn R?)	2	
MacKenzie R	Bob	OR	1918-19	Bradford C	4	
McQuillan J	Jack	LB	1916-17	Hull C	4	
Marshall JH	Jim	RH	1916-17	Bradfor C.	5	
Martin F*	Frank	HB	1915-19	GTFC. Footballers Battalion.	58	5
Martin J		OL	1919	Lincoln C war apps	1	
Mayson TF*	Tommy	IL	1916	GTFC. Leeds C 'guest'.	1	
Minney H		OR	1919	Navy. Standard Engineering Co FC,Leics	1	
Murray		RB	1919	vs. Lincoln C & Hull C (both away)	2	
Nash HE	Harry	IR	1917	Aston Villa	1	
Nevins R	Ralph	LB	1916	Brother of Hull C back, Tom	2	
Newton A	Albert	CF	1918-19	Barnsley amat. 3rd Mancs Rgmt (L Corp)	2	1
Nicholson		OL	1918	Army Pte	1	
Ormiston AP	Alec	CH	1915-16	Chelsea. Ex. Lincoln C	40	
Osmond		IR	1917	Army Pte	1	
Pace A	Arthur	IL	1917	Hull C	2	
Pattison JM	John	FB	1915-17	Hull C	2	
Pennington J	Jesse	RB	1917	WBA & England Int.	1	
Peplow		OL	1917	Birmingham works league	1	

Player		Pos	Years	War Details	A	G
Pickering FG*	Frank	CF	1917-18	Ex-GTFC	12	4
Pickering J	John	CF	1917	Sutton T. Chesterfield WW1.Frank's brother	8	1
Price F		IR	1917	Aston Villa ? vs. Birmingam (a)	1	
Pykett B		IR	1917	Notts Co. Leicester F 'guest'	1	
Rampton G*	George	CF	1915-18	Ex-GTFC. Lived in Midlands WW1	8	1
Rawlinson H		G	1917-18	4th Mancs Rgmt (Sgt)	5	
Raybould T	Tom	IR	1917	Ex-Wolves & GTFC. S Yorks based WW1	2	
Richards		CF	1918		1	
Richmond W		OR	1918		1	
Rippon T*	Pip	IR	1915-19	GTFC. Brother of Willis	67	21
Rippon W*	Willis	IL	1915-18	Rotherham Co, ex-GTFC. Army.	43	11
Ritchie A		HB	1917	Both apps vs. Notts Co/F (a)	2	
Robinson		G	1918	3rd Mancs Rgmt (Sgt)	1	
Robinson RW*	Ray	OR	1916	Scotswood,later Newcastle U. L Corp in 2/1st Nth Cyclists Corps	2	
Rudd AC*	Archie	OR	1918	Ex-GTFC	1	
Rushby W*	Billy	RH	1915-18	GTFC. Army Pte.	38	
Sagar		IR	1918	vs. Huddersfield T (a)	1	
Sandlin		IR	1918	Ex-Grimsby lge player. WW1 in Coventry area	2	1
Sankey T*	Tom	IL	1918-19	Huthwaite Colliery. Later signed for GTFC.	33	8
Scott JG*	Jack	OL	1918-19	Ex-GTFC	2	
Scrimshaw		OR	1919		1	
Searson		RH	1919	From Mansfield area	1	
Sewell WR	Ronnie	G	1915-16	Burnley. England Int. after war.	44	
Slide R	Bob	IL	1917	Hull C	1	
Smith JE	Stan	OR	1916-19	Ex-Hull C & Bury. Pte in Army	5	
Smith WE*	Walter	G	1917	Manchester C.'Guest' for Fulham,Leicester	1	
Sparham		OR	1915	vs. Derby Co (a)	1	
Spendiff MN*	Martin	G	1915-19	GTFC. WW1 'Stoker'.	4	
Spink J	Jimmy	RH	1916	Newcastle U. Durham Light Infantry WW1	12	
Spink TW*	Tommy	OR	1916-19	GTFC. Brother of Jim,served in Durham Light Infantry, Portsmouth guest	30	1
Spotiswood J		OL	1917	3rd Mancs Rgmt (Pte)	3	
Stainsby C	Colin	IF	1918-19	Grimsby Rov.Borrowed by Leicester F	15	4
Stainsby ST		IF	1917-18	Local. Brother of Colin	15	5
Storer H*	Harry	CF	1919	Eastwood. Later signed for GTFC	8	2
Summers		OL	1919	Bristol C. Hull C 'guest'	1	
Summers P*	Percy	G	1918	GTFC. Footballers Battalion. Sheffield Wed. guest	1	
Sutcliffe CT		G	1916-17	Ex-York C. Army Instructor (Sgt)	34	
Talbot		CF	1918	Borrowed vs. Sheffield U (a)	1	
Taylor		OR	1917	vs. Birmingham (a). Poss. Aston Villa ?	1	
Thompson A*	Alf	IR	1918-19	Grimsby T. 10th Lincs Rgmt ('Chums')	17	4
Thorpe E	Edwin	RB	1918-19	Sheffield Wed, later Lincoln C	4	
Towlson		OL	1918	vs. Sheffield Wed (a)	1	
Waine		CF	1918	CSM in Army	1	
Walker		LH	1917	vs. Leeds C (a)	1	
Walsh P		OR	1915-18	Grimsby T	7	
Ward F	Yaffer	LB	1917-19	Lincoln C	27	3
Warren		OR	1917	Accompanied Benfield. Army Sgt	1	
Webster F	Fred	RB	1915-19	Ex-Gainsborough Trin & Chelsea. L Corp.	88	
Wheelhouse S*	Sid	RB	1915	GTFC. Killed in action. Pte in Ftballrs Batt.	2	
Whitchurch E*	Ernie	LH	1915-18	GTFC. Badly injured elbow during WW1	65	1
White C		OL	1917	Army Pte. Played vs. Barnsley (a)	1	
Whittaker		LH	1917	vs. Birmingham (a). Aston Villa ?	1	
Whitworth		OR	1918	Both apps vs. Hull C	2	
Wightman H		LH	1917	Barnsley,also Chesterfield & Nottm F WW1	1	
Wild		RH	1916	Recruited from Yorks,vs.Bradford C (a). Guest for several clubs	1	
Wilkinson J		RH	1918-19	GTFC	27	1
Wilkinson R		OR	1917	Sgt in Army	3	
Willett HA		IL	1918	Sgt 3rd Dublin Fusiliers. Ex-Irish Inter-Lge fwd. Club Bohemians	1	
Williams T*	Trevor	W	1918	Local,ex-GTFC T amat	2	1
Wilson R		W	1917-18		2	
Wilson W		LB	1917-19	2 apps vs. Hull C (a)	6	
Winship T	Wee	OL	1917	Darlington. Leeds C 'guest'	1	
Woulds S	Sammy	IR	1915-16	Haycroft Rov (Gy),ex-Cleethorpes T	5	1
Young C*	Chris	CF	1915-18		47	35

Opponents are listed in some cases above, as very often during WW1, host clubs loaned their players to away teams.

*Also made Football League appearances for 'The Mariners'

Players of the Second World War (1939-1946)

Sheet 1 **Allard to Fleetwood**

Player		Pos	Years	War Details	A	G
Allard HC	Harry	CF	1942	Ex-GTFC 'A' & YMCA. Aircraftsman	1	1
Allen S	Sid	OL	1940-41	Scunthorpe U	11	
Annables W*	Wally	CF	1940	Carlisle U. Ex-GTFC	1	1
Archer GW	Bill	OL	1942	Lincoln C	1	
Arthur G		IL	1944	Signed after summer trial. From north	1	
Atkinson WH	Bill	IL	1945	Wrexham	1	
Bainbridge R		OR	1940-45	GTFC, 'guested' for Newcastle U	2	1
Baines PC	Peter	IL	1943-46	Wrexham. Ex. Oldham Ath. Amateur	16	5
Baird HHC	Harry	IL	1945	Huddersfield T. N.Ire Int.	4	
Bartholomew R*	Roland	OL	1939-40	Guest' for GTFC	6	3
Bateman A*	Arthur	IL	1944-45	Ex-GTFC.Grimsby Hotspurs.Policeman	7	1
Beattie JM*	Jock	IR	1939-40	Guest' for GTFC	14	4
Bell E	Ernie	IL	1945	Aldershot. POW until Nov 1943. Ex-Hull C & Mansfield T	3	
Bellamy R		G	1945	Sheffield Jnr Lge. GTFC 'A'& Dobsons U	2	
Bellas WJ*	Bill	RH	1945	Notts Co. Later signed after war	1	
Bestall JG*	Jackie	IR	1940	Birmingham Trainer. Ex-GTFC	2	
Betmead HA*	Harry	CH	1939-46	GTFC. Army PTI	40	5
Birch A		IL	1944	Played vs. Sheffield Wed (h). Pos. on books of a Yorks club.	1	
Black A	Andy	IR	1942-43	Hearts & Scotland Int	9	6
Blenkinsopp TW*	Tom	CH	1942-46	GTFC	8	1
Blewitt R		LH	1945	Middlesbrough Amat.	1	
Boyd JM*	Jimmy	OR	1939	GTFC	1	
Bradley G	Gordon	G	1943	Leicester C	3	
Brain HWT	Harry	IR	1942-44	Aston Villa	18	5
Bray E	Eric	OL	1940	Barnsley	2	
Brown J	Jackie	OR	1945	Birmingham & Irish Int. Ex-Wolves & Coventry	2	
Browning F	Freddie	CF	1943-46	Grimsby T 'A'. A war Dock worker	8	3
Buck T*	Teddy	LH	1939-46	GTFC. Auxilliary Fire Service (AFS)	204	7
Burton S	Stan	OR	1940	West Ham U. Ex-Wolves	3	
Butler MP	Malcolm	CF	1942-43	Blackpool. RAF Sgt. Irish Int.	5	1
Bytheway GS	George	IR	1943-44	Ex-Mansfield T, WBA	2	
Candice		IR	1945	Played vs. Sheffield Wed (a)	1	
Canning L	Larry	IR	1944	Paget Rov & Aston Villa amat. Became TV sports presenter	1	
Chadwick H#	Harry	OR	1940-46	GTFC signed from Blackpool. RAF	26	6
Chamberlain H	Harry	CF	1942	Waltham(1942/3).	1	
Charlesworth JSF*	Stan	CH	1939-46	Guest' for GTFC	39	1
Clewlow SJ	Sid	IR	1942-43	Wolves. Based at North Cotes	2	2
Clifton H*	Harry	IR	1946	GTFC. From Newcastle U. England War Int.	13	5
Collins A	Alan	CF	1940	Kilmarnock	2	
Corbett WR	Willie	IR	1945	Celtic & Scotland Int. Royal Navy	1	
Courtier LJ		IR	1943	Burnley. RAF	1	
Crack FW*	Freddie	W	1939-46	GTFC. Royal Armoured Corps Instructor	11	4
D'Arcy W		IL	1944	Wolves. RAF Binbrook	1	
Darley R		CF	1944	Amateur	2	
Davies W	Billy	W	1941-45	Watford	52	12
Dodd RI	Ronnie	IL	1940	Shrewsbury T. Doncaster Rov & Barnsley 'guest'	5	3
Dodds LS*	Les	OL	1942	Hartlepools U.Ex-GTFC	11	
Doherty PD	Peter	IL	1941-43	Man City & N Ire capt. RAF Sgt PTI	26	20
Dolan P		IR	1945	Signed after summer trial. From north	2	
Dorsett R	Dickie	IL	1943-44	Wolves. Bomb rack maker in RAF	12	9
Dunderdale WL	Len	CF	1943-45	Leeds U	27	14
Eastham J		IR	1942-43	Capt of 'The Base' (Gy Lge). A Soldier.	15	3
Ely GBV	George	IR	1942	Grimsby T 'A'. Brother of Lou	1	
Ely L	Lou	CH	1943	Grimsby T 'A'. Royal Navy	1	
Ewing WF		HB	1944	Third Lanark. RAF	2	
Ferguson A	Archie	G	1942	Doncaster Rov	3	
Ferrier RJ	Ron	CF	1941-43	Oldham Ath. Ex GTFC pro,later trainer	29	15
Fields GE	Babs	G	1940-43	Grimsby YMCA	4	
Fisher FT*	Fred	RB	1945	GTFC. Munitions worker WW2	2	
Fleetwood ED	Eddie	IL	1941	Scunthorpe U. Ex Barnsley & Blackburn	4	

Player		Pos	Years	War Details	A	G
Flowers IJ	Ivan	IL	1940-41	Mansfield T. K.I.A. 1944 at Caen.	18	9
Forsyth JG	John	IF	1943-44	Luton T,also Waltham (Gy Lge)	19	4
Foulston JD		IL	1945	Grimsby T 'Colts' & 'A' team	1	1
Fraser HGD		IR	1944	Borrowed vs. Doncaster Rov (a)	1	
Frost J	Jack	G	1940-43	GTFC.4th Royal Engineers (see note)	3	
Gibson R	Reg	HB	1944	Manchester U, in Militia	3	
Gilchrist A	Alex	IL	1943	Cardiff C. Stationed at North Cotes camp	1	
Glaister G	George	IL	1943	Blackburn Rov, based at Waltham	1	
Glass FW		RH	1944-46	Cardiff C, RAF Binbrook	18	1
Gorman JH		CF	1940	A Guardsman	2	1
Gotts JH	Jim	OR	1940	Ashington	1	
Gray R	Ron	RH	1944	Watford, 'guested' for Notts Co & Dundee	7	
Green SS	Stan	IL	1944	Newcastle U, in RAF	7	1
Greenfield H		CF	1942	Dobsons U (Gy Lge)	1	
Grogan J	John	LH	1944-45	Leicester C	5	
Hall AF*	Alec	RH	1939-46	GTFC.Member of AFS	184	22
Harris JB	Jimmy	RH	1941-46	West Ham U. Also Dobsons U (Gy Lge). Boston 1945/6	13	
Harvey W#	Billy	OR	1945-46	GTFC. Royal Engineers Bomb Disposal	4	
Hillard J	Johnny	OR	1940	GTFC.	2	
Hodgson JV*	Jack	LB	1939-46	GTFC.	234	4
Hodgson S*	Sam	RH	1943-46	GTFC. Army PTI	23	
Holland C	Connie	IL	1940	Consol (Gy Lge).Welsh ex-GTFC pro & Swansea T.	2	
Holmes MM*	Max	OL	1939-40	Lincoln C. Ex-GTFC. School teacher. Later Grimsby Hotspurs	15	1
Horden L		CH	1945	Played vs. Lincoln C (h)	1	
Howe F*	Fred	CF	1939-46	GTFC. Navy	20	11
Howshall T	Tom	OR	1940	Stockport Co.,'guested' for 9 other clubs	1	
Hullett WA	Bill	CF	1941	Man U. RAF Corp	1	1
Hurley J		IL	1945	GTFC 'A' trialist	2	
Huxford H	Harry	OR	1944-45	Boston U. Ex-GTFC & Hull C. Son of Gus	7	6
Iggleden H	Ray	IR	1942	Leicester C amat.Royal Marines. RAF Pilot	1	
Jennings HW	Bill	IR	1940-41	Northampton T. RAF	30	10
Johnson H	Harry	CF	1940-44	Scunthorpe U, also Doncaster Rov 'guest'	51	29
Johnson JW*	Jack	OR	1939-46	GTFC. RAF Sgt	15	3
Johnson J*	Jim	CF	1945-46	GTFC, signed from York C	18	6
Johnson R		CF	1945	Watford	1	
Johnston JW	Willie	G	1942	Scottish Lieutenant in Royal Engineers. Morton	2	
Jones R		OL	1946	GTFC 'A'.Local	3	
Jones S	Sam	CH	1944	Blackpool & N Ireland	1	
Jones TW*	Tommy	IL	1939-46	GTFC, a WW2 engineer	19	4
Jones W	Bill	LB	1941	Barnsley reserve, Scunthorpe U.	1	
Joyce ES	Eric	CF	1940	Bradford C amat. WW2 Gunner	1	
Kippax FP	Peter	CF	1942	Burnley & England amat int. RAF Pilot.	4	1
Kurz FJ*	Freddie	CF	1939-45	GTFC.R Artillery at Woolwich Arsenal	17	10
Lamb HE	Harry	IR	1944-45	Tranmere Rov	30	11
Lear S		G	1942	Amateur	1	
Lewis G	Glyn	W	1944-46	C Palace. RAF	20	4
Lilley J	Joe	OR	1942-43	Young serviceman,from N East, war apps. For Sunderland	3	
Little G	George	OL	1940	Doncaster Rov	2	
Logie JT	Jimmy	OR	1940-41	Arsenal reserve, later Scottish int. Navy	5	
Lowrey J	Jim	OR	1944	GTFC Amat. 'Guest' Lincoln C.	1	
Lumby WCW*	Wally	RH	1940-42	Stockport Co. Ex-GTFC. Army PTI	12	2
Mackenzie R	Jock	G	1942	Waltham & RAF Binbrook,a serviceman	4	
Major BB		RH	1944	Grimsby T 'A' 16 year old	1	
Marlow GA	Geoff	IL	1941	Lincoln C	4	
Marsh FK	Frank	W	1941-42	Chester. Based at Waltham. RAF	2	1
Matthewson GT	George	CH	1944	Bury	2	
Maw A	Digger	IL	1940	Scunthorpe U. Ex Leicester & Notts Co	3	
Meek J	Joe	OL	1942	Swansea T. RAF Corp.	1	
Middleton F		G	1941-42	Scunthorpe U	4	
Miller WH		IF	1943	Played vs. Doncaster Rov (h & a)	2	
Millington M	Mal	CH	1940-45	Scunthorpe U. Ex Torquay U. 'Guest' Southport, Lincoln C & Mansfield T	150	
Minto J		RB	1945	Signed in summer after trial.From 'north'.	1	

Sheet 3 **Moody KG to Wood**

Player		Pos	Years	War Details	A	G
Moody KG*	Ken	RB	1941-45	GTFC from Humber U.CSM in REME	12	
Moody R	Ray	IL	1945	Grimsby T 'A',brother of Ken	1	
Moore NW*	Norman	IR	1941-46	Guest' for GTFC.PTI with Devon Rgmt	38	10
Moore TR*	Roy	CH	1941-45	Guest' for GTFC.RAF Bomb Armourer at Binbrook	3	1
Moralee MW*	Matt	IF	1939-43	Shrewsbury T. Ex-GTFC	29	17
Moulson C	Con	RH	1944	Notts Co,ex-GTFC & Lincoln C. Irish Int.	1	
Moulson GB*	George	G	1940-46	GTFC. Lincoln C & Nottm F 'guest'. Brother of Con	109	
Mouncer FE*	Frank	RB	1946	GTFC	3	
Murphy JJ	Jimmy	OR	1941	Man City. RAF	1	
Neish J		IL	1940	A young Scot in the RAF	2	
Nightingale S	Sammy	IF	1941-42	Scunthorpe U ,also Doncaster Rov 'guest'	10	6
Pashley E		OL	1945	A Sheffield youngster, on trial	2	
Pearson S		IR	1940	Man C. A Soldier	3	2
Pearson WGA*	Billy	W	1942-46	RAF,signed player.	25	4
Platts L	Lawrie	G	1942	Mansfield T & Nottingham F amat	3	
Ponting WT*	Wally	CF	1939-40	Ex-GTFC,Grimsby Bor Police	7	1
Pridmore AJ		W	1940-44	Signed from Worksop T 1939. Army. 'Guest' for Bradford C.	11	1
Ranshaw JW	Jack	OL	1942-45	Newark T.Lincoln & Mansfield 'guest'	89	30
Rayner FW	Frank	IF	1942	Notts Co. Ex-Rotherham, Mansfield & Burnley	2	
Reeve FW*	Fred	RH	1939	GTFC. 'Guest' for Southend U	2	
Reeve KE*	Ken	CF	1939-44	GTFC. Royal Marine Sgt Instructor	29	15
Roberts J	John	IR	1939	GTFC pro signed from Scottish Jnr Lge	4	1
Roberts N	Nooky	CF	1944	Humber Utd to GTFC 'A'.Dock worker	1	
Robertson J	Jock	OR	1941	Scotsman living in Scunthorpe	6	
Robertson LV	Len	OR	1945-46	Hartlepools U	4	
Robinson I*	Ike	OL	1940	Ex-GTFC. Grimsby Borough Police	1	
Rodi J#	Joe	CF	1945-46	East Fife.'Guest' then signed for GTFC	34	21
Rook L	Len	OR	1943-45	Young GTFC 'A',pro. Laceby born.	17	3
Rudkin TW	Tom	IL	1941-45	Peterborough U. Ex-Lincoln C, next Arsenal.	23	14
Sackett G		IL	1942	Played vs. Barnsley (a)	1	
Sampson HM	M	OL	1945	A Sheffield youngster, Grimsby T 'A'	1	
Scrimshaw S	Stan	IF	1940-41	Bradford C. RAF Binbrook. Ex-Hartlepool	19	3
Sears DR	Dougie	IR	1943	GTFC. 'Guest' for Portsmouth & Fulham. Later Reading	5	3
Smith J	Jack	G		Sheffield U.Sgt RAF. 'Guest' both Nottingham clubs & Lincoln C.	15	
Squires		CF		Notts Co. Army 'A' side in Gy Lge	1	
Stevenson E	Ernie	CF		Wolves	1	
Stocks C	Cyril	OR	1941	Grantham T. player. Ex Nottm F	3	1
Sweeney FT	Fred	IL	1944	War apps for Everton,Rochdale,Stockport	2	
Swinburne TA	Tom	G	1941	Newcastle U & England war Int	1	
Syred TG	Tom	IF	1940	Gillingham,ex-Burnley	2	2
Tallent EV		OR	1944	Amateur	3	
Taylor GN		G	1940	Ex-Boston U	4	
Taylor WB*	Wally	LB	1944	GTFC. Bevin boy at Cresswell Colliery	1	
Temple W*	Bill	CF	1946	GTFC	1	1
Thomas DWJ	David	IF	1941-42	Plymouth Arg. RAF Binbrook	27	9
Tweedy GJ*	George	G	1939-46	GTFC. Army Infantry	72	
Vincent NE*	Ned	RB	1939-46	GTFC. Auxilliary Fire Service (AFS)	220	21
Vinson SR	Stan	CF	1943-45	GTFC signed from Consol. Later Army	4	2
Wallbanks WH*	Horace	OR	1944	Aberdeen. Signed for GTFC after war	5	1
Ward TEG	Tommy	IR		Mansfield T. Ex-Palace, GTFC, P.Vale & Stoke. Hull C, Leeds U & Dobson (GY Lge)	5	
Wardle W	Billy	OL		GTFC. British Army. 'Guest' Stockport, Hartlepools, Southampton & Swansea	24	2
Wattam F	Frank	LH		GTFC. Later Consolidated FC (Gy Lge).	20	1
White F	Fred	G		Sheffield U. 'Guest' Wrexham, Rotherham U, Sheffield W, Mansfield T & Nott F	1	
Wildman FR	Frank	G	1942	Swindon T	5	
Wilkin LC		G	1940	Ex-Wintringham & England Sch Int.	1	
Williams A		OR	1944	Luton T	3	
Wilson CM	Charlie	OR	1941	Stockport Co. Millwall 'guest'	2	
Witcomb DF	Dougie	HB	1940-41	WBA & Wales Int	8	1
Wood D		LH	1945	Dobsons U & GTFC 'A'	3	

Players war apps and goals are calculated from matches where line-ups are given (including details from the abandoned 1939/40 season and 1945/46 F.A. Cup)

*Also made Football League appearances for 'The Mariners'

#Played in 1945/46 FA Cup, but not in the Football League for 'The Mariners'

Lincolnshire F.A. Senior Cup

Season	Round	Date		Opposition	Score	Goalscorers
1881-82	1	Jan	1	Brigg Ancholme	6-3	Atkinson(2), Marshall(2), Unknown(2)
	2	Feb	18	Louth District	2-2	Earle, Atkinson
	2r	Feb	25	LOUTH DISTRICT	3-0	Unknown
	SF	Mar	25	Brigg Town	0-5	
1882-83	1	Nov	11	BRIGG BRITANNIA	2-1	Monument, Tonge
	2	Jan	6	MAN. SHEFF. & LINCS RAILWAY (STEAMSHIP DEP.)	2-1	Read, Marshall
	SF	Mar	17	Brigg Town	0-3	
1883-84	1	Nov	25	MARKET RASEN	10-1	Noble(2), Monument, T.Atkinson(3), G.Atkinson(2), Grarnham(2)
	2	Jan	5	Brigg Town	3-1	Garnham(2), Monument
	3	Mar	8	BARTON	2-0	Noble, France
	SF	Mar	22	GAINSBOROUGH TRINITY	4-2	Garnham, France, T.Atkinson, Monument
	F	Apr	5	Spilsby (at Brigg)	2-4	Noble, Monument
1884-85	1	Oct	1	MAN. SHEFF. & LINCS RAILWAY (STEAMSHIP DEP.)	3-1*	Read, Unknown(2) *(*MS & LR team left the field during first half, score stood)*
	2	Nov	29	BARTON	2-0	Noble, Raynes
	3	Jan	10	Lough and District	2-1	Monument, Garnham
	SF	Jan	31	Gainsborough Trinity	1-2	Garnham
1885-86	1	Nov	7	GRANTHAM VICTORIA	2-0	H.Atkinson, Seal
	2	Nov	28	Lincoln Rangers	5-0	Seal, H.Atkinson, (Opp. OG)
	3	Jan	23	Grantham Town	3-1	Monument, Garnham, H.Atkinson
	SF	Mar	13	LINCOLN CITY	1-1*	Monument *(* Grimsby awarded match, Lincoln refused to play extra-time,)*
	F	Apr	3	Lincoln Lindum (at Grantham)	2-0	H.Atkinson(2) *(Trophy withheld)*
1886-87	1	Nov	27	LINCOLN ST. SWITHIN'S	15-0	Seal(3),Pearson(3),H.Atkinson(2),Garnham(2),H.Taylor(2),C.Atkinson,Hall,J.H.Taylor
	2	Jan	19	Morton St. Paul's (at Grimsby Rangers Ground)	19-0	Unknown
	3			Bye		
	4	Feb	19	GRANTHAM TOWN	5-1	Seal(2), Monument, Pearson, Chapman
	SF	Mar	12	BRIGG TOWN	4-0	Monument(3), Seal
	F	Apr	2	Lincoln City (at Gainsborough Trinity)	2-2	Chapman, H.Atkinson
	Fr	Apr	23	Lincoln City (at Gainsborough Trinity)	0-2	
1887-88	1	Oct	29	LINCOLN RANGERS	10-0	Soames(3), Seal(2), Monument(2), Smith, J.Chapman, Unknown
	2	Dec	8	Horncastle United	2-1	McBeth, H.Atkinson
	3	Jan	14	GAINSBOROUGH TRINITY	5-0	Lee(2), H.Atkinson, Soames, Monument
	SF	Feb	18	Cleethorpes Town	3-0 *	H.Atkinson(2), Lee *(*Grimsby Town resigned from Lincs. FA. Final not played)*
1888-89	1	Jan	26	GRANTHAM TOWN	2-1	J.Taylor, Lundie
	SF	Mar	2	Lincoln Ramblers	5-0	McBeth(2), Smith, Riddoch, Hunt
	F	Apr	13	Grantham Rovers (at Boston)	3-1	Hunt(2), Doyle
1889-90				Grimsby Town scratched.		
1890-91	SF	Feb	14	GAINSBOROUGH TRINITY	1-2	Reid
				Grimsby Town did not enter for 1891-92 to 1895-96 seasons inclusive		
1896-97	1	Mar	16	GAINSBOROUGH TRINITY	2-1	McCairns(2)
	SF	Apr	1	Grimsby All Saints (played at unknown venue)	2-1	Unknown
	F	Apr	29	LINCOLN CITY	6-2	Fletcher(3), Gray, McCairns, Higgins
1897-98	1	Feb	19	GRIMSBY ALL SAINTS	4-0 *	McCairns(2), Gray, Goldie *(* Match void - Grimsby included an ineligible player)*
	1r	Mar	28	Grimsby All Saints (played at unknown venue)	7-0	Emmerson(2), Rogers, McCairns(2), Unknown, OG
	SF	Apr	13	LINCOLN ADELAIDE	0-4	
1898-99	2	Mar	1	Horncastle United	6-1	Unknown
	SF	Apr	19	GRIMSBY ALL SAINTS	5-2	Cockshutt(2), Jenkinson, Richards
	F	Apr	27	Gainsborough Trinity (at Lincoln)	4-0	Unknown
1899-1900	SF	Apr	5	Gainsborough Trinity	0-0	
	SFr	Apr	19	GAINSBOROUGH TRINITY	4-1	Hemingfield(2), Ratcliffe(2)
	F	Apr	24	LINCOLN ADELAIDE	6-4	Hemingfield(2), Ratcliffe(2), Griffiths, Richards
1900-01	SF	Mar	21	GAINSBOROUGH TRINITY	3-1	Fletcher, Mellor, Richards
	F	Apr	29	Lincoln City	1-0	Watkins
1901-02	SF	Apr	7	Lincoln City	1-1	Fletcher
	SFr	Apr	17	LINCON CITY	3-0	Dean, Ronaldson, Hemingfield
	F	Apr	24	GAINSBOROUGH TRINITY	1-0	Fletcher
1902-03	SF	Mar	5	GAINSBOROUGH TRINITY	2-2	Gray, Mountain
	SFr	Mar	30	Gainsborough Trinity	2-1	Hall, Unknown
	F	Apr	29	Lincoln City	1-1	Unknown
	Fr	Apr	30	LINCOLN CITY	3-2	Wilkinson(2), Rouse
1903-04	SF	Mar	16	Lincoln City	1-2	Unknown
1904-05	SF	Mar	30	GRIMSBY RANGERS	2-2	Baker, Reynolds
	SFr	Apr	11	Grimsby Rangers	2-1	Baker(2)
	F	Apr	26	Gainsborough Trinity	0-1	
1905-06	SF	Mar	28	LINCOLN CITY	1-0	Padley
	F	Apr	24	GAINSBOROUGH TRINITY	4-1	Bisby, Robinson, Baker, Hooper
1906-07	SF	Feb	2	LINCOLN ADELAIDE	6-1	R.Morris(3), Burnett, Rodger, Hooper
	F	Apr	17	Gainsborough Trinity	0-1	
1907-08	SF	Nov	13	Gainsborough Trinity	0-3	
1908-09	SF	Sep	29	GAINSBOROUGH TRINITY	5-0	Leonard(2), Davidson, Coxon, Bradley
	F	Dec	28	Lincoln City	2-1	Appleyard, Satterthwaite
1909-10	SF	Nov	24	Gainsborough Trinity	1-0	Blackburn
	F	Feb	5	Lincon City	0-4	
1910-11	SF	Mar	7	LINCOLN CITY	2-1	Springthorpe, Hubbard
	F	Mar	21	GAINSBOROUGH TRINITY	0-1	

Season	Round	Date	Opposition	Score	Goalscorers
1911-12	SF	Jan 13	GRIMSBY ROVERS	6-0	Seeburg(3), Hubbard(2), Rippon
	F	Mar 6	LINCOLN CITY	0-1	
1912-13	SF	Mar 8	Boston United	7-1	Andrews(3), Mayson(2), Gordon, Duncan
	F	Apr 28	Lincoln City	3-2	Rippon(3)
1913-14	SF	Jan 31	Lincoln City	1-2	Unknown
1919-20	SF	Mar 29	Gainsborough Trinity	4-0	Storer(4)
	F	May 3	Lincoln City	0-7	
1920-21	SF	Mar 29	Gainsborough Trinity	0-0	
	SFr	Apr 12	GAINSBOROUGH TRINITY	1-0	Smith
	F	Apr 27	LINCOLN CITY	4-1	Smith, Macauley, Collier, Deacey
1921-22	SF	Mar 16	Lincoln City	2-2	Carmichael, Miller
	SFr	Mar 22	LINCOLN CITY	0-1	
1922-23	4	Jan 11	GRIMSBY ROVERS	3-0	J.Miller(3)
	SF	Mar 15	Boston United	1-0	J.Miller
	F	Apr 30	LINCOLN CITY	2-1	Carmichael(2)
1923-24	4	Feb 7	SCUNTHORPE UNITED	2-0	Carmichael(2)
	SF	Mar 6	CLEETHORPES TOWN	6-0	Casson(4), Marshall, Dent
	F	Apr 14	Lincoln City	0-1	
1924-25	4	Jan 22	Grantham Town	1-1	Thain
	4r	Feb 19	GRANTHAM TOWN	6-1	Carmichael(4), Burley(2)
	SF	Mar 19	Scunthorpe United	2-2	Carmichael(2)
	SFr	Apr 2	SCUNTHORPE UNITED	1-1	Marshall
	SF2r	Apr 20	Scunthorpe United	3-0	Carmichael(2), Marshall
	F	Apr 23	Boston United	1-0	Carmichael
1925-26	4	Jan 12	SCUNTHORPE UNITED	6-3	Robson(3), McKenna, Carmichael, Devan
	SF	Jan 26	LINCOLN CITY	0-1	
1926-27	3	Feb 1	LINCOLN CITY	1-3	Devan
1927-28	3	Jan 24	GAINSBOROUGH TRINITY	2-0	Coglin, Powell
	SF	Feb 28	SCUNTHORPE UNITED	7-1	Robson(6), Prior
	F	Apr 24	Lincoln City	3-1	Robson(3)
1928-29	SF	Mar 12	GAINSBOROUGH TRINITY	5-0	Coglin(2), Twell, Marshall, Prior
	F	May 11	Lincoln City	1-0	Robson
1929-30	SF	Feb 25	GAINSBOROUGH TRINITY	5-1	Glover(3), Prior, Coleman
	F	May 10	LINCOLN CITY	7-1	Robson(6), Marshall
1930-31	SF	Mar 14	GAINSBOROUGH TRINITY	4-1	Coleman(2), Bestall, Hall
	F	May 9	Lincoln City	2-2	Glover, Prior
	Fr	Sep 22	LINCOLN CITY	0-1	
1931-32	SF	Mar 15	GAINSBOROUGH TRINITY	7-1	Chalmers(3), Moralee(2), Craven(2)
	F	May 14	Lincoln City	1-1	Holmes
	Fr	Sep 13	LINCOLN CITY	3-4	Glover(2), Dodsworth
1932-33	SF	Mar 16	SCUNTHORPE UNITED	4-1	Moralee(2), Wilson, Glover
	F	Apr 25	LINCOLN CITY	3-1	Craven(2), Glover
1933-34	SF	Mar 20	SCUNTHORPE UNITED	7-1	Craven(3), Glover(2), Jennings, OG
	F	Apr 26	LINCOLN CITY	2-2	Glover, Craven
	Fr	May 3	Lincoln City	1-2	Holmes
1934-35	F	Sep 24	Lincoln City	0-5	
1935-36	F	Sep 24	LINCOLN CITY	4-0	Craven(2), Jennings, OG
1936-37	F	Sep 23	Lincoln City	6-1	Tomlinson(3), Lewis(2), Hinchcliffe
1937-38	F	Sep 28	LINCOLN CITY	4-1	Bestall(2), Hinchcliffe, Tomlinson
1938-39			Withdrew		
1945-46	F	May 1	LINCOLN CITY	1-1	N.Moore
	Fr	May 11	Lincoln City	1-4	Vincent
1946-47	F	May 21	Lincoln City	2-1	Clifton(2)
1947-48	F	May 8	LINCOLN CITY	0-2	
1948-49	F	May 14	Lincoln City	1-2	Cairns
1949-50	F	May 13	LINCOLN CITY	2-1	Cairns(2)
1950-51	F	May 19	Lincoln City	0-3	
1951-52	SF	Mar 31	Scunthorpe United	0-1	
1952-53	SF	Apr 15	Lincoln City	3-0	Maddison(2), Lord
	F	May 9	SCUNTHORPE UNITED	1-0	Hernon
1953-54	F	May 8	Scunthorpe United	2-4	Wright, F.Smith
1954-55	SF	Oct 19	Lincoln City	0-2	
1955-56	SF	Oct 18	LINCOLN CITY	1-2	Evans
1956-57	SF	Oct 16	BOSTON UNITED	0-2	
1957-58	SF	Oct 8	Boston United	3-1	Rafferty, Evans, Reeson
	F	May 5	SCUNTHORPE UNITED	2-3	Rafferty(2)
1958-59	SF	Oct 9	Scunthorpe United	1-2	Fell
1959-60	SF	Oct 27	Boston United	1-2	Rafferty
1960-61	SF	Nov 7	LINCOLN CITY	8-3	Rafferty(6), Scott, Williams
	F	Mar 6	SCUNTHORPE UNITED	0-4	
1961-62	SF	Oct 17	SCUNTHORPE UNITED	0-1	
1962-63			Not entered		
1963-64	SF	Apr 28	Scunthorpe United	0-3	
1964-65			Believed not entered		
1965-66	SF	Mar 29	Lincoln City	1-1*	Green *(*No replay date agreed, Lincoln City 'won' on toss of coin)*
1966-67	SF	Nov 7	SCUNTHORPE UNITED	2-3	Collins, Worthington

Season	Round	Date		Opposition	Score	Goalscorers
1967-68	SF	Nov	7	GAINSBOROUGH TRINITY	3-1	Collins, Boylen, OG
	F	Mar	26	Lincoln City	3-2	Boylen, Collins, Wilson
1968-69	1	Oct	23	LINCOLN CITY	0-0	
	1r	Oct	29	Lincoln City	1-1*	Rathbone *(*aet)*
	1,2r	Mar	31	Lincoln City	2-3	Brace, Williams
1969-70	1	Sep	22	Gainsborough Trinity	2-3	Fletcher, Oates
1970-71	SF	Mar	1	LINCOLN CITY	3-1	Brace(2), Lewis
	F	May	11	Gainsborough Trinity	0-1	
1971-72	SF	May	3	Grantham	1-2	Rathbone
1972-73	1	Oct	17	GRANTHAM	3-2	Lewis, Brace, Gauden
	SF	Dec	20	GAINSBOROUGH TRINITY	1-0	Chatterley
	F	May	1	BOSTON UNITED	2-1	Brace, Hubbard
1973-74	QF	May	7	Scunthorpe United	1-2	Hubbard
1974-75	QF	Jan	7	GRANTHAM	2-1	Barton, Lewis
	SF	Mar	11	GAINSBOROUGH TRINITY	2-0	Hubbard, Boylen
	F	Apr	29	Lincoln City	0-2	
1975-76	QF	Aug	2	LINCOLN CITY	3-2	Wigg(3)
	SF	Aug	7	Scunthorpe United	4-1	Partridge, Lewis, OG(2)
	F	Aug	12	Gainsborough Trinity	1-0	Partridge
From 1976-77 season, early round matches played in qualifying groups (GM - group matches)						
1976-77	GM	Jul	31	LINCOLN CITY	1-2	Waters
	GM	Aug	7	SCUNTHORPE UNITED	1-3	Lewis
1977-78	GM	Jul	30	LINCOLN CITY	2-2	Cumming, Drinkell
	GM	Aug	6	Scunthorpe United	1-4	Liddell
1978-79	GM	Aug	1	Scunthorpe United	0-1	
	GM	Aug	5	LINCOLN CITY	0-1	
1979-80	GM	Jul	3	SCUNTHORPE UNITED	2-1	Liddell, K.Moore
	GM	Aug	6	Lincoln City	0-0	
	F	Oct	16	GAINSBOROUGH TRINITY	1-0*	Brolly *(*aet)*
1980-81	GM	Jul	29	Lincoln City	0-1	
	GM	Jul	30	Scunthorpe United	2-1	Cumming, Drinkell
1981-82	GM	Aug	11	SCUNTHORPE UNITED	1-1	K.Moore
	GM	Aug	12	Lincoln City	0-1	
1982-83	GM	Aug	7	Scunthorpe United	1-1	Kilmore
	GM	Aug	9	LINCOLN CITY	0-4	
1983-84	GM	Jan	30	LINCOLN CITY	5-0	Drinkell(2), K.Moore(2), Emson
	GM	Mar	19	Boston United	3-2	Shearer(2), Drinkell
	F	May	14	GAINSBOROUGH TRINITY	2-2*	Lund, Bonnyman *(*Grimsby won 5-3 in penalty shoot out, no extra time played)*
1984-85	GM	Jul	31	Gainsborough Trinity	2-4	Lund, Wilkinson
	GM	Aug	7	SCUNTHORPE UNITED	1-1	Wilkinson
1985-86	GM	Aug	3	Boston United	3-5	Gilligan(2), Crombie
	GM	Aug	12	GRANTHAM TOWN	1-0	Peake
Group matches discontinued, knock out rounds started from 1986-87 season)						
1986-87	SF	Aug	13	Boston United	4-0	Walsh(2), Horwood(2)
	F	Nov	11	SCUNTHORPE UNITED	2-1	Rawcliffe(2)
1987-88	SF	Aug	4	LINCOLN CITY	1-3	Turner
1988-89	SF	Aug	10	Boston United	0-0*	*(*Boston United won 4-2 on penalties)*
1989-90	SF	Aug	16	Gainsborough Trinity	1-0	Gilbert
	F	May	1	SPALDING UNITED	2-0	Alexander, Gilbert
1990-91	GM	Jul	31	Boston United	2-1	Rees, Childs
	GM	Aug	4	Grantham Town	2-0	Hargreaves, Cunnington
	F	May	13	Lincoln City	2-3	Smith(2)
1991-92	1	Jul	30	GRANTHAM TOWN	4-0	Jobling, Cockerill, Lever, Smith
	SF	Aug	3	Lincoln City	2-1	Rees, Smith
	F*	Oct	16	Boston United	6-1	Hargreaves, Watson(2), Childs(2), Rees *(*'Final played in October 1992)*
1992-93	SF	Aug	11	GAINSBOROUGH TRINITY	2-0	Gilbert, Woods
	F*	Jul	31	Boston United	1-0	Rees *(*'92-93 matches played almost a year apart)*
1993-94	SF	Aug	10	SCUNTHORPE UNITED	2-0	Mendonca, Dobbin
	F	Nov	23	BOSTON UNITED	1-0	Futcher
1994-95	1	Jul	30	Grantham Town	3-2	OG, Gilbert, Lever
	SF	Aug	6	LINCOLN CITY	2-0	Groves, Livingstone
	F	Nov	9	Boston United	5-3	Rees(2), Lester(2), S.Buckley
1995-96	GM(N)	Jul	20	Scunthorpe United	3-0	Childs, Livingstone, Dobbin
	GM(N)	Aug	7	Gainsborough Trinity	0-0*	*(*Grimsby went through on toss of coin)*
	F	Dec	6	Boston United	4-1	Shakespeare(2), Walker, Forrester
1996-97	1	Jul	24	Gainsborough Trinity	1-0	OG
	SF	Aug	13	Grantham Town	3-0	Childs, Laws, Forrester
	F	Dec	10	Scunthorpe United	3-3*	Black, Wrack, Lester *(*No extra-time, Scunthorpe won 5-4 on penalties)*
1997-98	1	Jul	30	Lincoln City	1-3	Clare
1998-99	1	Jul	26	Boston United	1-0*	Wrack *(*aet)*
	SF	Aug	5	Stamford	0-3	
1999-2000	1	Jul	30	Gainsborough Trinity	0-0*	*(*Grimsby won 4-1 on penalties)*
	SF	Feb	9	Boston United	2-1	Rowan, McKenzie
	F	May	3	LINCOLN UNITED	3-3*	Clare, Black, Allen *(*Grimsby won 4-2 on penalties)*

Other Matches 1878 - 2000

This section includes friendly matches (where details are known), charity and invitation trophies, testimonial and benefit games in which 'The Mariners' have contested. Also included are minor tournaments (where a Reserve XI was usually fielded), and tour matches. (Grimsby Town score first)

1878/79

2 Nov v Britannia and Brigg (a) 0-2
v Britannia and Brigg (h) 1-4
(Goalscorer: Monument)

1879/80

2nd game v Hull Town (a) 1-2

P	W	D	L	F	A
15	6	3	6	21	15

(Games v Lincoln, Gainsborough, Brigg, Grantham & Spilsby)

1880/81

P	W	D	L	F	A
12	6	4	2	(unknown)	

(Games v Louth T)

1881/82

P	W	D	L	F	A
19	9	3	7	49	42

(Games v Hull T, Louth T, Brigg T, Barton, Spilsby & Basford Rovers)

1882/83

v Leicester Fosse
v Lincoln Albion (a)
21 Oct v Louth (a) 6-1
28 Oct v Lincoln Rovers 1-3 (a)
2 Dec v Brigg Town 5-0 (h)
16 Dec v Hull Town 0-6 (a)
23 Dec v Lincoln Rovers 7-1 (h)
30 Dec v Nottm. Forest 2-2 (a)
13 Jan v Spilsby 5-0 (h)
27 Jan v Hull Town 6-1 (h)
10 Feb v Louth 2-7 (a)
17 Feb v Sheffield Pyebank (a) 0-4
3 Mar v Brigg Town 3-5 (a)
17 Mar v Spilsby 1-1 (a)
26 Mar v Sheffield Pyebank (h) 2-0
31 Mar v Nottm. Forest 5-0 (h)

1883/84

v Nottingham F (h) 1-5

P	W	D	L	F	A
33	17	5	11	86	61

1884/85

(10 Notts. clubs visited Cleethorpes)
20 Sep v Blackburn Olympic (h) 0-9
v Manchester Greenways (h) 4-0

P	W	D	L	F	A
33	17	5	11	55	47

1885/86

26 Sep v Lincoln City (a) 2-2
v Gainsborough Trinity (h) 2-2

P	W	D	L	F	A
38	30	6	2	118	27

1886/87

24 Nov v Preston NE (h) 0-3
(att; 6,000 Clee Park record)
11 Dec v Blackburn Rovers (h) 1-1

P	W	D	L	F	A
42	26	6	10	152	50

1887/88

24 Sep v Lincoln City (a) 1-3
14 Apr v Gainsborough Trinity (h) 1-6

P	W	D	L	F	A
47	31	4	12	156	56

v Derby Co., Wolverhampton Wands., Bolton Wands., Stoke, Notts County, Nottingham Forest, Small Heath, Rossendale, Long Eaton Rangers, Lockwood Bros. (Sheffield), Mitchell St. Georges' and Owlerton (all at home).

1888/89

12 Jan v Staveley (h)
30 Mar v West Brom Alb (a) 0-4
9 Apr v Rotherham T (h) 8-0
(Floodlight trial)
16 Apr v Boston (h) 5-1
(Floodlight Trial)

1889/90

v Bolton W., Sunderland, Derby Co., Burnley, Motherwell & Clyde.
7 Sep v West Brom Alb (h) 6-1
(Abbey Park opening)
30 Sept v Sheffield United (a) 1-3
12 Oct v Sheffield United (h) 3-1
26 Oct v Middlesbrough (a) 2-5
16 Nov v Burton Wanderers (h) 3-1
14 Dec v Lincoln City (a) 0-0
25 Dec v Nottingham Jardines (h) 7-1
Christmas games v Small Heath, Nottingham Forest & London Casuals.
28 Dec v London Casuals (h) 5-2
2 Jan v Moss End Swifts (h) 1-0
4 Jan v Newton Heath (a) 1-4
11 Jan v Lincoln City (h) 3-1
15 Feb v. Sheffield United (h) 7-0
8 Mar v Rotherham Swifts (h) 3-2
15 Mar v Gainsborough Trinity (h) 3-1
29 Mar v Newcastle East End (h) 0-2
7 Apr v Clapton Orient (h) 2-0
9 Apr v Gainsborough Trinity (a) 0-0
24 Apr v Notts. County (h) 1-1
24 Apr v Notts Co (h) 1-1
26 Apr v Accrington (h) 1-1
3 May v Lincoln City (h) 0-1
24 May v Lincoln City (a) 1-1

1890/91

11 Oct v Lincoln City (a) 1-2
28 Oct v Lincoln City (h) 0-1
(Lundie Benefit)
8 Nov v Lincoln City (h) 3-5

1891/92

v 'A Canadian Team' (h) 4-0
5 Sept v Lincoln City (h) 3-3
9 Sept v Lincoln City (a) 0-1
30 Apr v Lincoln City (a) 1-0
Dec v Royal Scots of York (h), won
Dec v Cambuslang (h), won

1892/93

P	W	D	L	F	A
22	13	4	5	71	57

29 Sept v Lincoln City (at Mablethorpe) 2-2
20 Oct v Lincoln City (h) 5-3
26 Nov v Lincoln City (a) 6-3
24 Mar v Lincoln City (h) 4-2
26 Apr v Lincoln City (a) 3-2
29 Apr v Notts Co (h) 3-1
v Sheffield U (at Hull), lost.
(Hull Hospital Cup, floodlight trial)

1893/94

Played 16 friendlies
v Lincoln C (a) 2-1
21 Sep v Nottinghamshire XI (h) 5-1
(Ackroyd Benefit)
Xmas v Royal Scots (h) 2-1
17 Mar v Grimsby All Saints (h) 1-1
Apr v Long Eaton Rangers (h) 5-3
(Lincoln Cup, played at John O'Gaunts Ground, Lincoln)
28 Apr v Grimsby All Saints (a) 1-6

1894/95

v Blackburn Rovers (h) 4-0
Xmas v Royal Scots (h) 6-0
Feb v United Hull (a) 9-1
(Widows/Orphans Fund)
Feb v Kirkley (a) 12-0
Feb v Millwall (a) 2-2
Feb v Luton Town (a)2-4
2 Mar v Notts Co (h) 4-0
Apr v Woolwich Arsenal (a) 2-1
2 Apr v Blackburn Rovers (h) 4-0

1895/96

No records traced.

1896/97

13 Feb v Newcastle U (a) 0-4
v West Brom Alb (h) 5-2
(Higgins Benefit)

1897/98
7 Sep v Newcastle U (a) 2-6
15 Sep v Newcastle U (h) 4-4
8 Jan v Notts Co (h) 2-1
1898/99
1 Sep v Notts Co (h) 1-2
20 Oct v Notts Co (a) 1-3
1899/1900
1900/01 No records traced.
1901/02 No records traced.
1902/03 No records traced.
1903/04
8 Sep v Notts Co (h) 4-3
Xmas v Edinburgh St. Bernard's (h) 5-1
30 Apr v Notts Co (h) 2-2
1904/05
24 Nov v Hull City (a) 2-4
21 Apr v Hull City (h) 2-1
1905/06 No records traced.
1906/07
30 Apr v Notts Co (h) 0-2
1907/08 No records traced.
1908/09 No records traced.
1909/10 No records traced.
1910/11
13 Sep v Notts Co (h) 2-1
20 Sep v Hull C (h) 2-2
25 Oct v Leicester F (h) 3-1
17 Dec v Chesterfield T (a) 3-4
1911/12
20 Sep v Hull C (h) 2-2
1917/18
8 sep v 3rd Manchester Regt. 2-2
1919/20
9 May v Hull C (a) 1-3
(Hull Hospital Cup)
1921/22
27 Mar v Lincoln C (a) 3-3
(Wilson Lincoln Hospital Cup)
4 Apr v Lincoln C (h) 5-1 (replay)
24 Apr v Hull C (h) 0-2 *(Spink Benefit)*
1922/23
v New Hucknall Colliery (h) 2-1
6 Nov v Manchester C. (h) 1-1
(Hickson Benefit)
1923/24
Sept v Scunthorpe United (a) 3-2
(New Stand Opening)
28 Apr v Boston (a) 1-0
(Boston Hospital Cup)
1924/25
v Scunthorpe United 1-0 *
v Boston 2-0 *
v Lincoln City 0-3 *
* *(RAF Cranwell Memorial Trophy)*
(venues and dates unknown)
v Leeds United (h) 2-1
(Affleck Benefit)
16 Apr v Hull C (a) 0-0 *(Offside rule Trial)*

(1924/25 contd.)
21 Apr v Hull C (h) 2-4 *(Offside rule Trial)*
30 Apr v Boston (a) 0-0
(Boston Hospital Cup)
1925/26
v Scunthorpe United (a) 1-5
(RAF Cranwell Memorial Trophy)
Apr v Boston (a) 1-3
(Boston Hospital Cup)
27 Apr v Hull C (h) 0-4
(Carmichael Benefit)
1926/27
30 Sep v Hull C (a) 1-4
(Hamilton Benefit)
25 Apr v Boston (a) 2-1
(Boston Hospital Cup)
3 May v Hull C (h) 3-1
(Grimsby Hospital Cup)
1927/28
28 Jan v Burnley (h) 4-4
Apr v Scunthorpe United (a) 3-0
(Scunthorpe Utd. Debt Liquidation Fund)
Apr v Rotherham United (a) 5-0
(Benefit Match)
19 Apr v Boston (a) 3-1
(Boston Hospital Cup)
3 May v Leicester C (h) 4-5 (aet.)
(90 mins 3-3) *(Grimsby Hospital Cup)*
1928/29
v Rotherham (h) 6-3
(venue and date unknown)
Apr v Boston (a) 2-2
(Boston Hospital Cup)
5 May v Boston (a) 2-2
(Boston Hospital Cup)
6 May v Leicester C (h) 1-2
(aet. 90 mins 1-1) *(Grimsby Hospital Cup)*
1929/30
(Marshall Test)
29 Apr v Leicester C (h) 1-2
(Grimsby Hospital Cup) (Reserve team)
1930/31
20 Apr v Notts Co (h) 2-4
(Grimsby Hospital Cup)
28 Apr v Sheffield U (at Spalding) 6-0
(Spalding Nursing Cup)
1931/32
25 Apr v Northampton T (a) 2-5
(Maloney Benefit)
1932/33
27 Sep v Leicester C (@ Spalding) 2-7
(Spalding Nursery Cup)
3 May v Northampton T (h) 6-2
(Grimsby Hospital Cup)
4 May v Boston (a) 3-0
1933/34
26 Feb v Torquay U (a) 2-4
23 Apr v Hull C (a) 4-2
(Goldsmith Benefit)

(1933/34 contd.)
30 Apr v Gainsborough Trin (a) 2-2
(Kells Benefit)
1 May v Norwich C (h) 3-0
(Grimsby Hospital Cup)
7 May v Norwich C (a) 2-7
(Norwich Hospital Cup)
1934/35
6 May v Sheffield Wed (h) 3-0
(Grimsby Hospital Cup)
1935/36
30 Apr v Doncaster Rov (a) 3-1
(Emery/Smith Benefit)
9 May v Bolton W (h) 1-0
(Grimsby Hospital Cup)
1936/37
7 Apr v Scarborough (a) 3-3
10 Apr v Crystal Palace (a) 3-6
28 Apr v Lincoln C (a) 2-2
(MacPhail/ Whyte Benefit)
4 May v Leicester C (h) 5-2
(Grimsby Hospital Cup)
1937/38
22 Jan v Newcastle U (a) 3-3
9 May v Hull C (h) 7-3
(Grimsby Hospital Cup)
1938/39
20 Aug v Lincoln C (a) 1-2
(Football League Jubilee Fund)
22 Aug v Chesterfield (a) 0-0
(Markham Colliery Disaster Fund)
29 Apr v Chelmsford C (a) 2-4
8 May v Newcastle U (h) 3-2
(Grimsby Hospital Cup)
1939/40
19 Aug v Lincoln C (h) 3-2
v Leeds U (h) 5-5
30 Sep v Bradford PA (a) 2-4
7 Oct v Barnsley (a) 2-2
14 Oct v Leeds U (a) 2-2
25 Dec v Hull C (h) 1-5
26 Dec v Hull C (a) 0-0
13 Jan v Huddersfield T (a) 0-1
2 Mar v Hull C (a) 2-4
1940/41
4 Oct v Peterborough U (h) 6-0
3 Apr v RAF (at Scunthorpe Utd)
1941/42
v RAF XI (h) 2-2
1945/46
2 May v Scunthorpe Utd. (a) 0-5
1946/47
26 May v Hull C (a) 0-1
(E.Riding Co FA Invitation Trophy)
1947/48
24 Jan v Rotherham U (at Doncaster) 3-4
28 Feb v Barnsley (h) 0-2
3 May v Hull C (a) 3-1 (aet. 90 mins 1-1)
(E.Riding Co FA Invitation Cup)

1948/49
19 Feb v Glasgow Celtic (h) 0-1
1949/50
11 Feb v Blackburn Rov (a) 4-4
1 May v Wigan Ath (a) 5-3
1950/51
10 Feb v Chesterfield (a) 3-1
30 Feb v Boston U (a) 2-0
12 May v Saarbrucken (Germany) (h) 1-2
(Festival of Britain)
1951/52
1 May v Lincoln C (h) 1-2
10 May v St. Mirren (a) *(Paisley Cup)* 3-4
1952/53
11 Mar v Blackburn Rov (h) 3-4
(Opening Floodlights)
24 Mar v Falkirk (h) 3-1
20 Apr v Preston N.E. *(Tweedy Ben.)* (h)
1953/54
13 Oct v Burnley (h) 1-0
27 Oct v Norwich C (h) 1-1
4 Nov v Luton T (h) 1-2
17 Nov v Rotherham U (h) 2-2
23 Feb v Army North Command (h) 3-0
23 Mar v Lincoln C (h) 1-1
22 Apr v Past Mariners XI (h) 4-4
26 Apr v Hull C (h) 1-0
(E.Riding Co FA Invit.Trophy - 1st leg)
27 Apr v Scottish Command (h) 2-2
29 Apr v Hull C (a) 1-0
(E.Riding Co FA Invit. Trophy - 2nd leg)
1954/55
5 Oct v RAC Catterick (h) 6-2
2 Nov v International XI (h) 6-4
17 Nov v Linfield (h) 2-0
23 Nov v Army Northern Command (h) 2-4
2 May v All Star XI (h) 4-4
(Johnston/Maddison Benefit)
1955/56
13 Mar v All Star XI (h)*(Brown Ben.)* 3-4
1956/57
30 Oct v Hull C (a) 1-1
22 Jan v Army Northern Command (h) 7-1
4 Mar v Akademisk Boldclub(Den)(h) 3-0
26 Mar v Hull C (h) 5-1 *(Conner Test)*
27 Apr v Sheffield Wed (h) 1-1
29 Apr v Scunthorpe U *(Benefit)* (a) 1-2
1957/58
Czechoslovakia Tour
6 May v Czech World Cup XI 1-1
13 May v Tartan Prezov 0-2
22 May v Spartak Pilsen 1-2
24 May v Spartak Usti 2-2
1958/59
16 Oct v Prague Dynamo (Czech.) 0-1
1959/60
30 Jan v Lincoln C (a) 2-1
5 May v Scunthorpe U (h) 1-1
(Refugee Appeal)

1960/61
18 Oct v All Star XI (h) 4-3
(Evans Memorial)
25 Nov v Millwall (a) 4-2
9 Jan v Bishop Auckland (h) 6-4
4 May v Gainsborough Trin (a)
(Oxby Benefit)
1961/62
12 Aug v Scunthorpe United (h) 2-2
4 Dec v British Police XI (h) 4-0
Czechoslovakian Tour
11 May v Pilsner Spartak 2-0
13 May v Slovan Liberec 4-0
14 May v Jiskra 9-1
16 May v Pardubice 1-2
18 May v SONP Kladno 2-2
20 May v Slovan Teplice 2-1
1962/63
10 Aug v Lincoln C (a) 2-0
26 Jan v Sheffield Wed (h) 2-2
1 Mar v Millwall (a) 0-3
1963/64
14 Aug v Lincoln C (a) 3-4
19 Aug v Leicester C (h) 1-1
25 Jan v Hibernian (h) 3-0
9 Mar v All Star XI (h) 4-5
1964/65
12 Aug v Lincoln C (a) 6-2
14 Aug v Lincoln C (h) 5-1
26 Apr v Oxford U (a) 1-0
1965/66
7 Aug v Bishop Auckland (h) 4-1
9 Aug v Darlington (a) 3-1
13 Aug v Darlington (h) 0-1
1966/67
6 Aug v Huddersfield T (h) 2-0
13 Aug v Bishop Auckland (h) 0-2
15 Aug v Derby Co (h) 1-1
17 Aug v Brigg T (a) 6-0
11 Mar v Queen of the South (h) 1-1
13 Mar v Boston U (a)
1967/68
4 Aug v Queen of the South (a) 3-4
8 Aug v Gainsborough Trin. (a) 2-0
9 Aug v York City (h) 2-4
12 Aug v Bishop Auckland (h) 3-0
27 Jan v Darlington (h) 2-1
17 Feb v Sunderland (h) 2-2
1968/69
27 Jul v Nottingham F (h) 3-1
29 Jul v Rotherham U (h) 2-0
v Brigg T (a)
5 Aug v Skegness T (a) 3-1
24 Mar Ron Cockerill XI v Sunderland
(Cockerill Testimonial) 2-2
23 Apr v Phonix Lubeck (h) 2-1
1969/70
31 Aug v Immingham T (a)
14 Sep v Anglia TV XI (a)

1970/71
29 Jul v Scunthorpe U (a) 4-3
1 Aug v Kilmarnock (h) 3-1
5 Aug v Boston U (a) 0-4
8 Aug v Barnsley (h) 2-1
v Alfreton T (a) 4-2
12 Dec v Preston NE (h) 2-3
13 Jan v Bolton W (h) 2-0
1971/72
29 Jul v Gainsborough Trin. (a) 5-0
3 Aug v York C (h) 0-0
7 Aug v Worksop Town (a) 2-2
10 Aug v Japan National XI (h) 7-2
18 May v Barton T (a)
1972/73
29 Jul v Prague Bohemians (h) 0-1
1 Aug v Norwich C (h)
3 Aug v Immingham Town (a) 5-0
7 Aug v Skegness Town (a) 2-2
10 Aug v Winterton Rangers (a)
3 Apr v All Stars XI (h) 3-3
(Wainman Test)
12 May v Barton T (a)
1973/74
14 Aug v Coventry C (h) 3-1
18 Aug v Hartlepool U (a) 1-1
20 Aug v Middlesbrough (h) 1-2
9 May v Ashby Institute (a)
(Taylor Benefit)
1974/75
1 Aug v Scarborough (a) 1-0
3 Aug v Yarmouth Town (h) 7-0
6 Aug v Hull C (h) 1-0
10 Aug v York City (h) 0-1
1975/76
9 Aug v Southampton (h) 2-2
17 Nov v Coventry C *(Boylen Test)* (h) 3-3
1976/77 No matches.
1977/78
3 Aug v Ayr U (h) 2-1
1978/79
29 Jul v Sheffield U (h) 4-1
22 Apr v Top Ten XI
(At King Edward VI Stadium. Grimsby.)
14 May v All Stars XI (h) 5-4
(Stratford Memorial)
1979/80
4 Aug v St. Mirren (h) 1-1
Aug v Brigg T (a)
13 Nov v Derby Co (h) 1-3 *(Booth Test)*
10 Mar v Boston U (a) *(Howells Test)*
27 Apr v Grimsby League XI
1980/81
21 Jul v Denaby U (a) 2-2
1 Aug v York C (a) 1-2
5 Aug v Sunderland (h) 0-2
3 Feb v Leeds U (h) 2-1
(Wainman Benefit)
26 Apr George Kerr XI v Radio Humberside

(1980/81 contd.)
4 May v Hull C (a) 2-1
(Humber Bridge Festival)
5 May v Skegness T (a) 2-0 *(Carter Test)*
1982/83
Aug v Winterton Rangers (a) 0-3
19 Aug v Denaby U (a)
8 Dec v Heanor T (a) *(New Floodlights)*
9 Feb v Worksop T (a)
11 Apr v Nottingham F (h) 0-0
(Fraser Benefit).
1983/84
5 Aug v Doncaster Rovers (a) 0-2
6 Aug v Winterton Rangers (a) 4-1
8 Aug v Retford T (a) 2-2
9 Aug v Grimsby Pelham (a)
10 Aug v Coventry C (h) 0-2
13 Aug v Notts Co (h) 1-1
16 Aug v Norwich C (h) 2-1
18 Aug v Whitby T (a) 2-1
22 Aug v Alfreton T (a)
18 Feb v Hull C (a) 3-2
1984/85
4 Aug v Clee Bor (a) 4-0
6 Aug v East Lincs Combination XI (at Louth Utd) 4-0
8 Aug v Worksop T (a) 6-2
9 Aug v Skegness T (a) 2-0
11 Aug v Sheffield Wed (h) 2-0
15 Aug v Scunthorpe U (a) 2-1
16 Aug v Brigg T (a) 1-0
17 Aug v Ross Sports (a) 6-1
21 Aug v Watford (h) 2-2
17 Sep v West Brom Alb (h) 1-2
(Waters Test)
19 Jan v Scunthorpe U (h) 1-2
16 Apr v Southampton (h) 1-1
1985/86
Aug v Lincoln U (a) 3-2
5 Aug v N Ferriby U (a) 3-0
7 Aug v Ross Sports (a) 2-0
10 Aug v Leicester C (h) 1-2
29 Aug v Immingham T (a)
(K.Moore Test)
18 Feb v Scunthorpe U (h) 1-2
1986/87
29 Jul v Immimgham T (a) 4-1
Iceland Tour
6 Aug v Akranes 5-2
9 Aug v Trotur Neskaupstadur 6-0
11 Aug v IBV (Westland Isles) 2-1
15 Aug v Louth U (a) 2-2
13 Oct v Sheffield Wed (h) 3-9
(K.Moore Test)
21 Feb v Brondby IF (Denmark) (h) 1-2

1987/88
7 Aug v Scunthorpe U (a) 1-0
11 Au g v Barnsley (a) 2-0
Played behind closed doors
30 Nov v Southampton (h) 3-1
(Heward Benefit)
1988/89
2 Aug v Goole T (a) 2-0
4 Aug v Charltons (Grimsby) (a) 1-2
9 Aug v Immingham T (a)1-0
13 Aug v Halifax T (h) 0-1 *
16 Aug v Bradford C (h) 1-1 *
20 Aug v Rotherham U (a) 1-0 *
* *Yorkshire & Humberside Cup (Group B)*
1989/90
29 Jul v Ilkeston T (a)
2 Aug v Oldham Ath (h) 1-1
5 Aug v Huddersfield T (a) 0-1 *
8 Aug v York C (h) 0-2 *
12 Aug v Barnsley (h) 2-0 *
* *Yorkshire & Humberside Cup (Group B)*
9 Oct v Long Sutton U (a) 4-0
(New Floodlights)
1990/91
26 Jul v Oadby T (a) 7-1
11 Aug v Halifax T (h) 0-1
Diamik Yorks. & Humber. Cup (Group B)
14 Aug v Whitby T (h) 0-0
15 Aug v Grimsby Bor (a) 0-0
18 Aug v Bradford C (a) 1-1
15 Oct v Bourne T (a) *(Needham Benefit)*
5 Mar v Sheffield U (h) 2-0
(Fraser Benefit)
12 May v Ciba-Geiby (h) 8-5
1991/92
1 Aug v Long Sutton U (a)
1 Aug v Immingham T (a) Res
6 Aug v York City (h) 3-0
10 Aug v Sheffield United (h) 0-1
1992/93
17 Jul v Oadby T (a) 3-0
23 Jul v N Ferriby U (a)
23 Jul v Immingham T (a) 2-0 (Res.)
1 Aug v Barnet (h) 1-0
4 Aug v Kettering (a) 2-1
7 Aug v Hull City (a) 1-1
27 Apr v Southampton (h) 1-3
(J.Cockerill Test)
1993/94
26 Jul v Kettering T (a)
27 Jul v Friar Lane O.B. (a) 2-0
28 Jul v Northampton T 1-0 *(at Wellingborough T)*
31 Jul v Halifax T (h) 0-0 *
7 Aug v Scarborough (a) 0-0 *
* *Yorkshire Electricity. Cup*

(1993/94 contd.)
Aug v Winterton (a) 4-1
3 Aug v Hull C (a) 0-1
6 Aug v Leeds U (h) 0-1 *(Bridge Test.)*
1994-95
26 Jul v Linfield (a) 3-0
27 Jul v Bangor (a) 1-0
28 Jul v Glentoran (a) 2-0
3 Aug v Birmingham C (h) 3-3
9 Aug v Scunthorpe U (a) 1-0
1995/96
29 Jul v Larne (a) 0-0
31 Jul v Ards (a) 3-0
2 Aug v Cliftonville (a) 3-0
5 Aug v Hull City (a) 1-2
1996/97
22 Jul v Winterton Rangers (a) 6-0
27 Jul v Dunfermline Ath (a) 3-3
29 Jul v East Fife (a) 1-0
31 Jul v Queen of the South (a) 2-0
3 Aug v Blackpool (a) 2-2
6 Aug v Hartlepool U (a) 4-4
10 Aug v Leeds U (h) 0-2
(McDermott Test)
1997/98
16 Jul v Winterton Rangers (a) 2-0
23 Jul v Aberdeen (h) 2-1
26 Jul v Darlington (at Billingham T) 2-0
29 Jul v Heart of Midlothian (h) 2-0
31 Jul v VS Rugby (a) 4-1
2 Aug v Mansfield T (a) 2-0
5 Aug v Leeds U (at Wetherby) 0-1
1998/99
10 Jul v Winterton Rangers (a) 2-0
14 Jul v Ilkeston T (a) 4-1
18 Jul v Isle of Man XI
(At Douglas Bowl) 2-0 *
20 Jul v Stockport Co (at Ramsey) 0-1 *
24 Jul v Huddersfield T.
(At NSC, Douglas) 1-0 *
* *(Isle of Man Tournament)*
27 Jul v Louth U (a) 2-2
28 Jul v Lincoln C (a) 2-2
31 Jul v Mansfield T (a) 0-0
3 Aug v Hull C (a) 2-0
5 Oct v Nottingham F (h) 3-3
(Lever Test)
10 May v Leicester C (h) 3-2
1999/2000
10 Jul v Winterton Rangers (a) 1-1
16 Jul v Halifax T (a) 0-3
19 Jul v Linfield (a) 0-0
21 Jul v Derry C (a) 1-1
24 Jul v Lincoln C (a) 2-0
28 Jul v Scunthorpe U (a) 0-1
31 Jul v York C (h) 1-0
2 Aug v Brigg T (a) 2-1

1888-89 The Combination

							Holtby	Lundie	Taylor H	Taylor JH	Smith H	Ogilvie	Mudie	Hunt	Riddoch	Lee	Pearce	Doyle	Hopewell	Reid	Sutherland	McBeth	Plumtree	Taylor J (Jnr)	Sanderson	Thickett	Hall	Croft	Beckett	Twyman	Child
1	Sep	1	LONG EATON RANGERS	1-3	Mudie	1200	1	2	3	4	5	6	7	8	9	10	11														
2	Dec	8	GAINSBOROUGH TRINITY	4-2	Reid, McBeth, Doyle, Unknown		1	2		4	5			11	9			3	6	7	8	10									
3		22	DERBY MIDLAND	1-0	OG	1500	1	2		4	5			11	9			3	6	7	8	10									
4		24	NORTHWICH VICTORIA	2-2	McBeth, Hunt	1500	1	2		7	5			11		8		3	6	4	9	10									
5		25	BURSLEM PORT VALE	6-2	Doyle(4), McBeth, Hunt	1500	1	2		4	5			11	8			9	6	3	7	10									
6		26	HALLIWELL	1-1	Doyle	1500	1	2		4	5			11	9			7		3	8	10	6								
7	Mar	9	NOTTINGHAM FOREST	4-0	Doyle, Hunt, Sutherland, Unknown		1	2		4	5			11	9			3		6	8	10		7							
8	Apr	1	Gainsborough Trinity	7-1	J.H.Taylor(2),J.Taylor,Sutherland,Hunt,Unknown,OG	4000	1	2		4	5			10	9			3		6	8			7	11						
9		6	Burslem Port Vale	1-2	Unknown			2		1	5			10	9					3	8			7	11	4	6				
10		20	CREWE ALEXANDRA	3-1	J.H.Taylor, Sanderson, Unknown	1500	1	2		4	5	6								3			9	7	11			8	10		
11		27	Bootle	1-2	Riddoch		1	2		4	5	6		11	9					3	8	10		7							
12	May	4	Newton Heath	3-0	?Taylor, Riddoch, McBeth	1000	1	2		4	5	6		11	9					3	8	10		7							
13		11	BOOTLE	7-1	?Taylor(2),Sutherland(2),Riddoch(2),OG	800		2		4	5	6		11	9					3	8	10		7						1	
						Apps.	11	13	1	13	13	5	1	12	11	2	1	7	4	12	11	9	2	7	3	1	1	1	1	1	
						Goals				3			1	4	4			7		1	4	4		1	1						

F.A. Cup

							Holtby	Lundie	Taylor H	Taylor JH	Smith H	Ogilvie	Mudie	Hunt	Riddoch	Lee	Pearce	Doyle	Hopewell	Reid	Sutherland	McBeth	Plumtree	Taylor J (Jnr)	Sanderson	Thickett	Hall	Croft	Beckett	Twyman	Child
P1	Oct	6	LINCOLN CITY	1-1	Sutherland	2500	1	2	3	4	5	6		11	9	8					7	10									
P1r		13	Lincoln City	1-1	McBeth	4000	1	2		4	5	6	7	11	9			3			8	10									
P12r		24	Lincoln City *	3-1	McBeth, Hunt, Unknown	1500	1	2		3	5	4	8	11	9	7						10									6
P2		27	Newark	4-4	Lee, McBeth, 2 Unknown	1500	1	2		3	5	4	8	11	9	7						10									6
P2r	Nov	3	NEWARK	9-0	#	2000	1	2		3	5	4	6	11	9	7					8	10									
P3		17	CLEETHOPES TOWN	5-0	McBeth, 4 Unknown		1	6		3	5	4		11	9	7		2			8	10									
R1	Dec	15	SUNDERLAND ABLION	3-1	J.Taylor, McBeth(2)		1	2		4	5			11	9			3		6	8	10		7							
R2	Feb	16	PRESTON NORTH END	0-2		8000	1	2		4	5			11	9			3		6	8	10		7							

* Played at Bramall Lane, Sheffield

Goalscorers: Sutherland(2), Lee(2), Riddoch, Hunt, 3 Unknown

1888/89 Season

Back: Burnham (Schooltmaster), Maddison (Confectioner), G.Smith (Ship Builder), Twyman, Patmore (Schoolmaster), Brocklesby (Fish Curer)
Middle: Hall, Reid, J.H.Taylor, Lundie, C.Smith, Ogilvie, Chapman (Asst Sec)
Front: Sutherland, J.Taylor (Jnr.), Riddoch, McBeth, Hunt

1889-90 4th in Football Alliance

					Att	Turnbull	Lundie	Reid	Taylor JH	Smith H	Ogilvie	McDill	Riddoch	McKnight	McBeth	Black	Stovin	Langley	Ross	Findley	Sutherland	Rose A	Walker	Rose H	Hughes	Haines	May	Mundahl
1	Sep 14	LONG EATON RANGERS	4-1	Riddoch, Black, McKnight, McDill	2000	1	2	3	4	5	6	7	8	9	10	11												
2	21	NOTTINGHAM FOREST	4-0	McBeth, Sutherland(2), Black		1	2	3	4	5	6	7		9	10	11					8							
3	28	Walsall Town Swifts	2-2	McKnight, McDill		1	2	3	4	5	6	7	10	9		11					8							
4	Oct 5	Nottingham Forest	2-1	McBeth, OG	2000	1	2	3	4	5			10	9	8	11					6	7						
5	19	Birmingham St. George's	3-3	McBeth(2), A.Rose		1	2	3	4	5			10	9	8	11					6	7						
6	Nov 2	SUNDERLAND ALBION	1-2	McKnight	4000		2	3	4	5			10	9	8	11	1				6	7						
7	9	Crewe Alexandra	0-6		2000		2	3	4	5			8	9		11	1				6		7					10
8	23	Small Heath	1-3	McKnight		1	2	3	4	5			8	9	10	11					6	7						
9	30	WALSALL TOWN SWIFTS	4-0	McBeth,McKnight,Ross,Riddoch		1	2	3	4	5			8	9	10	11			7		6							
10	Dec 7	SHEFFIELD WEDNESDAY	0-4			1	2	3		5	4		8	9	10	11			7		6							
11	21	DARWEN	7-3	McKnight(3),Reid(2),Black,J.H.Taylor	1500	1	2	3	4	5			8	9	10	11			7		6							
12	26	SMALL HEATH	4-0	McBeth(2), Riddoch, A.Rose		1	2	3	4				8	9	10	11			5		6	7						
13	Jan 25	Darwen	0-3				2	3	4	5	1		10	11					8	9	6	7						
14	Feb 8	NEWTON HEATH	7-0	H.Rose(2),McBeth(2),Black,Riddoch,McKnight	2400		2		4	3	1		8	9	10	11				5	6			7				
15	22	Bootle	1-2	Reid			2	3	4	5	1		8	7	10	11				9	6							
16	Mar 1	Sunderland Albion	0-4				2	3	4		1		8	9	10	11				5	6	7						
17	22	Sheffield Wednesday	3-4	Black, Hughes, Reid	6500		2	7	4	5	1				10	11		3			6				8		9	
18	Apr 4	BIRMINGHAM ST. GEORGE'S	5-4	McBeth(3), Reid, May	2500		2	7	4	5	1		8		10	11		3			6						9	
19	5	CREWE ALEXANDRA	3-1	McBeth, Reid, May			2	7	4	5	1		8		10	11		3			6						9	
20	12	BOOTLE	3-2	Reid(2), Black			2	7	4	5	1			9	10	11		3			6					8		
21	14	Newton Heath	1-0	McBeth	3000		2	7	4	5	1			9	10	11		3			6						8	
22	19	Long Eaton Rangers	3-2	McBeth(2), McKnight			2	7	4	5	1			9	10	11		3			6			8				
					Apps.	10	22	21	21	20	14	3	17	19	19	21	2	6	5	4	21	7	1	2	1	1	4	1
					Goals			8	1			2	4	10	16	6			1		2	2		2	1		2	

F.A. Cup

					Att	Turnbull	Lundie	Reid	Taylor JH	Smith H	Ogilvie	McDill	Riddoch	McKnight	McBeth	Black	Stovin	Langley	Ross	Findley	Sutherland	Rose A	Walker	Rose H	Hughes	Haines	May	Mundahl
R1	Jan 18	Newcastle West End	2-1	McBeth, Black			2	3	4	5	1		10	9	8	11			6		7							
R2	Feb 1	Blackburn Rovers	0-3		3000		2	3	4	5	1		10	7	8	11				9	6							

The Combination: 1888-89 Season

	P	W	D	L	F	A	W	D	L	F	A	Pts	Pts/game
Newton Heath	14	7	0	1	21	6	3	2	1	13	9	22	1.571
GRIMSBY TOWN	8	4	2	1	19	10	1	0	0	7	1	12	1.500
Northwich Victoria	9	4	0	0	10	3	2	1	2	9	11	13	1.444
Notts Rangers	16	4	0	2	21	12	7	1	2	26	16	23	1.438
Bootle	15	6	1	1	21	8	3	2	2	15	14	21	1.400
Small Heath	11	5	1	0	16	7	1	2	2	8	10	15	1.364
Long Eaton Rangers	16	5	2	1	21	9	3	2	3	13	17	20	1.250
Walsall Town Swifts	17	5	2	2	19	14	4	0	4	15	20	20	1.176
Halliwell	13	4	0	1	21	9	2	2	4	14	19	14	1.077
Birmingham St.George's	13	2	4	1	12	11	2	1	3	10	10	13	1.000
Darwen	15	5	2	1	26	13	0	2	5	7	20	14	0.933
Crewe Alexandra	16	4	0	4	24	17	1	4	3	12	16	14	0.875
South Shore	14	4	1	1	17	5	1	1	6	9	28	12	0.857
Lincoln City	12	1	2	3	6	11	3	0	3	6	11	10	0.833
Derby Midland	17	1	4	2	8	12	3	1	6	12	18	13	0.765
Derby Junction	12	2	0	4	13	12	0	4	2	11	13	8	0.667
Burslem Port Vale	25	6	2	4	24	15	0	2	11	14	41	16	0.640
Leek Town	15	2	1	4	12	18	1	0	7	7	26	7	0.467
Gainsborough Trinity	11	1	2	4	11	21	0	1	3	5	13	5	0.455
Blackburn Olympic	5	0	2	0	2	2	0	0	3	1	11	2	0.400

The above table was never officially published. This is as the final table may have appeared when the Combination was wound up on 5 April 1889. Some assumptions have been made as to whether fixtures were Combination games or Friendlies. Clubs ranked in points per game order. © *Tony Brown.*

Football Alliance 1889-90 Season

	P	W	D	L	F	A	W	D	L	F	A	Pts
Sheffield Wednesday	22	10	0	1	48	19	5	2	4	22	20	32
Bootle	22	11	0	0	49	8	2	2	7	17	31	28
Sunderland Albion	22	9	0	2	43	13	3	2	6	24	31	28*
GRIMSBY TOWN	22	9	0	2	42	17	3	2	6	16	30	26
Crewe Alexandra	22	6	2	3	42	27	5	0	6	26	32	24
Darwen	22	8	1	2	46	29	2	1	8	24	47	22
Birmingham St. George's	22	7	2	2	36	22	3	1	7	31	30	21*
Newton Heath	22	7	0	4	27	11	2	2	7	13	33	20
Walsall Town Swifts	22	6	3	2	27	19	2	0	9	17	40	19
Small Heath	22	5	3	3	33	18	1	2	9	11	49	17
Nottingham Forest	22	3	4	4	19	20	3	1	7	12	42	17
Long Eaton Rangers	22	3	1	7	18	28	1	1	9	17	45	10

* Sunderland Albion awarded 2 points, Birmingham St. George's deducted 2 points

1890-91 3rd in Football Alliance

No.	Date	Opponent	Score	Scorers	Att.	Ogilvie	Lundie	Langley	Reid	Smith H	Sutherland	McNichol	Rose H	Walker	Cosgrove	Black	Taylor JH	Rose A	Riddoch	Haines	Mundahl	Frith	Shaw	Arnold	Hughes	Murrell
1	Sep 13	NEWTON HEATH	3-1	Cosgrove(3)	2000	1	2	3	4	5	6	7	8	9	10	11										
2	20	Stoke	1-2	Walker		1	2	3	4	5	6	7	8	9	10	11										
3	27	SMALL HEATH	3-1	Cosgrove(2), unknown	2500	1	2	3		5		7	8	9	11		4				6				10	
4	Oct 4	STOKE	1-1	Cosgrove	3000	1	2	3	6	5		7	8	9	10	11	4									
5	18	Newton Heath	1-3	Unknown	4000	1	2		3	5	6		7	9	10	11	4		8							
6	25	BOOTLE	1-0	Unknown	500	1	2	4	3	5			8	9	10	11		7								6
7	Nov 1	Darwen	1-1	Cosgrove or Black	4000	1	2	3	5				7	9	10	11	4		8			6				
8	15	Sheffield Wednesday	1-2	H.Rose	8000	1	2	3	4		6		7	9	10	11			8				5			
9	22	Bootle	0-0			1	2	3	5				7	9	10	11	4		8			6				
10	Dec 6	Birmingham St. George's	0-2			1	2	3	6				7	9	10	11	4		8				5			
11	13	Sunderland Albion	1-2	Unknown		1	2	3	6				7	9	10	11	4						5	8		
12	27	Nottingham Forest	1-1	Cosgrove	1500	1	2	3	5		6		7	9	10	11	4		8							
13	Jan 3	Crewe Alexandra	3-4	Cosgrove(2), OG	2000	1	2	3	5		6		7	9	10	11	4		8							
14	Feb 21	Small Heath	2-1	Hughes, Riddoch		1	2	3	5				7	9		11			10		6	4			8	
15	28	WALSALL TOWN SWIFTS	3-0	H.Rose, Langley, Black	1500	1	2	3		5			8			11	4	7	9	10		6				
16	Mar 7	SHEFFIELD WEDNESDAY	3-0	H.Rose, Riddoch, Black	2000	1	2	3	6	5			8			11		7	9	10	4					
17	14	DARWEN	4-1	Black(3), Haines	2500	1	2		3	5			8	4		11		7	9	10		6				
18	21	Walsall Town Swifts	1-0	Unknown		1	2		3	5			7	9		11	4		8	10		6				
19	27	BIRMINGHAM ST. GEORGE'S	5-3	Black(2), Haines(2), Riddoch	4000	1	2	3	6	5			8	4		11		7	9	10						
20	28	CREWE ALEXANDRA	3-3	H.Rose, Reid, Riddoch	1500	1	2	3	6	5			8	4		11		7	9	10						
21	Apr 4	SUNDERLAND ALBION	2-0	H.Rose, Walker	1500	1	2	3	6	5			8	4		11		7	9	10						
22	9	NOTTINGHAM FOREST	3-0	Riddoch, Haines, Unknown	4000	1	2	3	6	5			8	4		11		7	9	10						
					Apps.	22	22	19	20	14	6	4	22	20	13	21	11	8	16	8	3	6	3	1	2	1
					Goals			1	1				5	2	8	6			5	4					1	

1 own goal

F.A.Cup

No.	Date	Opponent	Score	Scorers
R1	Oct 11	Ecclesfield	2-8	Smith(2)

Grimsby played the Reserve team as a protest in having to play in the qualifying rounds. Team: Holtby, Winter, T.Frith, Harvey, Waring, Walton, W.Smith, Hollingsworth, C.Frith, Haines, Hughes

1891-92 10th in Football Alliance

No.	Date	Opponent	Score	Scorers	Att.	Ogilvie	Lundie	Gray	Walker	Reid	Murrell	Devlin	Rose H	Riddoch	Ackroyd	McBeth	Frith T	Haines	Rose A	Elliman	Frith C	Hopewell	Bellamy	Smalley	Blythe	Dore	Smith H	McUrich	Taylor JH	Hughes
1	Sep 19	Sheffield Wednesday	2-4	H.Rose, Riddoch	10000	1	2	3	4	5	6	7	8	9	10	11														
2	Oct 10	BOOTLE	4-1	Unknown(4)	500	1	2	3	4	5	6	7	8	9	10			11												
3	17	NEWTON HEATH	2-2	Ackroyd, Unknown	3000	1	2	3	4	5	6		8	9	10			11	7											
4	31	Walsall Town Swifts	0-2			1	2	3	4	5	6	7	8	9	10			11												
5	Nov 21	Nottingham Forest	3-3	H.Rose(2), A.Rose		1	2	3	4	5			8	9	10			11	7		6									
6	28	BURTON SWIFTS	0-1			1	2	3			4		8	9	10			11	7		6						5			
7	Dec 12	Lincoln City	2-3	Ackroyd, Unknown		1	2	3	5		6		8	9	10		4	11	7											
8	19	SMALL HEATH	1-2	Ackroyd		1	2	3	4	5	6		8	9	10			11	7											
9	25	Ardwick	1-3	Ackroyd		1	2	3	4	5	6		8	9	10			11	7											
10	26	CREWE ALEXANDRA	1-1	Unknown		1		3	4	5	6			9			2	11	7							10		8		
11	Jan 2	Burton Swifts	1-2	Unknown		1			4	5	6			9			2	11			7	8	10						3	
12	30	ARDWICK	4-0	Smalley(3), H.Rose		1	2		4	5	6	11	8	9	10		3							7						
13	Feb 13	Crewe Alexandra	0-1			1	2		4	5	6		8	9	10		3						11	7						
14	20	Birmingham St. George's	0-0			1	2		9	5	4	7	8	10	11		3					6								
15	Mar 5	LINCOLN CITY	6-1	Ackroyd(4), Riddoch, H.Rose	2000	1	2		5	6	4	7	8	9	10		3			11										
16	12	Bootle	1-6	Ackroyd		1	2	4		6	5	7	8	9	10		3			11										
17	19	SHEFFIELD WEDNESDAY	1-0	Elliman		1	2		4	5	6	7	8	9	10		3			11										
18	26	Newton Heath	3-3	Ackroyd, Riddoch(2,1pen)	6000	1	2		5		4		8	9	10		3			11		6			7					
19	Apr 2	Small Heath	0-3			1	2		5	6	4		8	9	10		3			11			7							
20	15	BIRMINGHAM ST. GEORGE'S	5-0	Ackroyd, Devlin, Elliman(3)		1	2		5	6	4	7	8	9	10		3			11										
21	16	WALSALL TOWN SWIFTS	2-0	Ackroyd, Riddoch		1	2				4	7	8	9	10		3			11	5	6								
22	28	NOTTINGHAM FOREST	1-1	Ackroyd		1	2		5		4	7	8	9	10		3			11	6									
					Apps.	22	20	11	19	17	21	11	20	22	20	1	14	10	7	8	5	4	3	2	1	1	1	1	1	
					Goals							1	5	5	13				1	4				3						

1 own goal

F.A.Cup

F A Cup scorers: Reid(3), Haines, Ackroyd, Riddoch,(2), H.Rose,(2), Devlin.

No.	Date	Opponent	Score	Scorers	Ogilvie	Lundie	Gray	Walker	Reid	Murrell	Devlin	Rose H	Riddoch	Ackroyd	McBeth	Frith T	Haines	Rose A	Elliman	Frith C	Hopewell	Bellamy	Smalley	Blythe	Dore	Smith H	McUrich	Taylor JH	Hughes
Q1	Oct 3	LONG EATON RANGERS	2-1	Devlin, Ackroyd	1	2	3	6	5	4	7	8	9	10	11														
Q2	24	BOSTON TOWN	10-C	#	1	2	3	6	5	4	11	10	9	8			7												
Q3	Nov 14	SHEFFIELD UNITED	1-2	Haines	1	2	3	4	5			7		10			11	8		6									9

Football Alliance: 1890-91 Season

		P	W	D	L	F	A	W	D	L	F	A	Pts
1	Stoke City	22	9	2	0	33	15	4	5	2	24	24	33
2	Sunderland Albion	22	9	2	0	47	6	3	4	4	22	22	30
3	GRIMSBY TOWN	22	9	2	0	31	9	2	3	6	12	18	27
4	Birmingham St. George's	22	9	0	2	41	22	3	2	6	23	40	26
5	Nottingham Forest	22	6	4	1	39	15	3	3	5	27	24	23
6	Darwen	22	7	3	1	45	20	3	0	8	19	39	23
7	Walsall Town Swifts	22	6	1	4	22	22	3	2	6	12	39	21
8	Crewe Alexandra	22	5	1	5	28	29	3	3	5	31	38	20
9	Newton Heath	22	5	3	3	25	22	2	0	9	12	33	17
10	Small Heath	22	6	0	5	34	23	1	2	8	24	43	16
11	Bootle	22	3	6	2	28	18	0	1	10	12	43	13
12	Sheffield Wednesday	22	4	3	4	30	26	0	2	9	9	40	13

Nottingham Forest 2 points deducted

Football Alliance: 1891-92

		P	W	D	L	F	A	W	D	L	F	A	Pts
1	Nottingham Forest	22	8	3	0	38	6	6	2	3	21	16	33
2	Newton Heath	22	7	4	0	41	14	5	3	3	28	19	31
3	Small Heath	22	8	2	1	32	11	4	3	4	21	25	29
4	Sheffield Wednesday	22	10	0	1	45	16	2	4	5	20	19	28
5	Burton Swifts	22	8	1	2	38	23	4	1	6	16	29	26
6	Crewe Alexandra	22	6	2	3	28	16	1	2	8	16	33	18
7	Ardwick	22	5	3	3	28	21	1	3	7	11	30	18
8	Bootle	22	7	1	3	27	19	1	1	9	15	45	18
9	Lincoln City	22	4	4	3	23	20	2	1	8	14	45	17
10	GRIMSBY TOWN	22	6	3	2	27	9	0	3	8	13	30	16
11	Walsall Town Swifts	22	6	1	4	28	18	0	2	9	5	41	15
12	Birmingham St.George's	22	4	2	5	22	19	1	1	9	12	45	11

Grimsby Town and Birmingham St. George's 2 points deducted

1892-93 4th in Division 2

Captain: Jimmy Lundie

							Whitehouse	Lundie	Frith T	Murrell	Walker	Oglivie	Higgins	Henderson	Brayshaw	Ackroyd	Riddoch	Reid	McHardy	Fairley	Rose H	Smith W	Mullen	Fletcher	Linton	Holtby
1	Sep	3	NORTHWICH VICTORIA	2-1	Riddoch(2)	2000	1	2	3	4	5	6	7	8	9	10	11									
2		10	Crewe Alexandra	0-1		2000	1	2	3	4	5	6	8	9		10	11				7					
3		17	DARWEN	0-1		3000	1	2	3	4	5	6	7	8		10	11	9								
4		26	Sheffield United	0-2		5000	1	2	3	4	5	6	11	8		10				9		7				
5	Oct	1	SMALL HEATH	3-2	Higgins(3)		1	2		4	5	6	7	8		10	11	3		9						
6		8	BOOTLE	3-0	Ackroyd(2), Higgins		1	2		4	5	6	7	8		10	11	3		9						
7		22	Walsall Town Swifts	1-3	Ackroyd(pen)	2000	1	2	3		5	6	7	8		10	11	4					9			
8	Nov	5	ARDWICK	2-0	Mullen, Higgins	3000	1	2	3	4	5	6	7	8			11						9	10		
9	Dec	3	BURTON SWIFTS	4-0	Ackroyd(2), Riddoch, Mullen		1	2		4	5	3	8			7	11			6			9	10		
10		17	Bootle	1-3	Riddoch		1	2		4	5	3	8			7	11			6			9	10		
11		24	CREWE ALEXANDRA	4-0	Mullen, Ackroyd, Fletcher, Riddoch	2000	1			4	5	3		8	2	7	11			6			9	10		
12	Jan	7	Northwich Victoria	3-5	Mullen, Unknown(2)		1			4	5	3	7	8			11	2		6			9	10		
13		14	BURSLEM PORT VALE	2-0	Higgins, Unknown	500	1	2		4		5	8			7	11	3		6			9	10		
14		30	Ardwick	3-0	Riddoch, Fletcher(2)	2000	1	2		4		5	8			7	11	3		6			9	10		
15	Feb	11	Burslem Port Vale	1-0	Ackroyd		1	2		4		5		8		7	11	3		6			9	10		
16		18	LINCOLN CITY	2-2	Ackroyd, Murrell	2000	1	2		4		5	10	8		7	11	3		6			9			
17		25	Small Heath	3-8	Ackroyd(2), Mullen	3000	1	2		4		5	8			7	11	3		6			9	10		
18	Mar	4	Lincoln City	3-1	Riddoch, Fletcher, Mullen	5000	1	2	3	4		5	8			7	11			6			9	10		
19		18	Darwen	1-6	Smith		1	2	3	4	5		8			11				6		7	9	10		
20		31	SHEFFIELD UNITED	0-1		4000	1	2		4		3	8			7			5	6			9	10	11	
21	Apr	1	WALSALL TOWN SWIFTS	3-0	Ackroyd, Higgins(2)		1	2		4		3	8			7	11		5	6			9	10		
22		8	Burton Swifts	1-5	Ackroyd		1	2		4		3	8			7	11		5	6			9	10		
						Apps.	22	20	8	21	13	21	20	12	2	20	19	10	3	17	1	2	16	14	1	
						Goals				1			8			12	7					1	6	4		

F.A. Cup

							Whitehouse	Lundie	Frith T	Murrell	Walker	Oglivie	Higgins	Henderson	Brayshaw	Ackroyd	Riddoch	Reid	McHardy	Fairley	Rose H	Smith W	Mullen	Fletcher	Linton	Holtby
Q1	Oct	15	Attercliffe	2-0	Higgins, Mullen		1	2		4	5	6	7			11	10	3			8		9			
Q2	Nov	10	Doncaster Rovers *	2-1	Higgins (2)	1500	1	2	3	4	5	6	7	8			11						9	10		
Q3		19	GAINSBOROUGH TRINITY	1-0	Higgins			2		4	5	6	7	8		10	11	3					9			1
Q4	Dec	10	LINCOLN CITY	5-0	Higgins, Mullen(3), Fletcher	3000	1	2		4	5	3	8			7	10			6			9	11		
R1	Jan	21	STOCKTON	5-0	Ackroyd, Higgins, Mullen(2), OG	3000	1	2		4		5	8			7	11	3		6			9	10		
R2	Feb	3	Darwen	0-2			1	2		4	5	6	8			7	11	3					9	10		

*** 29 October: Match abandoned (score 1-1, attendance 3000)**

		P	W	D	L	F	A	W	D	L	F	A	F	A	Pts
1	Small Heath	22	10	1	0	57	16	7	1	3	33	19	90	35	36
2	Sheffield United	22	10	1	0	35	8	6	2	3	27	11	62	19	35
3	Darwen	22	10	0	1	43	15	4	2	5	17	21	60	36	30
4	GRIMSBY TOWN	22	8	1	2	25	7	3	0	8	17	34	42	41	23
5	Ardwick	22	6	3	2	27	14	3	0	8	18	26	45	40	21
6	Burton Swifts	22	7	1	3	30	18	2	1	8	17	29	47	47	20
7	Northwich Victoria	22	7	0	4	25	26	2	2	7	17	32	42	58	20
8	Bootle	22	8	1	2	35	20	0	2	9	14	43	49	63	19
9	Lincoln City	22	6	2	3	30	18	1	1	9	15	33	45	51	17
10	Crewe Alexandra	22	6	1	4	30	24	0	2	9	12	45	42	69	15
11	Burslem Port Vale	22	4	1	6	16	23	2	2	7	14	34	30	57	15
12	Walsall Town Swfts	22	4	3	4	25	24	1	0	10	12	51	37	75	13

1893-94 5th in Division 2

Captain: Jimmy Lundie

							Whitehouse	Lundie	Frith T	Murrell	Graham	Riddoch	Ackroyd	Crawford	Russell	Fletcher	Jones	Higgins	Gregory	Frith C	Rose	McCairns	Robinson	West	Cleator
1	Sep	2	NORTHWICH VICTORIA	7-0	Russell(3),Fletcher(2),Ackroyd,Crawford		1	2	3	4	5	6	7	8	9	10	11								
2		9	Rotherham Town	3-4	Crawford(2), Jones		1	2	3	4	5	6	7	10	9		11	8							
3		16	BURTON SWIFTS	2-1	Fletcher(2)	5000	1	2	3	4		6	7	8	9	10	11			5					
4		23	Lincoln City	2-1	Crawford(2)	6000	1	2	3	4	5	10	7	8			11			6		9			
5		25	Woolwich Arsenal	1-3	C.Frith	2000	1	2	3	4	5		7	8		10	11			6		9			
6		30	WALSALL TOWN SWIFTS	5-2	McCairns(2),Jones,Higgins,Crawford	2500	1	2	3	4	5	6		8		10	11	7				9			
7	Oct	5	Notts County	0-3		4000	1	2	3	4	5	10	7	8	6		11					9			
8		7	Small Heath	2-5	Fletcher, Higgins		1	2	3	4			7		6	10	11	8		5		9			
9		21	NOTTS COUNTY	5-2	McCairns(2), Higgins, Fletcher, Ackroyd	4000	1	2	3	4	5		7		6	10	11	8				9			
10		28	LINCOLN CITY	2-4	McCairns(2)	4000	1	2	3	4	5		7		6	10	11	8				9			
11	Nov	11	Middlesbrough Ironopolis	6-2	McCairns(2), Fletcher, Ackroyd, Jones, OG		1	2		4	5	8	7		6	10	11	3				9			
12	Dec	2	BURSLEM PORT VALE	4-0	McCairns,Jones,Ackroyd,Riddoch	2000	1	2			5	8	7		6	10	11	3		4		9			
13		4	Burslem Port Vale	1-6	McCairns		1	2			5	8	7		6	10	11	3		4		9			
14		9	Ardwick	1-4	McCairns	3000	1	2			5	8			6	10	11	7	3	4		9			
15		26	WOOLWICH ARSENAL	3-1	McCairns(2), Jones	3000	1	2	3		5	8	7		6	10	11	4				9			
16		30	Liverpool	0-2		2000	1	2	3		5	8	7		6	10	11	4				9			
17	Jan	13	ARDWICK	5-0	McCairns(2), Fletcher(2), Robinson		1	2	3		5		7		6	8	11	4				9	10		
18		20	Crewe Alexandra	3-3	Riddoch, Fletcher, Russell	2000	1	2	3		5	10	7		6	8	11	4				9			
19	Feb	3	MIDDLESBROUGH IRONOPOLIS	2-1	Riddoch, Ackroyd		1	2	3		5	10	7		6	8	11	4				9			
20		10	ROTHERHAM TOWN	7-1	Robinson(3),Fletcher,McCairns,OG,Unknown	1500	1	2	3		5				6	8	11	7		4		9	10		
21		17	Northwich Victoria	1-0	McCairns		1	2	3		5	10			6	8	11	4			7	9			
22		24	Newcastle United	1-4	H.Rose	4000	1	2	3		5	10			6	8	11	4			7	9			
23	Mar	3	SMALL HEATH	2-1	H.Rose, McCairns	3000	1	2	3		5	10			6	8	11	4			7	9			
24		10	CREWE ALEXANDRA	3-2	Fletcher(3)	1500	1	2	3		5	10			6	8	11	4			7	9			
25		24	Walsall Town Swifts	0-5			1	2	3		5	10			6	8	11	4			7	9			
26		31	LIVERPOOL	0-1			1	2	3		5	8			6	10	11	4			7	9			
27	Apr	7	Burton Swifts	3-0	H.Rose, Jones, Riddoch		1	2	3		5	8			6	10	11	4			7	9			
28		14	NEWCASTLE UNITED	0-0		2000	1	2	3				8		6	10	11	4		5	7	9			
						Apps.	28	28	24	11	25	21	18	7	25	25	28	23	1	9	8	25	2		
						Goals						4	5	6	4	14	6	3		1	3	18	4		

2 own goals

F.A. Cup

							Whitehouse	Lundie	Frith T	Murrell	Graham	Riddoch	Ackroyd	Crawford	Russell	Fletcher	Jones	Higgins	Gregory	Frith C	Rose	McCairns	Robinson	West	Cleator
Q1	Oct	14	KILNHURST	5-1	Ackroyd, Crawford, McCairns(2), Cleator	1500	1		3		5	6	7	8	4		11					9		2	10
Q2	Nov	4	Lincoln City	5-2	Riddoch(2), McCairns(3)		1	2	3	4	5	8	7		6	10	11					9			
Q3		25	Grantham Rovers	6-2	Acroyd(2), McCairns(2), Fletcher(2)	1000	1	2	3		5	8	7		6	10	11	4				9			
Q4	Dec	16	GAINSBOROUGH TRINITY	6-1	Riddoch(2), McCairns(2), Fletcher, Jones	1500	1	2	3		5	8	7		6	10	11	4				9			
R1	Jan	27	Liverpool	0-3			1	2	3		5	10	7		6		11	4			8	9			

		P	W	D	L	F	A	W	D	L	F	A	F	A	Pts
1	Liverpool	28	14	0	0	46	6	8	6	0	31	12	77	18	50
2	Small Heath	28	12	0	2	68	19	9	0	5	35	25	103	44	42
3	Notts County	28	12	1	1	55	14	6	2	6	15	17	70	31	39
4	Newcastle United	28	12	1	1	44	10	3	5	6	22	29	66	39	36
5	GRIMSBY TOWN	28	11	1	2	47	16	4	1	9	24	42	71	58	32
6	Burton Swifts	28	9	1	4	52	26	5	2	7	27	35	79	61	31
7	Burslem Port Vale	28	10	2	2	43	20	3	2	9	23	44	66	64	30
8	Lincoln City	28	5	4	5	31	22	6	2	6	28	36	59	58	28
9	Woolwich Arsenal	28	9	1	4	33	19	3	3	8	19	36	52	55	28
10	Walsall Town Swfts	28	8	1	5	36	23	2	2	10	15	38	51	61	23
11	Middlsbro Irnoplis	28	7	4	3	27	20	1	0	13	10	52	37	72	20
12	Crewe Alexandra	28	3	7	4	22	22	3	0	11	20	51	42	73	19
13	Ardwick	28	6	1	7	32	20	2	1	11	15	51	47	71	18
14	Rotherham Town	28	5	1	8	28	42	1	2	11	16	49	44	91	15
15	Northwich Victoria	28	3	3	8	17	34	0	0	14	13	64	30	98	9

1894-95 5th in Division 2

Captain: Billy Lindsay

	Date	Opponent	Score	Scorers	Att.	Whitehouse	Lindsay	Frith T	Higgins	Stott	Waterson	Rose	Eccleston	McCairns	Fletcher	Frost	Lundie	Graham	Murrell	Murray	Riddoch	Fairburn	Cooper
1	Sep 1	LEICESTER FOSSE	4-3	McCairns, Fletcher(2), OG	5000	1	2	3	4	5	6	7	8	9	10	11							
2	8	Walsall Town Swifts	3-4	McCairns, Eccleston(2)		1	2	3	4	5	6	7	8	9	10								11
3	10	Woolwich Arsenal	3-1	Fletcher(2), Eccleston		1	2	3	4	5	6	7	8	9	10						11		
4	15	NEWCASTLE UNITED	3-0	McCairns, Eccleston(2)	4000	1	2	3		5	6	7	8	9	10			4			11		
5	19	Burton Swifts	1-2	McCairns	4000	1	2	3	4	5		7	8	9	10			6			11		
6	22	Manchester City	5-2	McCairns,Eccleston,Fletcher(2),Rose	5000	1	2	3	4	5	6	7	8	9	10						11		
7	29	BURTON WANDERERS	7-2	McCairns(2),Eccleston(2),Fletcher,Stott,Riddoch	4000	1	2	3	4	5	6	7	8	9	10						11		
8	Oct 4	Notts County	2-3	Eccleston, Fletcher	5000	1	2	3	4	5	6	7	8	9	10						11		
9	6	Bury	1-5	Rose	5000	1	2	3		5	6	7	8	9	10	11		4					
10	20	Lincoln City	5-1	Riddoch,Higgins,Frost,Rose,OG	3000	1	2	3	4	5	6	7	8		10	11					9		
11	27	ROTHERHAM TOWN	4-1	Riddoch,Rose,Fletcher,Frost	3000	1	2	3	4	5	6	7	8		10	11					9		
12	Nov 10	LINCOLN CITY	3-0	Fairburn, Frost, OG	4000	1	2	3	4	5	6	7	8		10	11						9	
13	17	NEWTON HEATH	2-1	Fairburn, Stott	3000	1	2		4	5		7	8		10	11	3	6				9	
14	Dec 1	Newcastle United	4-1	McCairns, Riddoch, Fletcher, Higgins	2000	1	2	3	7	5	6		8	9	10			4			11		
15	8	CREWE ALEXANDRA	5-0	McCairns(2,1pen), Fletcher, Eccleston(2)	2000	1	2		3	5	6	7	8	9	10			4			11		
16	26	WOOLWICH ARSENAL	4-2	McCairns(2), Riddoch, Stott	5000	1	2		3	5	6	7	8	9	10			4			11		
17	Jan 5	BURY	3-2	McCairns, Riddoch, Fletcher	5000	1	2		3	5	6	7	8	9	10			4			11		
18	7	Rotherham Town	2-3	McCairns, Higgins		1	2	3	7	5	4	11	8	9	10			6					
19	12	Darwen	1-4	McCairns		1	2		3	5	6	7	8	9	10			4			11		
20	26	BURSLEM PORT VALE	4-1	Higgins(3), Fletcher		1	2	3	7	5	6		8	9	10			4			11		
21	Feb 5	NOTTS COUNTY	0-1		4000	1	2	3	7	5	6		8	9	10			4			11		
22	9	Crewe Alexandra	1-2	McCairns		1	2		3	5	6		8	9	10			4		7	11		
23	Mar 9	BURTON SWIFTS	7-1	McCairns,Fletcher(2),Eccleston(2),Stott,Frost	2000	1	2	3	4	5		7	8	9	11	10		6					
24	16	WALSALL TOWN SWIFTS	1-0	McCairns	3000	1	2	3	4	5			8	9	11	10		6		7			
25	23	Newton Heath	0-2		9000	1	2	3	4	5		7	8	9	11	10		6					
26	30	DARWEN	2-1	Frost, Riddoch	4000	1	2	3	4				7	9	8	11		6	5		10		
27	Apr 6	Burslem Port Vale	0-5		500	1	2	3		5			7	9	8	11		6	4		10		
28	13	Burton Wanderers	0-0			1	2	3	5	10		7		9	8	11		6	4				
29	15	Leicester Fosse	0-1		10000	1	2	3	5	6			7	9	8	11		4					10
30	20	MANCHESTER CITY	2-1	Fletcher, Higgins	2000	1	2	3	5	6		7	4	9	8	11					10		
					Apps.	30	30	24	27	29	20	22	29	26	30	14	1	20	3	2	19	2	2
					Goals				7	4		4	13	18	16	5					7	2	

3 own goals

F.A. Cup

	Date	Opponent	Score	Scorers	Att.	Whitehouse	Lindsay	Frith T	Higgins	Stott	Waterson	Rose	Eccleston	McCairns	Fletcher	Frost	Lundie	Graham	Murrell	Murray	Riddoch	Fairburn	Cooper
Q1	Oct 13	Lincoln City	3-0	Scott, Fletcher, Frost	5000	1	2	3	4	5	6	7	8	9	10	11							
Q2	Nov 3	ATTERCLIFFE	2-2	Higgins, Riddoch	2000		3	2	4	5	1	7	8		10	11		6			9		
Q2r	5	ATTERCLIFFE	8-0	Higgins, Stott,Eccleston,Riddoch(2),Frost(3)	1000	1	3	2	4	5		7	8		10	11		6			9		
Q3	24	WORKSOP TOWN	0-1		2500	1	3		9	5	4	7	8		10		2	6			11		

	P	W	D	L	F	A	W	D	L	F	A	F	A	Pts
1 Bury	30	15	0	0	48	11	8	2	5	30	22	78	33	48
2 Notts County	30	12	2	1	50	15	5	3	7	25	30	75	45	39
3 Newton Heath	30	9	6	0	52	18	6	2	7	26	26	78	44	38
4 Leicester Fosse	30	11	2	2	45	20	4	6	5	27	33	72	53	38
5 GRIMSBY TOWN	30	14	0	1	51	16	4	1	10	28	36	79	52	37
6 Darwen	30	13	1	1	53	10	3	3	9	21	33	74	43	36
7 Burton Wanderers	30	10	3	2	49	9	4	4	7	18	30	67	39	35
8 Woolwich Arsenal	30	11	3	1	54	20	3	3	9	21	38	75	58	34
9 Manchester City	30	9	3	3	56	28	5	0	10	26	44	82	72	31
10 Newcastle United	30	11	1	3	51	28	1	2	12	21	56	72	84	27
11 Burton Swifts	30	9	2	4	34	20	2	1	12	18	54	52	74	25
12 Rotherham Town	30	10	0	5	37	22	1	2	12	18	40	55	62	24
13 Lincoln City	30	8	0	7	32	27	2	0	13	20	65	52	92	20
14 Walsall Town Swfts	30	8	0	7	35	25	2	0	13	12	67	47	92	20
15 Burslem Port Vale	30	6	3	6	30	23	1	1	13	9	54	39	77	18
16 Crewe Alexandra	30	3	4	8	20	34	0	0	15	6	69	26	103	10

SEASON 1894/95
Back: Shephard (Sec) Whitehouse, Lindsay, Stott, Bellamy (Dir), Higgins, Murrell, Frith, Allen (Train), McCormack (Asst Train)
Middle: Rose, Graham, Riddoch. Front: Murray, Eccleston, McCairns, Fletcher, Pratt

SEASON 1895/96
Back: Shephard (Sec), Hall (Asst Train), White (Vice Pres), Coulson (Pres), Jennison, Bellamy (Treas), Allen (Train)
Middle: Blair, Munn, Higgins, Graham, Lindsay, Whitehouse, Frith, Hudson, Davis,
Front: Bailey, Bell, Pratt, McCairns, Fletcher, Gray

1895-96 3rd in Division 2

			Opponent	Score	Scorers	Att.	Whitehouse	Lindsay	Davis	Higgins	Blair	Graham	Bell	Pratt	McCairns	Fletcher	Gray	Hudson	Frith	Munn	Bailey	Robinson	Rose	Mountain
1	Sep	2	Woolwich Arsenal	1-3	McCairns	8000	1	2	3	4	5	6	7	8	9	10	11							
2		7	LINCOLN CITY	4-2	McCairns(4)	4000	1	2		4		6	7		9	10	11		3	5	8			
3		14	Darwen	3-3	Bell(2), Gray	3000	1	2		5		6	7	8	9	10	11	4	3					
4		21	MANCHESTER CITY	5-0	Fletcher(2), Gray(2), Pratt	5000	1	2		5		6	7	8	9	10	11		3	4				
5		28	Lincoln City	5-2	McCairns,Higgins,Fletcher,Gray,Pratt	5000	1	2		5		6	7	8	9	10	11		3	4				
6	Oct	3	Notts County	3-5	Pratt, Fletcher, Unknown	3500	1	2	3	5		6	7	8	9	10	11			4				
7		5	Burton Wanderers	1-2	Gray	4000	1	2		5		6	7	8	9	10	11	3		4				
8		19	LIVERPOOL	1-0	Gray		1	2		5		6	7	8	9	10	11		3	4				
9		26	Manchester City	1-2	Bell	14000	1	2		5		6	7	8	9	10			3	4				11
10	Nov	9	Burton Swifts	1-2	Unknown		1	2		5		6	9	8		10	11		3	4	7			
11		16	Burslem Port Vale	4-1	McCairns(2), Gray, Pratt	300	1	2		5		6	7	8	9	10	11		3	4				
12		30	LOUGHBOROUGH	2-0	Pratt(2)		1			5		6	7	8	9	10	11	2	3	4				
13	Dec	21	Loughborough	1-0	McCairns		1	2		5		6	7	8	9	10	11		3	4				
14		26	NEWCASTLE UNITED	2-1	Pratt(2)	4000	1	2		5		6	7	8	9	10	11		3	4				
15		28	BURTON SWIFTS	3-0	Bell(2), Higgins	3000	1	2		5		6	7	8	9	10	11		3	4				
16	Jan	1	Newton Heath	2-3	McCairns, Fletcher	8000	1	2		5		6	7	8	9	10	11		3	4				
17		4	BURSLEM PORT VALE	6-1	Fletcher(2),McCairns(2),Pratt,Davis	2000	1	2	11	5		6	7	8	9	10			3	4				
18		11	Newcastle United	5-1	McCairns,Fletcher,Higgins(2),Pratt	5000	1	2		5		6	7	8	9	10	11		3	4				
19		25	DARWEN	5-0	McCairns,Fletcher,Robinson(2),Pratt	4000	1	2	3	5		6	7	8	9	11				4		10		
20	Feb	8	Rotherham Town	0-1		2000	1	2	3			6	7	5	9	10	11			4		8		
21		22	Liverpool	1-3	Gray	10000	1	2	3	5		6	7	8	9	10	11			4				
22		29	CREWE ALEXANDRA	2-0	Robinson, Higgins		1	2	7	5		6		8	9	11		3		4		10		
23	Mar	3	ROTHERHAM TOWN	4-0	Pratt(2), Fletcher, OG		1	2	3	5		6	9	8		11				4		10	7	
24		7	Crewe Alexandra	1-0	McCairns		1	2	3	5		6	10	8	9	11				4			7	
25		14	NEWTON HEATH	4-2	McCairns, Pratt(2), Graham	2000	1	2	3	5		6	7	8	9	11				4		10		
26		21	NOTTS COUNTY	3-0	McCairns(2), Bell	3000	1	2	3			6	7	8	9	11		5		4			10	
27		28	BURTON WANDERERS	2-1	McCairns, Fletcher		1	2	3	5		6	7	8	9	10	11			4				
28	Apr	4	WOOLWICH ARSENAL	1-1	Higgins	6000	1	2	3	5		6	7	8	9	10	11			4				
29		6	Leicester Fosse	2-1	McCairns, Gray		1	2	3	5		6	7	8	9	10	11			4				
30		11	LEICESTER FOSSE	7-1	McCairns(6), Higgins		1	2	3	5		6	7	8	9	10	11			4				
						Apps.	30	19	15	28	1	30	29	29	28	30	22	5	15	28	2	5	3	1
						Goals			1	7		1	6	15	26	11	9					3		

1 own goal

F.A. Cup

			Opponent	Score	Scorers	Att.	Whitehouse	Lindsay	Davis	Higgins	Blair	Graham	Bell	Pratt	McCairns	Fletcher	Gray	Hudson	Frith	Munn	Bailey	Robinson	Rose	Mountain
Q1	Oct	12	Staveley	5-0	McCairns(3), Gray(2)	1000	1	2	4			6	7	8	9	10	11	3		5				
Q2	Nov	2	Kilnhurst	4-1	Davis, Graham, McCairns(2)	1000	1		4	2	5	6	7	8	9	10	11		3					
Q3		23	Lincoln City	4-2	McCairns(3), Fletcher	5000	1	2		5		6	7	8	9	10	11		3	4				
Q4	Dec	14	ROTHERHAM TOWN	4-0	Munn, Bell(2), OG	3000	1	2		5		6	7	8	9	10	11		3	4				
R1	Feb	1	Darwen	2-0	Graham, Pratt	4000	1	2	3	5		6	7	8	9	10	11			4				
R2		15	WEST BROM. ALB.	1-1	Gray	7500	1	2	3	5		6	7	8	9	10	11			4				
R2r		20	West Bromwich Albion	0-3		11000	1	2	3	5		6	7	8	9	10	11			4				

		P	W	D	L	F	A	W	D	L	F	A	F	A	Pts
1	Liverpool	30	14	1	0	65	11	8	1	6	41	21	106	32	46
2	Manchester City	30	12	3	0	37	9	9	1	5	26	29	63	38	46
3	GRIMSBY TOWN	30	14	1	0	51	9	6	1	8	31	29	82	38	42
4	Burton Wanderers	30	12	1	2	43	15	7	3	5	26	25	69	40	42
5	Newcastle United	30	14	0	1	57	14	2	2	11	16	36	73	50	34
6	Newton Heath	30	12	2	1	48	15	3	1	11	18	42	66	57	33
7	Woolwich Arsenal	30	11	1	3	42	11	3	3	9	16	31	58	42	32
8	Leicester Fosse	30	10	0	5	40	16	4	4	7	17	28	57	44	32
9	Darwen	30	9	4	2	55	22	3	2	10	17	45	72	67	30
10	Notts County	30	8	1	6	41	22	4	1	10	16	32	57	54	26
11	Burton Swifts	30	7	2	6	24	26	3	2	10	15	43	39	69	24
12	Loughborough	30	7	3	5	32	25	2	2	11	8	41	40	66	23
13	Lincoln City	30	7	1	7	36	24	2	3	10	17	51	53	75	22
14	Burslem Port Vale	30	6	4	5	25	24	1	0	14	18	54	43	78	18
15	Rotherham Town	30	7	2	6	27	26	0	1	14	7	71	34	97	17
16	Crewe Alexandra	30	5	2	8	22	28	0	1	14	8	67	30	95	13

1896-97 3rd in Division 2

Captain: Billy Lindsay

							Cain	Lindsay	Frith	Higgins	Chapman	Graham	Bell	Morris	McCairns	Fletcher	Gray	Wallace	Daw	Hardie	Davis	Rogers	Munn	Hogan
1	Sep	2	Loughborough	4-1	Fletcher(2), McCairns, OG	2000	1	2	3	4	5	6	7	8	9	10	11							
2		5	GAINSBOROUGH TRINITY	1-1	Gray		1	2	3	4	5	6	7	8	9	10	11							
3		12	Burton Wanderers	1-5	Rogers			2			5	6		8	9	10		1			3	7	4	11
4		19	NEWTON HEATH	2-0	Rogers, Fletcher	3000		2		5		6		8	9	10	11	1			3	7	4	
5		26	LINCOLN CITY	3-1	Rogers, Fletcher, Lindsay	5000		2		5	6			8	9	10	11	1			3	7	4	
6	Oct	1	Notts County	3-1	Rogers(2), Gray	10000		2		5	6			8	9	10	11	1			3	7	4	
7		3	Gainsborough Trinity	1-1	McCairns	4000		2		5	6			8	9	10	11	1			3	7	4	
8		10	Newcastle United	0-3		4000		2		5	6		7	8		10	11	1			3	9	4	
9		17	LOUGHBOROUGH	8-1	McCairns(3),Higgins(2),Fletcher,Rogers,Bell	3000		2		5	6		8	11	9	10		1			3	7	4	
10		24	MANCHESTER CITY	3-1	McCairns, Fletcher(2)	4000		2		5	6		8	11	9	10		1			3	7	4	
11		31	Small Heath	1-0	Rogers	7000		2		5	6		8	11	9	10		1			3	7	4	
12	Nov	7	Newton Heath	2-4	Rogers, Fletcher	5000		2			6	5	8	11	9	10		1			3	7	4	
13		21	NOTTS COUNTY	3-1	McCairns, Fletcher, Bell	7000		2		5	6		8		9	10	11	1			3	7	4	
14		28	Woolwich Arsenal	2-4	McCairns, Fletcher	8000		2		5	6		8	11	9	10		1			3	7	4	
15	Dec	5	Leicester Fosse	2-4	Gray, Fletcher	8000		2	3	5		6	8	7	9	10	11		1				4	
16		12	SMALL HEATH	2-1	Gray, Bell	3500		2	3	5		6	8		9	10	11	1				7	4	
17		19	Manchester City	1-3	Gray	10000		2	3	5	6			8	9	10	11	1				7	4	
18		26	NEWCASTLE UNITED	3-2	McCairns, Rogers(2)	10000		2	3	5	6			8	9	10	11	1				7	4	
19	Jan	1	Blackpool	0-1		5000		2	3	5	6			8	9	10	11	1				7	4	
20		2	BURTON WANDERERS	3-0	Rogers, Bell, Fletcher	2000		2	3	5	6		8	11	9	10		1				7	4	
21		9	Lincoln City	3-0	McCairns, Rogers, Morris	2000		2	3	5	6			8	9	10	11	1				7	4	
22		16	Burton Swifts	0-0				2	3	5	6			8	9	10	11	1				7	4	
23		23	LEICESTER FOSSE	4-1	McCairns, Gray(2), Fletcher	3000		2	3	5	6			8	9	10	11	1				7	4	
24	Feb	20	BLACKPOOL	2-2	Fletcher, Bell	5000			3	5	6		8		9	10	11		1		2	7	4	
25		27	Walsall Town Swifts	1-0	McCairns	6000			3	5	6		7	8	9	10	11			1		2	4	
26	Mar	6	DARWEN	4-2	McCairns(3), Fletcher	5000			3	5	6		8	7	9	10	11			1		2	4	
27		13	WALSALL TOWN SWIFTS	0-1		5000		2	3	5	6		8		9	10	11			1		7	4	
28		20	Darwen	1-3	OG	1000		2	3	5	6		8		9	10	11			1	7		4	
29	Apr	3	BURTON SWIFTS	3-0	Fletcher(2), Graham	3000			3	2	6	5	8		9	10	11			1		7	4	
30		8	WOOLWICH ARSENAL	3-1	Gray(2), Rogers	10000			3	2	6	5	8		9	10	11			1		7	4	
						Apps.	2	25	18	28	27	9	19	23	29	30	23	20	2	6	14	26	28	1
						Goals		1		2		1	5	1	15	17	9					13		

2 own goals

F.A. Cup

							Cain	Lindsay	Frith	Higgins	Chapman	Graham	Bell	Morris	McCairns	Fletcher	Gray	Wallace	Daw	Hardie	Davis	Rogers	Munn	Hogan
1	Jan	28	BOLTON WANDERERS	0-0		10000		2	3	5	6			8	9	10	11	1				7	4	
1r	Feb	3	Bolton Wanderers	3-3	Rogers, Bell, McCairns	7000		2	3	5	6		8		9	10	11	1				7	4	
1r2r		11	Bolton Wanderers*	2-3	Fletcher, OG	10000		2	3	5	6		8		9	10	11	1				7	4	

*** Played at Bramall Lane, Sheffield.**

		P	W	D	L	F	A	W	D	L	F	A	F	A	Pts
1	Notts County	30	12	1	2	60	18	7	3	5	32	25	92	43	42
2	Newton Heath	30	11	4	0	37	10	6	1	8	19	24	56	34	39
3	GRIMSBY TOWN	30	12	2	1	44	15	5	2	8	22	30	66	45	38
4	Small Heath	30	8	3	4	36	23	8	2	5	33	24	69	47	37
5	Newcastle United	30	13	1	1	42	13	4	0	11	14	39	56	52	35
6	Manchester City	30	10	3	2	39	15	2	5	8	19	35	58	50	32
7	Gainsborough Trin.	30	10	2	3	35	16	2	5	8	15	31	50	47	31
8	Blackpool	30	11	3	1	39	16	2	2	11	20	40	59	56	31
9	Leicester Fosse	30	11	2	2	44	20	2	2	11	15	37	59	57	30
10	Woolwich Arsenal	30	10	1	4	42	20	3	3	9	26	50	68	70	30
11	Darwen	30	13	0	2	54	16	1	0	14	13	45	67	61	28
12	Walsall	30	8	2	5	37	25	3	2	10	17	44	54	69	26
13	Loughborough	30	10	0	5	37	14	2	1	12	13	50	50	64	25
14	Burton Swifts	30	7	4	4	33	20	2	2	11	13	41	46	61	24
15	Burton Wanderers	30	8	1	6	22	22	1	1	13	9	45	31	67	20
16	Lincoln City	30	4	2	9	17	27	1	0	14	10	58	27	85	12

1897-98 12th in Division 2

Captain: Billy Lindsay

	Date		Opponent	Score	Scorers	Att.	Whittaker	Lindsay	Frith	Munn	McLean	Chapman	Rogers	Richardson W	McCairns	Fletcher	Gray	Leaning	Parker	Mountain	Brocklesby	Mount	Bell	Johnston	Hyde	Chatburn	Taylor F	Goldie	Robinson H	Frost	Blythe	Barton
1	Sep	1	Woolwich Arsenal	1-4	Fletcher	6000	1	2	3	4	5	6	7	8	9	10	11															
2		4	GAINSBOROUGH TRINITY	4-2	Fletcher, Rogers(2), OG	5000	1	2	3	4	5	6	7		9	10	11											8				
3		11	DARWEN	5-0	Robinson(2), Rogers(2), Goldie	4000	1	2	3		5		7			10				4		6			11			8	9			
4		18	LEICESTER FOSSE	0-0		3000	1	2	3		5		7		9	10				4		6			11			8				
5		25	Gainsborough Trinity	0-2		4000	1	2	3	4	6	5	7		9	10	11											8				
6	Oct	2	LINCOLN CITY	4-2	Gray(3), Goldie	5000	1	2	3	4	6	5	7		9	10	11											8				
7		9	Manchester City	0-3		12000	1	2	3	4	6	5	7		9	10	11			8												
8		16	Darwen	0-1		3000		2	3	4	6	5			9	10	8	1		7												11
9		23	BURNLEY	2-1	Rogers, Goldie	4000	1	2	3	4	6	5	7		9	10												8				11
10	Nov	6	NEWCASTLE UNITED	2-0	McCairns, Fletcher	4000	1	2	3		4	5	7		9	10	11							6				8				
11		13	SMALL HEATH	3-1	Fletcher(2), Mountain	2000		2	3		4	5			9	10	11	1		7				6				8				
12		20	Walsall	1-1	OG		1	2	3		4	5	7		9	10								6	11			8				
13		27	Newton Heath	1-2	Rogers	3000	1	2	3		4	5	7		9	10	11							6				8				
14	Dec	1	Burton United	0-4			1	2	3		4	5	7		9	10	11							6				8				
15		4	LOUGHBOROUGH	7-0	Fletcher(4),Goldie,Rogers,Barton	700	1	2			4	5	7		9	10						3		6				8				11
16		11	Burnley	0-6		4000	1	2	3		4	5	7		9	10	11							6				8				
17		18	MANCHESTER CITY	3-4	McCairns(2), Gray	5000	1	2			4	5	7		9	10	11					3		6				8				
18		25	Lincoln City	1-1	McLean	5000	1	2	3		6	5	7		9	10	11			4								8				
19		27	Luton Town	0-6			1	2	3		5		7		9	10	11			4					6			8				
20	Jan	22	LUTON TOWN	1-3	Gray	5000	1	2	3		4				9	10	11						5			6		7	8			
21	Feb	5	BURTON UNITED	7-2	McCairns(4), Gray(2), Rogers	2000	1	2	3		6		7		9	10	11			4			5					8				
22		12	WOOLWICH ARSENAL	1-4	Rogers	4000	1	2	3		6		7		9	10	11			4			5					8				
23	Mar	5	WALSALL	1-2	Goldie	2000	1		3		6	5	7		9	10	11		2	4								8				
24		12	Small Heath	2-0	McCairns, Fletcher	2500	1		3		4	6	7		9	8	11			2			5					10				
25		19	BLACKPOOL	3-0	McCairns, Fletcher, Rogers	2500	1		3		4	6	7		9	8	11			2			5							10		
26		26	Newcastle United	0-4		4000	1		3		4	6	7		9		11			2			5					8		10		
27	Apr	2	NEWTON HEATH	1-3	Blyth	3000	1		3		4	6	7		9		11			2			5					8			10	
28		9	Loughborough	1-2	McLean	1500	1		3		4	6	7		9		11				2		5					8			10	
29		11	Leicester Fosse	0-1			1		3		4	6	7		9		11			10	2		5					8				
30		16	Blackpool	1-1	Bell	1000	1		3		4		7		9					10	2		5				6	8			11	
						Apps.	28	22	28	7	30	23	27	1	29	25	24	2	1	16	3	4	10	8	4	1	1	26	2	2	3	3
						Goals					2		10		9	11	7			1			1				2	5	2		1	1

2 own goals

F.A. Cup

	Date		Opponent	Score	Scorers	Att.	Whittaker	Lindsay	Frith	Munn	McLean	Chapman	Rogers	Richardson W	McCairns	Fletcher	Gray	Leaning	Parker	Mountain	Brocklesby	Mount	Bell	Johnston	Hyde	Chatburn	Taylor F	Goldie	Robinson H	Frost	Blythe	Barton
1	Jan	29	Nottingham Forest	0-4		7000		2			3	6	7		9	10	11	1		4			5					8				

	P	W	D	L	F	A	W	D	L	F	A	F	A	Pts
1 Burnley	30	14	1	0	64	13	6	7	2	16	11	80	24	48
2 Newcastle United	30	14	0	1	43	10	7	3	5	21	22	64	32	45
3 Manchester City	30	10	4	1	45	15	5	5	5	21	21	66	36	39
4 Newton Heath	30	11	2	2	42	10	5	4	6	22	25	64	35	38
5 Woolwich Arsenal	30	10	4	1	41	14	6	1	8	28	35	69	49	37
6 Small Heath	30	11	1	3	37	18	5	3	7	21	32	58	50	36
7 Leicester Fosse	30	8	5	2	26	11	5	2	8	20	24	46	35	33
8 Luton Town	30	10	2	3	50	13	3	2	10	18	37	68	50	30
9 Gainsborough Trin.	30	10	4	1	30	12	2	2	11	20	42	50	54	30
10 Walsall	30	9	3	3	42	15	3	2	10	16	43	58	58	29
11 Blackpool	30	8	4	3	32	15	2	1	12	17	46	49	61	25
12 GRIMSBY TOWN	30	9	1	5	44	24	1	3	11	8	38	52	62	24
13 Burton Swifts	30	7	3	5	25	21	1	2	12	13	48	38	69	21
14 Lincoln City	30	6	3	6	27	27	0	2	13	16	55	43	82	17
15 Darwen	30	4	1	10	21	32	2	1	12	10	44	31	76	14
16 Loughborough	30	5	2	8	15	26	1	0	14	9	61	24	87	14

1898-99 10th in Division 2

Captain: Paddy Gray

No.	Month	Day	Opponent	Score	Scorers	Att.	Bagshaw	Pennington	Frith	Cherry	Gray P	Griffiths	Greenwood	Chapman	Cockshutt	Ratcliffe	Nelmes	Mountain	Stewart	Nidd	Lockie	Lowe	Bell	Jenkinson	Richards	Blythe	Pangbourne	Richardson	Robinson	Chatburn
1	Sep	3	Manchester City	2-7	Chapman(2)	10000	1	2	3	4	5	6	7	8	9	10	11													
2		10	GLOSSOP NORTH END	1-1	Jenkinson	2500	1		3			6		8	9	10		2				4	5	7			11			
3		17	Walsall Town Swifts	1-4	Cockshutt	5000	1				5	6	7	8	9			2				3	4	11			10			
4		24	BURTON SWIFTS	1-3	Chapman	3000	1		3		5	4	7	9		8	6	2						11			10			
5	Oct	1	Burslem Port Vale	0-2			1					5	9	8		10	6	11	2	3			4	7						
6		8	SMALL HEATH	2-0	Greenwood, Cockshutt	4000	1				5	11	8		9	10	6	2		3			4	7						
7		22	BLACKPOOL	2-1	Greenwood(2)	4000	1				5	11	8		9	10	6	2		3			4	7						
8	Nov	5	Newton Heath	2-3	Jenkinson, Ratcliffe	5000	1				5	11	8		9	10	6	2		3			4	7						
9		12	NEW BRIGHTON TOWER	2-2	Greenwood, Cockshutt	4500	1				5	11	8		9	10	6	2		3			4	7						
10		26	WOOLWICH ARSENAL	1-0	Gray		1				5	11	8		9	10	6	2		3			4	7						
11	Dec	3	Luton Town	1-3	Griffiths		1			4	5	11	8		9	10	6	2		3				7						
12		17	Darwen	2-0	Chapman, OG	300	1		3	4	5	11	8	10	9		6			2				7						
13		24	GAINSBOROUGH TRINITY	0-2		3500	1		3	7	5	11	8	10	9		6			2			4							
14		26	BARNSLEY	0-1		4500	1		3	4	5	11		8	10		6			2				7		9				
15	Jan	7	Glossop North End	2-4	Greenwood(2)		1		3	4		5	11	10	9		6			2				7	8					
16		14	WALSALL TOWN SWIFTS	2-1	Greenwood, Griffiths	4000	1		3	4	5	11	7	8		10	6			2					9					
17		21	Burton Swifts	2-1	Ratcliffe, Richards		1				5	4	11		9	10	6	2		3				7	8					
18	Feb	4	Small Heath	1-2	Cockshutt(pen)	2000	1				5		11		9	10	6	2		3			4	7	8					
19		11	LOUGHBOROUGH	5-0	Richards(3),Jenkinson,Greenwood	3500	1				5	4	11		9		6	2		3				7	8			10		
20		18	Blackpool	6-3	Greenwood(2),Jenkinson(2),Cockshutt(p),Richards	2000	1				5	4	11		9	10	6	2		3				7	8					
21		21	BURSLEM PORT VALE	3-1	Jenkinson, Cockshutt, Richards	2500	1				5	4	11		9	10	6	2		3				7	8					
22		25	Barnsley	2-2	Cockshutt, Richards	2000	1				5	4	11		9	10	6	2		3				7	8					
23	Mar	4	NEWTON HEATH	3-0	Cockshutt(3)	4000	1				5	4	11		9	10	6	2		3				7	8					
24		11	New Brighton Tower	0-2		6000	1				5	4	11		9	10	6	7		3	2				8					
25		18	LINCOLN CITY	1-1	Cockshutt	5000	1				5		11		9	10	6	7		3	2		4		8					
26		25	Woolwich Arsenal	1-1	Richards	4000	1				5	4	11		9	10	6	2		3				7	8					
27		31	LEICESTER FOSSE	1-0	Jenkinson	5000	1					4	11		9	10	6	2		3			5	7	8					
28	Apr	1	LUTON TOWN	5-0	Ratcliffe(2),Richards,Cockshutt,Bell	5000	1					4	11		9	10	6			3	2		5	7	8					
29		3	Leicester Fosse	0-2		6000	1					4	11		9	10	6	2		3			5	7	8					
30		8	Lincoln City	6-1	Ratcliffe(3),Richards,OG,Greenwood		1					4	11		9	10	6	2		3			5	7	8					
31		11	MANCHESTER CITY	1-2	Richards		1					4	11		9	10	6	2		3			5	7	8					
32		15	DARWEN	9-2	Jenkinson(3),Cockshutt(3),Chatburn,Richards,Bell	2500	1					4			9		6			3	2		5	7	8				10	11
33		17	Loughborough	3-1	Jenkinson(2), Richards		1				5		11		9	10	6			3	2		4	7	8					
34		22	Gainsborough Trinity	1-5	Cockshutt		1				5	4	11		9	10	6	2			2			7	8					
						Apps.	34	1	8	7	25	31	31	10	31	27	32	25	1	29	6	2	18	29	20	1	3	1	1	1
						Goals					1	2	11	4	16	7							2	12	13					1

2 own goals

F.A. Cup

Round	Month	Day	Opponent	Score	Scorers	Att.	Bagshaw	Pennington	Frith	Cherry	Gray P	Griffiths	Greenwood	Chapman	Cockshutt	Ratcliffe	Nelmes	Mountain	Stewart	Nidd	Lockie	Lowe	Bell	Jenkinson	Richards	Blythe	Pangbourne	Richardson	Robinson	Chatburn
Q1	Oct	29	MEXBOROUGH	5-0	Greenwood,(2),Cockshutt,Griffiths(2)	4000	1				5	11	8		9	10	6	2		3			4	7						
Q2	Nov	19	LINCOLN CITY	2-1	Gray, Griffiths	8000	1				5	11	8		9	10	6	2		3			4	7						
Q3	Dec	10	Barnsley	0-0			1		3	4	5	11	8	10	9		6			2				7						
Q3r		14	BARNSLEY	2-1	Jenkinson, Cockshutt	2000	1		3	4	5	11	8	10	9		6			2				7						
R1	Jan	28	Preston North End	0-7		4517	1				5	4	11		9	10	6	2		3				8	7					

		P	W	D	L	F	A	W	D	L	F	A	F	A	Pts
1	Manchester City	34	15	1	1	64	10	8	5	4	28	25	92	35	52
2	Glossop	34	12	1	4	48	13	8	5	4	28	25	76	38	46
3	Leicester Fosse	34	12	5	0	35	12	6	4	7	29	30	64	42	45
4	Newton Heath	34	12	4	1	51	14	7	1	9	16	29	67	43	43
5	New Brighton T.	34	13	2	2	48	13	5	5	7	23	39	71	52	43
6	Walsall	34	12	5	0	64	11	3	7	7	15	25	79	36	42
7	Woolwich Arsenal	34	14	2	1	55	10	4	3	10	17	31	72	41	41
8	Small Heath	34	14	1	2	66	17	3	6	8	19	33	85	50	41
9	Burslem Port Vale	34	12	2	3	35	12	5	3	9	21	22	56	34	39
10	GRIMSBY TOWN	34	10	3	4	39	17	5	2	10	32	43	71	60	35
11	Barnsley	34	11	4	2	44	18	1	3	13	8	38	52	56	31
12	Lincoln City	34	10	5	2	31	16	2	2	13	20	40	51	56	31
13	Burton Swifts	34	7	5	5	35	25	3	3	11	16	45	51	70	28
14	Gainsborough Trin.	34	8	4	5	40	22	2	1	14	16	50	56	72	25
15	Luton Town	34	8	1	8	37	31	2	2	13	14	64	51	95	23
16	Blackpool	34	6	3	8	35	30	2	1	14	14	60	49	90	20
17	Loughborough	34	5	4	8	31	26	1	2	14	7	66	38	92	18
18	Darwen	34	2	4	11	16	32	0	1	16	6	109	22	141	9

SEASON 1897/98
Back: Leach (Train), Lindsay, Whittaker, Mount, Coulson (Pres), Richardson
Middle: Munn, Johnston, Chapman Front: Rogers, Goldie, McCairns, Fletcher, Gray

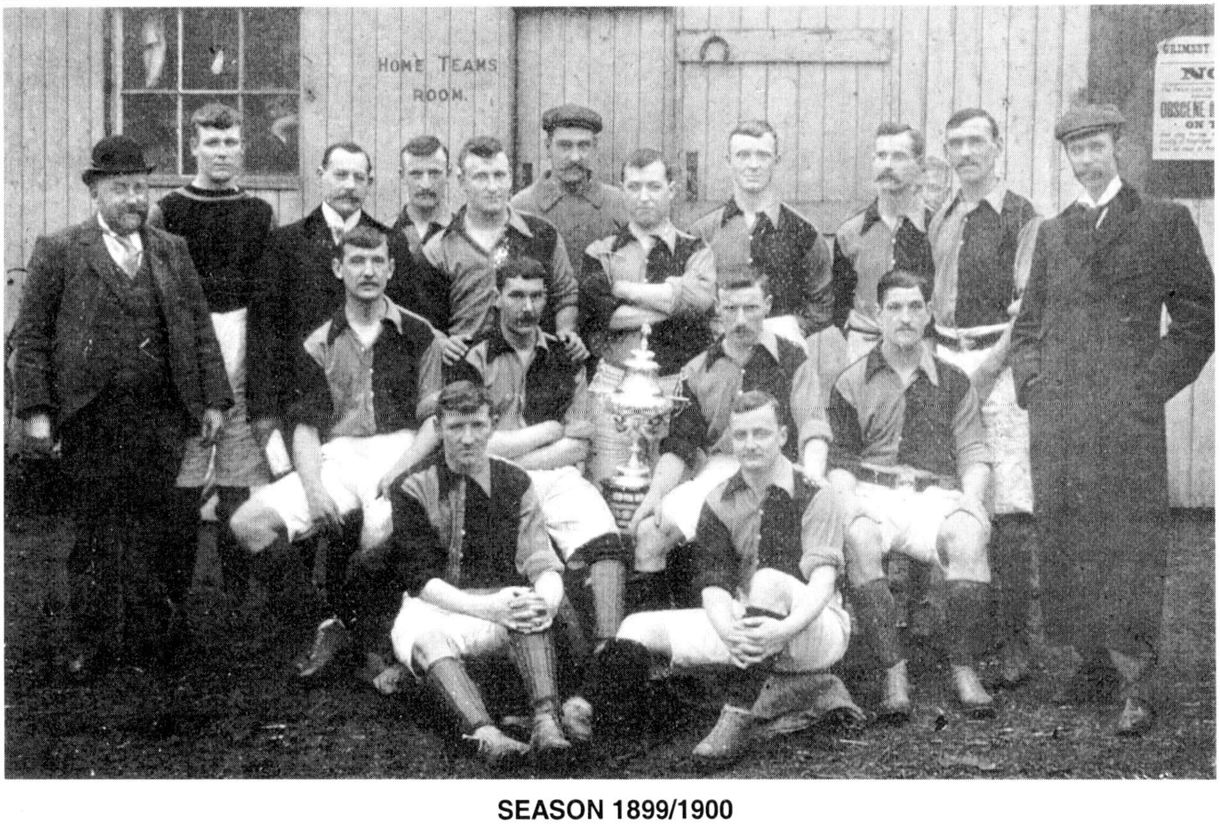

HOME TEAMS ROOM.

SEASON 1899/1900
Back: Whitehouse, Bellamy, Craddock (Trainer), Gray, Nidd, Nelmes
2nd Row: Hickson (Sec), Friend (Sec), Mountain, Cockshutt, White (Chair)
3rd Row: Jenkinson, Richards, Ratcliffe, Lukey Front: Hemingfield, Greenfield.

1899-00 6th in Division 2

Captain: Paddy Gray

No.	Month	Day	Opponent	Score	Scorers	Att.	Whitehouse	Beveridge	Nidd	Griffiths	Gray	Nelmes	Jenkinson	Richards	Cockshutt	Ratcliffe	Greenwood	Mountain	Finlayson	McAvoy	Hemingfield	Lakey	Robinson
1	Sep	2	LUTON TOWN	3-3	Cockshutt, Nidd, Ratcliffe	4000	1	2	3	4	5	6	7	8	9	10	11						
2		9	Burslem Port Vale	3-2	Jenkinson(2), Richards	3000	1	2		4	5	6	7	8	9	10			3			11	
3		16	WALSALL	4-2	Richards(2), Jenkinson, Ratcliffe	4500	1		3	4	5	6	7	8	9	10	11	2					
4		23	Middlesbrough	0-1		4000	1		3	4	5	6		8	9	10	11	2			7		
5	Oct	7	Gainsborough Trinity	3-2	Beveridge(2), Ratcliffe	2500	1	7	3	4	5	6		8	9	10	11	2					
6		14	BOLTON WANDERERS	0-0		5000	1	7	3	4	5	6		8	9	10	11	2					
7		21	Loughborough Town	0-0		2000	1	7	3	4	5	6		8	9	10	11	2					
8	Nov	11	LINCOLN CITY	5-2	Mountain,Jenkinson,Nelmes,Richards(2pens)	5000	1		3		5	6	7	8	9	11	4	2			10		
9		25	NEW BRIGHTON TOWER	1-2	Richards	4500	1		3		5	6	7	8		10	4	2			9	11	
10	Dec	2	Burton Swifts	2-1	Jenkinson, Ratcliffe		1		3	4	5	6	7	8	9	10			2		11		
11		16	BARNSLEY	8-1	* goalscorers - see below	2500	1		3	4	5	6	7	8	9	10		2			11		
12		23	Leicester Fosse	0-3			1				5	6	7	8	9	10	4	2	3		11		
13		25	CHESTERFIELD TOWN	0-3		6000	1				5	6	7	8	9	10	4	2	3		11		
14		26	NEWTON HEATH	0-7		4500	1			8	5	6	7		9	10	4		2			11	3
15		30	Luton Town	4-0	Richards(3), Ratcliffe		1			3	5	6	7	8	9	10	11	2			4		
16	Jan	2	Sheffield Wednesday	1-2	Richards	15000	1			3	5	6	7	8	9	10	11	2			4		
17		6	BURSLEM PORT VALE	1-1	Greenwood		1		3	5		6	7	8	9	10	11	4		2			
18		13	Walsall	1-1	OG	2000	1			4	5	6	7	8	9		11	2		3		10	
19		20	MIDDLESBROUGH	2-0	Richards, OG	3500	1			4	5	6	7	8	9		10	2		3	11		
20	Feb	3	Chesterfield Town	1-3	Lakey	1000			1	4		6	7	8	9	10		2		3	5	11	
21		10	GAINSBOROUGH TRINITY	3-0	Cockshutt, Richards(2)	2000	1			4		6	7	8	9	10		2		3	5	11	
22		12	Small Heath	1-0	Ratcliffe		1		7	4		6			9	10	8	2		3	5	11	
23		17	Bolton Wanderers	2-1	Ratcliffe, OG	3000	1		3	4	5		7	10	9	8	11	2			6		
24		24	LOUGHBOROUGH TOWN	3-0	Ratcliffe, Richards, Griffiths	2500	1		3	4	5		7	10	9	8	11	2			6		
25	Mar	3	Newton Heath	0-1		8000	1			4		6	7	8	9	10	11	2		3	5		
26		24	SMALL HEATH	2-0	Greenwood, Hemingfield	3000	1			4	5	6	7	8	9		11	2		3	10		
27		31	New Brighton Tower	1-2	Nelmes		1			4	5	6	7	8	9		11	2		3	10		
28	Apr	7	BURTON SWIFTS	6-0	Richards(3),Jenkinson,Cockshutt,OG	2000	1				5	6	7	8	9	10	11	2		3	4		
29		13	SHEFFIELD WEDNESDAY	1-2	Richards	7000			1	4	5	6	7	8	9	10	11	2		3			
30		14	WOOLWICH ARSENAL	1-0	Richards				1	4	5	6	7	8	9	10	11	2		3			
31		16	Woolwich Arsenal	0-2		3000			1	3	5	6	7	8	9	10	11	2				4	
32		21	Barnsley	1-0	Jenkinson				1	4	5	6	7	8		10		2		3	9	11	
33		27	Lincoln City	1-1	Lakey	3000			1	4	5	6	7	8		10		2		3	9	11	
34		28	LEICESTER FOSSE	6-1	Hemingfield(2),Ratcliffe(2),Lakey,Jenkinson	3000			1	4	5	6	7	8		10		2		3	9	11	

* Jenkinson(2),Ratcliffe(2),Cockshutt(2),Richards,Hemingfield

	Whitehouse	Beveridge	Nidd	Griffiths	Gray	Nelmes	Jenkinson	Richards	Cockshutt	Ratcliffe	Greenwood	Mountain	Finlayson	McAvoy	Hemingfield	Lakey	Robinson
Apps.	27	5	21	29	29	32	29	32	30	30	26	30	5	15	22	11	1
Goals		2	1	1		2	10	20	5	12	2	1			4	3	

4 own goals

F.A. Cup

Rd	Month	Day	Opponent	Score	Scorers	Att.	Whitehouse	Beveridge	Nidd	Griffiths	Gray	Nelmes	Jenkinson	Richards	Cockshutt	Ratcliffe	Greenwood	Mountain	Finlayson	McAvoy	Hemingfield	Lakey	Robinson
Q3	Oct	28	DONCASTER ROVERS	3-1	Jenkinson, Richards, Cockshutt		1		3	4	5	6	7	8	9	10		2			11		
Q4	Nov	21	BARNSLEY	3-2	Richards, Cockshutt, Ratcliffe	3000	1		3		5	6	7	8	9	11	4	2			10		
Q5	Dec	9	CHESTERFIELD TOWN	3-2	Jenkinson(2), Hemingfield	5000	1		3	4	5	6	7	8		10	9		2		11		
R1	Jan	27	Nottingham Forest	0-3		7000	1			4	5	6	7	8	9	10		3		2	11		

		P	W	D	L	F	A	W	D	L	F	A	F	A	Pts
1	Sheffield Wed.	34	17	0	0	61	7	8	4	5	23	15	84	22	54
2	Bolton Wanderers	34	14	2	1	47	7	8	6	3	32	18	79	25	52
3	Small Heath	34	15	1	1	58	12	5	5	7	20	26	78	38	46
4	Newton Heath	34	15	1	1	44	11	5	3	9	19	16	63	27	44
5	Leicester Fosse	34	11	5	1	34	8	6	4	7	19	28	53	36	43
6	GRIMSBY TOWN	34	10	3	4	46	24	7	3	7	21	22	67	46	40
7	Chesterfield	34	10	4	3	35	24	6	2	9	30	36	65	60	38
8	Woolwich Arsenal	34	13	1	3	47	12	3	3	11	14	31	61	43	36
9	Lincoln City	34	11	5	1	31	9	3	3	11	15	34	46	43	36
10	New Brighton T.	34	9	4	4	44	22	4	5	8	22	36	66	58	35
11	Burslem Port Vale	34	11	2	4	26	16	3	4	10	13	33	39	49	34
12	Walsall	34	10	5	2	35	18	2	3	12	15	37	50	55	32
13	Gainsborough Trin.	34	8	4	5	37	24	1	3	13	10	51	47	75	25
14	Middlesbrough	34	8	4	5	28	15	0	4	13	11	54	39	69	24
15	Burton Swifts	34	8	5	4	31	24	1	1	15	12	60	43	84	24
16	Barnsley	34	8	5	4	36	23	0	2	15	10	56	46	79	23
17	Luton Town	34	5	3	9	25	25	0	5	12	15	50	40	75	18
18	Loughborough	34	1	6	10	12	26	0	0	17	6	74	18	100	8

1900-01 1st in Division 2

Captain: Joe Leiper

	Date		Opponent	Score	Scorers	Att.	Harris	Mountain	Leiper	Griffiths	Gray	Nelmes	Jenkinson	Richards	Leigh	Mellor	Hemingfield	Leaning	McFarlane	McAvoy	Brumley	Watkins	Fletcher	Hall	Lakey
1	Sep	1	Burnley	0-3			1	2	3	4	5	6	7	8	9	10	11								
2		8	BURSLEM PORT VALE	6-1	Lakey(2),Leigh(2),Hemingfield(2)	4000	1	2	3	4	5	6		8	9	10	7								11
3		15	Leicester Fosse	0-4			1	2	3	4	5		7	8	9	10	6								11
4		22	NEW BRIGHTON TOWER	5-2	Richards(2),Jenkinson, Nelmes,OG	4500	1		3	4	5	6	7	8	9	10				2					11
5		29	Gainsborough Trinity	1-0	Jenkinson	5000	1		3	4	5	6	7	8	9	10				2					11
6	Oct	6	WALSALL	0-0			1	2	3	4	5	6	7	8	9	10									11
7		13	Burton Swifts	2-1	Nelmes, Lakey		1		3	4	5	6	7	8	9	10				2					11
8		20	BARNSLEY	1-0	Hemingfield				3	4	5	6	7	8			9	1		2			10		11
9		27	Woolwich Arsenal	1-1	Richards	8000	1		3	4	5	6		8	9	10	11			2			7		
10	Nov	3	Burslem Port Vale	0-0		3000	1		3	4	5	6		8	9	10	11			2			7		
11		10	STOCKPORT COUNTY	5-1	Richards(2,1p),Mellor,Hemingfield,Gray	5000	1		3	4	5	6		8	9	10	11			2			7		
12		17	SMALL HEATH	1-1	Griffiths	5000	1		3	4	5	6	7	8		10				2			9		11
13		24	CHESTERFIELD TOWN	5-2	Lakey,Leigh,Griffiths,Mellor,OG	6000		2	3	4	5	6		8	9	10		1					7		11
14	Dec	1	LINCOLN CITY	4-0	Richards, Leigh(3)	7000		2	3	4	5	6		8	9	10		1					7		11
15		8	NEWTON HEATH	2-0	Richards, Lakey	6000	1	2		4	5	6		8	9	10				3			7		11
16		15	Glossop	0-0		1500		2	3	4	5	6		8	9	10			1				7		11
17		22	MIDDLESBROUGH	2-0	Lakey, Nelmes	5000		2	3	4	5	6		8	9	10			1				7		11
18		25	Lincoln City	1-0	Lakey	7000		2	3	4	5	6		8	9	10			1				7		11
19		29	BURNLEY	2-1	Lakey, OG	7000		2		4		6		8	9	10	5		1	3			7		11
20	Jan	12	LEICESTER FOSSE	4-1	Mellor(2), Lakey, Hall	5000		2		4		6			9	10	5		1	3			7	8	11
21		19	New Brighton Tower	0-5				2	3	4		6		8	9	10	5		1				7		11
22		26	BLACKPOOL	2-0	Leigh, OG			2	3	4	5	6		8	9	10			1				7		11
23	Feb	9	Walsall	0-0				2	3	4		6		8	9	10	5		1				7	11	
24		16	BURTON SWIFTS	5-2	Watkins(2), Brumley, Nelmes, Fletcher	3000		2	3			6			9	10	4		1		5	11	7	8	
25		23	Barnsley	3-2	Richards, Hall, Brumley	2000		2	3			6		8		10	4		1		5	11	7	9	
26	Mar	2	WOOLWICH ARSENAL	1-0	Nelmes	4000		2	3		5	6		8	9	10	4		1			11	7		
27		9	Blackpool	1-0	Richards	2000		2	3		5			8	9	10	4		1			6	7		11
28		16	Stockport County	1-0	Watkins	5000		2	3		5	6		8	9	10	4		1			11	7		
29		30	Chesterfield Town	3-3	Watkins, Fletcher, Nelmes	3000		2	3		5	6		8	9	10	4		1			11	7		
30	Apr	1	Small Heath	1-2	Watkins			2	3		5	6			9	10	4		1			11	7	8	
31		5	GAINSBOROUGH TRINITY	0-0		8000	1	2	3		5	6			9	10	4					11	7	8	
32		13	Newton Heath	0-1		3000		2	3	4	5	6			9	10	8		1			11	7		
33		20	GLOSSOP	1-0	Leigh	6000		2	3		5	6		8	9	10	4		1			11	7		
34		27	Middlesbrough	0-0		8000		2	3		5	6			9	10	4		1			11	7	8	
						Apps.	13	26	31	24	28	32	8	28	31	33	22	3	18	11	2	11	27	7	19
						Goals				2	1	6	2	9	8	4	4				2	5	2	2	9

4 own goals

F.A. Cup

	Date		Opponent	Score	Scorers	Att.	Harris	Mountain	Leiper	Griffiths	Gray	Nelmes	Jenkinson	Richards	Leigh	Mellor	Hemingfield	Leaning	McFarlane	McAvoy	Brumley	Watkins	Fletcher	Hall	Lakey
Sup.	Jan	5	MIDDLESBROUGH	0-1		5000		2		4		6	7		9	10	5		1	3			8		11

		P	W	D	L	F	A	W	D	L	F	A	F	A	Pts
1	GRIMSBY TOWN	34	14	3	0	46	11	6	6	5	14	22	60	33	49
2	Small Heath	34	14	2	1	41	8	5	8	4	16	16	57	24	48
3	Burnley	34	15	2	0	39	6	5	2	10	14	23	53	29	44
4	New Brighton T.	34	12	5	0	34	8	5	3	9	23	30	57	38	42
5	Glossop	34	11	2	4	34	9	4	6	7	17	24	51	33	38
6	Middlesbrough	34	11	4	2	38	13	4	3	10	12	27	50	40	37
7	Woolwich Arsenal	34	13	3	1	30	11	2	3	12	9	24	39	35	36
8	Lincoln City	34	12	3	2	39	11	1	4	12	4	28	43	39	33
9	Burslem Port Vale	34	8	6	3	28	14	3	5	9	17	33	45	47	33
10	Newton Heath	34	11	3	3	31	9	3	1	13	11	29	42	38	32
11	Leicester Fosse	34	9	5	3	30	15	2	5	10	9	22	39	37	32
12	Blackpool	34	7	6	4	20	11	5	1	11	13	47	33	58	31
13	Gainsborough Trin.	34	8	4	5	26	18	2	6	9	19	42	45	60	30
14	Chesterfield	34	6	5	6	25	22	3	5	9	21	36	46	58	28
15	Barnsley	34	9	3	5	34	23	2	2	13	13	37	47	60	27
16	Walsall	34	7	7	3	29	23	0	6	11	11	33	40	56	27
17	Stockport County	34	9	2	6	25	21	2	1	14	13	47	38	68	25
18	Burton Swifts	34	7	3	7	16	21	1	1	15	18	45	34	66	20

1901-02 15th in Division 1

Captain: Joe Leiper

							Tennant	Mountain	Leiper	Hemingfield	Bellingham	Nelmes	Dean	Harper	Ronaldson	Leigh	Gardner	Clutterbuck	Whittaker	McConnell	Hall	Griffiths	Gray	Brumley	Skinner	Fletcher	Stevenson	Appleyard	Long
1	Sep	3	DERBY COUNTY	1-1	Leigh	7000	1	2	3	4	5	6	7	8	9	10	11												
2		7	Sheffield Wednesday	1-3	Dean		1		3	4	5	6	7	8	9	10	11			2									
3		14	NOTTINGHAM FOREST	1-0	Ronaldson	8000	1	2	3	4		6	7		9	8	11						5			10			
4		21	Notts County	0-3		7000	1	2	3	4		6	7	10	9	8	11						5						
5		28	BURY	2-0	Ronaldson, Leigh	7000	1	2	3	4		6			9	8	11						5			7	10		
6	Oct	5	Bolton Wanderers	0-4		5000	1	2	3	4		6	7		9	8	11						5				10		
7		12	BLACKBURN ROVERS	2-1	Leigh(2)	7000	1	2	3	4		6	7		9	8	11						5				10		
8		19	Manchester City	0-3		20000	1	2	3	4	6		7		8	9	11						5				10		
9		26	STOKE	1-2	Stevenson	6000	1	2	3	6			10		9	11						4	5			7	8		
10	Nov	2	Wolverhampton Wands.	0-2			1	2		4		6	7	10	9	11				3			5				8		
11		9	EVERTON	0-2		5000	1	2		4		6	7	10	9	11				3			5				8		
12		23	SUNDERLAND	3-3	Harper(2), Hemingfield			2	3	4		6	7	10	8	9	11	1					5						
13		30	Newcastle United	1-5	Gray	15000	1	2		4			7	10		9	11			3			5		6		8		
14	Dec	7	SMALL HEATH	1-0	Harper	4500	1	2	3	4		6	7	10	8	9	11						5						
15		14	Aston Villa	1-4	Gardner	12000		2	3	4		6	7	10	8	9	11		1				5						
16		25	Blackburn Rovers	0-2		10000		2	3	4		6	7		8	10	11		1				5					9	
17		28	SHEFFIELD UNITED	0-1		4000		2	3	4	5	6	7	10	8		11		1									9	
18	Jan	1	Bury	1-1	Ronaldson	8199		2		4		6		10	8		11		1	3			5			7		9	
19		4	SHEFFIELD WEDNESDAY	3-1	Ronaldson, Appleyard, Fletcher			2		4		6		10	8		11		1	3			5			7		9	
20		11	Nottingham Forest	1-0	Gardner	8000		2		4		6		10	8		11		1	3			5			7		9	
21		18	NOTTS COUNTY	1-0	Fletcher	7000		2		4		6		10	8		11		1	3			5			7		9	
22	Feb	1	BOLTON WANDERERS	4-1	Ronaldson(2), Appleyard, Nelmes			2		4		6			8	10	11		1	3			5			7		9	
23		11	Sheffield United	2-2	Long, Fletcher			2		4		6			8		11		1	3			5			7		9	10
24		15	MANCHESTER CITY	3-2	Appleyard(2), Fletcher	4500		2				6			8		11		1	3	4		5			7		9	10
25		22	Small Heath	0-6		10000		2					6		8		11		1	3	4		5			7		9	10
26	Mar	1	WOLVERHAMPTON WANDS.	3-0	Appleyard(2), Ronaldson	5000		2				6			8		11		1	3	4		5			7		9	10
27		8	Everton	1-0	Nelmes	10000		2				6			8		11		1	3	4			5		7		9	10
28		15	LIVERPOOL	1-1	Gardner	6000		2		4		6			8		11		1	3			5			7		9	10
29		22	Sunderland	1-3	Ronaldson	10000		2		4		6			8		11		1	3			5			7		9	10
30		28	NEWCASTLE UNITED	3-0	Gardner, Ronaldson, Long	7000		2		4		6			8		11		1	3			5			7		9	10
31	Apr	1	Derby County	0-2		4000		2	3	4		6			8		11		1				5			7		9	10
32		12	ASTON VILLA	4-1	Appleyard(3,1pen), Ronaldson	6000		2		4					8		11		1	6	3		5			7		9	10
33		14	Stoke	0-2				2		4					8		11		1	6	3		5			7		9	10
34		21	Liverpool	2-2	Long, Gray			2		4					8		11		1	3	6		5			7		9	10
						Apps.	13	33	15	30	4	27	17	14	33	17	31	1	20	20	7	1	30	1	1	20	8	19	12
						Goals				1		2	1	3	10	4	4						2			4	1	9	3

F.A. Cup

							Tennant	Mountain	Leiper	Hemingfield	Bellingham	Nelmes	Dean	Harper	Ronaldson	Leigh	Gardner	Clutterbuck	Whittaker	McConnell	Hall	Griffiths	Gray	Brumley	Skinner	Fletcher	Stevenson	Appleyard	Long
1	Jan	25	PORTSMOUTH	1-1	Appleyard	10000		2				6		10	8		11		1	3		4	5			7		9	
1r		29	Portsmouth	0-2		12000		2				6		10	8		11		1	3		4	5			7		9	

		P	W	D	L	F	A	W	D	L	F	A	F	A	Pts
1	Sunderland	34	12	3	2	32	14	7	3	7	18	21	50	35	44
2	Everton	34	11	2	4	31	11	6	5	6	22	24	53	35	41
3	Newcastle United	34	11	3	3	41	14	3	6	8	7	20	48	34	37
4	Blackburn Rovers	34	12	2	3	36	16	3	4	10	16	32	52	48	36
5	Nottingham Forest	34	11	4	2	32	13	2	5	10	11	30	43	43	35
6	Derby County	34	11	5	1	26	10	2	4	11	13	31	39	41	35
7	Bury	34	11	5	1	31	9	2	3	12	13	29	44	38	34
8	Aston Villa	34	9	5	3	27	13	4	3	10	15	27	42	40	34
9	Sheffield Wed.	34	9	5	3	30	14	4	3	10	18	38	48	52	34
10	Sheffield United	34	10	5	2	38	13	3	2	12	15	35	53	48	33
11	Liverpool	34	8	3	6	28	16	2	9	6	14	22	42	38	32
12	Bolton Wanderers	34	10	6	1	38	17	2	2	13	13	39	51	56	32
13	Notts County	34	12	2	3	44	19	2	2	13	7	38	51	57	32
14	Wolverhampton W.	34	12	3	2	32	13	1	3	13	14	44	46	57	32
15	GRIMSBY TOWN	34	11	3	3	33	16	2	3	12	11	44	44	60	32
16	Stoke	34	10	4	3	31	12	1	5	11	14	43	45	55	31
17	Small Heath	34	8	5	4	31	14	3	3	11	16	31	47	45	30
18	Manchester City	34	10	3	4	28	17	1	3	13	14	41	42	58	28

SEASON 1901/02

Back: White (Vice Pres), Hickson (Sec), Withers (Dir), Page (Dir), Bellingham, Tennant, Craddock(Train)
Middle (standing): Brocklesby, Nelmes, Mountain, Hemingfield, Gray, Blythe, Fletcher, Griffiths, Colbrook (Asst Train), Unknown
Middle (seated): Mellor, Watkins, Harris, Hall, Harper, A.McConnell, Leiper, Appleyard. Front: Ronaldson, Leigh, Lakey, McAvoy

SEASON 1902/03

Back: Craddock (Train), Whittaker. 2nd Row: Withers (Dir), A.McConnell, Nelmes, Gray, Hickson (Sec) Burnham (Dir)
3rd Row: Paterson, Page (Dir), Hall, Gardner, Brumley, Blythe, Colbrook (Asst Train)
4th Row: Bellingham, Spendiff, Dunn, Glen, Hemingfield, Brusey (Dir)
Seated: White (Vice Pres), Ronaldson, Long, Atherton, Harper, Singleton, Bellamy (Hon Fin Sec)
Front: Mountain, Appleyard, Fletcher

1902-03 17th in Division 1

Captain: Dave Gardner

						Whittaker	Gardner	McConnell	Hemingfield	Gray	Nelmes	Fletcher	Ronaldson	Appleyard	Long	Glen	Spendiff	Mountain	Dunn	Hall	Morgan	Brumley	Atherton	Harper	Hogg	Rouse	Paterson	Singleton	McLatchie
1	Sep	9 NOTTINGHAM FOREST	0-1		5000	1	2	3	4	5	6	7	8	9	10	11													
2		13 Bury	1-2	Appleyard	5000	1	2	3	4	5	6	7	8	9	10													11	
3		20 BLACKBURN ROVERS	4-1	Appleyard(2,1p),Fletcher,Singleton	6000	1		3	4	5	6	7	8	9	10			2										11	
4		27 Sunderland	1-5	Singleton			3		5		6	7	8	9			1	2		4				10				11	
5	Oct	4 STOKE	2-2	Ronaldson, Gray	4000	1	3			5	6	7	8	9				2		4				10				11	
6		11 Everton	2-4	Long, Nelmes	14000		3		4	5	6	7		9	10		1	2						8				11	
7		18 SHEFFIELD WEDNESDAY	0-1			1	3		4	5	6	7	10	9				2		11				8					
8		25 West Bromwich Albion	0-1		15000	1	3		4	5	6		11	9				2					7	8			10		
9	Nov	1 NOTTS COUNTY	1-1	Nelmes	3000	1	3		4		6	7	11	9				2		10	5			8					
10		8 BOLTON WANDERERS	1-1	Fletcher	3000	1	3		4	5	6	7	9					2		10			11	8					
11		15 MIDDLESBROUGH	2-2	Appleyard(2)		1	3		4	5	6	7	8	9				2									10	11	
12		22 Newcastle United	0-1		8000	1		3	4		6	7	8	9	10			2		5								11	
13		29 WOLVERHAMPTON WANDS.	1-2	Ronaldson	4000	1		3	4		6	7	8	9	10			2		5								11	
14	Dec	6 Liverpool	2-9	Appleyard, Hogg	10000	1		3	4		6	10	7	9					2	5					8				11
15		13 SHEFFIELD UNITED	1-2	Ronaldson	4000	1	3	2			6	7	8	9	10				4	5									11
16		20 DERBY COUNTY	4-1	Appleyard(2),McLatchie,Fletcher	4000	1	3	2				7	8	9	10			4	6	5									11
17		25 EVERTON	0-0		6000	1	3	2	4			7	8	9	10				6	5									11
18		27 Aston Villa	2-2	Fletcher, Mountain	20000	1	3	2	4			7	9			10		8	6	5									11
19	Jan	2 Bolton Wanderers	1-0	Mountain	16000	1	3	2			6	7	9			10		8	4	5									11
20		3 Nottingham Forest	1-2	Ronaldson		1	3	2			6	7	9			10		8	4	5									11
21		10 BURY	2-1	Glen, Ronaldson	6000	1	3	2			6	7	8	9		10			4	5									11
22		17 Blackburn Rovers	0-2		10000	1	3	2			6	7	8	9		10			4	5									11
23		24 SUNDERLAND	2-4	Appleyard(2,1pen)		1	3	2			6	7	8	9		10			4	5								11	
24		31 Stoke	1-1	Hall	6000		3		4				7	9		10	1	2	6	5					8			11	
25	Feb	14 Sheffield Wednesday	1-1	Fletcher	9000		3		4			7	8	9		10	1	2	6	5								11	
26		28 Notts County	1-0	Fletcher	8000		3	2	4			7		9	11	10	1	8	6	5									
27	Mar	14 Middlesbrough	0-2		12000		3	2	4			7		9		11	1		6	5					10	8			
28		21 NEWCASTLE UNITED	1-0	Hall	4000	1	3				6	7	8	9		10		2	4	5								11	
29		28 Wolverhampton Wands.	0-3		3000	1		3			6	7	10	9				2	4	5						8		11	
30	Apr	4 LIVERPOOL	3-1	Ronaldson(2), Rouse	2500	1	3	2			6	7	9		10				4	5						8		11	
31		10 WEST BROMWICH ALBION	4-0	Ronaldson, Rouse, Long	6000	1	3	2			6	7	9		10				4	5						8		11	
32		11 Sheffield United	0-3			1		3	4		6	7	9		10			2	5							8		11	
33		22 Derby County	2-2	Long(2)	5000	1	3	2			6	7	9		10				4			5				8		11	
34		25 ASTON VILLA	0-2		1500		3	2			6	7	9		10	8	1		4			5						11	
					Apps.	27	28	23	20	9	27	32	31	25	15	13	7	21	21	25	1	2	2	7	3	6	2	18	9
					Goals					1	2	6	9	10	4	1		2		2					1	2		2	1

F.A. Cup

						Whittaker	Gardner	McConnell	Hemingfield	Gray	Nelmes	Fletcher	Ronaldson	Appleyard	Long	Glen	Spendiff	Mountain	Dunn	Hall	Morgan	Brumley	Atherton	Harper	Hogg	Rouse	Paterson	Singleton	McLatchie
1	Feb	7 NEWCASTLE UNITED	2-1	Fletcher, Ronaldson	7000		3		4			7	8	9		10	1	2	6	5								11	
2		21 NOTTS COUNTY	0-2		9000		3		4			7	8	9		10	1	2	6	5								11	

		P	W	D	L	F	A	W	D	L	F	A	F	A	Pts
1	Sheffield Wed.	34	12	3	2	31	7	7	1	9	23	29	54	36	42
2	Aston Villa	34	11	3	3	43	18	8	0	9	18	22	61	40	41
3	Sunderland	34	10	5	2	27	11	6	4	7	24	25	51	36	41
4	Sheffield United	34	11	0	6	36	22	6	5	6	22	22	58	44	39
5	Liverpool	34	11	3	3	48	21	6	1	10	20	28	68	49	38
6	Stoke	34	11	2	4	29	11	4	5	8	17	27	46	38	37
7	West Bromwich Alb.	34	10	2	5	37	27	6	2	9	17	26	54	53	36
8	Bury	34	14	1	2	41	14	2	2	13	13	29	54	43	35
9	Derby County	34	13	2	2	34	11	3	1	13	16	36	50	47	35
10	Nottingham Forest	34	10	3	4	33	22	4	4	9	16	25	49	47	35
11	Wolverhampton W.	34	12	2	3	34	17	2	3	12	14	40	48	57	33
12	Everton	34	10	2	5	28	18	3	4	10	17	29	45	47	32
13	Middlesbrough	34	10	3	4	27	16	4	1	12	14	34	41	50	32
14	Newcastle United	34	12	1	4	31	11	2	3	12	10	40	41	51	32
15	Notts County	34	8	5	4	25	16	4	2	11	16	33	41	49	31
16	Blackburn Rovers	34	9	2	6	27	24	3	3	11	17	39	44	63	29
17	GRIMSBY TOWN	34	6	5	6	28	22	2	4	11	15	40	43	62	25
18	Bolton Wanderers	34	6	2	9	18	20	2	1	14	19	53	37	73	19

1903-04 6th in Division 2

Captain: Dave Gardner

							Spendiff	McConnell A	Gardner	Dunn	Roberts	Nelmes	Nichol	Rouse	Miller	Long	Lappin	Harmsworth	McDiarmid	Hodgkinson	Phillips	Grant	Baker	Elkins	Wilkinson	Speight	Williams	McConnell J	Horner
1	Sep	1	BRADFORD CITY	2-0	Dunn, Rouse	4000	1	2	3	4	5	6	7	8	9	10	11												
2		5	Lincoln City	1-2	Lappin	6000	1	2	3	4	5	6	7	8	9		11								10				
3		12	STOCKPORT COUNTY	2-1	Nichol(2)	4000	1	2	3	4	5	6	7	8	9		11								10				
4		19	Chesterfield Town	1-0	Rouse	3000	1	2	3	4	5		7	8		9	11		6						10				
5		26	BOLTON WANDERERS	0-0		5000	1	2	3	4	5		7	8	9		11		6						10				
6	Oct	3	Burnley	0-2		5000	1	2	3	4	5		7	8		9	11		6							10			
7		10	PRESTON NORTH END	1-1	Speight	4000	1	2	3	4	5	6	7	8		9	11									10			
8		17	BURSLEM PORT VALE	3-1	Long, Rouse, Roberts(pen)	3000	1	2	3	4	5	6	7	8		9	11									10			
9		24	Leicester Fosse	1-1	Roberts	5000	1	2	3	4	5		7	8		9	11		6							10			
10		31	Preston North End	0-2		10000	1	2	3	4	5		7	8		9	11		6							10			
11	Nov	21	Bristol City	0-4		8000	1	2	3	4	5		7	8		9			6	11						10			
12	Dec	5	Glossop	1-1	Hodgkinson	1000	1	2	3	4	5			9		7			6	8					10		11		
13		19	Woolwich Arsenal	1-5	Rouse	12000	1	2	3	4	5			9		7			6	8					10		11		
14		26	BARNSLEY	5-1	Hodgkinson(2),Long,Lappin,Wilkinson	4000	1	2	3	4		6		9		7	11		5	8					10				
15	Jan	2	LINCOLN CITY	1-1	Rouse	5000	1	2	3	4	5			9		7	11		6	8					10				
16		9	Stockport County	1-1	Rouse	3000	1	2	3	4	5			9		7	11		6	8					10				
17		16	CHESTERFIELD TOWN	1-0	Williams	3000	1	2		4	5			9		7			6	8					10		11	3	
18		23	Bolton Wanderers	0-4		6000	1	2	3		5	6		9		7	8		4	11				10					
19		30	BURNLEY	0-0		4000	1	2			5	6	7	9		8		3	4	11					10				
20	Feb	13	Burslem Port Vale	2-1	Rouse, Elkins(pen)		1	2		3	5	6	7	8		10	11		4					9					
21		20	LEICESTER FOSSE	4-3	Lappin, Nelmes, Elkins, Roberts	4000	1	2		3	5	6	7	8		10	11		4					9					
22		27	Blackpool	0-3		2000	1	2	3		5	6		8		10	11		4	7				9					
23	Mar	5	GAINSBOROUGH TRINITY	3-1	Lappin, Nichol, Hodgkinson		1	2	3	4	5		7			10	11		6	8				9					
24		12	Burton United	0-1			1	2	3		5		7			10	11	4	6			8		9					
25		19	BRISTOL CITY	2-0	Rouse, Elkins	4000	1	2	3	4		6		8		7		5		11				9	10				
26		26	Manchester United	0-2		10000	1	2	3		5	6		8		7		4		11				9	10				
27	Apr	1	BURTON UNITED	4-0	Rouse(3), Roberts		1	2	3		5	6		8		7		4		11	9		10						
28		2	GLOSSOP	2-0	Rouse, Baker	4000	1	2		3	5	6		10		7	11		4				8	9					
29		4	BLACKPOOL	4-0	Long(2), Elkins, Roberts	4500	1	2			5	6		10		7			4	11			8	9				3	
30		6	Gainsborough Trinity	2-4	Elkins(2,1pen)		1	2		3	5	6		10		7			4	11	9			8					
31		9	Bradford City	0-1		8000	1	2			5	6		10					4		7		8	9			11	3	
32		12	MANCHESTER UNITED	3-1	Rouse(2), Long	3000	1	2			5	6		10		7			4		9		8		11			3	
33		16	WOOLWICH ARSENAL	2-2	Phillips, Long		1	2			5	6		10		7			4		9		8		11			3	
34		23	Barnsley	1-3	Phillips			2		5		6				7			4		9		8	10	11			3	1
						Apps.	33	34	23	24	31	21	16	31	4	30	20	5	26	16	6	1	7	13	16	6	4	6	1
						Goals				1	4	1	3	13		6	4			4	2		1	7	2	1	1		

Game 4: Spendiff injured, replaced in goal by Nichol.

F.A. Cup

							Spendiff	McConnell A	Gardner	Dunn	Roberts	Nelmes	Nichol	Rouse	Miller	Long	Lappin	Harmsworth	McDiarmid	Hodgkinson	Phillips	Grant	Baker	Elkins	Wilkinson	Speight	Williams	McConnell J	Horner
Sup	Dec	12	BARNSLEY	2-0	Hodgkinson, Wilkinson		1	2	3	4	5			9		7			6	8					10		11		
1	Feb	6	Preston North End	0-1		9500	1	2		3	5	6	7	8		10	11		4					9					

		P	W	D	L	F	A	W	D	L	F	A	F	A	Pts
1	Preston North End	34	13	4	0	38	10	7	6	4	24	14	62	24	50
2	Woolwich Arsenal	34	15	2	0	67	5	6	5	6	24	17	91	22	49
3	Manchester United	34	14	2	1	42	14	6	6	5	23	19	65	33	48
4	Bristol City	34	14	2	1	53	12	4	4	9	20	29	73	41	42
5	Burnley	34	12	2	3	31	20	3	7	7	19	35	50	55	39
6	GRIMSBY TOWN	34	12	5	0	39	12	2	3	12	11	37	50	49	36
7	Bolton Wanderers	34	10	3	4	38	11	2	7	8	21	30	59	41	34
8	Barnsley	34	10	5	2	25	12	1	5	11	13	45	38	57	32
9	Gainsborough Trin.	34	10	2	5	34	17	4	1	12	19	43	53	60	31
10	Bradford City	34	8	5	4	30	25	4	2	11	15	34	45	59	31
11	Chesterfield	34	8	5	4	22	12	3	3	11	15	33	37	45	30
12	Lincoln City	34	9	4	4	25	18	2	4	11	16	40	41	58	30
13	Burslem Port Vale	34	10	3	4	44	20	0	6	11	10	32	54	52	29
14	Burton United	34	8	6	3	33	16	3	1	13	12	45	45	61	29
15	Blackpool	34	8	2	7	25	27	3	3	11	15	40	40	67	27
16	Stockport County	34	7	7	3	28	23	1	4	12	12	49	40	72	27
17	Glossop	34	7	4	6	42	25	3	2	12	15	39	57	64	26
18	Leicester Fosse	34	5	8	4	26	21	1	2	14	16	61	42	82	22

SEASON 1903/04

Back: Hickson (Sec), E. Smith 2nd Row: Roberts, Spendiff, Nelmes, McDiarmid 3rd Row: Horner, D.Gardner, J.McConnell, Colebrook (Asst.Train) Middle: Wheeler (Trainer), Lappin, Barwick, Elkins, Fleet Seated: Page (Dir), Nichol, Rouse, Miller, Long, Wilkinson, McAllister, Rushworth (Dir) Front: Dunn, A.McConnell

SEASON 1904/05

Back: J.Reynolds, A.McConnell, Spendiff, J.McConnell, Higgins
Middle: McDiarmid, Coles, Nelmes. Front: Hunter, Morley, Phillips, Turner, Ross

1904-05 13th in Division 2

Captain: 'Happy' Nelmes

						Spendiff	McConnell A	McConnell J	McDairmid	Coles	Nelmes	Reynolds J	Baker	Morley	Turner	Ross	Cartledge	McGregor	Ayre	Mochan	Higgins	Hunter	Phillips	Elkins	Butler	Padley	Oakes	Thompson AJ
1	Sep 3	BARNSLEY	0-0		4500	1	2	3	4	5	6	7	8	9	10	11												
2	10	West Bromwich Albion	2-0	Ross, Morley	10000	1	2	3	4	5	6	7	8	9	10	11												
3	17	BURNLEY	1-0	Ross	5000	1	2	3	4	5	6	7	8	9	10	11												
4	24	Bolton Wanderers	1-4	Ross	12000	1	2	3	4	5	6	7		9	10	11					8							
5	Oct 1	Blackpool	1-1	Ross	2000	1	2		4	5	6	7		9	10	11			3		8							
6	8	DONCASTER ROVERS	2-1	Ross, Baker	3000	1	2		4	5	6	7	8	9		11			3		10							
7	15	Gainsborough Trinity	1-2	Phillips	6000	1		3	4	5	6	7	8	2		11					10		9					
8	22	BURTON UNITED	1-0	Baker		1	2		4	5	6	7	8	3	10	11					9							
9	29	Liverpool	0-5		14000	1			5	2	6	7	8	3	10	11					4		9					
10	Nov 5	BURSLEM PORT VALE	0-3			1			4	5	6		7	2	10	11			3		8			9				
11	12	Bristol City	0-5		10000	1			4	5	6	7		3	10	11		2			8			9				
12	19	MANCHESTER UNITED	0-1		3000				8	5	6	7		2		11	1	4		3	10			9				
13	Dec 3	CHESTERFIELD TOWN	3-1	Higgins(2), Phillips	2000	1			8	5	6	7		2		11		4		3	10		9					
14	17	LINCOLN CITY	1-0	Phillips	4000	1			8	5	6			2		11		4		3	10	7	9					
15	24	Leicester Fosse	1-5	Higgins					6	5		7	8	2		11	1	4		3	10		9					
16	26	Burnley	0-1						6	5		7	8	2		11	1	4		3	10		9					
17	27	Bradford City	0-0		15000			3	6	5		7		2	8	11	1	4			10		9					
18	31	Barnsley	2-2	Ross, Hunter	3000			3	6	5				2	8	11	1	4			10	7	9					
19	Jan 7	WEST BROMWICH ALBION	1-3	Higgins	4000			3	6		5		8	2		11	1	4			10	7	9					
20	21	BOLTON WANDERERS	2-2	McDairmid, Baker		1			5		6	7	8	2		11		4		3		10	9					
21	2?	BLACKPOOL	2-0	Ross, Baker	3000				9	5	6	7	8	2		11	1	4		3		10						
22	Feb 11	GAINSBOROUGH TRINITY	0-0			1			5		6		8	2	10	11		4		3		7		9				
23	18	Burton United	0-1		3000	1			5		6	7	8	2	10	11		4		3				9				
24	25	LIVERPOOL	0-1			1			5		6	7	9	2	10	11		4		3	8							
25	Mar 4	Burslem Port Vale	0-2		2000	1			5			7	9	2		10		4		3	6		8				11	
26	11	BRISTOL CITY	4-0	Butler(2), Reynolds, Baker	4000	1		3	5		6	7	8	2		11		4			10				9			
27	18	Manchester United	1-2	Butler	14000	1		3	5		6	7	8	2		11		4			10				9			
28	25	GLOSSOP	3-0	Phillips(2), Reynolds(pen)		1		3	5		6	7	8	2				4			10		11		9			
29	Apr 1	Chesterfield Town	0-0			1		3	5		6	7	8	2				4				10			9			11
30	8	BRADFORD CITY	0-2		6000				5		6	7	8	2		9	1	4		3		10						11
31	15	Lincoln City	0-0		5000	1		3	8	5	6	7	10	2		11		4							9			
32	22	LEICESTER FOSSE	2-0	Padley(2)	2500	1		3	4	5	6	7	8	2		11							10			9		
33	24	Doncaster Rovers	2-0	Reynolds, Phillips	3000	1		3	4	5	6	7	8	2		11							10			9		
34	29	Glossop	0-2			1		3	6	5		7	8	2		11		4					10			9		
					Apps.	26	7	16	34	23	28	29	26	34	14	32	8	22	3	12	21	8	15	5	5	3	1	2
					Goals				1			3	5	1		7					4	1	7		2	2		

F.A. Cup

						Spendiff	McConnell A	McConnell J	McDairmid	Coles	Nelmes	Reynolds J	Baker	Morley	Turner	Ross	Cartledge	McGregor	Ayre	Mochan	Higgins	Hunter	Phillips	Elkins	Butler	Padley	Oakes	Thompson AJ
Pre	Jan 14	GAINSBOROUGH TRINITY	2-0	Reynolds, Baker	3000	1			5		6	7	8	2		11		4		3	10		9					
1	Feb 14	Stoke	0-2		10600	1			5		6	7	8	2		11		4		3		10	9					

		P	W	D	L	F	A	W	D	L	F	A	F	A	Pts
1	Liverpool	34	14	3	0	60	12	13	1	3	33	13	93	25	58
2	Bolton Wanderers	34	15	0	2	53	16	12	2	3	34	16	87	32	56
3	Manchester United	34	16	0	1	60	10	8	5	4	21	20	81	30	53
4	Bristol City	34	12	3	2	40	12	7	1	9	26	33	66	45	42
5	Chesterfield	34	9	6	2	26	11	5	5	7	18	24	44	35	39
6	Gainsborough Trin.	34	11	4	2	32	15	3	4	10	29	43	61	58	36
7	Barnsley	34	11	4	2	29	13	3	1	13	9	43	38	56	33
8	Bradford City	34	8	5	4	31	20	4	3	10	14	29	45	49	32
9	Lincoln City	34	9	4	4	31	16	3	3	11	11	24	42	40	31
10	West Bromwich Alb.	34	8	2	7	28	20	5	2	10	28	28	56	48	30
11	Burnley	34	10	1	6	31	21	2	5	10	12	31	43	52	30
12	Glossop	34	7	5	5	23	14	3	5	9	14	32	37	46	30
13	GRIMSBY TOWN	34	9	3	5	22	14	2	5	10	11	32	33	46	30
14	Leicester Fosse	34	8	3	6	30	25	3	4	10	10	30	40	55	29
15	Blackpool	34	8	5	4	26	15	1	5	11	10	33	36	48	28
16	Burslem Port Vale	34	7	4	6	28	25	3	3	11	19	47	47	72	27
17	Burton United	34	7	2	8	20	29	1	2	14	10	55	30	84	20
18	Doncaster Rovers	34	3	2	12	12	32	0	0	17	11	49	23	81	8

1905-06 8th in Division 2

Captain: Herbert Morley

#	Month	Day	Opponent	Score	Scorers	Att.	Cartledge	Morley	McConnell J	McGregor	McDairmid	Nelmes	Swarbrick	Baker	Burnett	Grant	Johnson	Horner	Butler	Coles	Openshaw	Milnes	Higgins	Hooper	Bisby	Fletcher	Robinson	Pynegar	Padley	Young	Reynolds
1	Sep	2	Chesterfield Town	4-1	Swarbrick, Grant, Baker, Morley	5000	1	2	3	4	5	6	7	8	9	10	11														
2		9	MANCHESTER UNITED	0-1		6000	1	2		4	5	6	7	8	9	10	11			3											
3		16	Burslem Port Vale	2-2	Burnett, Nelmes	2000	1	2	3	4	5	6	7	8	9	10	11														
4		23	GLOSSOP	1-1	Burnett	4000	1	2	3	4	5	6	7	8	9	10	11														
5		30	Barnsley	0-2			1	2		4		6			10	8	11			5	3			7					9		
6	Oct	7	STOCKPORT COUNTY	2-0	Baker(2)	3000	1	2		4			10	8	9		11			5	3		6	7							
7		14	Clapton Orient	2-1	Baker, Swarbrick		1	2		4			10	8	9		11			5	3		6	7							
8		21	BLACKPOOL	1-1	Baker		1	2		4		6	10	8	9		11			5	3			7							
9		28	Burnley	0-0		4000	1	2	3	4		6	10	8	9		11			5				7							
10	Nov	4	BRADFORD CITY	1-0	Burnett	4000	1	2	3	4			10	8	9		11			6		5		7							
11		11	Leeds City	0-3		7000	1	2	3	4			10	8	9		11		5	6				7							
12		25	Burton United	0-1			1	2	3	4			11		10					6			5	7		8		9			
13	Dec	2	LEICESTER FOSSE	1-1	Padley	3000	1	2	3	4			11		10					6			5	7		8			9		
14		9	Chelsea	0-2		3000	1	2	3	4					10		11			5			6	7		8			9		
15		16	Hull City	1-0	Johnson	8000	1	2	3	4				9	10		11			5			6		7		8				
16		23	GAINSBOROUGH TRINITY	2-0	Burnett(2)		1	2	3	4		6		9	10		11			5					7		8				
17		25	Lincoln City	1-3	Johnson		1		3	4				9	10		11		2	5			6		7		8				
18		27	BRISTOL CITY	1-1	Fletcher	4000	1	2	3	4			10		9		11					5	6			7	8				
19		30	CHESTERFIELD TOWN	2-0	Swarbrick, Baker	3000	1	2	3	4			11	8								5	6			7			9		10
20	Jan	6	Manchester United	0-5		15000	1	2	3	4			11	8	9		7					5	6								10
21		20	BURSLEM PORT VALE	5-0	Padley(2),Baker(2,1p),McGregor	3000	1	2	3	4			11	8	10							5	6			7			9		
22		27	Glossop	0-2			1	2	3	4			11	8	5								6			7	10		9		
23	Feb	3	WEST BROMWICH ALBION	3-2	Hooper, Padley, Baker(pen)		1	2		4			11	8					3			5	6	7			10		9		
24		10	Stockport County	2-2	Baker(pen), McGregor	1000		2		4			11	8				1	3			5	6	7			10		9		
25		17	CLAPTON ORIENT	4-1	Robinson(2), Swarbrick, Hooper			2		4			11	8				1	3			5	6	7			10		9		
26		24	Leicester Fosse	0-2				2		4			11	8	9			1	3			5	6	7			10				
27	Mar	3	BURNLEY	2-0	Young(2,1pen)	4000		2		4		6	11					1	3			5				7	10	8		9	
28		7	Blackpool	0-2				2		4		6	11		8			1	3			5				7	10			9	
29		17	LEEDS CITY	1-1	Milnes	3000		2	3	4		6	11	8				1				5				7				9	10
30		24	West Bromwich Albion	0-2			1	2	3	4		6	11		9	8						5				7					10
31		31	BURTON UNITED	1-0	Grant		1	2	3	4		6	11			8						5		7					9		10
32	Apr	5	BARNSLEY	2-1	Hooper, Robinson	1500	1		3	4		6	11			8			2			5		7					9		10
33		7	Bradford City	1-0	Johnson	9000	1	2	3	4		6	10		9		11					5		7			8				
34		13	LINCOLN CITY	2-2	Burnett, Robinson	6000	1		3	4		6	10		9		11		2			5		7			8				
35		14	CHELSEA	1-1	Robinson		1	2	3	4		6	11	8	9							5		7			10				
36		17	Bristol City	0-2		6000	1	2	3	4		6	11	8	9							5		7			10				
37		21	HULL CITY	1-0	Robinson	6000	1	2	3	4		6	10	8								5		7	11		9				
38		28	Gainsborough Trinity	0-1			1		3	4		6	10	8					2			5		7	11		9				
						Apps.	32	34	27	38	4	20	33	26	28	8	19	6	11	14	4	21	16	22	5	11	17	2	11	3	6
						Goals		1		2		1	4	10	6	2	3					1		3		1	6		4	2	

F.A. Cup

#	Month	Day	Opponent	Score	Scorers	Att.	Cartledge	Morley	McConnell J	McGregor	McDairmid	Nelmes	Swarbrick	Baker	Burnett	Grant	Johnson	Horner	Butler	Coles	Openshaw	Milnes	Higgins	Hooper	Bisby	Fletcher	Robinson	Pynegar	Padley	Young	Reynolds
1	Jan	16	NEWCASTLE UNITED*	0-6		23672	1	5	3	4			11	8	10				2				6			7			9		

* Played at St. James' Park, Newcastle

		P	W	D	L	F	A	W	D	L	F	A	F	A	Pts
1	Bristol City	38	17	1	1	43	8	13	5	1	40	20	83	28	66
2	Manchester United	38	15	3	1	55	13	13	3	3	35	15	90	28	62
3	Chelsea	38	13	4	2	58	16	9	5	5	32	21	90	37	53
4	West Bromwich Alb.	38	13	4	2	53	16	9	4	6	26	20	79	36	52
5	Hull City	38	10	5	4	38	21	9	1	9	29	33	67	54	44
6	Leeds City	38	11	5	3	38	19	6	4	9	21	28	59	47	43
7	Leicester Fosse	38	10	3	6	30	21	5	9	5	23	27	53	48	42
8	GRIMSBY TOWN	38	11	7	1	33	13	4	3	12	13	33	46	46	40
9	Burnley	38	9	4	6	26	23	6	4	9	16	30	42	53	38
10	Stockport County	38	11	6	2	36	16	2	3	14	8	40	44	56	35
11	Bradford City	38	7	4	8	21	22	6	4	9	25	38	46	60	34
12	Barnsley	38	11	4	4	45	17	1	5	13	15	45	60	62	33
13	Lincoln City	38	10	1	8	46	29	2	5	12	23	43	69	72	30
14	Blackpool	38	8	3	8	22	21	2	6	11	15	41	37	62	29
15	Gainsborough Trin.	38	10	2	7	35	22	2	2	15	9	35	44	57	28
16	Glossop	38	9	4	6	36	28	1	4	14	13	43	49	71	28
17	Burslem Port Vale	38	10	4	5	34	25	2	0	17	15	57	49	82	28
18	Chesterfield	38	8	4	7	26	24	2	4	13	14	48	40	72	28

Back: Directors. Middle (Standing): Kinnear (Trainer), Director, Nelmes, A.McConnell, Cartledge, Horner, McDiarmid, J.McConnell, Unknown, Hickson (Sec.)
Middle (Seated): Goodwin (Hon.Sec.), Unknown, Baker, Morley, 3 Unknowns, F.Bisby, Unknown, McGregor, Director
Front: Swarbrick, 2 Unknowns, Butler, Burnett, Higgins

1906-07 11th in Division 2

Captain: Herbert Morley

No.	Month	Date	Opponent	Score	Scorers	Att.	Cartledge	Morley	MacDonald	McGregor	Milnes	Higgins	Rodger	Robinson	Hakin	Morris R	Swarbrick	Horner	Carmichael	Butler	Coles	Openshaw	Lee	Fleet	Bisby J C	Hooper	Chantry	Cook	Barr	Fletcher	Burnett	Bisby F	Morris T
1	Sep	1	NOTTINGHAM FOREST	3-1	Robinson,R.Morris,Swarbrick(p)	7000	1	2	3	4	5	6	7	8	9	10	11																
2		3	Leicester Fosse	0-2			1	2		4	5	6	7	8	9	10	11																3
3		8	Lincoln City	1-2	F.Bisby	5000	1			4	5	6	7	8	9	10				2												11	3
4		15	BURTON UNITED	1-1	Swarbrick	5000	1	2	3	4			7	8	9	10	11				5			6									
5		22	Chesterfield Town	3-1	Hakin, R.Morris, Rodger	4000	1	2	3	4	5		7	8	9	10	11							6									
6		29	Burslem Port Vale	2-3	Fletcher, Hakin		1		3	4	5		7		9	10	11							6						8			2
7	Oct	6	BURNLEY	1-0	McGregor(pen)	4000	1		3	4	5		7	10	9		11							6						8			2
8		13	Leeds City	3-4	Morris, Rodger, Hakin	10000	1	2	3	4	5	6	7	8	9	10	11																
9		20	BARNSLEY	1-0	Rodger			3		4	5	6	7	8	9	10	11	1		2													
10		27	Chelsea	0-2		15000	1	3		4	5	6	7		9	10				2											8	11	
11	Nov	3	WOLVERHAMPTON WANDS.	2-1	Hakin, Swarbrick		1	3		4		6	7		9	10	11			2											8		5
12		10	Clapton Orient	0-1		5000		3				6	7		9	10	11	1		2			4								8		5
13		17	Gainsborough Trinity	1-2	Morley		1	3	2		5	6		10	9		11						4			7	8						
14		24	Stockport County	0-3		4000	1	3				4	8		10		11			2	5				6	7	9						
15	Dec	1	HULL CITY	1-3	Hakin	7000		3		4	5	6	7	10	9	8	11	1		2													
16		15	BLACKPOOL	0-0				2		4		6	8		10		11	1		3							7				9		5
17		22	Bradford City	0-1		10000		2		4		6	8			10	11	1		3							7				9		5
18		25	West Bromwich Albion	1-6	Robinson	19047		2		4		6		10	9			1		3						7				8		11	5
19		26	GAINSBOROUGH TRINITY	2-0	R.Morris, Rodger			2		4		6	8			10	11		1	3						7					9		5
20		29	Nottingham Forest	3-0	Rodger(2), Hooper			2		4		6	8			10	11		1	3						7					9		5
21	Jan	5	LINCOLN CITY	4-0	Swarbrick,Rodger,Burnett,R.Morris			2		4		6	8			10	11		1	3						7					9		5
22		19	Burton United	3-2	Rodger, Burnett, R.Morris			2	3	4		6	8			10	11		1							7					9		5
23		26	CHESTERFIELD TOWN	3-1	Rodger, Higgins, Burnett	2000		2		4		6	8			10	11		1	3						7					9		5
24	Feb	9	Burnley	0-2				2		4		6	8			10	11		1	3						7					9		5
25		12	Glossop	0-1					2	4		6	8			10	11	1		3						7					9		5
26		16	LEEDS CITY	4-0	R.Morris, Rodger, Hooper, Burnett	4000			2	4		6	8			10	11		1	3						7					9		5
27	Mar	2	CHELSEA	2-1	Swarbrick(pen), Burnett			2		4	6		8			10	11		1	3								7			9		5
28		9	Wolverhampton Wands.	0-5				2		4	6		7			8			1	3	5				10						9	11	
29		16	CLAPTON ORIENT	1-2	Swarbrick(pen)			2		4	6		7	10		8	11		1			3									9		5
30		21	BURSLEM PORT VALE	2-0	Fletcher(2)			2		4		6	7		10		11		1	3										8	9		5
31		29	WEST BROMWICH ALBION	2-1	Hakin, Burnett				2	4		6	8		10		11		1	3								7			9		5
32		30	STOCKPORT COUNTY	3-1	Rodger(3)				2	4		6	8		10		11		1	3									7		9		5
33	Apr	1	LEICESTER FOSSE	0-1					2	4		6	8		10		11		1	3								7			9		5
34		6	Hull City	2-4	Swarbrick(pen), Hakin	10000			2	4		6	7	8	10		11		1	3											9		5
35		11	Barnsley	1-1	Hakin									8	10		11		1	3	2		4		6			7			9		5
36		13	GLOSSOP	2-1	J.C.Bisby, Swarbrick							10		8	9		11		1	3	2		4		6			7					5
37		20	Blackpool	3-4	Burnett, Barr, Hakin				2	4		6	8		10		11		1	3									7		9		5
38		27	BRADFORD CITY	0-2					2	4		6	7	9	10		11		1	3										8			5

	Cartledge	Morley	MacDonald	McGregor	Milnes	Higgins	Rodger	Robinson	Hakin	Morris R	Swarbrick	Horner	Carmichael	Butler	Coles	Openshaw	Lee	Fleet	Bisby J C	Hooper	Chantry	Cook	Barr	Fletcher	Burnett	Bisby F	Morris T
Apps.	12	25	16	33	14	30	34	16	26	24	34	7	19	28	5	1	4	4	4	11	4	5	2	5	23	4	28
Goals		1		1		1	13	2	9	7	8								1	2			1	3	7	1	

F.A. Cup

Rd	Month	Date	Opponent	Score	Scorers	Att.	Cartledge	Morley	MacDonald	McGregor	Milnes	Higgins	Rodger	Robinson	Hakin	Morris R	Swarbrick	Horner	Carmichael	Butler	Coles	Openshaw	Lee	Fleet	Bisby J C	Hooper	Chantry	Cook	Barr	Fletcher	Burnett	Bisby F	Morris T
1	Jan	12	WOOLWICH ARSENAL	1-1	Hooper	9000		2		4		6	8			10	11		1	3						7					9		5
1r		16	Woolwich Arsenal	0-3		13500		2		4		6	8			10	11		1	3						7					9		5

		P	W	D	L	F	A	W	D	L	F	A	F	A	Pts
1	Nottingham Forest	38	16	2	1	43	13	12	2	5	31	23	74	36	60
2	Chelsea	38	18	0	1	55	10	8	5	6	25	24	80	34	57
3	Leicester Fosse	38	15	3	1	44	12	5	5	9	18	27	62	39	48
4	West Bromwich Alb.	38	15	2	2	62	15	6	3	10	21	30	83	45	47
5	Bradford City	38	14	2	3	46	21	7	3	9	24	32	70	53	47
6	Wolverhampton W.	38	13	4	2	49	16	4	3	12	17	37	66	53	41
7	Burnley	38	12	4	3	45	13	5	2	12	17	34	62	47	40
8	Barnsley	38	14	2	3	56	21	1	6	12	17	34	73	55	38
9	Hull City	38	11	2	6	41	20	4	5	10	24	37	65	57	37
10	Leeds City	38	10	5	4	38	26	3	5	11	17	37	55	63	36
11	GRIMSBY TOWN	38	13	2	4	34	16	3	1	15	23	46	57	62	35
12	Stockport County	38	8	8	3	26	12	4	3	12	16	40	42	52	35
13	Blackpool	38	9	4	6	25	19	2	7	10	8	32	33	51	33
14	Gainsborough Trin.	38	12	3	4	33	20	2	2	15	12	52	45	72	33
15	Glossop	38	10	4	5	32	21	3	2	14	21	58	53	79	32
16	Burslem Port Vale	38	11	5	3	45	26	1	2	16	15	57	60	83	31
17	Clapton Orient	38	9	7	3	25	13	2	1	16	20	54	45	67	30
18	Chesterfield	38	10	3	6	36	26	1	4	14	14	40	50	66	29
19	Lincoln City	38	10	2	7	29	24	2	2	15	17	49	46	73	28
20	Burton United	38	7	3	9	24	23	1	4	14	10	45	34	68	23

SEASON 1906/07

Back: Kinnear (Trainer), McConnell (Manager), Morley, Morris, Openshaw, Cartledge, Betmead (Asst.Train) Macdonald, Hickson (Sec)
2nd Row: Cooper (Dir), McGregor, Butler, Lee, Coles, Milnes, Fleet, Higgins, Westcott (Dir),
3rd Row: Dickinson (Dir), Goodwin (Fin.Sec), Robinson, Hooper, Hakin, Burnett, J.Bisby, Morris, F.Bisby, Doig (Dir), Cronshaw (Dir)
Front: Rodger, Cook, Swarbrick, Fletcher

SEASON 1907/08

Back: Wheelhouse, Scott, Carmichael, Crapper, Vincett, Betmead (Asst Train)
Middle (back): A.McConnell (Res Team Train), J.C.Bisby, J.McConnell, Coles, Bowden, Lee, Higgins, Hickson (Sec)
Middle (front): Athersmith (Train), Coulbeck, Cook, Fletcher, Stokes, Jewell, Hatton
Front: Young, Jack, Pattison, Kilbourne, Hakin, F.Bisby

1907-08 18th in Division 2

Captain: Harry Fletcher

No	Month	Day	Opponent	Score	Scorers	Att	Carmichael	Wheelhouse	Crapper	Lee	Bowden	Higgins	Pattinson	Kilbourne	Jack	Hakin	Jewel	Scott	Blanchard	McConnell J	Vincent	McDairmid	Hatton	Cook	Fletcher	Stokes	Bradley	Bisby F	Bush	Blanthorne	Coles	Bisby JC	Young	Coulbeck
1	Sep	3	GAINSBOROUGH TRINITY	1-4	Kilbourne		1	2	3	4	5	6	7	8	9	10	11																	
2		7	Lincoln City	0-1			1	2	3	4	5		7	8		9	11						6			10								
3		9	Stockport County	0-3			1	2	3	4			7	9		10	11						6									5		8
4		14	STOCKPORT COUNTY	2-1	Hakin, Pattinson	5000	1	2		4		5	7	8		9	11				3		6		10									
5		21	Fulham	1-0	Pattinson	24000	1	2		4		5	7	8		9	11				3		6		10									
6		28	GLOSSOP	4-0	Fletcher(3), Hakin	5000	1	2		4		5	7	8		9	11				3		6		10									
7	Oct	5	Barnsley	1-2	Hakin	4500	1	2		4	5		7	8		9	11				3		6		10									
8		12	LEICESTER FOSSE	1-1	Jewel	4500	1	2		4	5		7	8		9	11				3		6		10									
9		19	Chesterfield Town	0-0			1	2		4	5	6	7	8			11				3					10							9	
10		26	BLACKPOOL	2-2	Blanthorne(2)	4500	1	2		4	5	6	7	8			11				3					10				9				
11	Nov	2	Burnley	1-5	Blanthorne	4000	1	2		4		6	7	8							3	10						11		9	5			
12		9	STOKE	1-0	Jewel		1	2		4			7	10			11				3	5	6		8					9				
13		16	Oldham Athletic	0-2		8000		2		4			7	8		10	11	1			3	5	6							9				
14		23	WEST BROMWICH ALBION	2-2	Blanthorne(2)	4000		2		4	5		7	8		10	11	1			3		6							9				
15		30	Clapton Orient	1-2	Blanthorne	5000		2		4	5			8		10	11	1			3		6	7						9				
16	Dec	7	BRADFORD CITY	0-1		4000		2				5	7	4		8		1			3		6					11		9				
17		14	Leeds City	1-4	Kilbourne	6000		2		4		5		8		10		1		3			6		7			11		9				
18		21	Hull City	2-4	Blanthorne(2)	5000		2		4		5		8		10	11	1		3			6		7					9				
19		25	Derby County	0-4		12000	1	2		4		5		8		10	11				3		6		7					9				
20		26	Gainsborough Trinity	2-3	Blanthorne, Hakin	4000	1	2		4		5		8		10	11					3	6		7					9				
21		28	Wolverhampton Wands.	1-5	Kilbourne		1	2				5		8		10	11				3	4	6		7					9				
22	Jan	4	LINCOLN CITY	0-2		3000		2				6	7			10	11	1	5		3	4								9			8	
23		18	FULHAM	0-4		5000		2		4		5		8		10		1			3		6		11	7				9				
24		25	Glossop	2-1	Blanthorne, Kilbourne	1500		2		4	5			8		10		1			3		6	7	11					9				
25	Feb	8	Leicester Fosse	1-1	Hakin		1	2			5	4		8		10					3			7	11					9		6		
26		29	BURNLEY	0-1		3000	1			4	5			8		10			2		3		6		11	7								
27	Mar	14	OLDHAM ATHLETIC	2-0	Stokes, Hakin	6000		2		4		5		8		10		1			3		6			7			11	9				
28		19	Stoke	0-5				2				4	7	8		10		1			3	5	6						11	9				
29		21	West Bromwich Albion	2-1	Kilbourne, Bush	10000		2			5	4	7	8		10		1			3		6						11	9				
30		28	CLAPTON ORIENT	0-0				2			5	4	7	8		10		1			3		6						11	9				
31	Apr	1	Blackpool	0-3				2		4	5	6		8		10		1			3				7				11	9				
32		4	Bradford City	1-1	Blanthorne	17000				4	5	10				8		1		2	3				7				11	9		6		
33		9	BARNSLEY	4-1	Blanthorne,Kilbourne,Hakin,Bush	3000				4	5	6		10		8		1		2	3				7				11	9				
34		11	LEEDS CITY	2-0	Kilbourne, Higgins(pen)	4000				4	5	6		10		8		1		2	3				7				11	9				
35		17	WOLVERHAMPTON WANDS.	0-1						4	5	6		10		8		1			3				7				11	9				
36		18	HULL CITY	1-1	Higgins	6000				4	5	6		8				1			3		7				10		11	9	2			
37		20	DERBY COUNTY	1-0	Blanthorne	6000				4		5		7		10		1	2		3		6				8		11	9				
38		29	CHESTERFIELD TOWN	4-3	Blanthorne,Kilbourne,Higgins,Bradley					4		5		10				1		2	3		6		7		8		11	9				
						Apps.	17	30	3	31	19	28	19	36	1	32	19	21	3	6	32	7	27	3	21	6	3	3	12	28	2	3	2	1
						Goals						3	2	8		7	2								3	1	1		2	14				

Additional players: Glennon 10/16, Burkinshaw 9/26, Rudd 2/35

F.A. Cup

No	Month	Day	Opponent	Score	Scorers	Att	Carmichael	Wheelhouse	Crapper	Lee	Bowden	Higgins	Pattinson	Kilbourne	Jack	Hakin	Jewel	Scott	Blanchard	McConnell J	Vincent	McDairmid	Hatton	Cook	Fletcher	Stokes	Bradley	Bisby F	Bush	Blanthorne	Coles	Bisby JC	Young	Coulbeck
1	Jan	11	Bristol City	0-0		10000		2		4		5		8		10		1			3		6		11	7				9				
1r		15	BRISTOL CITY	2-1	Lee, Blanthorne	7000		2		4		5		8		10		1			3		6		11	7				9				
2	Feb	1	CARLISLE UNITED	6-2	Kilbourne, Blanthorne(5)	6000	1	2			5	4		8		10					3		6		11	7				9				
3		22	CRYSTAL PALACE	1-1	Blanthorne	9000	1	2		4	5	10		8							3		6		11	7				9				
4	Mar	7	Newcastle United	1-5	Kilbourne	45000		2		4	5	6		8		10		1			3				11	7				9				

		P	W	D	L	F	A	W	D	L	F	A	F	A	Pts
1	Bradford City	38	15	2	2	58	16	9	4	6	32	26	90	42	54
2	Leicester Fosse	38	14	2	3	41	20	7	8	4	31	27	72	47	52
3	Oldham Athletic	38	15	4	0	53	14	7	2	10	23	28	76	42	50
4	Fulham	38	12	2	5	50	14	10	3	6	32	35	82	49	49
5	West Bromwich Alb.	38	13	3	3	38	13	6	6	7	23	26	61	39	47
6	Derby County	38	15	1	3	50	13	6	3	10	27	32	77	45	46
7	Burnley	38	14	3	2	44	14	6	3	10	23	36	67	50	46
8	Hull City	38	15	1	3	50	23	6	3	10	23	39	73	62	46
9	Wolverhampton W.	38	11	4	4	34	11	4	3	12	16	34	50	45	37
10	Stoke	38	11	5	3	43	13	5	0	14	14	39	57	52	37
11	Gainsborough Trin.	38	9	4	6	31	28	5	3	11	16	43	47	71	35
12	Leeds City	38	9	6	4	33	18	3	2	14	20	47	53	65	32
13	Stockport County	38	9	4	6	35	26	3	4	12	13	41	48	67	32
14	Clapton Orient	38	10	5	4	28	13	1	5	13	12	52	40	65	32
15	Blackpool	38	11	3	5	33	19	0	6	13	18	39	51	58	31
16	Barnsley	38	8	3	8	41	31	4	3	12	13	37	54	68	30
17	Glossop	38	9	5	5	36	26	2	3	14	18	48	54	74	30
18	GRIMSBY TOWN	38	8	5	6	27	24	3	3	13	16	47	43	71	30
19	Chesterfield	38	6	6	7	33	38	0	5	14	13	54	46	92	23
20	Lincoln City	38	7	2	10	27	28	2	1	16	19	55	46	83	21

1908-09 13th in Division 2

Captain: 'Chopper' Lee

No	Month	Day	Opponent	Score	Scorers	Att.	Scott	Wheelhouse	Bidmead	Lee	Davidson	Forster	Bradley M	Owens	Springthorpe	Kilbourne	Coxon	Lonsdale	Henderson CG	Glennon	Hargreaves	Kelly	Hatton	Leonard	Stokes	Bacon	Beadling	Satterthwaite	Burkinshaw	Appleyard	Fletcher
1	Sep	1	STOCKPORT COUNTY	3-0	Coxon, Owens, Springthorpe	5000	1	2	3	4	5	6	7	8	9	10	11														
2		5	WEST BROMWICH ALBION	1-1	Bradley		1	2		4	5	6	7	9	10	7	11		3												
3		12	Birmingham	1-3	Kilbourne	15000	1	2		4	5	6	8	10		7	11		3					9							
4		19	GAINSBOROUGH TRINITY	1-2	Springthorpe		1	2		4	5	6	10		9	8	11		3					7							
5		26	Bolton Wanderers	0-2			1	2		4	5		8	9			11		3				6	10	7						
6	Oct	3	Fulham	2-5	Owens(2)	16000	1	2		4	5		8	9			11		3				6	10	7						
7		10	BURNLEY	0-1			1	2		4	5		8	9	10		11		3				6		7						
8		17	Bradford PA	2-0	Burkinshaw, Coxon	9000	1	2			5	4	8				11		3		6			10	7				9		
9		24	WOLVERHAMPTON WANDS.	3-0	Burkinshaw, Bradley(2)		1	2		4	5		8				11		3		6			10	7				9		
10		31	Oldham Athletic	0-4		15000	1	2		4	5		8				11		3		6			10	7				9		
11	Nov	7	CLAPTON ORIENT	1-0	Burkinshaw		1	2		4	5		8				11		3		6			10	7				9		
12		14	Leeds City	1-4	Stokes	3000	1	2		4	5		9				11		3		6			10	7			8			
13		21	BARNSLEY	0-0		6500	1	2		4	5						11		3		6			10			7	8		9	
14		28	Tottenham Hotspur	0-2		14000	1	2		4	5				10				3		6						7	8		9	11
15	Dec	5	HULL CITY	0-0		7000		2		4	5		8		10			1	3				6				7			9	11
16		12	Derby County	1-2	Bradley(pen)	5000	1	2		4	5		8				11		3				6	9			7	10			
17		19	BLACKPOOL	2-1	Appleyard(pen), Springthorpe		1	2			5				8		11		3	4			6				7	10		9	
18		26	CHESTERFIELD TOWN	1-0	Satterthwaite	7000	1	2			5						11		3	4			6	8			7	10		9	
19	Jan	1	Stockport County	1-0	Beadling		1	2		4	5						11		3				6	8			7	10		9	
20		2	West Bromwich Albion	0-7		5177	1	2		4	5						11		3				6	8			7	10		9	
21		9	BIRMINGHAM	0-3			1	2		4	5				8		11		3				6				7	10		9	
22		23	Gainsborough Trinity	3-0	Coxon, Leonard(2)	5000	1	2		4	5		8				11		3				6	9			7	10			
23		30	BOLTON WANDERERS	1-0	Leonard	4000	1	2		4	5		8				11		3				6	9			7	10			
24	Feb	6	Chesterfield Town	2-1	Leonard, Bradley	5000	1	2		4	5		8				11		3				6	9			7	10			
25		13	Burnley	0-2			1	2		4	5		8				11		3				6	9			7	10			
26		20	BRADFORD PA	1-1	Satterthwaite	6000	1	2			5		8				11		3	4			6	9			7	10			
27		27	Wolverhampton Wands.	0-0		8000	1	2			5						11		3	4			6	8			7	10		9	
28	Mar	13	Clapton Orient	1-2	Appleyard(pen)		1	2			5						11		3	4			6	8			7	10		9	
29		16	Glossop	0-1			1	2			5						11		3	4			6	8			7	10		9	
30		20	LEEDS CITY	0-1		5500	1	2			5					8	11		3	4			6				7	10		9	
31		25	FULHAM	2-2	Beadling, Coxon	4000	1	2			5		8			10	11		3	4			6	9			7				
32		27	Barnsley	1-3	Little(OG)		1	2					8			10	11		3	4	5		6	9			7				
33	Apr	3	TOTTENHAM HOTSPUR	1-2	Coxon		1	2					8			10	11		3		4	5	6			7				9	
34		10	Hull City	1-0	Kilbourne	12000	1	2		4			8			10	11		3			5	6	9			7				
35		12	GLOSSOP	2-0	Beadling(2)		1	2		4			8			10	11		3			5	6	9			7				
36		17	DERBY COUNTY	2-0	Kilbourne, Leonard	5000	1	2		4			8			10	11		3			5	6	9			7				
37		20	OLDHAM ATHLETIC	2-0	Beadling, Leonard	6000	1	2		4						10	11		3			5	6	9			7	8			
38		24	Blackpool	2-2	Kelly, Coxon		1	2		4						10	11		3			5	6	9			7	8			

	Scott	Wheelhouse	Bidmead	Lee	Davidson	Forster	Bradley M	Owens	Springthorpe	Kilbourne	Coxon	Lonsdale	Henderson CG	Glennon	Hargreaves	Kelly	Hatton	Leonard	Stokes	Bacon	Beadling	Satterthwaite	Burkinshaw	Appleyard	Fletcher
Apps.	37	38	1	27	31	5	25	6	8	13	36	1	37	9	9	6	27	29	8	1	25	20	4	13	2
Goals							5	3	3	3	6					1		6	1		5	2	3	2	

1 own goal

F.A. Cup

No	Month	Day	Opponent	Score	Scorers	Att.	Scott	Wheelhouse	Bidmead	Lee	Davidson	Forster	Bradley M	Owens	Springthorpe	Kilbourne	Coxon	Lonsdale	Henderson CG	Glennon	Hargreaves	Kelly	Hatton	Leonard	Stokes	Bacon	Beadling	Satterthwaite	Burkinshaw	Appleyard	Fletcher
1	Jan	20	STOCKPORT COUNTY	0-2		5000	1	2		4	5		8	9	7		11		3				6					10			

		P	W	D	L	F	A	W	D	L	F	A	F	A	Pts
1	Bolton Wanderers	38	14	3	2	37	8	10	1	8	22	20	59	28	52
2	Tottenham Hotspur	38	12	5	2	42	12	8	6	5	25	20	67	32	51
3	West Bromwich Alb.	38	13	5	1	35	9	6	8	5	21	18	56	27	51
4	Hull City	38	14	2	3	44	15	5	4	10	19	24	63	39	44
5	Derby County	38	13	5	1	38	11	3	6	10	17	30	55	41	43
6	Oldham Athletic	38	14	4	1	39	9	3	2	14	16	34	55	43	40
7	Wolverhampton W.	38	10	6	3	32	12	4	5	10	24	36	56	48	39
8	Glossop	38	11	5	3	35	17	4	3	12	22	36	57	53	38
9	Gainsborough Trin.	38	12	3	4	30	20	3	5	11	19	50	49	70	38
10	Fulham	38	8	4	7	39	26	5	7	7	19	22	58	48	37
11	Birmingham	38	10	6	3	35	21	4	3	12	23	40	58	61	37
12	Leeds City	38	12	3	4	35	19	2	4	13	8	34	43	53	35
13	GRIMSBY TOWN	38	9	5	5	23	14	5	2	12	18	40	41	54	35
14	Burnley	38	8	4	7	33	28	5	3	11	18	30	51	58	33
15	Clapton Orient	38	7	7	5	25	19	5	2	12	12	30	37	49	33
16	Bradford Park Ave.	38	9	2	8	30	25	4	4	11	21	34	51	59	32
17	Barnsley	38	11	3	5	36	19	0	7	12	12	38	48	57	32
18	Stockport County	38	11	2	6	25	19	3	1	15	14	52	39	71	31
19	Chesterfield	38	10	3	6	30	28	1	5	13	7	39	37	67	30
20	Blackpool	38	9	6	4	30	22	0	5	14	16	46	46	68	29

SEASON 1908/09

Back: Wheelhouse, Owens, Henderson, Hull, Scott, Lonsdale, Rudd, Hatton
Middle (standing): Lee, Forster, Davidson, J.C.Bisby, Coxon, Bidmead, Glennon
Middle (seated): Salter, Stokes, Kilbourne, Bradley, Burkinshaw, Leonard, Appleton Front: Raybould, Hargreaves, Bacon

SEASON 1909/10

Back: Jenkinson, Wheelhouse, Scott, Lonsdale, C.Henderson. Middle: Dart, Lee, Kelly, Porter, Bacon, Hatton, Coxon
Front: Blackburn, Gildea, Leonard, Brooks, Kilbourne, Bell.

1909-10 19th in Division 2

Unsuccessful in re-election application

Captain: 'Chopper Lee

No	Month	Day	Opponent	Score	Scorers	Att	Scott	Wheelhouse	Henderson	Lee	Porter	Hatton	Blackburn	Gildea	Warren	Bell TD	Coxon	Davidson	Leonard	Gates	Kelly	Kilbourne	Lonsdale	Rowston	Springthorpe	Beadling	Coulbeck	Bacon	Brooks	Hargreaves	Ramsden	Shaw J	Dart	Leafe	Ainsworth
1	Sep	1	BRADFORD PA	0-1			1	2	3	4	5	6	7	8	9	10	11																		
2		4	Lincoln City	0-0		6000	1	2	3	4		6	7	8		10	11		9		5														
3		11	CLAPTON ORIENT	2-0	Leonard, Kilbourne	5000	1	2	3	5		6				10	11		9			8		7									4		
4		18	Blackpool	0-1		4000	1	2	3	5			7			10	11		9	4		8											6		
5		25	HULL CITY	2-3	Leonard, Bell	10000	1	2	3	5		6				10	11		9	5		8		7											
6	Oct	2	Derby County	0-6		5000	1	2	3					8		10	11		9	5		6		7									4		
7		9	STOCKPORT COUNTY	0-1		4000	1	2	3							10	11			5		4		7						6				8	
8		16	Glossop	0-3		4000	1	2	3							9		5		4				7	10		8			6					11
9		23	BIRMINGHAM	0-2		5000	1	2	3	4						11		6			5			7	10		8					9			
10		30	West Bromwich Albion	3-4	Coulbeck, Leonard(2)	8000	1	2	3	4						11		6	9		5			7	10		8								
11	Nov	6	OLDHAM ATHLETIC	0-0		5000	1	2	3	4						11		6	9	10	5			7			8								
12		13	Barnsley	1-2	Kelly(pen)	5000	1	2	3	4						10	11	6	9		5				8		7								
13		20	FULHAM	0-2		4000	1	2	3	4			7			10	11	6	9		5						8								
14		27	Burnley	1-3	Springthorpe		1	2	3	4			7				11	6			5	10			8							9			
15	Dec	4	LEEDS CITY	3-1	Kilbourne, Springthorpe, Gates	3000	1	2	3	4			7				11	6		9	5	10			8										
16		11	Wolverhampton Wands.	1-8	Hargreaves		1		3	4								5		9		10			8	7				6					11
17		18	GAINSBOROUGH TRINITY	2-1	Kilbourne(2)	3000	1	2		4								5		9		10			8	7				6	3				11
18		25	Leicester Fosse	1-3	Bell	10000	1	2		4						10	11	5				8				7				6	3	9			
19		27	Manchester City	0-2			1	2		4						10	11	5				8				7				6	3	9			
20	Jan	1	Hull City	1-5	Bell	7000	1	2		4						10	11	5				8				7				6	3	9			
21		8	LINCOLN CITY	1-2	Rowston	4000	1	2		4							11		10		5			7	8					6	3	9			
22		22	Clapton Orient	0-0			1	2		4						10		5	9	3				7	8					6					
23	Feb	8	Bradford PA	1-6	Brooks		1	2		4		6				10		5		3		8	1			7		11	9						
24		12	DERBY COUNTY	1-1	Gates	3000		2	3	4		6				10		5		9			1		8	7		11							
25		15	BLACKPOOL	0-1				2	3	4		6					11	5		9			1	7				10	8						
26		19	Stockport County	1-2	Bell			2	3	4		6				10		5	7	9			1					11	8						
27		26	GLOSSOP	4-0	Kilbourne, Leonard(3)			2	3	4		6				10	11		9			8	1					7							
28	Mar	5	Birmingham	4-2	Bell(3), Leonard			2	3			6				10	11	5	9		4	8	1					7							
29		12	WEST BROMWICH ALBION	3-0	Leonard(2), Hatton			2	3			6				10	11	5	9		4		1		8			7							
30		19	Oldham Athletic	1-4	Leonard	12000		2	3			6				10	11	5	9		4		1		8			7							
31		25	MANCHESTER CITY	0-1		10000		2	3			6				10	11	5	9		4		1		8			7							
32		26	LEICESTER FOSSE	0-0				2	3			6				10	11		9		4	8	1			7									
33	Apr	2	Fulham	2-3	Leonard, Coulbeck	10000		2	3			6						5	9		4	10	1	11			8								
34		9	BURNLEY	5-3	Leonard(3,1p),Coulbeck,Bamford(OG)			2	3			6				10		5	9		4		1	11			8								
35		16	Leeds City	1-3	Leonard	5000		2	3			6				10	11	5	9		4		1	7			8								
36		23	WOLVERHAMPTON WANDS	1-0	Leonard			2				6				10	11	5	9	3	4		1	7			8								
37		26	BARNSLEY	7-0	Bell(2),Coulbeck(2),Kelly(p),Little(OG),Brooks	2000		2				6				10	11	5		3	4		1			7	8		9						
38		30	Gainsborough Trinity	1-1	Hatton			2				6				10		5	9	3	4		1			7	8								
						Apps.	22	37	28	24	1	20	6	3	1	31	25	28	24	17	20	17	16	15	14	10	12	9	4	9	5	6	3	1	3
						Goals						2				9			17	2	2	5		1	3		4		2	1					

Additional players: Blanchard 2/16; Fletcher 11/22; Gordon 5/27 & 32; Robinson 7/33 & 34; Huxford 11/38

2 own goals

F.A. Cup

No	Month	Day	Opponent	Score	Scorers	Att	Scott	Wheelhouse	Henderson	Lee	Porter	Hatton	Blackburn	Gildea	Warren	Bell TD	Coxon	Davidson	Leonard	Gates	Kelly	Kilbourne	Lonsdale	Rowston	Springthorpe	Beadling	Coulbeck	Bacon	Brooks	Hargreaves	Ramsden	Shaw J	Dart	Leafe	Ainsworth
1	Jan	15	BRISTOL ROVERS	0-2		5000	1	2	3	4							11	5		9		10		7			8			6					

		P	W	D	L	F	A	W	D	L	F	A	F	A	Pts
1	Manchester City	38	15	2	2	51	17	8	6	5	30	23	81	40	54
2	Oldham Athletic	38	15	2	2	47	9	8	5	6	32	30	79	39	53
3	Hull City	38	13	4	2	52	19	10	3	6	28	27	80	46	53
4	Derby County	38	15	2	2	46	15	7	7	5	26	32	72	47	53
5	Leicester Fosse	38	15	2	2	60	20	5	2	12	19	38	79	58	44
6	Glossop	38	14	1	4	42	18	4	6	9	22	39	64	57	43
7	Fulham	38	9	7	3	28	13	5	6	8	23	30	51	43	41
8	Wolverhampton W.	38	14	3	2	51	22	3	3	13	13	41	64	63	40
9	Barnsley	38	15	3	1	48	15	1	4	14	14	44	62	59	39
10	Bradford Park Ave.	38	12	1	6	47	28	5	3	11	17	31	64	59	38
11	West Bromwich Alb.	38	8	5	6	30	23	8	0	11	28	33	58	56	37
12	Blackpool	38	7	7	5	24	18	7	1	11	26	34	50	52	36
13	Stockport County	38	9	6	4	37	20	4	2	13	13	27	50	47	34
14	Burnley	38	12	2	5	43	21	2	4	13	19	40	62	61	34
15	Lincoln City	38	7	6	6	27	24	3	5	11	15	45	42	69	31
16	Clapton Orient	38	10	4	5	26	15	2	2	15	11	45	37	60	30
17	Leeds City	38	8	4	7	30	33	2	3	14	16	47	46	80	27
18	Gainsborough Trin.	38	8	3	8	22	21	2	3	14	11	54	33	75	26
19	GRIMSBY TOWN	38	8	3	8	31	19	1	3	15	19	58	50	77	24
20	Birmingham	38	7	4	8	28	26	1	3	15	14	52	42	78	23

1910-11 1st in Midland League

Captain: 'Chopper' Lee

No.	Month	Date	Opponent	Score	Scorers	Att.	Lonsdale	Wheelhouse	Arrowsmith	Kelly	Gordon	Henderson	Hobson	Jackson	Leonard	Bell	Worth	Bradley	Lee	North	Bacon	Hubbard	Springthorpe	Young	Huxford
1	Sep	1	Nottingham Forest Res.	1-0	Leonard		1	2	3	4	5	6	7	8	9	10	11								
2		3	BARNSLEY RES.	1-1	Kelly	3000	1	2	3	4	5	6	7	8	9	10	11								
3		10	Castleford Town	0-2			1	2	3	4	5	6	7	8	9	10	11								
4		17	LEICESTER FOSSE RES.	8-1	Leonard(5),Jackson,Worth,Springthorpe		1	2	3		5	6	7	8	9		11		4				10		
5		24	DENABY UNITED	4-0	Leonard(2), Hobson, Worth	3000	1	2	3		5	6	7	8	9		11		4				10		
6	Oct	1	SHEFFIELD UNITED RES.	4-2	Leonard, Hobson, Springthorpe(2)		1	2	3	4	5	6	7	8	9		11						10		
7		13	Hull City Res.	0-1			1	2	3	6	5	10	7	8	9		11		4						
8		15	LEEDS CITY RES.	4-0	Leonard(2), Jackson, Kelly			2	3	4	5	6	7	8	9	10	11	1							
9		22	Sheffield United Res.	0-0				2	3	6	5		7	8	9	10	11	1	4						
10		29	Lincoln City Res.	1-1	Leonard(pen)	2500		2	3	6	5		7		9	10	11	1	4		8				
11	Nov	5	Leicester Fosse Res.	2-1	Gordon,Worth			2	3	9	5	6	7		8	10	11	1	4						
12		12	MEXBOROUGH TOWN	6-0	Hubbard(2),Worth(2),Springthorpe,Leonard	3000		2	3	6	5		7		9		11	1	4			8	10		
13		19	GAINSBOROUGH TRINITY RES	3-1	Hubbard, Worth(2)			2	3	6	5		7		9		11	1	4			8	10		
14		26	WORKSOP TOWN	7-0	Bell(4), Leonard(2), Worth			2	3	4	5	6	7		9	10	11	1				8			
15	Dec	10	LINCOLN CITY RES.	4-1	Henderson(2),Hubbard,Leonard	2000		2	3	4	5	6	7		9	10	11	1				8			
16		24	CHESTERFIELD TOWN	2-1	Leonard(2)			2	3	4	5	6	7		9	10	11	1				8			
17		26	HULL CITY RES.	2-2	Leonard, Hubbard	7000		2	3	4	5		7		9	10	11	1	6			8			
18		27	Barnsley Res.	1-2	Leonard			2	3	6	5		7		9	10	11	1	4			8			
19		31	NOTTS COUNTY RES.	4-2	Leonard(2), Huxford(2)			2	3	6	5		7		9		11	1	4			8			10
20	Jan	2	Chesterfield Town	0-1			1	2	3	6	5		7		9		11		4			8			10
21		7	ROTHERHAM TOWN	3-2	Springthorpe,Hubbard(2,1pen)	3000	1	2	3	4	5	6	7			10	11					9	8		
22		21	CASTLEFORD TOWN	4-2	Leonard,Springthorpe,Hubbard,Worth		1	2	3	6	5		7		9		11		4			8	10		
23		28	Huddersfield Town Res.	1-0	Leonard		1	2	3		5	6	7		9	10	11		4			8			
24	Feb	11	Rotherham County	0-0			1	2	3	6	5		7			10	11		4			8		9	
25		18	Leeds City Res.	3-0	Young(2), Springthorpe		1	2	3	6	5		7				11		4			8	10	9	
26	Mar	4	Huddersfield Town Res.	3-1	Huxford(2), Hobson		1	2	3	6	5		7				11		4			8		9	10
27		11	Sheffield Wednesday Res.	1-2	Springthorpe		1	2	3	6	5		7		9		11		4			8	10		
28		18	Doncaster Rovers Res.	3-0	Gordon(2), Hubbard		1	2	3	6	5	4	7		9		11					8	10		
29		25	Gainsborough Trinity Res.	0-0			1	2	3	6	5		7		9		11		4			8	10		
30		29	Notts County Res.	1-2	Huxford		1	2	3	6	5		7		9		11		4			8			10
31	Apr	1	Mexborough Town	1-0	Bell		1	2	3	6	9	5	7			10			4			8			11
32		8	Denaby United	3-1	Gordon, Hobson, Huxford		1	2	3	6	9	5	7			10			4			8			11
33		14	SHEFFIELD WED. RES.	2-0	Hobson, Young	7000	1	2	3		5	6	7			10	11		4			8		9	
34		15	DONCASTER ROVERS RES.	3-2	Hubbard, Worth(2)		1	2	3		5	6	7			10	11		4			8		9	
35		17	NOTTINGHAM FOREST RES.	2-0	Bell, Gordon		1	2	3		5	6	7			10	11		4			8		9	
36		18	Rotherham Town	0-0			1	2	3		9	6	7			10	11		4	5		8			
37		22	Worksop Town	6-1	Hubbard(3),Gordon(2),Hubbard			2	3	6	9	5	7				11	1	4			8			10
38		27	ROTHERHAM COUNTY	4-0	Huxford, Young(3)			2	3	6	8	5	7				11	1	4					9	10
						Apps.	24	38	38	31	38	23	38	9	26	21	36	14	28	1	1	26	11	7	8
						Goals				2	7	2	5	2	24	6	11					13	8	6	8

F.A. Cup

Rd	Month	Date	Opponent	Score	Scorers	Att.	Lonsdale	Wheelhouse	Arrowsmith	Kelly	Gordon	Henderson	Hobson	Jackson	Leonard	Bell	Worth	Bradley	Lee	North	Bacon	Hubbard	Springthorpe	Young	Huxford
R1	Jan	26	CROYDON COMMON*	8-1	Hubbard(2),Leonard(3),Springthorpe,Worth(2)	5000	1	2	3	6	5		7		9		11		4			8	10		
R2	Feb	4	Crewe Alexandra	5-1	Gordon,Hubbard(2),Leonard(p),Springthorpe	10000	1	2	3	6	5		7		9		11		4			8	10		
R3		25	Bradford City	0-1		24000	1	2	3	6	5		7				11		4			8	10	9	

* Replay of match declared void on 14 January (Won 3-0).

	P	W	D	L	F	A	Pts
1 GRIMSBY TOWN	38	25	7	6	94	32	57
2 Sheffield Wed. Reserves	38	24	8	6	84	41	56
3 Doncaster Rovers	38	23	4	11	106	63	50
4 Hull City Reserves	38	20	9	9	105	63	49
5 Chesterfield Town	38	20	5	13	80	61	45
6 Rotherham County	38	19	7	12	81	73	45
7 Huddersfield T. Reserves	38	18	5	15	83	65	41
8 Barnsley Reserves	38	15	8	15	82	70	38
9 Notts County Reserves	38	18	2	18	88	81	38
10 Lincoln City Reserves	38	15	5	18	59	83	37
11 Mexborough Town	38	13	10	15	70	65	36
12 Gainsborough T. Reserves	38	15	6	17	51	63	36
13 Leeds City Reserves	38	13	9	16	66	70	35
14 Sheffield United Reserves	38	14	4	20	73	89	32
15 Castleford Town	38	14	3	21	72	110	31
16 Rotherham Town	38	11	7	20	57	72	29
17 Leicester Fosse Reserves	38	11	7	20	62	80	29
18 Denaby United	38	13	3	22	60	92	29
19 Nottingham F. Reserves	38	10	7	21	56	82	27
20 Worksop Town	38	10	2	26	54	107	22

SEASON 1910/11

Back: Cooper (Chair), Bradley, Wheelhouse, Lonsdale, Arrowsmith, Holden (Train), Hickson (Sec)
Middle: Clarke (Dir), Kelly, Lee, Gordon, Henderson
Front: Hobson, Jackson, Leonard, Bell, Huxford, Worth

SEASON 1911/12

Back: Wheelhouse, Lonsdale, Arrowsmith
2nd Row: Holden (Train), Director, Gordon, Rampton, Nocton, Fulljames, Director, Clarke (Dir), A.McConnell (Asst Train)
Middle: Hickson (Sec), Hall, Martin, Pearce (Dir), Bradley, Director, Hodgkinson, Speak, Huxford
Front: Seeburg, Staniforth, Hubbard, Rippon, Cooper (Chair), Mounteney, Mayson, Bell, Worth. Laying: Blanchard, Higgins

1911-12 9th in Division 2

Captain: Sid Wheelhouse

	Date		Opponent	Score	Scorers	Att.	Lonsdale	Wheelhouse	Arrowsmith	Seeburg	Gordon	Martin	Staniforth	Hubbard	Mounteney	Springthorpe	Worth	Bradley	Blanchard	Bacon	Henderson	Speak	Browell	Fulljames	Higgins	Hodgkinson	Rippon T	Rampton	Mayson	Bell	Huxford	Ashton
1	Sep	2	WOLVERHAMPTON WANDS.	0-0		6000	1	2	3	4	5	6	7	8	9	10	11															
2		9	Leicester Fosse	2-0	Rampton, Hubbard(pen)		1	2	3	4	5	6	7	8			11									9		10				
3		16	GAINSBOROUGH TRINITY	3-3	Hubbard(2,1pen), Staniforth		1	2	3	4	5	6	7	8			11									9		10				
4		23	Burnley	1-1	Hodgkinson		1	2	3	4	5	6	7	8			11				9					10						
5		26	BARNSLEY	0-0		5000	1	2	3	4	5	6	7	8			11				9					10						
6		30	Nottingham Forest	0-1			1	2	3	4	5	6	7	8												9		10			11	
7	Oct	7	CHELSEA	2-1	Huxford, Staniforth	7000	1	2	3	4	5	6	7	8	9											10					11	
8		14	Clapton Orient	0-1		13000	1	2	3	4	5	6	7	8	9											10					11	
9		21	BRISTOL CITY	3-0	Gordon, Hubbard(2,1pen)	6000	1	2	3	4	5	6	7	8	9														10		11	
10		28	Birmingham	2-2	Gordon, Hubbard	15000	1	2	3	4	5	6	7	8	9														10		11	
11	Nov	4	HUDDERSFIELD TOWN	1-2	Hubbard		1	2	3	4	5		7	8	9										6				10		11	
12		11	Blackpool	2-1	Mayson(2)	3000		2	3	4	5	6	7	8	9		11	1											10			
13		25	Hull City	0-1		15000		2	3	4	5	6	7	8	9		11	1											10			
14	Dec	2	BRADFORD PA	0-0			1	2	3	4	5	6	7		9		11									8			10			
15		4	Leeds City	2-1	Hodgkinson(2)	3000	1	2	3		5	6	7		9		11						4			8			10			
16		9	Bradford PA	1-4	Wheelhouse(pen)	5000	1	2	3		5	6	7		9		11						4			8			10			
17		16	FULHAM	1-0	Rampton	5000	1	2	3		5	6	7		8								4					9	10		11	
18		23	DERBY COUNTY	0-3		7000	1	2	3		5	6	7		8								4					9	10		11	
19		25	Derby County	1-2	Mayson	15000	1	2	3		5	6	7	9	8								4						10		11	
20		26	STOCKPORT COUNTY	2-2	Hubbard, Staniforth	8000	1	2	3		5	6	7	9	8								4						10		11	
21		30	Wolverhampton Wands.	2-1	Mounteney, Hubbard	6000	1	2	3	9	5	6	7	10	8								4						11			
22	Jan	6	LEICESTER FOSSE	4-0	Gordon, Staniforth, Mounteney, Martin	3000	1	2	3	9	5	6	7	10	8								4						11			
23		20	Gainsborough Trinity	3-2	Hubbard(2), Mounteney		1	2	3	9	5	6	7	10	8								4						11			
24		23	LEEDS CITY	1-2	Hubbard	3000	1	2	3		5	6	7	10	8								4			9			11			
25		27	BURNLEY	1-0	T.Rippon		1	2	3		5	6	7	10	8								4				9		11			
26	Feb	10	Chelsea	1-4	Mounteney(pen)	25000	1	2	3	9	5	6	7	10	8								4						11			
27		17	CLAPTON ORIENT	2-1	Mounteney(pen), Staniforth		1		2	9	5	6	7		8							3	4				10		11			
28		24	Bristol City	0-3		6000	1	2	3			6	7		8		11						4	5			9		10			
29	Mar	2	BIRMINGHAM	1-0	Worth		1		3		5	6	7		8		11		2				4						9	10		
30		9	Huddersfield Town	0-2		5500	1		2		5	6	7	9			11					3	4				8		10			
31		16	BLACKPOOL	1-0	Mounteney	4000	1	2	3		5	6	7	9	8		11						4						10			
32		20	NOTTINGHAM FOREST	1-4	Mounteney	3000	1		3		5	6	7		8	10	11			2			4				9					
33		23	Glossop	2-5	Mounteney(pen), T.Rippon		1	2		4	5	6	7		8		11					3				10	9					
34		30	HULL CITY	1-0	Worth	6000	1	2	3		5	6	7		8		11						4				9		10			
35	Apr	5	Stockport County	0-3		7000	1	2	3		5	6	7	10	8		11						4				9					
36		6	Barnsley	2-2	Mounteney, Hubbard	5000	1		3		5	6	7	10	8		11				2		4				9					
37		8	GLOSSOP	0-0			1		3		5	6	7		8		11				2		4				9					10
38		20	Fulham	3-1	Mounteney(3)	8000	1	2	3		5	6	7		8								4				9		10		11	
						Apps.	36	32	37	20	37	37	38	25	32	2	20	2	1	1	4	3	23	1	1	12	11	5	25	1	11	1
						Goals		1			3	1	5	13	12		2									3	2	2	3		1	

F.A. Cup

	Date		Opponent	Score	Scorers	Att.	Lonsdale	Wheelhouse	Arrowsmith	Seeburg	Gordon	Martin	Staniforth	Hubbard	Mounteney	Springthorpe	Worth	Bradley	Blanchard	Bacon	Henderson	Speak	Browell	Fulljames	Higgins	Hodgkinson	Rippon T	Rampton	Mayson	Bell	Huxford	Ashton
Pre	Nov	18	Lincoln City	2-3	Hubbard, Mayson	8000		2	3	4	5	6	7	8	9		11	1											10			

		P	W	D	L	F	A	W	D	L	F	A	F	A	Pts
1	Derby County	38	15	2	2	55	13	8	6	5	19	15	74	28	54
2	Chelsea	38	15	2	2	36	13	9	4	6	28	21	64	34	54
3	Burnley	38	14	5	0	50	14	8	3	8	27	27	77	41	52
4	Clapton Orient	38	16	0	3	44	14	5	3	11	17	30	61	44	45
5	Wolverhampton W.	38	12	3	4	41	10	4	7	8	16	23	57	33	42
6	Barnsley	38	10	5	4	28	19	5	7	7	17	23	45	42	42
7	Hull City	38	12	3	4	36	13	5	5	9	18	38	54	51	42
8	Fulham	38	10	3	6	42	24	6	4	9	24	34	66	58	39
9	GRIMSBY TOWN	38	9	6	4	24	18	6	3	10	24	37	48	55	39
10	Leicester Fosse	38	11	4	4	34	18	4	3	12	15	48	49	66	37
11	Bradford Park Ave.	38	10	5	4	30	16	3	4	12	14	29	44	45	35
12	Birmingham	38	11	3	5	44	29	3	3	13	11	30	55	59	34
13	Bristol City	38	11	4	4	27	17	3	2	14	14	43	41	60	34
14	Blackpool	38	12	4	3	24	12	1	4	14	8	40	32	52	34
15	Nottingham Forest	38	9	3	7	26	18	4	4	11	20	30	46	48	33
16	Stockport County	38	8	5	6	31	22	3	6	10	16	32	47	54	33
17	Huddersfield Town	38	8	5	6	30	22	5	1	13	20	42	50	64	32
18	Glossop	38	6	8	5	33	23	2	4	13	9	33	42	56	28
19	Leeds City	38	7	6	6	21	22	3	2	14	29	56	50	78	28
20	Gainsborough Trin.	38	4	6	9	17	22	1	7	11	13	42	30	64	23

1912-13 7th in Division 2

Captain: Sid Wheelhouse

No.	Month	Day	Opponent	Score	Scorers	Att.	Bradley	Wheelhouse	Arrowsmith	Andrews	Gordon	Martin	Staniforth	Mounteney	Quin	Mayson	Birch	Lonsdale	Speak	Blanchard	Rushby	Whitchurch	Rippon T	Rampton	Armstrong	Johnson	Pickering	Springthorpe	Ashton	Duncan	Cassidy
1	Sep	3	BLACKPOOL	1-1	Mounteney		1	2	3	4	5	6	7	8	9	10	11														
2		7	Bury	2-4	Birch, T.Rippon	7000	1	2	3	4	5	6	7		9	10	11						8								
3		9	Blackpool	1-2	Mounteney		1	2	3	4	5	6	7	8		10							9						11		
4		14	FULHAM	2-1	Mounteney(pen), T.Rippon	6000		2	3	4	5	6	7	8		10		1					9						11		
5		21	Barnsley	0-3		7000		2	3	4	5	6	7	8				1					9		10				11		
6		28	BRADFORD PA	3-0	Staniforth(2), Mayson	4000		2	3	4	5	6	7	8	9	10		1											11		
7	Oct	5	Wolverhampton Wands.	0-3		12000		2	3	4	5	6	7	8	9	10		1											11		
8		12	LEICESTER FOSSE	2-0	T.Rippon, Staniforth			2	3	4	5	6	7	8		10		1					9						11		
9		19	Stockport County	1-1	Mayson	4000		2	3	4	5	6	7	8		10	11	1					9								
10		26	PRESTON NORTH END	0-0				2	3	4	5	6	7	8				1					9					10	11		
11	Nov	2	Burnley	2-3	Mounteney(pen), Mayson	12000		2	3	4	5	6	7	8	9	10	11	1													
12		9	HULL CITY	2-0	Mounteney, Gordon	8000		2	3	4	5	6	7	8	9	10	11	1													
13		16	Glossop	0-2				2	3	4	5	6	7	8	9	10	11	1													
14		23	CLAPTON ORIENT	1-2	Mayson			2	3	4	5	6	7	8	9	10	11	1													
15	Dec	7	NOTTINGHAM FOREST	0-0				2	3	4	5	6	7		9	10	11	1					8								
16		14	Bristol City	2-2	Mayson, T.Rippon	4000		2	3	4	5	6	7		9	10	11	1					8								
17		21	BIRMINGHAM	2-2	Rampton, Crossthwaite(OG)			2	3	4	5	6	7			10	11	1					8	9							
18		25	Leeds City	2-1	Armstrong, Gordon	16000		2	3	4	5	6	7			10	11	1					8		9						
19		26	Huddersfield Town	2-0	T.Rippon(2)	9500		2	3	4	5	6	7			10	11	1					8		9						
20		28	BURY	4-0	Mayson(2),T.Rippon,Wheelhouse(pen)	10000		2	3	4	5	6	7			10	11	1					8	9							
21	Jan	4	Fulham	1-0	Mayson	7000		2	3	4	5	6	7			10	11	1					8	9							
22		18	BARNSLEY	1-1	Rampton			2	3		5	6	7			10	11	1			4		8	9							
23		25	Bradford PA	0-3				2	3	4	5	6	7			10	11	1					8	9							
24	Feb	1	Lincoln City	0-3		13000	1	2	3	4	5	6	7			10	11						8			9					
25		8	WOLVERHAMPTON WANDS.	2-1	T.Rippon, Mayson			2	3	4	5	6	7			10	11	1					8				9				
26		15	Leicester Fosse	0-1				2	3		5	6			7	10	11	1			4		8				9				
27		22	STOCKPORT COUNTY	4-1	Mayson(3,1pen),T.Rippon(pen)				2	4	5				7	10		1	3			6	8	9						11	
28	Mar	1	Preston North End	0-2		10000		2	3	4	5				7	10		1				6	8		9					11	
29		11	BURNLEY	2-0	Rampton, Mayson			2	3	4	5	6			7	10	11	1					8	9							
30		15	Hull City	0-5		7000		2	3		5	6			7	10	11	1				4	8	9							
31		21	LEEDS CITY	3-2	Mayson, T.Rippon(2)	8000		2	3	4	5	6			7	10	11	1					8	9							
32		22	GLOSSOP	0-0				2	3	4	5	6			7	10	11	1					8	9							
33		24	HUDDERSFIELD TOWN	0-0		7000		2		4	5	6			7	10	11	1		3			8	9							
34		29	Clapton Orient	3-1	Rampton, Mayson, T.Rippon			2		4	5	6			7	10	11	1		3			8	9							
35	Apr	5	LINCOLN CITY	0-0				2	3	4	5	6	7			10	11	1					8	9							
36		12	Nottingham Forest	2-1	Rampton(2)	7000		2	3	4	5	6	7			10	11	1					8	9							
37		19	BRISTOL CITY	3-0	T.Rippon, Quin, Nicholson(OG)	4000		2	3		5	6	7		9		11	1			4		8	10							
38		26	Birmingham	1-2	Quin			2	3		5	6	7		9		11				4		8	10							1
						Apps.	4	37	36	33	38	36	29	13	21	34	29	33	1	2	4	3	31	16	4	1	2	1	7	2	1
						Goals		1			2		3	5	3	15	1						13	6	1						

2 own goals

F.A. Cup

No.	Month	Day	Opponent	Score	Scorers	Att.	Bradley	Wheelhouse	Arrowsmith	Andrews	Gordon	Martin	Staniforth	Mounteney	Quin	Mayson	Birch	Lonsdale	Speak	Blanchard	Rushby	Whitchurch	Rippon T	Rampton	Armstrong	Johnson	Pickering	Springthorpe	Ashton	Duncan	Cassidy
1	Jan	18	Sheffield Wednesday	1-5	T.Rippon	26442		2	3	4	5	6	7			10	11	1					8	9							

		P	W	D	L	F	A	W	D	L	F	A	F	A	Pts
1	Preston North End	38	13	5	1	34	12	6	10	3	22	21	56	33	53
2	Burnley	38	13	4	2	58	23	8	4	7	30	30	88	53	50
3	Birmingham	38	11	6	2	39	18	7	4	8	20	26	59	44	46
4	Barnsley	38	15	3	1	46	18	4	4	11	11	29	57	47	45
5	Huddersfield Town	38	13	5	1	49	12	4	4	11	17	28	66	40	43
6	Leeds City	38	12	3	4	45	22	3	7	9	25	42	70	64	40
7	GRIMSBY TOWN	38	10	8	1	32	11	5	2	12	19	39	51	50	40
8	Lincoln City	38	10	6	3	31	16	5	4	10	19	36	50	52	40
9	Fulham	38	13	5	1	47	16	4	0	15	18	39	65	55	39
10	Wolverhampton W.	38	10	6	3	34	16	4	4	11	22	38	56	54	38
11	Bury	38	10	6	3	29	14	5	2	12	24	43	53	57	38
12	Hull City	38	12	2	5	42	18	3	4	12	18	37	60	55	36
13	Bradford Park Ave.	38	12	4	3	47	18	2	4	13	13	42	60	60	36
14	Clapton Orient	38	8	6	5	25	20	2	8	9	9	27	34	47	34
15	Leicester Fosse	38	12	2	5	34	20	1	5	13	15	45	49	65	33
16	Bristol City	38	7	9	3	32	25	2	6	11	14	47	46	72	33
17	Nottingham Forest	38	9	3	7	35	25	3	5	11	23	34	58	59	32
18	Glossop	38	11	2	6	34	26	1	6	12	15	42	49	68	32
19	Stockport County	38	8	4	7	32	23	0	6	13	24	55	56	78	26
20	Blackpool	38	8	4	7	22	22	1	4	14	17	47	39	69	26

1913-14 15th in Division 2

Captain: Sid Wheelhouse

	Date		Opponent	Score	Scorers	Att.	Spendiff	Wheelhouse	Lee	Andrews	Gordon	Martin	Miller	Rippon T	Kenny	Rampton	Birch	Lonsdale	Arrowsmith	Gregson	Quin	Rippon W	Scott	Mayson	McKenna	Whitchurch	Gimblett	Chalmers	Blanchard	Hodgson	Rushby	Thompson	Whelpton
1	Sep	6	NOTTS COUNTY	0-0		**5000**		2	3	4	5	6	7	8	9	10	11	1															
2		10	Bradford PA	0-3		8000	1	2		4	5	6	7	8	9	10	11		3														
3		13	Leicester Fosse	0-2		17000	1	2		4	5		7	10					3	8	9		11								6		
4		20	WOLVERHAMPTON WANDS.	1-0	Miller	7000	1	2		4	5	6	7	10					3	8	9		11										
5		27	Hull City	1-2	Gregson	14000	1	2		4	5	6	7	10					3	8	9		11										
6	Oct	14	BARNSLEY	1-1	Gregson	8000	1	2		4	5	6	7	8		9			3	10			11										
7		11	Bury	1-3	Gregson	12000	1	2		4	5	6		8		9			3	10	7		11										
8		18	HUDDERSFIELD TOWN	2-1	Gregson, T.Rippon	6000	1	2		4	5	6		8	9				3	10	7		11										
9		25	Lincoln City	3-1	Gregson, T.Rippon, Gordon	12000	1	2		4	5	6		8					3	10	7	9	11										
10	Nov	1	BLACKPOOL	2-0	W.Rippon, Jones(OG)	8000	1	2		4	5	6		8					3	10	7	9	11										
11		8	Nottingham Forest	1-4	T.Rippon		1	2		4	5	6		8			11		3	10	7	9											
12		15	WOOLWICH ARSENAL	1-1	W.Rippon	8000	1	2		4	5	6							3	8	7	9	11	10									
13		22	Fulham	2-2	W.Rippon, Rampton	16000	1	2			5	6				10			3	8	7	9	11			4							
14		29	Birmingham	2-1	W.Rippon(2)	20000	1	2		4	5	6				10			3	8	7	9	11										
15	Dec	6	BRISTOL CITY	1-0	Rampton	6000	1	2		4	5	6				10			3	8	7	9	11										
16		13	Leeds City	1-4	Quin	10000	1	2			5	6				10			3	8	9		11		4		7						
17		20	CLAPTON ORIENT	2-0	Gregson(2)		1	2			5	6				10			3	8	7	9	11		4								
18		25	STOCKPORT COUNTY	2-0	Fagan(OG), W.Rippon	10000	1	2			5	6				10			3	8	7	9	11		4								
19		26	Stockport County	2-2	Gregson(2)		1	2		4	5								3	8	7	9	11	10	6								
20		27	Notts County	0-4			1	2		10	5	6							3		7	9	11	8	4								
21	Jan	3	LEICESTER FOSSE	3-0	W.Rippon(2), Gregson		1		2	4	5	6		8					3	10		9	11				7						
22		17	Wolverhampton Wands.	1-4	W.Rippon	8000	1		2	4	5	6				10	11		3	8		9					7						
23		24	HULL CITY	1-3	Mayson	12000	1	2		4	5	6					11		3	8		9		10			7						
24	Feb	7	Barnsley	1-3	T.Rippon		1	2		4	5	6		8					3	10	7	9	11										
25		14	BURY	1-0	W.Rippon		1	2		4	5	6		8					3	10	7	9	11										
26		21	Huddersfield Town	2-1	T.Rippon(2)	3500	1	2		4		6		8	5				3	10	7	9	11										
27		24	BRADFORD PA	0-0			1	2		4		6		8	5				3	10	7	9	11										
28		28	LINCOLN CITY	1-3	W.Rippon(pen)		1	2		4	5			8		10			3		7	9		11	6								
29	Mar	7	Blackpool	1-1	W.Rippon	4000	1	2	3	4	5			8						10	7	9	11			6							
30		14	NOTTINGHAM FOREST	3-0	T.Rippon(2), Gregson	8000	1	2		4	5			8					3	10	7	9	11			6							
31		28	FULHAM	0-3		8000	1	2		4	5	7		8					3	10		9	11			6							
32	Apr	4	BIRMINGHAM	0-2				2		4	5	6		8					3	7				10				9				11	1
33		10	Glossop	0-3			1	2		4	5	6		8					3	10	7	9	11										
34		11	Bristol City	0-1		12000	1	2		4	5	6		8		9			3	10	7		11										
35		13	GLOSSOP	3-0	Rampton(2), T.Rippon		1	2		4	5	6		8		9			3	10	7		11										
36		18	LEEDS CITY	0-1		9000	1	2		4	5	6		8		9			3	10	7		11										
37		23	Woolwich Arsenal	0-2			1	2		4	5	6		8		9			3	10	7		11										
38		25	Clapton Orient	0-0		10000		2		4	5	6		8					3	10	7							9	1	11			
						Apps.	35	36	4	34	36	33	6	27	5	16	5	1	36	34	30	23	30	6	6	4	4	2	1	1	1	1	1
						Goals					1		1	9		4				11	1	12		1									

2 own goals

F.A. Cup

	Date		Opponent	Score	Scorers	Att.	Spendiff	Wheelhouse	Lee	Andrews	Gordon	Martin	Miller	Rippon T	Kenny	Rampton	Birch	Lonsdale	Arrowsmith	Gregson	Quin	Rippon W	Scott	Mayson	McKenna	Whitchurch	Gimblett	Chalmers	Blanchard	Hodgson	Rushby	Thompson	Whelpton
1	Jan	10	West Bromwich Albion	0-2		14000	1	2		4	5	6				9			3	8	7		11	10									

	P	W	D	L	F	A	W	D	L	F	A	F	A	Pts
1 Notts County	38	16	2	1	55	13	7	5	7	22	23	77	36	53
2 Bradford Park Ave.	38	15	1	3	44	20	8	2	9	27	27	71	47	49
3 Woolwich Arsenal	38	14	3	2	34	10	6	6	7	20	28	54	38	49
4 Leeds City	38	15	2	2	54	16	5	5	9	22	30	76	46	47
5 Barnsley	38	14	1	4	33	15	5	6	8	18	30	51	45	45
6 Clapton Orient	38	14	5	0	38	11	2	6	11	9	24	47	35	43
7 Hull City	38	9	5	5	29	13	7	4	8	24	24	53	37	41
8 Bristol City	38	12	5	2	32	10	4	4	11	20	40	52	50	41
9 Wolverhampton W.	38	14	1	4	33	16	4	4	11	18	36	51	52	41
10 Bury	38	12	6	1	30	14	3	4	12	9	26	39	40	40
11 Fulham	38	10	3	6	31	20	6	3	10	15	23	46	43	38
12 Stockport County	38	9	6	4	32	18	4	4	11	23	39	55	57	36
13 Huddersfield Town	38	8	4	7	28	22	5	4	10	19	31	47	53	34
14 Birmingham	38	10	4	5	31	18	2	6	11	17	42	48	60	34
15 GRIMSBY TOWN	38	10	4	5	24	15	3	4	12	18	43	42	58	34
16 Blackpool	38	6	10	3	24	19	3	4	12	9	25	33	44	32
17 Glossop	38	8	3	8	32	24	3	3	13	19	43	51	67	28
18 Leicester Fosse	38	7	2	10	29	28	4	2	13	16	33	45	61	26
19 Lincoln City	38	8	5	6	23	23	2	1	16	13	43	36	66	26
20 Nottingham Forest	38	7	7	5	27	23	0	2	17	10	53	37	76	23

SEASON 1913/14
Back: Spink, W.Rippon, Andrews, Wheelhouse, Lonsdale, Arrowsmith, Martin, Lee
Middle (standing): Holden (Asst Train), Sudds, Gordon, Spendiff, McKenna, Whitchurch, Gregson, McConnell (Trainer)
Middle (seated): Miller, T.Rippon, Kenny, Johnson, Rampton, Quin, Mayson, Birch
Front: Rushby, Jowet, Scott

SEASON 1914/15
Back: Kenny, Holden (Train), Andrews, Wheelhouse, W. Rippon, Lee, Summers, Martin
Front: Spink, T. Rippon, Rampton, Mayson, Thompson

1914-15 17th in Division 2

Captain: Sid Wheelhouse

							Summers	Wheelhouse	Arrowsmith	Andrews	Gordon	Martin	Spink	Rippon T.	Chalmers	Mayson	Scott	Blanchard	Spendiff	Atkin	McKenna	Lee	Kenny	Whitchurch	Quin	Gregson	Rampton	Padley	Thompson	Huxford
1	Sep	1	PRESTON NORTH END	2-2	T.Rippon, Gordon	5000	1	2	3	4	5	6	7	8	9	10	11													
2		5	Nottingham Forest	2-4	Mayson(2)		1	2	3	4	5	6	7	8	9	10	11													
3		7	Preston North End	0-3			1	2	3	4	5	6	7	8	9	10											11			
4		12	LEICESTER FOSSE	1-0	Rampton		1	2	3	4	5	6		8		10	11								7		9			
5		19	Barnsley	0-0			1	2	3	4	5	6	7	8			11									10	9			
6		26	GLOSSOP	1-0	Rampton	5000	1		3	4	5		7	8			11			2				6		10	9			
7	Oct	3	Wolverhampton Wands.	1-0	T.Rippon	8000	1		3	4	5		7	8			11			2				6		10	9			
8		10	FULHAM	1-1	Quin	8000	1		3	4	5		7	8			11			2				6	9		10			
9		17	Stockport County	1-1	Rampton		1		3	4	5		7	8						2				6	9	10	11			
10		24	HULL CITY	1-1	Quin	9000	1	5	3	4		6	7	8						2					9	10	11			
11		31	Leeds City	0-5		5000	1		3	4		6	7	8						2			5		9	10	11			
12	Nov	7	CLAPTON ORIENT	2-1	T.Rippon, Rampton		1	2	3	4	5	6	7	8		10											9		11	
13		14	Woolwich Arsenal	0-6			1	2	3	4	5	6	7	8		10											9		11	
14		21	DERBY COUNTY	1-2	Rampton	8000	1	2	3	4	5		7	8		11								6	9		10			
15		28	Lincoln City	1-2	Rampton		1	2	3	4			7	9			11						5	6		8	10			
16	Dec	5	BIRMINGHAM	1-0	T.Rippon		1	2	3	4			7	8			11						5	6		10	9			
17		12	BLACKPOOL	2-0	Rampton(2)		1	2	3	4			7	8			11						5	6		10	9			
18		19	Huddersfield Town	1-3	Scott	3500	1	2	3	4			7	8			11						5	6		10	9			
19		25	BRISTOL CITY	2-3	T.Rippon(2,1pen)	11000	1	2	3	4			7	8			11						5	6		10	9			
20		26	Bristol City	0-7			1	2	3	4			7	8			11						5	6		10	9			
21	Jan	2	NOTTINGHAM FOREST	4-0	Mayson,Rampton,T.Rippon,Andrews		1			4	5	6	7	8		10	11			2		3					9			
22		16	Leicester Fosse	0-2			1		3	4		5	7	8						2				6	9	10	11			
23		23	BARNSLEY	2-3	Padley, Gregson	4000	1		3	4			7							2	6		5		9	8	11	10		
24		30	Glossop	0-0		500			3	4			7				11	1		2	6		5			8	9	10		
25	Feb	6	WOLVERHAMPTON WANDS.	1-4	Padley				3	4			7	8			11	1		2	6		5				9	10		
26		13	Fulham	1-2	T.Rippon	3000			3	4			7	8			11	1		2	6		5				9	10		
27		20	STOCKPORT COUNTY	6-1	Andrews,Rampton(3),Mayson(2)		1	2	3	4			7	8		10					6		5				9			11
28	Mar	6	LEEDS CITY	2-5	Mayson, T.Rippon	4000	1	2	3	4			7	8		10					6		5				9			11
29		13	Clapton Orient	1-2	Mayson	7000	1	2		4			7	8		10					6	3	5				9			11
30		20	WOOLWICH ARSENAL	1-0	Rampton		1	2		4			7	8		10					6	3	5				9		11	
31		27	Derby County	1-1	Mayson	6000	1	2		4		6	7	8		10						3	5				9		11	
32	Apr	2	Bury	2-2	Rampton, Wheelhouse(pen)	4000	1	2		4		6	7	8		10						3	5				9		11	
33		3	LINCOLN CITY	5-1	Rampton(3), Mayson, T.Rippon		1	2		4		6		8		10						3	5		7		9		11	
34		5	BURY	1-0	T.Rippon	7000	1	2		4		6		8		10						3	5		7		9		11	
35		10	Birmingham	0-3			1	2		4		6	7	8		10						3	5				9		11	
36		17	Blackpool	0-5		4000	1		2	4		6	7	8		10						3	5				9		11	
37		24	HUDDERSFIELD TOWN	0-0		4000				4		6	7	8		10			1		2	3	5				9		11	
38		29	Hull City	1-4	Rampton	3000	1			4		6	7	8		10					2	3	5				9		11	
						Apps.	34	24	28	38	13	19	35	36	3	20	17	3	1	12	10	11	23	12	10	15	36	4	11	3
						Goals		1		2	1			11		9	1								2	1	18	2		

F.A. Cup

							Summers	Wheelhouse	Arrowsmith	Andrews	Gordon	Martin	Spink	Rippon T.	Chalmers	Mayson	Scott	Blanchard	Spendiff	Atkin	McKenna	Lee	Kenny	Whitchurch	Quin	Gregson	Rampton	Padley	Thompson	Huxford
1	Jan	9	NORTHAMPTON TOWN	0-3		8000	1		3	4	5	6	7	8		10	11			2							9			

		P	W	D	L	F	A	W	D	L	F	A	F	A	Pts
1	Derby County	38	14	3	2	40	11	9	4	6	31	22	71	33	53
2	Preston North End	38	14	4	1	41	16	6	6	7	20	26	61	42	50
3	Barnsley	38	16	2	1	31	10	6	1	12	20	41	51	51	47
4	Wolverhampton W.	38	12	4	3	47	13	7	3	9	30	39	77	52	45
5	Arsenal	38	15	1	3	52	13	4	4	11	17	28	69	41	43
6	Birmingham	38	13	3	3	44	13	4	6	9	18	26	62	39	43
7	Hull City	38	12	2	5	36	23	7	3	9	29	31	65	54	43
8	Huddersfield Town	38	12	4	3	36	13	5	4	10	25	29	61	42	42
9	Clapton Orient	38	12	5	2	36	17	4	4	11	14	31	50	48	41
10	Blackpool	38	11	3	5	40	22	6	2	11	18	35	58	57	39
11	Bury	38	11	5	3	39	19	4	3	12	22	37	61	56	38
12	Fulham	38	12	0	7	35	20	3	7	9	18	27	53	47	37
13	Bristol City	38	11	2	6	38	19	4	5	10	24	37	62	56	37
14	Stockport County	38	12	4	3	33	19	3	3	13	21	41	54	60	37
15	Leeds City	38	9	3	7	40	25	5	1	13	25	39	65	64	32
16	Lincoln City	38	9	4	6	29	23	2	5	12	17	42	46	65	31
17	GRIMSBY TOWN	38	10	4	5	36	24	1	5	13	12	52	48	76	31
18	Nottingham Forest	38	9	7	3	32	24	1	2	16	11	53	43	77	29
19	Leicester Fosse	38	6	4	9	31	41	4	0	15	16	47	47	88	24
20	Glossop	38	5	5	9	21	33	1	1	17	10	54	31	87	18

1915/16 13th in Midland Section (Principle Comp)

							1	2	3	4	5	6	7	8	9	10	11
1	Sep	4	NOTTINGHAM FOREST	1-1	Young	4000	Sewell	Wheelhouse	McGuire	Hatton	Johnson	Whitchurch	Walsh	Rippon T	Young	Coulbeck	Rippon W
2		11	Barnsley	2-3	Woulds, T.Rippon	3000	"	Green	"	Hesseltine	"	"	"	"	Woulds	"	Birch
3		18	LEICESTER FOSSE	0-0		3000	"	Webster	"	"	"	"	Hooper	"	Young	"	"
4		25	Sheffield United	1-6	T.Rippon	6000	"	"	"	Whitchurch	"	Graham	"	"	"	"	"
5	Oct	2	BRADFORD CITY	3-1	Young(2), Coulbeck	4000	"	"	"	Rushby	"	Whitchurch	"	"	"	"	Huxford
6		9	Huddersfield Town	1-4	Young	3000	"	"	"	"	Ormiston	"	"	"	"	"	"
7		16	Lincoln City	0-1			"	"	Lee JW	Martin F	"	"	"	"	"	"	"
8		23	NOTTS COUNTY	2-2	T.Rippon, Young	4000	"	Wheelhouse	Lee JA	Rushby	"	"	"	"	"	"	"
9		30	Derby County	2-3	Coulbeck, Young	2000	"	Pattison	"	"	"	"	Sparham	"	"	"	"
10	Nov	6	SHEFFIELD WED.	2-1	Young(2)	3000	"	Webster	Lee JW	"	"	"	Walsh	"	"	"	"
11		13	Bradford P.A.	0-2			"	Johnson	Graham	"	"	"	"	"	"	"	"
12		20	LEEDS CITY	0-0		3000	"	Webster	McGuire	"	"	"	Hooper	"	"	"	"
13		27	Hull City	1-4	Young	3000	"	"	"	"	"	"	Rippon T	Woulds	"	"	"
14	Dec	4	Nottingham Forest	0-2		1000	"	"	"	"	"	"	"	"	Rampton	"	"
15		11	BARNSLEY	4-1	Huxford,Young,T.Rippon,McGuire (pen)		"	Lee JW	"	"	"	"	"	Birch	Young	"	"
16		18	Leicester Fosse	0-2		3000	"	Lee JA	"	"	"	"	"	Woulds	Rampton	"	"
17		25	SHEFFIELD UNITED	2-1	Hooper, Rampton	1000	Spendiff	"	"	"	"	"	Hooper	Rippon T	Young	Rampton	"
18	Jan	1	Bradford City	0-0*		1000	Sewell	"	"	"	Johnson	"	Rippon T	Woulds	Rampton	Coulbeck	"
19		8	HUDDERSFIELD TOWN	0-1		1000	"	"	"	"	Ormiston	"	"	Rampton	Butler R	"	"
20		15	LINCOLN CITY	1-0	McGuire(pen)	2000	"	Webster	"	"	"	"	Hooper	Rippon T	Young	"	"
21		22	Notts County	2-1	Young, T.Rippon	3000	"	Lee JA	"	"	"	"	McIver	"	"	"	"
22		29	DERBY COUNTY	2-1	Huxford, Coulbeck		"	"	"	"	Johnson	"	"	"	"	"	"
23	Feb	5	Sheffield Wednesday	1-2	T.Rippon		"	"	"	"	"	"	Spink T	"	"	"	"
24		12	BRADFORD P.A.	1-1	Young		"	Webster	"	"	"	"	Hooper	"	"	"	Birch
25		19	Leeds City	1-3	Young	5000	"	Lee JA	"	"	"	"	Spink T	"	"	"	Huxford
26		26	HULL CITY	2-3	McGuire(2,1pen)	2000	"	"	"	Marshall	Ormiston	"	"	"	"	"	"

*Abandoned (65 mins). Score stood.

1st in Midland Section (Subsidiary Comp)

27	Mar	4	Rotherham County	2-3	Young(2)		Cooper J	Lee JA	McGuire	Rushby	Johnson	Whitchurch	Spink T	Rippon T	Young	Rippon W	Huxford
28		11	SHEFFIELD WED.	0-0			Spendiff	Webster	"	"	Ormiston	"	Robinson R	"	"	Butler R	"
29		18	Hull City	5-2	Young(2),McGuire(2),W.Rippon	3000	Heath	"	"	"	"	"	Spink T	"	"	Rippon W	"
30		25	SHEFFIELD UNITED	0-1			Sewell	"	"	"	"	"	Robinson R	"	"	Butler R	"
31	Apr	1	Lincoln City	2-1	Young, T.Rippon		"	"	"	"	"	"	Spink T	"	"	Rippon W	"
32		8	ROTHERHAM COUNTY	7-1	Young(5), W.Rippon, Huxford		"	"	"	"	"	"	"	"	"	"	"
33		15	Sheffield Wednesday	1-2	Young(pen)		"	"	"	"	"	"	"	"	"	"	"
34		22	HULL CITY	5-0	Young(3), W.Rippon, Huxford	4000	"	"	"	"	"	"	"	"	"	"	"
35		24	LINCOLN CITY	3-0	Young, W.Rippon, T.Rippon		"	"	"	"	"	"	"	"	"	"	"
36		29	Sheffield United	0-0			"	"	"	"	Johnson	"	"	"	Rippon W	Mayson	"

Final League Table: 1915-16
War League Midland Section: Principal Tournament

		P	W	D	L	F	A	Pts
1	Nottingham Forest	26	15	5	6	48	25	35
2	Sheffield United	26	12	7	7	51	36	31
3	Huddersfield Town	26	12	5	9	43	36	29
4	Bradford City	26	12	4	10	52	32	28
5	Leicester Fosse	26	11	6	9	42	34	28
6	Barnsley	26	12	4	10	46	55	28
7	Sheffield Wednesday	26	11	5	10	46	43	27
8	Notts County	26	10	6	10	39	36	26
9	Lincoln City	26	12	2	12	54	54	26
10	Leeds City	26	10	5	11	39	43	25
11	Hull City	26	10	3	13	42	58	23
12	Bradford P.A.	26	9	4	13	46	46	22
13	GRIMSBY TOWN	26	7	6	13	31	46	20
14	Derby County	26	7	2	17	39	74	16

Final League Table: 1915-16
War League Midland Division: Subsidiary Tournament

		P	W	D	L	F	A	Pts
1	GRIMSBY TOWN	10	5	2	3	25	10	12
2	Sheffield United	10	4	3	3	17	11	11
3	Rotherham County	10	5	1	4	20	24	11
4	Hull City	10	5	0	5	18	27	10
5	Sheffield Wednesday	10	3	3	4	10	13	9

Back: Hickson (Dir), Bellamy (Dir), Holden (Train), Wheelhouse, Sewell, McGuire, Hooton (Sec), Plastow (Dir)

Middle: Rushby, Johnson, Ormiston, Whitchurch, Webster

Front: Spink, T. Rippon, Young, Coulbeck, Huxford

1916/17 14th in Midland Section (Principal Comp)

							1	2	3	4	5	6	7	8	9	10	11
1	Sep	2	Barnsley	2-2	T.Rippon(2)	1000	Sewell	Webster	Lee JW	Rushby	Johnson	Whitchurch	Smith J	Rippon T	Rippon W	Bratley P	Huxford
2		9	LEEDS CITY	1-6	Young	4000	"	"	Lee JA	"	Ormiston	"	"	"	Young	Rippon W	"
3		16	Sheffield United	3-5	W.Rippon, T.Rippon, Charles	8000	"	"	"	Bratley H	"	"	"	"	Rippon W	Charles	"
4		23	BRADFORD CITY	1-3	W.Rippon(pen)		"	"	"	"	"	"	Rushby	"	"	Coulbeck	"
5		30	Leicester Fosse	0-0			"	"	Bratley P	Rushby	"	"	Spink T	"	Hall B	Rippon W	"
6	Oct	7	CHESTERFIELD	1-3	P.Bratley	300	"	"	Lee JA	"	"	"	Cooney	"	Bratley P	"	"
7		14	NOTTS COUNTY	3-3	T.Rippon(3)	2000	"	"	Bratley P	"	"	"	Spink T	"	Young	"	"
8		21	Rotherham County	0-3			"	"	"	Spink J	"	"	"	"	"	Huxford	Cooney
9		28	HUDDERSFIELD TOWN	2-1	W.Rippon, Young	1000	"	"	"	"	Johnson	"	"	"	"	Rippon W	Huxford
10	Nov	4	Lincoln City	1-1	W.Rippon		"	"	Butler J	"	Ormiston	"	"	"	"	"	"
11		11	SHEFFIELD WED.	1-0	Young		"	"	Nevins	"	"	"	"	"	"	"	"
12		18	Bradford P.A.	0-9			Holden	"	"	"	"	"	"	"	"	"	"
13		25	BIRMINGHAM	3-0	T.Rippon(2),Young		Sewell	Butler J	Webster	"	"	"	"	"	"	Benfield	"
14	Dec	2	Hull City	0-2		3000	Sutcliffe	"	"	"	"	"	"	"	"	Rippon W	"
15		9	BARNSLEY	2-2	Huxford, Whitchurch		"	"	"	"	Johnson	"	"	"	"	"	"
16		16	Leeds City	0-1		5000	"	"	"	"	Ormiston	"	"	"	Rippon W	Bratley C	Cooney
17		23	SHEFFIELD UNITED	2-0	Colebrook, Benfield		"	"	"	"	"	Johnson	"	Benfield	Young	Colebrook	Huxford
18		25	Nottingham Forest	1-5	Huxford		"	"	McQuillan	"	"	Whitchurch	"	Rippon T	Ashling	Rippon W	"
19		26	NOTTINGHAM FOREST	1-1	T.Rippon	3000	"	Webster	"	"	"	"	"	"	Young	"	"
20		30	Bradford City	0-3			"	"	"	Wild	Butler J	"	Rippon T	Fearnley	Ashling	"	Colebrook
21	Jan	6	LEICESTER FOSSE	1-3	T.Rippon		"	"	"	Rushby	Johnson	"	Colebrook	Rippon T	Young	"	Huxford
22		13	Chesterfield	5-4	T.Rippon,Hadley(og),Colebrook(2),Allott		"	Butler J	Webster	Butler W	"	"	Allott	"	Pickering J	"	Colebrook
23		20	Notts County	3-2	J.Pickering, W.Rippon, Langley	1200	"	"	"	"	Langley	"	"	"	"	"	"
24		27	ROTHERHAM COUNTY	1-0	Young		"	"	"	"	Johnson	"	"	"	Young	"	"
25	Feb	3	Huddersfield Town	0-1		2000	"	"	"	"	Hall E	"	"	"	Pickering J	"	Huxford
26		10	LINCOLN CITY	1-0	Young		"	"	"	Johnson	"	"	Wilkinson R	"	Young	"	Colebrook
27		17	Sheffield Wednesday	1-3	Colebrook		"	"	"	Butler W	Halley	"	Allott	Raybould	Pickering J	"	"
28		24	BRADFORD P.A.	0-2			"	"	"	Johnson	"	"	Wilkinson R	Benfield	Ashling	"	"
29	Mar	3	Birmingham	0-3		10000	"	Lyons	Butler J	Booth R	Crutchley	Whittaker	Taylor	Nash	Rampton	Humphries	Peplow
30		10	HULL CITY	2-3	Colebrook, Young	2000	"	Butler J	Webster	Johnson	Hall E	Cheetham	Colebrook	Rippon T	Young	Rippon W	Huxford

1 own goal

8th in Midland Section (Subsidiary Comp)

							1	2	3	4	5	6	7	8	9	10	11
31		17	LINCOLN CITY	1-1	Isherwood		Sutcliffe	Butler J	Butler W	Johnson	Hall E	Graham	Warren	Benfield	Rippon W	Isherwood	Huxford
32		31	CHESTERFIELD	2-3	Benfield (2)		"	"	Webster	Butler W	Johnson	"	Benfield	Stainsby S	Pickering J	Rippon W	Colebrook
33	Apr	6	HULL CITY	2-1	Benfield, Colebrook	1500	"	"	"	"	Hall E	Johnson	Colebrook	Rippon T	Benfield	"	Huxford
34		7	Lincoln City	3-1	T.Rippon, W.Rippon, Huxford		"	Webster	Atkinson	"	Johnson	Graham	"	"	Pickering J	"	"
35		9	Hull City	2-2	T.Rippon, Johnson	2000	"	Atkinson	Rippon W	Walsh	"	"	"	"	"	Pace	"
36		21	Chesterfield	2-3	Ashling, W.Rippon	1000	"	Webster	Atkinson	Butler W	"	Clarke	Gladwin	Ashling	"	Rippon W	Colebrook

Final League Table: 1916-17
War League Midland Section: Principal Tournament

		P	W	D	L	F	A	Pts
1	Leeds City	30	18	10	2	68	29	46
2	Barnsley	30	15	8	7	65	41	38
3	Birmingham	30	14	9	7	56	38	37
4	Huddersfield Town	30	15	6	9	41	31	36
5	Bradford P.A.	30	14	6	10	51	32	34
6	Nottingham Forest	30	14	5	11	57	39	33
7	Notts County	30	13	6	11	47	52	32
8	Bradford City	30	12	7	11	41	41	31
9	Rotherham County	30	12	6	12	53	52	30
10	Sheffield United	30	11	7	12	43	47	29
11	Hull City	30	10	7	13	36	57	27
12	Chesterfield Town	30	11	4	15	59	62	26
13	Sheffield Wednesday	30	9	6	15	36	48	24
14	GRIMSBY TOWN	30	8	6	16	38	71	22
15	Leicester Fosse	30	6	7	17	29	53	19
16	Lincoln City	30	5	6	19	38	65	16

Final League Table: 1916-17
War League Midland Section: Subsidiary Tournament

		P	W	D	L	F	A	Pts
1	Bradford P.A.	6	3	2	1	10	5	8
2	Sheffield United	6	4	0	2	12	7	8
3	Birmingham	6	3	2	1	17	12	8
4	Leicester Fosse	6	4	0	2	12	12	8
5	Chesterfield Town	6	4	0	2	15	16	8
6	Huddersfield Town	6	3	1	2	6	4	7
7	Leeds City	6	2	2	2	8	7	6
8	GRIMSBY TOWN	6	2	2	2	12	11	6
9	Hull City	6	2	2	2	13	12	6
10	Sheffield Wednesday	6	2	2	2	12	12	6
11	Barnsley	6	1	3	2	8	9	5
12	Rotherham County	6	2	1	3	9	13	5
13	Lincoln City	6	1	2	3	11	12	4
14	Nottingham Forest	6	1	2	3	12	14	4
15	Notts County	6	1	2	3	9	12	4
16	Bradford City	6	0	3	3	5	13	3

1917/18 12th in Midland Section (Principal Comp)

						1	2	3	4	5	6	7	8	9	10	11
1	Sep	15 BARNSLEY	1-3	Round(og)		Sutcliffe	Webster	Ward	Marshall	Johnson	Martin F	Wilkinson R	Knighton	Ashling	Benfield	Spotiswood
2		22 Barnsley	0-4			"	"	Wilson W	"	Bryan	Wightman	Spotiswood	Raybould	"	Hobson	White
3		29 BRADFORD P.A.	1-2	Benfield(pen)		"	"	Ward	"	Johnson	Martin F	Benfield	Knighton	"	Huxford	Spotiswood
4	Oct	6 Bradford P.A.	1-4	W.Butler		"	"	"	"	Martin F	Barraclough	Allott	Fearnley	Butler W	Hobson	Isherwood
5		13 Sheffield United	0-5		7000	"	"	"	Butler W	Johnson	Martin F	Harris	"	Ashling	"	"
6		20 SHEFFIELD UNITED	0-0			"	"	"	"	"	"	"	Hollings	"	"	"
7		27 Leeds City	2-2	Goodfellow, Hollings	2000	"	"	"	Johnson	Hendrie	Walker	"	"	Goodfellow	"	"
8	Nov	3 LEEDS CITY	0-4			"	"	"	"	"	Martin F	"	"	"	Andrews	Wilson R
9		10 Nottingham Forest	0-5			"	"	"	"	Ritchie	"	"	"	"	Lees J	Codd
10		17 NOTTINGHAM FOREST	1-1	Johnson		"	"	"	"	Hendrie	"	Isherwood	Osmond	"	Hobson	Huxford
11		24 Leicester Fosse	1-6	Knighton	2000	"	"	"	Dawson F	Hall B	"	Burton	Knighton	Ashling	Lees J	Winship
12	Dec	1 LEICESTER FOSSE	1-1	Fenney	1500	Hinton	"	"	Johnson	Hendrie	"	Harris	Ashling	Fenney	Stainsby S	Isherwood
13		8 Birmingham	1-0	Brooks		Rawlinson	Pennington	"	Ducat	Kenny	"	Harrold	Price	Battersby	Bell	Brooks
14		15 BIRMINGHAM	2-2	Hendrie(2)		"	Webster	"	Johnson	Cordall	"	Forman	Stainsby C	Hendrie	McDermott	Huxford
15		22 Notts County	0-8		2000	"	"	Ritchie	Hawley	"	"	Harris	Pykett	Fearnley	Pickering F	Lees J
16		26 Hull City	1-7	Hendrie	1000	Smith W	Johnson	Pattison	Elvin	"	Pace	Goodfellow	Stainsby S	Hendrie	Slide	Huxford
17		29 NOTTS COUNTY	2-0	Johnson, Knighton		Rawlinson	Webster	Gaskell	Johnson	"	Martin F	Benfield	Knighton	"	McDermott	"
18	Jan	5 Huddersfield Town	0-2			"	"	Atkinson	"	"	Clarke	"	"	"	"	Walsh
19		12 HUDDERSFIELD TOWN	1-0	F.Martin	1000	Robinson	"	"	"	"	Martin F	Black	Stainsby S	Ashling	"	Huxford
20		26 SHEFFIELD WED.	0-0			Branston	"	Ward	Martin F	Johnson	Graham	Walsh	"	Richards	Fearnley	"
21	Feb	2 ROTHERHAM COUNTY	2-2	Huxford(2)		Spendiff	"	"	Johnson	Cordall	Martin F	Wilson R	"	Hendrie	"	"
22		9 Rotherham County	1-1	Wild(og)		Cooper J	"	"	Wilkinson J	Butler W	Clarke	Rippon W	Smith J	Pickering F	Sankey	Summers J
23		16 LINCOLN CITY	4-1	F.Pickering(2),Huxford,S.Stainsby		Branston	"	"	"	Martin F	"	Forman	Stainsby S	"	Fearnley	Huxford
24		23 Lincoln City	0-1			"	"	"	"	"	"	"	Cavanagh	Fearnley	Sankey	Howarth
25	Mar	2 Bradford City	1-0	S.Stainsby		"	"	"	"	Butler W	"	MacKenzie	Stainsby S	Pickering F	"	Rippon W
26		9 BRADFORD CITY	0-0		1500	"	"	"	"	Martin F	"	Forman	"	Hendrie	Fearnley	Huxford
27	Apr	13 HULL CITY	0-0		500	"	"	Cookson	"	"	"	Cooper E	"	Pickering F	Sankey	"
28		27 Sheffield Wednesday	1-1	Sankey	4000	"	Thorpe	Binks	"	"	"	"	"	"	"	Towlson

2 own goals

1st in Midland Section (Subsidiary Comp)

						1	2	3	4	5	6	7	8	9	10	11
29	Mar	16 GAINSBOROUGH	4-0	Ward(2), C.Stainsby(2)		Branston	Webster	Cooper A	Wilkinson J	Martin F	Clarke	Forman	Stainsby C	Hendrie	Sankey	Ward
30		23 Gainsborough	3-0	F.Pickering, S.Stainsby, Clarke	2000	"	Hobson	Ward	"	"	"	Cooper E	Danesborough	Pickering F	Stainsby S	Scott
31		29 HULL CITY	2-0	Williams, S.Stainsby	2000	"	Webster	"	Graham	"	"	Richmond	Stainsby S	"	Sankey	Williams
32		30 Lincoln City	0-1			"	"	"	Wilkinson J	"	"	Brown	"	"	"	Bavin
33	Apr	1 Hull City	2-2	F.Pickering, S.Stainsby	3000	"	Johnson	Wilson W	"	"	"	Hendrie	"	"	"	Huxford
34		6 LINCOLN CITY	2-0	E.Cooper, F.Martin		"	Webster	Ward	Johnson	"	"	Cooper E	Stainsby C	"	"	"

Final League Table: 1917-18
War League Midland Section: Principal Tournament

	P	W	D	L	F	A	Pts
1 Leeds City	28	23	1	4	75	23	47
2 Sheffield United	28	20	1	7	66	27	41
3 Birmingham	28	14	6	8	59	38	34
4 Hull City	28	15	4	9	67	50	34
5 Nottingham Forest	28	13	4	11	41	28	30
6 Bradford P.A.	28	13	4	11	40	29	30
7 Leicester Fosse	28	13	3	12	52	43	29
8 Huddersfield Town	28	12	2	14	49	46	26
9 Rotherham County	28	8	9	11	42	52	25
10 Notts County	28	7	9	12	43	54	23
11 Sheffield Wednesday	28	9	5	14	45	59	23
12 GRIMSBY TOWN	28	5	11	12	24	62	21
13 Bradford City	28	8	4	16	34	55	20
14 Lincoln City	28	7	5	16	25	62	19
15 Barnsley	28	8	2	18	40	74	18

Final League Table: 1917-18
War League Midland Section: Subsidiary Tournament

	P	W	D	L	F	A	Pts
1 GRIMSBY TOWN	6	4	1	1	13	3	9
2 Notts County	6	4	0	2	19	9	8
3 Sheffield Wednesday	6	3	2	1	15	8	8
4 Hull City	6	3	2	1	12	9	8
5 Leeds City	6	3	2	1	8	6	8
6 Lincoln City	6	3	1	2	11	8	7
7 Huddersfield Town	6	3	1	2	13	11	7
8 Barnsley	6	3	1	2	14	12	7
9 Braford City	6	1	4	1	8	8	6
10 Birmingham	6	2	2	2	6	9	6
11 Sheffield United	6	2	1	3	9	12	5
12 Leicester Fosse	6	2	1	3	6	10	5
13 Nottingham Forest	6	2	1	3	4	7	5
14 Rotherham County	6	1	2	3	4	10	4
15 Bradford P.A.	6	1	1	4	8	12	3
16 Gainsborough Trinity	6	0	0	3	3	19	0

1918/19 15th in Midland Section (Principal Comp)

No	Month	Day	Opponent	Score	Scorers	Att	1	2	3	4	5	6	7	8	9	10	11
1	Sep	7	Coventry City	4-7	Sankey,Hooper,Sandlin,Ballance	10000	Branston	Gray G	Webster	Wilkinson J	Martin F	Crane	Rampton	Sandlin	Ballance	Sankey	Hooper
2		14	COVENTRY CITY	1-1	Sankey		"	Webster	Cookson	"	"	Clarke	Hooper	Stainsby C	"	"	Huxford
3		21	Barnsley	4-2	Hooper(2),Ballance,Burkinshaw		"	"	Dawson S	"	Johnson	"	"	Burkinshaw	"	"	Cooke
4		28	BARNSLEY	0-0			"	"	"	"	"	"	"	Stainsby C	"	"	Huxford
5	Oct	5	Leicester Fosse	3-5	J.Wilkinson, Knighton, Sankey		"	"	"	"	Martin F	"	Sandlin	"	Knighton	"	Cooke
6		12	LEICESTER FOSSE	4-1	Kitchen,Sankey(2),C.Stainsby		"	Johnson	"	"	"	Wilson W	Kitchen	"	Ballance	"	Huxford
7		19	NOTTINGHAM FOREST	0-2			"	"	"	"	"	"	Cooke	Ballance	Sankey	Willett	"
8		26	Nottingham Forest	1-6	Bertie	4000	"	Gray G	"	"	"	Clarke	Bertie	"	Knighton	Sankey	Cooke
9	Nov	2	LEEDS CITY	0-2		2000	"	Johnson	"	Dawson F	"	"	Rudd	Stainsby C	Waine	Laws	Nicholson
10		9	Leeds City	1-3	Thompson	2000	"	Gray G	"	Wilkinson J	"	"	Thompson	Hill	Pickering F	Whitchurch	Dunn
11		16	SHEFFIELD UNITED	2-2	F.Martin(2 pens)		"	Webster	"	Rushby	"	"	Finneran	Whitchurch	Henderson	Sankey	"
12		23	Sheffield United	1-3	Knighton	5000	"	Gray G	"	Wilkinson J	"	Beach	Hill	Knighton	Talbot	"	Dodds
13		30	BRADFORD P.A.	4-0	Thompson(3), C.Stainsby		"	"	"	"	"	Clarke	"	Thompson	Stainsby C	"	Kirkman
14	Dec	7	Bradford P.A.	0-5			"	"	"	"	Kenny	Martin F	Williams	"	"	"	"
15		14	HUDDERSFIELD TOWN	1-1	Knighton	2000	"	"	Ward	"	Martin F	Clarke	Spink T	Knighton	"	"	Huxford
16		21	Huddersfield Town	0-1		2000	"	"	Dawson S	Andrews	Kenny	Martin F	Beswick	Sagar	Thompson	"	Hooper
17		25	HULL CITY	1-1	Sankey	3000	"	"	"	Martin F	"	Clarke	Whitworth	Thompson	Young	"	Huxford
18		26	Hull City	0-2		7500	"	Lee JA	"	"	"	"	"	"	Stainsby C	"	"
19		28	SHEFFIELD WED.	0-2			"	Gray G	"	Day	Martin F	"	Newton	"	"	"	"
20	Jan	11	Bradford City	3-1	Battiste, Sankey, Newton	5000	"	"	"	Battiste	"	"	MacKenzie	"	Newton	"	Farrah
21		18	BRADFORD CITY	3-2	Huxford, Knighton(2)		"	"	"	Wilkinson J	Battiste	"	"	"	Knighton	"	Huxford
22		25	Lincoln City	1-0	Ward		"	"	"	"	"	"	Smith J	"	"	"	Ward
23	Feb	1	LINCOLN CITY	1-2	Battiste		"	Webster	"	"	Martin F	"	Scrimshaw	Stainsby C	Battiste	"	Huxford
24		8	ROTHERHAM COUNTY	1-0	Huxford		"	Gray G	"	Martin F	Kenny	"	Holt	Thompson	"	MacKenzie	"
25		15	Rotherham County	0-2			"	"	"	"	"	"	Rippon T	"	Storer	Battiste	Booth J
26		22	BIRMINGHAM	1-4	Ball(og)		Lawrence	"	"	"	"	"	Battiste	Rippon T	"	Thompson	Huxford
27	Mar	1	Birmingham	0-4		20000	Branston	"	"	Battiste	"	Martin F	Holt	Thompson	"	Sankey	Clarke
28		8	NOTTS COUNTY	0-0			"	"	"	"	"	Clarke	"	"	"	"	Huxford
29		15	Notts County	1-3	Storer	8000	Summers P	"	"	"	"	"	"	Horton	"	Knighton	Scott
30	Apr	22	Sheffield Wednesday	2-5	Battiste, Kenny		Branston	Thorpe	Wilson W	Clarke	"	Martin F	Spink T	Stainsby C	Broom	Gregson	Gray AE

1 own goal

3rd in Midland Section (Subsidiary Comp) Section D

No	Month	Day	Opponent	Score	Scorers	Att	1	2	3	4	5	6	7	8	9	10	11
31	Mar	22	COVENTRY CITY	1-1	Clarke		Branston	Gray G	Dawson S	Bailey	Kenny	Clarke	Holt	Davis	Storer	Battiste	Gray AE
32		29	Coventry City	1-2	Gregson	8000	"	"	"	Searson	"	Martin F	Battiste	"	Rampton	Gregson	Clarke
33	Apr	5	LINCOLN CITY	2-1	T.Spink, Battiste		"	"	"	Clarke	"	"	Spink T	Battiste	Storer	"	Gray AE
34		12	Lincoln City	2-1	Battiste(2)		"	Murray	Thorpe	"	"	"	Minney	Thompson	Battiste	Gray AE	Martin J
35		19	HULL CITY	1-2	F.Martin(pen)	7000	"	Gray G	Brelsford	"	"	"	Spink T	"	Broom	Battiste	Gray AE
36		26	Hull City	1-3	Storer	6000	Spendiff	Thorpe	Wilson W	Murray	"	"	"	Battiste	Storer	Gray AE	Clarke

Final League Table: 1918-19
War League Midland Section: Principal Tournament

		P	W	D	L	F	A	Pts
1	Nottingham Forest	30	18	6	6	59	31	42
2	Birmingham	30	20	1	9	72	36	41
3	Notts County	30	16	9	5	65	38	41
4	Leeds City	30	17	4	9	55	38	38
5	Bradford P.A.	30	15	7	8	53	41	37
6	Huddersfield Town	30	13	8	9	45	45	34
7	Hull City	30	12	7	11	48	42	31
8	Sheffield United	30	12	6	12	56	47	30
9	Coventry City	30	13	4	13	55	59	30
10	Leicester Fosse	30	13	3	14	53	53	29
11	Sheffield Wednesday	30	11	6	13	49	49	28
12	Lincoln City	30	10	4	16	38	59	24
13	Bradford City	30	9	4	17	48	56	22
14	Barnsley	30	9	3	18	45	79	21
15	GRIMSBY TOWN	30	7	6	17	40	69	20
16	Rotherham County	30	2	8	20	23	60	12

Final League Table: 1918-19
War League Midland Section: Subsidiary Tourn. Section D

		P	W	D	L	F	A	Pts
1	Hull City	6	4	0	2	11	7	8
2	Coventry City	6	3	2	1	7	6	8
3	GRIMSBY TOWN	6	2	1	3	8	10	5
4	Lincoln City	6	1	1	4	6	9	3

1919-20 22nd in Division 2

Captain: Dave Kenny

							Spendiff	Dawson	McEachran	Battiste	Kenny	Whitchurch	Spink	Clarke	Storer	Golightly	Smith Albert	Jennings	Scott	Martin	Affleck	Welsh	Gillow	Burton	Duke	Brooks	Rippon T	Thompson	Kemp	Bird	Broom	Wainwright	Huxford	Abbott	Gray
1	Aug	30	STOCKPORT COUNTY	0-3			1	2	3	4	5	6	7	8	9	10	11																		
2	Sep	1	Wolverhampton Wands.	1-6	Storer	12000	1	2	3	4	5	6	7	8	9	10	11																		
3		6	Stockport County	2-1	Storer(2)		1	2	3	4	5	6	7	8	9	10	11																		
4		8	WOLVERHAMPTON WAND	0-1			1	2	3	4	5	6	7	8	9	10	11																		
5		13	HUDDERSFIELD TOWN	1-0	Smith	5000	1	2	3	4	5	6	7	8	9	10	11																		
6		20	Huddersfield Town	0-3		4000	1	2	3	4	5	6		8	9	10	11									7									
7		27	BLACKPOOL	1-1	Storer		1		3	4	5	6	7	8	9	10	11			2															
8	Oct	4	Blackpool	0-2			1	2	3	4	5	6	7				11										8				9		10		
9		11	WEST HAM UNITED	0-1		6000	1	2	3		5	6	7		9		11					4					8								10
10		18	West Ham United	0-1		20000	1	2	3		5	6	7		9	10	11					4					8								
11		25	HULL CITY	2-1	Storer, Rippon	10000	1	2	3		5		7	10	9		11			6		4					8								
12	Nov	1	Hull City	1-4	Wainwright	12000	1	2			5		7		9		11			6	3	4					8					10			
13		8	ROTHERHAM COUNTY	0-1			1	2		4	5		7		9		11			6	3						8					10			
14		15	Rotherham County	1-3	Wainwright		1	2		4	5	6	7		9		11				3						8					10			
15		22	Stoke	0-3		8000	1	2		4	5		7		9		11			6	3						8					10			
16		29	STOKE	2-0	Smith, Rippon		1	2	3	4	5		7		9		11			6							8					10			
17	Dec	6	Bristol City	1-3	Storer	8000	1	2	3	4	5				9		11			6						7	8					10			
18		13	BRISTOL CITY	2-2	Smith, Broom	4000	1	2	3	4	5		7		9		11			6							8				10				
19		20	BIRMINGHAM	0-3			1	2	3	8					10		11			6		4		5		7		9							
20		25	Fulham	1-2	Storer	12000	1	2	3		5		7		10		11			4				6			8					9			
21		27	Birmingham	0-4		20000	1	2	3	7	5				10		11			4				6			8					9			
22	Jan	1	COVENTRY CITY	0-1		4000		10	3	7	5				9		11	1		4	2			6			8								
23		3	LEICESTER CITY	1-2	Broom(pen)			2	3	7	5				9		11	1		4				6			8				10				
24		17	Leicester City	0-2				2	3	4	5		7	9	10		11		1	6								8							
25		24	BARNSLEY	1-1	Storer	4000		2	3	4	5		7	8	10		11		1	6									9						
26	Feb	7	NOTTINGHAM FOREST	1-0	Clarke	7000		2	3		5		7	9			11		1	6			4				8		10						
27		9	Barnsley	1-0	Huxford	4000		2	3	8	5		7	9	10				1	6			4										11		
28		14	Nottingham Forest	0-2		5000			3	4	5		7	9	10				1	6	2								8				11		
29		21	LINCOLN CITY	2-2	Clarke, Kemp			2	3	4	5		7	9	10		11		1	6									8						
30		28	Lincoln City	0-2				2			5		7	9			11		1	6	3		4						10	8					
31	Mar	6	Bury	1-1	Clarke	2884		2		7				9			11		1	5	3		4	6					10	8					
32		13	BURY	1-2	Smith	8000		2		10			7	9			11		1	5	3		4	6						8					
33		20	Port Vale	1-2	Storer	10000		2					7	9	10		11		1	5	3		4	6					8						
34		27	PORT VALE	2-0	Storer, Spink			2		8			7		9		11		1	5	3		4	6										10	
35	Apr	2	FULHAM	0-2		10000		2		8	5		7		9		11		1		3		4	6					10						
36		3	Clapton Orient	0-3		10000		2		8			7		9	10	11		1	5	3		4	6											
37		6	Coventry City	0-2		18000			3	8			7		9		11		1	5	2		4	6					10						
38		10	CLAPTON ORIENT	2-0	Smith(pen), Spink				3	8			7		9		11		1	6	2		4		5									10	
39		17	Tottenham Hotspur	1-3	Storer	35000		2					7		9		11		1	6	3		4		5					8				10	
40		24	TOTTENHAM HOTSPUR	2-0	Storer, Bird			2	3				7		9		11		1	6			4		5					8				10	
41		26	South Shields	0-2				2					7		9		11		1	6	3		4		5					8				10	
42	May	1	SOUTH SHIELDS	3-1	Thompson,Bird,Cresswell(OG)			2		10			7				11		1	4	3			6	5			9		8					
						Apps.	21	38	28	31	30	11	35	18	36	9	40	2	19	31	18	5	14	13	5	3	16	3	9	7	3	8	3	5	1
						Goals							2	3	12		5										2	1	1	2	2	2	1		

Game 17: Spendiff injured, replaced in goal by Storer.

1 own goal

F.A. Cup

							Spendiff	Dawson	McEachran	Battiste	Kenny	Whitchurch	Spink	Clarke	Storer	Golightly	Smith Albert	Jennings	Scott	Martin	Affleck	Welsh	Gillow	Burton	Duke	Brooks	Rippon T	Thompson	Kemp	Bird	Broom	Wainwright	Huxford	Abbott	Gray
1	Jan	10	BRISTOL CITY	1-2	Thompson	10000		2	3	4	5			9	10		7	1		6								8					11		

		P	W	D	L	F	A	W	D	L	F	A	F	A	Pts
1	Tottenham Hotspur	42	19	2	0	60	11	13	4	4	42	21	102	32	70
2	Huddersfield Town	42	16	4	1	58	13	12	4	5	39	25	97	38	64
3	Birmingham	42	14	3	4	54	16	10	5	6	31	18	85	34	56
4	Blackpool	42	13	4	4	40	18	8	6	7	25	29	65	47	52
5	Bury	42	14	4	3	35	15	6	4	11	25	29	60	44	48
6	Fulham	42	11	6	4	36	18	8	3	10	25	32	61	50	47
7	West Ham United	42	14	3	4	34	14	5	6	10	13	26	47	40	47
8	Bristol City	42	9	9	3	30	18	4	8	9	16	25	46	43	43
9	South Shields	42	13	5	3	47	18	2	7	12	11	30	58	48	42
10	Stoke	42	13	3	5	37	15	5	3	13	23	39	60	54	42
11	Hull City	42	13	4	4	53	23	5	2	14	25	49	78	72	42
12	Barnsley	42	9	5	7	41	28	6	5	10	20	27	61	55	40
13	Port Vale	42	11	3	7	35	27	5	5	11	24	35	59	62	40
14	Leicester City	42	8	6	7	26	29	7	4	10	15	32	41	61	40
15	Clapton Orient	42	14	3	4	34	17	2	3	16	17	42	51	59	38
16	Stockport County	42	11	4	6	34	24	3	5	13	18	37	52	61	37
17	Rotherham County	42	10	4	7	32	27	3	4	14	19	56	51	83	34
18	Nottingham Forest	42	9	4	8	23	22	2	5	14	20	51	43	73	31
19	Wolverhampton W.	42	8	4	9	41	32	2	6	13	14	48	55	80	30
20	Coventry City	42	7	7	7	20	26	2	4	15	15	47	35	73	29
21	Lincoln City	42	8	6	7	27	30	1	3	17	17	71	44	101	27
22	GRIMSBY TOWN	42	8	4	9	23	24	2	1	18	11	51	34	75	25

1920-21 13th in Division 3

Captain: Wilf Gillow

No	Month	Date	Opponent	Score	Scorers	Att.	Whalley	Dawson	Affleck	Gillow	Carmichael	Broom	Spink	Collier	Storer	Macauley	Bache	Moody	Smith Frank	Irvine	McEachran	Smith A	Bradford	Duke	Deacey	Martin	Blake	Sykes	Clarke	Morrall	Bell	Johnston	Sankey	Talks	Kent
1	Aug	28	NORTHAMPTON TOWN	2-0	Macauley(2)	10594	1	2	3	4	5	6	7	8	9	10	11																		
2		30	SOUTHEND UNITED	1-0	Bache	10000	1	2	3	4	5	6	7	8	9		10					11													
3	Sep	4	Northampton Town	1-4	Storer	10000	1	2	3	4	5	6	7	8	9		10					11													
4		6	Southend United	1-3	Collier	7000			3	4	5		7	8	9		10	1	2							6	11								
5		11	Bristol Rovers	0-2		20000			2	4	9		7	8	10			1			3			5		6	11								
6		18	BRISTOL ROVERS	3-1	Morrall, Clarke(2)		1	2	3	4		5	7	8			11						6						9	10					
7		25	Reading	1-4	Clarke		1	2	3		5	4	7	8									6						9	10					11
8		29	Brighton & Hove Albion	3-1	Clarke(2), Collier	8000	1	2	3		5		7	8	11								4				6		9	10					
9	Oct	2	READING	2-0	Collier(2)		1	2	3		5		7	9	6								4				11		8	10					
10		9	Luton Town	1-3	Storer		1	2	3		5		7	8	6								4				11		9	10					
11		16	LUTON TOWN	0-1			1	2	3	4	5		7	8	6												11		9	10					
12		23	Merthyr Town	1-3	Morrall	15000	1		3	4	5		7		6	10				2							11		9	8					
13		30	MERTHYR TOWN	1-1	Clarke		1		2		5				7	8					3	11	4			6			9	10					
14	Nov	6	Swansea Town	1-3	Storer	15000			2	4	5	6			9	8		1			3	11						7		10					
15		13	SWANSEA TOWN	0-2					2	4	5			7	9			1			3	11	6						8	10					
16		20	QUEENS PARK RANGERS	2-1	Macauley, A.Smith(pen)		1		2	4	5			7	9	10					3	11	6							8					
17		27	Queens Park Rangers	0-2			1		2	4	5		7		9	10					3	11	6							8					
18	Dec	4	Southampton	1-0	Collier	12000	1		2	4	5			7	6	10					3	11								8			9		
19		11	SOUTHAMPTON	3-0	Macauley, Collier, A.Smith		1		2	4	5			7	6	10					3	11								8			9		
20		25	NORWICH CITY	1-1	Collier		1		2	4	5			7	6	10					3	11								8			9		
21		27	Norwich City	0-0			1		2	4	9			7	6	10					3	11			5					8					
22	Jan	1	BRIGHTON & H.A.	2-2	Carmichael, A.Smith	9000	1		2	4	9			7	6	10					3	11			5					8					
23		15	Plymouth Argyle	0-0		12000	1		2					7	6						3	11	4		5				9	8			10		
24		22	PLYMOUTH ARGYLE	1-1	Storer		1		2					7	6	10					3	11	4		5				9	8					
25	Feb	5	CRYSTAL PALACE	1-0	Talks				2	4			7	8	6			1			3	11			5					10				9	
26		9	Crystal Palace	0-2					2	4			7	8	6			1			3	11			5					10				9	
27		12	Exeter City	1-1	Clarke	6000			2	4			7		6			1			3	11			5				8	10				9	
28		19	EXETER CITY	2-0	Storer, Morrall			2		4			7	8	6			1			3	11			5					10				9	
29		26	Millwall	1-0	Storer	20000				4				8	6			1		2	3	11			5				7	10				9	
30	Mar	5	MILLWALL	0-2		10000				4				8	6			1		2	3	11			5				7	10				9	
31		12	Newport County	1-2	Clarke	8000			2	4				7		8		1			3	11	6		5				9	10					
32		19	NEWPORT COUNTY	1-1	A.Smith(pen)				2	4		6	7					1			3	11			5				9	10	8				
33		25	BRENTFORD	2-0	Collier, Elliott(OG)	8000			2	4			7	8				1			3	11	6		5				9	10					
34		26	GILLINGHAM	2-0	Deacey, A.Smith(pen)				2	4			7	8				1			3	11	6		5					10	9				
35		28	Brentford	0-5		7000			2	4				7				1			3	11	6		5				9	10	8				
36	Apr	2	Gillingham	1-2	Talks	5000			2	4				7		10		1			3	11	6		5							8		9	
37		9	SWINDON TOWN	3-0	Clarke, A.Smith(2)		1		2	4				7		10					3	11	6		5				9	8					
38		16	Swindon Town	0-0			1		2	4				7		10					3	11	6		5				9	8					
39		23	PORTSMOUTH	0-3			1		2	4			7	8							3	11	6		5				9	10					
40		30	Portsmouth	1-2	Collier	12000			2	4	7			8				1			3	11	6		5					10				9	
41	May	2	WATFORD	3-0	Carmichael,Morrall,A.Smith(pen)				2	4	8			7				1			3	11	6		5					10				9	
42		7	Watford	2-4	Collier, Morrall	5000			2	4	8			7				1			3	11	6		5					10				9	
						Apps.	23	10	39	35	24	7	21	36	28	16	5	19	1	3	31	32	22	1	22	3	7	1	21	36	3	1	4	10	1
						Goals					2			10	6	4	1					8			1				9	5				2	

1 own goal

F.A. Cup

Rd	Month	Date	Opponent	Score	Scorers	Att.	Whalley	Dawson	Affleck	Gillow	Carmichael	Broom	Spink	Collier	Storer	Macauley	Bache	Moody	Smith Frank	Irvine	McEachran	Smith A	Bradford	Duke	Deacey	Martin	Blake	Sykes	Clarke	Morrall	Bell	Johnston	Sankey	Talks	Kent
Q6	Dec	18	Kettering Town	4-2	Storer, Sankey, A.Smith(2pens)		1		2	4	5			7	6	10					3	11								8			9		
1	Jan	8	NORWICH CITY	1-0	A.Smith(pen)	11000	1		2	4				7	6	10					3	11			5				9	8					
2		29	SOUTHAMPTON	1-3	Storer	14000	1		2	4	5		7	8	6						3	11								10			9		

		P	W	D	L	F	A	W	D	L	F	A	F	A	Pts
1	Crystal Palace	42	15	4	2	45	17	9	7	5	25	17	70	34	59
2	Southampton	42	14	5	2	40	10	5	11	5	18	18	64	28	54
3	Queen's Park Rgs.	42	14	4	3	38	11	8	5	8	23	21	61	32	53
4	Swindon Town	42	14	5	2	51	17	7	5	9	22	32	73	49	52
5	Swansea Town	42	9	10	2	32	19	9	5	7	24	26	56	45	51
6	Watford	42	14	4	3	40	15	6	4	11	19	29	59	44	48
7	Millwall	42	11	5	5	25	8	7	6	8	17	22	42	30	47
8	Merthyr Town	42	13	5	3	46	20	2	10	9	14	29	60	49	45
9	Luton Town	42	14	6	1	51	15	2	6	13	10	41	61	56	44
10	Bristol Rovers	42	15	3	3	51	22	3	4	14	17	35	68	57	43
11	Plymouth Argyle	42	10	7	4	25	13	1	14	6	10	21	35	34	43
12	Portsmouth	42	10	8	3	28	14	2	7	12	18	34	46	48	39
13	GRIMSBY TOWN	42	12	5	4	32	16	3	4	14	17	43	49	59	39
14	Northampton Town	42	11	4	6	32	23	4	4	13	27	52	59	75	38
15	Newport County	42	8	5	8	20	23	6	4	11	23	41	43	64	37
16	Norwich City	42	9	10	2	31	14	1	6	14	13	39	44	53	36
17	Southend United	42	13	2	6	32	20	1	6	14	12	41	44	61	36
18	Brighton & Hove A.	42	11	6	4	28	20	3	2	16	14	41	42	61	36
19	Exeter City	42	9	7	5	27	15	1	8	12	12	39	39	54	35
20	Reading	42	8	4	9	26	22	4	3	14	16	37	42	59	31

Back: Unknown, Affleck, Jones, McEachran, Golightly (Trainer)
Middle: Jeffries (Dir), Moore (Dir), Plastow (Chair), Wilson (Dir), Pearce (Dir), Harborne (Dir), Gillow, Carmichael, Storer, Hooton (sec), Newby (Dir), Lonsdale (Asst. Train), Stokes (Dir), Hickson (Dir), E.Smith (Dir)
Front: Collier, Morrall, Unknown, Unknown, A.Smith

1921-22 3rd in Division 3 (North)

Captain: Charlie Deacey

No			Opponent	Score	Scorers	Att	Moody	Affleck	McEachran	Gillow	Deacey	Bradford	Spink	Carmichael	Miller J	Morrall	Smith Albert	Jones	Harrison	Hughes	Stevenson	Felton	Millar H	Coupland	Smith Frank	Robinson	Collier	Casson	Barrass	Talks	Raby	Laws
1	Aug	27	Ashington	0-1		9000	1	2	3	4	5	6	7	8	9	10	11															
2	Sep	3	ASHINGTON	6-1	J.Miller(3),Deacey,Gillow,Carmichael		1	2	3	4	5	6	7	8	9	10	11															
3		6	WALSALL	3-1	Carmichael,Deacey,Gillow		1	2	3	4	5	6	7	8	9	10	11															
4		10	Stalybridge Celtic	0-3		4000	1	2	3	4	5	6	7	8	9	10	11															
5		17	STALYBRIDGE CELTIC	1-1	Collier			2	3	4	5			10	9		11	1						6		7	8					
6		24	Wigan Borough	1-1	Carmichael		1			4	5	6	7	8	9	10	11				2	3										
7	Oct	1	WIGAN BOROUGH	1-1	Carmichael		1			4	5	6	7	8		10	11				2	3							9			
8		8	HARTLEPOOLS UNITED	2-0	Talks, A Smith(pen)		1			4	5		7	8			11				2	3			6				10	9		
9		15	Hartlepools United	0-0		9000	1			4	5		7	8			11				2	3			6				10	9		
10		22	Southport	1-7	Talks	4000	1			4	5		7	8			11				2	3			6				10	9		
11		29	SOUTHPORT	0-0		9000	1	2	3	6	5		7											4			8			9	10	11
12	Nov	5	Stockport County	1-0	Carmichael		1	2		6	5		7	8			10					3		4						9		11
13		12	STOCKPORT COUNTY	2-1	Carmichael, J.Miller		1	2		6	5		7	8	9		10					3		4								11
14		19	Rochdale	2-0	A.Smith, Carmichael		1	2			5	6	7	8	9	10	11					3		4								
15		26	ROCHDALE	3-0	Carmichael, J.Miller(2)		1	2			5	6	7	8	9	10	11					3		4								
16	Dec	10	Walsall	1-2	Raby			2			5	6	7	8	9		11	1					3	4							10	
17		24	HALIFAX TOWN	4-1	Carmichael(4,1pen)			2			5	6	7	9		10			1				3	4			8					11
18		26	CHESTERFIELD	2-2	Collier(2)	9000		2			5	6	7	9		10			1				3	4			8					11
19		27	Chesterfield	1-4	Carmichael	8000		2			5	4	7	9		10			1				3		6		8					11
20		31	Tranmere Rovers	2-2	Carmichael, Morrall	5000		2			5	6		9	10	8	11	1					3	4			7					
21	Jan	14	TRANMERE ROVERS	5-1	Laws(2),Carmichael(2),J.Miller			2		4	5	6		9	10	8				1		3					7					11
22		16	Halifax Town	0-2				2		4	5	6		9	10	8				1		3					7					11
23		21	Barrow	2-2	Carmichael(2)			2		4	5	6		9	10	8				1		3				7						11
24		28	BARROW	4-0	Carmichael(4)			2		4	5	6		9	10	8				1		3				7						11
25	Feb	4	Durham City	2-1	Carmichael(2)	1400		2		4	5	6		9	10	8				1		3				7						11
26		11	DURHAM CITY	5-2	Carmichael,J.Miller(3),Morrall			2		4	5	6		9	10	8				1		3				7						11
27		18	Wrexham	1-0	Carmichael	7000		2		4	5	6		9	10	8				1		3				7						11
28		25	WREXHAM	2-0	Carmichael, J.Miller			2		4	5	6		9	10	8				1		3				7						11
29	Mar	4	Nelson	0-3				2		4	5	6		9	10	8				1		3				7						11
30		11	NELSON	3-1	Casson, Carmichael(2,1pen)			2		4	5	6		9	10					1		3				7		8				11
31	Apr	1	CREWE ALEXANDRA	3-0	Carmichael(2,1pen), Laws			2		4	5	6		9	10	8	7			1		3										11
32		8	Crewe Alexandra	2-1	Laws(2)			2		4	5	6	7	9	10	8				1		3										11
33		14	LINCOLN CITY	3-1	J.Miller, Carmichael, Morrall			2		4	5	6	7	9	10	8				1		3										11
34		15	ACCRINGTON STANLEY	2-1	Carmichael, Spink	10000		2		4	5	6	7	9	10	8				1		3										11
35		17	Lincoln City	2-0	Carmichael(2,1pen)			2	3	4	5		7	9	10	8				1				6								11
36		22	Accrington Stanley	0-1		6000		2		4	5		7	9	10	8				1		3		6								11
37		29	DARLINGTON	3-1	J.Miller, Carmichael(2)			2		4	5		7	9	10	8			1			3		6								11
38	May	6	Darlington	0-2				2		4	5		7	9	10	8			1			3		6								11
						Apps.	14	33	7	31	38	27	25	37	29	29	17	3	5	16	5	26	5	14	4	9	8	1	4	5	2	24
						Goals				2	2		1	37	13	3	2										3	1		2	1	5

F.A. Cup

Rd			Opponent	Score	Scorers	Att	Moody	Affleck	McEachran	Gillow	Deacey	Bradford	Spink	Carmichael	Miller J	Morrall	Smith Albert	Jones	Harrison	Hughes	Stevenson	Felton	Millar H	Coupland	Smith Frank	Robinson	Collier	Casson	Barrass	Talks	Raby	Laws
Q5	Dec	3	KETTERING TOWN	1-1	J.Miller	7000	1				5	6	7	8	9	10	11				2		3	4								
Q5r		8	Kettering Town	2-0	A.Smith, OG	7850		2			5	6		8	9		11	1					3	4	7						10	
Q6		17	TUFNELL PARK	1-1	Spink			2			5	6	7	8			11	1					3	4						9	10	
Q6r		22	Tufnell Park	2-1	Coupland, Collier			2			5	6	7	9		10		1					3	4			8					11
R1	Jan	7	NOTTS COUNTY	1-1	Carmichael	12000		2		4	5	6		9	10		11	1				3		8			7					
R1r		12	Notts County	0-3		16381		2		4	5	6		9	10	8	11	1				3					7					

		P	W	D	L	F	A	W	D	L	F	A	F	A	Pts
1	Stockport County	38	13	5	1	36	10	11	3	5	24	11	60	21	56
2	Darlington	38	15	2	2	52	7	7	4	8	29	30	81	37	50
3	GRIMSBY TOWN	38	15	4	0	54	15	6	4	9	18	32	72	47	50
4	Hartlepools United	38	10	6	3	33	11	7	2	10	19	28	52	39	42
5	Accrington Stanley	38	15	1	3	50	15	4	2	13	23	42	73	57	41
6	Crewe Alexandra	38	13	1	5	39	21	5	4	10	21	35	60	56	41
7	Stalybridge Celtic	38	14	3	2	42	15	4	2	13	20	48	62	63	41
8	Walsall	38	15	2	2	52	17	3	1	15	14	48	66	65	39
9	Southport	38	11	6	2	39	12	3	4	12	16	32	55	44	38
10	Ashington	38	13	2	4	42	22	4	2	13	17	44	59	66	38
11	Durham City	38	14	0	5	43	20	3	3	13	25	47	68	67	37
12	Wrexham	38	12	4	3	40	17	2	5	12	11	39	51	56	37
13	Chesterfield	38	12	2	5	33	15	4	1	14	15	52	48	67	35
14	Lincoln City	38	11	2	6	32	20	3	4	12	16	39	48	59	34
15	Barrow	38	11	2	6	29	18	3	3	13	13	36	42	54	33
16	Nelson	38	7	6	6	27	23	6	1	12	21	43	48	66	33
17	Wigan Borough	38	9	4	6	32	28	2	5	12	14	44	46	72	31
18	Tranmere Rovers	38	7	5	7	41	25	2	6	11	10	36	51	61	29
19	Halifax Town	38	9	4	6	37	28	1	5	13	19	48	56	76	29
20	Rochdale	38	9	2	8	34	24	2	2	15	18	53	52	77	26

SEASON 1921/22

Back: Hickson (Sec), Hooton (Dir), Coupland, Felton, Moody, Fraser (Manager), Jones, McEachran Affleck, Pearce (Dir), Moore (Dir), Haith (Dir), E.Smith (Dir)
Middle (standing): Stokes (Dir), Fish (Dir), Newby (Dir), Collier, Spink, Stevenson, Carmichael, Deacey, Lewis, J.Miller, A.Smith, Gillow, Baker (Dir), Plastow (Chair), Harborne (Dir)
Middle (seated): Robinson, Talks, Morrall, A. Miller, Raby
Front: McMillan (Asst. Train), Bradford, Laws, F. Smith, Golightly (Trainer)

SEASON 1922/23

Back: Felton, Cook, Harrison, Hilton, Coupland, McKenna
Middle: Hickson (Sec), J.Miller, Crozier, Richardson, H.Millar, Affleck, Casson, Middleston, Morgan, Carmichael, Graver, Bradford, Fraser (Manager)
Front: Golightly (Trainer), Ritchie, Kettle, Cumming, Deacey, Laws, Kirsopp, Stevenson, Binks, McMillan (Asst.Train)

1922-23 14th in Division 3 (North)

Captain: Charlie Deacey

						Hughes	Affleck	Felton	Coupland	Deacey	Bradford	Cumming	Graver	Carmichael	Miller J	Laws	Harrison	Smith WE	Atter	Millar H	Stevenson	Binks	Crozier	Hilton	Cook	Ritchie	Kettle	Kirsopp	McKenna	Casson
1	Aug 26	WREXHAM	4-0	Carmichael(2,1pen), J.Miller(2)		1	2	3	4	5	6	7	8	9	10	11														
2	Sep 2	Wrexham	1-1	Graver	8000	1	2	3	4	5	6	7	8	9	10	11														
3	9	Durham City	3-0	Coupland(2), J.Miller	2000	1	2	3	4	5	6	7	8	9	10	11														
4	16	DURHAM City	1-0	J.Miller		1	2	3	4	5	6	7	8	9	10	11														
5	23	WIGAN BOROUGH	0-0			1	2	3	4	5	6	7	8	9	10	11														
6	30	Wigan Borough	0-1		12000	1	2	3	4	5	6	7		9	10	11												8		
7	Oct 7	CHESTERFIELD	3-1	Carmichael, Kirsopp(2)	10000	1	2	3	4	5	6			9	10	11										7		8		
8	14	Chesterfield	2-3	Carmichael, Ritchie	8000	1	2	3	4	5	6			9	10	11										7		8		
9	21	ROCHDALE	1-1	Carmichael		1	2	3	4	5				9	10	11							6			7		8		
10	28	Rochdale	1-0	Casson		1	2	3	4	5				8	10	11							6			7				9
11	Nov 4	CREWE ALEXANDRA	2-3	Casson, Deacey		1	2	3	4	5				8	10	11							6			7				9
12	11	Crewe Alexandra	0-3		6000	1	2	3		5	6			9	10	11							4				7			8
13	18	WALSALL	1-2	Carmichael		1	2	3		5	6			9	10	11							4			7				8
14	25	Walsall	0-1					3	4	5			8	9		11	1			2			6					7	10	
15	Dec 23	HALIFAX TOWN	0-1				2	3	4	5				9	10	11	1						6			7			8	
16	25	ACCRINGTON STANLEY	7-1	McKenna(3,1p),Carmichael(2),Ritchie,J.Miller			2	3	4	5				9	10	11	1						6			7			8	
17	30	BRADFORD PA	0-1			1	2	3	4	5				9	10	11							6			7			8	
18	Jan 1	Accrington Stanley	0-4		7000	1	2		4	5				9	10	11				3			6			7			8	
19	6	Bradford PA	1-2	J.Miller	10000		2		4	5				9	10	11		1		3			6			7			8	
20	20	TRANMERE ROVERS	0-0				2		4	5	6			9	10	11		1		3						7		8		
21	22	Halifax Town	0-1				2		4	5	6			8	10	11		1		3						7				9
22	27	Tranmere Rovers	2-3	Casson, Carmichael			2		4	5	6			8	10	11		1		3						7				9
23	Feb 3	BARROW	2-0				2		4	5	6			8	10	11		1				3				7				9
24	10	Barrow	0-2				2		4	5	6			9	10			1				3				7	11			8
25	17	Ashington	1-2	J.Miller(pen)	1000		2		4	5	6			9	10			1				3				7	11			8
26	24	ASHINGTON	7-4	Carmichael(4),J.Miller(2,1p),Kettle			3		4		6			9	8	11		1			2			5			7		10	
27	Mar 3	SOUTHPORT	2-1	Carmichael(2)	8000		3				6			9	8	11		1			2		4	5			7		10	
28	10	Southport	1-3	Kettle	4000		3		4		6			9	8	11		1			2			5			7		10	
29	17	Stalybridge Celtic	2-3	Carmichael, J.Miller	2000		3		4		6			9	10	11			1	2				5		8	7			
30	24	STALYBRIDGE CELTIC	3-0	Carmichael, J.Miller, McKenna			3				6			9	10	11			1	2			4	5			7		8	
31	30	DARLINGTON	0-1				3							9	10	11			1	2			4	5	6		7		8	
32	31	Nelson	1-1	Ritchie			3				4			9	10				1	2				5	6	7	11		8	
33	Apr 2	Darlington	3-1	Carmichael(2,1pen), Kettle			3			5	4			9	10				1	2					6	7	11		8	
34	7	NELSON	0-2				3			5	4			9	10				1	2					6	7	11		8	
35	14	Lincoln City	2-1	Carmichael(2)			3			5	4			9	10				1	2					6	7	11		8	
36	21	LINCOLN CITY	1-0	McKenna			3		6	5	4			9	10				1	2						7	11		8	
37	28	Hartlepools United	0-2		3000		3		6	5	4			9	10				1	2						7	11		8	
38	May 5	HARTLEPOOLS UNITED	1-0	Carmichael	5000		3		6		4			9	10				1	2				5		7	11			8
					Apps.	15	37	17	29	30	28	6	6	38	37	29	3	10	10	16	3	3	14	8	5	25	16	6	17	10
					Goals				2	1			1	23	11											4	3	2	5	3

F.A. Cup

						Hughes	Affleck	Felton	Coupland	Deacey	Bradford	Cumming	Graver	Carmichael	Miller J	Laws	Harrison	Smith WE	Atter	Millar H	Stevenson	Binks	Crozier	Hilton	Cook	Ritchie	Kettle	Kirsopp	McKenna	Casson
Q5	Dec 22	WORKSOP TOWN	0-2					3	4	5			9		10	11	1			2				6				7	8	

		P	W	D	L	F	A	W	D	L	F	A	F	A	Pts
1	Nelson	38	15	2	2	37	10	9	1	9	24	31	61	41	51
2	Bradford Park Ave.	38	14	4	1	51	15	5	5	9	16	23	67	38	47
3	Walsall	38	13	4	2	32	14	6	4	9	19	30	51	44	46
4	Chesterfield	38	13	5	1	49	18	6	2	11	19	34	68	52	45
5	Wigan Borough	38	14	3	2	45	11	4	5	10	19	28	64	39	44
6	Crewe Alexandra	38	13	3	3	32	9	4	6	9	16	29	48	38	43
7	Halifax Town	38	11	4	4	29	14	6	3	10	24	32	53	46	41
8	Accrington Stanley	38	14	2	3	40	21	3	5	11	19	44	59	65	41
9	Darlington	38	13	3	3	43	14	2	7	10	16	32	59	46	40
10	Wrexham	38	13	5	1	29	12	1	5	13	9	36	38	48	38
11	Stalybridge Celtic	38	13	2	4	32	18	2	4	13	10	29	42	47	36
12	Rochdale	38	8	5	6	29	22	5	5	9	13	31	42	53	36
13	Lincoln City	38	9	7	3	21	11	4	3	12	18	44	39	55	36
14	GRIMSBY TOWN	38	10	3	6	35	18	4	2	13	20	34	55	52	33
15	Hartlepools United	38	10	6	3	34	14	0	6	13	14	40	48	54	32
16	Tranmere Rovers	38	11	4	4	41	21	1	4	14	8	38	49	59	32
17	Southport	38	11	3	5	21	12	1	4	14	11	34	32	46	31
18	Barrow	38	11	2	6	31	17	2	2	15	19	43	50	60	30
19	Ashington	38	10	3	6	34	33	1	5	13	17	44	51	77	30
20	Durham City	38	7	9	3	31	19	2	1	16	12	40	43	59	28

1923-24 11th in Division 3 (North)

Captain: Jimmy Carmichael

No	Month	Day	Opponent	Score	Scorers	Att.	Atter	Ackroyd	Affleck	Gillow	Leddy	Bradford	McKenna	Thomson	Carmichael	Miller J	Flanaghan	Archibald	Arch	McClennon	Millar H	Davies	Wilson	Hilton	Dixon	Honeyman	Boylen	Shaw	Kitching	Dent	Casson	Marshall
1	Aug	25	Tranmere Rovers	1-2	Carmichael		1	2	3	4	5	6	7	8	9	10	11															
2		27	BRADFORD PA	2-0	J.Miller(2)		1	2	3	4	5	6	7	8	9	10	11															
3	Sep	1	TRANMERE ROVERS	0-0			1	2	3	4	5	6	7	8	9	10	11															
4		3	Bradford PA	1-2	Carmichael		1	2	3	4		6		8	9	10								5		7						11
5		8	Halifax Town	3-1	Carmichael, J.Miller(2)	8000	1	2	3	4		6		8	9	10								5		7						11
6		15	HALIFAX TOWN	1-1	J.Miller		1	2	3	4		6		8	9	10								5		7						11
7		22	Lincoln City	3-1	Carmichael(3)	7000	1		3	4	5	6			9	10			2							7			8			11
8		29	LINCOLN CITY	2-2	J.Miller, Honeyman		1		3	4	5	6			9	10			2							7			8			11
9	Oct	6	Hartlepools United	1-1	J.Miller	4351	1		3			6	7			10			2			4		5		8					9	11
10		13	HARTLEPOOLS UNITED	0-1		10000	1		3			6	7		9	10			2			4		5		8						11
11		20	New Brighton	0-0		6000			3	4		6			9	10		1	2					5		7			8			11
12		27	NEW BRIGHTON	0-0					3	4		6			9	10		1	2					5		7			8			11
13	Nov	3	Wolverhampton Wands.	1-4	Carmichael				3	4		6		8	9	10		1	2					5		7						11
14		10	WOLVERHAMPTON WANDS.	2-0	Carmichael, Marshall				3			6		8	9			1	2				4	5		7				10		11
15		17	WALSALL	1-0	Carmichael				3			6		8	9			1	2				4	5		7				10		11
16		24	Walsall	0-2					3			6		8	9			1	2				4	5		7				10		11
17	Dec	8	Ashington	0-1					3			6	7	8	9	10		1	2				4	5								11
18		22	Wigan Borough	0-4		2000			3			6	7	8	9	10		1	2				4	5								11
19		25	CREWE ALEXANDRA	2-0	Carmichael(2)	9000						6		8	9	10		1	2		3		4	5		7						11
20		26	Crewe Alexandra	0-0		5000						6		8	9	10		1	2		3		4	5		7						11
21		29	DURHAM CITY	1-0	Carmichael(pen)							6		8	9	10		1	2		3		4	5		7						11
22	Jan	1	Accrington Stanley	0-2		6000						6	10	8	9			1	2		3		4	5		7						11
23		5	Durham City	1-0	Thomson	3600			3			6	10	8	7			1	2				4	5							9	11
24		19	Chesterfield	2-4	Thomson, McKenna	7373			3			6	10	8				1	2				4	5			7				9	11
25		26	CHESTERFIELD	0-0		7000			3	4		6	10	8				1	2					5			7				9	11
26	Feb	2	Rotherham County	1-2	Wilson	6000			3			6	10	8		9		1	2				4	5			7					11
27		9	ROTHERHAM COUNTY	1-1	Marshall				3			6	8		9	10		1	2				4	5			7					11
28		16	Wrexham	1-1	J.Miller	4000			3		4	6	7	8	9	10		1	2					5								11
29		23	WREXHAM	0-0					3		4	6	7	8		10		1	2					5							9	11
30	Mar	1	Doncaster Rovers	1-2	Dent	4500			3			6				10		1	2				4	5		7				8	9	11
31		8	DONCASTER ROVERS	1-1	McKenna				3		6		10					1	2				4	5		7				8	9	11
32		15	ROCHDALE	1-0	Carmichael				3		5	6	10		9			1	2				4			7				8		11
33		22	Rochdale	2-4	Carmichael, Dent	6000			3		6		10		9			1	2				4	5		7				8		11
34		27	WIGAN BOROUGH	1-1	Thomson				3		6		7	8	9			1	2				4	5						10		11
35		29	SOUTHPORT	1-0	Dent	4000			3		6		8		9			1	2		7		4	5						10		11
36	Apr	5	Southport	0-3		4100			3		6		10		9			1		2			4	5				7	8	11		
37		8	ASHINGTON	4-0	Carmichael(3), Dent					8					9			1	3	2		6	4	5				7		10		11
38		12	DARLINGTON	3-0	Carmichael, Gillow(2)				3	8					9			1	2			6	4	5				7		10		11
39		18	ACCRINGTON STANLEY	2-0	Carmichael, Davies				3	8					9			1	2			6	4	5				7		10		11
40		19	Darlington	0-1		3000			3	8					9			1		2		6	4	5				7		10		11
41		26	BARROW	5-0	Gillow, Dent(3), Carmichael				3	8				7	9			1	2				4	5	6					10		11
42	May	3	Barrow	1-3	Casson	2000			3					7	9			1	2				4	5	6					10	8	11
						Apps.	10	6	37	17	13	31	21	25	35	23	3	32	34	3	5	6	26	36	2	21	4	5	5	16	8	38
						Goals				3			2	3	20	8						1	1			1				7	1	2

F.A. Cup

Rd	Month	Day	Opponent	Score	Scorers	Att.	Atter	Ackroyd	Affleck	Gillow	Leddy	Bradford	McKenna	Thomson	Carmichael	Miller J	Flanaghan	Archibald	Arch	McClennon	Millar H	Davies	Wilson	Hilton	Dixon	Honeyman	Boylen	Shaw	Kitching	Dent	Casson	Marshall
Q5	Dec	1	Hinckley	3-0	Thompson, J.Miller(2)	4000			3			6		8	9	10		1	2				4	5		7						11
Q6		15	Chesterfield	0-0		10000			3			6	7	8	9	10		1	2				4	5								11
Q6r		18	CHESTERFIELD	2-0	Carmichael(pen), J.Miller	12176			3			6	7	8	9	10		1	2				4	5								11
R1	Jan	12	Exeter City	0-1		8250			3			6	7	8	9	10		1	2				4	5								11

		P	W	D	L	F	A	W	D	L	F	A	F	A	Pts
1	Wolverhampton W.	42	18	3	0	51	10	6	12	3	25	17	76	27	63
2	Rochdale	42	17	4	0	40	8	8	8	5	20	18	60	26	62
3	Chesterfield	42	16	4	1	54	15	6	6	9	16	24	70	39	54
4	Rotherham County	42	16	3	2	46	13	7	3	11	24	30	70	43	52
5	Bradford Park Ave.	42	17	3	1	50	12	4	7	10	19	31	69	43	52
6	Darlington	42	16	5	0	51	19	4	3	14	19	34	70	53	48
7	Southport	42	13	7	1	30	10	3	7	11	14	32	44	42	46
8	Ashington	42	14	4	3	41	21	4	4	13	18	40	59	61	44
9	Doncaster Rovers	42	13	4	4	41	17	2	8	11	18	36	59	53	42
10	Wigan Borough	42	12	5	4	39	15	2	9	10	16	38	55	53	42
11	GRIMSBY TOWN	42	11	9	1	30	7	3	4	14	19	40	49	47	41
12	Tranmere Rovers	42	11	5	5	32	21	2	10	9	19	39	51	60	41
13	Accrington Stanley	42	12	5	4	35	21	4	3	14	13	40	48	61	40
14	Halifax Town	42	11	4	6	26	17	4	6	11	16	42	42	59	40
15	Durham City	42	12	5	4	40	23	3	4	14	19	37	59	60	39
16	Wrexham	42	8	11	2	24	12	2	7	12	13	32	37	44	38
17	Walsall	42	10	5	6	31	20	4	3	14	13	39	44	59	36
18	New Brighton	42	9	9	3	28	10	2	4	15	12	43	40	53	35
19	Lincoln City	42	8	8	5	29	22	2	4	15	19	37	48	59	32
20	Crewe Alexandra	42	6	7	8	20	24	1	6	14	12	34	32	58	27

1924-25 12th in Division 3 (North)

Captain: Jimmy Carmichael

	Date	Opponent	Score	Scorers	Att.	Archibald	Arch	Affleck	Wilson	Hilton	Davies	Thain	Burley	Carmichael	Dent	Marshall	Atter	Pearson	McClennon	Coverdale	Field	Dixon	Thompson	Oakton	Kitching	Cooper	Gillow	Robson	McKenna	Gray	Reay
1	Aug 30	DARLINGTON	0-2			1	2	3	4	5	6	7	8	9	10	11															
2	Sep 1	HARTLEPOOLS UNITED	2-1	Thain, Carmichael		1	2	3	4	5		7	8	9		11					6								10		
3	6	Bradford PA	1-0	Thain	12000	1	2	3	4	5		7	8	9		11					6								10		
4	10	Hartlepools United	1-2	Marshall	4200	1	2	3	4	5		7	8	9		11					6								10		
5	13	WREXHAM	0-1			1	2	3	4	5		7		8	10	11					6							9			
6	20	Rotherham County	0-3		6000	1	2	3	4	5			8	9		11					6		7						10		
7	27	CHESTERFIELD	0-0		8000		2	3	4	5				9	10	11	1				6		7			8					
8	Oct 4	Accrington Stanley	3-0	Cooper, Dent(2)			2	3	4	5				9	10	11	1			6			7			8					
9	11	HALIFAX TOWN	1-1	Dent			2	3	4	5		7		9	10	11	1			6							8				
10	18	New Brighton	2-3	Dent, Gray	8000		2	3		5					10		1			4		6	7			8		9		11	
11	25	Lincoln City	0-0				2	3		5				7		11	1			4		6				8		9		10	
12	Nov 1	BARROW	2-1	Robson, Carmichael(pen)			2	3		5				7		11	1			4		6				8		9		10	
13	8	Nelson	0-1				2	3		5				7			1			4		6				8		9	10	11	
14	15	ROCHDALE	1-1	Cooper			2	3		5		7		9		11	1			4	6					8	10				
15	22	Southport	1-3	Dent	2900		2	3	4	5				9	10	11	1					6	7			8					
16	Dec 6	Durham City	1-6	Marshall	2000		2		4	5	6	7		9		11	1	3								8			10		
17	13	CREWE ALEXANDRA	0-0		5000	1	2		4	5	6			9		11			3				7			8			10		
18	20	Wigan Borough	1-3	Carmichael	5000	1	2			5	6			9					3	8	4		7						10		11
19	25	WALSALL	2-1	Kitching, Thain		1	2			5	6	7		9		11			3		4				8		10				
20	26	Walsall	0-2			1	2	3		5	6	7		9		11					4				8		10				
21	27	Darlington	0-0		2000	1	2	3		5		7		9		11				6	4					8	10				
22	Jan 1	DONCASTER ROVERS	1-1	Marshall		1	2	3		5		7		9		11				6	4				8		10				
23	3	BRADFORD PA	2-0	Robson, Cooper		1	2	3		5		7				11				6	4				8	10		9			
24	10	ASHINGTON	1-3	Robson		1	2	3		5		7				11				6	4				8	10		9			
25	17	Wrexham	2-1	Carmichael, Marshall	4000	1				5		7		9		11		2	3	6	4					8			10		
26	24	ROTHERHAM COUNTY	3-1	Carmichael, Marshall, Cooper		1				5		7		9		11		2	3	6	4					8			10		
27	Feb 7	ACCRINGTON STANLEY	4-0	Cooper,Carmichael(2),McKenna		1	2			5		7		9		11			3	6	4					8			10		
28	14	Halifax Town	0-1		2000	1	2		4			7		9		11			3	6	5					8			10		
29	21	NEW BRIGHTON	2-3	Carmichael(2)		1	2		4			7		9		11			3	6	5					8			10		
30	28	LINCOLN CITY	1-2	Carmichael		1	2	3	4			7		9		11				6	5					8			10		
31	Mar 7	Barrow	2-3	McKenna, Carmichael	2000	1	2	3	4			7		9		11				6	5					8			10		
32	14	NELSON	2-0	Cooper, McKenna		1	2	3	4					9		11				6	5			7		8			10		
33	21	Ashington	2-0	McKenna, Marshall		1	2	3	4			7		9		11				6	5					8			10		
34	28	SOUTHPORT	3-1	Cooper, Carmichael, Marshall	6000	1	2	3	4					9		11				6	5			7		8			10		
35	Apr 4	Doncaster Rovers	2-2	Marshall, Thain	5100	1		3	4			7				11		2		6	5					8		9	10		
36	10	Tranmere Rovers	3-2	Marshall, Cooper, McKenna	10000	1	2	3	4					9		11				6	5				7	8			10		
37	11	DURHAM CITY	1-1	Cooper		1	2	3	4					9		11				6	5				7	8			10		
38	13	TRANMERE ROVERS	6-1	Coverdale,Carmichael(2),Cooper(2),McKenna			2	3	4					9		11	1			6	5				7	8			10		
39	14	Chesterfield	0-2		4161		2	3	4			7		9		11	1			6	5					8			10		
40	18	Crewe Alexandra	1-3	Carmichael	5000		2	3	4			7		9		11	1			6	5					8			10		
41	25	WIGAN BOROUGH	4-0	Carmichael(3), McKenna			2	3	4					9		11	1			6	5				7	8			10		
42	May 1	Rochdale	0-2		3000		2	3	4			7		9	8	11	1			6	5								10		
					Apps.	27	39	33	27	27	6	26	5	38	8	39	15	4	8	30	32	5	7	2	9	30	6	8	26	4	1
					Goals							4		18	5	9				1					1	11		3	7	1	

F.A. Cup

	Date	Opponent	Score	Scorers	Att.	Archibald	Arch	Affleck	Wilson	Hilton	Davies	Thain	Burley	Carmichael	Dent	Marshall	Atter	Pearson	McClennon	Coverdale	Field	Dixon	Thompson	Oakton	Kitching	Cooper	Gillow	Robson	McKenna	Gray	Reay
Q5	Nov 29	CHESTERFIELD	1-2	Carmichael	10000		2	3	4	5				9	10	11	1				6		7			8					

		P	W	D	L	F	A	W	D	L	F	A	F	A	Pts
1	Darlington	42	16	4	1	50	14	8	6	7	28	19	78	33	58
2	Nelson	42	18	2	1	58	14	5	5	11	21	36	79	50	53
3	New Brighton	42	17	3	1	56	16	6	4	11	19	34	75	50	53
4	Southport	42	17	2	2	41	7	5	5	11	18	30	59	37	51
5	Bradford Park Ave.	42	15	5	1	59	13	4	7	10	25	29	84	42	50
6	Rochdale	42	17	2	2	53	16	4	5	12	22	37	75	53	49
7	Chesterfield	42	14	3	4	42	15	3	8	10	18	29	60	44	45
8	Lincoln City	42	13	4	4	39	19	5	4	12	14	39	53	58	44
9	Halifax Town	42	11	5	5	36	22	5	6	10	20	30	56	52	43
10	Ashington	42	13	4	4	41	24	3	6	12	27	52	68	76	42
11	Wigan Borough	42	10	7	4	39	16	5	4	12	23	49	62	65	41
12	GRIMSBY TOWN	42	10	6	5	38	21	5	3	13	22	39	60	60	39
13	Durham City	42	11	6	4	38	17	2	7	12	12	51	50	68	39
14	Barrow	42	14	4	3	39	22	2	3	16	12	52	51	74	39
15	Crewe Alexandra	42	11	7	3	35	24	2	6	13	18	54	53	78	39
16	Wrexham	42	11	5	5	37	21	4	3	14	16	40	53	61	38
17	Accrington Stanley	42	12	5	4	43	23	3	3	15	17	49	60	72	38
18	Doncaster Rovers	42	12	5	4	36	17	2	5	14	18	48	54	65	38
19	Walsall	42	10	6	5	27	16	3	5	13	17	37	44	53	37
20	Hartlepools United	42	9	8	4	28	21	3	3	15	17	42	45	63	35
21	Tranmere Rovers	42	11	3	7	40	29	3	1	17	19	49	59	78	32
22	Rotherham County	42	6	5	10	27	31	1	2	18	15	57	42	88	21

SEASON 1924/25
Back: Field, Arch, Archibald, Affleck, Davies.
Front: Thain, Kitching, Carmichael, Gillow (Player/Man), Marshall, Hilton.

SEASON 1925/26
Back: Director, Director, Wilson, Archibald, Jacobson, Drewry (Dir), Lonsdale (Asst Train), Gillow (Manager)
Middle: Director, Director, Bellamy (Dir), Fish (Dir), McLachlan, Hardy, Pugsley, Pearce (Dir), Wilson (Dir)
Front: Jeffries (Dir), Devan, Gardner, Cooper, Plastow (Chair)?, Carmichael, McKenna, Marshall, Hickson (Dir), Clarke (Dir)

1925-26 1st in Division 3 (North)

Captain: Jack Hardy

	Date		Opponent	Score	Scorers	Att.	Atter	Arch	Jacobson	Wilson	Hardy	Pugsley	Foster	Cooper	Carmichael	McKenna	Marshall	Archibald	Pearson	Jackson	Evans	McLachlan	Wrack	Dixon	Devan	Kitching	Gardner	Robson
1	Aug	29	DONCASTER ROVERS	3-0	Carmichael(2), McKenna	9012	1	2	3	4	5	6	7	8	9	10	11											
2		31	WALSALL	5-1	McKenna(3),Marshall,Carmichael	8225	1	2	3	4		6	7	8	9	10	11						5					
3	Sep	5	Rotherham United	1-2	Carmichael	5388	1	2	3	4	5	6	7	8	9	10	11											
4		7	Walsall	2-2	Carmichael(2)	3605	1	2	3	4	5	6	7		9	10	11									8		
5		12	HALIFAX TOWN	1-0	Carmichael	7722	1	2	3	4	5	6	7	8	9	10	11											
6		14	TRANMERE ROVERS	8-0	Carmichael,Cooper(3),McKenna(2),Devan,Marshall	7109	1	2	3	4	5	6		8	9	10	11								7			
7		19	Accrington Stanley	0-1		2981	1	2	3	4		6			9	10	11						5		7	8		
8		26	DURHAM CITY	3-1	Cooper, Carmichael, McKenna	6817	1	2	3			6		8	9	10	11				4		5		7			
9	Oct	1	Tranmere Rovers	0-0		4604	1	2	3			6			8	10	11				4		5		7			9
10		3	Hartlepools United	1-1	Carmichael(pen)	6096	1	2	3			6		8	9	10	11				4		5		7			
11		10	ROCHDALE	3-0	Carmichael(2), Cooper	11602	1	2	3	4		6		8	9	10	11						5		7			
12		17	SOUTHPORT	3-2	McKenna, Marshall, Tyler(OG)	7339	1	2	3	4		6		8	9	10	11						5		7			
13		24	Lincoln City	1-4	Carmichael	13078	1	2	3	4		6	7	8	9	10	11						5					
14		31	COVENTRY CITY	2-0	Carmichael(2,1pen)	9318		2	3	4			7	8	9		11	1					5	6			10	
15	Nov	7	Wrexham	1-4	Carmichael	5774		2	3	4			7	8	9		11	1					5	6			10	
16		14	WIGAN BOROUGH	1-1	Foster	7763		2	3		5	6	7	8	9	10	11	1			4							
17		21	Ashington	2-4	Carmichael, Gardner	4537		2	3	4	5	6	7		9	10	11	1									8	
18	Dec	5	Nelson	1-1	Cooper	5675			3	4	5	6		8	9	10	11	1	2						7			
19		19	New Brighton	4-1	Robson(3), Mehaffy(OG)	4101				2	5	6				10	11	1		3		4			7		8	9
20		25	BRADFORD PA	3-0	Robson(3)	13230			3	2	5	6				10	11	1				4			7		8	9
21		26	Bradford PA	1-0	Devan	18599			3	2	5	6				10	11	1				4			7		8	9
22	Jan	16	ROTHERHAM UNITED	3-0	Carmichael, Hardy, Devan	7059			3	2	5	6		8	9	10	11	1				4			7			
23		23	Halifax Town	2-0	Hardy, Devan	7896			3	2	5	6			8	10	11	1				4			7			9
24		30	ACCRINGTON STANLEY	5-2	Carmichael(3),McKenna,Cooper	8573			3	2	5	6		8	9	10	11	1				4			7			
25	Feb	6	Durham City	0-0		2869			3	2	5	6		8	9	10	11	1				4			7			
26		13	HARTLEPOOLS UNITED	2-0	Marshall, Hardy	7859			3	2	5	6			9	10	11	1				4			7		8	
27		20	Rochdale	2-5	Marshall, McKenna	7544			3	2		6		8	9	10	11	1				4	5		7			
28		25	BARROW	4-0	Marshall,McKenna,Devan,Cooper	5350				2		6		8	9	10	11	1		3		4	5		7			
29		27	Southport	1-0	Cooper	4099				2		6		8	5	10	11	1		3		4			7			9
30	Mar	6	LINCOLN CITY	4-0	Carmichael(2), McKenna, Devan	12575				2	5	6		8	9	10	11	1		3		4			7			
31		13	Coventry City	1-1	Devan	11695				2	5	6		8	9	10	11	1		3		4			7			
32		20	WREXHAM	1-0	Carmichael	9319				2	5	6		8	9	10	11	1		3		4			7			
33		25	CREWE ALEXANDRA	2-0	Carmichael, Cooper	8355			3	2	5	6		8	4	10	11	1							7			9
34		27	Wigan Borough	2-2	Carmichael, McKenna	6689		2	3	4	5	6			9	10	11	1			8				7			
35	Apr	2	CHESTERFIELD	1-0	Marshall	16086			3	2	5	6		8	9	10	11	1				4			7			
36		3	ASHINGTON	3-1	Carmichael(2), Cooper	10284			3	2	5	6		8	9	10	11	1				4			7			
37		5	Chesterfield	0-2		11867			3	2	5	6		8	9	10	11	1				4			7			
38		10	Barrow	3-0	Carmichael(2), McKenna	1910				2	5	6			9	10	11	1		3		4			7		8	
39		17	NELSON	3-0	Carmichael, Gardner, Marshall	9641				2	5	6			9	10	11	1		3		4			7		8	
40		22	Doncaster Rovers	4-1	Carmichael,Marshall,Devan,Gardner	9711			3	2	5	6			9	10	11	1				4			7		8	
41		24	Crewe Alexandra	1-1	Devan	5571			3	2	5	6			9	10	11	1				4			7		8	
42	May	1	NEW BRIGHTON	1-0	Carmichael	14548			3	2	5	6		8	9	10	11	1				4			7			
						Apps.	13	18	34	38	29	40	10	28	39	40	42	29	1	8	5	22	12	2	32	2	11	7
						Goals					3		1	11	33	14	9								8		3	6

3 own goals

F.A. Cup

	Date		Opponent	Score	Scorers	Att.	Atter	Arch	Jacobson	Wilson	Hardy	Pugsley	Foster	Cooper	Carmichael	McKenna	Marshall	Archibald	Pearson	Jackson	Evans	McLachlan	Wrack	Dixon	Devan	Kitching	Gardner	Robson
R1	Nov	18	Walsall	1-0	McKenna	4982			3	4	5	6		8	9	10	11	1	2						7			
R2	Dec	12	Kettering Town	1-1	Carmichael	7074			3	4	5	6		8	9	10	11	1	2						7			
R2r		15	KETTERING TOWN	3-1	Devan, Carmichael, McKenna	7000			3	4	5	6			9	10	11	1	2						7		8	
R3	Jan	9	Birmingham	0-2		36000			3	2	5	6				10	11	1				4			7		8	9

		P	W	D	L	F	A	W	D	L	F	A	F	A	Pts
1	GRIMSBY TOWN	42	20	1	0	61	8	6	8	7	30	32	91	40	61
2	Bradford Park Ave.	42	18	2	1	65	10	8	6	7	36	33	101	43	60
3	Rochdale	42	16	1	4	55	25	11	4	6	49	33	104	58	59
4	Chesterfield	42	18	2	1	70	19	7	3	11	30	35	100	54	55
5	Halifax Town	42	12	5	4	34	19	5	6	10	19	31	53	50	45
6	Hartlepools United	42	15	5	1	59	23	3	3	15	23	50	82	73	44
7	Tranmere Rovers	42	15	2	4	45	27	4	4	13	28	56	73	83	44
8	Nelson	42	12	8	1	67	29	4	3	14	22	42	89	71	43
9	Ashington	42	11	6	4	44	23	5	5	11	26	39	70	62	43
10	Doncaster Rovers	42	11	7	3	52	25	5	4	12	28	47	80	72	43
11	Crewe Alexandra	42	14	3	4	43	23	3	6	12	20	38	63	61	43
12	New Brighton	42	13	4	4	51	29	4	4	13	18	38	69	67	42
13	Durham City	42	14	5	2	45	19	4	1	16	18	51	63	70	42
14	Rotherham United	42	13	3	5	44	28	4	4	13	25	64	69	92	41
15	Lincoln City	42	14	2	5	42	28	3	3	15	24	54	66	82	39
16	Coventry City	42	13	6	2	47	19	3	0	18	26	63	73	82	38
17	Wigan Borough	42	12	5	4	53	22	1	6	14	15	52	68	74	37
18	Accrington Stanley	42	14	0	7	49	34	3	3	15	32	71	81	105	37
19	Wrexham	42	9	6	6	39	31	2	4	15	24	61	63	92	32
20	Southport	42	9	6	6	37	34	2	4	15	25	58	62	92	32
21	Walsall	42	9	4	8	40	34	1	2	18	18	73	58	107	26
22	Barrow	42	4	2	15	28	49	3	2	16	22	49	50	98	18

1926-27 17th in Division 2

Captain: Jack Hardy/Charlie Wrack

	Date	Opponent	Score	Scorers	Att.	Archibald	Wilson	Jacobson	McLachlan	Hardy	Pugsley	Devan	Cooper	Carmichael	McKenna	Marshall	Prout	Cowell	Jackson	Harris	Newton	Wrack	Hunter	Swaby	Parry	Ferguson	Bestall	Prior	Gardner	Robson	Williamson	Coglin	Gray
1	Aug 28	Barnsley	1-2	Hardy	7004	1	2	3	4	5	6	7	8	9	10	11																	
2	30	SWANSEA TOWN	0-1		14926	1		3	4	5	6	7	8	9		11				2											10		
3	Sep 4	MANCHESTER CITY	2-2	Devan, Carmichael	16559	1		3	4	5		7	10	9		11				2	6								8				
4	6	Nottingham Forest	1-1	Devan	4659	1		3	4	5		7	10	9		11				2	6								8				
5	11	Darlington	3-2	Cooper(2), Carmichael	7982	1		3	4	5	6	7	10	9		11				2									8				
6	13	Swansea Town	1-1	Carmichael	14229	1		3	4	5	6	7		9		10				2									8				11
7	18	PORTSMOUTH	0-0		14503	1		3	4	5	6	7	10	9		11				2									8				
8	25	Oldham Athletic	1-3	Cooper	9384	1		3	4	5	6	7	10	9		11				2									8				
9	Oct 2	FULHAM	2-0	Cooper, McKenna	12162	1		3	4	5	6	7	8	9	10	11				2													
10	9	Preston North End	2-3	McKenna, Carmichael	12529	1		3	4	5	6	7	8	9	10	11				2													
11	16	HULL CITY	0-1		16023	1		3	4	5	6		8	9	10	11				2					7								
12	23	South Shields	2-3	McKenna, Devan	4871	1		3	4	5	6	7		9	10	11				2									8				
13	30	CHELSEA	0-0		12423	1		3	4	5	6	7	10	8		11			2											9			
14	Nov 6	Bradford City	2-2	Cooper, Gardner	5786	1		3		5	6		8	9		11			2		4					7			10				
15	13	SOUTHAMPTON	0-1		9196	1		3		5	6		8	9		11			2		4					7			10				
16	20	Port Vale	1-6	Pugsley(pen)	5327	1		3	4	5	6	7	8		10	11			2											9			
17	Dec 4	Clapton Orient	4-2	Marshall, Cooper(2), Bestall	11859	1		3	4		6	7	10			11			2			5					8			9			
18	18	Wolverhampton Wands.	4-3	Robson,Pugsley(pen),Cooper(2)	9869			3			6		10		7	11	1		2		4	5					8			9			
19	25	BLACKPOOL	2-1	Cooper, Bestall	15492			3			6		10		7	11	1		2		4	5					8			9			
20	27	Blackpool	2-6	Robson(2)	13980			3			6		10		7	11	1		2		4	5					8			9			
21	Jan 1	NOTTINGHAM FOREST	1-1	Bestall	13406			3			6		10			11	1		2		4	5				7	8			9			
22	15	BARNSLEY	1-3	Robson	10596	1		3		5	6	7			10	11			2		4						8			9			
23	22	Manchester City	0-2		21212	1	2	3			6	7	10			11					4	5					8			9			
24	29	NOTTS COUNTY	1-4	Marshall	9347	1	2				6	7	10	9		11			3		4		5				8						
25	Feb 5	Portsmouth	2-5	Devan, Robson	13969	1	2	3	4		6	7	10			11							5				8			9			
26	8	MIDDLESBROUGH	4-7	Robson(3), Pugsley(pen)	10288	1	2	3	4		6					11							5				8	7		9		10	
27	12	OLDHAM ATHLETIC	2-5	Pugsley(pen), Robson	11313	1	2	3			6					11					4		5				8	7		9		10	
28	19	Fulham	5-0	Bestall, Coglin, Robson(3)	6617		2	3	4		6					11		1					5				8	7		9		10	
29	26	PRESTON NORTH END	5-2	Coglin(2), Prior, Robson(2)	15183		2	3	4		6					11		1				5					8	7		9		10	
30	Mar 5	Hull City	3-2	Jacobson, Robson, Bestall	22274		2	3	4		6					11		1				5					8	7		9		10	
31	12	SOUTH SHIELDS	1-1	Robson	15190		2	3	4		6					11		1				5					8	7		9		10	
32	19	Chelsea	0-2		35239		2	3	4		6					11		1				5					8	7		9		10	
33	26	BRADFORD CITY	4-2	Robson, Bestall, Coglin, Prior	9940		2		4		6					11		1	3			5					8	7		9		10	
34	29	DARLINGTON	2-1	Bestall, Robson	11161		2		4		6					11		1		3		5					8	7		9		10	
35	Apr 2	Southampton	0-0		5713		2		4		6					11		1		3		5					8	7		9		10	
36	9	PORT VALE	4-4	Prior, Robson(2), Wilson	8717		2		4		6		8			11		1		3		5						7		9		10	
37	15	READING	0-1		18040		2				6					11		1		3	4	5					8	7		9		10	
38	16	Middlesbrough	0-3		22503		2				6		10			11		1		3	4	5					8	7		9			
39	18	Reading	1-1	Pugsley	16378		2		4		6		8			11		1		3		5					7	9				10	
40	23	CLAPTON ORIENT	2-2	Pugsley, Cooper	10003		2		4		6		8			11		1		3		5						7		9		10	
41	30	Notts County	0-3		9196		2		4		6		10			11		1		3				5			8	7		9			
42	May 7	WOLVERHAMPTON WANDS.	6-0	Robson(4,1pen), Prior(2,1pen)	9218		2		4		6		8			11		1		3		5						7		9		10	
					Apps.	23	21	31	30	17	40	18	28	16	10	42	4	15	12	20	14	19	5	1	1	3	23	17	9	26	1	15	1
					Goals		1	1		1	6	4	11	4	3	2											7	5	1	24		4	

F.A. Cup

	Date	Opponent	Score	Scorers	Att.	Archibald	Wilson	Jacobson	McLachlan	Hardy	Pugsley	Devan	Cooper	Carmichael	McKenna	Marshall	Prout	Cowell	Jackson	Harris	Newton	Wrack	Hunter	Swaby	Parry	Ferguson	Bestall	Prior	Gardner	Robson	Williamson	Coglin	Gray
R1	Nov 17	HALIFAX TOWN	3-2	Pugsley(pen),McKenna,Marshall	8500			3	4		6	7	8		10	11	1		2			5								9			
R2	Dec 11	YORK CITY	2-1	Bestall, Robson	10000	1		3	4		6		10		7	11			2			5					8			9			
R3	Jan 9	Burnley	1-3	Hardy	19556	1		3		5	6		10	9		11			2		4					7	8						

		P	W	D	L	F	A	W	D	L	F	A	F	A	Pts
1	Middlesbrough	42	18	2	1	78	23	9	6	6	44	37	122	60	62
2	Portsmouth	42	14	4	3	58	17	9	4	8	29	32	87	49	54
3	Manchester City	42	15	3	3	65	23	7	7	7	43	38	108	61	54
4	Chelsea	42	13	7	1	40	17	7	5	9	22	35	62	52	52
5	Nottingham Forest	42	14	6	1	57	23	4	8	9	23	32	80	55	50
6	Preston North End	42	14	4	3	54	29	6	5	10	20	43	74	72	49
7	Hull City	42	13	4	4	43	19	7	3	11	20	33	63	52	47
8	Port Vale	42	11	6	4	50	26	5	7	9	38	52	88	78	45
9	Blackpool	42	13	5	3	65	26	5	3	13	30	54	95	80	44
10	Oldham Athletic	42	12	3	6	50	37	7	3	11	24	47	74	84	44
11	Barnsley	42	13	5	3	56	23	4	4	13	32	64	88	87	43
12	Swansea Town	42	13	5	3	44	21	3	6	12	24	51	68	72	43
13	Southampton	42	9	8	4	35	22	6	4	11	25	40	60	62	42
14	Reading	42	14	1	6	47	20	2	7	12	17	52	64	72	40
15	Wolverhampton W.	42	10	4	7	54	30	4	3	14	19	45	73	75	35
16	Notts County	42	11	4	6	45	24	4	1	16	25	72	70	96	35
17	GRIMSBY TOWN	42	6	7	8	39	39	5	5	11	35	52	74	91	34
18	Fulham	42	11	4	6	39	31	2	4	15	19	61	58	92	34
19	South Shields	42	10	8	3	49	25	1	3	17	22	71	71	96	33
20	Clapton Orient	42	9	3	9	37	35	3	4	14	23	61	60	96	31
21	Darlington	42	10	3	8	53	42	2	3	16	26	56	79	98	30
22	Bradford City	42	6	4	11	30	28	1	5	15	20	60	50	88	23

1927-28 11th in Division 2

Captain: Charlie Wrack

No.	Month	Day	Opponent	Score	Scorers	Att.	Cowell	Wilson	Jacobson	Cowper	Hunter	Powell	Prior	Cooper	Robson	Coglin	Marshall	Read	Harris	Calderwood	Coupland	Tyler	Wrack	Meikle	Bestall	Twell	Wright
1	Aug	27	CLAPTON ORIENT	2-2	Marshall, Robson	15051	1	2	3	4	5	6	7	8	9	10	11										
2		30	READING	3-3	Coglin(3)	13431	1	2	3	4		6	7		9	10	11						5		8		
3	Sep	3	West Bromwich Albion	1-3	Prior	16525	1	2	3	4		6	7		9	10	11						5		8		
4		10	BRISTOL CITY	1-4	Robson	13006	1	2	3	4		6	7		9	10	11						5		8		
5		14	Reading	2-2	Prior(2)	6295	1					6	7		9	10	11		2	3	4		5		8		
6		17	Stoke City	0-0		15216	1					6	7		9	10	11		2	3	4		5		8		
7		24	SOUTHAMPTON	2-2	Prior, Robson	11298	1					6	7		9	10	11		2	3	4		5		8		
8	Oct	1	Notts County	2-3	Robson(2)	7174	1					6	7		9	10	11		2	3	4		5		8		
9		8	OLDHAM ATHLETIC	1-2	Bestall	10400	1					6			9	10	11		2	3	4		5	7	8		
10		15	Hull City	1-0	Bestall	18862	1		3			6			9	10	11			2	4		5	7	8		
11		22	LEEDS UNITED	3-2	Coglin, Meikle, Robson	11909	1	2	3			6			9	10	11				4		5	7	8		
12		29	Nottingham Forest	2-5	Coglin(pen), Meikle	14546	1	2	3						9	10	11			6	4		5	7	8		
13	Nov	5	MANCHESTER CITY	4-1	Marshall, Robson(2), Bestall	12522	1		3						9	10	11		2	6	4		5	7	8		
14		12	South Shields	2-1	Coglin, Marshall	6430	1		3						9	10	11		2	6	4		5	7	8		
15		19	PORT VALE	3-0	Bestall, Marshall, Harris	10119	1		3			6			9	10	11		2	4			5	7	8		
16		26	Fulham	2-2	Robson, Coglin	6395	1		3			6			9	10	11		2	4			5	7	8		
17	Dec	3	BARNSLEY	3-1	Coglin, Robson, Marshall	10241	1		3			6			9	10	11		2	4			5	7	8		
18		10	Wolverhampton Wands.	1-0	Marshall	7431	1		3			6			9	10	11		2	4			5	7	8		
19		17	SWANSEA TOWN	1-2	Robson	9581	1		3			6			9	10	11		2	4			5	7	8		
20		24	Preston North End	0-3		12706	1		3			6			9	10	11		2	4			5	7	8		
21		26	CHELSEA	1-1	Coglin(pen)	18630	1		3			6			9	10	11		2	4			5	7	8		
22		31	Clapton Orient	2-1	Coglin, Marshall	8738	1		3			6	7			10	11			2	4		5		8	9	
23	Jan	2	Blackpool	5-4	Bestall(4), Twell	10347	1		3			6	7			10	11			2	4		5		8	9	
24		7	WEST BROMWICH ALBION	0-6		12242	1		3			6	7			10	11			2	4		5		8	9	
25		21	Bristol City	0-0		11690		4	3			6	7	10	9		11	1	2				5		8		
26	Feb	4	Southampton	0-5		7180		4	3			6	7	10	9	11		1	2				5		8		
27		11	NOTTS COUNTY	1-0	Prior	7666		4	3			6	7	10	9	11		1		2			5		8		
28		18	Oldham Athletic	0-1		15701		4	3			6	7	10	9		11	1		2			5		8		
29		25	HULL CITY	1-1	Coglin	15986		4	3			6	7		9	10	11	1		2			5		8		
30	Mar	3	Leeds United	0-0		23567		4	3			6	7		9	10	11	1		2			5		8		
31		6	STOKE CITY	1-2	Wrack	8279			3			6	7	10	9	11		1		2		4	5		8		
32		10	NOTTINGHAM FOREST	2-1	Robson(2)	7466			3			6	7		9	10		1	2	4			5		8		11
33		14	Chelsea	0-4		14278			3			6	7		9	10		1	2	4			5		8		11
34		17	Manchester City	0-2		49185			3			6	7	10	9			1	2	4			5		8		11
35		24	SOUTH SHIELDS	4-1	Robson(2), Prior, Wright	7868			3			6	7	10	9			1	2	4			5		8		11
36		31	Port Vale	2-2	Robson, Bestall	9125			3			6	7	10	9			1	2	4			5		8		11
37	Apr	6	BLACKPOOL	3-3	Prior, Robson, Cooper	15097			3			6	7	10	9			1	2	4			5		8		11
38		7	FULHAM	1-0	Robson	9005		4	3				7	10	9		11	1	2	6			5		8		
39		14	Barnsley	4-1	Robson(3), Marshall	4516		4	3				7	10	9		11	1	2	6			5		8		
40		21	WOLVERHAMPTON WANDS.	0-1		7248		4	3				7	10	9		11	1	2	6			5		8		
41		28	Swansea Town	2-3	Robson(2)	9208			3				7	4	9	10	11	1	2	6			5		8		
42	May	5	PRESTON NORTH END	4-6	Robson(3), Bestall	8747		4	3			6	7	10	9		11	1	2				5		8		
						Apps.	24	16	37	4	1	35	29	15	39	32	33	18	27	34	13	1	41	13	41	3	6
						Goals							7	1	26	11	8		1				1	2	10	1	1

F.A. Cup

Rd	Month	Day	Opponent	Score	Scorers	Att.	Cowell	Wilson	Jacobson	Cowper	Hunter	Powell	Prior	Cooper	Robson	Coglin	Marshall	Read	Harris	Calderwood	Coupland	Tyler	Wrack	Meikle	Bestall	Twell	Wright
R3	Jan	14	Reading	0-4		19007	1	4	3			6			9	10	11		2				5	7	8		

		P	W	D	L	F	A	W	D	L	F	A	F	A	Pts
1	Manchester City	42	18	2	1	70	27	7	7	7	30	32	100	59	59
2	Leeds United	42	16	2	3	63	15	9	5	7	35	34	98	49	57
3	Chelsea	42	15	2	4	46	15	8	6	7	29	30	75	45	54
4	Preston North End	42	15	3	3	62	24	7	6	8	38	42	100	66	53
5	Stoke City	42	14	5	2	44	17	8	3	10	34	42	78	59	52
6	Swansea Town	42	13	6	2	46	17	5	6	10	29	46	75	63	48
7	Oldham Athletic	42	15	3	3	55	18	4	5	12	20	33	75	51	46
8	West Bromwich Alb.	42	10	7	4	50	28	7	5	9	40	42	90	70	46
9	Port Vale	42	11	6	4	45	20	7	2	12	23	37	68	57	44
10	Nottingham Forest	42	10	6	5	54	37	5	4	12	29	47	83	84	40
11	GRIMSBY TOWN	42	8	6	7	41	41	6	6	9	28	42	69	83	40
12	Bristol City	42	11	5	5	42	18	4	4	13	34	61	76	79	39
13	Barnsley	42	10	5	6	43	36	4	6	11	22	49	65	85	39
14	Hull City	42	9	8	4	25	19	3	7	11	16	35	41	54	39
15	Notts County	42	10	4	7	47	26	3	8	10	21	48	68	74	38
16	Wolverhampton W.	42	11	5	5	43	31	2	5	14	20	60	63	91	36
17	Southampton	42	11	3	7	54	40	3	4	14	14	37	68	77	35
18	Reading	42	9	8	4	32	22	2	5	14	21	53	53	75	35
19	Blackpool	42	11	3	7	55	43	2	5	14	28	58	83	101	34
20	Clapton Orient	42	9	7	5	32	25	2	5	14	23	60	55	85	34
21	Fulham	42	12	7	2	46	22	1	0	20	22	67	68	89	33
22	South Shields	42	5	5	11	30	41	2	4	15	26	70	56	111	23

SEASON 1926/27

Back: Wilson, Archibald, Jacobson,
Middle: McLachlan, Hardy, Pugsley
Front: Devan, Gardner, Carmichael, McKenna, Marshall

SEASON 1928/29

1928-29 2nd in Division 2

Captain: Jock Priestley

							Read	Calderwood	Jacobson	Priestley	Wrack	Powell	Prior	Bestall	Robson	Coglin	Marshall	Wilson	Swaby	Hair	Cooper	Coleman	Wright	Poskett
1	Aug	25	Bristol City	2-2	Robson(2)	16083	1	2	3	4	5	6	7	8	9	10	11							
2		27	BARNSLEY	2-1	Robson, Bestall	12967	1	2	3	4	5	6	7	8	9	10	11							
3	Sep	1	NOTTINGHAM FOREST	2-2	Priestley, Robson	12330	1	2	3	4	5	6	7	8	9	10	11							
4		8	West Bromwich Albion	0-1		13888	1	2	3	4	5	6	7	8	9	10	11							
5		15	CLAPTON ORIENT	6-1	Coglin(4), Robson(2)	10280	1	2	3	4	5	6	7	8	9	10	11							
6		22	Stoke City	2-1	Robson, Prior	15538	1	2	3	4	5	6	7	8	9	10	11							
7		29	HULL CITY	0-1		17048	1	2	3	4	5	6	7	8	9	10	11							
8	Oct	6	BRADFORD PA	4-2	Robson(3), Cooper	11360	1	2	3	4	5	6	7		9	10	11				8			
9		13	Swansea Town	1-2	Cooper	10443	1	2	3	4	5	6	7		9	10	11				8			
10		20	Tottenham Hotspur	1-2	Marshall	22218	1	2	3	4	5	6	7	8	9		11				10			
11		27	READING	4-0	Bestall,Robson,Prior,Cooper	6293	1	2	3	4	5	6	7	8	9		11				10			
12	Nov	3	Preston North End	2-5	Bestall, Cooper	18819	1	2	3	4	5	6	7	8	9		11				10			
13		10	PORT VALE	3-1	Robson(3)	9017	1	2	3	4	5	6		8	9	10	11			7				
14		17	Oldham Athletic	3-0	Coglin, Robson(2)	9396	1	2	3	4	5	6		8	9	10	11			7				
15		24	SOUTHAMPTON	2-1	Robson, Hair	9663	1	2	3	4	5	6		8	9	10	11			7				
16	Dec	1	Wolverhampton Wands.	2-2	Marshall, Bestall	12545	1	2	3	4	5	6		8	9	10	11			7				
17		8	NOTTS COUNTY	2-2	Robson(2)	12381	1	2	3	4	5	6		8	9	10	11			7				
18		15	Millwall	1-4	Hair	12576	1	2	3	4	5	6		8	9	10	11			7				
19		22	MIDDLESBROUGH	1-4	Bestall	10984	1	2	3	4	5	6	7	8	9	10	11							
20		25	BLACKPOOL	1-4	Robson	15457	1	2	3	4	5	6	7	8	9	10	11							
21		26	Blackpool	1-1	Powell(pen)	15337	1	2	3			6	7	8	9		11	4	5		10			
22		29	BRISTOL CITY	3-2	Robson(2), Prior	8018	1	2	3			6	7	8	9		11	4	5		10			
23	Jan	1	Barnsley	2-0	Cooper, Marshall	9049	1	2	3			6	7	8	9		11	4	5		10			
24		5	Nottingham Forest	1-0	Robson	7361	1	2	3			6	7	8	9		11	4	5		10			
25		19	WEST BROMWICH ALBION	3-1	Robson, Swaby, Coglin(pen)	9276	1	2	3		5		7	8	9	10	11	4	6					
26	Feb	2	STOKE CITY	2-1	Coglin(2)	9706	1		3	4	5		7	8	9	10	6	2					11	
27		9	Hull City	3-2	Bestall, Robson, Marshall	10453	1		3	4	5		7	8	9	10	11	2	6					
28		23	SWANSEA TOWN	4-1	Marshall, Robson(2), Coglin	9422	1		3	4	5	6	7	8	9	10	11	2						
29	Mar	2	TOTTENHAM HOTSPUR	2-0	Robson(2)	13850	1		3	4	5	6	7	8	9	10	11	2						
30		4	Clapton Orient	1-3	Robson	5209	1		3	4	5	6	7	8	9	10	11	2						
31		9	Reading	3-1	Bestall(2), Prior	9620	1	2	3		5	6	7	8	9	10	11	4						
32		16	PRESTON NORTH END	1-0	Robson	13268	1		3	4	5	6	7	8	9	10	11	2						
33		23	Port Vale	3-0	Robson, Bestall, Coglin	13085	1	6	3	4	5		7	8	9	10	11	2						
34		29	CHELSEA	1-0	Bestall	23644	1	6	3	4	5		7	8	9	10	11	2						
35		30	OLDHAM ATHLETIC	1-0	Coleman	13915	1		3	4	5	6	7	8		10		2				9	11	
36	Apr	1	Chelsea	2-3	Coleman, Wrack	25079	1		3	4	5	6	7	8		10		2				9	11	
37		6	Southampton	1-3	Coleman	17057	1		3	4	5	6	7	8		10		2				9	11	
38		13	WOLVERHAMPTON WANDS.	2-0	Bestall, Coglin	12699	1	2	3	4	5	6	7	8	9	10						11		
39		20	Notts County	2-1	Coleman(2)	28139	1		3	4	5	6	7	8		10		2				9	11	
40		27	MILLWALL	3-0	Coleman(2), Wright	16658	1		3	4	5	6	7	8		10		2				9	11	
41		29	Bradford PA	0-1		12143	1	6	3	4	5		7		9	10		2				8	11	
42	May	4	Middlesbrough	0-3		36503		6	3	4	5		7	8		10		2				9	11	1
						Apps.	41	31	42	36	38	35	36	39	36	35	34	21	6	6	9	8	8	1
						Goals				1	1	1	4	11	32	11	5		1	2	5	7	1	

F.A. Cup

							Read	Calderwood	Jacobson	Priestley	Wrack	Powell	Prior	Bestall	Robson	Coglin	Marshall	Wilson	Swaby	Hair	Cooper	Coleman	Wright	Poskett
R3	Jan	12	WEST BROMWICH ALBION	1-1	Cooper	16000	1	2	3			6	7	8	9		11	4	5		10			
R3r		16	West Bromwich Albion	0-2		21190	1	2	3			6	7	8	9		11	4	5		10			

		P	W	D	L	F	A	W	D	L	F	A	F	A	Pts
1	Middlesbrough	42	14	4	3	54	22	8	7	6	38	35	92	57	55
2	GRIMSBY TOWN	42	16	2	3	49	24	8	3	10	33	37	82	61	53
3	Bradford Park Ave.	42	18	2	1	62	22	4	2	15	26	48	88	70	48
4	Southampton	42	12	6	3	48	22	5	8	8	26	38	74	60	48
5	Notts County	42	13	4	4	51	24	6	5	10	27	41	78	65	47
6	Stoke City	42	12	7	2	46	16	5	5	11	28	35	74	51	46
7	West Bromwich Alb.	42	13	4	4	50	25	6	4	11	30	54	80	79	46
8	Blackpool	42	13	4	4	49	18	6	3	12	43	58	92	76	45
9	Chelsea	42	10	6	5	40	30	7	4	10	24	35	64	65	44
10	Tottenham Hotspur	42	16	3	2	50	26	1	6	14	25	55	75	81	43
11	Nottingham Forest	42	8	6	7	34	33	7	6	8	37	37	71	70	42
12	Hull City	42	8	8	5	38	24	5	6	10	20	39	58	63	40
13	Preston North End	42	12	6	3	58	27	3	3	15	20	52	78	79	39
14	Millwall	42	10	4	7	43	35	6	3	12	28	51	71	86	39
15	Reading	42	12	3	6	48	30	3	6	12	15	56	63	86	39
16	Barnsley	42	12	4	5	51	28	4	2	15	18	38	69	66	38
17	Wolverhampton W.	42	9	6	6	41	31	6	1	14	36	50	77	81	37
18	Oldham Athletic	42	15	2	4	37	24	1	3	17	17	51	54	75	37
19	Swansea Town	42	12	3	6	46	26	1	7	13	16	49	62	75	36
20	Bristol City	42	11	6	4	37	25	2	4	15	21	47	58	72	36
21	Port Vale	42	14	1	6	53	25	1	3	17	18	61	71	86	34
22	Clapton Orient	42	10	4	7	29	25	2	4	15	16	47	45	72	32

1929-30 18th in Division 1

Captain: Jock Priestley

							Read	Wilson	Jacobson	Priestley	Wrack	Powell	Prior	Bestall	Robson	Coglin	Marshall	Bateman	Calderwood	Hall	Swaby	Buck	Coleman	Barley	Cooper	Glover	Wright
1	Aug	31	Sheffield United	3-2	Marshall, Bestall(2)	22683	1	2	3	4	5	6	7	8	9	10	11										
2	Sep	4	PORTSMOUTH	1-1	Robson	19329	1	2	3	4	5	6	7	8	9	10	11										
3		7	NEWCASTLE UNITED	4-0	Robson,Coglin(pen),Priestley,Swaby	22390	1	2	3	4				8	9	10	11		6		5		7				
4		11	Portsmouth	1-1	Robson	12211	1	2	3	4				8	9	10	11		6		5		7				
5		14	Blackburn Rovers	1-4	Robson	18187	1	2	3	4				8	9	10	11		6		5		7				
6		21	MIDDLESBROUGH	0-3		15863	1	2	3	4		6		8	9	10	11				5		7				
7		24	HUDDERSFIELD TOWN	4-2	Robson(2), Bestall, Marshall	14989	1	2	3	4		6		8	9	10	11				5		7				
8		28	Liverpool	0-2		41960	1	2	3	4		6	7	8	9	10	11				5						
9	Oct	5	WEST HAM UNITED	2-2	Bestall, Coglin	15542	1	2	3	4		6	7	8	9	10	11				5						
10		12	Manchester United	5-2	Robson(2),Coglin,Bestall,Coleman	21494	1	2	3			6		8	9	10	11		4		5		7				
11		19	Arsenal	1-4	Robson	43794	1	2	3	4		6		8	9	10	11				5		7				
12		26	ASTON VILLA	0-2		20225	1	2	3	4	5			8	9	10	11				6		7				
13	Nov	2	Leeds United	0-6		24013	1	2	3	4			7	8	9	10	11	6			5						
14		9	MANCHESTER CITY	2-2	Robson, Prior	14311	1	2	3	4			7		9	10	11		6		5		8				
15		16	Burnley	1-3	Marshall	11660	1	2	3	4			7	8	9		11		6		5		10				
16		23	SUNDERLAND	0-1		10640	1	2	3	4			7	8	9	10	11		6		5						
17		30	Bolton Wanderers	3-2	Marshall(2), Robson	8506	1	2	3	4					9	10	11		6		5			7	8		
18	Dec	7	EVERTON	0-3		9503	1	2	3	4					9	10			6		5			7	8		11
19		14	Derby County	4-5	Bestall,Carr(OG),Wright,Robson	13880	1	2	3	4	6			8	9						5		10	7			11
20		25	LEICESTER CITY	1-4	Barley	16173	1	2	3	4				8	9						5	6	10	7			11
21		26	Leicester City	0-1		35644	1	2	3	4	5			8	9	10	11					6	7				
22		28	SHEFFIELD UNITED	4-1	Coglin(2pens), Robson(2)	13267	1	2	3	4	5			8	9	10	11					6	7				
23	Jan	4	Newcastle United	1-3	Coleman	31803	1	2	3	4	5			8	9	10	11					6	7				
24		18	BLACKBURN ROVERS	5-3	Bestall,Prior,Coglin,Robson(2)	11773	1	2	3	4	5		7	8	9	10	11					6					
25	Feb	1	LIVERPOOL	3-2	Coglin(3)	11184	1	2	3	4	5		7	8	9	10	11					6					
26		5	SHEFFIELD WED.	0-5		12514	1	2	3	4	5		7	8	9	10	11					6					
27		8	West Ham United	0-2		15034	1	2	3	4			7	8		10	11				5	6				9	
28		15	MANCHESTER UNITED	2-2	Robson, Prior	9337	1	2	3	4	5		7	8	9	10						6	11				
29		22	ARSENAL	1-1	Robson	17151	1	2	3	4			7	8	9		11				5	6	10				
30	Mar	5	Middlesbrough	5-1	Robson(2),Marshall,Coglin,Bestall	8880	1	2	3	4			7	8	9	10	11				5	6					
31		8	LEEDS UNITED	1-2	Coglin(pen)	16951	1	2	3	4			7	8	9	10	11				5	6					
32		15	Manchester City	1-3	Robson	26462	1	2		4	5		7	8	9	10	11	3				6					
33		22	BURNLEY	4-0	Coglin(2), Robson, Marshall	11262	1	2		4			7	8	9	10	11	3			5	6					
34		29	Sunderland	0-2		23842	1	2		4			7	8	9	10	11	3			5	6					
35	Apr	2	Aston Villa	1-4	Bestall	8965	1	2		4	5			8	9	10	11	3				6	7				
36		5	BOLTON WANDERERS	1-1	Robson	12081	1	2		4	5		7	8	9	10	11	3				6					
37		12	Everton	4-2	Robson(4)	47407	1	2	3	5			7	8	9		11			4		6			10		
38		18	BIRMINGHAM	2-1	Cooper, Robson	19884	1	2	3	5			7	8	9		11			4		6			10		
39		19	DERBY COUNTY	2-1	Robson, Marshall	14829	1	2	3	5			7	8	9		11			4		6			10		
40		22	Birmingham	2-0	Marshall, Robson	18482	1	2	3	5			7	8	9		11			4		6			10		
41		26	Sheffield Wednesday	0-1		22524	1	2	3	5			7	8	9		11			4		6			10		
42	May	3	Huddersfield Town	1-0	Bestall	14525	1	2	3	5			7	8	9		11			4		6			10		
						Apps.	42	42	37	41	14	8	26	39	41	32	38	6	9	6	24	23	18	4	8	1	3
						Goals				1			3	10	30	13	9				1		2	1	1		1

1 own goal

F.A. Cup

R3	Jan	11	Brighton & Hove Albion	1-1	Prior	10000	1	2	3	4	5		7	8		10	11					6	9				
R3r		14	BRIGHTON & HOVE ALBION	0-1			1	2	3	4	5		7	8		10	11					6	9				

		P	*W*	*D*	*L*	*F*	*A*	*W*	*D*	*L*	*F*	*A*	*F*	*A*	*Pts*
1	Sheffield Wed.	42	15	4	2	56	20	11	4	6	49	37	105	57	60
2	Derby County	42	16	4	1	61	32	5	4	12	29	50	90	82	50
3	Manchester City	42	12	5	4	51	33	7	4	10	40	48	91	81	47
4	Aston Villa	42	13	1	7	54	33	8	4	9	38	50	92	83	47
5	Leeds United	42	15	2	4	52	22	5	4	12	27	41	79	63	46
6	Blackburn Rovers	42	15	2	4	65	36	4	5	12	34	57	99	93	45
7	West Ham United	42	14	2	5	51	26	5	3	13	35	53	86	79	43
8	Leicester City	42	12	5	4	57	42	5	4	12	29	48	86	90	43
9	Sunderland	42	13	3	5	50	35	5	4	12	26	45	76	80	43
10	Huddersfield Town	42	9	7	5	32	21	8	2	11	31	48	63	69	43
11	Birmingham	42	13	3	5	40	21	3	6	12	27	41	67	62	41
12	Liverpool	42	11	5	5	33	29	5	4	12	30	50	63	79	41
13	Portsmouth	42	10	6	5	43	25	5	4	12	23	37	66	62	40
14	Arsenal	42	10	2	9	49	26	4	9	8	29	40	78	66	39
15	Bolton Wanderers	42	11	5	5	46	24	4	4	13	28	50	74	74	39
16	Middlesbrough	42	11	3	7	48	31	5	3	13	34	53	82	84	38
17	Manchester United	42	11	4	6	39	34	4	4	13	28	54	67	88	38
18	GRIMSBY TOWN	42	8	6	7	39	39	7	1	13	34	50	73	89	37
19	Newcastle United	42	13	4	4	52	32	2	3	16	19	60	71	92	37
20	Sheffield United	42	12	2	7	59	39	3	4	14	32	57	91	96	36
21	Burnley	42	11	5	5	53	34	3	3	15	26	63	79	97	36
22	Everton	42	6	7	8	48	46	6	4	11	32	46	80	92	35

SEASON 1929/30

Back: Woods (Train), Swaby, Bell, Priestley, Prior, Williams, Poskett, Read, Wilson, Gillow (Man), Jacobson, Powell, Bateman, Calderwood, Wattam, Golightly (Asst Train)
Front: Hall, Barley, Coglin, Bestall, Coleman, Robson, Munnings, Glover, Cooper, Marshall, Wright, Wrack

SEASON 1930/31

Back: Priestly, Prior, Wilson, Read, Bateman, Woods (Trainer), Buck.
Front: Coleman, Bestall, Robson, Coglin, Marshall, Wrack.

1930-31 13th in Division 1

Captain: Jock Priestley

No	Date	Opponent	Score	Scorers	Att.	Read	Wilson	Jacobson	Hall	Priestley	Buck	Prior	Bestall	Robson	Cooper	Marshall	Poskett	Bell	Bateman	Wrack	Swaby	Coleman	Fielding	Craven	Ponting	Barley	Glover	Coglin
1	Aug 30	CHELSEA	0-1		20294	1	2	3	4	5	6	7	8	9	10	11												
2	Sep 1	Huddersfield Town	2-2	Marshall(2)	11690	1	2	3	4	5	6		8	9		11						7						10
3	6	Newcastle United	2-1	Robson(2)	27155	1	2	3	4	5	6		8	9		11						7						10
4	9	ASTON VILLA	1-2	Bestall	19224	1	2	3	4	5	6		8	9		11						7						10
5	13	SHEFFIELD WED.	2-3	Prior(2)	17310	1	2	3	4	5	6	7	8			11						9		10				
6	15	Aston Villa	0-2		22301	1	2		4		6	7	8			11			3	5		9		10				
7	20	Derby County	0-1		13207	1	2	3	4	5	6	7	8			11						9		10				
8	27	Manchester United	2-0	Coleman, Fielding	14695	1	2	3	4	5	6		8		10	11						9	7					
9	Oct 4	WEST HAM UNITED	4-0	Marshall, Coleman(2), Cooper	14423	1	2	3	4	5	6		8		10	11						9	7					
10	11	Bolton Wanderers	2-4	Coleman(2)	14979	1	2	3	4	5	6		8		10	11						9	7					
11	18	PORTSMOUTH	0-3		13095	1	2	3	4	5	6		8		10	11						9	7					
12	25	Manchester City	0-1		24770	1	2	3	4	5	6	7	8			10						9	11					
13	Nov 1	LEICESTER CITY	8-2	Coleman(4),Prior(2),Priestley,Fielding	9868	1	2	3	4	5	6	7	8			10						9	11					
14	8	Sunderland	2-3	Coleman(2)	21225	1	2	3	4	5	6	7	8			10						9	11					
15	15	BLACKBURN ROVERS	2-0	Marshall, Bestall	9715	1	2	3	4	5	6	7	8			10						9	11					
16	22	Birmingham	1-4	Coleman	13639	1	2	3	4	5	6	7	8			10						9	11					
17	29	LEEDS UNITED	2-0	Bestall, Prior	6783	1	2	3		4	6	7	8			10					5	9	11					
18	Dec 13	SHEFFIELD UNITED	2-1	Bestall, Coleman	11735	1	2	3		4	6		8			10					5	9	11	7				
19	20	Blackpool	1-3	Priestley	11427	1	2	3		4	6		8			10					5	9	11	7				
20	25	LIVERPOOL	0-0		18564	1	2	3		4	6	7	8			10					5	9	11					
21	26	Liverpool	1-1	Coleman	38203	1	2	3	4		6		8			10					5	9	11		7			
22	27	Chelsea	0-5		23467	1	2	3	4		6		8		10	9					5		11		7			
23	Jan 1	Middlesbrough	1-2	Glover	23845		4	3			6		8			10	1	2			5		11			7	9	
24	3	NEWCASTLE UNITED	2-2	Bestall(pen), Prior	10565	1	4	3			6	7	8		10			2			5		11				9	
25	17	Sheffield Wednesday	1-4	Glover	19729	1	4	3			6	7	8			11		2			5	10					9	
26	28	Arsenal	1-9	Prior	15751	1				4	6	7	8			11		2	3		5	9						10
27	31	MANCHESTER UNITED	2-1	Bestall, Cooper	9305	1	2	3	4	5	6	7	8		10	11						9						
28	Feb 3	DERBY COUNTY	5-3	Bestall,Coleman(2),Marshall,Prior	8308	1	2	3	4	5	6	7	8		10	11						9						
29	7	West Ham United	4-3	Coleman(3), Marshall	15559	1	2	3	4	5	6	7	8		10	11						9						
30	17	BOLTON WANDERERS	4-1	Coleman(2), Cooper, Prior	5741	1	2	3	4	5	6	7	8		10	11						9						
31	21	Portsmouth	3-4	Cooper,Marshall,Coleman(pen)	12522	1	2	3	4	5	6	7	8		10	11						9						
32	28	MANCHESTER CITY	3-5	Coleman, Marshall, Bestall	12611	1	2	3	4	5	6	7	8		10	11						9						
33	Mar 7	Leicester City	1-0	Coleman	12163	1	2	3	4	5	6	7	8		10	11						9						
34	21	Blackburn Rovers	2-5	Coleman(2)	8890	1	2	3	4	5	6	7	8			11						9		10				
35	24	SUNDERLAND	2-1	Marshall, Coleman	9396	1		3	4	5	6	7	8		10	11		2				9						
36	28	BIRMINGHAM	4-1	Coleman(3), Prior	10994	1	2	3	4	5	6	7	8		10	11						9						
37	Apr 3	MIDDLESBROUGH	4-1	Cooper, Coleman(2), Prior	19821	1	2	3	4	5	6	7	8		10	11						9						
38	4	Leeds United	0-0		14951	1	2	3	4	5	6	7	8		10	11						9						
39	11	ARSENAL	0-1		22394	1	2	3	4	5	6	7	8		10	11						9						
40	18	Sheffield United	1-2	Cooper	9103	1	2	3	4	5	6	7	8		10	11						9						
41	25	BLACKPOOL	6-2	Coleman(3),Craven,Prior,Marshall	8042	1	2	3	4	5		7	8			11					6	9		10				
42	May 2	HUDDERSFIELD TOWN	2-1	Bestall(2)	16583	1	2	3	4	5	6	7	8			11						9		10				
					Apps.	41	40	40	34	36	41	30	42	4	20	41	1	5	2	1	11	38	17	8	2	1	3	4
					Goals					2		12	10	2	6	10						35	2	1			2	

F.A. Cup

Rd	Date	Opponent	Score	Scorers	Att.	Read	Wilson	Jacobson	Hall	Priestley	Buck	Prior	Bestall	Robson	Cooper	Marshall	Poskett	Bell	Bateman	Wrack	Swaby	Coleman	Fielding	Craven	Ponting	Barley	Glover	Coglin
R3	Jan 10	Scarborough	2-1	Prior, Bestall	8158	1	4	3			6	7	8			11		2			5	10					9	
R4	24	MANCHESTER UNITED	1-0	Marshall	15000	1		3		4	6	7	8		10	11		2			5	9						
R5	Feb 14	Everton	3-5	Bestall, Coleman, Marshall	65534	1	2	3	4	5	6	7	8		10	11						9						

		P	W	D	L	F	A	W	D	L	F	A	F	A	Pts
1	Arsenal	42	14	5	2	67	27	14	5	2	60	32	127	59	66
2	Aston Villa	42	17	3	1	86	34	8	6	7	42	44	128	78	59
3	Sheffield Wed.	42	14	3	4	65	32	8	5	8	37	43	102	75	52
4	Portsmouth	42	11	7	3	46	26	7	6	8	38	41	84	67	49
5	Huddersfield Town	42	10	8	3	45	27	8	4	9	36	38	81	65	48
6	Derby County	42	12	6	3	56	31	6	4	11	38	48	94	79	46
7	Middlesbrough	42	13	5	3	57	28	6	3	12	41	62	98	90	46
8	Manchester City	42	13	2	6	41	29	5	8	8	34	41	75	70	46
9	Liverpool	42	11	6	4	48	28	4	6	11	38	57	86	85	42
10	Blackburn Rovers	42	14	3	4	54	28	3	5	13	29	56	83	84	42
11	Sunderland	42	12	4	5	61	38	4	5	12	28	47	89	85	41
12	Chelsea	42	13	4	4	42	19	2	6	13	22	48	64	67	40
13	GRIMSBY TOWN	42	13	2	6	55	31	4	3	14	27	56	82	87	39
14	Bolton Wanderers	42	12	6	3	45	26	3	3	15	23	55	68	81	39
15	Sheffield United	42	10	7	4	49	31	4	3	14	29	53	78	84	38
16	Leicester City	42	12	4	5	50	38	4	2	15	30	57	80	95	38
17	Newcastle United	42	9	2	10	41	45	6	4	11	37	42	78	87	36
18	West Ham United	42	11	3	7	56	44	3	5	13	23	50	79	94	36
19	Birmingham	42	11	3	7	37	28	2	7	12	18	42	55	70	36
20	Blackpool	42	8	7	6	41	44	3	3	15	30	81	71	125	32
21	Leeds United	42	10	3	8	49	31	2	4	15	19	50	68	81	31
22	Manchester United	42	6	6	9	30	37	1	2	18	23	78	53	115	22

1931-32 21st in Division 1

Captain: Jock Priestley

	Date	Opponents	Res	Scorers	Att	Read	Wilson	Jacobson	Hall	Priestley	Buck	Prior	Bestall	Chalmers	Coleman	Marshall	Bell	Bateman	Dow	Gardner	Betmead	Seddon	Donaldson	Craven	Fielding	Dyson	Ponting	Glover	Holmes	Cooper	Wilson	Moralee	Dodds	Swaby
1	Aug 29	Huddersfield Town	1-1	Coleman	13668	1	2	3	4	5	6	7	8	10	9	11																		
2	31	Sheffield Wednesday	1-4	Chalmers	16734	1	2	3	4	5	6	7	8	10	9	11																		
3	Sep 5	NEWCASTLE UNITED	1-2	Fairhurst(OG)	12248	1	2	3	4		6	7	8	10	9	11																		5
4	9	Bolton Wanderers	3-5	Marshall, Coleman(2)	9700	1	2	3			6			10	9	11			4				7	8										5
5	12	Aston Villa	0-7		18753	1	2	3	5		6		8	10	9	11			4					7										
6	15	BOLTON WANDERERS	2-0	Glover, Prior	10857	1	2	3			6	7	8			11				4	5							9		10				
7	19	LEICESTER CITY	3-0	Glover(2), Marshall	13156	1	2	3			6	7	8			11				4	5							9		10				
8	26	Liverpool	0-4		26153	1	2	3			6	7	8			11				4	5							9		10				
9	Oct 3	ARSENAL	3-1	Marshall, Glover(2)	17840	1	2	3		5	6	7	8			11				4								9		10				
10	10	CHELSEA	1-2	Glover	16050	1		3		5	6	7	8			11	2			4								9		10				
11	17	Birmingham	1-2	Glover	16313	1	2	3		5	6	7			8	11				4								9		10				
12	24	SHEFFIELD UNITED	0-2		9063	1	2	3	4	5	6		8		7	11								10				9						
13	31	Blackburn Rovers	2-3	Coleman(2)	8102	1	2	3	6	5		7	8		9					4				10	11									
14	Nov 7	PORTSMOUTH	3-1	Prior, Fielding, Coleman	7247	1	2	3	6	5		7			9					4				8	11					10				
15	14	Manchester City	1-4	Fielding	20352	1	2	3	6	5		7	8		9					4					11					10				
16	21	EVERTON	1-2	Prior	16508	1	2	3		4	6	7	8		9						5				11					10				
17	28	Blackpool	3-4	Priestley(pen), Coleman, Glover	12700	1	2	3		4	6	7			9	10					5				11			8						
18	Dec 5	SUNDERLAND	1-3	Priestley(pen)	8962	1	2	3		4	6	7			9	10					5				11			8						
19	12	Derby County	3-3	Fielding(3)	10695	1	2	3			6	7	8		9	10				4	5				11									
20	19	WEST BROMWICH ALBION	0-0		9225	1	2	3			6	7	8		9	10				4	5				11									
21	25	WEST HAM UNITED	2-1	Bestall, Glover	15132	1	2	3			6	7	8			10				4	5				11			9						
22	26	West Ham United	1-3	Glover	23859	1	2	3		4	6		8			11					5				7			9		10				
23	Jan 2	HUDDERSFIELD TOWN	1-4	Coleman	7921	1	2	3				7	8		10	6				4	5				11			9						
24	16	Newcastle United	0-2		27837	1	2	3	4	5	6	7	8		9	11														10				
25	30	Leicester City	2-1	Marshall, Coleman	13907	1			4	5	6		8		9	11	2	3							7					10				
26	Feb 2	ASTON VILLA	2-2	Bestall, Coleman	11132	1			4	5	6		8		9	11	2	3							7					10				
27	6	LIVERPOOL	5-1	Buck,Coleman(3),Priestley(pen)	13124	1	2	3	4	5	6		8		9	11									7					10				
28	17	Arsenal	0-4		20980	1		3	4	5	6		8		9	11	2							10	7									
29	20	Chelsea	1-4	Betmead	24422	1	2	3	4		6		8		9	11					5			10	7									
30	27	BIRMINGHAM	1-1	Cooper	9454	1	2	3	4	5	6		8		9	11									7					10				
31	Mar 5	Sheffield United	1--2	Betmead	19284	1		3		4	6	7	8				2				5				11			9		10				
32	12	BLACKBURN ROVERS	4-3	Holmes, Marshall, Hall, Glover	10531	1		3	4	5			8			11	2								7			9	10		6			
33	19	Portsmouth	0-2		13961	1	2	3		4	6		8			11					5					7			9		10			
34	25	MIDDLESBROUGH	2-0	Holmes, Dyson	19005	1	2	3		4			8			11					5					7		9	10		6			
35	26	MANCHESTER CITY	2-1	Marshall, Glover	11481	1	2	3	4	5			8			11										7		9	10		6			
36	28	Middlesbrough	0-4		8373	1	2	3		5	4		8			11										7		9	10		6			
37	Apr 2	Everton	2-4	Graven, Dyson	28456	1	2	3	4				10									5		8		7		9			6		11	
38	9	BLACKPOOL	0-0		8651	1	2	3	4	5		7	10											8				9			6		11	
39	16	Sunderland	0-2		17614	1	2	3					8	10							4	5					7	9			6		11	
40	23	DERBY COUNTY	2-1	Dyson(2)	7386	1	2	3					8								4	5				7			9		6	10	11	
41	30	West Bromwich Albion	6-5	Holmes(3), Dyson(3)	13101	1		3	4				8			11		2				5				7			9		6	10		
42	May 7	SHEFFIELD WED.	3-1	Holmes(2), Dyson	16049	1	2	3	4				8			11						5				7			9		6	10		
					Apps.	42	35	40	21	26	29	22	37	6	23	33	6	3	2	13	17	5	1	9	19	8	1	20	8	16	11	3	4	2
					Goals				1	3	1	3	2	1	13	6					2			1	5	8		12	7	1				

1 own goal

F.A. Cup

	Date	Opponents	Res
R3	Jan 9	EXETER CITY	4-1
R4	23	BIRMINGHAM	2-1
R5	Feb 13	Liverpool	0-1

		P	W	D	L	F	A	W	D	L	F	A	F	A	Pts
1	Everton	42	18	0	3	84	30	8	4	9	32	34	116	64	56
2	Arsenal	42	14	5	2	52	16	8	5	8	38	32	90	48	54
3	Sheffield Wed.	42	14	4	3	60	28	8	2	11	36	54	96	82	50
4	Huddersfield Town	42	11	8	2	47	21	8	2	11	33	42	80	63	48
5	Aston Villa	42	15	1	5	64	28	4	7	10	40	44	104	72	46
6	West Bromwich Alb.	42	12	4	5	46	21	8	2	11	31	34	77	55	46
7	Sheffield United	42	13	3	5	47	32	7	3	11	33	43	80	75	46
8	Portsmouth	42	14	2	5	37	21	5	5	11	25	41	62	62	45
9	Birmingham	42	13	5	3	48	22	5	3	13	30	45	78	67	44
10	Liverpool	42	13	4	4	56	38	6	2	13	25	55	81	93	44
11	Newcastle United	42	13	5	3	52	31	5	1	15	28	56	80	87	42
12	Chelsea	42	12	4	5	43	27	4	4	13	26	46	69	73	40
13	Sunderland	42	11	4	6	42	29	4	6	11	25	44	67	73	40
14	Manchester City	42	10	5	6	49	30	3	7	11	34	43	83	73	38
15	Derby County	42	13	5	3	51	25	1	5	15	20	50	71	75	38
16	Blackburn Rovers	42	12	3	6	57	41	4	3	14	32	54	89	95	38
17	Bolton Wanderers	42	15	1	5	51	25	2	3	16	21	55	72	80	38
18	Middlesbrough	42	12	3	6	41	29	3	5	13	23	60	64	89	38
19	Leicester City	42	11	3	7	46	39	4	4	13	28	55	74	94	37
20	Blackpool	42	9	4	8	42	40	3	5	13	23	62	65	102	33
21	GRIMSBY TOWN	42	11	4	6	39	28	2	2	17	28	70	67	98	32
22	West Ham United	42	9	5	7	35	37	3	2	16	27	70	62	107	31

SEASON 1931/32
Back: Gillow (Man), Wilson (Dir), Drysdale, Gardner, Bell, Priestley, Wilson, Read, Jacobson, Tweedy, Chalmers, Poskett, Dow, Hopkins (Train), Hooton (Sec), Golightly (Asst Train) Middle: Fielding, Betmead, Moralee, Cooper, Armitage, Marshall, Buck Front: Prior, Ponting, Bestall, Dodsworth, Glover, Coleman, Dodds, Craven, Bateman

SEASON 1932/33
Back: Armitage, Annables, Hodgson, Craven, Betmead, Dodsworth, Read, C.('Tug') Wilson, Dyson, Seddon
Front: Moralee, Wright, Dodds, Jacobson, Bateman, Tweedy, Waring, Bestall, Homes, Buck

1932-33 13th in Division 2

Captain: Jackie Bestall

No.	Date	Opponent	Score	Scorers	Att.	Read	Bateman	Jacobson	Hall	Seddon	Wilson C	Dyson	Bestall	Holmes	Moralee	Fielding	Tweedy	Wilson CH	Wright	Kelly	Annables	Betmead	Hodgson	Buck	Wattam	Jennings	Craven	Ponting	Dodds	Dodsworth	Glover
1	Aug 27	NOTTINGHAM FOREST	1-1	Holmes	13423	1	2	3	4	5	6	7	8	9	10	11																
2	31	Plymouth Argyle	0-4		22760	1	2	3		5	6	7	8	9	10	11							4								
3	Sep 3	Charlton Athletic	3-2	Craven, Holmes, Dyson(pen)	8416	1	2	3		5	6	7	8	9		11							4				10				
4	6	PLYMOUTH ARGYLE	2-3	Craven, Dyson	9140	1	2	3		5	6	7	8										4					10	9	11		
5	10	STOKE CITY	0-1		9173	1		3			6	7	8					2				5					10	9	11	4	
6	17	Manchester United	1-1	Fielding	17662	1		3			10	7	8			11		2				5		6						4	9
7	24	TOTTENHAM HOTSPUR	3-2	Dyson, Glover(2)	9597	1		3			10	7	8			11		2				5		6						4	9
8	Oct 1	Lincoln City	3-6	Glover, Wilson, Dodsworth	14102	1	2	3		5	10	7	8											6		11				4	9
9	8	Oldham Athletic	1-0	Glover	4208	1		3		4	10	7	8					2				5		6		11					9
10	15	PRESTON NORTH END	5-5	Glover(4), Dyson	8166	1		3		4	10	7	8					2				5		6		11					9
11	22	BURY	1-0	Glover	8187	1		3	4			7	8	10					2			5		6		11					9
12	29	Southampton	0-3		10081	1		3	4			7	8	10					2			5		6		11					9
13	Nov 5	MILLWALL	1-1	Craven	7996	1		3	4			7	10						2			5		6		11	8				9
14	12	West Ham United	2-5	Dyson, Wilson(pen)	11481	1		3	4	5	10	7				11			2					6			8				9
15	19	BRADFORD CITY	1-1	Fielding	6594			3	4		10	7		9		11	1		2				5	6			8				
16	26	Swansea Town	0-1		9304			3	4	6			8			11	1		2				5			7	10				9
17	Dec 3	NOTTS COUNTY	1-1	Jennings	6065			3	4	5			8			11	1		2					6		7	10				9
18	10	Chesterfield	2-1	Jennings, Fielding	8138			3	4	5			8			11	1		2					6		7	10				9
19	17	FULHAM	1-0	Jennings	6006			3	4	5			8			11	1		2					6		7	10				9
20	24	Port Vale	2-4	Armitage(OG), Bestall	8342			3	4		10		8	9		11	1		2				5	6		7					
21	26	BURNLEY	1-2	Bestall	11186			3	4		5		8	9		11	1		2					6		7	10				
22	27	Burnley	0-2		13602			3	4			7	8			11	1		2			5			6		10				9
23	31	Nottingham Forest	2-3	Glover, Craven	9641			3	4			7	8				1		2			5		6		11	10				9
24	Jan 7	CHARLTON ATHLETIC	5-5	Glover(2),Craven,Fielding,Dyson	5697	1		3	4			7	8			11			2			5		6			10				9
25	21	Stoke City	0-2		8724	1		3	4			7	8			11			2			5		6			10				9
26	31	MANCHESTER UNITED	1-1	Jennings	4020	1		3	4				8			11			2			5		6		7	10				9
27	Feb 4	Tottenham Hotspur	3-4	Craven, Glover, Jennings	33395	1		3	4	6			8			11			2			5				7	10				9
28	11	LINCOLN CITY	3-3	Jennings(3)	11088	1		3	4	6			8			11			2			5				7	10				9
29	18	OLDHAM ATHLETIC	5-1	Craven(3), Bestall, Jennings	5026	1		3	4				8			11			2			5			6	7	10				9
30	Mar 2	Preston North End	2-4	Craven, Jennings(pen)	7449	1	3		4				8			11			2			5			6	7	10				9
31	4	Bury	1-4	Robinson(OG)	9039	1	3		4		10		8	9		11			2			5		6		7					
32	11	SOUTHAMPTON	2-2	Craven, Seddon	7257	1				4	3	7	8			6			2			5					11	10	9			
33	18	Millwall	1-0	Glover	17355	1		3	4				8			11				2		5		6		7	10				9
34	25	WEST HAM UNITED	2-1	Glover(2)	8546	1		3	4				8			11				2		5		6		7	10				9
35	Apr 1	Bradford City	2-2	Glover, Jennings	10272	1		3	4				8			11				2		5		6		7	10				9
36	8	Swansea Town	2-1	Bestall, Jennings	7809	1		3	4				8			11				2		5		6		7	10				9
37	14	BRADFORD P.A.	5-1	Craven(2),Jennings,Betmead,Glover	16836	1		3	4				8			11				2		5		6		7	10				9
38	15	Notts County	3-1	Bestall, Craven, Jennings(pen)	9230	1		3	4				8			11				2		5		6		7	10				9
39	17	Bradford P.A.	1-1	Glover	8961	1			4				8			11				2	3	5		6		7	10				9
40	22	CHESTERFIELD	1-1	Craven	7351	1			4				8			11				2	3	5		6		7	10				9
41	29	Fulham	1-0	Glover	17467	1			4			7	8			11		2		3		5		6			10				9
42	May 6	PORT VALE	6-1	Glover(2),Craven,Fielding,Betmead,Hall	6349	1			4			7	8			11		2		3		5		6			10				9
					Apps.	33	7	35	32	15	16	22	40	9	2	33	9	7	22	10	2	30	5	30	3	28	31	3	2	4	32
					Goals					1	1	2	6	5	2		5						2				14	16			1	22

2 own goals

F.A. Cup

Rd	Date	Opponent	Score	Scorers	Att.	Read	Bateman	Jacobson	Hall	Seddon	Wilson C	Dyson	Bestall	Holmes	Moralee	Fielding	Tweedy	Wilson CH	Wright	Kelly	Annables	Betmead	Hodgson	Buck	Wattam	Jennings	Craven	Ponting	Dodds	Dodsworth	Glover
R3	Jan 14	PORTSMOUTH	3-2	Dyson, Glover(2)	9200	1		3	4			7	8			11			2			5		6			10				9
R4	28	Bolton Wanderers	1-2	Craven	25866			3	4				8			11	1		2			5		6			10	7			9

		P	W	D	L	F	A	W	D	L	F	A	F	A	Pts
1	Stoke City	42	13	3	5	40	15	12	3	6	38	24	78	39	56
2	Tottenham Hotspur	42	14	7	0	58	19	6	8	7	38	32	96	51	55
3	Fulham	42	12	5	4	46	31	8	5	8	32	34	78	65	50
4	Bury	42	13	7	1	55	23	7	2	12	29	36	84	59	49
5	Nottingham Forest	42	9	8	4	37	28	8	7	6	30	31	67	59	49
6	Manchester United	42	11	5	5	40	24	4	8	9	31	44	71	68	43
7	Millwall	42	11	7	3	40	20	5	4	12	19	37	59	57	43
8	Bradford Park Ave.	42	13	4	4	51	27	4	4	13	26	44	77	71	42
9	Preston North End	42	12	2	7	53	36	4	8	9	21	34	74	70	42
10	Swansea Town	42	17	0	4	36	12	2	4	15	14	42	50	54	42
11	Bradford City	42	10	6	5	43	24	4	7	10	22	37	65	61	41
12	Southampton	42	15	3	3	48	22	3	2	16	18	44	66	66	41
13	GRIMSBY TOWN	42	8	10	3	49	34	6	3	12	30	50	79	84	41
14	Plymouth Argyle	42	13	4	4	45	22	3	5	13	18	45	63	67	41
15	Notts County	42	10	4	7	41	31	5	6	10	26	47	67	78	40
16	Oldham Athletic	42	10	4	7	38	31	5	4	12	29	49	67	80	38
17	Port Vale	42	12	3	6	49	27	2	7	12	17	52	66	79	38
18	Lincoln City	42	11	6	4	46	28	1	7	13	26	59	72	87	37
19	Burnley	42	8	9	4	35	20	3	5	13	32	59	67	79	36
20	West Ham United	42	12	6	3	56	31	1	3	17	19	62	75	93	35
21	Chesterfield	42	10	5	6	36	25	2	5	14	25	59	61	84	34
22	Charlton Athletic	42	9	3	9	35	35	3	4	14	25	56	60	91	31

1933-34 1st in Division 2

Captain: Jackie Bestall

							Read	Kelly	Jacobson	Hall	Betmead	Buck	Jennings	Bestall	Glover	Craven	Dodds	Tweedy	Waring	Dyson	Lewis	Ponting	Holmes	Moralee
1	Aug	24	BURNLEY	1-0	Jennings	10501	1	2	3	4	5	6	7	8	9	10	11							
2		29	BOLTON WANDERERS	2-3	Glover, Jennings	9961	1	2	3	4	5	6	7	8	9	10	11							
3	Sep	2	Oldham Athletic	5-1	Glover(3), Bestall, Craven	7449	1	2	3	4	5	6	7	8	9	10	11							
4		4	Bolton Wanderers	4-0	Glover,Jennings,Bestall,Dodds	9370	1	2	3	4	5	6	7	8	9	10	11							
5		9	PRESTON NORTH END	3-0	Glover(2), Bestall	13025	1	2	3	4	5	6	7	8	9	10	11							
6		16	Bradford P.A.	1-2	Glover	15672	1	2	3	4	5	6	7	8	9	10	11							
7		23	PORT VALE	1-2	Craven	10503	1	2	3	4	5	6	7	8	9	10	11							
8		30	NOTTINGHAM FOREST	2-1	Dyson, Glover	9103	1	2	3	4	5	6	11	8	9	10				7				
9	Oct	7	West Ham United	1-3	Glover	23481	1	2	3	4	5	6	11	8	9	10				7				
10		14	PLYMOUTH ARGYLE	5-1	Glover(2),Jennings,Dyson,Bestall	8394	1	2	3	4	5	6	11	8	9	10				7				
11		21	Notts County	2-1	Glover(2)	16890	1	2	3	4	5	6	11	8	9	10				7				
12		28	SWANSEA TOWN	3-1	Jennings, Bestall, Craven	6378	1	2	3	4	5	6	11	8	9	10				7				
13	Nov	4	Millwall	1-0	Ponting	10931		2	3	4	5	6	11	8		10		1		7		9		
14		11	LINCOLN CITY	3-0	Glover, Craven(2)	11791		2	3	4	5	6	11	8	9	10	7	1						
15		18	Bury	3-1	Glover(2), Jennings	8693		2	3	4	5	6	7	8	9	10		1					11	
16		25	HULL CITY	4-1	Glover(2), Craven, Holmes	16631		2	3	4	5	6	7	8	9	10		1					11	
17	Dec	2	Fulham	0-1		14650		2	3	4	5	6	7	8	9	10		1					11	
18		9	SOUTHAMPTON	3-1	Glover, Bestall, Jennings	8604		2	3	4	5	6	7	8	9	10		1					11	
19		16	Blackpool	4-3	Jennings, Holmes, Bestall(2)	15332		2	3	4	5	6	7	8	9	10		1					11	
20		23	BRADFORD CITY	1-4	Glover	10353		2	3	4	5	6	7	8	9	10		1					11	
21		25	Manchester United	3-1	Glover(3)	29443		2	3	4	5	6	7	8	9	10		1					11	
22		26	MANCHESTER UNITED	7-3	Holmes,Glover(2),Jennings,Bestall(2),Craven	15801		2	3	4	5	6	7	8	9	10		1					11	
23		30	Burnley	0-2		9598		2	3	4	5	6	7	8	9	10		1					11	
24	Jan	6	OLDHAM ATHLETIC	2-1	Glover,Craven	9071		2	3	4	5	6	7	8	9	10		1					11	
25		20	Preston North End	2-1	Glover(2)	24312	1	2	3	4	5	6	7	8	9	10							11	
26		30	BRADFORD P.A.	3-2	Glover(2), Craven	7486	1	2	3	4	5	6	7	8	9	10							11	
27	Feb	5	Port Vale	1-0	Craven	12662	1	2	3	4	5	6	7	8	9	10							11	
28		10	Nottingham Forest	2-4	Holmes, Glover	12230	1	2	3	4	5	6	7	8	9	10							11	
29		17	WEST HAM UNITED	1-1	Glover	10627	1	2	3	4	5	6	7	8	9	10							11	
30		24	Plymouth Argyle	2-0	Glover, Craven	18301	1	2	3	4	5	6	11	8	9	10				7				
31	Mar	3	NOTTS COUNTY	2-2	Jennings, Kelly(pen)	10918	1	2	3	4	5	6	11	8	9	10				7				
32		10	Swansea Town	1-1	Bestall	10029	1	2	3	4	5	6	11	8	9	10			7					
33		17	MILLWALL	5-2	Craven, Glover(3), Kelly(pen)	8101	1	2	3	4	5	6	11	8	9	10			7					
34		24	Lincoln City	3-3	Craven(2), Kelly(pen)	8723	1	2	3	4	5	6	11	8	9	10					7			
35		30	BRENTFORD	2-2	Craven, Glover	23233	1	2	3	4	5	6	11	8	9	10					7			
36		31	BURY	2-0	Dyson, Glover	10975	1	2	3	4	5	6	11	8	9	10				7				
37	Apr	2	Brentford	2-1	Moralee, Glover	26934	1	2	3	4	5	6		8	9	10				7				11
38		7	Hull City	1-0	Ponting	20077	1	2	3	4	5	6	11	8		10				7		9		
39		14	FULHAM	3-1	Craven, Glover, Lewis	9340	1	2	3	4	5	6	11	8	9	10					7			
40		21	Southampton	2-4	Jennings(2)	8843	1	2	3	4	5	6	11	8	9	10					7			
41		28	BLACKPOOL	7-0	Holmes(3),Craven(2),Moralee,Jennings	7090	1	2	3	4	5	6	7	8		10							9	11
42	May	5	Bradford City	1-2	Glover	8571	1	2	3	4	5	6	11	8	9	10					7			
						Apps.	30	42	42	42	42	42	41	42	39	42	8	12	2	11	5	2	16	2
						Goals		3					13	11	42	18	1			3	1	2	7	2

F.A. Cup

							Read	Kelly	Jacobson	Hall	Betmead	Buck	Jennings	Bestall	Glover	Craven	Dodds	Tweedy	Waring	Dyson	Lewis	Ponting	Holmes	Moralee
R3	Jan	13	CLAPTON ORIENT	1-0	Glover	13500		2	3	4	5	6	7	8	9	10		1					11	
R4		27	Portsmouth	0-2		34565	1	2	3	4	5	6	7	8	9	10							11	

		P	W	D	L	F	A	W	D	L	F	A	F	A	Pts
1	GRIMSBY TOWN	42	15	3	3	62	28	12	2	7	41	31	103	59	59
2	Preston North End	42	15	3	3	47	20	8	3	10	24	32	71	52	52
3	Bolton Wanderers	42	14	2	5	45	22	7	7	7	34	33	79	55	51
4	Brentford	42	15	2	4	52	24	7	5	9	33	36	85	60	51
5	Bradford Park Ave.	42	16	2	3	63	27	7	1	13	23	40	86	67	49
6	Bradford City	42	14	4	3	46	25	6	2	13	27	42	73	67	46
7	West Ham United	42	13	3	5	51	28	4	8	9	27	42	78	70	45
8	Port Vale	42	14	4	3	39	14	5	3	13	21	41	60	55	45
9	Oldham Athletic	42	12	5	4	48	28	5	5	11	24	32	72	60	44
10	Plymouth Argyle	42	12	7	2	43	20	3	6	12	26	50	69	70	43
11	Blackpool	42	10	8	3	39	27	5	5	11	23	37	62	64	43
12	Bury	42	12	4	5	43	31	5	5	11	27	42	70	73	43
13	Burnley	42	14	2	5	40	29	4	4	13	20	43	60	72	42
14	Southampton	42	15	2	4	40	21	0	6	15	14	37	54	58	38
15	Hull City	42	11	4	6	33	20	2	8	11	19	48	52	68	38
16	Fulham	42	13	3	5	29	17	2	4	15	19	50	48	67	37
17	Nottingham Forest	42	11	4	6	50	27	2	5	14	23	47	73	74	35
18	Notts County	42	9	7	5	32	22	3	4	14	21	40	53	62	35
19	Swansea Town	42	10	9	2	36	19	0	6	15	15	41	51	60	35
20	Manchester United	42	9	3	9	29	33	5	3	13	30	52	59	85	34
21	Millwall	42	8	8	5	21	17	3	3	15	18	51	39	68	33
22	Lincoln City	42	7	7	7	31	23	2	1	18	13	52	44	75	26

SEASON 1933/34
Back: Hooton (Sec), Hodgson, Kelly, Tweedy, Read, Jacobson, Ponting, Womack (Manager)
Middle: Dyson, Moralee, Bestall, Glover, Craven, Jennings, Dodds
Front: Hall, Betmead, Buck

SEASON 1934/35
Back: Annables, Rogers, Kelly, Jacobson, Wright, Wattam, Holden (Asst.Trainer)
Middle (standing): Hooton (Sec), Atherton (Trainer), Vincent, Dodsworth, Tweedy, Theacker, Read, Tomlinson, Ferrier, Hinchliffe, Womack (Manager)
Middle (seated): Moralee, Dyson, Ponting, Bestall, Glover, Craven, Jennings, Dodds, Swain
Front: Lewis, Waring, Hodgson, Betmead, Buck, Hall

1934-35 5th in Division 1

Captain: Jackie Bestall

							Tweedy	Kelly	Jacobson	Hall	Betmead	Buck	Lewis	Bestall	Glover	Craven	Jennings	Vincent	Wright J	Hodgson	Dyson	Moralee	Burley	Holmes	Annables
1	Aug	25	Preston North End	0-1		26805	1	2	3	4	5	6	7	8	9	10	11								
2		28	SUNDERLAND	0-0		15604	1	2	3	4		6	7	8	9	10	11			5					
3	Sep	1	PORTSMOUTH	3-0	Glover(2), Bestall	14552	1	2	3	4		6		8	9	10	7			5			11		
4		5	Sunderland	0-3		27753	1	2	3	4		6		8	9	10	7			5			11		
5		8	EVERTON	0-0		16343	1	2	3	4	5	6		8	9	10	7						11		
6		15	Huddersfield Town	5-1	Jennings, Glover(4)	10011	1	2	3	4	5	6		8	9	10	7						11		
7		22	WOLVERHAMPTON WANDS.	2-1	Burley, Bestall	9594	1	2	3	4	5	6		8	9	10	7						11		
8		29	Chelsea	0-2		25373	1	2	3	4	5	6		8	9	10	7						11		
9	Oct	6	ASTON VILLA	5-1	Craven(3), Burley, Glover	17732	1	2	3	4	5	6		8	9	10					7		11		
10		13	Derby County	4-1	Bestall, Glover(3)	21139	1	2	3	4	5	6		8	9	10					7		11		
11		20	Liverpool	1-1	Dyson	28047	1	2	3	4	5	6		8	9	10					7		11		
12		27	LEEDS UNITED	3-2	Glover(2), Craven	10940	1	2	3	4	5	6		8	9	10					7		11		
13	Nov	3	Blackburn Rovers	2-2	Glover, Craven	13308	1	2	3	4	5	6		8	9	10					7		11		
14		10	ARSENAL	2-2	Burley, Glover(pen)	26288	1	2	3	4	5	6		8	9	10					7		11		
15		17	Birmingham	2-3	Craven(2)	18604	1	2	3	4	5	6		8	9	10					7		11		
16		24	STOKE CITY	3-1	Glover(2), Dyson	14656	1	2	3	4	5	6		8	9	10					7		11		
17	Dec	1	Manchester City	0-1		31642	1	2	3	4	5	6		8	9	10					7		11		
18		8	MIDDLESBROUGH	2-2	Dyson, Betmead	12174	1	2	3	4	5	6		8	9	10	11				7				
19		15	West Bromwich Albion	2-4	Glover(2)	17262	1	2	3	4	5	6		8	9	10					7		11		
20		22	SHEFFIELD WEDNESDAY	3-1	Craven, Dyson, Glover	10438	1	2		4	5	6		8	9	10			3		7		11		
21		25	TOTTENHAM HOTSPUR	3-0	Craven, Buck, Glover	19706	1	2		4	5	6		8	9	10			3		7		11		
22		26	Tottenham Hotspur	1-2	Glover	45512	1	2		4	5	6		8	9	10	11		3		7				
23		29	PRESTON NORTH END	3-1	Jennings, Moralee, Glover	10007	1	2		4		6		8	9		11		3	5	7	10			
24	Jan	5	Portsmouth	0-1		18821	1	2		4		6		8	9	10	11		3	5	7				
25		19	Everton	1-3	Craven	24493	1	3		4	5	6		8	9	10	11	2			7				
26	Feb	2	Wolverhampton Wands.	3-0	Burley, Craven, Glover	21383	1	3		4	5	6			9	8		2			7	10	11		
27		9	CHELSEA	3-1	Bestall, Holmes, Glover(pen)	12442	1	3		4	5	6		8	9	10		2			7			11	
28		16	Aston Villa	2-3	Glover(2)	32020	1	3		4	5	6		8	9	10		2			7			11	
29		23	DERBY COUNTY	1-3	Dyson	12742	1	3		4	5	6		8	9	10		2			7	11			
30	Mar	2	LIVERPOOL	3-2	Burley, Glover(2)	10691	1	3		4	5	6		8	9	10		2			7		11		
31		9	Leeds United	1-3	Glover(pen)	15458	1	3		4		6		8	9	10		2		5	7		11		
32		16	BLACKBURN ROVERS	1-2	Glover	10778	1	3		4	5	6		8	9	10		2			7		11		
33		23	Arsenal	1-1	Glover	33591	1	3		4		6		8	9	10	11	2		5	7				
34		30	BIRMINGHAM	4-3	Glover(2), Dyson(2)	9837	1			4		6		8	9	10	3	2		5	7			11	
35	Apr	2	HUDDERSFIELD TOWN	1-1	Glover	8073	1			4		6		8	9	10	3	2		5	7			11	
36		6	Stoke City	0-0		13442	1			4		6		8	9	10		2		5	7	11			3
37		13	MANCHESTER CITY	1-1	Moralee	13394	1			4		6		8	9	10		2		5	7	11			3
38		19	LEICESTER CITY	3-1	Craven(2), Dyson	19531	1			4		6		8	9	10		2		5	7	11			3
39		20	Middlesbrough	2-0	Lewis, Craven	12124	1			4		6	7	8	9	10		2		5		11			3
40		22	Leicester City	2-2	Craven(2)	25195	1		2	4		6	7	8	9	10	3			5		11			
41	May	1	WEST BROMWICH ALBION	3-0	Craven(2), Bestall	12304	1		3	4		6	7	8	9	10		2		5		11			
42		4	Sheffield Wednesday	1-0		21046	1		3	4		6	7	8	9	10		2		5		11			
						Apps.	42	33	22	42	26	42	6	41	42	41	17	17	5	16	30	10	22	4	4
						Goals					1	1	1	5	34	18	2				8	2	5	1	

F.A. Cup

							Tweedy	Kelly	Jacobson	Hall	Betmead	Buck	Lewis	Bestall	Glover	Craven	Jennings	Vincent	Wright J	Hodgson	Dyson	Moralee	Burley	Holmes	Annables
R3	Jan	12	Everton	3-6	Glover(2), Graven	44850	1	2		4		6		8	9	10	11		3	5	7				

	P	W	D	L	F	A	W	D	L	F	A	F	A	Pts
1 Arsenal	42	15	4	2	74	17	8	8	5	41	29	115	46	58
2 Sunderland	42	13	4	4	57	24	6	12	3	33	27	90	51	54
3 Sheffield Wed.	42	14	7	0	42	17	4	6	11	28	47	70	64	49
4 Manchester City	42	13	5	3	53	25	7	3	11	29	42	82	67	48
5 GRIMSBY TOWN	42	13	6	2	49	25	4	5	12	29	35	78	60	45
6 Derby County	42	10	4	7	44	28	8	5	8	37	38	81	66	45
7 Liverpool	42	13	4	4	53	29	6	3	12	32	59	85	88	45
8 Everton	42	14	5	2	64	32	2	7	12	25	56	89	88	44
9 West Bromwich Alb.	42	10	8	3	55	33	7	2	12	28	50	83	83	44
10 Stoke City	42	12	5	4	46	20	6	1	14	25	50	71	70	42
11 Preston North End	42	11	5	5	33	22	4	7	10	29	45	62	67	42
12 Chelsea	42	11	5	5	49	32	5	4	12	24	50	73	82	41
13 Aston Villa	42	11	6	4	50	36	3	7	11	24	52	74	88	41
14 Portsmouth	42	10	5	6	41	24	5	5	11	30	48	71	72	40
15 Blackburn Rovers	42	12	5	4	42	23	2	6	13	24	55	66	78	39
16 Huddersfield Town	42	11	5	5	52	27	3	5	13	24	44	76	71	38
17 Wolverhampton W.	42	13	3	5	65	38	2	5	14	23	56	88	94	38
18 Leeds United	42	10	6	5	48	35	3	6	12	27	57	75	92	38
19 Birmingham	42	10	3	8	36	36	3	7	11	27	45	63	81	36
20 Middlesbrough	42	8	9	4	38	29	2	5	14	32	61	70	90	34
21 Leicester City	42	9	4	8	39	30	3	5	13	22	56	61	86	33
22 Tottenham Hotspur	42	8	8	5	34	31	2	2	17	20	62	54	93	30

1935-36 17th in Division 1

Captain: Jackie Bestall

							Tweedy	Vincent	Kelly	Hall	Hodgson	Buck	Dyson	Bestall	Glover	Craven	Moralee	Betmead	Jennings	Baldry	Lewis	Ponting	Smailes	Tomlinson	Robertson	Theaker	Crack
1	Aug	31	Blackburn Rovers	0-1		14035	1	2	3	4	5	6	7	8	9	10	11										
2	Sep	3	ARSENAL	1-0	Craven	25978	1	2	3	4	5	6	7	8	9	10	11										
3		7	CHELSEA	1-3	Moralee	14917	1	2	3	4	5	6	7	8	9	10	11										
4		11	Arsenal	0-6		33633	1	2	3	4		6	7	8		10	11	5				9					
5		14	Liverpool	2-7	Craven, Dyson	24180	1	2	3	4	5	6	7	8		10			11			9					
6		21	BOLTON WANDERERS	3-1	Glover(2,1pen), Craven	12768	1	2	3	4		6		8	9	10		5	7				11				
7		28	LEEDS UNITED	0-1		11236	1	2	3	4		6		8	9	10		5	7				11				
8	Oct	5	West Bromwich Albion	1-4	Ponting	20821	1	2	3	4		6		8	9	10		5	7				11				
9		12	SUNDERLAND	4-0	Glover(3), Craven	11751	1	2		4	3	6		8	9	10		5	7				11				
10		19	Huddersfield Town	0-1		10687	1	2		4	3	6		8	9	10		5	7				11				
11		26	MIDDLESBROUGH	0-1		12108	1	2		4	3	6	8	11	9	10		5	7								
12	Nov	2	Aston Villa	6-2	Glover(4), Dyson, Craven	35311	1	2		4	3	6	7	8	9	10		5	11								
13		9	WOLVERHAMPTON WANDS.	2-1	Dyson, Glover	10207	1	2		4	3	6	7	8	9	10		5	11								
14		16	Sheffield Wednesday	0-3		19376	1	2		4	3	6	7	8	9	10		5	11								
15		23	EVERTON	0-4		10247	1	2		4	3	6	7		9	8	10	5	11								
16		30	Preston North End	0-1		17103	1	2		4	3	6		11	9	8	10	5		7							
17	Dec	7	BRENTFORD	6-1	Glover(3,1p),Baldry,Craven(2)	5276	1	2		4	3	6		8	9	10		5		7	11						
18		14	Derby County	0-2		17113	1	2		4	3	6		8	9	10		5		7	11						
19		21	PORTSMOUTH	1-2	Glover	7772	1	2		4	3	6		8	9	10		5		7	11						
20		25	BIRMINGHAM	1-0	Baldry	11810	1	2		4	3	6		8	9	10		5		7	11						
21		26	Birmingham	1-1	Baldry	28978	1	2		4	3	6		8		10		5		7	11	9					
22		28	BLACKBURN ROVERS	1-1	Lewis	8068	1	2		4	3	6		8		10		5	9	7	11						
23	Jan	1	Manchester City	3-0	Craven(2), Lewis	32470	1		2	4	3	6		8		10		5	7		11	9					
24		4	Chelsea	2-0	Lewis, Baldry	30381	1		2	4	3	6		8	9	10		5		7	11						
25		18	LIVERPOOL	0-0		9289	1		2	4	3	6		8	9	10		5		7	11						
26		29	Bolton Wanderers	0-4		10068	1		2	4	3	6		8	9	10		5		7	11						
27	Feb	1	Leeds United	2-1	Glover, Baldry	24212	1		2	4	3	6		8	9	10		5		7	11						
28		8	WEST BROMWICH ALBION	4-2	Lewis, Baldry, Glover(2)	11122	1		2	4	3	6		8	9	10		5		7	11						
29		19	Sunderland	1-3	Glover(pen)	12108	1		2	4	3	6		8	9	10				7			11		5		
30		22	HUDDERSFIELD TOWN	1-1	Glover(pen)	10994	1		2	4	3	6		8	9	10		5		7			11				
31	Mar	4	Wolverhampton Wands.	0-1		8633	1		2	4	3	6		8		10		5		7			11	9			
32		7	PRESTON NORTH END	0-0		9172			2	4	3	6		8		10		5		7			11	9		1	
33		14	Middlesbrough	1-5	Tomlinson	14174	1		2	4	3	6		8		10		5		7			11	9			
34		24	SHEFFIELD WEDNESDAY	4-0	Bestall, Craven(2), Glover	7887	1	2	3	4	5	6	7	8	9	10	11										
35		28	Everton	0-4		24720	1	2	3	4	5	6	7	8	9	10	11										
36	Apr	4	ASTON VILLA	4-1	Callaghan(OG),Glover(2,1p),Baldry	10413	1		2	4	3	6		8	9	10		5		7	11						
37		10	STOKE CITY	3-0	Glover(2), Craven	19575	1		2	4	3	6		8	9	10	11	5		7							
38		11	Brentford	0-3		24830	1		2	4	3	6		8	9	10	11	5		7							
39		13	Stoke City	0-1		22882	1		2	4	3	6	7	8	9	10		5			11						
40		18	DERBY COUNTY	4-1	Glover(3), Bestall	11860	1		2	4	3	6	7	8	9	10		5			11						
41		25	Portsmouth	2-3	Glover, Craven	8918	1		2	4	3	6	7	8	9	10		5			11						
42	May	2	MANCHESTER CITY	3-1	Craven, Glover(2,1pen)	8974	1		2	4	3	6		8	9	10		5			7						11
						Apps.	41	24	28	42	38	42	15	41	34	42	10	35	13	20	17	4	10	3	1	1	1
						Goals							3	2	31	14	1			7	4	1		1			

1 own goal

F.A. Cup

							Tweedy	Vincent	Kelly	Hall	Hodgson	Buck	Dyson	Bestall	Glover	Craven	Moralee	Betmead	Jennings	Baldry	Lewis	Ponting	Smailes	Tomlinson	Robertson	Theaker	Crack
R3	Jan	11	Hartlepools United	0-0		15064	1		2	4	3	6		8	9	10		5		7	11						
R3r		14	HARTLEPOOLS UNITED	4-1	Buck, Bestall, Glover(2)	11500	1		2	4	3	6		8	9	10		5		7	11						
R4		25	Port Vale	4-0	Baldry(2), Bestall, Craven	13350	1		2	4	3	6		8	9	10		5		7	11						
R5	Feb	15	MANCHESTER CITY	3-2	Lewis(2), Glover	25997	1		2	4	3	6		8	9	10		5		7	11						
R6		29	MIDDLESBROUGH	3-1	Glover, Craven, Smailes	21000	1		2	4	3	6		8	9	10		5		7			11				
SF	Mar	21	Arsenal *	0-1		63210	1	2	3	4	5	6		8	9	10				7			11				

* Played at Leeds Road, Huddersfield.

		P	W	D	L	F	A	W	D	L	F	A	F	A	Pts
1	Sunderland	42	17	2	2	71	33	8	4	9	38	41	109	74	56
2	Derby County	42	13	5	3	43	23	5	7	9	18	29	61	52	48
3	Huddersfield Town	42	12	7	2	32	15	6	5	10	27	41	59	56	48
4	Stoke City	42	13	3	5	35	24	7	4	10	22	33	57	57	47
5	Brentford	42	11	5	5	48	25	6	7	8	33	35	81	60	46
6	Arsenal	42	9	9	3	44	22	6	6	9	34	26	78	48	45
7	Preston North End	42	15	3	3	44	18	3	5	13	23	46	67	64	44
8	Chelsea	42	11	7	3	39	27	4	6	11	26	45	65	72	43
9	Manchester City	42	13	2	6	44	17	4	6	11	24	43	68	60	42
10	Portsmouth	42	14	4	3	39	22	3	4	14	15	45	54	67	42
11	Leeds United	42	11	5	5	41	23	4	6	11	25	41	66	64	41
12	Birmingham	42	10	6	5	38	31	5	5	11	23	32	61	63	41
13	Bolton Wanderers	42	11	4	6	41	27	3	9	9	26	49	67	76	41
14	Middlesbrough	42	12	6	3	56	23	3	4	14	28	47	84	70	40
15	Wolverhampton W.	42	13	7	1	59	28	2	3	16	18	48	77	76	40
16	Everton	42	12	5	4	61	31	1	8	12	28	58	89	89	39
17	GRIMSBY TOWN	42	13	4	4	44	20	4	1	16	21	53	65	73	39
18	West Bromwich Alb.	42	12	3	6	54	31	4	3	14	35	57	89	88	38
19	Liverpool	42	11	4	6	43	23	2	8	11	17	41	60	64	38
20	Sheffield Wed.	42	9	8	4	35	23	4	4	13	28	54	63	77	38
21	Aston Villa	42	7	6	8	47	56	6	3	12	34	54	81	110	35
22	Blackburn Rovers	42	10	6	5	32	24	2	3	16	23	72	55	96	33

SEASON 1935/36
Back: Hall, Vincent, Tweedy, Betmead, Buck, Kelly
Front: Dyson, Bestall, Glover, Craven, Lewis

SEASON 1936/37
Back: Atherton (Train), Vincent, Robinson, Swain, Holden (Asst Train)
Middle (standing): Lumby, Wattam, Tweedy, Theaker, Hinchcliffe, Tomlinson, Moralee
Middle (seated): Hodgson, Dyson, Bestall, Glover, Craven Lewis, Kelly
Front: Hall, Whitaker, Betmead, Robertson, Buck

1936-37 12th in Division 1

Captain: Jackie Bestall

			Opponent	Score	Scorers	Att.	Tweedy	Kelly	Hodgson	Hall	Betmead	Buck	Dyson	Bestall	Glover	Craven	Lewis	Robertson	Vincent	Wattam	Quigley	Hinchcliffe	Tomlinson	Swain	Crack	Robinson
1	Aug	29	CHARLTON ATHLETIC	0-1		12696	1	2	3	4	5	6	7	8	9	10	11									
2	Sep	3	Chelsea	2-3	Lewis, Glover	25671	1	2	3	4	5		7	8	9	10	11			6						
3		5	Bolton Wanderers	2-1	Craven, Glover	21207	1	2	3	4	5		7	8	9	10	11			6						
4		8	CHELSEA	3-0	Craven, Lewis, Dyson	12667	1	2	3	4	5		7	8	9	10	11			6						
5		12	Liverpool	1-7	Craven	20972	1	2	3	4	5		7	8	9	10	11			6						
6		14	Stoke City	0-2		18332	1		3	4	5		7	8	9	10	11	2		6						
7		19	LEEDS UNITED	4-1	Lewis, Dyson, Glover(2)	11217	1	2	3	4	5		7	8	9	10	11			6						
8		26	Birmingham	3-2	Lewis, Craven, Glover(pen)	21985	1	2	3	4	5		7	8	9	10	11			6						
9	Oct	3	MIDDLESBROUGH	5-1	Dyson, Glover(4)	13073	1	2	3	4	5		7	8	9	10	11			6						
10		10	West Bromwich Albion	2-4	Lewis(2)	24447	1	2	3	4	5		7	8	9	10	11			6						
11		17	BRENTFORD	2-0	Lewis, Craven	11858	1	2	3	4	5		7	8		10	11			6			9			
12		24	Arsenal	0-0		51202	1	2	3	4	5		7	8	9	10	11			6						
13		31	PRESTON NORTH END	6-4	Lewis(4), Dyson, Craven	12341	1	2	3	4	5		7	8	9	10	11			6						
14	Nov	7	Sheffield Wednesday	0-2		19636	1	2	3	4	5		7	8	9					6		10		11		
15		14	MANCHESTER UNITED	6-2	Lewis(3),Bestall,Glover,Craven	9844	1	2	3	4	5		7	8	9	10	11			6						
16		21	Derby County	1-3	Dyson	17504	1	2	3	4	5		7	8	9	10	11			6						
17		28	WOLVERHAMPTON WANDS.	1-1	Lewis	10776	1	2	3	4	5		7	8	9	10	11			6						
18	Dec	5	Sunderland	1-5	Glover	25040	1	2	3		5	4	7	8	9	10	11			6						
19		12	HUDDERSFIELD TOWN	2-2	Glover(pen), Craven	8580	1	2	3		5	4	7		9	10	11			6		8				
20		19	Everton	0-3		21616	1	3	5			6	7	8	9	10	11		2	4						
21		25	MANCHESTER CITY	5-3	Lewis(2), Glover(2), Craven	17921	1	3		4	5	6	7	8	9	10	11		2							
22		26	Charlton Athletic	0-1		30733	1	3	5	4	9	6	7	8		10	11		2							
23		28	Manchester City	1-1	Lewis	16146	1	3		4	5	6	7	8	9	10	11		2							
24	Jan	2	BOLTON WANDERERS	3-1	Bestall, Dyson, Glover	9719	1	3		4	5	6	7	8	9	10	11		2							
25		9	LIVERPOOL	2-1	Glover, Hobson(OG)	10015	1	3		4	5	6	7	8	9	10	11		2							
26		23	Leeds United	0-2		11752	1	2	5	4		6	7	8	9	10	11									3
27	Feb	2	BIRMINGHAM	1-1	Lewis	6773	1	3	5	4		6	7		9	8	11		2			10				
28		6	Middlesbrough	0-0		20457	1	2	5	4		6	7	8	9	10	11									3
29		13	WEST BROMWICH ALBION	2-3	Glover, Swain	9898	1	2		4	5	6	7	8	9	10								11		3
30		27	ARSENAL	1-3	Craven	18216	1	2	3	4	5	6	7	8	9	10	11									
31	Mar	3	Brentford	3-2	Betmead, Glover(2)	14103	1	2	3	4	5	6	8		9	10					7				11	
32		10	Preston North End	2-3	Glover, Buck	9557	1	2	3	4	5	6	8		9	10					7				11	
33		13	SHEFFIELD WEDNESDAY	5-1	Bestall,Craven,Glover,Crack(2)	9978	1		3	4	5	6		8	9	10			2		7				11	
34		20	Manchester United	1-1	Crack	26636	1		3	4	5	6		8	9	10			2		7				11	
35		26	PORTSMOUTH	1-0	Craven	18141	1	2	3	4	5	6	8		9	10					7				11	
36		27	DERBY COUNTY	3-4	Craven(2), Crack	13418	1	2	3		5	6	4	8	9	10	7								11	
37		29	Portsmouth	1-2	Dyson	21219	1	2	3	4	5	6	7		9	10	11					8				
38	Apr	3	Wolverhampton Wands.	2-5	Dyson, Hinchcliffe	16413	1	2	3	4	5	6	7		9	10						8			11	
39		12	SUNDERLAND	6-0	Glover(5), Swain	8306	1	2	3	4	5	6	8		9	10					7			11		
40		17	Huddersfield Town	3-0	Glover(2), Craven	6189	1	2	3	4	5	6	8		9	10					7			11		
41		24	EVERTON	1-0	Glover	9773	1	2	3	4	5	6	8		9	10					7			11		
42	May	1	STOKE CITY	1-3	Swain	6585	1	2	3	4	5	6	8		9	10					7			11		
						Apps.	42	39	37	38	38	26	40	31	40	41	30	1	9	19	9	5	1	6	7	3
						Goals					1	1	9	3	29	15	19					1		3	4	

F.A. Cup

			Opponent	Score	Scorers	Att.	Tweedy	Kelly	Hodgson	Hall	Betmead	Buck	Dyson	Bestall	Glover	Craven	Lewis	Robertson	Vincent	Wattam	Quigley	Hinchcliffe	Tomlinson	Swain	Crack	Robinson
R3	Jan	16	Cardiff City	3-1	Glover, Craven, Lewis	36245	1	3	5	4		6	7	8	9	10	11		2							
R4		30	WALSALL	5-1	Buck, Glover(3), Lewis	11000	1	3	5	4		6	7	8	9	10	11		2							
R5	Feb	20	WOLVERHAMPTON WANDS.	1-1	Craven	31651	1	2	3	4	5	6	7	8	9	10	11									
R5r		24	Wolverhampton Wands.	2-6	Craven, Lewis	56799	1	2	3	4	5	6	7	8	9	10	11									

		P	W	D	L	F	A	W	D	L	F	A	F	A	Pts
1	Manchester City	42	15	5	1	56	22	7	8	6	51	39	107	61	57
2	Charlton Athletic	42	15	5	1	37	13	6	7	8	21	36	58	49	54
3	Arsenal	42	10	10	1	43	20	8	6	7	37	29	80	49	52
4	Derby County	42	13	3	5	58	39	8	4	9	38	51	96	90	49
5	Wolverhampton W.	42	16	2	3	63	24	5	3	13	21	43	84	67	47
6	Brentford	42	14	5	2	58	32	4	5	12	24	46	82	78	46
7	Middlesbrough	42	14	6	1	49	22	5	2	14	25	49	74	71	46
8	Sunderland	42	17	2	2	59	24	2	4	15	30	63	89	87	44
9	Portsmouth	42	13	3	5	41	29	4	7	10	21	37	62	66	44
10	Stoke City	42	12	6	3	52	27	3	6	12	20	30	72	57	42
11	Birmingham	42	9	7	5	36	24	4	8	9	28	36	64	60	41
12	GRIMSBY TOWN	42	13	3	5	60	32	4	4	13	26	49	86	81	41
13	Chelsea	42	11	6	4	36	21	3	7	11	16	34	52	55	41
14	Preston North End	42	10	6	5	35	28	4	7	10	21	39	56	67	41
15	Huddersfield Town	42	12	5	4	39	21	0	10	11	23	43	62	64	39
16	West Bromwich Alb.	42	13	3	5	45	32	3	3	15	32	66	77	98	38
17	Everton	42	12	7	2	56	23	2	2	17	25	55	81	78	37
18	Liverpool	42	9	8	4	38	26	3	3	15	24	58	62	84	35
19	Leeds United	42	14	3	4	44	20	1	1	19	16	60	60	80	34
20	Bolton Wanderers	42	6	6	9	22	33	4	8	9	21	33	43	66	34
21	Manchester United	42	8	9	4	29	26	2	3	16	26	52	55	78	32
22	Sheffield Wed.	42	8	5	8	32	29	1	7	13	21	40	53	69	30

1937-38 20th in Division 1

Captain: 'Ginger' Hall

						Tweedy	Kelly	Hodgson	Hall	Betmead	Buck	Quigley	Hinchcliffe	Glover	Craven	Swain	Vincent	Dyson	Shaw J	Robertson	Theaker	Lewis	Bestall	Beattie	Tomlinson	Lumby	Gallacher	Coulter	Crack	Shaw H
1	Aug 28	Preston North End	1-4	Swain	22098	1	2	3	4	5	6	7	8	9	10	11														
2	31	CHARLTON ATHLETIC	1-1	Buck	13347	1	2	3	4	5	6	7			10	11		8							9					
3	Sep 4	BOLTON WANDERERS	0-1		10642	1		3	4	5	6				10	11	2	7					8		9					
4	6	Charlton Athletic	0-0		16471	1	5	3	4		6		10		9		2	7					8						11	
5	11	LEEDS UNITED	1-1	Craven	9328	1	5	3	4	9	6		10		8		2	7											11	
6	15	Chelsea	0-1		15617	1		3	4	5	6		10		9		2	7					8						11	
7	18	Liverpool	1-2	Hinchcliffe	26350	1		3	4	5	6		10		7	11	2						8		9					
8	25	WEST BROMWICH ALBION	1-4	Quigley	9410	1		3	4	5	6	7	10		8	11	2								9					
9	Oct 2	Birmingham	2-2	Craven(2)	25644	1		3	4	5	6		8		10		2	7					11		9					
10	9	MIDDLESBROUGH	2-1	Hinchcliffe, Craven	10569	1	2	3	4	5	6		8		10			7					11		9					
11	16	Huddersfield Town	2-1	Craven, Coulter	15408	1		3	4	5	6		8		10		2	7							9			11		
12	23	EVERTON	2-1	Craven, Coulter	10308	1		3	4	5	6		8		10		2					7			9			11		
13	30	Wolverhampton Wands.	1-1	Craven	28032	1		3	4	5	6		8		10		2					7			9			11		
14	Nov 6	ARSENAL	2-1	Hinchcliffe, Coulter	20244	1		3	4	5	6		8		10		2	7							9			11		
15	13	Sunderland	2-2	Dyson, Coulter	23171	1		3	4	5	6		8		10		2	7							9			11		
16	20	BRENTFORD	0-1		13206	1		3	4	5	6		8		10		2	7							9			11		
17	27	Manchester City	1-3	Coulter	27526	1		3	4	5	6		8		10		2					7			9			11		
18	Dec 4	LEICESTER CITY	2-1	Tomlinson, Lewis	8246	1		3	4	5	6		8		10		2					7			9			11		
19	11	Blackpool	2-2	Coulter, Craven	12880	1		3	4	5	6		8		10		2						7		9			11		
20	18	DERBY COUNTY	0-0		8649	1		3	4	5	6		8		10		2						7		9			11		
21	25	STOKE CITY	1-5	Coulter	17673	1		3	4	5	6		8		10		2						7			9		11		
22	27	Stoke City	1-1	Craven	34114	1	2			5	6	7			8	10	3	4								9		11		
23	Jan 1	PRESTON NORTH END	1-1	Lewis	9427	1		3		5	6	7			8		2	4				11				9		10		
24	15	Bolton Wanderers	1-3	Hinchcliffe	14342	1		3	4	5	6	7	9		10		2						8					11		
25	26	Leeds United	1-1	Craven	10512	1		3		5	6		8		10		2		4								9	11		7
26	29	LIVERPOOL	0-0		9750	1		3		5	6		8		10		2		4								9	11		7
27	Feb 5	West Bromwich Albion	1-2	Hall	20067			3	8	5	6				10		2		4		1						9	11		7
28	12	BIRMINGHAM	4-0	Coulter,H.Shaw,Beattie,Betmead	9256			3	4	5	6				10		2				1			8			9	11		7
29	19	Middlesbrough	0-1		20156	1		3	4	5	6				10		2							8			9	11		7
30	26	HUDDERSFIELD TOWN	4-2	Craven, H.Shaw, Gallacher(2)	12085	1	2	3	4	5	6				10									8			9	11		7
31	Mar 5	Everton	2-3	Coulter, Gallacher	35637	1	2	3	4	5	6				10									8			9	11		7
32	12	WOLVERHAMPTON WANDS.	1-0	Coulter	17259	1		3	4	5	6				10		2							8			9	11		7
33	19	Arsenal	1-5	Coulter	40701	1		3	4	5	6				10		2							8			9	11		7
34	29	SUNDERLAND	0-2		11393	1		3	4	5	6				10		2							8			9	11		7
35	Apr 2	Brentford	1-6	Craven	17994	1		3	4	5	6				10		2							8			9	11		7
36	9	MANCHESTER CITY	3-1	Glover(2), Quigley	11413	1		3	4	5	6	7		9	10		2							8					11	
37	15	PORTSMOUTH	1-0	Glover	21197	1		3	4	5	6	7		9	10		2							8					11	
38	16	Leicester City	0-1		16733	1		3	4		6	7		9	10		2			5		11	8							
39	18	Portsmouth	0-3		30616	1		3	4		6				10		2			5		7		8			9		11	
40	23	BLACKPOOL	1-0	Lewis	10042	1		3	4		6	7		9	10		2			5		11		8						
41	30	Derby County	2-1	Hodgson, Lewis	8035	1		3	4	5	6	7		9	10		2					11		8						
42	May 7	CHELSEA	2-0	Beattie, Glover	14601	1		3	4	5	6	7		9	10		2					11		8						
					Apps.	40	8	41	38	38	42	12	22	7	42	6	37	13	3	3	2	10	11	14	16	3	12	25	6	11
					Goals			1	1	1	1	2	4	4	12	1		1				4		2	1		3	11		2

F.A. Cup

						Tweedy	Kelly	Hodgson	Hall	Betmead	Buck	Quigley	Hinchcliffe	Glover	Craven	Swain	Vincent	Dyson	Shaw J	Robertson	Theaker	Lewis	Bestall	Beattie	Tomlinson	Lumby	Gallacher	Coulter	Crack	Shaw H
R3	Jan 8	SWINDON TOWN	1-1	Tomlinson	14000	1	3	5			6		8		10		2	4					7		9			11		
R3r	12	Swindon Town *	1-2	Tomlinson	23101	1		3	4	5	6				10		2	7					8		9			11		

* a.e.t.

		P	W	D	L	F	A	W	D	L	F	A	F	A	Pts
1	Arsenal	42	15	4	2	52	16	6	6	9	25	28	77	44	52
2	Wolverhampton W.	42	11	8	2	47	21	9	3	9	25	28	72	49	51
3	Preston North End	42	9	9	3	34	21	7	8	6	30	23	64	44	49
4	Charlton Athletic	42	14	5	2	43	14	2	9	10	22	37	65	51	46
5	Middlesbrough	42	12	4	5	40	26	7	4	10	32	39	72	65	46
6	Brentford	42	10	6	5	44	27	8	3	10	25	32	69	59	45
7	Bolton Wanderers	42	11	6	4	38	22	4	9	8	26	38	64	60	45
8	Sunderland	42	12	6	3	32	18	2	10	9	23	39	55	57	44
9	Leeds United	42	11	6	4	38	26	3	9	9	26	43	64	69	43
10	Chelsea	42	11	6	4	40	22	3	7	11	25	43	65	65	41
11	Liverpool	42	9	5	7	40	30	6	6	9	25	41	65	71	41
12	Blackpool	42	10	5	6	33	26	6	3	12	28	40	61	66	40
13	Derby County	42	10	5	6	42	36	5	5	11	24	51	66	87	40
14	Everton	42	11	5	5	54	34	5	2	14	25	41	79	75	39
15	Huddersfield Town	42	11	3	7	29	24	6	2	13	26	44	55	68	39
16	Leicester City	42	9	6	6	31	26	5	5	11	23	49	54	75	39
17	Stoke City	42	10	7	4	42	21	3	5	13	16	38	58	59	38
18	Birmingham	42	7	11	3	34	28	3	7	11	24	34	58	62	38
19	Portsmouth	42	11	6	4	41	22	2	6	13	21	46	62	68	38
20	GRIMSBY TOWN	42	11	5	5	29	23	2	7	12	22	45	51	68	38
21	Manchester City	42	12	2	7	49	33	2	6	13	31	44	80	77	36
22	West Bromwich Alb.	42	10	5	6	46	36	4	3	14	28	55	74	91	36

SEASON 1937/38
Back: Vincent, J.Shaw, Theaker, Atherton (Trainer), Hodgson, Betmead
Front: Hall, H.Shaw, Gallacher, Craven, Coulter, Buck

SEASON 1938/39
Back: Shaw, Betmead, Vincent, Tweedy, Atherton (Train), Hodgson, Buck, Spencer (Man)
Middle: Boyd, Beattie, Howe, Jones, Lewis, Crack Front: Hall

1938-39 10th in Division 1

Captain: 'Ginger' Hall

						Tweedy	Vincent	Hodgson	Hall	Betmead	Buck	Boyd	Temple	Beattie	Jones	Bartholomew	Theaker	Glover	Anderson	Fisher	Taylor	Charlesworth	Shaw J	Wattam	Kurz	Howe	Swain	Crack	Lewis	Shaw H	Quigley	Moulson
1	Aug 27	ASTON VILLA	1-2	Jones	19177	1	2	3	4	5	6	7	8	9	10	11																
2	31	Everton	0-3		25017	1	2	3	4	5	6	7	8	9	10	11																
3	Sep 3	Sunderland	1-1	H.Shaw	23318	1	2	3	4	5	6	8		9	10													11		7		
4	6	PORTSMOUTH	2-1	Beattie, Boyd	11289	1	2	3	4	5	6	8		9	10												11			7		
5	10	MANCHESTER UNITED	1-0	Betmead	14077	1	2	3	4	5	6	8		9	10												11			7		
6	17	DERBY COUNTY	1-1	Swain	12451	1	2	3	4	5	6			8	10										9		11		7			
7	24	Blackpool	1-3	Beattie	27349	1	2	3	4	5	6	7		8	10										9		11					
8	Oct 1	BRENTFORD	0-0		12106		2	3	4	5	6	7		8	10		1								9		11					
9	8	Arsenal	0-2		39174		2	3	4	5	6	7		8	10		1									9	11					
10	15	Middlesbrough	2-3	Beattie, Bartholomew	21720	1	2	3	4	5	6	7		8	10	11										9						
11	22	BIRMINGHAM	1-0	Bartholomew	11022	1	2	3	4		6	7		8	10	11					5					9						
12	27	Stoke City	2-1	Howe, Boyd	19990	1	2	3	4	5	6	7		8		11										9	10					
13	Nov 5	CHELSEA	2-1	Howe, Beattie	11461	1	2	3	4	5	6	7		8		11										9	10					
14	12	Preston North End	1-1	Beattie	15506	1	2	3	4	5	6	7		8	10	11										9						
15	19	CHARLTON ATHLETIC	1-0	Bartholomew	11691	1	2	3	4	5	6	7		8	10	11										9						
16	26	Bolton Wanderers	1-1	Howe	16229	1	2	3	4	5	6	7		8	10	11										9						
17	Dec 3	LEEDS UNITED	3-2	Howe, Boyd, Beattie	11202	1	2	3	4	5	6	7		8	10	11										9						
18	10	Liverpool	2-2	Boyd, Betmead	26343	1	2	3	4	5	6	7		8	10	11										9						
19	17	LEICESTER CITY	6-1	Boyd, Howe(4), Beattie	9389	1	2	3	4	5	6	7		8	10											9			11			
20	24	Aston Villa	2-0	Lewis(2)	25195	1	2	3	4	5	6	7		8	10											9			11			
21	26	WOLVERHAMPTON WANDS.	2-4	Howe, Beattie	18655	1	2	3	4	5	6			8	10											9			11	7		
22	27	Wolverhampton Wands.	0-5		44131	1	2	3	4	5	6			8	10											9		7	11			
23	31	SUNDERLAND	1-3	Howe	11565	1	2	3	4	5	6	7		8	10											9			11			
24	Jan 14	Manchester United	1-3	Hodgson	25654	1	2	3	4	5	6	7		8	10											9			11			
25	28	BLACKPOOL	2-0	Glover, Swain	12126	1	2	3	4	5	6	7		8	10			9									11					
26	Feb 1	Derby County	1-4	Jones	11165	1	2	3	4		5	7		8	10			9					6				11					
27	4	Brentford	2-1	Jones, Bartholomew	17380	1	2		4		5	7		8	10	11		9		3			6									
28	18	MIDDLESBROUGH	0-2		11717	1	2	3	4	5	6			8	10			9										11			7	
29	21	ARSENAL	2-1	Howe, Boyd	10845	1	2	3	4	5		7		8	10								6			9		11				
30	25	Birmingham	1-1	Beattie	23231	1	2	3	4	5				8	10								6			9		11			7	
31	Mar 7	STOKE CITY	3-1	Howe(2), Crack	9452	1	2	3	4		5	7		8	10									6		9		11				
32	11	Chelsea	1-5	Boyd	17102	1	2	3	4		5	7		8	10									6		9		11				
33	18	PRESTON NORTH END	1-1	Howe	10600	1	2	3	4	5	6	7		8	10											9		11				
34	29	Charlton Athletic	1-3	Boyd	8469		2	3	4	5	6	7		8	10			1								9		11				
35	Apr 1	BOLTON WANDERERS	1-1	Jones	8558		2	3	4	5	6	7		8	10				1							9		11				
36	7	HUDDERSFIELD TOWN	3-3	Beattie, Betmead, Hall	18835	1	2	3	4	5		7		8	10			9						6		11						
37	8	Leeds United	1-0	Glover	19700	1	2	3	4	5		7		8	10			9						6		11						
38	11	Huddersfield Town	0-2		21747	1	2	3	4	5		7		8	10			9						6		11						
39	16	LIVERPOOL	2-1	Howe, Jones	6164	1	2	3	4	5	6	7		8	10											9		11				
40	19	Portsmouth	1-2	Beattie	16514	1	2	3	4		6	7		8	10							5				9		11				
41	22	Leicester City	2-0	Crack(2)	17326	1	2	3	4	5	6	7		8	10											9		11				
42	May 6	EVERTON	3-0	Glover(2), Boyd	11016	1	2	3	4	5	6	7		8	10			9										11				
					Apps.	38	42	41	42	36	37	37	2	42	40	12	2	9	1	1	1	1	4	5	3	29	10	14	7	4	2	
					Goals			1	1	3		9		11	5	4		4								15	2	3	2	1		

FAC SF: Moulson injured, replaced in goal by Hodgson

F.A. Cup

						Tweedy	Vincent	Hodgson	Hall	Betmead	Buck	Boyd	Temple	Beattie	Jones	Bartholomew	Theaker	Glover	Anderson	Fisher	Taylor	Charlesworth	Shaw J	Wattam	Kurz	Howe	Swain	Crack	Lewis	Shaw H	Quigley	Moulson
R3	Jan 10	TRANMERE ROVERS	6-0	Vincent(pen),Beattie(2),Howe(2),Lewis	10000	1	2	3	4	5	6	7		8	10											9			11			
R4	21	Millwall	2-2	Howe(2)	38447	1	2	3	4	5	6	7		8	10											9			11			
R4r	24	MILLWALL	3-2	Boyd, Howe, Jones	14400	1	2	3	4	5	6	7		8	10											9	11					
R5	Feb 11	Sheffield United	0-0		62022	1	2	3	4	5	6	7		8	10	11		9														
R5r	14	SHEFFIELD UNITED	1-0	Howe	14500	1	2	3	4	5	6	7		8	10											9		11				
R6	Mar 4	Chelsea	1-0	Crack	45409	1	2	3	4	5	6	7		8	10											9		11				
SF	25	Wolverhampton Wands. *	0-5		76962		2	3	4	5	6	7		8	10											9		11				1

*** Played at Old Trafford, Manchester.**

		P	W	D	L	F	A	W	D	L	F	A	F	A	Pts
1	Everton	42	17	3	1	60	18	10	2	9	28	34	88	52	59
2	Wolverhampton W.	42	14	6	1	55	12	8	5	8	33	27	88	39	55
3	Charlton Athletic	42	16	3	2	49	24	6	3	12	26	35	75	59	50
4	Middlesbrough	42	13	6	2	64	27	7	3	11	29	47	93	74	49
5	Arsenal	42	14	3	4	34	14	5	6	10	21	27	55	41	47
6	Derby County	42	12	3	6	39	22	7	5	9	27	33	66	55	46
7	Stoke City	42	13	6	2	50	25	4	6	11	21	43	71	68	46
8	Bolton Wanderers	42	10	6	5	39	25	5	9	7	28	33	67	58	45
9	Preston North End	42	13	7	1	44	19	3	5	13	19	40	63	59	44
10	GRIMSBY TOWN	42	11	6	4	38	26	5	5	11	23	43	61	69	43
11	Liverpool	42	12	6	3	40	24	2	8	11	22	39	62	63	42
12	Aston Villa	42	11	3	7	44	25	5	6	10	27	35	71	60	41
13	Leeds United	42	11	5	5	40	27	5	4	12	19	40	59	67	41
14	Manchester United	42	7	9	5	30	20	4	7	10	27	45	57	65	38
15	Blackpool	42	9	8	4	37	26	3	6	12	19	42	56	68	38
16	Sunderland	42	7	7	7	30	29	6	5	10	24	38	54	67	38
17	Portsmouth	42	10	7	4	25	15	2	6	13	22	55	47	70	37
18	Brentford	42	11	2	8	30	27	3	6	12	23	47	53	74	36
19	Huddersfield Town	42	11	4	6	38	18	1	7	13	20	46	58	64	35
20	Chelsea	42	10	5	6	43	29	2	4	15	21	51	64	80	33
21	Birmingham	42	10	5	6	40	27	2	3	16	22	57	62	84	32
22	Leicester City	42	7	6	8	35	35	2	5	14	13	47	48	82	29

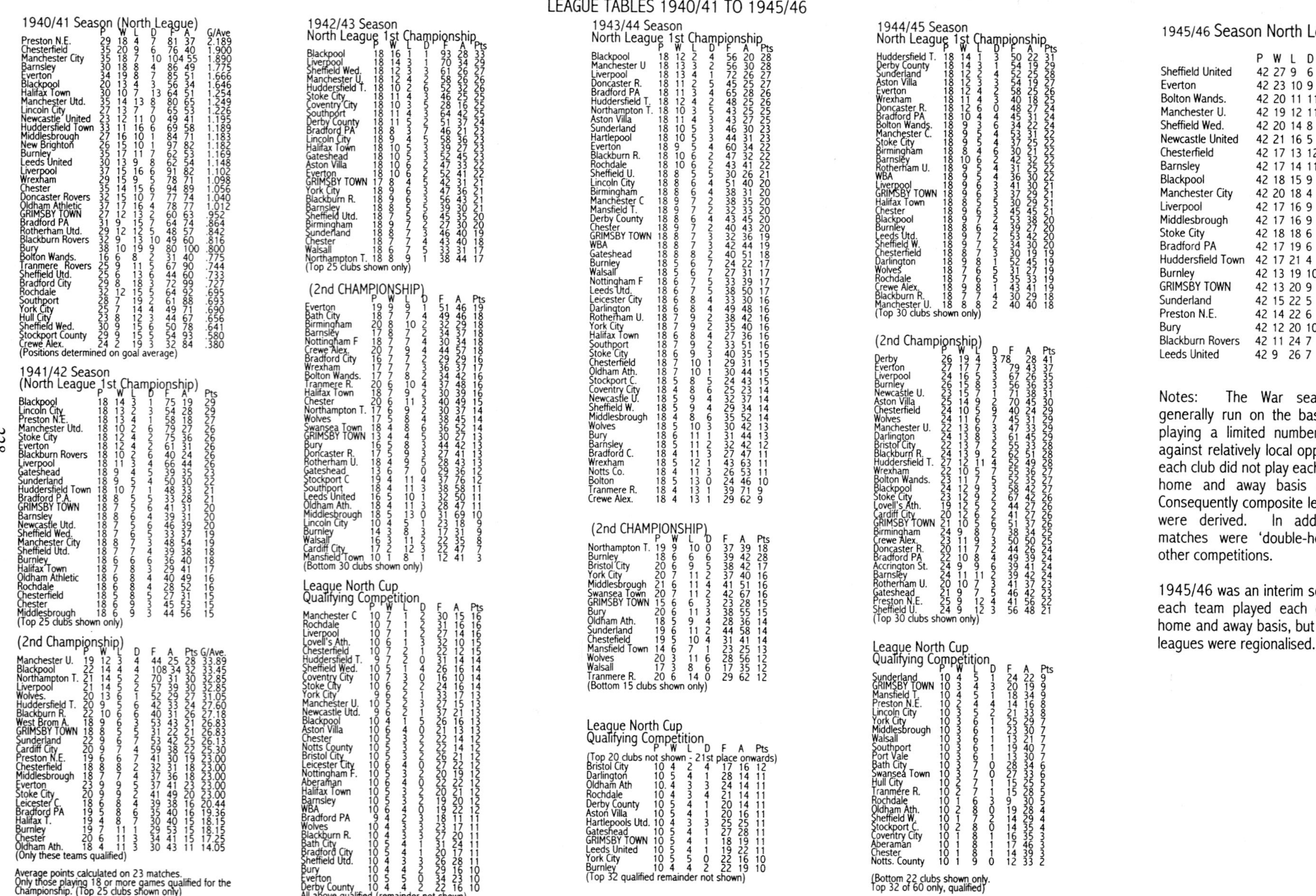

LEAGUE TABLES 1940/41 TO 1945/46

1940/41 Season (North League)

	P	W	L	D	F	A	G/Ave
Preston N.E.	29	18	4	7	81	37	2.189
Chesterfield	35	20	9	6	76	40	1.900
Manchester City	35	18	7	10	104	55	1.890
Barnsley	30	18	8	4	86	49	1.775
Everton	34	19	8	7	85	51	1.666
Blackpool	20	13	4	3	56	34	1.646
Halifax Town	30	10	7	13	64	51	1.254
Manchester Utd.	35	14	13	8	80	65	1.249
Lincoln City	27	13	7	7	65	53	1.226
Newcastle United	23	12	11	0	49	41	1.195
Huddersfield Town	33	11	16	6	69	58	1.189
Middlesbrough	27	16	10	1	84	71	1.183
New Brighton	26	15	10	1	97	82	1.182
Burnley	35	17	11	7	62	53	1.169
Leeds United	30	13	9	8	62	54	1.148
Liverpool	37	15	16	6	91	82	1.102
Wrexham	29	15	9	5	78	71	1.098
Chester	35	14	15	6	94	89	1.056
Doncaster Rovers	32	15	10	7	77	74	1.040
Oldham Athletic	37	17	16	4	78	77	1.012
GRIMSBY TOWN	27	12	13	2	60	63	.952
Bradford PA	31	9	15	7	64	74	.864
Rotherham Utd.	29	12	12	5	48	57	.842
Blackburn Rovers	32	9	13	10	49	60	.816
Bury	38	10	19	9	80	100	.800
Bolton Wands.	16	6	8	2	31	40	.775
Tranmere Rovers	25	9	11	5	67	90	.744
Sheffield Utd.	25	6	13	6	44	60	.733
Bradford City	29	8	18	3	72	99	.727
Rochdale	32	12	15	5	64	92	.695
Southport	28	7	19	2	61	88	.693
York City	25	7	14	4	49	71	.690
Hull City	23	8	12	3	44	67	.656
Sheffield Wed.	30	9	15	6	50	78	.641
Stockport County	29	9	15	5	54	93	.580
Crewe Alex.	24	2	19	3	32	84	.380

(Positions determined on goal average)

1941/42 Season (North League 1st Championship)

	P	W	L	D	F	A	Pts
Blackpool	18	14	3	1	75	19	29
Lincoln City	18	13	2	3	54	28	29
Preston N.E.	18	13	4	1	58	18	27
Manchester Utd.	18	10	2	6	79	27	26
Stoke City	18	12	4	2	75	36	26
Everton	18	12	4	2	61	31	26
Blackburn Rovers	18	10	2	6	40	24	26
Liverpool	18	11	3	4	66	44	26
Gateshead	18	9	4	5	39	35	23
Sunderland	18	9	5	4	50	30	22
Huddersfield Town	18	10	7	1	48	33	21
Bradford P.A.	18	8	5	5	33	28	21
GRIMSBY TOWN	18	7	5	6	41	31	20
Barnsley	18	8	6	4	39	31	20
Newcastle Utd.	18	7	5	6	46	39	20
Sheffield Wed.	18	7	6	5	33	37	19
Manchester City	18	8	7	3	48	54	19
Sheffield Utd.	18	7	7	4	39	38	18
Burnley	18	6	6	6	36	40	18
Halifax Town	18	7	8	3	29	41	17
Oldham Athletic	18	6	8	4	40	49	16
Rochdale	18	6	8	4	28	52	16
Chesterfield	18	5	8	5	27	31	15
Chester	18	6	9	3	45	53	15
Middlesbrough	18	6	9	3	44	56	15

(Top 25 clubs shown only)

(2nd Championship)

	P	W	L	D	F	A	Pts	G/Ave.
Manchester U.	19	12	3	4	44	25	28	33.89
Blackpool	22	14	4	4	108	34	32	33.45
Northampton T.	21	14	5	2	70	31	30	32.85
Liverpool	21	14	5	2	57	39	30	32.85
Wolves.	20	13	6	1	52	29	27	31.05
Huddersfield T.	20	9	5	6	42	33	24	27.60
Blackburn R.	22	10	6	6	40	31	26	27.18
West Brom A.	18	9	6	3	53	43	21	26.83
GRIMSBY TOWN	18	8	5	5	31	22	21	26.83
Sunderland	22	9	6	7	53	42	25	26.13
Cardiff City	20	9	7	4	59	38	22	25.30
Preston N.E.	19	6	6	7	41	30	19	23.00
Chesterfield	18	8	8	2	32	31	18	23.00
Middlesbrough	18	7	7	4	37	36	18	23.00
Everton	23	9	9	5	37	41	23	23.00
Stoke City	20	9	9	2	41	49	20	23.00
Leicester C.	18	6	8	4	39	38	16	20.44
Bradford PA	19	5	8	6	35	40	16	19.36
Halifax T.	19	4	8	7	30	40	15	18.15
Burnley	19	7	11	1	29	53	15	18.15
Chester	20	6	11	3	34	41	15	17.25
Oldham Ath.	18	4	11	3	30	43	11	14.05

(Only these teams qualified)

Average points calculated on 23 matches.
Only those playing 18 or more games qualified for the Championship. (Top 25 clubs shown only)

1942/43 Season North League 1st Championship

	P	W	L	D	F	A	Pts
Blackpool	18	16	1	1	93	28	33
Liverpool	18	14	3	1	70	34	29
Sheffield Wed.	18	12	3	3	61	26	27
Manchester U.	18	12	4	2	58	26	26
Huddersfield T.	18	10	2	6	52	32	26
Stoke City	18	11	4	3	46	25	25
Coventry City	18	10	3	5	28	16	25
Southport	18	11	4	3	64	42	25
Derby County	18	11	5	2	51	37	24
Bradford PA	18	8	3	7	46	21	23
Lincoln City	18	9	4	5	58	36	23
Halifax Town	18	10	5	3	39	27	23
Gateshead	18	10	5	3	52	45	23
Aston Villa	18	10	6	2	47	33	22
Everton	18	10	6	2	52	41	22
GRIMSBY TOWN	17	8	4	5	42	31	21
York City	18	9	6	3	47	36	21
Blackburn R.	18	9	6	3	56	43	21
Barnsley	18	8	5	5	39	30	21
Sheffield Utd.	18	7	5	6	45	35	20
Birmingham	18	9	7	2	27	30	20
Sunderland	18	8	7	3	46	40	19
Chester	18	7	7	4	43	40	18
Walsall	18	6	7	5	33	31	17
Northampton T.	18	8	9	1	38	44	17

(Top 25 clubs shown only)

(2nd CHAMPIONSHIP)

	P	W	L	D	F	A	Pts
Everton	19	9	9	1	51	46	19
Bath City	18	7	7	4	49	46	18
Birmingham	20	8	10	2	32	29	18
Barnsley	17	8	7	2	34	37	18
Nottingham F	18	7	7	4	30	34	18
Crewe Alex.	20	7	9	4	44	57	18
Bradford City	16	7	7	2	29	29	16
Wrexham	17	7	7	3	36	37	17
Bolton Wands.	17	7	8	2	34	42	16
Tranmere R.	20	6	10	4	37	48	16
Halifax Town	18	7	9	2	30	39	16
Chester	20	6	11	3	40	49	15
Northampton T.	17	6	9	2	30	37	14
Wolves	17	5	8	4	38	45	14
Swansea Town	18	4	8	6	36	52	14
GRIMSBY TOWN	13	4	4	5	30	27	13
Bury	16	5	8	3	44	42	13
Doncaster R.	17	5	9	3	27	41	13
Rotherham U.	18	4	9	5	28	43	13
Gateshead	13	6	7	0	29	36	12
Stockport C	19	4	11	4	37	76	12
Southport	18	4	11	3	38	58	11
Leeds United	16	5	10	1	32	50	11
Oldham Ath.	18	4	11	3	28	47	11
Middlesbrough	18	5	13	0	31	69	10
Lincoln City	10	4	5	1	23	18	9
Burnley	14	3	8	3	17	31	9
Walsall	16	3	11	2	22	35	8
Cardiff City	17	2	12	3	22	47	7
Mansfield Town	10	1	8	1	12	41	3

(Bottom 30 clubs shown only)

League North Cup Qualifying Competition

	P	W	L	D	F	A	Pts
Manchester C	10	7	1	2	30	15	16
Rochdale	10	7	1	2	31	16	16
Liverpool	10	7	1	2	27	14	16
Lovell's Ath.	10	6	1	3	32	10	15
Chesterfield	10	7	2	1	22	12	15
Huddersfield T.	9	7	2	0	31	14	14
Sheffield Wed.	10	5	1	4	26	16	14
Coventry City	10	7	3	0	16	10	14
Stoke City	10	6	2	2	24	16	14
York City	9	6	2	1	33	17	13
Manchester U.	10	5	2	3	27	15	13
Newcastle Utd.	9	6	2	1	37	21	13
Blackpool	10	4	1	5	26	16	13
Aston Villa	10	6	4	0	21	13	13
Chester	10	5	3	2	22	14	12
Notts County	10	5	3	2	22	14	12
Bristol City	10	5	3	2	26	21	12
Leicester City	10	6	4	0	27	22	12
Nottingham F.	10	5	3	2	20	19	12
Aberaman	10	6	4	0	22	22	12
Halifax Town	10	5	3	2	20	21	12
Barnsley	10	5	3	2	19	20	12
WBA	10	6	4	0	19	22	12
Bradford PA	9	4	2	3	18	11	11
Wolves	10	4	3	3	23	17	11
Blackburn R.	10	4	3	3	27	20	11
Bath City	10	5	4	1	31	24	11
Bradford City	10	5	4	1	20	17	11
Sheffield Utd.	10	4	3	3	26	28	11
Bury	10	4	4	2	29	16	10
Everton	10	5	5	0	34	23	10
Derby County	10	4	4	2	22	16	10
All above qualified (remainder not shown)							
GRIMSBY TOWN	10	3	3	4	22	20	10

1943/44 Season North League 1st Championship

	P	W	L	D	F	A	Pts
Blackpool	18	12	2	4	56	20	28
Manchester U	18	13	3	2	56	30	28
Liverpool	18	13	4	1	72	26	27
Doncaster R.	18	11	2	5	45	25	27
Bradford PA	18	11	3	4	65	28	26
Huddersfield T.	18	12	4	2	48	25	26
Northampton T.	18	10	3	5	43	25	25
Aston Villa	18	11	4	3	43	27	25
Sunderland	18	10	5	3	46	30	23
Hartlepool	18	10	5	3	44	31	23
Everton	18	9	5	4	60	34	22
Blackburn R.	18	10	6	2	47	32	22
Rochdale	18	10	6	2	43	41	22
Sheffield U.	18	8	5	5	30	26	21
Lincoln City	18	8	6	4	51	40	20
Birmingham	18	8	6	4	38	31	20
Manchester C	18	9	7	2	38	35	20
Mansfield T.	18	9	7	2	32	33	20
Derby County	18	8	6	4	43	45	20
Chester	18	9	7	2	40	43	20
GRIMSBY TOWN	18	8	7	3	32	36	19
WBA	18	8	7	3	42	44	19
Gateshead	18	8	8	2	40	51	18
Burnley	18	5	6	7	24	22	17
Walsall	18	5	6	7	27	31	17
Nottingham F	18	6	7	5	33	39	17
Leeds Utd.	18	6	7	5	38	50	17
Leicester City	18	6	8	4	33	30	16
Darlington	18	6	8	4	49	48	16
Rotherham U.	18	7	9	2	38	42	16
York City	18	7	9	2	35	40	16
Halifax Town	18	6	8	4	27	36	16
Southport	18	7	9	2	33	51	16
Stoke City	18	6	9	3	40	35	15
Chesterfield	18	7	10	1	29	31	15
Oldham Ath.	18	7	10	1	30	44	15
Stockport C.	18	5	8	5	24	43	15
Coventry City	18	4	8	6	25	23	14
Newcastle U.	18	5	9	4	32	37	14
Sheffield W.	18	5	9	4	29	34	14
Middlesbrough	18	4	8	6	35	52	14
Wolves	18	5	10	3	30	42	13
Bury	18	6	11	1	31	44	13
Barnsley	18	5	11	2	32	42	12
Bradford C.	18	4	11	3	27	47	11
Wrexham	18	5	12	1	43	63	11
Notts Co.	18	4	11	3	26	53	11
Bolton	18	5	13	0	24	46	10
Tranmere R.	18	4	13	1	39	71	9
Crewe Alex.	18	4	13	1	29	62	9

(2nd CHAMPIONSHIP)

	P	W	L	D	F	A	Pts
Northampton T.	19	9	10	0	37	39	18
Burnley	18	6	6	6	39	42	28
Bristol City	20	6	9	5	38	42	17
York City	20	7	11	2	37	40	16
Middlesbrough	21	6	11	4	41	51	16
Swansea Town	20	7	11	2	42	67	16
GRIMSBY TOWN	15	6	6	3	23	28	15
Bury	20	6	11	3	38	55	15
Oldham Ath.	18	5	9	4	28	36	14
Sunderland	19	6	11	2	44	58	14
Chestefield	19	5	10	4	31	41	14
Mansfield Town	14	6	7	1	23	25	13
Wolves	20	3	11	6	28	56	12
Walsall	17	3	8	6	17	35	12
Tranmere R.	20	6	14	0	29	62	12

(Bottom 15 clubs shown only)

League North Cup Qualifying Competition

	P	W	L	D	F	A	Pts
(Top 20 clubs not shown - 21st place onwards)							
Bristol City	10	4	2	4	17	16	12
Darlington	10	5	4	1	28	14	11
Oldham Ath	10.	4	3	3	24	14	11
Rochdale	10	4	3	4	21	14	11
Derby County	10	5	4	1	20	14	11
Aston Villa	10	5	4	1	20	16	11
Hartlepools Utd.	10	4	3	3	25	25	11
Gateshead	10	5	4	1	27	28	11
GRIMSBY TOWN	10	5	4	1	18	19	11
Leeds United	10	5	4	1	19	22	11
York City	10	5	5	0	22	16	10
Burnley	10	4	4	2	22	19	10

(Top 32 qualified remainder not shown)

1944/45 Season North League 1st Championship

	P	W	L	D	F	A	Pts
Huddersfield T.	18	14	1	3	50	22	31
Derby County	18	14	3	1	54	19	29
Sunderland	18	12	2	4	52	25	28
Aston Villa	18	12	3	3	54	19	27
Everton	18	12	4	2	58	25	26
Wrexham	18	11	4	3	40	18	25
Doncaster R.	18	12	6	0	48	27	24
Bradford PA	18	10	4	4	45	31	24
Bolton Wands.	18	9	3	6	34	22	24
Manchester C.	18	9	5	4	53	31	22
Stoke City	18	9	5	4	37	25	22
Birmingham	18	8	4	6	30	21	22
Barnsley	18	10	6	2	42	32	22
Rotherham U.	18	9	5	4	31	25	22
WBA	18	9	5	4	36	30	22
Liverpool	18	9	6	3	41	30	21
GRIMSBY TOWN	18	9	6	3	37	29	21
Halifax Town	18	8	5	5	30	29	21
Chester	18	9	6	3	45	45	21
Blackpool	18	9	7	2	53	38	20
Burnley	18	8	6	4	39	27	20
Leeds Utd.	18	9	7	2	53	42	20
Sheffield W.	18	9	7	2	34	30	20
Chesterfield	18	8	7	3	30	19	19
Darlington	18	9	8	1	52	45	19
Wolves	18	7	6	5	31	27	19
Rochdale	18	7	6	5	35	33	19
Crewe Alex.	18	9	8	1	43	41	19
Blackburn R.	18	7	7	4	30	29	18
Manchester U.	18	8	8	2	40	40	18

(Top 30 clubs shown only)

(2nd Championship)

	P	W	L	D	F	A	Pts
Derby	26	19	4	3	78	28	41
Everton	27	17	7	3	79	43	37
Liverpool	24	16	5	3	67	26	35
Burnley	26	15	8	3	56	36	33
Newcastle U.	23	15	7	1	71	38	31
Aston Villa	25	14	9	2	70	45	30
Chesterfield	24	10	5	9	40	24	29
Wolves	24	11	6	7	45	31	29
Manchester U.	22	13	6	3	47	33	29
Darlington	24	13	8	3	61	45	29
Bristol City	22	13	7	2	55	33	28
Blackburn R.	24	13	9	2	62	51	28
Huddersfield T.	27	12	11	4	52	49	28
Wrexham	22	10	5	7	55	36	27
Bolton Wands.	23	11	7	5	52	35	27
Blackpool	24	12	9	3	58	42	27
Stoke City	23	12	9	2	67	42	26
Lovell's Ath.	19	12	5	2	44	27	26
Cardiff City	20	12	6	2	41	27	26
GRIMSBY TOWN	21	10	5	6	51	37	26
Birmingham	24	9	8	7	38	34	25
Crewe Alex.	23	11	9	3	50	50	25
Doncaster R.	20	11	7	2	44	26	24
Bradford PA	22	10	8	4	49	39	24
Accrington St.	24	9	9	6	39	41	24
Barnsley	24	11	11	2	39	42	24
Rotherham U.	20	10	7	3	41	37	23
Gateshead	21	9	7	5	46	42	23
Preston N.E.	25	9	12	4	41	56	22
Sheffield U.	24	9	12	3	56	48	21

(Top 30 clubs shown only)

League North Cup Qualifying Competition

	P	W	L	D	F	A	Pts
Sunderland	10	4	5	1	24	22	9
GRIMSBY TOWN	10	3	4	3	20	19	9
Mansfield T.	10	4	5	1	18	34	9
Preston N.E.	10	2	4	4	14	16	8
Lincoln City	10	3	5	2	21	33	8
York City	10	3	6	1	25	29	7
Middlesbrough	10	3	6	1	23	30	7
Walsall	10	3	6	1	13	21	7
Southport	10	3	6	1	19	40	7
Port Vale	10	3	6	1	13	30	7
Bath City	10	3	7	0	28	34	6
Swansea Town	10	3	7	0	27	33	6
Hull City	10	2	7	1	15	25	5
Tranmere R.	10	2	7	1	15	28	5
Rochdale	10	1	6	3	9	30	5
Oldham Ath.	10	2	8	0	19	28	4
Sheffield W.	10	1	7	2	14	29	4
Stockport C.	10	2	8	0	14	35	4
Coventry City	10	1	8	1	16	35	3
Aberaman	10	1	8	1	17	46	3
Chester	10	1	8	1	14	39	3
Notts. County	10	1	9	0	12	33	2

(Bottom 22 clubs shown only.
Top 32 of 60 only, qualified)

1945/46 Season North League

	P	W	L	D	F	A	Pts
Sheffield United	42	27	9	6	112	62	60
Everton	42	23	10	9	88	54	55
Bolton Wands.	42	20	11	11	67	45	51
Manchester U.	42	19	12	11	98	62	49
Sheffield Wed.	42	20	14	8	67	60	48
Newcastle United	42	21	16	5	106	70	47
Chesterfield	42	17	13	12	68	49	46
Barnsley	42	17	14	11	76	68	45
Blackpool	42	18	15	9	94	92	45
Manchester City	42	20	18	4	78	75	44
Liverpool	42	17	16	9	80	70	43
Middlesbrough	42	17	16	9	75	87	43
Stoke City	42	18	18	6	88	79	42
Bradford PA	42	17	19	6	71	84	40
Huddersfield Town	42	17	21	4	90	89	38
Burnley	42	13	19	10	63	84	36
GRIMSBY TOWN	42	13	20	9	61	89	35
Sunderland	42	15	22	5	55	83	35
Preston N.E.	42	14	22	6	70	77	34
Bury	42	12	20	10	60	85	34
Blackburn Rovers	42	11	24	7	60	111	29
Leeds United	42	9	26	7	66	118	25

Notes: The War seasons were generally run on the basis of clubs playing a limited number of games against relatively local opponents, i.e. each club did not play each other on a home and away basis as normal. Consequently composite league tables were derived. In addition some matches were 'double-headers' for other competitions.

1945/46 was an interim season when each team played each other on a home and away basis, but the various leagues were regionalised.

1939/40 Division 1

Football League abandoned (outbreak of WW2). Position at cessation 14th

							1	2	3	4	5	6	7	8	9	10	11
1	Aug	26	Manchester United	0-4		22357	Tweedy	Vincent	Hodgson J	Hall	Betmead	Buck	Boyd	Beattie	Howe	Jones T	Crack
2		29	WOLVERHAMPTON W.	0-0		12192	"	"	"	Reeve F	"	"	Johnson JW	"	"	"	Wardle
3	Sep	2	PRESTON NORTH END	2-0	Howe(2)	6932	"	"	"	"	"	"	"	"	"	"	"

4th in Regional League (E Midland Div)

1	Oct	21	MANSFIELD TOWN	2-1	J.Roberts, Kurz	1400	Tweedy	Vincent	Hodgson J	Buck	Betmead	Wattam	Johnson JW	Roberts J	Kurz	Jones T	Crack
2	Nov	4	SHEFFIELD WED.	3-2	Holmes, Hall, J.W.Johnson		"	"	"	Hall	"	Buck	"	"	Reeve K	Holmes	Bartholomew
3		11	LINCOLN CITY	7-3	K.Reeve(3),Moralee,Bartholomew,Vincent,J.W.Johnson	6936	"	"	"	"	"	"	"	"	"	Moralee	"
4		18	Rotherham United	1-2	Buck	3000	"	"	"	"	"	Wattam	"	"	"	Buck	"
5	Dec	2	Notts County	2-1	Bartholomew(2)	7000	"	"	"	"	Charlesworth	"	"	Ward	Ponting	Holmes	"
6		9	CHESTERFIELD	1-0	Betmead	3000	"	"	"	"	Betmead	"	"	"	"	Howe	Wardle
7		23	Barnsley	1-4	Howe	2000	"	"	"	"	"	Buck	"	"	Howe	Holmes	Bartholomew
8	Jan	6	Doncaster Rovers	0-2		2215	"	"	"	"	Charlesworth	Wattam	"	Lumby	Reeve K	"	"
9	Mar	9	Lincoln City	1-4	Vincent	2000	Taylor G	"	"	"	"	"	Hillard	"	"	"	Pridmore
10		16	ROTHERHAM UNITED	3-1	Vincent(pen), Dodd, Hall	2000	"	"	"	Lumby	"	"	Pridmore	Hall	Ponting	Dodd	Little
11		22	SHEFFIELD UNITED	2-0	Ponting, Dodd	3000	Tweedy	"	"	"	"	"	Johnson JW	"	"	"	"
12		23	Sheffield Wednesday	1-2	Hall	4000	"	"	"	"	"	"	"	"	"	"	Holmes
13		30	NOTTS COUNTY	3-2	Dodd, Crack(2)	2000	"	"	"	Hall	Buck	"	Lumby	Bestall	"	"	Crack
14	Apr	6	Chesterfield	0-5		6000	"	"	"	"	Charlesworth	Buck	"	"	Collins	Ponting	Moralee
15		13	BARNSLEY	0-0		3000	"	"	"	"	"	"	Burton	Beattie	Howe	Moralee	Dodd
16	May	7	Mansfield Town	1-4	Beattie	1000	Taylor G	"	Buck	"	"	Wattam	Hillard	"	Collins	Reeve K	Pridmore
17		13	Nottingham Forest	1-1	Beattie	2255	"	"	Hodgson J	"	"	"	Lumby	"	Reeve K	Buck	"
18		18	Sheffield United	0-3		2500	Tweedy	"	"	Buck	"	"	"	Moralee	Pearson S	Neish	"
19	Jun	1	DONCASTER ROVERS	7-4	Lumby,Howe(3),Hall(2),Moralee	500	"	"	"	Hall	Betmead	Buck	"	"	Howe	Pearson S	Robinson
20		8	NOTTINGHAM FOREST	4-3	S.Pearson(2), Lumby, Hall	500	"	"	"	Buck	"	Wattam	"	Hall	"	"	Neish

War League Cup

R1L2	Apr	20	Middlesbrough	1-4	Howe	8000	Tweedy	Vincent	Hodgson J	Hall	Charlesworth	Buck	Burton	Beattie	Howe	Moralee	Bray
R2L2		27	MIDDLESBROUGH	3-1	Moralee,Howe 2(1p)	4000	"	"	"	"	"	"	"	"	Jones T	"	"

(Lost 5-4 on agg.)

Final League Table: 1939-40
Regional League (East Midland Division)

		P	W	D	L	F	A	Pts
1	Chesterfield	20	14	2	4	69	23	30
2	Sheffield United	20	12	1	7	46	34	25
3	Barnsley	20	10	5	5	43	39	25
4	GRIMSBY TOWN	20	10	2	8	40	44	22
5	Mansfield Town	20	9	3	8	49	48	21
6	Doncaster Rovers	20	7	4	9	37	45	18
7	Lincoln City	20	9	0	11	42	53	18
8	Rotherham United	20	7	4	9	24	42	18
9	Sheffield Wednesday	20	5	5	10	33	42	15
10	Nottingham Forest	20	5	4	11	37	43	14
11	Notts County	20	6	2	12	40	57	14

1940/41 21st in North Regional League

							1	2	3	4	5	6	7	8	9	10	11
1	Aug	31	Lincoln City	2-2	Annables, Scrimshaw	2500	Tweedy	Vincent	Hodgson J	Hall	Betmead	Buck	Logie	Scrimshaw	Annables	Holland	Holmes
2	Sep	7	LINCOLN CITY	2-1	J.W.Johnson, Hall	1000	Fields	"	"	"	"	"	Johnson JW	Logie	Joyce	Scrimshaw	"
3		14	Rotherham United	0-1		2000	Tweedy	"	"	"	Buck	Wattam	Howshall	"	Reeve K	"	"
4		21	Sheffield United	1-6	Scrimshaw	3000	Wilkin	"	"	"	Betmead	Buck	Chadwick	Scrimshaw	"	Wattam	"
5		28	MIDDLESBROUGH	1-3	K.Reeve	1000	Tweedy	"	"	"	"	"	Logie	"	"	Maw	"
6	Oct	12	SHEFFIELD UNITED	3-1	K.Reeve, Betmead, Jennings	2000	"	"	"	"	Buck	Wattam	Reeve K	Jennings	Betmead	Scrimshaw	Maw
7		19	DONCASTER ROVERS	3-2	Syred(2), Jennings	2000	"	"	"	"	"	"	"	"	Syred	Maw	Holmes
8		26	Rotherham United	2-3	Betmead,K.Reeve	1800	"	"	"	"	"	"	"	Witcomb	Betmead	Syred	Scrimshaw
9	Nov	9	BRADFORD CITY	3-2	Gorman,Jennings,Betmead(pen)	600	"	"	"	"	Betmead	Buck	Gotts	Jennings	Gorman	Scrimshaw	Holmes
10		16	Newcastle United	1-3	K.Reeve	5000	"	"	"	"	"	"	Reeve K	"	"	"	"
11		23	Doncaster Rovers	0-6		2500	"	"	"	Witcomb	"	"	"	Scrimshaw	Hall	Holland	"
12		30	CHESTERFIELD	4-5	H.Johnson,Wattam,Hall,K.Reeve	3490	Fields	"	"	Hall	Millington	"	"	Jennings	Johnson H	Scrimshaw	Wattam
13	Dec	7	Chesterfield	3-0	Flowers(2), H.Johnson	2500	Moulson G	"	"	"	"	"	"	"	"	Flowers	Allen
14		14	Middlesbrough	1-2	H.Johnson	2000	Frost	"	"	Scrimshaw	"	"	"	"	"	"	"
15		25	HULL CITY	1-1	H.Johnson	4500	Fields	"	"	Hall	"	"	"	Scrimshaw	"	"	"
16		28	Newcastle United	2-5	H.Johnson, Flowers	4000	Frost	"	"	"	"	"	Bainbridge	Jennings	"	"	Crack
17	Jan	4	SHEFFIELD UNITED	3-2	H.Johnson,Nightingale,Jennings	2000	Tweedy	"	"	Witcomb	"	"	Hall	"	"	Nightingale	Allen
18		11	NEWCASTLE UNITED	4-0	H.Johnson(3), Witcomb	3500	"	"	"	"	"	"	"	"	"	Scrimshaw	"
19		18	SHEFFIELD WED.	2-1	H.Johnson, Jennings	1500	"	"	"	Hall	"	"	Witcomb	"	"	"	"
20	Feb	1	BRADFORD P.A.	0-3		2000	"	"	"	"	"	"	"	"	"	Logie	"
21	Mar	22	Hull City	8-2	K.Reeve(3),Flowers,H.Johnson(2),Jennings,Buck	1000	"	"	"	"	"	"	Reeve K	"	"	Flowers	"
22		29	HULL CITY	0-1		1200	Middleton	"	"	"	"	"	"	"	"	"	"
23	Apr	5	Bradford City	4-2	H.Johnson,Jennings,Crack,K.Reeve	1000	Tweedy	"	"	"	"	Witcomb	"	"	"	"	Crack
24		12	York City	2-3	H.Johnson, Jennings	3000	Swinburne	"	"	"	Charlesworth	"	"	"	Kurz	Johnson H	Flowers
25		19	ROTHERHAM UNITED	5-3	Rudkin(3), H.Johnson, Flowers	1000	Tweedy	"	"	"	Millington	Buck	"	Nightingale	Johnson H	Rudkin	"
26		26	YORK CITY	2-0	Jennings, H.Johnson	1100	"	"	"	"	"	"	"	Jennings	"	Ward	Allen
27	May	10	Mansfield Town*	1-3	Flowers	600	"	"	"	"	"	"	"	Ward	"	Flowers	"

*Inter-League match.

The Mariners played home games at Scunthorpe United's - The Old Showground - during WW2. The 1st match was on 30/11/1940 v Chesterfield. Town didn't return to Blundell Park until 1/1/1944.

War Cup

R1L1	Feb	15	DONCASTER ROVERS	1-0	Flowers	2766	Tweedy	Vincent	Hodgson J	Hall	Millington	Buck	Scrimshaw	Jennings	Johnson H	Flowers	Marlow
R1L2	Mar	1	Doncaster Rovers	0-0		3608	Middleton	"	"	"	"	"	"	Fleetwood	"	"	"
R2L1		8	Barnsley	1-1	Jennings	2838	Tweedy	"	"	"	"	"	"	"	"	Jennings	"
R2L2		15	BARNSLEY*	2-2*	H.Johnson, Scrimshaw	3642	"	"	"	"	"	"	"	"	"	"	"

*aet (1-1 after 90 mins). after 161 mins play, the match was abandoned due to the referee returning to RAF duty. Barnsley were awarded tie through higher league ranking.

1941/42 13th in Football League North (1st Comp)

							1	2	3	4	5	6	7	8	9	10	11
1	Aug	30	Barnsley	1-2	Stocks	3000	Tweedy	Vincent	Hodgson J	Hall	Millington	Buck	Stocks	Jennings	Johnson H	Flowers	Rudkin
2	Sep	6	BARNSLEY	1-1	Rudkin	2500	"	"	Hall	Harris	"	"	"	"	"	Fleetwood	"
3		13	SHEFFIELD WED.	1-1	Vincent(pen)	2000	"	"	Jones W	Hall	"	"	"	"	"	Davies	"
4		20	Sheffield Wednesday	2-0	Rudkin, H.Johnson	3000	"	"	Hodgson J	"	"	"	Davies	"	"	Thomas	"
5		27	Rotherham United	3-2	H.Johnson(2), Davies	2800	Moore TR	"	"	"	"	"	"	Thomas	"	Flowers	Crack
6	Oct	4	ROTHERHAM UNITED	6-2	Rudkin,Thomas(3),Flowers(2)	2000	Tweedy	"	"	"	"	"	"	Jennings	Thomas	"	Rudkin
7		11	Huddersfield Town	1-5	Rudkin	2268	"	"	"	"	"	"	"	"	Johnson H	Thomas	"
8		18	HUDDERSFIELD TOWN	2-2	Thomas(2)	2000	"	"	"	"	"	"	Wilson	"	"	"	"
9		25	LINCOLN CITY	1-3	Thomas	4000	"	"	"	"	"	"	Jennings	Thomas	"	Flowers	"
10	Nov	1	Lincoln City	1-1	Hullett	5500	"	"	"	"	"	"	Johnson H	"	Hullett	"	"
11		8	Doncaster Rovers	3-1	Rudkin, Ferrier, Thomas(pen)	2515	"	"	"	"	"	"	Ferrier	"	Kurz	"	"
12		15	DONCASTER ROVERS	2-0	Buck, Rudkin	3400	"	"	"	"	"	"	Robertson J	Jennings	Ferrier	Thomas	"
13		22	SHEFFIELD UNITED	7-1	Rudkin(3), Ferrier(3), Doherty	2000	"	"	"	"	"	"	"	Thomas	"	Doherty	"
14		29	Sheffield United	0-0		3500	"	"	"	"	"	"		Jennings	"	Thomas	"
15	Dec	6	Mansfield Town	3-1	Ferrier, Doherty(2,1pen)	500	"	"	"	"	"	"	Johnson H	Robertson J	"	Doherty	Moore N
16		13	MANSFIELD TOWN	4-5	J.Hodgson, Doherty, Ferrier(2)	1500	"	"	"	"	"	"	Murphy	Thomas	"	"	Rudkin
17		20	Chesterfield	1-1	Marsh	1000	"	"	"	"	"	"	Johnson H	"	"	"	Marsh
18		25	CHESTERFIELD	2-3	H.Johnson(2)	2237	"	Hall	"	Wilson	"	"	"	Robertson J	"	Thomas	Ferrier

Various matches were 'double headers', I.e. were also considered for League Cup qualification. Grimsby Town finished 11th (top 32 qualified)

9th in Football League North (2nd Comp)

							1	2	3	4	5	6	7	8	9	10	11
19	Dec	27	YORK CITY	0-0		2000	Tweedy	Moody K	Hodgson J	Hall	Millington	Buck	Robertson J	Thomas	Johnson H	Ferrier	Davies
20	Jan	3	York City	2-3	Doherty(2)	4500	"	Vincent	"	"	"	"	Butler	"	Ferrier	Doherty	Wardle
21		10	Barnsley	0-0		3000	"	"	"	"	"	"	Lumby	"	"	"	Davies
22		17	BARNSLEY	2-0	Nightingale, Davies	1500	"	"	"	"	"	"	Davies	Nightingale	"	Thomas	Dodds
23		24	Lincoln City	2-1	Ferrier(2)	3000	"	"	"	"	"	"	"	Thomas	"	Doherty	Pridmore
24	Feb	21	Doncaster Rovers	2-1	Thomas, Hall	871	Johnston JW	"	"	"	"	"	"	"	Johnson H	Ferrier	Dodds
25		28	Halifax Town	2-2	H.Johnson, Doherty	3000	"	"	"	Moore N	"	Nightingale	Johnson H	"	Ferrier	Doherty	"
26	Mar	14	HUDDERSFIELD TOWN	1-2	Ferrier	1500	Platts	"	"	Hall	"	Buck	Davies	Iggleden	"	Johnson H	"
27		21	HALIFAX TOWN	1-3	Davies	2000	Middleton	"	"	"	"	"	"	Moore N	"	"	"
28		28	LINCOLN CITY	4-2	Doherty(2), Ferrier(2)	1500	"	"	"	"	"	"	"	Thomas	"	Doherty	"

League War Cup

							1	2	3	4	5	6	7	8	9	10	11
R1L1	Apr	4	Barnsley	2-1	Davies, Nightingale	7550	Ferguson	Vincent	Hodgson J	Hall	Millington	Buck	Davies	Nightingale	Ferrier	Thomas	Dodds
R1L2		6	BARNSLEY	1-1	Hall	2800	"	"	"	"	"	"	"	"	"	"	"
R2L1		11	NOTTINGHAM FOREST	3-1	Nightingale(2), Ferrier	3400	"	"	"	"	"	"	"	"	"	"	Crack
R2L2		18	Nottingham Forest	5-1	Doherty,Ferrier,Davies,Thomas,Vincent	8473	Wildman	"	"	"	"	"	"	Thomas	"	Doherty	Dodds
R3L1		25	Norwich City	0-1		11088	"	"	"	"	"	"	"	"	"	"	Rudkin
R3L2	May	2	NORWICH CITY	2-0	Ferrier, Buck	8000	"	"	"	"	"	"	"	Nightingale	"	"	Dodds
SFL1		9	Sunderland	0-0		20500	"	"	"	"	"	"	"	"	"	"	"
SFL2		16	SUNDERLAND	2-3	Doherty, Nightingale	11896	"	"	"	"	"	"	"	"	"	"	Meek

1942/43 16th in Football League North (1st Comp)

							1	2	3	4	5	6	7	8	9	10	11
1	Aug	29	Chesterfield	0-2		2500	Smith	Vincent	Hodgson J	Blenkinsopp	Millington	Buck	Davies	Ely G	Chamberlain	Doherty	Archer
2	Sep	5	CHESTERFIELD	3-1	Butler, Doherty(2)	1250	"	"	"	Hall	"	"	"	Kurz	Butler	"	Ranshaw
3		12	LINCOLN CITY	5-2	Kurz,Davies,Clewlow,Ranshaw(2)	2150	"	"	"	"	"	"	"	Clewlow	Kurz	Moore N	"
4		19	Lincoln City	2-2	Ranshaw, Doherty	3639	"	Moody K	"	"	"	"	"	Marsh	Johnson H	Doherty	"
5		26	Barnsley	3-1	Vincent, Davies, Ranshaw	4482	"	Vincent	"	"	"	"	"	Eastham	Kippax	Sackett	"
6	Oct	3	BARNSLEY	1-1	Doherty(pen)	2750	Platts	"	"	"	"	"	"	"	"	Doherty	"
7		10	SHEFFIELD WED.	2-0	Kippax, Doherty	2370	"	"	"	"	"	"	"	Black	"	"	"
8		17	Sheffield Wednesday	0-2		6000	Smith	"	"	"	"	"	Crack	Eastham	"	Moralee	"
9		24	York City	2-5	Black, Crack	5000	"	"	"	"	"	"	"	Black	Moralee	Rayner	"
10		31	YORK CITY	0-1		2000	"	Moody K	"	"	"	"	Davies	Rayner	Squires	Moralee	"
11	Nov	7	LINCOLN CITY	2-2	Davies, Moralee	2500	"	Vincent	"	"	"	"	"	Black	Moralee	Eastham	"
12		14	Lincoln City	2-2	Doherty, Moralee	5000	"	"	"	Butler	"	"	Eastham	Moralee	Reeve K	Doherty	"
13		21	Sheffield United	3-3	Ranshaw(2), Moralee	7000	Mackenzie	"	"	Hall	"	"	Davies	Eastham	Greenfield	Moralee	"
14		28	SHEFFIELD UNITED	4-3	Moralee,Eastham,Ranshaw,Vincent	2000	Lear	"	"	"	"	"	"	"	Moralee	Brain	"
15	Dec	5	Rotherham United	6-1	Allard, Ranshaw(4), Black	2000	Mackenzie	"	"	"	"	"	"	Black	Allard	Moralee	"
16		12	ROTHERHAM UNITED	4-1	N.Moore(2),Ranshaw,Moralee	1711	"	"	"	"	"	"	"	"	Moore N	"	"
17		19	DONCASTER ROVERS	3-2	Eastham, Vincent(pen), Hall	1400	Smith	"	"	"	"	"	Lilley	Eastham	Moralee	Davies	"

Various matches were 'double headers', I.e. were also considered for League Cup qualification. Grimsby Town did not qualify

16th in Football League North (2nd Comp)

							1	2	3	4	5	6	7	8	9	10	11
18	Dec	26	SHEFFIELD UNITED	3-3	H.Johnson(3,2pens)	3326	Mackenzie	Vincent	Hodgson J	Hall	Millington	Buck	Davies	Eastham	Johnson H	Moralee	Ranshaw
19	Jan	2	Sheffield United	3-5	Doherty(p),Moralee,A.Nightingale(og)	6000	Fields	"	"	"	"	"	"	Doherty	Ferrier	"	"
20		9	Rotherham United	3-1	Kurz(2), Black	1000	White	"	"	"	"	"	"	Black	Kurz	"	"
21		16	ROTHERHAM UNITED	3-3	Black(3)	1200	Bradley	"	"	"	Ely L	"	"	"	Johnson H	"	"
22		23	DONCASTER ROVERS	5-2	Moralee(5)	2000	"	"	"	"	Millington	"	Johnson H	"	Moralee	Miller	"
23		30	Doncaster Rovers	0-1		3074	"	"	"	"	"	"	Lilley	"	Miller	Doherty	"
24	Feb	6	Lincoln City	1-1	Doherty	5500	Moulson G	"	"	Moody K	"	"	Johnson H	Moralee	Butler	"	"
25		13	LINCOLN CITY	1-0	Doherty	2000	"	"	"	Hall	"	"	Eastham	"	"	"	"
26		20	Sheffield Wednesday	2-2	Davies, Kurz	10000	Smith	"	"	"	"	"	Davies	"	Kurz	"	"
27		27	SHEFFIELD WED.	1-2	N.Moore	4000	"	"	"	"	"	"	"	Moore N	Moralee	"	"
28	Mar	27	Doncaster Rovers	2-3	Moralee, Clewlow	2000	Frost	Moody K	"	"	"	"	Pridmore	Clewlow	"	Gilchrist	Pridmore
29	Apr	3	DONCASTER ROVERS	2-0	Browning(2)	700	Smith	Vincent	"	"	"	"	Davies	Eastham	Browning	Moralee	Pearson W
30		26	Nottingham Forest	4-3	Ranshaw,Browning,Moralee(2)	2876	"	"	"	"	"	"	Lilley	"	"	"	Ranshaw

1 own goal

1943/44 21st in Football League North (1st Comp)

						1	2	3	4	5	6	7	8	9	10	11
1	Aug 28	YORK CITY	3-1	Rudkin(2), Dunderdale	1100	Moulson G	Vincent	Hodgson J	Hall	Millington	Buck	Rudkin	Eastham	Dunderdale	Glaister	Ranshaw
2	Sep 4	York City	0-2		4182	"	"	"	"	"	"	"	Forsyth	"	Baines	Pearson W
3	11	CHESTERFIELD	0-0		1500	"	"	"	"	"	"	Forsyth	Courtier	"	"	Ranshaw
4	18	Chesterfield	2-1	Vincent(pen), Dunderdale		"	"	"	"	"	"	Rudkin	Browning	"	"	"
5	25	BARNSLEY	1-0	Pridmore	2300	"	"	"	"	"	"	Pridmore	"	"	"	"
6	Oct 2	Barnsley	0-3		4162	"	"	"	"	"	"	"	"	"	Forsyth	"
7	9	Lincoln City	2-2	Ranshaw, Baines	3000	"	"	"	"	"	"	Forsyth	Eastham	"	Baines	"
8	16	LINCOLN CITY	3-2	Eastham,Ranshaw,Vincent(pen)	2000	"	"	"	"	"	"	Sears	"	Ferrier	"	"
9	23	Sheffield Wednesday	3-2	Dunderdale(3)	10000	"	"	"	"	"	"	Rook	Moody K	Dunderdale	"	"
10	30	SHEFFIELD WED.	1-3	H.Johnson	2500	"	"	"	"	"	"	Johnson H	Forsyth	"	"	"
11	Nov 6	Lincoln CITY	0-4		4000	"	"	"	"	"	"	Rudkin	Sears	"	Forsyth	"
12	13	LINCOLN City	3-2	Ranshaw, H.Johnson, Sears	2500	"	"	"	Hodgson S	"	"	Johnson H	"	"	Hall	"
13	20	SHEFFIELD UNITED	4-2	Hall, Sears(2), Dorsett	2500	"	"	"	"	"	"	"	"	Hall	Dorsett	"
14	27	Sheffield United	1-1	Dorsett	7000	"	"	"	"	"	"	Rook	"	Forsyth	"	"
15	Dec 4	ROTHERHAM UNITED	4-1	Ranshaw,Dorsett,Brain,Forsyth	2500	"	"	"	Hall	"	"	"	Brain	"	"	"
16	11	Rotherham United	3-4	Dorsett, Vinson(2)	2000	"	"	"	"	"	"	"	Forsyth	Vinson	"	"
17	18	Doncaster Rovers	1-2	Dorsett	2914	"	"	"	"	"	"	Bytheway	Brain	Forsyth	"	"
18	25	DONCASTER ROVERS	1-3	Forsyth	3000	"	"	"	Moore N	"	"	Rook	"	"	"	"

Various matches were 'double headers', I.e. were also considered for League Cup qualification. Grimsby Town qualified.

42nd in Football League North (2nd Comp)

						1	2	3	4	5	6	7	8	9	10	11
19	Dec 27	Doncaster Rovers	0-1			Moulson G	Vincent	Hodgson J	Moore N	Millington	Buck	Rook	Brain	Forsyth	Dorsett	Ranshaw
20	Jan 1	DONCASTER ROVERS	1-1	Dorsett	5000	"	"	"	Hall	"	"	"	"	Dorsett	Baines	"
21	8	SHEFFIELD UNITED	2-0	Hall, Rook	5000	"	"	"	"	"	"	"	"	Kurz	Dorsett	"
22	15	Sheffield United	1-3	Ranshaw	10000	"	"	Forsyth	Moulson C	"	"	"	Bytheway	Roberts N	Brain	"
23	22	Lincoln City	3-1	Rook, Ranshaw, Forsyth	3000	"	"	Hodgson J	Ewing	"	"	"	Canning	Johnson H	Forsyth	"
24	29	LINCOLN CITY	3-0	Ranshaw, H.Johnson, Vincent	6000	"	"	"	Gibson	"	"	"	Brain	"	"	"
25	Feb 5	ROTHERHAM UNITED	2-1	Rook, Brain	5000	"	"	"	"	"	Ewing	"	"	"	"	"
26	12	Rotherham United	1-6	Brain	7000	"	Moody K	"	Hall	"	Gibson	"	"	Forsyth	Dorsett	"
27	19	Chesterfield	1-5	W.Pearson	1500	"	Vincent	"	"	"	Buck	Pearson W	"	Johnson H	Forsyth	"
28	26	CHESTERFIELD	4-1	Dorsett(2),Vincent(pen),Ranshaw	4000	"	"	"	"	"	"	"	"	Kurz	Dorsett	"
29	Apr 10	Lincoln City	1-0	Dunderdale	5000	"	"	"	Major	"	"	Rook	"	Dunderdale	Arthur	"

Match 20, returned to Blundell Park.

Football League North Cup

						1	2	3	4	5	6	7	8	9	10	11
R1L1	Mar 4	Rotherham United	2-2	Dorsett, Brain	9700	Moulson G	Vincent	Hodgson J	Hall	Millington	Buck	Pearson W	Brain	Johnson H	Dorsett	Ranshaw
R1L2	11	ROTHERHAM UNITED	2-1	Brain, Forsyth	8000	"	"	"	"	"	"	Sweeney	"	Kurz	Forsyth	"
R2L1	18	Sheffield United	0-4		18000	"	"	"	"	"	"	Lowrey	"	Johnson H	Sweeney	"
R2L2	25	SHEFFIELD UNITED	0-1		7000	"	"	"	"	"	"	Rook	"	Vinson	Pearson W	"

1944/45 17th in Football League North (1st Comp)

							1	2	3	4	5	6	7	8	9	10	11
1	Aug	26	MANSFIELD TOWN	5-1	K.Reeve(2),Hall,W.Pearson,Lewis	6000	Moulson G	Vincent	Hodgson J	Gray	Millington	Buck	Rook	Hall	Reeve K	Lewis	Pearson W
2	Sep	2	Mansfield Town	1-1	K.Reeve	3000	"	"	"	"	"	Hall	Pridmore	Williams	"	"	"
3		9	Doncaster Rovers	3-1	Hall, Vincent, W.Pearson	6000	"	"	"	"	"	Buck	Williams	Fraser	Hall	Green	"
4		16	DONCASTER ROVERS	2-1	Kurz(2)	2000	"	"	"	"	Matthewson	"	Wallbanks	Green	Kurz	Rudkin	"
5		23	ROTHERHAM UNITED	1-1	Kurz	5000	"	"	"	Millington	"	"	Huxford	Williams	"	Green	"
6		30	Rotherham United	0-2		10000	"	"	"	Gray	Millington	"	Wallbanks	Hall	Dunderdale	"	"
7	Oct	7	Derby County	2-3	Dunderdale, Lamb	10000	"	"	"	"	"	Hall	"	Lamb	"	"	"
8		14	DERBY COUNTY	3-1	Lamb(2), Green	5000	"	"	"	Hall	"	Buck	"	"	Darley	"	Ranshaw
9		21	LINCOLN CITY	4-0	Dunderdale(p),Wallbanks,Lamb,Hall	4000	"	Gray	"	"	Jones S	"	"	"	Dunderdale	Lewis	"
10		28	Lincoln City	2-5	Bean(og), Johnston(og)	4000	"	Vincent	"	"	Millington	"	Lewis	"	"	Green	"
11	Nov	4	Sheffield United	1-3	Ranshaw	10000	"	"	Taylor W	"	Hodgson J	"	Tallent	"	"	Lewis	"
12		11	SHEFFIELD UNITED	1-0	Dunderdale	5000	"	"	Hodgson J	"	Millington	"	"	"	"	D'Arcy	"
13		18	SHEFFIELD WED.	1-2	Dunderdale	5000	"	"	"	"	"	"	Kurz	"	"	Birch	"
14		25	Sheffield Wednesday*	3-2	Lamb, Lewis(2)	4000	"	"	"	"	"	"	Huxford	"	"	Lewis	"
15	Dec	2	Hull City	3-4	Symons(og), Lamb, Huxford	5000	"	"	"	"	"	"	"	"	"	"	"
16		9	HULL CITY	0-0		4000	"	"	"	"	"	"	Tallent	"	Darley	"	"
17		16	NOTTINGHAM FOREST	3-1	Hall, Dunderdale, Huxford	2000	"	"	"	Glass	"	"	Huxford	Hall	Dunderdale	"	"
18		23	Nottingham Forest	2-1	Lamb(2)	6000	"	"	"	Grogan	Blenkinsopp	"	Lamb	Beattie	"	"	"

*Played at Doncaster Rovers — 3 own goals

Various matches were 'double headers', I.e. were also considered for League Cup qualification. Grimsby Town did not qualify

20th in Football League North (2nd Comp)

							1	2	3	4	5	6	7	8	9	10	11
19	Dec	25	LINCOLN CITY	2-2	Huxford, T.R.Moore	5000	Moulson G	Vincent	Hodgson J	Moore TR	Millington	Buck	Huxford	Lamb	Hall	Lewis	Ranshaw
20		30	Lincoln City	2-0	Dunderdale(2)	4000	"	"	"	Glass	"	Grogan	Lamb	Hall	Dunderdale	Bateman	"
21	Jan	6	SHEFFIELD WED.	4-1	Vincent,Lamb,Bateman,Dunderdale	3000	"	"	"	"	"	"	"	"	"	"	"
22		13	Sheffield Wednesday	2-2	J.Hodgson, Beattie	6000	"	"	"	"	"	"	"	"	Beattie	"	"
23		20	DONCASTER ROVERS	1-2	Ranshaw	4000	"	"	"	"	"	"	"	"	Johnson R	"	"
24		27	Doncaster Rovers	1-5	Ranshaw	5272	"	"	"	Hall	"	Buck	"	Corbett	Stevenson	"	"
25	Feb	3	Sheffield United	2-2	Ranshaw(2)	13500	"	"	"	"	"	"	"	Beattie	Dunderdale	Atkinson	"
26		10	SHEFFIELD UNITED	1-2	Beattie	7000	"	"	"	"	"	"	Kurz	"	"	Lamb	"
27		17	ROTHERHAM UNITED	5-0	Ranshaw,Vincent(p),Huxford(3)	5000	"	"	"	Glass	"	"	Brown	Hall	Huxford	Rudkin	"
28		24	Rotherham United	0-3		8000	"	"	"	"	"	"	"	"	"	Rodi	"
29	Mar	3	Hull City	1-3	J.Johnson	4000	"	"	"	"	"	Blewitt	Robertson L	Dolan	Johnson J	Hurley	Pashley
30		10	BRADFORD CITY	3-2	Hall, Rodi(2)	3000	Bellamy	"	"	"	"	Wood	Ranshaw	Hall	Rodi	Moody R	Sampson
31		17	HULL CITY	4-0	Hall(2), Vincent(pen), Rodi	3000	"	"	"	"	"	"	Lamb	"	"	Hurley	Ranshaw
32		24	Leeds United	1-1	Rodi	7000	Moulson G	"	"	Hall	"	Buck	"	Robertson L	Johnson J	Rodi	Pashley
33		31	LINCOLN CITY	4-2	Rodi,Ranshaw,J.Johnson,Hall	3000	"	"	"	"	"	"	"	Beattie	"	"	Ranshaw
34	Apr	2	Lincoln City	3-3	Ranshaw,J.Johnson,Bainbridge	5000	"	"	"	Glass	Moore TR	Wood	Bainbridge	Dolan	"	Beattie	"
35		7	LEEDS UNITED	3-0	Rodi(2), Glass	6000	"	"	"	"	Millington	Hall	Chadwick	Browning	Rodi	Lamb	"
36		14	LINCOLN CITY	4-3	Hall(p),Ranshaw,Rodi,J.Hodgson	4000	"	Minto	"	"	Horden	"	"	Millington	"	Bateman	"
37		21	Lincoln City	2-2	Foulston, Rodi	3000	"	Vincent	"	"	Millington	Buck	Harvey	Hall	"	Foulston	"
38	May	5	NOTTS COUNTY	3-1	Rodi(3)	4000	"	"	"	"	Charlesworth	"	Chadwick	Moore N	"	Hall	"
39		12	Notts County	3-1	Rodi, Chadwick, Vincent	2000	"	"	"	Bellas	Millington	"	"	Lamb	"	"	"

1945/46 17th in Football League North

						1	2	3	4	5	6	7	8	9	10	11
1	Aug	25 Blackburn Rovers	2-3	Chadwick, Lamb	18000	Moulson G	Vincent	Hodgson J	Hall	Betmead	Buck	Chadwick	Lamb	Rodi	Bell	Davies
2	Sep	1 BLACKBURN ROVERS	2-0	Betmead, Chadwick	6000	"	"	"	Harris	"	"	"	"	"	Hall	"
3		8 BRADFORD P.A.	2-1	Kurz, Chadwick	8950	"	"	"	Hall	"	"	"	Moore N	Kurz	Rodi	Pearson W
4		15 Bradford P.A.	3-2	Hepworth(og), Rodi, Kurz	10669	"	"	"	"	Charlesworth	"	"	Lamb	"	"	Davies
5		22 Manchester City	2-0	Wardle, Lamb	20000	"	"	"	Harris	Betmead	"	Davies	"	Pearson W	"	Wardle
6		29 MANCHESTER CITY	0-2		12620	"	"	"	Hall	"	"	Chadwick	Rodi	"	Baird	"
7	Oct	6 NEWCASTLE UNITED	0-2		13000	Tweedy	"	"	"	"	"	"	Lamb	Rodi	Bell	Davies
8		13 Newcastle United	2-6	Blenkinsopp, Davies	45000	Moulson G	"	"	Harris	"	"	"	Rodi	Blenkinsopp	Baird	"
9		20 Sheffield Wednesday	1-4	Rodi	18000	"	"	"	"	"	"	Bell	Candice	Rodi	"	"
10		27 SHEFFIELD WEDNESDAY	1-2	Davies	10083	"	Moody K	"	"	"	"	Harvey	Lamb	"	"	"
11	Nov	3 HUDDERSFIELD TOWN	5-3	Rodi,J.Johnson,Chadwick(2),Davies	10275	"	"	"	"	"	"	Chadwick	Moore N	Johnson J	Rodi	"
12		10 Huddersfield Town	2-3	N.Moore, Rodi	10774	"	"	"	"	"	"	"	"	"	"	"
13		17 Chesterfield	2-0	N.Moore, Rodi	15000	"	"	"	"	"	"	"	"	"	"	Vinson
14		24 CHESTERFIELD	3-3	Rodi, J.Hodgson, Buck	12000	"	"	"	"	Blenkinsopp	"	Kurz	"	"	"	Pearson W
15	Dec	1 BARNSLEY	0-0		11000	"	Vincent	"	"	Charlesworth	"	Chadwick	"	"	"	"
16		8 Barnsley	0-2		11000	"	"	"	Hodgson S	"	"	"	"	"	"	"
17		15 Everton	1-2	W.Pearson	25000	"	"	"	"	"	"	"	"	"	Jones T	"
18		22 EVERTON	1-2	N.Moore	11000	"	"	"	"	"	"	"	"	"	"	Rudkin
19		25 BOLTON WANDERERS	0-2		10000	"	"	"	Harris	"	"	"	"	Rodi	Bateman	Vinson
20		29 Preston North End	2-1	Rodi, Buck	9000	"	"	"	Hodgson S	"	"	Rook	"	Browning	Rodi	Pearson W
21	Jan	1 Bolton Wanderers	0-0		20000	"	Mouncer	"	Harris	"	"	Harvey	Glass	"	"	Jones R
22		12 Manchester United	0-5		20789	"	Vincent	"	Hodgson S	"	Glass	Johnson J	Moore N	Pearson W	Jones T	Wardle
23		19 MANCHESTER UNITED	1-0	Charlesworth	9000	"	"	"	"	"	Buck	Robertson L	"	"	Rodi	Jones R
24		26 LEEDS UNITED	3-2	N.Moore(2), Howe	9750	"	"	"	"	"	"	Chadwick	"	Howe	"	Pearson W
25	Feb	2 Sunderland	0-2		18000	"	"	"	"	"	"	Johnson J	Clifton	"	Moore N	Jones R
26		9 Sheffield United	1-7	Buck	20000	Tweedy	"	"	"	Betmead	"	Moore N	"	"	Robertson L	Pearson W
27		16 SHEFFIELD UNITED	1-6	Howe	11000	Moulson G	Mouncer	"	Glass	"	"	Chadwick	"	Moore N	Rodi	Howe
28		23 MIDDLESBROUGH	1-1	Vincent(pen)	9000	"	Vincent	"	Hodgson S	Charlesworth	Betmead	"	"	"	Baines	Wardle
29	Mar	2 Middlesbrough	1-3	Baines	11000	"	"	"	"	"	Blenkinsopp	"	"	"	"	"
30		9 Leeds United	2-2	Wardle, Vincent	8000	"	"	"	"	"	Betmead	"	Moore N	Howe	Jones T	"
31		16 STOKE CITY	0-2		15000	"	"	"	"	"	Buck	Crack	"	"	"	"
32		23 BURNLEY	1-1	N.Moore	9000	"	"	"	Hall	"	"	"	Baines	Moore N	"	"
33		26 SUNDERLAND	4-1	Baines(2),Clifton,Vincent(pen)	5000	"	"	"	"	"	"	Lewis	Clifton	Blenkinsopp	Baines	"
34		30 Burnley	2-1	Baines, Clifton	15000	"	Fisher	"	Moore N	"	"	"	Baines	Howe	Clifton	"
35	Apr	6 BLACKPOOL	4-2	T.Jones(2), Clifton(2)	12000	"	Vincent	"	"	"	"	"	Clifton	"	Jones T	"
36		13 Blackpool	3-5	T.Jones(2), Clifton	10000	"	"	"	"	"	"	"	"	"	"	"
37		15 Stoke City	2-4	Vincent(pen), Lewis		Tweedy	"	"	Hodgson S	"	"	"	"	"	"	"
38		19 Liverpool	0-2		45000	"	"	"	"	"	Blenkinsopp	Johnson JW	"	"	"	"
39		20 BURY	1-1	Temple	12000	"	Fisher	"	"	Betmead	Buck	Lewis	Moore N	Temple	Baines	"
40		22 LIVERPOOL	1-1	J.Johnson	14000	"	Vincent	"	"	"	Hall	"	Baines	Johnson J	Jones T	"
41		27 Bury	1-1	J.Johnson	4000	"	"	"	"	"	"	"	Clifton	"	"	"
42	May	4 PRESTON NORTH END	1-0	A.Beattie(og)	11000	"	"	"	Hall	"	Moore N	Johnson JW	"	"	Lewis	"

2 own goals

FA Cup

R3L1	Jan	5 SUNDERLAND	1-3	Rodi	12050	Moulson G	Mouncer	Hodgson J	Hall	Hodgson S	Jones T	Chadwick	Moore N	Johnson J	Rodi	Wardle
R3L2		9 Sunderland	1-2	N.Moore	9000	"	Vincent	"	Hodgson S	Charlesworth	Blenkinsopp	Harvey	Rodi	Moore N	Jones T	"

1946-47 16th in Division 1

Captain: Harry Clifton

							Tweedy	Vincent	Hodgson JV	Hodgson S	Charlesworth	Reeve FW	Johnson Jack	Clifton	Johnson Jim	McGowan	Wardle	Moulson	Chisholm	Mouncer	Fisher	Blenkinsopp	Hall	Taylor RE	Penrose	Whitfield	Betmead	Pearson	Wallbanks	Jones	Hansen	Moore N	Cairns	Reeve K	Keeble
1	Aug	31	Manchester United	1-2	McGowan	41025	1	2	3	4	5	6	7	8	9	10	11																		
2	Sep	3	WOLVERHAMPTON WANE	0-0		18327	1	2	3	4			7		9	10	11					6					5			8					
3		7	PRESTON NORTH END	2-3	Jones(2)	18571	1	2	3	4			7		9	10	11					6					5			8					
4		14	Sheffield United	1-1	Vincent	31777	1	2	3	4			7	8								6					5	11		10		9			
5		21	CHELSEA	2-1	Jones, N.Moore	21932	1	2		4				8			11				3	6					5	7		10		9			
6		23	Wolverhampton Wands.	0-2		30537	1			4			7	8			11			2	3	6					5			10		9			
7		28	Bolton Wanderers	2-1	Clifton(2)	30547	1	2		4				8			11				3	6		5				7		10		9			
8	Oct	5	LIVERPOOL	1-6	Wardle(pen)	20189	1	2		4				8			11				3	6					5	7		10		9			
9		12	Leeds United	0-1		28877	1		3			6	7	8			11				2	4					5					9			10
10		19	Sunderland	2-1	Blenkinsopp(2)	42763	1		3			6	7	10			11				2	9	4			8	5								
11		26	PORTSMOUTH	3-2	Clifton, Cairns, Blenkinsopp	16885	1		3			6	7	8			11				2	9	4				5						10		
12	Nov	2	Everton	3-3	Blenkinsopp(2), Whitfield	48817	1		3	4		6					11				2	9				8	5		7				10		
13		9	HUDDERSFIELD TOWN	1-0	Blenkinsopp	14815	1		3	4				8			11				2	9		6			5		7				10		
14		16	Blackpool	3-2	Wardle, Cairns(2)	17511	1		3			6		8			11				2	9		4			5		7				10		
15		23	BRENTFORD	2-2	Blenkinsopp, Wallbanks	16570	1		3			6		8			11				2	9		4			5		7				10		
16		30	Blackburn Rovers	1-1	Cairns	22677	1		3			6		8			11				2	9	4				5		7				10		
17	Dec	7	ASTON VILLA	0-3		18257	1		3			6		8			11				2	9		4			5		7				10		
18		14	Derby County	1-4	Wardle	18809	1		3			6	7	8			11				2	9			4		5						10		
19		21	ARSENAL	0-0		13308	1		3				7	8	9		11				2	6	4				5						10		
20		25	CHARLTON ATHLETIC	3-1	Clifton(2), Cairns	17841	1		3			6	7	8			11				2	9	4				5						10		
21		26	Charlton Athletic	0-0		30804	1	2				6	7								3	9				4	5	11			8		10		
22		28	MANCHESTER UNITED	0-0		17183	1	2				6	7	8			11				3	9					5						10		
23	Jan	1	Middlesbrough	0-3		39947	1	2				6	7	10			11				3	9	4			8	5								
24		4	Preston North End	0-3		27262	1	2	5			6	7				11				3	9	4							8			10		
25		18	SHEFFIELD UNITED	2-1	J.Johnson, Vincent	17691	1	2				6		8	9		11				3		4	5					7						10
26	Feb	1	BOLTON WANDERERS	2-2	Clifton(2)	11467	1	2				6		10			11				3	9	4	5					7			8			
27		8	Chelsea	0-0		17896	1						7	8						2	3	6	4	5				11					9		10
28		12	Liverpool	0-5		20648	1						7	8						2	3	6	4	5				11						9	10
29	Mar	1	Portsmouth	1-4	Wardle(pen)	27099	1	2					7	8			11				3	6	4	5									9		10
30		8	EVERTON	2-2	Keeble, Cairns	11277	1	2					7	8			11				3	6	4				5						9		10
31		15	Huddersfield Town	2-3	Cairns(2)	17201	1						7	8			11			2	3	6	4				5						9		10
32		22	BLACKPOOL	2-3	Cairns, Wardle(pen)	13452	1		3				7	8		10	11				2	6	4				5						9		
33		29	Brentford	1-0	Cairns	19778	1					6	7	8			11			2	3	10		4			5						9		
34	Apr	4	STOKE CITY	2-5	Clifton, Wardle(pen)	26537						6		8			11	1		2	3	10		4			5		7				9		
35		5	BLACKBURN ROVERS	2-1	Cairns, K.Reeve	12975						6		8			11		1	2	3		4				5	7					10	9	
36		7	Stoke City	0-3		34386						6	7	8			11		1	2	3		4				5						10	9	
37		12	Aston Villa	3-3	J.Johnson, Clifton(2)	37741	1			4		6	7	8			11			2	3						5						10	9	
38		19	DERBY COUNTY	2-0	Clifton, Cairns	16200	1			4		6	7	8			11			2	3						5						10	9	
39		26	Arsenal	3-5	Cairns, K.Reeve, Clifton	42100	1			4		6	7	8			11			2	3						5						10	9	
40	May	3	MIDDLESBROUGH	4-0	Cairns(2), Whitfield, K.Reeve	13376	1					6	7				11			2	3		4			8	5						10	9	
41		10	SUNDERLAND	1-2	K.Reeve	12777	1					6	7	8			11			2	3		4				5						10	9	
42		17	LEEDS UNITED	4-1	Cairns(3), Wardle(pen)	10795	1					6	7	8			11			2	3	9				4	5						10		
						Apps.	39	15	18	13	1	27	29	36	5	4	38	1	2	14	38	33	20	12	1	6	34	8	9	8	1	7	28	8	7
						Goals							1	12	1	1	7					7				2		1	1	3		1	18	4	

F.A. Cup

							Tweedy	Vincent	Hodgson JV	Hodgson S	Charlesworth	Reeve FW	Johnson Jack	Clifton	Johnson Jim	McGowan	Wardle	Moulson	Chisholm	Mouncer	Fisher	Blenkinsopp	Hall	Taylor RE	Penrose	Whitfield	Betmead	Pearson	Wallbanks	Jones	Hansen	Moore N	Cairns	Reeve K	Keeble
R3	Jan	11	Reading	2-2	Cairns(2)	22890	1	2					7	8			11				3	6	4	5						10			9		
R3r		14	READING	3-1	Cairns(2), Keeble		1	2									11				3	6	4	5		8			7				9		10
R4		25	Liverpool	0-2		42000	1							8			11			2	3	6	4	5					7				9		10

		P	W	D	L	F	A	W	D	L	F	A	F	A	Pts
1	Liverpool	42	13	3	5	42	24	12	4	5	42	28	84	52	57
2	Manchester United	42	17	3	1	61	19	5	9	7	34	35	95	54	56
3	Wolverhampton W.	42	15	1	5	66	31	10	5	6	32	25	98	56	56
4	Stoke City	42	14	5	2	52	21	10	2	9	38	32	90	53	55
5	Blackpool	42	14	1	6	38	32	8	5	8	33	38	71	70	50
6	Sheffield United	42	12	4	5	51	32	9	3	9	38	43	89	75	49
7	Preston North End	42	10	7	4	45	27	8	4	9	31	47	76	74	47
8	Aston Villa	42	9	6	6	39	24	9	3	9	28	29	67	53	45
9	Sunderland	42	11	3	7	33	27	7	5	9	32	39	65	66	44
10	Everton	42	13	5	3	40	24	4	4	13	22	43	62	67	43
11	Middlesbrough	42	11	3	7	46	32	6	5	10	27	36	73	68	42
12	Portsmouth	42	11	3	7	42	27	5	6	10	24	33	66	60	41
13	Arsenal	42	9	5	7	43	33	7	4	10	29	37	72	70	41
14	Derby County	42	13	2	6	44	28	5	3	13	29	51	73	79	41
15	Chelsea	42	9	3	9	33	39	7	4	10	36	45	69	84	39
16	GRIMSBY TOWN	42	9	6	6	37	35	4	6	11	24	47	61	82	38
17	Blackburn Rovers	42	6	5	10	23	27	8	3	10	22	26	45	53	36
18	Bolton Wanderers	42	8	5	8	30	28	5	3	13	27	41	57	69	34
19	Charlton Athletic	42	6	6	9	34	32	5	6	10	23	39	57	71	34
20	Huddersfield Town	42	11	4	6	34	24	2	3	16	19	55	53	79	33
21	Brentford	42	5	5	11	19	35	4	2	15	26	53	45	88	25
22	Leeds United	42	6	5	10	30	30	0	1	20	15	60	45	90	18

SEASON 1946/47

Back: F.Reeve, S.Hodgson, Mouncer, Vincer, Tweedy, Fisher, Blenkinsopp, McIlwarne (Trainer)
Front: J.W.Johnson, Clifton, N.Moore, Jones, Wardle, Betmead

1947-48 22nd in Division 1

Captain: Harry Clifton

							Tweedy	Fisher	Hodgson JV	Blenkinsopp	Taylor RE	Reeve FW	Johnson Jack	Clifton	Briggs	Cairns	Wardle	Chisholm	Mouncer	Moody	Sibley	Hall	Penrose	Hodgson S	Galley	Whitfield	Wilson	Burnett	Armitage	McGowan	Reeve K	Boulton	Pearson
1	Aug	23	ASTON VILLA	3-0	Cairns(2), J.Johnson	20532	1	2	3	4	5	6	7	8	9	10	11																
2		27	Wolverhampton Wands.	1-8	Cairns	43289	1	2	3	4	5	6	7	8	9	10	11																
3		30	Sunderland	2-4	Cairns, Clifton	35937	1	3		4	5	6	7	8		10	11		2												9		
4	Sep	3	WOLVERHAMPTON WANDS.	0-4		21173	1	3		4	5	6				10	11		2							8	7				9		
5		6	SHEFFIELD UNITED	0-3		18103	1	3		4	5	6				10	11		2							8	7				9		
6		10	Huddersfield Town	1-5	Briggs	20145	1	2	3	6	5		7	8	9	10	11					4											
7		13	MANCHESTER CITY	1-0	Clifton	16766	1	2	3	6	5			8	9	10	11						4				7						
8		17	HUDDERSFIELD TOWN	3-0	Clifton, Cairns(2)	17658	1	2	3	6	5			8	9	10	11						4				7						
9		20	Blackburn Rovers	0-4		24254		2	3	6	5			8	9	10	11	1					4				7						
10		27	BLACKPOOL	0-1		25576		2	3	6	5			8	9	10	11	1					4				7						
11	Oct	4	Derby County	1-4	Cairns	24274		2	3	6	5				9	10	11	1					4				7			8			
12		11	Manchester United	4-3	Cairns(3), Blenkinsopp	41202	1	2	3	9	5	6				10	11						4				7			8			
13		18	PRESTON NORTH END	1-1	Wilson	17915	1	2	3	9	5	6				10	11						4				7			8			
14		25	Stoke City	1-2	Cairns	29980	1	2	3	9	5	6				10	11						4				7			8			
15	Nov	1	BURNLEY	1-2	Cairns	17697	1	2	3	9	5	6				10	11							4			7			8			
16		8	Liverpool	1-3	K.Reeve	36796	1	2	3	6	5				9	10	11							4			7				8		
17		15	MIDDLESBROUGH	0-5		14812	1	2	3	6	5		7	8		10	11							4							9		
18		22	Portsmouth	0-4		23459		2	3	5		6				10	11	1							4	8	7				9		
19		29	BOLTON WANDERERS	0-2		11901		3		5		6				10	11	1	2					4			7	8			9		
20	Dec	6	Charlton Athletic	3-2	Wardle(2), Cairns	14667	1	3		5		6	7			10	11				2				4			8			9		
21		13	ARSENAL	0-4		18700	1	3		5		6	7		9	10	11				2				4			8					
22		20	Aston Villa	2-2	Wardle, Briggs	31577	1	3		5		6			9	10	11				2				4			8					7
23		25	CHELSEA	0-0		19666	1	2	3	5		6	7		9	10	11							4				8					
24		27	Chelsea	3-2	Wardle, Briggs, Whitfield	34068	1	3		5		6			9	10	11				2			4		8		7					
25	Jan	3	SUNDERLAND	1-2	Whitfield	15882	1	3		5		6			9	10	11				2				4	8		7					
26		17	Sheffield United	0-4		27930	1	3			5	6	7			10	11				2				4	8			9				
27		31	Manchester City	1-3	Whitfield	36971	1	3		5		6				10	11				2				4	8		7	9				
28	Feb	7	BLACKBURN ROVERS	2-2	Cairns(2)	14231	1	3		6	5					9	10				2				4	8			7				11
29		14	Blackpool	1-3	Pearson	21612	1	3		6	5					9	10		2					4					7		8		11
30		21	DERBY COUNTY	2-3	Armitage, Cairns	11607	1	3		6	5					9	10		2						4				7		8		11
31	Mar	6	Preston North End	1-2	Armitage	25534	1	3		6						10	11		2						5	4	7		9		8		
32		13	STOKE CITY	0-0		9631	1	3		6			7				11				2				5	4			9		8		10
33		17	MANCHESTER UNITED	1-1	McGowan	12284	1	3		6					8					2					5	4	7		9	10			11
34		20	Burnley	1-4	Pearson	19522	1	3		6	5				8					2						4	7			10	9		11
35		26	EVERTON	3-0	Blenkinsopp, Pearson(2)	18279	1	3		6			7		9					2					5	4				10	8		11
36		27	LIVERPOOL	0-2		15781	1	3		6			7		9					2					5	4				10	8		11
37		29	Everton	1-3	Blenkinsopp	37926	1	3		6			7	8	9					2					5	4					10		11
38	Apr	3	Middlesbrough	1-4	Clifton	24130		3		6	5		7	8	9		11	1		2						4				10			
39		10	PORTSMOUTH	1-0	Briggs	10400	1	3		6				8	9		11			2					5	4				10			7
40		17	Bolton Wanderers	0-2		23378	1	3		6				8	9					2					5	4		7		10			11
41		24	CHARLTON ATHLETIC	1-3	Briggs	8655	1	3		6				8	9					2					5	4		7				10	11
42	May	1	Arsenal	0-8		34644	1	3		6			7		9		10			2				4	5					8			11
						Apps.	36	42	16	41	23	19	15	14	24	31	35	6	7	10	9	1	8	8	19	19	17	10	8	13	16	1	14
						Goals				3			1	4	5	16	4									3	1		2	1	1		4

F.A. Cup

							Tweedy	Fisher	Hodgson JV	Blenkinsopp	Taylor RE	Reeve FW	Johnson Jack	Clifton	Briggs	Cairns	Wardle	Chisholm	Mouncer	Moody	Sibley	Hall	Penrose	Hodgson S	Galley	Whitfield	Wilson	Burnett	Armitage	McGowan	Reeve K	Boulton	Pearson
R3	Jan	10	EVERTON	1-4	Whitfield	19000	1	3			5	6			9	10	11				2				4	8		7					

		P	W	D	L	F	A	W	D	L	F	A	F	A	Pts
1	Arsenal	42	15	3	3	56	15	8	10	3	25	17	81	32	59
2	Manchester United	42	11	7	3	50	27	8	7	6	31	21	81	48	52
3	Burnley	42	12	5	4	31	12	8	7	6	25	31	56	43	52
4	Derby County	42	11	6	4	38	24	8	6	7	39	33	77	57	50
5	Wolverhampton W.	42	12	4	5	45	29	7	5	9	38	41	83	70	47
6	Aston Villa	42	13	5	3	42	22	6	4	11	23	35	65	57	47
7	Preston North End	42	13	4	4	43	35	7	3	11	24	33	67	68	47
8	Portsmouth	42	13	5	3	44	17	6	2	13	24	33	68	50	45
9	Blackpool	42	13	4	4	37	14	4	6	11	20	27	57	41	44
10	Manchester City	42	13	3	5	37	22	2	9	10	15	25	52	47	42
11	Liverpool	42	9	8	4	39	23	7	2	12	26	38	65	61	42
12	Sheffield United	42	13	4	4	44	24	3	6	12	21	46	65	70	42
13	Charlton Athletic	42	8	4	9	33	29	9	2	10	24	37	57	66	40
14	Everton	42	10	2	9	30	26	7	4	10	22	40	52	66	40
15	Stoke City	42	9	5	7	29	23	5	5	11	12	32	41	55	38
16	Middlesbrough	42	8	7	6	37	27	6	2	13	34	46	71	73	37
17	Bolton Wanderers	42	11	2	8	29	25	5	3	13	17	33	46	58	37
18	Chelsea	42	11	6	4	38	27	3	3	15	15	44	53	71	37
19	Huddersfield Town	42	7	6	8	25	24	5	6	10	26	36	51	60	36
20	Sunderland	42	11	4	6	33	18	2	6	13	23	49	56	67	36
21	Blackburn Rovers	42	8	5	8	35	30	3	5	13	19	42	54	72	32
22	GRIMSBY TOWN	42	5	5	11	20	35	3	1	17	25	76	45	111	22

SEASON 1947/48
Back: J.V.Hodgson, Galley, Sibley, Tweedy, Fisher, F.Reeve
Front: Pearson, Burnett, Briggs, Cairns, Wardle, Blenkinsopp

SEASON 1948/49
Back: Dawson (Trainer), McKenna, Moody, Tweedy, Galley, Forrest, Fisher, Clifton
Front: Lloyd, Whitfield, Briggs, McGowan, Pearson

1948-49 11th in Division 2

Captain: Billy Cairns

	Date		Opponent	Score	Scorers	Att.	Tweedy	Moody	Sibley	McKenna	Galley	Forrest	McStay	Clifton	Cairns	Lloyd	Pearson	Chisholm	Fisher	Johnston	Robinson N	Moore R	MacMillan	Boulton	Whitfield	Shearer	Duthie	Briggs	McGowan	Lynn	Hair	Mouncer
1	Aug	21	FULHAM	2-3	Clifton, Cairns	19271	1	2	3	4	5	6	7	8	9	10	11															
2		24	NOTTINGHAM FOREST	1-2	Cairns	18298	1	2	3	4		6	7	8	10		11				5							9				
3		28	Plymouth Argyle	2-0	Briggs, Pearson	24618	1	2	3	4		6	7			8	11				5							9	10			
4	Sep	1	Nottingham Forest	0-0		21897	1	2	3	4		6	7			8	11				5							9	10			
5		4	BLACKBURN ROVERS	1-2	McStay(pen)	15671	1	2	3	4	5	6	7			8	11											9	10			
6		8	Chesterfield	3-0	Cairns, McKenna, Pearson	11846	1	2		4	5	6	7	10	9	8	11		3													
7		11	Cardiff City	0-3		32156	1	2		4	5		7	6	9	8	11		3										10			
8		14	CHESTERFIELD	3-3	Clifton(2), McGowan	14838	1	2		4	5	6	7	8	9		11		3										10			
9		18	QUEENS PARK RANGERS	4-1	McGowan,Pearson,Cairns, Forrest	15141	1	2		4		6	7	8	9		11		3		5								10			
10		25	Luton Town	1-1	Clifton	18173	1	2		4		6		8	9	7			3		5								10	11		
11	Oct	2	BRADFORD P.A.	0-3		15931	1	2		4	5	6		8	9	7			3										10	11		
12		9	LINCOLN CITY	2-2	Briggs, McKenna	22169	1	2		4	5	6		8		7	11		3									9	10			
13		16	Sheffield Wednesday	1-4	Briggs	34095	1	2		4	5	6				7	11		3						8			9	10			
14		23	COVENTRY CITY	4-1	Briggs(3), Clifton	13334	1	2		4	5	6	7	8		11			3									9	10			
15		30	Leeds United	3-6	Lloyd(pen), Galley, Briggs	33581	1	2		4	5	6	7	8		11			3									9	10			
16	Nov	6	LEICESTER CITY	1-0	Galley	14774		2		4	5	6	7	8		11		1	3									9	10			
17		13	Brentford	0-2		24992		2		4	5	6	7	8		11		1	3									9	10			
18		20	TOTTENHAM HOTSPUR	1-1	Lloyd	15863		2		4	5	6	7			11		1	3						8			9	10			
19	Dec	4	BURY	2-3	Lloyd (2 pens)	13523		2		4		6	7	8		11		1	3			5						9	10			
20		11	West Bromwich Albion	2-5	Briggs, Pearson	22664		2		4		6	7			8	11	1	3			5						9	10			
21		18	Fulham	1-3	Lloyd	19996		2	5	4		6	7		9	8	11	1	3					10								
22		25	BARNSLEY	3-0	Briggs, Cairns, Clifton	18369		2	5	4		6	7	8	10	11		1	3									9				
23		27	Barnsley	1-2	Clifton	19848		2	5	4		6	7	8	10	11		1	3									9				
24	Jan	1	PLYMOUTH ARGYLE	2-2	Briggs, Cairns	12175		2	5	4		6	7	8	10	11		1	3									9				
25		15	Blackburn Rovers	3-3	Whitfield, Cairns, Lloyd	13418		2	5	4		6	7		10	11		1	3						8			9				
26		22	CARDIFF CITY	2-2	Whitfield, Cairns	15210		2	5	4		6	7		10	11		1	3						8			9				
27	Feb	5	Queens Park Rangers	2-1	Briggs(2)	19813		2	5	4		6	7			8		1	3	10								9			11	
28		12	West Ham United	0-1		20795		2		4		5	7	10		8		1	3	6								9			11	
29		26	Bradford P.A.	1-0	Briggs	15139		2		4		5	7		10			1	3	6						8		9			11	
30	Mar	5	Lincoln City	3-2	Briggs(3)	23146		2		4		5	7		10			1	3	6						8		9			11	
31		12	SHEFFIELD WEDNESDAY	2-0	Briggs, Shearer	18425		2		4		5	7			10		1	3	6						8		9			11	
32		19	Coventry City	1-4	Lloyd	22278		2		4		5	7			10		1	3	6						8		9			11	
33		26	LEEDS UNITED	5-1	Briggs(2),Shearer,Cairns,Lloyd	15848		2		4		5			10	7		1	3	6						8		9			11	
34	Apr	2	Leicester City	1-1	Briggs	35847		2		4		5			10	7		1	3	6						8		9			11	
35		9	BRENTFORD	3-0	Briggs, McStay, Cairns	15695		2		4			7		10			1	3	6			5			8		9			11	
36		15	SOUTHAMPTON	0-1		25931		2		4			7		10			1	3	6			5			8		9			11	
37		16	Tottenham Hotspur	2-5	Cairns, Hair	25808		2		4			7	8	10			1	3	6			5					9			11	
38		18	Southampton	0-0		26064		2	6	8					10			1	3	4			5	7				9			11	
39		23	WEST HAM UNITED	3-0	Briggs(2),Shearer	15803			2	4					10	7		1	3	6			5			8		9			11	
40		30	Bury	1-5	Briggs	9036				4					10	7		1	3	6			5				8	9			11	2
41	May	3	LUTON TOWN	2-1	Briggs, Cairns	13809		2		4			7		10	8		1	3	6			5					9			11	
42		7	WEST BROMWICH ALBION	1-0	Briggs	18564		2		4			7		10	8		1	3	6			5					9			11	
						Apps.	15	40	14	42	13	33	33	19	26	33	13	27	37	16	5	2	8	2	4	9	1	34	17	2	16	1
						Goals				2	2	1	2	7	12	8	4								2	3		26	2		1	

F.A. Cup

	Date		Opponent	Score	Scorers	Att.	Tweedy	Moody	Sibley	McKenna	Galley	Forrest	McStay	Clifton	Cairns	Lloyd	Pearson	Chisholm	Fisher	Johnston	Robinson N	Moore R	MacMillan	Boulton	Whitfield	Shearer	Duthie	Briggs	McGowan	Lynn	Hair	Mouncer
R3	Jan	18	EXETER CITY	2-1	Whitfield, Cairns	15210		2	5	4		6	7		10	11		1	3						8			9				
R4		29	HULL CITY	2-3	Forrest, Briggs	26505		2	5	4		6	7		10	11		1	3						8			9				

	P	W	D	L	F	A	W	D	L	F	A	F	A	Pts
1 Fulham	42	16	4	1	52	14	8	5	8	25	23	77	37	57
2 West Bromwich Alb.	42	16	3	2	47	16	8	5	8	22	23	69	39	56
3 Southampton	42	16	4	1	48	10	7	5	9	21	26	69	36	55
4 Cardiff City	42	14	4	3	45	21	5	9	7	17	26	62	47	51
5 Tottenham Hotspur	42	14	4	3	50	18	3	12	6	22	26	72	44	50
6 Chesterfield	42	9	7	5	24	18	6	10	5	27	27	51	45	47
7 West Ham United	42	13	5	3	38	23	5	5	11	18	35	56	58	46
8 Sheffield Wed.	42	12	6	3	36	17	3	7	11	27	39	63	56	43
9 Barnsley	42	10	7	4	40	18	4	5	12	22	43	62	61	40
10 Luton Town	42	11	6	4	32	16	3	6	12	23	41	55	57	40
11 GRIMSBY TOWN	42	10	5	6	44	28	5	5	11	28	48	72	76	40
12 Bury	42	12	5	4	41	23	5	1	15	26	53	67	76	40
13 Queen's Park Rgs.	42	11	4	6	31	26	3	7	11	13	36	44	62	39
14 Blackburn Rovers	42	12	5	4	41	23	3	3	15	12	40	53	63	38
15 Leeds United	42	11	6	4	36	21	1	7	13	19	42	55	63	37
16 Coventry City	42	12	3	6	35	20	3	4	14	20	44	55	64	37
17 Bradford Park Ave.	42	8	8	5	37	26	5	3	13	28	52	65	78	37
18 Brentford	42	7	10	4	28	21	4	4	13	14	32	42	53	36
19 Leicester City	42	6	10	5	41	38	4	6	11	21	41	62	79	36
20 Plymouth Argyle	42	11	4	6	33	25	1	8	12	16	39	49	64	36
21 Nottingham Forest	42	9	6	6	22	14	5	1	15	28	40	50	54	35
22 Lincoln City	42	6	7	8	31	35	2	5	14	22	56	53	91	28

1949-50 11th in Division 2

Captain: Billy Cairns

No	Date		Opponent	Score	Scorers	Att	Chisholm	Moody	Fisher	McKenna	MacMillan	Johnston	McStay	Lloyd	Briggs	Cairns	Hair	Bircham	Tweedy	Harnby	Taylor W	Moore R	Duthie	MacKenzie	Bloomer	Mulholland	Rankin	Barney	Shearer	Johnson Jim
1	Aug	20	Southampton	2-1	Briggs(2)	26222	1	2	3	4	5	6	7	8	9	10	11													
2		24	Preston North End	0-2		30935	1	2	3	4	5	6	7	8	9	10	11													
3		27	COVENTRY CITY	3-2	Briggs(3)	18635	1	2	3	4	5	6	7	8	9	10	11													
4		31	PRESTON NORTH END	1-3	Briggs	24190	1	2	3	4	5	6	7	8	9	10	11													
5	Sep	3	Luton Town	0-0		16717	1	2	3	4	5	6		7	9	10	11											8		
6		7	SWANSEA TOWN	2-1	Briggs(2)	19465	1	2	3	4	5	6		7	9	10	11											8		
7		10	BARNSLEY	2-2	Briggs, Hair	19071	1	2	3	4	5	6		7	9	10	11											8		
8		17	West Ham United	3-4	Briggs(2), Shearer	28194	1	2	3	4	5	6		7	9	10	11												8	
9		24	SHEFFIELD UNITED	4-0	Lloyd(pen), Cairns(2), Briggs	18348	1	2	3		5	4		7	9	10	11							6					8	
10	Oct	1	Hull City	2-2	Shearer, Briggs	46282	1	2	3		5	4		7	9	10	11							6					8	
11		8	SHEFFIELD WEDNESDAY	4-1	Lloyd(3,2pens), Cairns	24822	1	2	3		5	4		7	9	10	11							6					8	
12		15	Plymouth Argyle	2-4	Briggs(2)	24276	1	2	3		5	4		7	9	10	11							6					8	
13		22	CHESTERFIELD	5-2	MacKenzie,Briggs(2),Cairns(2)	17055	1	2	3		5	4		7	9	10	11							6					8	
14		29	Bradford P.A.	1-4	Briggs	15474	1	2	3		5	4		7	9	10	11							6					8	
15	Nov	5	LEICESTER CITY	2-1	Cairns, Briggs	14114	1	2	3		5	4		7	9	10	11							6					8	
16		12	Bury	1-3	Cairns	10287	1	2	3			4		7	9	10	11					5		6				8		
17		19	TOTTENHAM HOTSPUR	2-3	Hair, Briggs	22580	1	2	3		5	4		7	9	10	11							6				8		
18		26	Cardiff City	0-1		22664	1	2	3		5	4	7		9	10	11							6				8		
19	Dec	3	BLACKBURN ROVERS	1-2	Briggs	15005	1	2	3		5	4			9	10	11							6	7				8	
20		10	Brentford	0-1		16273		2				4			9	10	11	1		3			5	6		7			8	
21		17	SOUTHAMPTON	1-1	Cairns	12818		2			5	4		7	9	10	11	1		3			6						8	
22		24	Coventry City	1-1	Briggs	24058		2			5	4	11	7	9	10		1		3			6						8	
23		26	QUEENS PARK RANGERS	1-1	Briggs	22336		2			5	4	11	7	9	10		1		3			6						8	
24		27	Queens Park Rangers	2-1	Shearer, Briggs	22884			2		5	4	11	7	9	10		1		3			6						8	
25		31	LUTON TOWN	6-1	Briggs(3), Hair, Cairns, Shearer	16932			2		5	4	7		9	10	11	1		3			6						8	
26	Jan	14	Barnsley	2-7	Cairns, Shearer	18519			2		5	4	7		9	10	11	1		3			6						8	
27		21	WEST HAM UNITED	2-0	Briggs(2)	17046			2		5	4	7		9	10	11	1		3			6						8	
28	Feb	4	Sheffield United	1-3	Cairns	33108	1		2		5	4		7	9	10	11			3				6				8		
29		18	HULL CITY	1-0	Cairns	26476	1	2			5	4		7	9	10	11				3			6					8	
30	Mar	4	PLYMOUTH ARGYLE	2-2	Briggs, Johnston	15551	1	2			5	4	7		9	10	11				3			6					8	
31		11	Chesterfield	1-2	Bloomer	11703	1	2			5	4	7			10	11				3			6	8					9
32		18	BRADFORD P.A.	4-0	Hair(2), Cairns, Briggs	15346	1	2	3		5	4		7	9	10	11							6	8					
33		25	Leicester City	0-1		31635	1	2	3		5	4		7	9	10	11							6	8					
34	Apr	1	CARDIFF CITY	0-0		14922	1	2	3		5	4		7	9	10	11							6	8					
35		7	LEEDS UNITED	2-0	MacKenzie(pen), OG	21469	1	2	3		5	4		7	9	10	11							6	8					
36		8	Blackburn Rovers	0-3		15363	1	2	3		5	4		7	9	10	11							6	8					
37		10	Leeds United	0-1		17991	1	2	3		5	4	11		9	10								6	8		7			
38		15	BURY	4-2	Shearer, Cairns(2), Briggs	14232	1	2	3		5	4		7	9	10	11							6					8	
39		22	Tottenham Hotspur	2-1	Cairns, Briggs	46423	1	2	3		5	4		7	9	10	11							6					8	
40		26	Sheffield Wednesday	0-4		40862	1	2	3		5	4		7	9	10	11							6					8	
41		29	BRENTFORD	4-1	Briggs(2), Cairns, Hair	12585		2	3		5	4	7		9	10	11		1					6					8	
42	May	6	Swansea Town	1-2	Briggs	18723	1	2	3		5	4		7	9	10	11							6					8	
						Apps.	33	37	35	8	40	42	15	32	41	42	38	8	1	9	3	1	8	27	8	1	1	7	24	1
						Goals						1		4	36	17	6							2	1				6	

1 own goal

F.A. Cup

Rd	Date		Opponent	Score	Scorers	Att	Chisholm	Moody	Fisher	McKenna	MacMillan	Johnston	McStay	Lloyd	Briggs	Cairns	Hair	Bircham	Tweedy	Harnby	Taylor W	Moore R	Duthie	MacKenzie	Bloomer	Mulholland	Rankin	Barney	Shearer	Johnson Jim
R3	Jan	7	Luton Town	4-3	Briggs(4)	18843			2		5	4	7		9	10	11	1		3			6						8	
R4		28	Portsmouth	0-5		39364			2		5	4	7		9	10	11	1		3			6					8		

		P	W	D	L	F	A	W	D	L	F	A	F	A	Pts
1	Tottenham Hotspur	42	15	3	3	51	15	12	4	5	30	20	81	35	61
2	Sheffield Wed.	42	12	7	2	46	23	6	9	6	21	25	67	48	52
3	Sheffield United	42	9	10	2	36	19	10	4	7	32	30	68	49	52
4	Southampton	42	13	4	4	44	25	6	10	5	20	23	64	48	52
5	Leeds United	42	11	8	2	33	16	6	5	10	21	29	54	45	47
6	Preston North End	42	12	5	4	37	21	6	4	11	23	28	60	49	45
7	Hull City	42	11	8	2	39	25	6	3	12	25	47	64	72	45
8	Swansea Town	42	11	3	7	34	18	6	6	9	19	31	53	49	43
9	Brentford	42	11	5	5	21	12	4	8	9	23	37	44	49	43
10	Cardiff City	42	13	3	5	28	14	3	7	11	13	30	41	44	42
11	GRIMSBY TOWN	42	13	5	3	53	25	3	3	15	21	48	74	73	40
12	Coventry City	42	8	6	7	32	24	5	7	9	23	31	55	55	39
13	Barnsley	42	11	6	4	45	28	2	7	12	19	39	64	67	39
14	Chesterfield	42	12	3	6	28	16	3	6	12	15	31	43	47	39
15	Leicester City	42	8	9	4	30	25	4	6	11	25	40	55	65	39
16	Blackburn Rovers	42	10	5	6	30	15	4	5	12	25	45	55	60	38
17	Luton Town	42	8	9	4	28	22	2	9	10	13	29	41	51	38
18	Bury	42	10	8	3	37	19	4	1	16	23	46	60	65	37
19	West Ham United	42	8	7	6	30	25	4	5	12	23	36	53	61	36
20	Queen's Park Rgs.	42	6	5	10	21	30	5	7	9	19	27	40	57	34
21	Plymouth Argyle	42	6	6	9	19	24	2	10	9	25	41	44	65	32
22	Bradford Park Ave.	42	7	6	8	34	34	3	5	13	17	43	51	77	31

SEASON 1949/50
Back: McGowan, C.P.Johnston, Mackenzie, McMillan, W.Taylor, Mouncer, Hair, Benson, Mulholland
Middle (standing): Jacobson (Asst Train), McStay, McKenna, Campbell, Bennett, Platt, Briggs, Jim Johnson, Coyle, Barney, McCoy (Physio), Dawson (Train)
Middle (seated): Spencer (Man), Osmond (Dir), Hooton (Dir), Fish (Vice Chair), Pearce (Chair), Drewdy (Dir), Harborne (Dir), Walker (Dir), J.Smith (Dir), Hammond (Sec)
Front: Lloyd, Fisher, Shearer, Bircham, Chisholm, Tweedy, Garbutt, Daley, Moody, Bloomer, Cairns

SEASON 1950/51
Back: Jacobson,(Asst.Train), Beasley (Clerk), Hammond (Sec), Watkin, Bloomer, MacMillan, Cairns, Briggs, Moody, Dawson (Trainer), McCoy (Physio), Tweedy (Asst.Man)
Middle: Mulholland, Gray, Mackenzie, Rankin, Chisholm, Hair, Maddison, Lloyd, C.P.Johnston
Front: McStay, Fisher, Shearer, Duthie, Taylor, Jim Johnson, Harnby

1950-51 22nd in Division 2

Captain: Billy Cairns

	Date	Opponent	Score	Scorers	Att.	Chisholm	Moody	Fisher	Johnston	MacMillan	MacKenzie	Bloomer	Squires	Briggs	Cairns	Hair	Turnbull	Hayhurst	Harnby	Taylor W	Greetham	Gray G	Barratt A	Scotson	Duthie	Walker	McStay	Lloyd	Mulholland	Rankin	Jenkin	Shearer	Maddison	Wood	Mouncer
1	Aug 19	CARDIFF CITY	0-0		20803	1	2	3	4	5	6	7	8	9	10	11																			
2	21	Chesterfield	2-2	Briggs, Hair	15910	1	2	3	4	5	6		8	9	10	11											7								
3	26	Birmingham City	1-1	Briggs	33017	1	2	3	4	5	6		8	9	10	11											7								
4	30	CHESTERFIELD	1-2	MacKenzie(pen)	18268	1	2	3	4	5	6		8	9	10	11											7								
5	Sep 2	Hull City	1-2	Briggs	38332	1	2	3	4	5	6		8	9	10	11											7								
6	6	MANCHESTER CITY	4-4	Cairns, OG, MacMillan, Briggs	18529	1	2	3	4	5	6			9	10	11												7				8			
7	9	NOTTS COUNTY	1-4	Cairns	21432	1	2	3	4	5	6	8		9	10	11												7							
8	16	Preston North End	0-2		24461	1	2			5	4		8	9	10	11			3						6				7						
9	23	BURY	2-1	Squires, Cairns	14956	1	2	3		5	4		8	9	10	11									6		7								
10	30	Queens Park Rangers	1-7	Briggs	16331	1	2	3	4	5			8	9	10	11									6			7							
11	Oct 7	Barnsley	1-3	Briggs	18417	1	2			5		7	8	9	10				3			4			6								11		
12	14	SHEFFIELD UNITED	2-2	Cairns(2)	12643	1	2			5		7	8	9	10				3			4			6								11		
13	21	Blackburn Rovers	0-2		23235	1	2			5	10	7	8	9					3			4			6								11		
14	28	SOUTHAMPTON	4-2	Bloomer(4)	13383	1	2			5	10	9	8						3				4		6		7						11		
15	Nov 4	Doncaster Rovers	1-3	MacKenzie	23197	1	2			5	10	9	8						3				4		6		7						11		
16	11	BRENTFORD	7-2	Bloomer(3),MacKenzie(2),Rankin,Squires	14985	1	2			5	10	9	8							3			4		6					7			11		
17	18	Luton Town	0-4		12144	1	2			5	10	9	8							3			4		6					7			11		
18	25	LEEDS UNITED	2-2	MacKenzie(2,1pen)	15561	1	2			5	10	9	8							3			4		6					7			11		
19	Dec 2	West Ham United	1-2	Cairns	18518	1	4	2			10		8		9					3			6		5					7			11		
20	9	SWANSEA TOWN	4-2	Briggs(2), Lloyd, MacKenzie	13754	1	2				10		8	9						3			6	4	5			7					11		
21	16	Cardiff City	2-5	Briggs(2)	15364	1	2	3			10		8	9									6	4	5			7					11		
22	23	BIRMINGHAM CITY	1-1	Briggs	13141	1	2				10		8	9						3			6	4	5			7					11		
23	25	LEICESTER CITY	0-2		17565	1	2		4		10		8	9						3			6		5			7					11		
24	26	Leicester City	0-0		28296			2				9	8		10	11	1			3			6	4	5			7							
25	30	HULL CITY	1-1	Maddison	20268			2			10	9	8				1			3			6	4	5			7					11		
26	Jan 13	Notts County	2-3	Cairns, Maddison	24849	1					10		8		9				2	3			6	4	5			7					11		
27	20	PRESTON NORTH END	0-4		16836							9	8		10			1	2	3			6	4	5			7					11		
28	Feb 3	Bury	3-2	Cairns(2), Lloyd	12775							9	8		10			1	2	3			6	4	5			7					11		
29	17	QUEENS PARK RANGERS	2-2	Cairns, Lloyd	14005						10		8		9			1	2	3			6	4	5			11			7				
30	24	BARNSLEY	3-1	Cairns, MacKenzie(pen), Lloyd	14862						10	9			8			1	2	3			6	4	5			11			7				
31	Mar 3	Sheffield United	2-4	Cairns, MacKenzie(pen)	23558						10		8		9			1	2	3			6	4	5			11			7				
32	10	BLACKBURN ROVERS	1-1	Cairns	13216							9	8		10			1	2	3			6	4	5			7					11		
33	17	Southampton	1-5	Cairns	14598							9	8		10			1	3	2			6	4	5			7					11		
34	23	COVENTRY CITY	1-2	Cairns	18841					5			8		9			1	3	2			4		6		7	10					11		
35	24	DONCASTER ROVERS	1-0	Bloomer	18754		2			5	4	9	8					1	3						6		7	10					11		
36	27	Coventry City	0-1		26441		2			5	4	9	8					1	3						6		7	10					11		
37	31	Brentford	1-5	Cairns	15777		2			5	6				8			1	3					4	9		7	10					11		
38	Apr 7	LUTON TOWN	0-2		12435		2				6	9	8					1	3					4	5		7	10					11		
39	14	Leeds United	0-1		15524					5	8	9						1	3		2			4		6	7	10					11		
40	21	WEST HAM UNITED	0-1		10674					5	8	9				11		1	3		2			4		6		10			7				
41	28	Swansea Town	3-1	Wood(2), Bloomer	14485					5		9	8			11		1	3		2		4			6		7						10	
42	May 5	Manchester City	2-2	Bloomer, Lloyd	20293					5		9	8			11		1	3		2		4			6		7						10	
					Apps.	24	27	13	9	26	31	24	36	17	24	14	2	16	23	18	4	3	23	17	31	4	13	26	1	4	4	1	25	2	
					Goals					1	9	10	2	11	16	1												5		1			2	2	

1 own goal

F.A. Cup

	Date	Opponent	Score	Scorers	Att.	Chisholm	Moody	Fisher	Johnston	MacMillan	MacKenzie	Bloomer	Squires	Briggs	Cairns	Hair	Turnbull	Hayhurst	Harnby	Taylor W	Greetham	Gray G	Barratt A	Scotson	Duthie	Walker	McStay	Lloyd	Mulholland	Rankin	Jenkin	Shearer	Maddison	Wood	Mouncer
R3	Jan 6	EXETER CITY	3-3	Scotson,Bloomer,MacKenzie	13823						10	9	8				1			3			6	4	5			7					11		2
R3r	10	Exeter City	2-4	Squires, Bloomer	18177						10	9	8				1		2	3			6	4	5			7					11		

		P	W	D	L	F	A	W	D	L	F	A	F	A	Pts
1	Preston North End	42	16	3	2	53	18	10	2	9	38	31	91	49	57
2	Manchester City	42	12	6	3	53	25	7	8	6	36	36	89	61	52
3	Cardiff City	42	13	7	1	36	20	4	9	8	17	25	53	45	50
4	Birmingham City	42	12	6	3	37	20	8	3	10	27	33	64	53	49
5	Leeds United	42	14	4	3	36	17	6	4	11	27	38	63	55	48
6	Blackburn Rovers	42	13	3	5	39	27	6	5	10	26	39	65	66	46
7	Coventry City	42	15	3	3	51	25	4	4	13	24	34	75	59	45
8	Sheffield United	42	11	4	6	44	27	5	8	8	28	35	72	62	44
9	Brentford	42	13	3	5	44	25	5	5	11	31	49	75	74	44
10	Hull City	42	12	5	4	47	28	4	6	11	27	42	74	70	43
11	Doncaster Rovers	42	9	6	6	37	32	6	7	8	27	36	64	68	43
12	Southampton	42	10	9	2	38	27	5	4	12	28	46	66	73	43
13	West Ham United	42	10	5	6	44	33	6	5	10	24	36	68	69	42
14	Leicester City	42	10	4	7	42	28	5	7	9	26	30	68	58	41
15	Barnsley	42	9	5	7	42	22	6	5	10	32	46	74	68	40
16	Queen's Park Rgs.	42	13	5	3	47	25	2	5	14	24	57	71	82	40
17	Notts County	42	7	7	7	37	34	6	6	9	24	26	61	60	39
18	Swansea Town	42	14	1	6	34	25	2	3	16	20	52	54	77	36
19	Luton Town	42	7	9	5	34	23	2	5	14	23	47	57	70	32
20	Bury	42	9	4	8	33	27	3	4	14	27	59	60	86	32
21	Chesterfield	42	7	7	7	30	28	2	5	14	14	41	44	69	30
22	GRIMSBY TOWN	42	6	8	7	37	38	2	4	15	24	57	61	95	28

1951-52 2nd in Division 3 (N)

Captain: Bill Brown

						Hayhurst	Brown	Harnby	Scotson	Bellas	Wheatley	Lloyd	McKenzie Don	Cairns	Johnston	McCue	Tweedy	Daley	Galbraith	Freeburn	MacMillan	Wood	Bloomer	Jenkin	Campbell	Marlow	Hernon	Goodwin	Green K	Maddison	Walker
1	Aug 18	Chesterfield	1-3	Cairns	10625	1	2	3	4	5	6	7	8	9	10	11															
2	22	LINCOLN CITY	2-3	Cairns(2)	21479	1	2	3	4			7	8	9	6	11					5						10				
3	25	BRADFORD P.A.	3-0	Marlow, Cairns(2)	14476		2		4		6	7		9	3		1				5					8	10			11	
4	29	Lincoln City	2-0	Hernon, Marlow	19522		2		4		6	7		9	3			1			5					8	10			11	
5	Sep 1	Halifax Town	0-3		9879		2		4		6	7		9				1	3		5					8	10			11	
6	5	BARROW	1-0	Cairns	16250		2		4					9	6			1	3		5		7			8	10			11	
7	8	MANSFIELD TOWN	1-1	Marlow	17574		2		4		6			9	3			1			5		7			8	10			11	
8	13	Barrow	1-3	Marlow	7821		2		4			10			6			1	3		5		9	7		8				11	
9	15	Rochdale	0-0		6181		2		4			10		9	6			1	3		5			7		8				11	
10	22	ACCRINGTON STANLEY	2-1	Marlow, Cairns	13095		2		4					9	6			1	3		5			7		8	10			11	
11	29	Carlisle United	2-1	Marlow, Jenkins	14114		2			5		11		9	6		1		3		4			7		8	10				
12	Oct 6	TRANMERE ROVERS	1-0	OG	14500		2			5		11		9	6		1		3		4			7		8	10				
13	13	Southport	0-2		7015		2			5				9	6		1		3		4			7		8	10			11	
14	20	CREWE ALEXANDRA	0-1		12772		2			5		11		10	6		1		3		4		9	7			8				
15	27	Gateshead	1-1	Hernon	11398	1	2		4					10	6	11			3		5		9		7		8				
16	Nov 3	DARLINGTON	3-0	McCue, Hernon, Bloomer	12803	1	2		4					9	6	11			3		5		8		7		10				
17	10	Oldham Athletic	1-1	Cairns	21502	1	2		4					9	6	11			3		5		8		7		10				
18	17	HARTLEPOOLS UNITED	2-0	Cairns(2)	12296	1	2		4					9	5	11			3			6	8		7		10				
19	Dec 1	YORK CITY	0-0		12398	1	2		4					9	6	11			3		5		8		7		10				
20	8	Chester	3-0	Cairns(2), Hernon	4935	1	2		4					9	6				3		5		8		7		10			11	
21	22	Bradford P.A.	2-3	Cairns, Bloomer	12169	1	2		4			7		9	6				3		5		8				10			11	
22	25	SCUNTHORPE UNITED	3-2	Cairns, Bloomer, Maddison	19351	1	2		4			7		9	6				3		5		8				10			11	
23	26	Scunthorpe United	3-1	Cairns, Bloomer(2)	15734	1	2		4			7		9	6				3		5		8				10			11	
24	29	HALIFAX TOWN	8-1	John'n(2p),Hernon(2),Cairns(2),Madd'n,Bloom'	13548	1	2		4			7		9	6				3		5		8				10			11	
25	Jan 5	Mansfield Town	2-2	Bloomer(2)	9471	1	2		4			7		9	6				3		5		8				10			11	
26	12	Wrexham	0-2		9755		2		4			7			6		1		3		5		8				10	9		11	
27	19	ROCHDALE	4-0	Bloomer(2),Maddison,Johnston	12780		2		4			7		9	6		1		3		5		8				10			11	
28	26	Accrington Stanley	3-0	Bloomer, Cairns, Maddison	4210		2		4			7		9	6		1		3		5		8				10			11	
29	Feb 2	WREXHAM	1-0	Hernon	14162		2		4			7			6		1		3		5		8				10		9	11	
30	9	CARLISLE UNITED	4-1	Bloomer(2),Hernon,Johnston(pen)	16148		2		4			7		9	6		1		3		5		8				10			11	
31	16	Tranmere Rovers	3-2	Johnson(pen), Bloomer, Hernon	9160		2		4			7		9	6		1		3		5		8				10			11	
32	23	Workington	4-2	Cairns(2), Hernon, Lloyd	6736		2		4			7		9	6		1		3		5		8				10			11	
33	Mar 1	SOUTHPORT	4-1	Cairns(3), Lloyd	15639		2		4			7		9	6		1		3		5		8				10			11	
34	8	Crewe Alexandra	2-1	Bloomer, Maddison	6959		2		4			7		9	6		1		3		5		8				10			11	
35	15	GATESHEAD	2-0	Hernon, Cairns	16306		2		4			7		9	6		1		3		5		8				10			11	
36	22	Darlington	2-0	Bloomer, Cairns	6707		2		4			7		9	6		1		3		5		8				10			11	
37	29	OLDHAM ATHLETIC	3-1	Cairns, Hernon, Maddison	12402		2		4			7		9	6		1		3		5		8				10			11	
38	Apr 5	Hartlepools United	1-2	Cairns	9063		2		4			7		9	6		1		3		5		8				10			11	
39	11	STOCKPORT COUNTY	4-0	Johnston(p),Maddison,Lloyd,Bloomer	26605		2		4			7		9	6		1		3		5		8				10			11	
40	12	BRADFORD CITY	2-1	Maddison, Cairns	16892		2		4			7		9	6		1			3	5					8	10			11	
41	14	Stockport County	1-1	Hernon	16300		2		4			7		9	6		1		3		5		8				10			11	
42	19	York City	1-1	Hernon	11335		2		4					9	6	7	1		3		5		8				10			11	
43	23	Bradford City	2-0	Johnston(pen), Cairns	8961		2		4				8	9	6	7	1		3		5						10			11	
44	26	CHESTER	2-1	Hernon, McCue	12434		2		4				8	9	6	7	1		3		5						10			11	
45	30	CHESTERFIELD	2-0	Johnston (pen), Maddison	10162	1	2		4			8		9	5	7			3								10			11	6
46	May 3	WORKINGTON	5-0	Cairns(2),Hernon,Brown,Jenkin	7591	1	2		4					9	6	8			3		5			7			10			11	
					Apps.	15	46	2	42	5	5	32	4	43	45	12	24	7	40	1	43	1	31	8	6	12	43	1	1	36	1
					Goals		1					3		31	8	2							17	2		6	16			9	

Game 2: Hayhurst injured, replaced in goal by Brown.

1 own goal

F.A. Cup

						Hayhurst	Brown	Harnby	Scotson	Bellas	Wheatley	Lloyd	McKenzie Don	Cairns	Johnston	McCue	Tweedy	Daley	Galbraith	Freeburn	MacMillan	Wood	Bloomer	Jenkin	Campbell	Marlow	Hernon	Goodwin	Green K	Maddison	Walker
R1	Nov 24	DARLINGTON	4-0	Bloomer, Cairns(3)	14309	1	2		4					9	6	11			3		5		8		7	10					
R2	Dec 15	Lincoln City	1-3	Cairns	21757	1	2		4					9	6				3		5		8		7	10			11		

		P	W	D	L	F	A	W	D	L	F	A	F	A	Pts
1	Lincoln City	46	19	2	2	80	23	11	7	5	41	29	121	52	69
2	GRIMSBY TOWN	46	19	2	2	59	14	10	6	7	37	31	96	45	66
3	Stockport County	46	12	9	2	47	17	11	4	8	27	23	74	40	59
4	Oldham Athletic	46	19	2	2	65	22	5	7	11	25	39	90	61	57
5	Gateshead	46	14	7	2	41	17	7	4	12	25	32	66	49	53
6	Mansfield Town	46	17	3	3	50	23	5	5	13	23	37	73	60	52
7	Carlisle United	46	10	7	6	31	24	9	6	8	31	33	62	57	51
8	Bradford Park Ave.	46	13	6	4	51	28	6	6	11	23	36	74	64	50
9	Hartlepools United	46	17	3	3	47	19	4	5	14	24	46	71	65	50
10	York City	46	16	4	3	53	19	2	9	12	20	33	73	52	49
11	Tranmere Rovers	46	17	2	4	59	29	4	4	15	17	42	76	71	48
12	Barrow	46	13	5	5	33	19	4	7	12	24	42	57	61	46
13	Chesterfield	46	15	7	1	47	16	2	4	17	18	50	65	66	45
14	Scunthorpe United	46	10	11	2	39	23	4	5	14	26	51	65	74	44
15	Bradford City	46	12	5	6	40	32	4	5	14	21	36	61	68	42
16	Crewe Alexandra	46	12	6	5	42	28	5	2	16	21	54	63	82	42
17	Southport	46	12	6	5	36	22	3	5	15	17	49	53	71	41
18	Wrexham	46	14	5	4	41	22	1	4	18	22	51	63	73	39
19	Chester	46	13	4	6	46	30	2	5	16	26	55	72	85	39
20	Halifax Town	46	11	4	8	31	23	3	3	17	30	74	61	97	35
21	Rochdale	46	10	5	8	32	34	1	8	14	15	45	47	79	35
22	Accrington Stanley	46	6	8	9	30	34	4	4	15	31	58	61	92	32
23	Darlington	46	10	5	8	39	34	1	4	18	25	69	64	103	31
24	Workington	46	8	4	11	33	34	3	3	17	17	57	50	91	29

SEASON 1951/52
Back: Dawson (Train), Johnston, MacMillan, Bellas, Tweedy, Marlow, Jenkin, Lloyd
Front: Cairns, Hernon, Brown, Galbraith, Maddison

SEASON 1952/53
Back: Hart, Galbraith, Scotson, Hayhurst, MacMillan, Johnston, Shankly (Manager)
Front: Dawson (Train), Lloyd, McCue, Brown, Hernon, Maddison

1952-53 5th in Division 3 (N)

Captain: Bill Brown

	Date	Opponent	Score	Scorers	Att	Tweedy	Brown	Galbraith	Scotson	MacMillan	Johnston	Lloyd	Bloomer	Cairns	Hernon	Maddison	Hayhurst	Daley	Freeburn	Robson	Player	Grant	Walker	Jenkin	McCue	Millar	Hart	Lord	Smith F	Rayner	Williams C	Smith D	Cadden
1	Aug 23	WREXHAM	2-0	Cairns, Bloomer	16676	1	2	3	4	5	6	7	8	9	10	11																	
2	28	Scunthorpe United	1-0	Johnston (pen)	18794	1	2	3	4	5	6	7	8	9	10	11																	
3	30	Bradford P.A.	3-0	Cairns(2), Bloomer	16998	1	2	3	4	5	6	7	8	9	10	11																	
4	Sep 3	SCUNTHORPE UNITED	1-0	Bloomer	22213	1	2	3	4	5	6	7	8	9	10	11																	
5	6	OLDHAM ATHLETIC	1-0	Bloomer	20013	1	2	3	4	5	6	7	8	9	10	11																	
6	8	Barrow	1-1	Lloyd	6275	1	2	3	4	5	6	7	8	9	10	11																	
7	13	Mansfield Town	1-1	Bloomer	12980	1	2	3	4	5	6	7	8	9	10	11																	
8	17	BARROW	2-1	F.Smith(2)	16990		2	3	4	5	6	7	8		10	11	1												9				
9	20	HALIFAX TOWN	2-0	F.Smith, Bloomer	17862		2	3	4	5	6	7	8		10	11	1												9				
10	25	Carlisle United	0-3		9528		2	3	4	5	6	7	8		10	11	1												9				
11	27	Accrington Stanley	3-1	Cairns, F.Smith	5774		2	3	4	5	6		8	10		11	1							7					9				
12	Oct 1	TRANMERE ROVERS	3-1	Cairns(2), F.Smith	14398		2	3	4	5	6		7	8	10	11	1												9				
13	4	WORKINGTON TOWN	2-0	F.Smith, Maddison	16223		2		4	5	6		7	8	10	11	1			3									9				
14	11	Stockport County	2-2	Cairns, Scotson	13260		2		4	5		7		8	10	11	1			3			6						9				
15	18	BRADFORD CITY	0-0		16043		2	3	4	5				8	10	11	1						6	7					9				
16	25	Rochdale	2-0	McCue(2)	12291		2	3	4	5	6		8		10	11	1								7				9				
17	Nov 1	DARLINGTON	2-0	Bloomer, Johnston(pen)	14618		2	3	4	5	6		8		10	11	1								7				9				
18	8	Gateshead	0-2		11451		2	3	4	5	6		8	9	10	11	1								7								
19	15	HARTLEPOOLS UNITED	7-0	F.Smith(4),Hernon,Millar,Johnston(pen)	13096		2	3	4	5	6				10	11	1								7	8			9				
20	29	SOUTHPORT	1-0	McCue	12312		2	3	4	5	6	8				11	1								7	10			9				
21	Dec 13	PORT VALE	1-1	MacMillan	13801		2	3	4	5	6	7			10	11	1								8				9				
22	20	Wrexham	1-3	Maddison	9420		2	3	4	5	6			8	10	11	1								7					9			
23	25	CHESTERFIELD	0-0		18848		2	3	4	5	6			9	10	11	1								7		8						
24	27	Chesterfield	2-3	Hart, Maddison	15519		2	3	4	5	6				10	11	1								7		8			9			
25	Jan 1	Tranmere Rovers	1-2	McCue	8769				4	5	6					11	1		2	3		8			7		10		9				
26	3	BRADFORD P.A.	2-3	Grant, Rayner	12201				4	5	6					11	1		2	3		8			7		10			9			
27	13	CHESTER	5-4	McCue(2),Hernon,F.Smith, Johnston(p)	6204			3	4	5	6	7			10	11	1		2						8				9				
28	17	Oldham Athletic	1-1	Johnston (pen)	26840		2	3	4	5	6	7			10	11	1								8		9						
29	24	MANSFIELD TOWN	5-1	McCue(2), Hart(2), Hernon	13890		2	3	4	5	6	7			10	11	1								8		9						
30	31	Chester	2-0	Maddison, McCue	4005		2	3	4	5	6	7			10	11	1								8		9						
31	Feb 7	Halifax Town	2-3	Maddison, Lloyd	9038		2	3	4	5	6	7			10	11	1								8		9						
32	14	ACCRINGTON STANLEY	3-0	Jenkin, Hernon, McCue	11118		2	3	4	5	6				10	11	1							7	8		9						
33	21	Workington Town	1-3	McCue	10454		2	3	4		6				10	11	1							7	8		9						5
34	28	STOCKPORT COUNTY	0-1		13148		2	3	4	5	6				10	11	1							7	8		9						
35	Mar 7	Bradford City	0-1		13651		2	3	4	5	6			8	10	11	1								7		9						
36	14	ROCHDALE	3-2	McCue(2), Scotson	10578			3	4	5	6	7		9		11	1		2						8		10						
37	21	Darlington	1-1	Hernon	6613			3	4	5	6	7		9	10	11	1		2						8								
38	28	GATESHEAD	0-0		10445			3	4	5	6	7		9	10	11	1		2						8								
39	Apr 3	YORK CITY	2-1	Grant, Lloyd	18551	1		3	4	5	10	7		9					2			8	6		11								
40	4	Hartlepools United	0-2		8714			3		5	4	7		9	10			1	2			8	6		11								
41	6	York City	0-2		12356			3		5				9		11		1	2		4	8	6	7		10							
42	11	CARLISLE UNITED	2-3	Lord, Jenkin	10260					5				9		11		1	2	3	4	6		7		10		8					
43	18	Southport	3-4	Cairns(2), Millar	6687					5				9		11		1	2	3	6	4		7		10		8					
44	25	CREWE ALEXANDRA	1-0	Cairns	8187					5				10		11		1	2	3	6	4		7				8	9				
45	29	Crewe Alexandra	2-1	F.Smith, Johnston	4162					5	10	7				11			2	3		4	6					8	9		1		
46	30	Port Vale	0-4		7964					5	10	7				11		1		3		4	6					8	9			2	
					Apps.	8	32	37	39	45	40	25	16	25	34	44	31	6	13	9	4	10	7	9	25	5	13	5	18	3	1	1	1
					Goals				2	1	6	3	7	10	5	5						2		2	13	2	3	1	12	1			

F.A. Cup

	Date	Opponent	Score	Scorers	Att	Tweedy	Brown	Galbraith	Scotson	MacMillan	Johnston	Lloyd	Bloomer	Cairns	Hernon	Maddison	Hayhurst	Daley	Freeburn	Robson	Player	Grant	Walker	Jenkin	McCue	Millar	Hart	Lord	Smith F	Rayner	Williams C	Smith D	Cadden
R1	Nov 22	Darlington	3-2	Johnston, Rayner, Millar	9452		2	3	4	5	6		8			11	1								7	10				9			
R2	Dec 6	BATH CITY	1-0	Johnston	15175		2	3	4	5	6				10	11	1								7	8			9				
R3	Jan 10	BURY	1-3	McCue	15291			3	4	5	6	7			10	11	1		2						8				9				

		P	W	D	L	F	A	W	D	L	F	A	F	A	Pts
1	Oldham Athletic	46	15	4	4	48	21	7	11	5	29	24	77	45	59
2	Port Vale	46	13	9	1	41	10	7	9	7	26	25	67	35	58
3	Wrexham	46	18	3	2	59	24	6	5	12	27	42	86	66	56
4	York City	46	14	5	4	35	16	6	8	9	25	29	60	45	53
5	GRIMSBY TOWN	46	15	5	3	47	19	6	5	12	28	40	75	59	52
6	Southport	46	16	4	3	42	18	4	7	12	21	42	63	60	51
7	Bradford Park Ave.	46	10	8	5	37	23	9	4	10	38	38	75	61	50
8	Gateshead	46	13	6	4	51	24	4	9	10	25	36	76	60	49
9	Carlisle United	46	13	7	3	57	24	5	6	12	25	44	82	68	49
10	Crewe Alexandra	46	13	5	5	46	28	7	3	13	24	40	70	68	48
11	Stockport County	46	13	8	2	61	26	4	5	14	21	43	82	69	47
12	Tranmere Rovers	46	16	4	3	45	16	5	1	17	20	47	65	63	47
13	Chesterfield	46	13	6	4	40	23	5	5	13	25	40	65	63	47
14	Halifax Town	46	13	5	5	47	31	3	10	10	21	37	68	68	47
15	Scunthorpe United	46	10	6	7	38	21	6	8	9	24	35	62	56	46
16	Bradford City	46	14	7	2	54	29	0	11	12	21	51	75	80	46
17	Hartlepools United	46	14	6	3	39	16	2	8	13	18	45	57	61	46
18	Mansfield Town	46	11	9	3	34	25	5	5	13	21	37	55	62	46
19	Barrow	46	15	6	2	48	20	1	6	16	18	51	66	71	44
20	Chester	46	10	7	6	39	27	1	8	14	25	58	64	85	37
21	Darlington	46	13	4	6	33	27	1	2	20	25	69	58	96	34
22	Rochdale	46	12	5	6	41	27	2	0	21	21	56	62	83	33
23	Workington	46	9	5	9	40	33	2	5	16	15	58	55	91	32
24	Accrington Stanley	46	7	9	7	25	29	1	2	20	14	60	39	89	27

1953-54 17th in Division 3 (N)

Captain: Reg Scotson

No.	Date	Opponent	Result	Scorers	Att.	Williams C	Brown	Robson	Scotson	MacMillan	Johnston	Bloomer	Wright	Smith F	Hernon	Maddison	Nicholson	Freeburn	Smith D	Jobling	Tucker	Grant	Walker	Williams D	Stroud	Jenkin	Dubois	Newton	Cairns	Lord	Connor	Rayner	Sowerby	Player
1	Aug 19	YORK CITY	3-0	Maddison(2), F.Smith	16320	1	2	3	4	5	6	7	8	9	10	11																		
2	22	SCUNTHORPE UNITED	0-1		18246	1	2	3	4	5	6	7	8		10	11													9					
3	26	CARLISLE UNITED	3-2	F.Smith(2), Hernon	14516	1	2	3	4	5	6	7	8	9	10	11																		
4	29	Stockport County	2-3	F.Smith, Stroud	8698	1	2	3	4	5	6	8	10	9		11									7									
5	Sep 1	Carlisle United	3-3	Jenkin(2), Maddison	10267	1	2	3	4	5	6	8	10	9		11										7								
6	5	ROCHDALE	3-2	Wright(2), F.Smith	12305	1	2	3	4	5	6	8	10	9		11										7								
7	9	ACCRINGTON STANLEY	2-0	Bloomer, Dubois	11357	1		3	4	5	6	8	10	9		11		2									7							
8	12	Wrexham	0-4		13748	1		3	4	5	6	8	10	9		11		2									7							
9	16	Accrington Stanley	1-3	Wright	7591			3	4		5		10	9		11	1	2					6				7		8					
10	19	MANSFIELD TOWN	0-2		9929			3	4		5	8	10	9		11	1	2					6				7							
11	23	HALIFAX TOWN	2-1	Grant(2)	7752	1	2	3	4		5		10	9		11						8	6				7							
12	26	Barrow	0-4		8006	1	2	3	4		5	7	10	9		11						8	6											
13	28	Halifax Town	0-2		3710	1	2	3	4		5		10	9		11						8	6		7									
14	Oct 3	BRADFORD CITY	1-0	F.Smith	8677	1	2	3	4		5	8	10	9		11							6					7						
15	10	GATESHEAD	2-0	F.Smith, Stroud	9166	1	2	3	4		5		10	9		11							6		7			8						
16	17	Hartlepools United	0-3		9039	1	2	3	4		5		10	9		11							6		7			8						
17	24	DARLINGTON	1-0	Robson	8907	1	2	10	4		5		8	9		11			3				6		7									
18	31	Barnsley	0-0		8438	1	2	3	4		5	9	10			11							6		7					8				
19	Nov 7	BRADFORD P.A.	0-0		8551	1	2	3	4		5	9	10			11						8	6		7									
20	14	Port Vale	0-2		14889	1	2	3	4		5	9	10			11							6		7							8		
21	28	Chester	1-1	Bloomer	5327	1	2	3	4	5		8	10	9		11							6		7									
22	Dec 5	SOUTHPORT	1-2	Bloomer	7469	1	2	3	4	5		8	10	9		11							6		7									
23	19	Scunthorpe United	1-2	Bloomer	9985	1	2	3	4	5		8	10			11							6		7							9		
24	25	TRANMERE ROVERS	1-0	Bloomer	12054	1	2	3	4	5		8	10			11							6		7							9		
25	26	Tranmere Rovers	4-2	Wright(2), Stroud, Bloomer	8662	1	2	3	4	5		8	10			11							6		7							9		
26	Jan 2	STOCKPORT COUNTY	1-0	Wright	8683	1	2	3	4	5		8	10			11							6		7							9		
27	16	Rochdale	1-4	F.Smith	4934	1	2	3	4	5		9	10	8		11							6		7									
28	23	WREXHAM	0-0		7744	1	2	3	4	5	8	9	10			11							6				7							
29	30	WORKINGTON TOWN	1-0	Stroud	5590	1	2	3	4	5	6	9	10			11									7						8			
30	Feb 6	Mansfield Town	1-5	Maddison	6513	1	2	3	4	5	6	9	10			11									7						8			
31	13	BARROW	1-0	Wright	6882	1		3	4		6	9	8			11		2		5					7								10	
32	20	Bradford City	0-3		11996			3	4			9	8			11	1	2		5				6	7								10	
33	27	Gateshead	1-7	Wright	4922			3	4				8	9		11	1	2		5				6	7								10	
34	Mar 6	HARTLEPOOLS UNITED	3-0	F.Smith(2), Robson	5628			3	4			7	8	9		11	1	2		5				6									10	
35	13	Darlington	0-3		4652			3	4				8	9		11	1	2		5				6	7								10	
36	17	Workington Town	0-2		7458			3	4				8	9	10	11	1	2		5				6	7									
37	20	BARNSLEY	0-1		6616			3	4				8	9	10	11	1	2		5			6		7									
38	27	Bradford P.A.	1-4	Grant	5302			3	5				7	9	10	11	1	2		4		6			8									
39	Apr 3	PORT VALE	2-2	F.Smith, Hernon	9952		2	3	4					8	10	11	1			5			6		7							9		
40	10	Crewe Alexandra	1-1	Rayner	3415		2	3	4	5				8	10	11	1						6		7							9		
41	12	York City	2-1	Rayner, Maddison	3826		2	3	4	5				8	10	11	1						6		7							9		
42	16	CHESTERFIELD	1-1	F.Smith(pen)	11913		2	3	4	5				8	10	11	1						6		7							9		
43	17	CHESTER	0-0		7330		2		4	5				8	10	11	1		3				6		7								9	
44	19	Chesterfield	0-1		7475		2		4						10	11	1		3		5		6		7					8			9	
45	24	Southport	1-2	Sowerby	2887		2	3	6					8	10	11	1				5				7								9	4
46	28	CREWE ALEXANDRA	3-1	Scotson, Wright, Stroud	4963		2	3	6				8	9	10	11	1				5				7									4
					Apps.	29	34	44	46	22	24	27	39	32	14	46	17	12	3	9	3	5	27	5	32	2	6	3	2	2	2	9	8	2
					Goals			2	1			6	9	12	2	5						3			5	2	1					2	1	

F.A. Cup

Rd	Date	Opponent	Result	Scorers	Att.	Williams C	Brown	Robson	Scotson	MacMillan	Johnston	Bloomer	Wright	Smith F	Hernon	Maddison	Nicholson	Freeburn	Smith D	Jobling	Tucker	Grant	Walker	Williams D	Stroud	Jenkin	Dubois	Newton	Cairns	Lord	Connor	Rayner	Sowerby	Player
R1	Nov 21	ROCHDALE	2-0	F.Smith, Maddison	8509	1	2	3	4	5		8	10	9		11							6		7									
R2	Dec 12	Witton Albion	1-1	Rayner	7573	1	2	3	4	5		8	10			11							6		7							9		
R2r	15	WITTON ALBION	6-1	Bloomer,Rayner(3),Wright,Maddison	5564	1	2	3	4	5		8	10			11							6		7							9		
R3	Jan 9	FULHAM	5-5	Scotson,Bloomer(3),OG	14772	1	2	3	4	5	8	9	10			11							6		7									
R3r	13	Fulham*	0-0		12000	1	2	3	4	5		8	10			11							6		7							9		
R3r	18	Fulham	1-3		18729	1	2	3	4	5		8	10	9		11							6		7									

* Abandoned at half-time, ground waterlogged.

		P	W	D	L	F	A	W	D	L	F	A	F	A	Pts
1	Port Vale	46	16	7	0	48	5	10	10	3	26	16	74	21	69
2	Barnsley	46	16	3	4	54	24	8	7	8	23	33	77	57	58
3	Scunthorpe United	46	14	7	2	49	24	7	8	8	28	32	77	56	57
4	Gateshead	46	15	4	4	49	22	6	9	8	25	33	74	55	55
5	Bradford City	46	15	6	2	40	14	7	3	13	20	41	60	55	53
6	Chesterfield	46	13	6	4	41	19	6	8	9	35	45	76	64	52
7	Mansfield Town	46	15	5	3	59	22	5	6	12	29	45	88	67	51
8	Wrexham	46	16	4	3	59	19	5	5	13	22	49	81	68	51
9	Bradford Park Ave.	46	13	6	4	57	31	5	8	10	20	37	77	68	50
10	Stockport County	46	14	6	3	57	20	4	5	14	20	47	77	67	47
11	Southport	46	12	5	6	41	26	5	7	11	22	34	63	60	46
12	Barrow	46	12	7	4	46	26	4	5	14	26	45	72	71	44
13	Carlisle United	46	10	8	5	53	27	4	7	12	30	44	83	71	43
14	Tranmere Rovers	46	11	4	8	40	34	7	3	13	19	36	59	70	43
15	Accrington Stanley	46	12	7	4	41	22	4	3	16	25	52	66	74	42
16	Crewe Alexandra	46	9	8	6	30	26	5	5	13	19	41	49	67	41
17	GRIMSBY TOWN	46	14	5	4	31	15	2	4	17	20	62	51	77	41
18	Hartlepools United	46	10	8	5	40	21	3	6	14	19	44	59	65	40
19	Rochdale	46	12	5	6	40	20	3	5	15	19	57	59	77	40
20	Workington	46	10	9	4	36	22	3	5	15	23	58	59	80	40
21	Darlington	46	11	3	9	31	27	1	11	11	19	44	50	71	38
22	York City	46	8	7	8	39	32	4	6	13	25	54	64	86	37
23	Halifax Town	46	9	6	8	26	21	3	4	16	18	52	44	73	34
24	Chester	46	10	7	6	39	22	1	3	19	9	45	48	67	32

SEASON 1953/54

Back: Newton, Thompson, Jobling, Tucker, K.Richardson, D.Smith, A.Walker, Nicholson, C.Williams, Daley, Lord, Dubois
Middle (Standing): Dawson (Train), Robinson (Sec), Shankly (Man), Thomlin, Scotson, MacMillan, Cairns, Brown, Bloomer, Johnston, Grant, David Williams, F.Smith, McCoy (Physio), Ashworth, Jacobson (Asst.Train)
Middle (Seated): Would, Bacon, Harborne, R.Walker, Baker, Pearce (Chair), Fish, Boyers, J.Smith, Drewry (Directors)
Front: Cousins, Stroud, Freeburn, Robson, Wright, Hernon, Maddison

SEASON 1954/55

Back: Bloomer, Hughes, C.Williams, Player, Brown, Johnston
Front: Conner, Stroud, Higgins, Harrison, Maddison

1954-55 23rd in Division 3 (N)

Captain: George Higgins

							Archer	Brown	Higgins	Scotson	MacMillan	Conner	Stroud	Pringle	Harrison	Hughes	DeGruchy	Williams	Maddison	Freeburn	Johnston	Robson	Jobling	Player	Redding	Chilton	Sowerby	Walker	Lowry	Harbertson	Faulkner	Bloomer	Slater	Phillips	Weatherall	Tinsley	Stokes
1	Aug	21	Rochdale	3-0	Hughes(2), DeGruchy	6915	1	2	3	4	5	6	7	8	9	10	11																				
2		24	SCUNTHORPE UNITED	1-4	Harrison	19736	1	2	3	4	5		7	8	9	10	11										6										
3		28	TRANMERE ROVERS	2-2	Hughes(2,1pen)	10669	1	2	3	4	5	6	8		9	10	11												7								
4	Sep	2	Scunthorpe United	0-1		15547	1	2	3	4		6	8		9	10			11					5					7								
5		4	Stockport County	0-0		10400	1	2	3	4		6			9	10			11					5			8		7								
6		8	CHESTER	3-1	Stroud, Lowry, Harrison	10128	1	2	3	4		6	8		9	10			11					5					7								
7		11	HARTLEPOOLS UNITED	1-0	Stroud	10117		2	3	4		6	8		9	10		1	11					5					7								
8		15	Chester	0-1		5133		2	3	4		6	8		9	10		1	11					5					7								
9		18	Gateshead	0-1		6698		2	3			4	10		9	6		1	11					5					7	8							
10		22	CREWE ALEXANDRA	2-1	Harbertson, Hughes(pen)	8134		2	3			4	10		9	6		1				11		5					7	8							
11		25	DARLINGTON	0-2		8727		2	3			4	10		9	6		1				11		5					7	8							
12		27	Crewe Alexandra	0-2		4519			2		5	4	10		9	6		1			3	11							7	8							
13	Oct	2	Chesterfield	0-1		11125			2			6	8		9	10		1	11			3	4	5						7							
14		9	WREXHAM	1-3	Harbertson	8291	1	2	3				7		10	6			11				4	5					8	9							
15		16	Accrington Stanley	0-3		8416	1	2	3	8		6	7			10			11				4	5						9							
16		23	MANSFIELD TOWN	3-2	Hughes(2,1pen), Stroud	7359	1	2	3	8		6	7		9	10			11				4	5													
17		30	Workington Town	2-2	Hughes(2)	9430	1	2	3	8		6	7		9	10			11				4	5													
18	Nov	6	BARROW	1-0	Stroud	6192		2	3	8		4	7			10		1	11		6			5						9							
19		13	Southport	2-2	Maddison(2)	3026		2	3			4	7		9	10		1	11		6			5								8					
20		27	Halifax Town	2-3	Conner, Stroud	8589		2	3			4	7		9			1	11		10		6	5								8					
21	Dec	4	OLDHAM ATHLETIC	1-1	Bloomer	5950		2	3			4	7		9	10		1	11		6			5								8					
22		18	ROCHDALE	1-1	Hughes	7853		2	3			4	7		8	10		1	11		6			5						9							
23		25	BARNSLEY	1-3	Harbertson	10400		2	3			4	7		9	10		1	11		6			5						8							
24		27	Barnsley	3-1	Stokes, Stroud, Maddison	16887		2	3			4	7					1	11						5			6		8			10				9
25	Jan	1	Tranmere Rovers	0-2		4806		2	3			4	7					1	11		6				5					8			10				9
26		15	STOCKPORT COUNTY	1-0	Harrison	5611		2				4	7		10			1	11		5	3						6		8							9
27		29	Carlisle United	1-3	Harbertson	5082		2	3			4	7		10			1	11		5				6					8							9
28	Feb	5	GATESHEAD	1-1	Stokes	6982		2	3			4	7		10			1	11		5							6		8							9
29		12	Darlington	3-1	Harrison(2), Maddison	4588		2	3			4			10			1	11		5							6		7			8				9
30		19	CHESTERFIELD	1-2	Harrison	5513			3			4			10			1	11	2	5							6		7			8				9
31	Mar	5	ACCRINGTON STANLEY	2-1	Harrison, Stokes	6672			3			4			10			1	11	2	5							6		8	7						9
32		8	CARLISLE UNITED	2-0	Faulkner, OG	3690			3			4			10			1	11	2	5							6		8	7			9			
33		12	Mansfield Town	0-3		6250			3			4			10			1	11	2	5							6		8	7						9
34		19	WORKINGTON TOWN	0-1		10519			3			4			10			1	11	2	6					5				8	7						9
35		23	Hartlepools United	2-3	Phillips, Harbertson(pen)	4134			3			4	7		10			1	11	2	6					5				8				9			
36		26	Barrow	0-2		2825			3			4	7		10			1	11	2	6					5				8				9			
37	Apr	2	SOUTHPORT	0-1		7088			3				7		10			1	11	2	4					5		6		8				9			
38		8	BRADFORD P.A.	1-0	Hughes	11610		2	3	4			7			8			11		6					5	10								9	1	
39		9	York City	0-0		12436		2	3	4			7			10			11		6					5	8								9	1	
40		11	Bradford P.A.	1-2	Harbertson	5850		2	3	4			7			10			11		6					5				8					9	1	
41		16	HALIFAX TOWN	0-1		5916		2	3	4			7		10				11		6					5				8				9		1	
42		20	Bradford City	0-4		5937		2	3	4			7		9				11		10			6		5								8		1	
43		23	Oldham Athletic	0-4		4296		2	3	4			7				10		11		6					5									8	1	9
44		27	YORK CITY	2-1	Stroud, Scotson	7184		2	3	4			7		9		10		11		6					5									8	1	
45		30	BRADFORD CITY	1-4	DeGruchy	6879		2	3	4			7		9		10		11		6					5									8	1	
46	May	4	Wrexham	0-5		2927		2	3				7		9		10				6			5		4					11				8	1	
						Apps.	10	36	45	20	4	34	39	2	38	25	7	27	39	8	29	5	6	21	3	13	4	9	11	26	5	3	4	6	7	9	11
						Goals				1		1	7		7	11	2		4										1	6	1	1		1			3

1 own goal

F.A. Cup

							Archer	Brown	Higgins	Scotson	MacMillan	Conner	Stroud	Pringle	Harrison	Hughes	DeGruchy	Williams	Maddison	Freeburn	Johnston	Robson	Jobling	Player	Redding	Chilton	Sowerby	Walker	Lowry	Harbertson	Faulkner	Bloomer	Slater	Phillips	Weatherall	Tinsley	Stokes
R1	Nov	30	HALIFAX TOWN	2-1	Hughes, Maddison	10174		2	3			4	7			10		1	11				6	5						9		8					
R2	Dec	11	SOUTHAMPTON	4-1	Harbertson(2),Harrison(2)	10075		2	3			4	7		9	10		1	11				6	5						8							
R3	Jan	8	WOLVERHAMPTON WAND	2-5	Harrison, Stokes	25964		2	3			4	7		10			1	11		5							6		8							9

		P	W	D	L	F	A	W	D	L	F	A	F	A	Pts
1	Barnsley	46	18	3	2	51	17	12	2	9	35	29	86	46	65
2	Accrington Stanley	46	18	2	3	65	32	7	9	7	31	35	96	67	61
3	Scunthorpe United	46	14	6	3	45	18	9	6	8	36	35	81	53	58
4	York City	46	13	5	5	43	27	11	5	7	49	36	92	63	58
5	Hartlepools United	46	16	3	4	39	20	9	2	12	25	29	64	49	55
6	Chesterfield	46	17	1	5	54	33	7	5	11	27	37	81	70	54
7	Gateshead	46	11	7	5	38	26	9	5	9	27	43	65	69	52
8	Workington	46	11	7	5	39	23	7	7	9	29	32	68	55	50
9	Stockport County	46	13	4	6	50	27	5	8	10	34	43	84	70	48
10	Oldham Athletic	46	14	5	4	47	22	5	5	13	27	46	74	68	48
11	Southport	46	10	9	4	28	18	6	7	10	19	26	47	44	48
12	Rochdale	46	13	7	3	39	20	4	7	12	30	46	69	66	48
13	Mansfield Town	46	14	4	5	40	28	4	5	14	25	43	65	71	45
14	Halifax Town	46	9	9	5	41	27	6	4	13	22	40	63	67	43
15	Darlington	46	10	7	6	41	28	4	7	12	21	45	62	73	42
16	Bradford Park Ave.	46	11	7	5	29	21	4	4	15	27	49	56	70	41
17	Barrow	46	12	4	7	39	34	5	2	16	31	55	70	89	40
18	Wrexham	46	9	6	8	40	35	4	6	13	25	42	65	77	38
19	Tranmere Rovers	46	9	6	8	37	30	4	5	14	18	40	55	70	37
20	Carlisle United	46	12	1	10	53	39	3	5	15	25	50	78	89	36
21	Bradford City	46	9	5	9	30	26	4	5	14	17	29	47	55	36
22	Crewe Alexandra	46	8	10	5	45	35	2	4	17	23	56	68	91	34
23	GRIMSBY TOWN	46	10	4	9	28	32	3	4	16	19	46	47	78	34
24	Chester	46	10	3	10	23	25	2	6	15	21	52	44	77	33

1955-56 1st in Division 3 (N)

Captain: Allenby Chilton

							Williams	Brown	DeGruchy	Johnston	Chilton	Richardson	Priestley	Evans	Crosbie	Reeson	Maddison	Conner	Pell	Anderson	Stokes	Weatherall	Player	Higgins	Lowry
1	Aug	20	ROCHDALE	1-1	Evans	11694	1	2	3	4	5	6	7	8	9	10	11								
2		23	CHESTER	6-1	Crosbie(4), Reeson(2)	10573	1	2	3	4	5	6	7	8	9	10	11								
3		27	Chesterfield	0-1		8881	1	2	3	4	5	6	7	8	9	10	11								
4		31	Chester	0-2		6193	1	2	3	4	5	6	7	8	9	10	11								
5	Sep	3	TRANMERE ROVERS	1-0	Richardson	9852	1	2	3	4	5	6	7	8		10	11					9			
6		6	CARLISLE UNITED	1-0	Weatherall	12194	1	2	3	4	5	6	7	8		10	11					9			
7		10	Southport	0-2		3650	1	2	3	4		6	7	8		10	11					9	5		
8		13	Carlisle United	2-1	Evans, Reeson	12294	1	2	3	4	5	6	7	8	9	10	11								
9		17	GATESHEAD	3-1	Maddison,Reeson,Crosbie(pen)	11266	1	2	3	4	5	6	7	8	9	10	11								
10		21	Bradford City	2-0	Priestley, Crosbie	11547	1	2	3		5	6	7	8	9	10	11	4							
11		24	Darlington	1-0	Evans	9270	1	2	3		5	6	7	8	9	10	11	4							
12		27	BARROW	3-0	Crosbie(2), Reeson	19874	1	2	3		5	6	7	8	9	10	11	4							
13	Oct	1	ACCRINGTON STANLEY	3-0	Maddison, Reeson, Crosbie	19069	1	2	3		5	6	7	8	9	10	11	4							
14		8	Oldham Athletic	1-1	Crosbie	10300	1	2	3		5	6	7	8	9	10	11	4							
15		15	HALIFAX TOWN	4-0	Evans,Crosbie,Maddison,Reeson	13092	1		3		5	6		8	9	10	11	4		2					7
16		22	York City	4-3	Reeson(3), Evans	14566	1		3		5	6	7	8	9	10	11	4		2					
17		29	DERBY COUNTY	2-1	Maddison, Crosbie	19874	1		3		5	6	7	8	9	10	11	4		2					
18	Nov	5	Crewe Alexandra	0-0		6165	1	2	3		5	6	7	8	9	10	11	4							
19		12	HARTLEPOOLS UNITED	1-0	Crosbie	14481	1	2	3		5	6	7	8	9	10	11	4							
20		26	MANSFIELD TOWN	2-0	Crosbie, Priestley	12572	1	2	3		5	6	7	8	9	10	11	4							
21	Dec	3	Wrexham	0-1		7654	1	2	3		5	6	7	8		10	11	4			9				
22		17	Rochdale	0-2		4547	1	2	3		5	6	7	8	9	10	11	4							
23		24	CHESTERFIELD	3-0	Crosbie(3)	13304	1	2	3		5	6	7	8	9	10	11	4							
24		26	BRADFORD P.A.	2-0	Crosbie(pen), Maddison	17908	1	2	3		5	6	7	8	9	10	11	4							
25		27	Bradford P.A.	1-2	Crosbie	12102	1	2			5	6	7	8	9	10	11	4						3	
26		31	Tranmere Rovers	1-0	Maddison	9005	1	2	3		5	6	7	8	9	10	11	4							
27	Jan	2	Barrow	0-0		11329	1	2	3		5	6	7	8	9	10	11	4							
28		21	Gateshead	0-2		4247	1	2	3		5	6	7	8	9	10	11	4							
29		28	WORKINGTON TOWN	1-2	Crosbie	10772	1	2	3		5	6	7	8	9	10	11	4							
30	Feb	11	Accrington Stanley	1-0	Evans	13305	1	2	3		5	6	7	8	9		11	4			10				
31		15	Stockport County	0-0		4000	1	2	3		5	6	7	8	9		11	4			10				
32		18	OLDHAM ATHLETIC	5-1	Reeson, Pell, Crosbie(3)	10070	1	2	3		5	6	7	8	9	11		4	10						
33	Mar	3	YORK CITY	2-1	Reeson, Crosbie	14529	1	2	3		5	6	7	8	9	10		4	11						
34		10	Derby County	3-1	OG, Crosbie, Priestley	33330	1	2	3		5	6	7	8	9	10	11	4							
35		17	STOCKPORT COUNTY	3-0	Reeson, Crosbie, Evans	13958	1	2	3		5	6	7	8	9	10	11	4							
36		24	Hartlepools United	2-1	Evans, Crosbie	10360	1	2	3		5	6	7	8	9	10	11	4							
37		30	SCUNTHORPE UNITED	0-1		23399	1	2	3		5	6	7	8	9	10	11	4							
38		31	CREWE ALEXANDRA	5-1	Crosbie(4), Reeson	12615	1	2	3	6			7	8	9	10	11	4					5		
39	Apr	2	Scunthorpe United	1-0	Evans	19067	1	2	3	6			7	8	9	10	11	4					5		
40		7	Mansfield Town	2-0	Priestley, Reeson	15562	1	2	3	6	5		7	8	9	10	11	4							
41		14	WREXHAM	1-0	Crosbie	14560	1	2	3	6	5		7	8	9	10	11	4							
42		17	DARLINGTON	1-0	Crosbie	16803	1	2	3	6	5		7	8	9	10	11	4							
43		21	Workington Town	0-0		8605	1	2	3	6	5		7	8	9	10	11	4							
44		25	SOUTHPORT	2-0	Evans, Crosbie	23056	1	2	3	6	5		7	8	9	10	11	4							
45		28	BRADFORD CITY	2-0	Evans, Maddison	15733	1	2	3	6	5		7	8	9	10	11	4							
46		30	Halifax Town	1-0	Crosbie	4315	1	2	3	6			7	8	9	10	11	4					5		
						Apps.	46	43	45	18	42	37	45	46	42	44	44	37	2	3	3	3	4	1	1
						Goals						1	4	11	35	15	7		1			1			

1 own goal

F.A. Cup

							Williams	Brown	DeGruchy	Johnston	Chilton	Richardson	Priestley	Evans	Crosbie	Reeson	Maddison	Conner	Pell	Anderson	Stokes	Weatherall	Player	Higgins	Lowry
R1	Nov	19	Netherfield	5-1	Evans,Crosbie(2),Reeson(2)	5161	1	2	3		5	6	7	8	9	10	11	4							
R2	Dec	10	Southport	0-0		9000	1	2	3		5	6	7	8		10	11	4	9						
R2r		14	SOUTHPORT	3-2	Priestley,Crosbie(pen),Reeson	6960	1	2	3		5	6	7	8	9	10	11	4							
R3	Jan	7	Portsmouth	1-3	Maddison	34598	1	2	3		5	6	7	8	9	10	11	4							

		P	W	D	L	F	A	W	D	L	F	A	F	A	Pts
1	GRIMSBY TOWN	46	20	1	2	54	10	11	5	7	22	19	76	29	68
2	Derby County	46	18	4	1	67	23	10	3	10	43	32	110	55	63
3	Accrington Stanley	46	17	4	2	61	19	8	5	10	31	38	92	57	59
4	Hartlepools United	46	18	2	3	47	15	8	3	12	34	45	81	60	57
5	Southport	46	12	9	2	39	18	11	2	10	27	35	66	53	57
6	Chesterfield	46	18	1	4	61	21	7	3	13	33	45	94	66	54
7	Stockport County	46	16	4	3	65	22	5	5	13	25	39	90	61	51
8	Bradford City	46	16	5	2	57	25	2	8	13	21	39	78	64	49
9	Scunthorpe United	46	12	4	7	40	26	8	4	11	35	37	75	63	48
10	Workington	46	13	4	6	47	20	6	5	12	28	43	75	63	47
11	York City	46	12	4	7	44	24	7	5	11	41	48	85	72	47
12	Rochdale	46	13	5	5	46	39	4	8	11	20	45	66	84	47
13	Gateshead	46	15	4	4	56	32	2	7	14	21	52	77	84	45
14	Wrexham	46	11	5	7	37	28	5	5	13	29	45	66	73	42
15	Darlington	46	11	6	6	41	28	5	3	15	19	45	60	73	41
16	Tranmere Rovers	46	11	4	8	33	25	5	5	13	26	59	59	84	41
17	Chester	46	10	8	5	35	33	3	6	14	17	49	52	82	40
18	Mansfield Town	46	13	6	4	59	21	1	5	17	25	60	84	81	39
19	Halifax Town	46	10	6	7	40	27	4	5	14	26	49	66	76	39
20	Oldham Athletic	46	7	12	4	48	36	3	6	14	28	50	76	86	38
21	Carlisle United	46	11	3	9	45	36	4	5	14	26	59	71	95	38
22	Barrow	46	11	6	6	44	25	1	3	19	17	58	61	83	33
23	Bradford Park Ave.	46	13	4	6	47	38	0	3	20	14	84	61	122	33
24	Crewe Alexandra	46	9	4	10	32	35	0	6	17	18	70	50	105	28

SEASON 1955/56
Back: Dukes (Dir), Pell, Richardson, Daley, De Gruchy, Williams, Stokes, Stockwood (Dir)
Middle (Standing): Lambton (Trainer), Dr.Carson, S.Smith (Dir), Redding, Player, Brown, Crosbie, Conner, Johnston, Wilson (Dir), McCoy (Physio), Humpston (Asst.Train), Robinson (Sec)
Middle (Seated): Pearce, Walker, Webb, Osmond (Directors), Chilton (Play/Man), Would (Chair), J.Evans, Winters, J.Smith (Directors)
Front: Priestley, W.Evans, Reeson, Maddison, Laverick, Higgins

SEASON 1956/57
Back: Crosbie, Player, Pell, DeGruchy, Richardson, Tucker, Redding
Middle: Humpston (Asst Train), Brown, Connor, Jobling, Daley, Williams, Stokes, Anderson, McCoy, Lambton (Train)
Front: Maddison, Higgins, Priestley, Reeson, Chilton (Man), Evans, Laverick, Johnston, Scott Inset: Rafferty

1956-57 16th in Division 2

Captain: Bill Brown

						Att	Williams C	Brown	DeGruchy	Conner	Chilton	Johnston	Priestley	Evans	Crosbie	Reeson	Maddison	Richardson	Tucker	Scott	Player	Walker	Jobling	Pell	Hodgson B	Stokes	Rafferty	Fell	Daley	Redding	Williams D.	Higgins
1	Aug	18	Bristol Rovers	0-0		27818	1	2	3	4	5	6	7	8	9	10	11															
2		20	Stoke City	0-1		20921	1	2	3	4	5	6	7	8	9	10	11															
3		25	NOTTS COUNTY	2-1	Reeson, Scott	18241	1	2	3	4	5	6		8	9	10	11			7												
4		28	STOKE CITY	4-1	Evans(2), Scott, Crosbie	17922	1	2	3	4	5	6		8	9	10	11			7												
5	Sep	1	Liverpool	2-3	Crosbie(2)	43222	1	2	3	4	5	6		8	9	10	11			7												
6		4	MIDDLESBROUGH	3-2	Crosbie, Evans, Maddison	20296	1	2	3	4	5	6		8	9	10	11			7												
7		8	LEYTON ORIENT	0-0		18251	1	2	3	4	5	6		8	9	10	11			7												
8		12	Middlesbrough	1-2	Crosbie	15999	1	2	3	4		6		8	9	10	11			7	5											
9		15	Huddersfield Town	1-2	Maddison	18312	1	2	3	4		6	8	10	9		11			7	5											
10		22	BURY	0-1		15698	1	2	3	4	5	6	9	8		10	11			7												
11		29	Lincoln City	0-1		18973	1	2	3	4		6	8		9	10	11			7	5											
12	Oct	6	SWANSEA TOWN	5-0	Crosbie(2),Evans(2),Johnston(pen)	13295	1	2	3	4		6	10	8	9		11			7	5											
13		13	Fulham	1-3	Scott	31727	1	2	3	4		6	10	8	9		11			7	5											
14		20	PORT VALE	1-0	Scott	13879	1	2	3	4		6	10	8	9		11			7	5											
15		27	West Ham United	1-0	Hodgson	24236	1	2	3	4		6	10	8			11			7	5				9							
16	Nov	3	BLACKBURN ROVERS	1-3	Maddison	16616	1	2	3	4		6	10	8			11			7	5				9							
17		10	Bristol City	2-0	Scott, Maddison	18976	1	2	3	4		5	10	8			11	6		7					9							
18		17	SHEFFIELD UNITED	1-2	Evans	15601	1	2	3	4		5	10	8			11	6		7					9							
19		24	Barnsley	0-2		11281	1	2	3	4		5	10	8			11	6		7					9							
20	Dec	1	NOTTINGHAM FOREST	0-0		13814	1	2		4		6				10	11	3	5	7				8		9						
21		8	Rotherham United	1-2	Maddison	10642	1	2		4		6		8	9	10	11		5	7										3		
22		15	BRISTOL ROVERS	3-2	Priestley, Evans, Crosbie	10460	1	2		4		6	7	8	9	10	11	3	5													
23		22	Notts County	1-0	Reeson	4869	1	2		4		6	7	8	9	10	11	3	5													
24		25	LEICESTER CITY	2-2	Maddison(2,1pen)	16381	1	2		4			7	8	9	10	11	3	5			6										
25		29	LIVERPOOL	0-0		15504	1	2		4			7	8	9	10	11	3	5			6										
26	Jan	12	Leyton Orient	1-1	Maddison	16400	1	2		4		6		8		10	11	3	5								9				7	
27		19	HUDDERSFIELD TOWN	1-2	Reeson	14929		2		4		6		8		10	11	3	5								9		1		7	
28		26	Leicester City	3-4	Rafferty(2), OG	34773	1	2					8			10	11	3	5	7		6					9					4
29	Feb	2	Bury	3-2	Scott, Rafferty(2)	12623	1	2		4			8			10	11	3	5	7		6					9					
30		9	LINCOLN CITY	2-0	OG, Rafferty	18523	1	2		4			8			10	11	3	5	7		6					9					
31		16	Swansea Town	1-3	Scott	17569	1	2		4			8			10	11	3	5	7		6					9					
32		23	FULHAM	3-1	Fell, Crosbie, Scott	13060	1	2		4		6	8		9			3	5	7							10	11				
33	Mar	2	Port Vale	0-3		15293	1	2		4		6	8					3	5	7						9	10	11				
34		9	WEST HAM UNITED	2-1	Fell, Crosbie	13996	1	2		4			8		9			3	5	7			6				10	11				
35		16	Blackburn Rovers	0-2		23195	1	2		4			8		9			3	5	7			6				10	11				
36		23	BRISTOL CITY	0-3		12692	1	2	3	4			8		9		11		5	7			6				10					
37		30	Sheffield United	0-2		18380	1	2		4			8		9		11	3	5	7			6				10					
38	Apr	6	BARNSLEY	4-1	Reeson, Rafferty, Evans(2)	10307	1	2		4				8		10		3	5	7			6				9	11				
39		13	Nottingham Forest	1-2	Rafferty	21316	1	2		4				8		10		3	5	7			6				9	11				
40		19	DONCASTER ROVERS	4-2	Rafferty(2), Evans, Scott	15393	1	2		4				8				3	5	7		6			10		9	11				
41		20	ROTHERHAM UNITED	3-2	Rafferty, Scott(2)	13474	1	2		4				8				3	5	7		6			10		9	11				
42		22	Doncaster Rovers	1-0	Conner	8981	1	2		4				8		10		3	5	7		6					9	11				
						Apps.	41	42	20	41	8	27	27	30	23	25	33	24	23	34	8	9	6	1	7	2	17	9	1	1	2	1
						Goals				1		1	1	10	10	4	8			11					1		10	2				

2 own goals

F.A. Cup

						Att	Williams C	Brown	DeGruchy	Conner	Chilton	Johnston	Priestley	Evans	Crosbie	Reeson	Maddison	Richardson	Tucker	Scott	Player	Walker	Jobling	Pell	Hodgson B	Stokes	Rafferty	Fell	Daley	Redding	Williams D.	Higgins
R3	Jan	7	West Ham United	3-5	Conner, Priestley, Rafferty	24500	1	2		4		6	7	8		10	11	3	5								9					

		P	W	D	L	F	A	W	D	L	F	A	F	A	Pts
1	Leicester City	42	14	5	2	68	36	11	6	4	41	31	109	67	61
2	Nottingham Forest	42	13	4	4	50	29	9	6	6	44	26	94	55	54
3	Liverpool	42	16	1	4	53	26	5	10	6	29	28	82	54	53
4	Blackburn Rovers	42	12	6	3	49	32	9	4	8	34	43	83	75	52
5	Stoke City	42	16	2	3	64	18	4	6	11	19	40	83	58	48
6	Middlesbrough	42	12	5	4	51	29	7	5	9	33	31	84	60	48
7	Sheffield United	42	11	6	4	45	28	8	2	11	42	48	87	76	46
8	West Ham United	42	12	4	5	31	24	7	4	10	28	39	59	63	46
9	Bristol Rovers	42	12	5	4	47	19	6	4	11	34	48	81	67	45
10	Swansea Town	42	12	3	6	53	34	7	4	10	37	56	90	90	45
11	Fulham	42	13	1	7	53	32	6	3	12	31	44	84	76	42
12	Huddersfield Town	42	10	3	8	33	27	8	3	10	35	47	68	74	42
13	Bristol City	42	13	2	6	49	32	3	7	11	25	47	74	79	41
14	Doncaster Rovers	42	12	5	4	51	21	3	5	13	26	56	77	77	40
15	Leyton Orient	42	7	8	6	34	38	8	2	11	32	46	66	84	40
16	GRIMSBY TOWN	42	12	4	5	41	26	5	1	15	20	36	61	62	39
17	Rotherham United	42	9	7	5	37	26	4	4	13	37	49	74	75	37
18	Lincoln City	42	9	4	8	34	27	5	2	14	20	53	54	80	34
19	Barnsley	42	8	7	6	39	35	4	3	14	20	54	59	89	34
20	Notts County	42	7	6	8	34	32	2	6	13	24	54	58	86	30
21	Bury	42	5	3	13	37	47	3	6	12	23	49	60	96	25
22	Port Vale	42	7	4	10	31	42	1	2	18	26	59	57	101	22

1957-58 13th in Division 2

Captain: Bill Brown

No	Month	Day	Opponent	Score	Scorers	Att.	Williams	Brown	Richardson	Conner	Tucker	Walker	Priestley	Evans	Rafferty	Stockin	Fell	Fleming	Player	Jobling	Whitefoot	Scott	Briggs	Reeson	Welbourne	DeGruchy	Sinclair	Laverick	Maddison	Tinsley
1	Aug	24	LEYTON ORIENT	7-2	Fell,Evans,Rafferty,Stockin,Conner,Priestley(2)	14274	1	2	3	4	5	6	7	8	9	10	11													
2		27	CARDIFF CITY	1-1	Evans	18014		2	3	4	5	6	7	8	9	10	11													1
3		31	Charlton Athletic	0-2		19969		2	3	4	5	6	7	8	9	10	11													1
4	Sep	4	Cardiff City	3-1	Rafferty, Fell, Evans	13433			3	4	5	6	7	8	9	10	11	2												1
5		7	DONCASTER ROVERS	3-1	Stockin(2), Rafferty	16575			3	4	5	6	7	8	9	10	11	2												1
6		10	Bristol City	2-2	Rafferty, Stockin	19887			3	4	5	6	7	8	9	10	11	2												1
7		17	BRISTOL CITY	1-1	Priestley	12004		2	3	4	5	6	7	8	9	10	11													1
8		21	HUDDERSFIELD TOWN	4-1	Scott, Evans, Rafferty(2)	14380		2	3	4	5			8	9	10	11					7			6					1
9		28	Lincoln City	4-1	Rafferty, Fell(2), Reeson	17221		2	3	4	5			8	9		11					7		10	6					1
10	Oct	5	Stoke City	1-4	Conner	18540		2	3	4	5			8	9		11					7		10	6					1
11		12	NOTTS COUNTY	2-0	Rafferty, Fell	14055		2	3	4	5			8	9		11					7		10	6					1
12		19	Ipswich Town	2-3	Rafferty(2)	18577		2	3	4	5			8	9							7		10	6				11	1
13		26	BLACKBURN ROVERS	3-4	Conner, Rafferty(2)	14761		2	3	4	5			8	9		11					7		10	6					1
14	Nov	2	Sheffield United	1-3	Fell	19675		2	3	4	5	6	8		9		11					7		10						1
15		9	WEST HAM UNITED	1-2	Evans	11878		2	6	4			7	8	9		11		5					10		3				1
16		16	Barnsley	3-3	Stockin, Rafferty(2)	16091	1		3	4			8		9	10	11		5		6	7				2				
17		23	FULHAM	3-1	Stockin, Rafferty(2)	15102	1	2	3	4			8		9	10	11		5		6	7								
18		30	Swansea Town	2-0	Whitefoot, Fell	12573	1	2	3	4			8		9	10	11		5		6	7								
19	Dec	7	DERBY COUNTY	3-2	Scott, Rafferty, Fell	12246	1	2	3	4			8		9	10	11		5		6	7								
20		14	Bristol Rovers	7-0	Stockin(2),Scott(2),Rafferty(p),Fell,Priestley	14577	1	2	3	4			8		9	10	11		5		6	7								
21		21	Leyton Orient	1-5	Whitefoot	13274	1	2	3	4			8		9	10	11		5		6	7								
22		25	LIVERPOOL	3-1	Scott, Whitefoot, Fell	17705	1	2	3	4			8		9	10	11		5		6	7								
23		26	Liverpool	2-3	Priestley, Rafferty	47776	1	2	3	4			8	10	9		11		5		6	7								
24		28	CHARLTON ATHLETIC	4-2	Rafferty(2), Whitefoot(pen), Fell	17537	1	2	3	4			8	10	9		11		5		6	7								
25	Jan	11	Doncaster Rovers	3-3	Fell(2), Scott	10817	1	2	3	4			8	10	9		11		5		6	7								
26		18	ROTHERHAM UNITED	3-1	Rafferty, Fell, Whitefoot	12278	1	2	3	4			8	10	9		11			5	6	7								
27	Feb	1	Huddersfield Town	0-1		14333	1	2	3	4			8	10	9		11			5	6	7								
28		8	LINCOLN CITY	4-0	Priestley, Evans(2), Rafferty	13464	1	2	3	4			8	10	9		11			5	6	7								
29		15	Rotherham United	0-2		9864	1	2	3	4			8	10	9		11			5	6	7								
30		22	Fulham	0-6		21316	1	2	3	4			8	10	9		11			5	6	7								
31	Mar	1	IPSWICH TOWN	0-2		13263	1		3				8		9		11	2		5	6	7			4			10		
32		8	Blackburn Rovers	0-3		27923	1	2	3	4			8		9	10			5		6	7							11	
33		15	SHEFFIELD UNITED	1-3	Briggs	16701	1	2	3	4			7		8	10	11		5		6		9							
34		22	West Ham United	0-2		25900	1	2	3	4			8		10		11		5		6	7	9							
35		29	BARNSLEY	2-1	Rafferty, Briggs	9622	1	2	3	4			8		10		11		5		6	7	9							
36	Apr	4	MIDDLESBROUGH	4-1	Briggs(3), Rafferty	17233	1	2	3	4					10	8	11			5	6	7	9							
37		5	Notts County	0-2		11555	1	2	3	4					10	8	11			5	6	7	9							
38		7	Middlesbrough	1-5	Stockin	22204			3	4				8		10	11	2		5	6	7	9							1
39		12	SWANSEA TOWN	2-2	Stockin, Scott	11275	1		3	4				8		10		2		5	6	7	9						11	
40		19	Derby County	0-1		13549	1		3	4			8		10		11	2		5	6	7	9							
41		22	STOKE CITY	0-0		10841	1		3	4				8	10		11	2		5	6	7	9							
42		26	BRISTOL ROVERS	3-2	Sinclair, Conner, Rafferty	10030	1		3	4				8	10		11	2		5		7			6		9			
						Apps.	27	32	42	41	14	8	30	26	40	21	39	9	15	13	26	33	9	7	8	2	1	1	3	15
						Goals				4			6	7	26	10	14				5	7	5	1			1			

F.A. Cup

Rd	Month	Day	Opponent	Score	Scorers	Att.	Williams	Brown	Richardson	Conner	Tucker	Walker	Priestley	Evans	Rafferty	Stockin	Fell	Fleming	Player	Jobling	Whitefoot	Scott	Briggs	Reeson	Welbourne	DeGruchy	Sinclair	Laverick	Maddison	Tinsley
R3	Jan	4	Sheffield United	1-5	Evans	27459	1	2	3	4			8	10	9		11		5		6	7								

		P	W	D	L	F	A	W	D	L	F	A	F	A	Pts
1	West Ham United	42	12	8	1	56	25	11	3	7	45	29	101	54	57
2	Blackburn Rovers	42	13	7	1	50	18	9	5	7	43	39	93	57	56
3	Charlton Athletic	42	15	3	3	65	33	9	4	8	42	36	107	69	55
4	Liverpool	42	17	3	1	50	13	5	7	9	29	41	79	54	54
5	Fulham	42	13	5	3	53	24	7	7	7	44	35	97	59	52
6	Sheffield United	42	12	5	4	38	22	9	5	7	37	28	75	50	52
7	Middlesbrough	42	13	3	5	52	29	6	4	11	31	45	83	74	45
8	Ipswich Town	42	13	4	4	45	29	3	8	10	23	40	68	69	44
9	Huddersfield Town	42	9	8	4	28	24	5	8	8	35	42	63	66	44
10	Bristol Rovers	42	12	5	4	52	31	5	3	13	33	49	85	80	42
11	Stoke City	42	9	4	8	49	36	9	2	10	26	37	75	73	42
12	Leyton Orient	42	14	2	5	53	27	4	3	14	24	52	77	79	41
13	GRIMSBY TOWN	42	13	4	4	54	30	4	2	15	32	53	86	83	40
14	Barnsley	42	10	6	5	40	25	4	6	11	30	49	70	74	40
15	Cardiff City	42	10	5	6	44	31	4	4	13	19	46	63	77	37
16	Derby County	42	11	3	7	37	36	3	5	13	23	45	60	81	36
17	Bristol City	42	9	5	7	35	31	4	4	13	28	57	63	88	35
18	Rotherham United	42	8	3	10	38	44	6	2	13	27	57	65	101	33
19	Swansea Town	42	8	3	10	48	45	3	6	12	24	54	72	99	31
20	Lincoln City	42	6	6	9	33	35	5	3	13	22	47	55	82	31
21	Notts County	42	9	3	9	24	31	3	3	15	20	49	44	80	30
22	Doncaster Rovers	42	7	5	9	34	40	1	6	14	22	48	56	88	27

SEASON 1957/58

Back: Maddison, Scott, Richardson, C.Williams, Stockin, Walker, Fell, Fleming
Middle: Derek Williams, Laverick, Rafferty, Jobling, De Gruchy, Player., Tucker, Locking, Burgess
Front: Priestley, Conner, Dunn, Brown, Chilton (Manager), Evans, Reeson, Anderson, Bratley

SEASON 1958/59

Back: Dukes (Dir), Rafferty, Priestley, Bell, C.Williams, White, Stockin, Stockwood (Dir)
Middle (Standing): Humpston (Trainer), W.Evans (Asst.Train), Donovan, Ritchie, Briggs, Locking, Jobling, Richardson, Player, Barrett, Cockerill, McCoy (Physio), Robinson (Sec)
Middle (Seated): Chilton (Manager), Wilson, Winters, Walker, Would (Chair.), Drewry, Osmond, Webb, J.Evans, J.Smith (Directors)
Front: Scott, Maddison, Cullen, Conner, Fleming, Welbourne, Fell

1958-59 21st in Division 2

Captain: Dick Conner

No.	Date	Opponent	Score	Scorers	Att.	Williams C	Donovan	Richardson	Conner	Jobling	Cockerill	Scott	Cullen	Rafferty	Priestley	Fell	Barnett	Bell	White	Bratley	Fleming	Burnett	Welbourne	Player	Paul	Williams D	Briggs	Pearce	Barratt	Stockin	Ritchie	Maddison	Bemrose
1	Aug 23	Liverpool	3-3	Fell, Scott, Rafferty	47502	1	2	3	4	5	6	7	8	9	10	11																	
2	26	LINCOLN CITY	4-2	Cullen(2), Scott(2)	22261		2	3	4	5	6	7	8	9	10	11		1															
3	30	MIDDLESBROUGH	3-2	Cullen(2), Rafferty	21004		2	3	4	5	6	7	8	9	10	11		1															
4	Sep 3	Lincoln City	4-4	Rafferty(4)	19759		2	3	4	5	6	7	8	9		11		1												10			
5	6	Charlton Athletic	1-2	Fell	18609		2	3	4	5	6	7	8	9		11		1												10			
6	10	Brighton & Hove Albion	0-2		20880		2	3	4	5	6	7	8	9	10	11		1															
7	13	BRISTOL CITY	2-0	Cockerill, Fell	15298		2	3	4	5	6	7	10	9		11		1									8						
8	16	BRIGHTON & HOVE ALBION	1-1	Briggs	15349		2	3	4	5	6	7	10	9		11		1									8						
9	20	Cardiff City	1-4	Cullen	22007		2	3	4	5	6	7	8	9		11		1													10		
10	27	HUDDERSFIELD TOWN	2-1	Cullen(2)	14401	1	2	3	4	5	6	7	8	9		10																11	
11	Oct 4	Barnsley	1-3	Scott	10157	1		3	4	5	6	7	8	9		10				2												11	
12	11	FULHAM	2-2	Cockerill, Fell	16644	1	2	3	4	6	10	7	8	9		11								5									
13	18	Sheffield Wednesday	0-6		29866		2	3	4	6	10		8	9	7	11			1					5									
14	25	SCUNTHORPE UNITED	1-1	Briggs	16753	1	2		4	6			8	10		11						3		5	7		9						
15	Nov 1	Sunderland	0-1		23045	1	2	3	4	6	5		8	10	7	11											9						
16	8	DERBY COUNTY	3-0	OG, Briggs, Fell	11044	1	2	3	4	6	5		8	10	7	11											9						
17	15	Bristol Rovers	3-7	Briggs, Cullen Rafferty	15733	1	2	3	4	6	5		8	10	7	11											9						
18	22	IPSWICH TOWN	2-3	Rafferty(2)	9499	1	2	3	4	6	5	7	8	10		11											9						
19	29	Swansea Town	1-1	Cullen	14244	1	2	3	6	5	10		7	8		11							4				9						
20	Dec 6	STOKE CITY	2-2	Cockerill, Rafferty	9255	1	2	3	6	5	10		7	8		11							4				9						
21	13	Leyton Orient	1-0	Scott(pen)	7632	1	2	3	6	5	10	7	8	9		11							4										
22	20	LIVERPOOL	2-3	Rafferty, Cullen	10402	1	2	3	6	5	10	7	8	9		11							4										
23	25	SHEFFIELD UNITED	1-2	Scott(pen)	13946		2	3	6	5	10	7	8	9		11	1						4										
24	27	Sheffield United	1-2	Rafferty	27555		2	3		5	6	7	8	9		11	1						4							10			
25	Feb 7	CARDIFF CITY	5-1	Scott(p),Fell,Cockerill,Rafferty(2)	9662		2	3		5	6	7	8	9		11	1						4							10			
26	14	Huddersfield Town	0-2		11389		2	3		5	6	7	8			11	1						4				9			10			
27	21	BARNSLEY	3-3	Scott(pen), Cullen, Welbourne	8130		2	3		5	6	10	8	9		11	1						4			7							
28	24	Bristol City	0-1		15138		2			5	6	10	8			11	1				3		4			7			9				
29	28	Derby County	0-3		22293		2			5	6	8	10			11	1				3		4			7			9				
30	Mar 7	SHEFFIELD WEDNESDAY	0-2		13109		2			5	6	7	8	10		11	1				3		4						9				
31	11	Middlesbrough	0-1		11799		2		8	5	6	7		9		11	1				3		4							10			
32	14	Scunthorpe United	3-1	Conner, Stockin, Rafferty	13539		2	3	8	5	6	7		9		11	1						4							10			
33	21	SUNDERLAND	1-1	Stockin	10193		2	3	8	5	6			9		11	1						4			7				10			
34	27	ROTHERHAM UNITED	1-1	Rafferty	14797		2		8	5	6	7		9		11	1				3		4							10			
35	28	Fulham	0-3		25517		2	3		5	6		8	9			1						4			7				10			11
36	30	Rotherham United	1-2	Stockin	8815		3		4	5	6	7		9		11	1			2								8		10			
37	Apr 4	BRISTOL ROVERS	1-2	Rafferty	9217		2	3		5	6	7	8	9		11	1						4							10			
38	11	Ipswich Town	1-2	Fell	12202		2	3		5	6	7	8	9		11	1						4							10			
39	14	CHARLTON ATHLETIC	1-5	Fell	11009		2	3		5	6	7	8	9		11	1						4							10			
40	18	SWANSEA TOWN	0-1		8818		4	3	10	5	6	7	8	9		11	1				2												
41	21	LEYTON ORIENT	4-1	Conner, Rafferty(2), Stockin	7754		4	3	8	5	6	7		9		11	1				2									10			
42	25	Stoke City	0-4		6855		4	3	8	5	6	7		9		11	1				2									10			
					Apps.	13	41	35	31	42	41	33	35	39	8	41	20	8	1	2	8	1	20	3	1	5	10	1	3	16	1	2	1
					Goals				2		4	8	11	19		8							1				4			4			

Game 1: C.Williams injured, replaced in goal by Fell.

1 own goal

F.A. Cup

Rd	Date	Opponent	Score	Scorers	Att.	Williams C	Donovan	Richardson	Conner	Jobling	Cockerill	Scott	Cullen	Rafferty	Priestley	Fell	Barnett	Bell	White	Bratley	Fleming	Burnett	Welbourne	Player	Paul	Williams D	Briggs	Pearce	Barratt	Stockin	Ritchie	Maddison	Bemrose
R3	Jan 10	MANCHESTER CITY	2-2	Cullen,Stockin	14964		2	3		5	6	7	8	9		11	1						4							10			
R3r	24	Manchester City	2-1	Cockerill(2)	35000		2	3		5	6	7	8	9		11	1						4							10			
R4	28	Nottingham Forest	1-4	Scott	39289			3		5	6	7	8	9		11	1			2			4							10			

		P	W	D	L	F	A	W	D	L	F	A	F	A	Pts
1	Sheffield Wed.	42	18	2	1	68	13	10	4	7	38	35	106	48	62
2	Fulham	42	18	1	2	65	26	9	5	7	31	35	96	61	60
3	Sheffield United	42	16	2	3	54	15	7	5	9	28	33	82	48	53
4	Liverpool	42	15	3	3	57	25	9	2	10	30	37	87	62	53
5	Stoke City	42	16	2	3	48	19	5	5	11	24	39	72	58	49
6	Bristol Rovers	42	13	5	3	46	23	5	7	9	34	41	80	64	48
7	Derby County	42	15	1	5	46	29	5	7	9	28	42	74	71	48
8	Charlton Athletic	42	13	3	5	53	33	5	4	12	39	57	92	90	43
9	Cardiff City	42	12	2	7	37	26	6	5	10	28	39	65	65	43
10	Bristol City	42	11	3	7	43	27	6	4	11	31	43	74	70	41
11	Swansea Town	42	12	5	4	52	30	4	4	13	27	51	79	81	41
12	Brighton & Hove A.	42	10	9	2	46	29	5	2	14	28	61	74	90	41
13	Middlesbrough	42	9	7	5	51	26	6	3	12	36	45	87	71	40
14	Huddersfield Town	42	12	3	6	39	20	4	5	12	23	35	62	55	40
15	Sunderland	42	13	4	4	42	23	3	4	14	22	52	64	75	40
16	Ipswich Town	42	12	4	5	37	27	5	2	14	25	50	62	77	40
17	Leyton Orient	42	9	4	8	43	30	5	4	12	28	48	71	78	36
18	Scunthorpe United	42	7	6	8	32	37	5	3	13	23	47	55	84	33
19	Lincoln City	42	10	5	6	45	37	1	2	18	18	56	63	93	29
20	Rotherham United	42	9	5	7	32	28	1	4	16	10	54	42	82	29
21	GRIMSBY TOWN	42	7	7	7	41	36	2	3	16	21	54	62	90	28
22	Barnsley	42	8	4	9	34	34	2	3	16	21	57	55	91	27

1959-60 4th in Division 3

Captain: Keith Jobling

	Date	Opponent	Score	Scorers	Att.	Barnett	Donovan	Richardson	Welbourne	Jobling	Birbeck	Scott	Cullen	Rafferty	Hunt	Fell	Keeble	Williams C	Fleming	Stockin	Pearce	Carrington	Cockerill	Knights	Williams D	Sinclair	Laverick	Duff
1	Aug 22	CHESTERFIELD	5-1	Hunt(2), Refferty(2), Cullen	11794	1	2	3	4	5	6	7	8	9	10	11												
2	24	Colchester United	2-2	Rafferty, Hunt	9683	1	2	3	4	5	6	7	8	9	10	11												
3	29	Newport County	2-0	Hunt, Scott(pen)	9511	1	2	3	4	5	6	7	8	9	10	11												
4	Sep 1	COLCHESTER UNITED	4-1	Scott, Hunt(3)	14455		2	3	4	5	6	7	8	9	10	11		1										
5	5	ACCRINGTON STANLEY	4-0	Rafferty, Hunt, OG, Scott(pen)	14528	1	2	3	4	5	6	7	8	9	10	11												
6	9	Swindon Town	2-3	Hunt, Rafferty	22678	1	2	3	4	5	6	7	8	9	10	11												
7	12	Bournemouth	2-4	Hunt, Scott	12292		2	3		5	6	7	8	9	10	11		1		4								
8	15	SWINDON TOWN	3-0	Hunt Scott(2,1pen)	11608		2	3		5	6	7	8	9	10	11		1		4								
9	19	TRANMERE ROVERS	1-1	Hunt	13227		2	3		5	6	7	8	9	10	11		1		4								
10	21	York City	3-3	Rafferty, Hunt(2)	11500	1	2	3	4	5	6	7	8	9	10	11												
11	26	Wrexham	1-2	Cullen	10184	1	2	3	4	5	6	7	8	9	10	11												
12	29	YORK CITY	2-2	Scott, Hunt	11500	1	2	3	4		6	7	8	9	10	11	5											
13	Oct 3	BRENTFORD	1-3	Hunt	11209	1	2	3	4	5	6	11	8	9	10										7			
14	5	Queens Park Rangers	0-0		15257	1	2	6	4	5			7	10			3			8						9	11	
15	10	Southend United	0-3		10462	1	2	6	4	5		7	8	10			3									9	11	
16	13	QUEENS PARK RANGERS	3-1	Rafferty(2), Duff	6024	1	2	6	4	5		7	8	9			3			10								11
17	17	MANSFIELD TOWN	2-1	Rafferty(2)	11207	1		3	4	5		7	8	9			2			10			6					11
18	24	Halifax Town	2-1	OG, Fell	6147	1		3	4	5		7	8	10		11	2						6			9		
19	31	NORWICH CITY	1-1	Cullen	15018	1	4	6		5		7	8	9		11	2		3	10								
20	Nov 7	Barnsley	3-3	Cullen, Rafferty, Fell	6521	1	4	6		5		7	8	9		11	2		3	10								
21	21	Reading	2-1	Rafferty, Donovan	11987	1	4	3		5	6	7	8	9	10	11	2											
22	28	SHREWSBURY TOWN	2-1	Fell, Scott(pen)	10958	1	4	3		5	6	7	8	9	10	11	2											
23	Dec 12	BURY	2-2	Scott(pen), Hunt	9899	1	4	3		5		7		8	9	11	2			10				6				
24	19	Chesterfield	2-2	Hunt(2)	3863	1	4	3		5	6	7		8	9	11	2			10								
25	26	Bradford City	1-3	Hunt	14207	1	4	3		5	6	7		8	9	11	2			10								
26	28	BRADFORD CITY	2-2	Hunt, Rafferty	18033	1	6	3	4			7	10	8	9	11	2					5						
27	Jan 2	NEWPORT COUNTY	0-1		9188	1		3	4		6	7		8	9	11	2			10		5						
28	16	Accrington Stanley	4-2	Rafferty, Scott, Hunt, Fell	4243	1	6	3	4			7		8	9	10	2					5						11
29	23	BOURNEMOUTH	1-1	Rafferty	7779	1	6	3	4	5		7	8	9	10	11	2											
30	Feb 10	Port Vale	1-2	Hunt	22987	1	6	3	4	5		7	8	9	10	11	2											
31	13	WREXHAM	3-1	Hunt, Rafferty, Scott	7002	1	6	3	4	5		7	8	9	10	11	2											
32	20	Brentford	2-0	Scott(2)	10900	1	6	3	4	5		7	8	9	10	11	2											
33	22	Tranmere Rovers	0-2		8909	1	6	3	4	5		7	8	9	10	11	2											
34	27	SOUTHEND UNITED	1-1	Rafferty	8860	1	6	3	4	5		7	8	9	10	11	2											
35	Mar 5	Mansfield Town	2-3	Fell, Rafferty	9111	1	6	3	4	5		7	8	9	10	11	2											
36	12	HALIFAX TOWN	3-2	Hunt(2), Rafferty	7116	1	6	3	4	5		7	8	9	10	11	2											
37	19	Shrewsbury Town	2-5	Hunt(2)	6107	1		3	4	5		7	8	9	10	11	2							6				
38	26	BARNSLEY	2-0	Hunt(2)	4621	1	2		4	5		7	8	9	10	11	3							6				
39	Apr 2	Southampton	1-1	Rafferty	20367	1	2		4	5		7	9	8	10	11	3							6				
40	9	READING	0-1		7389	1	2		4	5		7	9	8	10	11	3							6				
41	15	COVENTRY CITY	3-0	Rafferty, Fell, Cullen	11819	1	2		4	5		7	9	8	10	11	3							6				
42	16	Norwich City	1-1	Hunt	33720	1	2			5		7	9	8	10	11	3				4			6				
43	19	Coventry City	2-0	OG, Rafferty	16737	1	2			5		7	9	8	10	11	3				4			6				
44	23	PORT VALE	1-1	Hunt	8186	1	2			5		7	9	8	10	11	3				4			6				
45	26	SOUTHAMPTON	3-2	Rafferty(2), Hunt	11550	1	2			5		7	9	8	10	11	3				4			6				
46	30	Bury	1-1	Scott(pen)	4430	1	2			5		7	9	8	10	11	3				4			6				
					Apps.	42	42	37	31	42	18	45	41	46	39	41	34	4	2	12	5	3	2	11	1	3	2	3
					Goals		1					14	5	24	33	6												1

3 own goals

F.A. Cup

	Date	Opponent	Score	Scorers	Att.	Barnett	Donovan	Richardson	Welbourne	Jobling	Birbeck	Scott	Cullen	Rafferty	Hunt	Fell	Keeble	Williams C	Fleming	Stockin	Pearce	Carrington	Cockerill	Knights	Williams D	Sinclair	Laverick	Duff
R1	Nov 14	Rhyl	2-1	OG(2)	4405	1	4	3		5	6	7	8	9		11	2			10								
R2	Dec 5	WREXHAM	2-3	Rafferty, Hunt	11472	1	4	3		5	6	7	8	9	10	11	2											

		P	W	D	L	F	A	W	D	L	F	A	F	A	Pts
1	Southampton	46	19	3	1	68	30	7	6	10	38	45	106	75	61
2	Norwich City	46	16	4	3	53	24	8	7	8	29	30	82	54	59
3	Shrewsbury Town	46	12	7	4	58	34	6	9	8	39	41	97	75	52
4	GRIMSBY TOWN	46	12	7	4	48	27	6	9	8	39	43	87	70	52
5	Coventry City	46	14	6	3	44	22	7	4	12	34	41	78	63	52
6	Brentford	46	13	6	4	46	24	8	3	12	32	37	78	61	51
7	Bury	46	13	4	6	36	23	8	5	10	28	28	64	51	51
8	Queen's Park Rgs.	46	14	7	2	45	16	4	6	13	28	38	73	54	49
9	Colchester United	46	15	6	2	51	22	3	5	15	32	52	83	74	47
10	Bournemouth	46	12	8	3	47	27	5	5	13	25	45	72	72	47
11	Reading	46	13	3	7	49	34	5	7	11	35	43	84	77	46
12	Southend United	46	15	3	5	49	28	4	5	14	27	46	76	74	46
13	Newport County	46	15	2	6	59	36	5	4	14	21	43	80	79	46
14	Port Vale	46	16	4	3	51	19	3	4	16	29	60	80	79	46
15	Halifax Town	46	13	3	7	42	27	5	7	11	28	45	70	72	46
16	Swindon Town	46	12	6	5	39	30	7	2	14	30	48	69	78	46
17	Barnsley	46	13	6	4	45	25	2	8	13	20	41	65	66	44
18	Chesterfield	46	13	3	7	41	31	5	4	14	30	53	71	84	43
19	Bradford City	46	10	7	6	39	28	5	5	13	27	46	66	74	42
20	Tranmere Rovers	46	11	8	4	50	29	3	5	15	22	46	72	75	41
21	York City	46	11	5	7	38	26	2	7	14	19	47	57	73	38
22	Mansfield Town	46	11	4	8	55	48	4	2	17	26	64	81	112	36
23	Wrexham	46	12	5	6	39	30	2	3	18	29	71	68	101	36
24	Accrington Stanley	46	4	5	14	31	53	7	0	16	26	70	57	123	27

SEASON 1959/60

Back: Newmarch, Barnett, Fell, Stockin, Williams, Rafferty, Richardson, Keeble
Middle (standing): Lambton (Train), Jobling, Cockerill, White, Barrett, Robinson (Sec), McCoy (Physio)
Middle (seated): Donovan, Cullen, Drewry (Pres), Would (Chair), Hunt, Scott Front: Birbeck, Fleming, Welbourne

SEASON 1960/61

Back: Pearce, Fleming, Richardson, Cullen, Rafferty, Carrington, Donovan, Cockerill, Fell
Middle (Standing): McCoy (Physio), Newmarch, Jobling, Barnett, Keeble, White, Hunt, Renwick, Horsley, Robinson (Sec), Lambton (Train)
Middle (Seated): Ward (Manager), Webb, Wilson, Stockwood, Would (Chair), Walker, J.Smith, Winters (Directors)
Front: Scott, Laverick, Welbourne, Catley, Mills, Brader

1960-61 6th in Division 3

Captain: Keith Jobling

						White	Donovan	Keeble	Pearce	Jobling	Knights	Scott	Rafferty	Cullen	Hunt	Fell	Barnett	Fleming	Welbourne	Cockerill	Williams	Marklew	Carrington	Mills	Brader	Bemrose	Sinclair	Laverick	Hill
1	Aug 20	CHESTERFIELD	0-0		11282	1	2	3	4	5	6	7	8	9	10	11													
2	22	Colchester United	1-1	OG	7194	1	2	3	4	5	6	7	8	9	10	11													
3	27	Hull City	3-3	Hunt, Rafferty, OG	14252	1	2	3	4	5	6	7	8	9	10	11													
4	30	COLCHESTER UNITED	2-1	Cullen, Rafferty	16122	1	2	3	4	5		7	8	9		11				6								10	
5	Sep 3	READING	3-1	Rafferty, Cullen, Scott	10846	1	2	3	4	5		7	8	9		11				6							10		
6	6	BRADFORD CITY	1-0	Cullen	10811	1	2	3	4	5	6	7	8	9		11									10				
7	10	Coventry City	0-0		13906	1	2	3	4	5	6	7	8	9		11											10		
8	13	Bradford City	3-1	Rafferty, Scott, Williams	7546	1	2	3	4	5		7	8	9		11			6		10								
9	17	BRISTOL CITY	5-2	Rafferty(2), Scott, Williams, Fell	11839	1	2	3	4	5		7	8	9		11			6		10								
10	20	NEWPORT COUNTY	2-1	Williams, Cullen	12500	1	2	3	4	5		7	8	9		11			6		10								
11	24	Queens Park Rangers	0-2		11042	1	2	3	4	5		7	8	9		11			6		10								
12	26	Newport County	1-1	Rafferty	9233	1	2	3	4	5		7	8	9		11			6		10								
13	Oct 1	NOTTS COUNTY	1-1	Rafferty	12448	1	2	3	4	5		7	8	9		11			6		10								
14	5	Bournemouth	1-2	Rafferty	5987	1	2	3	4			7	8	9		11			6		10		5						
15	8	WALSALL	3-1	Rafferty, Williams, Jobling	10068	1	2	3	4	5		7	8	9		11			6		10								
16	15	Shrewsbury Town	1-2	OG	7184	1	2	3	4			7	8	9		11			6	5	10								
17	22	HALIFAX TOWN	6-1	Williams(2),Rafferty(2),Cullen,Scott(p)	10423	1	2	3	4	5		7	8	9		11			6		10								
18	29	Tranmere Rovers	6-3	Williams(4), Marklew, Fell(pen)	8991	1	2	3	4	5			8	9		11			6		10	7							
19	Nov 12	Brentford	1-0	Fell	8120	1	2	3	4	5		7	8	9		11			6		10								
20	28	SWINDON TOWN	3-2	Williams(2), Fell	7234	1	2	3	4	5		7	8	9		11			6		10								
21	Dec 3	PORT VALE	0-5		8843	1	2	3	4	5		7	8	9		11			6		10								
22	10	Southend United	1-1	Fell	5952		2	3		5		7	8	9		11	1		4	6	10								
23	17	Chesterfield	3-2	Williams, Cullen, Rafferty	4451		2	3		5		7	8	9		11	1		4	6	10								
24	20	BARNSLEY	3-2	Rafferty(3)	5915		2	3		5		7	8	9		11	1		4	6	10								
25	26	Barnsley	2-3	Cockerill(2)	10725		2	3		5		7	8	9		11	1		4	6	10								
26	31	HULL CITY	2-0	Cockerill, Williams	12712		2			5		7	8	9		11	1	3	4	6	10								
27	Jan 14	Reading	1-3	Rafferty	7304		2			5		7	8	9		11	1	3	4	6	10								
28	28	WATFORD	1-3	Scott	6692	1	2		6			7	8	9		11		3	4	5	10								
29	Feb 4	Bristol City	1-2	Cullen	11141	1	2	3	6			7	8	9		11			4	5	10								
30	6	Torquay United	0-0		5328	1	2	3	6			7	8	9	10	11			4	5									
31	11	QUEENS PARK RANGERS	3-1	Hunt, Cullen, Rafferty	10599	1	2	3	6			7	9	8	10	11			4	5									
32	18	Notts County	1-0	Welbourne	22292	1	2	3	6			7	9	8	10	11			4	5									
33	25	Port Vale	2-3	Rafferty(2)	9367	1	2	3	6			7	9	8	10	11			4	5									
34	Mar 4	SHREWSBURY TOWN	0-2		9388	1	2	3	6			7		8	10	11			4	5	9								
35	11	Halifax Town	0-0		4089	1	2	3	6			7	9	10		11			4	5	8								
36	18	TRANMERE ROVERS	4-1	Rafferty(3), Williams	6117	1	2	3		5		7	9	10		11			4	6	8								
37	25	Watford	0-2		10384	1	2	3		5		7	9	10					4	6	8	11							
38	31	BURY	2-2	Cockerill, Williams	14779	1	2	3		5		7	10	9					4	6	8	11							
39	Apr 1	BRENTFORD	0-0		14779	1	2	3		5		7	10	9					4	6	8	11							
40	4	Bury	0-2		13306	1	2	3		5		7	9		10				4	6	8	11							
41	8	Swindon Town	0-3		10117	1	2	3		5		11	8	9	10				4	6	7								
42	15	TORQUAY UNITED	4-2	Hunt(3), Hill	5437	1	2	3	6	5		7	9	8	10				4										11
43	18	COVENTRY CITY	2-3	Cullen, Hunt	5694	1	2	3		5		7	9	8	10				4	6									11
44	22	Walsall	1-2	Rafferty	16446	1	2	3		5		7	9	8	10					6	11			4					
45	25	BOURNEMOUTH	0-1		4679	1	2	3		5		7	9	8	10					6				4		11			
46	29	SOUTHEND UNITED	1-0	Williams	3852	1	2	3		5		7	9						4	6	10	11			8				
					Apps.	40	46	43	30	36	5	45	45	44	14	36	6	3	37	27	32	6	1	2	2	1	2	1	2
					Goals					1		5	24	9	6	5			1	4	17	1							1

3 own goals

F.A. Cup

						White	Donovan	Keeble	Pearce	Jobling	Knights	Scott	Rafferty	Cullen	Hunt	Fell	Barnett	Fleming	Welbourne	Cockerill	Williams	Marklew	Carrington	Mills	Brader	Bemrose	Sinclair	Laverick	Hill
R1	Nov 15	Darlington	0-2		12357	1	2	3	4	5			8	9		11			6		10	7							

League Cup

						White	Donovan	Keeble	Pearce	Jobling	Knights	Scott	Rafferty	Cullen	Hunt	Fell	Barnett	Fleming	Welbourne	Cockerill	Williams	Marklew	Carrington	Mills	Brader	Bemrose	Sinclair	Laverick	Hill
R1		Bye																											
R2	Oct 26	Bolton Wanderers	2-6	Rafferty(2)	7992	1	2	3	4	5			8	9		11		10	6			7							

	P	W	D	L	F	A	W	D	L	F	A	F	A	Pts
1 Bury	46	18	3	2	62	17	12	5	6	46	28	108	45	68
2 Walsall	46	19	4	0	62	20	9	2	12	36	40	98	60	62
3 Queen's Park Rgs.	46	18	4	1	58	23	7	6	10	35	37	93	60	60
4 Watford	46	12	7	4	52	27	8	5	10	33	45	85	72	52
5 Notts County	46	16	3	4	52	24	5	6	12	30	53	82	77	51
6 GRIMSBY TOWN	46	14	4	5	48	32	6	6	11	29	37	77	69	50
7 Port Vale	46	15	3	5	63	30	2	12	9	33	49	96	79	49
8 Barnsley	46	15	5	3	56	30	6	2	15	27	50	83	80	49
9 Halifax Town	46	14	7	2	42	22	2	10	11	29	56	71	78	49
10 Shrewsbury Town	46	13	7	3	54	26	2	9	12	29	49	83	75	46
11 Hull City	46	13	6	4	51	28	4	6	13	22	45	73	73	46
12 Torquay United	46	8	12	3	37	26	6	5	12	38	57	75	83	45
13 Newport County	46	12	7	4	51	30	5	4	14	30	60	81	90	45
14 Bristol City	46	15	4	4	50	19	2	6	15	20	49	70	68	44
15 Coventry City	46	14	6	3	54	25	2	6	15	26	58	80	83	44
16 Swindon Town	46	13	6	4	41	16	1	9	13	21	39	62	55	43
17 Brentford	46	10	9	4	41	28	3	8	12	15	42	56	70	43
18 Reading	46	13	5	5	48	29	1	7	15	24	54	72	83	40
19 Bournemouth	46	8	7	8	34	39	7	3	13	24	37	58	76	40
20 Southend United	46	10	8	5	38	26	4	3	16	22	50	60	76	39
21 Tranmere Rovers	46	11	5	7	53	50	4	3	16	26	65	79	115	38
22 Bradford City	46	8	8	7	37	36	3	6	14	28	51	65	87	36
23 Colchester United	46	8	5	10	40	44	3	6	14	28	57	68	101	33
24 Chesterfield	46	9	6	8	42	29	1	6	16	25	58	67	87	32

1961-62 2nd in Division 3

Captain: Keith Jobling

	Date	Opponent	Score	Scorers	Att.	White	Donovan	Keeble	Welbourne	Jobling	Cockerill	Scott	Portwood	Rafferty	Cullen	Jones	Barnett	Wealthall	Pearce	Knights	Waite	Fidler	Purvis	Williams	Hill
1	Aug 19	Newport County	2-0	Cullen(2)	11018	1	2	3	4	5	6	7	8	9	10	11									
2	22	TORQUAY UNITED	2-3	Cullen, Scott	10995	1	2	3	4	5	6	7	8	9	10	11									
3	26	SOUTHEND UNITED	3-1	Rafferty, Cullen, Jones	8834	1	2	3	4	5	6	7	8	9	10	11									
4	30	Torquay United	2-1	Rafferty, Portwood	7637	1		3	4	5	6	7	8	9	10	11		2							
5	Sep 2	Notts County	0-2		9289			3	4	5	6	7	8	9	10	11	1	2							
6	5	BRENTFORD	1-0	Portwood	8800			3	4	5	6	7	8	9	10	11	1	2							
7	9	SHREWSBURY TOWN	2-1	Portwood, Cockerill	7650			3	4	5	6	7	8	9	10	11	1	2							
8	16	Peterborough United	1-2	Cullen	14804			3	4	5	6	7	8	9	10	11	1	2							
9	20	Reading	2-1	Williams(2)	17265		2	3	4	5	6	7		9	10	11	1							8	
10	23	PORT VALE	1-1	Cullen	8715		2	3	4	5	6	7		9	10	11	1							8	
11	26	READING	4-0	Rafferty(3), Welbourne	9846		2	3	4	5	6	7		9	10	11	1							8	
12	29	Bristol City	0-3		10976		2	3	4	5	6	7		9	10	11	1							8	
13	Oct 3	Swindon Town	0-0		11308		2	3	4	5	6	7	8	9	10	11	1								
14	7	LINCOLN CITY	4-1	Portwood(3), Cullen	8820		2	3	4	5	6	7	8	9	10	11	1								
15	10	SWINDON TOWN	0-1		8930		2	3	4	5	6	7	8	9	10	11	1								
16	14	Northampton Town	0-7		11201		2	3	4	5	6	7	8	9	10		1					11			
17	21	QUEENS PARK RANGERS	1-1	Rafferty	6420		2	3	4	5	6	7	8	9	10		1					11			
18	28	Halifax Town	3-3	Rafferty, Fidler(2)	4776		2	3	4	5	6	7	8	9	10		1					11			
19	Nov 11	Crystal Palace	1-4	Rafferty	13661		2	3	4	5	6	7	8	9	10		1					11			
20	18	PORTSMOUTH	1-0	Rafferty	6889		2	3	4	5	6	7	8	9		11	1					10			
21	Dec 2	HULL CITY	1-0	Rafferty	6647		2	3	4	5	6		8	9		11	1				7	10			
22	9	Watford	1-2	Fidler	8910		2	3	4	5			8	9		11	1			6	7	10			
23	16	NEWPORT COUNTY	1-0	Jones	4575		2	3	4	5		7	8	9		11	1			6		10			
24	23	Southend United	0-2		4365		2	3	4	5				10	8	11	1			6		7	9		
25	26	Coventry City	0-2		11199		2	3	4	5		7		10	8		1			6			9		11
26	Jan 6	BOURNEMOUTH	3-0	Purvis, Rafferty, Jones	5367		2	3		5		7		10	8	11	1		4	6			9		
27	13	NOTTS COUNTY	2-1	Rafferty(2)	5773		2	3		5		7		10	8	11	1		4	6			9		
28	20	Shrewsbury Town	2-1	Purvis, Rafferty	7576		2	3		5		7		10	8	11	1		4	6			9		
29	27	Barnsley	3-0	Rafferty(2), Portwood	8086		2	3		5		7	9	10	8	11	1		4	6					
30	Feb 3	PETERBOROUGH UNITED	2-1	Rafferty(2)	11465		2	3		5		7	9	10	8	11	1		4	6					
31	10	Port Vale	2-0	Rafferty(2)	10071		2	3		5		7	9	10	8	11	1		4	6					
32	17	BRISTOL CITY	1-0	Rafferty	11662		2	3		5		7	9	10	8	11	1		4	6					
33	23	Lincoln City	1-1	Rafferty	13795		2	3		5			9	10	8	11	1		4	6			7		
34	Mar 3	NORTHAMPTON TOWN	3-2	Rafferty, Keeble, Portwood	9086		2	3		5		7	9	10	8	11	1		4	6					
35	10	Queens Park Rangers	2-3	Rafferty(2)	8374		2	3		5		7	9	10	8	11	1		4	6					
36	17	HALIFAX TOWN	3-0	Portwood(2), Jones	8000		2	3	4	5		7	9	10	8	11	1			6					
37	24	Bournemouth	3-2	Rafferty(2), Portwood	12620		2	3	4	5		7	9	10	8	11	1			6					
38	30	CRYSTAL PALACE	0-0		12611		2	3		5	4		9	10	8	11	1			6	7				
39	Apr 7	Portsmouth	2-0	Rafferty, Cockerill(pen)	19285		2	3		5	4		9	10	8	11	1			6	7				
40	10	COVENTRY CITY	2-0	Rafferty, Portwood	12760		2	3		5	4		9	10	8	11	1			6	7				
41	14	BARNSLEY	4-0	Jones(2), Rafferty, Waite	11022		2	3		5	4		9	10	8	11	1			6	7				
42	21	Hull City	1-2	Portwood	11404		2	3		5	4		9	10	8	11	1			6	7				
43	23	BRADFORD P.A.	3-2	Cullen, Jones, Scott(pen)	14170		2	3		5		7	9	10	8	11	1		4	6					
44	24	Bradford P.A.	1-0	Rafferty	11783		2	3		5		7	9	10	8	11	1		4	6					
45	28	WATFORD	5-3	Rafferty(2), Scott(2), Jones	14229		2	3		5	4	7	9	10	8	11	1			6					
46	May 1	Brentford	2-0	Portwood, Rafferty	19080		2	3		5	4	7	9	10	8	11	1			6					
					Apps.	4	41	46	27	46	28	37	37	46	42	41	42	5	12	25	7	9	6	4	1
					Goals			1	1		2	4	14	34	8	8					1	3	2	2	

F.A. Cup

	Date	Opponent	Score	Scorers	Att.	White	Donovan	Keeble	Welbourne	Jobling	Cockerill	Scott	Portwood	Rafferty	Cullen	Jones	Barnett	Wealthall	Pearce	Knights	Waite	Fidler	Purvis	Williams	Hill
R1	Nov 4	Mansfield Town	2-3	Portwood, Rafferty	10127		2	3	4	5	6	7	8	9	10		1					11			

League Cup

	Date	Opponent	Score	Scorers	Att.	White	Donovan	Keeble	Welbourne	Jobling	Cockerill	Scott	Portwood	Rafferty	Cullen	Jones	Barnett	Wealthall	Pearce	Knights	Waite	Fidler	Purvis	Williams	Hill
R1	Sep 13	Doncaster Rovers	2-3	Scott(pen), Rafferty	4000			3	4	5	6	7	8	9	10	11	1	2							

		P	W	D	L	F	A	W	D	L	F	A	F	A	Pts
1	Portsmouth	46	15	6	2	48	23	12	5	6	39	24	87	47	65
2	GRIMSBY TOWN	46	18	3	2	49	18	10	3	10	31	38	80	56	62
3	Bournemouth	46	14	8	1	42	18	7	9	7	27	27	69	45	59
4	Queen's Park Rgs.	46	15	3	5	65	31	9	8	6	46	42	111	73	59
5	Peterborough Utd.	46	16	0	7	60	38	10	6	7	47	44	107	82	58
6	Bristol City	46	15	3	5	56	27	8	5	10	38	45	94	72	54
7	Reading	46	14	5	4	46	24	8	4	11	31	42	77	66	53
8	Northampton Town	46	12	6	5	52	24	8	5	10	33	33	85	57	51
9	Swindon Town	46	11	8	4	48	26	6	7	10	30	45	78	71	49
10	Hull City	46	15	2	6	43	20	5	6	12	24	34	67	54	48
11	Bradford Park Ave.	46	13	5	5	47	27	7	2	14	33	51	80	78	47
12	Port Vale	46	12	4	7	41	23	5	7	11	24	35	65	58	45
13	Notts County	46	14	5	4	44	23	3	4	16	23	51	67	74	43
14	Coventry City	46	11	6	6	38	26	5	5	13	26	45	64	71	43
15	Crystal Palace	46	8	8	7	50	41	6	6	11	33	39	83	80	42
16	Southend United	46	10	7	6	31	26	3	9	11	26	43	57	69	42
17	Watford	46	10	9	4	37	26	4	4	15	26	48	63	74	41
18	Halifax Town	46	9	5	9	34	35	6	5	12	28	49	62	84	40
19	Shrewsbury Town	46	8	7	8	46	37	5	5	13	27	47	73	84	38
20	Barnsley	46	9	6	8	45	41	4	6	13	26	54	71	95	38
21	Torquay United	46	9	4	10	48	44	6	2	15	28	56	76	100	36
22	Lincoln City	46	4	10	9	31	43	5	7	11	26	44	57	87	35
23	Brentford	46	11	3	9	34	29	2	5	16	19	64	53	93	34
24	Newport County	46	6	5	12	29	38	1	3	19	17	64	46	102	22

SEASON 1961/62

Back: Ward (Manager), Lambton (Trainer), Donovan, Keeble, White, Cockerill, Rafferty, Barnett, Jobling, McCoy (Physio), Wealthall, Higgins (Asst.Train)
Middle: Scott, D.Williams, Welbourne, Cullen, Prestwood, Jones Front: Mills, Hill

SEASON 1962/63

Back: Wealthall, Purvis, Barnett, White, Rafferty, Donovan, Young
Middle (Standing): Johnston (Manager), Portwood, Keeble, Renwick, Jobling, Cockerill, Wheaton, Mills, Higgins (Trainer)
Middle (Seated): Williams (Youth Trainer), Scott, Fidler, Brader, Cullen, Knights, Jones, McCoy (Physio)
Front: Taylor, Hill, Catley, Thompson

1962-63 19th in Division 2

Captain: Keith Jobling

							Barnett	Donovan	Keeble	Cockerill	Jobling	Knights	Scott	Cullen	Portwood	Rafferty	Jones	White	Wright	Thompson J	Wealthall	Welbourne	Wheaton	Clifton	Waite	Catley	Pennington	Foster	Young	McLean	Purvis	Hill	Pearce
1	Aug	18	Plymouth Argyle	0-2		17090	1	2	3	4	5	6	7	8	9	10	11																
2		21	PORTSMOUTH	1-1	Scott(pen)	14778	1	2		4	5	6	7	8	9	10	11				3												
3		25	SCUNTHORPE UNITED	3-0	Cullen, Portwood, Scott(pen)	16533	1	2		4	5	6	7	8	9	10	11				3												
4		29	Portsmouth	1-2	Rafferty	19087	1	2		4	5	6	7	8	9	10	11				3												
5	Sep	1	NORWICH CITY	0-2		12873	1	2	3	4	5	6	7	8	9	10																11	
6		8	Walsall	1-4	Portwood	10691	1	2	3	4	5	6	8		10										7				9			11	
7		12	Cardiff City	3-5	Portwood(2), Knights	14426		2	3	4	5	6		10	8		7	1											9			11	
8		15	NEWCASTLE UNITED	0-1		12721		2	3	4	5	6		8	10		7	1												9		11	
9		18	CARDIFF CITY	1-2	Hill	10962		2	3	4	5	6		8	10		7	1												9		11	
10		22	Derby County	4-2	Young(3), Jones	12807		2	3	4	5	6		8		10	7	1											9			11	
11		29	MIDDLESBROUGH	3-4	Rafferty(2), Cullen	11853		2	3	4	5	6		10		8	7	1											9			11	
12	Oct	6	Bury	0-2		9962		2	3	4	5	6		10		8	7	1											9			11	
13		13	ROTHERHAM UNITED	1-2	McLean	10255		2	3	6	4		7		8		11	1					5							9	10		
14		20	Charlton Athletic	3-0	McLean(2), Jobling	14028		2	3		4	6	7	8	10			1					5							9		11	
15		27	STOKE CITY	1-1	Rafferty	14656		2	3		4	6	7			8		1					5	10						9		11	
16	Nov	3	Sunderland	2-6	McLean, Portwood	43087		2			4	6		8	7	10		1			3		5							9		11	
17		10	LEEDS UNITED	1-1	Cockerill	9329		2	3	6	4		7	8		10		1					5							9		11	
18		17	Swansea Town	0-1		5606		2	3	6		4	7	10	8			1					5							9		11	
19		24	CHELSEA	0-3		10823		2	3	6	4		7	8		10		1					5							9		11	
20	Dec	1	Luton Town	2-2	Portwood, McLean	7202		2	3	6	5				8	4	7	1										10		9		11	
21		8	SOUTHAMPTON	4-1	Hill(2), Portwood, McLean	7188		2	3	6	5				8	4	7	1										10		9		11	
22		15	PLYMOUTH ARGYLE	1-1	OG	8833		2	3	6	5				8	4	7	1										10		9		11	
23		21	Scunthorpe United	1-1	McLean	12698		2	3	6	5				8	4	7	1										10		9		11	
24		29	HUDDERSFIELD TOWN	1-1	Portwood	9814		2	3		5				8	4	7	1				6						10		9		11	
25	Feb	16	Middlesbrough	1-0	Clifton	17804		2	3		5				8	4			1					6		7		10		9		11	
26	Mar	9	CHARLTON ATHELTIC	2-1	McLean, Portwood(pen)	7623		2	3		5				8	4			1					6		7		10		9		11	
27		16	Stoke City	1-4	Portwood	24950		2	3		5		7		8	4			1					6				10		9		11	
28		23	SUNDERLAND	1-2	Foster	12332		3			5				7	8			1	2		4		6				10		9		11	
29		27	Newcastle United	0-0		27884		3			5	9			7	8			1	2		4		6				10				11	
30		30	Leeds United	0-3		13938		3			5				7	8			1	2		4		6				10		9		11	
31	Apr	6	SWANSEA TOWN	1-0	Rafferty	8670		3		4	5					10			1	2				6			7	8		9		11	
32		12	PRESTON NORTH END	2-0	Rafferty, McLean	14115		3		4	5					10			1	2				6			7	8		9		11	
33		13	Chelsea	1-2	McLean	21768			3	4	5				10		7		1	2				6				8		9		11	
34		15	Preston North End	0-0		11487		3		4	5					10			1	2				6			7	8		9		11	
35		20	LUTON TOWN	3-1	McLean, Pennington, Rafferty	9504		3		4	5					10			1	2				6			7	8		9		11	
36		24	Huddersfield Town	0-0		14281		3			5	4				10			1	2				6			7	8		9		11	
37		30	WALSALL	3-1	Foster, Rafferty, OG	12502		3		4	5					10			1	2				6			7	8		9		11	
38	May	4	DERBY COUNTY	0-0		12141		3		4	5					10			1	2				6			7	8		9		11	
39		7	Rotherham United	0-0		7765		3		4	5					10			1	2				6			7	8		9		11	
40		11	Norwich City	0-0		10295		3		4	5				10				1	2				6			7	8		9		11	
41		13	Southampton	1-4	Foster	9220		3		4	5	6						1		2				10			7	8		9		11	
42		18	BURY	5-1	McLean(4), Foster	8080		3		4	5				10			1		2				6			7	8		9		11	
						Apps.	6	41	24	31	41	19	13	16	27	31	17	20	16	15	4	4	7	19	1	2	11	23	5	31	1	37	
						Goals				1	1	1	2	2	10	8	1							1			1	4	3	15		3	

2 own goals

F.A. Cup

							Barnett	Donovan	Keeble	Cockerill	Jobling	Knights	Scott	Cullen	Portwood	Rafferty	Jones	White	Wright	Thompson J	Wealthall	Welbourne	Wheaton	Clifton	Waite	Catley	Pennington	Foster	Young	McLean	Purvis	Hill	Pearce
R3	Jan	8	LEICESTER CITY	1-3	Scott(pen)	15325	1	2	3	6	5		7		8	4												10		9		11	

League Cup

							Barnett	Donovan	Keeble	Cockerill	Jobling	Knights	Scott	Cullen	Portwood	Rafferty	Jones	White	Wright	Thompson J	Wealthall	Welbourne	Wheaton	Clifton	Waite	Catley	Pennington	Foster	Young	McLean	Purvis	Hill	Pearce
R2	Sep	25	Barnsley	2-3	Rafferty, Young	5408		2	3		5	6		10		8	7	1											9			11	4

		P	W	D	L	F	A	W	D	L	F	A	F	A	Pts
1	Stoke City	42	15	3	3	49	20	5	10	6	24	30	73	50	53
2	Chelsea	42	15	3	3	54	16	9	1	11	27	26	81	42	52
3	Sunderland	42	14	5	2	46	13	6	7	8	38	42	84	55	52
4	Middlesbrough	42	12	4	5	48	35	8	5	8	38	50	86	85	49
5	Leeds United	42	15	2	4	55	19	4	8	9	24	34	79	53	48
6	Huddersfield Town	42	11	6	4	34	21	6	8	7	29	29	63	50	48
7	Newcastle United	42	11	8	2	48	23	7	3	11	31	36	79	59	47
8	Bury	42	11	6	4	28	20	7	5	9	23	27	51	47	47
9	Scunthorpe United	42	12	7	2	35	18	4	5	12	22	41	57	59	44
10	Cardiff City	42	12	5	4	50	29	6	2	13	33	44	83	73	43
11	Southampton	42	15	3	3	52	23	2	5	14	20	44	72	67	42
12	Plymouth Argyle	42	13	4	4	48	24	2	8	11	28	49	76	73	42
13	Norwich City	42	11	6	4	53	33	6	2	13	27	46	80	79	42
14	Rotherham United	42	11	3	7	34	30	6	3	12	33	44	67	74	40
15	Swansea Town	42	13	5	3	33	17	2	4	15	18	55	51	72	39
16	Portsmouth	42	9	5	7	33	27	4	6	11	30	52	63	79	37
17	Preston North End	42	11	6	4	43	30	2	5	14	16	44	59	74	37
18	Derby County	42	10	5	6	40	29	2	7	12	21	43	61	72	36
19	GRIMSBY TOWN	42	8	6	7	34	26	3	7	11	21	40	55	66	35
20	Charlton Athletic	42	8	4	9	33	38	5	1	15	29	56	62	94	31
21	Walsall	42	7	7	7	33	37	4	2	15	20	52	53	89	31
22	Luton Town	42	10	4	7	45	40	1	3	17	16	44	61	84	29

1963-64 21st in Division 2

Captain: Keith Jobling

				Scorers	Att.	Wright	Donovan	Thompson	Cockerill	Jobling	Clifton	Pennington	Foster	McLean	Tees	Hill	Taylor Graham	Keeble	Welbourne	Walker	Howells	Knights	Portwood	Young	Ham	Collins	Bogie
1	Aug 24	Swansea Town	1-1	Tees	10740	1	2	3	4	5	6	7	8	9	10	11											
2	27	SWINDON TOWN	1-2	McLean	15085	1	3	2	4	5	6	7	8	9	10	11											
3	31	SOUTHAMPTON	2-2	Clifton(pen), Tees	11526	1	3	2		5	6	7	8	9	10	11			4								
4	Sep 3	Swindon Town	1-2	Hill	22059	1	3	2		5	6	7	8	9	10	11			4								
5	7	Middlesbrough	0-6		21458	1	2	3		5	6	7	8	9	10	11			4								
6	10	CHARLTON ATHLETIC	0-2		11619	1	3	2		5	6	7	10	9		11				4			8				
7	14	NEWCASTLE UNITED	2-1	Young, Foster	10106	1		2		5	6	7	10			11	3			4			8	9			
8	17	Charlton Athletic	1-2	Portwood	13326	1		2	6	5		7	8	9	10		3			4			11				
9	21	Huddersfield Town	2-1	Portwood, Tees	14258	1		2	6	5		7	8		10		3			4			11	9			
10	28	DERBY COUNTY	1-3	Portwood	9061	1		2	6	5		7	8	9			3			4			10				11
11	Oct 2	Cardiff City	0-0		10903	1		2	6	5		7	10				3			4			8	9		11	
12	5	Plymouth Argyle	2-3	Hill, Portwood	9729	1		2	6	5		7	8			11		3		4			10	9			
13	12	MANCHESTER CITY	1-1	Portwood	9754	1		2	6	5		7	10			11	3			4			8	9			
14	19	Bury	1-1	Young	6878	1	2	3		4	8	7			10	11				6	5			9			
15	26	NORWICH CITY	3-1	Young,Pennington,Walker(pen)	8981	1		2		4		7			10	11	3			6	5		8	9			
16	Nov 2	Sunderland	0-3		29044	1	2			4		7			10	11	3			6	5		8	9			
17	9	LEEDS UNITED	0-2		12369	1	2			4		7	10			11	3			6	5		8	9			
18	16	Rotherham United	0-1		7601	1	2			4		7	10	9		11	3			6	5		8				
19	23	PORTSMOUTH	0-3		7979	1	2			6		7	8		10	11	3			4	5			9			
20	30	Scunthorpe United	2-2	McLean, Pennington	8403	1	2		6	5		7	10	9		11	3			4			8				
21	Dec 7	NORTHAMPTON TOWN	4-1	McLean(2), Cockerill(2,1pen)	6305	1	2		4	5		7	10	9		11	3					6	8				
22	13	SWANSEA TOWN	1-1	Foster	6762	1	2		4	5		7	10	9		11	3					6	8				
23	21	Southampton	0-6		19242	1	2		4	5		7	10	9		11	3					6	8				
24	26	LEYTON ORIENT	1-1	McLean	8834	1	2		4	5		7	10	9		11	3					6	8				
25	28	Leyton Orient	0-0		9589	1	2		4	5		7	10	9		11	3					6	8				
26	Jan 11	MIDDLESBROUGH	3-1	Young(2), Foster	6681	1	2		4	5		7	10	9		11	3					6		8			
27	18	Newcastle United	0-4		23681	1	2		4	5		7	10	9		11	3					6		8			
28	Feb 1	HUDDERSFIELD TOWN	2-2	**Hill, Foster**	7266	1	2		4	5		7	8	9		11	3					6				10	
29	8	Derby County	0-0		10229	1	2		4	5		7	10	9		11	3					6		8			
30	15	PLYMOUTH ARGYLE	1-1	McLean	6774	1	2		4	5		7		9		11	3					6		8		10	
31	22	Manchester City	4-0	Portwood(2), Hill, Tees	11411	1	2		4	5		7		9	8	11	3					6	10				
32	29	ROTHERHAM UNITED	1-3	Portwood	7623	1	2		4	5		7		9	8	11	3					6	10				
33	Mar 7	Norwich City	0-2		11461	1	2		4	5		7		9	8	11	3					6	10				
34	21	Leeds United	1-3	Ham	23351	1	2		4	5		7	10	9		11	3	6							8		
35	27	PRESTON NORTH END	0-3		12138	1	2		4	5		7	10	9		11	3	6							8		
36	28	BURY	1-0	Portwood	4949	1		2	4	5			8		10	11		3				6	7	9			
37	30	Preston North End	0-1		24125	1		2	4	6	5	11	10		8			3					7	9			
38	Apr 4	Portsmouth	2-2	Young, Portwood	8207	1		2	4	5	6		10		8	11		3					7	9			
39	11	SCUNTHORPE UNITED	2-0	Young, Tees	10656	1		2	4	5	6		10		8	11		3					7	9			
40	15	CARDIFF CITY	0-2		8914	1		2	4	5	6		10		8	11		3					7	9			
41	18	Northampton Town	2-1	McLean, Young	10285	1		2	4		5			10	8	11		3				6	7	9			
42	25	SUNDERLAND	2-2	Portwood, Hill	16442	1		2	4	6	5			9	10	11		3					7	8			
					Apps.	42	27	22	31	41	14	36	33	27	21	37	27	10	3	15	6	15	28	21	2	3	1
					Goals				2		1	2	4	7	5	5				1			11	8	1		

F.A. Cup

				Att.	Wright	Donovan	Thompson	Cockerill	Jobling	Clifton	Pennington	Foster	McLean	Tees	Hill	Taylor Graham	Keeble	Welbourne	Walker	Howells	Knights	Portwood	Young	Ham	Collins	Bogie
R3	Jan 24	Blackburn Rovers	0-4	22887	1	2		4	5		7	10	9		11	3					6	8				

League Cup

					Att.	Wright	Donovan	Thompson	Cockerill	Jobling	Clifton	Pennington	Foster	McLean	Tees	Hill	Taylor Graham	Keeble	Welbourne	Walker	Howells	Knights	Portwood	Young	Ham	Collins	Bogie
R1	Sep 25	ROTHERHAM UNITED	1-3	Young	6829	1	4	2	6	5		7	8		10		3						11	9			

		P	W	D	L	F	A	W	D	L	F	A	F	A	Pts
1	Leeds United	42	12	9	0	35	16	12	6	3	36	18	71	34	63
2	Sunderland	42	16	3	2	47	13	9	8	4	34	24	81	37	61
3	Preston North End	42	13	7	1	37	14	10	3	8	42	40	79	54	56
4	Charlton Athletic	42	11	4	6	44	30	8	6	7	32	40	76	70	48
5	Southampton	42	13	3	5	69	32	6	6	9	31	41	100	73	47
6	Manchester City	42	12	4	5	50	27	6	6	9	34	39	84	66	46
7	Rotherham United	42	14	3	4	52	26	5	4	12	38	52	90	78	45
8	Newcastle United	42	14	2	5	49	26	6	3	12	25	43	74	69	45
9	Portsmouth	42	9	7	5	46	34	7	4	10	33	36	79	70	43
10	Middlesbrough	42	14	4	3	47	16	1	7	13	20	36	67	52	41
11	Northampton Town	42	10	2	9	35	31	6	7	8	23	29	58	60	41
12	Huddersfield Town	42	11	4	6	31	25	4	6	11	26	39	57	64	40
13	Derby County	42	10	6	5	34	27	4	5	12	22	40	56	67	39
14	Swindon Town	42	11	5	5	39	24	3	5	13	18	45	57	69	38
15	Cardiff City	42	10	7	4	31	27	4	3	14	25	54	56	81	38
16	Leyton Orient	42	8	6	7	32	32	5	4	12	22	40	54	72	36
17	Norwich City	42	9	7	5	43	30	2	6	13	21	50	64	80	35
18	Bury	42	8	5	8	35	36	5	4	12	22	37	57	73	35
19	Swansea Town	42	11	4	6	44	26	1	5	15	19	48	63	74	33
20	Plymouth Argyle	42	6	8	7	26	32	2	8	11	19	35	45	67	32
21	GRIMSBY TOWN	42	6	7	8	28	34	3	7	11	19	41	47	75	32
22	Scunthorpe United	42	8	8	5	30	25	2	2	17	22	57	52	82	30

SEASON 1963/64
Back: Welbourne, Clifton, Wright, Bogie, Taylor, Thompson
Middle: Portwood, Cockerill, Jobling, Donovan, Keeble
Front: Johnston (Man), Unknown, Foster, McLean, Tees, Hill, Higgins (Train)

SEASON 1964/65
Back: Caterer, Sorensen, Wainmen, Wilson, Wright, McLean, Swift
Middle (Standing): Higgins (Trainer), Williams (Youth Train), Allen, Cockerill, Keeble, Tees, Jobling, Clifton, Donovan, McCoy (Physio), Johnston (Manager)
Middle (Seated): Lakin, Taylor, Young, Hill, Foster, Thompson, Howells, Robinson Front: Pennington, Barratt, Collins

1964-65 10th in Division 3

Captain: Brian Clifton

No	Date	Opponent	Result	Scorers	Att	Wright	Thompson J	Keeble	Cockerill	Jobling	Clifton	Pennington	Tees	McLean	Foster	Hill	Taylor G	Haydock	Lancaster	Young	Barratt	Allen	Beckers	Collins	Wainman	Lakin	Donovan
1	Aug 22	Oldham Athletic	5-1	McLean(4), Tees	11420	1	2	3	4	5	6	7	8	9	10	11											
2	25	BRISTOL ROVERS	1-1	Foster	11302	1	2	3	4	6	5	7	8	9	10	11											
3	29	EXETER CITY	2-1	OG, Jobling	7658	1	2	3	4	6	5	7	8	9	10	11											
4	Sep 1	Bristol Rovers	3-5	Hill, Tees, Pennington	15542	1	2	3	4	5		7	8	9	10	11	6										
5	5	Bournemouth	2-1	Pennington(2)	8872	1	2	3	4	6	5	7	8	9	10	11											
6	9	BRENTFORD	2-1	Tees, McLean	9629	1	2	3	4	6	5	7	8	9	10	11											
7	12	PETERBOROUGH UNITED	2-0	Tees, Hill	10912	1	2	3	4	6	5	7	8	9	10	11											
8	15	Brentford	0-2		12759	1	2	3	4	6	5	7	8	9	10	11											
9	19	BARNSLEY	3-2	Foster, McLean(2)	7613	1	2	3	4	6	5	7	8	9	10	11											
10	26	Mansfield Town	2-2	McLean, Cockerill	10620	1	2	3	4	6	5	7	8	9	10	11											
11	30	COLCHESTER UNITED	2-0	McLean(2)	8686	1	2	3	4	6	5	7	8	9	10	11											
12	Oct 3	LUTON TOWN	2-2	Foster, Young	8410	1	2	3	4	6	5	7		9	8	11				10							
13	5	Colchester United	1-0	Foster	3837	1	2	3	4	6	5	7		9	10	11				8							
14	10	Walsall	0-1		5157	1	2	3	4	6	5	7		9	10	11				8							
15	17	WATFORD	1-0	Tees	7116	1	2	3	4	6	5	7	9		10	11				8							
16	21	CARLISLE UNITED	1-1	Young	5345	1	2		4	6	5	7		9	10	11	3			8							
17	24	Workington Town	2-2	Hill, Barratt	6434	1	2		4	6	5	7		9		11	3			8	10						
18	28	SOUTHEND UNITED	1-0	Jobling	5729	1	2		4	6	5	7		9	10	11	3			8							
19	31	HULL CITY	3-0	McLean(2), Pennington	9650	1	2		4	6	5	7		9	10	11	3				8						
20	Nov 7	Gillingham	0-0		11087	1	2		4	6	5	7		9	10	11	3				8						
21	21	Queens Park Rangers	1-1	Foster	6213	1	2		4	6	5	7	9		10	11	3				8						
22	28	SHREWSBURY TOWN	2-2	McLean, Tees	7006	1	2		4	6	5	7	8	9	10	11	3										
23	Dec 12	OLDHAM ATHLETIC	3-1	Foster, Haydock(2)	6158	1	2		4	5		7	9		10	11	3	8	6								
24	19	Exeter City	1-4	Tees	5438	1	2		4	5		7	9		10	11	3	8	6								
25	26	Scunthorpe United	1-2	Foster	10867	1	2		4	5		7	9		10	11	3	8	6								
26	Jan 2	BOURNEMOUTH	2-2	McLean(2)	7228	1	2			6	5	7		9	10	11	3	8	4								
27	9	Carlisle United	1-3	Foster	7144	1	2			6	5		8	9	10	11	3	7	4								
28	16	Peterborough United	1-3	McLean	13343		2			6	5	7		9	10	11	3	8	4						1		
29	Feb 6	MANSFIELD TOWN	1-1	Hill	6546		2		4	6	5	7		9	10	11	3	8							1		
30	13	Luton Town	1-1	Cockerill	5160		2		4	6	5	7			10	11	3	8	9						1		
31	20	WALSALL	2-2	Cockerill, McLean	5064		2		4	6	5	7		9	10	11	3	8							1		
32	27	Watford	1-1	Foster	6931	1	2		4	6	5	7		9	10	11	3	8									
33	Mar 6	READING	1-1	Allen	4955	1	2		4	6	5	7		9		11	3	10				8					
34	9	BRISTOL CITY	0-2		5973	1	2		4	5	6	7		9	10	11	3					8					
35	13	Hull City	3-3	Clifton, McLean, Cockerill	26564	1	2		4	5	6	7		9	10	11	3					8					
36	20	GILLINGHAM	1-1	McLean	4191	1	2		4	5	6	7		9	10	11	3					8					
37	24	Reading	0-2		6326	1	2		4	5	6			9	10	11	3	7				8					
38	26	Bristol City	0-4		11464	1	2		4	5	6			9	10	11	3	7				8					
39	30	Barnsley	0-1		2633	1	2		4	5	6		8	9	10	11	3	7									
40	Apr 3	QUEENS PARK RANGERS	0-0		4207	1	2		4	5	6	7	9			11	3	8						10			
41	6	SCUNTHORPE UNITED	3-0	Tees, Foster, Cockerill	6756	1	2		4	5	6	7	9		10	11	3	8									
42	10	Shrewsbury Town	3-1	Pennington, Clifton, Haydock	3868	1	2		4	5	6	7	9			10	3	8						11			
43	16	PORT VALE	2-0	Cockerill(2,1pen)	8325	1	2		4	5	6	7	9			10	3	8						11			
44	17	WORKINGTON TOWN	0-1		5542	1	2		4	5	6	7	9			10	3	8						11			
45	20	Port Vale	3-2	Tees, Collins, Haycock	3569	1	2		4	5	6	7	9			10	3	8						11			
46	24	Southend United	0-4		6550	1	2		4	5	6	7	9			10	3	8					11				
					Apps.	42	46	15	43	46	42	42	26	33	38	46	32	21	7	7	4	6	1	5	4		
					Goals				7	2	2	5	9	19	10	4		4		2	1	1		1			

1 own goal

F.A. Cup

Rd	Date	Opponent	Result	Scorers	Att	Wright	Thompson J	Keeble	Cockerill	Jobling	Clifton	Pennington	Tees	McLean	Foster	Hill	Taylor G	Haydock	Lancaster	Young	Barratt	Allen	Beckers	Collins	Wainman	Lakin	Donovan
R1	Nov 14	Barrow	1-1	Barratt	3675	1	2		4	6	5	7		9	10	11					8						3
R1r	17	BARROW	2-2*	Cockerill(pen), Foster	4193	1	2		4	6	5	7			10	11				9	8						3
R12r	23	Barrow ~	2-0	Pennington, Tees	9292	1	2		8	6	5	7	9		10	11	3										4
R2	Dec 5	Stockport County +	0-0			1	2		4	6	5	7	8	9	10	11	3										
R2	7	Stockport County	0-1		10163	1	2		4	5		7	8		10	11	3			9							6

* After extra time. ~ Played at Old Trafford, Manchester. + Abandoned after 50 minutes.

League Cup

Rd	Date	Opponent	Result	Scorers	Att	Wright	Thompson J	Keeble	Cockerill	Jobling	Clifton	Pennington	Tees	McLean	Foster	Hill	Taylor G	Haydock	Lancaster	Young	Barratt	Allen	Beckers	Collins	Wainman	Lakin	Donovan
R1	Sep 23	OLDHAM ATHLETIC	3-1	Young(2), McLean	5775	1	2	3	4	6	5	7		9	10	11				8							
R2	Oct 19	LEICESTER CITY	0-5		7270	1	2		4	6	5	7		9	10	11					8					3	

		P	W	D	L	F	A	W	D	L	F	A	F	A	Pts
1	Carlisle United	46	14	5	4	46	24	11	5	7	30	29	76	53	60
2	Bristol City	46	14	6	3	53	18	10	5	8	39	37	92	55	59
3	Mansfield Town	46	17	4	2	61	23	7	7	9	34	38	95	61	59
4	Hull City	46	14	6	3	51	25	9	6	8	40	32	91	57	58
5	Brentford	46	18	4	1	55	18	6	5	12	28	37	83	55	57
6	Bristol Rovers	46	14	7	2	52	21	6	8	9	30	37	82	58	55
7	Gillingham	46	16	5	2	45	13	7	4	12	25	37	70	50	55
8	Peterborough Utd.	46	16	3	4	61	33	6	4	13	24	41	85	74	51
9	Watford	46	13	8	2	45	21	4	8	11	26	43	71	64	50
10	GRIMSBY TOWN	46	11	10	2	37	21	5	7	11	31	46	68	67	49
11	Bournemouth	46	12	4	7	40	24	6	7	10	32	39	72	63	47
12	Southend United	46	14	4	5	48	24	5	4	14	30	47	78	71	46
13	Reading	46	12	8	3	45	26	4	6	13	25	44	70	70	46
14	Queen's Park Rgs.	46	15	5	3	48	23	2	7	14	24	57	72	80	46
15	Workington	46	11	7	5	30	22	6	5	12	28	47	58	69	46
16	Shrewsbury Town	46	10	6	7	42	38	5	6	12	34	46	76	84	42
17	Exeter City	46	8	7	8	33	27	4	10	9	18	25	51	52	41
18	Scunthorpe United	46	9	8	6	42	27	5	4	14	23	45	65	72	40
19	Walsall	46	9	4	10	34	36	6	3	14	21	44	55	80	37
20	Oldham Athletic	46	10	3	10	40	39	3	7	13	21	44	61	83	36
21	Luton Town	46	6	8	9	32	36	5	3	15	19	58	51	94	33
22	Port Vale	46	7	6	10	27	33	2	8	13	14	43	41	76	32
23	Colchester United	46	7	6	10	30	34	3	4	16	20	55	50	89	30
24	Barnsley	46	8	5	10	33	31	1	6	16	21	59	54	90	29

1965-66 11th in Division 3

Captain: Graham Taylor

	Date	Opponent	Score	Scorers	Att.	Wright	Thompson J	Taylor Graham	Cockerill	Jobling	Clifton	Ross	Tees	Green	Foster	Hill	Collins	Wainman	Bloomer	Lancaster	Davidson	Wilkinson	Fielding	Garland	Taylor George	Kerry	Morgan
1	Aug 21	BRISTOL ROVERS	1-1	Tees	5606	1	2	3	4	5	6	7	8	9	10	11											
2	24	BRENTFORD	3-2	Tees, Cockerill(pen), Green	5238	1	2	3	4	5	6	7	8	9	10	11											
3	27	York City	1-1	Green	8764	1	2	3	4	5	6	7	8*	9	10	11				12							
4	Sep 4	OXFORD UNITED	1-1	Foster	5720	1	2	3	4	5	6	7	8	9	10	11											
5	11	Swansea Town	0-1		7620	1	2	3		5	6	7	8	9	10	11				4							
6	15	BRIGHTON & HOVE ALBION	3-1	Tees, Foster, Ross	5374	1	2	3	6	5		7	8	9	10	11				4							
7	18	WALSALL	3-0	Tees(2), Hill	5292	1	2	3	6	5		7	8	9	10	11	12			4*							
8	25	Workington Town	0-1		2328	1	2	3	6	5	4	7	8	9	10	11											
9	Oct 2	BOURNEMOUTH	2-0	Tees, Clifton	5780	1	2	3	6	5	4	7	8	9	10	11											
10	5	Brighton & Hove Albion	2-1	Tees(2)	14070	1	2	3*	6	5		4	8	9	10	7	11								12		
11	9	WATFORD	2-1	Cockerill, Tees	7195	1	2		6	5		4	8	9	10	7	11					3					
12	16	Oldham Athletic	4-1	Tees(2), Green(2)	6445	1	2	3	6	5		4	8	9	10	7	11										
13	23	GILLINGHAM	3-1	Tees(2), Foster	8176	1	2	3	6	5		4	8	9	10	7	11										
14	30	Millwall	1-2	Hill	17299	1	2	3	6	5		4	8	9	10	7	11										
15	Nov 6	PETERBOROUGH UNITED	3-0	Tees, Green, Ross	9982	1	2	3		5	6	4	8	9	10	11	7										
16	20	READING	3-3	Tees, Green, Foster	7715	1	2	3		5	6		8	9	10	11	7				4						
17	24	Brentford	2-3	Hill, Green	5180	1	2	3		5	6	4*	8	9	10	11	7				12						
18	27	Hull City	1-1	Tees	20681	1	2	3		5	6		8	9	10	11	7				4						
19	Dec 11	Queens Park Rangers	0-3		6671	1	2	3		5	6	4	8	9	10	11	7										
20	18	OLDHAM ATHLETIC	3-1	Hill(2), Tees	6242	1	2	3		5	6		8	9*	10	11	7				4					12	
21	27	SWINDON TOWN	2-2	Hill, Fielding	13518	1	2	3		5	6	9	8*		10	11	12				4		7				
22	Jan 1	Watford	1-1	Foster	7022	1	2	3		5	6	9			10	11	7				4		8				
23	8	EXETER CITY	1-1	Ross	7737	1	2	3	4	5	6	9	8		10	11							7				
24	29	Bristol Rovers	1-2	Ross	8303	1	2	3	4	5		6	8	9	10	11	7										
25	Feb 5	YORK CITY	3-1	Tees(2), Foster	7549	1	2	3	6	5		4	8	9	10	11	7										
26	19	Oxford United	0-2		7661	1	2	3	6		5	7		9	10	11				4			8				
27	26	SWANSEA TOWN	2-2	Tees(2)	6867	1	2	3	6		5	4	8	9	10	11							7				
28	Mar 5	Gillingham	2-3	Green, Fielding	7915	1	2	3	6		5	4*	8	9	10	11	12						7				
29	12	Walsall	0-1		9228	1*	2	3	6		5		8	9	10	11	12			4			7				
30	19	WORKINGTON TOWN	1-0	Tees	5691		2	3	6	5	4		8	9		10	11	1					7				
31	26	Bournemouth	0-1		6703		2	3	6	5	4		8	10		11		1					7	9			
32	Apr 2	Peterborough United	1-1	Tees	5601		2	3	6	5	4		8	9		10	11	1					7				
33	8	SCUNTHORPE UNITED	1-3	Fielding	10960		2	3*	6	5	4		8	9		10	11	1		12			7				
34	9	MANSFIELD TOWN	0-1		4228				6	5	4		8	10			11	1	2			3	7	9			
35	12	Scunthorpe United	2-2	Tees(2)	7783		4		6	5	10		8	9			11	1	2			3	7				
36	23	HULL CITY	1-0	Fielding	18018		2		6	5	4		8*	9	10	11	12	1				3	7				
37	25	Southend United	1-3	Hill	7526		2		6	5	4			9	10	8	11	1				3	7				
38	30	Mansfield Town	1-2	Thompson	4961		2	3	6	5	4*		8	9	10	11	12	1					7				
39	May 2	Shrewsbury Town	1-3	Fielding	3012			3	6	5		4*	8	9		10	11	1	2			12	7				
40	4	SHREWSBURY TOWN	2-1	Cockerill(pen), Fielding	3417		4	3	6	5			8	9		10	11	1	2				7				
41	7	QUEENS PARK RANGERS	4-2	Collins(2), Fielding, Tees	5586		4	3	6	5			8	9		10	11	1	2				7				
42	10	Swindon Town	0-0		8226		4		6	5			8		9	10	11	1	2			3	7				
43	17	SOUTHEND UNITED	1-0	OG	4554		2	3	6	5		4	8	9		10	11	1					7				
44	21	Exeter City	0-2		3770		4	3	6	5			8	9		10	11	1	2				7				
45	23	Reading	0-0		5432		4	3	6	5			8	9	10	11		1	2				7				
46	28	MILLWALL	2-0	Tees(2)	6008		4	3	6	5			8	9	10	11		1	2				7				
					Apps.	29	44	40	37	42	29	27	43	42	35	44	26	17	9	5	5	6	24	2			
					Subs.												6			2	1	1			1	1	
					Goals		1		3		1	4	28	8	6	7	2						7				

Game 29: Wright injured, replaced in goal by Green.

1 own goal

F.A. Cup

	Date	Opponent	Score	Scorers	Att.	Wright	Thompson J	Taylor Graham	Cockerill	Jobling	Clifton	Ross	Tees	Green	Foster	Hill	Collins	Wainman	Bloomer	Lancaster	Davidson	Wilkinson	Fielding	Garland	Taylor George	Kerry	Morgan
R1	Nov 13	Barrow	2-1	Tees, Foster	8656	1	2	3		5	6		8	9	10	11	7										4
R2	Dec 4	Barnsley	1-1	Green(pen)	8112	1	2	3		5	6		8	9	10	11	7				4						
R2r	8	BARNSLEY	2-0	Tees(2)	10664	1	2	3		5	6	4	8	9	10	11	7										
R3	Jan 22	PORTSMOUTH	0-0		10204	1	2	3	6	5		4	8	9	10	11	7										
R3r	26	Portsmouth	3-1	Tees(2), Green	23735	1	2	3	6	5		4	8	9	10	11	7										
R4	Feb 12	Manchester City	0-2		37918	1	2	3	6	5		4	8	9	10	11	7										

League Cup

	Date	Opponent	Score	Scorers	Att.	Wright	Thompson J	Taylor Graham	Cockerill	Jobling	Clifton	Ross	Tees	Green	Foster	Hill	Collins	Wainman	Bloomer	Lancaster	Davidson	Wilkinson	Fielding	Garland	Taylor George	Kerry	Morgan
R2	Sep 22	Crystal Palace	1-0	Green	13285	1	2	3	6	5	4	7	8	9	10	11											
R3	Oct 13	BOLTON WANDERERS	4-2	Ross, Green(2), Foster	8844	1	2	3	6	5		4	8	9	10	11	7										
R4	Nov 13	PRESTON NORTH END	4-0	Tees(3), Foster	10340	1	2	3		5	6	4	8	9	10	11	7										
R5	17	WEST HAM UNITED	2-2	Tees, Green	16281	1	2	3		5	6		8	9	10	11	7				4						
R5r	Dec 15	West Ham United	0-1		17500	1	2	3		5	6		8	9	10	11	7				4						

		P	W	D	L	F	A	W	D	L	F	A	F	A	Pts
1	Hull City	46	19	2	2	64	24	12	5	6	45	38	109	62	69
2	Millwall	46	19	4	0	47	13	8	7	8	29	30	76	43	65
3	Queen's Park Rgs.	46	16	3	4	62	29	8	6	9	33	36	95	65	57
4	Scunthorpe United	46	9	8	6	44	34	12	3	8	36	33	80	67	53
5	Workington	46	13	6	4	38	18	6	8	9	29	39	67	57	52
6	Gillingham	46	14	4	5	33	19	8	4	11	29	35	62	54	52
7	Swindon Town	46	11	8	4	43	18	8	5	10	31	30	74	48	51
8	Reading	46	13	5	5	36	19	6	8	9	34	44	70	63	51
9	Walsall	46	13	7	3	48	21	7	3	13	29	43	77	64	50
10	Shrewsbury Town	46	13	7	3	48	22	6	4	13	25	42	73	64	49
11	GRIMSBY TOWN	46	15	6	2	47	25	2	7	14	21	37	68	62	47
12	Watford	46	12	4	7	33	19	5	9	9	22	32	55	51	47
13	Peterborough Utd.	46	13	6	4	50	26	4	6	13	30	40	80	66	46
14	Oxford United	46	11	3	9	38	33	8	5	10	32	41	70	74	46
15	Brighton & Hove A.	46	13	4	6	48	28	3	7	13	19	37	67	65	43
16	Bristol Rovers	46	11	10	2	38	15	3	4	16	26	49	64	64	42
17	Swansea Town	46	14	4	5	61	37	1	7	15	20	59	81	96	41
18	Bournemouth	46	9	8	6	24	19	4	4	15	14	37	38	56	38
19	Mansfield Town	46	10	5	8	31	36	5	3	15	28	53	59	89	38
20	Oldham Athletic	46	8	7	8	34	33	4	6	13	21	48	55	81	37
21	Southend United	46	15	1	7	43	28	1	3	19	11	55	54	83	36
22	Exeter City	46	9	6	8	36	28	3	5	15	17	51	53	79	35
23	Brentford	46	9	4	10	34	30	1	8	14	14	39	48	69	32
24	York City	46	5	7	11	30	44	4	2	17	23	62	53	106	27

SEASON 1965/66
Back: Collins, Lancaster, Cockerill, Wright, Jobling, Thompson, Graham Taylor, Higgins (Train)
Front: Ross, Tees, Green, Clifton, Foster, Hill

SEASON 1966/67
Back: Higgins (Trainer), McCoy (Physio), Lancaster, J.Bloomer, Jobling, Wainman, Cockerill, Green, Hill, Tees, McGuigan (Manager)
Front: Thompson, Worthington, Rudd, Graham Taylor, Fielding, Ross, Collins

1966-67 17th in Division 3

Captain: Graham Taylor

			Opponent	Score	Scorers	Att.	Wainman	Bloomer	Taylor Graham	Thompson	Jobling	Cockerill	Fielding	Ross	Green	Rudd	Hill	Oakley	Worthington	Smith R.W.	Lancaster	Rathbone	Collins	Housley	Tees	Moore G	Wilson	Martin	Boylen
1	Aug	20	Workington Town	1-2	Thompson	2645	1	2	3	4	5	6	7	8	9	10	11												
2		27	WALSALL	3-1	Worthington, Fielding, Hill	5864	1	2	3	4	5	6	7	8		10	11		9										
3	Sep	3	Peterborough United	1-2	Ross	6958	1	2	3	4	5	6	7	8		10	11		9										
4		7	SCUNTHORPE UNITED	7-1	Tees, Green(3), Hill(3)	8255	1		3	2	5	6		4	9	10	11		7						8				
5		10	TORQUAY UNITED	1-0	Tees	6861	1		3	2	5	6		4	9	10	11		7						8				
6		17	Briston & Hove Albion	2-0	Tees(2)	9762	1		3	2		6		4	9	10	11		7		5				8				
7		24	DARLINGTON	4-1	Hill(2), Worthington, Taylor	6558	1		3	2		6		4	9	10	11		7		5				8				
8		27	Scunthorpe United	0-0		11373	1		3	2		6		4	9	10	11		7		5				8				
9	Oct	1	Queens Park Rangers	1-5	Green	9097	1		3	2*		6	12	4	9	10	11		7		5				8				
10		8	OLDHAM ATHLETIC	1-0	Green	8321	1	2	3		5	6		4	9	10	11		7						8				
11		15	Oxford United	1-3	Collins	6707	1	2	3		5	6		4		10	11		9				7		8				
12		19	READING	2-0	Tees. Green	6140	1		3	2	5	6		4	9	10	7						11		8				
13		22	BRISTOL ROVERS	0-0		7271	1		3	2	5	6		4	9	10			7				11		8				
14		29	Colchester United	0-4		6330	1		3	2	5	6		4	9	10	7						11		8				
15	Nov	5	SHREWSBURY TOWN	1-1	Worthington	5309	1		3	2	5	6		4	9	10			7						8			11	
16		12	Middlesbrough	1-0	Tees	14162	1		3	2	5	6		4	9	10			7						8			11	
17		16	Reading	0-6		4355	1		3	2		6		4	9	10			7			5			8			11	
18		19	SWANSEA TOWN	2-1	Cockerill(pen), Martin	4475	1		3	2	4	6			9	10			7			5			8			11	
19	Dec	3	LEYTON ORIENT	1-2	Rudd	3744	1		3	2	4	6		7	9	10						5			8			11	
20		10	Gillingham	0-2		5327			3	2	4	6		7	9	10		1				5			8			11	
21		17	WORKINGTON TOWN	4-1	Rudd, Green(2), Martin	2936			3	2	6			4	9	10		1				5	7		8			11	
22		23	Doncaster Rovers	2-3	Green(pen), Tees	9185			3	2	6			4	9	10		1				5	7		8			11	
23		26	DONCASTER ROVERS	4-1	Tees, Green,(2), Jobling	9182			3	2	6			4	9	10		1	7			5			8			11	
24		31	Walsall	0-1		8812			3	2	6			4	9	10		1	7			5			8			11	
25	Jan	14	Torquay United	1-3	Tees	8872			3	2		6			9	10		1	7	4		5			8			11	
26		21	BRIGHTON & HOVE ALBION	2-3	Worthington, Green	5094	1		3	2	6				9	10			7	4		5			8			11	
27	Feb	4	Darlington	0-1		5258	1		3	2		6	7	9		10			8	4		5						11	
28		11	QUEENS PARK RANGERS	1-1	Rudd	7157	1		3	2	4	6	7	9		10				8		5						11	
29		24	Oldham Athletic	1-0	Rudd	9411	1		3	2		6		9		10			8	4		5		7				11	
30		28	Swindon Town	1-3	Cockerill(pen)	11620	1		3	2		6				10			8	4		5		7		9		11	
31	Mar	4	OXFORD UNITED	1-0	Moore	6033	1		3	2		6				10				4		5		7		8	9	11	
32		18	Bristol Rovers	0-0		9474	1	2	3			6		7		10				4		5				9	8	11	
33		24	MANSFIELD TOWN	1-2	Rudd	10017	1	2	3			6		7		10				4		5				9	8	11	
34		25	COLCHESTER UNITED	0-0		4682	1	2	3			6		7		10				4		5				9	8	11	
35		28	Mansfield Town	0-4		11734	1	2	3			6		7		10				4		5				9	8	11	
36	Apr	1	Shrewsbury Town	1-0	Rathbone	4035	1	2	3			6				10				4		5	7			9	8	11	
37		5	SWINDON TOWN	3-4	Wilson, Moore, Rudd	4948	1	2	3			6				10				4		5	7			9	8	11	
38		8	MIDDLESBROUGH	2-1	Collins, Moore	5106		2	3			6				10		1		4		5	7			9	8	11	
39		12	WATFORD	0-2		4662		2	3			6		12		10		1		4		5	7			9*	8	11	
40		15	Swansea Town	0-2		4821			3			6		8		10		1	2	4		5	11	7			9		
41		22	BOURNEMOUTH	1-0	Wilson	3668			3			6		10		8		1	2	4		5	7				9	11	
42		25	Watford	1-3	Wilson	8902			3			6		10		7		1	2	4		5	11			8	9		
43		29	Leyton Orient	1-1	Wilson	6459			3			6		10				1	2	4		5	8	7			9	11	
44	May	2	PETERBOROUGH UNITED	1-1	Ross	3661			3			6		10				1	2	4		5	8	7			9	11	
45		6	GILLINGHAM	4-0	Collins, Wilson(3)	3658			3			6		8				1	2	4		5	7				9	11	10
46		13	Bournemouth	0-0		3411			3			6		8				1	2	4		5	7				9	11	10
						Apps.	31	13	46	29	21	41	5	37	23	42	13	15	29	22	4	30	17	6	23	11	16	30	2
						Subs.							1	1															
						Goals			1	1	1	2	1	2	12	6	6		4			1	3		9	3	7	2	

F.A. Cup

			Opponent	Score	Scorers	Att.	Wainman	Bloomer	Taylor Graham	Thompson	Jobling	Cockerill	Fielding	Ross	Green	Rudd	Hill	Oakley	Worthington	Smith R.W.	Lancaster	Rathbone	Collins	Housley	Tees	Moore G	Wilson	Martin	Boylen
R1	Nov	26	Crewe Alexandra	1-1	Tees	6000	1		3	2	4	6			9	10			7			5			8			11	
R1r		30	CREWE ALEXANDRA	0-1		5414	1		3	2	4	6			9	10			7			5			8			11	

League Cup

			Opponent	Score	Scorers	Att.	Wainman	Bloomer	Taylor Graham	Thompson	Jobling	Cockerill	Fielding	Ross	Green	Rudd	Hill	Oakley	Worthington	Smith R.W.	Lancaster	Rathbone	Collins	Housley	Tees	Moore G	Wilson	Martin	Boylen
R1	Aug	24	Barnsley	2-1	Worthington, Hill	2495	1	2	3	4	5	6	7	8		10	11		9										
R2	Sep	14	Bradford P.A.	0-0		3384	1		3	2	5	6		4	9	10	11		7						8				
R2r		21	BRADFORD P.A.	3-1	Worthington,Tees,Green	6877	1		3	2		6		4	9	10	11		7		5				8				
R3	Oct	5	WORKINGTON TOWN	3-0	Cockerill(pen),Worthington,Hill	6104	1	2	3		5	6		4	9	10	11		7						8				
R4		26	BIRMINGHAM CITY	2-4	Cockerill, Tees	11298	1		3	2	5	6		4	9*	10	11		7				12		8				

		P	W	D	L	F	A	W	D	L	F	A	F	A	Pts
1	Queen's Park Rgs.	46	18	4	1	66	15	8	11	4	37	23	103	38	67
2	Middlesbrough	46	16	3	4	51	20	7	6	10	36	44	87	64	55
3	Watford	46	15	5	3	39	17	5	9	9	22	29	61	46	54
4	Reading	46	13	7	3	45	20	9	2	12	31	37	76	57	53
5	Bristol Rovers	46	13	8	2	47	28	7	5	11	29	39	76	67	53
6	Shrewsbury Town	46	15	5	3	48	24	5	7	11	29	38	77	62	52
7	Torquay United	46	17	3	3	57	20	4	6	13	16	34	73	54	51
8	Swindon Town	46	14	5	4	53	21	6	5	12	28	38	81	59	50
9	Mansfield Town	46	12	4	7	48	37	8	5	10	36	42	84	79	49
10	Oldham Athletic	46	15	4	4	51	16	4	6	13	29	47	80	63	48
11	Gillingham	46	11	9	3	36	18	4	7	12	22	44	58	62	46
12	Walsall	46	12	8	3	37	16	6	2	15	28	56	65	72	46
13	Colchester United	46	14	3	6	52	30	3	7	13	24	43	76	73	44
14	Orient	46	10	9	4	36	27	3	9	11	22	41	58	68	44
15	Peterborough Utd.	46	12	4	7	40	31	2	11	10	26	40	66	71	43
16	Oxford United	46	10	8	5	41	29	5	5	13	20	37	61	66	43
17	GRIMSBY TOWN	46	13	5	5	46	23	4	4	15	15	45	61	68	43
18	Scunthorpe United	46	13	4	6	39	26	4	4	15	19	47	58	73	42
19	Brighton & Hove A.	46	10	8	5	37	27	3	7	13	24	44	61	71	41
20	Bournemouth	46	8	10	5	24	24	4	7	12	15	33	39	57	41
21	Swansea Town	46	9	9	5	50	30	3	6	14	35	59	85	89	39
22	Darlington	46	8	7	8	26	28	5	4	14	21	53	47	81	37
23	Doncaster Rovers	46	11	6	6	40	40	1	2	20	18	77	58	117	32
24	Workington	46	9	3	11	35	35	3	4	16	20	54	55	89	31

1967-68 22nd in Division 3

Captain: Graham Taylor

	Date		Opponent	Score	Scorers	Att.	Wainman	Worthington	Taylor Graham	Ross	Rathbone	Cockerill	Collins	Boylen	Wilson	Rudd	Martin	Harker	Bloomer	SmithR.W.	Davidson	Jobling	Moore	Housley	Wilkinson	Bartlett	Taylor George
1	Aug	19	LEYTON ORIENT	0-0		6233	1	2	3	4	5	6	7	8	9	10	11										
2		26	Northampton Town	0-3		10206	1	2	3	4	5	6	7	8*	9	10	11			12							
3	Sep	2	WALSALL	3-0	Rudd(2), Wilson	4989	1	2	3	4	5	6	7		9	8	11			10							
4		6	STOCKPORT COUNTY	3-1	Wilson, Martin, Rudd	5711	1	2	3		5	6	7		8	10	11			4			9				
5		9	Gillingham	0-1		4568	1	2	3		5	6	7		10	8	11			4			9				
6		16	SCUNTHORPE UNITED	2-1	Collins, Moore	7825	1	2	3	4	5	6	7		10	8	11						9				
7		23	TORQUAY UNITED	1-1	Cockerill(pen)	5465	1	2	3	10	5	6	7			8	11				4		9				
8		25	Stockport County	1-1	Cockerill(pen)	8747	1	7	3	10	5	6				8	11		2	9	4						
9		30	Reading	0-3		7784	1	2	3	10	5	6	12		7	8	11*			9	4						
10	Oct	4	BRIGHTON & HOVE ALBION	4-2	Moore,Boylen,Cockerilll(pen),OG	4933	1	2	3	8		6		10	7		11				4	5	9				
11		7	Bristol Rovers	0-3		6626	1	2	3	8		6		10	7		11				4	5	9				
12		14	BARROW	0-1		4453		2		8		6		10	7	12	11	1		3	4*	5	9				
13		21	Oxford United	1-2	Rathbone	6202		2		4	5		7		8	10	11	1		3			9		6		
14		23	Brighton & Hove Albion	1-3	Wilson	13185		2	9	4	5	12	7		8	10	11	1		6					3*		
15		28	BURY	3-1	Martin, Moore, Ross(pen)	4307		2	3	4	5		7		8	10	11	1		6			9				
16	Nov	4	Bournemouth	0-1		4237		2	3	4	5		7		8	10	11	1		6			9				
17		11	COLCHESTER UNITED	1-2	Moore	3964		2	3	4	5		7		8	10	11	1		6			9				
18		14	Walsall	0-2		13354		2	3	4	5		11		8	10		1		6			9	7			
19		18	Peterborough United	2-3	Moore, OG	7243		2	3	4	5			10	7	11		1		6			9	8			
20		25	MANSFIELD TOWN	0-0		3263			3	4	5		9	10	8	11		1	2	6				7			
21	Dec	2	Watford	1-7	Ross	9074		2	3	8	5			11*	9			1		10	4	6	12	7			
22		16	Leyton Orient	0-1		3690	1	9	3	6				11	8				2	12	4	5*	10	7			
23		23	NORTHAMPTON TOWN	0-0		3595	1	8	3	6	5		7		10		11		2		4		9				
24		26	Shrewsbury Town	2-3	Worthington, OG	7208	1	9	3	6	5		7	10	8		11		2		4						
25		30	SHREWSBURY TOWN	0-1		3116	1	9	3	10	5		7	8			11		2	6	4						
26	Jan	20	Scunthorpe United	3-0	Moore(2), Wilson	6881	1	2	3	6	5		7	10	8		11			4			9				
27	Feb	3	Torquay United	0-1		7499	1	2	3	6	5		7	10	8		11			4			9				
28		10	READING	1-1	Moore	3800	1	2	3	6	5		7	10	8		11			4			9				
29		24	BRISTOL ROVERS	3-2	Moore, Taylor, Boylen	3512	1	2	3	6	5		7	10	8		11			4			9				
30		27	Swindon Town	0-5		12962	1	2	3	6	5		7	10	8		11			4			9				
31	Mar	2	Barrow	0-2		6009	1	2	3	6	5		7	10	8		11			4			9				
32		13	GILLINGHAM	1-1	Wilson	3504	1	2	3	6	5		7	10	8		11			4			9				
33		16	OXFORD UNITED	0-1		3070	1	2	3	4	5		7	10	8		11			6			9				
34		20	TRANMERE ROVERS	3-0	Wilson(2), Boylen	2805	1	2	3	4	5			10	8		11					6	9			7	
35		23	Bury	0-2		7718	1	2	3	4	5			10	8		11			7		6	9				
36		30	BOURNEMOUTH	2-1	Wilson, Boylen	2458	1	2	3	4	5		7	10	8		11					6	9				
37	Apr	6	Colchester United	3-1	Wilson(2), Moore	3231	1	2	3	4	5		7	10	8		11					6	9				
38		12	OLDHAM ATHLETIC	0-1		7048	1	2	3	4	5		7	10	8		11		12			6	9*				
39		13	PETERBOROUGH UNITED	1-1	Boylen	4101	1	7	3	4	5		8	10	9		11		2			6					
40		16	Oldham Athletic	1-2	Wilson	4821	1	2	3	6			8	10	9		11				4	5		7			
41		20	Mansfield Town	1-1	Ross(pen)	6277	1	2	3	6			7		9		11			10	4	5		8			
42		24	SOUTHPORT	2-0	Collins, Martin	2750	1	2	3	4	5		10		9		11				8	6		7			
43		27	WATFORD	0-1		3027	1	2	3	10	5		8		9		11			12	6*	4		7			
44		29	Tranmere Rovers	2-1	Worthington(2)	5187	1	4	3	8	5		10		9		11		2			6		7			
45	May	3	Southport	1-0	Smith	4788	1	4	3*	8	5		10		9		11		2	12		6		7			
46		11	SWINDON TOWN	3-2	Wilson, Housley, Collins	4798	1	4	3	8	5		10		9		11		2			6		7			
						Apps.	36	45	44	44	40	12	36	26	43	17	41	10	10	26	15	18	28	12	2	1	
						Subs.						1	1			1			1	4			1				
						Goals		3	1	3	1	3	3	5	12	3	3			1			10	1			

3 own goals

F.A. Cup

	Date		Opponent	Score	Scorers	Att.	Wainman	Worthington	Taylor Graham	Ross	Rathbone	Cockerill	Collins	Boylen	Wilson	Rudd	Martin	Harker	Bloomer	SmithR.W.	Davidson	Jobling	Moore	Housley	Wilkinson	Bartlett	Taylor George
R1	Dec	9	BRADFORD P.A.	1-1	Ross(pen)	2388	1	9	3	4	5		11	12	8	10			2	6				7*			
R1r		11	Bradford P.A.	1-4	Worthington	5243	1	9		10					7				2	6	4	5	8		3		11

League Cup

	Date		Opponent	Score	Scorers	Att.	Wainman	Worthington	Taylor Graham	Ross	Rathbone	Cockerill	Collins	Boylen	Wilson	Rudd	Martin	Harker	Bloomer	SmithR.W.	Davidson	Jobling	Moore	Housley	Wilkinson	Bartlett	Taylor George
R1	Aug	23	CHESTERFIELD	1-0	Rudd	5354	1	2	3	4	5	6	7	8	9	10	11*			12							
R2	Sep	12	BURY	2-2	Worthington, Collins	7017	1	2	3	4	5	6	7		10	8	11						9				
R2r		19	Bury	0-2		6564	1	2	3		5	6				8	11			10	4		9				7

		P	W	D	L	F	A	W	D	L	F	A	F	A	Pts
1	Oxford United	46	18	3	2	49	20	4	10	9	20	27	69	47	57
2	Bury	46	19	3	1	64	24	5	5	13	27	42	91	66	56
3	Shrewsbury Town	46	14	6	3	42	17	6	9	8	19	32	61	49	55
4	Torquay United	46	15	6	2	40	17	6	5	12	20	39	60	56	53
5	Reading	46	15	5	3	43	17	6	4	13	27	43	70	60	51
6	Watford	46	15	3	5	59	20	6	5	12	15	30	74	50	50
7	Walsall	46	12	7	4	47	22	7	5	11	27	39	74	61	50
8	Barrow	46	14	6	3	43	13	7	2	14	22	41	65	54	50
9	Peterborough Utd.	46	14	4	5	46	23	6	6	11	33	44	79	67	50
10	Swindon Town	46	13	8	2	51	16	3	9	11	23	35	74	51	49
11	Brighton & Hove A.	46	11	8	4	31	14	5	8	10	26	41	57	55	48
12	Gillingham	46	13	6	4	35	19	5	6	12	24	44	59	63	48
13	Bournemouth	46	13	7	3	39	17	3	8	12	17	34	56	51	47
14	Stockport County	46	16	5	2	49	22	3	4	16	21	53	70	75	47
15	Southport	46	13	6	4	35	22	4	6	13	30	43	65	65	46
16	Bristol Rovers	46	14	3	6	42	25	3	6	14	30	53	72	78	43
17	Oldham Athletic	46	11	3	9	37	32	7	4	12	23	33	60	65	43
18	Northampton Town	46	10	8	5	40	25	4	5	14	18	47	58	72	41
19	Orient	46	10	6	7	27	24	2	11	10	19	38	46	62	41
20	Tranmere Rovers	46	10	7	6	39	28	4	5	14	23	46	62	74	40
21	Mansfield Town	46	8	7	8	32	31	4	6	13	19	36	51	67	37
22	GRIMSBY TOWN	46	10	7	6	33	21	4	2	17	19	48	52	69	37
23	Colchester United	46	6	8	9	29	40	3	7	13	21	47	50	87	33
24	Scunthorpe United	46	8	9	6	36	34	2	3	18	20	53	56	87	32

SEASON 1967/68

Back: Ross, J.Bloomer, Rathbone, Jobling, Wainman, Harker, Cockerill, Moore, Wilkinson, Wilson
Front: Worthington, Rudd, George Taylor, Martin, Graham Taylor, Boylen, Collins, Davidson, Housley

SEASON 1968/69

Back:Martin, Wilson, Wainman, Macey, J.Bloomer, Ross, Kemplay
Middle: Butler, Hickman, Jobling, Moore, Campbell, Rathbone, Wigginton, Crampton
Front: Davidson, Boylen, Collins, Housley, Duncliffe, Worthington

1968-69 23rd in Division 4

Captain: Graham Rathbone

No	Month	Day	Opponent	Score	Scorers	Att.	Wainman	Worthington	Duncliffe	Hickman	Rathbone	Jobling	Ross	Wilson	Moore	Boylen	Collins	Macey	Bloomer	Davidson	Kennedy	Campbell F	Wigginton	Housley	Brace	Oates	Walker	Cockburn
1	Aug	10	NEWPORT COUNTY	3-0	Wilson(2), Moore	4943	1	2	3	4	5	6	7	8	9	10	11											
2		17	Darlington	0-0		5024	1	2	3	4	5	6	7	8	9	10	11											
3		24	SWANSEA TOWN	1-2	Wilson	4878	1	2	3	4	5	6	7	8*	9	10	11		12									
4		27	WORKINGTON TOWN	0-1		3717	1	4	3	8	5	6	7		9	10	11*		2	12								
5		31	Wrexham	0-2		6866	1	7	3	4	5	6	8	9			11		2	10								
6	Sep	7	Bradford P.A.	1-1	OG	2263	1	4	3		5	6			8		11		2	10		9		7				
7		10	ALDERSHOT	0-2		3146		4	3		5	6			9	10	11	1	2	8				7				
8		17	NOTTS COUNTY	2-0	Worthington, Moore	2361		4	3		5	6			9	10	11	1	2	8				7				
9		21	Lincoln City	0-3		9140		4*	3	12	5	6			9	10	11	1	2	8				7				
10		28	SOUTHEND UNITED	0-0		2368		4	3	8	5	6			9	10		1	2	11				7				
11	Oct	4	Colchester United	1-2	Housley	7543		2	3	8	5	6	4		9	10		1		11				7				
12		9	Workington Town	0-2		3055		2	3	8	5	6	4		9	10*		1	12	11				7				
13		12	CHESTERFIELD	1-2	Rathbone	3177		2	3	8	5	6	4		9*			1	12	10				7		11		
14		19	Peterborough United	1-1	Ross(pen)	5783		2	3	8	5	6	4		9	12		1		10*				7		11		
15		26	CHESTER	0-0		2828		2	3	9	5	6	4			10		1		8				7		11		
16	Nov	2	Exeter City	2-2	Hickman, Ross	5180		4	3	9	5		6			10		1	2	12				11*	7	8		
17		6	Scunthorpe United	2-1	Oates, Housley	5368		4	3	9	5	6				10		1	2					11	7	8		
18		9	YORK CITY	3-0	Worthington, Boylen, Brace	3627		4	3	9	5	6				10		1	2					11	7	8		
19		23	PORT VALE	1-1	Walker	3313		4	3	8	5	6				10		1	2						7	11	9	
20		29	Doncaster Rovers	1-2	Brace	8935		2	3	8	5	6	4			10		1							7	11	9	
21	Dec	7	ROCHDALE	2-0	Walker(2)	2714		2	3	8	5	6				10		1		4					7	11	9	
22		14	Chesterfield	0-0		4674		2	3	8	5	6						1		4				11	7	10	9	
23		21	PETERBOROUGH UNITED	2-2	Walker, Davidson	3609		2	3	8	5	6						1		4				11	7	10	9	
24		26	COLCHESTER UNITED	2-4	Oates, Hickman	5990		2	3	8	5		6			10		1		4					7	11	9	
25	Jan	4	Rochdale	1-6	Ross(pen)	2038		2	3	8	5	6	4			12		1		10					7	11*	9	
26		11	EXETER CITY	1-2	Cockburn	3073		2	3		5	6	8			10		1		4					7		9	11
27		18	York City	5-2	Brace(3), Rathbone, OG	3807		4	3	8*	5	6				12		1	2						7	10	9	11
28		25	SCUNTHORPE UNITED	0-1		5983		4	3	8*	5	6				12		1	2						7	10	9	11
29	Feb	1	BRADFORD CITY	1-5	Brace	2844		2	3	6	5					8		1		4					7	10	9	11
30		22	Brentford	2-4	Brace, Walker	5697	1	2	3	12	5		6			8*				4					7	10	9	11
31		28	Newport County	0-2		1846	1	10	3				6			8			2	4			5		7	11	9	
32	Mar	8	DARLINGTON	1-1	OG	5007		2	3	10		5	6					1		8	4				7	11	9	
33		12	Bradford City	1-1	Hickman	5034		2	3	8	6	5	10					1			4				7	11	9	
34		15	Swansea Town	1-1	Brace	3380		2	3	8	6	5	10					1		12	4				7	11	9*	
35		22	WREXHAM	1-1	Rathbone	3895		2	3	9	6	5	10			12		1		8*	4				7	11		
36		26	Chester	1-0	OG	4051		2	3	9	6	5	10			8		1			4				7	11		
37		29	BRADFORD P.A.	2-0	Rathbone, Ross(pen)	4540		2	3	9	6	5	10			8		1			4				7	11		
38	Apr	4	HALIFAX TOWN	0-1		7844		2	3	10		5	6			8		1			4				7		9	11
39		5	Southend United	1-0	Brace	9934		2	3	9*		5	6			10		1		8		4			7		12	11
40		7	Notts County	1-2	Cockburn	6307		4	3			5	6			10		1	2	8					7		9	11
41		12	LINCOLN CITY	1-1	Brace	5113		2	3	8		6	4			10		1					5		7		9	11
42		15	Halifax Town	0-0		6492	1	2	3	9	5	6	10			8						4		11	7			
43		19	Aldershot	1-3	Kennedy	4001	1	2		9	5	6	10						3	8	4				7	11		
44		21	Port Vale	0-1		2679		2	3	9	5	6	10			8		1			4				7			11
45	May	3	BRENTFORD	0-2		1833		2	3	4	5	6				8		1		12					7*	10	9	11
46		5	DONCASTER ROVERS	1-3	Boylen	5310		2	3	9	5	6				8		1		10		4				7		11
						Apps.	10	46	45	38	40	41	30	4	13	32	9	36	16	26	9	4	2	16	30	27	20	12
						Subs.				2						5			3	4							1	
						Goals		2		3	4		4	3	2	2				1	1			2	10	2	5	2

4 own goals

F.A. Cup

Rd	Month	Day	Opponent	Score	Scorers	Att.	Wainman	Worthington	Duncliffe	Hickman	Rathbone	Jobling	Ross	Wilson	Moore	Boylen	Collins	Macey	Bloomer	Davidson	Kennedy	Campbell F	Wigginton	Housley	Brace	Oates	Walker	Cockburn
R1	Nov	16	Darlington	0-2		6082		4	3	8	5	6				10		1	2					11	7	9		

League Cup

Rd	Month	Day	Opponent	Score	Scorers	Att.	Wainman	Worthington	Duncliffe	Hickman	Rathbone	Jobling	Ross	Wilson	Moore	Boylen	Collins	Macey	Bloomer	Davidson	Kennedy	Campbell F	Wigginton	Housley	Brace	Oates	Walker	Cockburn
R1	Aug	14	NOTTS COUNTY	0-0		4627	1	2	3	4	5	6	7	8	9	10	11											
R1r		21	Notts County	1-0	Hickman	6082	1	2	3	4	5	6	7	8	9	10	11											
R2	Sep	4	BURNLEY	1-1	Hickman	8762	1	2	3	8	5	6	4*		9		11		12	10				7				
R2r		10	Burnley	0-6		5926		4	3		5	6			9	11	8	1	2	10				7				

		P	W	D	L	F	A	W	D	L	F	A	F	A	Pts
1	Doncaster Rovers	46	13	8	2	42	16	8	9	6	23	22	65	38	59
2	Halifax Town	46	15	5	3	36	18	5	12	6	17	19	53	37	57
3	Rochdale	46	14	7	2	47	11	4	13	6	21	24	68	35	56
4	Bradford City	46	11	10	2	36	18	7	10	6	29	28	65	46	56
5	Darlington	46	11	6	6	40	26	6	12	5	22	19	62	45	52
6	Colchester United	46	12	8	3	31	17	8	4	11	26	36	57	53	52
7	Southend United	46	15	3	5	51	21	4	10	9	27	40	78	61	51
8	Lincoln City	46	13	6	4	38	19	4	11	8	16	33	54	52	51
9	Wrexham	46	13	7	3	41	22	5	7	11	20	30	61	52	50
10	Swansea Town	46	11	8	4	35	20	8	3	12	23	34	58	54	49
11	Brentford	46	12	7	4	40	24	6	5	12	24	41	64	65	48
12	Workington	46	8	11	4	24	17	7	6	10	16	26	40	43	47
13	Port Vale	46	12	8	3	33	15	4	6	13	13	31	46	46	46
14	Chester	46	12	4	7	43	24	4	9	10	33	42	76	66	45
15	Aldershot	46	13	3	7	42	23	6	4	13	24	43	66	66	45
16	Scunthorpe United	46	10	5	8	28	22	8	3	12	33	38	61	60	44
17	Exeter City	46	11	8	4	45	24	5	3	15	21	41	66	65	43
18	Peterborough Utd.	46	8	9	6	32	23	5	7	11	28	34	60	57	42
19	Notts County	46	10	8	5	33	22	2	10	11	15	35	48	57	42
20	Chesterfield	46	7	7	9	24	22	6	8	9	19	28	43	50	41
21	York City	46	12	8	3	36	25	2	3	18	17	50	53	75	39
22	Newport County	46	9	9	5	31	26	2	5	16	18	48	49	74	36
23	GRIMSBY TOWN	46	5	7	11	25	31	4	8	11	22	38	47	69	33
24	Bradford Park Ave.	46	5	8	10	19	34	0	2	21	13	72	32	106	20

1969-70 16th in Division 4

Captain: Graham Rathbone

No	Month	Date	Opponent	Score	Scorers	Att.	Wainman	Worthington	Mobley	Kennedy	Rathbone	Ross	Brace	Fletcher	Walker	Hickman	Oates	Boylen	Wigginton	Duncliffe	Lewis	Chapman	Cockburn	Williams	Marsden	Macey
1	Aug	9	Workington Town	0-0		2344	1	2	3	4	5	6	7	8	9	10	11									
2		16	HARTLEPOOL	2-0	Hickman, Brace	3507	1	2	3	4	5	6	7	9		10	8	11								
3		23	Bradford P.A.	1-1	Ross(pen)	3384	1	2	3	4	5	6	7	9		10	8	11								
4		25	Southend United	3-1	Brace(3)	11826	1	2	3	4	5	6	7	9		10	8	11								
5		30	WREXHAM	0-0		5986	1	2	3	4	5	6	7	9		10	8	11*		12						
6	Sep	6	Notts County	1-2	Brace	4991	1	2	3	4	5	6	7	9	11	10*	8						12			
7		13	SCUNTHORPE UNITED	1-1	Brace	7161	1	2	3	4	5	6	7	9		10	8	11								
8		16	CHESTER	4-1	Brace(2), Fletcher, Hickman	4186	1	2	3	4	5	6	7	9		10	8	11								
9		20	Port Vale	0-1		8787	1	2	3	4	5	6	7	9		10	8	11								
10		27	LINCOLN CITY	0-2		6718	1	2	3	4		6	7	9	12	10	8	11*	5							
11		30	NEWPORT COUNTY	1-1	Hickman	3672	1	2	3	4	5	6	7		9	10	8	11								
12	Oct	4	Crewe Alexandra	0-3		2616	1	2	3	4	5	6	7	9		10	8	11								
13		6	Hartlepool	1-0	Hickman	2758	1	2	3	4	5	6	7		9	8		10				11				
14		11	DARLINGTON	0-1		3427	1	2	3	4	5	6	7		9	8		10				11				
15		18	PETERBOROUGH UNITED	0-0		3869	1	2	3	4		6	7			9	8	10	5			11*	12			
16		25	Exeter City	1-0	Brace	5459	1	2	3	4		6	7			9	8	10	5	11						
17	Nov	1	OLDHAM ATHLETIC	4-1	Brace(2), Oates, Worthington	4463	1	2	3	4		6	7			9	8	10	5	11						
18		8	Chesterfield	2-1	Brace, Hickman	9254	1	2	3	4		6	7			11	8	10	5						9	
19		22	Colchester United	2-3	Brace, Hickman	3474	1	2	3	4		6	7			11	8	10	5						9	
20		24	Brentford	0-3		7630	1	2	3	4		6	7			9	8	10	5				11			
21	Dec	13	Scunthorpe United	1-1	Brace	7340	1	2	3	4		6	7			9	8	10	5	11						
22		26	BRADFORD P.A.	2-2	Hickman(2)	6805	1	2	3	4		6	7			9	8	10	5				11			
23	Jan	3	NOTTS COUNTY	2-1	Worthington, Brace	3791	1	2	3	4	5	10	7			9	8*	11	6				12			
24		10	PORT VALE	2-0	Hickman, Brace	4654	1	2		6*	5	8	7			9		10	4	3			12	11		
25		17	Lincoln City	0-2		7269	1	4	2		5		8			9		11	6	3		10		7*		12
26		24	SWANSEA TOWN	0-2		4460	1	10	2*		5	4	7			9	8	11	6	3		12				
27		31	CREWE ALEXANDRA	0-2		4252	1	2			5	4	7			9	8	11	6	3	10					
28	Feb	7	Darlington	0-0		2371	1	2			5	4	7			9	8	11	6	3	10					
29		14	WORKINGTON TOWN	1-1	Brace	3228	1	2		4	5	6	7			9	8	11		3	10					
30		21	EXETER CITY	2-0	Lewis, Boylen	2093	1	2		4	5	6	7			9	8	11	12	3	10*					
31		28	Oldham Athletic	2-0	Brace, Lewis	5530	1	2		4	5	6	7			9	8	11		3	10					
32	Mar	2	York City	1-1	Lewis	3090	1	2		4	5	6	7			9	8	11		3	10					
33		10	ALDERSHOT	2-2	Rathbone, Oates	4399	1	2		4	5	6	7			9	8	11		3	10					
34		14	Northampton Town	1-3	Brace	4537	1	2		4	5	6	7			9	8	11		3	10					
35		17	Swansea Town	0-2		10633	1	2		10	5	4	7			9	8	11	6	3						
36		21	YORK CITY	0-0		3335	1	2		4	5	6	7			9	8	11		3	10					
37		27	CHESTERFIELD	1-0	Lewis	7801	1	2		4	5	10	7				8	11	6	3	9					
38		28	Aldershot	2-2	Brace, Wigginton	7740	1	2		4	5	10	7				12	11	6	3	9	8*				
39		30	Peterborough United	0-1		4715	1	2		6	5	8	7					10	4	3	9	11				
40	Apr	4	SOUTHEND UNITED	2-2	Hickman, Brace	3202	1	2		4	5	6	7			9	11	10		3	8					
41		7	BRENTFORD	2-1	Brace(2)	3793	1	2		4	5	6	7			9	11	10		3	8					
42		15	Chester	1-3	Brace	2186	1	2		4	5	6	7			9	11	10		3	8					
43		18	NORTHAMPTON TOWN	0-1		3445	1	2		4	5	6	7			9	11	10		3	8					
44		20	Wrexham	2-3	Boylen, Brace	8671	1	2	12	6	5	8*	7				11	10	4	3	9					
45		25	Newport County	0-1		998	1	4	2	6			7			9	10		5	3	8		11			
46		28	COLCHESTER UNITED	5-3	Hickman(3), Oates(2)	2393	1	2		4	5		7			9	11	10	6	3	8					
						Apps.	46	46	26	42	36	43	46	11	5	42	40	43	22	26	19	6	3	2	2	
						Subs.			1						1		1		1	1		1	4			1
						Goals		2			1	1	25	1		13	4	2	1		4					

F.A. Cup

Rd	Month	Date	Opponent	Score	Scorers	Att.	Wainman	Worthington	Mobley	Kennedy	Rathbone	Ross	Brace	Fletcher	Walker	Hickman	Oates	Boylen	Wigginton	Duncliffe	Lewis	Chapman	Cockburn	Williams	Marsden	Macey
R1	Nov	15	Bradford City	1-2	Boylen	8134	1	2	3	4		6	7			9	8	10	5				11			

League Cup

Rd	Month	Date	Opponent	Score	Scorers	Att.	Wainman	Worthington	Mobley	Kennedy	Rathbone	Ross	Brace	Fletcher	Walker	Hickman	Oates	Boylen	Wigginton	Duncliffe	Lewis	Chapman	Cockburn	Williams	Marsden	Macey
R1	Aug	13	DONCASTER ROVERS	0-2		6243	1	2	3	4	5	6	7	8	9		11	10								

		P	W	D	L	F	A	W	D	L	F	A	F	A	Pts
1	Chesterfield	46	19	1	3	55	12	8	9	6	22	20	77	32	64
2	Wrexham	46	17	6	0	56	16	9	3	11	28	33	84	49	61
3	Swansea Town	46	14	8	1	43	14	7	10	6	23	31	66	45	60
4	Port Vale	46	13	9	1	39	10	7	10	6	22	23	61	33	59
5	Brentford	46	14	8	1	36	11	6	8	9	22	28	58	39	56
6	Aldershot	46	16	5	2	52	22	4	8	11	26	43	78	65	53
7	Notts County	46	14	4	5	44	21	8	4	11	29	41	73	62	52
8	Lincoln City	46	11	8	4	38	20	6	8	9	28	32	66	52	50
9	Peterborough Utd.	46	13	8	2	51	21	4	6	13	26	48	77	69	48
10	Colchester United	46	14	5	4	38	22	3	9	11	26	41	64	63	48
11	Chester	46	14	3	6	39	23	7	3	13	19	43	58	66	48
12	Scunthorpe United	46	11	6	6	34	23	7	4	12	33	42	67	65	46
13	York City	46	14	7	2	38	16	2	7	14	17	46	55	62	46
14	Northampton Town	46	11	7	5	41	19	5	5	13	23	36	64	55	44
15	Crewe Alexandra	46	12	6	5	37	18	4	6	13	14	33	51	51	44
16	GRIMSBY TOWN	46	9	9	5	33	24	5	6	12	21	34	54	58	43
17	Southend United	46	12	8	3	40	28	3	2	18	19	57	59	85	40
18	Exeter City	46	13	5	5	48	20	1	6	16	9	39	57	59	39
19	Oldham Athletic	46	11	4	8	45	28	2	9	12	15	37	60	65	39
20	Workington	46	9	9	5	31	21	3	5	15	15	43	46	64	38
21	Newport County	46	12	3	8	39	24	1	8	14	14	50	53	74	37
22	Darlington	46	8	7	8	31	27	5	3	15	22	46	53	73	36
23	Hartlepool	46	7	7	9	31	30	3	3	17	11	52	42	82	30
24	Bradford Park Ave.	46	6	5	12	23	32	0	6	17	18	64	41	96	23

SEASON 1969/70
Back: Hickman, Ross, Rathbone, Walker
Middle: McCoy (Physio), Duncliffe, Fletcher, Wainman, Macey, Worthington, Mobley, Higgins (Train)
Front: Oates, Brace, Kennedy (Play/Man), Boylen, Cockburn

SEASON 1970/71
Back: Kennedy (Man), Worthington, Wigginton, Rathbone, Wainman, Ross, Kirkland, Higgins (Train)
Front: Woodward, Brace, Lewis, Oates, Boylen, Hickman

1970-71 19th in Division 4

Captain: Dave Worthington

						Wainman	Worthington	Kirkland	Ross	Rathbone	Kennedy	Woodward	Brace	Hickman	Lewis	Boylen	Gray	Tees	Campbell A	Oates	Short	Wigginton	Moore A	Gadsby	Crampton	Carroll
1	Aug 15	OLDHAM ATHLETIC	4-1	Ross(p),Boylen,Brace,Woodward	4301	1	2	3	4	5	6	7	8	9	10	11										
2	22	Bournemouth	1-2	Brace	7029	1	2	3	4	5	6	7	8	9*		11				10		12				
3	29	HARTLEPOOL	1-1	Woodward	4500	1	2	3	8	5	6	9	7			10				11		4				
4	Sep 1	Newport County	1-0	Ross(pen)	2569	1	2	3	4	5	6	7	8	9		10				11						
5	8	Southport *	0-1		3790	1*	2	3	4	5	10		7	9		11				8		6			12	
6	12	NORTHAMPTON TOWN	0-2		4483		2	3	10	5	6	7	8	9		11	4							1		
7	19	Peterborough United	1-1	Woodward	5473		2	3		5	10	7	8	9		11	4					6		1		
8	23	Lincoln City	0-3		8844	1	2	3		5	10	7	8	9		11	4					6				
9	26	Southport	1-2	Hickman	3469	1	2	3		5	6	7	8	9		10	4			11						
10	29	SOUTHEND UNITED	2-0	Oates, Hickman	3824	1	2		3	5	6	7	8	9		10	4			11						
11	Oct 3	Scunthorpe United	2-1	Oates(2)	6945	1	2		3	5	6	7	8	9		10	4			11						
12	7	Chester	0-5		4596	1	2		3		6	7	8	9		10	4			11		5				
13	10	NOTTS COUNTY	2-1	Boylen, Brace	5384	1	2		3	5	6	7	8	9		10	4			11						
14	17	Oldham Athletic	0-1		9100	1	2		3	5	6	7	8	9		10	4			11						
15	21	Exeter City	0-4		4087	1	2		3	5	6	7	8	9		10	4			11						
16	24	YORK CITY	3-1	Boylen(pen), Woodward, Brace	4052	1	2			5	6	8	7	9		10	4		3	11						
17	31	Workington Town	0-1		2025	1	2			5	6	8	7	9		10	4		3	11						
18	Nov 7	CAMBRIDGE UNITED	2-0	Tees, Boylen(pen)	7295	1	2			5	6	11	7	8		10	4	9	3							
19	10	BARROW	3-1	Woodward, Rathbone, Tees	6661	1	2			5	6	11	7	8		10	4	9	3							
20	14	Brentford	0-2		5490	1	2		12	5	6	7		8	11	10*	4	9	3							
21	28	Aldershot	2-3	Lewis, Tees	4540	1	2			5	6	7	11	4	8		10	9	3							
22	Dec 5	STOCKPORT COUNTY	1-2	Tees	3862	1	2		4	5	6	7	11		8		10	9	3							
23	19	BOURNEMOUTH	1-0	Brace	2968	1	2		6	5		7	11	9	12	10*	4	8	3							
24	26	Darlington	1-5	Tees	4265	1	2		6	5		7	11		9	10	4	8	3							
25	Jan 8	Southend United	1-1	Woodward	6805	1	2		6	5		7	11	9*	12	10	4	8	3							
26	16	EXETER CITY	1-2	Lewis	2926	1	2		6	5		7	11	8	9	10	4		3							
27	30	ALDERSHOT	0-2		1955		4		6	5	8	7	11		9	10	2		3		1					
28	Feb 5	Stockport County	0-1		1777		2			5	4	7	11	9		10	6	8	3		1					
29	20	Barrow	1-0	Hickman	1825		2	3		5	4	7	11	9		10	6	8			1					
30	22	Colchester United	0-1		7253		2	3		5	4	7	11	9		10	6	8			1					
31	27	WORKINGTON TOWN	1-0	Tees	2295		2			5	4*	7	11	8	12	10	6	9	3		1					
32	Mar 5	York City	1-4	Lewis	3514		2	3*	12	5	4	7	11	8	9	10	6				1					
33	9	LINCOLN CITY	1-1	Tees	4217		2		3	5	4	7	12	8	11	10*	6	9			1					
34	13	BRENTFORD	1-5	Lewis	3167		2		3	5	4	11*		8	10		6	9			1	12	7			
35	17	Crewe Alexandra	0-4		2827		2			5	4		7*	8	11	10	6	9	3		1		12			
36	20	Cambridge United	3-2	Hickman, Boylen, Lewis	3929		2			5	4		7	9	11	10	8		3		1	6				
37	27	CHESTER	2-2	Brace, OG	2591	1	2			5	4	8	7	9	11	10	6		3							
38	Apr 3	Hartlepool	2-2	OG, Lewis	1764	1	2		3	5		8	7	4	11	10	6	9								
39	9	SCUNTHORPE UNITED	1-0	Rathbone	7639	1	2			5		7	11	4	9	10	6	8	3							
40	10	DARLINGTON	1-1	Woodward	3059	1	2		12	5		9	7	4	11*	10	6		3				8			
41	13	Northampton Town	4-0	Boylen, Woodward, Brace, Tees	6538	1	2		8	5		11	7	4		10	6	9	3							
42	17	Notts County	0-1		12182	1	2		8	5		11	7	4*		10	6	9	3			12				
43	20	COLCHESTER UNITED	3-1	Brace, Lewis, Ross(pen)	4166	1	2		4	5		11	7		8	10	6	9	3							
44	24	PETERBOROUGH UNITED	2-1	Brace, Tees	3012	1	2		4	5		11	7		8	10	6	9	3							
45	27	NEWPORT COUNTY	2-0	Boylen, Woodward	4710	1	2		4	5		11	7		8*	10	6	9	3			12				
46	May 4	CREWE ALEXANDRA	2-0	Ross, Tees	4739	1	2		4			11	7	8		10	6	9	3*			5				12
					Apps.	34	46	12	27	44	33	43	43	39	19	43	41	23	25	13	10	7	2	2		
					Subs.				3				1		3							4	1		1	1
					Goals				4	2		9	9	4	7	7		10		3						

* Wainman injured, replaced in goal by Worthington

2 own goals

F.A. Cup

						Wainman	Worthington	Kirkland	Ross	Rathbone	Kennedy	Woodward	Brace	Hickman	Lewis	Boylen	Gray	Tees	Campbell A	Oates	Short	Wigginton	Moore A	Gadsby	Crampton	Carroll
R1	Nov 21	BURY	0-1		7191	1	2			5	6	11	7	8		10	4	9	3							

League Cup

						Wainman	Worthington	Kirkland	Ross	Rathbone	Kennedy	Woodward	Brace	Hickman	Lewis	Boylen	Gray	Tees	Campbell A	Oates	Short	Wigginton	Moore A	Gadsby	Crampton	Carroll
R1	Aug 14	Lincoln City	1-2	Hickman	7665	1	2	3	4	5	6	7	8	9	10*	11				12						

		P	W	D	L	F	A	W	D	L	F	A	F	A	Pts
1	Notts County	46	19	4	0	59	12	11	5	7	30	24	89	36	69
2	Bournemouth	46	16	5	2	51	15	8	7	8	30	31	81	46	60
3	Oldham Athletic	46	14	6	3	57	29	10	5	8	31	34	88	63	59
4	York City	46	16	6	1	45	14	7	4	12	33	40	78	54	56
5	Chester	46	17	2	4	42	18	7	5	11	27	37	69	55	55
6	Colchester United	46	14	6	3	44	19	7	6	10	26	35	70	54	54
7	Northampton Town	46	15	4	4	39	24	4	9	10	24	35	63	59	51
8	Southport	46	15	2	6	42	24	6	4	13	21	33	63	57	48
9	Exeter City	46	12	7	4	40	23	5	7	11	27	45	67	68	48
10	Workington	46	13	7	3	28	13	5	5	13	20	36	48	49	48
11	Stockport County	46	12	8	3	28	17	4	6	13	21	48	49	65	46
12	Darlington	46	15	3	5	42	22	2	8	13	16	35	58	57	45
13	Aldershot	46	8	10	5	32	23	6	7	10	34	48	66	71	45
14	Brentford	46	13	3	7	45	27	5	5	13	21	35	66	62	44
15	Crewe Alexandra	46	13	1	9	49	35	5	7	11	26	41	75	76	44
16	Peterborough Utd.	46	14	3	6	46	23	4	4	15	24	48	70	71	43
17	Scunthorpe United	46	9	7	7	36	23	6	6	11	20	38	56	61	43
18	Southend United	46	8	11	4	32	24	6	4	13	21	42	53	66	43
19	GRIMSBY TOWN	46	13	4	6	37	26	5	3	15	20	45	57	71	43
20	Cambridge United	46	9	9	5	31	27	6	4	13	20	39	51	66	43
21	Lincoln City	46	11	4	8	45	33	2	9	12	25	38	70	71	39
22	Newport County	46	8	3	12	32	36	2	5	16	23	49	55	85	28
23	Hartlepool	46	6	10	7	28	27	2	2	19	6	47	34	74	28
24	Barrow	46	5	5	13	25	38	2	3	18	26	52	51	90	22

1971-72 1st in Division 4

Captain: Dave Worthington

	Date		Opponent	Score	Scorers	Att.	Wainman	Worthington	Campbell	Thomson JA	Rathbone	Gray	Brace	Lewis	Tees	Boylen	Woodward	Wigginton	Hickman	Chatterley	Gauden	Smith Bob	Simpson	Cuff	Ferguson	Turner	Czuczman
1	Aug	14	SCUNTHORPE UNITED	4-1	Tees(3), Lewis	7497	1	2	3	4	5	6	7	8	9	10	11										
2		21	Exeter City	4-3	OG, Brace, Tees, OG	4052	1	2	3	4	5	6	7	8	9	10*	11		12								
3		28	WORKINGTON TOWN	1-1	Tees	8427	1	2	3	4	5	6	7	8	9	10	11										
4		31	DONCASTER ROVERS	3-1	Woodward(2), Lewis	10236	1	2	3	4	5	6	7	8	9*	10	11		12								
5	Sep	4	Barrow	0-0		2686	1	2	3	4	5	6	7	8		10	11		9								
6		11	BRENTFORD	3-1	Rathbone, Brace, Hickman	11529	1	2	3	4	5	8	7			10	11	6	9								
7		17	Southend United	1-3	Hickman	6310	1	2	3	4	5	8	7			10	11	6	9								
8		25	STOCKPORT COUNTY	4-1	Hickman, Tees, Woodward(2)	9658	1	2	3	4	5	6	7		9	10	11		8								
9		29	Lincoln City	0-3		15015	1	2	3	12	5	6	7		9	10	11		8*				4				
10	Oct	2	Reading	3-1	Boylen, Hickman, Tees	5183	1	2	3		5	6	7		9	10	11		8				4				
11		9	GILLINGHAM	2-1	Hickman, Tees	10381	1	2	3		5	6	7		9	10	11		8				4				
12		16	Scunthorpe United	2-1	Tees(2)	11510	1	2	3	4	5	6	7		9	10			8				11				
13		19	CREWE ALEXANDRA	2-3	Brace, Tees	11010	1	2	3	4	5	6	7		9	10		12	8				11*				
14		23	SOUTHPORT	0-1		10640	1	2	3*	12	5	6	7	8	9	10			4				11				
15		30	Northampton Town	0-3		6220	1	2		4*		6	7	10	9	11		5	8			3					12
16	Nov	6	HARTLEPOOL	3-2	Tees, Brace, Lewis	8589		2				6	7	8	9	11		5	10			3		1	4		
17		13	Darlington	2-3	Tees, Hickman	2284		2			5	3	7*	8	9	11		6	10			4		1	12		
18		27	Aldershot	1-1	Brace	4000	1	2	3*	4		6	7	10	9	12		5	8			11					
19	Dec	4	BURY	4-1	Thomson(2pens),Hickman,Tees	6779	1	2	3	4		6	7	10	9			5	8			11					
20		18	BARROW	2-0	Tees, Hickman	6890	1	2	3	4		6	7	8	9			5	11			10					
21		27	Cambridge United	1-3	Thomson	8691	1	2	3*	4		6	7	8	9	12		5	10			11					
22	Jan	1	SOUTHEND UNITED	4-1	Thomson(p),Lewis,Brace,Hickman	9137	1	2	3	4*		6	7	8	9	12		5	10			11					
23		8	Workington Town	0-0		2460	1	2	3	4	5	6	7		9	10			8			11					
24		15	NEWPORT COUNTY	4-2	Brace(2), OG, Rathbone	8112	1	2	3	4	5	6	7	8	9	10						11					
25		22	LINCOLN CITY	2-2	Worthington, Brace	15564	1	2	3	4	5	6	7	8	9	10			11								
26		29	Crewe Alexandra	1-0	Brace	1960	1	2	3	4	5	6	7	8	9	10			11								
27	Feb	5	CHESTER	1-0	Brace	9431	1	2	3	4	5	6	7	8	9	10			11								
28		12	Southport	0-1		2670	1	2	3	4	5	6	7	8*	9	10		12	11								
29		19	NORTHAMPTON TOWN	4-2	Hickman, Brace(2,1pen), Tees	10000	1	2	3	4*	5	6	7		9	10			8		11		12				
30		26	Hartlepool	1-0	Tees	5194	1	2	3		5	6	7		9	10*		12	8	4	11						
31	Mar	4	DARLINGTON	2-0	Gauden, Tees	10388	1	2	3		5	6	7		9	10		12	8	4	11*						
32		11	Gillingham	1-0	Brace	4279	1	2	3		5	6	7	8	9	10			11	4							
33		13	Newport County	1-2	Gauden	2870	1	2	3		5	6	7	11	9	10		8		4							
34		21	COLCHESTER UNITED	3-0	Gauden, Tees, Brace	13288	1	2	3			6	7	12	9	10*		5	8	4	11						
35		25	Brentford	0-2		14620	1	2	3			6	7	12	9	10		5	8	4	11*						
36		27	Peterborough United	2-0	Hickman, Tees	4961	1	2	3			6	7		9	10		5	8	4	11						
37		31	READING	2-0	Boylen, Tees	16567	1	2	3			6	7		9	10		5	8	4	11						
38	Apr	1	CAMBRIDGE UNITED	2-1	Tees, HIckman	12583	1	2	3			6	7		9	10		5	8	4	11						
39		3	Stockport County	2-0	Brace (2,1pen)	4026	1	2	3			6	7		9	10		5	8	4	11						
40		8	Chester	2-1	Tees(2)	2823	1	2	3			6	7		9	10		5	8	4	11						
41		15	ALDERSHOT	3-3	Tees(2), Gauden	13414	1	2	3	12		6		8	9	10		5	11	4*	7						
42		17	Colchester United	1-0	Chatterley	5086	1	2	3			6		7	9	10		5	8	4	11*	12					
43		22	Bury	1-1	Wigginton	4977	1	2	3			6	11	7	9	10		5*	8	4	12						
44		25	Doncaster Rovers	1-2	Brace(pen)	12320	1	2	3			6	7		9	10		5	8	4	11						
45		29	PETERBOROUGH UNITED	3-2	Wigginton, Brace(pen), Gauden	14143		2	3			6	7	12	9*	10		5	8	4	11					1	
46	May	2	EXETER CITY	3-0	Tees, Hickman, Chatterley	22489	1	2	3			6	7		9	10		5	8	4	11						
						Apps.	43	46	43	23	26	46	44	24	43	41	11	24	40	17	15	10	6	2	1	1	
						Subs.				3				3		3		4	2		1	1	1		1		1
						Goals		1		4	2	1	19	4	27	2	4	2	13	2	4						

3 own goals

F.A. Cup

	Date		Opponent	Score	Scorers	Att.	Wainman	Worthington	Campbell	Thomson JA	Rathbone	Gray	Brace	Lewis	Tees	Boylen	Woodward	Wigginton	Hickman	Chatterley	Gauden	Smith Bob	Simpson	Cuff	Ferguson	Turner	Czuczman
R1	Nov	20	York City	2-4	Thomson(2pens)	6578	1	2		4	5	6	12	8	9	10			7			3	11*				

League Cup

	Date		Opponent	Score	Scorers	Att.	Wainman	Worthington	Campbell	Thomson JA	Rathbone	Gray	Brace	Lewis	Tees	Boylen	Woodward	Wigginton	Hickman	Chatterley	Gauden	Smith Bob	Simpson	Cuff	Ferguson	Turner	Czuczman
R1	Aug	17	DONCASTER ROVERS	4-3	Brace,Lewis,Tees,Woodward	8836	1	2	3	4	5	6	7	8	9	10	11										
R2	Sep	7	SHREWSBURY TOWN	2-1	Brace(2)	13596	1	2	3	4	5	6	7	8*		10	11		9				12				
R3	Oct	5	Gillingham	1-1	Brace	9038	1	2	3		5	6	7		9	10	11		8				4				
R3r		12	GILLINGHAM	1-0	Boylen(pen)	15801	1	2	3	12	5	6	7		9	10	11*		8				4				
R4		26	NORWICH CITY	1-1	Gray	22408	1	2		4		6	7	10	9	11		5	8				3				
R4r	Nov	3	Norwich City	1-3	Tees	27531	1	2		12	6	3	7	8	9	11		5	10*			4					

		P	W	D	L	F	A	W	D	L	F	A	F	A	Pts
1	GRIMSBY TOWN	46	18	3	2	61	26	10	4	9	27	30	88	56	63
2	Southend United	46	18	2	3	56	26	6	10	7	25	29	81	55	60
3	Brentford	46	16	2	5	52	21	8	9	6	24	23	76	44	59
4	Scunthorpe United	46	13	8	2	34	15	9	5	9	22	22	56	37	57
5	Lincoln City	46	17	5	1	46	15	4	9	10	31	44	77	59	56
6	Workington	46	12	9	2	34	7	4	10	9	16	27	50	34	51
7	Southport	46	15	5	3	48	21	3	9	11	18	25	66	46	50
8	Peterborough Utd.	46	14	6	3	51	24	3	10	10	31	40	82	64	50
9	Bury	46	16	4	3	55	22	3	8	12	18	37	73	59	50
10	Cambridge United	46	11	8	4	38	22	6	6	11	24	38	62	60	48
11	Colchester United	46	13	6	4	38	23	6	4	13	32	46	70	69	48
12	Doncaster Rovers	46	11	8	4	35	24	5	6	12	21	39	56	63	46
13	Gillingham	46	11	5	7	33	24	5	8	10	28	43	61	67	45
14	Newport County	46	13	5	5	34	20	5	3	15	26	52	60	72	44
15	Exeter City	46	11	5	7	40	30	5	6	12	21	38	61	68	43
16	Reading	46	14	3	6	37	26	3	5	15	19	50	56	76	42
17	Aldershot	46	5	13	5	27	20	4	9	10	21	34	48	54	40
18	Hartlepool	46	14	2	7	39	25	3	4	16	19	44	58	69	40
19	Darlington	46	9	9	5	37	24	5	2	16	27	58	64	82	39
20	Chester	46	10	11	2	34	16	0	7	16	13	40	47	56	38
21	Northampton Town	46	8	9	6	43	27	4	4	15	23	52	66	79	37
22	Barrow	46	8	8	7	23	26	5	3	15	17	45	40	71	37
23	Stockport County	46	7	10	6	33	32	2	4	17	22	55	55	87	32
24	Crewe Alexandra	46	9	4	10	27	25	1	5	17	16	44	43	69	29

SEASON 1971/72
Back: Rathbone, Czuczman, Gray, Wainman, Tees, Wigginton
Middle: Lewis, Brace, Boylen, Worthington, McMenemy (Man), Thomson, Woodward
Front: Park, Riley, Simpson, Hickman, Campbell

SEASON 1972/73
Back: Czuczman, Gray, Wainman, Turner, Chatterley, Rathbone
Middle (standing): Clunie (Train), Hickman, Booth, Wigginton, Lynch, Tees, Fraser (Physio)
Middle (seated): Boylen, Campbell, Worthington, McMenemy (Man), Lewis, Gauden, Brace Front: Marley, Robinson

1972-73 9th in Division 3

Captain: Dave Worthington

							Wainman	Worthington	Booth	Wigginton	Rathbone	Gray	Brace	Hickman	Tees	Lewis	Gauden	Turner	Campbell	Chatterley	Hubbard	Lynch	Boylen	Czuczman	Hooks
1	Aug	12	York City	0-0		6827	1	2	3	4	5	6	7	8	9	10	11								
2		19	ROTHERHAM UNITED	2-1	Brace(pen), Lewis	11969	1	2	3	4	5	6	7	8	9	10	11								
3		26	Bristol Rovers	1-2	Gauden	9095	1	2	3	4	5	6	7	8	9	10	11								
4		29	Plymouth Argyle	1-3	Hickman	8472	1	2*	3	4	5	6	7	8	9	10	11						12		
5	Sep	2	WATFORD	2-0	Brace(2)	8992		2	3		5	6	7	9		8	11	1		4			10		
6		9	Walsall	0-1		4174		2	3		5			7	9		11	1	12	4		6	10	8*	
7		16	BOLTON WANDERERS	2-0	Tees, Gauden	8858		2	3		5	8		7	9		11	1		4		6	10		
8		19	Oldham Athletic	2-1	Tees, Brace	5596		2	3		5	8	7		9	12	11	1		4		6	10*		
9		23	Scunthorpe United	2-1	Gray, Chatterley	10768		2	3		5	8	7	11	9	12		1		4		6*	10		
10		26	BLACKBURN ROVERS	2-0	Boylen, Brace	12994		2	3		5	7	9		8*	12	11	1		4		6	10		
11		30	ROCHDALE	1-0	Worthington	12173		2	3	9	5	8*	7			12	11	1		4		6	10		
12	Oct	7	Swansea City	2-6	Chatterley, Booth	3071		2	3	9	5	8	7			12	11*	1		4		6	10		
13		10	Shrewsbury Town	2-3	Gauden(2)	1763		2	3	9*	5	8	7				11	1		4		6	10		12
14		14	CHARLTON ATHLETIC	0-2		8646		2	3		5	6	7	9*		8	11	1		4		12	10		
15		21	Halifax Town	1-1	Lewis	3068			3	5		8	7			9	11*	1	2	4		6	10	12	
16		24	SOUTHEND UNITED	3-1	Hickman(2), Gauden(pen)	9964			3	5		6	7*	8		9	11	1	2	4		12	10		
17		28	BOURNEMOUTH	0-1		12370			3	5		6		8		7	11	1	2	4	9		10		
18	Nov	4	Blackburn Rovers	0-0		7676		12	3	5	4	6		8		7*	11	1	2		9		10		
19		11	OLDHAM ATHLETIC	6-2	Brace(4,1pen), Tees, Hubbard	9893			3	5	12	6	7	4	9*		11	1	2		8		10		
20		25	Wrexham	2-3	Brace(2,1pen)	3656			3*	5		6	7	8		12	11	1	2	4	9		10		
21	Dec	2	NOTTS COUNTY	3-1	Hubbard(3)	8963	1	2		5		6	7	8		12	11		3	4	9		10*		
22		16	BRENTFORD	4-0	Wigginton, Hickman, Chatterley, Worthington	8926	1	2	3	5		6	7	8*		12	11			4	9		10		
23		23	Chesterfield	1-2	Brace	5003	1	2	3	5		6	7	8			11			4	9		10		
24		26	SCUNTHORPE UNITED	1-0	Chatterley	16580	1	2	3	5		6	7	8			11			4	9		10		
25		30	Rotherham United	0-2		5691	1	2	3	5	4	6	7	8		12	11				9*		10		
26	Jan	6	BRISTOL ROVERS	2-0	Hubbard, Booth	8975	1	2	3	5		6	7	8			11			4	9		10		
27		20	Watford	2-1	Tees(2)	5864	1	2	3	6		5	7		10				4	8	9		11		
28		27	WALSALL	6-2	Chatterley(3), Gauden(2), Hubbard	11142	1	2	3	5		6	7		9		11			4	8		10		
29	Feb	10	Bolton Wanderers	0-2		16588	1	2	3	5		6	7	8	9		11*			4	12		10		
30		13	SHREWSBURY TOWN	3-2	Hubbard(2), Gauden	11382	1	2	3	5		6		8		7	11			4	9		10		
31		17	YORK CITY	1-2	Hubbard	12899	1	2	3	5		6		8		7	11			4	9		10		
32		24	Brentford	1-0	Brace	9300		2	3	5		6	7	8			11	1		4	9		10		
33	Mar	3	SWANSEA CITY	2-0	Brace(2)	11701		2*	3	5		6	7	8		12	11	1		4	9		10		
34		6	PORT VALE	0-1		13896			3	5		6	7		10	8	11	1	2	4	9				
35		10	Charlton Athletic	1-1	OG	5423			3	5		6	7		9	8	11	1	2	4*	10			12	
36		12	Southend United	0-2		4813			3	5		6	7	8		10	11*	1	2		9	12		4	
37		17	HALIFAX TOWN	0-0		10836			3	5		6	7	4		8	11	1	2		9		10		
38		19	Tranmere Rovers	1-1	Czuczman	5366			3	5		6	7	8		12	11	1	2		9*		10	4	
39		24	Bournemouth	1-1	Brace	11393			3	5		6	7	8		12	11	1*	2		9		10	4	
40		31	WREXHAM	0-1		9040	1	2		5		6	7	8*		12	11		3		9		10	4	
41	Apr	7	Notts County	0-4		16208	1	2		5		6	7	8		10			3		9	12	11	4*	
42		14	TRANMERE ROVERS	2-0	Hickman, OG	7211	1	2	3*	5		6	7	8		10				4	9		11	12	
43		20	CHESTERFIELD	2-1	Brace, Hickman	10353	1	2	3	5		6	7	8		10				4	9		11		
44		21	Port Vale	0-3		3772	1	2	3	5		6	7	8		10				4	9		11*	12	
45		23	Rochdale	2-3	Hubbard, Brace	1911	1	2	3	5		6	7	8	10					4*	9	11	12		
46		28	PLYMOUTH ARGYLE	1-1	Booth	7361	1	2	3	5		6		7*	9	12	11			4	8		10		
						Apps.	22	34	43	39	16	45	39	36	17	20	39	24	16	33	29	10	38	6	
						Subs.		1			1					14			1		1	4	2	4	1
						Goals		2	3	1		1	18	6	5	2	8			7	10		1	1	

2 own goals

F.A. Cup

							Wainman	Worthington	Booth	Wigginton	Rathbone	Gray	Brace	Hickman	Tees	Lewis	Gauden	Turner	Campbell	Chatterley	Hubbard	Lynch	Boylen	Czuczman	Hooks
R1	Nov	18	WIGAN ATHLETIC	2-1	Brace, Boylen	11560			3	5		6	7	4	9*	12	11	1	2		8		10		
R2	Dec	8	CHESTERFIELD	2-2	Hickman, Gauden	10646	1	2		5		6	7	8		12	11*		3	4	9		10		
R2r		13	Chesterfield	1-0	Brace	9658	1	2	3	5		6	7	8			11			4	9		10		
R3	Jan	13	PRESTON NORTH END	0-0		16000	1	2	3	5		6	7	8		12	11*			4	9		10		
R3r		15	Preston North End	1-0	Gauden	13175	1	2	3	5		6	7	8			11			8	9		10		
R4	Feb	3	Coventry City	0-1		38104	1	2	3	5		6	7	8	9		11			4			10		

League Cup

							Wainman	Worthington	Booth	Wigginton	Rathbone	Gray	Brace	Hickman	Tees	Lewis	Gauden	Turner	Campbell	Chatterley	Hubbard	Lynch	Boylen	Czuczman	Hooks
R1	Aug	16	Barnsley	0-0		4292	1	2	3	4	5	6	7*	8	9	10	11						12		
R1r		22	BARNSLEY	2-0	Tees(2)	12383	1	2	3	4	5	6	7	8*	9	10	11						12		
R2	Sep	5	Bury	0-1		3096		2	3	12	5	6*	7	9		8	11	1		4			10		

		P	W	D	L	F	A	W	D	L	F	A	F	A	Pts
1	Bolton Wanderers	46	18	4	1	44	9	7	7	9	29	30	73	39	61
2	Notts County	46	17	4	2	40	12	6	7	10	27	35	67	47	57
3	Blackburn Rovers	46	12	8	3	34	16	8	7	8	23	31	57	47	55
4	Oldham Athletic	46	12	7	4	40	18	7	9	7	32	36	72	54	54
5	Bristol Rovers	46	17	4	2	55	20	3	9	11	22	36	77	56	53
6	Port Vale	46	15	6	2	41	21	6	5	12	15	48	56	69	53
7	Bournemouth	46	14	6	3	44	16	3	10	10	22	28	66	44	50
8	Plymouth Argyle	46	14	3	6	43	26	6	7	10	31	40	74	66	50
9	GRIMSBY TOWN	46	16	2	5	45	18	4	6	13	22	43	67	61	48
10	Tranmere Rovers	46	12	8	3	38	17	3	8	12	18	35	56	52	46
11	Charlton Athletic	46	12	7	4	46	24	5	4	14	23	43	69	67	45
12	Wrexham	46	11	9	3	39	23	3	8	12	16	31	55	54	45
13	Rochdale	46	8	8	7	22	26	6	9	8	26	28	48	54	45
14	Southend United	46	13	6	4	40	14	4	4	15	21	40	61	54	44
15	Shrewsbury Town	46	10	10	3	31	21	5	4	14	15	33	46	54	44
16	Chesterfield	46	13	4	6	37	22	4	5	14	20	39	57	61	43
17	Walsall	46	14	3	6	37	26	4	4	15	19	40	56	66	43
18	York City	46	8	10	5	24	14	5	5	13	18	32	42	46	41
19	Watford	46	11	8	4	32	23	1	9	13	11	25	43	48	41
20	Halifax Town	46	9	8	6	29	23	4	7	12	14	30	43	53	41
21	Rotherham United	46	12	4	7	34	27	5	3	15	17	38	51	65	41
22	Brentford	46	12	5	6	33	18	3	2	18	18	51	51	69	37
23	Swansea City	46	11	5	7	37	29	3	4	16	14	44	51	73	37
24	Scunthorpe United	46	8	7	8	18	25	2	3	18	15	47	33	72	30

1973-74 6th in Division 3

Captain: Lew Chatterley

	Date	Opponent	Res	Scorers	Att	Wainman	Beardsley	Booth	Chatterley	Wigginton	Gray	Brace	Barton	Hubbard	Hickman	Sharp	Boylen	Czuczman	Lewis	Lumby	Fletcher	Freeman	Brown	Turner
1	Aug 25	HEREFORD UNITED	1-3	Chatterley	10709	1	2	3	4	5	6	7*	8	9	10	11			12					
2	Sep 1	Chesterfield	0-1		4977	1	2	3	4	5	6	7	8	9	10	11								
3	8	BRISTOL ROVERS	1-1	Chatterley(pen)	7640	1	2	3	4	5	6	7	8	9	10	11*	12							
4	11	HALIFAX TOWN	4-1	Chatterley(2,1p),Wigginton,Barton	7860	1	2	3	4	5	6		7	9	8	11	10							
5	14	Tranmere Rovers	0-0		6872	1	2	3	4	5	6		7	9*	8	11	10	12						
6	19	Blackburn Rovers	0-1		7975	1	2	3	4	5	6		7	9	8	11	10							
7	22	BRIGHTON & HOVE ALBION	0-0		7797	1	2	3	4	5	6		7	9	8	11	10*		12					
8	29	Shrewsbury Town	1-1	Chatterley	2306	1	2	3	4	5	6		7	9	8*	11	12	10						
9	Oct 2	BLACKBURN ROVERS	4-2	Chatterley(2),Hubbard,Czuczman	7608	1	2	3	4	5	6		7	9	8	11		10						
10	12	Southport	1-0	Hubbard	2294	1	2	3	4	5	6		7	9	8	11		10						
11	20	ALDERSHOT	1-0	Barton	7644	1	2	3	4	5	6		7	9	8	11		10						
12	27	Rochdale	1-1	Hubbard	1849	1	2	3	4	5	6		7	9	8	11		10						
13	Nov 3	CAMBRIDGE UNITED	1-0	Sharp	7011	1	2	3	4	5	6		7	9	8*	11		10	12					
14	6	WALSALL	1-0	Sharp	7869	1	2*	3	4	5	6		7	9		11		10	12		8			
15	10	Wrexham	1-1	Lewis	5066	1		3	4	5	6		7	9		11	12	10	2		8*			
16	13	Plymouth Argyle	0-1		7700	1	2	3	4	5	6		7	9		11	10		8					
17	17	BOURNEMOUTH	1-1	Lewis	8194	1	2	3	4	5	6		7	9		11*		10	8		12			
18	Dec 8	Port Vale	1-1	Lewis	3157	1	2	3	4	5	6		7*	9	8	11	10		12					
19	22	SHREWSBURY TOWN	1-2	Hubbard	5071	1	2	3	4*	5	6		7	9	8	11	10		12					
20	26	York City	1-1	Lewis	5527	1	2	3	4	5	6		7		8	11	10		9					
21	29	Bristol Rovers	1-1	Lewis	14317		2	3	4	5	6		7		8	11	10		9					1
22	Jan 1	CHESTERFIELD	1-1	Lewis	9308	1	2	3	4	5	6		7		8	11	10		9					
23	12	TRANMERE ROVERS	5-0	Hickman(2),Barton,Hubbard,Boylen	5200	1	2	3		5	6		7	4	8	11	10		9					
24	19	Hereford United	1-2	Booth	10287	1	2	3		5	6		7	4	8	11	10		9					
25	26	ROCHDALE	5-1	Lewis, Hickman(2), Hubbard(2)	5548	1	2	3	12	5	6*		7	4	8		10		9		11			
26	Feb 2	HUDDERSFIELD TOWN	2-1	Boylen(2)	7013	1	2	3		5	6		7	4	8		10		9		11			
27	9	Brighton & Hove Albion	1-1	Lewis	10469	1	2	3		5	6		7	4	8		10		9		11			
28	16	SOUTHPORT	2-1	Boylen, OG	7240	1	2	3		5	6		7	4	8		10		9		11			
29	23	Walsall	1-3	Hubbard	4071	1	2	3		5	6		7	4	8		10		9		11			
30	Mar 2	YORK CITY	1-2	Fletcher	7410	1	2	3		5	6		7	4	8	12	10		9		11*			
31	16	Aldershot	0-1		4005	1	2	3		5			7		4	11	10	6	9*	8	12			
32	20	Huddersfield Town	0-1		4473	1	2	3		5			7		4	11	10	6	9	8				
33	23	WREXHAM	1-1	Lumby	5383	1	2	3		5			7	4	8		11	6	9	10				
34	26	SOUTHEND UNITED	2-1	Lumby, Hubbard	5933	1	2	3		5			7	4	8		11	6	9	10				
35	30	Cambridge United	1-0	Lewis	3638	1	2	3		5			7	4	8		11	6	9	10				
36	Apr 2	Oldham Athletic	1-3	Lewis	12338	1	2	3		5			7	4	8	12	11	6	9	10*				
37	6	PLYMOUTH ARGYLE	3-0	Lumby(3)	5102	1	2	3		5			7	4	8		11	6	9	10				
38	9	Halifax Town	2-1	Hubbard, Lumby	1624	1	2	3		5			7	4	8		11	6	9	10				
39	12	CHARLTON ATHLETIC	5-0	Lumby(2),Brown,Wigginton,Barton	8168	1	2	3		5			7	4		12	8	6	9	10*			11	
40	13	Bournemouth	1-1	Boylen(pen)	6223	1	2	3		5			7	4			8	6	9	10*	12		11	
41	15	Charlton Athletic	1-2	Hickman	3366	1	2	3		5			7	4	8		11	6	9	10				
42	20	PORT VALE	2-0	Lumby, Boylen	6166		2	3		5			7	4	8		11	6	9	10		1		
43	22	Southend United	1-4	Hickman	5335		2	3		5			7	4	8		11	6	9	10		1		
44	24	OLDHAM ATHLETIC	2-1	Hickman(2)	7820		2	3		5			7	4	8		11	6	9	10		1		
45	27	Watford	2-1	Lewis, Hickman	6935		2	3		5			7	4	8		11	6	9	10		1		
46	29	WATFORD	2-2	Lewis(2)	8813		2	3		5			7	4	8		11	6	9	10		1		
					Apps.	40	45	46	22	46	30	3	46	41	40	26	34	25	30	16	8	5	2	1
					Subs.				1							3	3	1	6		3			
					Goals			1	7	2			4	10	9	2	6	1	13	9	1		1	

1 own goal

F.A. Cup

	Date	Opponent	Res	Scorers	Att	Wainman	Beardsley	Booth	Chatterley	Wigginton	Gray	Brace	Barton	Hubbard	Hickman	Sharp	Boylen	Czuczman	Lewis	Lumby	Fletcher	Freeman	Brown	Turner
R1	Nov 14	Runcorn	1-0	Barton	3934	1	2	3	4	5	6		7	9		11		10			8			
R2	Dec 15	BLYTH SPARTANS	1-1	Hickman	5724	1	2	3	4	5	6		7	9*	8	11		10	12					
R2r	18	Blyth Spartans	2-0	Hickman, Hubbard	2500	1	2	3	4	5	6		7	9	8	11		10						
R3	Jan 5	BURNLEY	0-2		14152	1	2	3	4	5	6		7	12	8	11*		10	9					

League Cup

	Date	Opponent	Res	Scorers	Att	Wainman	Beardsley	Booth	Chatterley	Wigginton	Gray	Brace	Barton	Hubbard	Hickman	Sharp	Boylen	Czuczman	Lewis	Lumby	Fletcher	Freeman	Brown	Turner
R1	Aug 28	NORTHAMPTON TOWN	2-1	Brace, Sharp	7829	1	2	3	4	5	6	7	8	9	10	11								
R2	Oct 10	Luton Town	1-1	Chatterley	9656	1	2	3	4	5	6		7	9	8	11*		10	12					
R2r	16	LUTON TOWN	0-0		13643	1	2	3	4	5	6		7	9	8	11*		10	12					
R22r	23	LUTON TOWN *	0-2		15365	1	2	3	4	5	6		7	9	8	11*		10	12					

* Grimsby won choice of venue on toss of coin

		P	W	D	L	F	A	W	D	L	F	A	F	A	Pts
1	Oldham Athletic	46	13	6	4	50	23	12	6	5	33	24	83	47	62
2	Bristol Rovers	46	15	6	2	37	15	7	11	5	28	18	65	33	61
3	York City	46	13	8	2	37	15	8	11	4	30	23	67	38	61
4	Wrexham	46	15	6	2	44	15	7	6	10	19	28	63	43	56
5	Chesterfield	46	14	6	3	31	16	7	8	8	24	26	55	42	56
6	GRIMSBY TOWN	46	14	6	3	48	21	4	9	10	19	29	67	50	51
7	Watford	46	12	6	5	34	21	7	6	10	30	35	64	56	50
8	Aldershot	46	13	6	4	47	22	6	5	12	18	30	65	52	49
9	Halifax Town	46	9	11	3	23	15	5	10	8	25	36	48	51	49
10	Huddersfield Town	46	14	5	4	37	16	3	8	12	19	39	56	55	47
11	Bournemouth	46	11	5	7	25	23	5	10	8	29	35	54	58	47
12	Southend United	46	10	7	6	40	30	6	7	10	22	32	62	62	46
13	Blackburn Rovers	46	13	4	6	38	21	5	6	12	24	43	62	64	46
14	Charlton Athletic	46	13	5	5	43	29	6	3	14	23	44	66	73	46
15	Walsall	46	11	7	5	37	19	5	6	12	20	29	57	48	45
16	Tranmere Rovers	46	10	8	5	31	15	5	7	11	19	29	50	44	45
17	Plymouth Argyle	46	13	6	4	37	17	4	4	15	22	37	59	54	44
18	Hereford United	46	10	5	8	31	25	4	10	9	22	32	53	57	43
19	Brighton & Hove A.	46	10	3	10	31	31	6	8	9	21	27	52	58	43
20	Port Vale	46	12	6	5	37	23	2	8	13	15	35	52	58	42
21	Cambridge United	46	11	7	5	36	27	2	2	19	12	54	48	81	35
22	Shrewsbury Town	46	7	7	9	24	24	3	4	16	17	38	41	62	31
23	Southport	46	4	14	5	19	20	2	2	19	16	62	35	82	28
24	Rochdale	46	1	12	10	24	38	1	5	17	14	56	38	94	21

SEASON 1973/74
Back: Hickman, Chatterley, Lewis, Czuczman
Middle (standing):Clunie (Train),Beardsley,Gray, Wigginton, Ross, Roberts, Hall, Booth,Fleming (Yth. Coach),Fraser (Physio)
Middle (seated): Brace, Gauden, Hubbard, Wainman, Ashman (Man), Turner, Boylen, Sharp, Barton
Front: Harris, Marley, Cumming

SEASON 1974/75
Back: Marley, Young, Beardsley, Wainman, Czuczman, Freeman, Gray, Wigginton, Brown, Cumming
Front: Hubbard, Fletcher, Barton, Hickman, Ashman (Man), Appleton (Train), Booth, Lewis, Lumby, Boylen

1974-75 16th in Division 3

Captain: Dave Booth

						Wainman	Beardsley	Cumming	Hubbard	Wigginton	Czuczman	Gray	Hickman	Lewis	Lumby	Boylen	Freeman	Booth	Govier	Marley	Young	Coyle	Barton	Partridge	Wigg	Fletcher	Brown
1	Aug	17 BLACKBURN ROVERS	1-2	Lewis	7293	1	2	3	4	5	6	7	8	9	10	11*											12
2		24 Plymouth Argyle	1-2	Lewis	8531	1	2		4	5		7	8	9		6		3					11			10	
3		31 PORT VALE	3-0	Lumby, Lewis, Boylen(pen)	5200	1	2		4	5	8	6		9	10	11		3					7				
4	Sep	7 Bury	1-1	Lewis	3428	1	2		4	5	10	6	8	9		11		3					7				
5		14 PETERBOROUGH UNITED	1-2	Hubbard	6379	1	2		4	5	10	6	8	9	12	11*		3					7				
6		17 WATFORD	2-2	Czuczman, Lewis	5003	1	2		4	5	6		8	9	10	11		3					7				
7		21 Chesterfield	0-2		4364	1	2		4*	5	6		8	9	10	11		3			12		7				
8		28 ALDERSHOT	2-0	Lewis(2)	4342	1	2			5	6		8	9	12	11		3			4		7				10
9	Oct	1 Crystal Palace	0-3		19105	1	2			5	6	12	8	9*		11		3			4		7				10
10		5 HUDDERSFIELD TOWN	1-2	Boylen(pen)	4901	1	2			5	6		8		9*	10		3			12	4	7				11
11		8 BRIGHTON & HOVE ALBION	3-2	Barton(2), Hubbard	4795				8	5	2	6			9	10	1	3				4	7				11
12		12 Wrexham	3-2	Brown(2), Hubbard	5415				8	5	2	6		9		10	1	3				4	7				11
13		16 Brighton & Hove Albion	1-3	Lewis	8172				8	5	2	6		9		10	1	3				4	7				11
14		19 GILLINGHAM	2-1	Lewis(2)	5131				8	5	2	6		9		10	1	3				4	7				11
15		23 Bournemouth	1-0	Hubbard	4254				8	5	2	6		9		10	1	3				4	7				11
16		26 Preston North End	0-2		9934				8	5	2	6		9		10	1	3				4	7				11
17	Nov	2 Swindon Town	2-3	Hubbard(pen), Lewis	7198				8	5	2	6	12	9		10	1	3				4*	7				11
18		9 TRANMERE ROVERS	3-2	Barton(2), Hubbard	4723	1			8	5	2	6		9		10		3				4	7				11
19		15 Colchester United	0-5		4489	1		3	8	5	2	6	4	9		10							7				11
20		29 Southend United	0-3		4992		7		8	5	2	6	4			10	1	3					9				11
21	Dec	7 HALIFAX TOWN	2-1	Hubbard, Lewis	4331		11		8	5	2	6		9		10	1	3				4	7				
22		21 CHARLTON ATHETIC	1-1	Barton	4991		2		8		6			9	10	11	1	3	5			4	7				
23		26 Peterborough United	3-1	OG, Lumby, Hubbard	10163		2		8		6		12	9	10*	11	1	3			5	4	7				
24		28 WALSALL	0-0		6051		2		8		6			9	10*	11	1	3			5	4	7				12
25	Jan	4 Watford	2-3	Coyle, Lewis	5669		2		8		6			9		10	1	3			5	4	7				11
26		11 Halifax Town	1-1	Lewis	2063		2		8		6		12	9		10*	1	3			5	4	7				11
27		14 Walsall	0-2		5036		2		8		6			9		10	1	3			5	4	7				11
28		18 SOUTHEND UNITED	0-0		4904		2		8		6		10*	9		11	1	3			5	4	7				12
29		31 Tranmere Rovers	1-3	Wigg	2940		2	3	8		6			9			1				5	4	7		10		11
30	Feb	8 SWINDON TOWN	2-0	Barton, Hubbard	5121			3	10	5	2			7		11	1		6			4	8		9		
31		15 Hereford United	2-3	Lewis(2)	5445	1		3	8	5	2			7		10		11	6				4		9		
32		22 COLCHESTER UNITED	1-1	Lewis	5608	1			10	5	2			7		11		3	6			4*	8		9		12
33	Mar	1 Port Vale	0-1		3335	1	2		10		8	6		7				3			5	4	11		9*		12
34		4 HEREFORD UNITED	0-0		5445	1			9		2	6		7		10		3			5	4	8				11
35		8 BOURNEMOUTH	0-0		5781	1			9		2	6		7		10		3			5	4	8		12		11*
36		15 Aldershot	0-0		3499	1			8		2	6				10		3			5	4*	7	9	12		11
37		19 Blackburn Rovers	1-1	Czuczman	13062	1			4		2	6		8		10		3			5		7	9			11
38		22 BURY	2-0	Young, Hubbard	5432	1			4		2	6		7		10		3			5		8	9			11
39		28 CHESTERFIELD	2-0	Lewis, Brown	8693	1			4*		2	6		7		10			3	12	5		8	9			11
40		29 Charlton Athletic	1-1	Boylen(pen)	11277	1			4		2	6		7		10			3		5		8	9			11
41	Apr	5 PRESTON NORTH END	2-1	Lewis, Hubbard	6211	1			4		2	6		7		10			3		5		8	9			11
42		8 CRYSTAL PALACE	2-1	Brown, Lumby	8381	1			4		2	6		7*	12	10			3		5		8	9			11
43		12 Huddersfield Town	0-1		3961	1			4		2	6			7	10			3		5		8	9			11
44		19 WREXHAM	2-0	Lewis(2)	5837	1			4			6		7	9	10			3	2			5	8			11
45		22 PLYMOUTH ARGYLE	1-1	Boylen	9052	1			4			6		7	9*	10		11	3	2			5	8			12
46		26 Gillingham	0-2		5165	1			4			6		7		10		11	3	2			5	8			9
					Apps.	28	21	5	43	24	42	30	12	41	12	44	18	36	12	3	20	24	45	11	5	1	29
					Subs.							1	3		3					1	2				2		6
					Goals				11		2			21	3	4					1	1	6		1		4

1 own goal

F.A. Cup

						Wainman	Beardsley	Cumming	Hubbard	Wigginton	Czuczman	Gray	Hickman	Lewis	Lumby	Boylen	Freeman	Booth	Govier	Marley	Young	Coyle	Barton	Partridge	Wigg	Fletcher	Brown
R1	Nov	23 HUDDERSFIELD TOWN	1-0	OG	5541				8	5	2	6	4	9		10	1	3					7				11
R2	Dec	14 BURY	1-1	Barton	5927		11		8	5	2	6		9		10	1	3				4	7				
R2r		17 Bury	1-2	Lewis	4546		11		8	5	2	6		9		10	1	3				4	7				

League Cup

						Wainman	Beardsley	Cumming	Hubbard	Wigginton	Czuczman	Gray	Hickman	Lewis	Lumby	Boylen	Freeman	Booth	Govier	Marley	Young	Coyle	Barton	Partridge	Wigg	Fletcher	Brown
R1	Aug	31 Chesterfield	0-3		4159	1	2		4	5	6	7	8	9	10*	11		3					12				

		P	W	D	L	F	A	W	D	L	F	A	F	A	Pts
1	Blackburn Rovers	46	15	7	1	40	16	7	9	7	28	29	68	45	60
2	Plymouth Argyle	46	16	5	2	38	19	8	6	9	41	39	79	58	59
3	Charlton Athletic	46	15	5	3	51	29	7	6	10	25	32	76	61	55
4	Swindon Town	46	18	3	2	43	17	3	8	12	21	41	64	58	53
5	Crystal Palace	46	14	8	1	48	22	4	7	12	18	35	66	57	51
6	Port Vale	46	15	6	2	37	19	3	9	11	24	35	61	54	51
7	Peterborough Utd.	46	10	9	4	24	17	9	3	11	23	36	47	53	50
8	Walsall	46	15	5	3	46	13	3	8	12	21	39	67	52	49
9	Preston North End	46	16	5	2	42	19	3	6	14	21	37	63	56	49
10	Gillingham	46	14	6	3	43	23	3	8	12	22	37	65	60	48
11	Colchester United	46	13	7	3	45	22	4	6	13	25	41	70	63	47
12	Hereford United	46	14	6	3	42	21	2	8	13	22	45	64	66	46
13	Wrexham	46	10	8	5	41	23	5	7	11	24	32	65	55	45
14	Bury	46	13	6	4	38	17	3	6	14	15	33	53	50	44
15	Chesterfield	46	11	7	5	37	25	5	5	13	25	41	62	66	44
16	GRIMSBY TOWN	46	12	8	3	35	19	3	5	15	20	45	55	64	43
17	Halifax Town	46	11	10	2	33	20	2	7	14	16	45	49	65	43
18	Southend United	46	11	9	3	32	17	2	7	14	14	34	46	51	42
19	Brighton & Hove A.	46	14	7	2	38	21	2	3	18	18	43	56	64	42
20	Aldershot	46	13	5	5	40	21	1	6	16	13	42	53	63	38
21	Bournemouth	46	9	6	8	27	25	4	6	13	17	33	44	58	38
22	Tranmere Rovers	46	12	4	7	39	21	2	5	16	16	36	55	57	37
23	Watford	46	9	7	7	30	31	1	10	12	22	44	52	75	37
24	Huddersfield Town	46	9	6	8	32	29	2	4	17	15	47	47	76	32

1975-76 18th in Division 3

Captain: Dave Booth

					Att	Freeman	Booth	Govier	Gray	Young	Cumming	Lewis	Partridge	Wigg	Boylen	Hubbard	Wainman	Baker	Czuczman	Marley	Barton	Walton	Waters	Ford	Parkin	Brown	Oldridge
1	Aug 16	CARDIFF CITY	2-0	Lewis, Hubbard	6283	1	2	3*	4	5	6	7	8	9	10	11										12	
2	23	Gillingham	0-2		4407		3		4*	5	12	7	8	9	10	11		1	2		6						
3	30	SHREWSBURY TOWN	3-2	Lewis(2), Barton	4709				4	5	3	11	8	9	10	7	1		2		6						
4	Sep 6	Chester	2-1	Lewis, Boylen	4902				4	5	3	7	8	9	10	11	1		2		6						
5	13	MILLWALL	2-1	Czuczman, Wigg	6466				6	5	3	7	8	11	10	9	1		2		4						
6	20	Sheffield Wednesday	0-4		11345		11		6	5	3	7			10	9	1		2	8	4						
7	23	HALIFAX TOWN	2-2	Hubbard, Lewis	6130		8		6	5	3	7			10	9	1			2	4					11	
8	27	ALDERSHOT	1-0	Partridge	5139		8		6	5	3	7	11		10	9	1			2	4						
9	Oct 4	Walsall	0-2		4113		10		6	5	3	7	11	9		8*	1			2	4			12			
10	11	Crystal Palace	0-3		15552		8		6	5	3	7	9	11	10		1		2	4							
11	18	BRIGHTON & HOVE ALBION	2-1	Wigg, Lewis	4938		8		6	5	3	7		11	10*	9	1		2	4				12			
12	25	Swindon Town	0-3		5873		3	12	6		11	8		9		10*	1		5	2	4			7			
13	Nov 1	BURY	0-0		5189		10		6		3*	8	9	11		12	1		5	2	4			7			
14	4	Peterborough United	2-4	Partridge(2)	7646		3		6			8	9	11	10		1		5	2	4			7			
15	8	Hereford United	2-3	Wigg, Barton	6391	1	3		6	5		8	9	11	10					2	4			7			
16	11	WREXHAM	3-2	Boylen, Young, Lewis	4850	1	3		6	5		8	9	11	10	4				2	7						
17	15	MANSFIELD TOWN	4-1	Partridge(2), Wigg, Lewis	4659	1	3		6	5		7	9	11	10	8				2	4						
18	29	PRESTON NORTH END	0-0		4519	1	3	6		4		7	9	11	10	8			5	2							
19	Dec 5	Southend United	2-5	Partridge, Lewis	2925	1	3	6		4		7	9	11	10	8*			5	2				12			
20	20	Port Vale	3-4	Lewis, OG, Wigg	2789	1	3	6		5	4	7	9	11	10	8			2								
21	26	ROTHERHAM UNITED	4-1	Partridge,Boylen,Lewis,Oldridge	6919		3	6		5	4*	7	9	11	10	8	1		2								12
22	27	Colchester United	0-1		3136		3	6		5		7	9	11	10	8	1		2			4					
23	Jan 3	CHESTERFIELD	3-0	Boylen(pen), Walton, Marley	4024		3		6		12	7		9	10	8	1		5	2		4*					11
24	10	Shrewsbury Town	0-1		3334		3		6		11	7		9	10	8	1		5	2	4						
25	17	SHEFFIELD WEDNESDAY	1-1	Wigg	7167		3		6		12	7	8	9	10		1		5	2	4						11*
26	24	Millwall	1-1	Waters	5486		3		6		11*	7	9	12	10		1		5	2	4		8				
27	31	Wrexham	0-1		2808		3	6			11	7	9	10			1		5	2	4		8				
28	Feb 7	PETERBOROUGH UNITED	1-1	Partridge	5482		3		6			7	9	11	10		1		5	2	4		8				
29	14	HEREFORD UNITED	1-0	Lewis	5944		3		6		12	7*	9	11	10		1		5	2	4		8				
30	21	Mansfield Town	0-1		6094		3		6		12	7	9	11	10	8*	1		5	2	4						
31	24	Halifax Town	1-2	Czuczman(pen)	2229		3		6	4	11	7	9	12	10		1		5	2*	8						
32	28	SWINDON TOWN	1-0	Partridge	5218		3		6			7	9	11	10		1		5	2	4		8				
33	Mar 6	Bury	1-1	Barton	4821		3		6			7	9	11	10		1		5	2	4		8				
34	9	WALSALL	1-2	Partridge	4942		3		6			7	9	11	10*		1		5	2	4		8	12			
35	13	CRYSTAL PALACE	1-2	Hubbard	8412		3		6			7	8	11	10	9	1		5	2			4				
36	17	Brighton & Hove Albion	2-4	Marley, Hubbard	17384		10	3	6	4		7	11	12		9*	1		5	2			8				
37	20	Preston North End	0-0		6586			3	6	4		7	11	12	10	9	1		5	2*			8				
38	27	SOUTHEND UNITED	2-2	Waters, Booth	4518		3		6		12	8	11*		10	9	1		5	2			4	7			
39	30	PORT VALE	1-1	Lewis	4322		3		6	4	11*	10		12		9	1		5	2			8	7			
40	Apr 3	Cardiff City	1-2	Lewis	9645		3		6	5	12	10*				9	1		2		4		8	7	11		
41	7	Aldershot	3-0	Barton(2), Booth	3069		3		6	5	11					9	1			2	4		8	7	10		
42	10	CHESTER	2-0	Hubbard, Cumming	4644		3		6	5	11					9	1			2	4		8	7	10		
43	16	Chesterfield	3-4	Booth, Hubbard, Lewis	5483		3*		6	5	11	7	12			9	1			2	4		8		10		
44	17	Rotherham United	0-3		4414	1		3	6	5	11*	9		12						2	4		8	7	10		
45	19	COLCHESTER UNITED	0-1		4682	1	3		6	5	11*	10		12		9				2	4		8	7			
46	24	GILLINGHAM	2-1	Cumming, Booth	4415	1	3		6	5*	11	10	9	12					2		4		8		7		
					Apps.	10	41	10	40	30	25	44	33	30	33	31	35	1	34	36	32	2	19	11	6	1	2
					Subs.			1			7		1	8		1								4		1	1
					Goals		3			1	2	15	10	7	4	6			2	2	5	1	2				1

1 own goal

F.A. Cup

					Att	Freeman	Booth	Govier	Gray	Young	Cumming	Lewis	Partridge	Wigg	Boylen	Hubbard	Wainman	Baker	Czuczman	Marley	Barton	Walton	Waters	Ford	Parkin	Brown	Oldridge
R1	Nov 22	GATESHEAD	1-3	Booth	5120	1	3		6	5		11	8		10	7				2	4			12		9*	

League Cup

					Att	Freeman	Booth	Govier	Gray	Young	Cumming	Lewis	Partridge	Wigg	Boylen	Hubbard	Wainman	Baker	Czuczman	Marley	Barton	Walton	Waters	Ford	Parkin	Brown	Oldridge
R1/1	Aug 19	Doncaster Rovers *	1-3	Wigg	3218	1*	3		4	5	6		8	9	10	7			2			12				11	
R1/2	25	DONCASTER ROVERS	0-0		5552		3		4	5		11	8	9	10	7	1		2		6						

Grimsby Town lost on aggregate scores

* Freeman injured, replaced in goal by Hubbard

		P	W	D	L	F	A	W	D	L	F	A	F	A	Pts
1	Hereford United	46	14	6	3	45	24	12	5	6	41	31	86	55	63
2	Cardiff City	46	14	7	2	38	13	8	6	9	31	35	69	48	57
3	Millwall	46	16	6	1	35	14	4	10	9	19	29	54	43	56
4	Brighton & Hove A.	46	18	3	2	58	15	4	6	13	20	38	78	53	53
5	Crystal Palace	46	7	12	4	30	20	11	5	7	31	26	61	46	53
6	Wrexham	46	13	6	4	38	21	7	6	10	28	34	66	55	52
7	Walsall	46	11	8	4	43	22	7	6	10	31	39	74	61	50
8	Preston North End	46	15	4	4	45	23	4	6	13	17	34	62	57	48
9	Shrewsbury Town	46	14	2	7	36	25	5	8	10	25	34	61	59	48
10	Peterborough Utd.	46	12	7	4	37	23	3	11	9	26	40	63	63	48
11	Mansfield Town	46	8	11	4	31	22	8	4	11	27	30	58	52	47
12	Port Vale	46	10	10	3	33	21	5	6	12	22	33	55	54	46
13	Bury	46	11	7	5	33	16	3	9	11	18	30	51	46	44
14	Chesterfield	46	11	5	7	45	30	6	4	13	24	39	69	69	43
15	Gillingham	46	10	8	5	38	27	2	11	10	20	41	58	68	43
16	Rotherham United	46	11	6	6	35	22	4	6	13	19	43	54	65	42
17	Chester	46	13	7	3	34	19	2	5	16	9	43	43	62	42
18	GRIMSBY TOWN	46	13	7	3	39	21	2	3	18	23	53	62	74	40
19	Swindon Town	46	11	4	8	42	31	5	4	14	20	44	62	75	40
20	Sheffield Wed.	46	12	6	5	34	25	0	10	13	14	34	48	59	40
21	Aldershot	46	10	8	5	34	26	3	5	15	25	49	59	75	39
22	Colchester United	46	9	6	8	25	27	3	8	12	16	38	41	65	38
23	Southend United	46	9	7	7	40	31	3	6	14	25	44	65	75	37
24	Halifax Town	46	6	5	12	22	32	5	8	10	19	29	41	61	35

SEASON 1975/76
Back: Cumming, Wigg, Govier, Czuczman, Partridge, Hubbard
Middle: Fraser (Physio), Booth, Freeman, Wainman, Gray, Young, Aitken (Train)
Front: Marley, Lewis, Barton, Casey (Man), Boylen, Brown, Coyle

SEASON 1976/77
Back: Aitken, Gray, Govier, Batch, Booth, Wainman, Partridge, Young, Wigg
Middle: Boylen, Cumming, Fraser (Physio), Casey (Man), Conner (Train), Waters, Lewis, Hubbard
Front: Oldridge, K.Moore

1976-77 23rd in Division 3

Captain: Dave Booth

	Date	Opponent	Score	Scorers	Att.	Wainman	Cumming	Moore K	Young	Blant	Govier	Whitehead	Waters	Lewis	Booth	Oldridge	Batch	Yates	Harper	Partridge	Donovan	Harding	Hanvey	Gray	Ford	Liddell	Wigg	Drinkell	Boylen	Brolly
1	Aug 21	Bury	0-2		4107	1	2	3	4	5	6*	7	8	9	10	11				12										
2	24	CRYSTAL PALACE	0-1		5841	1	2	3	4	5		7	8	11	6*	12				9									10	
3	28	PETERBOROUGH UNITED	2-2	Partridge, Waters(pen)	4057	1	2	3	5	6		7	4	9		11				8									10	
4	Sep 4	Mansfield Town	0-3		5220	1	2*	3	6	5		12	4	9		10				8	11				7					
5	11	BRIGHTON & HOVE ALBION	2-0	Partridge, Waters	4481	1	2	3	4	5			8	7						9		6							10	11
6	18	Oxford United	2-5	Brolly, Waters(pen)	3791	1	2	3	4	5			8	7						9		6							10	11
7	25	PRESTON NORTH END	1-0	Boylen	3896	1	2	3	4	5			8	7						9		6					12		10*	11
8	Oct 2	Rotherham United	2-3	Partridge, Lewis	3925	1	2	3	4	5*			8	7		12				9		6							10	11
9	9	CHESTER	0-0		3910	1	2	3	4	5			8*	7		12				9		6							10	11
10	16	YORK CITY	1-0	Lewis	4237	1		3	5				2	9		7*				4	8			6			12		10	11
11	22	Tranmere Rovers	0-2		3580	1	2	3	5				4	7		12				8				6			9		10*	11
12	30	Port Vale	0-2		3714	1	2	3	4							8				10	7	5		6			9			11
13	Nov 2	Gillingham	1-1	Partridge	4279	1	3		4				2			8				10	7	5		6			9			11
14	6	CHESTERFIELD	1-2	Partridge	3131	1	3		4*				2	12		8				10	7	5		6			9			11
15	13	Shrewsbury Town	1-2	Lewis	4639	1	3	6	4				2	7						8				5			9		10	11
16	27	PORTSMOUTH	1-0	Lewis	3836	1	2	3	5				4	7*						8	12			6			9		10	11
17	30	WREXHAM	3-0	Donovan(2), Wigg	4820	1	2	3	5				4							8	7			6*	12		9		10	11
18	Dec 18	READING	2-1	Waters, Lewis	3080	1	2*		6				4	7					3	8	12			5			9		10	11
19	27	Lincoln City	0-2		11645	1	3		4				2	7					6	8				5	12		9		10*	11
20	28	SHEFFIELD WEDNESDAY	1-1	Donovan	8000				5				2	7			1		3	8	4			6			9		10	11
21	Jan 3	PORT VALE	2-4	Partidge, Wigg	5666		2		5				4	7*	3		1			8	12			6			9		10	11
22	15	Crystal Palace	1-2	Wigg	13638		2		5				4		3		1			8	7			6			9		10	11
23	22	BURY	2-0	Donovan, Wigg	3638		2		5				4		3		1			8	7			6			9		10	11
24	29	NORTHAMPTON TOWN	0-1		3676		2		5				4		3	12	1			8	7			6			9		10*	11
25	Feb 1	Walsall	0-1		4405		2	10	5				4		3		1			8	7			6			9			11
26	5	Peterborough United	1-3	Brolly	5753		2	12	5				4		3		1			8	7			6			9*		10	11
27	12	MANSFIELD TOWN	0-1		5322		2		12				4	7	3		1			8	9*		5	6					10	11
28	16	Chesterfield	1-0	Donovan	3250	1	2		10				4	7	3					8	9		5	6						11
29	19	Brighton & Hove Albion	0-3		20412	1	2		10				4	7	3					8	9		5	6						11
30	26	OXFORD UNITED	1-2	Partridge	3865	1	2		12				4	8	3					9			5	6	7*				10	11
31	Mar 5	Preston North End	1-2	Young	7278	1			12				4	7	3			2		8	9*		5	6					10	11
32	8	Swindon Town	1-4	Lewis	6980	1			9				4	7	3			2		8			5	6					10	11
33	12	ROTHERHAM UNITED	1-1	Liddell	5792	1		3					4	7				2		8			5	6		9			10	11
34	19	Chester	0-2		3246	1	3						4	7				2		8			5	6		9			10	11
35	26	York City	1-1	Lewis	2798	1	10	3	6				4	7	12			2		8			5*			9				11
36	Apr 2	TRANMERE ROVERS	1-0	Partridge	2690	1	7	3					4	8	6			2		9			5			10				11
37	8	LINCOLN CITY	1-2	Partridge(pen)	8506	1	10	3					4	7	6			2		8			5			9				11
38	9	Sheffield Wednesday	0-1		10182	1	10	3					4		6			2		8	7		5			9				11
39	11	GILLINGHAM	1-1	Partridge	2820	1	10	3					4		6			2		8			5			7		9		11
40	16	Wrexham	2-3	Drinkell(2)	7878	1	10	3					4		6			2*		8			5			7		9	12	11
41	19	Northampton Town	0-0		5699	1	2						4	7	3					8			5	6		11		9	10	
42	23	SHREWSBURY TOWN	2-1	Donovan, Brolly	2430	1	2						4	7	3*					8	12		5	6		9			10	11
43	30	Portsmouth	2-1	Liddell, OG	10155	1	2	3					4	7						8			5	6		9			10	11
44	May 3	WALSALL	2-2	Waters, Partridge(pen)	2500	1	2*	3					4	7						8			5	6	12	9			10	11
45	7	SWINDON TOWN	2-0	Lewis, Liddell	3027	1	2	3					4	7*						8			5	6	12	9			10	11
46	14	Reading	0-2		3816	1	2	3					4	7						8			5	6		9		12	10*	11
					Apps.	38	41	27	30	9	1	3	45	34	21	7	8	10	3	45	17	8	20	31	2	14	16	3	32	41
					Subs.			1	3			1		1	1	5				1	4				4		2	1	1	
					Goals				1				5	8						11	6					3	4	2	1	3

1 own goal

F.A. Cup

	Date	Opponent	Score	Scorers	Att.	Wainman	Cumming	Moore K	Young	Blant	Govier	Whitehead	Waters	Lewis	Booth	Oldridge	Batch	Yates	Harper	Partridge	Donovan	Harding	Hanvey	Gray	Ford	Liddell	Wigg	Drinkell	Boylen	Brolly
R1	Nov 20	Droylsden	0-0		5000	1	3	5	4				2	9						7				6			8		10	11
R1r	24	DROYLSDEN	5-3	Gray,Lewis,Partridge(2,1p),Wigg	4464	1	3	6	4				2	7						8				5			9		10	11
R2	Dec 11	CHESTER	0-1		5729	1	2	3	5				4	12						7	8			6			9		10	11*

League Cup

	Date	Opponent	Score	Scorers	Att.	Wainman	Cumming	Moore K	Young	Blant	Govier	Whitehead	Waters	Lewis	Booth	Oldridge	Batch	Yates	Harper	Partridge	Donovan	Harding	Hanvey	Gray	Ford	Liddell	Wigg	Drinkell	Boylen	Brolly
R1/1	Aug 14	SHEFFIELD WEDNESDAY	0-3		6222	1	2	3	4		5		8	11	6					9				10	7					
R1/2	18	Sheffield Wednesday	0-0		10207	1	2	3	4	5	6		8*	11	10	7				9					12					

		P	W	D	L	F	A	W	D	L	F	A	F	A	Pts
1	Mansfield Town	46	17	6	0	52	13	11	2	10	26	29	78	42	64
2	Brighton & Hove A.	46	19	3	1	63	14	6	8	9	20	26	83	40	61
3	Crystal Palace	46	17	5	1	46	15	6	8	9	22	25	68	40	59
4	Rotherham United	46	11	9	3	30	15	11	6	6	39	29	69	44	59
5	Wrexham	46	15	6	2	47	22	9	4	10	33	32	80	54	58
6	Preston North End	46	15	4	4	48	21	6	8	9	16	22	64	43	54
7	Bury	46	15	2	6	41	21	8	6	9	23	38	64	59	54
8	Sheffield Wed.	46	15	4	4	39	18	7	5	11	26	37	65	55	53
9	Lincoln City	46	12	9	2	50	30	7	5	11	27	40	77	70	52
10	Shrewsbury Town	46	13	7	3	40	21	5	4	14	25	38	65	59	47
11	Swindon Town	46	12	6	5	48	33	3	9	11	20	42	68	75	45
12	Gillingham	46	11	8	4	31	21	5	4	14	24	43	55	64	44
13	Chester	46	14	3	6	28	20	4	5	14	20	38	48	58	44
14	Tranmere Rovers	46	10	7	6	31	23	3	10	10	20	30	51	53	43
15	Walsall	46	8	7	8	39	32	5	8	10	18	33	57	65	41
16	Peterborough Utd.	46	11	4	8	33	28	2	11	10	22	37	55	65	41
17	Oxford United	46	9	8	6	34	29	3	7	13	21	36	55	65	39
18	Chesterfield	46	10	6	7	30	20	4	4	15	26	44	56	64	38
19	Port Vale	46	9	7	7	29	28	2	9	12	18	43	47	71	38
20	Portsmouth	46	8	9	6	28	26	3	5	15	25	44	53	70	36
21	Reading	46	10	5	8	29	24	3	4	16	20	49	49	73	35
22	Northampton Town	46	9	4	10	33	29	4	4	15	27	46	60	75	34
23	GRIMSBY TOWN	46	10	6	7	29	22	2	3	18	16	47	45	69	33
24	York City	46	7	8	8	25	34	3	4	16	25	55	50	89	32

1977-78 6th in Division 4

Captain: Joe Waters

							Wainman	Cooper	Moore K	Waters	Barker	Partridge	Brolly	Liddell	Drinkell	Donovan	Batch	Mawer	Cumming	Booth	Hanvey	Lester	Ford	Boylen
1	Aug	20	DARLINGTON	2-0	Donovan(2)	3182	1	2	3	4	5	6	7*	8	9	10			12					11
2		26	Stockport County	0-2		3054	1	2	3	4	5	6	7	8	9	10								11
3	Sep	3	ROCHDALE	2-1	Partridge(pen), Waters	2516	1	2	3	4	5	6	7	8	9	10			11*				12	
4		6	Watford	0-1		6850	1		3	4	5	6	12	7*	9	8		2	10				11	
5		10	York City	2-1	Liddell, Brolly	1872	1		3	4	5	6	11	8	9			2	10				7	
6		13	HARTLEPOOL UNITED	2-1	Liddell, Drinkell	3790	1		3	4	5	6	11	8	9			2	10				7	
7		16	Swansea City	0-2		7402	1		3*	4	5	6	11	8	9	12		2	10				7	
8		24	DONCASTER ROVERS	0-0		4758	1		3	4	5	6	11	8*	9	12		2	10				7	
9		27	Southport	2-2	Drinkell, Waters	1843	1		3	4	5	6	11	8*	9	12		2	10				7	
10	Oct	1	Newport County	0-3		2746	1		3	4	5	6	11	8	9			2	10				7	
11		4	WIMBLEDON	3-1	Drinkell(2), Liddell	4048	1		3	4	5	6	11	8	9			2	10				7	
12		8	SCUNTHORPE UNITED	0-0		5249	1		3	4	5	6	11	8	9*	12		2	10				7	
13		14	Barnsley	2-1	Liddell, Cumming	6151	1		3	4	5	10	7	8	9			2	11		6			
14		22	ALDERSHOT	1-0	Cumming	4283	1		3	4	5	10	7	8	9	12		2	11*		6			
15		29	Huddersfield Town	3-1	Donovan(2), Liddell	5871	1		3	4	5	10	7	8		9		2	11		6			
16	Nov	5	Torquay United	1-3	Donovan	2301	1		3*	4	5	10	7	8		9		2	11		6		12	
17		12	READING	0-1		3762	1		3	4	5	10	7	8		9*		2	11		6		12	
18		19	Crewe Alexandra	2-0	Ford, Liddell	2227			12	4	5	10*	11	8	9		1	2	3		6		7	
19	Dec	3	BOURNEMOUTH	0-2		3767				4	5	10	11	8	9	12	1	2	3*		6		7	
20		10	Brentford	1-3	Liddell	5760			3	4	5	10	7	8	9*		1	2	11		6	12		
21		26	HALIFAX TOWN	0-0		6051	1		3	4	5	10	11	8*	12	9		2			6	7		
22		27	Northampton Town	1-2	Liddell	3518	1		3	4	5	10	11	8		9		2			6	7		
23		31	TORQUAY UNITED	3-1	Partridge(pen), Donovan(2)	3707	1		3	4	5	10	11	8	12	9		2			6	7*		
24	Jan	2	Southend United	1-1	Waters	9973	1		3	4	5	10	11	8		9		2			6		7	
25		14	Darlington	2-1	Cumming, Liddell	2265			3	4	5	9	11	10	12	8*	1	2	7		6			
26		21	STOCKPORT COUNTY	0-0		4716			3	4	5		11	10	9*	12	1	2	7		6	8		
27	Feb	4	YORK CITY	3-2	Hanvey, Donovan(2)	3282			3	4	5	10	7	8*	12	9	1	2	11		6			
28		25	NEWPORT COUNTY	1-0	Liddell	3937			3	4	5	10	7	8		9	1	2			6		11	
29		28	Doncaster Rovers	1-0	Waters	4280			3	4	5	10	7	8		9	1	2			6		11	
30	Mar	3	Scunthorpe United	1-2	Donovan	7612			3	4	5	10	7	8		9	1	2			6		11	
31		7	Hartlepool United	1-3	Liddell	2554			3	4	5	10	7	8		9	1	2			6		11	
32		11	BARNSLEY	1-0	Brolly	5005	1		3	4	5	10	7	8		9		2			6		11	
33		17	Aldershot	2-4	Brolly, Donovan	3606	1		3	4	5	10	7	8		9		2			6		11	
34		20	Rochdale	3-1	Drinkell, Waters, Ford	1042	1			4	5		7		8	9		2		3	6	10	11	
35		24	HUDDERSFIELD TOWN	1-0	Hanvey	7718	1			4	5		7		8	9		2		3	6	10	11	
36		25	NORTHAMPTON TOWN	0-1		4835	1			4	5	10*	7	8	12	9		2		3	6		11	
37		27	Halifax Town	0-0		2481	1		10	2	5*		11	8	12	9				3	6	4	7	
38	Apr	1	SOUTHEND UNITED	2-0	Brolly, Donovan	3505	1		5	4			11	8		9		2	10	3	6		7	
39		4	Wimbledon	2-2	Partridge, Lester	2380	1		5	4		12	11			9*		2	10	3	6	8	7	
40		8	Reading	0-0		3378	1		5	4		10	11	8				2		3	6	9	7	
41		11	WATFORD	1-1	Partridge	7189	1		5	4		10	11			8		2		3	6	9	7	
42		15	CREWE ALEXANDRA	2-2	Donovan, Lester	3826	1		5	4		10	11			8		2		3	6	9	7	
43		18	SWANSEA CITY	2-1	Donovan, Waters	5692	1		5	4		10	11			8		2		3	6	9	7	
44		22	Bournemouth	0-1		2515	1		5	4		10	11*			8		2	12	3	6	9	7	
45		25	SOUTHPORT	2-0	Waters, Lester	3966	1		3	4	5		11			8		2	10		6	9	7	
46		29	BRENTFORD	2-1	Waters, Brolly	4469	1		5	4			11	12		8		2	10	3*	6	9	7	
						Apps.	36	3	41	46	38	38	45	37	20	31	10	42	25	12	34	15	31	2
						Subs.			1			1	1	1	6	7			2			1	3	
						Goals				8		4	5	11	5	14			3		2	3	2	

F.A. Cup

							Wainman	Cooper	Moore K	Waters	Barker	Partridge	Brolly	Liddell	Drinkell	Donovan	Batch	Mawer	Cumming	Booth	Hanvey	Lester	Ford	Boylen
R1	Nov	26	Workington Town	2-0	Waters, Liddell	1200				4	5	10	11	8	9		1	2	3		6		7	
R2	Dec	17	BARNSLEY	2-0	Donovan(2)	6171	1		3	4	5	9	7	10		8		2	11		6			
R3	Jan	7	SOUTHAMPTON	0-0		16582			3*	4	5	10	11	8	12	9	1	2	7		6			
R3r		11	Southampton	0-0		22462			3	4	5	9	11	10*	12	8	1	2	7		6			
R32r		17	Southampton*	1-4	Waters	11556			3	4	5	8	11	10	12	9*	1	2	7		6			

* Played at Filbert Street, Leicester

League Cup

							Wainman	Cooper	Moore K	Waters	Barker	Partridge	Brolly	Liddell	Drinkell	Donovan	Batch	Mawer	Cumming	Booth	Hanvey	Lester	Ford	Boylen
R1/1	Aug	13	HARTLEPOOL UNITED	3-0	Waters(3,1pen)	2318	1	2	3	4	5	6	11	9	8	7								10
R1/2		16	Hartlepool United	2-1	Drinkell, Donovan	2733	1	2	3	4	5	6	7	8	9	10								11
R2		30	WATFORD	1-2	Donovan	4345	1	2	3	4	5	6	7	8	9*	10			11				12	

		P	W	D	L	F	A	W	D	L	F	A	F	A	Pts
1	Watford	46	18	4	1	44	14	12	7	4	41	24	85	38	71
2	Southend United	46	15	5	3	46	18	10	5	8	20	21	66	39	60
3	Swansea City	46	16	5	2	54	17	7	5	11	33	30	87	47	56
4	Brentford	46	15	6	2	50	17	6	8	9	36	37	86	54	56
5	Aldershot	46	15	8	0	45	16	4	8	11	22	31	67	47	54
6	GRIMSBY TOWN	46	14	6	3	30	15	7	5	11	27	36	57	51	53
7	Barnsley	46	15	4	4	44	20	3	10	10	17	29	61	49	50
8	Reading	46	12	7	4	33	23	6	7	10	22	29	55	52	50
9	Torquay United	46	12	6	5	43	25	4	9	10	14	31	57	56	47
10	Northampton Town	46	9	8	6	32	30	8	5	10	31	38	63	68	47
11	Huddersfield Town	46	13	5	5	41	21	2	10	11	22	34	63	55	45
12	Doncaster Rovers	46	11	8	4	37	26	3	9	11	15	39	52	65	45
13	Wimbledon	46	8	11	4	39	26	6	5	12	27	41	66	67	44
14	Scunthorpe United	46	12	6	5	31	14	2	10	11	19	41	50	55	44
15	Crewe Alexandra	46	11	8	4	34	25	4	6	13	16	44	50	69	44
16	Newport County	46	14	6	3	43	22	2	5	16	22	51	65	73	43
17	Bournemouth	46	12	6	5	28	20	2	9	12	13	31	41	51	43
18	Stockport County	46	14	4	5	41	19	2	6	15	15	37	56	56	42
19	Darlington	46	10	8	5	31	22	4	5	14	21	37	52	59	41
20	Halifax Town	46	7	10	6	28	23	3	11	9	24	39	52	62	41
21	Hartlepool United	46	12	4	7	34	29	3	3	17	17	55	51	84	37
22	York City	46	8	7	8	27	31	4	5	14	23	38	50	69	36
23	Southport	46	5	13	5	30	32	1	6	16	22	44	52	76	31
24	Rochdale	46	8	6	9	29	28	0	2	21	14	57	43	85	24

SEASON 1977/78
Back: Brolly, Cumming, Liddell, Donovan, Ford
Middle: Cooper, Booth, Barker, Wainman, Batch, Partridge, Hanvey, Young
Front: K.Moore, Waters, Newman (Man), Boylen, Drinkell

SEASON 1978/79
Back: Young, Partridge, Lester, Barker, K.Moore
Middle: Fraser (Physio), Liddell, Cumming, Batch, Wainman, Ford, D.Moore, Mitchell
Front: Donovan, Booth, Waters, Newman (Man), Drinkell, Mawer, Brolly

1978-79 2nd in Division 4

Captain: Joe Waters

							Batch	Mawer	Moore K	Waters	Barker	Crombie	Ford	Donovan	Lester	Mitchell	Cumming	Moore D	Wigginton	Brolly	Liddell	Drinkell	Young	Partridge
1	Aug	19	READING	2-1	Lester	3918	1	2	3	4	5	6	7	8	9	10*	11				12			
2		23	Wigan Athletic	3-0	Donovan(2), K.Moore	9227	1	2	3	4	5	6	7	8	9	10	11*				12			
3		26	Halifax Town	2-1	Donovan, Ford	2038	1	2	3	4	5	6	7	8	9	10				11				
4	Sep	2	TORQUAY UNITED	3-0	OG, Brolly, K.Moore	3934	1	2	3	4	5	6	7	8	9		10*			11	12			
5		9	Darlington	1-0	Brolly	2220	1	2	3	4	5	6	7		9					11	8		10	
6		12	WIMBLEDON	2-2	Waters(pen), OG	6974	1	2	3	4	5	6	7*		9					11	8		10	12
7		16	HARTLEPOOL UNITED	0-1		4729	1		3	2	5	6	7		9*	10				11	8	12	4	
8		23	Crewe Alexandra	3-0	K.Moore, Liddell(2)	2000	1	2	3	4	5	6	7							11	8	9		10
9		26	Huddersfield Town	0-2		4238	1	2	3	4	5	6	7							11	8	9		10
10		30	ROCHDALE	4-0	Brolly(2), Liddell(2)	3681	1	2	3	4	5	6	7							11	8	9	12	10*
11	Oct	7	Port Vale	1-1	Liddell	3433	1	2	3	4	5	6	7							11	8	9		10
12		14	PORTSMOUTH	1-0	K.Moore	5141	1	2	3	4	5	6	7							11	8	9	12	10*
13		17	NORTHAMPTON TOWN	4-3	Drinkell(2), Young, Brolly	5529	1	2	3	4	5	6	7							11	8	9	10	
14		21	Bournemouth	0-0		3399	1	2	3	4	5	6	7				12			11	8	9	10*	
15		28	HEREFORD UNITED	1-1	Drinkell	5349	1	2	3	4	5	6*	7				12			11	8	9	10	
16	Nov	4	Aldershot	0-2		3536	1	2	3	4	5	6	7				12			11	8*	9	10	
17		11	Torquay United	1-3	Drinkell	3136	1		3	4	5	6				11	10	2		7		9		8
18		18	HALIFAX TOWN	2-1	Cumming, K.Moore	4128	1		3	4	5	6	12			11	10	2		7		9		8*
19	Dec	4	Stockport County	1-2	K.Moore	3300	1		3	4	5	6	12		8	10	11	2		7		9*		
20		9	NEWPORT COUNTY	1-0	Barker	3667	1		3	4	5	6	7		9	8	10	2		11				
21		23	YORK CITY	3-0	Cumming(3,1pen)	4339	1		3	4	5	6	7		9	8	10	2		11				
22		26	Scunthorpe United	1-2	Cumming	8165	1		3	4	5	6	7		9	8	10	2		11*		12		
23	Jan	9	BRADFORD CITY	5-1	Ford(3), Mitchell, Cumming	4995	1		3	4	5	6	7		9	8	10	2		11*		12		
24		16	DARLINGTON	7-2	Lester(4), Ford, Waters, K.Moore	5387	1		3	4	5	6	7		9	8	10	2		11				
25		20	Hartlepool United	0-1		2212	1		3	4	5	6	7		9	8	10*	2		11		12		
26	Feb	3	HUDDERSFIELD TOWN	2-1	Waters, Ford	4921	1		3	4	5	6	8		9	10	11	2		7				
27		24	Portsmouth	3-1	Ford(2), Brolly	12782	1		3	4	5	6	8		9	10	11*	2		7		12		
28		27	CREWE ALEXANDRA	2-2	Ford, Cumming	6598	1		3	4	5	6	8		9*	10	11	2		7		12		
29	Mar	3	BOURNEMOUTH	1-0	Waters	5428	1		3	4		6	8		9	10	11	2	5	7*		12		
30		10	Hereford United	1-0	OG	2939	1		3	4		6	8			10	11	2	5	7		9		
31		13	Rochdale	5-2	Ford, Brolly, Liddell, Waters(pen), Mitchell	2395	1		3	4		6	8			10	11	2	5	7	9			
32		17	ALDERSHOT	0-0		6121	1		3	4		6	8			10	11	2	5	7	9			
33		20	Wimbledon	1-0	Waters	3452	1		3	4		6	8			10	11	2	5	7	9			
34		24	WIGAN ATHLETIC	3-1	Waters, Brolly, Ford	8252	1		3	4		6	8		11	10		2	5	7	9			
35		28	Reading	0-4		8394	1		3	4		6	8		11	10*		2	5	7	9	12		
36		31	Doncaster Rovers	1-0	Ford	4707	1		3	4		6	8		10		11	2	5	7	9*	12		
37	Apr	3	PORT VALE	1-0	Ford	7815	1		3	4		6	8		10		11	2	5	7	9			
38		7	STOCKPORT COUNTY	2-1	Cumming, Ford	7495	1		3	4		6	8		10		11	2	5	7	9*	12		
39		13	York City	0-0		5500	1		3	4		6	8		10		11	2	5	7	9			
40		14	SCUNTHORPE UNITED	1-1	Drinkell	10197	1		3*	4		6	8	12		10	11	2	5	7		9		
41		16	Bradford City	3-1	Waters, Ford, Drinkell	4505	1		3	4		6	8		10*		11	2	5	7	12	9		
42		21	BARNSLEY	2-0	Crombie, Lester	15585	1		3	4		6	8		10		11	2	5	7		9		
43		24	Northampton Town	2-1	Cumming, Waters	3450	1		3	4		6	8		10		11	2	5	7		9		
44		28	Newport County	1-1	Waters	3049	1		3	4		6	8		10		11	2	5	7		9		
45	May	5	DONCASTER ROVERS	3-4	Drinkell, Ford, Cumming	10243	1		3	4		6	8		10		11	2	5	7		9		
46		8	Barnsley	1-2	Lester	21261	1		3	4		6	8		10*		11	2	5	7	12	9		
						Apps.	46	15	46	46	28	46	43	4	30	24	31	30	18	44	21	20	7	7
						Subs.							2	1			3				5	10	2	1
						Goals			7	10	1	1	16	3	7	2	10			8	6	7	1	

3 own goals

F.A. Cup

							Batch	Mawer	Moore K	Waters	Barker	Crombie	Ford	Donovan	Lester	Mitchell	Cumming	Moore D	Wigginton	Brolly	Liddell	Drinkell	Young	Partridge
R1	Nov	25	Hartlepool United	0-1		3584	1		3	4	5	6	7		12	8	10	2		11*		9		

League Cup

							Batch	Mawer	Moore K	Waters	Barker	Crombie	Ford	Donovan	Lester	Mitchell	Cumming	Moore D	Wigginton	Brolly	Liddell	Drinkell	Young	Partridge
R1/1	Aug	12	YORK CITY	2-0	Waters(pen), Lester	3051	1	2	3	4	5	6	7	8	10	11	9							
R1/2		15	York City	3-0	Donovan, Mitchell, Cumming	2668	1	2	3	4	5	6	7	8	9*	10	11				12			
R2		29	Manchester City	0-2		21481	1	2	3	4	5	6	7	8	9	10	11*				12			

		P	W	D	L	F	A	W	D	L	F	A	F	A	Pts
1	Reading	46	19	3	1	49	8	7	10	6	27	27	76	35	65
2	GRIMSBY TOWN	46	15	5	3	51	23	11	4	8	31	26	82	49	61
3	Wimbledon	46	18	3	2	50	20	7	8	8	28	26	78	46	61
4	Barnsley	46	15	5	3	47	23	9	8	6	26	19	73	42	61
5	Aldershot	46	16	5	2	38	14	4	12	7	25	33	63	47	57
6	Wigan Athletic	46	14	5	4	40	24	7	8	8	23	24	63	48	55
7	Portsmouth	46	13	7	3	35	12	7	5	11	27	36	62	48	52
8	Newport County	46	12	5	6	39	28	9	5	9	27	27	66	55	52
9	Huddersfield Town	46	13	8	2	32	15	5	3	15	25	38	57	53	47
10	York City	46	11	6	6	33	24	7	5	11	18	31	51	55	47
11	Torquay United	46	14	4	5	38	24	5	4	14	20	41	58	65	46
12	Scunthorpe United	46	12	3	8	33	30	5	8	10	21	30	54	60	45
13	Hartlepool United	46	7	12	4	35	28	6	6	11	22	38	57	66	44
14	Hereford United	46	12	8	3	35	18	3	5	15	18	35	53	53	43
15	Bradford City	46	11	5	7	38	26	6	4	13	24	42	62	68	43
16	Port Vale	46	8	10	5	29	28	6	4	13	28	42	57	70	42
17	Stockport County	46	11	5	7	33	21	3	7	13	25	39	58	60	40
18	Bournemouth	46	11	6	6	34	19	3	5	15	13	29	47	48	39
19	Northampton Town	46	12	4	7	40	30	3	5	15	24	46	64	76	39
20	Rochdale	46	11	4	8	25	26	4	5	14	22	38	47	64	39
21	Darlington	46	8	8	7	25	21	3	7	13	24	45	49	66	37
22	Doncaster Rovers	46	8	8	7	25	22	5	3	15	25	51	50	73	37
23	Halifax Town	46	7	5	11	24	32	2	3	18	15	40	39	72	26
24	Crewe Alexandra	46	3	7	13	24	41	3	7	13	19	49	43	90	26

1979-80 1st in Division 3

Captain: Joe Waters

	Date	Opponent	Score	Scorers	Att.	Batch	Moore D	Moore K	Waters	Wigginton	Stone	Brolly	Ford	Liddell	Mitchell	Cumming	Crombie	Kilmore	Drinkell	Cawthorne	Crosby	Mawer	Lester
1	Aug 18	EXETER CITY	4-1	Cumming, Liddell(2), Waters(pen)	5937	1	2	3	4	5	6	7	8	9	10	11							
2	22	Chester	1-3	K.Moore	3779	1	2	3	4	5	6	7	8	9	10	11							
3	25	BLACKPOOL	4-3	Waters(pen), Cumming(2), K.Moore	7306	1	2	3	4	5	6	7	8	9	10	11							
4	Sep 1	Blackburn Rovers	0-0		8877	1	2	3	4	5	6	7	8	9	10	11							
5	8	PLYMOUTH ARGYLE	1-0	Cumming	7244	1	2	3	4	5	6	7	8	9*	10	11							12
6	15	Brentford	0-1		7121	1	2	3	4	5	6	7	8*	9	10	11	12						
7	18	Bury	1-1	Kilmore	3176	1	2	3	4	5		7		9	10	11	6	8					
8	22	COLCHESTER UNITED	1-2	Kilmore	6962	1	2	3	4	5	6*	7		9	10	11		8					12
9	29	Swindon Town	0-3		6825	1	2	3	4	5		7	8*	9	10	11	6	12					
10	Oct 2	BURY	1-0	Cumming	7109	1	2	3	4	5		7		8	10	11*	6	9	12				
11	6	Millwall	0-2		5057	1	2	3	4	5		7		9	10	11	6	8*	12				
12	9	CHESTER	0-2		8007	1	2	3	4	5		7	8	9	10*	11	6	12					
13	13	CHESTERFIELD	1-1	Kilmore	6559	1	2	3	4	5			7		10	11	6	8	9				
14	20	Gillingham	1-0	Kilmore	6378	1	2	3	4	5		7		12	10	11	6	8*	9				
15	23	Sheffield Wednesday	0-2		13885	1	2	3	4	5		7			10	11	6	8	9				
16	27	ROTHERHAM UNITED	2-0	Waters, Cumming	7702	1		3	4	5	2	7	8	12	10*	11	6		9				
17	Nov 3	Exeter City	2-1	Ford, OG	4356	1		3	4	5	2	7	8*	12	10	11	6		9				
18	6	SHEFFIELD WEDNESDAY	3-1	Drinkell, Wigginton, Ford	14900	1		3	4	5	2	7	8		10	11	6		9				
19	9	Southend United	0-1		4119	1		3	4	5	2	7	8		10	11	6		9				
20	17	WIMBLEDON	1-0	Waters(pen)	6716	1		3	4	5	2	7	11	8	10		6	9					
21	Dec 1	Oxford United	1-0	Kilmore	3361	1		3	4	5	2	7		12	10	11	6	8	9*				
22	8	MANSFIELD TOWN	2-1	Ford, Waters(pen)	7663	1		3	4	5	2	7	11	12	10		6	8*	9				
23	21	Carlisle United	2-0	Kilmore, K.Moore	4663	1		3	4	5	2	7			10	11	6	8	9				
24	26	BARNSLEY	3-0	Kilmore(2), Cumming	14153	1		3	4	5	2	7	8*	12	10	11	6	9					
25	29	Sheffield United	1-1	Cumming	21800	1	2	3	4	5		7	8	9	10	11	6						
26	Jan 12	BLACKBURN ROVERS	1-2	Brolly	10965	1			4	5	2	7	11		10		6	8*	9		3	12	
27	15	READING	2-1	Drinkell, Kilmore	8532	1		3	4	5*	2	11	7		10		6	8	9			12	
28	19	Plymouth Argyle	1-1	**Cumming**	6310	1		3	4	5	2	7	8		10	11*	6	12	9				
29	26	Blackpool	3-0	Drinkell(2), Cumming	4932	1	2	3	4	5	6	7			10	11		8	9				
30	Feb 2	BRENTFORD	5-1	Brolly, Drinkell(2), Kilmore, Waters	9669	1		3	4	5	2	8	12		10	11*	6	7	9				
31	8	Colchester United	1-2	OG	5149	1		3	4	5	2	11	7		10		6	8	9				
32	16	SWINDON TOWN	2-0	Cumming, Ford	12675	1		3	4	5	2	7	12		10	11	6	8*	9				
33	23	Chesterfield	3-2	Drinkell, Cumming, Kilmore	13867	1		3	4	5	2	7	12		10	11	6	8	9*				
34	Mar 1	GILLINGHAM	1-0	Drinkell	11246	1	2		4	5		7	11		10	3	6	8*	9			12	
35	8	Rotherham United	0-0		9032	1	2	3	4	5		7	12		10	11	6	8*	9				
36	15	MILLWALL	2-0	Kilmore, Drinkell	10923	1	2	3	4	5		7	12		10	11*	6	8	9				
37	22	SOUTHEND UNITED	1-0	Ford	10532	1	2	5	4			7	11		10	3	6	8	9				
38	25	Hulll City	2-2	Brolly, Drinkell	14176	1		3*	4			7	11		10	2	6	8	9	5	12		
39	29	Wimbledon	6-3	Kilmore(3), Cumming, Drinkell, Mitchell	2485	1	2		4	5		7	11		10*	3	6	8	9		12		
40	Apr 4	CARLISLE UNITED	2-0	Mitchell, Drinkell	15121	1	2		4	5		7	11		10	3	6	8	9				
41	5	Barnsley	1-0	Brolly	16433	1	2		4	5		7	11		10	3	6	8*	9		12		
42	7	HULL CITY	1-1	Cumming	18363	1	2	3	4	5		7	8		10	11	6		9				
43	12	Reading	1-1	Waters	9549	1	2	3	4	5	12	7	8		10	11*	6		9				
44	19	OXFORD UNITED	2-0	K.Moore, Drinkell	11735	1	2	3	4	5	12	7	8		10	11*	6		9				
45	26	Mansfield Town	0-0		10100	1	2	3	4	5	11	7	8		10		6		9				
46	May 3	SHEFFIELD UNITED	4-0	Drinkell(3), Waters	19276	1	2	3	4	5	12	7	8		10*	11	6		9				
					Apps.	46	29	41	46	44	25	45	32	14	46	40	38	27	31	1	1		
					Subs.						3		5	6			1	3	2		3	3	2
					Goals			4	8	1		4	5	2	2	14		15	16				

2 own goals

F.A. Cup

	Date	Opponent	Score	Scorers	Att.	Batch	Moore D	Moore K	Waters	Wigginton	Stone	Brolly	Ford	Liddell	Mitchell	Cumming	Crombie	Kilmore	Drinkell	Cawthorne	Crosby	Mawer	Lester
R1	Nov 24	CHESTERFIELD	1-1	Waters	8406	1		3	4	5	2	7	8		10	11	6	9*	12				
R1r	27	Chesterfield	3-2	K.Moore, Drinkell, Kilmore	7820	1		3	4	5	2	7	8*		10	11	6	12	9				
R2	Dec 15	SHEFFIELD UNITED	2-0	Waters, Crombie	14849	1		3	4	5	2	11	7	12	10		6	8	9*				
R3	Jan 5	Liverpool	0-5		49706	1	2		4	5	6	7	12		10	11	3	8*	9				

League Cup

	Date	Opponent	Score	Scorers	Att.	Batch	Moore D	Moore K	Waters	Wigginton	Stone	Brolly	Ford	Liddell	Mitchell	Cumming	Crombie	Kilmore	Drinkell	Cawthorne	Crosby	Mawer	Lester
R1/1	Aug 11	SCUNTHORPE UNITED	2-0	Ford(2)	5083	1	2	3	4	5	6	7	8	9	10	11*			12				
R1/2	14	Scunthorpe United	0-0		3908	1	2	3	4	5	6	11	7	8	10				9				
R2/1	28	HUDDERSFIELD TOWN	1-0	Cumming	7803	1	2	3	4	5	6	7	8	9	10	11							
R2/2	Sep 4	Huddersfield Town	4-1	Lester, Ford, Cumming(2)	5550	1	2	3	4*	5	6	7	8	9	10	11							12
R3	25	NOTTS COUNTY	3-1	Ford, Liddell, Cumming	11881	1	2	3	4	5		7	8	9*	10	11	6		12				
R4	Oct 30	EVERTON	2-1	Brolly(2)	22043	1		3	4	5	2	7	8		10	11	6		9				
R5	Dec 4	WOLVERHAMPTON WANDS.	0-0		23115	1		3	4	5	2	7	8		10	11	6		9				
R5r	11	Wolverhampton Wands.	1-1	OG	28455	1		3	4	5	2	11	7	8	10		6		9				
R52r	18	Wolverhampton Wands. *	0-2		16475	1		3	4	5	2	7	8*	12	10	11	6		9				

*** Played at the Baseball Ground, Derby**

		P	W	D	L	F	A	W	D	L	F	A	F	A	Pts
1	GRIMSBY TOWN	46	18	2	3	46	16	8	8	7	27	26	73	42	62
2	Blackburn Rovers	46	13	5	5	34	17	12	4	7	24	19	58	36	59
3	Sheffield Wed.	46	12	6	5	44	20	9	10	4	37	27	81	47	58
4	Chesterfield	46	16	5	2	46	16	7	6	10	25	30	71	46	57
5	Colchester United	46	10	10	3	39	20	10	2	11	25	36	64	56	52
6	Carlisle United	46	13	6	4	45	26	5	6	12	21	30	66	56	48
7	Reading	46	14	6	3	43	19	2	10	11	23	46	66	65	48
8	Exeter City	46	14	5	4	38	22	5	5	13	22	46	60	68	48
9	Chester	46	14	6	3	29	18	3	7	13	20	39	49	57	47
10	Swindon Town	46	15	4	4	50	20	4	4	15	21	43	71	63	46
11	Barnsley	46	10	7	6	29	20	6	7	10	24	36	53	56	46
12	Sheffield United	46	13	5	5	35	21	5	5	13	25	45	60	66	46
13	Rotherham United	46	13	4	6	38	24	5	6	12	20	42	58	66	46
14	Millwall	46	14	6	3	49	23	2	7	14	16	36	65	59	45
15	Plymouth Argyle	46	13	7	3	39	17	3	5	15	20	38	59	55	44
16	Gillingham	46	8	9	6	26	18	6	5	12	23	33	49	51	42
17	Oxford United	46	10	4	9	34	24	4	9	10	23	38	57	62	41
18	Blackpool	46	10	7	6	39	34	5	4	14	23	40	62	74	41
19	Brentford	46	10	6	7	33	26	5	5	13	26	47	59	73	41
20	Hull City	46	11	7	5	29	21	1	9	13	22	48	51	69	40
21	Bury	46	10	4	9	30	23	6	3	14	15	36	45	59	39
22	Southend United	46	11	6	6	33	23	3	4	16	14	35	47	58	38
23	Mansfield Town	46	9	9	5	31	24	1	7	15	16	34	47	58	36
24	Wimbledon	46	6	8	9	34	38	4	6	13	18	43	52	81	34

SEASON 1979/80

Back: Wainwright, D.Moore, Collins, Shelton
Middle (standing): King (Comm Man), Kerr (Man), Lester, Liddell, Stone, Batch, Wainman, Young, Wiggington, K.Moore, Booth (Yth Coach), Dowse (Sec)
Middle (seated): Crombie, Mawer, Cumming, Waters, Brolly, Ford, Mitchell
Front: Fell, Crosby, O'Dell, Nicholson

SEASON 1980/81

Back: Kerr (Man), Fraser (Physio), Steeples, Beacock, Wainwright, Crombie, Cawthorne, Wigginton, Stone, K.Moore, D.Moore, Bridges (Groundsman), King (Comm.Man), Booth (Coach)
Middle: Dowse (Sec), Batch, Liddell, Mawer, Ford, Drinkell, Waters, Cumming, Mitchell, Brolly, Kilmore, Wainman
Front: Fell, Nicholson, O'Dell, Crosby

1980-81 7th in Division 2

Captain: Joe Waters

							Batch	Stone	Moore K	Waters	Wigginton	Crombie	Brolly	Ford	Drinkell	Mitchell	Cumming	Crosby	Whymark	Kilmore	Czuczman	Moore D	Liddell	Steeples	Beacock
1	Aug	16	Shrewsbury Town	1-1	Drinkell	4998	1	2	3	4	5	6	7	8	9	10	11								
2		19	PRESTON NORTH END	0-0		10461	1	2	3	4	5	6	7	8	9	10	11								
3		23	WREXHAM	1-0	Ford	9175	1	2	3	4	5	6	7	8		10	11			12			9*		
4		30	Bristol Rovers	2-2	Cumming(2)	4461	1	2	3	4	5	6	7	8	9	10	11								
5	Sep	6	Orient	0-2		4506	1	2	3	4	5	6	7	8*	9	10	11						12		
6		13	DERBY COUNTY	0-1		15502	1	2	3	4	5	6	7		9	10	11			8*			12		
7		20	Blackburn Rovers	0-2		10838	1	2	3	4	5	6	7*	12	9	10	11						8		
8		27	LUTON TOWN	0-0		9044	1		6	4	5			7	9	10	11	3			2		8		
9	Oct	4	BRISTOL CITY	1-0	Drinkell	8781	1		6	4	5		12	7	9	10	11	3		8*	2				
10		7	Notts County	0-0		8017	1		6	4	5		12	7	9	10	11	3		8*	2				
11		11	Chelsea	0-3		15206	1		6	4	5		12	7	9	10	11*	3		8	2				
12		18	WATFORD	1-1	K.Moore	8906	1	2	6	4	5		12	7*	9	10	11	3		8					
13		21	SHEFFIELD WEDNESDAY	0-0		10298	1	2	6	4	5		7	8	9	10	11	3							
14		24	Swansea City	0-1		12928	1	2	6	4	5		7	8	9	10	11	3							
15	Nov	1	QUEENS PARK RANGERS	0-0		10015	1	2	6	4	5		7*	8	9	10	11	3		12					
16		8	West Ham United	1-2	Stone	15468	1	2	6	4	5		7		9	10		3		8			11*	12	
17		15	SHREWSBURY TOWN	1-0	Cumming	8737	1	2	6	4	5	3	7	8*	9	10	11			12					
18		22	Bolton Wanderers	1-1	Stone	9031	1	2	6	4	5	3	7*	8	9	10	11			12					
19		29	CAMBRIDGE UNITED	3-1	Waters, Brolly, Cumming	7592	1	2	6	4	5	3	7	8*	9	10	11			12					
20	Dec	2	Preston North End	4-2	Cumming, Ford, Brolly(2)	5209	1	2	6	4	5	3	7	8	9	10	11*			12					
21		6	Cardiff City	1-1	Waters(pen)	6023	1	2	6	4	5	3	7	11	9	10			8*	12					
22		13	CHELSEA	2-0	Whymark, Ford	14708	1		6	4	5	3	7	11	9	10			8*	12		2			
23		20	Watford	1-3	Kilmore	10209	1		6	4	5	3	7	11*	9	10			8	12		2			
24		26	NEWCASTLE UNITED	0-0		17623	1	2	6	4		3	7	11*	9	10	12		8		5				
25		27	Oldham Athletic	2-1	Waters, Ford	7183	1	2		4		6	7*	8	9	10	11	3	12		5				
26	Jan	10	BOLTON WANDERERS	4-0	Cumming, Drinkell(2), Waters(pen)	9320	1	2	6	4	5	3	7	8	9	10	11*						12		
27		17	BRISTOL ROVERS	2-0	Cumming, Drinkell	9601	1	2	6	4	5	3	7*	8	9	10	11		12						
28		21	Wrexham	2-0	Cumming(2)	5619	1	2	6	4	5	3	7		9	10	11		8						
29	Feb	7	Derby County	1-2	Waters(pen)	19691	1	2	6	4	5	3	7*		9	10	11		8	12					
30		14	ORIENT	2-0	Waters(2pens)	10190	1	2	6	4	5	3	7		9	10	11		8						
31		21	Luton Town	2-0	Cumming, Waters	9217	1	2	6	4	5	3	7		9*	10	11		8	12					
32		28	BLACKBURN ROVERS	0-0		12210	1		6	4	5	3	7		9	10	11		8			2			
33	Mar	10	Bristol City	1-1	Cumming	5881	1		6	4	5	3	7		9	10	11		8			2			
34		14	NOTTS COUNTY	2-1	Whymark, Brolly	12184	1	2	6	4	5	3	7		9	10			8	11*				12	
35		28	SWANSEA CITY	1-0	Whymark	12166	1	2	6	4	5	3	7		9	10			8	12				11*	
36	Apr	4	Queens Park Rangers	0-1		8906	1	2	6	4	5	3	7*		9	10	11		8	12					
37		11	WEST HAM UNITED	1-5	Waters(pen)	17924	1	2	6	4	5	3	7	12	9	10	11		8						
38		18	OLDHAM ATHLETIC	0-0		10634	1	2	6	4	5	3*	7	12	9	10			8					11*	
39		20	Newcastle United	1-1	Drinkell	13215	1	2	6	4	5	3	11	7	9	10			8*	12					
40		25	CARDIFF CITY	0-1		7377	1	2	6	4	5	3			9	10	11		8	12				7*	
41		28	Sheffield Wednesday	2-1	Drinkell, Kilmore	16747	1	2	6	4	5	3	11		9*	10			8	7					12
42	May	2	Cambridge United	1-5	Waters(pen)	4528	1		6	4	5	3	11		9	10			8	7*		2			12
						Apps.	42	33	41	42	40	33	36	25	41	42	31	10	19	9	6	5	4	3	
						Subs.							4	3			1		2	15			3	2	2
						Goals		2	1	10			4	4	7		11		3	2					

F.A. Cup

							Batch	Stone	Moore K	Waters	Wigginton	Crombie	Brolly	Ford	Drinkell	Mitchell	Cumming	Crosby	Whymark	Kilmore	Czuczman	Moore D	Liddell	Steeples	Beacock
R3	Jan	3	West Bromwich Albion	0-3		22477	1	2	6	4	5	3	7*	12	9	10	11		8						

League Cup

							Batch	Stone	Moore K	Waters	Wigginton	Crombie	Brolly	Ford	Drinkell	Mitchell	Cumming	Crosby	Whymark	Kilmore	Czuczman	Moore D	Liddell	Steeples	Beacock
R1/1	Aug	9	NOTTS COUNTY	1-0	Waters	7402	1	2	3	4	5	6	7	8	9	10	11								
R1/2		12	Notts County	0-3		4718	1	2	3	4	5	6	7	8	9	10	11								

Anglo Scottish Cup

							Batch	Stone	Moore K	Waters	Wigginton	Crombie	Brolly	Ford	Drinkell	Mitchell	Cumming	Crosby	Whymark	Kilmore	Czuczman	Moore D	Liddell	Steeples	Beacock
Q1	Jul	28	Hull City	0-1		4848	1	2	3	4	5	6	7	8	9*	10	11						12		
Q2	Aug	2	CHESTERFIELD	3-3	Brolly, Drinkell, Ford	3148	1	2	3	4	5	6	7	8	9	10	11								
Q3		5	Sheffield Wednesday	1-0	Waters	4921	1	2		4	5	6	7	8	9	10	3			12			11*		

	P	W	D	L	F	A	W	D	L	F	A	F	A	Pts
1 West Ham United	42	19	1	1	53	12	9	9	3	26	17	79	29	66
2 Notts County	42	10	8	3	26	15	8	9	4	23	23	49	38	53
3 Swansea City	42	12	5	4	39	19	6	9	6	25	25	64	44	50
4 Blackburn Rovers	42	12	8	1	28	7	4	10	7	14	22	42	29	50
5 Luton Town	42	10	6	5	35	23	8	6	7	26	23	61	46	48
6 Derby County	42	9	8	4	34	26	6	7	8	23	26	57	52	45
7 GRIMSBY TOWN	42	10	8	3	21	10	5	7	9	23	32	44	42	45
8 Queen's Park Rgs.	42	11	7	3	36	12	4	6	11	20	34	56	46	43
9 Watford	42	13	5	3	34	18	3	6	12	16	27	50	45	43
10 Sheffield Wed.	42	14	4	3	38	14	3	4	14	15	37	53	51	42
11 Newcastle United	42	11	7	3	22	13	3	7	11	8	32	30	45	42
12 Chelsea	42	8	6	7	27	15	6	6	9	19	26	46	41	40
13 Cambridge United	42	13	1	7	36	23	4	5	12	17	42	53	65	40
14 Shrewsbury Town	42	9	7	5	33	22	2	10	9	13	25	46	47	39
15 Oldham Athletic	42	7	9	5	19	16	5	6	10	20	32	39	48	39
16 Wrexham	42	5	8	8	22	24	7	6	8	21	21	43	45	38
17 Orient	42	9	8	4	34	20	4	4	13	18	36	52	56	38
18 Bolton Wanderers	42	10	5	6	40	27	4	5	12	21	39	61	66	38
19 Cardiff City	42	7	7	7	23	24	5	5	11	21	36	44	60	36
20 Preston North End	42	8	7	6	28	26	3	7	11	13	36	41	62	36
21 Bristol City	42	6	10	5	19	15	1	6	14	10	36	29	51	30
22 Bristol Rovers	42	4	9	8	21	24	1	4	16	13	41	34	65	23

1981-82 17th in Division 2

Captain: Joe Waters

	Date		Opponent	Score	Scorers	Att.	Batch	Stone	Crombie	Waters	Wigginton	Moore K	Brolly	Whymark	Drinkell	Mitchell	Kilmore	Moore D	Crosby	Cooper	Ford	Cumming	Beacock	Czuczman	O'Dell	Ward	Steeples	Grotier
1	Aug	29	LEICESTER CITY	2-2	Kilmore, Drinkell	11032	1	2	3	4	5	6	7*	8	9	10	11				12							
2	Sep	1	Watford	2-0	Ford(2)	11257	1	2	3	4	5	6	7	8*	9	10	11				12							
3		5	Orient	2-1	Ford, Kilmore	3764	1	2	3	4	5	6	7		9	10	11*				8	12						
4		12	QUEENS PARK RANGERS	2-1	Cumming(2)	9490	1	2	3	4	5	6	7		9	10*	12				8	11						
5		19	Charlton Athletic	0-2		6875	1	2	3*	4	5	6		8	9	10	12				7	11						
6		22	NORWICH CITY	1-2	Whymark	10185	1	2	3*	4	5	6	7	8	9	10	12					11						
7		26	SHEFFIELD WEDNESDAY	0-1		13110	1		3	4	5	6	7	8	9	10	12	2				11*						
8	Oct	3	Bolton Wanderers	2-1	Drinkell, Mitchell	7217	1		3	4	5	6	7	8	9	10		2			12	11*						
9		10	CAMBRIDGE UNITED	1-2	Ford	7450	1		3	4		6	7	8	9*	10		2			12	11		5				
10		17	Luton Town	0-6		9090	1		3	4		6	7	8	9	10	12	2			11*			5				
11		24	BLACKBURN ROVERS	1-1	Wigginton	7159	1	2*	3	4	5	6		9		10	12				8	11					7	
12		31	Derby County	1-1	K.Moore	11706	1		3	4*	5	6	12	9		10		2			7	11				8		
13	Nov	7	Wrexham	0-2		3351	1		3		5	6	4	9		10	8	2			7	11*	12					
14		21	Chelsea	1-1	Ford	11931	1				5	3	7	9	12	10		2			11			6	4*	8		
15		28	NEWCASTLE UNITED	1-1	Mitchell	9256	1		3		5	6	7	9		10		2			8	11			4*	12		
16	Dec	5	Oldham Atheltic	1-3	Ford	5907	1		3		5	6	7	9	12	10		2			8	11			4*			
17	Jan	9	ORIENT	1-2	Waters	6877	1		3	4	5	6	7*	9		10	12	2			8	11						
18		30	CHARLTON ATHLETIC	3-3	Drinkell(2), K.Moore	7088	1	4	3			5	12		9	10	8	2	6		7		11*					
19	Feb	6	Queens Park Rangers	0-1		8753	1	4		12	5	6	11		9	10	8	2	3		7*							
20		9	ROTHERHAM UNITED	1-2	Waters(pen)	8629	1	7		4	5	6	11*		9	10	8	2	3		12							
21		20	Sheffield Wednesday	1-1	Waters(pen)	14654	1	7	3	4	5	6	11		9	10		2			8							
22		27	Cambridge United	2-2	Brolly, Drinkell	3542	1	7	3	4	5	6	11		9	10		2			8							
23	Mar	2	BOLTON WANDERERS	1-1	Waters(pen)	6525	1		3	4	5	6	11		9	10		2*			8		7				12	
24		6	LUTON TOWN	0-0		7733	1		3	4		6	7		9	10		2		5	8	11						
25		13	Blackburn Rovers	0-2		8676	1		3	4		6	7	12	9			2		5	8*	11	10					
26		16	WATFORD	0-2		6146	1		3	4		6	7	12	9		8	2		5		11*	10					
27		20	DERBY COUNTY	1-0	Kilmore	7573	1		3	4		6	7	12	9		8*	2		5		11	10					
28		23	Barnsley	2-3	Drinkell, Whymark	15383	1		3	4		6	7	12	9		8	2		5		11*	10					
29		27	WREXHAM	1-1	Kilmore	6216	1		3	4		6	7	12	9		8	2		5		11	10*					
30		30	Cardiff City	1-2	Whymark(pen)	3924	1	4	3			6	7	9		10	8	2		5*	12	11						
31	Apr	3	Crystal Palace	3-0	Kilmore, K.Moore, Whymark	7541	1	5	3*	4		6	7	9		10	8	2	12			11						
32		9	BARNSLEY	3-2	Whymark, K.Moore, Waters	12218	1	5		4		6	7*	9		10	8	2	3		12	11						
33		10	Rotherham United	2-2	Whymark, Ford	10011	1		6	4			11	9*		10	8	2	3	5	7		12					
34		17	CHELSEA	3-3	D.Moore, Cooper, Kilmore	9164	1		6	4			11	9	12	10	8	2*	3	5	7							
35		20	CRYSTAL PALACE	0-1		7696	1		6	4			11	9	12	10*	8	2	3	5	7							
36		24	Newcastle United	1-0	Brolly, Drinkell	14011	1	7	6	4			11	9			8*	2	3	5	12		10					
37		27	SHREWSBURY TOWN	5-1	Whymark,Waters(p),Crosby,Brolly,D.Moore	7051	1	7	6	4		10*	11	9			8	2	3	5	12							
38	May	1	OLDHAM ATHLETIC	2-1	Whymark, Waters(pen)	7656	1	7	6	4		10	11*	9			8	2	3	5	12							
39		5	Norwich City	1-2	Whymark	18360	1	2	6	4		10*	11	9			8		3	5	7		12					
40		8	Shrewsbury Town	0-2		4036	1	10	6	4			12	9	8			2	3	5	7	11*						
41		12	Leicester City	2-1	Whymark(2)	13941	1	7	6	4				9			8	2	3	5	11		10					
42		15	CARDIFF CITY	0-1		8148	1		6	4		5		9	12		8	2	3		7	11	10*					
						Apps.	42	21	38	35	20	36	35	28	23	30	23	34	14	16	25	23	10	3	3	2	1	
						Subs.				1			3	5	5		7		1		10	1	3			1	1	
						Goals				7	1	4	3	11	6	2	6	2	1	1	7	2						

F.A. Cup

	Date		Opponent	Score	Scorers	Att.	Batch	Stone	Crombie	Waters	Wigginton	Moore K	Brolly	Whymark	Drinkell	Mitchell	Kilmore	Moore D	Crosby	Cooper	Ford	Cumming	Beacock	Czuczman	O'Dell	Ward	Steeples	Grotier
R3	Jan	5	Millwall	6-1	Brolly,Whymark,Drinkell(2),Cumming(2)	5824	1		3	4*	5	6	7	8	9	10		2			12	11						
R4		23	Newcastle United	2-1	Kilmore, Drinkell	25632	1	4	3			5		9*	12	10	8	2	6		7		11					
R5	Feb	13	Queens Park Rangers	1-3	K.Moore	13334	1	11	3	4	5	6	7		9	10*		2			8		12					

League Cup

	Date		Opponent	Score	Scorers	Att.	Batch	Stone	Crombie	Waters	Wigginton	Moore K	Brolly	Whymark	Drinkell	Mitchell	Kilmore	Moore D	Crosby	Cooper	Ford	Cumming	Beacock	Czuczman	O'Dell	Ward	Steeples	Grotier
R2/1	Oct	6	WATFORD	1-0	K.Moore	7044	1		3	4	5	6	7	8	9	10		2			12	11*						
R2/2		27	Watford	1-3	Whymark	13213	1		3	4	5	6	7	8	9	10	11*					2			12			

League Group Cup

(preliminary rounds played in groups of four)

	Date		Opponent	Score	Scorers	Att.	Batch	Stone	Crombie	Waters	Wigginton	Moore K	Brolly	Whymark	Drinkell	Mitchell	Kilmore	Moore D	Crosby	Cooper	Ford	Cumming	Beacock	Czuczman	O'Dell	Ward	Steeples	Grotier
C1	Aug	15	CHESTERFIELD	1-0	Waters	1772	1	2	3	4	5		7	8*	9	10	12					11+		6		13		
C2		18	SHEFFIELD UNITED	2-0	Whymark, Mitchell	2314	1	2	3	4	5		7	8	9*	10	11				12			6				
C3		22	Doncaster Rovers	2-0	K. Moore, Brolly	4097	1	2	3	4	5	6	7*	8	9	10	11							12				
QF	Dec	8	Newport County	2-0	Beacock, Drinkell	2206	1		3	4	5	6	7	8*	9	13		2				11	10+			12		
SF	Jan	19	SHREWSBURY TOWN	2-1	Kilmore(2)	3253	1	7	3	4*		6		9		10	8	2			11		12	5				
F	Apr	6	WIMBLEDON	3-2	Cumming, Ford(2)	3423	1+			2		6	12	9		10		5	3		8	11			4		7*	13

		P	W	D	L	F	A	W	D	L	F	A	F	A	Pts
1	Luton Town	42	16	3	2	48	19	9	10	2	38	27	86	46	88
2	Watford	42	13	6	2	46	16	10	5	6	30	26	76	42	80
3	Norwich City	42	14	3	4	41	19	8	2	11	23	31	64	50	71
4	Sheffield Wed.	42	10	8	3	31	23	10	2	9	24	28	55	51	70
5	Queen's Park Rgs.	42	15	4	2	40	9	6	2	13	25	34	65	43	69
6	Barnsley	42	13	4	4	33	14	6	6	9	26	27	59	41	67
7	Rotherham United	42	13	5	3	42	19	7	2	12	24	35	66	54	67
8	Leicester City	42	12	5	4	31	19	6	7	8	25	29	56	48	66
9	Newcastle United	42	14	4	3	30	14	4	4	13	22	36	52	50	62
10	Blackburn Rovers	42	11	4	6	26	15	5	7	9	21	28	47	43	59
11	Oldham Athletic	42	9	9	3	28	23	6	5	10	22	28	50	51	59
12	Chelsea	42	10	5	6	37	30	5	7	9	23	30	60	60	57
13	Charlton Athletic	42	11	5	5	33	22	2	7	12	17	43	50	65	51
14	Cambridge United	42	11	4	6	31	19	2	5	14	17	34	48	53	48
15	Crystal Palace	42	9	2	10	25	26	4	7	10	9	19	34	45	48
16	Derby County	42	9	8	4	32	23	3	4	14	21	45	53	68	48
17	GRIMSBY TOWN	42	5	8	8	29	30	6	5	10	24	35	53	65	46
18	Shrewsbury Town	42	10	6	5	26	19	1	7	13	11	38	37	57	46
19	Bolton Wanderers	42	10	4	7	28	24	3	3	15	11	37	39	61	46
20	Cardiff City	42	9	2	10	28	32	3	6	12	17	29	45	61	44
21	Wrexham	42	9	4	8	22	22	2	7	12	18	34	40	56	44
22	Orient	42	6	8	7	23	24	4	1	16	13	37	36	61	39

SEASON 1981/82

Back: Fell, K.Moore, Batch, Cawthorne, Robinson, Czuczman, D.Moore
Middle (standing): Kerr (Man), Fraser (Physio), Steeples, Crosby, Ford, Beacock, Ward, Stone, Crombie, Wigginton, Kilmore, Booth (coach), Wainman (Yth Coach)
Middle (seated): O'Dell, Mitchell, Drinkell, Waters, Cumming, Brolly, Whymark
Front: Wilkinson, Thorpe

SEASON 1982/83

Back: Crosby, Crombie, Beacock, K.Moore, D.Moore Middle: Ford, Stone, Batch, Grotier, Cooper, Kilmore
Seated: Steeples, O'Dell, Waters, Drinkell, Whymark, Cumming

1982-83 19th in Division 2

Captain: Mick Speight(Aug-Nov), Joe Waters(Nov-May)

	Date	Opponent	Score	Scorers	Att.	Batch	Moore D	Crombie	Waters	Cooper	Moore K	Ford	Kilmore	Drinkell	Bonnyman	Whymark	Grotier	Speight	Crosby	Cumming	Stone	Whitlock	Saxby	Wilkinson	O'Dell	Beacock	Steeples
1	Aug 28	LEEDS UNITED	1-1	Kilmore	16137	1	2	3	4	5	6	7*	8	9	10	11										12	
2	Sep 4	Carlisle United	3-2	Waters(pen), Drinkell (2,1pen)	4683	1	2	3	4	5	6	7*	8	9	10	11		12									
3	7	BLACKBURN ROVERS	5-0	Drinkell,Kilmore(2),Waters,Ford	7567	1		3	4	5	6	7	8	9	10	11		2									
4	11	SHREWSBURY TOWN	2-0	Drinkell, Waters(pen)	7599	1			4	5	6	7	8	9	10	11*		2	3	12							
5	18	Charlton Athletic	1-0	Kilmore	4361	1	2	3	4	5	6		12	9	10	8*		11		7							
6	25	BOLTON WANDERERS	1-0	Cumming	7583	1	2	3	4	5	6			9	10	8		11		7							
7	28	Middlesbrough	4-1	Waters(2pens),Cooper,Crombie	5927	1	2	3	4	5	6		12	9	10	8*		11		7							
8	Oct 2	Chelsea	2-5	Drinkell, Cumming	10019	1	2*	3	4	5	6		12	9	10	8		11		7							
9	9	Leicester City	0-2		9640	1		3*	4	5	6	7	8	9	10			2		11						12	
10	16	DERBY COUNTY	1-1	Waters	7572		2		4	5	6		8	9	10	12	1	11*	3	7							
11	23	Sheffield Wednesday	0-2		17904		2		4	5	6	12	8	9	10	11	1		3*	7							
12	30	CAMBRIDGE UNITED	1-0	Drinkell	5738		2					11	7	9	10	8	1	6		3	5	4					
13	Nov 6	Wolverhampton Wands.	0-3		12701		2					11	7*	9	10	8	1	6	12	3	5	4					
14	13	FULHAM	0-4		6952	1	2		4	7		11		9	10	8			3		5	6					
15	20	BARNSLEY	1-2	Whymark	7219	1	2		4	5		11	12	9	10*	8		7		3		6					
16	27	Oldham Athletic	1-1	Ford	5508	1	2		4	5	3	7		9	10	8				11*	12	6					
17	Dec 4	CRYSTAL PALACE	4-1	Drinkell(3), Cumming	5295	1	2		4	5	3	7		9	10	8				11		6					
18	11	Queens Park Rangers	0-4		9811	1	2		4	5	3	7		9	10	8					11	6					
19	18	BURNLEY	3-2	Cumming, Bonnyman, Drinkell	5448	1	2	3	4		6	7		9	10	8				11	5						
20	27	Rotherham United	0-3		9231	1	2	3	4		6	7		9	10	8				11	5						
21	28	NEWCASTLE UNITED	2-2	Drinkell(2)	14983	1	2	3	4	5	6	7		9	10	8				11*		12					
22	Jan 1	Barnsley	0-4		12318	1	2	3	4	5	6	7		9		8				11					10		
23	3	CARLISLE UNITED	2-1	Drinkell, Ford	6377	1	2	3	4	5	6	7		9		8				11					10		
24	15	Leeds United	0-1		13583	1	2	3	4		6	7		9	11	8					5				10		
25	22	CHARLTON ATHLETIC	1-1	Wilkinson	5990	1	2	3	4		6	7		9	11*	8					5			12	10		
26	Feb 5	Blackburn Rovers	1-2	Cumming	4724	1	2	3	4	5	6	7		9	10			11		8							
27	12	CHELSEA	2-1	Drinkell(2)	6711	1	2	3	4	5	6	7		9	10					8					11		
28	19	LEICESTER CITY	2-0	Ford, Drinkell	6963	1	2	3	4	5	6	7		9	10					8					11		
29	26	Derby County	0-2		12775	1	2	3	4	5	6	7		9	10					8					11		
30	Mar 5	SHEFFIELD WEDNESDAY	1-1	Cumming	9472	1	2	3	4		6	7		9	10				5	8					11		
31	12	Cambridge United	0-1		3337	1	2	3	4		6	7			9				10*	8	12		5		11		
32	19	WOLVERHAMPTON WANDS.	1-1	Waters(pen)	7600	1	2	3	4		6	7			8				5	11	10*			9	12		
33	26	Fulham	0-4		8906	1	2	12	4		6	7			8				3	11			5*	9	10		
34	Apr 2	Newcastle United	0-4		20143	1	2	3	4		6	7	12	9	8*				5	11					10		
35	4	ROTHERHAM UNITED	1-2	Waters	7117	1		12	4		6	7	8	9	10					3	2*		5		11		
36	8	Shrewsbury Town	0-0		4446	1	2	3	4		6	7		9	8					11			5		10		
37	16	MIDDLESBROUGH	0-3		5985	1	2	3	4		6	7		9	8					11			5*	12	10		
38	23	Crystal Palace	0-2		5909	1	2	3	4	7*	6	11	12	9	8								5		10		
39	30	OLDHAM ATHLETIC	0-2		4755	1	2	3	4		6	7	11*	9	10	8							5		12		
40	May 2	Bolton Wanderers	0-0		5866	1	2	3	4		6	7		9	10	8				11			5				
41	7	Burnley	1-1	Drinkell	7083	1	2	3	4		6	7		9	10	8				11			5				
42	14	QUEENS PARK RANGERS	1-1	Cumming	9590	1	2	3	4		6	7	12	9	10	8*				11			5				
					Apps.	38	38	30	40	24	38	36	11	39	40	27	4	12	9	32	10	7	10	2	15		
					Subs.			2				1	7			1		1	1	1	2	1		2	2	2	
					Goals			1	8	1		4	4	17	1	1				7				1			

F.A. Cup

	Date	Opponent	Score	Scorers	Att.	Batch	Moore D	Crombie	Waters	Cooper	Moore K	Ford	Kilmore	Drinkell	Bonnyman	Whymark	Grotier	Speight	Crosby	Cumming	Stone	Whitlock	Saxby	Wilkinson	O'Dell	Beacock	Steeples
R3	Jan 8	Scunthorpe United	0-0		11010	1	2	3	4	5	6	7		9		8				11					10		
R3r	11	SCUNTHORPE UNITED	2-0	Waters(pen), Ford	9509	1	2	3	4		6	7		9*	11	8					5			12	10		
R4	29	Ipswich Town	0-2		21455	1	2	3	4	5	6	7		9	10	8*		11						12			

League Cup

	Date	Opponent	Score	Scorers	Att.	Batch	Moore D	Crombie	Waters	Cooper	Moore K	Ford	Kilmore	Drinkell	Bonnyman	Whymark	Grotier	Speight	Crosby	Cumming	Stone	Whitlock	Saxby	Wilkinson	O'Dell	Beacock	Steeples
R1/1	Aug 31	Scunthorpe United	2-1	Drinkell(2)	2620	1	2	3	4	5	6	7	8	9	10	11											
R1/2	Sep 14	SCUNTHORPE UNITED	0-0		3347	1			4	5	6	7	8	9	10	11		2*	3	12							
R2/1	Oct 12	SHEFFIELD UNITED	3-3	Drinkell(3)	5295		2		4	5	6		8	9	10		1	11	3	7							
R2/2	26	Sheffield United	1-5	K.Moore	13367		2		4	5*	6	11		9		8	1		3	7	10				12		

League Trophy

Date	Opponent	Score	Scorers	Att.	Batch	Moore D	Crombie	Waters	Cooper	Moore K	Ford	Kilmore	Drinkell	Bonnyman	Whymark	Grotier	Speight	Crosby	Cumming	Stone	Whitlock	Saxby	Wilkinson	O'Dell	Beacock	Steeples
Aug 14	Sheffield United	3-1	Drinkell(3)	5831	1	2	3	4	5	6	7*		9	10+	8		11								13	12
18	Lincoln City	1-2	Drinkell	1430	1	2	11	4	5	6	12	7	9	10	8*			3								
21	SCUNTHORPE UNITED	2-0	K.Moore, Waters(pen)	2334	1	2	3	4	5	6	7*	13	9	10	8+		11		12							

		P	W	D	L	F	A	W	D	L	F	A	F	A	Pts
1	Queen's Park Rgs.	42	16	3	2	51	16	10	4	7	26	20	77	36	85
2	Wolverhampton W.	42	14	5	2	42	16	6	10	5	26	28	68	44	75
3	Leicester City	42	11	4	6	36	15	9	6	6	36	29	72	44	70
4	Fulham	42	13	5	3	36	20	7	4	10	28	27	64	47	69
5	Newcastle United	42	13	6	2	43	21	5	7	9	32	32	75	53	67
6	Sheffield Wed.	42	9	8	4	33	23	7	7	7	27	24	60	47	63
7	Oldham Athletic	42	8	10	3	38	24	6	9	6	26	23	64	47	61
8	Leeds United	42	7	11	3	28	22	6	10	5	23	24	51	46	60
9	Shrewsbury Town	42	8	9	4	20	15	7	5	9	28	33	48	48	59
10	Barnsley	42	9	8	4	37	28	5	7	9	20	27	57	55	57
11	Blackburn Rovers	42	11	7	3	38	21	4	5	12	20	37	58	58	57
12	Cambridge United	42	11	7	3	26	17	2	5	14	16	43	42	60	51
13	Derby County	42	7	10	4	27	24	3	9	9	22	34	49	58	49
14	Carlisle United	42	10	6	5	44	28	2	6	13	24	42	68	70	48
15	Crystal Palace	42	11	7	3	31	17	1	5	15	12	35	43	52	48
16	Middlesbrough	42	8	7	6	27	29	3	8	10	19	38	46	67	48
17	Charlton Athletic	42	11	3	7	40	31	2	6	13	23	55	63	86	48
18	Chelsea	42	8	8	5	31	22	3	6	12	20	39	51	61	47
19	GRIMSBY TOWN	42	9	7	5	32	26	3	4	14	13	44	45	70	47
20	Rotherham United	42	6	7	8	22	29	4	8	9	23	39	45	68	45
21	Burnley	42	10	4	7	38	24	2	4	15	18	42	56	66	44
22	Bolton Wanderers	42	10	2	9	30	26	1	9	11	12	35	42	61	44

1983-84 5th in Division 2

Captain: Joe Waters

							Batch	Cumming	Crombie	Waters	Nicholl	Moore K	Ford	Wilkinson	Drinkell	Bonnyman	Emson	Speight	Whymark	Moore A	Cooper	Lund	Henshaw	Agnew	Shearer
1	Aug	27	SHREWSBURY TOWN	1-1	Drinkell	5177	1	2	3	4	5	6	7	8	9	10	11								
2	Sep	3	Cardiff City	1-3	Waters	5135	1	2	3	4		6	7	8*	9	10	11		12		5				
3		6	LEEDS UNITED	2-0	Drinkell, Waters(pen)	7797	1		3	4	5	6	7		9	10	11		8		2				
4		10	NEWCASTLE UNITED	1-1	Speight	9000	1		3	4	5	6	7		9		11	10	8		2				
5		17	Middlesbrough	1-1	Waters	10239	1		3	4	5	6	7	8	9		11	10			2				
6		24	FULHAM	2-1	Wilkinson, Emson	5769	1	12	3	4	5	6	7	8	9*		11	10			2				
7		27	Barnsley	1-3	Wilkinson, Emson	10966	1	12	3	4	5	6	7	9			11	10			2	8*			
8	Oct	1	Manchester City	1-2	Emson	25080	1	12	3	4*	5	6	7	8	9		11	10			2				
9		8	Huddersfield Town	0-0		8897	1	2	3	4	5	6	7	8	9		11	10							
10		15	BRIGHTON & HOVE ALBION	5-0	Wilkinson(2),Ford,Lund,Emson	5969	1	2	3	4	5	6	7	9			11	10*				8	12		
11		22	CRYSTAL PALACE	2-0	Waters, Ford	6075	1	2	3	4	5	6	7	8	9	10	11								
12		29	Derby County	2-1	Drinkell(2)	11531	1	2	3	4	5	6	7	8	9		11	10							
13	Nov	5	Portsmouth	0-4		12906	1	2	3	4	5	6	7		9		11*	10	12						8
14		12	CHARLTON ATHLETIC	2-1	Drinkell, Whymark	5584	1	2	3	4		6	7	8	9		11	10	5						
15		19	Swansea City	1-0	K.Moore	6178	1	2	3	4	5	6	7	8	9		11	10							
16		26	CARLISLE UNITED	1-1	Waters(pen)	5665	1	2	3	4	5	6	7	8	9		11	10							
17	Dec	4	Blackburn Rovers	1-1	Bonnyman	6409	1	2	3	4	5	6	7	8*	9	12	11	10							
18		13	OLDHAM ATHLETIC	3-0	Ford, Speight, Wilkinson	4825	1	2	3	4	5	6	7	8		12	11	10*	9						
19		17	Chelsea	3-2	Waters, Emson, Ford	13151	1	2	3	4	5	6	7	8		10	11		9						
20		26	SHEFFIELD WEDNESDAY	1-0	Wilkinson	16197	1	3		4	5	6	7	8		10	11		9	2					
21		28	Cambridge United	2-2	Emson, Ford	4319	1	3		4	5	6	7	8	12	10	11		9*	2					
22		31	CARDIFF CITY	1-0	Emson	7164	1	2	3	4	5	6	7		9	10	11		8						
23	Jan	2	Fulham	1-1	Drinkell	7351	1	2	3	4	5	6	7		9	10	11		8						
24		14	Shrewsbury Town	2-1	Drinkell, Wilkinson	3343	1		3	4	5	6	7	8	9	10	11			2					
25		21	MIDDLESBROUGH	0-0		7342	1	2	3	4	5	6	7	8	9	10	11								
26	Feb	4	MANCHESTER CITY	1-1	Wilkinson	11986	1	2*	3	4	5	6	7	8	9	10	11	12							
27		11	Newcastle United	1-0	Drinkell	28526	1	2	3	4	5	6	7	8	9	10	11								
28		21	DERBY COUNTY	2-1	Wilkinson, Drinkell	8530	1	2	3	4	5	6	7	8	9	10	11								
29		25	Crystal Palace	1-0	Ford	5956	1	2	3	4	5	6	7	8	9	10	11								
30	Mar	3	PORTSMOUTH	3-4	Drinkell, Ford, Cumming	8729	1	2	3	4	5	6	7	8	9	10	11								
31		10	Charlton Athletic	3-3	Drinkell(2), Ford	7626	1	2	3	4	5	6	7	8	9	10	11*	12							
32		17	Leeds United	1-2	Wilkinson	14412	1		3	4	5	6	7	8	9	10	11	2							
33		31	HUDDERSFIELD TOWN	2-1	Waters(pen), Bonnyman	7541	1		3	4	5	6	7	8	9	10	11			2					
34	Apr	7	Brighton & Hove Albion	0-2		10610	1		3	4	5	6	7	8*	9	10	11			2					12
35		10	BARNSLEY	1-0	Wilkinson	6769	1		3	4	5	6	7	8	9	10*	11	2							12
36		14	SWANSEA CITY	3-0	Drinkell(3)	5851	1		3	4	5	6	7	8	9	10	11*	2							12
37		21	Sheffield Wednesday	0-1		25828	1		3	4*	5	6	7	8		10	11	2		12		9			
38		23	CAMBRIDGE UNITED	0-0		5828	1	2	3		5	6*	7	8	9		11	4				12	10		
39		28	Carlisle United	1-1	Wilkinson	3512	1	2	3		5	6	7	8	9	10	11	4							
40	May	5	BLACKBURN ROVERS	3-2	Bonnyman(pen), Lund(2)	4826	1	2*	3			6	7	8	9	10		4		5		12	11		
41		7	Oldham Athletic	1-2	Lund	4156	1		6		5		7	8	9	10		4		2		11		3	
42		12	CHELSEA	0-1		13000	1		3		5	6	7	8	9	10		4		2		12	11*		
						Apps.	42	27	40	37	39	41	42	37	35	27	39	23	9	8	7	4	3	1	1
						Subs.		3							1	2		2	2	1		3	1		3
						Goals			1	7		1	8	12	15	3	6	2	1			4			

F.A. Cup

							Batch	Cumming	Crombie	Waters	Nicholl	Moore K	Ford	Wilkinson	Drinkell	Bonnyman	Emson	Speight	Whymark	Moore A	Cooper	Lund	Henshaw	Agnew	Shearer
R3	Jan	7	Portsmouth	1-2	Drinkell	12707	1	2	3	4	5	6	7	8	9	10	11								

League Cup

							Batch	Cumming	Crombie	Waters	Nicholl	Moore K	Ford	Wilkinson	Drinkell	Bonnyman	Emson	Speight	Whymark	Moore A	Cooper	Lund	Henshaw	Agnew	Shearer
R1/1	Aug	30	York City	1-2	Wilkinson	3505	1	2	3	4	5	6	7	8	9	10	11								
R1/2	Sep	13	YORK CITY *	2-0	Drinkell(2)	3529	1	12	3	4	5	6	7	8	9		11	10			2*				
R2/1	Oct	4	COVENTRY CITY	0-0		6088	1	2	3	4	5	6	7	8	9		11						10		
R2/2		25	Coventry City	1-2	Wilkinson	8705	1	2	3	4	5	6	7	8	9	10	11								

* After extra time

		P	W	D	L	F	A	W	D	L	F	A	F	A	Pts
1	Chelsea	42	15	4	2	55	17	10	9	2	35	23	90	40	88
2	Sheffield Wed.	42	16	4	1	47	16	10	6	5	25	18	72	34	88
3	Newcastle United	42	16	2	3	51	18	8	6	7	34	35	85	53	80
4	Manchester City	42	13	3	5	43	21	7	7	7	23	27	66	48	70
5	GRIMSBY TOWN	42	13	6	2	36	15	6	7	8	24	32	60	47	70
6	Blackburn Rovers	42	9	11	1	35	19	8	5	8	22	27	57	46	67
7	Carlisle United	42	10	9	2	29	13	6	7	8	19	28	48	41	64
8	Shrewsbury Town	42	13	5	3	34	18	4	5	12	15	35	49	53	61
9	Brighton & Hove A.	42	11	6	4	42	17	6	3	12	27	43	69	60	60
10	Leeds United	42	13	4	4	33	16	3	8	10	22	40	55	56	60
11	Fulham	42	9	6	6	35	24	6	6	9	25	29	60	53	57
12	Huddersfield Town	42	8	6	7	27	20	6	9	6	29	29	56	49	57
13	Charlton Athletic	42	13	4	4	40	26	3	5	13	13	38	53	64	57
14	Barnsley	42	9	6	6	33	23	6	1	14	24	30	57	53	52
15	Cardiff City	42	11	3	7	32	27	4	3	14	21	39	53	66	51
16	Portsmouth	42	8	3	10	46	32	6	4	11	27	32	73	64	49
17	Middlesbrough	42	9	8	4	26	18	3	5	13	15	29	41	47	49
18	Crystal Palace	42	8	5	8	18	18	4	6	11	24	34	42	52	47
19	Oldham Athletic	42	10	6	5	33	27	3	2	16	14	46	47	73	47
20	Derby County	42	9	5	7	26	26	2	4	15	10	46	36	72	42
21	Swansea City	42	7	4	10	20	28	0	4	17	16	57	36	85	29
22	Cambridge United	42	4	7	10	20	33	0	5	16	8	44	28	77	24

SEASON 1983/84

Back: K.Moore, A.Moore, Grotier, Hannay, Batch, Wilkinson, Nicholl
Middle (standing): Fraser (Physio), Lund, Crombie, Bonnyman, Stone, Ford, Emson, Henshaw, Whymark, Booth (Man)
Middle (seated): Shearer, Drinkell, Waters, Cumming, Speight, Cooper
Front: Foster, Matthews, Holgeth, Topliss

SEASON 1984/85

Front: Crombie, Wilkinson, Grotier, Batch, A.Moore, Matthews
Middle: Booth (Man.), K.Moore, Lund, Emson, Rowbotham, Henshaw, Ford, Foley, Nicholl (Play/Ass.Man.)
Front: Hine, Bonnyman, Drinkell, Cumming, Seagraves, Agnew

1984-85 10th in Division 2

Captain: Kevin Moore

No.	Date	Opponent	Score	Scorers	Att.	Batch	Cumming	Crombie	Foley	Nicholl	Moore K	Ford	Lund	Wilkinson	Bonnyman	Emson	Drinkell	Seagraves	Robinson	Moore A	Felgate	Agnew	Hine	Henshaw	Grotier	Matthews	Rowbotham	Dawson
1	Aug 25	BARNSLEY	1-0	Wilkinson	6190	1	2	3	4	5	6	7	8*	9	10	11	12											
2	27	Manchester City	0-3		21137	1	2*	3	4	5	6	7		8	10	11	9	12										
3	Sep 1	Middlesbrough	5-1	Drinkell(2),Emson,Wilkinson,Ford	5179	1		3	4	5	6	7		8	10	11	9	2										
4	4	CHARLTON ATHLETIC	2-1	Drinkell, Ford	5692	1		3	4	5	6	7		8	10	11	9	2										
5	8	LEEDS UNITED	0-2		13290	1		3	4	5	6	7		8	10	11	9	2										
6	15	Blackburn Rovers	1-3	Wilkinson	5203	1		3	4	5	6	7		8	10	11	9	2*						12				
7	22	OXFORD UNITED	1-2	Bonnyman	5563	1		3	4	5	6	7	12	8	10		9		2					11*				
8	29	Sheffield United	3-2	Lund(3)	12438	1		3	4	5	6	7	9	8	10	11			2									
9	Oct 6	OLDHAM ATHLETIC	4-1	Emson(2), Wilkinson, Foley	5072	1		3	4	5	6	7	9	8	10	11			2									
10	13	Portsmouth	2-3	Wilkinson(2)	13624	1		3	4	5	6	7		8	10	11			2							9		
11	20	CARLISLE UNITED	1-0	Lund	4832	1		3	4	5	6	7	9	8	10	11		2										
12	27	Cardiff City	4-2	Lund, Wilkinson, Emson, Drinkell	4500	1		5	4		6	7	9	8	10	11*	12	2				3						
13	Nov 3	Notts County	1-1	K.Moore	5750	1			4	5	6	7	9*	8	10	11	12	2				3						
14	10	WOLVERHAMPTON WANDS.	5-1	Wilkinson,OG,Ford,Bonnyman,Drinkell	7220	1		3	4	5	6	7	9	8*	10	11	12	2										
15	17	FULHAM	2-4	Ford, Lund	6287	1		3	4	5	6	7	9	8	10	11	12	2*										
16	24	Wimbledon	1-1	K.Moore	3314	1		3	4	5	6	7		8	10	11	9	2										
17	Dec 1	SHREWSBURY TOWN	2-1	Wilkinson, Bonnyman	6146	1		3	4	5	6	7		8	10	11	9	2										
18	8	Brighton & Hove Albion	0-0		9367	1		3	4	5	6	7		8	10	11	9	2										
19	15	CRYSTAL PALACE	1-3	Wilkinson	5814	1		3	4	5	6	7	12	8	10	11	9	2*										
20	22	MIDDLESBROUGH	3-1	K.Moore, Wilkinson, Drinkell	5650	1			4	5	6	7	12	8*	10	11	9	2				3						
21	26	Birmingham City	1-2	Drinkell	14168	1	12	3	4	5	6	7		8	10	11*	9	2										
22	29	Charlton Athletic	1-4	K.Moore	3853	1	12	3	4	5	6	7		8	10	11	9*	2										
23	Jan 1	HUDDERSFIELD TOWN	5-1	Cumming(2),Lund,Foley,Wilkinson	8790	1		5	4		6	7	9	8	10	11		2				3						
24	12	BLACKBURN ROVERS	1-1	Lund	7851			5	4		6	7	9	8	10	11		2				3			1			
25	Feb 2	SHEFFIELD UNITED	0-2		7261		12	5	4		6	7	9	8	10	11*			2			3			1			
26	9	Leeds United	0-0		12517			3	4*		6	7	12	8	10	11	9		2	5								1
27	23	NOTTS COUNTY	2-0	Drinkell(2)	4966		12	3	4	5		7	8*		10	11	9		2	6	1							
28	Mar 2	CARDIFF CITY	6-3	Bonnyman(2,2pens),Drinkell(2),Ford,Lund	4285		12	3	4	5		7*	8		10	11	9		2	6	1							
29	5	Wolverhampton Wands.	1-0	Ford	6127		11	3	4	5	6	7		8	10		9		2		1							
30	9	CARLISLE UNITED	1-1	Wilkinson	3218		11	3	4	5	6*	7		8	10	12	9		2		1							
31	16	PORTSMOUTH	2-3	Cumming, Wilkinson	6197		11	3	4	5	6*	7		8	10	12	9		2		1							
32	23	Oldham Athletic	0-2		3388		11	6		5		7	12	8			9		2		1	3	10*				4	
33	30	Oxford United	0-1		8587		11	3		5		7	8				9	2		6	1		4	10				
34	Apr 5	BIRMINGHAM CITY	1-0	Henshaw(pen)	6926		11	3		5		7	8				9	2		6	1		4	10				
35	9	Huddersfield Town	0-0		5834		11*	3		5		7	8			12	9	2		6	1		4	10				
36	13	MANCHESTER CITY	4-1	Drinkell, Lund(2), Cumming	8362		11	3		5		7	8				9	2		6	1		4	10				
37	20	Fulham	1-2	Lund	3632		11	3			6	7	8		10	12	9		2*	5	1		4					
38	27	WIMBLEDON	2-1	Cumming, Bonnyman(pen)	4283		11				6	7	8*		10	12	9		2	5	1	3	4					
39	30	Barnsley	0-0		3261		11	6				7			10	8	9		2	5		3	4*		1		12	
40	May 4	Shrewsbury Town	1-4	Bonnyman	3450		11	6				7			10		9		2	5		3	12		1	8*	4	
41	7	BRIGHTON & HOVE ALBION	2-4	Bonnyman, Matthews	4034			6				7			10	11	9		2	5		3			1	8	4	
42	11	Crystal Palace	2-0	Drinkell(2)	4923		2	6				7			10	11	9			5		3		4	1	8		
					Apps.	23	15	39	31	31	31	42	19	30	37	30	30	22	17	13	12	12	8	6	6	4	3	1
					Subs.		5						5			5	5	1					1	1			1	
					Goals		5		2		4	6	12	14	8	4	14							1		1		

1 own goal

F.A. Cup

Rd	Date	Opponent	Score	Scorers	Att.	Batch	Cumming	Crombie	Foley	Nicholl	Moore K	Ford	Lund	Wilkinson	Bonnyman	Emson	Drinkell	Seagraves	Robinson	Moore A	Felgate	Agnew	Hine	Henshaw	Grotier	Matthews	Rowbotham	Dawson
R3	Jan 5	Notts County	2-2	Ford, Lund	6202	1	11*	5	4		6	7	9	8	10	12		2				3						
R3r	8	NOTTS COUNTY	4-2	Wilkinson, Lund(3)	6743	1	11	5	4		6	7	9	8	10			2				3						
R4	26	WATFORD	1-3	Foley	12989		12	5	4		6	7	9	8	10	11		2*				3			1			

League Cup

Rd	Date	Opponent	Score	Scorers	Att.	Batch	Cumming	Crombie	Foley	Nicholl	Moore K	Ford	Lund	Wilkinson	Bonnyman	Emson	Drinkell	Seagraves	Robinson	Moore A	Felgate	Agnew	Hine	Henshaw	Grotier	Matthews	Rowbotham	Dawson
R2/1	Sep 25	BARNSLEY	3-0	K.Moore,Wilkinson,Bonnyman(pen)	3577	1		3	4	5	6	7	9	8	10	11		2										
R2/2	Oct 9	Barnsley	1-1	Foley	5578	1		3	4	5	6	7	9*	8	10	11		2									12	
R3	30	Rotherham United	0-0		8413	1		5	4		6	7	9	8	10	11		2				3						
R3r	Nov 6	ROTHERHAM UNITED	6-1	Foley,Ford,Wilkinson,Lund,Bonnyman,Emson	7649	1		3	4	5	6	7	9	8*	10	11	12	2										
R4	20	Everton	1-0	Wilkinson	26298	1		3	4*	5	6	7	9	8	10	11	12	2										
QF	Jan 16	NORWICH CITY	0-1		15050	1		5	4*		6	7	9	8	10	11		2				3		12				

		P	W	D	L	F	A	W	D	L	F	A	F	A	Pts
1	Oxford United	42	18	2	1	62	15	7	7	7	22	21	84	36	84
2	Birmingham City	42	12	6	3	30	15	13	1	7	29	18	59	33	82
3	Manchester City	42	14	4	3	42	16	7	7	7	24	24	66	40	74
4	Portsmouth	42	11	6	4	39	25	9	8	4	30	25	69	50	74
5	Blackburn Rovers	42	14	3	4	38	15	7	7	7	28	26	66	41	73
6	Brighton & Hove A.	42	13	6	2	31	11	7	6	8	23	23	54	34	72
7	Leeds United	42	12	7	2	37	11	7	5	9	29	32	66	43	69
8	Shrewsbury Town	42	12	6	3	45	22	6	5	10	21	31	66	53	65
9	Fulham	42	13	3	5	35	26	6	5	10	33	38	68	64	65
10	GRIMSBY TOWN	42	13	1	7	47	32	5	7	9	25	32	72	64	62
11	Barnsley	42	11	7	3	27	12	3	9	9	15	30	42	42	58
12	Wimbledon	42	9	8	4	40	29	7	2	12	31	46	71	75	58
13	Huddersfield Town	42	9	5	7	28	29	6	5	10	24	35	52	64	55
14	Oldham Athletic	42	10	4	7	27	23	5	4	12	22	44	49	67	53
15	Crystal Palace	42	8	7	6	25	27	4	5	12	21	38	46	65	48
16	Carlisle United	42	8	5	8	27	23	5	3	13	23	44	50	67	47
17	Charlton Athletic	42	8	7	6	34	30	3	5	13	17	33	51	63	45
18	Sheffield United	42	7	6	8	31	28	3	8	10	23	38	54	66	44
19	Middlesbrough	42	6	8	7	22	26	4	2	15	19	31	41	57	40
20	Notts County	42	6	5	10	25	32	4	2	15	20	41	45	73	37
21	Cardiff City	42	5	3	13	24	42	4	5	12	23	37	47	79	35
22	Wolverhampton W.	42	5	4	12	18	32	3	5	13	19	47	37	79	33

1985-86 15th in Division 2

Captain: Kevin Moore

			Opponent	Score	Scorers	Att.	Felgate	Robinson	Agnew	Peake	Moore A	Crombie	Ford	Lund	Gilligan	Bonnyman	Emson	Hobson	Moore K	Lyons	Cumming	Hine	Henshaw	Barratt	Batch	Matthews	Grocock
1	Aug	17	Brighton & Hove Albion	2-2	Lund, Hobson	9787	1	2	3	4	5	6	7	8	9	10	11*	12									
2		20	HUDDERSFIELD TOWN	1-1	Lund	6180	1	2	3	4	5	6	7	8*	9	10	11	12									
3		24	CHARLTON ATHLETIC	2-2	Lund, Hobson	4260	1	2	3	4	5		7	8	9	10	11	6									
4		26	Fulham	1-2	Lund	4873	1	2	3	4	5	6	7	8	9	10		11*				12					
5		31	WIMBLEDON	0-1		3476	1			4	5	3	7	8	9	10		11	6					2			
6	Sep	4	Stoke City	1-1	Lund	7362	1	2		4	5	3	7	8	9	10		11	6								
7		7	Sunderland	3-3	Ford, Gilligan, Lund	14985	1	2*		4	5	3	7	8	9	10	12	11	6								
8		13	CARLISLE UNITED	1-0	Peake	4099	1	2*		4	5	3	7	8	9	10	12	11	6								
9		21	Barnsley	0-1		5356	1		3	4	5		7	8	12	10	11*	9	6					2			
10		28	BRADFORD CITY	2-0	Peake, Emson	5158	1		3	4	5		7		8		11	9	6			10		2			
11	Oct	5	Oldham Athletic	1-2	Gilligan	5301	1		3	4	5		7	12	8		11*	9	6			10		2			
12		12	SHEFFIELD UNITED	0-1		5935				4	5	3	7*	12	8		11	9	6			10		2	1		
13		19	Leeds United	1-1	Hobson	11244				4	5	3*	7	12	8	10		9	6		11			2	1		
14		26	MIDDLESBROUGH	3-2	Hobson, Gilligan(2)	4454				4	5	3	7		8	10	11	9	6					2	1		
15	Nov	2	MILLWALL	5-1	Hobson(3),A.Moore,Bonnyman	3658				4*	5	3	7	8		10	11	9	6		12			2	1		
16		9	Crystal Palace	1-2	Emson	4620				4	5	3	7	8*		10	11	9	6		12			2	1		
17		16	PORTSMOUTH	1-0	Bonnyman(pen)	6436				4		3	7		8	10	11	9	6	5				2	1		
18		23	Norwich City	2-3	OG, Emson	12018			3	4	12		7		8*	10	11	9	6	5				2	1		
19		30	BLACKBURN ROVERS	5-2	Ford, Hine, K.Moore, Hobson(2)	5016					4		7		8	10		9	6	5	3	11		2	1		
20	Dec	7	Huddersfield Town	2-2	Lyons, Hobson	4811			12		4		7		8*	10		9	6	5	3	11		2	1		
21		14	BRIGHTON & HOVE ALBION	0-2		5320					4	12	7		8*	10		9	6	5	3	11		2	1		
22		21	Charlton Athletic	0-2		3525					4	3	7		12	10	11*	9	6	5	8			2	1		
23		26	Hull City	0-2		12824					4	3	7	12		10		9	6	5*	11	8		2	1		
24	Jan	1	SHREWSBURY TOWN	3-1	Lyons(2), Lund	4750						3	7	8		10		9	6	5	11	4		2	1		
25		11	Carlisle United	2-1	Hobson, Emson	2483	1		3	4		6	7	8	12		11	9		5		10*		2			
26		18	Wimbledon	0-3		2770			3	4		6	7*	8	12	10	11	9		5				2	1		
27		25	STOKE CITY	3-3	Emson, Bonnyman, Ford	4523		2		4		6	7	8		10	11	9		5	3				1		
28	Feb	1	FULHAM	1-0	Peake	3576		2		4		6	7	8	12	10	11	9*		5	3				1		
29		8	LEEDS UNITED	1-0	Hobson	6382		2		4		6	7	8*	12	10	11	9		5	3				1		
30	Mar	1	Bradford City	1-0	Cumming	5185		2	3	4	5	6	7			10	11	9			8				1		
31		4	Middlesbrough	1-3	Crombie	4496		2	3	4	5	6	7			10	11	9			8				1		
32		8	OLDHAM ATHLETIC	1-4	Hobson	4178		2	3	4		6	7			10*	11	9	12	5	8				1		
33		15	Sheffield United	1-1	Henshaw	9165		10		4	2	3	12		8			9	6	5	11*		7		1		
34		22	SUNDERLAND	1-1	Lund	5339		10		4	2	3	12	8				9	6	5	11		7*		1		
35		29	Shrewsbury Town	2-0	Lyons, Henshaw(pen)	3097		10	3	4	2			8				9	6	5		7*	11	12	1		
36	Apr	1	HULL CITY	0-1		9121				4	2	3		8				9	6	5	11	10	7*	12	1		
37		5	Millwall	0-1		3612		2		4	12	3		8					6	5	11	10	9*	7	1		
38		12	CRYSTAL PALACE	3-0	Henshaw(2,1pen), Peake	4222		10		4	2	3		8				9	6	5	11*		7		1	12	
39		19	Portsmouth	1-3	Cumming	12967		10	12	4	2	3		8*				9	6	5	11		7		1		
40		22	BARNSLEY	1-2	Hobson	4009		10		4	2	3		8*				9	6	5	11		7		1	12	
41		26	NORWICH CITY	1-0	Hobson	8090		10		4	2	3		12				9	6	5	11		7		1	8*	
42	May	5	Blackburn Rovers	1-3	K.Moore	7600		10		4		3				2		9	6	5	11*		7		1	8	12
						Apps.	12	22	14	36	31	33	32	24	19	29	21	39	30	24	22	12	10	20	30	2	
						Subs.			2		2	1	2	5	6		2	2	1		2	1		2		2	1
						Goals				4	1	1	3	8	4	3	5	15	2	4	2	1	4				

1 own goal

F.A. Cup

			Opponent	Score	Scorers	Att.	Felgate	Robinson	Agnew	Peake	Moore A	Crombie	Ford	Lund	Gilligan	Bonnyman	Emson	Hobson	Moore K	Lyons	Cumming	Hine	Henshaw	Barratt	Batch	Matthews	Grocock
R3	Jan	4	ARSENAL	3-4	Lund, Lyons, Peake(pen)	12829			3	4		6	7	8	12		11*	9		5		10		2	1		

League Cup

			Opponent	Score	Scorers	Att.	Felgate	Robinson	Agnew	Peake	Moore A	Crombie	Ford	Lund	Gilligan	Bonnyman	Emson	Hobson	Moore K	Lyons	Cumming	Hine	Henshaw	Barratt	Batch	Matthews	Grocock
R2	Sep	24	YORK CITY	1-1	Gilligan	2908	1		3	4	5		7		8	10	11	9	6					2			
R2r	Oct	8	York City	3-2	Hobson(2), Gilligan	5030	1			4	5	3	7	12	8			9	6		11*	10		2			
R3		29	IPSWICH TOWN	0-2		6684				4	5	3	7	12	8*	10	11	9	6					2	1		

Full Members Cup

(Northern group mini League 3)

			Opponent	Score	Scorers	Att.	Felgate	Robinson	Agnew	Peake	Moore A	Crombie	Ford	Lund	Gilligan	Bonnyman	Emson	Hobson	Moore K	Lyons	Cumming	Hine	Henshaw	Barratt	Batch	Matthews	Grocock
NG	Sep	17	SUNDERLAND	3-2	Bonnyman, Hobson(2)	2435			3		5	6	7	8	9+	10	13	11			12	4		2*	1		
NG	Oct	1	Sunderland	1-2	Lund	11571			3	4	5		7	8	9		11		6			10		2	1		

Aggregate 4-4, Sunderland won 3-2 on penalties. Oldham Athletic and Middlesbrough withdrew from this group; only Grimsby and Sunderland competed.

		P	W	D	L	F	A	W	D	L	F	A	F	A	Pts
1	Norwich City	42	16	4	1	51	15	9	5	7	33	22	84	37	84
2	Charlton Athletic	42	14	5	2	44	15	8	6	7	34	30	78	45	77
3	Wimbledon	42	13	6	2	38	16	8	7	6	20	21	58	37	76
4	Portsmouth	42	13	4	4	43	17	9	3	9	26	24	69	41	73
5	Crystal Palace	42	12	3	6	29	22	7	6	8	28	30	57	52	66
6	Hull City	42	11	7	3	39	19	6	6	9	26	36	65	55	64
7	Sheffield United	42	10	7	4	36	24	7	4	10	28	39	64	63	62
8	Oldham Athletic	42	13	4	4	40	28	4	5	12	22	33	62	61	60
9	Millwall	42	12	3	6	39	24	5	5	11	25	41	64	65	59
10	Stoke City	42	8	11	2	29	16	6	4	11	19	34	48	50	57
11	Brighton & Hove A.	42	10	5	6	42	30	6	3	12	22	34	64	64	56
12	Barnsley	42	9	6	6	29	26	5	8	8	18	24	47	50	56
13	Bradford City	42	14	1	6	36	24	2	5	14	15	39	51	63	54
14	Leeds United	42	9	7	5	30	22	6	1	14	26	50	56	72	53
15	GRIMSBY TOWN	42	11	4	6	35	24	3	6	12	23	38	58	62	52
16	Huddersfield Town	42	10	6	5	30	23	4	4	13	21	44	51	67	52
17	Shrewsbury Town	42	11	5	5	29	20	3	4	14	23	44	52	64	51
18	Sunderland	42	10	5	6	33	29	3	6	12	14	32	47	61	50
19	Blackburn Rovers	42	10	4	7	30	20	2	9	10	23	42	53	62	49
20	Carlisle United	42	10	2	9	30	28	3	5	13	17	43	47	71	46
21	Middlesbrough	42	8	6	7	26	23	4	3	14	18	30	44	53	45
22	Fulham	42	8	3	10	29	32	2	3	16	16	37	45	69	36

SEASON 1985/86

Back: Crombie, Dawson, N.Woodward, Batch, Felgate, Gilligan
Middle (Standing): Grotier (Asst.Man), Fraser (Physio), Topliss, Robinson, Emson, Rowbotham, K.Moore, Lund, Bonnyman, Ford, Matthews, Booth (Manager), A.Woodward (Youth Coach)
Middle (Seated): Henshaw, Agnew, Hine, A.Moore, Cumming, Barratt, Hobson
Front: Gaughan, Storr, Leadbitter, Maloney, Thompson, Duckworth, Dixon, McDermott

SEASON 1986/87

Back: Simmonite (Youth Coach), Bonnyman (Player/Coach), A.Moore, Matthews, Batch, Felgate, Horwood, Rice, O'Riordan (Player/Asst. Man), Fraser (Physio)
Middle: Burgess, Henshaw, Straw, Crombie, Agnew, Walsh, Robinson, Dixon
Front: Hazel, Turner, Hobson, Lyons (Player/ Manager), K.Moore, Cumming, Rawcliffe

1986-87 21st in Division 2

Captain: Kevin Moore(Aug-Feb), Mick Halsall(Feb-May)

							Batch	Burgess	Cumming	Peake	Lyons	Moore K	Robinson	Walsh	Hobson	O'Riordan	Turner	Agnew	Felgate	Prudhoe	Halsall	Crombie	Rawcliffe	Henshaw	Bonnyman	McDermott	McGarvey	Hazel	Straw	Rice	Grocock	Moore A	Matthews	Moore D
1	Aug	23	Ipswich Town	1-1	Walsh	12455	1	2	3	4	5	6	7	8	9	10	11																	
2		30	BRADFORD CITY	0-0		6393	1	2	3	4	5	6	7	8	9	10	11																	
3	Sep	6	Brighton & Hove Albion	1-0	Hobson	7791	1	2	3	4	5	6		8	9	10	11							7*					12					
4		13	DERBY COUNTY	0-1		7305	1	2	12		5	6	4*	8	9	10	11					3		7										
5		20	Sheffield United	2-1	Hobson, K.Moore	9840	1	2			5	6		8	9	10	11	3						7					4					
6		27	BARNSLEY	0-1		4789	1	2	3		5			8	9*	10	11					6		7					4					
7	Oct	1	Reading	3-2	Henshaw, Turner, Walsh	6130	1	2	3		5*		9	8		10	11					6	12	7					4					
8		4	Shrewsbury Town	1-4	Walsh(pen)	2451	1	2	3				9	8		10	11					6	12	7					4*					
9		11	PLYMOUTH ARGYLE	1-1	K.Moore	4155	1	2	3		5*	6		8	9	10	11						12	7	4									
10		18	West Bromwich Albion	1-1	Rawcliffe	8618	1	2			5*	6		8		10	11	3					9	7	12				4					
11		25	LEEDS UNITED	0-0		7168		2			5	6		8	9	10		3	1				12		11*			7	4					
12	Nov	1	MILLWALL	1-0	K.Moore	3757		2			5	6			9	10		3	1				8					7	4	11				
13		8	Crystal Palace	3-0	Walsh, Hobson, O'Riordan	5052		2			5	6	4	8	9	10		3	1						12			7*		11				
14		15	SUNDERLAND	1-1	Walsh(pen)	7065		2			5	6	4	8	9			3	1				12		10			7		11*				
15		22	Portsmouth	1-2	Hazel	9517		2			5	6	4	8		10		3	1				9		11*			7	12					
16		29	BIRMINGHAM CITY	0-1		4734	1	2			5	6	4	8		10		3					9					7		11*	12			
17	Dec	2	BLACKBURN ROVERS	1-0	O'Riordan	3483	1	2			5	6	4	8		10		3					12					7			11		9*	
18		6	Hull City	1-1	Hazel	7217	1				5	6	4	8		10	11	3						9				7						2
19		13	STOKE CITY	1-1	Rawcliffe	4642					5	6	4	8		10	7	3	1				12	9							11*			2
20		21	Derby County	0-4		14440		2			5*	6	4	9		10	11	3	1				8	7					12					
21		26	OLDHAM ATHLETIC	2-2	O'Riordan, Henshaw	6469			11		5	6	2	8		10	4	3	1					9				7						
22		27	Sunderland	1-0	Walsh	13769			11		5	6	2	8		10	4	3	1					7	9									
23	Jan	1	Huddersfield Town	0-0		7530		12	11*		5	6	2	8		10	4	3	1					7	9									
24		3	BRIGHTON & HOVE ALBION	1-2	Henshaw	4729		8			5	6	2			10	4	3	1				12	7							11		9*	
25		17	Blackburn Rovers	2-2	Walsh(2,1pen)	4654		2	11*			6	7	8		10	4	3	1			5	12		9									
26		24	IPSWICH TOWN	1-1	Robinson	4981	1	2			5	6	7	8		10*	4	3					12	11	9									
27	Feb	7	Bradford City	2-4	K.Moore(2)	8413	1	2			5	6	11	8			4	3						10	9	7								
28		14	READING	3-2	Robinson(2), Turner	3579	1					6	7			10	4	3					8	11	9	2						5		
29		24	Barnsley	0-1		5136	1				9		7			10	4	3				6	11	8		2						5		
30		28	SHEFFIELD UNITED	1-0	O'Riordan	5051	1		11				7			10	4	3			6	5	12	8		2							9*	
31	Mar	7	Leeds United	0-2		14270	1	11					7			10	4	3			6	5		8		2	9							
32		14	WEST BROMWICH ALBION	3-1	Henshaw, O'Riordan, Cumming	5024	1		11				7	12		10	4	3			6	5		8*		2	9							
33		21	Plymouth Argyle	0-5		2671	1	12	11				7	9*		10	4	3			6	5		8		2								
34		28	SHREWSBURY TOWN	0-1		3437		12	11				7	8*		10		3		1	6	5		4		2	9							
35	Apr	4	CRYSTAL PALACE	0-1		3071			11*				7			10	4			1	6	5		8			9				12	3		2
36		11	Millwall	0-1		3881			12				2			10	4	3*		1	11	6	8	7			9					5		
37		18	HUDDERSFIELD TOWN	0-1		4198			11							10	4	3*		1	2	6	8	7	12		9					5		
38		21	Oldham Athletic	1-1	O'Riordan	7032		3	11							10	4			1	7	6			8	2	9					5		
39		25	PORTSMOUTH	0-2		5085		3	11							10	4			1	7	6		12	8*	2	9					5		
40	May	2	Birmingham City	0-1		4457		3	11				4	12		10	8			1	7*	6				2	9					5		
41		5	HULL CITY	2-2	Walsh, Turner	6757		3	7					8		10	4			1		6				2	9				11	5		
42		9	Stoke City	1-5	McGarvey	6407		2								10	4	3			8*	6		12	11	7	9					5		
						Apps.	21	28	21	3	26	25	30	28	11	40	34	29	12	8	12	19	9	27	13	13	11	9	7	4	4	10	3	3
						Subs.		3	2					2									11	2	3				3		2			
						Goals			1			5	3	9	3	6	3						2	4			1	2						

Additional players: Horwood 12/6, Dixon 5/8, Pratt 1/42

F.A. Cup

							Batch	Burgess	Cumming	Peake	Lyons	Moore K	Robinson	Walsh	Hobson	O'Riordan	Turner	Agnew	Felgate	Prudhoe	Halsall	Crombie	Rawcliffe	Henshaw	Bonnyman	McDermott	McGarvey	Hazel	Straw	Rice	Grocock	Moore A	Matthews	Moore D
R3	Jan	10	STOKE CITY	1-1	Walsh	7367		2	11		5	6	7	8		10	4	3	1						9									
R3r		26	Stoke City	1-1	K.Moore	14340	1	2			5	6	7	8		10	4	3					12	11	9*									
R32r		28	Stoke City *	0-6		12087	1	2			5	6	7	8		10	4	3					12	11*	9									

* At Stoke City. Grimsby lost at the toss of a coin for venue choice.

League Cup

							Batch	Burgess	Cumming	Peake	Lyons	Moore K	Robinson	Walsh	Hobson	O'Riordan	Turner	Agnew	Felgate	Prudhoe	Halsall	Crombie	Rawcliffe	Henshaw	Bonnyman	McDermott	McGarvey	Hazel	Straw	Rice	Grocock	Moore A	Matthews	Moore D
R1/1	Sep	2	Carlisle United	0-1		2861	1	2	3	4		6	7*	8+	9	10	11							12								5		
R1/2		9	CARLISLE UNITED	2-0	Walsh(2)	3902	1	2		4	5	6		8	9	10	11					3		7										
R2/1		23	Hull City	0-1		5115	1	2	12		5	6*		8	9	10	11	3						7					4					
R2/2	Oct	7	HULL CITY	1-1	Walsh	5471	1	2	3		5		4	8	9*	10	11					6	12	7										

Additional player: Harwood 13/R1/1

Full Members Cup

							Batch	Burgess	Cumming	Peake	Lyons	Moore K	Robinson	Walsh	Hobson	O'Riordan	Turner	Agnew	Felgate	Prudhoe	Halsall	Crombie	Rawcliffe	Henshaw	Bonnyman	McDermott	McGarvey	Hazel	Straw	Rice	Grocock	Moore A	Matthews	Moore D
	Oct	21	HULL CITY	1-3	Walsh	2460	1	2				6	13	8		10	11+	3					9	7*	5				4					

Additional player: Harwood 12

	P	W	D	L	F	A	W	D	L	F	A	F	A	Pts
1 Derby County	42	14	6	1	42	18	11	3	7	22	20	64	38	84
2 Portsmouth	42	17	2	2	37	11	6	7	8	16	17	53	28	78
3 Oldham Athletic	42	13	6	2	36	16	9	3	9	29	28	65	44	75
4 Leeds United	42	15	4	2	43	16	4	7	10	15	28	58	44	68
5 Ipswich Town	42	12	6	3	29	10	5	7	9	30	33	59	43	64
6 Crystal Palace	42	12	4	5	35	20	7	1	13	16	33	51	53	62
7 Plymouth Argyle	42	12	6	3	40	23	4	7	10	22	34	62	57	61
8 Stoke City	42	11	5	5	40	21	5	5	11	23	32	63	53	58
9 Sheffield United	42	10	8	3	31	19	5	5	11	19	30	50	49	58
10 Bradford City	42	10	5	6	36	27	5	5	11	26	35	62	62	55
11 Barnsley	42	8	7	6	26	23	6	6	9	23	29	49	52	55
12 Blackburn Rovers	42	11	4	6	30	22	4	6	11	15	33	45	55	55
13 Reading	42	11	4	6	33	23	3	7	11	19	36	52	59	53
14 Hull City	42	10	6	5	25	22	3	8	10	16	33	41	55	53
15 West Bromwich Alb.	42	8	6	7	29	22	5	6	10	22	27	51	49	51
16 Millwall	42	10	5	6	27	16	4	4	13	12	29	39	45	51
17 Huddersfield Town	42	9	6	6	38	30	4	6	11	16	31	54	61	51
18 Shrewsbury Town	42	11	3	7	24	14	4	3	14	17	39	41	53	51
19 Birmingham City	42	8	9	4	27	21	3	8	10	20	38	47	59	50
20 Sunderland	42	8	6	7	25	23	4	6	11	24	36	49	59	48
21 GRIMSBY TOWN	42	5	8	8	18	21	5	6	10	21	38	39	59	44
22 Brighton & Hove A.	42	7	6	8	22	20	2	6	13	15	34	37	54	39

1987-88 22nd in Division 3

Captain: Don O'Riordan

							Sherwood	McDermott	Agnew	Turner	Slack	Burgess	Robinson	Walsh	North	O'Riordan	McGarvey	Toale	Saunders	Dixon	Cunnington	Jobling	Watson	Curran	Grocock	Stubbs	Rawcliffe	Lever	Moore D	Stephenson
1	Aug	15	Doncaster Rovers	0-1		2482	1	2	3	4	5	6	7	8*	9	10	11	12	12											
2		22	GILLINGHAM	2-0	Walsh(2)	2901	1	2*	3	7	5	6	4	8	9	10	11	12												
3		29	Notts County	0-0		5322	1		3	4	5		7	8	9	10	11	2	6											
4		31	BRENTFORD	0-1		3361	1		3	4	5	6	7	8	9	10	11	2												
5	Sep	5	Preston North End	3-1	Saunders, Walsh, O'Riordan	5522	1		3	4	5	6		8		10	11	2	7				9							
6		12	MANSFIELD TOWN	2-3	O'Riordan, Grocock	3410	1	12	3	4	5	6		8*	9	10	11+	2					7		14					
7		15	Bury	2-0	McGarvey(2,1pen)	1899	1		3	4	5	6	9	12	8*	10	11	2					7							
8		19	Chester City	0-1		1897	1		3	4	5	6	9	12	8	10	11*	2					7*		14					
9		26	WALSALL	0-2		3314	1	2	3	4	5	6			8	10	11	7	9*						12					
10		29	Rotherham United	0-0		3375	1	2		4	5	6			8	10	11		9	3			7							
11	Oct	3	SOUTHEND UNITED	1-3	O'Riordan, Grocock	2544	1	2	3	4	5			12	8+	10	11	6	9				7*		14					
12		10	Chesterfield	3-0	North, Walsh(2,1pen)	2072	1	2		4	5		6	8	9	10	11	3					7							
13		17	BRISTOL CITY	1-4	McGarvey	3100	1		3	4	5	6	8	9*		10	11	2					7		12					
14		20	BLACKPOOL	1-1	Turner	2260	1		3	4	5	6	9		8	10	11	2					7*		12					
15		24	Northampton Town	1-2	Turner	5388	1		3	4+	5	6	8		9	10	11	2*		14			7		12					
16		31	BRIGHTON & HOVE ALBION	0-1		2711	1	2			5	6+	8		9	10	11		3	14			7*		4		12			
17	Nov	3	Fulham	0-5		3493	1	2			5		4		9	10	11		8	3			6+	7	12					
18		7	Sunderland	1-1	North	18197	1	2			5				9	10	11		8	3			4	7*	6		12			
19		21	YORK CITY	5-1	North(2),Robinson(2),O'Riordan	2973	1	2		4	5		6		9	10	11*		8	3				7	12					
20		28	Bristol Rovers	2-4	O'Riordan(2,1pen)	2787	1	2		4			6		9	10	11	7*	8	3					5				12	
21	Dec	12	WIGAN ATHLETIC	0-2		2196	1	2	3	4		5	6		9	10	11	7*	8					12						
22		19	Aldershot	2-3	Turner, Saunders	2405	1	2*	3	4	5		6			10	11	12	8	9				7+	14					
23		26	Walsall	2-3	McGarvey, North	6272	1		3	4	5*	6	7		9	10	11	14	8	2+				12						
24		28	PORT VALE	3-1	North(3)	3043	1		3	4		5	6		9	10	11		8	2				7						
25	Jan	1	NOTTS COUNTY	0-0		5297	1		3	4		5	6		9*	10	11		8	2			12	7						
26		2	Mansfield Town	0-1		3315	1		3	4		5	6			10	11	7+	8	2			12	9*	14					
27		16	CHESTER CITY	2-1	McGarvey(2)	2594	1		3	4		5	6		9	10	11		8	2			12	7*						
28		26	BURY	2-0	Turner, O'Riordan	2525	1		3	4		5	6			10	11*		8	2			12	7	9					
29	Feb	2	Gillingham	1-1	McDermott	2993	1	7	3	4		5	6		9	10	11		8	2										
30		6	PRESTON NORTH END	0-1		3790	1	7	3	4		5	6		9+	10	11		8	2*			14		12					
31		13	Port Vale	0-2		3417	1	3		4		5	7		9+	10		6*	8	2			12		11			14		
32		20	DONCASTER ROVERS	0-0		3890	1		3			5	11		9	10			8	2	4	6		7*	12					
33		23	Brentford	2-0	Jobling, Saunders	3534	1	12	3			5	7		9*	10	11		8	2	4	6								
34		26	Southend United	0-0		3409	1	9	3			5	7			10	11		8	2	4	6								
35	Mar	5	Bristol City	1-1	O'Riordan	8343	1	14	3			5	7		9*	10	11		8	2	4	6				12				
36		8	ROTHERHAM UNITED	2-1	Cunnington, North	3423	1		3			5	7		9	10	11		8	2	4	6								
37		12	CHESTERFIELD	1-1	Stubbs	3464	1	14	3			5	7		9*	10	11		8	2+	4	6				12				
38		19	Brighton & Hove Albion	0-0		7269	1	14	3			5	7		9*	10	11		8+	2	4	6				12				
39		26	NORTHAMPTON TOWN	2-2	Cunnington, Robinson	3406	1	12	3			5	7		9	10			8	2	4*	6			11					
40	Apr	2	SUNDERLAND	0-1		7001	1	14	3			5	7		9+	10			8*	2	4	6			11	12				
41		4	York City	2-0	Stubbs, Agnew	3315	1	8	3			5	7			10				2	4	6			11	9				
42		9	FULHAM	0-2		3123	1	9	3			5	7			10		12		2*	4	6			11	8				
43		23	Blackpool	0-3		2555	1		3			5	7		9*	10	11		8	2	4	6				12				
44		30	BRISTOL ROVERS	0-0		2505	1		3			5	7		9	10	12		8	2	4	6			11*					
45	May	2	Wigan Athletic	1-0	North	2705	1	9*	3			5	7		12	10	11+		8	2	4	6			14					
46		7	ALDERSHOT	1-1	North	5639	1	11	3			5	7		9	10			8	2*	4	6			12					
						Apps.	46	21	38	28	21	38	40	8	37	46	38	16	34	30	15	15	13	10	10	2				
						Subs.		7						3	1		1	4	1	2			6	2	15	5	2	1	1	
						Goals		1	1	4			3	5	11	8	6		3		2	1			1	2				

F.A. Cup

							Sherwood	McDermott	Agnew	Turner	Slack	Burgess	Robinson	Walsh	North	O'Riordan	McGarvey	Toale	Saunders	Dixon	Cunnington	Jobling	Watson	Curran	Grocock	Stubbs	Rawcliffe	Lever	Moore D	Stephenson
R1	Nov	14	Scarborough	2-1	McGarvey, North	3764	1	2		4	5		6		9	10	11		8	3				7*	12					
R2	Dec	5	HALIFAX TOWN	0-0		3239	1	2	3	4			6		9	10	11		8						7				5	
R2r		8	Halifax Town	0-2		2633	1	2	3	4		5	6		9	10	11	7*	8						12					

League Cup

							Sherwood	McDermott	Agnew	Turner	Slack	Burgess	Robinson	Walsh	North	O'Riordan	McGarvey	Toale	Saunders	Dixon	Cunnington	Jobling	Watson	Curran	Grocock	Stubbs	Rawcliffe	Lever	Moore D	Stephenson
R1/1	Aug	18	DARLINGTON	3-2	Walsh, McGarvey, North	2248	1	2	3	4	5	6	7	9	8	10	11													
R1/2		26	Darlington	1-2*	North	1237	1		3	4	5	6	7	8*	9	10	11	2	12											

* After extra-time (Darlington won on away-goals rule)

Sherpa Van Trophy

							Sherwood	McDermott	Agnew	Turner	Slack	Burgess	Robinson	Walsh	North	O'Riordan	McGarvey	Toale	Saunders	Dixon	Cunnington	Jobling	Watson	Curran	Grocock	Stubbs	Rawcliffe	Lever	Moore D	Stephenson
P	Oct	13	Scunthorpe United	0-2		1710	1			4	5	6	7	8	9*		11+	2		10					13		12			3
P		27	HALIFAX TOWN	2-1	Grocock, McGarvey	1316	1		3*		5	6	8		9+	10	11		13	12			7		4		2			
P	Dec	15	SCUNTHORPE UNITED #	1-2	Turner	970	1	2	3	4			6		9*	10	11	7	8				12	5						

\# play-off

		P	W	D	L	F	A	W	D	L	F	A	F	A	Pts
1	Sunderland	46	14	7	2	51	22	13	5	5	41	26	92	48	93
2	Brighton & Hove A.	46	15	7	1	37	16	8	8	7	32	31	69	47	84
3	Walsall	46	15	6	2	39	22	8	7	8	29	28	68	50	82
4	Notts County	46	14	4	5	53	24	9	8	6	29	25	82	49	81
5	Bristol City	46	14	6	3	51	30	7	6	10	26	32	77	62	75
6	Northampton Town	46	12	8	3	36	18	6	11	6	34	33	70	51	73
7	Wigan Athletic	46	11	8	4	36	23	9	4	10	34	38	70	61	72
8	Bristol Rovers	46	14	5	4	43	19	4	7	12	25	37	68	56	66
9	Fulham	46	10	5	8	36	24	9	4	10	33	36	69	60	66
10	Blackpool	46	13	4	6	45	27	4	10	9	26	35	71	62	65
11	Port Vale	46	12	8	3	36	19	6	3	14	22	37	58	56	65
12	Brentford	46	9	8	6	27	23	7	6	10	26	36	53	59	62
13	Gillingham	46	8	9	6	45	21	6	8	9	32	40	77	61	59
14	Bury	46	9	7	7	33	26	6	7	10	25	31	58	57	59
15	Chester City	46	9	8	6	29	30	5	8	10	22	32	51	62	58
16	Preston North End	46	10	6	7	30	23	5	7	11	18	36	48	59	58
17	Southend United	46	10	6	7	42	33	4	7	12	23	50	65	83	55
18	Chesterfield	46	10	5	8	25	28	5	5	13	16	42	41	70	55
19	Mansfield Town	46	10	6	7	25	21	4	6	13	23	38	48	59	54
20	Aldershot	46	12	3	8	45	32	3	5	15	19	42	64	74	53
21	Rotherham United	46	8	8	7	28	25	4	8	11	22	41	50	66	52
22	GRIMSBY TOWN	46	6	7	10	25	29	6	7	10	23	29	48	58	50
23	York City	46	4	7	12	27	45	4	2	17	21	46	48	91	33
24	Doncaster Rovers	46	6	5	12	25	36	2	4	17	15	48	40	84	33

SEASON 1987/88

Back: McDermott, Saunders, Dixon, Robinson, D.Moore
Middle: Fraser (Physio), Grocock, North, Sherwood, Burgess, Agnew, Slack, Roberts (Man)
Front: Rawcliffe, Turner, O'Riordan, McGarvey, Walsh, Toale

SEASON 1988/89

Back: Agnew, O'Kelly, North, Sherwood, Tillson, Reece, Alexander, Williams, Cunnington
Geeson (Physio), McGarvey, Stoutt, Dixon, Buckley (Man), Jobling, McDermott, Grocock, Mann (Asst Man)

1988-89 9th in Division 4

Captain: Tommy Williams

	Date	Opponents	Score	Scorers	Att.	Sherwood	Dixon	Agnew	Williams	Cunnington	Cockerill	Jobling	McDermott	O'Kelly	Stoutt	North	Tillson	Reece	Lever	Alexander	Saunders	Caldwell	Grocock	Watson	Stephenson	Banton	Gilbert	Smaller	McGarvey
1	Aug 27	Cambridge United	1-4	Stoutt	2290	1	2*	3	4	5	6	7	8	9	10	11	12												
2	Sep 3	TORQUAY UNITED	1-0	North	2889			3	4	6		7	12	9	10	8	5	1	2	11*									
3	10	Scunthorpe United	1-1	Alexander	6037			3	4	6		7		9		8	5	1	2	11	12	10*							
4	17	ROTHERHAM UNITED	0-4		3697			3	4	8	6	7	12	9*			5	1		11	14	10+	2						
5	20	Wrexham	2-1	Jobling, North	2267		2	3	4	6		7		9		8	5	1		11			10						
6	24	ROCHDALE	1-3	North	2939		2	3	4	6		7		9		8	5	1		11		12	10*						
7	Oct 1	Hereford United	1-2	O'Kelly	1888	1	2*	3	4	6	14	7	10	9		8	5			11+	12								
8	4	TRANMERE ROVERS	0-0		2288	1		3		6		7	2	9		8	4		5	11*	10		12						
9	8	PETERBOROUGH UNITED	0-0		2822	1		3		6		7*	2	9		8	4		5	11	10		12						
10	15	Exeter City	1-2	Alexander	2232	1	14	3		6	12	7*	2	9		8+	4		5	11			10						
11	22	YORK CITY	2-0	Cockerill, Alexander	2829	1		3	2*	6	10		7	9		12	4		5	11	8								
12	25	Crewe Alexandra	2-2	Saunders(2)	2311	1		3		6			2	9		7	4		5	11	8			10					
13	29	HALIFAX TOWN	3-2	Saunders(2), O'Kelly	3260	1		3	2	6			7	9			4		5	11	8			10					
14	Nov 5	Stockport County	1-3	McDermott	2064	1			2*	6	3		7	9			4		5	11	8		12	10					
15	8	DONCASTER ROVERS	5-0	Watson(2,1p),Alexander,Saunders,Cockerill	3382	1				6	10		2	9			4		5	11	8			7	3				
16	12	Hartlepool United	1-2	Watson(pen)	1782	1		12		6	10		2*	9+			4		5	11	8		14	7	3				
17	26	Carlisle United	1-2	Cockerill	2195			3		6	10		2	9		7	4	1	5	11*	8			12					
18	Dec 3	SCARBOROUGH	2-1	Alexander, Cockerill	3887	1		3		6	10		2	9		7	4		5	11	8								
19	17	LEYTON ORIENT	2-2	Lever, Saunders	3445	1		3		6	10	12	2	9*		7	4		5	11	8								
20	26	Lincoln City	2-2	Watson, Alexander	8038			3				10	2	9		7*	4	1	5	11	8		12	6					
21	31	Burnley	0-1		7367			3				10	2	9*		7	4	1	5	11	8		12	6					
22	Jan 2	COLCHESTER UNITED	2-2	O'Kelly, Alexander	4472			3		6	14	10+	2	9		12	4	1	5	11*	8			7					
23	14	Torquay United	2-2	North, Alexander	2251			3		6	10	7*	2			9	4	1	5	11	8			12					
24	21	CAMBRIDGE UNITED	4-0	O'Kelly,Saunders,Cunnington,Tillson	3644			3		6	10		2	9		7	4	1	5	11	8								
25	Feb 4	WREXHAM	0-1		5058			3		6	10	2		9		7	4	1	5*	11	8			12					
26	11	Rochdale	2-0	Alexander(2)	1621	1		3		6	10	7		9		2	4		5	11	8								
27	14	DARLINGTON	0-0		4628	1		3		6	10	7*		9		2	4		5	11	8			12					
28	25	EXETER CITY	2-1	O'Kelly, Lever	4684	1		3		6	10		2	9		7	4		5	11	8								
29	28	CREWE ALEXANDRA	0-0		5404	1		3		6		10	2	9		7	4		5	11*	8			12					
30	Mar 4	York City	3-0	Saunders, O'Kelly, North	3481	1				6		10	2	9		7	4		5		8			11	3				
31	7	Rotherham United	0-1		4888	1				6		10	2	9		7	4		5	12	8			11*	3				
32	11	STOCKPORT COUNTY	2-0	North, Jobling	4685	1				6		10	2	9		7	4		5	11	8				3				
33	14	Halifax Town	1-2	O'Kelly	1609	1				6		10	2	9		7	4		5	11	8			12	3*				
34	18	SCUNTHORPE UNITED	1-1	O'Kelly	9796	1		12		6		10	2	9		7	4		5	11	8				3*				
35	24	Colchester United	0-0		4507	1		3		6	10	7	2	9			4		5	11	8								
36	27	LINCOLN CITY	1-0	O'Kelly	8618	1		3		6	10	2		9			4		5	11	12					7*	8		
37	Apr 1	Leyton Orient	0-5		4149	1		3		6	10	7	2	9*			4		5+	11	12				14		8		
38	4	Darlington	1-1	Jobling	1840	1			5	6	10	7	2				4			11	9				3		8		
39	8	BURNLEY	1-0	Saunders	4856				2	6		10					4	1	5	11	7			12	3	9*	8		
40	15	HEREFORD UNITED	1-1	Gilbert	4036				2	6	14	10	9*				4	1	5+	11	7				3	12	8		
41	25	Peterborough United	2-1	Alexander, Jobling(pen)	2937	1		3	5	6	12	10	2	9*			4			11	7						8		
42	29	CARLISLE UNITED	0-0		3833	1		3	5+	6	10	7*	2	12			4			11	9					14	8		
43	May 1	Doncaster Rovers	3-2	Banton, Tillson, O'Kelly	2183	1		3*	5	6	10		2	9			4			14	7+			12		11	8		
44	6	Scarborough	3-2	Alexander(2), Saunders	3923	1			2	6	10		9				4		5	11	7			12	3*	14	8+		
45	9	Tranmere Rovers	2-3	Cockerill, Gilbert	6938	1			2	6	10		3				4+		5	11	9			7*	14	12	8		
46	13	HARTLEPOOL UNITED	3-0	Cockerill, Alexander, Gilbert	3801	1			4	6	10		2						5+	11	9			7*	3	12	8	14	
					Apps.	32	4	32	19	44	24	31	36	38	2	27	44	14	37	42	36	2	4	12	12	3	11		
					Subs.		1	2			5	1	2	1		2	1			2	5	1	6	9	2	5		1	
					Goals					1	6	4	1	10	1	6	2		2	14	10			4		1	3		

F.A.Cup

	Date	Opponents	Score	Scorers	Att.	Sherwood	Dixon	Agnew	Williams	Cunnington	Cockerill	Jobling	McDermott	O'Kelly	Stoutt	North	Tillson	Reece	Lever	Alexander	Saunders	Caldwell	Grocock	Watson	Stephenson	Banton	Gilbert	Smaller	McGarvey
R1	Nov 19	WOLVERHAMPTON WANDS.	1-0	Cockerill	7922	1		3		6	10		2	9		7	4		5	11	8								
R2	Dec 10	ROTHERHAM UNITED	3-2	North, Cunnington, OG	5676	1		3		6	10		2	9		7	4		5	11	8								
R3	Jan 7	Middlesbrough	2-1	North(2)	19190			3		6	10	7	2	9*		12	4	1	5	11	8								
R4	28	READING	1-1	North	9401			3		6	10		2	9		7	4	1	5	11	8								
R4r	Feb 1	Reading	2-1	Cunnington, Jobling	8541			3		6	10	12	2*	9		7	4	1	5	11	8								
R5	18	Wimbledon	1-3	Alexander	12517	1	12	3		6	10	7		9*		2	4		5	11	8								

League Cup

	Date	Opponents	Score	Scorers	Att.	Sherwood	Dixon	Agnew	Williams	Cunnington	Cockerill	Jobling	McDermott	O'Kelly	Stoutt	North	Tillson	Reece	Lever	Alexander	Saunders	Caldwell	Grocock	Watson	Stephenson	Banton	Gilbert	Smaller	McGarvey
R1L1	Aug 30	ROTHERHAM UNITED	0-1		2517		2*	3	4	6		7	8	9	10	11	5	1											12
R1L2	Sep 6	Rotherham United	0-1		3381			3	4	6		7	12	9	10*	8	5	1	2	11+	13								

Sherpa Van Trophy

	Date	Opponents	Score	Scorers	Att.	Sherwood	Dixon	Agnew	Williams	Cunnington	Cockerill	Jobling	McDermott	O'Kelly	Stoutt	North	Tillson	Reece	Lever	Alexander	Saunders	Caldwell	Grocock	Watson	Stephenson	Banton	Gilbert	Smaller	McGarvey
P	Nov 29	ROTHERHAM UNITED	1-0	Saunders	1192			3		6	10	12	2*	9		7	4	1	5	11	8								
P	Dec 6	Doncaster Rovers	1-1	Saunders	681	1		3		6*	10	12	2	9		7			5	11	8			4					
R1	Jan 17	HUDDERSFIELD TOWN	1-3	North	2116			3		6	10	12	2	13		9	4	1	5*	11	8			7+					

		P	W	D	L	F	A	W	D	L	F	A	F	A	Pts
1	Rotherham United	46	13	6	4	44	18	9	10	4	32	17	76	35	82
2	Tranmere Rovers	46	15	6	2	34	13	6	11	6	28	30	62	43	80
3	Crewe Alexandra	46	13	7	3	42	24	8	8	7	25	24	67	48	78
4	Scunthorpe United	46	11	9	3	40	22	10	5	8	37	35	77	57	77
5	Scarborough	46	12	7	4	33	23	9	7	7	34	29	67	52	77
6	Leyton Orient	46	16	2	5	61	19	5	10	8	25	31	86	50	75
7	Wrexham	46	12	7	4	44	28	7	7	9	33	35	77	63	71
8	Cambridge United	46	13	7	3	45	25	5	7	11	26	37	71	62	68
9	GRIMSBY TOWN	46	11	9	3	33	18	6	6	11	32	41	65	59	66
10	Lincoln City	46	12	6	5	39	26	6	4	13	25	34	64	60	64
11	York City	46	10	8	5	43	27	7	5	11	19	36	62	63	64
12	Carlisle United	46	9	6	8	26	25	6	9	8	27	27	53	52	60
13	Exeter City	46	14	4	5	46	23	4	2	17	19	45	65	68	60
14	Torquay United	46	15	2	6	32	23	2	6	15	13	37	45	60	59
15	Hereford United	46	11	8	4	40	27	3	8	12	26	45	66	72	58
16	Burnley	46	12	6	5	35	20	2	7	14	17	41	52	61	55
17	Peterborough Utd.	46	10	3	10	29	32	4	9	10	23	42	52	74	54
18	Rochdale	46	10	10	3	32	26	3	4	16	24	56	56	82	53
19	Hartlepool United	46	10	6	7	33	33	4	4	15	17	45	50	78	52
20	Stockport County	46	8	10	5	31	20	2	11	10	23	32	54	52	51
21	Halifax Town	46	10	7	6	42	27	3	4	16	27	48	69	75	50
22	Colchester United	46	8	7	8	35	30	4	7	12	25	48	60	78	50
23	Doncaster Rovers	46	9	6	8	32	32	4	4	15	17	46	49	78	49
24	Darlington	46	3	12	8	28	38	5	6	12	25	38	53	76	42

1989-90 2nd in Division 4

Captain: Shaun Cunnington

No.	Date	Opponent	Score	Scorers	Att.	Sherwood	McDermott	Agnew	Tillson	Lever	Cunnington	Childs	Gilbert	Rees	Cockerill	Alexander	Watson	Hargreaves	Williams	Reece	Birtles	Stephenson	Willis	Jobling	Smaller	Stoutt	Gabbiadini	Knight
1	Aug 19	CAMBRIDGE UNITED	0-0		4822	1	2	3	4	5	6	7	8	9+	10*	11	12	14										
2	26	Torquay United	3-0	Childs, Cunnington, Rees	2525	1	2*	3	4	5	6	7	8	9	10	11			12									
3	Sep 2	COLCHESTER UNITED	4-1	Rees(2), Watson, OG	4678		2	3	4	5	6	7	8	9		12	10			1	11*							
4	9	Carlisle United	1-1	Childs	3360		2	3	4	5	6	7	8	9	10	12				1	11*							
5	16	MAIDSTONE UNITED	2-3	Gilbert(2,1pen)	5198		2		4	5*	6	7	8		10	11	12			1	9	3+	14					
6	23	York City	1-0	Rees	3366	1	2		4	5	6	7	8	9		12	10				11*	3						
7	27	Exeter City	1-2	Lever	3702	1	2		4	5	6	7	8	9			10				11	3						
8	30	HEREFORD UNITED	0-2		4832	1	2		4	5	6	7	8	9		12	10+				11	3*		14				
9	Oct 7	ROCHDALE	1-2	Tillson	3996	1			4	5	6	7		9	10	11	2	12					8*	3				
10	14	Scarborough	1-3	Gilbert(pen)	2828		2		4	5	6	7*	8	9	10+	11	14	12		1				3				
11	17	GILLINGHAM	2-0	Jobling, Hargreaves	3447				4	5	6		8	9		11	7	2		1				10	3			
12	21	Lincoln City	1-1	Alexander	6251			3	4	5	6		8			11	7	2		1	9			10				
13	28	HALIFAX TOWN	1-1	Cunnington	4021		2		4	5	6	7	8			11*	10	12		1	9		14			3+		
14	Nov 1	Peterborough United	1-1	Gabbiadini	6827		2	3	4	5	6	7	8		10					1	9						11	
15	4	CHESTERFIELD	0-1		4513		2	3		5	6	7	8	9+	10			12		1	4*			14			11	
16	11	Wrexham	1-0	Birtles	1658	1	2	3	4	5	6	7	8		10						9		12				11*	
17	25	ALDERSHOT	2-1	Agnew, Birtles	3716		2	3	4	5	6	7	8		10	12		11*		1	9							
18	Dec 2	Burnley	1-1	Cockerill	5615		2	3	4	5	6	7	8		10	12		11*		1	9							
19	19	SOUTHEND UNITED	2-0	Cockerill(2 pens)	4001		2	3	4	5	6	7	8	9	10	11				1								
20	26	Scunthorpe United	2-2	Alexander, Agnew	8384		2	3	4+	5	6	7	8*	9	10	11				1	12			14				
21	30	Hartlepool United	2-4	Rees, Alexander	3398		2		4	5	6	7	8*	9		11	14			1	12	3+		10				
22	Jan 1	STOCKPORT COUNTY	4-2	Alexander, Rees, Gilbert(pen), Birtles	5717		2		4*	5	6	7	8	9		11	12			1	10			3				
23	13	TORQUAY UNITED	0-0		4586	1	2		4		6	7	8	9	10	11*		12						3				5
24	16	Doncaster Rovers	0-0		4338	1			4		6	7	8	9	10			11				3		2				5
25	20	Cambridge United	0-2		2623	1			4		6	7	8*	9	10		14	12			11	3+		2				5
26	27	CARLISLE UNITED	1-0	Alexander	4657	1	2		4		6	7+	8	9	10	12					11		14	3*				5
27	Feb 3	YORK CITY	3-0	Tillson, Rees, Alexander	5049	1	2		4*		6	7	8	9	10	12					11			3				5
28	10	Maidstone United	2-2	Childs, Alexander	2365	1	2*		4	14	6	7	8	9	10	12					11+			3				5
29	17	BURNLEY	4-2	Knight, Cunnington, Childs, Birtles	5973	1	2		4		6	7	8	9	10	12					11*			3				5
30	20	Colchester United	0-1		3026	1	2	14	4		6	7	8	9	10+	12					11			3				5*
31	24	Aldershot	0-0		1858	1	2		4	5	6	7	8		10	11					9			3				
32	Mar 3	DONCASTER ROVERS	2-1	Rees, Gilbert	5536	1	2+	14	4	5*	6	7	8	9	10	12					11			3				
33	7	Hereford United	1-0	Childs	3013	1	2	12	4		6	7	8	9	10*	5					11			3				
34	10	EXETER CITY	1-0	Gilbert	6629	1	2	12	4	5	6	7	8	9	10*						11			3				
35	17	Rochdale	1-0	Gilbert	3058	1	2	3	4*	5	6	7	8	9		12+		14			11			10				
36	20	SCARBOROUGH	3-0	Rees(2), Lever	7690	1	2	3	4	5	6	7	8	9		12					11*			10				
37	24	Gillingham	2-1	Alexander, Rees	4150	1		3	4	12	6*	7	8	9		5	2				11			10				
38	31	LINCOLN CITY	1-0	Gilbert(pen)	11427	1	2	3	4*	5		7	8	9	10						11		12	6				
39	Apr 7	Halifax Town	2-2	Rees, Alexander	3620	1	2	3		5		7	8*	9	10	11		12			4			6				
40	10	PETERBOROUGH UNITED	1-2	Alexander	8123	1	2	3+		14	6	7	8	9*	10	11		12			5			4				
41	14	Stockport County	4-2	Gilbert(2), Birtles, Hargreaves	4065	1	2*			5	6	7	8	9+	10	11		12			4		14	3				
42	17	SCUNTHORPE UNITED	2-1	Tillson, Cockerill	11894	1	2		4+	5	6	7*	8	9	10	14		12			11			3				
43	20	Southend United	2-0	Alexander(2)	4945	1	2		4	5	6	7	8		10	11					9*		12	3				
44	24	HARTLEPOOL UNITED	0-0		8687	1	2		4	5	6	7+	8		10	11*		12			9		14	3				
45	28	WREXHAM	5-1	Birtles(3), Cockerill, Rees	8431	1	2	12	4	5	6	7	8	9*	10	14					11+			3				
46	May 5	Chesterfield	0-2		7501	1		3+	4	5	6	7	8			11*	2	12			9			10				14
					Apps.	31	39	19	42	35	44	44	45	35	33	22	10	5		15	36	7	1	30	1	1	3	8
					Subs.			5		3						16	6	14	1		2		8	3				1
					Goals			2	3	2	3	5	10	13	5	12	1	2			8			1			1	1

1 own goal

F.A. Cup

Round	Date	Opponent	Score	Scorers	Att.	Sherwood	McDermott	Agnew	Tillson	Lever	Cunnington	Childs	Gilbert	Rees	Cockerill	Alexander	Watson	Hargreaves	Williams	Reece	Birtles	Stephenson	Willis	Jobling	Smaller	Stoutt	Gabbiadini	Knight
R1	Nov 18	York City	2-1	Hargreaves(2)	4128	1	2	3	4	5	6	7	8		10			11			9							
R2	Dec 9	DONCASTER ROVERS	1-0	Cockerill	6623		2	3	4	5	6	7	8	12	10	11*				1	9							
R3	Jan 6	Huddersfield Town	1-3	Gilbert	9901		2		4	5*	6	7	8	9	3	11		12		1	10+			14				

Littlewoods Cup

Round	Date	Opponent	Score	Scorers	Att.	Sherwood	McDermott	Agnew	Tillson	Lever	Cunnington	Childs	Gilbert	Rees	Cockerill	Alexander	Watson	Hargreaves	Williams	Reece	Birtles	Stephenson	Willis	Jobling	Smaller	Stoutt	Gabbiadini	Knight
R1/1	Aug 22	Hull City	0-1		5045	1		3	4	5	6	7	8	9		11*	10		2		12							
R1/2	29	HULL CITY *	2-0	Alexander, Childs	6753			3	4	5	6	7	8	9	10	11+	12		2*	1	14							
R2/1	Sep 19	COVENTRY CITY	3-1	Gilbert, Watson, Birtles	10150	1	2		4	5	6	7	8	9			10				11	3						
R2/2	Oct 4	Coventry City	0-3		15327	1	2		4	5	6	7	8	9	10	11							12	3*				

* After extra time

Leyland DAF Cup

Round	Date	Opponent	Score	Scorers	Att.	Sherwood	McDermott	Agnew	Tillson	Lever	Cunnington	Childs	Gilbert	Rees	Cockerill	Alexander	Watson	Hargreaves	Williams	Reece	Birtles	Stephenson	Willis	Jobling	Smaller	Stoutt	Gabbiadini	Knight
NPR, Grp 3	Nov 28	Doncaster Rovers	0-1		1551		2	3	4	5	6	7*	8		10	12		11		1	9							
NPR, Grp 3	Dec 12	HUDDERSFIELD TOWN	3-3	Alexander, Cockerill, Rees	992			3		5+	6	7	8	9	10	11	12	14		1	4*			2				

		P	W	D	L	F	A	W	D	L	F	A	F	A	Pts
1	Exeter City	46	20	3	0	50	14	8	2	13	33	34	83	48	89
2	GRIMSBY TOWN	46	14	4	5	41	20	8	9	6	29	27	70	47	79
3	Southend United	46	15	3	5	35	14	7	6	10	26	34	61	48	75
4	Stockport County	46	13	6	4	45	27	8	5	10	23	35	68	62	74
5	Maidstone United	46	14	4	5	49	21	8	3	12	28	40	77	61	73
6	Cambridge United	46	14	3	6	45	30	7	7	9	31	36	76	66	73
7	Chesterfield	46	12	9	2	41	19	7	5	11	22	31	63	50	71
8	Carlisle United	46	15	4	4	38	20	6	4	13	23	40	61	60	71
9	Peterborough Utd.	46	10	8	5	35	23	7	9	7	24	23	59	46	68
10	Lincoln City	46	11	6	6	30	27	7	8	8	18	21	48	48	68
11	Scunthorpe United	46	9	9	5	42	25	8	6	9	27	29	69	54	66
12	Rochdale	46	11	4	8	28	23	9	2	12	24	32	52	55	66
13	York City	46	10	5	8	29	24	6	11	6	26	29	55	53	64
14	Gillingham	46	9	8	6	28	21	8	3	12	18	27	46	48	62
15	Torquay United	46	12	2	9	33	29	3	10	10	20	37	53	66	57
16	Burnley	46	6	10	7	19	18	8	4	11	26	37	45	55	56
17	Hereford United	46	7	4	12	31	32	8	6	9	25	30	56	62	55
18	Scarborough	46	10	5	8	35	28	5	5	13	25	45	60	73	55
19	Hartlepool United	46	12	4	7	45	33	3	6	14	21	55	66	88	55
20	Doncaster Rovers	46	7	7	9	29	29	7	2	14	24	31	53	60	51
21	Wrexham	46	8	8	7	28	28	5	4	14	23	39	51	67	51
22	Aldershot	46	8	7	8	28	26	4	7	12	21	43	49	69	50
23	Halifax Town	46	5	9	9	31	29	7	4	12	26	36	57	65	49
24	Colchester United	46	9	3	11	26	25	2	7	14	22	50	48	75	43

SEASON 1989/90
Back: Agnew, Stoutt, Sherwood, Reece, Willis, Cunnington
Middle: Jellett (Physio), O'Kelly, Gilbert, Childs, Stephenson, Smaller, Watson, Jobling, McDermott, Mann (Asst Man)
Front: Williams, Cockerill, Alexander, Buckley (Man), Tillson, Birtles, Lever

SEASON 1990/91
Back: Jellett (Physio), Hargreaves, Lever, Tillson, Knight, Sherwood, Reece, Alexander, Cockerill, Willis, Birtles, Mann (Asst Man)
Front: Agnew, Rees, Cunnington, Watson, Buckley (Man), Childs, McDermott, Gilbert, Jobling

1990-91 3rd in Division 3

Captain: Shaun Cunnington

	Month	Day	Opponent	Result	Scorers	Att.	Sherwood	McDermott	Jobling	Tillson	Knight	Cunnington	Childs	Gilbert	Woods	Cockerill	Hargreaves	Rees	Watson	Alexander	Lever	Birtles	Agnew	Baraclough	Croft	Futcher	Smith M
1	Aug	25	Preston North End	3-1	Gilbert(pen), Hargreaves, Woods	6372	1	2	3	4	5	6	7	8	9	10	11										
2	Sep	1	WIGAN ATHLETIC	4-3	Childs, Hargreaves, Woods(2)	5162	1	2	3	4	5*	6	7		11	10	8+	9	12	14							
3		8	Crewe Alexandra	2-1	Woods, Cockerill	3265	1	2	3	4		6	7*	8	11	10		9	12		5						
4		15	BRADFORD CITY	1-1	Tillson	7960	1	2	3	4		6		8	11*	10		9	7		5	12					
5		18	HUDDERSFIELD TOWN	4-0	Rees, Watson, Cockerill(2)	6158	1	2	3	4		6		8	11	10		9	7		5						
6		22	Shrewsbury Town	2-1	Woods, Watson	2904	1	2	3	4		6		8	11	10	9		7		5						
7		29	Brentford	0-1		5951	1	2	3	4*	14	6		8	11	10	12	9	7		5+						
8	Oct	2	ROTHERHAM UNITED	2-1	Lever, Woods	6923	1	2	3	4		6		8	11*	10	12	9	7		5						
9		6	SWANSEA CITY	1-0	Gilbert	5974	1	2	3	4		6		8	11	10		9	7		5						
10		13	Chester City	2-1	Woods, OG	1875	1	2	3	4		6		8	11	10		9	7		5						
11		20	Birmingham City	0-0		10123	1	2	3	4		6	12	8	11	10		9	7*		5						
12		23	LEYTON ORIENT	2-2	Woods, Knight	6660	1	2	3*	4	14	6	7	8	11		12	9	10		5+						
13		27	STOKE CITY	2-0	Watson, Childs	10799	1	2	3	4		6	7	8	11			9	10		5						
14	Nov	3	Exeter City	0-0		4647	1		3	4	14	6	7+	8	11	10	12	9*	2		5						
15		10	Tranmere Rovers	2-1	Cunnington, Gilbert	6140	1		3	4		6		8	11	10	12		7		5	9*	2				
16		24	BOLTON WANDERERS	0-1		6240	1	2	3	4	5	6	12	8	11	10		9+	7*			14					
17	Dec	1	MANSFIELD TOWN	2-0	Gilbert(2,1pen)	5350	1	2	3	4	5	6	7	8	11	10		9									
18		15	Southend United	0-2		8126	1	2*	3	4		6		8	11	10	12	9	7+		5	14					
19		22	BOURNEMOUTH	5-0	Rees(2), Cunnington, Gilbert(2,1pen)	5651	1	2				6	7	8	11	10		9			5	4	3				
20		26	Reading	0-2		3045	1	2	12			6	7+	8	11	10	9*				5	4	3	14			
21		29	Cambridge United	0-1		5922	1	2	7			6	12	8	11	10*	9				5	4+	3	14			
22	Jan	1	FULHAM	3-0	Rees, Hargreaves, Childs	7492	1	2	10			6	7		11		8	9*	12		5	4	3				
23		5	BURY	0-1		6248	1	2	10		14	6	7	8	11		9		12		5	4+	3*				
24		12	Wigan Athletic	0-2		2868	1	2	3			6	7	8*	11		9		10		5	4+		14	12		
25		19	PRESTON NORTH END	4-1	Lever, Rees(2), Childs	5391	1		2			6	7	8	11		12	9*	10		5			3		4	
26		26	Bradford City	2-0	Watson, Gilbert	8314	1	2	3			6	7	8	11			9	10		5					4	
27	Feb	2	Huddersfield Town	1-1	Watson(pen)	6571	1	2	3			6	7	8*	11			9	10		5	12				4	
28		5	SHREWSBURY TOWN	1-0	Watson	5683	1	2	3			6	7	8	11*			9	10		5	12				4	
29		16	Bolton Wanderers	0-0		10318	1	2	3			6	7	8	11*			9	10		5	12				4	
30		23	TRANMERE ROVERS	0-1		6375	1	2	3			6	7	8	11	14	12	9	10*		5+					4	
31	Mar	2	Mansfield Town	1-1	Rees	3502	1	2	3			6	7	8				9	10		5	11				4	
32		9	SOUTHEND UNITED	1-0	Gilbert	9689	1	2	3			6	7*	8	14	10		9	12		5	11+				4	
33		12	ROTHERHAM UNITED	4-1	Rees(2), OG, Woods	5542	1	2	3			6		8	12	10		9	7		5	11*				4	
34		16	BRENTFORD	2-0	Woods(2)	6685	1	2	3			6		8	11	10		9	7		5					4	
35		20	CHESTER CITY	2-0	Woods, Watson	6012	1	2	3			6		8	11	10		9	7		5					4	
36		23	Swansea City	0-0		3203	1	2	3			6		8	11	10		9	7+		5		12			4	14*
37		30	READING	3-0	Cockerill(2), Gilbert(pen)	7219	1	2	3			6	12	8	11+	10		9	7		5*					4	14
38	Apr	2	Bournemouth	1-2	Watson	7021	1	2	3			6		8	11+	10		9	7*		5	12				4	14
39		6	CAMBRIDGE UNITED	1-0	Gilbert(pen)	8550	1	2	3			6		8		10		9	7		5					4	11
40		9	Bury	2-3	Rees, Gilbert(pen)	4748	1	2	3			6		8	11	10		9	7+		5*	12				4	14
41		13	Fulham	0-0		5464	1	2	3			6		8	11	10		9*	7			5				4	12
42		20	BIRMINGHAM CITY	0-0		8842	1	2	3			6	12	8	11	10		9+	7*			5				4	14
43		23	CREWE ALEXANDRA	0-1		7166	1	2	3			6		8	11	10	12		7+		5	9				4*	14
44		27	Leyton Orient	2-0	Birtles, Watson	4306	1	2	3			6+		8	11*	10	12		7		5	9				4	14
45	May	4	Stoke City	0-0		11832	1	2	3			6		8	11	10			7		5	9*				4	12
46		11	EXETER CITY	2-1	Cockerill(2)	14225	1	2	3			6		8	11	10		9*	7		5					4	12
						Apps.	46	43	44	18	4	46	20	44	42	34	8	36	36		40	15	6	1		22	1
						Subs.			1		4		5		2	1	10		5	1		8	1	3	1		10
						Goals				1	1	2	4	12	12	7	3	10	9		2	1					

2 own goals

F.A. Cup

	Month	Day	Opponent	Result	Scorers	Att.	Sherwood	McDermott	Jobling	Tillson	Knight	Cunnington	Childs	Gilbert	Woods	Cockerill	Hargreaves	Rees	Watson	Alexander	Lever	Birtles	Agnew	Baraclough	Croft	Futcher	Smith M
R1	Nov	17	Blackpool	0-2		4175	1	12	3	4		6		8	11	10		9	7		5+	14	2*				

Rumbelows Cup

	Month	Day	Opponent	Result	Scorers	Att.	Sherwood	McDermott	Jobling	Tillson	Knight	Cunnington	Childs	Gilbert	Woods	Cockerill	Hargreaves	Rees	Watson	Alexander	Lever	Birtles	Agnew	Baraclough	Croft	Futcher	Smith M
R1/1	Aug	28	CREWE ALEXANDRA	2-1	Rees, Gilbert	3882	1	2	3	4	5	6	7	8		10	11*	9		12							
R1/2	Sep	4	Crewe Alexandra	0-1		2781	1	2	3	4		6	7	8		10	11*	9	14	12	5+						

Leyland DAF Cup

	Month	Day	Opponent	Result	Scorers	Att.	Sherwood	McDermott	Jobling	Tillson	Knight	Cunnington	Childs	Gilbert	Woods	Cockerill	Hargreaves	Rees	Watson	Alexander	Lever	Birtles	Agnew	Baraclough	Croft	Futcher	Smith M
NPR, Grp7	Nov	6	YORK CITY	1-3	Cockerill	1362	1		3	4	14	6	7*	8	11	10	9		2		5+		12				
NPR, Grp7	Dec	11	Darlington	1-3	Woods	1106	1	2	10	4*		6		8	11		12	9	7		5		3				

		P	W	D	L	F	A	W	D	L	F	A	F	A	Pts
1	Cambridge United	46	14	5	4	42	22	11	6	6	33	23	75	45	86
2	Southend United	46	13	6	4	34	23	13	1	9	33	28	67	51	85
3	GRIMSBY TOWN	46	16	3	4	42	13	8	8	7	24	21	66	34	83
4	Bolton Wanderers	46	14	5	4	33	18	10	6	7	31	32	64	50	83
5	Tranmere Rovers	46	13	5	5	38	21	10	4	9	26	25	64	46	78
6	Brentford	46	12	4	7	30	22	9	9	5	29	25	59	47	76
7	Bury	46	13	6	4	39	26	7	7	9	28	30	67	56	73
8	Bradford City	46	13	3	7	36	22	7	7	9	26	32	62	54	70
9	Bournemouth	46	14	6	3	37	20	5	7	11	21	38	58	58	70
10	Wigan Athletic	46	14	3	6	40	20	6	6	11	31	34	71	54	69
11	Huddersfield Town	46	13	3	7	37	23	5	10	8	20	28	57	51	67
12	Birmingham City	46	8	9	6	21	21	8	8	7	24	28	45	49	65
13	Leyton Orient	46	15	2	6	35	19	3	8	12	20	39	55	58	64
14	Stoke City	46	9	7	7	36	29	7	5	11	19	30	55	59	60
15	Reading	46	11	5	7	34	28	6	3	14	19	38	53	66	59
16	Exeter City	46	12	6	5	35	16	4	3	16	23	36	58	52	57
17	Preston North End	46	11	5	7	33	29	4	6	13	21	38	54	67	56
18	Shrewsbury Town	46	8	7	8	29	22	6	3	14	32	46	61	68	52
19	Chester City	46	10	3	10	27	27	4	6	13	19	31	46	58	51
20	Swansea City	46	8	6	9	31	33	5	3	15	18	39	49	72	48
21	Fulham	46	8	8	7	27	22	2	8	13	14	34	41	56	46
22	Crewe Alexandra	46	6	9	8	35	35	5	2	16	27	45	62	80	44
23	Rotherham United	46	5	10	8	31	38	5	2	16	19	49	50	87	42
24	Mansfield Town	46	5	8	10	23	27	3	6	14	19	36	42	63	38

1991-92 19th in Division 2

Captain: Shaun Cunnington

							Sherwood	McDermott	Jobling	Futcher	Lever	Dobbin	Watson	Gilbert	Rees	Smith M	Woods	Jones	Agnew	Cockerill	Birtles	North	Childs	Cunnington	Hargreaves	Reece	Ford	Rodger	Mendonca	Knight
1	Aug	17	CAMBRIDGE UNITED	3-4	Watson, Rees(2)	7657	1	2	3	4	5	6+	7	8	9	10*	11	12	14											
2		24	Oxford United	2-1	Cockerill, McDermott	4511	1	2	3	4	5	6	7	8		14	11+	9*		10	12									
3		31	TRANMERE ROVERS	2-2	Woods(2)	7018	1	2	3	4	5	6	7+	8		14	11	9*		10	12									
4	Sep	4	Leicester City	0-2		16242	1	2	3	4	5	6	7	8		14	11	9*		10+	12									
5		7	Bristol Rovers	3-2	Jobling, Jones, Gilbert	4641	1	2	3	4	5	6	7+	8		14	11	9*	10		12									
6		14	PLYMOUTH ARGYLE	2-1	Jobling, Jones	5432	1	2	3	4	5	6	7+	8		14	11*	9	10			12								
7		17	PORTSMOUTH	1-1	Woods	5348	1	2	3	4	5	6		8		12	11	9	10				7*							
8		21	Sunderland	2-1	Dobbin, Cunnington	16535	1	2		4	5	10		8		11		9	3				7*	6	12					
9		28	IPSWICH TOWN	1-2	Gilbert	6621	1	2		4*	5	10		8	14	3	11	9+					7	6	12					
10	Oct	5	Watford	0-2		6930	1	2		4	5	10+		8	9	3	11	14			12		7*	6						
11		12	PORT VALE	1-2	Childs	8218	1	2*		4		10+	12	8	9	3	11	14			5		7	6						
12		19	MIDDLESBROUGH	1-0	Woods	10265	1	2	3	4	5		10	8	9		11						7	6						
13		26	Blackburn Rovers	1-2	Childs	11096	1	2	3	4	5		10+	8	9		11	12		14			7*	6						
14	Nov	2	CHARLTON ATHLETIC	1-0	Childs	4743	1	2			5		14	8		12	11		3	10+	4*		7	6	9					
15		6	Brighton & Hove Albion	0-3		4420	1	2		4	5			8*		11		12	3	10			7	6	9					
16		9	Newcastle United	0-2		16959	1	2*			5		10			8	11	9	3	12	4		7	6						
17		23	MILLWALL	1-1	Cunnington	5701			3	4		10			9	8	11*	12	5				7	6		1	2			
18		26	Wolverhampton Wanderers	1-2	Dobbin	9378			3	4		8			9	12	11		5	10			7	6*		1	2			
19		30	Swindon Town	1-1	Dobbin	8397			3	4		6		8*	9	12	11		5	10			7			1	2			
20	Dec	7	BRISTOL CITY	3-1	Woods, Jones, Smith	4866			3	4		6		8		9	11	12	5	10*			7			1	2			
21		14	Barnsley	1-4	Smith	6856			3	4+	14	10		8		9	11	12	5				7*	6		1	2			
22		26	Derby County	0-0		16392		2	10	4	5			8		11		9	3					6		1	7			
23		28	Tranmere Rovers	1-1	Ford	7900		2		4	5	6		8		10		9	3				11		12	1*	7			
24	Jan	1	WOLVERHAMPTON WANDERERS	0-2		9158	1	2		4+	5	6	14	8	9	3		10*					11		12		7			
25		11	OXFORD UNITED	1-0	Rees	5117		2	3		5	6		8	9*			12					7			1	11	4	10	
26		18	Cambridge United	1-0	Dobbin	6092		2	3		5	6		8	9			12					7			1	11	4	10*	
27	Feb	8	BLACKBURN ROVERS	2-3	Mendonca, Cunnington	10014		2+	3		5	11		8	9	12							7*	6		1	14	4	10	
28		15	Millwall	1-1	Rees	6807		2	3		5	11		8*	9	10	12						7	6		1		4		
29		18	SOUTHEND UNITED	3-2	Smith, Cunnington, Dobbin	5337		2	3		5	11		8*	9	10	12						7+	6		1	14	4		
30		22	SWINDON TOWN	0-0		6817		2	3		5	11		8	9	10*	12						7	6		1		4		
31		29	Bristol City	1-1	Woods	8992		2	3		5	11+		8	9	10	12		14				7*	6		1				4
32	Mar	3	Charlton Athletic	3-1	Smith, OG, Rees	3658		2	3		5	11*		8	9	10			12				7	6		1				4
33		7	BARNSLEY	0-1		6913		2	3		5*	11		8	9	10	12						7	6		1				4
34		10	BRIGHTON & HOVE ALBION	0-1		4583			2		5	11		8	9	10	12		3				7*	6		1	14			4+
35		17	LEICESTER CITY	0-1		6377		2	3		5+	8			9*	10	11						7	6	12	1	14	4		
36		21	NEWCASTLE UNITED	1-1	Cunnington	11613		2	3	4	5	9				8*	11	12						6		1	7		10	
37		28	Southend United	1-3	Woods	4591	1	2	3	4*	5	9+		8			11	12	14					6			7		10	
38		31	Plymouth Argyle	2-1	Mendonca, Woods	6274	1	2			5			8		9	11		3					6			7	4	10	
39	Apr	4	BRISTOL ROVERS	0-1		4859	1	2	14		5			8		9*	11	12	3+					6			7	4	10	
40		7	DERBY COUNTY	0-1		7040	1	2	3		5			8+		12	11	9						6	14		7*	4	10	
41		11	Portsmouth	0-2		10576			2		5		12	8		3	11	9*						6	14	1	7	4	10+	
42		18	SUNDERLAND	2-0	Dobbin, Mendonca	8864		2	3	5		9		8			11						7*	6		1	12	4	10	
43		21	Ipswich Town	0-0		22393		2	3	5			7	8		9	11		10					6		1		4		
44		25	WATFORD	0-1		6483		2	3	5			7	8*		9	11+	12						6	14	1	10	4		
45		28	Middlesbrough	0-2		18570		2	3	5			7	8	9*	12	11		10					6		1		4		
46	May	2	Port Vale	1-0	Watson	8678		2	3	5			7	8	9*	11	12		10					6		1		4		
						Apps.	21	39	35	29	35	32	13	41	22	28	30	14	20	8	3		29	33	2	25	17	16	10	4
						Subs.			1		1		4		1	12	7	14	4	2	5	1			8		5			
						Goals		1	2			6	2	2	5	4	8	3		1			3	5			1		3	

Game 23: Reece injured, replaced by Hargreaves, Jones went in goal

1 own goal

F.A. Cup

							Sherwood	McDermott	Jobling	Futcher	Lever	Dobbin	Watson	Gilbert	Rees	Smith M	Woods	Jones	Agnew	Cockerill	Birtles	North	Childs	Cunnington	Hargreaves	Reece	Ford	Rodger	Mendonca	Knight
R1	Nov	16	Blackpool	1-2	Cunnington	4074	1		2				4		9	8	11	12+	3	10	5*		7	6	14					

Rumbelows Cup

							Sherwood	McDermott	Jobling	Futcher	Lever	Dobbin	Watson	Gilbert	Rees	Smith M	Woods	Jones	Agnew	Cockerill	Birtles	North	Childs	Cunnington	Hargreaves	Reece	Ford	Rodger	Mendonca	Knight
R1/1	Aug	20	Rotherham United	3-1	Dobbin, Jones, Rees	3839	1	2	10	4	5+	6	7	8	9		11	12	3*		14									
R1/2		27	ROTHERHAM UNITED	1-0	Birtles	3637	1	2	3	4	5	6	7	8*		14	11			10	9+				12					
R2/1	Sep	25	ASTON VILLA	0-0		13835	1	2		4	5	10		8	14	12	11	9+	3*				7	6						
R2/2	Oct	9	Aston Villa	1-1	Gilbert(pen)	15338	1	2		4	5	10		8	9*	3	11	12					7	6						
R3		29	TOTTENHAM HOTSPUR	0-3		17017	1	2	3*	4+	5		14	8	9	12	11			10			7	6						

Zenith Data Systems Cup

							Sherwood	McDermott	Jobling	Futcher	Lever	Dobbin	Watson	Gilbert	Rees	Smith M	Woods	Jones	Agnew	Cockerill	Birtles	North	Childs	Cunnington	Hargreaves	Reece	Ford	Rodger	Mendonca	Knight
Nth R1	Oct	1	WOLVES	1-0	Rees	1593	1	2		4	5	10		8	9*	3	11	12					7	6						
Nth R2		22	Tranmere Rovers	1-5	OG	4053	1	2	3*	4	5+		10	8	9	12	11				14		7	6						

		P	W	D	L	F	A	W	D	L	F	A	F	A	Pts
1	Ipswich Town	46	16	3	4	42	22	8	9	6	28	28	70	50	84
2	Middlesbrough	46	15	6	2	37	13	8	5	10	21	28	58	41	80
3	Derby County	46	11	4	8	35	24	12	5	6	34	27	69	51	78
4	Leicester City	46	14	4	5	41	24	9	4	10	21	31	62	55	77
5	Cambridge United	46	10	9	4	34	19	9	8	6	31	28	65	47	74
6	Blackburn Rovers	46	14	5	4	41	21	7	6	10	29	32	70	53	74
7	Charlton Athletic	46	9	7	7	25	23	11	4	8	29	25	54	48	71
8	Swindon Town	46	15	3	5	38	22	3	12	8	31	33	69	55	69
9	Portsmouth	46	15	6	2	41	12	4	6	13	24	39	65	51	69
10	Watford	46	9	5	9	25	23	9	6	8	26	25	51	48	65
11	Wolverhampton W.	46	11	6	6	36	24	7	4	12	25	30	61	54	64
12	Southend United	46	11	5	7	37	26	6	6	11	26	37	63	63	62
13	Bristol Rovers	46	11	9	3	43	29	5	5	13	17	34	60	63	62
14	Tranmere Rovers	46	9	9	5	37	32	5	10	8	19	24	56	56	61
15	Millwall	46	10	4	9	32	32	7	6	10	32	39	64	71	61
16	Barnsley	46	11	4	8	27	25	5	7	11	19	32	46	57	59
17	Bristol City	46	10	8	5	30	24	3	7	13	25	47	55	71	54
18	Sunderland	46	10	8	5	36	23	4	3	16	25	42	61	65	53
19	GRIMSBY TOWN	46	7	5	11	25	28	7	6	10	22	34	47	62	53
20	Newcastle United	46	9	8	6	38	30	4	5	14	28	54	66	84	52
21	Oxford United	46	10	6	7	39	30	3	5	15	27	43	66	73	50
22	Plymouth Argyle	46	11	5	7	26	26	2	4	17	16	38	42	64	48
23	Brighton & Hove A.	46	7	7	9	36	37	5	4	14	20	40	56	77	47
24	Port Vale	46	7	8	8	23	25	3	7	13	19	34	42	59	45

SEASON 1991/92
Back: Jellett (Physio), Sherwood, Birtles, Jones, Baraclough, Knight, Lever, Cockerill, Woods, Futcher, Agnew, Reece, O'Kelly (Yth Coach)
Front: Gilbert, McDermott, Rees, Jobling, Cunnington, Buckley (Manager), Mann (Asst. Man), Hargreaves, Smith, Dobbin, Watson, Childs

SEASON 1992/93
Back: Agnew, Rees, Ford, Futcher, Reece, Woods, Smith, Dobbin
Middle: Reed (Physio), Baraclough, Rodger, Wilmot, Sherwood, Lever, Cockerill, Mann (Asst Man)
Front: Hargreaves, Jobling, McDermott, Childs, Buckley (Man), Gilbert, Watson, Burns, Croft

1992-93 9th in Division 1 *

* Divisions re-numbered (Former Division 2)

Captain: Graham Rodger

	Date	Opponent	Res	Scorers	Att	Wilmot	McDermott	Jobling	Baraclough	Rodger	Dobbin	Watson	Gilbert	Rees	Mendonca	Woods	Smith M	Groves	Agnew	Handyside	Hargreaves	Ford	Croft	Futcher	Tillson	Childs	Lever	Beasant	Sherwood	Daws
1	Aug 15	Charlton Athletic	1-3	Dobbin	4823	1	2	3	4	5	6	7	8	9*	10	11+	12	14												
2	22	WATFORD	3-2	Mendonca, Watson, Rodger	4772	1	2	3		4	6	7	8		10	11		9	5											
3	30	Birmingham City	1-2	Mendonca	6807	1	2	3			6	7			10	11	8*	9	5	4	12									
4	Sep 5	OXFORD UNITED	1-1	Mendonca(pen)	4546	1	2*	3			6	7		12	10	11		9	5	4		8								
5	12	Tranmere Rovers	1-1	Watson	5330	1		3		4	6	7	8	12	10	11*		9		5			2							
6	19	Bristol Rovers	3-0	Rees, Woods(2)	5320	1				5	6	7	8	9		11		10					3	2*	4	12				
7	26	CAMBRIDGE UNITED	1-1	Rodger	4848	1	2			5	6	7	8		9+	11	14	10*					3		4	12				
8	29	Swindon Town	0-1		5759	1				5	6	7*	8		9	11+	14	10					3	2	4	12				
9	Oct 3	PETERBOROUGH UNITED	1-3	Rodger	5208	1		3*		5	6	7	8		9	11	14	10					2+		4	12				
10	10	Notts County	0-1		6442	1				4	6	2		9	12	11*	14	10					3	8+		7	5			
11	17	SOUTHEND UNITED	1-0	Rodger	4117	1	2			4	6		8	9*	12	11		10					3			7	5			
12	24	Newcastle United	1-0	Dobbin	30088		2				6	7	8		10	11		9					3	4			5	1		
13	31	PORTSMOUTH	3-0	Gilbert, McDermott, Rees	5708		2				6	7	8	12	10	11*		9					3	4			5	1		
14	Nov 3	WEST HAM UNITED	1-1	Mendonca	9119		2				6	7	8	11*	10		12	9					3	4			5	1		
15	7	Luton Town	4-1	Groves(3), Rees	6928		2			14	6*	7	8	11	10		12	9					3	4			5+	1		
16	14	BRISTOL CITY	2-1	Watson, Mendonca	5651		2			14	6	7	8	11	10	12		9					3	4*			5+	1		
17	21	Brentford	3-1	Mendonca, Groves, Dobbin	7439		2				6	7	8	11*	10	12		9					3	4			5	1		
18	28	Wolverhampton Wanderers	1-2	Lever	14240	1	2			14	6	7	8	11*	10	12		9					3	4+			5			
19	Dec 5	LEICESTER CITY	1-3	Groves	7488	1	2			4		6	8	11	10+		12	9			14		3			7*	5			
20	12	Millwall	1-2	McDermott	6900	1	2			5	6	7*	8			11	10	9	12		14		3	4+						
21	20	DERBY COUNTY	0-2		6475		2			5	6	7	8	9		11+	12	10			14		3	4*					1	
22	26	BARNSLEY	4-2	Gilbert(2), Groves, Watson	8242		2			4	6	7	8	11*	10	12		9	3	5									1	
23	28	Sunderland	0-2		20771		2			4	6	7	8	11	10*	12	14	9	3	5+									1	
24	Jan 9	BRISTOL ROVERS	2-0	Dobbin, Rees	4922	1	2			5	6	7	8	11	10*		12	9	3					4						
25	16	Cambridge United	0-2		4137	1	2			5	6	7+	8	11			10	9	3			12	14	4*						
26	26	SWINDON TOWN	2-1	Rees, Groves	5207	1	2			5	6		8	11*	10		12	9	3					4		7				
27	30	Watford	3-2	Rodger, Mendonca, Groves	6613	1	2			5	6			11	10		8	9	3			12		4		7*				
28	Feb 6	CHARLTON ATHLETIC	1-0	Rodger	5403	1	2			5	6			11	10		8	9	3					4		7				
29	20	BIRMINGHAM CITY	1-1	Rodger	5237		2	14		5	6		8	11*	10		12	9	3					4		7+			1	
30	23	Oxford United	1-0	Gilbert	4944		2			5	6		8		10		11	9	3					4		7			1	
31	27	NOTTS COUNTY	3-3	Groves(3)	5871			14		5	6		8	12	10		11*	9	3				2	4+		7			1	
32	Mar 6	Peterborough United	0-1		6657		2			5+	6		8	12	10		11	9	3				14	4		7*			1	
33	9	West Ham United	1-2	Groves	13170	1	2	6					8+	10	12	11*		9	14			7	3	4			5			
34	13	LUTON TOWN	3-1	Ford(2), Mendonca	5193	1	2	6					8	11	10			9				7	3	4			5			
35	16	TRANMERE ROVERS	0-0		5686	1	2	6					8	11	10			9				7	3	4			5			
36	20	Leicester City	0-3		15930	1	2	6*					8	11+	10			9	14			7	3	4		12	5			
37	23	BRENTFORD	0-1		4384	1	2	6+		5			8		10	11*	12	9	3			7	14	4						
38	28	Bristol City	0-1		6755	1				5			8	11	10*	12		9	3			6	2+	4		7				14
39	Apr 3	WOLVERHAMPTON WANDS.	1-0	Dobbin	5080	1					6		8		12	11*		10	3	5		7	2	4						9
40	6	MILLWALL	1-0	Mendonca(pen)	4445	1	2				6		8		10			11	3	5		7		4						9
41	10	Barnsley	2-0	Mendonca, Dobbin	4958	1	2				6		8	14	10+	12		11	3	5		7		4						9*
42	12	SUNDERLAND	1-0	Woods	8090	1	2				6		8	14	10	12		11		5*		7	3	4						9+
43	17	Derby County	1-2	Woods	12428	1	2				6		8		10	9	12	11	3+	5*		7	14	4						
44	23	Southend United	0-1		5807	1	2	14			6		8*		10	9	12	11		5+		7	3	4						
45	May 4	NEWCASTLE UNITED	0-2		14402	1	2			5	6		8*		10	11	12	9				7	3	4+		14				
46	8	Portsmouth	1-2	Daws	24955	1	2			5	6		8*		10+	14	12	11				7	3	4						9
					Apps.	33	38	11	1	27	39	24	41	24	38	21	8	45	20	11		15	28	35	4	11	14	6	7	5
					Subs.			3		3				7	4	9	18	1	3		4	2	4			6				1
					Goals		2			7	6	4	4	5	10	4		12				2					1			1

F.A.Cup

	Date	Opponent	Res	Scorers	Att	Wilmot	McDermott	Jobling	Baraclough	Rodger	Dobbin	Watson	Gilbert	Rees	Mendonca	Woods	Smith M	Groves	Agnew	Handyside	Hargreaves	Ford	Croft	Futcher	Tillson	Childs	Lever	Beasant	Sherwood	Daws
R3	Jan 2	Brentford	2-0	Mendonca, Dobbin	6880	1		12		5	6	7*	8	11+	10		14	9	3			2		4						
R4	Feb 2	Swansea City	0-0		8307	1	2			5	6		8+	11	10		14	9	3*				12	4		7				
R4r	9	SWANSEA CITY	2-0	Mendonca, Gilbert	8452	1	2			5	6		8	11	10			9	3					4		7				
R5	13	Ipswich Town	0-4		17894	1	2			5	6		8	11+	10		12	9	3				14	4		7*				

Rumbelows Cup

	Date	Opponent	Res	Scorers	Att	Wilmot	McDermott	Jobling	Baraclough	Rodger	Dobbin	Watson	Gilbert	Rees	Mendonca	Woods	Smith M	Groves	Agnew	Handyside	Hargreaves	Ford	Croft	Futcher	Tillson	Childs	Lever	Beasant	Sherwood	Daws
R1/1	Aug 19	BARNSLEY	1-1	Mendonca	3927	1	2	3		4	6	7	8	9*	10	11		12	5											
R1/2	25	Barnsley	1-1*	Mendonca	4636	1	2	3			6	7			10	11*	8	9	5	4	12									
R2/1	Sep 23	Queens Park Rangers	1-2	Watson	7275	1	2			4	6	7	8	9*	12	11		10		5			3							
R2/2	Oct 6	QUEENS PARK RANGERS	2-1+	OG, Woods	8443	1				4	6	12	8	14	10+	11		9				2*	3			7	5			

* Won 5-3 on penalties + lost 5-6 on penalties

Anglo Italian Cup

Qualifying matches

	Date	Opponent	Res	Scorers	Att	Wilmot	McDermott	Jobling	Baraclough	Rodger	Dobbin	Watson	Gilbert	Rees	Mendonca	Woods	Smith M	Groves	Agnew	Handyside	Hargreaves	Ford	Croft	Futcher	Tillson	Childs	Lever	Beasant	Sherwood	Daws
Grp 2	Sep 2	Leicester City	0-4		4112	1	2	3			6*	7			10	11	8+	9	5	4	14					12				
Grp 2	16	NEWCASTLE UNITED	2-2	Rees, Groves	2159	1					6	7*	8	9+		11		10		5	14		3	2	4	12				

1993-94 16th in Division 1

Captain: Graham Rodger (Club), Paul Groves (Team)

	Date		Opponents	Score	Scorers	Att.	Crichton	McDermott	Croft	Futcher	Lever	Groves	Watson	Gilbert	Daws	Mendonca	Shakespeare	Dobbin	Rodger	Ford	Woods	Crosby	Jobling	Handyside	Childs	Jemson	Agnew	Okorie	Livingstone	Rees
1	Aug	14	BOLTON WANDERERS	0-0		8593	1	2	3	4	5	6	7*	8	9+	10	11	12	14											
2		21	Nottingham Forest	3-5	Mendonca(2), Dobbin	23225	1	2		4	5	9	12	8+		10	3	6	14	7*	11									
3		24	PORTSMOUTH	1-1	Mendonca(pen)	5259	1	2	3	4*	12	9		8		10		6	5		11	7								
4		28	TRANMERE ROVERS	0-0		4793	1	2	3+		5	9	12	8		10		6	4		11	7*	14							
5	Sep	4	Peterborough United	2-1	Mendonca, Groves	5962	1	2	3			11		8	9	10	12	6	4					5	7*					
6		11	WATFORD	2-2	Jemson(pen), Groves	4783	1	2	3			11		8	9		12	6	4*			14		5	7+	10				
7		18	Birmingham City	1-1	Gilbert	11302	1	2	3			11	7	8	9			6						5		10	4			
8		25	WOLVERHAMPTON WANDS.	2-0	Childs, Mendonca	6310	1	2	3*	4	5	9		8		10	12	6							7	11				
9		28	Sunderland	2-2	Groves, OG	15488	1	2		4	5	11				9	8	6							7*	10	3	12		
10	Oct	2	Oxford United	2-2	Jemson, Childs	4301	1	2		4	5*	11				9	8	6	12						7	10	3			
11		9	SOUTHEND UNITED	4-0	Mendonca(2,1pen), Childs(2)	4726	1	2		4		11		8*		9	12	6	5				14		7	10	3+			
12		16	Stoke City	0-1		14696	1	2		4	5	11		8*	9+	10	12	6					14		7		3			
13		23	CHARLTON ATHLETIC	0-1		5118	1	2		4	5+	11	12		9	10	8*	6					14		7		3			
14		30	Crystal Palace	0-1		12202	1	2*		4	5	11	12			10		6					3		7		8+	14	9	
15	Nov	2	LEICESTER CITY	0-0		6344	1		11	4	5	8				10		6		2			3		7			12	9*	
16		7	Barnsley	2-1	Mendonca(2,1pen)	5797	1		3	4	5	11		8		10		6+		2			14		7				9*	12
17		20	Derby County	1-2	Mendonca(pen)	13498	1	2*	3	4	5	11		8	9	10	6			12			14		7+					
18		27	Millwall	0-1		7691	1		3	4	5	11	12	8	10+		7*	6					2						9	14
19	Dec	4	BARNSLEY	2-2	Dobbin, Watson	8123	1		3	4	5	11	7*	8	10+		12	6					2						9	14
20		18	Bolton Wanderers	1-1	Dobbin	9431	1	2	3	4	5	11	7*	8		10	12	6											9	
21		27	NOTTS COUNTY	2-2	Livingstone, OG	7781	1	2	3	4	5+	11	7*	8		10	12	6											9	14
22		29	Luton Town	1-2	Groves	7234	1	2*	3	4		11		8+		10	12	6		7				5					9	14
23	Jan	1	BRISTOL CITY	1-0	Groves	5469	1	2	3	4		11		8		10		6		7				5					9	
24		3	Middlesbrough	0-1		10441	1	2	8	4		11				10	12	6+		7				5			3*		9	14
25		15	STOKE CITY	0-0		8577	1		3	4		9	7*	8+		10	11	6		2				5			12			14
26		22	Southend United	2-1	Dobbin, Livingstone	4367	1		3	4		11		8		10+	7*	6	14	2				5	12				9	
27	Feb	1	WEST BROMWICH ALBION	2-2	Shakespeare, Groves	4740	1		3	4	5	11		8+		10	12	6*		2					7				9	14
28		5	Charlton Athletic	1-0	Mendonca	7598	1		3	4		11				10	8	6	5	2					7				9	
29		12	CRYSTAL PALACE	1-1	Mendonca	6302	1		3	4		11		8	14	10	12	6*	5	2					7					9+
30		19	Portsmouth	1-3	Groves	7794	1	2	3	4		11				10	6		5	8					7*		12	14		9+
31	Mar	5	Tranmere Rovers	2-1	Childs, Shakespeare	6454	1		12	4		11		8		10	6*		5	2					7		3	14		9+
32		8	PETERBOROUGH UNITED	3-2	Groves, Livingstone, Childs	4504	1	2		4		11		8		10			5	6					7		3		9	
33		12	BIRMINGHAM CITY	1-0	Croft	5405	1	2	12	4		11		8*					5	6	14				7		3		9	10+
34		15	Watford	3-0	Gilbert(pen), Groves, Shakespeare	5109	1	2		4		11		8			6		5	7							3		9	10
35		19	Wolverhampton Wanderers	0-0		20224	1	2	3	4		11		8			6		5	7	12								9	10*
36		26	OXFORD UNITED	1-0	Mendonca	5025	1	2+	12	4		11		8		10	6		5	14					7*		3		9	
37		29	MIDDLESBROUGH	1-1	Groves	5709	1			4		11		8		10	6		5	2					7		3		9	
38	Apr	2	Notts County	1-2	Rodger	7205	1		3+			11		8		10+	6		5	2	14			12	7*		4		9	
39		4	LUTON TOWN	2-0	Gilbert(2)	5542	1		12			11		8		10	6		5	2	14			4	7*		3		9	
40		9	Bristol City	0-1		5480	1		12			11		8		10	6		5	2	14			4	7*		3		9+	
41		12	SUNDERLAND	0-1		4732	1		2	4*		11		8		10			5	6	12				7		3		9	
42		16	Leicester City	1-1	Mendonca	15859	1		2	4	6	11				10			5	8					7		3		9	
43		23	DERBY COUNTY	1-1	Groves	7451	1		2	4	5	11		8		10				6	12				7		3		9*	
44		30	West Bromwich Albion	0-1		16870	1		2	4	5	11		8		10				6	12			14	7		3+		9*	
45	May	3	NOTTINGHAM FOREST	0-0		11930	1		3	4	5	11		8		10	6			2					7				9*	12
46		8	MILLWALL	0-0		5355	1		3	4		11		8		10	6	12		2			14	5*	7+					9
						Apps.	46	26	31	39	21	46	6	37	9	39	21	27	20	27	3	2	4	11	30	6	21		27	7
						Subs.			5		1		5		1		12	2	4	2	8	1	7	2	1		2	5		9
						Goals			1			11	1	4		14	3	4	1						6	2			3	

2 own goals

F.A. Cup

	Date		Opponents	Score	Scorers	Att.	Crichton	McDermott	Croft	Futcher	Lever	Groves	Watson	Gilbert	Daws	Mendonca	Shakespeare	Dobbin	Rodger	Ford	Woods	Crosby	Jobling	Handyside	Childs	Jemson	Agnew	Okorie	Livingstone	Rees
R3	Jan	8	WIGAN ATHLETIC	1-0	Croft	4488	1	2	3	4		11		8*		10	14	6		7				5			12			9+
R4		29	ASTON VILLA	1-2	Groves	15771	1		3	4	12	11		8		10	14	6+		2				5*	7				9	

Coca-Cola Cup

	Date		Opponents	Score	Scorers	Att.	Crichton	McDermott	Croft	Futcher	Lever	Groves	Watson	Gilbert	Daws	Mendonca	Shakespeare	Dobbin	Rodger	Ford	Woods	Crosby	Jobling	Handyside	Childs	Jemson	Agnew	Okorie	Livingstone	Rees
R2/1	Sep	21	HARTLEPOOL UNITED	3-0	Dobbin, Mendonca(2)	2353	1	2	3		12	11	7+	8	9	10	14	6						5*			4			
R2/2	Oct	5	Harltepool United	2-0	Groves, Dobbin	1385	1	2		4		9		8*		10	11	6	5				12	3	7					
R3		26	Tranmere Rovers	1-4	Okorie	5204	1	2		4	5	11	12		9+	10	8*	6					3		7			14		

Anglo Italian Cup

Qualifying matches

	Date		Opponents	Score	Scorers	Att.	Crichton	McDermott	Croft	Futcher	Lever	Groves	Watson	Gilbert	Daws	Mendonca	Shakespeare	Dobbin	Rodger	Ford	Woods	Crosby	Jobling	Handyside	Childs	Jemson	Agnew	Okorie	Livingstone	Rees
Grp 2	Aug	31	MIDDLESBROUGH	2-1	Mendonca, Daws	996	1	2	3			9		8	12	10		6	4		11*			5	7					
Grp 2	Sep	14	Barnsley	1-2	Dobbin	1627	1	2	3			11		8	9+		12	6	4					5	7*	10	14			

		P	W	D	L	F	A	W	D	L	F	A	F	A	Pts
1	Crystal Palace	46	16	4	3	39	18	11	5	7	34	28	73	46	90
2	Nottingham Forest	46	12	9	2	38	22	11	5	7	36	27	74	49	83
3	Millwall	46	14	8	1	36	17	5	9	9	22	32	58	49	74
4	Leicester City	46	11	9	3	45	30	8	7	8	27	29	72	59	73
5	Tranmere Rovers	46	15	3	5	48	23	6	6	11	21	30	69	53	72
6	Derby County	46	15	3	5	44	25	5	8	10	29	43	73	68	71
7	Notts County	46	16	3	4	43	26	4	5	14	22	43	65	69	68
8	Wolverhampton W.	46	10	10	3	34	19	7	7	9	26	28	60	47	68
9	Middlesbrough	46	12	6	5	40	19	6	7	10	26	35	66	54	67
10	Stoke City	46	14	4	5	35	19	4	9	10	22	40	57	59	67
11	Charlton Athletic	46	14	3	6	39	22	5	5	13	22	36	61	58	65
12	Sunderland	46	14	2	7	35	22	5	6	12	19	35	54	57	65
13	Bristol City	46	11	7	5	27	18	5	9	9	20	32	47	50	64
14	Bolton Wanderers	46	10	8	5	40	31	5	6	12	23	33	63	64	59
15	Southend United	46	10	5	8	34	28	7	3	13	29	39	63	67	59
16	GRIMSBY TOWN	46	7	14	2	26	16	6	6	11	26	31	52	47	59
17	Portsmouth	46	10	6	7	29	22	5	7	11	23	36	52	58	58
18	Barnsley	46	9	3	11	25	26	7	4	12	30	41	55	67	55
19	Watford	46	10	5	8	39	35	5	4	14	27	45	66	80	54
20	Luton Town	46	12	4	7	38	25	2	7	14	18	35	56	60	53
21	West Bromwich Alb.	46	9	7	7	38	31	4	5	14	22	38	60	69	51
22	Birmingham City	46	9	7	7	28	29	4	5	14	24	40	52	69	51
23	Oxford United	46	10	5	8	33	33	3	5	15	21	42	54	75	49
24	Peterborough Utd.	46	6	9	8	31	30	2	4	17	17	46	48	76	37

SEASON 1993/94
Back: Dunlop, Woods, Handyside, Crichton, Wilmot, Rodger, Lever, Futcher
Middle: Reed (Physio), Ford, Shakespeare, Maddison, Agnew, Groves, Mendonca, Dobbin, O'Kelly (Yth Coach)
Front: Jobling, Rees, Watson, Childs, Mann (Asst. Man), Buckley (Man), Daws, Gilbert, McDermott, Croft

SEASON 1994/95
Back: Livingstone, Rodger, Lever, Handyside, Gowshall, Woods
Middle: Mitchell (Physio), Gilbert, Futcher, Groves, Dobbin, Crichton, Pearcey, Croft,
Agnew, S.Buckley, Mendonca, Shakespeare
Front: Cook, Lester, Jobling, Watson, Swain (Asst Man), Laws (Play/Man), Childs, McDermott, Lambert, Neil

1994-95 10th in Division 1

Captain: Paul Groves

							Crichton	Jobling	Croft	Futcher	Lever	Shakespeare	Watson	Gilbert	Livingstone	Mendonca	Groves	Agnew	Lester	Handyside	Woods	Childs	Dobbin	McDermott	Rodger	Laws	Forrester	Fickling	Pearcey
1	Aug	13	BOLTON WANDERERS	3-3	Mendonca(3,1pen)	8393	1	2	3	4	5	6	7*	8	9	10	11	12											
2		20	Watford	0-0		6324	1		2	4	5	6		8	9*	10	11	3		7	12								
3		27	TRANMERE ROVERS	3-1	Livingstone(2), Groves	4087	1		2	4	5	6		8	9	10	11	3	12			7*							
4		30	Sunderland	2-2	Childs, Mendonca(pen)	15788	1	3	2	4	5*	6		8	9+	10	11			12	14	7							
5	Sep	3	Derby County	1-2	Mendonca	12027	1	3	2	4	5	6		8	9+	10	11	12			14	7*							
6		10	CHARLTON ATHLETIC	0-1		3970	1		2		5	6		8*		10	11	3		4	9	7	12						
7		13	PORT VALE	4-1	Woods, Mendonca(2), Gilbert	3216	1		2		5	6		8	12	10	11	3		4	9*	7							
8		17	West Bromwich Albion	1-1	Shakespeare	14496	1		2		5	6		8	12	10	11	3		4	9*	7+	14						
9		24	Swindon Town	2-3	Woods, Groves	8219	1		2		5	6		8	12	10	11	3		4	9*		7						
10	Oct	1	PORTSMOUTH	2-0	Mendonca(pen), Woods	4172	1	12	2		5	6		8		10	11	3		4	9		7*						
11		8	SHEFFIELD UNITED	0-0		8930	1	3	2		5	6	8			10*	11		12	4	9		7						
12		15	Wolverhampton Wanderers	1-2	Groves	24447	1	3*	2	12	5	6	8+		10		11			4	9	14	7						
13		22	BRISTOL CITY	1-0	Childs	4024	1	3	2		5	11*	7		9		6			4	10	12	8						
14		29	Southend United	0-0		5086	1	3	2		5		7	11	9		6			4	10		8						
15	Nov	1	Luton Town	2-1	Gilbert(2)	5839	1	3	2*		5		7	11	9		6	12		4	10		8						
16		5	MIDDLESBROUGH	2-1	Woods, Dobbin	8488	1	3	2		5		7	11	9		6			4	10		8						
17		12	MILLWALL	1-0	Woods	5261	1	3	2		5		7	11	9		6			4	10		8						
18		19	Stoke City	0-3		12055	1	3	2		5		7*	11	9+		6			4	10	12	8	14					
19		26	BURNLEY	2-2	Woods, Gilbert	7084	1	3	2		5			11	9		6			4	10	7	8						
20	Dec	3	Bristol City	2-1	Gilbert, Childs	6030	1	3	2		5+			11	9		6		12	4	10*	7	8		14				
21		10	WATFORD	0-0		6288	1	3	2					11	9		6			4	10	7*	8	12	5				
22		17	Bolton Wanderers	3-3	Woods, Jobling, Groves	10522	1	3	2					11*	9		6			4	10	7	8	12	5				
23		26	Barnsley	1-4	Woods	8669	1	3	2			12		11	9+		6		14	4	10	7*	8	5					
24		27	OLDHAM ATHLETIC	1-3	Woods	6958	1		3	5		12	7	11+		14	6		9	4	10		8*	2					
25		31	Reading	1-1	Shakespeare	8526	1		3			8	7	11*		9	6		12	4	10			2	5				
26	Jan	14	SOUTHEND UNITED	4-1	Shakespeare, Groves, Woods, Croft	3915	1	2	3			8	7	11		9	6			4	10				5				
27		21	Middlesbrough	1-1	Woods	15360	1	2+	3		5		7*	11	12	10	6			4	9		8	14					
28		28	NOTTS COUNTY	2-1	Woods, Mendonca	5161	1	2	3		5*		7	11		10	6			4	9		8			12			
29	Feb	4	Millwall	0-2		7397	1	2	3		5		7	11*		10	6			4	9	12	8+			14			
30		11	LUTON TOWN	5-0	Dobbin, Gilbert, Woods, Watson(2)	4615	1	3			5+		7	11*		10	6			4	9	12	8	2		14			
31		18	Burnley	2-0	Mendonca(2)	10511	1	3					7*	11		10	6			4	9		8	2	5	12			
32		21	STOKE CITY	0-0		6384	1	3	2				7	11		10	6			4	9		8*		5	12			
33		25	Portsmouth	1-2	Rodger	8274	1	3	11				7*		12	10	6			4	9		8	2+	5	14			
34	Mar	4	SWINDON TOWN	1-1	Watson	4934	1	3	11				7			10	6			4	9		8	2	5				
35		7	DERBY COUNTY	0-1		5310	1	3	11				12	10	9		6			4		7*	8+	2	5	14			
36		11	Tranmere Rovers	0-2		15810	1	3	2					11	9		6			4		7*	8		5	12	10		
37		19	SUNDERLAND	3-1	Livingstone(2), Forrester	5697	1	3	2					11	9		6			4		7	8		5		10		
38		21	Charlton Athletic	1-2	Childs	9601	1	3	2					11	9		6			4*		7	8		5	12	10		
39		25	WEST BROMWICH ALBION	0-2		7393	1	3	2		4	12		11+	9		6					7	8*		5	14	10		
40	Apr	1	Port Vale	2-1	Livingstone, Laws	7150	1	3	11		4				9		6					7	8		5	2	10		
41		8	READING	1-0	Livingstone	4519	1	3	7		4			11	9		6		12				8		5	2	10*		
42		15	Oldham Athletic	0-1		6757	1	3	7					11	9*		6				12		8		5	2	10	4	
43		17	BARNSLEY	1-0	Woods	7277	1	3	7		4			11*	9		6				10+	12	8		5	2	14		
44		22	Notts County	2-0	Livingstone, OG	5286		3	7		4			11	10		6				9		8		5	2			1
45		29	WOLVERHAMPTON WANDS.	0-0		10112		3	7		4			11	10		6				9	12	8		5	2*			1
46	May	6	Sheffield United	1-3	Livingstone	14323		3	2		4	8		11*	10+		6				9	7	12		5		14		1
						Apps.	43	37	44	6	31	16	20	40	29	21	46	7	1	34	33	18	35	8	20	6	7	1	3
						Subs.		1		1		3	1		5	1		3	6	1	4	7	3	4	1	10	2		
						Goals		1	1			3	3	6	8	11	5				14	4	2		1	1	1		

1 own goal

F.A. Cup

							Crichton	Jobling	Croft	Futcher	Lever	Shakespeare	Watson	Gilbert	Livingstone	Mendonca	Groves	Agnew	Lester	Handyside	Woods	Childs	Dobbin	McDermott	Rodger	Laws	Forrester	Fickling	Pearcey
R3	Jan	7	NORWICH CITY	0-1		11198	1	12	3			8		11+		9	6		14	4	10	7*		2	5				

Coca Cola Cup

							Crichton	Jobling	Croft	Futcher	Lever	Shakespeare	Watson	Gilbert	Livingstone	Mendonca	Groves	Agnew	Lester	Handyside	Woods	Childs	Dobbin	McDermott	Rodger	Laws	Forrester	Fickling	Pearcey
R1/1	Aug	16	Bradford City	1-2	Gilbert	5983	1	2	3	4	5	6	7	8	9*	10	11				12								
R1/2		23	BRADFORD CITY	1-2	Groves	3498	1		2	4	5+	6		8	9	10	11	3	14		12	7*							

		P	W	D	L	F	A	W	D	L	F	A	F	A	Pts
1	Middlesbrough	46	15	4	4	41	19	8	9	6	26	21	67	40	82
2	Reading	46	12	7	4	34	21	11	3	9	24	23	58	44	79
3	Bolton Wanderers	46	16	6	1	43	13	5	8	10	24	32	67	45	77
4	Wolverhampton W.	46	15	5	3	39	18	6	8	9	38	43	77	61	76
5	Tranmere Rovers	46	17	4	2	51	23	5	6	12	16	35	67	58	76
6	Barnsley	46	15	6	2	42	19	5	6	12	21	33	63	52	72
7	Watford	46	14	6	3	33	17	5	7	11	19	29	52	46	70
8	Sheffield United	46	12	9	2	41	21	5	8	10	33	34	74	55	68
9	Derby County	46	12	6	5	44	23	6	6	11	22	28	66	51	66
10	GRIMSBY TOWN	46	12	7	4	36	19	5	7	11	26	37	62	56	65
11	Stoke City	46	10	7	6	31	21	6	8	9	19	32	50	53	63
12	Millwall	46	11	8	4	36	22	5	6	12	24	38	60	60	62
13	Southend United	46	13	2	8	33	25	5	6	12	21	48	54	73	62
14	Oldham Athletic	46	12	7	4	34	21	4	6	13	26	39	60	60	61
15	Charlton Athletic	46	11	6	6	33	25	5	5	13	25	41	58	66	59
16	Luton Town	46	8	6	9	35	30	7	7	9	26	34	61	64	58
17	Port Vale	46	11	5	7	30	24	4	8	11	28	40	58	64	58
18	Portsmouth	46	9	8	6	31	28	6	5	12	22	35	53	63	58
19	West Bromwich Alb.	46	13	3	7	33	24	3	7	13	18	33	51	57	58
20	Sunderland	46	5	12	6	22	22	7	6	10	19	23	41	45	54
21	Swindon Town	46	9	6	8	28	27	3	6	14	26	46	54	73	48
22	Burnley	46	8	7	8	36	33	3	6	14	13	41	49	74	46
23	Bristol City	46	8	8	7	26	28	3	4	16	16	35	42	63	45
24	Notts County	46	7	8	8	26	28	2	5	16	19	38	45	66	40

1995-96 17th in Division 1

Captain: Paul Groves

	Date	Opponents	Score	Scorers	Att.	Crichton	Laws	Jobling	Handyside	Rodger	Groves	Croft	Shakespeare	Woods	Livingstone	Southall	Lester	Jewell	Dobbin	Lever	Fickling	Pearcey	McDermott	Childs	Smith R	Watson	Bonetti	Forrester	Warner	Butler	Gambaro	Gallimore	Flatts	Mendonca
1	Aug 12	Millwall	1-2	Livingstone	8546	1	2*	3	4	5	6	7	8	9	10	11	12																	
2	19	PORTSMOUTH	2-1	Laws, Croft	4515	1	2	3	4	5	6	7	8	9	10	11																		
3	26	Derby County	1-1	Shakespeare(pen)	10564	1	2	3^	4	5	6	7	8	9	10	11*		12	13															
4	29	LUTON TOWN	0-0		4289	1	2		4		6	7	8	9	10	11			3*	5	12													
5	Sep 2	WATFORD	0-0		3933		2+		4		6	3	8	9	10	11		12	13	5^		1	14	7*										
6	9	Wolverhampton Wanderers	1-4	Groves	23656	1			4		6	3	8*	9^	10	11		12	13				2	7	5									
7	12	Reading	2-0	Woods, Livingstone	7283	1	12		4		6	3	8	9	10	11							2*	7	5									
8	16	PORT VALE	1-0	Livingstone	4066	1	2		4		6	3	8*	9	10	11			12					7^	5	13								
9	23	NORWICH CITY	2-2	Childs, Southall	5901	1			4		6	3		9	10	11			8				2	7*	5	12								
10	30	Southend United	0-1		4977	1			4		6	3	12	9		11	13	10^	8				2	7*	5									
11	Oct 7	Charlton Athletic	1-0	Jewell	8994	1	2		4		6	3				11		9	8					7	5		10							
12	14	OLDHAM ATHLETIC	1-1	Dobbin	5509	1	2*		4		6	3		9		11	12		8					7	5		10							
13	21	Birmingham City	1-3	Woods	16445	1	2		4		6	3		9		11^			8		12			7	5*		10	13						
14	28	STOKE CITY	1-0	Groves	5477	1	2		4		6	3		9	12	11^			8	5				7*			10	13						
15	Nov 4	Ipswich Town	2-2	Woods, Dobbin	10250	1	2		4		6	3		9	12	11			8	5				7				10*						
16	11	BARNSLEY	3-1	Lever, OG, Livingstone	6166	1	2		4		6	3		9	10				8	5				7			11							
17	18	WEST BROMWICH ALBION	1-0	Bonetti	8155	1	2		4		6	3			10				8	5				7			11	9						
18	21	Sheffield United	2-1	Southall, Childs	9884	1			4		6	3	12		10	11*			8	5			2	7				9						
19	25	Tranmere Rovers	1-0	Bonetti	7500	1	12			4	6	3			10				8	5			2	7			11	9*						
20	Dec 2	CHARLTON ATHLETIC	1-2	Groves	6881	1				4	6	3		12	10				8	5			2	7			11	9*						
21	9	Norwich City	2-2	Livingstone, Groves	13283	1	12		4		6	3			10				8	5			2	7			11	9*						
22	16	SOUTHEND UNITED	1-1	Forrester	5269	1	2		4		6	3		12	10*				8	5				7			11	9						
23	23	LEICESTER CITY	2-2	OG, Dobbin	7713	1	2		4		6	3			10	11			8	5				7				9						
24	Jan 1	HUDDERSFIELD TOWN	1-1	Livingstone	7524	1	2		4		6	3		12	10				8	5				7			11	9*						
25	13	Portsmouth	1-3	Groves	6958	1	2		4	5*	6	3	13	14	10				8^	12				7			11	9+						
26	20	MILLWALL	1-2	Livingstone	5218	1	12			4*	6	3	13		10	14			8^	5			2	7			11	9+						
27	24	Sunderland	0-1		14656	1	8			4	6	3	7	12	10					5			2	13			11*	9^						
28	Feb 3	DERBY COUNTY	1-1	Bonetti	7818	1				12	6	3		9			13			5*			2	7			11	10^	4	8				
29	10	Luton Town	2-3	Forrester(2)	7158	1	2				6	3		9		12	13			5				7*			11	10^	4	8				
30	17	READING	0-0		6546	1					6	3	8	9	12	11				5	4		2	7				10*						
31	Mar 3	SUNDERLAND	0-4		5318	1	12				6	3		13	10	11				5			2	7^				9*	4	8				
32	5	Crystal Palace	0-5		11548	1				4	6	3	8	9	10	11				5			2	7										
33	9	Leicester City	1-2	Livingstone	13784	1	12			4	6	3	8	9	10	11*				5			2	7^							13			
34	12	WOLVERHAMPTON WANDS.	3-0	Shakespeare, Groves, Forrester	5013	1	11			12	6	3	8		10					5*			2	7	4			9						
35	16	CRYSTAL PALACE	0-2		5059	1	11			5	6	3^	8		10	12					13		2	7*	4			9						
36	24	Huddersfield Town	3-1	Livingstone, Childs, Groves	12090	1				5	6	3	8		10	11							2	7	4			9						
37	30	BIRMINGHAM CITY	2-1	Groves, Livingstone	5475	1				5	6		8		10	11							2		4			9				3	7	
38	Apr 2	Oldham Athletic	0-1		5037	1				5	6		8	12	10	11^							2	13	4			9*				3	7	
39	6	Stoke City	2-1	Groves, Gallimore	12524	1			5		6		8	9		12					13		2^	11	4			14				3	7*	10+
40	8	IPSWICH TOWN	3-1	Mendonca(3)	5904	1			5		6		8*	9	12	13					2			11^	4+			14				3	7	10
41	13	West Bromwich Albion	1-3	Forrester	16116	1					6		8	9*	12	11					5		2		4			7^				3	13	10
42	16	Port Vale	0-1		5796	1			5		6		8	9		7							2		4		11					3		10
43	20	SHEFFIELD UNITED	0-2		7685	1			5		6		8		9	7^					12		2		4*		11					3		10
44	23	Watford	3-6	Groves, Livingstone, Walker	8909	1			4^		6		8	12	9				7	5*	13		2					11				3+		10
45	27	TRANMERE ROVERS	1-1	Mendonca(pen)	5408	1			5		6		8		9	7			12		4		2				11*					3		10
46	May 4	Barnsley	1-1	McDermott	6108				5		6			12	9				8		4	1	2					13				3		10

Additional players: Clare 43/13; Walker 44/14 (1 goal), 46/11^; Neil 46/7*

	Crichton	Laws	Jobling	Handyside	Rodger	Groves	Croft	Shakespeare	Woods	Livingstone	Southall	Lester	Jewell	Dobbin	Lever	Fickling	Pearcey	McDermott	Childs	Smith R	Watson	Bonetti	Forrester	Warner	Butler	Gambaro	Gallimore	Flatts	Mendonca
Apps.	44	21	3	30	14	46	36	24	24	33	28		2	21	23	5	2	27	33	18		19	23	3	3		10	4	8
Subs.		6			2			4	9	5	5	5	3	5	1	6		1	2		2		5			1		1	
Goals		1				10	1	2	3	11	2		1		1			1	3			3	5				1		4

2 own goals

F.A. Cup

	Date	Opponents	Score	Scorers	Att.	Crichton	Laws	Jobling	Handyside	Rodger	Groves	Croft	Shakespeare	Woods	Livingstone	Southall	Lester	Jewell	Dobbin	Lever	Fickling	Pearcey	McDermott	Childs	Smith R	Watson	Bonetti	Forrester	Warner	Butler	Gambaro	Gallimore	Flatts	Mendonca
R3	Jan 6	LUTON TOWN	7-1	Forrester(2),Livingstone(2),Bonetti,Southall,Woods	5387	1	2		4	5	6	3	13	12	10*	14			8^					7+		11	9							
R4	Feb 7	West Ham United	1-1	Laws	23030	1	4				6	3	8	9	12	13				5			2	7		11^	10*							
R4r	14	WEST HAM UNITED	3-0	Childs, Woods, Forrester	8382	1					6	3	8	9	12	11				5	4		2	7*			10							
R5	21	CHELSEA	0-0		9648	1	4				6	3	8	9	10	11				5			2	7										
R5r	28	Chelsea	1-4	Groves	28545	1	4*				6	3	8	9	10	11+			13	5	12		2	7^			14							

Coca Cola Cup

	Date	Opponents	Score	Scorers	Att.	Crichton	Laws	Jobling	Handyside	Rodger	Groves	Croft	Shakespeare	Woods	Livingstone	Southall	Lester	Jewell	Dobbin	Lever	Fickling	Pearcey	McDermott	Childs	Smith R	Watson	Bonetti	Forrester	Warner	Butler	Gambaro	Gallimore	Flatts	Mendonca
R2/1	Sep 20	Birmingham City	1-3	Woods	7466	1	2*		4		6	3		9	10	11	12		8		5					7								
R2/2	Oct 3	BIRMINGHAM CITY	1-1	Southall	3280	1	2		4		6	3				11		9	8		5			7*			10							

Additional player: Clare 1R2L/12

		P	W	D	L	F	A	W	D	L	F	A	F	A	Pts
1	Sunderland	46	13	8	2	32	10	9	9	5	27	23	59	33	83
2	Derby County	46	14	8	1	48	22	7	8	8	23	29	71	51	79
3	Crystal Palace	46	9	9	5	34	22	11	6	6	33	26	67	48	75
4	Stoke City	46	13	6	4	32	15	7	7	9	28	34	60	49	73
5	Leicester City	46	9	7	7	32	29	10	7	6	34	31	66	60	71
6	Charlton Athletic	46	8	11	4	28	23	9	9	5	29	22	57	45	71
7	Ipswich Town	46	13	5	5	45	30	6	7	10	34	39	79	69	69
8	Huddersfield Town	46	14	4	5	42	23	3	8	12	19	35	61	58	63
9	Sheffield United	46	9	7	7	29	25	7	7	9	28	29	57	54	62
10	Barnsley	46	9	10	4	34	28	5	8	10	26	38	60	66	60
11	West Bromwich Alb.	46	11	5	7	34	29	5	7	11	26	39	60	68	60
12	Port Vale	46	10	5	8	30	29	5	10	8	29	37	59	66	60
13	Tranmere Rovers	46	9	9	5	42	29	5	8	10	22	31	64	60	59
14	Southend United	46	11	8	4	30	22	4	6	13	22	39	52	61	59
15	Birmingham City	46	11	7	5	37	23	4	6	13	24	41	61	64	58
16	Norwich City	46	7	9	7	26	24	7	6	10	33	31	59	55	57
17	GRIMSBY TOWN	46	8	10	5	27	25	6	4	13	28	44	55	69	56
18	Oldham Athletic	46	10	7	6	33	20	4	7	12	21	30	54	50	56
19	Reading	46	8	7	8	28	30	5	10	8	26	33	54	63	56
20	Wolverhampton W.	46	8	9	6	34	28	5	7	11	22	34	56	62	55
21	Portsmouth	46	8	6	9	34	32	5	7	11	27	37	61	69	52
22	Millwall	46	7	6	10	23	28	6	7	10	20	35	43	63	52
23	Watford	46	7	8	8	40	33	3	10	10	22	37	62	70	48
24	Luton Town	46	7	6	10	30	34	4	6	13	10	30	40	64	45

SEASON 1995/96

Back: Mendonca, S.Buckley, Watson, Neil, Lester, Crichton, Pearcey, Fickling, Petchey, Gowshall, Brookes, McDermott
Middle: Bielby (Kit Man), Handyside, Woods, Shakespeare, Livingstone, Rodger, Lever,
Groves, Delahunt (Physio), Cockerill (Youth Coach)
Front: Jobling, Southall, Childs, Swain (Asst Man), Laws (Player/Manager), Gilbert, Croft, Dobbin

SEASON 1996/97

Back: Southall, Gallimore, Love, Pearcey, Crichton, Handyside, Woods
Middle: Bielby (Kit Man), Clare, Fickling, Smith, Livingstone, Lever, Rodger, Lester,
Gowshall, Neil, Harsley, Oster, Delahunt (Physio)
Front: Forrester, Jobling, Mendonca, Shakespeare, Walker, Swain (Asst Man), Laws (Player/Manager),
Cockerill (Youth Coach), McDermott, Black, Wrack, Widdrington, Childs

1996-97 22nd in Division 1

Captain: Peter Handyside(Aug-Sep), Graham Rodger(Sep-May)

	Date	Opponent	Score	Scorers	Att.	Pearcey	Laws	Gallimore	Handyside	Smith R	Widdrington	Shakespeare	Webb	Woods	Mendonca	Black	Southall	Wrack	McDermott	Livingstone	Childs	Forrester	Walker	Fickling	Trollope	Jobling	Lever	Rodger	Oster	Lester	Appleton	Miller	Love
1	Aug 17	WOLVERHAMPTON WANDS	1-3	Mendonca	7910	1	2*	3	4	5	6	7	8	9^	10	11	12	13															
2	23	Tranmere Rovers	2-3	Mendonca(pen), Handyside	6800	1		3	4		6	8	9^		10	11	12		2	5	7*	13											
3	27	Ipswich Town	1-1	Mendonca	9762	1		3	4		6^	5	8		10	11*	12		2	9	7+		13	14									
4	31	PORTSMOUTH	0-1		4747	1		3	4	5	6				10	11*	7		2	9	12				8								
5	Sep 7	SWINDON TOWN	2-1	Mendonca(2,1pen)	4089	1			4		6			9	10	11	12		2	5	7*				8	3							
6	10	Bolton Wanderers	1-6	Trollope	12448	1			4		6		12	9	10		11*	7	2	5^					8	3	13						
7	14	Port Vale	1-1	Southall	4892	1		12	4		6			9	10		11	7	2						8	3*	5						
8	21	OXFORD UNITED	0-2		4120	1		12	4*		6	13		9+	10	11		14	2		7				8^	3	5						
9	28	Barnsley	3-1	Shakespeare,Forrester,McDermott	8833	1		12			6	5			10	11*	13		2	9	7+	14		4	8	3^							
10	Oct 1	NORWICH CITY	1-4	Flickling	5266	1		12			6^	5		13	10	11			2	9	7	8+		4	14	3*							
11	5	QUEENS PARK RANGERS	2-0	Mendonca, Widdrington	5472	1		3			6	5		12	10	11	13		2	9	7^	8*		4									
12	12	Reading	1-1	Wrack	6656	1	5*	3			6				10	11	8	13	2	9	7^	12		4									
13	16	Southend United	0-1		3305	1	5+	3			6				10	11*	8	7	2	9^		12		4		14		13					
14	19	WEST BROMWICH ALBION	1-1	Fickling	7187	1		3			6				10	11	8	7	2		12	9*		4				5					
15	26	Crystal Palace	0-3		13665	1		3		12	6	7			10	11^	8	9	2*	13				4				5					
16	29	OLDHAM ATHLETIC	0-3		3532	1		3		12	6	8			9	11				13	7	10^		4*		2		5					
17	Nov 3	SHEFFIELD UNITED	2-4	Livingstone (2)	5935	1		3		4		10		6	9^	11		12		8	7*	13		2+		14		5					
18	16	STOKE CITY	1-1	Mendonca(pen)	5601	1		3		4	6	10			9	11				8	7^	13		12		2*		5					
19	23	Huddersfield Town	0-2		10590	1		3*		4	6	10^		13	9	11				8	7+	14		12		2		5					
20	26	Charlton Athletic	3-1	Mendonca(2), Livingstone	9435	1		3		4	6			11+	9		12			8	7	14		13		2^		5	10*				
21	30	CRYSTAL PALACE	2-1	Livingstone, Rodger	5115	1		3		4	6			11	9	12	13			8	7*					2		5	10^				
22	Dec 7	Birmingham City	0-0		17001	1		3		4	6			11	9					8	7					2		5	10				
23	21	BRADFORD CITY	1-1	Lester	5766	1		3		4	6			11	9	12		13			7^					2		5	10*	8			
24	26	BOLTON WANDERERS	1-2	Childs	8185	1		3		4	6	12		11	10						7					2*		5	9	8			
25	Jan 11	PORT VALE	1-1	Mendonca	3863	1		3			6*			9	10	11^	12	13	2					4			5		7	8			
26	18	Norwich City	1-2	Lester	16687	1		3						9^	10	12	11		2					4		6*	5		13	8	7		
27	25	Swindon Town	3-3	Gallimore, Appleton, Mendonca	9127	1		3						9	10		11^		2	12	13			4		6+	5		14	8*	7		
28	28	BARNSLEY	2-3	Oster, Appleton	6323			3						9+	10		11		2	13	12^			4		14	5		6	8*	7	1	
29	Feb 1	CHARLTON ATHLETIC	2-0	Mendonca(pen), Lester	4139			3			6			9	10				2		12						5	4	11	8*	7	1	
30	8	Oldham Athletic	3-0	Oster, Woods, Mendonca	6549			3			6			9	10				2	12							5	4	11	8*	7	1	
31	15	HUDDERSFIELD TOWN	2-2	Widdrington, Lester	6197	1		3+		5	6			9*	10		12		2	13						14		4	11	8^	7		
32	22	Sheffield United	1-3	Lester	17502	1		3		5	6			9	10		12		2	13								4	11	8^	7*		
33	Mar 1	BIRMINGHAM CITY	1-2	Southall	5166			3^			6	12		9+	10		7		2*	13		14		5				4	11	8			1
34	5	Stoke City	1-3	Livingstone	8621						6	3		9	10		5			8^	12			2				4	11*	13	7		1
35	8	Bradford City	4-3	Mendonca(2),Rodger,Livingstone	15219						6	3			10		11			8				2		9	5	4			7		1
36	15	MANCHESTER CITY	1-1	Appleton	8732	1		12			6	3*			10		11^			8				2		9	5	4			7		
37	18	Oxford United	2-3	Mendonca, Widdrington	6421	1		12			6	3			10		11^			8+	13			2		9	5*	4	7	14			
38	22	TRANMERE ROVERS	0-0		4353	1		3			6	9			10			12			7^					2	5	4	11*	8			
39	31	IPSWICH TOWN	2-1	Mendonca, Lee	6268	1		3			6	9			10		7			8*	12					2	5	4		11^			
40	Apr 5	Portsmouth	0-1		9854	1		3			6+	9			10		7			12	11^			13		2	5	4		14			
41	12	Queens Park Rangers	0-3		10765	1		3	12		13	9			10		7		2*							6+	5	4	11	14			
42	16	Manchester City	1-3	Shakespeare	23334	1		3*			6	9					7		2	10^				4		8	5		11	12			
43	19	READING	2-0	Southall, Widdrington	4392	1		3			6	9			10		7		2					4			5		11	8			
44	23	Wolverhampton Wanderers	1-1	Oster	25474	1		3			6	9			10	12	7		2								5	4	11^	8*			
45	26	West Bromwich Albion	0-2		15574	1		3			6	9*			10	12	7		2					13			5^	4	11	8+			
46	May 4	SOUTHEND UNITED	4-0	Southall,Mendonca(2,1pen),Lee	7367	1		3			6				10	8^	7		2	9+				12			5*	4	11	13			
Apps.						40	3	36	8	12	41	23	3	21	45	19	23	5	29	23	19	4		20	6	24	20	27	21	16	10	3	3
Subs.								6	1	2	1	3	1	3		5	11	7		9	8	9	1	7	1	4	1	1	3	6			
Goals								1	1		4	2		1	19		4	1	1	6	1	1		2	1			2	3	5	3		

Additional player: Neil 38/13

F.A. Cup

	Date	Opponent	Score	Scorers	Att.	Pearcey	Laws	Gallimore	Handyside	Smith R	Widdrington	Shakespeare	Webb	Woods	Mendonca	Black	Southall	Wrack	McDermott	Livingstone	Childs	Forrester	Walker	Fickling	Trollope	Jobling	Lever	Rodger	Oster	Lester	Appleton	Miller	Love
R3	Jan 4	Sheffield Wednesday	1-7	Oster	20590	1		3			6			9	10	11			12		7^		4		2*		5	13	8				

F.L. Cup (Coca Cola Cup)

	Date	Opponent	Score	Scorers	Att.	Pearcey	Laws	Gallimore	Handyside	Smith R	Widdrington	Shakespeare	Webb	Woods	Mendonca	Black	Southall	Wrack	McDermott	Livingstone	Childs	Forrester	Walker	Fickling	Trollope	Jobling	Lever	Rodger	Oster	Lester	Appleton	Miller	Love
R1/1	Aug 20	Oldham Athletic	1-0	Mendonca	2975	1		3	4	5*	6	10	8+		9	11	14		2	12	7^			13									
R1/2	Sep 3	OLDHAM ATHLETIC *	0-1		2371	1		3	4		6	5		9^	10	11	12		2	8	7*	13											

* Oldham won on penalties

		P	W	D	L	F	A	W	D	L	F	A	F	A	Pts
1	Bolton Wanderers	46	18	4	1	60	20	10	10	3	40	33	100	53	98
2	Barnsley	46	14	4	5	43	19	8	10	5	33	36	76	55	80
3	Wolverhampton W.	46	10	5	8	31	24	12	5	6	37	27	68	51	76
4	Ipswich Town	46	13	7	3	44	23	7	7	9	24	27	68	50	74
5	Sheffield Utd.	46	13	5	5	46	23	7	8	8	29	29	75	52	73
6	Crystal Palace	46	10	7	6	39	22	9	7	7	39	26	78	48	71
7	Portsmouth	46	12	4	7	32	24	8	4	11	27	29	59	53	68
8	Port Vale	46	9	9	5	36	28	8	7	8	22	27	58	55	67
9	Queens Park Rgs.	46	10	5	8	33	25	8	7	8	31	35	64	60	66
10	Birmingham City	46	11	7	5	30	18	6	8	9	22	30	52	48	66
11	Tranmere Rovers	46	10	9	4	42	27	7	5	11	21	29	63	56	65
12	Stoke City	46	15	3	5	34	22	3	7	13	17	35	51	57	64
13	Norwich City	46	9	10	4	28	18	8	2	13	35	50	63	68	63
14	Manchester City	46	12	4	7	34	25	5	6	12	25	35	59	60	61
15	Charlton Athletic	46	11	8	4	36	28	5	3	15	16	38	52	66	59
16	West Bromwich Alb.	46	7	7	9	37	33	7	8	8	31	39	68	72	57
17	Oxford United	46	14	3	6	44	26	2	6	15	20	42	64	68	57
18	Reading	46	13	7	3	37	24	2	5	16	21	43	58	67	57
19	Swindon Town	46	11	6	6	36	27	4	3	16	16	44	52	71	54
20	Huddersfield Town	46	10	7	6	28	20	3	8	12	20	41	48	61	54
21	Bradford City	46	10	5	8	29	32	2	7	14	18	40	47	72	48
22	GRIMSBY TOWN	46	7	7	9	31	34	4	6	13	29	47	60	81	46
23	Oldham Athletic	46	6	8	9	30	30	4	5	14	21	36	51	66	43
24	Southend United	46	7	9	7	32	32	1	6	16	10	54	42	86	39

1997-98 3rd in Division 2

Captain: Paul Groves

	Date	Opponent	Score	Scorers	Att	Davison	McDermott	Gallimore	Handyside	Lever	Widdrington	Donovan	Black	Livingstone	Nogan	Groves	Jobling	Woods	Southall	Gilbert	Lester	Pearcey	Butterfield	Holsgrove	Rodger	Clare	Burnett	Smith D	Wrack	Dobbin
1	Aug 9	BRISTOL CITY	1-1	Widdrington	6220	1	2	3*	4	5	6	7	8^	9	10	11	12	13												
2	16	Plymouth Argyle	2-2	Donovan(pen), Nogan	6002	1	2	3*	4	5		7		9^	10	11	12		6	8	13									
3	23	WREXHAM	0-0		4404	1	2		4	5		7		12	9	11	3		6	8*	10									
4	30	Brentford	1-3	Nogan	3875	1	2	12	4	5	13	7		14	9	11	3		6*	8^	10+									
5	Sep 2	Preston North End	0-2		9489	1	2*		4	5	12	7	13	9		11	3	14	6	8^	10+									
6	9	YORK CITY	0-0		5308			3	4	5	6	7	12	10^	9	11	14			8*	13	1	2+							
7	13	Fulham	2-0	Livingstone	6874		12	3	4	5		7	8	10	9^	11					13	1	2*	6						
8	20	MILLWALL	0-1		4267		2	3*	4	5	12	7	8^	10	9+	11		13			14	1		6						
9	27	Bournemouth	1-0	Groves	3712	1	2*	3	4	5	12	7	8	10	13	11					9^			6						
10	Oct 4	WIGAN ATHLETIC	2-1	Donovan(2pens)	4623	1	2	3	4	5	6	7	8+	12	9*	11		13			10^			14						
11	11	NORTHAMPTON TOWN	1-0	Donovan	4778			3	4		6+	7	8	12	9	11	13				10*	1	2^	14	5					
12	18	Blackpool	2-2	Nogan, Donovan(pen)	5234	1		3^	4+	5	6	7	8*	10	9	11	2				12			13	14					
13	21	Oldham Athletic	0-2		4520	1			4	5	6	7	8*	10^	9	11	3	12			13			14	2+					
14	25	WATFORD	0-1		5699	1	2	3	4*	5	6	7	8^	12	9	11		13			10									
15	Nov 1	SOUTHEND UNITED	5-1	Nogan(2), Lester, Groves, Widdrington	4501	1	2		4	5	6^	7	8		9*	11	3	12			10+			13		14				
16	4	Walsall	0-0		2599	1	2		4	5	6+	7	8^	12	9	11	3				10*			13		14				
17	8	Chesterfield	0-1		5004	1	2		4	5	6+	7	8*	10	9^	11	3		12		13			14						
18	22	BURNLEY	4-1	Groves, Widdrington, Lester, Nogan	4829	1	2	3	4		6	7	8	12	9^	11	13				10*				5					
19	29	Gillingham	2-0	Jobling, Black	4855	1	2	3	4			7	8	12	9	11	6				10*				5					
20	Dec 2	WYCOMBE WANDERERS	0-0		4160	1	2	3	4		12	7	8^	13	9	11	6				10*				5+	14				
21	12	Bristol Rovers	4-0	Gallimore, Livingstone(2), Donovan	4801	1	2	3	4		8	7		12	9*	11	6				10^		13		5+	14				
22	20	CARLISLE UNITED	1-0	McDermott	6222	1	2	3	4		8*	7	12	9		11	6						13		5	10^				
23	26	York City	0-0		7093	1	2	3	4		8	7	10	9		11	6*								5	12				
24	28	PRESTON NORTH END	3-1	Donovan(2), Black	6725	1	2	3	4	12	6^	7	8	9		11	13						14		5*	10+				
25	Jan 10	Bristol City	1-4	Groves	12567	1	2	3		5		7	8	9		11	6	12							4^	10*	13			
26	17	BRENTFORD	4-0	Groves, Smith, Donovan, Clare	4624	1	2	3+		5	12	7	13	9		11	14	4^								10	6*	8		
27	31	FULHAM	1-1	Burnett	6785	1	2	3^	4	5*		7	12	9		11	13				10+					14	6	8		
28	Feb 7	Millwall	1-0	Livingstone	6020	1	2	3	4	5^		7	12	9	13	11					10*						6	8		
29	14	Wigan Atheltic	2-0	Nogan, Donovan	3548	1	2	3	4	5		7		10	9*	11					12						6	8		
30	21	BOURNEMOUTH	2-1	OG, Groves	5456	1	2	3	4	5^		7	12	10	9+	11					13					14	6	8*		
31	24	BLACKPOOL	1-0	Clare	4924	1	2			5		7	8	4	9*	11	3				10					12	6			
32	28	Northampton Town	1-2	Donovan	6932	1	2			5		7	8^	4	9	11	3				10*					12	6		13	
33	Mar 3	CHESTERFIELD	0-0		4940	1	2		12	5		7	8*	4	9^	11	3				13					10	6			
34	7	Southend United	1-0	Clare	4829	1	2	3	12	5		7	8*	4	9^	11					13					10	6			
35	14	WALSALL	3-0	Nogan, Donovan(2)	4916	1	2	3*	4	5		7	12		9^	11	13				14					10+	6	8		
36	21	Luton Town	2-2	Gallimore, Donovan	5700	1	2	3	4	5		7		12	9*	11					10						6	8		
37	24	PLYMOUTH ARGYLE	1-0	Groves	4661	1	2	3*	4	5		7	12	13	9^	11					10						6	8		
38	28	Burnley	1-2	Lester	8256	1	2		4	5		7	8^	9	12	11	13				10*					14		3		6+
39	31	Wrexham	0-0		5421	1	2	3	4	5		7		12	9	11					10*						6	8		
40	Apr 4	GILLINGHAM	0-0		5190	1	2*	3	4	5		7	12	9^		11					10					13	6	8		
41	7	LUTON TOWN	0-1		4455	1		3	4	5+		7	12			11		13			10*		2			9	6	8^		14
42	10	Wycombe Wanderers	1-1	Lester	5846	1	2	3*	4	5		7	12		9	11					10						6	8		
43	13	BRISTOL ROVERS	1-2	Donovan(pen)	5484	1	2	3+	4	5		7	12		9*	11	13				10					14	6^	8		
44	21	Carlisle United	1-0	Donovan(pen)	3956	1	2		4			7	8	5	9	11					10*					12	6	3		
45	25	Watford	0-0		14002	1	2	3	4	5		7*	12	10^	9+	11	14				13						6	8		
46	May 2	OLDHAM ATHLETIC	0-2		8054	1	2	3*	4^	5		7	12	10		11	13				9+					14	6	8		
					Apps.	42	40	34	40	37	15	46	24	28	33	46	17	1	4	5	27	4	4	3	10	8	20	17		1
					Subs.		1	1	2	1	6		15	13	3		13	9	1		13		3	7	1	14	1		1	1
					Goals		1	2			3	16	2	5	8	7	1				4					3	1	1		

F.A. Cup

	Date	Opponent	Score	Scorers	Att	Davison	McDermott	Gallimore	Handyside	Lever	Widdrington	Donovan	Black	Livingstone	Nogan	Groves	Jobling	Woods	Southall	Gilbert	Lester	Pearcey	Butterfield	Holsgrove	Rodger	Clare	Burnett	Smith D	Wrack	Dobbin
R1	Nov 15	Shrewsbury Town	1-1	Southall	3193	1	2	3	4			7	8*	12	9	11			6		10				5					
R1r	25	SHREWSBURY TOWN	4-0	Nogan, OG, Lester, Jobling	3242	1	2	3	4			7	8	12	9+	11^	6		13		10				5	14				
R2	Dec 6	CHESTERFIELD	2-2	Rodger, Nogan	4762	1	2	3	4		8^	7		12	9	11	6				10*				5	13				
R2r	16	Chesterfield	2-0	Lester, Groves	4553	1	2	3	4		8	7		9		11	6				10*				5	12				
R3	Jan 3	NORWICH CITY	3-0	McDermott, Woods, Donovan	8161	1	2	3	4	12		7+	8		9^	11	6	13					14		5	10*				
R4	24	Leeds United	0-2		29598	1	2	3	4	5		7	10	9		11	6*									12		8		

Rumbelows Cup

	Date	Opponent	Score	Scorers	Att	Davison	McDermott	Gallimore	Handyside	Lever	Widdrington	Donovan	Black	Livingstone	Nogan	Groves	Jobling	Woods	Southall	Gilbert	Lester	Pearcey	Butterfield	Holsgrove	Rodger	Clare	Burnett	Smith D	Wrack	Dobbin
R1L1	Aug 12	Oldham Athletic	0-1		5656	1	2	3	4	5	6+	7	8*	9^	10	11	12	13							14					
R1L2	26	OLDHAM ATHLETIC	5-0	Lester(3), Livingstone, Donovan	5078	1	2		4	5	12	7		13	9^	11	3	14	6*	8	10+									
R2L1	Sep 17	SHEFFIELD WEDNESDAY	2-0	Groves, Livingstone	6429		2	3	4	5	6	7	8	10	9*	11					12	1								
R2L2	Oct 1	Sheffield Wednesday	2-3	Nogan, Groves	11120	1	2	3	4	5	6	7	8	10*	9	11					12									
R3	14	LEICESTER CITY	3-1	Jobling, Livingstone(2)	7738	1		3	4		6	7	8*	12	9	11	13				10		2^		5					
R4	Nov 18	Liverpool	0-3		28515	1	2	3	4	5	6	7	8+	12	9	11^	13		14		10*									

Auto Windscreens Shield

	Date	Opponent	Score	Scorers	Att	Davison	McDermott	Gallimore	Handyside	Lever	Widdrington	Donovan	Black	Livingstone	Nogan	Groves	Jobling	Woods	Southall	Gilbert	Lester	Pearcey	Butterfield	Holsgrove	Rodger	Clare	Burnett	Smith D	Wrack	Dobbin
Nth R1	Dec 9	Chesterfield	1-0	Nogan	1128	1	2	3	4		8	7		10*	9+	11	6^				12		14		5	13				
Nth R2	Jan 6	HULL CITY	1-0	Butterfield	4778	1	2^	3	4	5			8			11	6	9*					7+			10			12	
Nth QF	27	Scunthorpe United	2-0	Groves, Burnett	4596	1	2	3	4	5		7	8^	9		11	13				12					10*	6			
Nth SF	Feb 17	BLACKPOOL	1-0	Burnett	8027	1	2	3	4	5*		7		10	9	11					12						6	8		
Nth Fl1	Mar 10	BURNLEY	1-1	Groves, Burnett	6064	1	2	3+	14	5^		7	13	4	9*	11					12					10	6	8		
Nth Fl2	17	Burnley	2-0	Nogan, Donovan	10257	1	2	3	4	5		7			9	11					10						6	8		
F	Apr 19	Bournemouth#	2-1	Black, Burnett	62432	1	2	3^	4	5		7	13	12	9+	11	14									10*	6	8		

Played at Wembley, after extra time 'Golden Goal'

Additional players: Bloomer Nth R2/13; Chapman Nth R2/14

Division 2 Play-Off

	Date	Opponent	Score	Scorers	Att	Davison	McDermott	Gallimore	Handyside	Lever	Widdrington	Donovan	Black	Livingstone	Nogan	Groves	Jobling	Woods	Southall	Gilbert	Lester	Pearcey	Butterfield	Holsgrove	Rodger	Clare	Burnett	Smith D	Wrack	Dobbin
SFL1	May 9	Fulham	1-1	Smith	13954	1	2	3	4	5+		7	13		9*	11	14				10^					12	6	8		
SFL2	13	FULHAM	1-0	Donovan	8689	1	2	3*	4	5		7	13	12	9^	11					10						6	8		
F	23	Northampton Town	1-0	Donovan	62988	1	2	3	4	5		7	13	12	9*	11					10						6	8^		

SEASON 1997/98

Back: Groves, Woods, Rodger, Davison, Lever, Handyside, Livingstone
Middle: Bielby (Kit Man), Lester, Jobling, Fickling, Black, Brown, Neil, Stephenson, Chapman, Delahunt (Physio)
Front: Gallimore, Southall, McDermott, Wrack, Buckley (Man), Cockerill (Asst Man), Clare, Widdrington, Bloomer

			Home					Away							
		P	W	D	L	F	A	W	D	L	F	A	F	A	Pts.
1	Watford	46	13	7	3	36	22	11	9	3	31	19	67	41	88
2	Bristol City	46	16	5	2	41	17	9	5	9	28	22	69	39	85
3	GRIMSBY TOWN	46	11	7	5	30	14	8	8	7	25	23	55	37	72
4	Northampton Town	46	14	5	4	33	17	4	12	7	19	20	52	37	71
5	Bristol Rovers	46	13	2	8	43	33	7	8	8	27	31	70	64	70
6	Fulham	46	12	7	4	31	14	8	3	12	29	29	60	43	70
7	Wrexham	46	10	10	3	31	23	8	6	9	24	28	55	51	70
8	Gillingham	46	13	7	3	30	18	6	6	11	22	29	52	47	70
9	Bournemouth	46	11	8	4	28	15	7	4	12	29	37	57	52	66
10	Chesterfield	46	13	7	3	31	19	3	10	10	15	25	46	44	65
11	Wigan Athletic	46	12	5	6	41	31	5	6	12	23	35	64	66	62
12	Blackpool	46	13	6	4	35	24	4	5	14	24	43	59	67	62
13	Oldham Athletic	46	13	7	3	43	23	2	9	12	19	31	62	54	61
14	Wycombe Wanderers	46	10	10	3	32	20	4	8	11	19	33	51	53	60
15	Preston North End	46	10	6	7	29	26	5	8	10	27	30	56	56	59
16	York City	46	9	7	7	26	21	5	10	8	26	37	52	58	59
17	Luton Town	46	7	7	9	35	38	7	8	8	25	26	60	64	57
18	Millwall	46	7	8	8	23	23	7	5	11	20	31	43	54	55
19	Walsall	46	10	8	5	26	16	4	4	15	17	36	43	52	54
20	Burnley	46	10	9	4	34	23	3	4	16	21	42	55	65	52
21	Brentford	46	9	7	7	33	29	2	10	11	17	42	50	71	50
22	Plymouth Argyle	46	10	5	8	36	30	2	8	13	19	40	55	70	49
23	Carlisle United	46	8	5	10	27	28	4	3	16	30	45	57	73	44
24	Southend United	46	8	7	8	29	30	3	3	17	18	49	47	79	43

1998-99 11th in Division 1

Captain: Paul Groves

	Date	Opponent	Score	Scorers	Att.	Davison	McDermott	Gallimore	Handyside	Smith R	Widdrington	Coldicott	Black	Nogan	Lester	Groves	Smith D	Burnett	Ashcroft	Livingstone	Clare	Lever	Dobbin	Donovan	Butterfield	Bloomer	Love	Buckley	Croudson	Chapman
1	Aug 9	IPSWICH TOWN	0-0		7211	1	2	3	4	5	6	7	8*	9	10	11	12													
2	15	Bolton Wanderers	0-2		16584	1	2	3+	4	5		7	12	10^	13	11	8	6*	9	14										
3	22	HUDDERSFIELD TOWN	1-0	Groves(pen)	6974	1	2	3	4	5	12	7		9^	10	11	8	6*			13									
4	29	Oxford United	0-0		5587	1	2	3	4	5	12	7			10	11	8*	6	9											
5	31	WEST BROMWICH ALBION	5-1	Handyside,Burnett,D.Smith,Groves(p),Black	7931	1	2	3*	4	5		7	12	13	10^	11	8	6	9											
6	Sep 5	Stockport County	0-2		6199	1	2	3*	4+	5		7^	12	13	10	11	8	6	9			14								
7	8	Sheffield United	2-3	Lester, Burnett	12293	1	2	3		4^		7*	12		10	11	8	6	9	13		5								
8	12	BARNSLEY	1-2	Ashcroft	8149	1	2	3		4	7		12	13	10	11	8*	6^	9	14		5+								
9	19	Birmingham City	1-0	D.Smith	17563	1	2	3		5		7	12	10^	13	11	8	6*	9	4										
10	26	PORT VALE	2-2	Clare(2)	5747	1	2+	3		5			8		10	11		6^	9*	4	12	13	14	7						
11	29	CREWE ALEXANDRA	1-1	Nogan	5024	1	2	3+		4	6^		8	9*	12	11					10	5	13	7	14					
12	Oct 3	Queens Park Rangers	2-1	D.Smith, Black	10240	1	2	3		5	12	6*	10	9		11	8					4		7						
13	17	BRADFORD CITY	2-0	Nogan, Groves	7473	1	2	3		4	6		10	9		11	8					5	12	7*						
14	20	BRISTOL CITY	2-1	Groves(2,1pen)	5082	1	2	3		4	6		10	9	12	11	8*			13		5		7^						
15	24	Wolverhampton Wanderers	0-2		18480	1	2	3	12	4	6+		7^	9	10	11	8			13		5*	14							
16	31	CRYSTAL PALACE	2-0	Widdrington, Lester	6948	1		3	4		6	7	12	9*	10	11	8			5					2^	13				
17	Nov 7	Sunderland	1-3	Groves	40077	1	2	3	4		6*	7	12	9+	10	11	8^		14	5		13								
18	14	PORTSMOUTH	1-1	Groves	6236		2	3	4		6	7^	12	9*	10	11	8+		14	5		13					1			
19	21	Bury	0-1		4198	1		3+	4		6	7*		9^	10	11	8		13	5	14	12			2					
20	28	SWINDON TOWN	1-0	Lester	5657	1	2	3	4		6	12	13	14	10	11	8^		9+	5	7*									
21	Dec 2	Norwich City	1-3	D.Smith	12024	1	2	3	4		6	12	5*	13	10	11	8		9^		7+			14						
22	5	Tranmere Rovers	2-1	Groves(pen), Ashcroft	4937	1	2	3*	4			6	12	9	10^	11	8		13	5				7						
23	13	Portsmouth	1-0	Groves	8180	1	2	3	4	12		6	13	9^		11	8		10	5*				7						
24	19	WATFORD	2-1	D.Smith, Groves	6679	1	2	3	4	5	12	6*	10^	9		11	8		7		13									
25	26	Huddersfield Town	0-2		16186	1	2		4	5	12	6	3+	9^	13	11	8		10	14				7*						
26	28	STOCKPORT COUNTY	1-0	Groves	8058	1	2		4	5	6		8		10	11	3			9				7						
27	Jan 9	Ipswich Town	1-0	Handyside	15575	1	2	3	4	5	12	6	10^	9*		11	8				13			7						
28	16	OXFORD UNITED	1-0	Groves	6626	1	2*	3	4	5	12	6	10^	9	13	11	8							7						
29	30	West Bromwich Albion	1-1	Black	17843	1	2	3	4	5		6	10*	9		11	8				12			7						
30	Feb 6	**BOLTON WANDERERS**	0-1		8674	1	2	3+	4	5	12	6	10	9		11	8*				14	13		7^						
31	20	Barnsley	0-0		16343	1	2		4		8	6	10	9		11	3*					5		7	12					
32	27	BIRMINGHAM CITY	0-3		7807	1	2	3		4	12	6*	8	9^		11		13	10		14	5+		7						
33	Mar 13	SUNDERLAND	0-2		9528	1	2	3	4	5	6			12		11	8*		9		10			7						
34	16	Crewe Alexandra	0-0		4855	1	2	3	4	5	12	6	8^			11			9		10*	13		7						
35	20	Crystal Palace	1-3	Groves	15228	1	2	3	4^	5	10	6	8+			11		12	9*		13	14		7						
36	23	Port Vale	1-0	Groves	4980	1	2	3	4	5		6	10	9		11	8*			12				7						
37	Apr 3	Bradford City	0-3		14522		2	3	4	5*		6	10^	9	8+	11		13	14	12				7			1			
38	5	**NORWICH CITY**	0-1		6302		2	3				6	12	9+	10*	11		13	8	4	14	5^		7			1			
39	10	**Bristol City**	1-4	Ashcroft	11616		2+	3				7	8	12	10*	11		6^	9	4	13	5			14		1			
40	13	QUEENS PARK RANGERS	1-0	Lester	4789			3				7*	8	10	12	11		6	9	4		5			2		1			
41	17	BURY	0-0		5132			3		5			8*	12	10^	11		6	9+	4	13	14		7	2		1			
42	20	SHEFFIELD UNITED	1-2	Black	5109			3+				5	8*	9^	10	11		6	12	4	13			7	2	14	1			
43	24	Swindon Town	0-2		7197			3^				4	8+	9	10*	11		6			12	5		7	2	13	1	14		
44	May 1	TRANMERE ROVERS	1-0	Clare	5916			3	4			6	8	9^	10	11		12			13	5*		7	2		1			
45	4	WOLVERHAMPTON WANDS	0-0		7009			3	4			6	8		10	11		5			9			7	2				1	
46	9	Watford	0-1		20303			3+	4			6	8*		10	11					9^	5		7	2	12		13	1	14
					Apps.	35	37	43	30	29	16	35	29	30	26	46	30	15	21	15	7	15		27	9		9		2	
					Subs.				1	1	10	2	13	8	7		1	5	6	8	15	9	4	1	3	4		2		1
					Goals				2		1		4	2	4	14	5	2	3		3									

F.A. Cup

	Date	Opponent	Score	Scorers	Att.	Davison	McDermott	Gallimore	Handyside	Smith R	Widdrington	Coldicott	Black	Nogan	Lester	Groves	Smith D	Burnett	Ashcroft	Livingstone	Clare	Lever	Dobbin	Donovan	Butterfield	Bloomer	Love	Buckley	Croudson	Chapman
R1	Jan 2	Bradford City	1-2	McDermott	13870	1	2	3	4	5	13	6+	12		10	11	8^			9		14		7*						

Worthington Cup

	Date	Opponent	Score	Scorers	Att.	Davison	McDermott	Gallimore	Handyside	Smith R	Widdrington	Coldicott	Black	Nogan	Lester	Groves	Smith D	Burnett	Ashcroft	Livingstone	Clare	Lever	Dobbin	Donovan	Butterfield	Bloomer	Love	Buckley	Croudson	Chapman
R1L1	Aug 12	PRESTON NORTH END	0-0		3008	1	2	3*	4	5	6^	7	8+	9	10	11	12	13		14										
R1L2	18	Preston North End#	0-0		5650	1	2	3	4	5	12	7		9+	10^	11	8	6*		14	13									
R2L1	Sep 15	Sheffield United	1-2	Ashcroft	4689	1	2	3^		5	7		8+	12	10*	11	13	6	9	6					14					
R2L2	22	SHEFFIELD UNITED~	2-0	Groves, Clare	4287	1	2	3		5	6*		7		10	11	8+		9^	4	13		12	14						
R3	Oct 27	Sunderland	1-2	Nogan	18676	1	2	3	13	4*	12		8	9	10	11				6		5			7^					

after extra time, won 7-6 on penalties

~ after extra time.

		P	W	D	L	F	A	W	D	L	F	A	F	A	Pts
1	Sunderland	46	19	3	1	50	10	12	9	2	41	18	91	28	105
2	Bradford	46	15	4	4	48	20	11	5	7	34	27	82	47	87
3	Ipswich Town	46	16	1	6	37	15	10	7	6	32	17	69	32	86
4	Birmingham City	46	12	7	4	32	15	11	5	7	34	22	66	37	81
5	Watford	46	12	8	3	30	19	9	6	8	35	37	65	56	77
6	Bolton	46	13	6	4	44	25	7	10	6	34	34	78	59	76
7	Wolverhampton W.	46	11	10	2	37	19	8	6	9	27	24	64	46	73
8	Sheffield United	46	12	6	5	42	29	6	7	10	29	37	71	66	67
9	Norwich City	46	7	12	4	34	28	8	5	10	28	33	62	61	62
10	Huddersfield Town	46	11	9	3	38	23	4	7	12	24	48	62	71	61
11	GRIMSBY TOWN	46	11	6	6	25	18	6	4	13	15	34	40	52	61
12	West Bromwich Alb	46	12	4	7	43	33	4	7	12	26	43	69	76	59
13	Barnsley	46	7	9	7	35	30	7	8	8	24	26	59	56	59
14	Crystal Palace	46	11	10	2	43	26	3	6	14	15	45	58	71	58
15	Tranmere Rovers	46	8	7	8	37	30	4	13	6	26	31	63	61	56
16	Stockport County	46	7	9	7	24	21	5	8	10	25	39	49	60	53
17	Swindon Town	46	7	8	8	40	44	6	3	14	19	37	63	81	50
18	Crewe Alexandra	46	7	6	10	27	35	5	6	12	27	43	54	78	48
19	Portsmouth	46	10	5	8	34	26	1	9	13	23	47	57	73	47
20	Queens Park Rgs.	46	9	7	7	34	22	3	4	16	18	39	52	61	47
21	Port Vale	46	10	3	10	22	28	3	5	15	23	47	45	75	47
22	Bury	46	9	7	7	24	27	1	10	12	11	33	35	60	47
23	Oxford United	46	7	8	8	31	30	3	6	14	17	41	48	71	44
24	Bristol City	46	7	8	8	35	36	2	7	14	22	44	57	80	42

SEASON 1998/99

Back: Lester, Burnett, Livingstone, Lever, Love, Wrack, Davison, Gallimore, Handyside, R.Smith, Groves
Middle: Bielby (Kit Man), Nogan, Clare, Widdrington, Donovan, Croudson, Black, McDermott, Dobbin, D.Smith, Mitchell (Physio)
Front: Bloomer, Oswin, Oakes, Alan Buckley (Man), Cockerill (Asst.Man), Adam Buckley, Butterfield, Chapman

SEASON 1999/2000

Back: Knight (Yth Coach), Groves, R.Smith, Livingstone, Croudson, Coyne, Love, Lever, Handyside, McKenzie, Mitchell (Physio)
Middle: Bielby (Kit Man), Allen, Clare, Black, Bloomer, Gallimore, Ashcroft, Coldicott, D.Smith
Front: Butterfield, Chapman, Goodhand, Oswin, Cockerill (Asst Man), Alan Buckley (Man), Adam Buckley, Donovan, Lester, Burnett

1999-00 20th in Division 1

G = Goalkeeper, RB = Right back, LB = Left back, CD = Central defender,
CM = Central midfield, RM = Right midfield, LM = Left midfield, CF = Central forward, (S) = Substitute.

Captain: Paul Groves

							G	RB	LB	CD	CD	CM	CM	RM	LM	CF	CF	(S)
1	Aug	7	STOCKPORT COUNTY	0-1		5528	1	12(2)	8	5	14	11	16	7	17(26)	9	25(10)	
2		14	Nottingham Forest	1-2	Groves(pen)	17121	1	12(2)	3	5	14	11	16	7	8(26)	9	25(10)	
3		21	FULHAM	1-1	Black	6196	1	2	8	5	15	11	16	7	17	9(26)	10	
4		27	Crewe Alexandra	1-1	Lester	5444	1	2	8	5	15(14)	11	16	7	17(26)	9	10	
5		30	SWINDON TOWN	1-0	Groves(pen)	5705	1	2	8	5	14	11	16	7	17(3)	9	10	
6	Sep	5	Port Vale	1-3	Allen	3737	1	12(26)	3(25)	5	14	11	16	7	8	9	17	
7		11	WALSALL	1-0	Allen	6014	1	16	3	5	14	11	26	7	8(25)	9(17)	10	
8		18	Crystal Palace	0-3		13294	1	16	3	5	14(12)	11	26	7	8(6)	9(25)	10	
9		25	Portsmouth	2-1	Ashcroft, Coldicott	12073	1	12	3	5	11	6(26)	16	7	8(13*)	9(17)	10	
10	Oct	2	IPSWICH TOWN	2-1	Donovan, Ashcroft	6531	1	12	3	5	11	6	16	7	26	9	10	
11		16	Blackburn Rovers	1-1	Ashcroft(pen)	17575	1	12	3	5	11	6(25)	16	7	8(26)	9	10	
12		19	Tranmere Rovers	2-3	Allen(2)	5004	1	12	3	5	11	6(17)	16	7	18(26)	9(25)	10	
13		23	BIRMINGHAM CITY	1-1	Allen	6266	1	12	3	5	15	6	11	26	8	25	10	
14		26	PORTSMOUTH	1-0	Awford OG	5912	1	12	3(17)	5	15	6(16)	11	26	8	25(9)	10	
15		30	Ipswich Town	0-2		16617	1	12	3	11	15	6(17)	16	26	8(18)	25(9)	10	
16	Nov	6	Wolverhampton Wanderers	0-3		19036	1	12	3	5	15	11	16	28	8	9(25)	10	
17		12	CHARLTON ATHLETIC	2-5	Ashcroft(pen), Donovan	6849	1	12	3	5(6)	15	28(25)	16	7	8	9	10	
18		20	Bolton Wanderers	0-2		12415	1	12	8	3	15	28	16	7(14)	18(26)	9(25)	10	
19		23	QUEENS PARK RANGERS	2-1	Ashcroft(2pens)	4297	1	12	8	3	15	28(6)	16	7	18(17)	9	10	
20		28	NORWICH CITY	2-1	Ashcroft(2,1pen)	5333	1	12	8	3	15	28	16	7	18(17)	9	10	
21	Dec	4	Stockport County	1-2	Hamilton	5581	1	12	8	3	11	28	16(26)	7	18(25)	9(14)	10	
22		14	WEST BROMWICH ALBION	1-1	Allen	4036	13	2	3	5	15	11	16(26)	7	18(8)	14	25(17)	
23		18	Huddersfield Town	1-3	Groves	14065	13	2(12)	3	5	15	11	16(26)	7	8	14	25(10)	
24		26	BARNSLEY	0-3		8742	1	2	3	5	15	11	26	7(25)	18(16)	14	10(9)	
25		28	Manchester City	1-2	Coldicott	32607	1	2	3	14	15	11	16	7	18(17)	9	10	17(25)
26	Jan	3	SHEFFIELD UNITED	2-2	Lester, Ashcroft	7618	1	2	3	14	15(25)	11	16	7	8(18)	9	10	
27		15	NOTTINGHAM FOREST	4-3	Lester,Ashcroft(2,1p),Donovan	6738	1	2	3	14	15(26)	11	16	7	17(25)	9	10	
28		22	Fulham	1-0	Lester	10802	1	2	3	14	15	11	16	7	17	9(26)	10(25)	
29		29	CREWE ALEXANDRA	1-1	Allen	6147	1	2	3	11	15	26(12)	16	7	17(19)	14	25	
30	Feb	5	Swindon Town	1-0	Ashcroft	5784	1	2	8	14	15	11	16	7	17(19)	9	25(12)	
31		12	PORT VALE	2-0	Clare, Allen	6265	1	2	3(8)	14	15	11(26)	16	7	17(18)	19	25	
32		19	Norwich City	0-3		13583	1	2	8(12)	14	15	11	16	7	26	9(19)	25	
33		26	CRYSTAL PALACE	1-0	D.Smith(pen)	5421	1	2	8	14	15	11	16	7	17	10(26)	19	
34	Mar	4	Walsall	0-1		5384	1	2(12)	3	14	15	11	16	7	17(18)	10(26)	19	
35		7	WOLVERHAMPTON WANDS.	1-0	Clare	5575	1	2	3	11	15	26	16	7	8	10(17)	19	
36		11	Queens Park Rangers	0-1		10450	1	12	3(17)	11	15	26	16	7	8	10(14)	19	
37		18	BOLTON WANDERERS	0-1		5289	1	2	3	11	15	26	16	7	8	10(17)	19	
38		22	Charlton Athletic	0-4		19364	1	2	3	11	15	26	16	7	8(25)	17	19	
39		27	Barnsley	0-3		14613	1	12	3	14(20)	15	11	16	7	17	10(25)	19	
40	Apr	1	HUDDERSFIELD TOWN	0-0		6993	1	2(12)	3	11	15	26	16	7	8	9(25)	19	
41		8	Sheffield United	0-0		11612	1	12	3(14)	11	15	26	16	7	8	9	19(17)	
42		15	MANCHESTER CITY	1-1	Pouton	8116	1	12	3	11	15	26	16	7	8	9	19(14)	
43		22	BLACKBURN ROVERS	0-0		6558	1	12(2)	3	11	15	26(25)	16	7	8(17)	9	14	
44		24	West Bromwich Albion	1-2	Black	15291	1	2	3(12)	11	15	26	16	7	8(17)	9	25(19)	
45		29	TRANMERE ROVERS	1-2	Clare	5427	1	2	22	14	15	11	16	26	17(18)	9(20)	19(25)	
46	May	7	Birmingham City	0-0		25263	1	2	3	14	15	11	16	7	8	9	19(17)	

* (1) Coyne dismissed, (13) Croudson keeper replacement

1 own goal

F.A. Cup

							G	RB	LB	CD	CD	CM	CM	RM	LM	CF	CF	(S)
R3	Dec	11	STOCKPORT COUNTY	3-2	Livingstone(2), Allen	3400	13	12(2)	3	5	15	11	16(26)	7	18	14	10(25)	
R4	Jan	8	BOLTON WANDERERS	0-2		4270	1	2	22(12)	14	15	26	16	7	18(17)	9	10(25)	

Worthington Cup

							G	RB	LB	CD	CD	CM	CM	RM	LM	CF	CF	(S)
R1L1	Aug	10	Carlisle United	0-0		2327	1	12(2)	8	5	14	11	16	7	17(26)	9	10(25)	
R1L2		24	CARLISLE UNITED	6-0	Lester(3),Groves,Coldicott,Donovan	2696	1	2	8	5	14	11(26)	16	7	17	9(19)	10(25)	
R2L1	Sep	14	LEYTON ORIENT	4-1	Groves,D.Smith,Gallimore,Ashcroft(p)	2238	1	12	3	11	14	26	16	7(19)	8(18)	9	10(25)	
R2L2		21	Leyton Orient	0-1		1036	1	12	8	5	11	26(6)	16	7	17	9(25)	10	
R3	Oct	13	Leicester City	0-2		13701	13	12	3	5	11	6(8)	16	7	26	9(15)	10	

Squad	League App(Sub)	Gls	FA Cup App(Sub)	Gls	FL Cup App(Sub)	Gls	Squad	League App(Sub)	Gls	FA Cup App(Sub)	Gls	FL Cup App(Sub)	Gls
1 Coyne	44		1		4		16 Coldicott	43(2)	2	2		5	1
2 McDermott	23(3)		1(1)		1(1)		17 Black	15(16)	2	0(1)		3	
3 Gallimore	38(1)		1		2	1	18 Buckley	8(5)		2		0(1)	
4 Handyside							19 Clare	13(4)	3			0(2)	
5 Smith R	19		1		4		20 Bloomer	0(2)					
6 Burnett	7(3)				1(1)		21 Love						
7 Donovan	41	3	2		5	1	22 Chapman	1		1			
8 Smith D	34(2)	1			4(1)	1	23 McKenzie						
9 Ashcroft	31(3)	12	1		4	1	24 Oswin						
10 Lester	23(3)	4	2		5	3	25 Allen	12(19)	8	0(2)	1	0(4)	
11 Groves	43	3	1		5	2	26 Pouton	19(17)	1	1(1)		3(2)	
12 Butterfield	21(8)		1(1)		4		27 (Not allocated)						
13 Croudson	2(1)		1		1		28 Hamilton	6	1				
14 Livingstone	23(6)		2	2	3		(Replacement player)						
15 Lever	35		2		0(1)		10 Nicholls	6					

Grimsby Town Reserves

Seasonal Summaries 1901-02 to 1999-2000

	P	W	D	L	F	A	Pts	Pos
MIDLAND LEAGUE								
1901-02	28	16	3	9	76	38	35	4th
1902-03	32	12	4	16	51	47	28	13th
1903-04	34	15	4	15	55	62	34	8th
1904-05	Did not compete							
1905-06	34	24	6	4	88	31	54	2nd
1906-07	38	25	7	6	92	46	57	2nd
1907-08	38	18	8	12	68	57	44	5th
1908-09	38	16	5	17	70	71	37	11th
1909-10	42	20	4	18	107	81	44	7th
1910-11 First team played in the Midland League (no reserve side).								
1911-12	36	17	5	14	68	84	39	5th
1912-13	38	15	9	14	66	66	39	7th
1913-14	34	16	6	12	68	56	38	6th
1914-15	38	21	3	14	73	54	45	7th
First World War)								
1919-20	34	14	5	15	66	64	33	10th
1920-21	38	12	5	21	45	70	39	18th
1921-22	42	24	9	9	81	82	57	2nd
1922-23	42	21	9	12	77	59	51	5th
1923-24	42	25	6	11	98	46	56	2nd
MIDLAND COMBINATION								
1924-25	22	8	6	8	37	31	20	7th
MIDLAND COMBINATION SUBSIDIARY								
1924-25	10	6	2	2	28	10	14	1st
MIDLAND COMBINATION								
1925-26	24	14	5	5	72	26	33	1st
COMBINATION CUP								
1925-26	12	9	2	1	40	15	20	1st
MIDLAND COMBINATION								
1926-27	24	13	1	10	48	43	27	5th
MIDLAND COMBINATION SUBSIDIARY								
1926-27	12	7	4	1	29	12	18	2nd
MIDLAND LEAGUE								
1927-28	44	20	8	16	93	88	48	12th
1928-29	54	24	6	20	109	96	54	10th
1929-30	50	28	9	13	160	86	65	4th
1930-31	46	32	6	8	174	73	70	1st
1931-32	46	36	3	7	178	60	75	2nd
1932-33	46	36	1	9	189	66	73	1st
1933-34	32	25	4	3	127	47	54	1st
1934-35	38	20	8	10	114	54	48	3rd
1935-36	40	16	8	16	89	70	40	4th
1936-37	42	70	23	12	108	61	53	3rd
1937-38	42	22	5	15	88	57	49	5th
1938-39	42	23	6	13	120	74	52	5th
(Second World War)								
1946-47	42	29	8	5	133	54	66	1st
1947-48	42	18	10	14	101	88	46	10th
MIDLAND LEAGUE								
1948-49	42	21	9	12	87	65	51	5th
1949-50	46	29	7	10	98	58	65	2nd
1950-51	42	23	5	14	84	61	51	4th
1951-52	42	15	7	20	73	73	37	14th
1952-53	46	27	8	11	115	56	62	3rd
1953-54	46	20	8	18	74	64	48	10th
1954-55	46	16	9	21	89	98	41	17th
1955-56	46	19	6	21	88	76	44	12th
1956-57	46	18	7	21	108	86	43	15th
1957-58	46	22	10	14	88	75	54	5th

	P	W	D	L	F	A	Pts	Pos
NORTH REGIONAL LEAGUE								
1958-59	36	12	10	14	58	58	34	11th
1959-60	42	13	8	21	58	67	34	19th
1960-61	40	14	8	18	62	81	36	14th
1961-62	28	14	3	11	70	50	31	5th
1962-63	32	16	3	13	68	53	35	14th
1963-64	32	15	9	8	67	49	39	6th
1964-65	30	14	4	12	60	63	52	12th
NORTHERN INTERMEDIATE LEAGUE								
1965-66	32	18	8	6	84	44	44	4th
(This was the youth side - no reserve team fielded this season)								
MIDLAND COUNTIES LEAGUE								
1966-67	42	14	5	23	70	83	33	6th
1967-68	40	10	11	19	53	61	31	16th
NORTH MIDLANDS LEAGUE								
1968-69	26	8	4	14	36	51	20	11th
1969-70	28	8	2	18	31	53	18	14th
1970-71	26	3	9	14	30	56	15	13th
1971-72	28	10	6	12	40	52	26	9th
1972-73	28	7	11	10	42	58	25	10th
1973-74	28	15	4	9	48	37	34	4th
1974-75	28	10	7	11	38	39	27	7th
1975-76	24	8	6	10	32	40	22	7th
1976-77	22	7	5	10	25	42	19	7th
1977-78	28	11	6	11	38	32	28	8th
1978-79	30	15	7	8	60	37	37	2nd
1979-80	28	14	4	10	44	46	32	6th
1980-81	28	13	7	8	68	49	33	5th
1981-82	24	9	4	11	39	41	22	9th
1982-83	16	5	4	7	16	23	14	4th
CENTRAL LEAGUE (Division Two)								
1983-84	30	10	8	12	53	46	38	12th
1984-85	34	11	10	13	50	57	43	12th
1985-86	34	18	2	14	58	59	56	7th
1986-87	32	17	5	10	63	43	56	3rd
CENTRAL LEAGUE (Division One)								
1987-88	34	6	3	25	29	100	21	7th
CENTRAL LEAGUE (Division Two)								
1988-89	34	12	15	17	47	61	41	10th
1989-90	34	6	8	20	35	65	26	17th
PONTINS CENTRAL LEAGUE (Division Two)								
1990-91	34	10	5	19	28	56	35	15th
1991-92	34	10	8	16	39	45	38	13th
1992-93	34	13	7	14	51	45	46	10th
1993-94	34	11	7	16	48	61	40	12th
1994-95	34	10	7	17	47	62	37	12th
1995-96	34	10	9	15	59	68	39	13th
Re-organisation of Pontin's League (dropping 'Central' from title) for 1996-97. Introduction of four divisions. The Mariners being placed in Division Two, despite being demoted to the 'third' division.								
PONTINS LEAGUE (Division Two)								
1996-97	24	15	5	4	54	29	50	1st
PONTINS LEAGUE (Division One)								
1997-98	24	11	4	9	31	26	37	5th
1998-99	24	5	5	14	20	46	20	13th
Reorganised due to Premier League sides forming their own League.								
PONTINS LEAGUE (Premier Division)								
1999-00	22	2	9	11	23	41	15	12th
Relegated to Pontins League (Division One)								

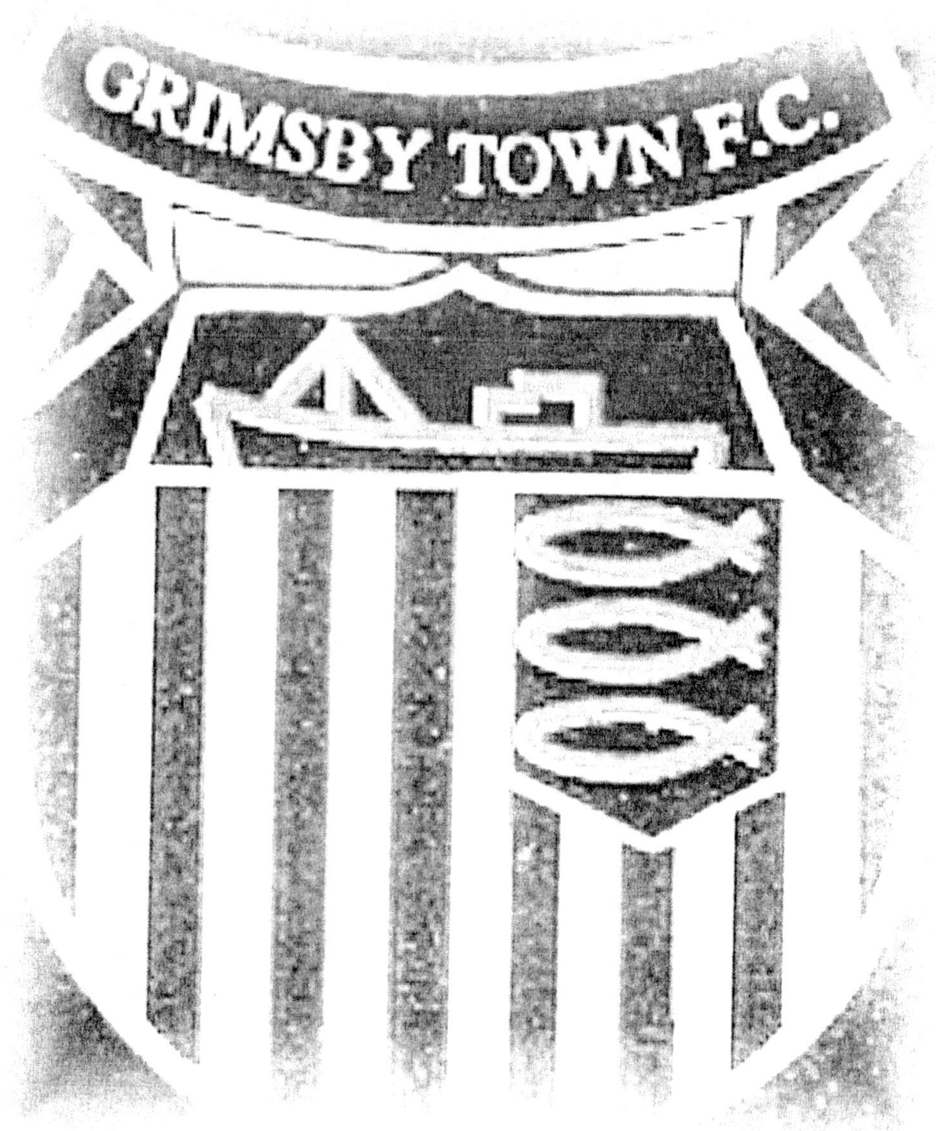
GRIMSBY TOWN F.C.

~ Advanced Subscribers ~

T.W. Knapton
Dave Burton
Daniel Lawrence Blackman, Grimsby
Roy Dowie, Isle of Man
Ian Fitzgerald, Chesterfield
B.W. Clark, Broughton
David Colin Gregory
Mark Edward Hill
Harold John Kemp Hall
Jack & Doreen Harrison
Roy Middleton, Tockington, Bristol
Geoff Milborn, Cleethorpes
Ted Riley, Cleethorpes
Gary Ladd, Cleethorpes
The Dring Family, Broughton
David Kenneth Webster, Keelby
Steven, Patricia, Neil Mapley
Thomas Edward Jenkinson, Binbrook
Paul Germaney, Grimsby
Allan Barrick, Goxhill, Lincs.
Victoria Barrick, Killamarsh, Sheffield
Simon Barrick, Assleby, Yorks.
Chris Potts, Doncaster
William Robert McIlveen, Grimsby
David Watford, Cleethorpes
Philip Waller, Comfort Match
Mike Day, Thorne
John Kirk, Horsington
Mike Cullen, Grimsby
M.D. Hearn, Gainsborough
Kristine Fitzjohn, Grimsby
Emma Gillingham
Ed Blackbourn
Janice Rooke, Waltham
Andy Plowman, Cleethorpes
David Tasker, Cumbria
Heather Tuck, Scartho
Mr. S. Burton
Matthew Barrick, Goxhill, Lincs.
William John Ladds, Grimsby
Mr. Timothy E. Cliff
Loyd Baker, Nottingham
Ray Head, Stickney Boston
Neil Sears, Bottesford
Dean Fitzsimons, Grimsby
Oliver Laws, Louth
Stan Laws, Louth
Jack Westerby, Louth
Tony Hand, Louth
Darren Chiumento, Legbourne
Mrs. I.E. Wherry, Louth
K.M. 'Ted' Wherry, Willoughby
Ken Simpson, Louth
Tom Simpson, Louth
Jack Corby, Louth
Steve Ellis, Australia
Janet Burnett, Grimsby
David Martin, Marske, Cleveland
Ian Martin, Leeds
Gavin Shufflebotham, Leigh-on-Sea
Tina Mountain, Maidstone
Harry McLellan, Louth
Laura McLellan, Louth
Julie McLellan, Louth
Russell McLellan, Louth
Daniel Taylor, Grimsby
Lee Taylor, Grimsby
Nicholas Elvidge, North Somercotes
Tim Jaines, Louth
Alistair Wood, Louth
Bill Armstrong, Louth
Mick Robinson, Louth
Bren Clarke, West Drayton
Pete Hawson, Fulham
Tez Leesing, Farnborough, Kent
John Robinson
Mike Robinson
James Morris
Roger Swindells
Jostein Jensen
Peter Bradford
Paul Vessey
Allen Vessey
Ian Parratt
Stuart Morton
Giles Sudderick
James & Terry Booth
Jeremy Edward Charles Baily
Gavin Gresswell
Bill Osborne
Tim & Matt Coombs
Robert Sedgwick
Nick Jackson
Lindsay Warren
James Bull
Keith R. Collins
David Peasgood
Adrian Small
Michael Jarvis
David Keats, Thornton Heath
Mr. R. Shaw, Sutton-in-Ashfield
George Painter, Castle Cary
Michael Grayson
Mr. L.A. Zammit
Derek Hyde
Graham Spackman
Barry Watson
Peter Cogle, Aberdeen
Bryan Spittlehouse, East Halton
Peter Miles, Southend, Essex
Allan Grieve
A. Timlin
Chas Sumner, Kelsall, Cheshire
Gordon Macey, Q.P.R. Historian
Steve Emms, Evesham
David E. Griffiths
Geoff Allman
Dave Windross
Jonny Stokkeland, Kvinesdal, Norway
George Mason
Phil Hollow, Plymouth Argyle
John Treleven
John Ringrose
Geoffrey Wright
Denis Manders, Sleaford
Keith & Kieron Coburn
Richard Owen, Portsmouth F.C.Historian
Richard Wells
Philip Pike, Penisarwaen, Caernarfon
Bob Lilliman
Chris Marsh, Chesterfield
J.R. Orton
Reg White
A & J.A. Waterman
Richard Lane, Norwell, Notts.
S. Metcalfe
Mr. M.J.W. Carr
Fred Lee, Plymouth Argyle
Richard Stocken, Cheshire
David J. Godfrey
Willy Østby, Proud Potter
Martin Cripps, Sussex
Raymond Koerhuis
David Pease
John Coyle
David Jowett, Keighley
James Jordan
Roger Wash
Terry Frost
Mark Tyler, Billericay Town F.C.
Ray Bickel
Mick McConkey, Luton
Alan Hindley
Don Starr
Gareth A. Evans
John Rawnsley
Phil Martin, Knutsford, Cheshire
Christer Svensson, Ödeshög, Sweden
Arran & Nicholas Matthews